THE DUXBURY SERIES IN STATISTICS AND DECISION SCIENCES

Applications, Basics, and Computing of Exploratory Data Analysis, Velleman and Hoaglin

Applied Regression Analysis for Business and Economics, Dielman

Elementary Statistics, Fifth Edition, Johnson

Elementary Statistics for Business, Second Edition, Johnson and Siskin

Essential Business Statistics: A Minitab Framework, Bond and Scott

Fundamental Statistics for the Behavioral Sciences, Second Edition, Howell

Fundamentals of Biostatistics, Third Edition, Rosner

Introduction to Mathematical Programming: Applications and Algorithms, Winston

Introduction to Probability and Statistics, Eighth Edition, Mendenhall and Beaver

Introduction to Statistical Methods and Data Analysis, Third Edition, Ott

Introductory Business Statistics with Microcomputer Applications, Shiffler and Adams

Introductory Statistical Methods: An Integrated Approach Using Minitab, Groeneveld

Introductory Statistics for Management and Economics, Third Edition, Kenkel

Making Hard Decisions: An Introduction to Decision Analysis, Clemen

Mathematical Statistics with Applications,
  Fourth Edition, Mendenhall, Wackerly, and Scheaffer

Minitab Handbook, Second Edition, Ryan, Joiner, and Ryan

Minitab Handbook for Business and Economics, Miller

Operations Research: Applications and Algorithms, Second Edition, Winston

Probability and Statistics for Engineers, Third Edition, Scheaffer and McClave

Probability and Statistics for Modern Engineering, Second Edition, Lapin

SAS Applications Programming: A Gentle Introduction, DiIorio

Statistical Methods for Psychology, Second Edition, Howell

Statistical Thinking for Managers, Third Edition, Hildebrand and Ott

Statistics: A Tool for the Social Sciences, Fourth Edition, Ott, Larson, and Mendenhall

Statistics for Business and Economics, Bechtold and Johnson

Statistics for Business: Data Analysis and Modelling, Cryer and Miller

Statistics for Management and Economics, Sixth Edition,
  Mendenhall, Reinmuth, and Beaver

Student Edition of Execustat, the authors of Statgraphics

Understanding Statistics, Fifth Edition, Ott and Mendenhall

THE DUXBURY ADVANCED SERIES IN STATISTICS AND DECISION SCIENCES

A First Course in the Theory of Linear Statistical Models, Myers and Milton

Applied Nonparametric Statistics, Second Edition, Daniel

Applied Regression Analysis and Other Multivariate Methods, Second Edition, Kleinbaum, Kupper, and Muller

Classical and Modern Regression with Applications, Second Edition, Myers

Elementary Survey Sampling, Fourth Edition, Scheaffer, Mendenhall, and Ott

Introduction to Contemporary Statistical Methods, Second Edition, Koopmans

Introduction to Probability and Its Applications, Scheaffer

Introduction to Probability and Mathematical Statistics, Bain and Engelhardt

Linear Statistical Models: An Applied Approach, Second Edition, Bowerman and O'Connell

Probability Modeling and Computer Simulation, Matloff

Quantitative Forecasting Methods, Farnum and Stanton

Time Series Analysis, Cryer

Time Series Forecasting: Unified Concepts and Computer Implementation, Second Edition, Bowerman and O'Connell

Statistics for Business: Data Analysis and Modelling

Jonathan D. Cryer
University of Iowa

Robert B. Miller
University of Wisconsin

PWS-KENT Publishing Company ■ *Boston*

PWS–KENT
Publishing Company

20 Park Plaza
Boston, Massachusetts 02116

To
Judy, Lee, Todd, and Jill
Lynette, Ann, Jeff, and Matt

PWS-KENT Publishing Company is a division of Wadsworth, Inc.

> ***About the Cover***
> *Clay model prototypes of new cars are designed by hand. These models are then placed in wind tunnels to test them aerodynamically and pinpoint the friction points. By modifying the design from these data, carmakers are able to reduce the vehicles' fuel consumption.*
>
> *Our thanks to General Motors and Ford for providing slides, photographs, and other props. The authors provided the scatterplot matrix and computer printouts comparing the gas consumption of various cars.*

Library of Congress Cataloging-in-Publication Data
Cryer, Jonathan D.
    Statistics for business: data analysis and modelling/by
  Jonathan D. Cryer and Robert B. Miller
      p. 840 cm.
      Includes bibliographical references (p. 760) and index.
      ISBN 0-534-92239-2
      1. Management—Statistical methods.   2. Commercial statistics.
  3. Business—Mathematical models.   I. Miller, Robert B. (Robert
  Burnham).   II. Title.
  HD30.215.C79   1990   519.5—dc20   90-7476

International Student Edition ISBN 0-534-98344-8

Printed in the United States of America
91 92 93 94 95—10 9 8 7 6 5 4 3 2 1

Sponsoring Editor: Michael R. Payne
Editorial Assistant: Tricia Schumacher
Production Editor: S. London
Manufacturing Coordinator: Margaret Sullivan Higgins
Interior and Cover Designer: S. London
Cover Photographer: Greg Bowl
Typesetter: Polyglot Pte. Ltd.
Cover Printer: John P. Pow Company
Printer and Binder: R. R. Donnelley & Sons

Contents

CHAPTER 2

PLOTTING PROCESS DATA   29

CHAPTER 3

DISTRIBUTION PLOTS   53

CHAPTER 4

METRIC DATA SUMMARIES   80

CHAPTER 5

DESCRIBING CATEGORICAL VARIABLES   106

CHAPTER 6

SUMMARIZING RELATIONSHIPS   132

CHAPTER 7

FITTING CURVES   179

PART TWO: MODELLING PROCESS VARIATION   219

C H A P T E R 8

NORMAL DISTRIBUTIONS   221

C H A P T E R 9

CONTROL CHARTS FOR METRIC VARIABLES   249

C H A P T E R 1 0

BINOMIAL DISTRIBUTIONS   283

C H A P T E R 1 1

CONTROL CHARTS FOR BINARY VARIABLES   310

Designed Data Analysis and Modelling

PART THREE: DATA BY DESIGN   323

C H A P T E R 1 2

DATA COLLECTION   325

C H A P T E R 1 3

INTRODUCTION TO SURVEYS   348

PART FOUR: PRINCIPLES OF PROBABILISTIC INFERENCE   439

PART FIVE: MODELLING MANY VARIABLES 535

C H A P T E R 2 0

INFERENCE IN REGRESSION MODELS 537

C H A P T E R 2 1

REGRESSION DIAGNOSTICS AND TRANSFORMATIONS 580

C H A P T E R 2 2

REGRESSION MODEL SELECTION 622

Statistics in Organizations

Preface

This book provides training in statistical thinking and statistical techniques for business students. Business schools have long recognized the importance of statistics training by making one or two statistics courses a required part of the curriculum for the BBA and MBA degrees. The American Assembly of Collegiate Schools of Business mandates statistical training for accreditation of schools of business.

The report by L. W. Porter and L. E. McKibbon, *Management Education and Development* (New York: McGraw-Hill, 1988), reaffirms the fundamental importance of quantitative subjects in business education but provocatively argues for placing these and other subjects in a broad perspective that acknowledges the complexity of our society and the problems it faces.

> In Chapter 2 we stressed two trends that already were occurring and which seem likely to accelerate in the years immediately ahead: the move from a primarily industrial to an increasingly service-oriented economy and the related development of a strong focus on the generation, distribution, and management of information... [B]usiness/management schools in the next decade will need to take a hard look at *how an information orientation can be incorporated into the entire curriculum and into fundamental research activities.* (pp. 320–321)
>
> A major issue that was discussed at some length in the Commentary section of Chapter 3 will be reemphasized here: the need for business/management education to provide sufficient attention—in the curriculum and in other activities—to an *integrated* approach to problems that cuts across specific functional areas. (p. 322)

In recent years the business community has gained a new appreciation of statistical thinking because of intensified international competition in major items such as motor vehicles, cameras, copiers, and integrated circuits, and in services such as banking, word processing, and computer software. In the international arena, quality is a major competitive factor, and the strategic use of statistical methods has become fundamental to designing and controlling the quality of goods and services. Statistical thinking has moved out of the backroom and into the boardroom.

In a series of annual conferences in 1986–1990, members of the business and academic communities met to exchange views on improving the effectiveness of statistics in schools of business.[†] The conferees agreed on the following points:

- Training in *techniques*, while necessary, is not sufficient for the person who must use statistical thinking for decision making; problem recognition and problem formulation precede the use of techniques.

- Training of users of statistics should be done in the context of scientific methods for problem solving rather than in the context of the mathematics of statistics.

- Training should stress the cross-disciplinary nature of complex problem solving and the importance of communication in a commonly understood vocabulary.

Writing a textbook according to these principles has been both exciting and perplexing. Our intended reader is the student enrolled in a one- or two-semester (or quarter) course in a university school of business, at either the BBA or the MBA level. While wishing to convey a realistic business-world context for the use of statistical methods, we do not necessarily presuppose that the reader has a great deal of practical experience in that world. Thus we have at times opted for examples that clearly exemplify a technique rather than convey the complexity of a business problem to which the technique may be applied. We have tried to use examples with which students can concretely identify. Having mastered the art of using statistical thinking to solve concrete problems, the student will, we hope, be able to expand the scope of applications to the myriad problems that arise in business practice.

We believe that skill in statistical thinking makes people better managers, accountants, marketers, manufacturers, health care providers, administrators, and so on. Statistics is a catalyst for creativity. It offers a formal framework for systematic clarification of ambiguous and uncertain processes. It provides efficiencies of thought that result in improved designs and cost savings that have measurable impact in the marketplace. Statistics, despite its reputation as an abstract and difficult subject, is an eminently practical one. We hope to convey some of the practical flavor in this text.

[†] At the University of Chicago, New York University, University of Wisconsin, University of Michigan, and University of Kansas.

The reader who works through this text may expect to accomplish the following goals:

- To understand and apply basic statistical analysis techniques
- To use statistical techniques in the context of real data analysis
- To practice a scientific approach to problem formulation and solution
- To recognize and remedy defects in statistical analysis

We achieve these goals by sticking closely to the analysis of real data sets throughout the text. We also stress the critical link between the procedure for collecting data and the conclusions that can be realistically drawn from them. In addition to the analysis techniques, we have spent considerable time on design and collection issues. These help put analysis into proper context.

It is hard to imagine doing statistics today without access to a computer and to statistical software. Throughout the text we presuppose such access, but after much consideration we have chosen not to teach any particular computer system or any particular edition of statistical software. The varieties of both are staggering, and this very variety convinces us of the importance of conveying fundamental principles of statistics without tying them to a particular representation in a hardware/software combination. Computer-based systems can be time- and labor-saving devices, but they produce errors just as fast as they produce correct information. The user of statistics must rely on a firm grasp of the fundamentals of thought and common sense for protection against misuse. We concentrate on teaching these fundamentals, but this does not mean that we shy away from presenting computer-assisted analyses, nor do we avoid setting exercises that require machine computation. Far from recommending avoidance of computers, we positively encourage their use. In particular, nearly all of the graphs in the text were reproduced without artist intervention from camera ready copy produced by the Minitab statistical software system (release 7.2). The graphs were made assuming that a Hewlett–Packard plotter would be the output device but they were instead directed to a computer file and printed on a Hewlett–Packard LaserJet Series II printer using the PrintAPlot plotter emulation software from Insight Development Corporation. A small number of the graphs were produced by the Stata statistics/graphics/data management system. A disk containing nearly 100 data sets used in the exercises and elsewhere in the text is available from the publisher. The data files are self-documenting and set up for direct Minitab input. With minor editing they may be used with any statistical software. Numerous Minitab macros are also supplied on the disk to carry out calculations not directly supported by Minitab.

Section 1.8 gives an overview of the contents of the text. Courses with a variety of emphases and levels of mathematical sophistication are possible. In the Note to Instructors and in the *Instructor's Guide and Solutions Manual* that accompanies the text we have outlined a number of such courses.

It is our pleasure to acknowledge the help and support we have received during the writing of this book. We are blessed with families that have tolerated, taken an interest in, and even actively worked on the project. We are in debt to them in perpetuity. Our editor, Michael Payne, deserves credit for convincing us to undertake the project and then sticking with us over a long and uncertain course of trial and error. He has been extremely generous in his support. Susan London has been an outstanding production editor and Marcia Cole an enjoyable, as well as able, assistant editor. We also wish to thank our copy editor Sally Stickney for her critical analysis of every word, phrase, sentence, and cross reference. The text has been reviewed and class tested by a large number of people, and we have benefited from their painstaking, and sometimes painful, comments. The reviewers for this text include:

Bruce L. Bowerman
Miami University

Michael Broida
Miami University

Sangit Chatterjee
Northeastern University

Delores Conway
University of Southern California

Nicholas R. Farnum
California State University-Fullerton

Mark Ferris
Washington University

Anil Gulati
Western New England College

George Heitmann
Pennsylvania State University

Steven Hillmer
University of Kansas

Burt Holland
Temple University

Thomas Johnson
North Carolina State University
at Raleigh

Stuart and Marie Klugman
Drake University

Johannes Ledolter
University of Iowa

Joseph A. Machak
University of Michigan

John D. McKenzie, Jr.
Babson College

William Q. Meeker, Jr.
Iowa State University

Joe Megeath
Metropolitan State College

Kim I. Melton
Virginia Commonwealth University

Joseph Murray
Community College of Philadelphia

Harry V. Roberts
University of Chicago

Stanley L. Sclove
University of Illinois at Chicago

Sandra Strasser
University of Colorado at Boulder

Peter Swank
University of Southern California

Andrew M. Welki
John Carroll University

Dean W. Wichern
Texas A&M University

Othmar W. Winkler
Georgetown University

Mustafa R. Yilmaz
Northeastern University

Mary Sue Younger
University of Tennessee at Knoxville

Douglas A. Zahn
The Florida State University

We are especially grateful to Steve Hillmer, Mary Sue Younger, and Doug Zahn in this regard because they acted as a focus group that gave the project a much needed shot of enthusiasm at a critical moment. A special word of thanks goes to the library at the University of Dubuque for generously allowing us to use a private room for many meetings during the preparation of the text. Finally, we wish to thank all the students who were subjected to earlier drafts of the text for their comments and their patience with all the flaws preliminary drafts are heir to. We trust that our new readers will prove as diligent in pointing out the remaining flaws, so we can correct them.

Jonathan D. Cryer and Robert B. Miller

A NOTE TO INSTRUCTORS ON POSSIBLE COURSE OUTLINES

A variety of courses can be structured from this text. We outline six plans to illustrate the flexibility available. These courses assume a traditional 15 week semester. Instructors on other systems will need to make appropriate adjustments. Note that Chapter 25: *A Perspective on Statistics in Organizations* may be used any time after Chapter 6. We recommend covering that material between Chapters 6 and 7.

- **Plan 1:** *Introduction to Statistics*—Traditional emphasis
  Chapters 1–8, 10, 12–14, 17, 19

- **Plan 2:** *Introduction to Statistics*—Quality improvement emphasis
  Chapters 1–6, 25, 7–15

- **Plan 3:** *Introduction to Statistics*—Theoretical emphasis
  Chapters 1–8, 10, 12–14, 17–19

- **Plan 4:** *Introduction to Statistics*—Regression emphasis
  Chapters 1–8, 10, 19, 20–23

- **Plan 5:** *A Second Course in Statistics*—Methods emphasis
  Chapters 8–16, 19–24

- **Plan 6:** *Two-semester Sequence*
  Chapters 1–25

Observational Data and Modelling

PART 1

Process Analysis

## CHAPTER 1

Data Analysis and Model Building: An Introduction

SCIENCE AND ITS METHODS

Science, with a capital *s*, and a scientific community are usually regarded as phenomena of relatively recent origin. The fables of science involving Galileo, Kepler, Newton, Laplace, Pasteur, Darwin, and Einstein date from the seventeenth through the twentieth centuries. Yet the ancient world had sufficient "scientific" knowledge to construct pyramids, treat illnesses, and govern empires. Modern science, the systematic discovery of order in the natural world through observation and theory, indeed began with the Renaissance, but the methods of modern science are applications of mental activities common to all intellectual pursuits. What originally distinguished science from other studies was the emphasis on the natural, rather than the spiritual, world and the requirement that theories be testable by repeated observation. These concepts are so common today that we have difficulty appreciating how revolutionary and controversial they were in the seventeenth century.

In this section logical rather than technical scientific methods are discussed. Technical methods are methods of measurement and manipulation that permit fruitful investigation of phenomena. They are specific to the material under investigation and are so varied that they cannot be summarized completely. On the other hand, the logical methods of science are techniques for reasoning from available evidence and are common to all scientific investigation. They are the core of the scientific method. Few scientists subscribe to the notion that science uses a single method; yet many authorities summarize scientific investigation in the steps of *observation, hypothesis, deduction,* and *experimental verification*. Although scientists may follow these steps more or less unconsciously because they are trained to do so, it is important not to look upon the steps as part of a mechanical procedure. Actual scientific investigations involve a great deal of trial and error, outright guess-work, backtracking, and starting over again. Yet when an investigation is completed, hindsight often reveals a progression that corresponds in some degree to these four steps.

■ **EXAMPLE 1.1A:** A passage[†] published in 1946, will help to illustrate the four steps. The article describes the work of Frederick Winslow Taylor, who was employed as an engineer by the Midvale Steel Company in Pennsylvania, and who is credited with founding scientific management.

> *No doubt, most of us when we first hear of such a thing as the science of shovelling by hand, are apt to be amused; shovelling is labour which anybody is supposed to be fitted for if he is sufficiently strong and phlegmatic. So far as is known, no one ever made a systematic study of shovelling, until Taylor, whose personal experience in manual work had been only as a machinist and pattern-maker, undertook to develop the science of shovelling in a large steel plant where many kinds of material were being handled, the heaviest being iron ore, the lightest, small size anthracite coal. Taylor selected a few of the better shovellers whom he placed under the instruction of trained observers; these men worked on various materials, using several sizes of shovels under differing conditions. Careful records were kept of every phase of the work; the effect of rest periods of different lengths and frequency was noted. It was finally determined that the best results were obtained when the shovel load was kept as close as possible to 21 lb., which was much less than the usual load for the heavier materials and much more than for the lighter ones, in other words, shovels had been regularly over-loaded for the heavy iron ore and much under-loaded for the lighter coal. Special shovels were then secured, each designed to hold 21 lbs. of the material for which it was to be used. Teaching and supervision were maintained, and when the new plan was in full operation, the average wages of the shovellers were 63% higher, though the cost of handling had decreased 54%. During the first year the total savings to the works in the cost of shovelling, including all increased overhead, amounted to $36,417.69.*

Taylor's initial observation was to notice the shovelling operations. Somehow he formed the hypothesis that the shovelling operations were not as efficient as they could be. The article does not mention how he came to be concerned about

---

[†] From "Scientific Management" in *Encyclopaedia Britannica* 14th Ed (1946), 20:123.

shovelling or what raised the question of efficiency.[†] We are told that as he observed the men shovelling he made the deduction that their efficiency was influenced by a variety of conditions, including the frequency and length of rest periods and the weight of a shovel-load of material. The passage describes in some detail the process of experimental verification that Taylor used. The conclusions of his investigations were that the weight of the load was the critical factor in efficiency and that standardizing the shovel-loads at 21 pounds created a situation that was beneficial for both the steel company and the workers. ■

SECTION 1.2

SCIENCE AND PRACTICAL AFFAIRS

The methods of science seek to discover order in natural phenomena. Strictly speaking, scientists seek *explanations*, that is, models, for how and why things work. Explanations need not have great predictive power to be valuable from a strictly scientific point of view, but people with practical concerns, such as managers, engineers, doctors, and farmers, tend to value explanations that can be put to use.

For example, psychologists have learned a great deal about human preferences by studying everything from overt behavior to brain waves. But all this knowledge helps very little in predicting what products people will purchase. Although the diligence of psychological researchers and the elegance of their theories may be very impressive, the only way to find out if products will be purchased is to offer them in the marketplace. In the same vein, F. W. Taylor might have tried to discover the optimal weight of a shovel-load of coal by studying the literature on human physiology, but we have no doubt that the method he chose was preferable.

Phenomena of practical interest can be seen as systems of interrelated processes. The emphasis on relationships helps keep each process in perspective. The emphasis on process helps keep the focus on dynamic and evolutionary issues. This seems to be critical in understanding practical applications, because they often need to be expressed in terms of predictions or expectations or "trends." Because the idea of a process is so fundamental, it is discussed in some detail in the next section.

SECTION 1.3

WHAT IS A PROCESS?

DEFINITION OF PROCESS

In simplest terms, a **process** is a sequence of steps taken to achieve a goal. In industry, processes are sequences of steps taken to produce goods and services. In business, the process may be a series of negotiations that lead to a sale or a merger, or a plan for building a shopping center. In medicine, the process may be a treatment with the

---

[†] We know from Taylor's writings that he was quite concerned with workers' welfare, and he believed it was in a firm's interest to create the best possible working conditions. This may have been his concern when he conceived the shovelling experiment.

goal of curing a patient. And in agriculture, the process may be the steps that lead to a bumper harvest of soybeans. Practical processes can be exceedingly complex, and studying and managing them can command considerable resources. In this chapter some elementary processes are introduced to help you become familiar with this basic concept.

A relatively simple process is the sequence of steps you take to brew a pot of coffee. An incredibly complex process is the sequence of steps taken to produce the output of the economy of the United States.[†]

Even a relatively simple process consists of subprocesses. Consider the following steps in brewing a pot of coffee:

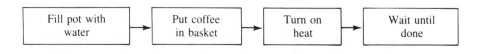

These steps presuppose the choice of coffee pot, type of water, brand of coffee, amount of coffee, and the strength setting on the pot (if it has one), but each of these is a process as well.[††] Once we purchase a coffee pot, we use it until it fails or someone gives us a new one. But we may experiment frequently with the type of water, the brand of coffee, the amount, and the strength setting. These processes can become quite elaborate or can be kept simple. Think about the process of choosing a brand of coffee. How elaborate can you make it?

In brewing a pot of coffee we control all the steps in the process because we make the choices. In complex processes no individual controls all the steps, so the behavior of such processes is the collective behavior of the people, machines, materials, and methods involved in it.

PROCESSES YIELD RESULTS

If the appropriate sequence of steps is followed, a pot of coffee is obtained. The coffee is the result of the process. The goods and services produced by the U.S. economy are the results of the economic efforts of the people. Every process produces results. We are seldom content simply to note the results of a process; we are usually interested in their quality. After you make a pot of coffee, you pour a cup, drink it, and register your satisfaction or dissatisfaction with it. If you share your coffee with someone else, your satisfaction may be determined by your friend's comments.

It is likewise with GNP. When the U.S. Department of Commerce reports the quarterly GNP, we instinctively compare it to the GNP for the previous quarter and to the GNP for the same quarter a year ago. Only within such a context is a GNP figure meaningful. If GNP is substantially higher than it was in the previous quarter and in the same quarter a year ago, the productivity of the economy is applauded.

[†] In the following discussion gross national product, a measure of a country's economic production invented by economists, is referred to. GNP is the standard abbreviation for gross national product.
[††] This example assumes that an automatic coffee pot that stops when the coffee is brewed is used. The brewing process is quite different if a "manual" pot is used.

If the growth in GNP is slight or negative, not only the poor showing but also the future of the economy are of concern.

PROCESSES YIELD DATA

Data are measures of characteristics of a process. For example, Matt brews a pot of coffee every morning. If each morning Matt records the date and the number of cups of coffee he makes, then Matt is collecting data on his coffee-brewing process. Other data Matt might record are the number of tablespoons of coffee used and the brand of coffee. Even though coffee brand is not naturally a numerical measure, coffee brands may be analyzed as data called *categorical data*; the coffee brands are treated as categories of coffee. If Matt faithfully records the data each day, he soon has a lengthy record of numerical and other measures that may be processed statistically to give insight into his coffee-making habits.

In the coffee-making example, Matt may attempt to measure the quality of the coffee numerically. The simplest scheme is to record a 1 if he is satisfied and a 0 if he is not. This is a *binary coding* of the quality of the coffee he makes. An alternative is to use a more discriminating five-point scale:

$$0 = \text{very unsatisfactory}$$
$$1 = \text{unsatisfactory}$$
$$2 = \text{neither unsatisfactory or satisfactory}$$
$$3 = \text{satisfactory}$$
$$4 = \text{very satisfactory}$$

Matt is free to measure the quality of the coffee in any way he sees fit. As long as he faithfully records his data, he will be able to analyze it to obtain insights into the coffee-making process.

The GNP is the result of two processes: the economy that produces actual goods and services and the process that measures the dollar values of the goods and services and forms them into the GNP. The production of goods and services is analogous to brewing a pot of coffee, and the GNP is analogous to a measure of the quality of the coffee those goods and services.

Many measures are needed to give insights into such a complex process as the economy. Most of them are reported monthly in the *Survey of Current Business*, which is published by the U.S. Department of Commerce.

PROCESS RESULTS VARY

Processes often involve creating and communicating information. In many organizations processing documents accounts for a substantial portion of expenses. Improvements in the management of document flow and office automation can yield significant savings.

As a simple illustration of data from an information process, consider some counts collected daily from a copy machine at the University of Wisconsin in 1987.

Only weekdays are included in this study. The process is the sequence of steps taken to produce photocopies. One of the important characteristics of the process is the number of photocopies made each day. A reading of the counter on the machine is taken at 7:45 A.M. and at 4:30 P.M. each workday. The difference between the two readings is the number we require. Exhibit 1.3A reports 30 such numbers.

EXHIBIT 1.3A

Number of Photocopies by Day

Date	Number of Copies	Date	Number of Copies
10/12	416	11/2	616
10/13	556	11/3	797
10/14	395	11/4	456
10/15	447	11/5	364
10/16	238	11/6	589
10/19	532	11/9	607
10/20	349	11/10	780
10/21	390	11/11	374
10/22	579	11/12	456
10/23	274	11/13	393
10/26	621	11/16	1199
10/27	362	11/17	362
10/28	447	11/18	547
10/29	440	11/19	530
10/30	505	11/20	741

You can see that the number of copies varies from day to day. The largest number of copies, 1199, was made on November 16. The smallest number was 238, made on October 16. How might these data be displayed to get more insights into the process? We shall see in Chapter 2.

Exhibit 1.3B lists quarterly U.S. GNP figures (in billions of current dollars) for the years 1984, 1985, and 1986. The figures are seasonally adjusted; that is, seasonal effects such as the Christmas-buying binge was removed.

EXHIBIT 1.3B

Quarterly U.S. GNP, 1984–1986, Seasonally Adjusted (in billions of current dollars)

Quarter	Year		
	1984	**1985**	**1986**
I	3553.3	3917.5	4149.2
II	3644.7	3960.6	4175.6
III	3694.6	4016.9	4240.7
IV	3758.7	4059.3	4258.7

Source: Survey of Current Business, June, 1985 p. 5; June, 1986, p. 3; June, 1987, p. 3

As you can see, the GNP figures vary from quarter to quarter. How might the figures be displayed to convey the pattern of variability? One useful display is the sequence plot, which is introduced in Chapter 2.

STATISTICS IN SCIENCE

Statistical tools help with efficient acquisition, analysis, and presentation of data. They are valuable in a scientific context because one of the hallmarks of science is the development and testing of theories on the basis of data. Looking at the four steps of the methods of science—observation, hypothesis, deduction, and experimental verification—we see that statistics should be more prominent in the first and fourth steps than in the second and third. Much of modern statistical research and practice concentrates on the experimental-verification step, the step in which new explanations and predictions are tested. Significant findings in this step can lead to process improvements that lower costs, as they did in Taylor's shovelling experiments, or to new products that can be successfully marketed, as they did when nylon was discovered at Du Pont. Since experimental verification is the "payoff step," it is only natural that efforts are devoted to improving statistical tools for this step.

We shall often emphasize the "diagnostic" aspects of statistics, the aspects that help put explanations and theories to the test. When we collect data from a process, we are always on the lookout for measurements that appear exceptional. Unusual measurements may hint at a point where the process went out of control, where the measuring instruments failed, or even where something unusually beneficial occurred.

One of the major risks in using scientific methods is that the data are subject to bias that can completely invalidate conclusions drawn from the data. Statisticians have contributed much to the methods of experimental design and to the design and execution of sample surveys. These tools help us collect data that are free of bias and hence help us draw proper conclusions.

To illustrate, a sampling scheme that consists of measuring the air temperature at noon each day for a year tells us nothing about the variations in temperature within a day. Using the range of the daily noon temperatures as an estimate of the range of temperatures within a day would lead to a vast overestimate for most locations. It is hard to imagine someone making this elementary error, but subtle errors of comparable magnitude are quite possible. For example, a panel marketing survey consists of selecting a cross section of consumers and tracking their purchasing behavior over an extended period of time. A danger in this design is that the panel may, through age or loss of panel members to follow-up, become atypical of consumers in the marketplace as a whole. If this occurs, a large number of observations on the panel can be as useless in estimating the range of variation in the market as noon temperatures are in estimating the range of temperatures in a day. For this reason, the constant updating of marketing panels is an established part of modern market-research practice.

PROCESS ANALYSIS AND PROCESS CONTROL

Recall that a process is a sequence of steps taken to achieve a goal. At each step, something happens to the material, paper, or information that constitutes input to the step; the transformed material, paper, or information is output from the current step and becomes input for the next step.

Scientific study of a process seeks to model each step and the relationships among the steps. A successful model yields understanding of the fundamental causes of the variations in the process. Activities leading to such an understanding are called **process analysis**.

Ideally a model also yields accurate predictions of the future behavior of the process. If so, the model can be used as a basis for **process control**. Control may mean keeping the process outcomes near a predetermined "target" so the output from the process is dependable. This kind of control, which is also called *process regulation*, is typical in manufacturing, agriculture, and some management applications. Another kind of control seeks to change the steps in the process so that it operates more efficiently, produces superior output, or both. This kind of control is also called *process improvement* or *quality improvement*. It is applicable to processes found in all walks of life.

PDCA — THE DEMING WHEEL

Walter A. Shewhart was a pioneer in the development of the concept of process improvement. He noted that process improvement is never a "one-shot" proposition but rather cycle after cycle of painstaking planning, experimenting, checking, setting new standards, looking for new ways to improve, and so on. W. Edwards Deming elaborated Shewhart's ideas and popularized them in Japan in the 1950s and more recently in the United States.

Exhibit 1.5A displays a diagram that Deming calls "Shewhart's cycle" but that is more widely known as *Deming's wheel*.[†] It is an outline of the application of the methods of science to process improvement. It involves repeated application of the steps of **PDCA**: planning (P), doing (D), checking (C), and acting (A). Notice the emphasis on prediction in Step 4 of the cycle. This is typical of applications in which we wish to achieve objectives. Also note the suggestion that the cycle is repeated over and over again, as the wheel revolves, an illustration of the concept called "never-ending improvement."

Step 1 in Exhibit 1.5A is the planning step. Here the current situation is evaluated, goals are set, and a test, experiment, or survey is planned. Statistical experimental design or survey design can play a major role in this step. Step 2 is the doing step, in which the plan is carried out. If the experiment or survey is complicated, statistical methods may be used to audit work in progress to ensure ad-

---

[†] Shewhart was an engineer employed by Bell Telephone Labs. His book *Economic Control of Quality of Manufactured Product* (New York: Van Nostrand, 1931) sets forth much of the scientific approach to quality control in use today. See W. Edwards Deming, *Out of the Crisis* (New York: Wiley, 1986) for commentary. Another useful reference is Masaaki Imai, *Kaizen* (New York: Random House, 1986).

EXHIBIT 1.5A

Deming's Wheel (PDCA)

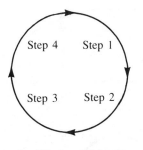

Step 1   What could be the most important accomplishments of this team? What changes
         might be desirable? What data are available? Are new observations needed? If yes,
         plan a change or test. Decide how to use the observations.
Step 2   Carry out the change or test decided upon, preferably on a small scale.
Step 3   Observe the effects of the change or test.
Step 4   Study the results. What did we learn? What can we predict?
Step 5   Repeat Step 1, with knowledge accumulated.
Step 6   Repeat Step 2, and onward.

herence to the work plan. Step 3 is checking. Do the data suggest that substantial
change has taken place? Statistical methods are usually needed to answer such a
question. Step 4 is the action step. Here the implications of the experiment or survey are studied. In particular, we want to know if a significant change found in the
experiment or survey may be projected into the future. This returns us to the
planning step and repetition of the cycle.

Every process can be improved. Improvement comes about by eliminating
unnecessary steps, using better equipment, developing better definitions of work
required, involving workers in decision making, redesigning products and services
to meet customer needs, and so on. The advantage of a scientific approach to
improvement is that both efforts and achievements are documented through the
collection and presentation of data. This tends to eliminate ambiguity and misunderstanding and to focus attention on those aspects of problems that are most
difficult and most in need of attention. In other words, using scientific methods
speeds up the process of improvement.

Exhibit 1.5B is a diagram of the organization of research and development at
AT&T. The core of this diagram is the PDCA wheel. The activities arranged around
the wheel are the ones needed for the productive pursuit of research and development at AT&T.

In terms of our discussion about the methods of science, how do the steps of
observation, hypothesis, deduction, and experimental verification fit into the PDCA
wheel? The observation step may precede the PDCA cycle, as when a step in a
process that needs improvement is noticed. Observation may well take place during
the planning step, as the process needing improvement is evaluated. Formulations
of hypotheses and deduction also take place during the planning step. Experimental
verification is the doing and checking steps, in which the hypotheses are put to the
test. Although the action step may seem more germane to a decision-making setting,
it also occurs in science, though it is not listed in the usual paradigm called scientific
method. The steps of observation, hypothesis, deduction, and verification are not

Source: Gundaker, Martinich, and Tortorella, "Quality Technology in Product Realization Systems," *AT&T Technical Journal* 66(5) (September/October 1987): 7.

ends in themselves but means for learning and gaining understanding. Thus even in science the questions in Step 4 of the Deming wheel come up: What have we learned? Where do we go next? In science these questions are answered on the basis of the desire to explain natural phenomena better, whereas in practical affairs they are answered on the basis of the desire to achieve a commercial advantage, a new cure, a better crop, and so on.

STATISTICS: LISTENING TO PROCESSES

To improve processes we "listen" to them, that is, collect data and take appropriate actions on the information we receive. While it is obvious that the quality of decisions is affected by the quality of data, it may not be so obvious that collecting good-quality data is in practice very difficult. We are so bombarded with data that we are in danger of accepting the fallacy that because data are abundant they must be right. Nothing could be further from the truth! Our society's ability to collect quantities of data is far ahead of its ability to collect trustworthy data.

Data vary in accuracy, reliability, quantity, and relevance. Thus to use data effectively, we must learn not only how to analyze data but also how to evaluate the trustworthiness of the data.

SIMPLE OBSERVATION

The simplest scheme for collecting data is to record every outcome generated by the process as it evolves. These outcomes can be measured systematically at predetermined instants. This entire process is called **simple observation**.

■ **EXAMPLE 1.6A:** Data on business operations must be collected for accounting and other management reports. Records of sales, inventories, accounts receivable, expenses, and so on result in huge data bases that are summarized and reported in a variety of ways. ■

■ **EXAMPLE 1.6B:** Dimensions of important parts in an assembly operation must be measured to make sure that the finished product meets design specifications. For critical assemblies *every* part is measured for conformance to specifications. ■

■ **EXAMPLE 1.6C:** For each departure and arrival of an airplane at an airport, many pieces of data are recorded, including time, crew, weather, and so on. ■

It is not always necessary to collect every possible piece of data to monitor a process for decision making. To take an extreme example, when we go to a clinic for a checkup, we need give only a small amount of blood for testing—fortunately the small sample tells about all the blood in our bodies. Many of the quantities studied in physics are like this. The laws of motion, thermodynamics, and atomic behavior are the same everywhere, so their discovery in the lab, wind tunnel, or cyclotron is as good as learning them anywhere else. Few characteristics of human behavior are so stable or predictable. On the other hand, it is wasteful to take more measurements than are needed to make the appropriate decisions.

■ **EXAMPLE 1.6D:** In a well-managed manufacturing operation a typical sampling scheme is to take batches of product from a work location at five or six set times each workday, once every hour, or some other systematic scheme. The sampled items are inspected and the resulting measurements put into a special sequence plot called a control chart. As long as the control chart signals that the process is operating normally, the process is allowed to continue. Only when the chart signals trouble, referred to as a "special cause of variation," is corrective action taken. This procedure assures the smooth functioning of the process, with minimal interruption, while simultaneously providing sufficient basis for detecting trouble in a timely fashion. Control charts, their application and interpretation, are the subject of Chapters 9 and 11. ■

SURVEYS

In practice collecting data can be time consuming and expensive when the environment from which the data are collected is complex. In such situations advanced methods of data collection are helpful because they attempt to gain the maximum information at minimum cost. The most commonly used advanced method is the sample **survey**, in which a sample of elements is selected from a universe of elements for measurement. The subject of surveying is covered in detail in Chapters 13–16, but some examples are given here as an introduction.

In this discussion **universe** refers to the collection of all elements of interest, such as customers who purchase a product during a given time period, inventory of items in stock, people in a country, and so on. A **sample** is a collection of elements drawn from the universe and studied by collecting data, such as answers to questions, observation of certain behaviors, and so on.

■**EXAMPLE 1.6E:** Opinion polls are prominent examples of surveys that receive a great deal of media attention. A number of polling organizations, such as Gallup, Roper, ABC-*Washington Post*, and NBC-*New York Times*, take polls at regular intervals (many of them weekly). These polls are conducted by "random digit dialing" telephone-survey techniques. Telephone numbers are drawn using probability methods in such a way that the information obtained from the people at these numbers (the sample) may be inferred, within limits, to be true about the universe of people who can be reached by telephone. Certain questions, such as those about the president's popularity, are asked each time a poll is conducted. In this way a pollster can track the evolution of public opinion on a particular question. The polls are analogous to a series of snapshots. Telephone surveying is relatively inexpensive, so the pollster can afford to survey frequently.

Market researchers also use telephone surveying extensively because it is relatively inexpensive and data can be collected rapidly. One serious difficulty with surveying by telephone is the ease with which a respondent can refuse to cooperate, simply by hanging up the phone. Even a fairly small number of refusals can seriously damage survey data, and the telephone surveyor has few options for correcting for this "nonresponse bias."   ■

■**EXAMPLE 1.6F:** Another survey technique is the personal interview. Surveyors typically use housing units as elements in the universe. Interviewers visit the chosen units and interview specified occupants. The personal interview allows more extensive questioning than the telephone survey, but it is expensive. An example of a survey conducted by personal interview is the Current Population Survey, which is a monthly survey of about 60,000 households done by the Census Bureau for the Bureau of Labor Statistics. It is the basis for monthly estimates of population, labor force, employment, and unemployment.   ■

EXPERIMENTS

In simple observation and surveying, the discovery of characteristics of a process or a universe is emphasized. Observation and surveying are passive listening devices. Experiments, on the other hand, are active listening devices because with them we attempt to discern what *would be* true of a process or universe if it were changed. An **experiment** is the study of the effects of change in a limited environment that is, to some degree, under the control of the experimenter. Although experiments help explain the effects of changes, their results cannot always be immediately generalized to practical situations because the control exercised in the experiment may not be replicated in the real world.

Much research effort goes into conducting experiments in realistic settings to increase the practical value of the experiments. Experimenters distinguish between *laboratory experiments* in which they create the experimental environment and *field experiments* in which a real-world setting, such as a supermarket or an actual production process, provides the environment. Field experiments produce results more readily applicable to immediate problems, but they may be quite expensive to conduct and may not yield the level of control needed to isolate the effects of different experimental conditions. Designing a relevant and affordable experiment requires the experimenter's utmost ingenuity and intimate knowledge of the process under study.

In industrial experiments especially there is a heavy emphasis on experimentation to help create products that work under a wide variety of conditions. Such products are called "robust." As an example, consider the task of an automobile maker who wants to sell automobiles in the United States. The automobiles must be capable of functioning in a bewildering variety of climates and under an incredible variety of driving and care practices of their owners. It is not sufficient to make an automobile that runs only in the laboratory or on the test track!

Many people think experimentation takes place only in a laboratory setting, as is characteristic of "pure" sciences such as physics and chemistry. On the contrary, experimentation is a staple of practical science.

SECTION 1.7

DESIGNED AND OBSERVATIONAL STUDIES

In this section two terms that are crucial for the proper interpretation of statistical analyses are defined: designed study and observational study. The distinction between the two is whether randomization is used in collecting the data.

RANDOMIZATION

Randomization means actions that can be modelled by the mathematics of probability.

■**EXAMPLE 1.7A:** The simplest randomization device is an ordinary coin. If we place the coin on our thumb, flip it in the air, and let it fall to a table or the floor, we find that the coin falls either heads up or tails up. Call this activity a *trial*. It is an example of a process. A sequence of trials constitutes the evolution of the process. We find that in a large number of trials the coin tends to yield about 50% heads and 50% tails. Even though the outcome of a *particular* trial cannot be predicted with certainty, a collection of trials exhibits predictable behavior.

Exhibit 1.7A is a plot of the cumulative proportion of heads for 50 flips. The trials are numbered $1, 2, \ldots, 50$. At the first trial we get a tail (T), and the proportion of heads to date is $0/1 = 0$. At the second trial we get another tail (T), and the proportion of heads to date is $0/2 = 0$. At the third trial we get a head (H), and the proportion of heads to date is $1/3 = 0.3333$. Continuing this way we obtain the sequence of fractions plotted in the exhibit. The solid horizontal line in the middle of the plot marks the value 0.5.[†] For 50 or fewer trials the deviations of the cumulative proportions from 0.5 (which means 50% heads) can be quite large.

[†] The plot in Exhibit 1.7A is a sequence plot. Sequence plots, important statistical tools in the study of processes, are the topic of Chapter 2.

EXHIBIT 1.7A

Sequence Plot of
Cumulative Proportions
of Heads versus
Number of Flips
For 50 Flips of
an Ordinary Coin

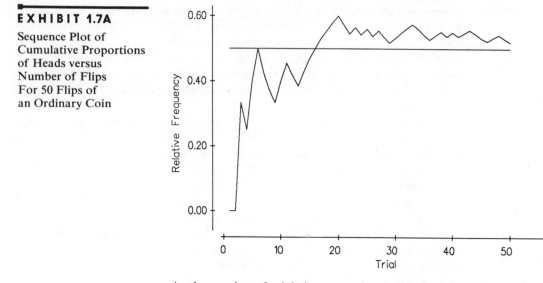

As the number of trials increases the cumulative proportion of heads tends to stabilize in the neighborhood of 0.5 (or 50%). The proportions vary from trial to trial, but the amount of deviation from 0.5 tends to decrease as the number of trials increases. Exhibit 1.7B shows the results of 200 trials; the tendency to decrease in the deviations from 0.5 is evident.

EXHIBIT 1.7B

Sequence Plot of
Cumulative Proportions
of Heads versus
Number of Flips
For 200 Flips of
an Ordinary Coin

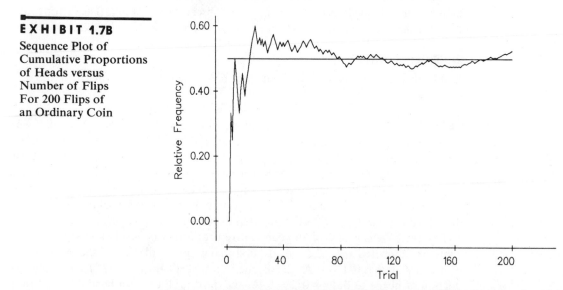

The variation exhibited by the coin in Example 1.7A is the type of variation that can be modelled by the mathematics of probability. If the variation in a ratio that is the proportion of occurrences of an event, such as the number of heads, divided by the number of trials tends to stabilize as the number of trials increases, then a "limiting value" of the ratio is hypothesized as the number of trials increases indefinitely, and this value is called the **probability** of the event.

More information about probability models is presented in Chapters 8, 10, 17, and 18. In this introductory treatment, only the intuitive notion of a limiting value of a ratio is used.

▪ **EXAMPLE 1.7B:** Consider a bowl containing 10 chips of identical physical makeup except that they are numbered $0, 1, \ldots, 9$. Let a trial be the thorough mixing of the chips and the random drawing of a chip. The outcome of the trial is the number on the chip. To perform a second trial, return the chip to the bowl, mix thoroughly, and draw a chip. This is the process of interest. Exhibit 1.7C is a table showing the outcomes of 1000 trials. Analysis shows that each of the digits $0, 1, 2, \ldots, 9$, accounts for about 10% of them. We can say that the probability of getting a 0 from a trial is 1/10, the probability of getting a 1 is 1/10, and so on. Each digit has the same probability of being drawn in a trial.

A table of equally likely digits, such as the one in Exhibit 1.7C, is called a **table of random digits**. The digits can be grouped to form random numbers with any desired number of digits. To illustrate, group the numbers in groups of three. Reading across the first row, the first five three-digit numbers are $219, 463, 955, 717$, and 244.

There are 1000 three-digit numbers: $000, 001, 002, \ldots, 999$. Were we to go through a very large table of random numbers and form the three-digit numbers, as just illustrated for the small table, we would find that each of the 1000 possible numbers accounts for about 1/1000 of the outcomes; that is, each of the possible three-digit numbers has probability 1/1000 of being formed in a table of random digits. The same argument applies to two- and four-digit numbers, in fact to numbers with any desired number of digits. ▪

DESIGNED STUDIES

In statistical studies the objects that are measured to produce data are called **elements**. A **designed study** is one in which the elements are chosen or assigned by a randomization device. The typical device is a table of random digits, such as the one in Exhibit 1.7C.

A **probability survey** is a designed study in which a sample of elements is chosen at random from the universe.

▪ **EXAMPLE 1.7C:** A professor has a class of 279 students. He wishes to select a random sample of 10 students. He plans to look up the cumulative grade point average of the 10 students selected.

To illustrate how the professor might proceed, refer to row 5 of the table of random digits in Exhibit 1.7C. Form groups of three-digit numbers until 10 numbers that fall between 000 and 278 are obtained. These 10 numbers will pick corresponding entries from the class roster. The first entry on the roster is numbered 000, the second 001, and so on. The last entry is numbered 278. This procedure will draw the 10 entries from the class roster so that each entry has the same chance of being drawn, namely 1/279. Ignoring the numbers 279 through 999 does not affect the equal probability property of the numbers 000 through 278.

EXHIBIT 1.7C

A Table of 1000
Random Digits

Row	1	2	3	4	5	6	7	8	9	10	11	12	13	14	15	16	17	18	19	20
1	2	1	9	4	6	3	9	5	5	7	1	7	2	4	4	6	7	1	7	8
2	9	5	5	6	6	0	3	0	7	3	5	5	7	0	8	4	2	8	9	6
3	2	5	2	3	2	0	0	4	5	3	1	4	8	1	3	7	7	6	4	0
4	3	9	4	4	3	8	5	4	3	9	0	2	8	4	6	4	9	7	7	6
5	6	4	0	9	4	6	8	0	5	5	7	6	1	1	9	8	1	5	4	1
6	1	3	7	3	8	1	9	9	8	7	5	8	0	3	7	0	1	4	2	1
7	0	3	0	9	9	6	9	1	2	1	4	7	4	7	5	5	2	3	1	9
8	9	7	8	2	2	1	1	6	7	6	0	9	7	8	0	1	2	5	2	1
9	9	9	3	6	1	3	3	9	7	6	8	5	9	1	2	4	9	7	0	1
10	7	5	0	3	6	8	9	5	4	9	9	4	6	5	0	4	9	7	4	9
11	7	8	5	7	1	7	9	3	7	1	1	7	1	9	1	5	7	8	1	1
12	4	2	6	8	1	1	8	7	6	0	5	6	7	1	2	1	9	8	3	4
13	0	0	7	5	9	4	1	8	6	4	4	0	6	6	8	4	0	9	7	8
14	0	4	6	0	5	3	8	7	9	0	7	1	0	2	4	7	4	7	5	7
15	0	4	0	1	8	0	6	8	8	7	5	5	1	2	1	5	8	7	7	4
16	5	4	8	5	3	4	1	9	1	5	0	1	9	5	3	0	3	3	9	1
17	0	5	4	8	7	9	0	4	9	9	0	0	5	0	8	8	1	4	0	3
18	6	2	4	8	9	9	0	2	2	5	0	1	6	0	8	7	7	6	4	0
19	0	1	8	4	2	2	3	5	9	2	5	7	8	0	6	1	9	4	9	0
20	8	9	8	2	4	1	0	0	9	6	8	9	5	4	3	9	1	4	9	6
21	4	9	8	1	1	9	0	6	0	6	9	9	7	3	7	0	4	2	7	2
22	2	9	4	1	8	2	9	9	3	3	8	2	8	3	5	0	3	5	4	3
23	5	3	4	1	0	3	2	0	4	1	2	5	3	5	3	5	5	8	5	2
24	9	6	4	5	4	4	6	0	9	7	9	8	5	5	2	5	2	6	1	4
25	3	4	1	5	1	3	0	2	1	3	3	1	2	9	4	8	9	8	2	8
26	7	7	2	9	6	2	4	6	3	2	1	3	6	7	3	9	4	1	6	7
27	5	3	9	2	7	8	2	6	7	6	6	9	1	5	9	2	5	4	4	3
28	6	7	7	8	7	7	8	1	0	4	1	7	0	6	4	3	6	8	0	6
29	6	4	6	0	6	0	2	3	3	0	6	7	3	5	0	7	3	9	8	7
30	0	7	2	6	5	9	1	7	4	2	2	7	9	2	9	5	2	9	5	0
31	1	3	7	8	4	5	2	4	2	6	7	3	2	9	9	3	5	1	6	4
32	1	8	5	6	6	3	7	7	0	0	1	9	2	6	1	4	2	1	0	9
33	0	7	6	5	0	3	8	2	6	0	1	0	4	4	0	1	1	4	9	7
34	7	1	7	3	2	6	6	4	5	0	6	2	6	6	9	3	6	8	8	4
35	1	0	5	9	9	6	7	7	6	3	5	1	3	3	7	4	4	0	6	1
36	9	9	6	7	7	2	8	3	9	8	8	0	1	8	8	8	0	2	1	2
37	5	3	4	9	7	9	2	9	2	9	9	1	1	1	5	3	5	0	6	5
38	0	4	6	6	8	5	2	9	3	5	2	9	2	0	0	7	3	1	3	6
39	6	9	8	4	0	3	4	2	8	2	8	0	9	1	7	3	0	8	9	6
40	3	0	3	0	5	0	7	8	0	9	1	3	0	7	8	6	8	6	0	8
41	9	5	1	2	8	1	8	2	6	3	9	9	0	1	0	7	7	2	3	3
42	5	3	2	2	2	4	0	0	3	9	6	8	9	1	7	4	2	7	6	8
43	2	1	6	1	3	3	1	6	5	7	7	3	5	1	7	4	5	7	3	8
44	5	7	1	4	4	7	1	2	9	1	8	5	9	9	7	7	9	8	7	9
45	9	0	0	5	4	6	3	6	1	5	0	0	4	8	3	5	9	5	3	2
46	0	5	0	0	0	2	1	9	2	3	0	1	0	2	8	6	6	3	6	7
47	0	2	4	1	1	5	0	2	5	5	7	7	8	2	2	9	0	4	0	9
48	4	0	1	7	9	7	7	3	0	2	0	7	0	0	1	2	3	2	2	6
49	1	6	0	8	0	7	8	6	6	6	6	5	2	7	1	1	8	2	1	7
50	5	9	9	9	5	0	7	4	7	1	1	5	4	6	3	5	9	7	5	6

The first three-digit number in line 5 of the table is 640. Because this number is greater than 278, ignore it and go on to the next number, which is 946. This too is ignored. The first usable three-digit number occurs in columns 13, 14, and 15 of row 5. It is 119. It chooses the name on the class roster coded as 119.

Continuing to the end of row 5, we end with columns 19 and 20. We move down to row 6 and use the number in column 1 to complete the three-digit number 411, which must be ignored. The next usable number, 142, occurs in columns 17, 18, and 19 of row 6. We continue through the table, finding the usable numbers 103, 99 (which looks like 099 in the table), 214, 221, 107, 125, 219, and 133. The last number is in columns 5, 6, and 7 of row 9.

Using this procedure it is possible for the table to yield the same three-digit number more than once. If this happens, the number is ignored the second and all subsequent times it comes up.

Now that the sample is drawn, the professor goes to the registrar's office and looks up the grade point averages of the students whose entries in the class roster have been chosen. He has drawn a random sample from the universe of students. The set of grade point averages of all the students in the universe is called the **population** of grade point averages. The sample of 10 grade point averages he looks up is a random sample from the population. ■

In an experiment the goal is to compare the impact of different treatments on the elements. A **treatment** is a set of conditions set up by the experimenter and applied to an element. A **designed experiment** is a designed study in which a randomization device is used to determine which treatment is applied to which elements.

■**EXAMPLE 1.7D:** The simplest experiment uses two treatments. Here is an example. A computer manufacturer maintains a staff of telephone order takers and wishes to evaluate the effectiveness of a program of process improvement training that has been designed for the staff by a consultant. The members of the staff are divided into two groups at random. One-third of the members are chosen at random to receive the program of training, which is to last six weeks. The rest of the staff members are to continue their activities as usual. After the training period, the manufacturer will collect data on the staff members' performance for three months. Several measures of productivity will be maintained, including speed with which telephone calls are answered, volume of sales, and customer satisfaction as determined by questionnaires filled out by the customers themselves. Data from the two groups will be compared for signs of substantial difference.

Because the two groups are chosen at random, the differences between them can be attributed to the training program. If instead staff members are allowed to volunteer or are chosen by management for the training program, the differences could be attributed to factors other than the training program. For example, volunteers might be exceptionally ambitious employees and have superior performance at the outset. Staff members chosen by management could be exceptionally good, or management might choose people who have poor records in hopes that the training would improve their performance. In the latter case, the benefits of the training program could be masked by the fact that more or less capable staff members receive the training. The randomization eliminates these possibilities and allows objective evaluation of the training program. ■

OBSERVATIONAL STUDIES

Observational studies are those in which randomization is not used to select elements for observation. Examples 1.6A through 1.6D all illustrated observational studies.

In some observational studies all available data are collected. In others samples are collected but randomization is not used, as illustrated in Example 1.6D. In Example 1.7D, if the staff members had not been divided into groups at random, the study would have been observational.

In practice, studies often have both designed and observational aspects. An example is a sequence of weekly opinion polls. Each week a probability survey, a designed study, is conducted and an estimate of public opinion formed. But the study of the sequence of polls to discern trends is observational. The study of the evolution of a process is necessarily observational, even when measurements are taken from the process using randomization.

If a process evolves in a stable fashion, however, the measurements taken from the process over time may be treated *as if* they were random. When this is possible the process is said to be in statistical control. This notion will be defined more precisely in Chapter 9. It forms the basis for a great deal of practical data analysis.

Another study common in practice is the **quasi-experimental design** study. In this study an experimental treatment, called an *intervention*, is applied to a process; then the behavior of the process before the intervention is compared to the behavior of the process after the intervention. Such studies are used, for example, to document the effects of actions intended to improve processes. They are also common in public policy studies. For example, the legislation that changed the speed limit on U.S. highways to 55 miles per hour appeared to result in decreases in deaths due to highway accidents. But the change in the speed limit coincided with large increases in gasoline prices due to the actions of OPEC. Motorists responded by driving less, which could have accounted for the decrease in deaths. This illustrates the weakness of quasi-experimental studies. It is not always possible to isolate the cause of an observed effect. For many problems, however, quasi-experimental studies are the only ones available.

SECTION 1.8

EXERCISES

1.8A Obtain an ordinary thumbtack. Toss the thumbtack in the air, let it fall to the table or floor, and determine whether it falls point up or point down. Let one repetition of this process be a trial. Perform 50 trials, keeping track of whether the tack falls point up or point down on each trial. Prepare a sequence plot like the one in Exhibit 1.7A for your data. What probability would you assign to the event "tack lands point up"? Do you feel you need more data to answer this question? How much more?

1.8B Obtain an ordinary die. Roll the die and determine the number of spots on the up face. Let one repetition of this process be a trial. Perform 360 trials, keeping track of the outcome on each trial. Prepare a sequence plot like the one in Exhibit 1.7A for the event "one spot on the up face." What probability would you assign to this event? Do you feel you need more data to answer this question? Why?

1.8C Obtain a record of the closing price of the Dow Jones 30 Industrials average for 61 consecutive days. The process of interest is the set of transactions that lead to the average. Define a trial as the determination of whether the average increased or decreased from one day to the next. Let the event of interest be "the average increased." The data you have collected allow you to perform 60 trials. Prepare a plot like the one in Exhibit 1.7A for your data. What probability would you assign to the event "the average increased"? Do you feel you need more data to answer this question? How much more?

You are offered two lotteries. The first one pays $1 if an ordinary coin is tossed and lands heads up. The second one pays $1 if the Dow Jones 30 Industrials average increases tomorrow. Which lottery offers you a better chance of winning $1? Why?

1.8D Obtain an ordinary coin. Hold the coin on its edge on a table with the index finger of one hand. With the index finger of the other hand, flick the coin so it spins. Record whether the coin comes to rest heads up or tails up. Let one repetition of this process be a trial. Perform 60 trials, keeping track of whether the coin lands heads up or tails up on each trial. Prepare a sequence plot like the one in Exhibit 1.7A for the event "heads up." What probability would you assign to the event "heads up"? Do you feel that 1/2 is a reasonable probability? Do you feel you need more data to answer this question? How much more?

1.8E Here are the names of 20 people in a department.

John	Norman
Bob M.	Jed
Kam	Zack
Bob W.	Gouri
Probal	Dave
George	Mary
Murray	Candy
Doug	Gloria
Wei-Yin	Mary Ann
Richard	Alice

A committee of five people is to be formed to discuss the adoption of rules for flexible work schedules. Use the table of random digits in Exhibit 1.7C to select a committee. The last five names in the list above are women. How many women are included in your sample? Is it possible to select a committee at random that has all women? Is it possible to select a committee at random that has all men? Mathematics can be used to show that it is possible to form 15,504 different committees. If a committee is formed at random, then each possible committee has the same probability as any other of being chosen. What, therefore, is the probability of selecting a committee of five women?

1.8F Reconsider the setup in Exercise 1.8E. Suppose it has been decided that the committee should consist of exactly 4 men and 1 woman. To accomplish this, 4 men will be selected at random from the group of 15 men, and 1 woman will be selected at random from the group of 5 women. Use the table of random digits in Exhibit 1.7C to select such a sample. In sampling work, this is called a *stratified sample*. The men form a stratum and the women form a stratum. A random sample is selected from each stratum. This guarantees that each stratum will contribute a predetermined number of elements to the sample. Mathematics can be used to show that there are 6825 possible stratified samples with 4 men and 1 woman. Stratification reduces the number of samples from the number possible in Exercise 1.8E. Identify at least two samples that are possible in Exercise 1.8E that are not possible in this exercise.

1.8G On Friday, September 25, 1987, the *Wisconsin State Journal* carried a story with the headline "People-meters add perspective to ratings" in section 4, page 6. Here are some excerpts from the article:

The people-meter is a new, hand-held device that viewers punch in on when they watch TV. The device, according to Nielsen, will provide more accurate and more detailed information about the age and sex of viewers. Nielsen switched to the new people-meter device as of last week.

CBS's "Wiseguy," a male-oriented crime drama, was 21st in the overall audience rankings, but it was a top-10 show, at seventh, among men [aged] 18–49.

NBC's "St. Elsewhere" was a top-10 show among women [aged] 18–49, who placed it eighth. With overall audiences, it was 16th overall, and 21st with males [aged] 18–49.

Grouping TV watchers by age and gender is an example of stratification. Why was stratification necessary in this application?

1.8H The department studying flexible work hours in Exercise 1.8E is to be divided into two groups, one to receive a long questionnaire and the other to receive a short questionnaire. The long-form group is to contain 7 people, the short-form group 13.
(a) Why is this an experiment?
(b) What has to be done to make it a designed experiment?
(c) Use a table of random digits to select the two experimental groups.

1.8I A professor wants to evaluate class performance on two different tests over the same material. He divides the class into two equal groups. The groups take the exams in different rooms.
(a) Why is this an experiment?
(b) What must be done to make it a designed experiment? Would it be sufficient for the professor to form the groups by taking the students with last names in the top half of the alphabet as one group? Why?

1.8J Look up and read Toshio Sugiman and Jyuji Misumi, "Development of a New Evacuation Method for Emergencies: Control of Collective Behavior by Emergent Small Groups," *Journal of Applied Psychology* 73(1) (1988): 3–10. Explain the experimental plans used in the reported study. What treatments were applied? Discuss some of the limitations of the study. Explain the concept of an emergent small group. What additional studies would you like to see done to test the authors' conclusions?

S E C T I O N 1.9

OUTLINE OF THE BOOK

This book is divided into three major segments. The first is on the analysis and modelling of observational data; the second on the analysis and modelling of designed data; the third on the organizational context of statistics. The first segment is divided into two parts. Part 1, Chapters 1–7, is a survey of statistical methods for collecting and reporting data. In this first part ideas and tools that play a role in virtually all applications of statistics are emphasized. By way of example the concept of variation and how statistical tools document the nature and sources of variation are discussed.

Part 2, Chapters 8–11, presents two basic classes of models for variation: normal distributions and binomial distributions. These models underlie many statistical applications, one of the most important of which is the construction of process control charts. Chapter 8, on normal distribution theory, is followed by a presentation of standard deviation and mean control charts in Chapter 9. Chapter 10, on binomial distribution theory, is followed by a presentation of proportion control charts. The applications chapters help put the theory in Chapters 8 and 10 into a practical context. The control charts are especially useful examples because they illustrate the role of prediction in process improvement.

The second segment is divided into three parts. Part 3, Chapters 12–16, is an extensive unit on data collection, with emphasis on designed methods. Chapter 12 introduces the subject, while Chapters 13–16 provide a substantial tutorial on surveys.

Accurate information can be elicited from complex processes with surveys, but the methods require both delicate statistical theory and painstaking management to achieve success. Although the presentation in Chapters 13–16 is elementary, such thorny issues as coverage error, nonresponse, auditing fieldwork, interviewer bias, and sampling design are addressed. Because surveys are a major source of information, Chapter 15 devotes considerable attention to reading results published by a professional survey outfit. Even for someone who never conducts a survey, the material in Chapters 13–16 is essential to intelligent consumption of survey results.

Part 4, Chapters 17–19, forms a bridge between the less technical chapters in Parts 1–3 and the more technical chapters in Part 5. Using the techniques of simulation and mathematical modelling, we offer the reader a deeper understanding of process and sampling variation than was possible in the earlier chapters. This part culminates in a discussion of the concept of significance testing, which plays a role in the model-building material that follows.

In Part 5 two tools that are needed for more advanced applications are presented: regression analysis and time series analysis. We have chosen to concentrate on these tools because they are the most valuable for those who need to work at a more advanced level.

The last segment of the book offers a perspective on the use of statistics in organizations. While statistics has many uses in everyday life and in scientific labs and fieldwork, it also is part of the language of organizations, especially now that we live in the "information age," and some thinkers believe organizations will be centered increasingly on the processing of information.[†] In Chapter 25 some statistical tools that have proven valuable in identifying, formulating and solving problems in organizations are presented. They are quite elementary, more so than many of the tools presented in other chapters. Experience supports the notion that widespread application of these simple tools leads to substantial improvements in processes. In the case of business and industrial firms, these improvements are associated with increased profits and dividends. In the case of not-for-profit organizations, such as government agencies, most hospitals, and the like, the improvements are associated with increased quality and levels of services even as budgets tighten. While it has not been the custom for introductory statistics books to introduce the simple tools presented in Chapter 25 or to discuss organizational issues, we include both because of the impact they have had in improving organizations of all types in many countries. Chapter 25 could be read after Chapter 6 or any time later. It is placed at the end of the book because of its nontraditional flavor. We believe that for many readers it is the most important chapter in the book.

[†] See, for example, Peter F. Drucker, "The Coming of the New Organization," *Harvard Business Review* (January/February 1988): 45–53.

You will need statistical tools not discussed in this book for specific applications, especially multivariate techniques, advanced time series analysis, and econometric methods. A mastery of the material in this book will give you a good foundation for learning these additional tools. We believe, though, that the material in Chapters 1–15 and 25 is a truly essential foundation. It is there that we attempt to sharpen your ability to think statistically, and we believe that your ability to think this way will pay handsome dividends.

SECTION 1.10

ON USING COMPUTERS

By vastly increasing the speed with which enormous quantities of data can be stored and retrieved, the speed with which complicated computations can be performed, and the sophistication with which information can be displayed, computers have changed how we think and act. Not only does the computer increase our ability to communicate, it also places that ability in the hands of more people through the miracle of miniature chips. You can place on your desk a small, inexpensive computer that outperforms the large, expensive computers available just a few years ago. And you can fairly quickly learn to use an array of software packages that let you take advantage of the products of decades of painstaking research and development.

The impact of the computer revolution pervades the field of statistics, which is the study of the collection, analysis, and presentation of data. In view of this, we believe that today's textbooks on statistics must reflect the essential role of computers in statistical applications. We have chosen to do this by using statistical software throughout the text.

We do not teach you how to use any particular software package, however. The exhibits we display can be made by many packages, but to teach the mechanics of a particular package is to limit access to the statistical material that is our primary subject. The package we use most is Minitab®.[†] We also show output from other popular packages, such as SAS, MYSTAT, StatGraphics, Stata, and SPSS.

To use this book most effectively you will need to be familiar with a computing system, to have access to a statistical software package and a word processor or editor. We encourage you throughout the text to use the computer to gain insights that can hardly be achieved from reading alone or from working problems by hand. As you examine computer output you will find occasions for doing some hand calculation and even more occasions for doing some hard thinking. The computer does not do the thinking for us!

[†] Minitab is distributed by Minitab, Inc., 3081 Enterprise Drive, State College, Pennsylvania 16801. It is an interactive system that runs on computers of all sizes: micro, mini, and mainframe. Minitab was designed as a teaching language, so it has many pedagogical advantages, but it has many advanced capabilities also. Some Minitab commands in footnotes and some computer output from other statistical systems are included.

SUPPLEMENTARY EXERCISES FOR CHAPTER 1

1A The process of interest is dealing a five-card hand from a well-shuffled standard deck of 52 cards. The event of interest is a hand with exactly one face card (jack, queen, or king of any suit). Repeat the process 100 times, keeping track of whether the hand does or does not contain exactly one face card. Use your data to construct a sequence plot like the one in Exhibit 1.7A. What probability would you assign to the event?

1B **(a)** Use a table of random digits to select a sample of 10 people from your class. How many of them are men? Measure the heights of the people in your sample and average the resulting numbers.

   (b) Repeat part (a) four more times. On the basis of your data, what is your best guess at the average height of all the members of the class?

   (c) Have all the members of the class report their heights. Average the numbers and compare the average with the guess you came up with in part (b).

1C **(a)** Divide your class into two groups: men and women. Use a table of random digits to draw a stratified sample consisting of five men and five women. Refer to Exercise 1.8F for the definition of stratified random sample. Average the five men's heights. Average the five women's heights. Average all 10 of the heights.

   (b) Repeat part (a) four more times. On the basis of your data, what is your best guess at the average height of the men in your class? The average height of the women in your class? The average height of all the people in your class? Is the average of the 10 people in a stratified sample the best estimate of the average height of all the people in the class? If not, suggest a better estimate.

   (c) Ask all the members of the class to report their height and their gender. Average the men's heights and the women's heights and compare them with the guesses you came up with in part (b). Average all the people's heights and compare the average you came up with in part (b).

GLOSSARY FOR CHAPTER 1

Designed experiment A designed study in which a randomization device is used to determine which treatment is applied to which elements.

Designed study A study in which the elements are chosen or assigned by a randomization device.

Element An object that is measured in a statistical study.

Experiment The study of the effects of change in an environment that is, to some degree, under the control of the experimenter.

Observational study A study in which randomization is not used to select elements for observation.

PDCA Plan, Do, Check, Act. The steps in Deming's wheel taken over and over again to bring about improvement in processes.

Population The set of all measurements associated with a universe of elements.

Probability The hypothesized limiting value of the proportion of occurrences of an event in a large number of repetitions of a process that may yield the event.

Probability survey   A designed study in which a sample of elements is chosen at random from a larger collection of elements called a universe.

Process   A sequence of steps taken to achieve a goal or outcome.

Process analysis   Activities undertaken to understand and model the steps in a process and the relationships among the steps.

Process control   Activities undertaken to keep process outcomes as close as possible to a predetermined target or to effect an improvement in the performance of the process.

Quasi-experimental design   An intervention is applied to a process; then the behavior of the process before the intervention is compared to the behavior of the process after the intervention.

Randomization   Actions that can be modelled by the mathematics of probability.

Sample   A collection of elements drawn from a universe.

Simple observation   Observation of every outcome from a process or outcomes taken systematically at predetermined instants.

Survey   A data-collection tool in which a sample of elements is selected from a universe of elements for measurement.

Table of random digits   A table of the digits $0, 1, \ldots, 9$ constructed so that each of the digits has an equal chance of occurring in any location in the table.

Treatment   A set of conditions set up by an experimenter and applied to an element.

Universe   The collection of all elements that might be drawn into a sample for a survey.

## CHAPTER 2

Plotting Process Data

KNOWLEDGE THROUGH DATA

We seldom have complete knowledge of a process, nor can we expect to exercise complete control over every step in a process. Fortunately, most processes can be managed by exercising control at just a few critical steps. A key ingredient in managing and improving business and industrial processes is to stay in touch with the critical steps by collecting relevant measurements. Such measurements are called *data*.

Ideally data are collected systematically over a long period of time from the truly critical steps of the process. Studies of the evolution of a process over time are called **longitudinal**. More precisely, a longitudinal study consists of

- collection of measurements from a process over time
- comparison of measurements from different time periods
- documentation of variation over time
- evaluation of changes in behavior of the process.

By thinking longitudinally, we focus on those aspects of the process most important for decision making. By limiting our attention to the points that make the most difference, we work at peak efficiency, avoiding wasted effort.

A basic tool in studying the longitudinal aspects of a process is the sequence plot.

SEQUENCE PLOTS

Sequence plots are the basic tools for showing the evolution of a measured characteristic of a process. A **sequence plot** is a simple graph with time displayed on the horizontal axis and the corresponding quantity or quantities from the process displayed on the vertical axis.

ANALYSIS OF PHOTOCOPY DATA

Exhibit 2.2A shows a hand-drawn sequence plot of the photocopy counts that were given in Exhibit 1.3A. The vertical height of the dots represents the counts, and the horizontal positioning indicates time. The dots are joined by lines to reinforce the presentation of the passage of time. The letters M, T, W, R, and F code the days of the week. (R is the symbol for Thursday.)

EXHIBIT 2.2A

Hand-Drawn Sequence Plot of Photocopy Data

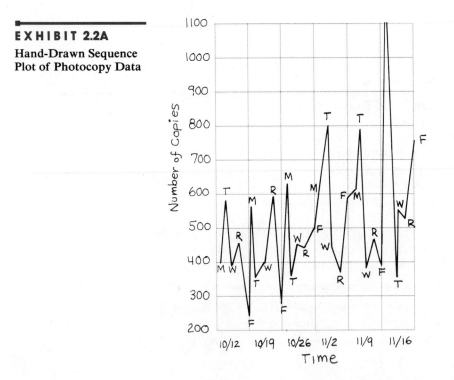

The sequence plot displays a process with a great deal of variation. On two days, fewer than 300 copies were made; on two other days almost 800 were made. Most of the numbers are between 300 and 650, but one day does not even fit on the graph. On this one day, November 16, an exception was made to allow students taking their master's degree oral examination to exceed the normal limit of 25 copies per job on the machine. This was done to accommodate the preparation of last-minute handouts for their exam.

Another exception to the 25-copy rule is the preparation of manuscripts to send to a central copy center for mass production. The office staff is authorized to exceed the limit in this case to minimize the time they must spend away from their workstations. Manuscripts are processed at irregular intervals, and this contributes to the variability and unpredictability in the photocopy process.

After looking at the sequence plot, we have a rough idea of how the process is likely to evolve. On most days the number of copies will be between 300 and 650, but occasionally such unpredictable events as manuscript preparation and other special exceptions may cause the number to be substantially greater than 650. If the machine is down for repairs, if the office closes for part of a day, or if many department members are out of town to attend a conference, then the number of copies can be below 300.

The data presented here are all that had been collected at the time of writing, but even they are useful for forming a tentative impression about the future of the process. Our impression of the process will be modified as we collect more data, but already we see one of the main functions of collecting data: *predicting future behavior.*

Making predictions allows us to look for changes in future behavior. Suppose, for example, that in the photocopy example, data collected for the first two weeks of December show that on most days the number of copies falls between 500 and 800. This would be a marked shift upward relative to the behavior observed in October and November. We would certainly look for reasons for the shift. The reason might be a sharp increase in the number of manuscripts being processed, or it might be that department members are reproducing their holiday letters on the machine, an unauthorized use! This illustrates another function of collecting data: *detecting changes in a process.*

A sequence plot such as the one in Exhibit 2.2A is posted above the copy machine, and it is updated every day. This allows the users of the machine to see the effects of their copying activity. If a major shift occurs, attention is called to it and reasons for the shift explained. The visual reporting of the data makes communication very easy. The data collected from the machine are also used as a basis for reporting department activity to the operations committee. We see yet another function of collecting data: *sharing information* (communication).

ANALYSIS OF GNP DATA

Exhibit 2.2B is a hand-drawn sequence plot of the GNP data in Exhibit 1.3B. The symbols I, II, III, and IV denote the quarters of the year. GNP figures from many years are available, and the long historical record provides a proper context for studying the behavior of GNP. The short series of figures in Exhibit 2.2B is presented for illustrative purposes only.

EXHIBIT 2.2B

Hand-Drawn Sequence
Plot of GNP Data

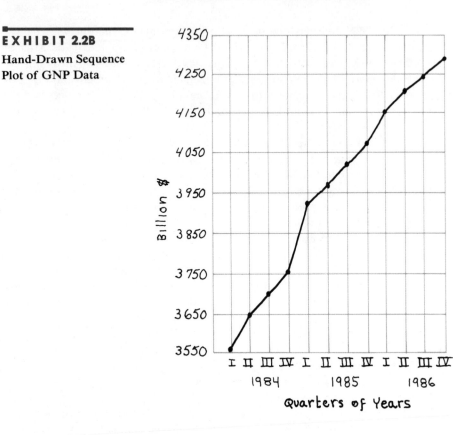

An obvious feature in the plot is the upward trend. The years 1984–1986 are a period of growth in the GNP. Notice, however, that the amount by which GNP grows varies from quarter to quarter. The largest change occurs between quarter IV of 1984 and quarter I of 1985, an increase of $158.8 billion. The smallest change occurs between quarters III and IV of 1986, an increase of only $18 billion.

Exhibit 2.2C gives a table of the twelve quarterly GNP figures from Exhibit 1.3B and the eleven quarterly *changes* that may be computed from them. Exhibit 2.2D shows sequence plots of both the original GNP figures and the changes. The plot of the changes is on a different scale from the original figures, easing the comparison of magnitudes.

The sequence plot of the original GNP figures in Exhibit 2.2B tempts us to predict that GNP will rise in future quarters, as GNP has done historically. The sequence plot of the changes in GNP suggests that the amount of growth from quarter to quarter is quite variable. Eight of the eleven changes fall between $30 billion and $110 billion. The two smallest changes are $18 billion and $26.4 billion, and the largest change is $158.8 billion. We feel uneasy about making predictions on the basis of so few observations. We would want to analyze a larger slice of the process before making predictions. (See Exercise 2.3A.)

The sequence plot is an ideal tool for displaying process data. It emphasizes the time dimension and provides a basis for making useful predictions about the evo-

EXHIBIT 2.2C

Quarterly U.S. GNP, 1984–1986, and the Quarterly Changes (in billions of current dollars)

Year	Quarter	GNP	Quarterly Change
1984	I	3553.3	*†
1984	II	3644.7	91.4
1984	III	3694.6	49.9
1984	IV	3758.7	64.1
1985	I	3917.5	158.8
1985	II	3960.6	43.1
1985	III	4016.9	56.3
1985	IV	4059.3	42.4
1986	I	4149.2	89.9
1986	II	4175.6	26.4
1986	III	4240.7	65.1
1986	IV	4258.7	18.0

† This change cannot be computed without knowledge of GNP in quarter IV of 1983.

EXHIBIT 2.2D

Hand-Drawn Sequence Plot of GNP Data and Changes

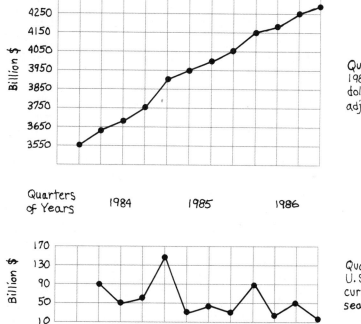

Quarterly U.S. GNP, 1984–1986, current dollar, seasonally adjusted

Quarterly changes in U.S. GNP, 1984–1986, current dollar, seasonally adjusted

lution of a process. It can be displayed in the workplace to promote communication, and it can also form the basis for higher-level reporting. The sequence plot is constructed from data collected regularly from an ongoing process and thus emphasizes the need to collect data carefully and faithfully. Despite its simplicity, the sequence plot is a fundamental statistical tool.

EXERCISES

2.3A Consult various issues of the *Survey of Current Business* and collect quarterly GNP figures for at least 10 years. Make a table showing the original GNP figures and the quarter-to-quarter changes. Plot both sequences in a plot like Exhibit 2.2D. What sorts of predictions are you willing to make about the future of the GNP process? As time passes, collect GNP data and compare them with the predictions you have made.

2.3B Collect the most recent 50 to 100 consecutive balances from your checkbook. Make a table showing the balances and the balance-to-balance changes. Plot both sequences in a plot like Exhibit 2.2D. What predictions are you willing to make about the future of your checkbook balances? Can you explain some of the large changes? Can you anticipate some of the large changes that will occur? (If this exercise is to be handed in, you may wish to add a constant such as $100 to all your data to protect the anonymity of your personal finances!)

An alternative data-collection scheme is to record the balance in the checkbook at the end of each day. Or the number of transactions made each day could be recorded. Try this scheme and make sequence plots of the end-of-day balances and the numbers of checks written. Compare these plots with the ones based on consecutive balances.

2.3C If you work in an office that keeps a log of photocopies, obtain a record of the number of copies for 200 to 300 consecutive jobs. Make a sequence plot of these figures. Can you give a reason for the highest and lowest figures? What predictions are you willing to make about the future of the process?

2.3D Collect a sequence of data from any process that interests you. Make a sequence plot and try to predict the future of the process. Collect new data from the process and compare it with your predictions.

2.3E Describe a simple repetitive process that is part of your daily personal life. Examples are driving a car, getting a child ready for nursery school, preparing breakfast, shooting baskets, jogging, and so on. What quantities could be measured to help describe aspects of the process?

2.3F Describe a repetitive process that is part of your school or workplace life. What quantities could be measured to help describe aspects of that process?

2.3G Describe a process where the results have *no variability*! Would there be any interest in studying such a process?

COMPUTER-ASSISTED SEQUENCE PLOTS

Hand-drawn sequence or time series plots were introduced in Section 2.2 as one means of displaying process data in a meaningful way. However, especially with large data sets, the plots are tedious to produce and manipulate. An interactive computer data analysis system (such as Minitab) allows us to do the plotting and to look at different aspects of process data with ease. Exhibits 2.4A and 2.4B display computer-produced plots corresponding to the hand-drawn Exhibits 2.2A and 2.2B.

Time series or process data often have an associated **period**, that is, a time span at which a sequence *may* tend to repeat its general behavior. For example, the photocopy data are collected for weekdays and, as such, the same day of the week repeats with a period of five days. The GNP series is measured quarterly and so has

EXHIBIT 2.4A

Computer Sequence Plot of Photocopy Process Data

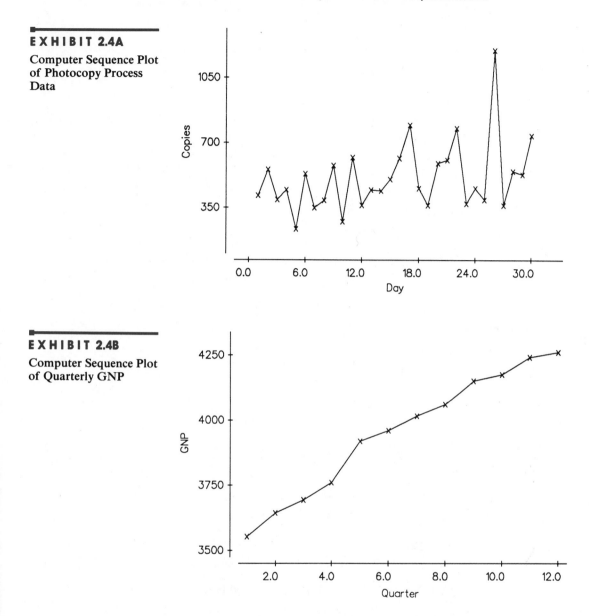

EXHIBIT 2.4B

Computer Sequence Plot of Quarterly GNP

an associated period of four measurements per year. If the same plotting symbol is used for the same day of the week, same quarter of the year, same month, and so on, process values that may be of interest can be easily compared. Do Monday counts tend to behave differently than Wednesday or Friday counts? Do fourth-quarter GNP values look any different from GNP values for other quarters? Exhibits 2.4C and 2.4D display the sequence plots corresponding to Exhibits 2.4A and 2.4B but with the period properly specified. In Exhibit 2.4C all Mondays are plotted as A's, Tuesdays as B's, and so forth. With monthly data the plotting symbols used are A, B, C, D, E, F, G, H, I, J, K, and L.

E X H I B I T 2.4C

**Sequence Plot of
Photocopy Data with
Period 5**

E X H I B I T 2.4D

**GNP Sequence Plot with
Period 4**

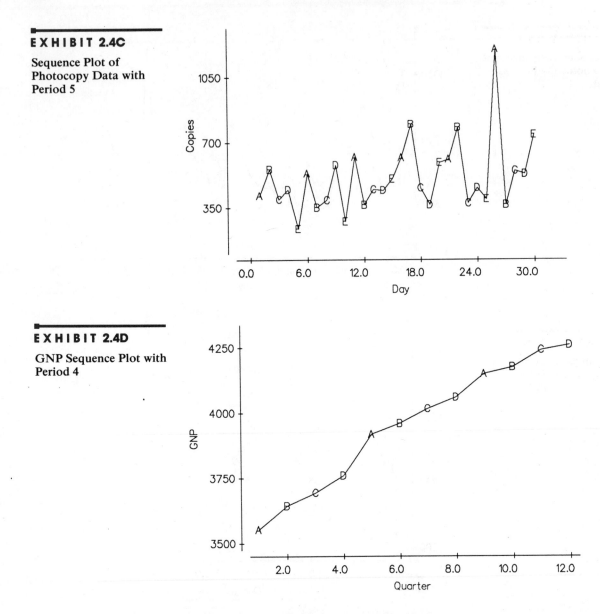

No particular day-of-the-week effect is evident in Exhibit 2.4C. However, Exhibit 2.4D seems to suggest that GNP jumps from the end of one year to the beginning of the next year—fourth quarter to first quarter. Of course, a longer record of GNP should be checked for similar patterns before such a conclusion could be drawn. For longer series, computer plotting is indispensable.

ANOTHER EXAMPLE: CHECKBOOK BALANCES

The top part of Exhibit 2.4E shows 120 consecutive balances recorded in a checkbook, and Exhibit 2.4F is a sequence plot of the balances. The high balances occur at the beginnings of months, when a paycheck is deposited. Then the balances rapidly decrease because a large number of bills are paid. Then follows a period of routine daily transactions, which may result in negative balances toward the end of the month. Small deposits may result to try to eliminate the negative balances. The sequence plot in Exhibit 2.4F shows two such cycles and the beginning of a third. Here we see a rather predictable pattern that recurs monthly.

EXHIBIT 2.4E

Checkbook Balances (top) and Balance-to-Balance Changes (bottom)

(Read across, row by row)
Balances

4847	4304	4029	3629	3191	3097	3076	2876	2845	2641
2627	2572	2290	760	650	630	599	561	477	454
409	373	338	331	-594	-597	-618	-705	-715	-738
635	617	609	604	590	534	529	432	426	421
289	261	241	323	225	214	122	120	116	401
376	382	356	345	343	318	198	183	75	63
4315	3772	3472	3035	2634	2570	2536	2497	2475	1923
1643	1588	1557	1519	1512	1494	1466	1066	1026	942
832	872	831	810	790	774	773	699	677	669
667	566	496	646	412	404	356	252	253	248
246	235	226	212	159	148	19	-3	-7	-14
-104	-111	-120	19	4262	3719	3688	3388	2951	2550

Changes

*	-543	-275	-400	-438	-94	-21	-200	-31	-204
-14	-55	-282	-1530	-110	-20	-31	-38	-84	-23
-45	-36	-35	-7	-925	-3	-21	-87	-10	-23
1373	-18	-8	-5	-14	-56	-5	-97	-6	-5
-132	-28	-20	82	-98	-11	-92	-2	-4	285
-25	6	-26	-11	-2	-25	-120	-15	-108	-12
4252	-543	-300	-437	-401	-64	-34	-39	-22	-552
-280	-55	-31	-38	-7	-18	-28	-400	-40	-84
-110	40	-41	-21	-20	-16	-1	-74	-22	-8
-2	-101	-70	150	-234	-8	-48	-104	1	-5
-2	-11	-9	-14	-53	-11	-129	-22	-4	-7
-90	-7	-9	139	4243	-543	-31	-300	-437	-401

Source: Confidential

EXHIBIT 2.4F

Sequence Plot of 120 Checkbook Balances

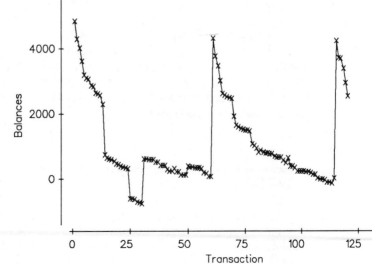

Many transactions may take place on a single day, so the transaction, not calendar time, is the unit on the horizontal axis. If you wanted to use days as the time units, you could record, for example, the number of transactions in a day and the balance in the checkbook after the last transaction of the day. This would be analogous to recording trading volume and closing price for a stock on a stock exchange. The sequence plot of such data would present quite a different appearance than the one in Exhibit 2.4F.

The bottom part of Exhibit 2.4E shows the balance-to-balance changes, which are the amounts of the transactions recorded in the checkbook. A deposit yields a positive change, and writing a check yields a negative change. Exhibit 2.4G shows the sequence plot of the changes. The major changes occur at the beginnings of months.

EXHIBIT 2.4G

Sequence Plot of 119
Balance-to-Balance
Changes

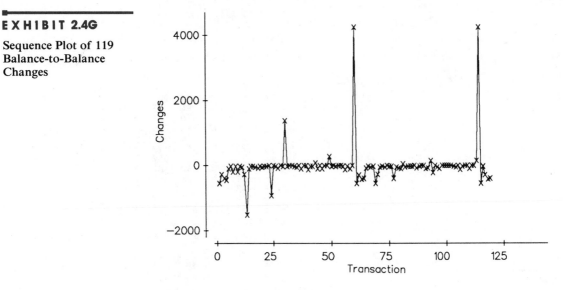

In the analysis of financial data, you will often encounter the types of sequence plots shown in Exhibits 2.2D, 2.4F, and 2.4G. The balances are called **levels** of the measured variable, which are the actual values of a sequence where the first differences or changes may be of primary interest. The changes from one data value to the next are called **first differences**. Plots of levels and first differences often yield useful insights into such processes.

SECTION 2.5

EXERCISES

2.5A The data below give 81 consecutive values for the amount of deviation (in 0.000025-inch units) from a specified target value that an industrial machining process at Deere & Co. produced under certain specified operating conditions. In this data 0 means that the value was right on target, and −3 means that the part produced measured 0.000075 inches below the target value. Plot the second line of values (beginning with −2 and ending with 2) by hand in a sequence plot. Repeat the sequence plot using all the values and a computer software package. Describe both the plots in words. Are there any unusual values that seem to be out of line with the rest of the values?

```
# filename: DEERE1.DAT
# Deere & Co. machining data, n=81
# (Source: Jerri Matchinsky, M.S. thesis,
# University of Iowa, 1988.)
# Coded in 0.000025 inch deviations from target
# (Read across, row by row)
   3  0 -1 -4  7  3  7  3  3 -1 -1  5 -4  1 -3  2 -3  1 -2 -3 -4
  -2  3  3  3  3 30  2  7 -7  3  2  3  0  3  0  3 -1  3  3  3  2
   3  3 -1  3  3  2  3  2  3  8  0 -1  0  0  1  2  2  0  8  0  1
  -2 -3  4  0  4 -1 -1  1 -7  3  1  3  1  0 -1 -4 -1 -1  3
```

2.5B The data file below gives the average hourly wage ($\times 100$) for U.S. workers in the manufacturing industries by month over the period from July 1981 to June 1987. Create a sequence plot of the data over the six-year period. Describe the plot. Form the month-to-month difference sequence. Plot the differences in a sequence plot. Are there any striking features of this plot?

```
# filename: MANWAGES.DAT
# Average hourly earnings per worker (X100)
# Manufacturing excluding overtime
# (Source: Survey of Current Business, September issues, 1981-1987)
# July 1981 through June 1987
# Jul Aug Sep Oct Nov Dec Jan Feb Mar Apr May Jun
  775 774 787 789 794 800 817 810 813 819 822 825 # 1981-1982
  831 826 833 831 836 842 846 850 847 848 849 849 # 1982-1983
  853 844 852 854 861 867 872 870 873 875 876 877 # 1983-1984
  883 878 885 887 893 900 907 907 909 913 913 913 # 1984-1985
  919 912 916 917 923 931 931 933 933 933 934 932 # 1985-1986
  935 927 931 932 937 942 944 944 944 948 945 944 # 1986-1987
```

2.5C The data file below gives the average hourly wage ($\times 100$) for workers in the apparel and other textile products industries. The data are given by month over the period from July 1981 to June 1987. Create a sequence plot of the data over the six-year period. Describe the plot. Form the month-to-month difference sequence. Plot the differences in a sequence plot. Are there any striking features of this plot?

```
# filename: APAWAGES.DAT
# Hourly wages (X100), apparel and other textile products
# (Source: Survey of Current Business, September issues, 1981-1987)
# July 1981 through June 1987
# Jul Aug Sep Oct Nov Dec Jan Feb Mar Apr May Jun
  492 496 504 505 504 504 518 513 515 518 516 518 # 1981-1982
  519 520 523 521 524 528 533 533 533 535 533 536 # 1982-1983
  535 535 539 540 543 544 550 546 548 549 548 550 # 1983-1984
  553 555 563 561 568 573 570 573 574 569 570 # 1984-1985
  570 569 575 574 575 580 582 579 580 581 578 579 # 1985-1986
  579 583 591 587 587 590 594 593 593 594 589 591 # 1986-1987
```

MONTHLY SALES DATA AND SEASONALITY

Exhibit 2.6A lists a set of sales data obtained from Deere & Co., a major worldwide manufacturer of John Deere tractors, other farm and construction machinery, and consumer products such as garden tractors and snowblowers. The data give monthly sales of a particular low-cost (approximately $10 in 1987) replacement oil filter from the manufacturer to John Deere dealers.[†] The series covers 48 months beginning in July 1983 and ending in June 1987. Exhibit 2.6B gives the sequence plot of these data. Notice that the plotting symbols have been selected to indicate the month of each observation. Since the first observation was taken in July, the first observation is plotted with a G. This makes it easy to keep track of actual monthly values and consider their patterns, if any. From the plot we see that higher sales tend to occur in January and February, months A and B, and lower sales occur in July through December, months G through L. Peak sales of 5862 units occurred in January of 1984, and December 1987 produced the lowest number of sales—1586 units. The oil-filter data exhibit **seasonality**, that is, there is a pattern that tends to repeat itself according to the period of the series. Another way to look at the sales data to see the seasonality is to plot sales versus month of the year, that is, plot all January values above the same horizontal position, all February values above a second horizontal position, and so forth. Exhibit 2.6C gives such a display. Here on the horizontal axis January = 1, February = 2, and so on.

EXHIBIT 2.6A

Wholesale Oil-Filter
Sales, Deere &
Company, Inc.

```
# filename: OILFILT.DAT
# Deere & Co. oil filter sales to dealers ($10 part)
# (Source: William Fullkerson, Deere & Co.,
# Technical Center, Moline, Illinois.)
# July 1983 through June 1987, n=48
# Jul  Aug  Sep  Oct  Nov  Dec  Jan  Feb  Mar  Apr  May  Jun
  2385 3302 3958 3302 2441 3107 5862 4536 4625 4492 4486 4005 # 1983-1984
  3744 2546 1954 2285 1778 3222 5472 5310 1965 3791 3622 3726 # 1984-1985
  3370 2535 1572 2146 2249 1721 5357 5811 2436 4608 2871 3349 # 1985-1986
  2909 2324 1603 2148 2245 1586 5332 5787 2886 5475 3843 2537 # 1986-1987
```

EXHIBIT 2.6B

Sequence Plot of Oil-
Filter Sales to Dealers

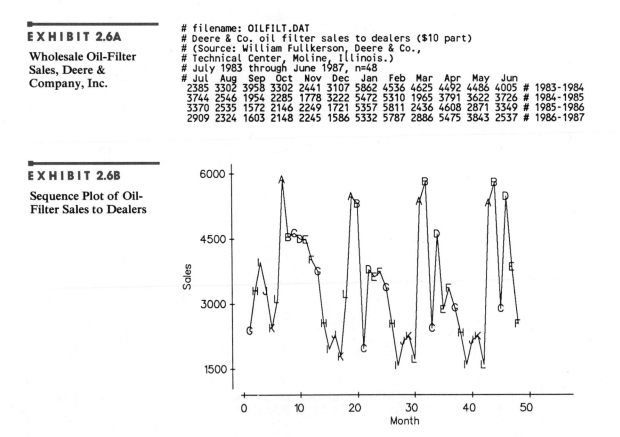

[†] Data courtesy of William F. Fulkerson, Deere & Co. Technical Center, Moline, Illinois.

EXHIBIT 2.6C

Plot of Sales versus
Month

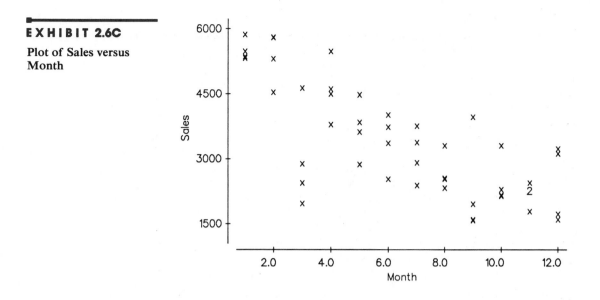

From this plot we again see that sales are nearly always higher in January and
February than later in the year. We also see an unusual drop in sales in March
relative to the other months for three of the four years. September and March
sales show substantial variability relative to other months. Note, however, that
Exhibit 2.6C does not provide information concerning which years produced which
values. Exhibit 2.6D displays the same sales information but by year rather than
by month. Note that the first and last year contain only 6 observations each, whereas the other years contain a full 12 observations. In this plot the information as to
which month the values pertain to has been lost.

EXHIBIT 2.6D

Plot of Sales versus
Year

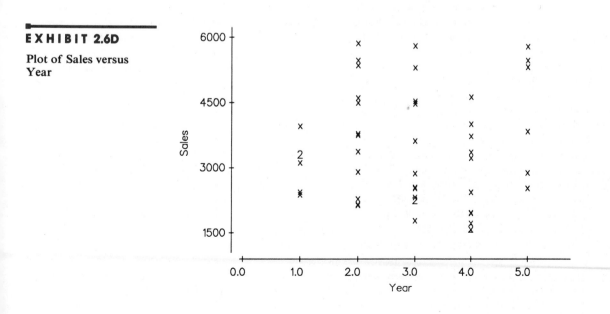

SECTION 2.7

EXERCISES

2.7A The data set below gives the monthly sales of a large part ($250 each) from the manufacturer, Deere & Co., to its John Deere distributors from July 1983 through June of 1987. Using these sales data, produce a sequence plot as in Exhibit 2.6B. Comment on any seasonal patterns that might be present. Are there any other distinctive features of the series that are apparent from the plot?

```
# filename: STRAW.DAT
# Deere & Co., straw walker sales to dealers ($250 item)
# (Source: William Fullkerson, Deere & Co.,
# Technical Center, Moline. Illinois.)
# July 1983 through June 1987, n=48
# Jul Aug Sep Oct Nov Dec Jan Feb Mar Apr May Jun
  392 251 264 535 127  33 114  72 165 132 112 240 # 1984
  285 275 294 517 379 124  94 147 131 180 152 253 # 1985
  363 290 270 591 381  93  60  65 131 329 113 226 # 1986
  339 374 276 592 381  93  60  65 134  34 168 746 # 1987
```

2.7B Using the data of Exercise 2.7A, produce plots of sales versus month and sales versus year as in Exhibits 2.6C and 2.6D. Comment on the displays. Any patterns, any unusual values, and so on? (Filename: STRAW.DAT.)

SECTION 2.8

SOME ASSEMBLY-LINE DATA AND TRANSFORMATIONS

Amana Refrigeration, Inc., is a major U.S. manufacturer of home appliances including freezers, refrigerators, air conditioning units, furnaces, and microwave ovens. Some assembly-line data from the manufacture of microwave ovens are presented here.[†] Some models of Amana microwave ovens use a stainless steel oven cavity wrapper—the box in which the food is actually cooked. Hidden inside the oven is another steel box, called the waveguide, which literally guides the microwaves created by an electronic device into the oven cavity where the cooking takes place. The waveguide must be physically attached to the top of the oven cavity wrapper by spot welding. The positioning of the waveguide is important to the proper operation of the oven. The microwaves must be properly guided into the oven cavity, and the other electronic equipment must fit near the waveguide. Exhibit 2.8A shows a simplified top view of the basic setup. Design specifications state that for proper assembly the distances labelled "Left" and "Right" in the figure should be 6.056 inches with a tolerance of plus or minus 0.045 inch. However, the two distances interact in the sense that it is also very important that the waveguide be parallel to the oven cavity wrapper. If the Left distance is a little long it is preferable that the Right distance also be a little long so that the waveguide is still parallel to the oven cavity wrapper. As a check on the quality of the assembly

---

[†] Data courtesy of Robert W. Cech, Director of Quality Assurance, Amana Refrigeration, Amana, Iowa.

process, for every 200–300 oven cavities coming down the assembly line, one oven cavity is selected and the Left and Right distances are measured and recorded. With a typical assembly line and production schedule this process produces about two pairs of Left and Right measurements per day. A partial data sheet is shown in Exhibit 2.8B, and the full data set is given in Appendix 2 and in data file AMANA.DAT.

EXHIBIT 2.8A

Waveguide Positioning on the Microwave Oven Cavity Wrapper

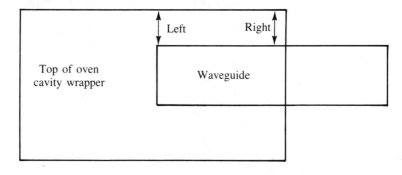

EXHIBIT 2.8B

Data Sheet for Waveguide Location

Waveguide Location on Oven Cavity Wrapper
Front edge of waveguide to front flange of oven cavity
wrapper is 6.056″ ± 0.045″

Date	Time	Card #	Left	Right
6–2–86	7:15	743	6.056	6.054
6–2–86	9:42	743	6.070	6.058
6–3–86	7:54	743	6.071	6.074
6–3–86	11:24	743	6.058	6.050

Card # refers to the timecard number of the employee taking the measurements.

The Left and Right measurements are typically of the form 6.050″, 6.073″, and so on. Usually they differ only in the hundredths and thousandths places. For entering the observations in a computer, it is easier to enter only the last two digits as an integer; that is, effectively 6 inches are subtracted from each measurement and then each value is multiplied by 1000. Thus 6.050 becomes 50 and 6.073 becomes 73. We say that we have **coded** the data. The data set used contains 120 pairs of coded Left and Right measurements recorded from June 2, 1986, to December 19, 1986. Exhibits 2.8C and 2.8D give separate sequence plots of the Left and Right values. Notice that the values obtained vary considerably over time. There are time periods with little variation of values and other time periods with considerable variation.

EXHIBIT 2.8C

Sequence Plot of the
Left Measurement

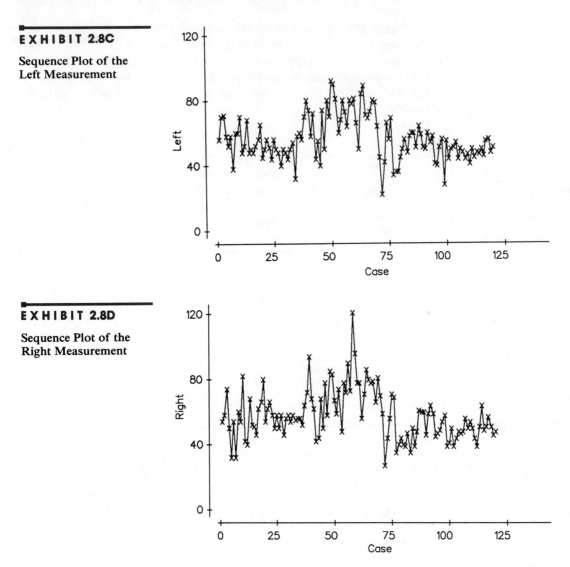

EXHIBIT 2.8D

Sequence Plot of the
Right Measurement

To compare the variation in the sequences with the tolerances that the product designers have specified for the process, it is useful to overlay on the sequence plots horizontal lines at the specification value and tolerance limits. With our coded data the specification or target value of 6.056 inches is coded as 56 and the upper and lower tolerances are then $56 + 45 = 101$ and $56 - 45 = 11$, respectively. Exhibits 2.8E and 2.8F display the results. Exhibit 2.8F clearly shows that the Right measurement at "time" 58 is above the upper specification limit. Looking back through the data sheets we see that this measurement was made on September 3, 1986. If we had been creating these plots immediately as the data came off the assembly line, we would be alerted to investigate the cause of the problem and correct it before possibly several hundred ovens were poorly assembled. The sequence plot also shows that whatever the difficulty was, it did not persist as a long-term production problem. Chapters 9 and 11 on control charts will deal extensively with such problems.

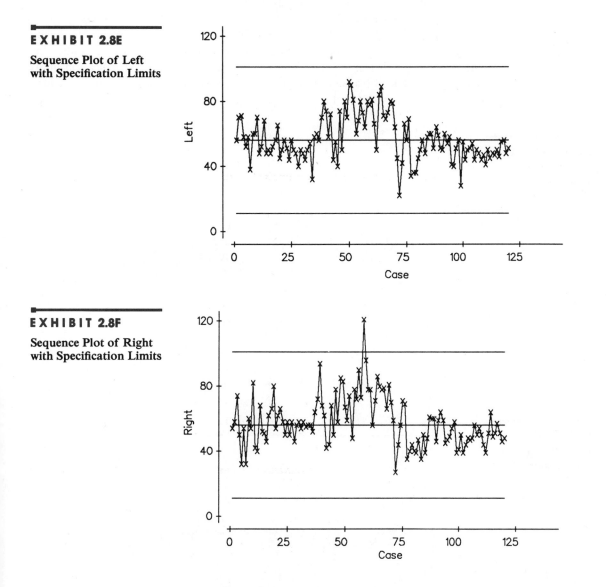

E X H I B I T 2.8E

Sequence Plot of Left with Specification Limits

E X H I B I T 2.8F

Sequence Plot of Right with Specification Limits

TRANSFORMATIONS

As stated earlier, the Left and Right dimensions interact—both are required to be similar so that the waveguide can be parallel to the oven cavity. This suggests that it might be better to investigate some different sequences that are computed from the given Left and Right measurements. In particular, the Left and Right measurements could be averaged to get a value representing the distance from the waveguide to the outer edge of the oven cavity halfway between the left and right positions. Call that distance Midvalue. We also let the difference of the Left and Right values be a measure of the parallelism of the waveguide—the closer the difference is to zero the better. Let Diff denote the variable Left − Right. The times series plots with specification limits for the sequences of Midvalue and Diff values are given in Exhibits 2.8G and 2.8H. The unusually high Midvalue value at time 58 is still noticeable. The sequence of Diff values varies around zero quite closely, indicating no problems with lack of parallelism in the waveguide. The specification limits of 6.056″ ± 0.045″ translate into limits of ±90 for the differences of the coded measurements.

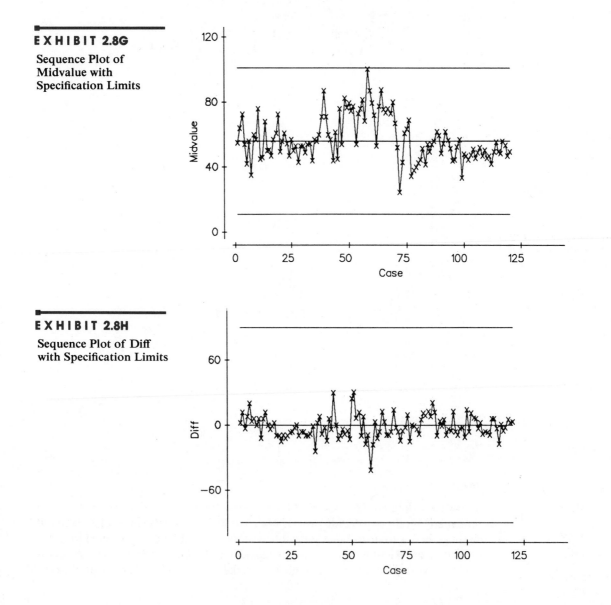

EXHIBIT 2.8G

Sequence Plot of
Midvalue with
Specification Limits

EXHIBIT 2.8H

Sequence Plot of Diff
with Specification Limits

SECTION 2.9

EXERCISE

2.9A The data file below gives some accounts receivable data for the Winegard Company of Burlington, Iowa—a worldwide manufacturer of electronic equipment. The data are the number of days for a particular independent retail electronics distributor, called XYZ Company to protect its anonymity, to pay its bills to Winegard. The terms of the account were 1%–10 days and net–30 days; that is, if the bill is paid within 10 days a 1% discount can be taken, but, in any case, the full bill is due within 30 days. The data cover January 1986 through December 1986 with about 10 bills coming due each month.

Construct a sequence plot of the data. Are there any isolated points that seem out of line with the rest of the values? Compare the first half of the values with the last half. Are there important differences? Do you think Winegard should be concerned about the pattern of bill paying that seems to be emerging near the end of the series?

```
# filename: XYZ1.DAT
# Number of days to pay account: XYZ Company
# Winegard, Inc. accounts receivable data
# (Source: Mark Sellergren, Winegard, Inc.
# Burlington, Iowa.)
# January 1986 through December 1986
# Terms: 10 days-1%, 30 days-net.  n=110
# (Read across, row by row)
  29 25 22 21 34 29 27 45 22 22 41 32 32 30 30
  30 30 22 17 15 25 28 22 22 22 20 20 18 32 31
  30 77 22 18 18 25 25 24 21 17 17 28 42 38 30
  30 30 30 27 21 68 31 23 23 23  1 20 29 31 31
  43 33 38 42 36 48 48 52 49 44 51 49 54 50 50
  50 50 50 49 62 62 62 61 60 55 61 59 54 54 62
  57 55 62 62 62 62 62 62 57 57 57 57 55 50 50
  44 44 43 43 41
```

SECTION 2.10

SOME REGIONAL ECONOMIC DATA AND ANALYSIS OF CHANGES

The data for an index of monthly flour prices in Buffalo, New York, for the period August 1972 through November 1980 are listed in Exhibit 2.10A. Exhibit 2.10B is a sequence plot that displays the movement of this flour price index during that time. The series exhibits no apparent seasonality or other discernible pattern. The series might best be described as meandering. A **meandering series** is one in which observations that are close in time are also close in value but observations that are far apart in time may be very different in value. Short-term variation is small but long-term variation may be quite large. The index grows for certain fairly long periods but then drops over other long periods only to begin another upward path later on. The peak price over this time span occurred in October 1974, and the lowest price appears at the beginning of the series, August 1972, which is nearly equalled by the June 1977 value. By the end of this time period, November 1980, the index was nearly back up to its peak level.

EXHIBIT 2.10A

Flour Price Index for
Buffalo, New York

```
# filename: BUFLOUR.DAT
# Flour price index (X10) at Buffalo, New York,
# August 1972 through November 1980.
# (Source: G.C.Tiao and R.S.Tsay, Technical Report 61,
# Graduate School of Business, University of Chicago.)
# (Read across, row by row)
# Aug  Sep  Oct  Nov  Dec  Jan  Feb  Mar  Apr  May  Jun  Jul
  1071 1135 1127 1147 1234 1236 1163 1185 1198 1203 1274 1251 # 1972-1973
  1276 1290 1246 1341 1465 1712 1786 1722 1715 1636 1856 1988 # 1973-1974
  1957 1903 2079 2128 1999 1853 1830 1735 1722 1653 1599 1703 # 1974-1975
  1722 1845 1850 1777 1691 1747 1694 1778 1701 1671 1714 1723 # 1975-1976
  1526 1441 1435 1356 1354 1345 1361 1356 1228 1190 1085 1133 # 1976-1977
  1148 1209 1237 1278 1254 1315 1277 1312 1452 1419 1393 1411 # 1977-1978
  1359 1365 1372 1438 1387 1339 1377 1438 1408 1534 1575 1795 # 1978-1979
  1775 1780 1768 1798 1742 1711 1759 1722 1647 1757 1774 1875 # 1979-1980
  1907 1904 1924 1929                                         # 1980
```

EXHIBIT 2.10B

Sequence Plot of Flour
Price Index for Buffalo,
New York

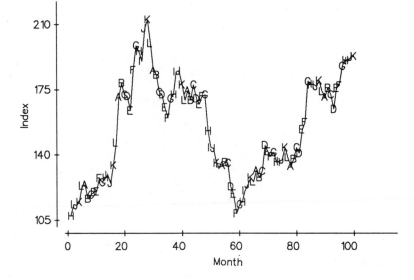

DIFFERENCES

For many series that meander, especially economic series, it is the month-to-month (or quarter-to-quarter or year-to-year) changes, or first differences, that are most easily described, modelled, and predicted. Changes in the GNP series were plotted in Exhibits 2.2C and 2.2D. Any computer data analysis system will allow easy calculation of the required differences. The sequence of changes or month-to-month differences of the flour price index is plotted in Exhibit 2.10C. Note that changes vary quite "randomly" from low values of about −20 to high values of about 25.

PERCENTAGE CHANGES

Series that tend to meander frequently also have the property that the variation in the changes associated with large values of the series is greater than the variation in the changes associated with small values of the series. In such situations it is most productive to investigate the **percentage changes** in the series, the relative changes from one data value to the next data value on a percentage basis and relative to the previous data value. The percentage change is 100 times the change divided by the previous value of the process. The following small table shows some illustrative calculations:

Time	Series Value	Change	Percentage Change	
1	126	*		*
2	132	6	$100(6)/126$ =	4.76%
3	128	−4	$100(-4)/132$ =	−3.03%
4	141	3	$100(3)/128$ =	2.34%

E X H I B I T 2.10C

Sequence Plot of Changes in Flour Price Index, Buffalo, New York

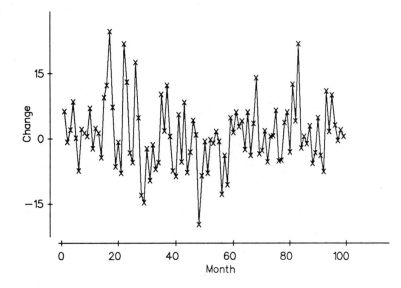

E X H I B I T 2.10D

Sequence Plot of Percentage Changes in Flour Price Index, Buffalo, New York

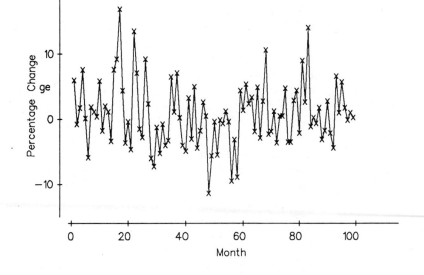

Exhibit 2.10D gives the sequence plot of the percentage changes for the flour price index series. No patterns or seasonalities are apparent in the plot. The percentage changes vary quite "randomly" between about −15% on the low end to about 15% on the high side.

EXERCISE

2.11A The data below are the monthly flour price index (× 10) in the Kansas City area for August 1972 through November 1980. Display a sequence plot for the 101 data points and compare it with the corresponding plot in Exhibit 2.10B. Compute the month-to-month changes in the index and plot them in a sequence plot. Compare them with Exhibit 2.10C. Finally, compute the percentage changes of the index and plot their sequence plot. Comment on the similarities and dissimilarities with Exhibit 2.10D.

```
# filename: KCFLOUR.DAT
# Kansas City monthly flour price index (X10)
# August 1972 through November 1980
# (Source: G.C.Tiao and R.S.Tsay, Technical Report 61,
#  Graduate School of Business, University of Chicago.)
# (Read across, row by row)
# Aug  Sep  Oct  Nov  Dec  Jan  Feb  Mar  Apr  May  Jun  Jul
  1109 1146 1155 1170 1350 1328 1226 1238 1289 1267 1393 1357 # 1972-1973
  1356 1460 1407 1470 1639 1943 2008 1934 1903 1880 1961 2150 # 1973-1974
  2016 2034 2221 2287 2161 2002 1896 1733 1697 1610 1517 1671 # 1974-1975
  1744 1897 1874 1784 1658 1649 1718 1754 1659 1573 1614 1592 # 1975-1976
  1428 1385 1342 1261 1242 1227 1235 1183 1123 1057 0977 1058 # 1976-1977
  1069 1100 1143 1188 1172 1261 1205 1256 1320 1346 1303 1370 # 1977-1978
  1366 1370 1384 1429 1404 1360 1401 1482 1464 1585 1635 1871 # 1978-1979
  1817 1815 1819 1909 1869 1801 1848 1748 1690 1784 1753 1782 # 1979-1980
  1820 1886 1908 1922                                         # 1980
```

SOME U.S. MACROECONOMIC DATA AND SEASONALITY

The U.S. Bureau of the Census regularly collects and reports many quantities of interest to the business community relating to the economic health of the nation. The *Survey of Current Business* gives monthly values broken down into categories such as manufacturing, construction, mining, and so on. Exhibit 2.12A shows the average weekly hours per worker on private, nonagricultural manufacturing payrolls by month for the time period July 1982 through June 1987. The sequence plot of data is shown in Exhibit 2.12B. By plotting the series with period 12, the seasonal nature of the series becomes readily apparent. High weekly hours occur most frequently in December (plotting symbol L), with low hours generally falling in July (symbol G). We also readily see the low weekly hours at the beginning of the series corresponding to the 1982 recession and the economic recovery during 1983. Models for seasonal sequences will be studied in Chapter 24.

EXHIBIT 2.12A

```
# filename: MANHOURS.DAT
# Average hours worked per week per worker (X10)
# Manufacturing (not seasonally adjusted)
# (Source: Survey of Current Business, September issues, 1982-1987.)
# July 1982 through June 1987
# Jul Aug Sep Oct Nov Dec Jan Feb Mar Apr May Jun
  389 390 389 390 393 397 392 388 396 398 399 403 # 1982-1983
  400 402 408 407 408 412 406 407 407 409 406 408 # 1983-1984
  403 404 407 405 407 412 403 397 404 401 403 406 # 1984-1985
  401 405 408 408 409 417 407 403 407 405 406 408 # 1985-1986
  402 407 410 407 410 415 408 408 409 404 409 411 # 1986-1987
```

EXHIBIT 2.12B

**Sequence Plot of
Average Hours Worked
per Week in
Manufacturing**

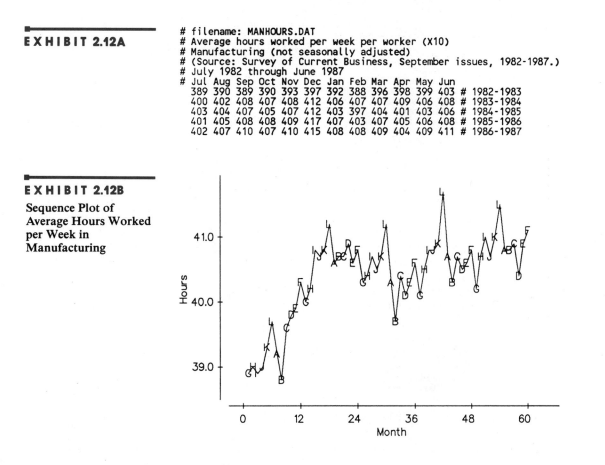

SECTION 2.13

DISCUSSION

In this chapter we have defined and given examples of processes. We have argued that processes yield results but that process results also vary. To describe and interpret this variation we have shown how to construct sequence plots of various kinds to display different aspects of process data. Always look for seasonality in monthly, quarterly, weekly, or daily data. Sometimes simple transformations of the data series, especially differences, changes, or percentage changes, will be much easier to analyze, understand, and predict than the original values.

SECTION 2.14

SUPPLEMENTARY EXERCISES FOR CHAPTER 2

2A Sequence data from an industrial process at Deere & Co. are listed below. (We will return to these data in the Supplementary Exercises for Chapter 23.)

(a) Construct a sequence plot of these data.

(b) Do values that are close in time tend to be close in value? That is, do the data meander?

```
# filename: DEERE2.DAT
# Deere & Co. machine data, n=102
# (Source: Jerri Matchinsky, M.S. thesis,
# University of Iowa, 1988.)
# Deviations from target in 0.00000125ths of an inch
# (Read across, row by row)
 -18 -24 -17 -27 -37 -34  -8  14  18   7   4  17  10  13  -1
   3  -4  -3  -3  -5  -8   0  -9  -4  -3   4   7  14   9  -2
   0   2   7   5 -18   8   3   1 -10   4   5  11   3  11   5
   6   6  -8  -8  -9  -7   0  -6  15  10  15 -14  -3  -5 -13
 -14  -3   0   7  10   4  -5   5   6  15   6  -5  -3  -8  -9
 -16 -10 -10  -6  -4  -6  -7   0  -5   2   5   6   2   8  17
  11  21   9  11   9   9   7   4  14  12  12  10
```

2B The data file below gives the monthly total of U.S retail sales (in billions of dollars) for 1983 through 1987. (We will return to these data in the Supplementary Exercises for Chapter 24.)

(a) Construct a sequence plot of these data without using any special plotting symbols. Describe any features of the plot.

(b) Now construct a sequence plot using monthly plotting symbols. Are there any patterns evident in this plot? Do the special plotting symbols help bring out the patterns?

```
# filename: RETAIL.DAT
# Monthly U.S. retail sales, 1983-1987
# (Source: Survey of Current Business,
# Washington, D.C., U.S. Government Printing Office, 1987.)
# in billions of dollars
# (Read across, row by row)
# Jan   Feb   Mar   Apr   May   Jun   Jul   Aug   Sep   Oct   Nov   Dec
 81.3  78.9  93.8  94.0  97.8 100.6  99.6 100.2  98.0 100.7 103.9 125.7
 93.1  93.7 104.3 104.3 111.3 112.0 106.6 110.7 103.9 109.2 113.3 131.8
 98.8  95.6 110.2 113.1 120.3 115.0 115.5 121.1 114.2 116.1 118.6 139.5
105.6  99.7 114.2 115.7 125.4 120.4 120.7 124.1 124.6 123.1 120.8 151.3
106.4 105.8 120.4 125.4 129.1 129.0 129.0 131.0 123.8 127.2 125.4 154.8
```

S E C T I O N 2.15

GLOSSARY FOR CHAPTER 2

Coded data	Replacing data by a code for simplicity.
First differences	The sequence of changes from one data value to the next.
Levels	The actual values of a sequence where the first differences or changes may be of primary interest.
Longitudinal study	A study of the evolution of a process over time.
Meandering series	A series whose observations close in time are also close in value but whose observations far apart in time may be quite different.
Percentage changes	The relative changes from one data value to the next data value on a percentage basis and relative to the previous data value.
Period	Time span at which a sequence *may* tend to repeat its general behavior — 12 for monthly data, 4 for quarterly data, and so on.
Seasonality	The tendency of a sequence to repeat its general behavior at regular time periods.
Sequence plot	A graph with time displayed on the horizontal axis and values of the variable of interest on the vertical axis.

## CHAPTER 3

Distribution Plots

INTRODUCTION

To be subjected to statistical analysis, data must be numerical or coded numerically. Even things that are not strictly "measurable" are reduced to cold figures. We are all familiar with this reality, having had our performance in the classroom converted to a grade point average and ultimately to a class rank! Yet measurements give us a concrete handle on problems that no amount of speculation can replace. We strive to be realistic enough about data to know they are not truth, but we need to be able to draw from data the valuable information they contain. We want to be skeptical but not cynical.

We are accustomed to obtaining numerical measurements on quantities like length, weight, temperature, and so on. This type of data is called *metric* data. Other somewhat different data, called *categorical* data, such as gender (1 = female, 0 = male), will be considered in Chapter 5.

When a collection of data values becomes available for analysis, it is important to gain an understanding of some basic characteristics of the collection. The sequence plots of Chapter 2 displayed the longitudinal aspects of a data set collected over time. In this chapter we ignore the time dimension, if any, of a data set. Instead we ask, What is a "typical" value? How far are the extreme values from the typical values? Are there gaps within the range of values where no data were observed? How spread out is the set of values? What proportion of the values is greater than the value for our own firm? When the time dimension is either absent or ignored, we say that we are considering the **cross-sectional** aspects of the data.

Most people cannot discern how the data are distributed over their range of values from a mere listing of the data. Summaries and, especially, graphical displays of the distribution of the data are needed to help us derive information.

In this chapter and the next, we show how to describe data collected on a single metric variable. We begin with a basic graphical display—the dotplot. Stem-and-leaf displays are then explored, followed by a discussion of various types of histograms. All these tools play an important role in statistical analysis. Generally speaking, dotplots are useful for small sets of data, stem-and-leaf displays for moderate-sized data sets, and histograms for large sets of data. Finally, the difference between the information displayed in a distribution display (a cross-sectional display) and in a time sequence plot (a longitudinal display) are emphasized.

S E C T I O N 3.2

DOTPLOTS

A **dotplot** consists of a horizontal scale upon which dots locate the numerical values of the data points. If a data value repeats, then the dots are piled up at that location, one dot for each repetition. Because this discussion uses the photocopy data of Exhibit 3.2A, the data in Exhibit 1.3A with the extreme values, those less than 300 and greater than 650, are repeated in parentheses for easy reference.

EXHIBIT 3.2A

Number of Photocopies by Date (Exhibit 1.3A repeated with extreme values in parentheses)

Date	Number of Copies	Date	Number of Copies
10/12	416	11/2	616
10/13	556	11/3	(797)
10/14	395	11/4	456
10/15	447	11/5	364
10/16	(238)	11/6	589
10/19	532	11/9	607
10/20	349	11/10	(780)
10/21	390	11/11	374
10/22	579	11/12	456
10/23	(274)	11/13	393
10/26	621	11/16	(1199)
10/27	362	11/17	362
10/28	447	11/18	547
10/29	440	11/19	530
10/30	505	11/20	741

Exhibit 3.2B shows a hand-drawn dotplot of the photocopy data set with the extremes excluded. However, statistical packages can also produce dotplots. Since a computer display, unlike a real number line, contains only a limited number of unique positions, observations that are nearly equal but actually different may have to be plotted at the same plotting position. (For example, the standard Minitab dotplot uses about 56 horizontal plotting positions.) To conserve space, a colon (:) is plotted if two observations need to be plotted in the same position. Thus the display in Exhibit 3.2C is not identical to the corresponding portion of the hand-drawn plot, but the general interpretations of the two displays are the same. The main impression left by the plot is the chaotic behavior of the observations between 300 and 650. We see little basis for predicting any particular value or range of values over others within these limits. As more data become available, we may be able to detect tendencies for the data to cluster about some value or within a subinterval of [300, 650], but on the basis of the data in Exhibit 3.2C, we would not be surprised by any number between 300 and 650 in the future. Statisticians say that the dotplot displays the *distribution* of the data. The dotplot is especially useful when the distribution behavior of a relatively small set of numbers needs to be displayed. It shows the position of the data points on a number line and displays the frequencies, but for large sets of data (say 100 or more observations) it is tedious to construct by hand. Furthermore, with larger data sets more useful distribution displays are available.

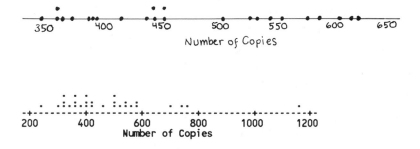

EXHIBIT 3.2B
Hand-Drawn Dotplot of Photocopy Data (extremes excluded)

EXHIBIT 3.2C
Computer-Drawn Dotplot of Photocopy Data (extremes included)

To see the detail of the dotplot display in the middle range of data more clearly, the dotplot can be redone with the extremes excluded. Exhibit 3.2D shows an example with the photocopy data but looking only at the values between 300 and 650.

EXHIBIT 3.2D
Computer-Drawn Dotplot of Photocopy Data (extreme values excluded)

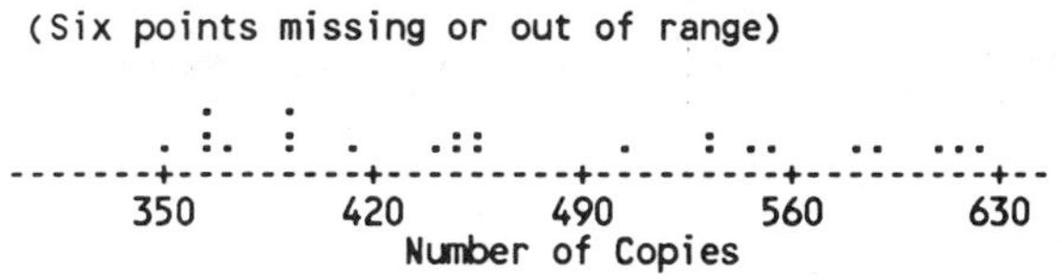

Dotplots may also be used to make easy visual comparisons among variables that have been categorized by another variable. Exhibit 3.2E shows a sequence of dotplots of the oil-filter sales data by month. Again the monthly effects that were observed earlier in sequence plots are seen.

```
       Dec
        . .                     ..
       -+---------+---------:---------+---------+---------+-----

       Nov
          .      : . .
       -+---------+---------+---------+---------+---------+-----

       Oct
              : .            .
       -+---------:---------+---------+---------+---------+-----

       Sep
         :  .                    .
       -+---------+---------+---------:---------+---------+-----

       Aug
              . :      .
  M    -+---------:---------+---------+---------+---------+-----
  o
  n    Jul
  t           .      .    .    .
  h    -+---------+---------+---------+---------+---------+-----

       Jun
              .      .       .
       -+---------+---------+---------+---------+---------+-----

       May
              .      .  .     .
       -+---------+---------+---------+---------+---------+-----

       Apr
                     .      .   ..       .
       -+---------+---------+---------+---------+---------+-----

       Mar
            .      .          .
       -+---------+---------+---------+---------+---------+-----

       Feb
                      .      .    ..
       -+---------+---------+---------+---------+--:------+-----

       Jan
                                      :.  .
       -+---------+---------+---------+---------:-+-------+-----
      1600      2400      3200      4000      4800      5600
                  Number of Oil Filters Sold
```

EXERCISES

3.3A Display a dotplot for the following 20 exam scores: 87, 78, 96, 91, 89, 74, 59, 88, 67, 82, 93, 72, 79, 84, 65, 81, 95, 85, 89, 91. (Filename: SCORES.DAT.)

3.3B Form a dotplot for the following weights (in grams): 243, 267, 253, 244, 246, 235, 239, 249, 251, 244, 238, 262, 248, 234, 253, 260, 247, 238, 251, 244, 244, 240, 253, 262, 233. (Filename: WEIGHTS.DAT.)

3.3C Prepare a dotplot of the 81 data values from the Deere & Co. machining process given in Exercise 2.5A. Describe the appearance of the distribution displayed in the dotplot. Does it appear symmetric? Are there gaps in the distribution? What values occur most frequently? Least frequently? (Filename: DEERE1.DAT.)

3.3D Compute the month-to-month differences for the wage data in Exercise 2.5B. Describe the appearance of the distribution displayed in the dotplot. Does it appear symmetric? Are there gaps in the distribution? What values occur most frequently? Least frequently? Do the differences associated with certain months tend to be located together in the dotplot? (Filename: MANWAGES.DAT.)

3.3E Prepare a dotplot of the Winegard accounting data in Exercise 2.9A. Compare the dotplot with the sequence plot of the data. What information does the dotplot convey? What information does the sequence plot convey? (Filename: XYZ1.DAT.)

3.3F Compute the percentage changes for the Kansas City flour price index data in Exercise 2.11A. Prepare a dotplot of the percentage changes and compare the information the dotplot provides to the information in the sequence plot. (Filename: KCFLOUR.DAT.)

SECTION 3.4

STEM-AND-LEAF DISPLAYS

With a moderate-to-large data set on a variable that may take on a large number of different values, the distribution is best displayed by grouping together data values that are reasonably close together and displaying the frequencies of the groups. Stem-and-leaf displays were invented by John Tukey to speed the hand construction of such grouped frequency plots. The emphasis is on simplicity, so that even a fairly large set of data (say 100 observations) can be processed and displayed reasonably quickly by hand. (Another more complicated display, the histogram, is discussed in the next section.) The stem-and-leaf technique is presented using the data in Exhibit 3.2A. The **stem-and-leaf display** is a combination table and graphical display, as it retains (essentially) the numerical values of the individual data points while at the same time producing a profile that graphically displays the frequencies of the grouped data values. The basic idea is to let the digits in the data values do the work of grouping the data while also displaying the frequencies. Usually only the two leading digits in the data values will actually be used, so the first step is to reduce all the numbers to two digits by chopping off the digits after the first two. If the data had consisted of four-digit numbers, two digits would have been chopped, keeping only two significant digits. The second step is to mentally separate each of the resulting two-digit numbers into a *stem* digit (the left-hand digit) and a *leaf* digit (the right-hand digit). Because in our example the original numbers were restricted to be between 300 and 650, the stem digits are 3, 4, 5, and 6. The first data value, 416, is then considered to be divided as

$$4 \mid 1 \mid 6$$

Stem Leaf Ignored

Stem = leading digit; Leaf = trailing digit; Ignored = digit chopped

The stems are then placed in numerical order on a vertical line. Frequently, a vertical bar is used to separate the stems from the leaves.

```
3 |
4 |
5 |
6 |
```

The next step is to go through the data values one by one and place the leaf digit directly to the right of the corresponding stem digit. The value 416 is plotted as

```
3 |
4 | 1
5 |
6 |
```

The next data value, 556, is then chopped to 55 and the leaf of 5 is placed next to the stem of 5, as in

```
3 |
4 | 1
5 | 5
6 |
```

Proceeding in this way the entire data set is gone through, building up the stem-and-leaf display:

```
3 | 94966796
4 | 144455
5 | 5370843
6 | 210
```

Since the widths of the leaf piles are intended to display the frequencies of the various stem groupings, it is important, when hand drawing a stem-and-leaf display, *to use the same horizontal space for all digits.* A "thin" 1 must use the same space as a "thick" 8, for example. After the basic stem-and-leaf display is constructed, most authors recommend ordering the leaves in increasing numerical order to make the final display:

Leaf unit = 10

```
3 | 46667999
4 | 144455
5 | 0233478
6 | 012
```

In our illustration the grouping of the data into just four groups may mask some of the detail in the distribution. To see more detail, divide the leaf digits into two equal-sized groups:

Group 1: 0, 1, 2, 3, 4 (code = *)

Group 2: 5, 6, 7, 8, 9 (code = .)

To display these two groups for each stem digit, write down each stem digit and attach the appropriate group code:

```
3*
 .
4*
 .
5*
 .
6*
 .
```

Now again move through the data in Exhibit 3.2A and record the leaf digits at the appropriate spots on the corresponding stems. The first data value is 416, which is chopped to 41. The leaf digit is in Group 1, so it goes next to the 4* in the stem. The second data value is 556, which is chopped to 55. The leaf digit is in Group 2, so it goes next to the 5. in the stem. These two values appear in the more detailed diagram as:

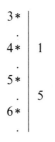

```
3*
 .
4*  | 1
 .
5*
 .  | 5
6*
 .
```

Continue through the data in this fashion until the whole display is created again:

Leaf unit = 10

23, 27   (← low extreme values)

```
3*  | 4
3.  | 9966796
4*  | 1444
4.  | 55
5*  | 3043
5.  | 578
6*  | 210
```

74, 78, 79, 119   (← high extreme values)

The extreme values have been included in the display with their ones digits chopped off. A final cleaning up of the display usually consists of ordering the leaves on each stem from smallest to largest.

Leaf unit = 10

23, 27   (← low extreme values)

```
3*  4
3.  6667999
4*  1444
4.  55
5*  0334
5.  578
6*  012
```

74, 78, 79, 119   (← high extreme values)

In this fashion a compact display of the complete set of data has been provided, with more detail than in the previous display. Because of the chopping and grouping of digits, the scale on which the data are displayed is still more compressed than it is in the dotplot. This is a desirable feature when a large amount of data needs to be displayed because retaining too much detail leads to clumsy manipulations. Within the limitations of the scale, though, the stem-and-leaf display presents the data in order, and it displays frequencies, so it is a frequency plot.

Exhibits 3.4A and 3.4B show computer-drawn stem-and-leaf displays. The first column in the exhibits shows the cumulative count of observations on that line or on lines toward the nearer extreme. Such counts are useful in determining the order statistics (see Chapter 4). The line containing the middle of the ordered values has its own count, which is shown in parentheses. Otherwise, the displays are the same as the hand-constructed displays.

EXHIBIT 3.4A

Computer-Drawn Stem-and-Leaf Display

```
Stem-and-leaf of Copies    N=30
Leaf unit=10

    2    2 37
   10    3 46667999
   (6)   4 144455
   14    5 0334578
    7    6 012
    4    7 489
    1    8
    1    9
    1   10
    1   11 9
```

EXHIBIT 3.4B

Computer-Drawn Stem-and-Leaf with Extreme Value Shown Separately

```
Stem-and-leaf of Copies    N=30
Leaf unit=10

    1     2 3
    2     2 7
    3     3 4
   10     3 6667999
   14     4 1444
   (2)    4 55
   14     5 0334
   10     5 578
    7     6 012
    4     6
    4     7 4
    3     7 89

         HI   119
```

The construction of an effective stem-and-leaf display depends on the choice of the stem digits. In the photocopy example, the hundreds digit was retained for the stem. Other choices will be indicated for other data sets. For example, if the observations consist of five-digit numbers of the form *abcde*, we may wish to retain the *ab* digits for the stem and use the *c* digits for the leaves. This means chopping the *de* digits. (See Exercise 3.7B for a numerical illustration.) There is no hard-and-fast rule for creating stems and leaves. The important thing is to get a good representation of the distribution without doing an excessive amount of work.

SECTION 3.5

EXERCISES

3.5A Display a stem-and-leaf diagram for the following 20 exam scores: 87, 78, 96, 91, 89, 74, 59, 88, 67, 82, 93, 72, 79, 84, 65, 81, 95, 85, 89, 91. Compare this display to the dotplot in Exercise 3.3A. (Filename: SCORES.DAT.)

3.5B Form a stem-and-leaf diagram for the following weights (in grams): 243, 267, 253, 244, 246, 235, 239, 249, 251, 244, 238, 262, 248, 234, 253, 260, 247, 238, 251, 244, 244, 240, 253, 262, 233. Compare the stem-and-leaf diagram to the dotplot constructed in Exercise 3.3B. (Filename: WEIGHTS.DAT.)

3.5C Prepare a stem-and-leaf display of the Deere & Co. machining data in Exercise 2.5A. Compare the information conveyed by the stem-and-leaf display and the dotplot of Exercise 3.3C. (Filename: DEERE1.DAT.)

3.5D Display a stem-and-leaf display of the month-to-month differences in the wage data given in Exercise 2.5B. Compare the information conveyed by the stem-and-leaf display and the dotplot of Exercise 3.3D. (Filename: MANWAGES.DAT.)

3.5E Make a stem-and-leaf display of the Winegard accounting data in Exercise 2.9A. Compare the information conveyed by the stem-and-leaf display and the dotplot of Exercise 3.3E. (Filename: XYZ1.DAT.)

3.5F Prepare a stem-and-leaf display of the Kansas City flour price index data listed in Exercise 2.11A. Compare the information conveyed by the stem-and-leaf display and the dotplot of Exercise 3.3F. (Filename: KCFLOUR.DAT.)

SECTION 3.6

HISTOGRAMS

Histograms are tools for displaying distributions of large sets of data. Histograms group the data into a relatively small number of classes and report the frequencies of the classes in a graphic display. In the statistical literature several somewhat different displays are called histograms. To avoid confusion, we use different adjectives when referring to the different kinds of histograms. We introduce three types: frequency histograms, relative frequency histograms, and density histograms.

FREQUENCY HISTOGRAMS

Frequency histograms, the most basic histograms, are a graphical display of a frequency distribution. All they require is grouping the data into *classes*, counting the number of observations in each class, and making a plot. Exhibit 3.6A shows a computer-generated histogram for a variable called Outlook, which will be covered more completely in Chapter 5. This variable is part of a large data set obtained in a survey of Wisconsin restaurant owners and assumes one of the values 1, 2, 3, ..., 6 according to the business outlook perceived by the owners. (See especially Exhibit 5.4A.) In Exhibit 3.6A asterisks (∗) have been stacked according to the count or **class frequency** of observations at each of the possible values 1 through 6. The frequencies are then easily seen and compared from the display. Sometimes the sizes of the frequencies are portrayed using *rectangles* instead of asterisks, as in Exhibit 3.6B. These displays are often turned on their side with the frequencies displayed vertically as in Exhibit 3.6J. The information conveyed is the same in all these types of displays.

EXHIBIT 3.6A

Computer-Generated Histogram of Business Outlook

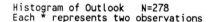

Histogram of Outlook   N=278
Each * represents two observations

Midpoint	Count	
1	37	********************
2	40	********************
3	66	***********************************
4	73	**************************************
5	49	**************************
6	13	*******

EXHIBIT 3.6B

Histogram of Business Outlook (alternative form)

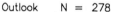

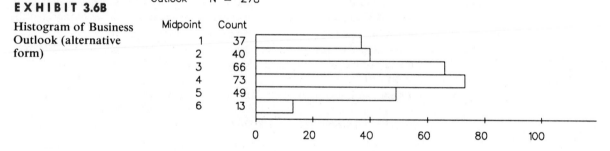

Outlook   N = 278

Midpoint	Count
1	37
2	40
3	66
4	73
5	49
6	13

With metric data that may assume a large number of possible values, the data must be grouped into **class intervals** to construct a histogram. To illustrate, let us divide the photocopy data in Exhibit 3.2A (extremes excluded) into five class intervals of equal length. The data range from a low value of 349 to a high value of 621, a difference of 272, so the class intervals need to be about $272/5 = 54.4$ in length. The determination of class intervals is somewhat arbitrary, because we can choose different starting values and interval lengths and obtain a system of intervals that covers the data. A common approach is to pick a starting value that has more decimal places than any data value. Then none of the data values will coincide with an interval endpoint. This avoids having to decide which interval such a data value belongs to. If we decide to use a fractional starting value, we can use an integral interval length, which simplifies the addition. We choose to start our system of intervals at 348.5 and to use an interval length of 55. The five intervals we need are [348.5, 403.5), [403.5, 458.5), [458.5, 513.5), [513.5, 568.5), and [568.5, 623.5). We show the intervals closed on the left and open on the right, so they cover all the values between 348.5 and 623.5 and they do not overlap. Now we need to count the number of data values that fall in each of the intervals, the class frequencies. The simplest way to do this is to move sequentially through the data and to place a tally mark by the interval that contains a data value. The first data value in Exhibit 3.2A is 416, and this puts a tally mark by the second interval because 416 falls between 403.5 and 458.5. The second data value in Exhibit 3.2A is 556, which falls in the fourth interval. The scheme below shows the results of tallying all the data values in Exhibit 3.2A.

Interval	Tally	Count	Histogram Display
[348.5, 403.5)	Ⅷ‖‖	8	********
[403.5, 458.5)	Ⅶ‖	6	******
[458.5, 513.5)	‖	1	*
[513.5, 568.5)	‖‖‖‖	4	****
[568.5, 623.5)	Ⅶ	5	*****
Total		24	

The count is also called the *frequency* of the interval. Also shown is a simple histogram display. This is all there is to a frequency histogram. Compare this frequency histogram with the stem-and-leaf displays in Section 3.4 and with the dotplots in Exhibits 3.2B and 3.2D. Each statistical tool displays the same data in a slightly different way. Remember that the histogram replaces the data with a system of intervals and their corresponding frequencies. It thus can reduce a sizable set of data to a small number of quantities that display the distribution of the data graphically.

COMPUTER-GENERATED HISTOGRAMS

Statistical computer packages can produce histograms at the touch of a few keys. Exhibit 3.6C shows such a histogram of the full photocopy data set. The software chose the class width of 100 and chose to use 11 class intervals to cover the complete data set. Exhibit 3.6D shows the corresponding histogram when values less than 300 and greater than 650 are excluded. Here the software chose to use 8 intervals each of width 40.

EXHIBIT 3.6C

Computer-Generated
Histogram of
Photocopy Data
(extremes included)

```
Histogram of Copies    N=30

Midpoint    Count
    200        1    *
    300        2    **
    400       11    ***********
    500        6    ******
    600        6    ******
    700        1    *
    800        2    **
    900        0
   1000        0
   1100        0
   1200        1    *
```

EXHIBIT 3.6D

Computer-Generated Histogram of Photocopy Data (extremes excluded)

```
Histogram of Copies    N=30
Two observations below the first class
Four observations above the last class

Midpoint    Count
     350        4  ****
     390        4  ****
     430        4  ****
     470        2  **
     510        1  *
     550        4  ****
     590        3  ***
     630        2  **
```

COMPARISONS

Histograms (and dotplots) are useful for comparing different distributions. Winegard Company, based in Burlington, Iowa, is a worldwide manufacturer of television-reception products, antennas, satellite dishes, and so forth. One of their many manufacturing processes involves a punching operation to produce end caps for a particular satellite-dish antenna system. The punching operation is intended to produce an end cap with a certain specified dimension (width outside, bend-to-bend). However, as always, variation is present in the dimension actually obtained. Using the present punch method, 50 end caps were produced and measured, resulting in the data set† given in Exhibit 3.6E.

EXHIBIT 3.6E

Punch Data Before Die Change

```
# filename: PUNCH_B.DAT
# Winegard punch data before die change
# (Source: Mark Sellergren, Winegard, Inc.,
# Burlington, Iowa)
# January 13, 1988. Width outside (in inches), bend-to-bend
 1.799  1.799  1.800  1.798  1.798  1.798  1.798  1.798  1.799  1.798
 1.799  1.797  1.800  1.800  1.800  1.800  1.797  1.798  1.799  1.798
 1.798  1.801  1.799  1.799  1.797  1.798  1.802  1.800  1.798  1.797
 1.798  1.798  1.798  1.800  1.799  1.799  1.799  1.799  1.798  1.799
 1.798  1.798  1.798  1.798  1.798  1.799  1.798  1.798  1.802  1.799
```

Exhibit 3.6F gives a histogram of these data. Most of the values are in the range from 1.798 to 1.800, with a few values below and a few above. Design specifications require that the measured dimension lie in the range $1.772 \pm .022$ inch. As the histogram clearly shows, none of the 50 parts meet those requirements. In order to reduce the dimension to more acceptable levels, a die change was introduced into the

EXHIBIT 3.6F

Histogram of Punch Data Before Die Change

```
Histogram of Before    N=50

Midpoint    Count
 1.79700        4  ****
 1.79800       22  **********************
 1.79900       14  **************
 1.80000        7  *******
 1.80100        1  *
 1.80200        2  **
```

† Data courtesy of Mark R. Sellergren, former Vice President—Finance, Winegard Company.

punch operation. Exhibit 3.6G lists the 50 data points observed after the change. The histogram of these data, given in Exhibit 3.6H, shows that the die change was indeed effective. The pair of histograms for both the before and after data in Exhibit 3.6I are done on the same scale to display the change even more dramatically.

EXHIBIT 3.6G

Punch Data After Die Change

```
# filename: PUNCH_A.DAT
# Winegard punch data after die change
# (Source: Mark Sellergren, Winegard, Inc.,
# Burlington, Iowa)
# January 13, 1988. Width outside (in inches), bend to bend
1.780  1.778  1.779  1.779  1.779  1.779  1.779  1.778  1.780  1.779
1.779  1.777  1.778  1.779  1.777  1.779  1.780  1.779  1.779  1.779
1.779  1.777  1.778  1.779  1.779  1.778  1.780  1.779  1.779  1.778
1.779  1.778  1.777  1.778  1.780  1.779  1.778  1.777  1.778  1.776
1.778  1.778  1.778  1.777  1.778  1.779  1.779  1.779  1.780  1.779
```

EXHIBIT 3.6H

Histogram of Punch Data After Die Change

```
Histogram of After    N=50

Midpoint   Count
1.77600      1   *
1.77700      6   ******
1.77800     14   **************
1.77900     23   ***********************
1.78000      6   ******
```

EXHIBIT 3.6I

Histograms on Same Scale for Comparisons

```
Histogram of Before    N=50

Midpoint   Count
1.776        0
1.778        0
1.780        0
1.782        0
1.784        0
1.786        0
1.788        0
1.790        0
1.792        0
1.794        0
1.796        4   ****
1.798       36   ************************************
1.800        8   ********
1.802        2   **
```

```
Histogram of After    N=50

Midpoint   Count
1.776        7   *******
1.778       37   *************************************
1.780        6   ******
1.782        0
1.784        0
1.786        0
1.788        0
1.790        0
1.792        0
1.794        0
1.796        0
1.798        0
1.800        0
1.802        0
```

RELATIVE FREQUENCY HISTOGRAMS

Relative frequency histograms can be used to compare the distributions of two sets of data for which the numbers of observations in the two data sets are different. To take a hypothetical case, suppose the counts for two sets of data are as follows:

Interval	Counts	
	Data Set A	Data Set B
I1	40	80
I2	59	118
I3	102	204
I4	69	138
I5	37	74
Total	307	614

For each interval the count in Data Set B is twice as large as the count in Data Set A, so the frequency histogram of Data Set B has piles of asterisks that are twice as high as the corresponding ones from Data Set A. Yet the two distributions are identical in terms of the proportions of observations allocated to the intervals. The proportions of observations allocated to the intervals are called *relative frequencies*. A histogram display in which the lengths of the piles of asterisks are equal to the relative frequencies of the intervals is called a **relative frequency histogram**. When two distributions allocate observations to the same intervals, then the relative frequency histograms may be compared to discover similarities or differences between the two distributions.

Because of the arbitrariness in choice of number of intervals, starting value, and length of intervals, histograms can be made to take on different shapes for the same set of data, especially if the data set is small. Histograms are thus best used for data sets with at least 100 observations. Exhibit 3.6J shows a histogram of the percent changes in the Buffalo, New York, flour price index series introduced in Chapter 2. Here there are 99 data points. The histogram uses eight class intervals and is drawn by the software package Stata.® For comparison purposes, Exhibit 3.6K shows

EXHIBIT 3.6J

Histogram for Percentage Change in Flour Price Index

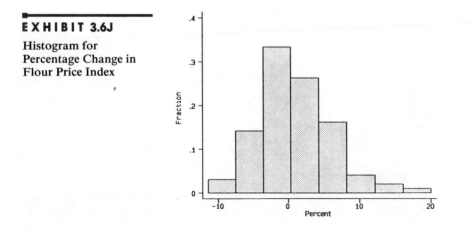

EXHIBIT 3.6K

EXHIBIT 3.6K   Histograms for Percentage Change in Flour Price Index—Various
Numbers of Intervals

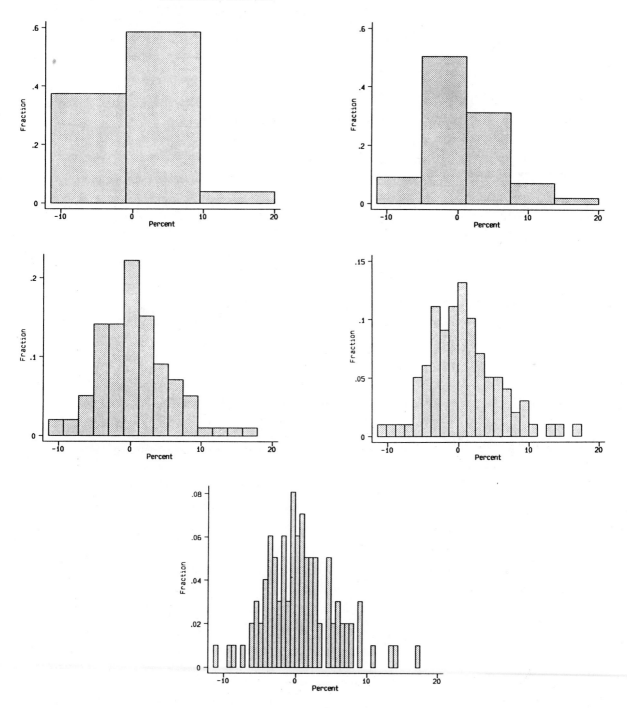

histograms of the same data set based on 3, 5, 15, 25, and 50 class intervals, respectively. As more and more intervals are used, more detail in the distribution is displayed but at the expense of producing a more jagged graph, which may obscure the underlying smoothness of the distribution. On the other hand, too few intervals, say three, produces too much smoothing and nearly all of the details in the distribution are lost. A reasonable guideline is to use about $\sqrt{n}$ intervals when dealing with n data points. In this case we have a data set of 99 points, so about 10 intervals should be used. Statistical smoothing methods beyond the scope of this book can be used to yield smooth histogram-type displays. Exhibit 3.6L shows such a curve for the percent changes of the flour price index.

E X H I B I T 3.6L

Smooth Histogram for Percentage Change in Flour Price Index

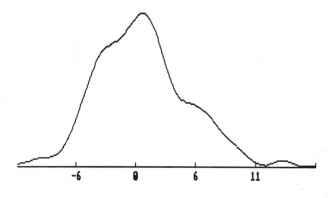

DENSITY HISTOGRAMS

Density histograms are the most general but also the most complex form of histogram. They use *area* to show relative frequency because the resulting scaling allows comparison of data sets that allocate different amounts of data to different intervals. If the adjustment is not used, the graphs will be misleading.

▪**E X A M P L E 3.6A:** The hypothetical data reported in Exhibit 3.6M will be used to illustrate the construction of a density histogram. The measured variable will be called "utility."

E X H I B I T 3.6M

Data for Construction of Density Histogram

Utility Interval	Frequency	Relative Frequency	Length of Interval	Relative Frequency Density
[20, 40)	5	0.05	20	0.0025
[40, 60)	10	0.10	20	0.0050
[60, 120)	45	0.45	60	0.0075
[120, 180)	30	0.30	60	0.0050
[180, 500)	10	0.10	320	0.0003125
Totals	100	1.00	480	

The interval frequencies 5, 10, 45, 30, and 10 are converted to relative frequencies by dividing them by their total of 100. The relative frequencies are simply the proportions of observations falling in the intervals. Find the lengths of the intervals by subtracting their lower endpoints from their upper endpoints. Find the relative frequency densities by dividing the relative frequencies by the corresponding interval lengths. Exhibit 3.6N shows how the data look displayed in a density histogram. Each interval of utility has a rectangle sitting on it, so the bases of the rectangles are equal to the lengths of the class intervals, that is, the intervals dividing up the values of a variable. The heights of the rectangles are chosen so that the areas of the rectangles are equal to the relative frequencies of the intervals. This means that

$$\text{Relative frequency} = \text{Area} = \text{Class interval length} \times \text{density}$$

because density = relative frequency/class interval length.

EXHIBIT 3.6N

Density Histogram for Utility Data

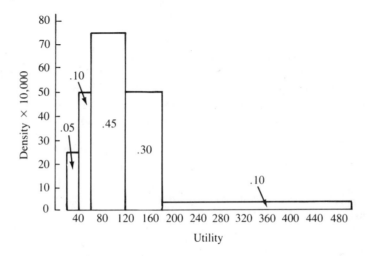

You see that density measures *the proportion of observations in the class interval per amount of interval length.* A wide interval with many observations may have the same density as a narrow interval with few observations. The intervals [40, 60) and [120, 180) in Exhibit 3.6N provide an example. Another important observation is that the total area of the rectangles in Exhibit 3.6N is 1.00. This is a property of density histograms by construction. The requirement that all density histograms have a total area of 1.00 normalizes the histograms and makes comparison between histograms meaningful even though the underlying data sets may have different numbers of observations and allocate observations to different intervals.

■**EXAMPLE 3.6B:** In this example two real data sets are compared using density histograms. The data are taken from U.S. Bureau of the Census, *Statistical Abstract of the United States: 1984* (104th ed.) Washington, D.C., 1983, 37 and 38. They are distributions of families in family income categories for the white and black populations in March 1982. See Exhibit 3.6O.

EXHIBIT 3.6O

Numbers of U.S.
Families in Income
Categories, by Race,
1982

| | Number of Families (in thousands) | |
Income Interval	White Population	Black Population
$0–$5,000	2,399	1,069
$5,000–$10,000	5,452	1,389
$10,000–$15,000	7,007	1,060
$15,000–$25,000	13,615	1,413
$25,000–$50,000	19,628	1,346
Subtotal	48,101	6,277
$50,000+	5,168	137
Grand total	53,269	6,414

Source: U.S. Bureau of the Census, *Statistical Abstract of the United States:*
1984 (104th ed.) Washington, D.C., 1983, 37 and 38.

All the families with incomes over $50,000 are grouped into an open-ended
category, one that has no upper limit. It is not possible to construct a density
histogram with open-ended intervals. The problem is simply avoided by using the
first five categories. The subtotals given in Exhibit 3.6O are used to compute relative
frequencies and densities. Exhibit 3.6P shows the computations.

EXHIBIT 3.6P

Computations for
Density Histograms for
Data in Exhibit 3.6O
(incomes in $1000 units)

White Population				
Income Interval (in $1000 units)	Frequency	Relative Frequency	Interval Length	Density
0–5	2,399	0.0498742	5	0.0099768
5–10	5,452	0.1133448	5	0.0226735
10–15	7,007	0.1456726	5	0.0291403
15–25	13,615	0.2830502	10	0.0283078
25–50	19,628	0.4080580	25	0.0163230
Total	48,101	1.0000000		

Black Population				
Income Interval (in $1000 units)	Frequency	Relative Frequency	Interval Length	Density
0–5	1,069	0.1703314	5	0.03407
5–10	1,389	0.2213193	5	0.04427
10–15	1,060	0.1688974	5	0.03379
15–25	1,413	0.2251434	10	0.02252
25–50	1,346	0.2144678	25	0.00858
Total	6,277	1.0000000		

Exhibit 3.6Q shows the histograms for the white and black populations in a back-to-back format that eases comparisons. The exhibit shows that the black population is more dense in the three lower income intervals and less dense in the two higher income intervals than the white population. The black population has the greatest density in the interval [$5000, $10,000), whereas the white population has the greatest density in the interval [$10,000, $15,000). These conclusions are quite difficult to draw from the frequencies because intervals are not all the same length. The interval with the greatest frequency in the black population is [$15,000, $25,000), while the interval with greatest frequency in the white population is [$25,000, $50,000), but these intervals are not of equal length. The conversion to densities clears up the problem.

EXHIBIT 3.6Q

Back-to-Back Density Histograms for Comparison. (Density × 10,000.)

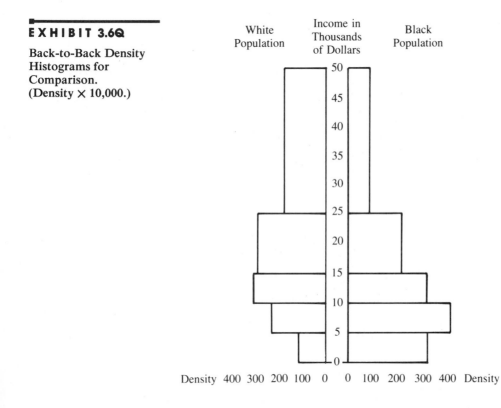

Density 400 300 200 100 0   0 100 200 300 400 Density

EXERCISES

3.7A Explain the meaning of the term *distribution*.

3.7B The following table shows median family incomes by state for the years 1969 and 1979. The incomes by state for a given year have no longitudinal component. Remember that statisticians call such data *cross-sectional*. If we try to compare the distributions of median incomes for the two years, then we encounter a longitudinal component.

PART I

In this part of the exercise we ask you to prepare frequency plots of the cross section of data from 1969.

(a) Prepare a stem-and-leaf display. Use the ten-thousands and thousands digits for the stem and the hundreds digits for the leaves. In other words, chop off the ones and tens digits. You may wish to write the names of the states near the lines where their leaves are located. This will serve to order the states by median income.

(b) Prepare a dotplot of the 1969 cross section. Compare the dotplot to the stem-and-leaf display in part (a). Do you gain insight from the additional detail in the dotplot?

State	Median Family Income 1969	1979	State	Median Family Income 1969	1979
Alabama	$ 7,263	$16,347	Montana	$ 8,509	$18,413
Alaska	12,441	28,395	Nebraska	8,562	19,122
Arizona	9,185	19,017	Nevada	10,687	21,311
Arkansas	6,271	14,641	New Hamsphire	9,682	19,723
California	10,729	21,537	New Jersey	11,402	22,906
Colorado	9,552	21,279	New Mexico	7,845	16,928
Connecticut	11,808	23,149	New York	10,609	20,180
Delaware	10,209	20,817	North Carolina	7,770	16,792
District of Columbia	9,576	19,099	North Dakota	7,836	18,023
Florida	8,261	17,280	Ohio	10,309	20,909
Georgia	8,165	17,414	Oklahoma	7,720	17,668
Hawaii	11,552	22,750	Oregon	9,487	20,027
Idaho	8,380	17,492	Pennsylvania	9,554	19,995
Illinois	10,957	22,746	Rhode Island	9,733	19,448
Indiana	9,966	20,535	South Carolina	7,620	16,978
Iowa	9,016	20,052	South Dakota	7,490	15,993
Kansas	8,690	19,707	Tennessee	7,446	16,564
Kentucky	7,439	16,444	Texas	8,486	19,618
Louisiana	7,527	18,088	Utah	9,320	20,024
Maine	8,205	16,167	Vermont	8,928	17,205
Maryland	11,057	23,112	Virginia	9,044	20,018
Massachusetts	10,833	21,166	Washington	10,404	20,018
Michigan	11,029	22,107	West Virginia	7,414	17,308
Minnesota	9,928	21,185	Wisconsin	10,065	20,915
Mississippi	6,068	14,591	Wyoming	8,944	22,430
Missouri	8,908	18,784			

(c) Prepare a density histogram of the 1969 cross section. Do you find it convenient to use intervals of equal length or do you prefer intervals of unequal length?

PART II

Repeat the items in Part I for the 1979 cross section. On the basis of the plots you have prepared, compare the 1969 to the 1979 cross section. If you ordered the states by median income, are the orderings the same in the two years? Do you feel the data provide a basis for predicting median family income in 1989? In 1980? Explain why or why not. (Filename: STATEINC.DAT.)

3.7C In Exercise 2.3A you computed a series of quarter-to-quarter changes in GNP. Prepare an appropriate frequency plot of these changes. Describe the distribution of the changes.

3.7D Graph a histogram of the percentage changes for the Kansas City flour price index. The data appear in Exercise 2.11A. Compare and contrast this histogram with the corresponding one for the Buffalo, New York, flour price index shown in Exhibit 3.6J. (Filename: KCFLOUR.DAT.)

3.7E The following data show the number of research articles published in statistical theory during the period 1980 through 1986 in nine leading journals.

Number of Articles	Journal
796	*Annals of Statistics*
611	*Biometrika*
34	*Econometric Theory*
80	*International Statistical Review*
610	*Journal of the American Statistical Association*
146	*Journal of Multivariate Analysis*
129	*Journal of Time Series Analysis*
286	*Journal of the Royal Statistical Society* (Series B)
135	*Sankhya* (Series A)

Source: Phillips, P. C. B, Choi, I., & Schochert, P. Z. (1988). Worldwide institutional and individual rankings in statistical theory by journal publications over the period 1980–1986. *Econometric Theory*, 4, 1–34.

(a) Display these data in a bar chart ordering the journals from most to least articles.

(b) Would a density histogram be appropriate for these data?

3.7F In Exercise 2.3B you collected a sequence of 50 to 100 checkbook balances and computed the balance-to-balance changes. Prepare appropriate histograms of the balances and the changes. For which sequence do you feel the histogram yields more useful insights, if any? Explain why.

3.7G Collect a set of cross-sectional data and make an appropriate histogram to display the distribution of the data. Describe the distribution. What predictive value do you feel the data have, if any? [*Suggestion:* Studying the price of a pound of coffee at the food outlets in your town or city makes for an interesting data set. You can study the variation across brands as well as across stores.]

SECTION 3.8

DISTRIBUTION DISPLAYS VERSUS SEQUENCE PLOTS

In this chapter graphic displays of the distribution of a set of data without regard to the time dimension of the data, if any, have been the focus. In Chapter 2 many ways of looking at that time aspect were presented. What kind of information about a data set is given through a histogram display compared with the information presented in a time sequence plot? Histograms of two (hypothetical) sequences are given in Exhibit 3.8A. Notice that the histograms are identical! As batches of numbers, the distributions of the data sets are the same. (In fact, if we listed the data, you would see that the data values are identical.)

E X H I B I T 3.8A

Histograms for Series 1 and 2

```
Histogram of Series 1   N=50          Histogram of Series 2   N=50

Midpoint   Count                      Midpoint   Count
    8.0      2   **                        8.0      2   **
    8.5      3   ***                       8.5      3   ***
    9.0      6   ******                    9.0      6   ******
    9.5      9   *********                 9.5      9   *********
   10.0     10   **********               10.0     10   **********
   10.5      9   *********                10.5      9   *********
   11.0      6   ******                   11.0      6   ******
   11.5      3   ***                      11.5      3   ***
   12.0      2   **                       12.0      2   **
```

However, Exhibits 3.8B and 3.8C give the sequence plots for each of the series. What a difference! Series 1 seems quite random over time, while Series 2 shows a steady upward pattern over its full extent. Be sure to remember that histograms give *no information whatsoever* about the time aspects of the series.

E X H I B I T 3.8B

Sequence Plot for Series 1

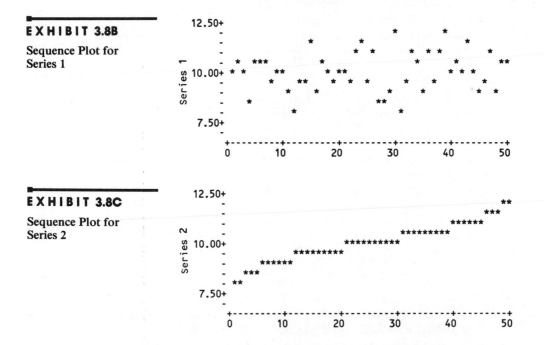

E X H I B I T 3.8C

Sequence Plot for Series 2

If the sequence plots of Exhibits 3.8B and 3.8C are entered as documents into a word processor or editor and all the horizontal spaces between the plotted data points and the vertical column above 0 are deleted, the asterisks are pulled toward the vertical axis and the histogram display in Exhibit 3.8D is produced.[†] By doing this, the time aspect of the series has been removed. Compare these displays to each other and to the histograms in Exhibit 3.8A. Except for the fact that the larger numbers are at the top the displays are identical!

E X H I B I T 3.8D

Collapsed "Histograms" from Sequence Plots

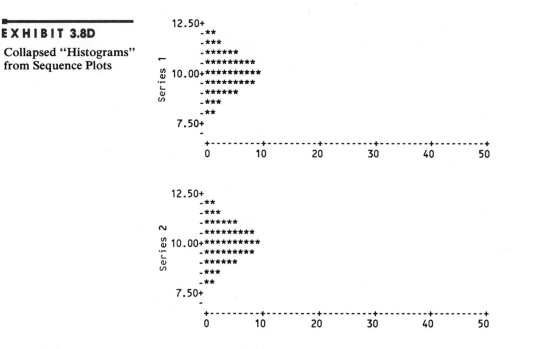

Think about predicting the next value of Series 1 and of Series 2. If you were given only the histogram, you could make a good guess at the next value in Series 1 because the sequence plot shows the series to be random. Your best guess is probably the middle value of the distribution, namely 10. For Series 2, however, the histogram is not a good guide to the future. The information in the sequence plot is vital to making a good prediction. When you are confronted with having to make a prediction or asked to use a prediction made by someone else, you will find the longitudinal context of the prediction to be an important issue. Always ask these questions: What is the longitudinal context? (Is a sequence plot available?) Has the prediction properly taken this context into account?

S E C T I O N 3.9

EXERCISES

3.9A Explain why frequency plots do not display the time dimension. Why is the time dimension important in decision making?

[†] Idea from Professor Harry V. Roberts, University of Chicago.

3.9B Compare and contrast the information given in the sequence plot of the Deere & Co. machining data in Exercise 2.5A with the distribution given in the dotplot of Exercise 3.3C or the stem-and-leaf display of Exercise 3.5C. (Filename: DEERE1.DAT.)

3.9C Prepare a histogram of the Buffalo, New York, flour price index data given in Exhibit 2.10A. Compare the information given in the histogram to the information given in the sequence plot in Exhibit 2.10B. Would the histogram help in guessing the next, that is December 1980, value of the index? (Filename: BUFLOUR.DAT.)

3.9D Compare and contrast the information given in the sequence plot of the percentage change in the Buffalo, New York, flour price index data in Exhibit 2.10D with the distribution given in Exhibit 3.6J. What is your guess for the next (that is, December 1980) percentage change in the series? What is your guess for the next value of the index? (Filename: BUFLOUR.DAT.)

S E C T I O N 3.10

DISCUSSION

In this chapter three tools for displaying the cross-sectional distribution of a data set were introduced: dotplots, stem-and-leaf displays, and histograms. Dotplots are most useful for small-sized data sets, stem-and-leaf displays for medium-sized data sets, and histograms for large-sized data sets. All of them convey, in one way or another, the frequencies with which numerical outcomes occur in the data set. This information is useful in understanding the nature of a process. For processes that evolve more-or-less randomly over time, such information is the most useful in making predictions about the future evolution of the process. For processes that have trends, that meander, or have cycles, however, the information in the cross-sectional distribution is not sufficient for making good predictions and may not even be relevant. Thus the longitudinal context of a cross-sectional distribution must be understood in order to use it properly for decision making.

S E C T I O N 3.11

SUPPLEMENTARY EXERCISES FOR CHAPTER 3

3A A data file showing the sizes of 84 football stadiums in the United States follows on page 77.
  (a) Display the stem-and-leaf diagram for these data. Divide the leaf digits into equal-sized groups as was done in Exhibit 3.4B.
  (b) Display the dotplot of these data.
  (c) Display a histogram of these data
  (d) Compare the three plots obtained in parts (a), (b), and (c). Which of the three displays best portrays the distribution of these data? Are there features that can be seen in one but not another?

```
# filename: STADIUMS.DAT
# Size of U.S. university football stadiums (in 1000's)
# (Source: The World Almanac and Book of Facts, 1985)
   59   Alabama                    50   North Carolina
   70   Arizona State              30   Northern Illinois
   52   Arizona                    50   Northwestern
   42   Arkansas                   60   Notre Dame
   72   Auburn                     85   Ohio State
   48   Baylor                     51   Oklahoma State
   32   Boston College             75   Oklahoma
   30   Bowling Green State        41   Oregon State
   66   Brigham Young              41   Oregon
   77   California-Berkeley        84   Penn State
   73   Clemson                    61   Pennsylvania
   52   Colorado                   56   Pittsburgh
   34   Duke                       46   Princeton
   35   East Carolina              69   Purdue
   55   Florida State              70   Rice
   72   Florida                    72   South Carolina
   58   Georgia Tech               33   Southern Mississippi
   82   Georgia                    85   Stanford
   37   Harvard                    50   Syracuse
   50   Hawaii                     91   Tennessee
   71   Illinois                   72   Texas A & M
   52   Indiana                    46   Texas Christian
   50   Iowa State                 52   Texas, El Paso
   66   Iowa                       47   Texas Tech
   42   Kansas State               80   Texas
   52   Kansas                     40   Tulsa
   30   Kent State                 47   U.S. Air Force Academy
   58   Kentucky                   39   U.S. Military Academy
   76   Louisiana State            30   U.S. Naval Academy
   36   Louisville                 30   Utah State
   45   Maryland                   35   Utah
   50   Memphis State              41   Vanderbilt
   76   Michigan State             52   Virginia Tech
  102   Michigan                   42   Virginia
   32   Mississippi State          30   Wake Forest
   42   Mississippi                40   Washington State
   62   Missouri                   60   Washington
   74   Nebraska                   50   West Virginia
   32   Nevada-Las Vegas           52   Wichita State
   30   New Mexico State           77   Wisconsin
   31   New Mexico                 34   Wyoming
   46   North Carolina State       71   Yale
```

3B The data file below lists the county population sizes for the 99 counties of Iowa in 1980.
  (a) Display the stem-and-leaf display for these data. Divide the leaf digits into equal-sized groups as was done in Exhibit 3.4B.
  (b) Display the dotplot of these data.
  (c) Display a histogram of these data.
  (d) Compare the three plots obtained in parts (a), (b), and (c). Which of the three displays best portrays the distribution of these data? Are there features that can be seen in one but not another?

```
# filename: COUNTIES.DAT
# Population of Iowa counties - 1980 census (in 1000's)
# (Source: The World Almanac and Book of Facts, 1985)
# (in alphabetical order)
  10 6 15 16 9 24 138 26 25 23 21 18 14 23 17 19 48 16 15 9 20 21 57 19
  30 9 10 19 46 16 94 13 25 20 13 9 12 14 12 18 14 22 16 19 11 12 9 15
  23 36 16 82 20 13 22 43 170 12 10 13 13 23 30 42 13 12 12 9 13 40 17
  8 19 13 25 11 303 87 19 6 14 160 15 31 72 20 8 14 9 40 35 20 8 46 13
  22 101 9 16
```

3C The data file which follows gives information on three variables—calories, sodium content, and percent edible—for eight brands of popcorn. In addition, these variables are reported for two different popping methods, hot-oil popped and hot-air popped, for each brand.

(a) Display a dotplot of the calorie content of all 16 data points. Comment on the display.

(b) Display the dotplots of calorie content separately for hot-oil popped and hot-air popped. Comment on these dotplots.

(c) Repeat parts (a) and (b) for sodium content and percent edible. Do any clear differences show up between the two popping methods for these variables?

```
# filename: POPCORN.DAT
# Popcorn data
# (Source: Consumer Reports, June 1989)
# calories, sodium, percent edible
# hot-oil popped=1, hot-air popped=0
  182 1 87 1
  133 1 98 1
  152 2 93 1
  141 1 93 1
  131 1 97 1
  135 1 97 1
  127 2 98 1
  138 1 96 1
   97 1 87 0
   81 1 92 0
   72 1 96 0
   71 1 97 0
   60 0 94 0
   79 2 91 0
   68 1 96 0
   79 1 95 0
```

3D The data file below shows the calories, sodium content, and percent saturated fat (all per tablespoon) for several brands of butter and margarine. There are 37 margarine brands and 9 butters.

(a) For the sodium content variable, construct histograms separately for butter and margarine. Since there are only 9 butters but 37 margarines, use relative frequency histograms so that the two may be compared.

(b) Repeat part (a) for the variables calories and percent saturated fat. Comment on the distributions.

```
# filename: BUTTER.DAT
# Butter and margarine data
# (Source: Consumer Reports, September 1989)
# calories, sodium, % saturated fat
# per tablespoon
# butter=1, margarine=0
  100 115 64  1        100 115   9 0
   63  75 65  1        100  95  18 0
  103  88 64  1        100   0  18 0
  103   0 64  1         90  90  10 0
   99 110 64  1        100  95  18 0
   99   0 64  1        100  95  18 0
  100   2 64  1        100   0  18 0
   96 115 66  1         60 100  14 0
   62   1 66  1         90 105  20 0
   90  95 20  0        100   0  18 0
  100 115 18  0         60 110  19 0
  100  95 18  0        100 100  18 0
   90  90 20  0         60 110  14 0
   60  75 14  0        100 120  18 0
  100 115  9  0         60 110  14 0
  100 100 18  0         80  70  25 0
  100 115 18  0        100  95  18 0
   80 110 22  0        100  95  18 0
  100 100 18  0         70 100  14 0
  100  95 27  0         50   0  17 0
  100  95 18  0        100 115  18 0
   90  90 20  0        100 110  18 0
  100 100 19  0         50  50  17 0
```

GLOSSARY FOR CHAPTER 3

Class frequencies	The frequencies or counts of data values within the class intervals.
Class intervals	Intervals dividing up the values of a variable.
Cross-sectional	Data where the time dimension is either absent or ignored.
Density histogram	A graphical display of a distribution especially useful with unequal-width class intervals.
Dotplot	The display of a distribution on a number line with no grouping.
Frequency histogram	A graphical display of a frequency distribution.
Relative frequency histogram	A graphical display of a relative frequency distribution especially useful for comparing distributions of different-sized data sets.
Stem-and-leaf display	A display of a distribution using the digits of the data to form the groupings and graphical display of frequencies.

## CHAPTER 4

Metric Data Summaries

INTRODUCTION

In the preceding chapters we saw how metric data may be presented in graphs. A time sequence plot may reveal important time-related aspects of a data set, for example, seasonality or trend. A dotplot, stem-and-leaf display, or histogram shows how the observations are distributed. Sometimes, however, certain aspects of data distributions must be summarized or described with just a few numbers.

In the first quarter of 1988, Nissan U.S.A. car sales were down 24% compared to the first quarter of the previous year—very bad news for Nissan. Although marketing and forecasting models aid in evaluating future market conditions, planners at Nissan also need to know current data on who buys their cars and for what reasons. A profile giving income, education, occupation, marital status, and other information on current buyers would be useful. Based on extensive market-survey research,[†] they found (among many other things) that the median age of

[†] Maritz and Rogers, 1988, "Early Model New Car Buyers' Study," as quoted in *PC Week*, June 28, 1988.

Nissan buyers was 43 years, median family income was $54,000, and the average family size of buyers was 2.6 persons.[†]

What aspects of the complete distributions do these single numbers describe? How can an average of 2.6 persons be interpreted? What other numbers portray different relevant characteristics of the distributions? This chapter investigates such numerical descriptors.

Numbers calculated from a data set are *statistics*. Statistics used to describe various features of a data distribution are typically called *descriptive statistics*.

SECTION 4.2

STATISTICS BASED ON ORDERED VALUES

Many useful statistics may be calculated from the data values once they have been put into numerical order, say from the smallest to the largest. With a small data set this is easily accomplished by hand. For larger sets a statistical computer package is used. Exhibit 4.2A gives the ordered values for the photocopy data presented in Exhibit 1.3A. Our first task is to define and discuss a statistic that measures the middle or center of a distribution.

EXHIBIT 4.2A

Photocopy Data, Ordered from Smallest to Largest

238	274	349	362	362	364	374	390	393	395	416
440	447	447	456	456	505	530	532	547	556	579
589	607	616	621	741	780	797	1199			

THE MEDIAN

Once the data have been sorted into order, the middle value in the ordered list can be identified. Such a value is called the **median** of the data set, of the variable, or of the distribution. From Exhibit 4.2A we see that there are 30 observations and that the 15th and 16th in order are both equal to 456. The median number of photocopies per day is thus 456 copies. In general, the specific value for the median depends on whether the data set contains an even or odd number of observations and, in the even case, whether or not the two middle values are the same or different. To find the median of a set of data,

(1) Arrange the numbers in numerical order from smallest to largest.

(2) If the number of data points, n, is odd, the median is the middle value in the ordered list. It is located by counting in $(n + 1)/2$ positions from either end of the ordered list.

(3) If n is even, then the median is the average of the two middle data points. That is, it is the average of the data points at positions $n/2$ and $(n/2) + 1$.

For the ordered data set 3, 5, 5, 6, 7, 9, 9, the median is 6. For the data set 1, 4, 5, 7, the median is $(4 + 5)/2 = 4.5$. *The median value has the property that, as nearly as possible, half the data are below and half the data are above that value.*

[†] It would also be helpful to separate this information by car model—Sentra, Stanza, Maxima, 300 ZX, and so forth—but for competitive reasons these data were not reported to the general public.

SOME NOTATION

In order to express and manipulate statistics it is convenient to use some mathematical notation or shorthand. Let n denote the size of the set of data and let the individual observations be written as $y_1, y_2, \ldots, y_n$. In general, y_i is the ith observation. If the data are collected over time, then the subscript is associated with time, y_1 being the first observation, y_2 the second, and so on. If the observations are taken over a certain cross section, say n regions of the country, then the subscripts are merely labels for the various regions, with no intrinsic meaning or ordering. The ordered data may be written as $y_{(1)} \leq y_{(2)} \leq \cdots \leq y_{(n-1)} \leq y_{(n)}$. For example, if $n = 4$, $y_1 = 3.1$, $y_2 = 1.6$, $y_3 = 2.0$, and $y_4 = 2.5$, then the ordered values are $1.6 < 2.0 < 2.5 < 3.1$, so that $y_{(1)} = 1.6$, $y_{(2)} = 2.0$, $y_{(3)} = 2.5$, and $y_{(4)} = 3.1$.

Let $m = (n + 1)/2$ if n is odd and let $m = n/2$ if n is even.[†] Then we may write

$$\text{Median} = \begin{cases} y_{(m)} & \text{if } n \text{ is odd} \\ \dfrac{y_{(m)} + y_{(m+1)}}{2} & \text{if } n \text{ is even} \end{cases}$$

The median may also be readily found from a stem-and-leaf display. Exhibit 4.2B repeats Exhibit 3.4A—the computer-generated stem-and-leaf display for the full photocopy data. The number of data points, $n = 30$, is shown. In addition, the first column gives a cumulative count of the number of data on that line or on lines toward the nearer extreme. The line that contains the median shows a non-cumulative count in parentheses of the values associated with that stem alone. Thus we need to look for the 15th and 16th observations in the stem labelled 4, which corresponds to 400. We see that the leaves for the 15th and 16th data points are both 5, corresponding to 50, so that, to the accuracy available due to the chopping of the tens digits, the median is 450.

E X H I B I T   4.2B

Stem-and-Leaf Display for Photocopy Data (Exhibit 3.4A repeated)

```
Stem-and-leaf of Copies    N=30
Leaf unit=10

    2      2 37
   10      3 46667999
   (6)     4 144455
   14      5 0334578
    7      6 012
    4      7 489
    1      8
    1      9
    1     10
    1     11 9
```

Note that the median uses order information in the data but does not use the actual numbers to any large extent. The extremely large number of photocopies, 1199, that occurred on one day has essentially no effect on the median number of photocopies. If that 1199 had been any other number above 456, for example, 1999 or 524, the median would be unchanged. Similarly, small extreme values have no

---

[†] An alternative description is that m is the *integer part* of $(n + 1)/2$.

effect on the median. *The median is not influenced at all by the extreme observations in a data set.* For this reason the median is often used as a typical or middle value for distributions that have many atypical extreme values, such as family income distributions as given in Exhibits 3.6O and 3.6Q, which contain a few very large values and a preponderance of smaller numbers.

THE RANGE

The median is very useful in characterizing the middle of a set of data. However, there is much more to a distribution than its center. Another aspect of a data set that is helpful in describing data is its *spread, dispersion,* or *variability* around its middle. Exhibit 4.2C gives simple dotplots of two small data sets that have exactly the same median but are grossly different in their dispersions around that middle value. If the median were used as a predictor of what might be observed in a future observation, we would surely be more confident in our prediction if Data Set 2 described the distribution than if Data Set 1 did.

EXHIBIT 4.2C

Distributions with the Same Median but Differing Dispersions

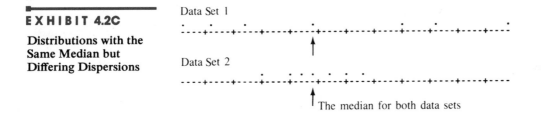

The simplest measure of variability of a distribution is its **range**, which is the difference between the largest and smallest data value.

$$\text{Range} = \text{largest } y - \text{smallest } y = y_{(n)} - y_{(1)}$$

The range for the photocopy data is $1199 - 238 = 961$ copies.

Although simple to compute, the range does have some rather undesirable features. By definition it is based only on the extreme observations. Thus it is highly sensitive to those extreme values and completely insensitive to the other observations and their spread or variability. The distributions shown in Exhibit 4.2D have the same range (and same median for ease of comparison) but clearly have different dispersions according to reasonable interpretations of dispersion.

EXHIBIT 4.2D

Distributions with the Same Range but Differing Dispersions

Data Set 1

Data Set 2

The median for both data sets

Measures of variability that are more sensible but also somewhat more difficult to calculate are based on the following discussion of quartiles. Another important dispersion measure, the standard deviation, is covered in Section 4.4.

QUARTILES AND INTERQUARTILE RANGE

The median splits the ordered data set down the middle into two parts, each containing about half the observations. The first and third quartiles further divide these halves each in half. The **first quartile** is one-quarter up from the bottom of the ordered list; the **third quartile** is one-quarter down from the top of the ordered list. Thus the three descriptive statistics—the first quartile, the median, and the third quartile—divide the data set into quarters (thus the term *quartiles*).

As is the case with the median, where it is not always possible to divide the ordered data into *exactly* two parts, it will also not always be possible to divide the data into exact quarters. For some values of n the task is easy. If $k = (n + 1)/4$ is an integer, then the first quartile, Q_1, is

$$Q_1 = y_{(k)}$$

and the third quartile, Q_3, is

$$Q_3 = y_{(3k)}$$

For example, if $n = 15$, then $k = (15 + 1)/4 = 4$, so that $Q_1 = y_{(4)}$ and $Q_3 = y_{(12)}$; if $n = 11$, then $k = (11 + 1)/4 = 3$, so that $Q_1 = y_{(3)}$ and $Q_3 = y_{(9)}$.

To do an example by hand, suppose there are seven data points: 2.5, 2.1, 1.9, 3.6, 2.4, 1.2, 3.0. First arrange the data into numerical order: 1.2, 1.9, 2.1, 2.4, 2.5, 3.0, 3.6. The median is $2.4 = y_{(4)}$; the first quartile is $1.9 = y_{(2)}$; and the third quartile is $3.0 = y_{(6)}$. Exhibit 4.2E shows the corresponding dotplot with these statistics marked.

EXHIBIT 4.2E

Quartiles and Median for a Small Data Set

First quartile   Median   Third quartile

But suppose that, as in the photocopy data set, $n = 30$, so that $(30 + 1)/4 = 7.75$. Presumably, the first quartile should be taken somewhere between the seventh and eighth ordered data values. Several slightly different rules have been advocated for defining the quartiles in this case.[†] One popular rule is to linearly interpolate between the seventh and eighth ordered values, that is, go three-quarters of the way from $y_{(7)}$ toward $y_{(8)}$. In the photocopy data set given in Exhibit 4.2A, $y_{(7)} = 374$ and $y_{(8)} = 390$, so that the first quartile is $Q_1 = 374 + 0.75(390 - 374) = 386$. Similarly, $3(n + 1)/4 = 23.25$, so that the third quartile is $Q_3 = y_{(23)} + 0.25(y_{(24)} - y_{(23)}) = 589 + 0.25(607 - 589) = 593.5$.

[†] Minitab uses the linear interpolation rule in its DESCRIBE command when computing quartiles. SAS has options for using any one of *five* slightly different definitions in its PROC UNIVARIATE.

To state the interpolation rule in general, we write

$$\tfrac{1}{4}(n + 1) = k + f$$

where k is an integer and f is a fraction with $0 \le f < 1$. Then the first quartile is

$$Q_1 = y_{(k)} + f(y_{(k+1)} - y_{(k)})$$

Similarly, writing

$$\tfrac{3}{4}(n + 1) = m + g$$

where m is an integer and g a fraction with $0 \le g < 1$, the third quartile is given by

$$Q_3 = y_{(m)} + g(y_{(m+1)} - y_{(m)})$$

However, it is important not to get bogged down in specific computational details and lose the essence of the quartile idea: *the quartiles and median divide the ordered data set into quarters.* Notice that the quartiles are essentially unaffected by the actual values of the data that are below the first quartile or above the third quartile. Thus they are quite insensitive to extremely large or small values in the observations.

With the quartiles defined, our new measure of dispersion is simply the distance between the quartiles—the **interquartile range**:

Interquartile range = third quartile − first quartile = $Q_3 - Q_1$

From the discussion above, this measure is resistant to extreme observations. For the photocopy data the interquartile range is equal to $593.5 - 386 = 207.5$ copies.

Exhibit 4.2F gives a display of the relationships among the median, quartiles, and interquartile range of a set of observations.

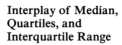

EXHIBIT 4.2F

Interplay of Median, Quartiles, and Interquartile Range

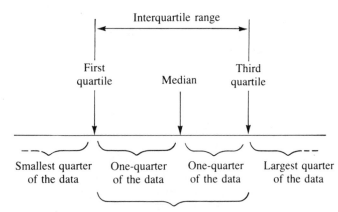

SYMMETRY AND SKEWNESS

Symmetry is a useful concept in data analysis. A distribution is **symmetric** if its left and right sides are mirror images of each other—every detail that appears on the left also appears on the right and at the same distance from the middle of the distribution. A substantial advantage of symmetric distributions is that the "middle" is then unambiguously defined. The median of a symmetric distribution is at the same place as other measures of the middle, which are discussed in Section 4.4. When data are far from symmetrically distributed, analysts may very well disagree on a proper definition of the middle of the distribution. For a symmetric distribution the first quartile, Q_1, is the same distance below the median as the third quartile, Q_3, is above the median. Finally, many statistical procedures work best with (approximately) symmetrically distributed data. Exhibit 4.2G gives dotplots of three symmetric distributions. Notice that even though the third one is piled up at either end with very little data in the middle, it is still symmetric. Algebraically, symmetry around the number c is obtained if $c - y_{(1)} = y_{(n)} - c, c - y_{(2)} = y_{(n-1)} - c$, and, generally, $c - y_{(i)} = y_{(n+1-i)} - c$ for $i = 1, 2, \ldots, n$. Of course these artificial data sets are too good to be true! Exact symmetry will never be observed with real data. The histogram in Exhibit 3.6J shows that the distribution of percentage change in the flour price index is approximately but not exactly symmetric.

EXHIBIT 4.2G

Dotplots of Symmetric Distributions

Data Set 1

```
      .     .     .     .    .  .           .     .
 :----+----+----+----+----+----+----+----+----+----
```

Data Set 2

```
        .      .      . .  .      .      .     .
  ---+----+----+----+----+----+----+----+----+----
```

Data Set 3

```
 . . .:: . .      .       .        .      .  .::  . .
 ---+----+----+----+----+----+----+----+----+----
```

Many real data sets are far from symmetric. The income distributions in Exhibit 3.6Q provide one example. Example 4.2A provides another.

■ **EXAMPLE 4.2A:** Consider the data in Exhibit 4.2H and the histogram in Exhibit 4.2I. The distribution of city sizes in Iowa is highly concentrated at the low end, with a few mid-sized cities and very few large cities. The median city size is computed as 8.5, that is, 8500 people. We say that the distribution is *skewed* to the right or higher values. A **skewed distribution** is an asymmetric distribution with values stretched out on either the high or low end. The skewness in this example is also indicated by the quartiles, $Q_1 = 7000$ and $Q_3 = 26,000$, which are far from being equally spaced around the median of 8500.

EXHIBIT 4.2H

Population of Iowa Cities—1980 Census (in thousands, only ≥ 5000 reported)

```
# filename: CITIES.DAT
# City populations of Iowa - 1980 census (in thousands, 5000 and over)
# (Source: The World Almanac and Book of Facts, 1985)
# (alphabetical order)
  6  6 46 15  8 27 13 30 10 36 110  7  5  9  7  5  7 33  6  8 56  8 103  8  7 191 62
  8  9 29 14  5  9  5  6 11 51  6 14  8  8  6 19 27 30  7 23  6 15  8 11 27  8  7
  7  5  6 82 12  8 18  5  6 76  8  9 22  6
```

Source: The World Almanac and Book of Facts, 1985.

EXHIBIT 4.2I

Distribution of City
Sizes in Iowa (in
thousands)

```
Histogram of Cities   N=68

Midpoint   Count
       0      38  **************************************
      20      17  *****************
      40       5  *****
      60       3  ***
      80       2  **
     100       1  *
     120       1  *
     140       0
     160       0
     180       0
     200       1  *
```

■ **EXAMPLE 4.2B:** Exhibit 4.2J gives the data on the exam scores of a class of 36 students. Exhibit 4.2K gives the histogram of these data, which are skewed toward the left or lower values in the distribution. Here the median is 82 and the quartiles are $Q_1 = 76$ and $Q_3 = 86.75$, showing the asymmetry with the distribution more spread out below the median than above it.

EXHIBIT 4.2J

Exam Scores
for 36
Undergraduates

```
# filename: EXAMS1.DAT
# First exam scores for an undergradute
# business statistics course, 1989, n=36
 54  62  69  69  72  72  76  74  75  76  76  76
 77  77  78  81  82  82  82  82  82  82  82  84
 84  86  86  87  89  90  90  92  92  92  94  96
```

EXHIBIT 4.2K

Distribution of Exam
Scores

```
Histogram of Exam 1   N=36

Midpoint   Count
      55       1  *
      60       1  *
      65       0
      70       4  ****
      75       8  ********
      80       9  *********
      85       5  *****
      90       6  ******
      95       2  **
```

SECTION 4.3

EXERCISES

4.3A Compute the median, quartiles, interquartile range, and range for each of the following data sets:

(a) 3, 5, 14, 9, 11, 6, 7   (b) 3, 5, 41, 9, 11, 6, 7   (c) 3, 4, 14, 9, 13, 6, 7

(d) Comment on the differences among the statistics for the three data sets.

4.3B A group of 50 employees has a median annual wage of $27,000. The highest-paid member of the group, Danforth, has an annual wage of $34,000. If Danforth gets a $4000 raise while all other wages increase by $1000, what now is the median annual wage for the employees?

4.3C Suppose a group contains half men and half women. If we know the median salary for the men and the median salary for the women, can we calculate the median salary for everyone taken together? Why or why not?

STATISTICS BASED ON MOMENTS

Moments are statistics that average a set of observations, their squares, their cubes, or higher powers. The most common moment statistic is the arithmetic average or mean. Such averages are encountered every day with average miles per gallon of gasoline, average score on a midterm exam, average family size of Nissan car buyers, grade point averages, and so on.

THE MEAN

The **mean** of a set of data $y_1, y_2, \ldots, y_n$, denoted by $\bar{y}$, is given by the arithmetic average:

$$\bar{y} = \frac{1}{n} \sum_{i=1}^{n} y_i = \frac{y_1 + y_2 + \cdots + y_n}{n}$$

(Read the symbol $\bar{y}$ as "y bar.") As a simple example, the mean of the five numbers 3, 5, 2, 3, and 4 is $\bar{y} = (3 + 5 + 2 + 3 + 4)/5 = 17/5 = 3.4$. In contrast to the median, the mean uses the actual value of each and every observation. The median of these data is 3. Since the mean adds the actual data values, it generally makes sense only for metric data.

An important exception occurs when we are dealing with binary variables. A *binary variable* assumes only the two values 0 and 1. For example, the variable might indicate gender with 1 = female, 0 = male. Here the total $y_1 + y_2 + \cdots + y_n$ is just the *number* of females in the data set. Thus the mean is the *proportion* or *rate* of females in the data. Even if we express the rate as a percentage, as we frequently do, we are still just working essentially with the mean of a very special type of data.

The mean, when applied to metric data, has a very simple but enlightening physical interpretation as a measure of the middle. Consider a dotplot of the small data set given above:

```
  .          :          .          .
  +----+----+----+----+----+----+----+
  2         3         4         5
```

Imagine the horizontal axis as a (weightless) stick with weights of equal size placed on the stick at the positions of each dot. Where will the stick balance? Arguments from elementary physics or mechanics show that the balance point will always be exactly at the mean:

```
  .          :          .          .
  +----+----+----+----+----+----+----+
  2         3  ↑      4         5
```
Balance point = mean = 3.4

If the observation (weight) at 5 were moved to the right, the mean (balance point) would also be moved to the right. Similarly, if the data point at 2 were to decrease to l the mean would also decrease. The mean and median measure the middle of a distribution in different ways. Notice that 60% of the observations lie below the mean in the case above and the dotplot does *not* balance at the median of 3.

For a perfectly symmetric distribution the balance point is the same as the median, so the mean and median agree in that case. As an example, refer to the percentage change in the flour price index. Here the mean may be calculated as 0.48%, which may be compared to the median value of 0.28%, very little difference for a distribution that covers the interval from −12.9% to 14.4%.

■**EXAMPLE 4.4A:** The city-size distribution given in Exhibit 4.2I gives an extreme example of how the mean and median may present quite different pictures of the middle. For that data set, the mean is 21,710 people compared with a median size of 8500 people. The few large cities have a large influence on the mean, as their actual numerical size is included in the numerator of the ratio used to find $\bar{y}$. As already noted, the median is resistant to the influence of extreme values. Which measure of the middle is correct? The answer depends on our purposes. As a typical value, the median is probably the best measure. However, if we are given only a measure of the middle and we wish to know the *total* population in the 68 cities, then 68 times the mean (68 × 21,710 = 1,476,280) will recover the total city population size. On the other hand, 68 times the median gives 578,000, a completely inappropriate total city population figure. ■

If a data set contains extreme values that are erroneous for some reason, then their strong influence on the mean is unfortunate. As a small example, suppose that the true data are 12, 15, 11, and 14 so that the mean is (12 + 15 + 11 + 14)/4 = 13. If when entering the data into a computer the 12 is mistakenly entered as 21, a typical error, then the mean changes to (21 + 15 + 11 + 14)/4 = 15.25, a substantial error. No statistic can protect against all errors in the data.

On several occasions the effects of extreme observations have been highlighted. Statisticians call observations that are separated from the main body of the data **outliers**. Outliers may simply be the result of errors in measuring or recording the data. Alternatively, outliers may indicate changes in processes that can lead to new discoveries. Regardless of their origin, outliers need to be detected and investigated.

THE STANDARD DEVIATION

The most widely used measure of dispersion, spread, or variability is the **standard deviation**, denoted by s. This statistic is the most complicated we have seen so far, so we need to spend some extra time understanding it. Fortunately we will compute s by hand only a few times for practice. In real applications a computer or a statistical calculator will do the work.

The standard deviation measures dispersion around the mean, so we need to obtain $\bar{y}$ first. The standard deviation is then based on the squared deviations of the observations from their mean. The steps are as follows on page 90.

(1) Find the deviations, $y_i - \bar{y}$, from $\bar{y}$ for all y_i, $i = 1, 2, \ldots, n$.

(2) Square all the deviations and add them up.

(3) Divide this sum by $n - 1$.

(4) Finally, take the positive square root to get the standard deviation s.

Some of the deviations from the mean will be positive and some negative. However, since the deviations are squared, the farther an observation is from the mean in either direction, the larger that observation's contribution is to the standard deviation. The more spread out a distribution is around its mean, the larger its standard deviation. In one big formula, we have

$$s = \sqrt{\frac{\sum_{i=1}^{n}(y_i - \bar{y})^2}{n - 1}}$$

▪ **EXAMPLE 4.4B:** A numerical example will help illustrate. We use the data set 3, 5, 2, 3, 4 with $n = 5$ for which we earlier found the mean to be 3.4. The calculations are best laid out in a table, as in Exhibit 4.4A.

EXHIBIT 4.4A

Calculations to Obtain the Standard Deviation

Observation	Deviation	Squared Deviation
3	$3 - 3.4 = -0.4$	$(-0.4)^2 = 0.16$
5	$5 - 3.4 = 1.6$	$(1.6)^2 = 2.56$
2	$2 - 3.4 = -1.4$	$(-1.4)^2 = 1.96$
3	$3 - 3.4 = -0.4$	$(-0.4)^2 = 0.16$
4	$4 - 3.4 = 0.6$	$(0.6)^2 = 0.36$
Sum $\underline{17}$	$\underline{(0.0)}$	$\underline{5.20}$

($\uparrow$ Use to get $\bar{y}$)

So for these data the standard deviation is $s = \sqrt{5.20/4} = \sqrt{1.3} \cong 1.140175425$, which we round off to $s = 1.14$. Whew!   ▪

Many calculators calculate the standard deviation almost automatically. Just enter the raw data and push the correct button to compute s. (The button may be labelled with the lowercase Greek letter sigma, σ.) Check yours with these data and see if you get the same answer. If not, your calculator may divide by n rather than $n - 1$.[†]

Notice also that the sum of the deviations from the mean is zero. This is no coincidence. The following algebra shows that this is always the case:

$$\sum_{i=1}^{n}(y_i - \bar{y}) = \left(\sum_{i=1}^{n} y_i\right) - n\bar{y} = n\bar{y} - n\bar{y} = 0$$

[†] There are theoretical arguments that support using $n - 1$ as the denominator in the definition of s. Other arguments support the choice of n as the denominator. For reasonably large n there is little difference in the final numerical result.

Thus if any $n - 1$ of the n deviations are given, the remaining deviation can be determined. We say that the n deviations have only $n - 1$ *degrees of freedom*. This partially explains the choice of $n - 1$ as the divisor in computing s.

To help interpret the standard deviation, observe the following facts:

(1) The units for the standard deviation are the same as the units for the observations. That is, if y is measured in inches (or dollars), then s is also in inches (or dollars).

(2) The standard deviation is never negative. It is zero if and only if all the data values are equal.

(3) The standard deviation is strongly influenced by extreme observations and outliers.

As an example of the influence of outliers on s, suppose that the true data are 12, 15, 11, and 14, so that the mean is $\bar{y} = 13$. With these data the standard deviation is found to be

$$ s = \sqrt{\frac{[(12 - 13)^2 + (15 - 13)^2 + (11 - 13)^2 + (14 - 13)^2]}{3}} = \sqrt{\frac{10}{3}} = 1.826 $$

If the 12 is mistakenly entered as 21, then, as we saw earlier, the mean changes to 15.25. In addition, the standard deviation changes to 4.193, more than double the correct value.

For distributions with an approximate mound shape, the standard deviation is especially useful for interpreting the spread of the observations. Consider once more the distribution of percentage changes in the flour price index. The histogram appears in Exhibit 3.6J. Because this distribution is approximately symmetric with a predominance of the data in the middle, the distribution has a mound-shaped appearance. For distributions of this kind, it may be argued theoretically (see Chapter 8) that *about 68% of the observations lie within one standard deviation of the mean*. For these 99 data points the mean is 0.476% and the standard deviation is 4.818%, so about 68% of the distribution should lie in the interval from $0.476 - 4.818 = -4.342\%$ to $0.476 + 4.818 = 5.294\%$. If we count the number of data points within this interval we find that 71 out of 99, or about 71%, are there. In addition, theory says that *about 95% lie within two standard deviations of the mean* and *nearly all of the data lie within three standard deviations of the mean*. For this set of data, the actual figures are 93 out of 99, or 94%, and 99 out of 99, or 100%, respectively. For mound-shaped frequency distributions the mean and standard deviation are a compact summary of the complete distribution.

SYMMETRY AND SKEWNESS

A numerical measure of lack of symmetry, or skewness, based on moments may be obtained by looking at the third power or cube of the deviations from the mean, $(y_i - \bar{y})^3$. Remember that the cube of a negative number is negative. Thus if the distribution is approximately symmetric, then the cube of the positive deviations should tend to be cancelled by corresponding cubes of negative deviations, at least on the average. Hence if we average the cubed deviations we should tend to get numbers near zero for symmetric distributions, positive numbers for distributions skewed to the right, and negative numbers for distributions skewed to the left. To obtain a unitless measure of skewness that may be compared across different distributions, we divide this average of cubed deviations by s^3. The Greek letter kappa, κ, is commonly used to denote this unitless *coefficient of skewness*. In a grand formula, we have

$$\text{Coefficient of skewness} = \kappa = \frac{1}{s^3}\left[\frac{\sum\limits_{i=1}^{n}(y_i - \bar{y})^3}{n-1}\right] = \sqrt{n-1}\,\frac{\left[\sum\limits_{i=1}^{n}(y_i - \bar{y})^3\right]}{\left[\sqrt{\sum\limits_{i=1}^{n}(y_i - \bar{y})^2}\right]^3}$$

$$= \frac{1}{n-1}\sum\limits_{i=1}^{n}\left[\frac{y_i - \bar{y}}{s}\right]^3$$

▪ **EXAMPLE 4.4C:** Consider the data set of Exhibit 4.4A. Adding a new column to that table, we get Exhibit 4.4B. The coefficient of skewness is then $\kappa = (\sqrt{4})1.44/[\sqrt{5.20}]^3 = (2)1.44/11.86 = 0.2429$. We would say that the distribution is very slightly skewed to the right.

EXHIBIT 4.4B

Calculations for Coefficient of Skewness (continuation of Exhibit 4.4A)

Observation	Deviation	Squared Deviation	Cubed Deviation
3	−0.4	0.16	−0.064
5	1.6	2.56	4.096
2	−1.4	1.96	−2.744
3	−0.4	0.16	−0.064
4	0.6	0.36	0.216
Sum 17	(0.0)	5.20	1.440

For the percentage changes in the flour price index we find that $\kappa = 0.2034$, a very small positive skewness, while for the Iowa city population size distribution we obtain $\kappa = 3.30$, indicating strong positive skewness. The exam scores whose distribution is depicted in Exhibit 4.2K have a coefficient of skewness of -0.634, documenting the mild negative skewness of that distribution.

SIMPSON'S PARADOX (OPTIONAL)

For magazine publishers, the renewals of expiring subscriptions are very important to the continuance of their business. The publisher of *American History Illustrated* noted in 1979 that the renewal rate increased from 51.2% in January to 64.1% in February.[†] However, it is also important to investigate the renewal rates among different categories of subscribers. The subscribers are categorized according to whether the previous subscription was a gift, a previous renewal, and so forth. To the publishers' surprise they discovered that when broken down by these subscriber categories the rates all *decreased* from January to February! How is this possible? The full data are given in Exhibit 4.4C.

[†] Clifford H. Wagner, "Simpson's Paradox in Real Life," *The American Statistican*, 36 (1982): 46–48.

EXHIBIT 4.4C

Magazine Renewal
Rates and Simpson's
Paradox

Month	Gift	Previous Renewal	Direct Mail	Subscription Service	Catalog Agent	Overall
January						
Total	3,594	18,364	2,986	20,862	149	45,955
Renewals	2,918	14,488	1,783	4,343	13	23,455
Rate	81.2%	78.9%	59.7%	20.8%	8.7%	51.2%
February						
Total	884	5,140	2,224	864	45	9,157
Renewals	704	3,907	1,134	122	2	5,869
Rate	79.6%	76.0%	51.0%	14.1%	4.4%	64.1%

(Category column spans Gift, Previous Renewal, Direct Mail, Subscription Service, Catalog Agent)

The overall rate of renewals for January and for February can be written as

$$\text{January rate} = \frac{3{,}594}{45{,}955} \times \frac{2{,}918}{3{,}954} + \frac{18{,}364}{45{,}955} \times \frac{14{,}488}{18{,}364} + \frac{2{,}986}{45{,}955} \times \frac{1{,}783}{2{,}986} + \frac{20{,}862}{45{,}955}$$

$$\times \frac{4{,}343}{20{,}862} + \frac{149}{45{,}955} \times \frac{13}{149}$$

$$= 0.08(0.81) + 0.40(0.79) + 0.06(0.60) + 0.45(0.21) + .00(0.09)$$

$$= 0.512$$

and

$$\text{February rate} = \frac{884}{9157} \times \frac{704}{884} + \frac{5140}{9157} \times \frac{3907}{5140} + \frac{2224}{9157} \times \frac{1134}{2224} + \frac{864}{9157} \times \frac{122}{864}$$

$$+ \frac{45}{9157} \times \frac{2}{45}$$

$$= 0.10(0.80) + 0.56(0.76) + 0.24(0.51) + 0.09(0.14) + 0.00(0.04)$$

$$= 0.641$$

Notice that in January a large percentage of the renewals were in the subscription service category ($20{,}862/45{,}955 = 45.4\%$), while in February only $864/9157 = 9.4\%$ were in that category. The overall renewal rate is a *weighted average* of the renewal rates for individual categories with weights given by the percentages that the categories represent of the total renewals. Changes in the weights together with changes in the renewal rates of the individual categories affect the overall renewal rate.

The direction of an effect may often be reversed once data are broken down by another variable. In general, **Simpson's paradox** refers to this reversal when data are either combined or broken down by another variable.

EXERCISES

4.5A Compute the mean and standard deviation for each of the following data sets:
(a) 3, 5, 14, 9, 11, 6, 7   (b) 3, 5, 41, 9, 11, 6, 7   (c) 3, 4, 14, 9, 13, 6, 7
(d) Comment on the differences among the statistics for the three data sets.

4.5B A group of 50 employees has a mean annual wage of $27,000. The highest-paid member of the group, Danforth, has an annual wage of $34,000. If Danforth gets a $4000 raise while all other wages increase by $1000, what now is the mean annual wage for the employees?

4.5C Suppose a group contains half men and half women. If we know the mean salary for the men and the mean salary for the women, can we calculate the mean salary for everyone taken together? Why or why not?

4.5D Recently the *Des Moines Register* carried a story headlined "Des Moines lowest in survey of home prices." The story reported on a 62-city survey released by the National Association of Realtors. According to the survey the median price of an existing Des Moines home was $55,000 and had fallen 2.1% from the previous year. However, local real estate experts disputed these figures. According to the Greater Des Moines Board of Realtors, Mike Knapp of Iowa Realty claimed that the average sale price of an existing Des Moines home increased from $61,012 a year earlier to $67,279 last month. "I guess it's a matter of how you keep your statistics," said Knapp.
(a) Comment on the apparent discrepancy between the two measures of home prices.
(b) What type of average must the Greater Des Moines Board of Realtors be using?
(c) Which measure provides a prospective buyer with a better typical value?
(d) Which measure would provide a tax assessor with a better typical value?

4.5E When data are reported as frequencies within intervals, as in Exhibit 3.6P, means, medians, standard deviations, and so on may only be approximated. Can you think of a reasonable way to approximate the mean of the underlying, but unreported, data that led to Exhibit 3.6P? The median? The standard deviation?

4.5F Suppose data are reported as in Exhibit 3.6O where an unbounded interval of the type $50,000+ occurs. Could we reasonably approximate the mean income in this situation? How about the median income?

4.5G If a data set is (roughly) symmetrically distributed, argue that the mean and median will be nearly equal.

4.5H Compute the mean and standard deviation of the number of photocopies made per day. The data are listed in Exhibit 4.2A. Recalculate the mean and standard deviation excluding the outlier at 1199. Do the values of the mean and standard deviation change much? (Filename: PHOTOCOP.DAT.)

4.5I Ten accounts have a mean balance of $562. If an 11th account with balance $721 is added to the group, what is the new mean balance?

4.5J Suppose 100 accounts have a mean balance of $562. If another account of size $721 is added to the group, what is the new mean balance? Compare with Exercise 4.5I.

LINEAR TRANSFORMATIONS AND STANDARDIZATION

The same variable can often be measured in different units—dollars or yen, miles or kilometers, pounds or kilograms, Fahrenheit or Celsius. If y is temperature measured in Celsius, then $y^* = 32 + \frac{9}{5}y$ is the corresponding temperature measured in Fahrenheit. For example, $20°$ Celsius corresponds to $32 + \frac{9}{5}(20) = 32 + 36 = 68°$ Fahrenheit. Similarly, if y is the number of photocopies made and each costs $0.05, then $0.05y$ is the cost of the copies.

Many similar transformations arise in practical applications. In general, the effect of **linear transformations** is

$$y^* = a + by \qquad (4.1)$$

where b is a positive number. Then the shape of the distribution of y^* is the same as the shape of the distribution of y, only the labelling of the values changes. Our discussion is limited to positive b values since nearly all practical examples satisfy this constraint.

▪**EXAMPLE 4.6A:** Exhibit 4.6A shows the histogram of photocopy costs at $0.05 per page. Compare this to the histogram of the photocopy counts shown in Exhibit 3.6C. The shapes are the same. Only the labelling of the values has changed.

EXHIBIT 4.6A

Histogram of Photocopy Costs

```
Histogram of Costs    N=30

Midpoint    Count
      10        1   *
      15        2   **
      20       11   ***********
      25        6   ******
      30        6   ******
      35        1   *
      40        2   **
      45        0
      50        0
      55        0
      60        1   *
```

▪

Although the shape of a distribution remains unchanged by a linear transformation, the descriptive statistics for the distribution will change in a predictable way. It is easy to show that the mean of the y^* values is given by

$$\bar{y}^* = a + b\bar{y} \qquad (4.2)$$

Similarly, the median, first and third quartiles, and minimum and maximum for y and y^* are related as in Equation (4.2). For example, the median of y^* is $a + b \times$ (median of y).

On the other hand, since measures of dispersion are all relative to a middle of a distribution, the standard deviation, range, and interquartile range are all multiplied by the coefficient b as in

$$s_{y^*} = bs_y \qquad (4.3)$$

but are *not* affected by the additive constant a.

▪**EXAMPLE 4.6B:** Exhibit 4.6B shows the descriptive statistics for both the photocopy counts and costs. Here $b = 0.05$ and, for example, $25.60 = 0.05(512.1)$ and $9.47 = 0.05(189.3)$ to the number of decimal places shown.

■━━━━━━━━
EXHIBIT 4.6B

Descriptive Statistics of
Photocopy Counts and
Costs

	Mean	Median	Standard Deviation
Copies	512.1	456.0	189.3
Costs	25.60	22.80	9.47

	Minimum	Maximum	Q_1	Q_3
Copies	238.0	1199.0	386.0	593.5
Costs	11.90	59.95	19.30	29.68

■

STANDARDIZATION

The particular linear transformation

$$z = \frac{y - \bar{y}}{s} \qquad \text{(4.4)}$$

applied case by case is called **standardization** of the variable y. Here $a = -\bar{y}/s$ and $b = 1/s$. The notation z is commonly used for standardized variables. From Equations (4.2) and (4.3) it follows that *all standardized variables have a mean of 0 and a standard deviation of 1*.

If y is measured in dollars, then $\bar{y}$ and s are also in dollars, so the corresponding standardized variable is *unitless*. This is true for any variable y regardless of the original units.

The standardized value z measures the number of standard deviations, s, that y is away from its mean, $\bar{y}$. A z value of 1.6 means that y is 1.6 standard deviations above its mean, $\bar{y}$. In general, a positive value for z indicates that y is above its mean, and a negative value of z indicates that y is below its mean.

If the distribution of y is mound shaped, then the distribution of z is also mound shaped and approximately 68% of the standardized values lie within the interval from -1 to 1, 95% within $(-2, 2)$, and nearly all within $(-3, 3)$. Standardized values will be especially important when we deal with normal distributions, beginning in Chapter 8. The normal distribution is a theoretical model for mound-shaped distributions.

SECTION 4.7

EXERCISES

4.7A Consider the Deere & Co. machining data given in Exercise 2.5A. The data were coded in 0.000025-inch deviations from a target value.
 (a) If y represents the coded value (as given), find the values of a and b so that $y^* = a + by$ represents the deviation from target *in inches*. [Answer: $a = 0$ and $b = 0.000025$]
 (b) Find the mean and standard deviation for the coded values and use Equations (4.2) and (4.3) to obtain the mean and standard deviation in inches.

4.7B The Amana microwave oven data of Section 2.8 were coded so that 6.050″ is written as 50, 6.073″ is 73, and so on.

(a) If y represents the coded value, find the values of a and b so that $y^* = a + by$ represents the actual measurement *in inches*. [Answer: $a = 6$ and $b = 0.001$]

(b) If y represents the actual value and y^* the coded value, find the values of a and b so that $y^* = a + by$. [Answer: $a = -6000$ and $b = 1000$]

4.7C On September 27, 1989, the rate of exchange for the Japanese yen was 140.60 per U.S. dollar. If on that day a data set is given in dollars and has a median value of $10,400 with an interquartile range of $2300, what were the corresponding median and interquartile range in yen on that date?

4.7D On September 28, 1989, a West German mark was worth 1.8815 U.S. dollars. If on that day a set of accounts payable had a mean of 640 marks and a standard deviation of 160 marks, what were the corresponding values in U.S. dollars?

4.7E In Exercise 4.5H you computed the mean and standard deviation of the number of photocopies made per day excluding the outlier at 1199. The data are in Exhibit 4.2A. Use that mean and standard deviation to obtain the standarized values for the photocopy data. Does the standardized value for the outlier seem out of line with the other standardized values? (*Hint:* Compare with what we expect for a mound-shaped distribution.) (Filename: PHOTOCOP.DAT.)

SECTION 4.8

DESCRIPTIVE STATISTICS AND THE COMPUTER

Statistical software packages include commands or menu selections to calculate the descriptive statistics we have discussed so far and many more.

Exhibit 4.8A displays the output obtained from the DESCRIBE command in the Minitab system applied to two of the variables we have been working with throughout the last few chapters. The data set count, together with the number of missing values, if any, is given for each variable "described." Three measures of the middle are reported: the mean, the median, and the trimmed mean (labelled TRMEAN). The trimmed mean is obtained by "trimming off" the 5% largest and 5% smallest observations and then calculating the arithmetic average of the middle 90% of the data. It can be considered as a compromise between the mean and median that attempts to maximize the advantages of each while minimizing the disadvantages. In addition, the standard deviation (STDEV) is given together with the standard error of the mean (SEMEAN), which is discussed in Chapters 8 and 14. Finally, the minimum, maximum, and quartiles are given. Similar output for StatGraphics and SPSS/PC+ is shown in Exhibits 4.8B and 4.8C. Although all are a little different, the overlap is considerable.

EXHIBIT 4.8A

An Example of the DESCRIBE Command in Minitab

	N	N*	MEAN	MEDIAN	TRMEAN	STDEV	SEMEAN
%Change	99	1	0.476	0.281	0.425	4.818	0.484

	MIN	MAX	Q1	Q3
%Change	-12.910	14.428	-2.976	3.205

	N	MEAN	MEDIAN	TRMEAN	STDEV	SEMEAN
Cities	68	21.71	8.50	17.05	30.82	3.74

	MIN	MAX	Q1	Q3
Cities	5.00	191.00	7.00	26.00

EXHIBIT 4.8B

Results from the STATS
Command in
StatGraphics

Variable:	Copies	Percent
Sample size	30	99
Average	512.067	0.475974
Median	456	0.2809
Mode	362	0.2703
Geometric mean	484.138	
Variance	35849.2	23.2137
Standard deviation	189.339	4.81806
Standard error	34.5684	0.484233
Minimum	238	-12.9096
Maximum	1199	14.4276
Range	961	27.3372
Lower quartile	390	-2.9757
Upper quartile	589	3.2055
Interquartile range	199	6.1812
Skewness	1.76549	0.207597
Standardized skewness	3.94776	0.843265
Kurtosis	4.90642	0.590332
Standardized kurtosis	5.48554	1.19897

EXHIBIT 4.8C

Output from the
DESCRIPTIVES
Command from
SPSS/PC+

Page 19	SPSS/PC+		7/12/90

Number of Valid Observations (Listwise) =   99.00

Variable PERCENT

Mean	.476	S.E. Mean	.484
Std Dev	4.818	Variance	23.214
Kurtosis	.590	S.E. Kurt	.481
Skewness	.208	S.E. Skew	.243
Range	27.337	Minimum	-12.91
Maximum	14.43	Sum	47.122

Valid Observations - 99   Missing Observations - 1

Very few statistics based on ordered data are included in the SPSS/PC+ DESCRIPTIVES command, but this system has other commands for obtaining quartiles. A large number of descriptive statistics are reported with the STATS command in StatGraphics, many of which we have not discussed.

SECTION 4.9

EXERCISES

4.9A Preferably using a statistical package, compute the mean and median of the city sizes given in Exhibit 4.2H. Which gives a better measure of typical value? Which would be more useful if interest centers on the total population of the cities? (Filename: CITIES.DAT.)

4.9B Compute the standard deviations of the "before" and "after" punch data given in Exhibits 3.6E and 3.6G. What are the units of measurement for these standard deviations? (Filenames: PUNCH_B.DAT. and PUNCH_A.DAT.)

4.9C Refer to the monthly Deere & Co. oil-filter sales reported in Exhibit 2.6A.
(a) Find the means and standard deviations for each of the 12 months.
(b) Do these statistics agree with the graphical displays in Exhibit 2.6C? (Filename: OILFILT.DAT.)

4.9D Refer to the Amana Refrigeration assembly data plotted in Exhibits 2.8C and 2.8D. The data are listed in Appendix 2 and are in file AMANA.DAT.
(a) Compute the mean and standard deviations of both the Left and Right values.
(b) Do the means and standard deviations appear comparable?

4.9E Find the mean, median, and standard deviation for the percentage changes in the Buffalo, New York, flour price index listed in Exhibit 2.10A. If the index stands at 172 this month, what would be a reasonable prediction for the index value for next month? Find standardized values for the percentage changes in the flour price index. Display a histogram for the standardized values and compare the shape of this histogram to that of the original values given in Exhibit 3.6J. (Filename: BUFLOUR.DAT.)

SECTION 4.10

AN EXTENDED EXAMPLE—LOS ANGELES TRAFFIC

A medium-sized retail firm is considering opening a store in the metropolitan Los Angeles area. One of many variables that will be of interest to them is the traffic volume in and near their proposed site. Fortunately, some general traffic data from 1987 in that area are available. Traffic volumes measured as vehicles per weekday were obtained at 396 sites in the greater Los Angeles area.[†] The data set is listed in Appendix 2 and is available in data file TRAFFIC.DAT. The first report said that there was an average (mean) of 37,663 vehicles per weekday passing any given location on "typical" Los Angeles roads. This seems like an enormous number of vehicles even for Los Angeles! Surely a further look at the data is necessary to understand what this average means.

With 396 numbers it is useless to look at the data directly. A histogram should tell a great deal about the traffic volume distribution. Exhibit 4.10A gives this display. The immediate reaction is to wonder about the extreme skewness of the distribution. Exhibit 4.10B gives the descriptive statistics for these data, and we see that the mean number of vehicles per weekday is indeed 37,663 while the median is only 15,268. Clearly, we need to dig deeper into this data set.

EXHIBIT 4.10A

Weekday Traffic
Volumes in Los Angeles

```
Histogram of Volume    N=396
Each * represents five observations

Midpoint   Count
       0      33   *******
   10000     158   *********************************
   20000      75   ***************
   30000       3   *
   40000       4   *
   50000       4   *
   60000      12   ***
   70000      14   ***
   80000      14   ***
   90000      21   *****
  100000      10   **
  110000      19   ****
  120000       8   **
  130000      15   ***
  140000       6   **
```

[†] Data courtesy of Lee Cryer, Barton-Aschman Associates, Inc., Pasadena, California.

EXHIBIT 4.10B

Descriptive Statistics
for Los Angeles Traffic
Volumes

	N	Mean	Median	Standard Deviation
Volume	396	37663	15268	41055

	Min	Max	Q_1	Q_3
Volume	954	137000	9086	70500

After going back to the data source, it was discovered that the traffic counts
include data from a number of different road types. Some of the values pertain to
freeways, some to major arterial roads, some to minor arterial roads, and some 50 of
the counts come from one major arterial road—Ventura Boulevard. The distribution portrayed in Exhibit 4.10A is really a mixture of volumes from some very
different road types, not all of which pertain to the problem at hand—the retail
store cannot be sited on a freeway!

Exhibits 4.10C–F show the histograms of the traffic volumes stratified according
to road type: freeway, major arterial, minor arterial, and Ventura Boulevard. The
dotplots in Exhibit 4.10G give a succinct display of the differences and similarities
among the four distributions.

EXHIBIT 4.10C

Freeway Traffic Volume
in Los Angeles

```
Histogram of Freeway    N=127

Midpoint   Count
  40000       4    ****
  50000       4    ****
  60000      12    ************
  70000      14    **************
  80000      14    **************
  90000      21    *********************
 100000      10    **********
 110000      19    *******************
 120000       8    ********
 130000      15    ***************
 140000       6    ******
```

EXHIBIT 4.10D

Major Arterial Traffic
Volume—Los Angeles

```
Histogram of Major      N=110

Midpoint   Count
   4000       4    ****
   6000       4    ****
   8000      12    ************
  10000       8    ********
  12000      17    *****************
  14000      19    *******************
  16000      21    *********************
  18000      16    ****************
  20000       4    ****
  22000       1    *
  24000       2    **
  26000       0
  28000       1    *
  30000       1    *
```

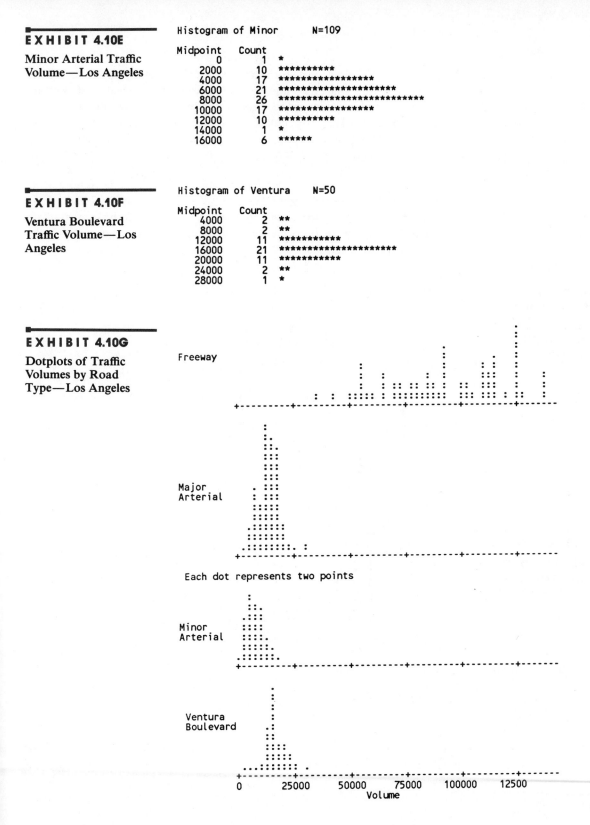

EXHIBIT 4.10E

Minor Arterial Traffic
Volume—Los Angeles

```
Histogram of Minor      N=109

Midpoint    Count
       0        1   *
    2000       10   **********
    4000       17   *****************
    6000       21   *********************
    8000       26   **************************
   10000       17   *****************
   12000       10   **********
   14000        1   *
   16000        6   ******
```

EXHIBIT 4.10F

Ventura Boulevard
Traffic Volume—Los
Angeles

```
Histogram of Ventura    N=50

Midpoint    Count
    4000        2   **
    8000        2   **
   12000       11   ***********
   16000       21   *********************
   20000       11   ***********
   24000        2   **
   28000        1   *
```

EXHIBIT 4.10G

Dotplots of Traffic
Volumes by Road
Type—Los Angeles

Notice that the dotplots for major arterial roads and for Ventura Boulevard are very similar. A little reflection and further investigation reveal that Ventura Boulevard is, in fact, a major arterial road. Exhibit 4.10H gives the descriptive statistics by road type. Here the similarities between major arterials and Ventura Boulevard may be examined more closely. The means are 13,789 and 15,802, respectively. The standard deviations are 4765 and 4838. Since both distributions are mound shaped, we would expect about 68% of traffic volumes to lie in the intervals 9074 to 18,554 and 10,964 to 20,640, respectively. The interquartile ranges, $16,695 - 10,646 = 6049$ and $19,121 - 13,074 = 6047$, are astonishingly close. In the absence of further information about where the store is to be located, there is no compelling reason to keep the Ventura Boulevard data separate from the other major arterials data.

EXHIBIT 4.10H

Descriptive Statistics for Different Road Types— Los Angeles

	N	Mean	Median	Standard Deviation
Freeway	127	92,898	92,000	26,282
Major	110	13,789	13,860	4,765
Minor	109	7,247	7,236	3,626
Ventura	50	15,802	15,146	4,838
	Min	**Max**	$Q1$	$Q3$
Freeway	36,000	137,000	72,000	114,000
Major	3,522	29,230	10,646	16,695
Minor	954	16,555	4,870	9,499
Ventura	2,970	29,370	13,074	19,121

EXHIBIT 4.10I

Combined Major Arterial Road Volumes—Los Angeles

```
Histogram of Combined    N=160

Midpoint   Count
   2000      1    *
   4000      4    ****
   6000      6    ******
   8000     12    ************
  10000     10    **********
  12000     24    ************************
  14000     31    *******************************
  16000     32    ********************************
  18000     18    ******************
  20000      9    *********
  22000      6    ******
  24000      4    ****
  26000      0
  28000      1    *
  30000      2    **
```

Exhibit 4.10I shows the distribution after combining the volumes from major arterials and Ventura Boulevard. A very symmetric distribution results. The descriptive statistics are given in Exhibit 4.10J. The mean and median are 14,418 and 14,748 with a standard deviation of 4863. The middle 50% lies in the interval from

	N	Mean	Median	Standard Deviation
Combined	160	14418	14748	4863
	Min	**Max**	**Q1**	**Q3**
Combined	2970	29370	11734	17086

EXHIBIT 4.10J

Combined Major Arterial Descriptive Statistics—Los Angeles

11,734 to 17,086. We should be willing to take an even bet that the traffic volume will be in this range. Exhibit 4.10H shows that the volume on minor arterial streets averages 7427 vehicles per weekday with a standard deviation of 3626 vehicles per weekday. The middle 50% runs from 4870 to 9499 vehicles per weekday.

Management has estimated that a weekday average traffic volume of at least 10,000 vehicles is desired to attract the required business volume at the new site. Locating the business on a major arterial road in Los Angeles would likely meet this criterion, but a minor arterial site would probably not generate enough traffic to meet their needs.

SECTION 4.11

DISCUSSION

In this chapter the importance of using a few numbers to describe various characteristics of distributions possibly involving many data points was emphasized. The two most important characteristics are measures of the middle and the dispersion in a distribution. Statistics based on ordered data include the median, range, quartiles, and interquartile range. Other important statistics, the mean and standard deviation, measure middle and dispersion in another way. The notions of distribution shape with respect to symmetry or skewness were also introduced.

SECTION 4.12

SUPPLEMENTARY EXERCISES FOR CHAPTER 4

4A Use the stadium-size data given in Supplementary Exercise 3A.
   (a) Find the mean and median stadium sizes. Which is larger? Does this ordering agree with the shape of the distribution as given in either the stem-and-leaf display, dotplot, or histogram in Supplementary Exercise 3A?
   (b) Find the first and third quartiles and the interquartile range for these data. Do the quartiles and median indicate that the distribution is symmetric or skewed? (Filename: STADIUMS.DAT.)

4B Use the Iowa county–size data given in Supplementary Exercise 3B.
   (a) Find the mean and median county sizes. Which is larger? Does this ordering agree with the shape of the distribution as given in either the stem-and-leaf display, dotplot, or histogram in Exercise 3.3B?
   (b) There are 99 counties in this data set. Is the mean or median more help in finding the total 1980 population of Iowa? Explain.

(c) Find the first and third quartiles and the interquartile range for these data. Do the quartiles and median indicate that the distribution is symmetric or skewed? (Filename: COUNTIES.DAT.)

4C In Supplementary Exercise 3C several variables for eight brands of popcorn were considered. Use those data here.

(a) Calculate the mean calories of the 16 data points for the eight brands and two popping methods.

(b) Calculate the mean calories separately for the two popping methods. Compare these with the value obtained in part (a).

(c) Consider the percent edible variable. Compare the overall mean with the means calculated separately for the two popping methods. Comment on clear differences or lack thereof. (Filename: POPCORN.DAT.)

4D In Supplementary Exercise 3D, butter and margarine were compared with respect to several variables. Using those data:

(a) Calculate the median and first and third quartiles for the calorie content of margarine.

(b) Using the numbers obtained in part (a), would you describe the distribution as symmetric or skewed? If skewed, is it skewed toward high values or low values?

(c) Do your conclusions in part (b) based on these descriptive statistics agree with the distribution plots obtained in Supplementary Exercise 3D?

(d) Repeat parts (a), (b), and (c) for percent saturated fat content of margarine. (Filename: BUTTER.DAT.)

4E A group of people contains 50 men and 50 women. The median salary for the men is $30,000, and the median salary for the women is $30,000. What can you say about the median salary for the group of 100 people?

4F A group of people contains 50 men and 50 women. The mean salary for the men is $30,000, and the mean salary for the women is $30,000. What can you say about the mean salary for the group of 100 people?

4G A group of people contains 25 men and 15 women. The mean salary for the men is $25,000, and the mean salary for the women is $30,000. What can you say about the mean salary for the group of 40 people?

4H During a December 1989 Hawkeye basketball game a TV announcer commented that last year an average of $\frac{1}{3}$ of a player fouled out per game. His partner, the color commentator, remarked that he thought it was impossible for $\frac{1}{3}$ of a player to foul out. Assuming that average here means the mean, explain the color commentator's mistake.

S E C T I O N   4.13

GLOSSARY FOR CHAPTER 4

First quartile	The data value one-quarter from the bottom of the ordered list.
Interquartile range	The difference between the third quartile and the first quartile.
Linear transformation	Replacing a variable y by $a + by$ for some choice of constants a and b.
Mean	The arithmetic average of the data values.
Median	The middle value for a data set ordered in magnitude.
Moment	A statistic formed as the average of a power of the data values.
Outlier	An observation that is separated from the main body of the data.

Range	The difference between the largest and smallest data value.
Simpson's paradox	A paradox where an overall average changes in a way opposite to the changes in the averages for component parts.
Skewed distribution	An asymmetric distribution with values stretched out on either the high or low end.
Standard deviation	The square root of the number obtained from the sum of the squared deviations of the observations from their mean divided by $n - 1$.
Standardization	Replacing a variable y by $(y - \bar{y})/s$, case by case.
Symmetric distribution	A distribution whose left and right sides are mirror images of one another.
Third quartile	The data value one-quarter from the top of the ordered list.

## CHAPTER 5

Describing Categorical Variables

SECTION 5.1

INTRODUCTION

In Chapters 2, 3, and 4 a number of tools for displaying and describing metric data were presented. Another important type of data is **categorical data**, data that are arranged in classes or categories.

Counting is a basic data-collection technique, and counts are important statistics in practical applications. For example, we may wish to know how many firms belong to a certain Standard Industrial Classification (SIC) category, or the number of units sold in a given day, week, month, or quarter, or how many firms responding to a questionnaire belong to a certain geographic region. Whenever we count, we deal with categorical data.

Another source of categorical data is the classification of elements into groups according to a common attribute. For example, we may group together firms with fewer than 100 employees and call them "small." Or we may group together persons according to gender or brand of coffee usually purchased.

The tools presented in this chapter will help you analyze and report categorical data. The basic tool is the multi-way table. In Section 5.4 the simplest table, a tally table for a single variable, is introduced. But first the notion of variables is discussed.

SECTION 5.2

VARIABLES

■ **EXAMPLE 5.2A:** Exhibit 5.2A displays a data set that is a prototype of many encountered in practice. The set is a small portion of one collected in the 1980 Wisconsin Restaurant Survey conducted by the University of Wisconsin Small Business Development Center.[†] It consists of seven columns of figures, each column representing a characteristic of a restaurant. There are 10 data entries in each column, each corresponding to a restaurant that returned a questionnaire. A given restaurant's responses to the seven questions make up a row in the table. (A realistic data set would have many more rows because a large number of restaurants would be surveyed.)

EXHIBIT 5.2A

A Small Data Set with 7 Columns (variables) and 10 Rows (cases)

Id	Outlook	Sales	Wages	Adv	Full	Part
1	2	480	25	2	8	30
2	4	507	20	5	6	25
3	5	210	24	3	0	17
4	5	246	30	1	2	13
5	2	148	35	1	*	*
6	3	135	30	10	2	*
7	2	72	10	5	0	5
8	3	99	25	1	1	8
9	4	160	*	*	2	10
10	4	243	15	2	2	19

Asterisk (*) denotes data not reported or reported incorrectly.

The first column is an identification number, in this case a serial number. The second column records the responses to a question on economic outlook. Respondents could give any number from 1 to 6, with 1 denoting very unfavorable outlook and 6 denoting very favorable. The third column records the sales, in thousands of dollars, the restaurant made in 1979. Columns four and five give wages and advertising, respectively, as a percentage of sales. Columns six and seven give the numbers of full-time and part-time employees.

[†] An extensive analysis of the full data set may be found in R. B. Miller, *Minitab Handbook for Business and Economics* (Boston: PWS-KENT, 1988), Chapter 4.

In a data set like this each column of figures corresponds to a **variable**, that is, a characteristic of the elements under study, which in this example are restaurants. The rows in a data table are called **cases**. Each restaurant is a case of a variable, that is, it contributes an observation on the variable in question.

Although each variable can be studied separately by manipulating the figures in a single column, groups of variables can also be studied. For example, the relationship among sales, wages, and advertising may be of interest.

Several of the entries in Exhibit 5.2A are asterisks (∗), which denote missing data. Sometimes respondents fail or refuse to answer some of the questions on a questionnaire, creating *partial nonresponse* because some of the questions are answered and some are not. Sometimes the responses are unreadable or are clearly in error. If such responses cannot be corrected, then they too must be coded as missing. In survey work, the problem of missing data almost always creeps in.   ▪

One of the most common statistical operations is the creation of new variables through arithmetic or functional operations on old variables. For example, in Chapter 2 the *averages* and the *differences* of the Left and Right measurements on microwave ovens were considered. Monthly differences of flour prices were also computed. Here are two more examples, using the data in Exhibit 5.2A.

▪**EXAMPLE 5.2B:** In Exhibit 5.2A a new variable, "full-time equivalent employees" (Fte), is defined by the rule Fte = Full + (.5) × Part; that is, full-time equivalent is the number of full-time employees plus half the part-time employees. This definition understates the effort of part-time employees who work more than half-time and overstates the effort of part-time employees who work less than half-time, but it is a simple definition and probably does not represent a substantial error. For the restaurant business, which tends to be labor intensive, Fte might be used as a measure of the magnitude of the business operation. The variable Fte may provide too fine a categorization for some analyses, and some grouping may be done to ease comparisons.

To illustrate, let us also define a variable Size by the following rule:

If Fte is between 1 and 9.5, set Size = 1.

If Fte is between 10 and 20, set Size = 2.

If Fte is greater than 20, set Size = 3.

Here the value of Size depends on the value of Fte. For each case, Size assumes only one of the three values 1, 2, and 3, which might for practical purposes be interpreted as "small," "medium," and "large," much as shirt and dress sizes are interpreted. Restaurants of different sizes are grouped into a category such as "medium" when the truly important differences are differences between the categories rather than between individual restaurants. For some problems this will be the case. For other problems, grouping will mask important distinctions between restaurants. The appropriateness of grouping must be decided in the context of the problem under attack.

Exhibit 5.2B is a repeat of Exhibit 5.2A with the variables Fte and Size added. Cases 5 and 6 have missing data for numbers of employees, so the values of the variables Fte and Size cannot be computed for these cases. Asterisks have been entered for these values. You see that missing data transmits itself to new variables.

If we agree to measure "size" of restaurant by number of employees, we can choose to use the variable Fte itself or we can use the Size variable we have defined. Size divides the restaurants into three size categories, based on the numbers of employees. We can think of Size as a variable that allocates restaurants to ordered categories. **Ordered categories** are those categories that cannot be displayed in an arbitrary order without losing some information. For example, Male and Female genders or brands of automobiles could be reported in any order. The Size variable in Exhibit 5.2B does not satisfy this condition. If the 1's and 2's in the Size column were interchanged, the order conveyed by the symbols would be destroyed.

EXHIBIT 5.2B

A Small Data Set with 9 Columns (variables) and 10 Rows (cases)

Id	Outlook	Sales	Wages	Adv	Full	Part	Fte	Size
1	2	480	25	2	8	30	23	3
2	4	507	20	5	6	25	18.5	2
3	5	210	24	3	0	17	8.5	1
4	5	246	30	1	2	13	8.5	1
5	2	148	35	1	*	*	*	*
6	3	135	30	10	2	*	*	*
7	2	72	10	5	0	5	2.5	1
8	3	99	25	1	1	8	5	1
9	4	160	*	*	2	10	7	1
10	4	243	15	2	2	19	11.5	2

Asterisk (*) denotes data not reported or reported incorrectly.

▪**EXAMPLE 5.2C:** In a variety of applications it is useful to apply mathematical functions to create new variables. To illustrate, a new variable, Logsales, can be created simply by taking the natural logarithm of each sales figure in Exhibit 5.2B. For example, in the first case, the Sales figure is 480 (representing $480,000), and its natural logarithm is Logsales = log(480) = 6.1738, to four decimal places. In the second case, the Sales figure is 507, and Logsales = log(507) = 6.2285, to four decimal places. Proceeding down the Sales column in this way the values of the new variable, Logsales, are created. Exhibit 5.2C displays this variable along with the Id, Outlook, and Sales variables from Exhibit 5.2B.

EXHIBIT 5.2C

A Small Data Set with 4 Columns (variables) and 10 Rows (cases)

Id	Outlook	Sales	Logsales
1	2	480	6.1738
2	4	507	6.2285
3	5	210	5.3471
4	5	246	5.5053
5	2	148	4.9972
6	3	135	4.9053
7	2	72	4.2767
8	3	99	4.5951
9	4	160	5.0752
10	4	243	5.4931

▪

EXERCISES

5.3A Add a variable named Sqrtsales, which is formed by taking the square root of the sales figure for each case, to Exhibit 5.2C.

5.3B Explain why the Size variable in Exhibit 5.2B is an ordered-category variable. List the cases in each of the strata defined by Size.

5.3C Suppose you wanted to stratify the cases in Exhibit 5.2B by Outlook *and* Size. How many strata are defined in this way? List the cases in each of the strata.

5.3D The data in the table below were collected as part of a study of real estate property valuation. They are part of a larger study that is presented in detail in Section 6.2. They are observations on 10 parcels that sold in a particular calendar year in a particular neighborhood.

   Sq.ft = Square feet of living area

   Grade = Type of construction (-1 = low, 0 = medium, 1 = high)

   Assessed = Most recent assessed value on city assessor's books (in thousands of dollars)

   Market = Selling price of parcel (in thousands of dollars)

Sq.ft	Grade	Assessed	Market
521	-1	7.80	26.0
538	-1	28.20	19.4
544	0	23.20	25.2
577	-1	22.20	26.2
661	-1	23.80	31.0
662	0	19.60	34.6
677	0	22.80	36.4
691	-1	22.60	33.0
694	0	28.00	37.4
712	0	21.20	42.4

(a) Separate the parcels into two groups determined by their grades of construction. Find average Sq.ft, Assessed, and Market for each group. Does there appear to be a difference between the two groups?

(b) Create a new variable by calculating for each case the ratio of Assessed to Market value. Such ratios are used extensively in property valuation work. Compute average ratios for the two groups formed in part (a). Is there a substantial difference in the averages?

TALLIES

PRODUCING TALLIES

Exhibit 5.4A shows a little more of the Wisconsin restaurant survey data introduced in Section 5.2. The full data set is listed in Appendix 2 and given in file RESTRNT.DAT. The survey was done by the University of Wisconsin Small

Business Development Center to provide data to educators, researchers, and public policy makers interested in the status of Wisconsin's restaurant sector. A second purpose was to develop data for small-business counselors who advise managers on how to plan and operate small restaurants.

EXHIBIT 5.4A

Excerpt of Restaurant Survey Data

```
# Wisconsin Restaurant Survey Data for 1979
# Variable:      Description
# ID Number:
# Business Outlook: categorized as
#   1=very unfavorable,..., 6=very favorable
# Sales: Gross 1979 sales in $1000's
# New Capital: invested in 1979 ($1000's)
# Value: Est. market value of business ($1000's)
# Cost of goods sold: as % of sales
# Wages: as % of sales
# Advertising: as % of sales
# Type: 1=fast food, 2=supper club, 3=other
# Seats: number of dining seats
# Owner: 1=sole proprietorship, 2=partnership, 3=corporation
# Full Time: # of full time employees
# Part Time: # of part time employees
# Size: Size of restaurant categorized as
#   1=1 to 9.5 full time equivalent employees
#   2=10 to 20 full time equivalent employees
#   3=more than 20 full time equivalent employees
#   (Full time equivalent=full time+(1/2)part time)
#
    1  2  480   0   600 35 25   2 2 200 3    8  30 3
    2  4  507  22   375 59 20   5 2 150 1    6  25 2
    3  5  210  25   275 40 24   3 1  46 1    0  17 1
    4  5  246   *    80 43 30   1 1  28 3    2  13 1
    5  2  148   *    85 45 35   1 3  44 1    *   *  *
    6  3   50   *   135 40 30  10 2  50 3    2   *  *
    7  2   72   0   125 85 10   5 2  50 1    0   5 1
    8  3   99   7   150 43 25   1 2 130 1    1   8 1
    9  4  160   5    85  *  *   *  *   *  2   2  10 1
   10  4  243   7   150 38 15   2 2  50 2    2  19 2
    :  :    :   :     :  :  :   :  :   :  :   :   :  :
  269  4  250   3     5 35 50   0 3  15 2    1   3 1
  270  5  215   1   100 36 33   2 3  98 3    5  17 2
  271  4    *   *     *  *  *   * 2  36 2    7   6 2
  272  3  733  35   500 53 21   0 1   0 1    6  40 3
  273  1    *   *     *  *  *   * 3   0 1    0   0 1
  274  1  200   1   210 50 20   5 2  70 *    *   *  *
  275  5  305   0   450 58 27   2 2  85 3    3  25 2
  276  1  110   5   175  *  *   * 2  99 1    0   7 1
  277  2    *   *   100  *  *   * 3  45 1    3   6 1
  278  3  100  20   250 24 30  10 3 100 3    0   7 1
  279  4  355   *    95 40 20   5 1 130 3    8  12 2
```

In this data set the variables Outlook and Size are ordered-categorical variables, and the variables Typefood and Owner are categorical but not ordered. An asterisk (*) indicates a missing measurement.

Exhibit 5.4B shows a tally of the variable Outlook produced by a statistical computer package. A **tally** is just a count of the number of cases in each category. The last line in the tally, "* = 1," indicates that one restaurant did not report a value for the variable Outlook. Outlook is a categorical variable taking values $1, 2, \ldots, 6$, meaning from very unfavorable to very favorable. However, the tally reveals four restaurants with Outlook value of 7. Clearly something is wrong with these values. Welcome to the real world! Errors like this are quite common in data sets, especially in large, complex ones. If we do not discover errors and either correct them or temper our analysis in light of the errors, then our conclusions will be affected.

```
Outlook   Count
   1        37
   2        40
   3        66
   4        73
   5        49
   6         9
   7         4
  N  =     278
  *  =       1
```

In this case there are at least two ways of dealing with the errors. We could set the suspect values equal to the missing value code, *, and not use those values in any subsequent analysis. We took another approach here and replaced the 7's with 6's. In Exercise 5.7A you are asked to try the first approach and investigate the consequences.

Other errors remain in the data. Several zero values are found among the variable Sales, Value, Wages, Costgoods, Ads, and Seats. Not all of these zeros make sense. We have set all the suspect 0's to the missing value code, *, before further analysis.

After correcting the Outlook values, a percentage tally is produced as in Exhibit 5.4C to tabulate the distribution of Outlook values over its six possible values. This exhibit shows that 13.31% of the 278 respondents viewed their business outlook as very unfavorable; only 4.68% thought their business outlook was very favorable. An Outlook value of 4 received the largest percent among the respondents, but a value of 3 was a close second. Exhibits 3.6A and 3.6B provide graphical displays of this information.

Outlook	Percent	Rounded Percent
1	13.31	13
2	14.39	14
3	23.74	24
4	26.26	26
5	17.63	18
6	4.68	5
Total	100.00	100

REPORTING TALLIES

Statistical software and spreadsheet software packages prepare tallies quickly and easily, but their output is usually not in a form that is most suitable for reporting the information in a memorandum or a meeting. Typically the software packages print out too many decimal places in percentages, asking the reader to absorb figures that have no bearing on the message in the tally. As an illustration, compare the ROUNDED PERCENT and PERCENT columns in Exhibit 5.4C. Does the latter convey more information than the former? We think not, and the former offers fewer figures for our eyes, and brains, to absorb. You very quickly pick up from the ROUNDED PERCENT column that the middle two categories contain 50% of the responses.

The display in Exhibit 5.4C is still not as informative as it could be because the categories are coded numerically. Numerical coding is useful for computer processing but not for reporting. The categories should be named, and the legend of the exhibit should explain where the data came from and other pertinent details that permit the reader to assess the relevance of the data. Exhibit 5.4D offers a fairly informative report. A Total row does not need to be included at the bottom of the tally because the number of responses is given in the legend, and the Percent column sums to 100 unless there is an error in the figures. For reporting, it is best to avoid redundant or extraneous symbols. Including them asks the reader to discount visible cues; leaving them out lets the important cues stand out. An even more compact report would result from reporting only the Percent column, leaving the reader to apply the percents to the reported total.

EXHIBIT 5.4D

Number and Percent Responding to Question Concerning Economic Outlook for the Coming Year

Response	Number	Percent
Very unfavorable	37	13
Unfavorable	40	14
Mildly unfavorable	66	24
Mildly favorable	73	26
Favorable	49	18
Very favorable	13	5

Source: 1980 Wisconsin Restaurant Survey conducted by the University of Wisconsin Small Business Development Center. A mail survey of a random sample of 1000 restaurants in 19 Wisconsin counties yielded 278 usable responses to the question.

SECTION 5.5

EXERCISES

5.5A Prepare a tally for the Size variable in Exhibit 5.2B. Include both counts and percents. Create a presentation-quality table.

5.5B Repeat Exercise 5.5A using the data on Size reported in Exhibit 5.4A.

5.5C Prepare a tally for the Grade variable in Exercise 3.3D. Include both counts and percents. Create a presentation-quality table.

TWO-WAY TABLES

COUNTS AND PERCENTS

A **two-way table** shows a breakdown of the number of respondents (or counts) in each category that is formed by intersecting the categories of two variables. Exhibit 5.6A displays a two-way table that shows a breakdown of the count of respondents in each Owner category by each Outlook category. Recall that Owner = 3 corresponds to corporation-owned restaurants. We see that there were 14 corporation-owned restaurants, indicating that the business outlook was very unfavorable (Outlook = 1). This entry is highlighted in the exhibit by a ☐. Each location in the table is called a **cell**, which is defined by the intersection of a category of one variable with the category of another variable. The highlighted cell corresponds to Owner = 3 and Outlook = 1.

EXHIBIT 5.6A

Two-Way Table: Count of Owner versus Outlook

ROWS: Owner	COLUMNS: Outlook						
	1	2	3	4	5	6	All
1	19	17	24	29	14	3	106
2	1	1	8	11	3	3	27
3	14	21	32	32	31	6	136
All	34	39	64	72	48	12	269

CELL CONTENTS—COUNT

The cells defined by all the combinations of categories of the variables in a table make up the **body** of the table. In Exhibit 5.6A the body of the table consists of $3 \times 6 = 18$ cells.

For an arbitrary two-way table, r denotes the number of categories of the variable whose categories define the *rows* in the table, and c denotes the number of categories of the variable whose categories define the *columns* in the table. The table is said to be an $r \times c$ table. The table in Exhibit 5.6A is a 3×6 table.

The cell in the lower right-hand corner of the table shows the total number of responses reported in the table. We see in Exhibit 5.6A that only 269 of the 279 questionnaires returned had complete data for both of the variables Outlook and Owner.

The counts in the ALL row and the ALL column are called *marginal counts* because they occur in the margins of the table. We see that 106 of the restaurants were owned under a sole proprietorship arrangement. In the other margin we see that 72 of the respondents viewed the business outlook at level 4.

Exhibit 5.6B presents the Owner-Outlook tabulation in another way. Instead of reporting counts, the table shows row percentages. The rows give the distribution of Outlook for each type of restaurant ownership. The ALL marginal row percentage distribution is essentially the same as that given in Exhibit 5.4C. The minor differences are due to additional missing data in the cross tabulation. Column percents can be computed analogously.

EXHIBIT 5.6B

Percent Outlook by Owner

ROWS: Owner	COLUMNS: Outlook						
	1	2	3	4	5	6	All
1	17.92	16.04	22.64	27.36	13.21	2.83	100.00
2	3.70	3.70	29.63	40.74	11.11	11.11	100.00
3	10.29	15.44	23.53	23.53	22.79	4.41	100.00
All	12.64	14.50	23.79	26.77	17.84	4.46	100.00

CELL CONTENTS—% OF ROW

The table in Exhibit 5.6B needs a lot of work to make it suitable for user-friendly reporting. The "100.00" figures in the right-hand column are redundant, too many figures are reported in the percents, and the numerical codes need to be interpreted. Exhibit 5.6C gives a more pleasing appearance and reports more information than Exhibit 5.6B. The Outlook categories have been placed down the side of the table and the Ownership categories across the top. Therefore, as our eyes move across the table we make comparisons among restaurants with different types of owners.

EXHIBIT 5.6C

Percent Responding to Question Concerning Economic Outlook for the Coming Year, by Type of Ownership (percents in columns sum to 100)

Outlook	Sole Proprietorship	Partnership	Corporation
Very unfavorable	18	4	10
Unfavorable	16	4	15
Mildly unfavorable	23	29	24
Mildly favorable	27	41	24
Favorable	13	11	23
Very favorable	3	11	4

Source: 1980 Wisconsin Restaurant Survey conducted by the University of Wisconsin Small Business Development Center. A mail survey of a random sample of 1000 restaurants in 19 Wisconsin counties yielded 269 usable responses to the table.

COLLAPSING TABLES

Exhibit 5.6A displays the distributions of Outlook responses for each of the three ownership categories: sole proprietorship (1), partnership (2), and corporation (3). The responses tend to cluster in the two middle Outlook responses, "mildly unfavorable" (3) and "mildly favorable" (4), with category 4 being the most frequent response. Looking at the group of restaurants as a whole, we see from Exhibit 5.6A that 137 out of the 269, approximately 51%, responded in one of the unfavorable categories.

Working with the six-category Outlook variable presents a fairly complex task. Perhaps we can gain insight by **collapsing** it, that is, combining categories of a variable to create a variable with fewer categories, into a two-category variable in which all the unfavorable categories are coded as 0 and all the favorable categories are coded as 1. This yields Exhibit 5.6D. The new table makes it easier to explore the relationship between the variables Outlook and Owner.

EXHIBIT 5.6D

Two-Way Table Showing the Relationship Between Ownership and Outlook

Data = Count (row percent)

| | Outlook | | |
Ownership	Unfavorable	Favorable	Total
Sole Proprietorship	60(57%)	46(43%)	106(100%)
Partnership	10(37%)	17(63%)	27(100%)
Corporation	67(49%)	69(51%)	136(100%)
Total	137(51%)	132(49%)	269(100%)

Exhibit 5.6D shows that only 43% of the sole proprietorships have a favorable outlook; but 63% of partnerships and 51% of corporations have a favorable outlook. Less than 50% of all respondents have a favorable outlook, but only *one* of the three ownership categories has less than 50% favorable responses. This example cautions us about applying conclusions about a group to its subgroups. (We saw this same message in the example of Simpson's paradox in Chapter 4.)

In Exhibit 5.6D it is redundant to report all the row percentages. We know that if 63% of the partnerships responded favorably, then 37% responded unfavorably. In other words, we could display percentages only in Exhibit 5.6D. We could then report only the ownership categories and the figures listed in the Favorable column and leave out the rest of the table.

When collecting categorical data, variables with many categories may be used. For purposes of analysis and reporting, however, we have the option of collapsing, or combining, some of the categories. If this operation yields no significant distortion of information, it is usually a good strategy, leading to both clarity and simplicity of analysis.

SECTION 5.7

EXERCISES

5.7A For the restaurant data set, recode all the Outlook responses of 7 to the missing data code. Now redo all the calculations outlined in Sections 5.4 and 5.6. What difference does the different coding make?

5.7B The data that follow are actual responses to a student survey done in a statistics class of about 250 students. For this exercise the first 20 responses were chosen from the data base.

The rows correspond to students (elements); the columns correspond to questions on the questionnaire (variables). Responses are shown for five items:

(1) What is your gender? (0 = male, 1 = female)

(2) I won't have much use for statistics beyond this course.

(3) I am worried about how well I will do in this course.

(4) I think statistics is a boring subject to learn.

(5) Large lecture courses offer little opportunity for individual attention.

For the last four questions, students responded with a number from 1 to 5. Response 1 meant "strongly agree" with the statement, 2 meant "agree," 3 meant "neutral," 4 meant "disagree," and 5 meant "strongly disagree."

```
# filename: STUDENTS.DAT
# Data from a survey of a statistics class
# 1. What is your gender? (0=male, 1=female)
# 2. I won't have much use for statistics beyond this course.
# 3. I am worried about how well I will do in this course.
# 4. I think statistics is a boring subject to learn.
# 5. Large lecture courses offer little opportunity for individual attention.
#  For the last 4 questions: 1=strongly agree, 2=agree, 3=neutral,
#  4=disagree, and 5=strongly disagree
 0 4 1 2 2
 1 3 4 2 2
 0 4 1 2 2
 1 2 2 1 1
 1 5 4 3 2
 0 5 4 3 3
 0 4 1 4 1
 0 3 4 1 1
 0 2 2 2 2
 0 4 5 4 4
 0 4 2 2 1
 0 4 4 2 3
 1 2 1 3 1
 0 3 2 1 3
 0 5 1 1 1
 0 4 5 1 3
 1 3 2 1 1
 0 4 5 4 3
 1 1 3 1 1
 0 3 1 1 1
```

(a) Prepare a 2 × 5 table of variables 1 and 2 (gender and future use). Compute the row percents. Do males and females seem to agree or disagree in their responses?

(b) Prepare a 5 × 5 table of variables 2 and 3 (future use and anxiety). Many of the cells have no data because there are only 20 cases. This illustrates the notion that a large number of cases are needed to study variables with many categories. When the number of cases is small, variables usually have to be collapsed into a small number of categories.

(c) Collapse the responses to variables 2 and 3 into two categories. Combine the original 1, 2, and 3 responses into a new category called "do not disagree." Combine the original 4 and 5 responses into a new category called "disagree." Prepare a 2 × 2 table using these new categories. How would you characterize the relationship between the two variables?

5.7C Use the data in Exercise 5.7B.

(a) Prepare a 2 × 5 table of variables 1 and 5 (gender and lecture size). Compute the row percents. Do males and females seem to agree or disagree in their responses?

(b) Prepare a 5 × 5 table of variables 2 and 5 (future use and lecture size). Many of the cells have no data because there are only 20 cases. This illustrates the notion that a large number of cases are needed to study variables with many categories. When the number of cases is small, variables usually have to be collapsed into a small number of categories.

(c) Collapse the responses to variables 2 and 5 into two categories. Combine the original 1, 2, and 3 responses into a new category called "do not disagree." Combine the original 4 and 5 responses into a new category called "disagree." Prepare a 2 × 2 table using these new categories. How would you characterize the relationship between the two variables? (Filename: STUDENTS.DAT.)

5.7D In the text we suggest that Exhibit 5.6D could be greatly simplified by reporting only percentages. Prepare a table following the guidelines set forth in the text. Make it presentation quality. (*Hint:* In the legend of the table you need to report the number of responses on which the percentages are based. Why?)

5.7E Use the data reported in Exhibit 5.4A.

(a) Make a 5 × 3 table of the Outlook and Size variables. Compute row percents. Do the different Size categories tend to have different outlooks?

(b) Collapse the Outlook variable into the two categories used in the text and make the resulting 2 × 3 table of Outlook and Size. Do the different Size categories tend to have different outlooks? (Filename: RESTRNT.DAT.)

5.7F Redo Exercise 5.7E using the same variables and all the cases in the restaurant data. Comment on the relationship between Outlook and Size. (Filename: RESTRNT.DAT.)

SECTION 5.8

OTHER DATA WITHIN CATEGORIES

OTHER CATEGORICAL DATA

The cells of a two-way table may be used to report other data in addition to the basic counts and percents presented in Section 5.6. To illustrate, let us use both ownership and the type of restaurant to create categories. Because there are three ownership categories and three types of restaurant [Fast Food (1), Supper Club (2), and Other (3)], there are nine categories in the two-way classification. Exhibit 5.8A shows the counts of restaurants in each of the nine categories and also the percentage of those restaurants giving a favorable Outlook response. Because Outlook is reported in only two categories, favorable and unfavorable, the information in the table in Exhibit 5.8A is reported very economically. If a six-category classification of Outlook had been used, the table would have been much more complex.

Within each Ownership category there is substantial variation in the percentages over the types of restaurants. In the Sole Proprietorship category, 55% of the Fast Food restaurants responded favorably, but only 33% of the Supper Clubs and 38% of the Others did. This has the effect of making the percentage of favorable responses in the Sole Proprietorship category less than 50%. Applying the 43% to the whole category would be misleading for the Fast Food restaurants, however. Similarly, the 62% favorable responses from the Partnerships overall is clearly inappropriate for the Fast Food Partnerships!

EXHIBIT 5.8A

Restaurants Classified
by Ownership and Type

$$\text{Data} = \begin{cases} \text{Number in category} \\ \text{Percent responding favorably on Outlook} \end{cases}$$

	Type of Restaurant			
Ownership	Fast Food	Supper Club	Other	Total
Sole Proprietorship	42	30	32	104
	55%	33%	38%	43%
Partnership	8	9	7	24
	38%	78%	71%	62%
Corporation	59	35	37	131
	52%	46%	54%	51%
Total	109	74	76	259
	52%	45%	49%	49%

METRIC DATA

Tables may also be used to display quantities on a third, metric, variable. In Exhibit 5.8B the average sales (in $1000s) are broken down by the values of the Owner and Size categorical variables. For example, in the cell corresponding to Owner = 1 and Size = 1, all the restaurants with these two characteristics were collected and their sales were recorded and averaged. Similar calculations were done for each cell. Notice that for each of the values of the nonordered variable Owner, the average sales increase as the value of the ordered categorical variable Size increases. Recall that Size is defined by number of employees. The table shows, at least on the average, that increasing Size is associated with increasing Sales.

EXHIBIT 5.8B

Average Sales by Owner
and Size

ROWS: Owner	COLUMNS: Size			
	1	2	3	All
1	117.11	237.94	579.00	150.07
2	88.12	321.25	695.00	228.12
3	231.50	313.84	887.96	507.78
All	147.45	291.57	861.74	340.41

CELL CONTENTS—Average Sales

The table in Exhibit 5.8B needs some work to make it more user friendly. The categories need names, the averages could be reported with fewer figures, and the table needs a legend. Exhibit 5.8C shows how Exhibit 5.8B might be improved. The averages have been reported only to two significant figures, sacrificing a bit of detail for clarity. But the main message of the table comes through more clearly despite, in fact because of, the loss of detail.

■
EXHIBIT 5.8C

Average Sales by
Ownership and Size of
Restaurant (sales are in
$10,000s)

| Ownership | Size | | | |
	Small	Medium	Large	All
Sole Proprietorship	12	24	58	15
Partnership	9	32	69	23
Corporation	23	31	89	51
All	15	29	86	34

Source: 1980 Wisconsin Restaurant Survey conducted by the University of Wisconsin Small Business Development Center. A mail survey of a random sample of 1000 restaurants in 19 Wisconsin counties yielded 261 usable responses to the table.

TIME SERIES DATA

Data collected in sequence, as considered in Chapter 2, are usefully tabled to display special features. The Deere & Co. oil-filter sales data reported in Chapter 2 might appear in a data table as shown in Exhibit 5.8D. The second and third columns might either appear in the file or else be created by a statistical computer package when analysis begins. In any case Exhibit 5.8E shows the same information displayed in a more useful tabular format. Here the sales can be tracked over individual years and also across the same month for different years. Exhibit 5.8F adds additional information to the table by displaying the row (monthly) averages and the column (yearly) averages. The seasonality observed in Chapter 2 is readily apparent in the variation of the monthly averages in this display.

■
EXHIBIT 5.8D

**Deere & Co. Oil-Filter
Sales: Number, Month,
and Year**

Number	Month	Year
2385	7	83
3302	8	83
3958	9	83
3302	10	83
2441	11	83
3107	12	83
5862	1	84
4536	2	84
4625	3	84
4492	4	84
⋮	⋮	⋮
5787	2	87
2886	3	87
5475	4	87
3843	5	87
2537	6	87

EXHIBIT 5.8E	Month/Year	83	84	85	86	87
Sales in Year-by-Month Layout	1	—	5862	5472	5357	5332
	2	—	4536	5310	5811	5787
	3	—	4625	1965	2436	2886
	4	—	4492	3791	4608	5475
	5	—	4486	3622	2871	3843
	6	—	4005	3726	3349	2537
	7	2385	3744	3370	2909	—
	8	3302	2546	2535	2324	—
	9	3958	1954	1572	1603	—
	10	3302	2285	2146	2148	—
	11	2441	1778	2249	2245	—
	12	3107	3222	1721	1586	—

EXHIBIT 5.8F	Month/Year	83	84	85	86	87	Average
Sales in Year-by-Month Layout with Averages	1	—	5862	5472	5357	5332	5505
	2	—	4536	5310	5811	5787	5361
	3	—	4625	1965	2436	2886	2978
	4	—	4492	3791	4608	5475	4591
	5	—	4486	3622	2871	3843	3705
	6	—	4005	3726	3349	2537	3404
	7	2385	3744	3370	2909	—	3102
	8	3302	2546	2535	2324	—	2676
	9	3958	1954	1572	1603	—	2271
	10	3302	2285	2146	2148	—	2470
	11	2441	1778	2249	2245	—	2178
	12	3107	3222	1721	1586	—	2409
	Average	3082	3627	3123	3103	4310	3387

SECTION 5.9

EXERCISES

5.9A Use Exhibit 5.9A to answer the following questions.

(a) Rearrange the Establishments with Payrolls data into a two-way table showing number of establishments and sales by kind of business and by year.

(b) Tidy up the figures in the table by displaying them to two significant digits only. Also arrange the kinds of business in decreasing order of 1977 sales.

(c) Prepare another table with the same categories as in parts (a) and (b) but showing number of establishments as a percentage of total number of establishments within each year and showing sales as a percentage of total sales within each year. Examine this table for substantial changes in the percentages between 1972 and 1977. Are both sets of percentages in decreasing order within each year? Can you explain why?

EXHIBIT 5.9A   Numbers of Establishments and Total Retail Sales in 1972 and 1977 for Various Kinds of Business (establishments with payroll shown for 1972; establishments with payroll and all establishments shown for 1977)

| | 1972 | | 1977 | | | |
| | Establishments with Payrolls | | All Establishments | | Establishments with Payrolls | |
Kind of Business	Number (in 1000s)	Sales (in millions of dollars)	Number (in 1000s)	Sales (in millions of dollars)	Number (in 1000s)	Sales (in millions of dollars)
Building materials, hardware garden supply, and mobile home dealers	62.0	22,958	90.4	38,860	65.8	37,793
General merchandise group stores	44.4	64,669	48.9	93,948	38.4	93,455
Food stores	173.1	96,375	252.0	157,940	171.6	152,745
Automotive dealers	85.1	88,491	139.0	149,952	94.8	147,202
Gasoline service stations	183.4	31,440	176.5	56,468	146.5	53,749
Apparel and accessory stores	105.7	24,115	140.1	35,564	114.8	34,719
Furniture, home furnishings, and equipment stores	82.5	21,505	138.6	33,176	91.7	31,568
Eating and drinking places	287.36	35,048	368.1	63,276	308.6	61,307
Drug and proprietary stores	47.6	15,420	49.6	23,196	47.2	23,196
Miscellaneous retail stores	193.9	40,202	452.0	70,753	242.2	64,038
Retail trade, Total	1,264.9	440,222	1,855.1	723,134	1,303.6	699,635

Source: Adapted from U.S. Bureau of the Census, "Table No. 1434—Establishments with Payroll, 1972, and Establishments, Sales and Employees, 1977, by Kind of Business," *Statistical Abstract of the United States: 1984* (104th ed.), Washington, D.C.: U.S. Government Printing Office, 1983.

     (d) Prepare another table with the same categories as in part (c) but showing the average sales per establishment. Examine this table for substantial changes in the averages. If you were to arrange the kinds of business in decreasing order of average sales in 1977, would the order be different from the one in your table? Can you explain why?

     (e) How would you go about obtaining more recent data so that the study begun in this exercise could be extended? What kinds of business would you most like to follow up on in an extended study?

5.9B Consider Exhibit 5.9A.

     (a) Collapse the Kind of Business categories into two: Eating and Drinking Places and Other. Make a two-way table showing number of establishments with payroll by Kind of Business and Year.

     (b) Calculate the row percents for this table.

     (c) Prepare a table showing row percents that would be appropriate for presentation in a report or a meeting.

5.9C Using the restaurant data, explain how you would construct a table showing the mean and standard deviation of sales in a Size by Type of Food classification. Do not carry out the calculations. Simply indicate the calculations needed. Design the table you would make to report the results in a meeting.

5.9D Redo the table in Exhibit 5.8F, reporting figures only to two significant figures. How does this change the information reported in the table?

MULTI-WAY TABLES

In Exhibit 5.6D the relationship between the two categorical variables Ownership and Outlook was examined. In Exhibit 5.8A outlook information for restaurants classified by Ownership and Type of Restaurant, a two-way classification, was reported. Another variable of interest in the survey is the Size of restaurant. If this variable is added to the analysis, a three-way classification of the restaurants will result. The Size variable has three categories: Small (1), Medium (2), and Large (3), so the table will be $3 \times 3 \times 3$.

Exhibit 5.10A shows one way to display the distributions of the Outlook variable across restaurant sizes within each of the nine categories defined by ownership and type of restaurant. The entries in the body of the table are sets of three numbers showing the percentages of favorable responses for Small, Medium, and Large restaurants within the nine categories. The dashes (—) indicate no restaurants in the category. This example illustrates how we can "run out of data" in categories as more and more of them are created. While the figures in Exhibit 5.10A are interesting and suggestive, some of them are based on precious few cases, making us uneasy about the conclusions we draw from them.

EXHIBIT 5.10A

Three-Way Classification of Restaurants

Data = { Percentage favorable of Small, Percentage favorable of Medium, Percentage favorable of Large }

| | Type of Restaurant | | | |
Ownership	Fast Food	Supper Club	Other	Total
Sole Proprietorship	50%	30%	35%	40%
	78%	43%	50%	61%
	—	—	—	—
Partnership	50%	50%	60%	56%
	—	—	—	—
	—	50%	100%	75%
Corporation	35%	44%	60%	42%
	68%	46%	56%	57%
	53%	45%	50%	50%
Total	45%	35%	45%	43%
	67%	54%	55%	59%
	50%	50%	52%	51%

The entries in the margins of the table in Exhibit 5.10A show the distributions of Outlook responses by Size within the categories of the ownership and type of restaurant variables. Specifically, at the bottom of the column labelled Fast Food, we see the numbers 45%, 67%, and 50%. The percentage of small fast food restaurants responding favorably is 45%; the percentage of medium-sized fast food restaurants responding favorably is 67%; and the percentage of large fast food restaurants responding favorably is 50%. These are the percentages that apply to fast food restaurants without regard to the style of ownership. Other entries are interpreted similarly. The distribution in the lower right-hand corner of the table applies to the Size categories without regard to style of ownership or to type of food. We see that the table displays Outlook responses at several different levels of categorization.

Another table could have been constructed using Size and Ownership as the marginal variables and type of food as the variable displayed within the body of the table. Then the distribution in the lower right-hand corner would have been the percentages that applied to the types of food service alone.

We may also wish to study relationships among the three variables Ownership, Type of Restaurant, and Size. This can be accomplished by looking at counts and

---

EXHIBIT 5.10B

Cell Counts in a Three-Way Table Based on Restaurant Data

PROP = Sole Proprietorship,
PART = Partnership, CORP = Corporation
S = Small, M = Medium, L = Large

Fast Food

	S	M	L	All
PROP	32	9	1	42
PART	6	2	0	8
CORP	20	19	19	58
All	58	30	20	108

Supper Clubs

	S	M	L	All
PROP	23	7	0	30
PART	2	4	2	8
CORP	9	13	11	33
All	34	24	13	71

Other

	S	M	L	All
PROP	26	2	1	29
PART	5	0	2	7
CORP	10	9	18	37
All	41	11	21	73

row or column percents within the cells of the $3 \times 3 \times 3$ classification. One possible format is shown in Exhibit 5.10B, which displays counts. Within each Type category, there is a 3×3 table for the variables Ownership and Size. Other formats are clearly possible. Exhibit 5.10C shows the row percents for the same classification.

EXHIBIT 5.10C

Row Percents in a Three-Way Table Based on Restaurant Data

PROP = Sole Proprietorship,
PART = Partnership,
CORP = Corporation
S = Small, M = Medium,
L = Large

Fast Food

	S	M	L
PROP	76	22	2
PART	75	25	—
CORP	34	32	32
All	53	27	18

Supper Club

	S	M	L
PROP	77	23	—
PART	25	50	25
CORP	27	40	33
All	48	34	18

Other

	S	M	L
PROP	90	7	3
PART	71	—	29
CORP	27	24	49
All	56	15	29

Comparisons in a three-way table are somewhat complex. The marginal distributions are usually a big help in judging the existence of patterns in the body of the table. For example, look at the FAST FOOD table in Exhibit 5.10C. The marginal row percents are 53%, 27%, and 18%. Do these percents apply to the different types of restaurants in the table? Clearly not! Corporations are about evenly divided among Small, Medium, and Large firms, but there are practically no large sole proprietorships or partnerships. About 75% of both sole proprietorships and partnerships are small.

The marginal row percents for SUPPER CLUBS are 48%, 34%, and 18%, not that different from the row percents for FAST FOOD. Again we find very different patterns within the body of the table.

When variables separate cases into categories, multi-way tables are the natural way to display relationships among the variables. As the number of variables grows, however, the size and complexity of the tables grow also, placing a premium on the ability to display the information efficiently. Tools for doing this use only as many significant figures as the reader can absorb (two significant figures is recommended) and display only the absolutely essential figures (eliminate redundant percentages, for example).[†]

SECTION 5.11

EXERCISES

5.11A The table below has the structure of Exhibit 5.10C except that column percents are displayed. Make as many comparisons as you can. How would you describe the relationships among the variables?

Fast Food	S	M	L	All
PROP	55	30	5	39
PART	10	7	—	7
CORP	35	63	95	54

Supper Club	S	M	L	All
PROP	68	29	—	42
PART	6	17	15	12
CORP	26	54	85	46

Other	S	M	L	All
PROP	63	18	5	40
PART	12	—	9	9
CORP	25	82	86	51

5.11B Verify the row percents in Exhibit 5.10C; that is, carry out the necessary calculations in Exhibit 5.10B to obtain Exhibit 5.10C.

[†] For further reading on the construction and use of multi-way tables, see Ottar Hellevik, *Introduction to Causal Analysis: Exploring Survey Data by Crosstabulation* (London: George Allen & Unwin, 1984) and A. S. C. Ehrenberg, *Primer in Data Reduction* (New York: Wiley, 1982).

5.11C The data below are part of a data set collected from a business statistics class at the University of Wisconsin. Students were asked to write on a card their gender, age, and academic classification, among other items. Female was coded as 2, male as 1. Age was coded as follows: $1 = $ age $< 18, 2 = 18 \leq $ age $< 21, 3 = 21 \leq $ age $< 24, 4 = 24 \leq $ age $< 26,$ and $5 = $ age $\geq 26.$ Academic classification was coded as follows: $1 = $ prebusiness, $2 = $ business undergraduate, $3 = $ business graduate, $4 = $ nonbusiness student.

```
# filename: CLASS.DAT
# Business statistics class data
# Gender: 2=female, 1=male
# Age coded as: 1=age less than 18, 2=ages 18 to 20, 3=ages 21 to 23
# 4=ages 24 to 25, and 5=ages greater than 25.
# Academic classification coded as: 1=prebusiness, 2=business undergraduate,
# 3=business graduate, 4=nonbusiness student
# variables: Gender, Age, Academic Classification
 1  5  4            1  2  1
 2  2  1            1  3  4
 2  2  1            1  2  1
 1  3  1            1  2  1
 2  2  1            2  2  1
 1  4  3            2  1  1
 2  2  1            1  2  1
 1  2  1            2  2  1
 1  2  1            2  1  1
 2  2  1            1  2  1
 2  3  1            2  2  1
 1  3  1            2  3  4
 2  2  1            2  4  4
 1  2  2            1  2  1
 1  2  1            1  4  1
 2  4  3            2  2  1
 1  2  2            2  3  2
 2  2  1            2  2  1
 1  3  2            2  2  1
 2  4  4            2  2  1
 2  2  1            2  2  1
 2  2  1            2  5  4
 1  2  1
```

(a) Make a $2 \times 5 \times 4$ table for these three variables. Show counts.
(b) From the table you made in part (a) make a table showing row percents.
(c) From the table you made in part (a) make a table showing column percents.
(d) Interpret the relationships among the variables.

5.11D Use the data in Exercise 5.11C. Collapse the age variable into two categories: age < 21 and age ≥ 21. Collapse the classification variable into two categories by combining the original 1 and 4 categories (call it "not in School of Business") and the original 2 and 3 categories (call it "in School of Business"). Now redo parts (a)–(d) in Exercise 5.11C.

SECTION 5.12

SUPPLEMENTARY EXERCISES FOR CHAPTER 5

5A The following data are taken from U.S. Bureau of the Census, Table No. 850 *Statistical Abstract of the United States: 1989* (109th ed.), Washington, D.C.: U.S. Government Printing Office, 1989. Displayed are the Total Business Receipts (income from sales and operations) and Total Business Deductions for the years 1982–1986. All figures are in millions of dollars.

Year	Receipts	Deductions
1982	433,665	383,092
1983	465,169	404,809
1984	516,037	445,270
1985	540,045	461,273
1986	559,384	468,960

(a) Net Income is the difference between Total Business Receipts and Total Business Deductions. Compute the values of this variable for the years 1982–1986.

(b) Compute the ratio of Net Income to Total Business Receipts and express the ratio as a percentage.

(c) Make a sequence plot of the ratio you computed in part (b). How has the ratio evolved over the years 1982–1986?

5B The data below are taken from U.S. Bureau of the Census, Table No. 857, *Statistical Abstract of the United States: 1989* (109th ed.), Washington, D.C.: U.S. Government Printing Office, 1989. Displayed are Current Assets and Current Liabilities for nonfinancial corporations in the United States for the years 1975–1986. All figures are in billions of dollars, as of December 31.

Year	Assets	Liabilities
1975	756.3	446.9
1976	823.1	487.5
1977	900.9	546.8
1978	1,028.1	661.9
1979	1,200.9	809.1
1980	1,281.6	877.2
1981	1,374.5	923.2
1982	1,425.4	977.8
1983	1,557.3	1,043.0
1984	1,703.0	1,163.6
1985	1,778.5	1,232.7

(a) Working Capital is the difference between Current Assets and Liabilities. Compute the values of Working Capital for the years 1975–1985. Compute the annual percentage increases in the three variables Current Assets, Liabilities, and Working Capital for the years 1976–1985. Put the sequence plots of the three percentage increase series on the same set of axes, using different plotting symbols for the three series. Compare the behaviors of the three series.

(b) The Current Ratio is the Current Assets divided by the Current Liabilities. Compute the Current Ratio for the years 1975–1985 and make a sequence plot of the resulting series. Describe the behavior of the series.

5C The following data are taken from U.S. Bureau of the Census, Table No. 859, *Statistical Abstract of the United States: 1989* (109th ed.), Washington, D.C.: U.S. Government Printing Office, 1989. Shown are numbers of establishments, numbers of employees, and annual payroll for selected industries and selected employment classes within industries, for the year 1986. To make the presentation of the table more compact, the following definitions are used:

E1 = Number of employees less than 20

E2 = Number of employees between 20 and 99

E3 = Number of employees between 100 and 499

E4 = Number of employees between 500 and 999

E5 = Number of employees 1000 or more

I1 = Agricultural services

I2 = Mining

I3 = Contract construction

I4 = Manufacturing

I5 = Transportation (and other public utilities)

I6 = Wholesale trade

I7 = Retail trade

I8 = Finance and insurance (including real estate)

I9 = Services

Counts are presented in units of 1000, payroll is presented in units of $1 billion.

Number of Establishments

Industry	E1	E2	E3	E4	E5	Total
I1	65	3	Z	Z	Z	68
I2	28	6	1	Z	Z	35
I3	445	42	5	Z	Z	492
I4	230	86	32	4	2	356
I5	170	32	7	.1	Z	210
I6	374	59	6	Z	Z	440
I7	1237	184	19	1	Z	1441
I8	450	45	7	1	Z	504
I9	1639	139	29	3	2	1811
Total	5082	605	107	8	5	5807

Note: Z stands for number of establishments surveyed in the class is less than 500 and hence not reported for reasons of confidentiality.

Number of Employees

Industry	E1	E2	E3	E4	E5	Total
I1	235	110	52	10	4	412
I2	141	240	278	103	85	847
I3	1877	1607	797	142	236	4659
I4	1420	3900	6525	2409	4888	19142
I5	823	1312	1352	418	980	4884
I6	2048	2231	1108	190	147	5725
I7	6418	7321	3230	346	235	17550
I8	1836	1807	1418	427	882	6371
I9	6746	5621	5499	1735	3277	22878
Total	22296	24311	20260	5780	10734	88380

Industry	Annual Payroll					Total
	E1	E2	E3	E4	E5	
I1	3.4	1.5	.7	Z	Z	5.8
I2	3.3	6.1	8.7	3.6	2.8	24.5
I3	37.0	37.3	20.3	3.7	6.2	104.5
I4	27.8	79.4	142.3	59.9	158.5	467.8
I5	16.3	30.1	35.8	13.0	32.4	127.7
I6	45.5	53.0	29.3	5.8	4.7	138.2
I7	68.0	76.4	38.4	5.6	5.0	193.0
I8	38.5	42.0	34.5	11.0	25.3	151.0
I9	21.8	86.8	80.7	29.5	62.6	381.4
Total	375	414	391	132	298	1609

Note: Z stands for total payroll in the class is less than $500 million and hence not reported for reasons of confidentiality.

(a) Collapse each table above into tables that report only three industry categories: manufacturing, services, and other. Compare manufacturing and services with respect to number of establishments, number of employees, and payroll. How are these quantities distributed within employment-size categories for manufacturing and services?

(b) For each of the tables you constructed in part (a), collapse the employment-size categories into three: under 100, between 100 and 999, and 1000 or more. Compare the information displayed in these doubly collapsed tables with the information displayed in the original tables. Has the collapsing suppressed any significant information?

5D Have each member of your class write the following information on an index card:

> Gender
> Classification
> Age
> Height
> Mother's height
> Amount of loose change in pocket or purse

Collapse classification into three categories and age into three categories (the choice of categories is up to you). Now make a $2 \times 3 \times 3$ table using gender, classification, and age as the variables. Within each cell of the table place height. Make another table that reports mother's height. Make a third table that reports amount of loose change in pocket or purse. For each table, average the data in each cell. Does there appear to be a difference in the averages for males and females? Does there appear to be a difference in the averages for people of different classifications? Different ages?

SECTION 5.13

GLOSSARY FOR CHAPTER 5

Body   The cells defined by all the combinations of categories of the variables in a table.

c   Symbol for number of columns in a two-way table.

Cases	Rows in a data table.
Categorical data	Data that are arranged in classes or categories.
Cell	Location in a table defined by the intersection of a category of one variable with a category of another variable.
Collapsing	Combining categories of a variable to create a variable with fewer categories.
Ordered categories	Those categories that cannot be displayed in an arbitrary order without losing some information.
r	Symbol for the number of rows in a two-way table.
Tally	A count of the number of cases in each category of a variable.
Two-way table	A breakdown of the number of respondents (or counts) in each category that is formed by intersecting the categories of two variables.
Variable	A characteristic of the elements under study.

## CHAPTER 6

Summarizing Relationships

INTRODUCTION

Statistical analysis is used to document relationships among variables. Relationships that yield dependable predictions can be exploited commercially or used to eliminate waste from processes. A marketing study done to learn the impact of price changes on coffee purchases is a commercial use. A study to document the relationship between moisture content of raw material and yield of usable final product in a manufacturing plant can result in finding acceptable limits on moisture content and working with suppliers to provide raw material reliably within these limits. Such efforts can improve the efficiency of the manufacturing process.

We strive to formulate statistical problems in terms of comparisons. For example, the marketing study in the preceding paragraph was conducted by measuring coffee purchases when prices were set at several different levels over a period of time. Similarly, the raw material study was conducted by comparing the yields from batches of raw materials that exhibited different moisture contents.

132

In this chapter some of the most important tools for documenting relationships among variables are presented: scatterplots, correlation, and measures of association.

SECTION 6.2

SCATTERPLOTS

Scatterplots display statistical relationships between two metric ·variables. In this section the details of scatterplotting are presented using the data in Exhibit 6.2A. The data were collected as part of a study of real estate property valuation. They are observations on 60 parcels that sold in a particular calendar year in a particular neighborhood. The city the data came from is stratified into a number of neighborhoods. Data like those displayed in Exhibit 6.2A are available for each neighborhood for a number of years. The data we work with are thus just a small part of a single cross section taken from a much larger data structure.

EXHIBIT 6.2A

Data on 60 Residential Parcels Sold in a Particular Year

Sq.ft = Square feet of living area
Grade = Type of construction (-1 = low, 0 = medium, 1 = high)
Assessed = Most recent assessed value on city assessor's books
Market = Selling price of parcel
Ft.cat = Categorization of Sq.ft (see text for details)
Mk.cat = Categorization of Market (see text for details)

Sq.ft	Grade	Assessed	Market	Ft.cat	Mk.cat
521	-1	7.80	26.0	1	7
538	-1	28.20	19.4	1	8
544	0	23.20	25.2	1	7
577	-1	22.20	26.2	1	6
661	-1	23.80	31.0	1	5
662	0	19.60	34.6	1	4
677	0	22.80	36.4	1	4
691	-1	22.60	33.0	1	5
694	0	28.00	37.4	1	4
712	0	21.20	42.4	2	2
721	0	21.60	32.8	2	5
722	-1	7.40	25.6	2	7
743	0	26.20	34.8	2	4
760	0	26.60	35.8	2	4
767	-1	22.20	33.6	2	5
780	-1	22.60	31.0	2	5
787	0	22.40	39.2	2	3
802	0	25.40	36.0	2	4
814	0	14.80	34.8	2	4
815	0	14.40	34.4	2	4
825	0	28.20	38.0	2	4
834	-1	18.00	34.6	2	4

(Continued)

	Sq.ft	Grade	Assessed	Market	Ft.cat	Mk.cat
EXHIBIT 6.2A	838	0	25.60	35.6	2	4
(*Continued*)	858	−1	22.40	35.8	2	4
	883	0	25.80	39.6	2	3
	890	0	20.20	35.0	2	4
	899	0	23.20	37.6	2	4
	918	0	32.20	41.2	3	3
	920	−1	20.80	31.2	3	5
	923	−1	4.60	30.0	3	6
	926	0	18.22	37.4	3	4
	931	0	24.60	38.0	3	4
	965	0	14.60	37.2	3	4
	966	0	30.20	44.0	3	2
	967	0	26.00	44.2	3	2
	1011	0	28.00	43.6	3	2
	1011	0	26.00	38.4	3	3
	1024	0	27.00	42.2	3	2
	1033	0	25.20	40.4	3	3
	1040	0	22.40	40.4	3	3
	1047	0	30.00	43.6	3	2
	1051	0	26.40	41.4	3	3
	1052	0	20.20	39.6	3	3
	1056	0	25.80	41.8	3	3
	1060	1	29.20	44.8	3	2
	1060	0	24.00	38.4	3	3
	1070	0	22.80	43.6	3	2
	1075	0	30.40	42.8	3	2
	1079	0	24.20	40.6	3	3
	1100	0	30.00	41.6	3	3
	1106	0	31.60	42.8	4	2
	1138	0	25.60	39.0	4	3
	1164	1	29.40	41.8	4	3
	1171	0	32.20	48.4	4	1
	1237	0	17.00	39.8	4	3
	1249	0	22.00	47.2	4	1
	1298	1	23.60	45.2	4	2
	1435	0	21.40	38.8	5	3
	1602	1	31.00	47.4	6	1
	1804	0	30.60	45.4	7	2

The purpose of our study is to document relationships that may exist among the listed variables. The purpose of the larger study is to document such relationships for all the neighborhoods in the city and also to document the stability or lack of stability of those relationships over time. Such a study is valuable to city and state governments, who must assess the value of each parcel of real estate each year for taxation. It is valuable to the real estate industry as a basis for pricing parcels as they come on the market and for documenting market trends. In this section longitudinal issues are not addressed; basic cross-sectional analysis is the focus.

Exhibit 6.2B shows the details of constructing a scatterplot using the first five cases in Exhibit 6.2A. In the scatterplot Market is plotted on the vertical axis and Sq.ft on the horizontal axis. For the first case, we find 521 on the horizontal axis (marked in the plot) and 26 on the vertical axis (also marked). Mentally pass a line parallel to the vertical axis through 521 on the horizontal axis, and mentally pass a line parallel to the horizontal axis through 26 on the vertical axis. Put a dot where these two lines intersect. (Our computer software uses an **x** as a plotting symbol.) This is the plot of the first case. Repeat this operation for each case, and you get the scatterplot.

EXHIBIT 6.2B

Scatterplot of Market versus Sq.ft for First Five Cases in Exhibit 6.2A

Sq.ft	Grade	Assessed	Market
521	−1	7.8	26.0
538	−1	28.2	19.4
544	0	23.2	25.2
577	−1	22.2	26.2
661	−1	23.8	31.0

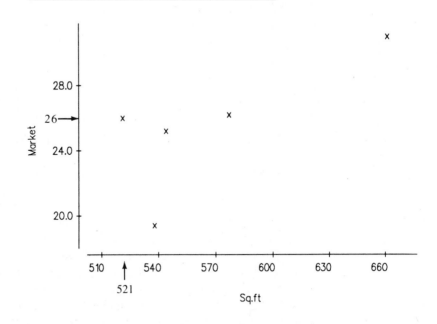

This kind of plotting procedure is standard in plotting mathematical functions. The scatterplot, however, shows the *variation* in the data. The points do not lie on a simple, smooth mathematical curve; hence the name *scatterplot*. Scatterplots are used to try to discover a tendency for the plotted variables to be related in a simple way. Thus the more the scatterplot reminds us of a mathematical curve, the more closely related we infer the variables are. Of course, with such a few points as in Exhibit 6.2B, we cannot be sure of any pattern that may suggest itself.

■ **EXAMPLE 6.2A:** Exhibit 6.2C shows the scatterplot of all 60 cases from Exhibit 6.2A. We see a distinct tendency for the higher values of Market to be associated with higher values of Sq.ft, and vice versa, despite the rather extensive amount of scatter in the plot. A *direct* relationship between the two variables is inferred. An *inverse* relationship means that higher values of one variable tend to be associated with lower values of another variable, and vice versa. Not every case satisfies this condition, but the preponderance of cases do, so our eyes see the "trend." Exhibit 2.6C displays an inverse relationship between oil-filter sales and month, indicating a tendency to have higher sales in the first part of the year, lower sales in the second part.

EXHIBIT 6.2C

Scatterplot of Market versus Sq.ft for All 60 Cases in Exhibit 6.2A

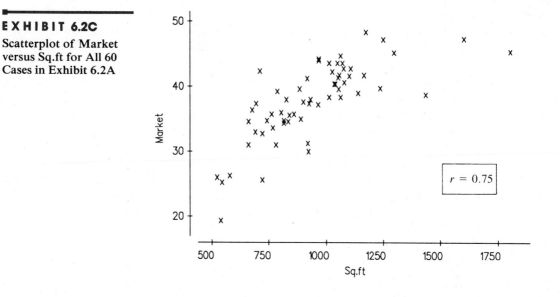

The boxed expression in Exhibit 6.2C, $r = 0.75$, gives the value of a measure of association between variables called the **product-moment correlation coefficient**, which is a measure of how linear the tendency in the scatterplot is. More details on r are given in Section 6.4. Notice that r has a positive value, which corresponds to the direct relationship between Market and Sq.ft. The correlation coefficient is negative when the relationship is inverse.   ■

■ **EXAMPLE 6.2B:** Exhibit 6.2D repeats the scatterplot in Exhibit 6.2C and overlays it with a set of axes whose origin is the point whose first coordinate is the mean of the Sq.ft variable and whose second coordinate is the mean of the Market variable: the point (941.7, 37.8).

EXHIBIT 6.2D

Scatterplot of Market versus Sq.ft for All 60 Cases in Exhibit 6.2A

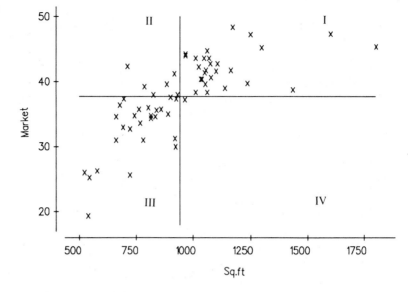

The four quadrants formed by this new axis system are labelled I, II, III, and IV. About equal numbers of points fall in quadrants I and III, a few points fall in quadrant II, and only one point falls in quadrant IV. This plot highlights the strong linear tendency in the points. The absence of points in quadrant IV also signals a lack of balance that could be caused by a certain lack of linearity in the plot. Indeed a slight "rainbow" shape is detected in the scatterplot.   ■

■ **E X A M P L E 6.2C:** The relationship between metric variables can be presented in tabular form, thus linking it to the presentation in Chapter 5. A tabular presentation is often required by those receiving a report (for example, by a planning committee or a court). In such cases, the metric variables must be categorized.

Exhibit 6.2E shows the results of a particular choice of categories. The variable Sq.ft has been broken into the eight classes of equal length $[18, 22)$, $[22, 26)$, ..., $[46, 50)$, and Market has been broken into the seven classes of equal length $[500, 700)$, $[700, 900)$, ..., $[1700, 1900)$. The first table in Exhibit 6.2E shows the numbers of parcels falling into the categories of the resulting cross-classification. The row and column labelled ALL show the marginal frequencies, and you can see that all 60 parcels are accounted for. To verify details, return to Exhibit 6.2A and identify the parcels in the various categories by using the columns labelled Ft.cat and Mk.cat. The former associates the numbers $1, 2, ..., 8$ with the eight classes of Sq.ft, while the latter associates the numbers $1, 2, ..., 7$ with the seven classes of Market.

The large number of zeros and the ALL summaries clutter the first table in Exhibit 6.2E. The second table repeats the first without the clutter. All the essential information is there, and the relationship between the variables is displayed semigraphically. The table thus performs double duty. It also displays the tendency of the plot to rainbow.

EXHIBIT 6.2E   Two Tabular Displays of the Relationship Between Sq.ft and Market Values for the 60 Parcels in Exhibit 6.2A

ROWS: Market values ($1000s)   COLUMNS: Square feet of living area

	500 ~ 700	700 ~ 900	900 ~ 1100	1100 ~ 1300	1300 ~ 1500	1500 ~ 1700	1700 ~ 1900	ALL
46 ~ 50	0	0	0	2	0	1	0	3
42 ~ 46	0	1	8	2	0	0	1	12
38 ~ 42	0	2	10	3	1	0	0	16
34 ~ 38	3	11	3	0	0	0	0	17
30 ~ 34	2	3	1	0	0	0	0	6
26 ~ 30	1	0	1	0	0	0	0	2
22 ~ 26	2	1	0	0	0	0	0	3
18 ~ 22	1	0	0	0	0	0	0	1
ALL	9	18	23	7	1	1	1	60

ROWS: Market values ($1000s)   COLUMNS: Square feet of living area

	500 ~ 700	700 ~ 900	900 ~ 1100	1100 ~ 1300	1300 ~ 1500	1500 ~ 1700	1700 ~ 1900
46 ~ 50				2		1	
42 ~ 46		1	8	2			1
38 ~ 42		2	10	3	1		
34 ~ 38	3	11	3				
30 ~ 34	2	3	1				
26 ~ 30	1		1				
22 ~ 26	2	1					
18 ~ 22	1						

Note the importance for the graphical display of arranging the Market categories from largest to smallest down the left-hand side of the table. The directions of the variables in the table correspond to the directions in the scatterplot.

It was also important to choose enough categories of Sq.ft and Market to allow the relationship to show up in the table. Using too few categories would have masked the essentials of the relationship. On the other hand, using too many categories is not really different from showing the scatterplot. Constructing tables like those in Exhibit 6.2E thus requires some experimentation with different categories and judgments on what will be acceptable to users and what constitutes a presentation that does not distort the relationship. The choices made here are analogous to choices of number of classes and class widths in constructing histograms. (See the discussion in Section 3.6.) ▪

▪**EXAMPLE 6.2D:** In the last two examples there has been a nonlinear, rainbow tendency in the scatterplot of market values versus square feet of living area. This tendency has some intuitive appeal. The desirability of increased living space is high when current living space is limited, but when current living space is plentiful an increase in living space is less attractive than other additions to assets.

This principle could be modelled by changing the scale of measurement of the Sq.ft variable. The change can be accomplished by transforming this variable and plotting Market values versus the transformed Sq.ft values. We want a transformation that discounts larger values of Sq.ft and leaves smaller and intermediate ones intact. The most common transformation with this property is the logarithm.

To see how it performs in our example we used a computer to calculate the natural logarithms of each of the Sq.ft values in Exhibit 6.2A. We then plotted the Market values versus the corresponding logarithms of Sq.ft values. Exhibit 6.2F shows the scatterplot and a set of axes with the origin determined by the means of the variables. Most of the points fall in quadrants I and III. Quadrants II and IV each contain four points, suggesting linearity, and the rainbow effect is much less pronounced than in Exhibit 6.2C. The product-moment correlation coefficient for this scatterplot is $r = 0.801$, which is larger than the 0.75 in Exhibit 6.2B, which means a greater degree of linearity in the plot. The logarithmic transformation has succeeded in increasing the linearity of the relationship.

E X H I B I T 6.2F

Scatterplot of Market versus log(Sq.ft) for All 60 Cases in Exhibit 6.2A

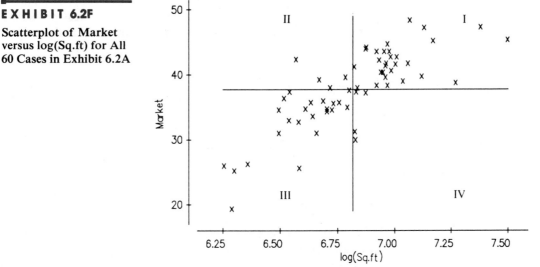

A *letter plot* is a special kind of scatterplot. It is simply two scatterplots drawn on one set of axes with different plotting symbols showing the different variables on the vertical axis. The variable on the horizontal axis is the same for both plots. Exhibit 6.2G shows a letter plot of Assessed and Market values versus Sq.ft. The A's show Assessed values, the M's Market values. It is clear from the plot that Assessed values tend to understate Market values, a predictable characteristic of a real estate market in which prices are rising. Assessments are done once a year and are based on historical data. The actual selling prices reflect market conditions at times of sale, which are distributed throughout the year.

EXHIBIT 6.2G

Letter Plot of Market
versus Sq.ft and
Assessed versus Sq.ft.

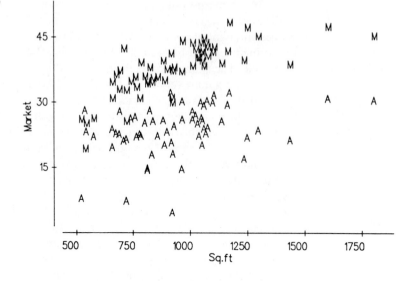

The discrepancy between Assessed and Market values is partially due to timing
(are assessments done at the beginning or middle of the year?) and the inflation
rate, among other factors. These factors make the valuation of real property a
never-ending struggle to account for variation. Data like these are analyzed constantly by those who must make decisions about real estate markets.

SECTION 6.3

EXERCISES

6.3A Using the data in Exhibit 6.2A, prepare a scatterplot of Market versus Assessed values.
How would you characterize the relationship between the variables? (Filename:
REALPROP.DAT.)

6.3B Use the data in Exhibit 6.2A. Select all the parcels associated with low-grade construction
(grade = −1). Prepare a scatterplot of Market versus Sq.ft for these parcels. Compare the
relationship in your scatterplot with that displayed in Exhibit 6.2C. Now do the same thing
for the other grades of parcels. Do the relationships in the grade categories appear consistent
with the overall relationship? What difficulties do you have in attempting to answer this
question? (Filename: REALPROP.DAT.)

6.3C Divide the Assessed values into classes and prepare tables like the ones in Exhibit 6.2E
showing the relationship between Assessed values and Market values. Explain how you
arrived at the choice of Assessed value classes. Discuss the pros and cons of displaying
the relationship by means of a scatterplot and by means of a table. (Filename:
REALPROP.DAT.)

6.3D Reproduce the scatterplot in Exhibit 2.6C. Describe the relationship in the plot. What factors
cause the relationship? (Filename: OILFILT.DAT.)

6.3E How would you characterize the relationship between oil-filter sales and years in Exhibit 2.6D? What would the scatterplot look like if there had been a strong upward trend
in sales over the years? A strong downward trend? (Filename: OILFILT.DAT.)

6.3F Consider Exhibits 2.8C and 2.8D, showing Amana manufacturing data. Suppose that for each case you plotted the Left reading on the horizontal axis and the Right reading on the vertical axis. Roughly what kind of relationship would be displayed? Suppose you plotted the Midvalue measurements in Exhibit 2.8G on the vertical axis instead of the Right reading. What kind of relationship would be displayed? What relationship would be displayed if you plotted the Diff measurements in Exhibit 2.8H on the vertical axis? Confirm your answers by preparing plots using the data reported in Appendix2. (Filename: AMANA.DAT.)

6.3G An economic survey yields information on households. Among other variables, income and percentage of income spent on food are obtained. What relationship do you expect to see if a scatterplot of these variables is constructed?

6.3H The four data sets below were constructed by Frank Anscombe ["Graphs in Statistical Analysis," *The American Statistician* 27 (February 1973): 17–21]. Draw scatterplots of the four data sets, and verbally characterize the four relationships. Plot x on the horizontal axis and y on the vertical. (Filename: ANSCOMBE.DAT.)

Data Set 1		Data Set 2		Data Set 3		Data Set 4	
x	y	x	y	x	y	x	y
10	8.04	10	9.14	10	7.46	8	6.58
8	6.95	8	8.14	8	6.77	8	5.76
13	7.58	13	8.74	13	12.74	8	7.71
9	8.81	9	8.77	9	7.11	8	8.84
11	8.33	11	9.26	11	7.81	8	8.47
14	9.96	14	8.10	14	8.84	8	7.04
6	7.24	6	6.13	6	6.08	8	5.25
4	4.26	4	3.10	4	5.39	19	12.50
12	10.84	12	9.13	12	8.15	8	5.56
7	4.82	7	7.26	7	6.42	8	7.91
5	5.68	5	4.74	5	5.73	8	6.89

6.3I Formulate a practical problem in which it would be useful to document the relationship between two variables. Design and implement a scheme for collecting data on the variables. Prepare a scatterplot and interpret the information it conveys about the relationship. Carefully keep track of any problems you encounter in carrying out this exercise. Comment on how those problems may affect the information conveyed in the scatterplot. What further information would you like to have on the variables you studied? How would you go about getting that information?

SECTION 6.4

CORRELATION

Relationships between metric variables (measurements such as length, weight, time, cost, and so on) are displayed in scatterplots, as explained in Section 6.2. The simplest relationship is one whose scatterplot looks like a straight line. The descriptive statistic most widely used to summarize a relationship between metric variables is a measure of the degree of *linearity* in the relationship. It is called

Pearson's **product-moment correlation coefficient** because many of its properties were reported by Karl Pearson.[†]

The product-moment correlation coefficient is denoted by the symbol r. Its computation is tedious, and although we demonstrate the computational algorithm we recommend that for practical work you use a calculator or computer that has been preprogrammed. You should never have to do more than enter the data and run a routine that computes r.

The data in Exhibit 6.2B, a data set that is not computationally taxing, are used to make the presentation concrete. The correlation coefficient r for the two variables Sq.ft and Market is computed using these steps:

(1) Compute the means and standard deviations for each variable.

(2) Standardize each observation, case by case.

(3) Multiply the standardized values of the observations together, case by case.

(4) Add the resulting products and divide by *one less than the number of cases*.

In symbols,

$$r = \frac{1}{n-1} \sum_{i=1}^{n} \left[\left(\frac{x_i - \bar{x}}{s_x} \right) \left(\frac{y_i - \bar{y}}{s_y} \right) \right]$$

where $\bar{x}$ and s_x are the mean and standard deviation of the x variable and $\bar{y}$ and s_y are the mean and standard deviation of the y variable.

▪ **EXAMPLE 6.4A:** Exhibit 6.4A shows the calculations for the data in Exhibit 6.2B. A value is standardized by subtracting the mean of the variable and dividing the resulting difference by the standard deviation of the variable. So to standardize the first case of Sq.ft, compute $(521 - 568.2)/55.7109 = -0.84723$. To standardize the fifth case of Market, compute $(31 - 25.56)/4.1313 = 1.3168$, and so on.

In Exhibit 6.4A the means of the standardized variables are 0, and their standard deviations are 1. This is a consequence of standardization. Standardized variables always have 0 mean and unit standard deviation. (See Section 4.6.) The practical implication is that a standardized variable is *free of the units of measurement* of the original variable.

The first case of the Product variable is found by multiplying the standardized values of Sq.ft and Market together, that is, $-0.0902 = (-0.8472)(0.1065)$. The second case of the Product variable is $0.8083 = (-0.5421)(-1.4910)$, and so on. Because standardized variables are multiplied, the result is free of units of measurement. If Sq.ft had been multiplied by Market, the quantity would have had units of thousands of dollars times square feet, units that are difficult to interpret and not essential to the question of relationship between the variables. Specifically, when the *standardized* variables are scatterplotted, the picture of the relationship is the same as when the original variables are plotted. All that changes are the units listed on the horizontal and vertical axes.

[†] See Karl Pearson, "Mathematical Contributions to the Theory of Evolution, III. Regression, Heredity, and Panmixia," *Philosophical Transcriptions of the Royal Society* A 187 (1896): 253–318. Other pioneer contributors to the development of the correlation coefficient are F. Galton and F. Y. Edgeworth.

			Standardized		
Case	Sq.ft	Market	Sq.ft	Market	Product
1	521	26.0	−0.8472	0.1065	−0.0902
2	538	19.4	−0.5421	−1.4910	0.8083
3	544	25.2	−0.4344	−0.0872	0.0378
4	577	26.2	0.1580	0.1549	0.0245
5	661	31.0	1.6657	1.3168	2.1934
Mean	568.2	25.56	0	0	—
Standard deviation	55.7109	4.1313	1	1	—

EXHIBIT 6.4A

Computation of
Product-Moment
Correlation Coefficient
for Data on Sq.ft and
Market in Exhibit 6.2

$$r = (-0.0902 + 0.8083 + 0.0378 + 0.0245 + 2.1934)/(5 - 1)$$
$$= 0.7434 \simeq 0.74$$

Note: Product = Standardized Sq.ft × Standardized Market

One less than the number of cases is $4 = 5 - 1$, so the computation of r is completed by dividing by 4:

$$r = (-0.0902 + 0.8083 + 0.0378 + 0.0245 + 2.1934)/4 \simeq 0.74$$

The correlation coefficient turns out to be essentially the average of the products of the standardized variables; hence its designation as the *product-moment* correlation coefficient. The divisor in the "average" is degrees of freedom, rather than the number of cases, using the same argument used in Chapter 4 regarding the standard deviation.   ■

Recent research has yielded algorithms to compute r that are relatively immune to round-off error, and these have been incorporated by software packages. These algorithms are not discussed in this book, because our concern is more with the interpretation and uses of r than with its computation.

The product-moment correlation coefficient has many properties, the most important of which are:

(1) Its numerical value lies between -1 and $+1$, inclusive.

(2) If $r = 1$, then the scatterplot shows that the data lie exactly on a straight line with a positive slope; if $r = -1$, then the scatterplot shows that the data lie on a straight line with a negative slope.

(3) An $r = 0$ indicates that there is no linear component in the relationship between the two variables.[†]

These properties emphasize the role of r as a measure of linearity. Essentially, the more the scatterplot looks like a positively sloping straight line, the closer r is to $+1$, and the more the scatterplot looks like a negatively sloping straight line, the closer r is to -1.

[†] If the points lie exactly on a vertical or horizontal line, then r is not defined.

■ **EXAMPLE 6.4B:** Exhibit 6.2C is a scatterplot of all 60 cases in the real estate data set. The correlation coefficient is $r = 0.75$. Although there is a trend in the plot, there is also plenty of scatter. Lay a piece of taut string or a thin pencil on the plot so that it best follows the trend. You see that most of the points do not lie under your string or pencil. For any given value of square feet of living area you can find a range of plausible market values, because many factors affect the market value. The scatter is due to the influence of market factors other than square feet of living area.

Earlier we discussed the tendency for the points to rainbow and noted that this effect may be the result of a *diminishing return* to additions of square feet of living area. This visual impression can be further documented by plotting only the first 57 parcels and computing the correlation coefficient. This is done in Exhibit 6.4B. The correlation coefficient for these parcels is 0.804, higher than the 0.75 for all 60 parcels. Taking out the parcels that are not consistent with the linear trend increases the correlation coefficient because the remaining points more nearly follow a linear relationship, though there is still plenty of scatter because other factors are at work.

EXHIBIT 6.4B

Scatterplot of First
57 Parcels of Real
Estate Data Set

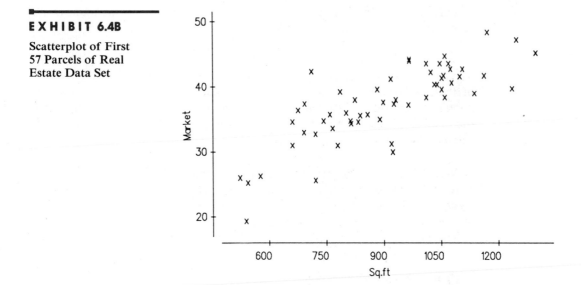

One of the factors at work is the grade of construction. In Exercise 6.3B you grouped the parcels by grade (yielding three groups) and made scatterplots of market values versus square feet of living area for each group. Computing the correlation coefficient for each group yields the following results:

Grade	Grade Code	Number of Parcels	Correlation Coefficient
Low	−1	12	0.69
Medium	0	44	0.66
High	1	4	0.73

The correlation coefficients for the three groups are lower than 0.75, which is the coefficient for the whole set. This suggests that the relationship between market value and square feet of living area may be somewhat different for the different groups. A graphical impression of this idea is conveyed through the letter plot in Exhibit 6.4C, which is a scatterplot of market value versus square feet of living area with letter codes showing the construction-grade groups. Low grade is shown by L's, medium grade by M's, and high grade by H's. It seems plausible to use different trend lines for the different groups, but this impression is based on so few cases in the low and high groups that it should be tested with other, hopefully larger, data sets before advancing it as a conclusion.[†]

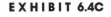

EXHIBIT 6.4C

Letter Plot of Market versus Square Feet of Living Area Showing Construction-Grade Groups Low (L), Medium (M), and High (H)

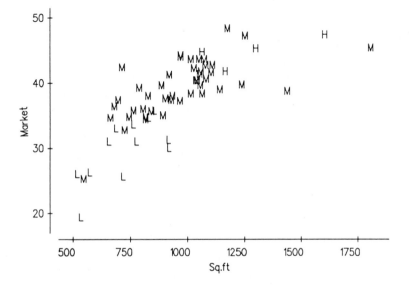

This section ends with a set of scatterplots, in Exhibit 6.4D, of artificially constructed data that display differing degrees of correlation. These data sets are constructed by simulation techniques, which are explained more fully in Chapter 17. Simulations are somewhat like laboratory studies: because the researcher has complete control over the conditions under which the data are generated, he or she can study the impact of deliberate changes in the environment under study. For each of the six simulations in Exhibit 6.4D, the variable on the horizontal axis, denoted by x, is exactly the same. A probability mechanism was used to generate the data on the vertical axes so that the scatterplots would display varying degrees of correlation. The actual correlation coefficients computed from the data sets, and rounded to two significant figures, are shown in the exhibit.

Pictures like these help interpret data collected from practical processes. For example, the tendency for the data to congregate along a line as the correlation

---

[†] In Example 6.2D we showed that another way to handle the nonlinear relationship between Market and Sq.ft is to apply a nonlinear logarithmic transformation to Sq.ft and to study the relationship between Market and log(Sq.ft). Even in this case there is scatter in the relationship. It is not exact.

EXHIBIT 6.4D   Scatterplots Showing Six Different Degrees of Correlation

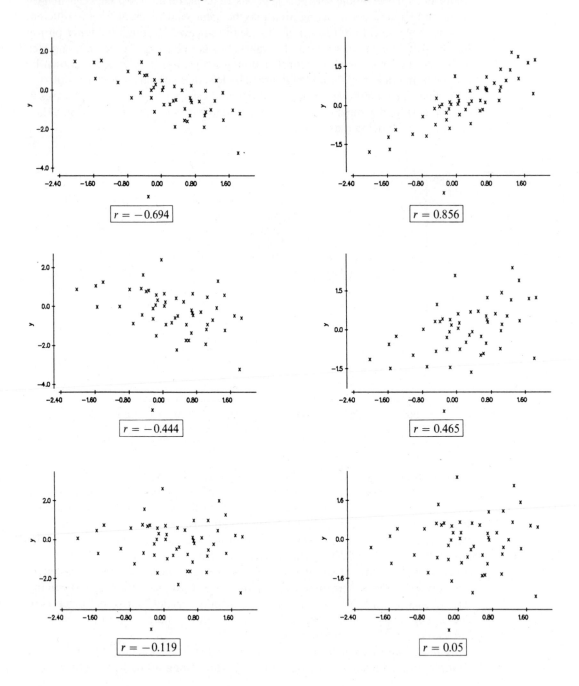

coefficient approaches -1 or $+1$ is quite clear. On the other hand, it is useful to see that even for correlation coefficients of $-.9$ and $+.9$ there can be considerable scatter in the scatterplot.

SECTION 6.5

EXERCISES

6.5A **(a)** For the real estate data set in Section 6.2, prepare scatterplots of market values versus assessed values and of assessed values versus square feet of living area. Compute the correlation coefficients corresponding to these two plots. To what extent do the correlation coefficients summarize the relationships displayed in the plots? What information should be conveyed in addition to that conveyed by the correlation coefficient?

(b) Both market and assessed values are correlated with square feet of living area, as is natural. What other factors besides square feet of living area would cause market and assessed values to be correlated? Suggest a method for determining the extent to which the correlation between assessed and market values is due to square feet and the extent to which it is due to other factors. (Filename: REALPROP.DAT.)

6.5B Compute the correlation coefficient that corresponds to the scatterplot of oil-filter sales versus months in Exhibit 2.6C. To what extent does the coefficient summarize the relationship between the variables? What information should be conveyed in addition to that conveyed by the correlation coefficient? (Filename: OILFILT.DAT.)

6.5C For the scatterplots suggested in Exercise 6.3F, what values for r would you estimate? What makes estimating r easy or hard for you in these examples?

6.5D For each of the four Anscombe data sets in Exercise 6.3H, compute the means and standard deviations of the variables and compute the correlation coefficient r. Compare the values you have computed for the four data sets. What implications do these results have for someone attempting to summarize data using descriptive statistics? What information would you recommend reporting in addition to the descriptive statistics, on the basis of your experience with the data sets in this exercise? (Filename: ANSCOMBE.DAT.)

6.5E For the data you collected for Exercise 6.3I, compute the means and standard deviations of the variables and compute the correlation coefficient r. To what extent do the descriptive statistics summarize the information in the data? What important aspects of the data are not conveyed by the descriptive statistics?

6.5F Select any scatterplot you have constructed. Standardize the variables in the plot and scatterplot the standardized variables. Describe the differences and similarities in the two plots. Does standardization affect the relationship between the variables? What does standardization do?

6.5G Use the last five cases in the data set in Exhibit 6.2A as data. Compute the means, standard deviations, and correlation coefficients for the following pairs of variables:
(a) Sq.ft and Market   **(b)** Sq.ft and Assessed   **(c)** Assessed and Market

6.5H Write a one- or two-page essay explaining the meaning of the correlation coefficient. Include three examples, each using five cases, that illustrate negative, near zero, and positive correlation.

6.5I Look at the formula for r. Explain why the formula treats the variables x and y symmetrically. In other words, explain why you can interchange x and y without changing the value of r.

LIMITATIONS OF CORRELATION

Correlation helps convey information about relationships between metric variables in a compact numerical form. It is useful when complex problems with many variables are being examined, for it helps us concentrate on patterns rather than detail. On the other hand, whenever summary measures are used, there is a risk of masking an important detail that hints at an important special feature of a relationship, as in Exercise 6.5D. One safeguard against errors in the use of descriptive statistics is to prepare plots that display relationships in detail. If descriptive statistics seem to summarize a scatterplot well, then they may be used in place of it. If not, then the unique features of the relationship as well as the descriptive statistics need to be reported.

THE EFFECT OF OUTLIERS

Recall that an outlier is a value separated from the main body of the data. Chapter 4 discussed some popular statistics, such as means and standard deviations, that are sensitive to outliers; that is, their values can change substantially if an extreme value in the data set changes. The correlation coefficient, being a moment-type statistic, is also sensitive to outliers, as you are asked to confirm in Exercise 6.7A This means that changes in one or two data values may change the numerical value of r substantially. When you are confronted with outliers, you should attempt to determine their origin. They could be caused by mistyping data or by a mistake in collecting the data. Or they could be due to your mixing data from two groups that differ significantly. Always follow up on outliers. They often indicate problems or hint at a useful structure in a process (for example, the existence of a heretofore unsuspected subgroup).

ECOLOGICAL CORRELATIONS

Ecological correlations are correlations computed from data that are aggregates of smaller units of study.

■ **EXAMPLE 6.6A:** Exhibit 6.6A shows data on bank deposits and assets in 1982 by state for nine midwestern states. The basic unit of study is the bank, but the data from all the banks in a given state are totalled, and only these totals are available in the data source. The scatterplot of the data shows a high degree of linearity, which is reflected in the correlation coefficient of $r = 0.998$. Do not infer, however, that such a high degree of linearity would be present if the original data on the banks were plotted. In fact, a great deal more variation would be expected in the data on banks than in the data on the states. The plot in Exhibit 6.6A displays the effect of a third variable, the population size of the state. In other words, totals for a large state, like Illinois, are naturally greater than totals for a small state, like Iowa. The sizes of the states and the totalling of bank data to the state level induce the very high degree of correlation in Exhibit 6.6A.

EXHIBIT 6.6A

Data on Assets and
Deposits in Banks by
State for Nine States
(All figures are in
billions of current
dollars)

State	Assets	Deposits
Nebraska	14.0	11.4
Kansas	19.6	16.5
Iowa	25.5	21.5
Wisconsin	30.0	24.3
Indiana	36.3	29.8
Minnesota	36.8	28.0
Michigan	56.6	46.0
Ohio	62.4	47.6
Illinois	130.2	91.8

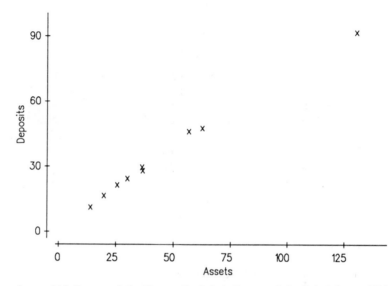

Source: U.S. Bureau of the Census, *Statistical Abstract of the United States: 1984*
(104th ed.) (Washington, D.C.: U.S. Government Printing Office, 1983) 511.   ■

There is nothing invalid about the correlation displayed in Exhibit 6.6A. The
potential error is inferring from it that the same degree of correlation exists for
individual banks. To solve a given problem, the ecological correlation may be just
what is needed, whereas to solve a different problem, the correlation at the bank level
may be needed.

■ **EXAMPLE 6.6B:** Consider a firm trying to assess the effect of a change in
advertising expenditures on sales. The data may consist of advertising expenditures
and total sales for a number of years (ideally adjusted for inflation, since inflation
tends to make more recent dollar figures larger). Advertising expenditures and sales
transactions are aggregated to an annual level in this example. A reasonably high

degree of correlation between sales and advertising expenditures would support the use of advertising to boost sales.[†]

On the other hand, such data would be of little use to an advertising executive who is trying to learn *how* advertising affects individual buying behavior. He or she needs data on the effect of a certain type of ad on customers, data that are both difficult and expensive to obtain. Moreover, even an ad that only slightly increases customers' willingness to buy a product can be beneficial from an ecological point of view, for if out of a population of 100,000 potential customers, an additional 100 can be interested in buying, then an ad may be profitable. But it can be difficult to detect such a small yet commercially advantageous relationship between variables. This example underlines a problem that is pervasive in practice: the evaluation of actions that affect individuals in terms of measures that are highly aggregated. Drawing correct conclusions in such situations is not simple.   ▪

NONLINEAR RELATIONSHIPS

As illustrated in Exhibit 6.2D, relationships can, and often do, have nonlinear as well as linear features. Computing correlation coefficients may be of little value in such situations and can be misleading. For example, a correlation of $r = 0.7$ might be very impressive until you learn that the data could be fitted almost perfectly with a nonlinear curve! As we have said before, there is no substitute for visual inspection of relationships. Only when descriptive statistics convey the important essentials of a relationship may they be substituted for graphs. But remember that in complex problems there is much to be gained from succinctly summarizing data patterns by using descriptive statistics. Techniques based on transformations of data that bring them into a form suitable for summarization by descriptive statistics are thus widely used in practice to attack complex problems. (See Example 6.2D.)

CORRELATION AND CAUSE

Correlation between two variables need not be the result of a causal link between them. Indeed it is possible to find correlation between variables that in truth may have nothing to do with each other.

▪ **E X A M P L E 6.6C:** Here are death rates and divorce rates in 1985 for nine regions in the United States.[††] The rates are numbers of deaths and divorces per 1000 of

---

[†] The situation can be more complicated than suggested here. For example, an increase in advertising can be part of launching a new product or improving an existing one. The increase in sales could be attributed to the quality of the product rather than the advertising. As usual, the truth is probably somewhere in the middle. High sales are due to product quality, but advertising helps inform the public about the availability of the product.

[††] This example comes from A. J. Jaffe and H. F. Spirer, *Misused Statistics: Straight Talk for Twisted Numbers* (New York: Marcel Dekker, 1987), 93. This book has a wealth of entertaining and instructive examples of statistical uses gone awry. We are indebted to Jaffe and Spirer for pointing out the discussion of cause by Mosteller and Tukey, cited in the footnote on page 151, which is summarized in the text.

population in the region.

Region	Death Rate	Divorce Rate
Mountain	6.9	7.0
Pacific	7.7	5.4
West South Central	7.9	7.0
East North Central	8.9	4.6
South Atlantic	9.0	5.2
West North Central	9.2	4.2
East South Central	9.3	5.7
New England	9.3	3.9
Mid Atlantic	9.9	3.7

Mountain: Montana, Idaho, Wyoming, Colorado, New Mexico, Arizona, Utah, Nevada

Pacific: Washington, Oregon, California, Alaska, Hawaii

West South Central: Arkansas, Louisiana, Oklahoma, Texas

East North Central: Ohio, Indiana, Illinois, Michigan, Wisconsin

South Atlantic: Delaware, Maryland, District of Columbia, Virginia, West Virginia, North Carolina, South Carolina, Georgia, Florida

West North Central: Minnesota, Iowa, Missouri, North Dakota, South Dakota, Nebraska, Kansas

East South Central: Kentucky, Tennessee, Alabama, Mississippi

Dakota, South Dakota, Nebraska, Kansas East South Central: Kentucky, Tennessee, Alabama, Mississippi

New England: Maine, New Hampshire, Vermont, Massachusetts, Rhode Island, Connecticut

Mid Atlantic: New York, New Jersey, Pennsylvania

Source: U.S. Bureau of the Census, Tables 112 and 134, *Statistical Abstract of the United States: 1989* (109th ed.) (Washington, D.C.: U.S. Government Printing Office, 1989).

The scatterplot of these data is shown in Exhibit 6.6B. The negative correlation is clear, with $r = -0.82$. Higher divorce rates are associated with lower death rates. Does divorce raise one's immunity to death? The proposition is difficult to accept, yet the correlation is strong. Almost surely the correlation points to an ignorable artifact. How might we argue for this conclusion?

According to Mosteller and Tukey[†], to establish cause one must establish *consistency*, *responsiveness*, and *mechanism*. To establish consistency one must show that the relationship holds in a number of contexts. For example, would the

[†] Frederick Mosteller and John W. Tukey, *Data Analysis and Regression* (Reading, Mass.: Addison-Wesley, 1977).

EXHIBIT 6.6B

Scatterplot of Death
Rates versus Divorce
Rates for Nine U.S.
Regions—1985

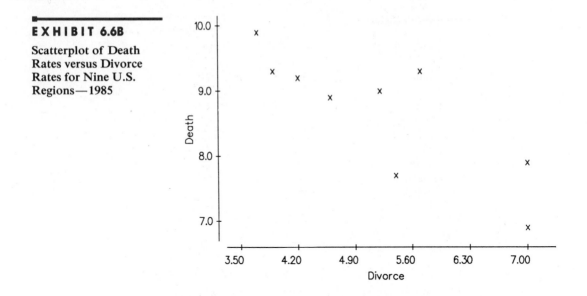

relationship in Exhibit 6.6B hold if the study were conducted in countries in Europe, Asia, or Africa? If so, then there is consistency across countries. But consistency is not enough. Even if the correlation in Exhibit 6.6B fails to point to a real relationship between divorce and death rates, a similar correlation may occur in studies of other countries for the same reason it occurred in the United States.

To establish responsiveness, one must show that a change in x leads to a change in y. In our example, we would have to show that groups of couples, alike in every way except divorce rate, have different death rates. Such a study would require us to conduct an experiment in which groups of couples that are alike except for divorce rate are formed—a tall order, and one that would require a great deal of time and expense. Absence of such an experiment considerably weakens the support that Exhibit 6.6B lends to a cause-and-effect relationship between divorce and immunity to death.

To establish mechanism, one must construct a model that shows step by step how the presumed cause leads to the presumed effect. Moreover, one must show that the presumed effect does not lead step by step to the presumed cause! We invite you to invent a convincing model for how divorce leads to higher immunity to death. If you do, you will have added plausibility to the relationship in Exhibit 6.6B.

Another test of a presumed cause-and-effect relationship is to identify a third variable, called a **lurking variable**, that plausibly explains the relationship. For the relationship in Exhibit 6.6B, a plausible explanation is that age of couples leads to the observed correlation. The divorce rate in the United States used to be quite a bit lower than it is today. Thus older couples in a study will tend to have lower divorce rates than younger couples. But they will also tend to have higher death rates than the younger couples.[†] It is therefore plausible to imagine that much, if not most, of

---

[†] This analysis presumes that older people are more highly concentrated in some parts of the country than in others.

the downward slope in Exhibit 6.6B is explained by a decrease in average age of couples as we move from left to right across the graph. This observation suggests that we try to find divorce rates and death rates grouped by age of couple and do the scatterplots of death rates versus divorce rates for different age groups.[†] If there is still a negative correlation, we have observed a *consistency* that would help support a cause-and-effect relationship between divorce and immunity to death. If the negative correlation is not apparent in the age-dependent scatterplots, then we have scotched the idea of cause and effect. We do not pursue this idea but invite you to do so if your interest warrants it. ■

When changes in a variable x do directly influence changes in a variable y, correlation in a scatterplot of y versus x may be plausibly expected. Yet substantial correlation between observed x's and y's will appear only if there is a strong linear component in the causal relationship. If the relationship is completely nonlinear and we observe the relationship over the range of its nonlinear behavior, then the correlation coefficient may be quite small. Naturally, the scatterplot will display the nonlinear relationship, but this relationship will not be summarized well by the correlation coefficient.

As you can see, cause can be studied with the help of correlation, but the study is subtle and full of pitfalls.[††]

SECTION 6.7

EXERCISES

6.7A Use the data set below.

Case	x	y	Case	x	y	Case	x	y
1	0	36	8	38	64	15	66	52
2	18	71	9	40	47	16	69	40
3	28	31	10	47	66	17	71	38
4	29	78	11	52	28	18	78	60
5	31	72	12	57	69	19	100	18
6	34	57	13	60	100			
7	36	29	14	64	34			

Construct a scatterplot of y versus x and compute the correlation coefficient. (Answer: $r = -0.205$) Now add a 20th case in which $x = 150$ and $y = 150$. Add the point to your scatterplot and compute r. (Answer: $r = 0.410$) The outlier makes a substantial difference! Experiment with the data set by making up a variety of 20th cases, constructing the

[†] See Exercise 6.7D for a crude analysis in this direction.

[††] For a common-sense discussion see A. S. C. Ehrenberg, Parts Four and Six in *A Primer in Data Reduction* (New York: Wiley, 1982).

scatterplot, and computing r. You may also wish to try adding several cases to the data set simultaneously and discovering the impact on r. For example, for some of the intermediate values of x, add some outlying y's. What would be the effect of doing this to the plot in Exhibit 6.6A? (Filename: EX6_7A.DAT.)

6.7B The scatterplot below displays a relationship between a variable y and a variable x. The correlation coefficient has value $r = -0.008$. Does this value convey any useful information about the relationship? Draw a curve through the data. Describe the curve in words.

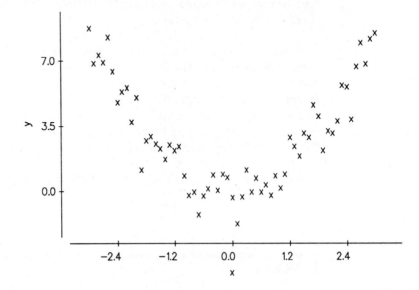

6.7C For the 50 cases below, the correlation coefficient between x and y is 0.095.

Case	x	y	Case	x	y	Case	x	y
1	−19	−4	18	−4	−1	35	3	12
2	−16	−15	19	−4	−14	36	3	−12
3	−13	−8	20	−3	15	37	4	10
4	−13	−4	21	−2	−1	38	4	−13
5	−11	3	22	−2	16	39	6	−9
6	−10	5	23	−2	28	40	6	5
7	−10	12	24	−2	1	41	7	8
8	−10	8	25	−2	2	42	12	11
9	−10	−7	26	−1	−2	43	12	1
10	−10	−3	27	−1	−7	44	13	0
11	−9	−3	28	−1	5	45	15	16
12	−8	0	29	0	4	46	17	−3
13	−8	11	30	0	−15	47	17	7
14	−6	8	31	0	−13	48	21	−19
15	−6	−19	32	1	−9	49	22	22
16	−4	6	33	2	0	50	23	−6
17	−4	23	34	2	−6			

(a) Make a scatterplot of y versus x and verify that $r = 0.095$.

(b) Form the cases into five subgroups: cases 1–10, cases 11–20, cases 21–30, cases 31–40, and cases 41–50. Find the averages of the x's and y's in each subgroup. Make a scatterplot with the x averages on the horizontal axis and the corresponding y averages on the vertical axis. Compute the correlation coefficient for this scatterplot. (Answer: $= 0.341$)

(c) Compare the two scatterplots and the two correlation coefficients you have made. How do they illustrate the concept of ecological correlation? (Filename: EX6_7C.DAT.)

6.7D This exercise is a continuation of Example 6.6C. Given below are the percent of population aged 65 or over in the nine regions given in Example 6.6C, and in the same order.

$$10.6 \quad 10.9 \quad 10.7 \quad 12.2 \quad 13.0 \quad 13.6 \quad 12.3 \quad 13.4 \quad 13.5$$

The source is Table 27 of the *Statistical Abstract* cited in Example 6.6C. These percentages are indexes of the age distributions in the regions; on average, a region with an older population has a higher percentage over the age of 65. Investigate this variable as a potential lurking variable. In other words, is it plausible to conclude that differing age distributions in the regions account for the relationship between death rates and divorce rates?

SECTION 6.8

AUTOCORRELATION

Planning for the future is a hallmark of practical decision making, so the ability to search data for clues about the future behavior of processes is a critical skill. In Chapter 2 the construction of sequence plots and the study of processes were introduced as basic notions in longitudinal data analysis. In this section the crucial idea of correlation is given a longitudinal focus as well. By analyzing data collected from repeated operations of a process in time sequence, the extent to which past behavior provides clues about future behavior can be documented.

By way of introduction, only the simplest case of a vast area of study known as *time series analysis* is covered. Predictive aspects are emphasized because of their obvious relevance to planning activities.

A **time series** is a sequence of observations collected from a process at fixed (and usually equally spaced) epochs of time. The sequence plots in Chapter 2 are graphical displays of time series. Because sales forecasting is basic to business planning,[†] the oil-filter sales data in Exhibit 2.6A are used for illustration in this section.

▪ EXAMPLE 6.8A: Exhibit 2.6B is a sequence plot of the series in which the plotting symbols A = January, B = February, and so on display months. As noted in Chapter 2, the sales data exhibit seasonality, that is, tendency for months to occupy a distinctive position in a pattern of sales throughout the year. Exhibit 2.6C

[†] Demand must be anticipated for budgeting, personnel decisions, production scheduling, order of raw materials and supplies, and a host of other business plans. Underestimating future demand results in lost sales, increased cost of overtime and limited-term workers needed to meet demand, and sometimes poor-quality products made hastily by inadequately trained workers. Overestimating future demand results in substantial costs of excess inventory and can even lead to bankruptcy in extreme cases.

EXHIBIT 6.8A

Deere & Co. Sales Data
and Lags

Row	Year	Month	Sales	Lag 12 Sales	Lag 1 Sales
1	1983	7	2385	*	*
2	1983	8	3302	*	2385
3	1983	9	3958	*	3302
4	1983	10	3302	*	3958
5	1983	11	2441	*	3302
6	1983	12	3107	*	2441
7	1984	1	5862	*	3107
8	1984	2	4536	*	5862
9	1984	3	4625	*	4536
10	1984	4	4492	*	4625
11	1984	5	4486	*	4492
12	1984	6	4005	*	4486
13	1984	7	3744	2385	4005
14	1984	8	2546	3302	3744
15	1984	9	1954	3958	2546
16	1984	10	2285	3302	1954
17	1984	11	1778	2441	2285
18	1984	12	3222	3107	1778
19	1985	1	5472	5862	3222
20	1985	2	5310	4536	5472
21	1985	3	1965	4625	5310
22	1985	4	3791	4492	1965
23	1985	5	3622	4486	3791
24	1985	6	3726	4005	3622
25	1985	7	3370	3744	3726
26	1985	8	2535	2546	3370
27	1985	9	1572	1954	2535
28	1985	10	2146	2285	1572
29	1985	11	2249	1778	2146
30	1985	12	1721	3222	2249
31	1986	1	5357	5472	1721
32	1986	2	5811	5310	5357
33	1986	3	2436	1965	5811
34	1986	4	4608	3791	2436
35	1986	5	2871	3622	4608
36	1986	6	3349	3726	2871
37	1986	7	2909	3370	3349
38	1986	8	2324	2535	2909
39	1986	9	1603	1572	2324
40	1986	10	2148	2146	1603
41	1986	11	2245	2249	2148
42	1986	12	1586	1721	2245
43	1987	1	5332	5357	1586
44	1987	2	5787	5811	5332
45	1987	3	2886	2436	5787
46	1987	4	5475	4608	2886
47	1987	5	3843	2871	5475
48	1987	6	2537	3349	3843

shows that sales tend to decrease gradually throughout the year, except for the rather severe drop that occurs in March, followed by an April recovery. Exhibits 2.6B and 2.6D show that there is little tendency for sales to rise or fall over the years, so a *time trend* in the data is not observed. We thus concentrate on documenting the seasonal pattern through correlation.

First arrange the data in a format that associates each July with the previous July, each August with the previous August, and so on. The resulting table is shown in Exhibit 6.8A. You see in the 13th row that the sales figure for July 1984 sits next to the sales figure for July 1983, in the 14th row the sales figure for August 1984 sits next to the sales figure for August 1983, and so on. The figures in the 5th column of the table are called the 12-month lagged value of the figures in the 4th column. **Lagging** is the name given to the operation of associating previous values in a time series with current values. A **lag** is an interval of time between observations in a time series. The 1-month lags of the sales figures are also displayed, in the 6th column of Exhibit 6.8A. For the 5th column, the lag length is 12; for the 6th column the lag length is 1. **Lag length** refers to the number of time periods skipped in associating a past value of the series with a current value. Lagging creates "missing" values at the beginning of the lagged series. For example, the sales figure for July 1982 is needed to compute the 12th lag for July 1983, but the former figure is not given in the data set. Missing values are denoted with asterisks (∗).

A graphical display of the relationship of the sales with its 12th lag is created by making a scatterplot with the 12th lag on the horizontal axis and sales on the vertical axis. (See the first graph in Exhibit 6.8B.) The scatterplot displays only 36 data points because the first 12 rows of the data are lost through the lagging operation. In Exhibit 6.8B the correlation coefficient is $r = 0.8$, confirming a high degree of linearity in the relationship between sales and its 12th lag.

EXHIBIT 6.8B

Scatterplots of Sales versus 12th Lag and Sales versus 1st Lag

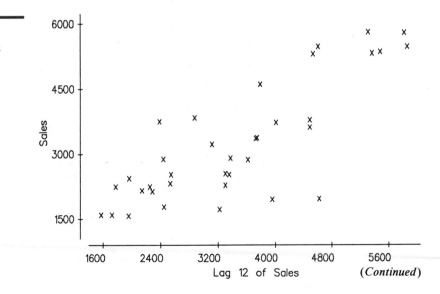

Lag 12 of Sales   *(Continued)*

EXHIBIT 6.8B
(*Continued*)

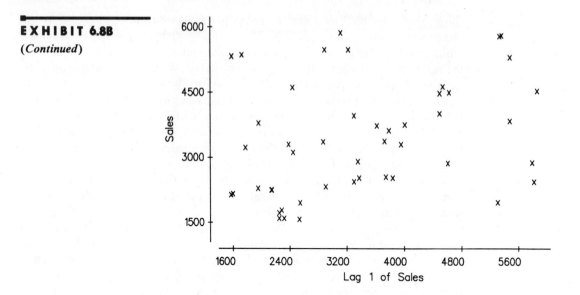

In contrast, the second graph in Exhibit 6.8B shows the scatterplot of sales versus its 1st lag. The correlation coefficient of $r = 0.3$ confirms a low degree of linearity, and the scatterplot displays relatively little relationship of any sort between sales and its 1st lag.

▪

The correlations in Exhibit 6.8B are called **autocorrelations** because they convey information about the relationship between a series and its own past history, just the kind of information needed to search for clues about the future behavior of a process in its past behavior. If the type of behavior observed in the sales figures for 1983–1987 were to continue into the future, then we are justified in looking at the 12th lag series for clues about future sales.

ANALYSIS OF PREDICTION RULES

In particular, the January 1987 sales of 5332 units might be a reasonable guess at the January 1988 sales, the February 1987 sales might be a reasonable guess at the February 1988 sales, and so on. These statements, applied to each month of 1988, constitute a prediction rule.

These statements are *predictive* because they make statements about data not yet known (the data for 1988 were not known when the data in Exhibit 2.6A were recorded). Notice that the statements are also *conditional*, because they say *if* the observed behavior continues into the future. However, in the absence of data for 1988 or beyond, we cannot check whether the condition holds.

Different prediction rules can be compared by applying them to the data on hand and comparing the prediction errors that would have been made if the rules had been used over the period of time covered by the data. This will give some indication of the expected performance of the rules if they are applied to predicting future observations and *if the process continues to behave about the way it has in the past.*

■**EXAMPLE 6.8B:** Applying the prediction rule to the 1984 data, we get predictions for sales in 1985. The prediction for January 1985 is the sales figure for January 1984, namely 5862. The actual sales figure for January 1985 is 5472. The *prediction error* is $5472 - 5862 = -390$; that is, the prediction was too high by 390. Similarly, the prediction for February 1985 is 4536, the actual value is 5310, and the prediction error is $5310 - 4536 = 774$; that is, the rule produced a prediction that was too low by 774. Continuing through the series in this way, we see that we are simply subtracting the 12th lag of the sales series from the sales series itself to produce the series of prediction errors. (See the top portion of Exhibit 6.8C.)

EXHIBIT 6.8C

Computation of
Prediction Errors for
Selected Cases

Case	Year	Month	Sales	Lag 12 Sales	Prediction Error
1	1983	7	2385	*	*
2	1983	8	3302	*	*
3	1983	9	3958	*	*
4	1983	10	3302	*	*
5	1983	11	2441	*	*
6	1983	12	3107	*	*
7	1984	1	5862	*	*
8	1984	2	4536	*	*
9	1984	3	4625	*	*
10	1984	4	4492	*	*
11	1984	5	4486	*	*
12	1984	6	4005	*	*
13	1984	7	3744	2385	1359
14	1984	8	2546	3302	−756
15	1984	9	1954	3958	−2004

Case	Year	Month	Sales	Lag 1 Sales	Prediction Error
1	1983	7	2385	*	*
2	1983	8	3302	2385	917
3	1983	9	3958	3302	656
4	1983	10	3302	3958	−656
5	1983	11	2441	3302	−861
6	1983	12	3107	2441	666
7	1984	1	5862	3107	2755
8	1984	2	4536	5862	−1326
9	1984	3	4625	4536	89
10	1984	4	4492	4625	−133
11	1984	5	4486	4492	−6
12	1984	6	4005	4486	−481
13	1984	7	3744	4005	−261
14	1984	8	2546	3744	−1198
15	1984	9	1954	2546	−592

For purposes of comparison, consider the prediction rule that uses the 1st lag of sales to predict sales; that is, January 1984 is used to predict February 1984, February 1984 is used to predict March 1984, and so on. The prediction errors for this rule are found by subtracting the 1st lag of sales from sales. (See the bottom portion of Exhibit 6.8C.)

Exhibit 6.8D shows dotplots and descriptive statistics for the two series of prediction errors. There are 36 prediction errors for the 12th lag prediction rule. Their average is −217, and their standard deviation is 808. There are 47 prediction errors for the 1st lag prediction rule. Their average is 3, and their standard deviation is 1526. The variability of the 12th lag rule is much less than the variability of the 1st lag rule. On the other hand, the 1st lag rule's prediction errors have an average closer to zero than the 12th lag prediction rule's prediction errors. This is appealing because a prediction error close to zero means a prediction that is close to the actual value of sales.

E X H I B I T 6.8D

Dotplots and Descriptive Statistics for Prediction Errors

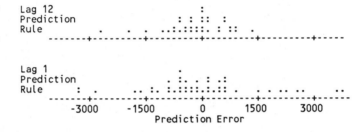

Descriptive Statistics

	n	Mean	Standard Deviation
Lag 12 rule	36	−217	808
Lag 1 rule	47	3	1526

Statisticians often use the concept of root mean square prediction error, which takes both the mean and the standard deviation of the prediction errors into account, to compare different prediction rules. The **root mean square prediction error** for a particular prediction rule is denoted by the notation RMSPE and is computed with the formula

$$\text{RMSPE} = \sqrt{(\text{Mean of PE})^2 + (\text{Standard deviation of PE})^2}$$

where PE stands for prediction error. Each prediction rule will have its own set of prediction errors and, thus, its own value for RMSPE.

▪**E X A M P L E 6.8C:** For the 12th lag prediction rule,

$$\begin{aligned}
\text{RMSPE} &= \sqrt{(-217)^2 + (808)^2} \\
&= \sqrt{47{,}089 + 652{,}864} = \sqrt{699{,}953} \\
&= 837
\end{aligned}$$

By a similar calculation for the 1st lag prediction rule we find that RMSPE = 1526, so by the RMSPE criterion, the 12th lag prediction rule is more accurate than the 1st lag prediction rule.

Even though the 12th lag rule's predictions are more off target on the average than the 1st lag rule's predictions, they are sufficiently less variable to win in the comparison based on the RMSPE. The autocorrelations in Exhibit 6.8B are consistent with this finding. The autocorrelation between 12th lags is much higher than the autocorrelation between 1st lags, suggesting that 12th lags have more predictive power than 1st lags.   ■

The average of the prediction errors is called the *prediction bias*, while the standard deviation of the prediction errors is, as usual, a measure of variation in the predictions. The RMSPE can be displayed symbolically as RMSPE = $\sqrt{\text{Bias}^2 + \text{Variation}^2}$, or, squaring both sides of the equation, MSPE = Bias^2 + Variation^2, where MSPE is called the *mean squared prediction error*. You will often see comparisons based on MSPE rather than RMSPE, but the latter has the advantage of giving a numerical value in the same units as the original measurements.

In this section autocorrelation, the relationship between observations on a process taken at different times, has been introduced. Such relationships form the basis for prediction and planning, so documenting them with data is a critical skill. We have seen that scatterplots and correlation coefficients are helpful tools in longitudinal data analysis, supplementing the sequence plots introduced in Chapter 2. Finally, we have looked at longitudinal analysis predictively and shown that the root mean square prediction error (RMSPE) can be used to compare prediction rules by applying them to data already on hand.

Such analysis may or may not be relevant to the future. It depends on if the process continues to behave about the same as before. In some applications this is not a realistic assumption. For example, a prediction of items in a budget based on historical records fails to take into account that a budget is a plan of action and that the items in the budget may reflect the desire of management to *deviate* from historical performance. Computing predictions based on history may be a first step in budgeting, to give a baseline report on past trends, but large deviations from the trends should not be surprising; in many cases they should be applauded.

S E C T I O N 6.9

EXERCISES

6.9A Here is the time series of annual exports from the United States of iron and steel (excluding scrap) in millions of tons for the years 1937–1980. (Read across the rows to follow the time order.)

3.89	2.41	2.80	8.72	7.12	7.24	7.15	6.05	5.21	5.03	6.88	4.70	5.06	3.16
3.62	4.55	2.43	3.16	4.55	5.17	6.95	3.46	2.13	3.47	2.79	2.52	2.80	4.04
3.08	2.26	2.17	2.78	5.94	8.14	3.55	3.61	5.06	7.13	4.15	3.86	3.22	3.50
3.76	5.11												

(a) List the series in a column. Then list the 1st and 2nd lags of the series.

(b) Prepare scatterplots of the exports versus 1st lag and of the exports versus 2nd lag.

(c) Compute the autocorrelations associated with the scatterplots in part (b).

(d) On the basis of the analysis you have done so far, which lag contains the most information about future values of the series? On the basis of your answer, state how confident you would be trying to predict the series one year ahead. What about two years ahead?

(e) Consider the following three prediction rules:

(1) Predict each future value with the value 4.4 (which happens to be the mean of the series). This is a naive prediction rule that ignores any information in the lags.

(2) Predict each future value with the previous value, that is, use the 1st lag series to predict the original series.

(3) Predict each value by computing $(1/2)(4.4) + (1/2)$ (previous value), that is, the average of the two prediction rules given in parts (1) and (2).

Compute RMSPEs for each of the prediction rules. Which rule produces the smallest RMSPE? Does this encourage you to use the "winning" rule for actual prediction? Under what conditions would the RMSPE be a valid guide to the best rule to use? (Filename: STEELEXP.DAT.)

SECTION 6.10

PEARSON'S X^2 STATISTIC FOR 2 × 2 TABLES

As was the case with metric variables, statistics that summarize relationships among categorical variables are needed. *Measures of association* are such statistics. In this section the simplest case is used to introduce the ideas: a two-way table with two categories per variable, that is, a 2 × 2 table. Exhibit 6.10A displays such a table, in which the frequencies in the categories of the cross-classification are denoted by a, b, c, and d. A parallel numerical example is included for concreteness. It is adapted from Exhibit 5.6A. A two-category Owner variable is created by combining categories 1 and 2 in Exhibit 5.6A. A two-category Outlook variable is created by combining categories 1, 2, and 3 and by combining categories 4, 5, and 6.

EXHIBIT 6.10A

Notation for a Simple Two-Way Table and a Numerical Example

		W		
		W_1	W_2	Total
V	V_1	a	c	$a + c = n_{1.}$
	V_2	b	d	$b + d = n_{2.}$
	Total	$a + b = n_{.1}$	$c + d = n_{.2}$	$a + b + c + d = n$

		Outlook		
		Unfavorable	Favorable	Total
Owner	Noncorporation	70	63	133
	Corporation	67	69	136
	Total	137	132	269

Source: Data come from Exhibit 5.6A.

The two variables are denoted by the symbols V and W, with V_1, V_2, W_1, and W_2 denoting the categories. Thus the symbol a denotes the number of cases that are in both categories V_1 and W_1, and so on. In the numerical example V = Owner, V_1 = Noncorporation, V_2 = Corporation, W = Outlook, W_1 = Unfavorable, and W_2 = Favorable.

The notation for the totals in the margins is defined in the exhibit. For example, $n_{.1} = a + b$ is the sum of the counts in the first column of the table; it is the number of cases in category W_1. Note that $n = a + b + c + d$ is the total number of cases in the table.

■**EXAMPLE 6.10A:** A numerical example will help introduce the discussion of measures of association. Ask yourself the following question: If I were given only the ownership status of a restaurant, what basis would I have for predicting its outlook status? In answering this question, it is helpful to have a table of the row percents. Such a table is displayed in Exhibit 6.10B.

EXHIBIT 6.10B

Table of Row Percents
for Numerical Example
in Exhibit 6.10A

		Outlook	
		Unfavorable	Favorable
Owner	Noncorporation	53	47
	Corporation	49	51
	All	51	49

The percentages of noncorporations and corporations in the unfavorable and favorable categories are not very different. If only two more of the corporations had given an unfavorable response, the percentages for that group would have been reversed, so we intuitively believe that the basis for predicting the outlook status from the ownership status is rather weak.

This belief is reinforced if the alternative data table displayed in Exhibit 6.10C is considered.

EXHIBIT 6.10C

Data Table with the
Same Marginal Counts
as the Table in Exhibit
6.10B but with Different
Frequencies in the Cross-
Classification (The table
also shows row percents
in parentheses.)

		Outlook		
		Unfavorable	Favorable	Total
Owner	Noncorporation	133	0	133
		(100)	(0)	(100)
	Corporation	4	132	136
		(3)	(97)	(100)
	Total	137	132	269
		(51)	(49)	(100)

Here we see that knowing the ownership status allows us to predict with certainty (noncorporation case) or very high probability (corporation case) the outlook status. Intuitively then, we deem the association between the variables in Exhibit 6.10C to be much greater than the association between the variables in Exhibits 6.10A and 6.10B.   ▪

A numerical measure of association whose value is close to zero for the data in Exhibit 6.10A and much larger than 0 for the data in Exhibit 6.10C is now introduced. The measure does not take into account any order implied in the categories.[†] The measure of association is called **Pearson's X^2 statistic**.[††] For the 2×2 table in Exhibit 6.10A it is calculated with the formula

$$X^2 = \frac{n(ad - bc)^2}{(a + b)(c + d)(a + c)(b + d)} \tag{6.1}$$

▪ **E X A M P L E 6.10B:** For the numerical example in Exhibit 6.10A,

$$X^2 = \frac{269(70 \times 69 - 67 \times 63)^2}{137 \times 132 \times 133 \times 136} = \frac{269(4830 - 4221)^2}{327,103,392}$$

$$= \frac{269(609)^2}{327,103,392} = 269(0.001133834) = 0.305$$ ▪

Now try your hand at a calculation. Apply the formula to the data in Exhibit 6.10C. You will get 253.5 for an answer, a number considerably larger than 0.305.

Also verify that if $b = c = 0$ or if $a = d = 0$, then the value of X^2 is n. The maximum possible value for X^2 is the sample size n. With $b = c = 0$ or with $a = d = 0$, there is a *maximum association* between the variables.

The minimum value of X^2 is 0, and this minimum is attained when the table exhibits *no association*. For example, consider the 2×2 table with $a = 50$, $b = 50$, $c = 100$, and $d = 100$. The variables are not associated, and you may verify that $X^2 = 0$. For there to be no association in a 2×2 table it must be true that $a/b = c/d$, which is equivalent to $ad = bc$, which implies $X^2 = 0$, because the numerator of X^2 involves the expression $ad - bc$.

▪ **E X A M P L E 6.10C:** Consider the following table:

		W		
		W_1	W_2	Total
V	V_1	60	120	180
	V_2	40	80	120
	Total	100	200	300

[†] The Owner categories are not ordered, but the Outlook categories are ordered from 1 to 6, with the numbers standing for increasing degrees of favorability. There are measures of association that take ordering into account, but they are not presented here. See L. A. Goodman and W. H. Kruskal, "Measures of Association for Cross-Classifications," *Journal of the American Statistical Association* 49 (1954): 732–764 for a discussion of such a measure.

[††] See K. Pearson, "On a Criterion That a Given System of Deviations from the Probable in the Case of a Correlated System of Variables Is Such That It Can Be Reasonably Supposed to Have Arisen from Random Sampling," *Philosophical Magazine* 50(5) (1900): 157–175.

Because $ad = bc = 4800$, we know that $X^2 = 0$. The corresponding table of row percents is

		W		
		W_1	W_2	Total
V	V_1	33%	67%	100%
	V_2	33%	67%	100%
	Total	33%	67%	100%

All three rows of row percents are the same. This is a consequence of the lack of association. ■

It can be shown in general that if $ad = bc$, then all three rows of row percents are the same. Conversely, it can be shown that if all three rows of row percents are the same, then there is no association in the table, that is, $ad = bc$, and $X^2 = 0$.

■ **EXAMPLE 6.10D:** The following table with specified marginal counts is given:

		W		
		W_1	W_2	Total
V	V_1			150
	V_2			150
	Total	100	200	300
	Row percent	33%	67%	

The marginal row percents (bottom row of the table) are $100(100/300)\% \simeq 33\%$ and $100(200/300)\% \simeq 67\%$. We wish to complete the body of the table so that there is no association between the variables. This can be done by making all rows of row percents the same. We thus complete the first row by placing 33% of the first row total in the $V_1 W_1$ cell, that is, we let $a = (1/3)(150) = 50$. This in turn requires us to use $b = 50$, $c = 100$, and $d = 100$. The table satisfies $ad = bc$ and all the row percent rows are the same. It follows that $X^2 = 0$. ■

SECTION 6.11

EXERCISES

6.11A Consider these two tables:

Row	Table I	Table II
First	50, 100	100, 50
Second	100, 50	50, 100

(a) Comment on the degree of association between the variables displayed in these tables.

(b) Compute the values of a/b and c/d.

(c) Compute the value of X^2 for each table. What do these values imply about the degree of association between the variables?

6.11B Consider 2×2 tables with the following counts in their bodies:

(1) First row: 250, 300   Second row: 0, 450

(2) First row: 550, 0   Second row: 0, 450

(3) First row: 165, 385   Second row: 135, 315

(a) Comment on the degree of association in each of the tables.

(b) Compute the value of X^2 for each table. What do these values imply about the degree of association between the variables?

6.11C The 2×2 table below is taken from J. I. Mann, M. P. Vessey, M. Thorogood, and R. Doll, "Myocardial Infarction in Young Women with Special Reference to Oral Contraceptive Practice," *British Medical Journal* 2 (1975): 241–245. (Myocardial infarction means heart attack.)

EXHIBIT 6.11A

Classification of 216 Women According to Incidence of Heart Attacks and Smoking Habits

		Heart Attack		
		Yes	No	Total
Smoker	Yes	45	83	128
	No	14	74	88
	Total	59	157	216

(a) Compute the row percents and comment on the association between the two variables. According to this table, does knowledge of smoking habits make much difference in predicting heart attacks?

(b) Cover the counts in the body of the table, leaving the marginal totals exposed. Now write counts in the body of the table that produce a table with no association. How does this table differ from the original one?

(c) Compute the values of a/b and c/d.

(d) Compute X^2 for the table above and for the one you constructed in part (b). What do they imply?

(e) The relationship between smoking and heart attacks has been controversial, frequently pitting the tobacco industry against a variety of claimants in expensive court battles. Even though data such as those in the table above often support a direct relationship, it is technically inappropriate to infer causality because people choose to smoke, and the propensity to smoke and the propensity to have heart attacks could be caused by some other factor, though such a factor has not yet been identified scientifically. If you are interested in this question, you may wish to track down newspaper articles, court testimony, papers in medical journals, and reports by the U.S. Surgeon General that deal with the controversy. It is an education in the widespread use of data and statistical methods on a problem with massive commercial and public health implications.

6.11D Consider a 2×2 table with

First row: $a, 400 - a$
Second row: $500 - a,$ $a + 100$

(a) The parameter a may assume any integer value between 0 and 400. Display the tables for $a = 0, 50, 100, 150, 200, 250, 300, 350,$ and 400. Include counts and row percents in the tables. Describe in words the degree of association you observe in these tables.

(b) Verify that for the general table,

$$X^2 = 1000[a(a + 100) - (500 - a)(400 - a)]^2/(500)^2(400)(600)$$

Compute X^2 for $a = 0, 50, 100, 150, 200, 250, 300, 350,$ and 400. Comment on how well these statistics reflect the degree of association you observed in part (a).

6.11E Suppose in a 2×2 table that $k = a/b = c/d$.

(a) Show that all three rows of row percents have the form

$$100b/(b + d) \qquad 100d/(b + d)$$

(b) Explain why this condition yields $X^2 = 0$.

6.11F Pearson's X^2 treats the variables in a 2×2 table symmetrically. This means the variables can be interchanged without affecting the value of X^2. It also means that column percents can be used in place of row percents in the discussion of Section 6.10. Demonstrate these remarks with numerical examples.

SECTION 6.12

REINTERPRETATION OF PEARSON'S X^2

The formula (6.1) given for X^2 is easy to compute with but it is not easy to interpret, and it applies only to 2×2 tables. Another version of the formula that is easier to interpret and that applies to any $r \times c$ table is presented in this section. The interpretation is given in terms of the 2×2 table to simplify the presentation.

The idea is to compare the counts in the body of the table with the counts in a table with the same marginal counts but with no association between the variables. Then X^2 will be interpreted as a measure of how "close" the two sets of counts in the bodies of the tables are to each other. This idea can be put into the context of the equation

$$\text{Observation} = \text{Fit} + \text{Residual}$$

The observations are the actual counts a, b, c, and d. The fitted values, denoted by $\hat{a}, \hat{b}, \hat{c},$ and $\hat{d}$, are the counts from the table with no association. The assumption of no association provides a base of comparison. The closer the observed counts are to the counts that yield no association, the closer the value of X^2 is to zero. The further the observed counts are from the counts that yield no association, the closer the value of X^2 is to n. The residuals are the observed values minus the fitted values: $a - \hat{a}, b - \hat{b}, c - \hat{c},$ and $d - \hat{d}$. It can be shown that X^2 is the following function of the residuals and the fitted values:

$$X^2 = \frac{(a - \hat{a})^2}{\hat{a}} + \frac{(b - \hat{b})^2}{\hat{b}} + \frac{(c - \hat{c})^2}{\hat{c}} + \frac{(d - \hat{d})^2}{\hat{d}} \qquad \textbf{(6.2)}$$

In words, this formula says to compute for each cell in the body of the table the square of the residual divided by the fitted value and then to add up the resulting ratios.

▪**EXAMPLE 6.12A:** Here is the 2 × 2 table introduced in Exhibit 6.10A:

		Outlook		Total
		Unfavorable	Favorable	
Owner	Noncorporation	70	63	133
	Corporation	67	69	136
	Total	137	132	269
	Row percent	50.93%	49.07%	

The marginal row percents are $50.93\% = 100(137/269)\%$ and $49.07\% = 100(132/269)\%$. More decimal places are carried here than in previous calculations because the accuracy is needed to implement Equation (6.2). To obtain the counts that yield no association in the table, apply the marginal row percents to the row totals 133 and 136. This yields a table with $\hat{a} = (137/269)(133) \simeq 67.7361$, $\hat{b} = (137/269)(136) \simeq 69.2639$, $\hat{c} = (132/269)(133) \simeq 65.2639$, and $\hat{d} = (132/269)(136) \simeq 66.7361$. These fitted values are displayed in a 2 × 2 table:

		Outlook		Total
		Unfavorable	Favorable	
Owner	Noncorporation	67.7361	65.2639	133
	Corporation	69.2639	66.7361	136
	Total	137	132	269
	Row percent	50.93%	49.07%	

With the four-decimal-place accuracy displayed in this table, we have $\hat{a}\hat{d} = 4520.4$ and $\hat{b}\hat{c} = 4520.4$ to one-decimal-place accuracy. If more decimal places had been carried in the table, the equality $\hat{a}\hat{d} = \hat{b}\hat{c}$ would have been even more accurate. The accuracy used is sufficient for hand calculation. A calculator or computer, which would typically be used in practice, achieves greater accuracy effortlessly.

Notice that the fitted "counts," though not whole numbers, do add up to the row and column totals given in the actual data table, and they satisfy the condition of no association. This is the condition we wished to achieve with the fitted values. Our next job is to compute the value of X^2 using Formula (6.2):

$$X^2 = \frac{(70 - 67.7361)^2}{67.7361} + \frac{(67 - 69.2639)^2}{69.2639} + \frac{(63 - 65.2639)^2}{65.2639} + \frac{(69 - 66.7361)^2}{66.7361}$$

$$= \frac{(2.2639)^2}{67.7361} + \frac{(-2.2639)^2}{69.2639} + \frac{(-2.2639)^2}{65.2639} + \frac{(2.2639)^2}{66.7361}$$

$$= 0.07566 + 0.07310 + 0.07853 + 0.07680 = 0.30409 \simeq 0.304$$

which is essentially the value obtained in Example 6.10B. The discrepancy between the values is due to the rounding done in the calculation just displayed.

This demonstrates by numerical example the assertion that Equation (6.2) yields the same value of X^2 as Formula (6.1). ■

Equation (6.2) is a measure of closeness between two sets of counts: the actual counts a, b, c, and d and the fitted counts $\hat{a}, \hat{b}, \hat{c}$, and $\hat{d}$. It was Karl Pearson's genius that discovered the formula for X^2, and subsequent applications have proven how profoundly appropriate the formula is. The formula compares the two set of counts by computing the squares of their differences, that is, the residuals, dividing these squared residuals by the fitted values, and adding up the ratios. The reason for the division by the fitted values is hard to explain intuitively. The advanced theory behind the calculation is not presented here. The theory states that cells with larger fitted values tend to have larger residuals. At this point, we must ask you to accept Pearson's formula as the appropriate adjustment.

Equation (6.2) can be transformed into another, equivalent, equation that is preferable for hand or calculator calculation:

$$X^2 = \frac{a^2}{\hat{a}} + \frac{b^2}{\hat{b}} + \frac{c^2}{\hat{c}} + \frac{d^2}{\hat{d}} - n \qquad \textbf{(6.3)}$$

■**EXAMPLE 6.12B:** Using the observed and fitted values calculated in Example 6.12A, substitute into Equation (6.3) to get

$$X^2 = \frac{70^2}{67.7361} + \frac{67^2}{69.2639} + \frac{63^2}{65.2639} + \frac{69^2}{66.7361} - 269$$

$$= \frac{4900}{67.7361} + \frac{4489}{69.2639} + \frac{3969}{65.2639} + \frac{4761}{66.7361} - 269$$

$$= 72.3396 + 64.8101 + 60.8146 + 71.3407 - 269 = 269.3014 - 269$$

$$= 0.3014$$

which is close to the value 0.304 obtained in Example 6.10A. The discrepancy is due to the rounding used in the calculation in this example. If more decimal places had been carried in the fitted values, a result closer to 0.304 would have been obtained. In calculating X^2 an error in the second or third decimal place is not a source of concern. Accuracy to one decimal place is adequate for practice. ■

SECTION 6.13

EXERCISES

6.13A Use the heart attack data in Exercise 6.11C.
  (a) Compute the value of X^2 using Equation (6.2), retaining four decimal places in your calculations.
  (b) Compute the value of X^2 using Equation (6.3), retaining four decimal places in your calculations.

(c) Compare the value of X^2 you got in parts (a) and (b) and in Exercise 6.11C. How could you have made them closer together?

6.13B Show algebraically that Equations (6.2) and (6.3) are equivalent. It will be helpful to use the fact that $a + b + c + d = \hat{a} + \hat{b} + \hat{c} + \hat{d} = n$.

SECTION 6.14

PEARSON'S X^2 FOR $r \times c$ TABLES

In Section 5.10 we saw that relationships among categorical variables are displayed in multi-way tables. But displaying more than three variables is rather complex. When working on a practical problem, we may collect data on and wish to understand the relationships among many more than three variables. One approach to such analysis is to use summary measures (descriptive statistics) to characterize the essentials of relationships. Using the numerical summaries, characterizations of large numbers of variables can be produced.

Equation (6.2) may be written schematically as

$$X^2 = \sum \frac{(\text{Observation} - \text{Fit})^2}{\text{Fit}} = \sum \frac{(\text{Residual})^2}{\text{Fit}} \tag{6.4}$$

where the symbol $\sum$ stands for adding up over the cells in the body of the table. This formula applies to any $r \times c$ table. The fitted values are computed so that:

(1) The row and column marginal totals are the same as in the original data table.

(2) The fitted values satisfy the condition of no association.

Both these conditions are satisfied if the marginal row percents are applied to the marginal row totals to compute the fitted values.

For purposes of hand calculation we use the alternative Equation (6.3), which may be written schematically as

$$X^2 = \sum \frac{(\text{Observation})^2}{\text{Fit}} - n \tag{6.5}$$

▪**EXAMPLE 6.14A:** Exhibit 6.14A displays the calculations for a 4×3 table ($r = 4$ rows and $c = 3$ columns). For example, the marginal row percents are 18.47%, 29.07%, and 52.46%. Applying these percentages to the row total for Alabama, we get fitted values $1,327.28 \simeq (2,695/14,591)(7,186)$, $2,088.67 \simeq (4,241/14,591)(7,186)$, and $3,770.05 \simeq (7,655/14,591)(7,186)$. The other fitted values are found similarly.

The value of X^2 is approximately 59, which is much closer to the minimum possible value of 0 than it is to the maximum value of $n = 14,591$. We conclude there is little association between the variables State and Year with regard to frequency of motor vehicle registrations. Another way to look at it is that the distribution of motor vehicle registrations varied pretty much the same over time in the four states examined. Exhibit 6.14B displays the row percents for all the rows in the table as well as the bottom margin. Although the rows are not exactly the same (in other words, there is some association), the degree of association is small.

E X H I B I T   6.14A

Calculation of Pearson's
X^2 Statistic for a 4 × 3
Table Showing a Cross-
Classification of Motor
Vehicle Registrations by
State and Year

$$\text{Data} = \begin{cases} \text{Observed count} \\ \text{Fitted count} \end{cases}$$

(Observed counts are in thousands of vehicles.)

State	Year			Total
	1960	1970	1980	
Alabama	1,282	1,966	3,938	7,186
	1,327.28	2,088.67	3,770.05	7,186
Alaska	81	139	226	446
	82.38	129.63	233.99	446
Arizona	624	1,093	1,917	3,634
	671.21	1,056.25	1,906.54	3,634
Arkansas	708	1,043	1,574	3,325
	614.14	966.44	1,744.42	3,325
Total	2,695	4,241	7,655	14,591
	2,695	4,241	7,655	14,591
Row percent	18.47%	29.07%	52.46%	

$$X^2 = \frac{1,282^2}{1,327.28} + \frac{1,966^2}{2,088.67} + \frac{3,938^2}{3,770.05} + \frac{81^2}{82.38} + \frac{139^2}{129.63} + \frac{226^2}{233.99} +$$

$$\frac{624^2}{671.21} + \frac{1,093^2}{1,056.25} + \frac{1,917^2}{1,906.54} + \frac{708^2}{614.14} + \frac{1,043^2}{966.44} + \frac{1,574^2}{1,744.42} \simeq 59$$

Source: Data from U.S. Bureau of the Census, Table No. 1062, *Statistical Abstract of the United States: 1984* (104th ed.) (Washington, D.C.: U.S. Government Printing Office, 1983).

E X H I B I T   6.14B

Table of Row Percents
for Table in
Exhibit 6.14A

State	Year		
	1960	1970	1980
Alabama	21%	32%	47%
Alaska	17%	29%	54%
Arizona	17%	30%	53%
Arkansas	22%	31%	47%
Total	20%	31%	49%

S E C T I O N   6.15

EXERCISES

6.15A Consider the table in Exhibit 6.15A. It is adapted from a case presented in G. A. Churchill, *Basic Marketing Research* (Chicago: Dryden Press, 1988), 587. The case concerns a survey conducted by a catalog sales department of a sporting goods manufacturer. A sample of 225 names was taken at random from a mailing list, and a questionnaire and a catalog were sent to each of these people. They were also offered a $3 coupon toward their next purchase as a reward for answering the questionnaire.

EXHIBIT 6.15A

Tabulation of Survey
Results—Catalog Sales
Case

$$\text{Data} = \begin{cases} \text{Counts} \\ \text{(Row percents)} \end{cases}$$

Willingness to Purchase

Order Status	Unwilling	Somewhat Willing	Very Willing	Total
Never ordered	20	7	16	43
	(47)	(16)	(37)	
Ever ordered but	20	11	8	39
not in last year	(52)	(28)	(20)	
Ordered within	10	17	15	42
last year	(24)	(40)	(36)	
Total	50	35	39	124
	(40.3)	(28.2)	(31.5)	

The response from this mailing was 124 questionnaires. Among the many questions asked, one requested information on whether the person had purchased something from the company's catalog never, ever but not within the last year, or within the last year. Another question asked if the person would be unwilling, somewhat willing, or very willing to make a purchase in the future. The market researchers wished to know if previous purchase behavior was associated with willingness to purchase in the future.

(a) Compute the fitted values that correspond to the condition of no association. Put them into a 3 × 3 table and verify that they yield the same row and column totals as shown in Exhibit 6.15A.

(b) Compute the value of X^2 using Equation (6.4). Comment on the degree of association indicated by X^2.

(c) Compute the value of X^2 using Equation (6.5). Why is it slightly different from the value you got in part (b)?

6.15B Consider the data in Exhibit 6.15A. A natural collapsing of the data occurs if we distinguish between people who have never bought from the catalog and those who have ever bought. Suppose we restrict our attention to those who have ever bought. Define one level of this variable as "bought more than one year ago" and the other level as "bought less than one year ago."

(a) Using the variable defined above and Willingness as the other variable, create a 2 × 3 table. This shows that when we restrict our attention to people who have ever bought, the time since last purchase appears to be a useful predictor of willingness to buy again. (This certainly makes sense; a higher percentage of those who have bought recently are favorably disposed than those who have let more than a year pass without buying.)

(b) Compute X^2 for the table you created in part (a). What degree of association does this value imply? How does this compare with the degree of association implied in Exercise 6.15A?

(c) By examining the row percents in Exhibit 6.15A, come up with an explanation for why the value of X^2 values differ so much in the two tables you compared in part (b). Then go on to try to develop reasons for why the responses follow the patterns they do. How might you try to obtain data that would support or refute the reasons you come up with? Perhaps the most striking information in the table is obvious from the row percents: 64.3% of the people who purchased within the last year are unwilling or only somewhat willing to purchase again. This suggests trying to contact these people and asking why they responded this way!

6.15C Exhibit 5.10B shows three 3×3 tables, one for each type of restaurant: fast food, supper club, and other. Each table displays the relationship between the variables Ownership and Size.
(a) For each 3×3 table compute the value of X^2.
(b) To what extent do the X^2 values suggest similarities or differences in the relationships between Ownership and Size over the different types of restaurant? Do these statistics adequately summarize your intuitive understanding of the relationships? Would you be willing to report only the values of X^2 by type of restaurant as a summary of the data? If so, you have effected a substantial reduction in the amount of material that must be reported!

SECTION 6.16

SUPPLEMENTARY EXERCISES FOR CHAPTER 6

6A The data below are taken from J. O. Ramsay, "Monotone Regression Splines in Action," *Statistical Science* 3(4) (November 1988): 425–441.

The variables in the first five columns are:

> Price ($100 U.S.)
> Engine displacement (liters)
> City gas consumption (liters/100 km)
> Expressway gas consumption (liters/100 km)
> Weight (100 kg)

Column 6 gives the make of automobile. Column 7 numbers the foreign makes, column 8 numbers all the makes, and column 9 numbers the domestic makes. This classification is a bit artbitrary because an automobile can be produced in a variety of countries!

56	1.6	13.3	6.8	10.0	# Chevrolet Chevette		1	1
74	1.6	10.5	5.5	10.2	# Chevrolet Nova		2	2
67	1.5	10.1	5.3	8.7	# Chevrolet Spectrum		3	3
56	1.5	11.0	5.6	9.9	# Dodge Colt		4	4
68	1.6	11.5	5.6	9.5	# Dodge Omni		5	5
61	1.9	12.0	6.2	10.9	# Ford Escort		6	6
56	1.5	11.5	6.5	9.2	# Honda Civic	1	7	
75	2.0	12.0	6.3	10.9	# Mitsubishi Tredia	2	8	
56	1.6	10.5	5.6	9.5	# Nissan Sentra	3	9	
60	1.4	12.0	5.6	9.1	# Renault Alliance	4	10	
80	1.8	12.0	5.6	10.4	# Subaru	5	11	
73	1.6	11.0	5.3	10.3	# Toyota Corolla	6	12	
56	1.5	11.0	5.5	9.7	# Toyota Tercel	7	13	
74	1.8	12.0	6.3	10.1	# Volkswagen Golf	8	14	

(Continues)

83	1.8	12.6	6.3	10.5	#Volkswagen Jetta	9	15	
94	2.2	15.8	7.4	12.7	#Chrysler Laser		16	7
73	1.5	9.4	5.6	9.0	#Honda Civic CRX	10	17	
110	1.8	10.5	6.5	10.6	#Honda Prelude	11	18	
109	1.9	14.9	6.8	12.4	#Isuzu Impulse	12	19	
89	2.0	12.0	6.3	11.2	#Mitsubishi Corida	13	20	
95	1.8	12.6	6.5	12.2	#Nissan 200SX	14	21	
87	1.6	9.7	5.1	9.2	#Nissan Pulsar NX	15	22	
89	2.5	12.6	6.7	11.5	#Pontiac Fiero		23	8
142	2.2	14.1	8.2	10.7	#Audi 4000S	16	24	
67	2.0	15.8	7.2	11.6	#Chevrolet Cavalier		25	9
74	2.3	13.3	6.2	11.8	#Ford Tempo		26	10
88	2.0	13.3	6.3	11.8	#Honda Accord	17	27	
92	2.0	12.6	6.7	11.8	#Mazda 626	18	28	
132	2.4	14.9	6.7	12.9	#Mitsubishi Galant	19	29	
101	2.0	11.0	5.6	11.1	#Nissan Stanza	20	30	
93	2.5	14.1	6.7	12.0	#Oldsmobile Calais		31	11
126	2.0	14.1	7.9	12.9	#Saab 900	21	32	
97	2.0	11.0	5.5	12.2	#Toyota Camry	22	33	
144	2.3	14.1	7.9	13.3	#Volvo	23	34	
101	2.5	16.9	6.5	12.6	#Buick Century		35	12
149	5.2	23.0	9.7	16.2	#Chrysler Fifth Avenue		36	13
100	2.2	13.3	7.9	11.7	#Chrylser Le Baron		37	14
72	2.2	13.3	7.9	11.5	#Dodge Aires		38	15
94	2.2	15.8	8.7	12.7	#Dodge Lancer		39	16
114	3.8	15.8	8.7	14.1	#Mercury Cougar		40	17
107	3.8	19.5	9.0	15.2	#Oldsmobile Cutlass		41	18
95	2.8	16.9	8.7	12.6	#Pontiac 6000		42	19
154	3.8	18.1	7.7	15.0	#Buick Electra		43	20
106	5.0	18.1	8.2	16.5	#Chevrolet Caprice		44	21

(a) Make scatterplots for each pair of variables and compute descriptive statistics and correlation coefficients. Which variables are most highly correlated?

(b) Repeat part (a) treating the foreign and domestic automobiles as two separate groups. Do the two groups differ in the behavior of the variables listed? (Filename: AUTOSPEC.DAT.)

6B The data below are annual U.S. GNP in trillions of dollars for the years 1978–1982. The current dollar figures are reported in dollars valued as of the reporting year. They do not take the effects of inflation into account. The constant dollar figures remove the effects of inflation by attributing to each dollar the value it would have had if it had been spent in 1972.

Year	Current Dollars	Constant Dollars
1978	2.13	1.40
1979	2.37	1.43
1980	2.63	1.48
1981	2.94	1.50
1982	3.06	1.48

(a) Compute the correlation coefficient between the Current Dollars and Constant Dollars variables.

(b) Define two new variables: $x = 5$ (Current Dollars) $- 3$ and $y = 3$ (Constant Dollars) $+ 5$. Compute the values of these two new variables for each year and add them to the table above.

(c) Compute the correlation coefficient between x and y. It should have the same value as the coefficient you computed in part (a). This illustrates a general property of the correlation coefficient: *its magnitude does not change if the variables are subject to linear transformations.*

(d) Linear transformations of the variables do not change the magnitude of the correlation coefficient, but they can change the sign. Verify this by defining and computing the values of the variable $z = -3$ (Constant Dollars) $+ 5$ and then computing the correlation coefficient between z and the variable x defined in part (b).

(e) Suppose you standardized two variables and computed the correlation coefficient between the standardized variables. How would this correlation coefficient relate to the correlation coefficient between the two original variables?

(f) Suppose you standardized y and computed the correlation coefficient between x and the standardized version of y. How would this correlation coefficient relate to the correlation coefficient between x and y?

6C Write a brief, one- to two-page, memo explaining the concept of ecological correlation. How does it arise in practice? What danger lurks in the interpretation of ecological correlations?

6D Suppose x helps to cause y but the relationship between x and y is statistical, that is, there is variation in the scatterplot.

(a) Sketch a scatterplot of a situation in which x is the only cause of y, the relationship is linear, but the scatter in the data is due to a mild degree of measurement error.

(b) Sketch a scatterplot of a situation in which x is the only cause of y, the relationship is quadratic, but the scatter in the data is due to a mild degree of measurement error.

(c) Sketch a scatterplot of a situation in which x is one of many causes of y, the relationship is linear, but the scatter is due to the influence of the many other causes as well as measurement error.

(d) Compare the values of the correlation coefficients you would get in the examples in parts (a), (b), and (c).

6E RMSPE is one tool for comparing prediction rules. Other performance measures are also used. A popular one is the *mean absolute prediction error (MAPE)*. To compute it, simply find the absolute values of the prediction errors and then average them. This is an extremely easy rule to implement. Simply form a column of prediction errors with the minus signs erased and average the numbers in the column. Compare the two prediction rules in Section 6.8 using the MAPE. How does the comparison based on the MAPE compare with the comparison based on the RMSPE? (Filename: OILFILT.DAT.)

6F This exercise refers to Section 6.8 and Exercise 6E. Some practitioners prefer to make comparisons based on the *relative prediction error*, defined as the prediction error divided by the actual value:

$$\text{Relative prediction error} = \frac{\text{Actual value} - \text{Predicted value}}{\text{Actual value}}$$

Let RPE stand for relative prediction error. Root mean square relative prediction errors (RMSRPE) and mean absolute relative prediction errors (MARPE) can be defined simply by applying the root mean square or mean absolute value calculations to the RPEs. Apply these calculations to the two prediction rules in Section 6.8. How do the evaluations compare with the RMSPE and MARPE comparisons? It can happen that the different evaluation criteria we have proposed disagree with each other as to the best prediction rule. When this happens there is no completely objective way to decide which rule is best. Reserving judgment may be the best course! (Filename: OILFILT.DAT.)

6G Compute the 1st lag autocorrelation coefficients for the two time series listed in Exercise 6B. Which series has a higher autocorrelation? Which series exhibits more variation over time?

6H As we shall see in Chapter 13, nonresponse is common in surveys. Nonresponse simply means that respondents fail to fill out questionnaires or refuse to answer questions over the phone. One often needs to conduct a pilot study of a set of potential respondents to get an indication of the magnitude of the nonresponse. Then appropriate plans can be made to handle the problem in a final survey. Here is the result of a pilot study on a sample of 100 insurance companies. The companies were divided into two groups (called *strata* in survey work): Large and Other. Size was measured by reported assets in the annual statements of the companies. Random samples of 30 Large and 70 Other companies were chosen and questionnaires sent. The table below shows the numbers of respondents and nonrespondents in each group.

| | Responded? | | |
Company Size	No	Yes	Total
Other	35	35	70
Large	10	20	30
Total	45	55	100

(a) Compute the row percents for the table. Do they suggest similar behavior by Large and Other companies?

(b) Compute Pearson's X^2 for the table. How does it compare with its minimum and maximum values of 0 and 100? Does it suggest similar behavior by the Large and Other companies?

(c) In planning the final survey, what precautions would you make, if any, in light of the data from the pilot study?

6I Write a one- to two-page essay explaining the concept of association of categorical variables. Use numerical examples to illustrate your points. In what sense is association between categorical variables analogous to correlation of metric variables?

6J The law school and the business school admissions committees provide the following summary of their activities for the previous academic year.

| | Law School | | |
Gender of Applicant	Number Admitted	Number Not Admitted	Total
Male	120	120	240
Female	180	180	360
Total	300	300	600

| | Business School | | |
Gender of Applicant	Number Admitted	Number Not Admitted	Total
Male	400	800	1200
Female	200	400	600
Total	600	1200	1800

(a) Compute the row percents for each table. Are the two schools consistent in their treatment of men and women in terms of admission rates?

(b) Compute the values of Pearson's X^2 for each table. What do the values of these statistics imply about the treatment of men and women by the two admissions committees?

(c) Aggregate the two tables, that is, add the figures in the corresponding cells of the tables to produce a table that reports the combined activity of the two schools. Compute the row percents and the value of Pearson's X^2 for the new table. What do these statistics imply about the treatment of men and women by the two schools combined? What causes the paradox?

6K A marketing research study consists of showing an ad for a new product on television stations in a limited, pilot market for four weeks. A random sample of households is then contacted and the head of the household is asked if he or she has heard of the new product. The respondent is also asked to state if his or her age falls in one of three ranges: under 30, between 30 and 50, and over 50. Here are the numbers of respondents categorized by age and "recall," that is, whether they say they have heard of the product.

| | Heard of Product? | | |
Age of Respondent	No	Yes	Total
Under 30	50	50	100
Between 30 and 50	300	150	450
Over 50	180	20	200
Total	530	220	750

Compute the value of Pearson's X^2 and interpret its meaning.

GLOSSARY FOR CHAPTER 6

Autocorrelation	Correlation between values of a time series at a given lag.
Ecological correlation	Correlation computed from data that are aggregates of smaller units of study.
Lag	An interval of time between observations in a time series.

Lagging	The operation of associating previous values in a time series with current values.
Lag length	The number of time periods skipped in associating a past value of a series with a current value.
Lurking variable	A third variable whose influence plausibly explains the correlation between two other variables.
Pearson's X^2 statistic	$$X^2 = \sum \frac{(\text{Observation} - \text{Fit})^2}{\text{Fit}} = \sum \frac{(\text{Residual})^2}{\text{Fit}}$$
Product-moment correlation coefficient	$$r = \frac{1}{n-1} \sum_{i=1}^{n} \left[\left(\frac{x_i - \bar{x}}{s_x} \right) \left(\frac{y_i - \bar{y}}{s_y} \right) \right]$$
Root mean square prediction error	$\text{RMSPE} = \sqrt{(\text{Mean of PE})^2 + (\text{Standard deviation of PE})^2}$ where PE denotes prediction error.
Scatterplot	An (x, y) plot that displays a statistical relationship between two variables.
Time series	A sequence of observations collected from a process at fixed epochs of time.

## CHAPTER 7

Fitting Curves

In Sections 6.4 and 6.6 we showed how to summarize relationships between metric variables using correlations. Although correlations are valuable tools, they are not powerful enough to handle many complex problems in practice. Correlations have two major limitations:

- They summarize only linearity in relationships.
- They do not yield *models* for how one variable influences another.

The tool of *regression analysis* overcomes these limitations by using mathematical curves to summarize relationships among several variables. A **regression model** consists of the mathematical curve summarizing the relationship together with measures of variation from that curve. Because any type of curve can be used, relationships may be nonlinear.

Regression analysis also easily accommodates transformation of variables and categorical variables, and it provides a host of diagnostic statistics that help assess the utility of variables and transformations and the impact of such features as outliers and missing data.

In this chapter the basic notions of regression analysis are introduced. More advanced techniques are discussed in later chapters.

MODELS

A model describes *how* a process works. For scientific purposes, the most useful models are statements of the form "*if* certain conditions apply, *then* certain consequences follow." The simplest of such statements assert that the list of conditions result in a single consequence without fail. For example, we learn in physics that if an object falls toward the earth, then it accelerates at about 981 centimeters per second per second.

A less simple statement is one that asserts a tendency: "Loss in competition tends to arouse anger."[†] While admitting the existence of exceptions, this statement is intended to be universal, that is, anger is the expected response to loss in competition.

Contrast the last two examples with the discussion of brand loyalty presented in H. Assael, *Consumer Behavior and Marketing Action*, 3rd ed. (Boston: PWS-KENT, 1987), 75–76. The discussion is summarized in the following if-then formulation:

If a person tends to

- be influenced by reference groups
- be self-confident in making choices
- perceive a high level of risk in a purchase
- be store loyal

then the person may be brand loyal.

Assael cites research that says that brand loyalty is not as common as it used to be, suggesting that only about 50% of repeat purchasers are truly loyal, while the other 50% purchase out of convenience or habit. Here is a set of conditions that yields a consequence only about 50% of the time, hardly the stuff of a universal statement. Yet many of the statements made about human behavior have this flavor, simply because behavior is so variable and subject to change over time. We are often quite happy to find a set of conditions that allows us to predict with 50% accuracy!

To be useful in documenting the behavior of processes, models must allow for a range of **consequences** or outcomes. They must also be able to describe a range of **conditions**, fixed levels of predictor variables, for it is impossible to hold conditions constant in practice. When a model describes the range of consequences corresponding to a fixed set of conditions, it describes *local* behavior. A summary of the local behaviors for a range of conditions is called *global* behavior. Models are most useful if they describe global behavior over the range of conditions encountered in practice. When they do, they allow us to make predictions about consequences corresponding to conditions that have not actually been observed. In such cases, the models help us reason about processes despite being unable to observe them in complete detail.

[†] George C. Homans, *Social Behavior: Its Elementary Forms* (New York: Harcourt Brace Jovanovich 1961), 123.

Exhibit 7.1A illustrates these remarks schematically with diagrams showing two common situations handled with regression methods. The first situation shows a quantitative conditions variable x that varies continuously over a range of values. For each observed value of x there is a corresponding observed value of the quantitative consequences variable y. The graph shows an observed x, x_0, and the corresponding observed y, y_0. The study illustrated in the graph involved 13 pairs of (x, y) observations. (This is the situation dealt with in the discussion of correlation in Chapter 6.)

EXHIBIT 7.1A

Stylized Plots of Two Situations Commonly Encountered in Regression Analysis

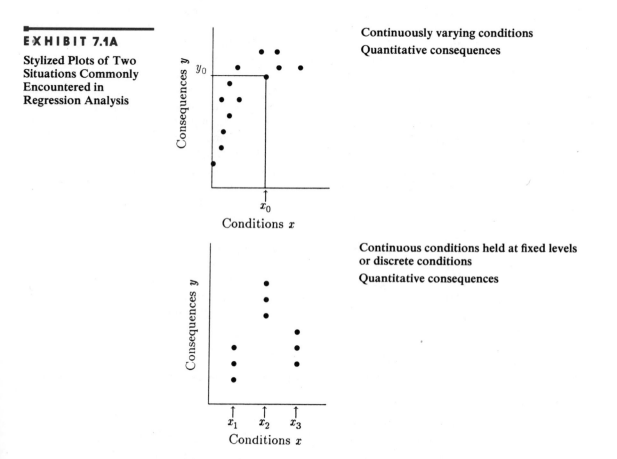

Continuously varying conditions
Quantitative consequences

Continuous conditions held at fixed levels or discrete conditions
Quantitative consequences

The diagram has been drawn to suggest a nonlinear relationship between x and y to reinforce the idea that correlation analysis would be of limited use for this study. For some levels of the conditions variable x there are different values of the consequence variable y. For a fixed condition level, multiple consequences display the local variation. The nonlinear shape of the graph overall is the global nature of the relationship between x and y.

The second diagram in Exhibit 7.1A shows quantitative consequences of a conditions variable that could be

- A continuous-type variable that is held at three fixed levels, with three consequences observed at each level
- A categorical variable with three categories that have been coded numerically for display on the graph

This second situation is not one that can be handled with correlation analysis. Correlation is most appropriate when both the x and y variables vary continuously, and then only if the relationship is predominantly globally linear.

Regression analysis is a flexible modelling tool, but it must be used with care and good judgment. The most serious pitfall is the failure to use x and y variables that can legitimately be interpreted as conditions and consequences. The most clear-cut *legitimate* case is cause and effect. If a model says x causes (or helps to cause) y, then we proceed to develop the model with no hesitation. The most clear-cut *inappropriate* situation is one in which there is no causal link between x and y, but a third variable, a lurking variable, affects x and y so that they appear to be related. (An example of this situation was given in Example 6.6C.) Most practical studies fall between the extremes. Usually, many conditions contribute to the observed behavior in a consequence variable y. Moreover, the conditions usually do not act independently of each other but rather interact with each other as well as with y. Regression models can help partially document complications, but certain complications that defy any attempts to sort them out are inherent in complex processes.

In the next few sections some basic mechanics of regression analysis are introduced. A variety of conditions that can be handled are illustrated by example. Section 7.13 presents two practical experiences.

Throughout the treatment of regression analysis in this and subsequent chapters, the consequences variable y is referred to as a *response* variable and the conditions variable x as a *predictor* variable. (See Section 7.10.) There is no universally adopted terminology. Different authors use different labels. Ours are fairly common.

ILLUSTRATIONS OF LINEAR REGRESSION

A SMALL-SAMPLE ILLUSTRATION

For our first illustration, we take a small subsample of the 60 parcels of real estate displayed in Exhibit 6.2A. It is much easier to introduce ideas with this small set of data. At the end of this section the ideas will be applied to the full set of 60 parcels.

To choose the subsample we rolled a die; the result was the face with three spots. We simply chose the third case and every sixth case thereafter from the data set in Exhibit 6.2A, a total of 10 cases.[†] Exhibit 7.2A shows the data on square feet of living area and market value for these 10 cases. The number of cases is denoted by n, so in this example $n = 10$.

[†] This is an application of *systematic sampling*, which is discussed in Section 16.5.

EXHIBIT 7.2A

Square Feet of Living Area and Market Values (Cases 3, 9, 15, 21, 27, 33, 39, 45, 51, and 57 in Exhibit 6.2A)

Sq.ft (x)	Market (y)
544	25.2
694	37.4
767	33.6
825	38.0
899	37.6
965	37.2
1033	40.4
1060	44.8
1106	42.8
1298	45.2

Exhibit 7.2B shows the scatterplot of the data in Exhibit 7.2A. Our eyes detect a marked linear trend in the plot. Before reading further, use a straight-edge to draw a line through the points that appear to you to be the best description of the trend. Roughly estimate the coordinates of two points (not necessarily points corresponding to data points) that lie on the line. From these two estimated points, estimate the slope and y intercept of the line.[†] Next, describe the manner in which the data points deviate from your estimated line. Finally, suppose you are told that a parcel has 923 square feet of living area, and you are asked to use your model to predict the market value of the parcel. Give your best guess at the range of plausible market values. If you do all these things, you will have performed the essential operations of a linear regression analysis of the data.

If you followed the suggestions in the previous paragraph, you were probably pleased to find that regression analysis is really quite simple. On the other hand, you may not be pleased with the prospect of analyzing many large data sets "by eye" or trying to determine a complex model that relates market values to square feet of living area, assessed values, and grade scores simultaneously. To do any but the most rudimentary analyses, the help of a computer is needed.

Statistical software does regression calculations quickly, reliably, and efficiently. Recent research has yielded algorithms especially suited to machine calculation, and these do not resemble algorithms used for hand calculation. In practice one never has to do more than enter data, manipulate data, issue commands that ask for calculations and graphs, and interpret output. Consequently, computational formulas are not presented here.

[†] Let (x_1, y_1) and (x_2, y_2) denote two points, with $x_1 \neq x_2$ on a line whose equation is $y = a + bx$. Then the slope of the line is

$$b = \frac{\text{Difference in } y \text{ coordinates}}{\text{Difference in } x \text{ coordinates}} = \frac{y_1 - y_2}{x_1 - x_2}$$

and the y intercept is

$$a = \frac{x_1 y_2 - x_2 y_1}{x_1 - x_2}$$

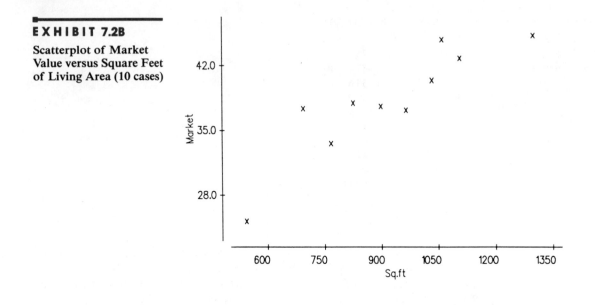

The most widely available routines for regression computations use *least squares* methods. In this chapter the ideas behind **ordinary least squares** (often referred to as **OLS**) are explained. Ordinary least squares fits a curve to data pairs (x_1, y_1), $(x_2, y_2), \ldots, (x_n, y_n)$ by minimizing the sum of the squared vertical distances between the y values and the curve. Ordinary least squares is the fundamental building block of most other fitting methods.

FITTING A LINE BY ORDINARY LEAST SQUARES

When a computer program is asked to fit a straight-line model to the data in Exhibit 7.2A using the method of ordinary least squares, this equation is obtained:

$$\hat{y} = 16.3 + .0239x$$

The symbol y stands for a value of Market, and the symbol $\hat{\ }$ over the y indicates that the model gives only an estimated value. The symbol x stands for a value of square feet of living area.

This result can be put into the representation

$$\text{Observation} = \text{Fit} + \text{Residual}$$

where y is the observation, $\hat{y}$ is the fit(ted) value, and $y - \hat{y}$ is the residual. Consider the parcel in Exhibit 7.2A that has square feet of living area $x = 965$. The corresponding observed market value is $y = 37.2$. The fitted value given by the ordinary least square line is

$$\hat{y} = 16.3 + .0239(965)$$
$$= 16.3 + 23.0 = 39.3$$

The vertical distance between the actual market value and the fitted market value is $y - \hat{y} = 37.2 - 39.3 = -2.1$, which is the residual. The negative sign indicates the actual market value is *below* the fitted line.

For the parcel with $x = 1060$ square feet of living area, the actual market value is $y = 44.8$, and the fitted value, that is, the value on the line, is $\hat{y} = 41.6$. (Confirm this.) Thus the residual is $y - \hat{y} = 44.8 - 41.6 = 3.2$. A positive residual means the observed market value is larger than the fitted value.

Exhibit 7.2C shows a scatterplot of the data with the ordinary least squares line fitted through the points. The actual market values are plotted with M's, the fitted values with F's. How does the line compare with the line you obtained by eye? It is probably pretty close, confirming that the computer can be "trained" to do the job of fitting a line.

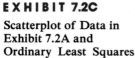

EXHIBIT 7.2C

Scatterplot of Data in Exhibit 7.2A and Ordinary Least Squares Line

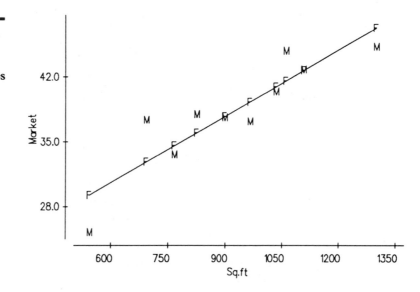

Another output from the statistical software is a measure of variation: $s = 2.8$. This measure of variation is the standard deviation of the vertical differences between the data points and the fitted line, that is, the standard deviation of the residuals. Exhibit 7.2D shows the data, fitted values, and residuals for the 10 parcels in the subsample.

You may verify that the numbers in the residual column sum to zero. This is a characteristic of the method of least squares: *for any data set, the residuals from fitting a straight line by the method of OLS sum to zero.*[†]

In statistical practice, to compute the standard deviation of a set of numbers, subtract their mean from each number, sum the squares of the resulting differences, divide by the degrees of freedom, and finally take the square root.

[†] This statement assumes the model includes a y-intercept term. If the model is forced to go through the origin, a different theory is called for.

Sq.ft	Market	Fitted	Residual
544	25.2	29.3	−4.1
694	37.4	32.8	4.6
767	33.6	34.6	−1.0
825	38.0	36.0	2.0
899	37.6	37.7	−0.1
965	37.2	39.3	−2.1
1033	40.4	40.9	−0.5
1060	44.8	41.6	3.2
1106	42.8	42.7	0.1
1298	45.2	47.2	−2.1

EXHIBIT 7.2D

Data, Fitted Values, and Residuals for 10 Real Estate Parcels

Because the mean of the OLS residuals is zero, their standard deviation is the square root of the sum of their squares divided by the degrees of freedom. *When fitting a straight line by OLS, the number of degrees of freedom is two less than the number of cases, denoted by $n - 2$.*[†]

In our example, then, degrees of freedom $= 10 - 2 = 8$. Thus the value of s is found by computing

$$s = \sqrt{[(-4.1)^2 + \cdots + (-2.1)^2]/8}$$
$$= \sqrt{62.3/8} = \sqrt{7.8}$$
$$= 2.8$$

We see that the model fitted to the data affects the number of degrees of freedom. In Chapter 4 the mean $\bar{y} = \hat{y}$ was fitted to the data, the residuals were of the form $y - \bar{y}$, and the residuals summed to zero, yielding $n - 1$ degrees of freedom. In linear regression, the model $\hat{y} = b_0 + b_1 x$ is fitted to the data, the residuals are of the form $y - \hat{y}$, and the residuals satisfy two mathematical constraints, yielding $n - 2$ degrees of freedom. Whenever the residuals sum to zero, the standard deviation of the residuals is found by dividing the sum of their squares by the degrees of freedom and taking the square root of the result.

ANALYSIS OF RESIDUALS

Two fundamental tests are applied to residuals from a regression analysis: a test for normality and a scatterplot of residuals versus fitted values. The first test can be

---

[†] Because the residuals sum to zero, 1 is deducted from n. This is analogous to the calculation of s in Chapter 4. The OLS residuals satisfy another constraint, which leads to the subtraction of another 1, yielding $n - 2$ degrees of freedom. The second constraint is that the sum of the products of the fitted values and the residuals, case by case, is zero. For the data in Exhibit 7.2D, the calculation is $(29.3)(-4.1) + \cdots + (47.2)(-2.1) \simeq 0$. The result is not exactly 0 because not enough decimal places are displayed. In the computer, many more decimal places are carried, and the numerical result is zero to the accuracy of the machine. The constraints mentioned here are mathematical results, but there are always questions of numerical accuracy in practical implementation. Note that division by degrees of freedom means that the value of the standard deviation depends on the model that has been fitted to the data. Different models applied to the same data have different standard deviations.

performed by checking the percentage of the residuals within one, two, and three standard deviations of their mean, which is zero.[†] The second test gives visual cues of model inadequacy. Neither test is very effective when the data set is small, as in the current example, but both are introduced here because they are easy to explain in the context of a small data set.

The interpretation of the standard deviation of the residuals from the linear regression model is essentially the same as the interpretation of the standard deviation given in Chapter 4. If the distribution of residuals is roughly mound shaped and the number of cases is sufficiently large, then approximately 68% of them are within one standard deviation of 0 (which is the mean), approximately 95% of them are within two standard deviations of 0, and approximately 99.7% of them are within three standard deviations of 0.

For the residuals in Exhibit 7.2D, the one-, two-, and three-standard-deviation intervals are $[-2.8, 2.8]$, $[-5.6, 5.6]$ and $[-8.4, 8.4]$. The percentages of residuals in each of these intervals are 70%, 100%, and 100%, indicating a fairly compact distribution of residuals. An analysis based on 10 observations rarely yields much insight.

To perform the second test, simply make a scatterplot of the Residual variable versus the Fitted variable[††] in Exhibit 7.2D. Exhibit 7.2E shows the result.

EXHIBIT 7.2E

Scatterplot of Residual versus Fitted from Exhibit 7.2D (based on linear regression model for 10 cases in Exhibit 7.2A)

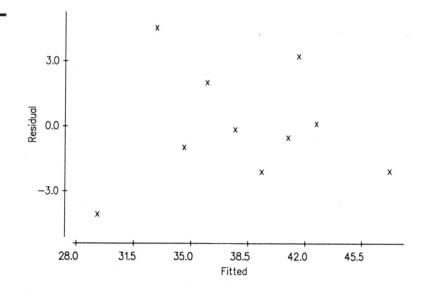

[†] This analysis can be supplemented with a normal probability plot, which is introduced in Chapter 8.

[††] It may appear more natural to plot the residuals versus the predictor variable x, because if the data follow a curved model then the curve should appear in this plot. That is correct, and such a plot is often done as part of a residual analysis. The plot of the residuals versus the fitted values is essentially the same plot, however, because the fitted values determined by the equation $\hat{y} = b_0 + b_1 x$ represent a linear transformation of the x's. Thus a trend that would show up in the plot of Residual versus x would also show up in the plot of Residual versus $\hat{y}$. The advantage of the latter plot is that it can be implemented for more complicated models than the straight-line model, as is illustrated later in the chapter.

What do we look for in a plot of residuals versus fitted values? We look for a plot that suggests *random scatter*. As noted in the footnote on page 186, the residuals satisfy the constraint

$$\sum (y - \hat{y})\hat{y} = 0$$

where the summation is done over all cases in the data set. The constraint, in turn, implies that the product-moment correlation coefficient between the residuals and the fitted values is zero. If the scatterplot is somehow not consistent with this fact because it exhibits trend or other peculiar behavior, then we have evidence that the model has not adequately captured the relationship between x and y. This is the primary purpose of residual analysis: to seek evidence of model inadequacy.

Exhibit 7.2F shows three stylized plots of residuals versus fitted values. The first plot is a prototype of a plot that would cause no concern. The points may be characterized as random scatter and are quite consistent with the verdict of no correlation. The second plot is consistent with the verdict of no correlation, but it casts serious doubt on the adequacy of the fitted model. There is a strong nonlinear

E X H I B I T 7.2F   **Three Stylized Residual Plots**

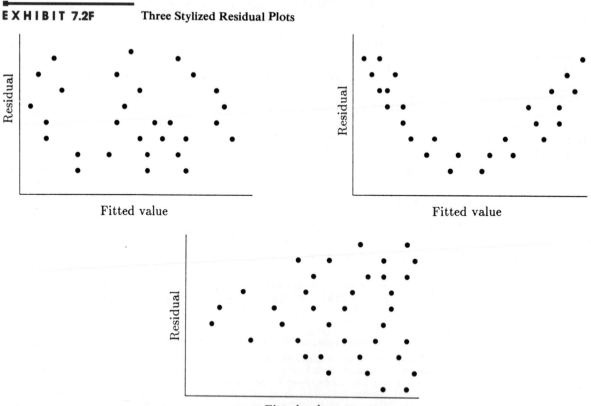

Note: The first plot shows no model inadequacy. The second shows that a nonlinear trend term is needed. The third shows that a trend in variability must be accounted for.

trend that the fitted model has not accounted for. The conclusion from this plot is that a more elaborate model is called for. The third plot displays a trend in the variability of the residuals. This, too, calls for modification of the model. Lack of constancy in the variability of the residuals can often be remedied by transforming the response variable or the predictor variable. (See Chapter 22 for a presentation of transformations.)

Because the plot in Exhibit 7.2E involves only 10 points, it provides scanty evidence for or against model inadequacy. On the basis of the plot, we would not be willing to make a strong statement in either direction.

PREDICTIONS

How does the linear regression model translate into predictions of parcels that are not part of the data used to determine the model? The data set in Exhibit 6.2A offers 50 test cases, those not drawn into the subsample. The model can be used to make the predictions for these cases. The predicted values can then be compared to the actual market values of the test cases.

Exhibit 7.2G shows the results. For each case in the test group, the x value was fed into the model and the two-standard-deviation prediction interval[†] computed. The exhibit shows the x value, the endpoints of the prediction interval, the actual market value, and an indicator that is 1 if the actual value falls inside the prediction interval, zero otherwise. We see that 43 of the prediction intervals contain the actual Market values, a success rate of $100(43/50)\% = 86\%$. Because two standard deviation prediction intervals were used, a 95% success rate might have been expected. As we shall see, though, the straight-line model does not adequately describe the relationship between y and x. We are making predictions from an inadequate model and so should not expect to achieve the success rate that using an adequate model would provide.

A LARGE-SAMPLE ILLUSTRATION

Having introduced the use of the linear regression model in the context of a small data set, we turn to fitting a straight line to all 60 cases in Exhibit 6.2A. Again $x =$ Sq.ft is used to predict $y =$ Market. Statistical software yields

$$\hat{y} = 20.5 + .018362x$$

with residual standard deviation $s = 3.981$.

Compare this model with the one fitted to the subsample in Exhibit 7.2A, namely, $\hat{y} = 16.3 + .0239x$ with $s = 2.8$. The y intercept and slope have changed, but they are the same orders of magnitude as those from the smaller data set. Moreover, they yield roughly comparable fitted values, as illustrated on page 191 for a few values of x.

[†] For a given case, the form of the prediction interval is

$$[\hat{y} - 2 \cdot predsd, \ \hat{y} + 2 \cdot predsd]$$

where **predsd** is the estimated standard deviation of the prediction errors and is computed by the formula given in Appendix A to this chapter. It is a function of values of the predictor variable x and of s.

| | | Prediction Limits | | | Hit = 1 |
EXHIBIT 7.2G	Case	Sq.ft (x)	Lower	Upper	Market (y)	Miss = 0
Predictions of Cases	1	521	21.0	36.4	26.0	1
from Exhibit 6.2A Not	2	538	21.5	36.8	19.4	0
Listed in Exhibit 7.2A	4	577	22.6	37.6	26.2	1
(based on linear	5	661	24.9	39.2	31.0	1
regression model for 10	6	662	24.9	39.3	34.6	1
cases in Exhibit 7.2A)	7	677	25.3	39.6	36.4	1
	8	691	25.7	39.9	33.0	1
	10	712	26.3	40.3	42.4	0
	11	721	26.5	40.5	32.8	1
	12	722	26.5	40.5	25.6	0
	13	743	27.1	41.0	34.8	1
	14	760	27.5	41.3	35.8	1
	16	780	28.0	41.8	31.0	1
	17	787	28.2	41.9	39.2	1
	18	802	28.6	42.2	36.0	1
	19	814	28.9	42.5	34.8	1
	20	815	28.9	42.5	34.4	1
	22	834	29.4	43.0	34.6	1
	23	838	29.5	43.0	35.6	1
	24	858	30.0	43.5	35.8	1
	25	883	30.6	44.1	39.6	1
	26	890	30.8	44.3	35.0	1
	28	918	31.5	44.9	41.2	1
	29	920	31.5	45.0	31.2	0
	30	923	31.6	45.0	30.0	0
	31	926	31.7	45.1	37.4	1
	32	931	31.8	45.2	38.0	1
	34	966	32.6	46.1	44.0	1
	35	967	32.6	46.1	44.2	1
	36	1011	33.6	47.2	43.6	1
	37	1011	33.6	47.2	38.4	1
	38	1024	33.9	47.5	42.2	1
	40	1040	34.3	47.9	40.4	1
	41	1047	34.4	48.1	43.6	1
	42	1051	34.5	48.2	41.1	1
	43	1052	34.5	48.2	39.6	1
	44	1056	34.6	48.3	41.8	1
	46	1060	34.7	48.4	38.4	1
	47	1070	34.9	48.7	43.6	1
	48	1075	35.1	48.8	42.8	1
	49	1079	35.1	48.9	40.6	1
	50	1100	35.6	49.5	41.6	1
	52	1138	36.4	50.5	39.0	1
	53	1164	36.9	51.2	41.8	1
	54	1171	37.1	51.4	48.4	1
	55	1237	38.4	53.2	39.8	1
	56	1249	38.6	53.5	47.2	1
	58	1435	42.1	58.9	38.8	0
	59	1602	45.1	64.0	47.4	1
	60	1804	48.4	70.2	45.4	0

x	$\hat{y} = 16.3 + .0239x$	$\hat{y} = 20.5 + .018362x$
600	30.6	31.5
800	35.4	35.2
1000	40.2	38.9
1200	45.0	42.5
1400	49.8	46.2

The major difference between the two models is in the measures of variation. The model based on 60 cases has $s = 3.981$; the model for 10 cases has $s = 2.8$. Comparing the scatterplots for the two data sets shows why. The scatterplot in Exhibit 6.2C displays a great deal more variation than the one in Exhibit 7.2B. The small subsample fails to capture the large amount of variation exhibited in the larger data set; we thus place greater assurance in the measure of variation $s = 3.981 \simeq 4.0$ as an index of deviation from the trend indicated by the fitted line.

Using a computer program and the model fitted to all 60 cases, we computed the two-standard-deviation prediction ranges for the 60 cases. We compared actual market values to the intervals and found that only three of the intervals, those for cases 2, 10, and 12, failed to contain the actual market values. The percentage of failures is $100(3/60)\% = 5\%$, which corresponds with the expectation that two-standard-deviation prediction ranges be correct about 95% of the time.

Recall that the prediction ranges are functions of the model, the value of x, and the value of s. We see that the large number of cases, and the larger value of s, yields predictions for the 60 cases that are quite close to expectation. We must temper our enthusiasm for this finding with the knowledge that we have predicted cases that were used to develop the model. The acid test would be predicting *new* cases collected after building the model.[†] We will return to this idea in Section 7.12. In the next section, we find reasons to be dissatisfied with the straight-line model developed in this section!

SECTION 7.3

EXERCISES

7.3A Refer to the Anscombe data in Exercise 6.3H. For each data set in that exercise, do the following:

(a) Use statistical software to fit a straight line to the data set using OLS; save the fitted values and residuals for further analysis.

[†] This is the test we put to the model built from the small sample. We have no new test cases to apply to the model built from the whole data set, so we applied a test that is unreasonably favorable to it, namely, prediction of cases used in fitting the model. Tests of this type are the source of much misunderstanding in practice. Analysis of the fitted values of a model tends to make one overly optimistic about the ability of the model to predict new cases. This in turn leads to disillusionment when the actual ability of the model is discovered. It is prudent to reserve judgment about any model that has not been tested against new cases.

(b) Make a multiple scatterplot showing the data points and the fitted values plotted versus the predictor variable on the same set of axes.

(c) Make a scatterplot of residuals versus the predictor variable.

(d) Comment on how the residual plot in part (c) does or does not display weaknesses in the fitted model.

Compare the y intercepts and slopes of the lines fitted to the four data sets. What important aspects of the data sets are not conveyed by these coefficients? (Filename: ANSCOMBE.DAT.)

7.3B Refer to Exercise 6.3I. On the basis of the scatterplot you constructed for that exercise, comment on the appropriateness of fitting a straight line. Now fit a straight line using OLS and plot the residuals versus the predictor variable. Do the residuals display any potential weaknesses in the fitted model? Can you think of any reasons why the straight-line model might not be appropriate?

7.3C Refer to Exercise 6.5A, which uses the real estate data. Repeat that exercise, computing the coefficients of the OLS straight line, computing the measure of variability s, making a scatterplot of the residuals versus the fitted values, and making a scatterplot of the residuals versus the predictor variable, instead of computing the correlation coefficient r. Compare the two scatterplots. Explain why they convey the same information. (Filename: REALPROP.DAT.)

7.3D Refer to the data in Exercise 6.7A. Redo that exercise fitting straight-line models instead of computing correlation coefficients. Notice the impact of the outliers on b_0, b_1, and s. (Filename: EX6_7A.DAT.)

7.3E Consider these two data sets:

Data Set 1		Data Set 2	
x	y	x	y
1	1	1	7
2	4	2	5
3	3	3	3
4	5	4	4
5	7	5	1

For each data set find a straight-line model using OLS, compute the fitted values and residuals, plot the residuals versus the fitted values, and plot the residuals versus the predictor variable x. On the basis of your work, comment on the effect of positively and negatively sloping lines on the residual plots.

7.3F Fit a straight-line model to the bank data in Exhibit 6.6A, using x = Assets and y = Deposits. Plot residuals versus fitted values. Do you see any evidence of model inadequacy? (Filename: DEPOSITS.DAT.)

S E C T I O N   7.4

ILLUSTRATION OF QUADRATIC REGRESSION

In Sections 6.2 and 6.4 a rainbow effect was evident in the plot of Market versus Sq.ft, a finding consistent with the idea of decreasing return to amount of square feet of living area. (The residual plot in Exhibit 21.2C confirms the inadequacy of the straight-line model.) Different grades of construction were mentioned as yet another possible source of variation. In this section a model that is quadratic in square feet of living area is investigated. And in Section 7.6 the incorporation of the Grade variable is examined.

The model considered in this section has the form

$$\hat{y} = b_0 + b_1 x + b_2 x^2$$

where x denotes a value of square feet of living area. Using statistical software, set up the squared variable and ask for the fit of the indicated model. The result for the 60 cases of real estate is

$$\hat{y} = 0.073 + 0.059729x - 0.000019604x^2$$

with measure of variation $s = 3.473$. A large number of decimal places is reported for computational accuracy. The fitted values should be reported to the same level of accuracy as the original data, which is hundreds of dollars. For example, for a value of square feet $x = 1000$, the fitted value is

$$\hat{y} = 0.073 + 0.059729(1000) - 0.000019604(1000)^2$$
$$= 0.073 + 59.729 - 19.604 = 40.198$$
$$\simeq 40.2$$

which means a market value of $40,200.

Exhibit 7.4A shows a scatterplot of Market versus Sq.ft with the fitted quadratic curve drawn through it. You see the slight bend in the curve made possible by the quadratic term. The residuals are simply the differences between the actual market values and the fitted values on the quadratic curve. (See Exhibit 21.2D for a residual plot.)

EXHIBIT 7.4A

Scatterplot of Market Values versus Square Feet of Living Area (60 residential parcels and quadratic curve fitted by OLS)

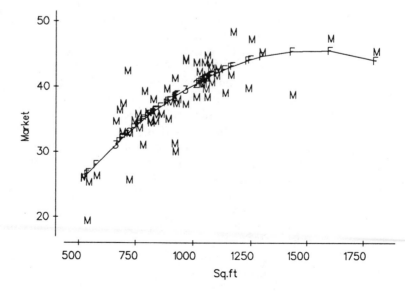

The standard deviation s is computed by the rules given in Section 7.2:

(1) Compute the fitted values for all the cases.

(2) Compute residuals by subtracting the fitted values from the actual values.

(3) Sum the squared residuals and divide the sum of squares by degrees of freedom.

(4) Take the square root of the resulting quantity to obtain s.

For the quadratic model, degrees of freedom equals $n - 3$ because the residuals may be shown to satisfy *three* mathematical constraints.

The value of $s = 3.473$ for the quadratic model is smaller than the value of s for the linear model (which was $s = 3.981$). The quadratic model accounts for more of the variation in the data than does the linear model. We therefore expect the prediction ranges based on the quadratic model to be smaller than the prediction ranges based on the linear model, and this is true. If it is also true that the prediction ranges based on the quadratic model predict reliably (for example, if the two-standard-deviation prediction ranges contain the actual market value about 95% of the time), then they are superior to the ranges based on the linear model because they are just as reliable even though they are shorter.

In the following display, the prediction ranges from the two models for selected values of square feet of living area are given, illustrating concretely that the quadratic model produces smaller ranges.

x	Linear Model	Quadratic Model
600	(23.4, 39.7)	(21.6, 36.1)
800	(27.1, 43.3)	(28.3, 42.3)
1000	(30.8, 46.9)	(33.2, 47.2)
1200	(34.4, 50.7)	(36.4, 50.6)
1400	(37.9, 54.5)	(38.0, 52.5)
1600	(41.4, 58.4)	(37.8, 53.2)

Remember that these ranges are computed by statistical software; the mathematical formulas that yield the ranges for the quadratic case are not displayed because they are too complicated to use for hand calculation.

The same test that was performed on the linear model was used on the quadratic model: prediction ranges were computed for all 60 cases and the intervals that did not contain the actual market values were found. Four cases, numbers 10, 12, 29, and 30, for which the ranges missed the actual market values were found. This yields a percentage of misses $100(4/60)\% = 6.67\%$, which is very close to 5%. Because they are smaller than the ranges from the linear model, we conclude that the quadratic model is superior to the linear model. This conclusion coincides with the impression we formed looking at the scatterplot.

Exhibit 7.4A points out another potential pitfall of using regression models blindly. Notice that the quadratic curve used to model the scatterplot starts to turn downward at about $x = 1500$ square feet. Is this really appropriate for the situation at hand? Should the market value of a house with 1800 square feet of living space tend to be less than the market value of a house with 1200 square feet of living space? For this data set no observations are available for houses larger than 1804 square feet, but common sense tells us that the market values do not decrease as the quadratic regression curve suggests. For the range of x values in the data set, the quadratic curve represents the situation reasonably well—the decrease in predicted market values over the range from $x = 1500$ to 1804 is very small. Perhaps a more complicated curve would provide an even better representation of the relationship.

This example does show that common sense and knowledge of the particular problem at hand should always be exercised in problem solving. In particular, regression models must be used very cautiously to predict y values associated with x values *outside* the range of x values used to fit the model. Such predictions are extremely dangerous because the model may not apply outside the observed range. Although this advice seems rather easy to follow, the situation gets much more complicated when several x variables are incorporated into the prediction equation, as is done in Section 7.6. Some statisticians[†] have said, All models are wrong, some models are useful! Models are "wrong" because they do not apply to all situations and to every detail. Those that are useful yield insight in relevant situations. Models are not responsible for errors that result from applying them to situations in which they have not been tested. That is the responsibility of the user.

SECTION 7.5

EXERCISES

7.5A Compute the 60 residuals for the quadratic model reported in Section 7.4.
  (a) Plot the residuals versus x.
  (b) Plot the residuals versus the fitted values $\hat{y}$.
  (c) Compare the residual plots in parts (a) and (b). Does either suggest model inadequacy?
  (d) The one-, two-, and three-standard-deviation intervals for the residuals are $[-3.473, 3.473]$, $[-6.946, 6.946]$, and $[-10.419, 10.419]$. What percentages of the residuals are in these intervals? Are they roughly consistent with the 68%, 95%, and 99.7% values associated with the normal distribution?
  (e) Verify that each of the following correlation coefficients is zero:

  ▪ Between the residuals and x

  ▪ Between the residuals and x^2

  ▪ Between the residuals and $\hat{y}$

  (Filename: REALPROP.DAT.)

7.5B Use computer software and the method of ordinary least squares to fit a quadratic model to the real estate data in Exhibit 7.2A. Obtain the coefficients b_0, b_1, and b_2, the fitted values, the residuals, and the residual standard deviation s.
  (a) Show numerically that $\sum_{i=1}^{10} \hat{y}_i = \sum_{i=1}^{10} y_i$ and hence that $\sum_{i=1}^{10} (y_i - \hat{y}_i) = 0$.
  (b) Show numerically that $\sum_{i=1}^{10} (y_i - \hat{y}_i)x_i = \sum_{i=1}^{10} (y_i - \hat{y}_i)x_i^2 = 0$.
  (c) Show why the facts in parts (a) and (b) imply that $\sum_{i=1}^{10} (y_i - \hat{y}_i)\hat{y}_i = 0$. (*Hint*: Remember that the fitted values are linear functions of x and x^2.)
  (d) Show why the facts in part (b) imply that the residuals are uncorrelated with the observed values of x and x^2, that is, the correlation coefficients are zero. (Filename: REALPROP.DAT.)

[†] George Box, "Robustness in the Strategy of Scientific Model Building," in R. L. Lanner and G. N. Wilkerson, eds., *Robustness in Statistics* (New York: Academic Press, 1979), 201–236.

7.5C Here are 20 cases of data for which there is an x measurement and a y measurement:

x	y	x	y
−296	214	17	−1
−167	76	27	5
−132	49	36	−7
−125	31	42	12
−105	9	60	16
−55	12	67	6
−27	−6	74	12
−16	9	88	20
−7	9	117	31
7	1	169	72

(a) Fit a straight line by OLS and plot the residuals versus the fitted values. What does the plot suggest?

(b) Using the straight-line model, for each value of the predictor variable obtain the two-standard-deviation prediction interval for the response variable. Use statistical software to do the computations. How many of the actually observed values fall outside the corresponding intervals?

(c) Fit a quadratic model by OLS and plot the residuals versus the fitted values. What does the plot suggest?

(d) Using the quadratic model, for each value of the predictor variable obtain the two-standard-deviation prediction interval for the response variable. How many of the actually observed values fall outside the corresponding intervals? (Filename: EX7_5C.DAT.)

7.5D Why is it possible for a straight-line model to perform predictively according to expectation (for example, to have about 95% of the predictions in the two-standard-deviation prediction limits) and still be unsatisfactory? Do you think it is possible to have a model that predicts perfectly? Do you think it is possible for an imperfect model to be useful? Cite examples to support your opinions.

SECTION 7.6

CATEGORICAL VARIABLES

The next step is to incorporate the Grade variable into the model. Grade is a categorical variable; its numerical values, −1, 0, and 1, stand for different grades of construction. These values carry no meaning other than the ordering of the categories, however, so Grade should not be treated as a metric variable. Instead, *two* binary variables are used to characterize *three* categories. This device makes it possible to incorporate the categorical variable into the regression framework.

Exhibit 7.6A shows the Grade variable along with three binary variables, Lo, Med, and Hi. The variable Lo is equal to 1 whenever Grade is equal to −1, and 0 otherwise; the variable Med is equal to 1 whenever Grade is equal to 0, and 0 otherwise; and the variable Hi is equal to 1 whenever Grade is equal to 1, and 0 otherwise. Only two of the three binary variables are needed to characterize Grade, and we choose to use Med and Hi. Note that when both Med $= 0$ and Hi $= 0$, then we know Grade $= -1$, which is why only two of the binaries are needed.

EXHIBIT 7.6A

Grade Variable and
Three Associated
Binary Variables

Case	Grade	Lo	Med	Hi	Case	Grade	Lo	Med	Hi
1	−1	1	0	0	31	0	0	1	0
2	−1	1	0	0	32	0	0	1	0
3	0	0	1	0	33	0	0	1	0
4	−1	1	0	0	34	0	0	1	0
5	−1	1	0	0	35	0	0	1	0
6	0	0	1	0	36	0	0	1	0
7	0	0	1	0	37	0	0	1	0
8	−1	1	0	0	38	0	0	1	0
9	0	0	1	0	39	0	0	1	0
10	0	0	1	0	40	0	0	1	0
11	0	0	1	0	41	0	0	1	0
12	−1	1	0	0	42	0	0	1	0
13	0	0	1	0	43	0	0	1	0
14	0	0	1	0	44	0	0	1	0
15	−1	1	0	0	45	1	0	0	1
16	−1	1	0	0	46	0	0	1	0
17	0	0	1	0	47	0	0	1	0
18	0	0	1	0	48	0	0	1	0
19	0	0	1	0	49	0	0	1	0
20	0	0	1	0	50	0	0	1	0
21	0	0	1	0	51	0	0	1	0
22	−1	1	0	0	52	0	0	1	0
23	0	0	1	0	53	1	0	0	1
24	−1	1	0	0	54	0	0	1	0
25	0	0	1	0	55	0	0	1	0
26	0	0	1	0	56	0	0	1	0
27	0	0	1	0	57	1	0	0	1
28	0	0	1	0	58	0	0	1	0
29	−1	1	0	0	59	1	0	0	1
30	−1	1	0	0	60	0	0	1	0

Before adding the binary variables to the model derived in Section 7.4, let us look at a model that contains just the binary variables. This will make clear the effect of including such variables in the model. The model using only the Grade information has the form

$$\hat{y} = b_0 + b_1 x_2 + b_2 x_3$$

where x_2 denotes Med and x_3 denotes Hi. Using statistical software yields the fitted model

$$\hat{y} = 29.783 + 9.567 x_2 + 15.017 x_3$$

with measure of variation $s = 4.229$. The value of s is larger than the s of 3.473 associated with the quadratic model, so if we had to choose between the two models, we would choose to use the quadratic model.

Because x_2 and x_3 take on only three combinations of values ($x_2 = x_3 = 0$, $x_2 = 1$ and $x_3 = 0$, and $x_2 = 0$ and $x_3 = 1$) this model produces only three distinct fitted values:

x_2	x_3	$\hat{y} = 29.783 + 9.567x_2 + 15.017x_3$
0	0	29.783
1	0	$29.783 + 9.567 = 39.35$
0	1	$29.783 + 15.017 = 44.8$

You may verify that 29.783 is the average of the market values of the parcels with Grade -1 construction, 39.35 is the average of the market values of the parcels with Grade 0 construction, and 44.8 is the average of the market values of the parcels with Grade 1 construction. In other words, the model uses the average of the market values in a category of construction as the fitted value for every parcel in that category. The model seems a complicated way of doing something simple, but the advantage of this formulation is the ease with which it fits into the regression context so that the Grade information can be combined with other information in the data set.

Now add the Grade information to the model in Section 7.4. The model has the form

$$\hat{y} = b_0 + b_1x_1 + b_2x_1^2 + b_3x_2 + b_4x_3$$

where x_1 denotes square feet of living area, x_2 denotes Med, and x_3 denotes Hi. Using statistical software, the model fitted by OLS is found to be

$$\hat{y} = 5.32 + 0.044311x_1 - 0.000014426x_1^2 + 5.339x_2 + 6.989x_3$$

with measure of variation $s = 2.941$. We note immediately that the measure of variation is considerably less than the s of 3.473 associated with the quadratic model in Section 7.4. The grade variable contains information about market values that is not contained in square feet of living area. In other words, knowing both square feet of living area and Grade, we expect to predict market value within a smaller range than we would knowing square feet of living area alone. In fact, when we compute the prediction ranges for the 60 cases in the data set, we find that they are indeed smaller than those obtained from the quadratic model, and only three of them, those for cases 10, 29, and 30, fail to contain the actual market values. By this test, then, the model that includes both square feet of living area and Grade information is superior to the other models considered so far.

In the following display the model for each possible combination of values for x_2 and x_3 is shown:

x_2	x_3	$\hat{y} =$ $5.32 + 0.044311x_1 - 0.000014426x_1^2 + 5.339x_2 + 6.989x_3$
0	0	$5.32 + 0.044311x_1 - 0.000014426x_1^2$ (low grade)
1	0	$10.659 + 0.044311x_1 - 0.000014426x_1^2$ (medium grade)
0	1	$12.309 + 0.044311x_1 - 0.000014426x_1^2$ (high grade)

For all combinations of x_2 and x_3, the coefficients on x_1 and x_1^2 are the same, but the y intercepts are different for the different combinations.

SECTION 7.7

EXERCISES

7.7A Compute the 60 residuals for the model reported in Section 7.6.
   (a) Plot the residuals versus x_1.
   (b) Plot the residuals versus the fitted values $\hat{y}$.
   (c) Compare the residual plots in parts (a) and (b). Do either suggest model inadequacy?
   (d) The one-, two-, and three-standard-deviation intervals for the residuals are $[-2.941, 2.941]$, $[-5.882, 5.882]$, and $[-8.823, 8.823]$. What percentages of the residuals are in these intervals? Are they roughly consistent with the 68%, 95%, and 99.7% values associated with the normal distribution?
   (e) Verify that each of the following correlation coefficients is zero:

   ■ Between the residuals and x_1
   ■ Between the residuals and x_1^2
   ■ Between the residuals and x_2
   ■ Between the residuals and x_3
   ■ Between the residuals and $\hat{y}$

   The standard deviation of the residuals for this model has $60 - 5 = 55$ degrees of freedom because the residuals satisfy five mathematical constraints. (Filename: REALPROP.DAT.)

7.7B The seasonality of the oil-filter sales data in Exhibit 2.6A was examined by plotting sales versus month (see Exhibit 2.6C). Eleven binary variables that characterize the month information can be defined: let $x_1 = 1$ if the month is January and $= 0$ otherwise, let $x_2 = 1$ if the month is February and $= 0$ otherwise, and so on until $x_{11} = 1$ if the month is November and $= 0$ otherwise is defined. Set up a data structure with sales and these 11 binary variables. Fit $y =$ sales to the 11 predictor variables $x_1, x_2, \ldots, x_{11}$. Determine the equations used to compute the fitted values for each of the months, and compute the fitted values. Do the fitted values appear to be reasonable? Compute the residuals and prepare a sequence plot of them. Is there any evidence of seasonality in the residuals? (Filename: OILFILT.DAT.)

7.7C Suppose you were asked to examine some quarterly data for seasonality. How would you set up binary variables to characterize the quarterly information?

7.7D Using a large data base created from company records for a certain year, a consultant derives the following model for salaried employees:

$$\hat{y} = b_0 + b_1 x_1 + b_2 x_2$$

where y denotes salary converted to an hourly rate, x_1 denotes years of employment with the company, and x_2 denotes gender of employee ($x_2 \doteq 1$ if male, $= 0$ if female). Explain the implied behavior of the fitted values of this model. In particular, what interpretation can you give the coefficient b_2?

SECTION 7.8

ADDITION OF A SECOND METRIC VARIABLE

So far the variables used to account for variation in market values are measures of physical characteristics that are more or less permanent, though square feet of living area and construction grade can change with improvements or deteriorations. These variables do not link up directly with economic factors in the marketplace, however. Regardless of the size of a house or the quality of its construction, it may be located in a neighborhood that is gaining or losing popularity with buyers or it may be located in a city that is attracting or failing to attract new industry and business. Such factors are critical in assessing the market value of a parcel, and they are factors that are supposedly captured in the assessed values of the parcels.

Assessed values, even though they are determined at most once a year, attempt to account not only for the physical characteristics of a parcel but also for the dynamics of the market. No realistic model for market values can fail to include the assessed values, giving ample reason to add a second metric variable to our model.

Letting x_4 denote assessed value, we propose to fit a model of the form

$$\hat{y} = b_0 + b_1 x_1 + b_2 x_1^2 + b_3 x_2 + b_4 x_3 + b_5 x_4$$

where x_1, x_2, and x_3 are as defined before. Using statistical software,

$$\hat{y} = 1.111 + 0.044883x_1 - 0.000015064x_1^2 + 4.15x_2 + 5.216x_3 + 0.22337x_4$$

with $s = 2.719$. This value of s is less than the $s = 2.941$ associated with the model in Section 7.6, indicating that the assessors indeed add information not contained in square feet of living area and grade.

Exhibit 7.8A shows the plot of residuals versus fitted values. The plot gives no obvious signal of model inadequacy. One-, two-, and three-standard-deviation intervals are marked around the mean of zero, which allows us to count the numbers of observations in these intervals. The percentages of observations in the three intervals are 75%, 97%, and 100%, which is comfortingly close to the 68%, 95%, and 99.7% we use as a standard of comparison.

EXHIBIT 7.8A

Scatterplot of Residuals versus Fitted Values for Model in Section 7.8

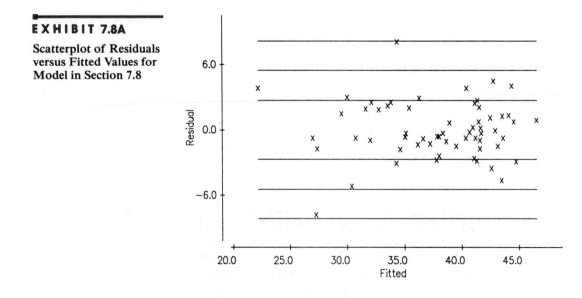

Exhibit 7.8B shows the two-standard-deviation prediction intervals for market value for the 60 cases in our data set. They are the smallest prediction ranges we have obtained; only the ranges for cases 2 and 10 fail to contain the actual market values. Although this is gratifying performance and commands confidence in the model, we would hesitate to expect this same level of performance if the model were asked to predict new cases.

EXHIBIT 7.8B Two-Standard-Deviation Prediction Ranges for the Model Including Square Feet of Living Area, Grade, and Assessed Value

Case	Sq.ft (x)	Low	High	Market (y)	Hit = 1 Miss = 0	Case	Sq.ft (x)	Low	High	Market (y)	Hit = 1 Miss = 0
1	521	16.1	28.2	26.0	1	31	926	32.4	43.6	37.4	1
2	538	21.2	33.2	19.4	0	32	931	34.0	45.0	38.0	1
3	544	24.5	36.3	25.2	1	33	965	32.1	43.5	37.2	1
4	577	21.2	32.7	26.2	1	34	966	35.7	46.9	44.0	1
5	661	23.8	35.2	31.0	1	35	967	34.9	45.9	44.2	1
6	662	27.0	38.5	34.6	1	36	1011	35.9	47.0	43.6	1
7	677	28.2	39.5	36.4	1	37	1011	35.5	46.6	38.4	1
8	691	24.3	35.7	33.0	1	38	1024	35.9	47.0	42.2	1
9	694	29.7	41.1	37.4	1	39	1033	35.6	46.7	40.4	1
10	712	28.7	39.9	42.4	0	40	1040	35.1	46.2	40.4	1
11	721	29.0	40.2	32.8	1	41	1047	36.9	48.0	43.6	1
12	722	21.4	33.2	25.6	1	42	1051	36.1	47.2	41.4	1
13	743	30.6	41.7	34.8	1	43	1052	34.7	45.9	39.6	1
14	760	31.0	42.2	35.8	1	44	1056	36.1	47.2	41.8	1
15	767	25.9	37.3	33.6	1	45	1060	37.3	49.7	44.8	1
16	780	26.3	37.7	31.0	1	46	1060	35.7	46.8	38.4	1
17	787	30.7	41.8	39.2	1	47	1070	35.6	46.7	43.6	1
18	802	31.7	42.8	36.0	1	48	1075	37.3	48.5	42.8	1
19	814	29.4	40.8	34.8	1	49	1079	36.0	47.1	40.6	1
20	815	29.3	40.7	34.4	1	50	1100	37.5	48.7	41.6	1
21	825	32.8	43.9	38.0	1	51	1106	37.9	49.2	42.8	1
22	834	26.4	37.8	34.6	1	52	1138	37.0	48.1	39.0	1
23	838	32.5	43.6	35.6	1	53	1164	38.6	50.9	41.8	1
24	858	27.8	39.3	35.8	1	54	1171	38.7	50.0	48.4	1
25	883	33.4	44.4	39.6	1	55	1237	35.8	47.2	39.8	1
26	890	32.2	43.3	35.0	1	56	1249	37.1	48.4	47.2	1
27	899	33.1	44.1	37.6	1	57	1298	38.3	50.6	45.2	1
28	918	35.3	46.6	41.2	1	58	1435	37.6	49.2	38.8	1
29	920	28.5	40.1	31.2	1	59	1602	40.1	52.8	47.4	1
30	923	24.6	36.8	30.0	1	60	1804	36.9	51.2	45.4	1

Note: "Hit" means range contains actual market value.

EXERCISES

7.9A Using a large data base created from company records for a certain year, a consultant derives the following model for salaried employees:

$$\hat{y} = b_0 + b_1 x_1 + b_2 x_2 + b_3 x_3$$

where y denotes salary converted to an hourly rate, x_1 denotes years of employment with the company, x_2 denotes age of employee, and x_3 denotes gender of employee ($x_3 = 1$ if male, $= 0$ if female). Explain the implied behavior of the fitted values of this model. In particular, what interpretation can you give the coefficient b_3?

7.9B Refer to the restaurant data in Exhibit 5.2B. Specify a model form that relates sales to wages, advertising, and type of food. Give a formula; no calculation is required. How would you specify a model form that relates sales to new capital, wages, number of full-time employees, and type of ownership?

7.9C The data for this exercise came from a study conducted by a company that was manufacturing printed electronic circuit boards. The purpose of the study was to develop a technique for predicting completion time for assembly of the boards, to be used for incentive rate calculation and cost estimation. The response variable y is an average time to completion based on actual assembly times of a number of boards (the numbers of boards contributing to each average is not given). The company's goal was to predict the y variable within 5% of true value. Use the data to construct a regression model. Do a residual analysis. Comment on the usefulness of your model, given the company's goal. The variables are defined as follows:

y: Mean time to completion (in hours)

x_1: Number of capacitors on the board

x_2: Number of integrated circuit sockets

x_3: Number of transistors

x_4: Number of hand-soldered leads

x_5: Total number of components on board

x_6: Number of types of components on board

x_7: Size of board, where 1 indicates small and 4 indicates large (The area of the large board is 4 times the area of the small board.)

```
# filename: BOARDS.DAT
# Printed circuit board assembly data
# (Source: Robert B. Miller, Minitab Handbook for
# Business & Economics, Boston: PWS-KENT, 1988)
# Eight variables: number of capacitors, number of sockets,
# number of transistors, number of hand-soldered leads,
# total number of components, number of types of components,
# size of board(1=small,4=large), and time to completion (hours)
87   9  5   0 320 75 4 2.62        0   0  0 14  23  4 1 0.12
36  16  0   0 132 28 4 0.84        0   3  0  0  88  0 1 0.79
43   0  0   0 171 32 4 0.98        0   0  0  0 132  2 1 0.64
43   0  0   0 155 32 4 0.86        0   0  0  0  67  2 1 0.51
39  12  0   0 176 60 4 1.10       16   8  0  0  55 12 1 0.33
72   0  0   0 318 35 4 1.98       14   0  0  0  59 14 1 0.35
72   0  0   0 318 35 4 1.89        0   0  0  0   6  4 1 0.10
75   4  8   0 280 68 4 1.72       22   0  0  0 100 14 1 0.52
70   6  0   0 297 42 4 1.70        8   0  0  0  73 20 1 0.47
37  16  1   0 156 41 4 0.89       14   1  4  0  79 30 1 0.55
53   2  0   0 229 46 4 1.37       12   1  0  0  26 11 1 0.25
57   8  1   0 246 55 4 1.54       27   2  8  0  90 31 1 0.81
76   4  9   0 280 68 4 2.08        2   0  2  0  41 13 1 0.26
 0   0  0  10  14  4 1 0.08       10   0  0  0  61 13 1 0.38
 0   0  0  12  17  4 1 0.11        2   0  1  0  19 12 1 0.34
 9   0  0  73  97 13 1 0.25       14   5  0  0  49 19 1 0.35
 0   0  0  24  36  2 1 0.10       12  16  0  0  25 11 1 0.32
                                  10  19  0  0  73 25 1 0.48
```

SUMMARY OF CURVE FITTING BY OLS

The mechanics of curve fitting by ordinary least squares are fairly easy to outline, though their mathematical and numerical implementation require a great deal of technical expertise. Some details are sketched here. For more complete information, see Appendix A at the end of this chapter. The elegance and generality of the theory of regression models is very impressive, but the value of regression models lies in their ability to yield insight into processes of practical interest. The notation in this section gives a useful framework in which to develop the specific models needed in practice; it is a means to an end.

THE GENERAL LINEAR MODEL

The notation for the **general linear model (GLM)** is

$$\hat{y} = b_0 + b_1 x_1 + b_2 x_2 + \cdots + b_k x_k$$

where the variable denoted by y is the *response* variable, and the variables denoted by $x_1, x_2, \ldots, x_k$ are the *predictor* variables. The model expresses a relationship between the response variable and the set of predictor variables. It is called the general linear model because it consists of a sum (or linear combination) of factors of the form bx, where x denotes a predictor variable and b denotes a *regression coefficient*.[†]

A regression coefficient may be thought of as a *partial slope* coefficient. For example, if the values of $x_2, \ldots, x_k$ are held *fixed* and the value of x_1 is allowed to vary,[††] b_1 is the slope of the resulting line. Some authors use the following language: b_1 measures the *effect* of x_1 on the fitted values, all other things being equal. This means holding all other variables in the model fixed, which is quite a bit less grandiose than holding all other things equal. Beware of grandiosity when interpreting regression models.

The GLM is quite flexible because the variables in the model can be transformations of other variables. For example, the quadratic model in Section 7.4 is a GLM with $x_2 = x_1^2$. In Section 7.6 two binary variables, x_3 and x_4, were used to characterize the ordered categorical variable Grade. It is common in practice to use transcendental functions of measured variables, such as logarithms, sines, and cosines. For example, y may be the natural logarithm of one of the variables in the original data structure. It can happen that predictions of the logarithm, or some other function, of a measured variable can be transformed into more accurate predictions of the original variable than the predictions obtained by modelling the original variable directly.

In some discussions the cases in the data table are referred to in the context of the GLM. The number of cases is denoted by n, and a general case is denoted by i. In

---

[†] Technically, the model is linear in the coefficients $b_0, b_1, \ldots, b_k$. An example of a nonlinear model is $\hat{y} = b_0 + b_1 x_1^{b_3} + b_2 x_2^{b_4}$ because the model cannot be represented as a linear combination of the b's. These coefficients are scrambled in a nonlinear fashion. Nonlinear regression models are not discussed in this text.

[††] This is impossible to do if any of the $x_2, \ldots, x_k$ is a function of x_1, for example, if $x_2 = x_1^2$.

other words, i can mean any of the cases $1, 2, \ldots, n$. The value of the response variable for the ith case is denoted by y_i. The value of the predictor variable x_j for the ith case is denoted by x_{ij}. A representation of the GLM for the ith case is

$$\hat{y}_i = b_0 + b_1 x_{i1} + b_2 x_{i2} + \cdots + b_k x_{ik}$$

The equations displayed so far give fitted values. As seen in earlier sections, the fitted values do not reproduce the observed values of the response variable, and the differences between observed and fitted values are called residuals. The symbol $\hat{e}$ denotes the residual $y - \hat{y}$, so the residual for the ith case is

$$\hat{e}_i = y_i - \hat{y}_i$$

The residuals express the variation left in the observations after the fitted values have been removed. They show the effect of variables not included in the model for the fitted values. Analysts frequently search various plots of the residuals for clues that point to ways the model can be improved. For example, if the residuals are correlated with a potential predictor variable that has not been included, this provides support for including that variable.

As seen in earlier sections, the residuals are used to compute the standard deviation s, which is a measure of variation about the fitted values and contributes to the computation of prediction intervals. For the GLM fitted by the method of ordinary least squares, the number of degrees of freedom in the residuals is $n - k - 1$, and the residual standard deviation is

$$s = \sqrt{\frac{1}{n-k-1} \sum_{i=1}^{n} \hat{e}_i^2}$$

because the mean of the residuals is zero.

The method of OLS is nothing more than a mathematical procedure for choosing the coefficients $b_0, b_1, \ldots, b_k$ so that the sum of the squared residuals, that is, the quantity $\sum_{i=1}^{n} \hat{e}_i^2$, is as small as it can be. Other criteria can be and are put forward for the choice of the b's, but none of them can yield a smaller sum of squared residuals than the OLS coefficients.[†] The sum of the squared residuals appears in the formula for s, so that in this sense the OLS fitted values result in the smallest possible measure of variation and therefore the closest fit to the observed y values.[††]

[†] For example, we could choose the coefficients to minimize the sum of the absolute values of the residuals. In this case, the OLS coefficients yield a larger sum of absolute values of the residuals, so each set of coefficients is "best" according to the criterion by which it is derived. We are faced with choosing a *principle* upon which to build the choice of coefficients. Ordinary least squares has proven to be the most popular principle, but it has had to be generalized and modified in complex problems to solve thorny technical problems. In this introductory chapter, we avoid a discussion of choice principles by simply presenting the most popular method.

[††] If you have studied analytic geometry, you will recognize the quantity $\sqrt{\sum_{i=1}^{n} \hat{e}_i^2}$ as the Euclidean distance between a point whose coordinates are the residuals and the origin, which is a point whose coordinates are all zero. Since the mean of the residuals is zero, the origin is a natural reference point for the residual point. The closer the point is to the origin, the smaller the Euclidean distance and the closer the fitted values are to the observed values by this criterion.

The computation of the appropriate quantities for a given GLM and a set of data are embodied in many statistical software packages, so the technical details can remain transparent to the analyst. The challenge in applications is to discover the appropriate GLM to describe the process of practical interest, and this may require a great deal of experimentation and analysis. Given the time-consuming nature of this kind of work, it is essential that an analyst be familiar with fruitful approaches to modelling and the capabilities of the software package but not necessarily with the mathematics or computer science aspects of the techniques. In this chapter, the use of GLMs, especially their use in prediction, is emphasized.

Given a model and a set of data, b coefficients and the value of s can be computed. Then for any set of values for the predictor variables, $x_1, x_2, \ldots, x_k$, the model equation yields a "fitted value"

$$\hat{y} = b_0 + b_1 x_1 + b_2 x_2 + \cdots + b_k x_k$$

which in a predictive context is treated as a prediction of the observed value of y the process would yield if the predictor variables assumed the specified values. The chosen set of x values need not be one that corresponds to any case in the data set, which is why "fitted value" is in quotation marks above.

Of course, we do not expect the prediction to be exactly equal to an observed y; process variability makes this virtually impossible. Thus we must state some limits on the magnitude of the difference between the value the process may actually produce and the prediction we have made. The most common way to do this is to compute a standard deviation of the prediction error and then to compute a two- or three-standard-deviation interval around the predicted value, that is

$$[\hat{y} - t \cdot predsd, \ \hat{y} + t \cdot predsd]$$

where t is equal to 2 or 3 and *predsd* denotes the standard deviation that appropriately measures the expected variation in prediction errors (*not* in the predictions themselves). The latter standard deviation is a function of the model, the value of s, and the values of $x_1, x_2, \ldots, x_k$. Its computation, while complicated, is programmed into the better software packages. (The formula for the simple linear regression case is in Appendix A.) Such software was used to do the computations reported in earlier sections of this chapter.

The most important qualitative characteristic of *predsd* is that it is larger than s. In fact, we can show mathematically that

$$predsd^2 = s^2 + fitsd^2$$
$$= s^2(1 + \text{a function of the } x \text{ variables})$$

where *fitsd* is a measure of variation in the prediction due to the fact that the coefficients $b_0, b_1, \ldots, b_k$ are derived from a sample of observations from the process. Another sample from the process would yield a slightly different set of coefficients, and *fitsd* is a measure of the variation that would be experienced from sample to sample. The standard deviation *predsd* depends on the values of $x_1, \ldots, x_k$ through *fitsd*, and this is why the endpoints of the prediction intervals vary with $x_1, \ldots, x_k$.

Generally speaking, in practice the major source of variation is s, the measure of process variation. This is why the value of s is a reasonable index of the predictive power of a model and why we recommend using it as a measure of the quality of a model. It is a much more concrete measure of the value of a fitted relationship than is the correlation coefficient between variables because it is related to the prediction interval that is actually produced by the model.

A NUMERICAL ILLUSTRATION OF COMPUTER-ASSISTED REGRESSION ANALYSIS

Each piece of statistical software prints out about the same information, but each arranges the output differently. Exhibit 7.10A shows a "generic" printout that includes the basic elements you would see using any software if you fitted the model in Section 7.8 to the 60 cases of real estate property data.

■━━━━━━━━━━
EXHIBIT 7.10A

Essentials of Computer Output for Fitting the Model in Section 7.8

Predictor Variable	Coefficient	
Constant	1.111	$(= b_0)$
Sq.ft $(= x_1)$	0.044883	$(= b_1)$
Sq.ft. sq $(= x_1^2)$	-0.000015064	$(= b_2)$
Med $(= x_2)$	4.150	$(= b_3)$
Hi $(= x_3)$	5.216	$(= b_4)$
Assessed $(= x_4)$	0.22337	$(= b_5)$

$s = 2.719$ $R\text{-sq} = 80.9\%$ $R\text{-sq(adj)} = 79.2\%$

Analysis of Variance

Source	SS	df	MS	F
Regression	1693.16	5	338.63	45.8
Error	399.24	54	7.39	
Total	2092.40	59		

The coefficients reported in Exhibit 7.10A are the same as the coefficients of the model reported in Section 7.8, and the value of s is the same. You also see some unfamiliar items in Exhibit 7.10A: R-sq, R-sq(adj), and an analysis of variance table. It is easiest to start with the analysis of variance table. The first column, labelled Source, lists the sources of variation, Regression, Error, and Total. The second column, labelled SS for sum of squares, gives measures of variation for the three sources. The Total sum of squares, 2092.40, is simply the sum of the squared residuals formed by using the average Market value as the fitted value for each parcel, that is

$$\text{Total } SS = \sum_{i=1}^{n} (y_i - \bar{y})^2$$

By dividing this quantity by $n - 1 = 60 - 1 = 59$ and then taking the square root, the standard deviation introduced in Chapter 4 is obtained. It is the residual standard deviation obtained if the information in the predictor variables is ignored and just the mean of the response variable is used as the fitted value for each case. This standard deviation is denoted by s_y.

The Error sum of squares, 399.24, is the residual sum of squares from the fitted model. In some computer printouts, it is called the residual sum of squares. By dividing this sum of squares by its degrees of freedom, $n - k - 1 = 60 - 5 - 1 = 54$, and taking the square root, the value of s is obtained. This is the measure of the variation left over after the fitted values are subtracted from the observed values of the response variable. The df column shows the degrees of freedom for each sum of squares. The MS column shows mean squares, that is, sums of squares divided by degrees of freedom. In the row labelled Error, $MS = SS/df = 399.24/54 = 7.39 = s^2$. The Error mean square is the square of the residual standard deviation.

In the analysis of variance table, you see that Total SS = Regression SS + Error SS, or $2092.40 = 1693.16 + 399.24$, and Total df = Regression df + Error df. The Total sum of squares and the Total degrees of freedom decompose into two components, one associated with the fit (Regression) and one associated with the residual (Error). The relatively large value of the Regression sum of squares is interpreted to mean that the model accounts for a substantial amount of the variation in the response variable, leaving relatively little variation behind in the residuals. One index of the importance of the variation in the fitted values relative to the variation in the residuals is F = Regression MS/Residual MS, where Regression MS = Regression SS/Regression df. The larger F is the greater the ability of the fitted values to mimic the observed values.

Another index that is widely used is the *multiple coefficient of determination*, $R^2 = 100[1 - (\text{Error } SS/\text{Total } SS)]\%$, which is close to 100% when the Error SS is small relative to the Total SS (that is, when the fitted values are close to the actual values), and is close to 0% when Error SS is large relative to Total SS (that is, when the fitted values are not close to the actual values, leaving a great deal of variation in the residuals). The value of R^2 for the model fitted in Exhibit 7.10A is 80.9%.

Although R^2 has some intuitive appeal, it is difficult to interpret predictively. It is also subject to misinterpretation because it can be made arbitrarily close to 100% by adding variables to the model, even extraneous ones. Ideally, useless variables would not be added to a model, but if a complex problem is not clearly understood, one may be "fishing" for useful predictor variables. Using R^2 as a guide to the usefulness of a variable or of a set of variables can actually lead to adopting complicated models that predict *worse* than less complicated ones. For this reason, we refrain from recommending R^2 as a useful index.

A more useful index is the R^2 adjusted for degrees of freedom, denoted by $R^2(\text{adj})$ in the computer output in Exhibit 7.10A. It is computed by the formula $R^2(\text{adj}) = 100[1 - (s^2/s_y^2)]\%$, which is the formula for R^2 with sums of squares replaced by squared standard deviations. You can see that $R^2(\text{adj})$ is just a complicated way of using s^2 as an index, for s^2 is the only quantity in the formula that changes if the model is changed. If a coefficient of determination must be used, however, $R^2(\text{adj})$ is the one to use because it does not automatically increase when a variable is added to the model.

The items explained in this illustration are the basic ones in any regression program output. Many others are typically printed out; they will be explained in the later chapters on regression modelling. In Appendix B of this chapter output from four statistical software packages is displayed.

EXERCISES

7.11A This is a continuation of Exercise 7.3A. Complete that exercise before doing this one. For each data set in Exercise 6.3H, compute R^2 and R^2(adj) and the analysis of variance table. Compare these items for the different data sets. (Filename: ANSCOMBE.DAT.)

7.11B Refer to the real estate data in Exhibit 6.3A. Split the data into five subsets of 12 cases each. To form the first subset, choose cases 1, 6, 11, 16, and so on to 56. To form the second subset, choose cases 2, 7, 12, 17, and so on to 57. Continue in this fashion. Now choose a GLM that you wish to fit to the data, possibly one that has been considered in the text. Fit your model to the data in each of the five subsets and make as many comparisons of the fits as you can think of. Note, for example, how much variation you find in the coefficients of your model from subset to subset. Try predicting "out of sample" values with models. Do they all perform equally well in this test? (This exercise lends itself well to breaking a class into teams, with each team responsible for one subset.) (Filename: REALPROP.DAT.)

7.11C Refer to the data in Exercise 7.5C. You have fitted straight-line and quadratic models to the data. Compare the coefficients, s, R^2, R^2(adj), analysis of variance tables, and residuals of the two fits. Which model is likely to give better predictions of future observations that come from the process that yielded the data? For a selected set of values of x, form the two-standard-deviation prediction intervals of the two models and compare them. (Filename: EX7_5C.DAT.)

7.11D You are given the following portion of an analysis of variance table from the fitting of a GLM to a set of data:

Source	SS	df
Regression	510.90	3
Error	127.33	6
Total		

Complete the analysis of variance table, and compute s_y, s, R^2, and R^2(adj).

7.11E Suppose that in the analysis of variance table in Exercise 7.11D the Error $df = 12$ instead of 6. What effect does this have on the statistics you computed in that exercise? What if the Error $df = 24$? What action is taken in practice to achieve a larger Error df?

7.11F You are given the following portion of an analysis of variance table from the fitting of a GLM to a set of data:

Source	SS	df
Regression	8.584	2
Error	126.879	
Total		223

Complete the analysis of variance table, and compute s_y, s, R^2, and R^2(adj).

7.11G In Appendix A it is shown that for the straight-line model $\hat{y} = b_0 + b_1 x$, the OLS coefficients are $b_0 = \bar{y} - b_1\bar{x}$ and $b_1 = rs_y/s_x$, where r is the correlation coefficient between x and y, s_x and s_y are the standard deviations of x and y, and $\bar{x}$ and $\bar{y}$ are the means of x and y.
  (a) Show that we may write $\hat{y} = \bar{y} + b_1(x - \bar{x})$.
  (b) Show that the expression in part (a) may be written as

$$\left(\frac{\hat{y} - \bar{y}}{s_y}\right) = r\left(\frac{x - \bar{x}}{s_x}\right)$$

SECTION 7.12

INTERNAL AND EXTERNAL PREDICTIVENESS

Decision making almost always involves predictive thinking. From deciding whether to pack an umbrella to setting an operating budget for a department, every decision forces us to assess the likelihoods of a menu of outcomes and the consequences resulting from different courses of action. Regression modelling is often used to summarize information needed for making complex decisions, so it is used predictively. In this section some of the subtleties of this predictive focus are explored.

INTERNAL PREDICTIVENESS

The sample of 60 parcels analyzed earlier in this chapter provides a concrete basis for discussion. The data are cross-sectional because they all come from a single year, and a model that proved to be internally consistent for that year was constructed. We showed, for example, that the model produced two-standard-deviation prediction intervals that contained 58 of the 60 actual market values. On the basis of this finding we can be quite confident that the model could have predicted other market values that might have been generated by sales during the study year. This is internal predictiveness. But, of course, that year has passed, and we are more interested in knowing if the model might successfully predict market values in future years.

EXTERNAL PREDICTIVENESS

What evidence supports the model's ability to predict market values for years other than the study year, that is, its external predictiveness? One characteristic that shows promise is the presence of assessed value as a predictor variable. If assessed values are updated every year, as is common in many municipalities, then this new information keeps the model updated to some extent. We still need to question the relevance of the coefficients in the model and the measure of variability s. As we noted, variation in the coefficients tends to have less impact than the process variation measured by s.

The most reliable way to assess the external predictiveness of a model is to compare its predictions to a truly external set of outcomes. This strategy could be implemented in the real estate study because the sales information is available over a series of years. Here are two tests that can be performed:

(1) Let T denote the study year, and let $T + 1, T + 2, \ldots, T + L$ denote the L subsequent years for which data are available. For each of the subsequent years, feed the predictor variables associated with the sales data into the model derived from the data from year T, and compute two-standard-deviation prediction intervals for the market values. For each year, compute the percentage of actual market values contained in the associated prediction intervals. These are truly external predictions, and if they are successful, that is, if about 95% of the intervals contain the actual market values, we conclude that the real estate market is stable and the updating of the assessed values is sufficient to track the market. If the predictions fail, then we conclude that the market is too volatile to be captured in the model, and we look for other ways and means of making successful predictions.

(2) For each of the subsequent years, build models based on the sales data for that year. Inspect the series of models for changes in form (that is, presence or absence of variables in different years), substantial differences in the values of the coefficients in different years, and, most important, substantial differences in the values of s over the different years. If large shifts in s are observed, we have documented a highly volatile market process for which accurate predictions may be only a dream. On the other hand, if fairly mild shifts in the models over the years are observed, we have documented a stable market process that can probably be successfully predicted.

The main point to remember from this discussion is that external predictiveness is impossible to document without comparing truly external cases. A model that performs internal predictions well may perform quite badly on external cases because the underlying process is volatile. Although the achievement of good internal predictive performance is important to model building, it does not guarantee good external predictive performance.

In practice, decision makers are frequently asked to make predictive analyses based on information from models built from a single cross section of data. In such situations, clues to the degree of volatility of the underlying process that generated the data should be sought. Lacking such clues, predictions made from the model should be made cautiously. If the predictive analysis is to be made repeatedly, the decision maker should insist that data to test the external predictiveness of the model be collected and the tests performed. No amount of speculation can settle the question of external predictiveness.

SECTION 7.13

PRACTICAL EXPERIENCES

To reinforce the usefulness of regression, two experiences from actual practice are illustrated.

■**EXAMPLE 7.13A:** The first experience is an example of macroeconomic analysis using time series data.[†] Rogers discusses the impact of revisions on data

[†] See R. Mark Rogers, "Tracking the Economy: Fundamentals for Understanding Data," *Economic Review* Federal Reserve Bank of Atlanta (March/April 1989): 30–41. Carefully read this article for useful advice on avoiding the pitfalls of using data supplied in government publications.

supplied by government agencies. Because data are collected by nationwide surveys, they can be subject to revision over periods of many months. The revisions are necessary because not all the elements in the sample report on time. Several revisions may be needed before a final figure is reached. For example, in a June publication a figure for the previous March may be different from the one reported in the April issue. When collecting data it is important to keep track of the revisions and to make sure that data in time series are reported on a consistent basis.

To illustrate this point, Rogers displays two regression equations, one based on data processed and made consistent by a professional data provider, the other based on data manually collected from a series of issues of the *Federal Reserve Bulletin* and not checked for consistency.

The two time series reported are quarterly percentage changes in U.S. GNP, y, and percentage changes in U.S. indices of industrial production, x. The series contain data from the second quarter of 1980 to the fourth quarter of 1987, a total of $n = 31$ observations.

The regression equation based on the consistent data is

$$\hat{y}_i = 1.396 - 0.339y_{i-1} + 0.046x_i$$

with $s = 2.224$ and $R^2(\text{adj}) = 75\%$. The symbol y_{i-1} implies that one of the predictor variables is the first lag value of the response variable. This sort of term arises often in regression analysis with time series data because of the presence of autocorrelation. (See Section 6.8 for a review of autocorrelation.)

The regression equation based on the manually collected data is

$$\hat{y}_i = 2.285 - 0.449y_{i-1} + 0.035x_i$$

with $s = 3.919$ and $R^2(\text{adj}) = 41\%$. The value of s is substantially higher and the adjusted R^2 substantially lower for this model than for the one based on consistent data, and the coefficients of the two models also differ substantially. The differences are due entirely to the different ways in which the data were processed before being fitted to the models.

This discussion is not intended to disparage the data reported by the Federal Reserve. Revision is a fact of life in large surveys. The discussion warns us to pay attention to the revisions reported by the Federal Reserve. If we do not, we may derive models that lead us to different conclusions than we would have gotten if we had paid attention to the revisions.   ■

■ **E X A M P L E 7.13B:** Even though we discuss this second example[†] only briefly, it is a prototype for many practical applications. The problem is the testing of a certain kind of telephone instrument for noise distortions, that is, disturbances that can be picked up by the human ear as a result of chance fluctuations in the electric current. The goal is to decide the extent to which distortion must be controlled, since controlling fluctuations that do not disturb the ear of the customer is not cost effective.

[†] The example is taken from W. A. Shewhart, *Economic Control of Quality of Manufactured Product* (Princeton, N. J.: D. Van Nostrand, 1931), 401–403.

Shewhart notes that tests can be performed by having people listen to the instruments, but doing this for all manufactured instruments is too costly. The idea, therefore, is to come up with a machine measurement that is correlated with ear measurements. The machine measurements are much cheaper, and if they give sufficiently precise predictions of ear measurements, then they can be used to judge the quality of the instruments.

Shewhart describes a study involving determinations of both ear and machine measurements for 942 instruments. He presents a scatterplot of the data but does not report the actual measurements. The straight-line model fitted to the data provides predictions that, according to Shewhart, justify the substitution of machine measurements for ear measurements. In this case the model serves two purposes:

■ It documents the usefulness of an appropriate machine measurement.

■ It gives the curve needed to perform the predictions.

In many practical problems the measurements that we would like to have are unavailable, either because they are too expensive or because we can measure only indirectly. As an illustration of the latter, consider customer loyalty or customer satisfaction. These are difficult things to measure directly, so we have to resort to eliciting responses to questionnaires or to observing behavior in relatively uncontrolled settings. For small samples of customers we may be able to obtain direct indications of loyalty or satisfaction. Such data are precious because they allow us to calibrate our indirect measures with the direct ones. Often, however, the most important measures are literally impossible to get. In such cases, we base our decisions on indirect measurements that are palpably second-best.   ■

SECTION 7.14

DISCUSSION

A model is a collection of if-then statements relating sets of conditions to ranges of consequences. For each set of conditions, the model describes the local behavior of the process, and the link between consequences and different sets of conditions constitutes the global behavior described by the model. Although this definition does not require the model to be embodied in a mathematical curve, many statistical applications are made easier by using curves. Note that the curve does not completely define the model. We must also, through measures of variability, describe how consequences may deviate from the tendency defined by the curve. The hallmark of regression models, in particular, is their ability to incorporate many variables and to provide clear-cut measures of variation.

SECTION 7.15

SUPPLEMENTARY EXERCISES FOR CHAPTER 7

7A Consider the data in Exercise 6A. Let City Gas Consumption be the response variable (y), and let Engine Displacement (x_1) and Weight (x_2) be predictors. Fit the following models:
(a) $\hat{y} = b_0 + b_1 x_1$ **(b)** $\hat{y} = b_0 + b_1 x_2$ **(c)** $\hat{y} = b_0 + b_1 x_1 + b_2 x_2$

(*Note*: The *b* coefficients do not have the same meaning or values in the three equations. We use *b* as a general symbol for coefficients in a fitted regression. The context of the fitted model determines the meaning and value of a coefficient.)

Compare the three fits in terms of the coefficients and the residuals. Which fit do you prefer? Why? (Filename: AUTOSPEC.DAT.)

7B Repeat Exercise 7A, treating the foreign and domestic automobiles as two separate groups. Note similarities and differences in the two groups in terms of the statistics.

7C In Exercise 7A add the variable

$$x_3 = \begin{cases} 0 & \text{if foreign make} \\ 1 & \text{if domestic make} \end{cases}$$

to each model. Compare these models to the models you obtained in Exercise 7B.

7D Repeat Exercises 7A–7C using Expressway Gas Consumption as the response variable. Compare and contrast the modelling of city and expressway gas consumption.

7E Repeat Exercises 7A–7C using Price as the response variable.

7F Consider the data in Exercise 6A. Some analysts analyze distance per unit of gas rather than the gas consumption variable reported there. In other words, if y = gas consumption in units of liters/100 km, some analysts would make the transformation $y' = 1/y$ and use y' in units of 100 km/liter as the response variable. Redo the analyses in Exercises 7A–7C using y' as the response. How does the analysis differ from that using y? Do you prefer one response variable to the other on statistical grounds? (Most analysts prefer y to y'.) (Filename: AUTOSPEC.DAT.)

7G Suppose a regression analysis yields the following fitted equation:

$$\hat{y} = b_0 + b_1 x_1 + b_2 x_2$$

where x_1 is a metric variable and x_2 is a binary (0–1) variable. Sketch the graph of the fitted values versus x_1 for each choice of x_2 values.

7H Suppose a regression analysis yields the following fitted equation:

$$\hat{y} = b_0 + b_1 x_1 + b_2 x_2 + b_3 x_1 x_2$$

where x_1 is a metric variable and x_2 is a binary (0–1) variable. Sketch the graph of the fitted values versus x_1 for each choice of x_2 values.

7I Suppose a regression analysis yields the following fitted equation:

$$\hat{y} = b_0 + b_1 x_1 + b_2 x_2 + b_3 x_1 x_2$$

where x_1 and x_2 are both metric variables. Sketch the graph of the fitted values versus x_1 and x_2.

7J A company tests three different safety programs by operating each program in 10 of its plants. The data available are y = number of accidents this year, x_1 = number of accidents last year,

$$x_2 = \begin{cases} 1 & \text{if safety plan 1 is in use} \\ 0 & \text{if safety plan 1 is not in use} \end{cases}$$

$$x_3 = \begin{cases} 1 & \text{if safety plan 2 is in use} \\ 0 & \text{if safety plan 2 is not in use} \end{cases}$$

Write a model that compares the safety plans, taking into account the ability of last year's number of accidents to predict this year's number of accidents.

7K You are given the following portion of an analysis of variance table from the fitting of a GLM to a set of data:

Source	SS	df
Regression	0.1379	5
Error		21
Total	0.2461	

Complete the analysis of variance table, and compute s_y, s, R^2, and $R^2(\text{adj})$.

7L A simple linear regression model is fitted to a set of data for which $\bar{y} = 100$, $s_y = 10$, $\bar{x} = 50$, and $s_x = 5$. For the value $x = 60$, the corresponding value of $\hat{y}$ is 90. Calculate the values of r, b_0, and b_1. See Exercise 7.11G.

7M Give an example that shows how changing the position of a single outlier in a scatterplot could change the sign of b_1 in the fitted regression line.

7N A coworker of yours likes to run regressions but thinks that supplementing them with scatterplots is a waste of time. Write a memo to your coworker presenting an example that demonstrates the danger of that approach.

SECTION 7.16

GLOSSARY FOR CHAPTER 7

b_i	Notation for coefficient on the ith predictor variable in a regression model.
Conditions	Fixed levels of predictor variables.
Consequences	Responses to a set of conditions in a model.
General linear model (GLM)	$\hat{y} = b_0 + b_1 x_1 + b_2 x_2 + \cdots + b_k x_k$
k	Notation for the number of predictors in a regression model.
n	Notation for the number of cases in a regression data set.
Ordinary least squares (OLS)	A method that fits a curve to data pairs $(x_1, y_1), \ldots, (x_n, y_n)$ by minimizing the sum of the squared vertical distances between the y-values and the curve.
predsd	Notation for the estimated standard deviation of a prediction error in a regression model.
R^2	Notation for the multiple coefficient of determination.
$R^2(\text{adj})$	Notation for the adjusted coefficient of determination.
Regression model	A mathematical curve summarizing a relationship among variables together with measures of variation from the curve.
s	Notation for residual standard deviation.
x	Notation for a predictor (conditions) variable.
y	Notation for a response (consequences) variable.
$\hat{y}$	Notation for fitted value.
$y - \hat{y} = \hat{e}$	Notation for residual.

MECHANICS OF ORDINARY LEAST SQUARES

The mechanics of OLS are sketched for the simple linear model to keep the algebra relatively simple. The formulas for the GLM require matrix notation, which is avoided in this introductory chapter. For a complete discussion, consult one of the many fine books on regression analysis.[†]

Let $\{(x_i, y_i): i = 1, 2, \ldots, n\} = \{(x_1, y_1), (x_2, y_2), \ldots, (x_n, y_n)\}$ denote the n data points formed by pairing the value of x and the value of y for each case. We wish to fit a straight-line model to these data points using the principle of ordinary least squares. To do this we define a family of lines by the expression

$$y^*(\beta_0, \beta_1) = \beta_0 + \beta_1 x$$

where for each choice of β_0 and β_1 we obtain a linear function of x with y intercept β_0 and slope β_1. We seek the choice $\beta_0 = b_0$ and $\beta_1 = b_1$ that best fits the data. To do this we define the *sum of squares function*

$$S(\beta_0, \beta_1) = \sum_{i=1}^{n} [y_i - y_i^*(\beta_0, \beta_1)]^2$$

$$= \sum_{i=1}^{n} [y_i - \beta_0 - \beta_1 x_i]^2$$

which is nothing more than the squared Euclidean distance between the point with coordinates $(y_1, y_2, \ldots, y_n)$ and the point with coordinates $(\beta_0 + \beta_1 x_1, \beta_0 + \beta_1 x_2, \ldots, \beta_0 + \beta_1 x_n)$. The point $(y_1, y_2, \ldots, y_n)$ is the observed data point; the point $(\beta_0 + \beta_1 x_1, \beta_0 + \beta_1 x_2, \ldots, \beta_0 + \beta_1 x_n)$ is the fitted values point. We find b_0 and b_1 so that $S(b_0, b_1)$ is the minimum value of $S(\beta_0, \beta_1)$ so the observed data point and the point of fitted values are as close as possible in the Euclidean sense.[††]

To find b_0 and b_1 treat $S(\beta_0, \beta_1)$ as a function of the two variables β_0 and β_1 and minimize it by setting its partial derivatives equal to zero and solving the resulting equations for β_0 and β_1. The solutions of the equations are b_0 and b_1. It is a standard exercise in calculus to show that these values minimize rather than maximize the sum of squares function.

[†] See N. R. Draper and H. Smith, *Applied Regression Analysis*, 2d ed. (New York: Wiley, 1981): R. H. Meyers, *Classical and Modern Regression Analysis*, 2d ed. (Boston: PWS-KENT, 1990); and S. Weisberg, *Applied Linear Regressions*, 2d ed. (New York: Wiley, 1985).

[††] Other fitting principles make these two points close in non-Euclidean senses. The basics of the theory are the same regardless of the fitting principle. What changes is the objective function. The sum of squares function is the objective function that yields OLS. Another possible objective function is $D(\beta_0, \beta_1) = \sum_{i=1}^{n} |y_i - y_i^*(\beta_0, \beta_1)|$. A very useful objective function is the weighted least squares function $WS(\beta_0, \beta_1) = \sum_{i=1}^{n} w_i [y_i - y_i^*(\beta_0, \beta_1)]^2$, where $w_1, w_2, \ldots, w_n$ are weights that enhance the importance of some cases and diminish the importance of others. In this scheme the fitted values tend to fit the cases with greater weights more closely than the cases with lesser weights.

The partial derivatives are easiest to take if we first reexpress the sum of squares function as follows:

$$S(\beta_0, \beta_1) = \sum_{i=1}^{n} [y_i - \beta_0 - \beta_1 x_i]^2$$

$$= \sum_{i=1}^{n} [y_i^2 + \beta_0^2 + (\beta_1 x_i)^2 - 2\beta_0 y_i - 2\beta_1 x_i y_i + 2\beta_0 \beta_1 x_i]$$

$$= \sum_{i=1}^{n} y_i^2 + n\beta_0^2 + \sum_{i=1}^{n} x_i^2 \beta_1^2 - 2 \sum_{i=1}^{n} y_i \beta_0 - 2 \sum_{i=1}^{n} x_i y_i \beta_1 + 2 \sum_{i=1}^{n} x_i \beta_0 \beta_1$$

The partial derivative of this expression with respect to β_0 is

$$2n\beta_0 - 2 \sum_{i=1}^{n} y_i + 2 \sum_{i=1}^{n} x_i \beta_1$$

The partial derivative of the sum of squares function with respect to β_1 is

$$2 \sum_{i=1}^{n} x_i^2 \beta_1 - 2 \sum_{i=1}^{n} x_i y_i + 2 \sum_{i=1}^{n} x_i \beta_0$$

Replace the β's with b's in these two expressions and set the expressions equal to zero. Solving the resulting two equations for the two unknowns b_0 and b_1 we get, after some algebra,

$$b_1 = r \frac{s_y}{s_x}$$

and

$$b_0 = \bar{y} - b_1 \bar{x}$$

where r is the correlation coefficient between x and y, s_x and s_y are the standard deviations of x and y, and $\bar{x}$ and $\bar{y}$ are the means of x and y.

From the discussion of the residual standard deviation in the body of the text, we see that $s^2 = S(b_0, b_1)/(n - 2)$. The theory extends to the prediction of an observation at a (possibly new) value of the predictor variable x^*. The predicted value of the response variable is $\hat{y}^* = b_0 + b_1 x^*$, and the standard error of the prediction error, $y^* - \hat{y}^*$, may be shown to be

$$predsd = s \sqrt{1 + \frac{1}{n} + \frac{(x^* - \bar{x})^2}{(n - 1)s_x^2}}$$

This formula holds whether or not the new x^* is part of the original data set. As stated in the body of the chapter, the t-standard-deviation prediction interval for the new value of y is $[\hat{y}^* - t \cdot predsd, \hat{y}^* + t \cdot predsd]$.

The decomposition of the total sum of squares in the analysis of variance is expressed algebraically as

$$\sum_{i=1}^{n} (y_i - \bar{y})^2 = \sum_{i=1}^{n} (\hat{y}_i - \bar{y})^2 + \sum_{i=1}^{n} (y_i - \hat{y}_i)^2$$

and in words as

Total sum of squares = Regression sum of squares + Error sum of squares

The decomposition of the degrees of freedom is $(n - 1) = 1 + (n - 2)$.

EXERCISES FOR APPENDIX A

7A.A Verify that equations that result from setting the first partial derivatives equal to zero, as explained in Appendix A, yield the stated solutions for b_0 and b_1.

7A.B Carry out the operations in Appendix A for the data set in which $x_1 = -1$, $x_2 = 0$, $x_3 = 1$, $y_1 = -1$, $y_2 = 1$, and $y_3 = 0.75$.

APPENDIX B

OUTPUT FROM STATISTICAL SOFTWARE

The regression analysis reported in Section 7.8 has been run through four statistical packages: Minitab, Stata, StatGraphics, and MYSTAT. Portions of the output from these packages are shown below. You will see all the basic quantities listed in Exhibit 7.10A plus others. Consult the reference manuals for the different packages to learn about the quantities not explained in the text.

Minitab Regression Results

```
The regression equation is
market = 1.11 + 0.0449 sq.ft - 0.000015 sq.ft.sq + 4.15 med
                            + 5.22 hi + 0.223 assessed

Predictor         Coef         Stdev     t-ratio          p
Constant         1.111         4.242        0.26      0.794
sq_ft         0.044883      0.008073        5.56      0.000
sq_ft_sq   -0.00001506    0.00000366       -4.12      0.000
med              4.150         1.081        3.84      0.000
hi               5.216         1.926        2.71      0.009
assessed       0.22337       0.06940        3.22      0.002

s = 2.719         R-sq = 80.9%      R-sq(adj) = 79.2%

Analysis of Variance

SOURCE         DF           SS          MS          F         p
Regression      5      1693.16      338.63      45.80     0.000
Error          54       399.24        7.39
Total          59      2092.40
```

Stata Regression Results

```
. regr market sq_ft sq_ft_2 med hi assessed
(obs=60)

   Source |       SS       df       MS              Number of obs =      60
----------+----------------------------           F(  5,    54) =   45.80
    Model | 1693.15672        5  338.631345        Prob > F      =  0.0000
 Residual | 399.243331       54  7.39339502        R-square      =  0.8092
----------+----------------------------           Adj R-square  =  0.7915
    Total | 2092.40005       59  35.4644077        Root MSE      =  2.7191

 Variable |  Coefficient  Std. Error       t    Prob > |t|        Mean
----------+----------------------------------------------------------------
   market |                                                        37.8
----------+----------------------------------------------------------------
    sq_ft |     .044883     .008073     5.560      0.000      941.7333
  sq_ft_2 |    -.0000151    3.66e-06    -4.117      0.000        944851
      med |     4.150356    1.080701     3.840      0.000      .7333333
       hi |     5.216019    1.926324     2.708      0.009      .0666667
 assessed |     .2233726    .0694006     3.219      0.002      23.56033
    _cons |     1.111179    4.241674     0.262      0.794
1
----------+----------------------------------------------------------------
```

StatGraphics Regression
Results

```
                              Model fitting results for: market
              --------------------------------------------------------------------
              Independent variable      coefficient  std. error    t-value   sig.level
              --------------------------------------------------------------------
              CONSTANT                    1.111177    4.241674      0.2620    0.7943
              sq_ft                       0.044883    0.008073      5.5597    0.0000
              sq_ft_2                    -0.000015 3.658916E-6     -4.1170    0.0001
              med                         4.150355    1.080701      3.8404    0.0003
              hi                          5.216018    1.926324      2.7078    0.0091
              assessed                    0.223373    0.069401      3.2186    0.0022
              --------------------------------------------------------------------
              R-SQ. (ADJ.) = 0.7915  SE= 2.719080  MAE=       1.980337  DurbWat=  1.908
              Previously:    0.0000     0.000000              0.000000            0.000
              60 observations fitted
```

MYSTAT Regression
Results

```
              DEP VAR:  MARKET    N: 60  MULTIPLE R: .900  SQUARED MULTIPLE R: .809
              ADJUSTED SQUARED MULTIPLE R:  .792  STANDARD ERROR OF ESTIMATE:  2.719

                  VARIABLE  COEFFICIENT  STD ERROR  STD COEF  TOLERANCE    T    P(2 TAIL)

                  CONSTANT      1.111      4.242      0.000   .            0.262   0.794
                    SQ_FT       0.045      0.008      1.830  0.0326046     5.560   0.000
                   SQ_FT_2     -0.000      0.000     -1.321  0.0343082    -4.117   0.000
                      MED       4.150      1.081      0.311  0.5395250     3.840   0.000
                       HI       5.216      1.926      0.220  0.5336893     2.708   0.009
                  ASSESSED      0.223      0.069      0.218  0.7671128     3.219   0.002

                                  ANALYSIS OF VARIANCE

                  SOURCE     SUM-OF-SQUARES   DF   MEAN-SQUARE   F-RATIO      P

                  REGRESSION     1693.157     5      338.631     45.802     0.000
                  RESIDUAL        399.243    54        7.393
```

EXERCISE FOR APPENDIX B

7B.A Identify the components of the "generic" output in Exhibit 7.10A in each of the outputs listed in Appendix B.

Modelling Process Variation

## CHAPTER 8

Normal Distributions

SECTION 8.1

INTRODUCTION

As discussed in Chapters 2, 3, and 4, many processes produce data whose distribution has a particularly distinctive shape. In this chapter that shape is further explored and related to indisputably the most important distribution in all of statistics, the *normal distribution*. Exhibit 8.1A displays a frequency histogram of the 99 percentage changes in the flour price index presented in a slightly different form in Exhibit 3.6J.

EXHIBIT 8.1A

Histogram of Percent Changes in Flour Price Index

```
Histogram of Percent    N=99

Midpoint    Count
   -12        1    *
   -10        2    **
    -8        1    *
    -6        6    ******
    -4       14    **************
    -2       13    *************
     0       18    ******************
     2       19    *******************
     4        8    ********
     6        8    ********
     8        5    *****
    10        1    *
    12        2    **
    14        1    *
```

This general histogram shape, with a predominance of data in the middle and less and less in both tails, is very common for individual values from processes (or transformations of them) or for common cross-sectional data. The histogram of Los Angeles traffic volumes for major arterial roads in Exhibit 4.10I also had this shape. Other examples of distributions with this general shape include the distributions of

- Heights of groups of adults of the same sex
- IQs of young adults
- Repeated measurements on a fixed dimension of a product

However, the most important situations in which this shape occurs are in the distributions of many statistics, such as the mean obtained from individual process values or from a sample survey.

▪**EXAMPLE 8.1A:** Consider calculating the mean of five consecutive observations from a process that at each time period selects one of the integers -5, -4, -3, -2, -1, 0, 1, 2, 3, 4, or 5 at random. For each nonoverlapping group of five observations on the process, a new value for the mean is obtained. If this is repeated for a sufficient time, a good picture of the distribution of the mean will be obtained. It is possible to obtain a value for the mean of -5, but this is rather unlikely since it will occur only if the process produces five -5's in a row in one group. Similarly, it is possible but unlikely to observe a mean of $+5$. However, many different groups of five will produce a mean of zero. For example, -5, -4, 0, 4, 5 and 0, -5, 3, 0, 2 both lead to a mean of zero. Thus a predominance of mean values near zero and very few around -5 or $+5$ is expected.

Simulation is a valuable technique for illustrating this important idea. (See Chapter 17 for a more extensive discussion of simulation methods.) Small simulations may be carried out by hand but such a task is quite tedious. The exercises in Section 8.2 ask you to do a simulation by hand, but doing this once in a lifetime is quite sufficient. Computer simulations, on the other hand, are easy to do and allow many examples to be examined in a short period of time.

To illustrate these ideas statistical software is used to simulate 5000 observations chosen randomly from the integers -5 to 5. To simulate the process of means of five, consecutive, nonoverlapping groups of five observations are then used to produce a sequence of 1000 means. Again, this seemingly large job is quite easily and quickly accomplished with a computer.

Exhibit 8.1B shows the histogram of the full set of 5000 data points to illustrate the uniform distribution on the integers -5 to 5, which describes the distribution of individual process values. Theoretically, each of these class intervals should contain 1/11 of the 5000 observations, or about 455 of them.

The goal is to look at the distribution of the means of five consecutive observations. Exhibit 8.1C shows the result. The effect is quite dramatic. The mound-shaped distribution of the means is quite different from the rectangular shape of the distribution of individual values.

Exhibit 8.1D gives various statistics for this distribution and for the underlying uniform distribution of individual process values. Notice that, to the accuracy displayed, the two means are equal and are also quite close to zero. Notice also that the standard deviation for the distribution of means is 1.4760, which is much smaller

EXHIBIT 8.1B

Histogram for Uniform
Process

```
Histogram of Uniform   N=5000
Each * represents 10 observations

Midpoint   Count
    -5      469   ******************************************************
    -4      459   ******************************************************
    -3      441   *****************************************************
    -2      463   *****************************************************
    -1      473   *******************************************************
     0      443   ***************************************************
     1      448   ****************************************************
     2      439   ****************************************************
     3      459   ******************************************************
     4      437   ****************************************************
     5      469   ******************************************************
```

EXHIBIT 8.1C

Histogram of Means of
Five from Uniform
Distribution

```
Histogram of Y bar   N=1000
Each * represents 10 observations

Midpoint   Count
  -4.00       7   *
  -3.00      42   *****
  -2.00     117   ************
  -1.00     206   *********************
   0.00     258   **************************
   1.00     223   ***********************
   2.00     103   ***********
   3.00      39   ****
   4.00       5   *
```

EXHIBIT 8.1D

Descriptive Statistics for
Uniform and Mean
Distributions

	N	Mean	Median	Standard Deviation
Uniform	5000	−0.0214	0.0000	3.1756
y bar	1000	−0.0214	0.0000	1.4760

than the standard deviation of the uniform distribution, 3.1756. Averaging five observations together pulls the means toward the middle and reduces the standard deviation of this distribution compared to the standard deviation of the uniform distribution from which the data were taken. In Section 8.5 the particular way in which this reduction occurs is discussed. ■

These observed distributions based on large data sets suggest that there may be a theoretical distribution that will conveniently describe many such situations and serve as a reference distribution for comparison purposes and convenient calculation. Such a distribution is the normal distribution or normal curve.[†]

SECTION 8.2

EXERCISES

8.2A Roll an ordinary six-sided die four times and record the total spots obtained in the four rolls. Repeat this experiment 50 times and produce a histogram of your 50 totals. Do your results produce a distribution that is mound shaped as in Exhibits 8.1A and 8.1C?

[†] In this context the word *normal* is not used as the opposite of abnormal.

8.2B Use a statistical software package to perform large-scale experiments similar to those reported in Exhibits 8.1B and 8.1C. Try different shapes for the distribution of individual values and different sample sizes, for example, 5, 10, and 30, to compute the means. Are your results similar to ours? Comment on the improvement, if any, in the mound-shapedness for larger sample sizes.

8.2C Repeat Exercise 8.2B but compute the standard deviation of each sample and display the distribution of the standard deviations. For $n = 5$ the distribution will not likely be very mound shaped. For $n = 30$ when sampling from a mound-shaped process distribution, the distribution of the standard deviation should itself be quite mound shaped.

8.2D Repeat Exercise 8.2B but compute the median of each sample and display the distribution of the medians.

8.2E Repeat Exercise 8.2B but compute the maximum value of each sample and display the distribution of the maximums. For neither $n = 5$ nor $n = 30$ will the distribution be very mound shaped.

S E C T I O N 8.3

THE NORMAL CURVE

The **normal curve** has been used since the early 1700s. It began as a tool for analyzing games of chance but was eventually discovered to apply to numerous situations involving uncertainty. It describes the theoretical histogram for an (infinite) collection of measurements along a continuous number line. In the real world, all measurements will be discrete, being selected from a certain finite (but possibly very large) collection of possible values. For example, prices are usually no finer than cents, stock prices are measured in eighths of a dollar, and even measurements of weight, length, and time are limited by measuring instruments (scales, rulers, or clocks, respectively).

However, even if the collection of possible values is small, perhaps only 10 different values, a continuous normal curve can frequently be used to describe the discrete distribution to an excellent and very useful approximation. The formula for the normal curve is

$$f(y) = \frac{1}{\sqrt{2\pi}\,\sigma} e^{-\frac{1}{2}\left[\frac{y-\mu}{\sigma}\right]^2} \tag{8.1}$$

where e is the base of the natural logarithms (about 2.71828) and π is the well-known constant from geometry (about 3.14159). Here μ is the mean of the theoretical distribution and $\sigma > 0$ is the standard deviation. They measure center and dispersion, respectively, for a theoretical distribution in a fashion analogous to the mean and standard deviation for a set of data.

Exhibit 8.3A displays a graph of the normal curve for the case where $\mu = 0$ and $\sigma = 1$. This curve is called the **standard normal curve**.

Exhibit 8.3B shows the normal curve with mean 100 and standard deviation 16. Note that the shape is really the same, only the center of the distribution and the scales on the two axes have changed. If normal curves with different standard deviations are plotted on the same scale, they appear to look different. Exhibit 8.3C

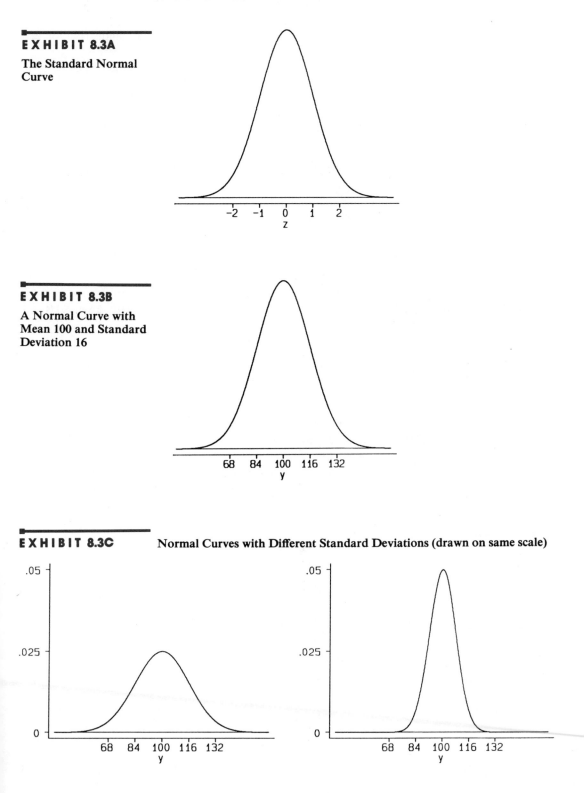

EXHIBIT 8.3A

The Standard Normal Curve

EXHIBIT 8.3B

A Normal Curve with Mean 100 and Standard Deviation 16

EXHIBIT 8.3C   Normal Curves with Different Standard Deviations (drawn on same scale)

gives an example. All calculations necessary for using any normal distribution can be related back to calculations for the standard normal curve.

Another unique way of picturing this curve is shown in Exhibit 8.3D.

E X H I B I T 8.3D   **The Normal Curve in Words**

```
                              THE
                            NORMAL
                         LAW OF ERROR
                     STANDS OUT IN THE
                   EXPERIENCE OF MANKIND
                  AS ONE OF THE BROADEST
               GENERALIZATIONS OF NATURAL
              PHILOSOPHY ⋆ IT SERVES AS THE
             GUIDING INSTRUMENT IN RESEARCHES
          IN THE PHYSICAL AND SOCIAL SCIENCES AND
        IN MEDICINE AGRICULTURE AND ENGINEERING ⋆
        IT IS AN INDISPENSABLE TOOL FOR THE ANALYSIS AND THE
INTERPRETATION OF THE BASIC DATA OBTAINED BY OBSERVATION AND EXPERIMENT
```

Source: W. J. Youden, in E. R. Tufte, *The Visual Display of Quantitative Information*. (Cheshire, Conn.: Graphics Press, 1983.)

The normal curve has two important features:

- The curve is symmetric about its mean μ.
- The total area between the curve and the horizontal axis is 1, or 100%.

The first feature is apparent from the graphs in Exhibits 8.3A, 8.3B, and 8.3C. The second one requires calculus applied to Equation (8.1). The area under a normal curve between two values a and b, as shown in Exhibit 8.3E, represents the proportion of values in the (theoretically infinite) collection of measurements that

---

E X H I B I T 8.3E

Areas Under a Normal Curve

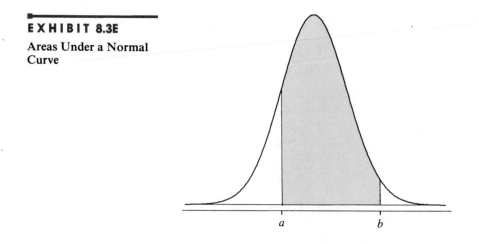

lie between a and b. For a standard normal curve,

- About 68% of the distribution values lie between -1 and $+1$.
- About 95% of the distribution values lie between -2 and $+2$.
- About 99.7% of the distribution values lie between -3 and $+3$.

See Exhibit 8.3F. The curve is very near zero outside of the interval from -3 to $+3$ and appears on the graph to be at zero height even though in theory it never really gets to zero but only approaches zero as a limit.

EXHIBIT 8.3F

Selected Areas Under a
Standard Normal Curve

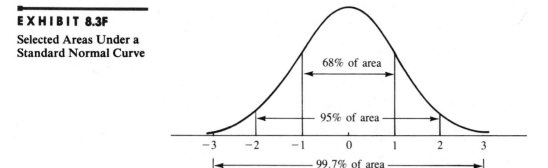

How are areas like these obtained? Unfortunately, even calculus is not helpful in finding such areas under the normal curve. Instead, tables such as the **normal distribution table** (see Exhibit 8.3G) are frequently used. Normal curve areas may also be obtained from statistical calculators or directly in most computer statistical software packages. In addition, we will see that by using standard units (or by standardizing), we really have to deal only with areas under the standard normal curve.

STANDARD UNITS

Key Result: If a variable y has a normal distribution with mean μ and standard deviation σ, then the new variable

$$z = \frac{y - \mu}{\sigma} \tag{8.2}$$

has a standard normal distribution, that is, a normal distribution with mean 0 and standard deviation 1.

We also say that z is measured in *standard units*. The variable z says how many standard deviations y is above (or below) the mean of y. This can be seen most easily by solving Equation (8.2) for y to obtain

$$y = \mu + z\sigma \tag{8.3}$$

If z is positive, then y is above its mean, and if z is negative, then y is below its mean. The quantity z is sometimes called a **z-score** or **z-value**.

EXHIBIT 8.3G

Normal Distribution Table

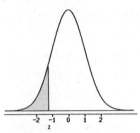

Plot for Normal Table

Each entry is the total area under the standard normal curve to the left of *z*.
Values were obtained by rounding the results from Minitab's CDF command.

z	0.00	0.01	0.02	0.03	0.04	0.05	0.06	0.07	0.08	0.09
-3.9	0.0000	0.0000	0.0000	0.0000	0.0000	0.0000	0.0000	0.0000	0.0000	0.0000
-3.8	0.0001	0.0001	0.0001	0.0001	0.0001	0.0001	0.0001	0.0001	0.0001	0.0001
-3.7	0.0001	0.0001	0.0001	0.0001	0.0001	0.0001	0.0001	0.0001	0.0001	0.0001
-3.6	0.0002	0.0002	0.0001	0.0001	0.0001	0.0001	0.0001	0.0001	0.0001	0.0001
-3.5	0.0002	0.0002	0.0002	0.0002	0.0002	0.0002	0.0002	0.0002	0.0002	0.0002
-3.4	0.0003	0.0003	0.0003	0.0003	0.0003	0.0003	0.0003	0.0003	0.0003	0.0002
-3.3	0.0005	0.0005	0.0005	0.0004	0.0004	0.0004	0.0004	0.0004	0.0004	0.0003
-3.2	0.0007	0.0007	0.0006	0.0006	0.0006	0.0006	0.0006	0.0005	0.0005	0.0005
-3.1	0.0010	0.0009	0.0009	0.0009	0.0008	0.0008	0.0008	0.0008	0.0007	0.0007
-3.0	0.0013	0.0013	0.0013	0.0012	0.0012	0.0011	0.0011	0.0011	0.0010	0.0010
-2.9	0.0019	0.0018	0.0018	0.0017	0.0016	0.0016	0.0015	0.0015	0.0014	0.0014
-2.8	0.0026	0.0025	0.0024	0.0023	0.0023	0.0022	0.0021	0.0021	0.0020	0.0019
-2.7	0.0035	0.0034	0.0033	0.0032	0.0031	0.0030	0.0029	0.0028	0.0027	0.0026
-2.6	0.0047	0.0045	0.0044	0.0043	0.0041	0.0040	0.0039	0.0038	0.0037	0.0036
-2.5	0.0062	0.0060	0.0059	0.0057	0.0055	0.0054	0.0052	0.0051	0.0049	0.0048
-2.4	0.0082	0.0080	0.0078	0.0075	0.0073	0.0071	0.0069	0.0068	0.0066	0.0064
-2.3	0.0107	0.0104	0.0102	0.0099	0.0096	0.0094	0.0091	0.0089	0.0087	0.0084
-2.2	0.0139	0.0136	0.0132	0.0129	0.0125	0.0122	0.0119	0.0116	0.0113	0.0110
-2.1	0.0179	0.0174	0.0170	0.0166	0.0162	0.0158	0.0154	0.0150	0.0146	0.0143
-2.0	0.0227	0.0222	0.0217	0.0212	0.0207	0.0202	0.0197	0.0192	0.0188	0.0183
-1.9	0.0287	0.0281	0.0274	0.0268	0.0262	0.0256	0.0250	0.0244	0.0239	0.0233
-1.8	0.0359	0.0351	0.0344	0.0336	0.0329	0.0322	0.0314	0.0307	0.0301	0.0294
-1.7	0.0446	0.0436	0.0427	0.0418	0.0409	0.0401	0.0392	0.0384	0.0375	0.0367
-1.6	0.0548	0.0537	0.0526	0.0516	0.0505	0.0495	0.0485	0.0475	0.0465	0.0455
-1.5	0.0668	0.0655	0.0643	0.0630	0.0618	0.0606	0.0594	0.0582	0.0571	0.0559
-1.4	0.0808	0.0793	0.0778	0.0764	0.0749	0.0735	0.0721	0.0708	0.0694	0.0681
-1.3	0.0968	0.0951	0.0934	0.0918	0.0901	0.0885	0.0869	0.0853	0.0838	0.0823
-1.2	0.1151	0.1131	0.1112	0.1093	0.1075	0.1056	0.1038	0.1020	0.1003	0.0985
-1.1	0.1357	0.1335	0.1314	0.1292	0.1271	0.1251	0.1230	0.1210	0.1190	0.1170
-1.0	0.1587	0.1562	0.1539	0.1515	0.1492	0.1469	0.1446	0.1423	0.1401	0.1379
-0.9	0.1841	0.1814	0.1788	0.1762	0.1736	0.1711	0.1685	0.1660	0.1635	0.1611
-0.8	0.2119	0.2090	0.2061	0.2033	0.2005	0.1977	0.1949	0.1921	0.1894	0.1867
-0.7	0.2420	0.2389	0.2358	0.2327	0.2296	0.2266	0.2236	0.2206	0.2177	0.2148
-0.6	0.2743	0.2709	0.2676	0.2643	0.2611	0.2578	0.2546	0.2514	0.2483	0.2451
-0.5	0.3085	0.3050	0.3015	0.2981	0.2946	0.2912	0.2877	0.2843	0.2810	0.2776
-0.4	0.3446	0.3409	0.3372	0.3336	0.3300	0.3264	0.3228	0.3192	0.3156	0.3121
-0.3	0.3821	0.3783	0.3745	0.3707	0.3669	0.3632	0.3594	0.3557	0.3520	0.3483
-0.2	0.4207	0.4168	0.4129	0.4090	0.4052	0.4013	0.3974	0.3936	0.3897	0.3859
-0.1	0.4602	0.4562	0.4522	0.4483	0.4443	0.4404	0.4364	0.4325	0.4286	0.4247
-0.0	0.5000	0.4960	0.4920	0.4880	0.4840	0.4801	0.4761	0.4721	0.4681	0.4641

EXHIBIT 8.3G (*Continued*)

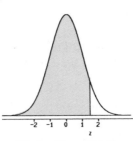

Plot for Normal Table

Each entry is the total area under the standard normal curve to the left of z.
Values were obtained by rounding the results from Minitab's CDF command.

z	0.00	0.01	0.02	0.03	0.04	0.05	0.06	0.07	0.08	0.09
0.0	0.5000	0.5040	0.5080	0.5120	0.5160	0.5199	0.5239	0.5279	0.5319	0.5359
0.1	0.5398	0.5438	0.5478	0.5517	0.5557	0.5596	0.5636	0.5675	0.5714	0.5753
0.2	0.5793	0.5832	0.5871	0.5910	0.5948	0.5987	0.6026	0.6064	0.6103	0.6141
0.3	0.6179	0.6217	0.6255	0.6293	0.6331	0.6368	0.6406	0.6443	0.6480	0.6517
0.4	0.6554	0.6591	0.6628	0.6664	0.6700	0.6736	0.6772	0.6808	0.6844	0.6879
0.5	0.6915	0.6950	0.6985	0.7019	0.7054	0.7088	0.7123	0.7157	0.7190	0.7224
0.6	0.7257	0.7291	0.7324	0.7357	0.7389	0.7422	0.7454	0.7486	0.7517	0.7549
0.7	0.7580	0.7611	0.7642	0.7673	0.7704	0.7734	0.7764	0.7794	0.7823	0.7852
0.8	0.7881	0.7910	0.7939	0.7967	0.7995	0.8023	0.8051	0.8078	0.8106	0.8133
0.9	0.8159	0.8186	0.8212	0.8238	0.8264	0.8289	0.8315	0.8340	0.8365	0.8389
1.0	0.8413	0.8438	0.8461	0.8485	0.8508	0.8531	0.8554	0.8577	0.8599	0.8621
1.1	0.8643	0.8665	0.8686	0.8708	0.8729	0.8749	0.8770	0.8790	0.8810	0.8830
1.2	0.8849	0.8869	0.8888	0.8907	0.8925	0.8944	0.8962	0.8980	0.8997	0.9015
1.3	0.9032	0.9049	0.9066	0.9082	0.9099	0.9115	0.9131	0.9147	0.9162	0.9177
1.4	0.9192	0.9207	0.9222	0.9236	0.9251	0.9265	0.9279	0.9292	0.9306	0.9319
1.5	0.9332	0.9345	0.9357	0.9370	0.9382	0.9394	0.9406	0.9418	0.9429	0.9441
1.6	0.9452	0.9463	0.9474	0.9484	0.9495	0.9505	0.9515	0.9525	0.9535	0.9545
1.7	0.9554	0.9564	0.9573	0.9582	0.9591	0.9599	0.9608	0.9616	0.9625	0.9633
1.8	0.9641	0.9649	0.9656	0.9664	0.9671	0.9678	0.9686	0.9693	0.9699	0.9706
1.9	0.9713	0.9719	0.9726	0.9732	0.9738	0.9744	0.9750	0.9756	0.9761	0.9767
2.0	0.9772	0.9778	0.9783	0.9788	0.9793	0.9798	0.9803	0.9808	0.9812	0.9817
2.1	0.9821	0.9826	0.9830	0.9834	0.9838	0.9842	0.9846	0.9850	0.9854	0.9857
2.2	0.9861	0.9864	0.9868	0.9871	0.9875	0.9878	0.9881	0.9884	0.9887	0.9890
2.3	0.9893	0.9896	0.9898	0.9901	0.9904	0.9906	0.9909	0.9911	0.9913	0.9916
2.4	0.9918	0.9920	0.9922	0.9925	0.9927	0.9929	0.9931	0.9932	0.9934	0.9936
2.5	0.9938	0.9940	0.9941	0.9943	0.9945	0.9946	0.9948	0.9949	0.9951	0.9952
2.6	0.9953	0.9955	0.9956	0.9957	0.9959	0.9960	0.9961	0.9962	0.9963	0.9964
2.7	0.9965	0.9966	0.9967	0.9968	0.9969	0.9970	0.9971	0.9972	0.9973	0.9974
2.8	0.9974	0.9975	0.9976	0.9977	0.9977	0.9978	0.9979	0.9979	0.9980	0.9981
2.9	0.9981	0.9982	0.9982	0.9983	0.9984	0.9984	0.9985	0.9985	0.9986	0.9986
3.0	0.9987	0.9987	0.9987	0.9988	0.9988	0.9989	0.9989	0.9989	0.9990	0.9990
3.1	0.9990	0.9991	0.9991	0.9991	0.9992	0.9992	0.9992	0.9992	0.9993	0.9993
3.2	0.9993	0.9993	0.9994	0.9994	0.9994	0.9994	0.9994	0.9995	0.9995	0.9995
3.3	0.9995	0.9995	0.9995	0.9996	0.9996	0.9996	0.9996	0.9996	0.9996	0.9997
3.4	0.9997	0.9997	0.9997	0.9997	0.9997	0.9997	0.9997	0.9997	0.9997	0.9998
3.5	0.9998	0.9998	0.9998	0.9998	0.9998	0.9998	0.9998	0.9998	0.9998	0.9998
3.6	0.9998	0.9998	0.9999	0.9999	0.9999	0.9999	0.9999	0.9999	0.9999	0.9999
3.7	0.9999	0.9999	0.9999	0.9999	0.9999	0.9999	0.9999	0.9999	0.9999	0.9999
3.8	0.9999	0.9999	0.9999	0.9999	0.9999	0.9999	0.9999	0.9999	0.9999	0.9999
3.9	1.0000	1.0000	1.0000	1.0000	1.0000	1.0000	1.0000	1.0000	1.0000	1.0000

Any area needed with respect to y can be reexpressed in terms of z, that is, in terms of standard units. The required area may then be found using the standard normal distribution tables. Given the *Key Result*, the selected areas displayed in Exhibit 8.3F can be rephrased as

- About 68% of the values in any normal distribution are within 1 standard deviation of its mean.
- About 95% of the values in any normal distribution are within 2 standard deviations of its mean.
- About 99.7% of the values in any normal distribution are within 3 standard deviations of its mean.

▪**EXAMPLE 8.3A:** An automatic machine is used to fill "one-pound" cans of coffee. In fact there is inherent variability in the filling process. Suppose we know from past experience that the distribution of actual fill amounts can be described approximately as a normal distribution with standard deviation $\sigma = 1$ ounce. The machine has an adjustment that allows the mean fill amount, μ, to be set at any value desired. If the mean fill amount is set at 16 ounces, what fraction of the cans will be underfilled, that is, contain less than 16 ounces? Exhibit 8.3H illustrates the desired area and also shows the appropriate standard units. An actual value of 16 corresponds to a standard unit of $(16 - 16)/1 = 0$. The area to the left of 0 is, by symmetry, equal to 0.5 without need for a table. Thus if the mean fill amount is set at 16, half of the cans will be underfilled.

EXHIBIT 8.3H

Area Below 16 Under a Normal Curve with Mean = 16 Ounces

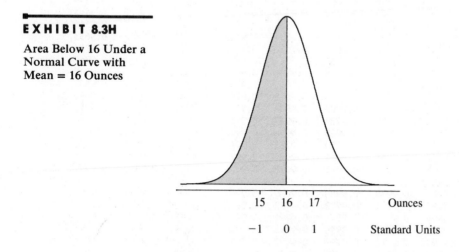

Suppose the mean fill amount is decreased to 15 ounces. What fraction will then be underfilled? Now the area below the standard value of $(16 - 15)/1 = 1$ is needed. Exhibit 8.3I shows the required area. Using the normal distribution table, we see that the value below $z = 1.00$ is 0.8413. That is, about 84% will be underfilled.

EXHIBIT 8.3I

Area Below 16 Under a
Normal Curve with
Mean = 15 Ounces

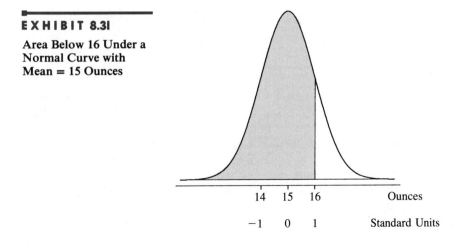

Suppose the mean fill amount is increased to 17 ounces. What fraction will now be underfilled? The area below the standard value of $(16 - 17)/1 = -1$ is needed. Exhibit 8.3J displays the required area. From the normal distribution table, the required area is 0.1587, or about 16%.

EXHIBIT 8.3J

Area Below 16 Under a
Normal Curve with
Mean = 17 Ounces

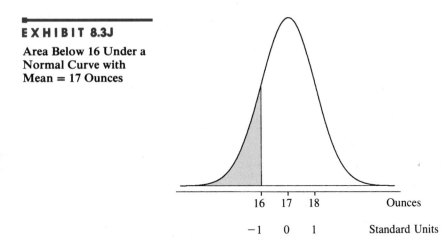

What percent will be underfilled if the mean fill amount is 18.32 ounces? Here the standard unit is $(16 - 18.32)/1 = -2.32$. Again using the normal distribution table, the area is 0.0102, or about 1% will be underfilled at this mean fill amount setting. Of course, cans that will hold more than 16 ounces of coffee must be used unless the frequent excess spilling over is acceptable.

Suppose that the filling machine can be adjusted (or a better model purchased) so that the standard deviation of fill amount is reduced to 0.1 ounce. What percentage of cans will be underfilled with a mean fill amount set at 16.3 ounces? In standard units, 16 ounces corresponds to $(16 - 16.3)/0.1 = -3$, and the area below -3 on the standard normal curve is needed. This area is 0.0013, or a little more than 1 in a thousand will be underfilled.

Studying this process from a statistical point of view provides many insights that will translate into less waste, less cost, and fewer dissatisfied customers. ▪

▪**EXAMPLE 8.3B:** A business that designs, manufactures, and sells women's coats needs information on the sizes of its customers. The heights of American women are normally distributed with mean 65 inches and standard deviation 2.5 inches. Assuming that the customers' heights follow a similar distribution, what fraction of the customers will be between 63 and 70 inches tall? Exhibit 8.3K shows the area required. In standardized terms, the area between $(63 - 65)/2.5 = -0.8$ and $(70 - 65)/2.5 = 2.0$ is needed. From the normal distribution table, the area below 2.0 is 0.9772 and that below -0.8 is 0.2119. The area required is thus $0.9772 - 0.2119 = 0.7653$, and about 77% of the customers' heights will fall into the range from 63 inches to 70 inches.

EXHIBIT 8.3K

Fraction of Women with Height Between 63 and 70 Inches

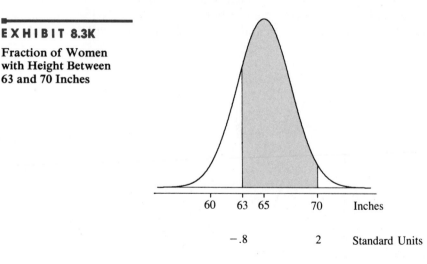

Statistical software has commands and procedures that allow the user to avoid referring to the normal distribution table. For example, Minitab has a command named CDF (cumulative distribution function) to find areas from $-\infty$ up to any given z-value.

PERCENTILES

The normal curve frequently needs to be used in a "backwards" fashion. That is, a fraction or area desired is given and the z-value that produces that area must be found. A **percentile** is a number below which a specified percent of a distribution's values lie. What is the 90th percentile of the standard normal distribution? Using a normal distribution table, we look through the body of the table to find an area as close as possible to 0.90. From the normal distribution table we find that 0.8997 corresponds to a z-score of 1.28 so that the 90th percentile of the standard normal distribution is 1.28. Exhibit 8.3L displays the required area and z-score. If now the 90th percentile of a normal distribution with mean μ and standard deviation σ is needed, this is given by $\mu + 1.28\sigma$.

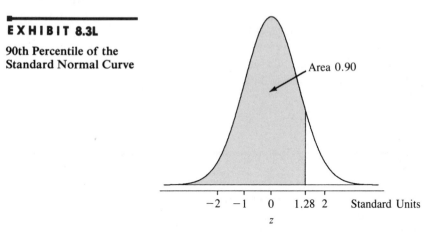

Area 0.90

−2 −1 0 1.28 2 Standard Units

z

▪ EXAMPLE 8.3C: In the coffee-filling example suppose that $\sigma = 0.1$ ounce and we want to set the mean fill adjustment so that in the long run only 1% of the cans will be underfilled. Equivalently, we want 16 ounces to be the 1% point, or first percentile, of the distribution of fill amount. We first find the point on a standard normal curve where 1% of the area is below. From the normal distribution table, the closest value is -2.33 and the 1% point of the fill amount distribution satisfies

$$16 = \mu + (-2.33)0.1$$

Solving for μ, the required mean fill amount is

$$\mu = 16 - (-2.33)0.1 = 16.233 \text{ ounces}$$

Exhibit 8.3M displays the ideas graphically.

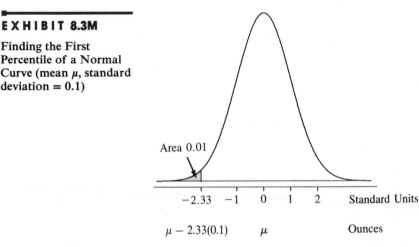

Area 0.01

−2.33 −1 0 1 2 Standard Units

$\mu - 2.33(0.1)$ μ Ounces

■**EXAMPLE 8.3D:** In the distribution of women's heights in Example 8.3B, what height represents the 95th percentile of the distribution? Using the normal distribution table we find areas of 0.9495 at $z = 1.64$ and 0.9505 at $z = 1.65$. In this case a simple interpolation is easy, so we take 1.645 as the 95th percentile of the standard normal distribution. The 95th percentile of the original distribution of heights is then $65 + 1.645(2.5) = 69.1125$, which is rounded to 69.1 inches.   ■

Statistical software can usually find percentiles (for many different distributions) very easily. For example, the Minitab command INVCDF (inverse CDF) does the job.

SECTION 8.4

EXERCISES

8.4A Find the following areas for the standard normal curve:
(a) Below 1.00   (c) Above 0.5   (e) Below -1.00
(b) Below 2.34   (d) Between 1.00 and 2.00   (f) Below -2.3

8.4B Find the following percentiles for a standard normal curve:
(a) 50th (b) 99th (c) 97.5th (d) 84.13th

8.4C Find the following percentiles for a standard normal curve:
(a) 1st (b) 5th (c) 25th (d) .1st

8.4D Consider a normal curve with $\mu = 100$ and $\sigma = 5$.
(a) What is the z-score corresponding to $y = 107.5$?
(b) What is the z-score corresponding to $y = 95$?
(c) What is the standard unit corresponding to $y = 112$?

8.4E Consider a normal curve with $\mu = 23$ and $\sigma = 1.2$.
(a) What is the y-value corresponding to a z-score of 2.1?
(b) What is the y-value corresponding to a standard unit value of -1?

8.4F For a standard normal curve, what is the area
(a) between 0 and 2?   (c) between -1 and 1?   (e) between -2.48 and -1.84?
(b) between 1.1 and 3.23?   (d) between -2 and 1?

8.4G Suppose that a distribution is normal with mean 10 and standard deviation 2. What is the area
(a) between 11 and 13? (c) above 11.2? (e) between 9 and 10?
(b) between 12 and 19? (d) below 9.5?   (f) between 8.4 and 11.7?

8.4H For a normal distribution with mean 100 and standard deviation 16, what is
(a) the 99th percentile?   (c) the 75th percentile (or third quartile)?
(b) the 50th percentile (or median)? (d) the 25th percentile (or first quartile)?

8.4I Recent experience indicates that monthly dollar sales of a certain nonseasonal product tend to follow a normal distribution with a mean of $12,000 and standard deviation of $1000. How would you react if sales next month turn out to be $15,000? $8000?

8.4J A tire manufacturer claims that under normal driving conditions the tread life of a certain tire follows a normal distribution with mean 50,000 miles and standard deviation 5000 miles.
(a) If *your* tires of this type wear out at 45,000 miles, would you consider this unusual?
(b) If the manufacturer sells 100,000 of these tires and warrants them to last *at least* 40,000 miles, about how many tires will wear out before their warranty expires?

SECTION 8.5

THE CENTRAL LIMIT EFFECT

Section 8.1 showed that the distribution of the means of five consecutive process values looks like a normal distribution even when the distribution of individual values is not normal. Exhibit 8.5A shows a similar result when the process selects values randomly from the asymmetric distribution shown in the exhibit. The latter process produces values from a triangularly shaped distribution with a predominance of values on the low end and very few on the high end. Here again, even though the distribution of individual process values is not normal, the distribution of the means of five consecutive process values resembles a normal distribution. (Simulations like these will be covered more fully in Chapter 17.)

EXHIBIT 8.5A

Triangular Process and
Distribution of Mean of
Five Observations

```
Histogram of Triangle   N=5000
Each * represents 35 observations

Midpoint   Count
     -2     1722   ********************************************************
     -1     1290   ****************************************
      0      983   ****************************
      1      655   *******************
      2      350   **********


Histogram of Ybar    N=1000
Each * represents 5 observations

Midpoint   Count
  -2.000     4    *
  -1.800     16   ****
  -1.600     34   *******
  -1.400     72   ***************
  -1.200     111  **********************
  -1.000     120  ************************
  -0.800     144  *****************************
  -0.600     151  *******************************
  -0.400     111  **********************
  -0.200     82   *****************
   0.000     67   **************
   0.200     43   *********
   0.400     16   ****
   0.600     19   ****
   0.800     4    *
   1.000     5    *
   1.200     0
   1.400     1    *


                N      Mean    Median    StDev
Triangle      5000   -0.6758  -1.0000   1.2610
Ybar          1000   -0.6758  -0.8000   0.5547
```

Both of these examples illustrate the **central limit effect**:

Central Limit Effect for Means. *If $\bar{y}$ is the mean of n process values $y_1, y_2, \ldots, y_n$ drawn independently[†] from a distribution with mean μ and standard deviation σ, then the distribution of $\bar{y}$ is approximately a normal distribution with mean μ and standard deviation $\sigma/\sqrt{n}$.*

[†] Independence means that there is no influence between process values. There are no tendencies for high values to follow high values, low values to follow low values, or any other systematic patterns. It is as if the observations are drawn randomly from a bowl and thoroughly remixed between draws.

The larger the value of n, the better the approximation. The practical meaning of this theoretical result is that the normal distribution allows predictions that are correct within limits for means of future process values from stable processes. This remarkable result was first established in a simpler setting by Abraham de Moivre in the early 1700s.[†] Note that the distribution of individual process values can have any shape.[††] The standard deviation of the distribution of $\bar{y}$, namely, $\sigma/\sqrt{n}$, is usually called the *standard error of the mean*, although $s/\sqrt{n}$ also goes by this name.

The central limit effect as stated requires that the mean be based on independent observations randomly selected from some fixed process distribution. In practice, hourly readings on some processes may very well be interrelated with perhaps another high value tending to follow a high value if there is "momentum" in the process. Alternatively, in another process, low values may tend to follow high values and vice versa, especially if the process is overcontrolled or tampered with, that is, readjusted too frequently. Fortunately, there are more complicated versions of the central limit effect that apply to many, but not all, cases with statistically dependent measurements. What is especially important is that several data are averaged together and that no few data dominate the average.

The accuracy of the approximating normal distribution depends in a complicated way on several factors. The following general statements can be made:

- Other things being equal, the larger the sample size n the better the approximation.
- The closer the distribution of the individual process values is to a normal distribution, the better the approximation.
- The approximation is always better when applied to the middle portion of the distribution of $\bar{y}$ as opposed to approximating areas in the extremes of the distribution.

In practice we will operate as if $\bar{y}$ has in fact a normal distribution with mean μ and standard deviation $\sigma/\sqrt{n}$ where n is the number of data points averaged and μ and σ are the mean and standard deviation of the distribution of individual process values. Notice how the standard deviation of $\bar{y}$, $\sigma/\sqrt{n}$, decreases as n increases but only at the rate of the square root of n. Notice also that the dispersion in $\bar{y}$ is directly proportional to σ, the dispersion in the process.

Returning to Exhibit 8.1D we can now see why certain descriptive statistics came out the way they did in our simulation. For the simple uniform process used there, it can be shown that the distribution of individual process values has $\mu = 0$ and $\sigma = \sqrt{10} \simeq 3.16$. Our simulated process of 5000 values had a mean of -0.0016 and standard deviation of 3.1916. For our simulated distribution of $\bar{y}$ we obtained a standard deviation of 1.4590, which agrees quite well with the value predicted by theory of $\sigma/\sqrt{n} = \sqrt{10}/\sqrt{5} = \sqrt{2} \simeq 1.41$.

Exhibit 8.5B gives a further example of the central limit effect. Here $n = 20$ data points from the same triangular process distribution seen in Exhibit 8.5A have been averaged and the sampling repeated until 1000 such averages were obtained.[§] The

---

[†] A fascinating history of statistics before 1900 is given in Stephen M. Stigler, *The History of Statistics* (Cambridge, Mass.: Harvard University Press, 1986).

[††] Technically speaking, the distribution must have a finite standard deviation.

[§] Note that $20 \times 1000 = 20,000$ observations are needed in this simulation. It was done by computer, not by hand!

histogram of these 1000 means in Exhibit 8.5B shows a strong resemblance to a normal distribution. In addition, in this case it may be shown that $\sigma \simeq 1.25$ so that statistical theory predicts that the standard deviation of $\bar{y}$ should be $\sigma/\sqrt{n} \simeq 1.25/\sqrt{20} \simeq 0.28$. The descriptive statistics in Exhibit 8.5B show a standard deviation of 0.28016 for the 1000 means obtained.

EXHIBIT 8.5B

Distribution of $\bar{y}$ with $n = 20$ from the Triangular Process Distribution

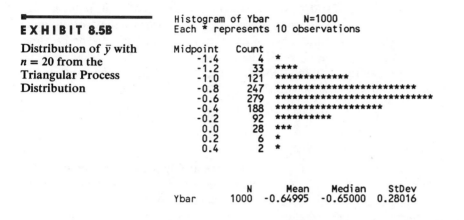

```
Histogram of Ybar        N=1000
Each * represents 10 observations

Midpoint    Count
   -1.4        4    *
   -1.2       33    ****
   -1.0      121    *************
   -0.8      247    *************************
   -0.6      279    ****************************
   -0.4      188    *******************
   -0.2       92    **********
    0.0       28    ***
    0.2        6    *
    0.4        2    *


              N      Mean     Median   StDev
Ybar        1000   -0.64995  -0.65000  0.28016
```

Many practical applications of the central limit effect are given throughout the remainder of the book. Here are two examples.

■**EXAMPLE 8.5A:** Return to the manufacturing of microwave ovens introduced in Section 2.8. The Left dimension of the waveguide positioning process has a historical mean of $\mu = 56.5$ and a standard deviation of $\sigma = 13.5$. If four ovens are sampled at random at 3:00 P.M. and if the process is operating as it has historically, what should be the expected average of the four Left measurements? For example, what fraction of the averages are below 70? The standard error of the mean in this case is $\sigma/\sqrt{n} = 13.5/2 = 6.75$ and the corresponding z-score is $(70 - 56.5)/6.75 = 2.00$. From the normal distribution table in Exhibit 8.3G, we obtain an area below 2.00 of 0.9772, or about 98% of the averages are below 70. What fraction of the averages are above 50? Here the z-score is $(50 - 56.5)/6.75 = -0.96$ to the nearest hundredth. Using the symmetry of the normal curve, the area above -0.96 is the same as the area below $+0.96$, which, from the normal distribution table, is 0.8315. Thus about 83% of the averages of four Left measurements will exceed 50.   ■

■**EXAMPLE 8.5B:** As a second example consider again the Winegard manufacturing process for producing a punched satellite dish antenna part first seen in Section 3.6 in the "Comparisons" subsection. After the die change the process appeared to be capable of producing parts well within the specifications the designers had agreed were acceptable for the part to function properly. The data set of 50 given in Exhibit 3.6G has a mean of 1.7785 and a standard deviation of 0.0009. This sample of 50 comes from a process that will produce many parts over a typical day, week, month, or longer period. For illustration suppose that the values for the continuing process are $\mu = 1.78$ inches and $\sigma = 0.001$ inches. These values are quite consistent with the calculated values for the 50 observations. Now suppose that we consider sampling the process at 11:00 A.M. one day and measuring the required width on five of the parts chosen at random. We then average the five observations to produce $\bar{y}$. What should we expect concerning the "behavior" of $\bar{y}$ in this case? For example, what fraction of the means exceed 1.785 inches? The standard error of the mean for $n = 5$ is $\sigma/\sqrt{n} = 0.001/\sqrt{5} = 0.000447$. The z-score corresponding to 1.785 is then $(1.785 - 1.78)/0.000447 = 11.2$ to the nearest tenth. The number 1.785 is 11.2 standard deviations above the mean of $\mu = 1.78$ inches in the distribution of $\bar{y}$. This of course is out of the range of the normal distribution table and such an occurrence is extremely unlikely. If the process continues to operate as it has historically, we can say that about 99.7% of the means of five of these dimensions are within $\mu \pm 3\sigma/\sqrt{n}$, that is, within

$$1.78 \pm (3 \times 0.000447) = 1.78 \pm 0.00134 = (1.779, 1.781) \qquad ■$$

THE CENTRAL LIMIT EFFECT FOR TOTALS

Sometimes we are interested in totals rather than averages. For example, if account errors have a distribution with mean $25 and standard deviation $5, what can we say about the distribution of the total error for 20 accounts selected at random? We already know that the distribution of the average $\bar{y}$ is approximately normal with mean $\mu = \$25$ and standard deviation $\sigma/\sqrt{n} = \$5/\sqrt{20}$. But the total in the 20 accounts is just the multiple $20 \times \bar{y}$. Multiplying by 20 does not change the shape of the distribution, only its mean and standard deviation. Thus the central limit effect also applies to totals. In particular, the mean of the total $n\bar{y}$ is $n\mu$ and the standard deviation is $n\sigma/\sqrt{n} = \sqrt{n}\sigma$.

> **Central Limit Effect for Totals.** *If $n\bar{y}$ is the total of n independent values from a distribution with mean μ and standard deviation σ, then the distribution of the total $n\bar{y}$ is approximately a normal distribution with mean $n\mu$ and standard deviation $\sqrt{n}\sigma$.*

■ **EXAMPLE 8.5C:** If 20 accounts are randomly selected from the distribution of errors with mean $25 and standard deviation $5, what can be said about the distribution of the total error in the 20 accounts? It will be approximately normal with mean $20 \times \$25 = \$500$ and standard deviation $\sqrt{20} \times \$5 = 4.472 \times \$5 = \$22.36$. Thus the fraction of total errors exceeding $550 is approximately the area above the z-value $(550 - 500)/22.36 = 2.24$ or below -2.24, which is 0.0125, or about 1.25%. ■

■ **EXAMPLE 8.5D:** A market study has suggested that shoppers at a particular large department store spend an average of $36 per shopping trip. The dispersion in the distribution of purchase amounts is measured by a standard deviation of $12. If during a particular morning 42 shoppers make purchases at the store, what is the total purchase value expected for these shoppers? The central limit effect applied to totals says that total purchases follow a normal distribution (approximately) with mean $42 \times \$36 = \$1512$ and standard deviation $\sqrt{42} \times \$12 = \$77.77$, which rounds to $78. About 95% of the time, the total purchase amount for 42 customers falls in the range from $1512 - (2 \times \$78) = \$1356$ to $1512 + (2 \times \$78) = \$1668$.

The fraction of purchase totals below \$1300 is (approximately) the area below $(1300 - 1512)/78 = -2.72$ in the standard normal curve. This fraction is 0.0033, or about 0.3%.   ■

The most common mistake in calculations relating to the central limit effect is to use the wrong standard deviation for a mean or total. If the process mean and standard deviation are denoted as μ and σ and the mean or total is based on n observations, then keep in mind that for *means*

$$\mu_{\bar{y}} = \mu \quad \text{and} \quad \sigma_{\bar{y}} = \frac{\sigma}{\sqrt{n}}$$

But for *totals*,

$$\mu_{n\bar{y}} = n\mu \quad \text{and} \quad \sigma_{n\bar{y}} = \sqrt{n}\,\sigma$$

SECTION 8.6

EXERCISES

8.6A Suppose that amounts spent at a grocery store have a distribution with mean \$55 and standard deviation \$5. If nine amounts spent are randomly selected, what is the approximate distribution of the mean of the nine values? What fraction of the means of nine values exceed \$60? What is the approximate distribution of the total of the nine measurements?

8.6B A small airplane has 30 seats. The distribution of weights of individual passengers with their baggage has a mean of 175 pounds and a standard deviation of 25 pounds. If the plane is full, what can be said about the distribution of total weight of the 30 passengers plus baggage? Discuss the implications with regard to safe carrying capacity of the plane.

8.6C Historically, the number of days until a certain distributor pays its accounts payable to a certain manufacturer has a distribution with mean 28.1 days and standard deviation 5.2 days. If five such accounts are randomly selected, what fraction of the means of the five accounts are less than 21 days?

8.6D A tire manufacturer claims that under normal driving conditions the tread life of a certain type of tire follows a normal distribution with mean 50,000 miles and standard deviation 5000 miles. A small company purchases 36 of these tires for a fleet of vehicles and carefully keeps track of the tire wear. After all the tires have worn out the company calculates that the mean tire lifetime was only 45,000 miles. If the tire-manufacturing process is stable, what fraction of sets of 36 tires will produce a mean of 45,000 miles or less wear? On the basis of this calculation, what would you recommend to the company?

SECTION 8.7

CHECKING FOR NORMALITY

How can we tell if a given set of data conforms to a normal distribution?[†] The first step should be to inspect a dotplot or histogram of the data to look for gross nonnormality. Look for skewness and asymmetry. Look for gaps in the distribution

[†] It is important for the distribution of the errors in regression and time series models to be normal. These models are considered in later chapters.

with no observations. These visual checks do not ways reveal observations that are extreme relative to what is expected from a normal distribution. If all the data are first converted to standard units, then such extreme values would be easier to spot. For the ith data point, y_i, the corresponding standardized value is just the z-score based on the mean and standard deviation of the data. That is,

$$\frac{y_i - \bar{y}}{s}$$

With a computer package the standardized data can be quickly obtained and their histogram plotted. Exhibit 8.7A gives the histogram of standardized values for the percent change in the Buffalo, New York, flour price index. Since we are now checking to see if a *standard* normal distribution fits the data, it is easier to relate to the scale of the numbers. For example, we know that values outside of ± 3 are quite unusual and about 95% of the values should lie within $(-2, +2)$. With 99 data points, we would expect about $0.05 \times 99 = 4.95$, or five, of the standardized points to be outside of ± 2, that is, farther than 2 standard deviations from the mean. This agrees quite well with the histogram shown in Exhibit 8.7A.

Exhibit 8.7B gives the histogram of the 1000 standardized $\bar{y}$ values with $n = 20$ from the triangular process. Again normality is substantiated to a large degree.

EXHIBIT 8.7A

Histogram of
Standardized Percent
Changes in Flour Price
Index

```
Histogram of Standardized Percent    N=99

Midpoint   Count
  -3.0       1    *
  -2.5       1    *
  -2.0       1    *
  -1.5       5    *****
  -1.0      15    ***************
  -0.5      15    ***************
   0.0      26    **************************
   0.5      12    ************
   1.0      12    ************
   1.5       7    *******
   2.0       1    *
   2.5       2    **
   3.0       1    *
```

EXHIBIT 8.7B

Distribution of
Standardized Values of
$\bar{y}$ with $n = 20$ from
Triangular Process

```
Histogram of Standard    N=1000
Each * represents 5 observations

Midpoint   Count
  -2.5       8    **
  -2.0      29    ******
  -1.5      46    **********
  -1.0     136    ****************************
  -0.5     186    *************************************
   0.0     208    ******************************************
   0.5     181    ************************************
   1.0     120    ************************
   1.5      35    *******
   2.0      34    *******
   2.5      11    ***
   3.0       4    *
   3.5       2    *
```

NORMAL COUNTS

Another way to check for normality is to count the number of observations within 1, 2, and 3 standard deviations of the mean and compare the results with what is expected for a normal distribution. Once the observations are ordered from smallest to largest, these counts are easy to obtain. A computer package can do all the hard work.

For the percent change in flour price index, 70.7% are found to be within 1 standard deviation of the mean, compared to 68.26% for a true normal distribution. Further counting shows that 93.9% lie within 2 standard deviations of the mean. This compares well with the normal value of 95.45%. Finally, *all* the data are within 3 standard deviations of the mean, while the figure is 99.73% for a normal distribution—again, good agreement.

For the simulated data sets shown in Exhibits 8.1C, 8.5A, and 8.5B, the corresponding percents are given in the following table. All the distributions checked agree well with the normal distribution.

	Data Set			Compare to Normal
Percent within Interval	Uniform $n = 5$	Triangular $n = 5$	Triangular $n = 20$	
$\bar{y} \pm 1s$	68.7%	71.9%	67.6%	68.26%
$\bar{y} \pm 2s$	94.8%	95.1%	96.3%	95.45%
$\bar{y} \pm 3s$	100.0%	99.4%	99.6%	99.73%

NORMAL SCORES

For n independent observations, it is mathematically possible to establish what the "ideal" values would be if they came from a standard normal distribution. Such numbers are called **normal scores**. There are minor differences in how various authors define normal scores, but the basic idea is illustrated in Exhibit 8.7C for a sample size of five. In general, the normal scores for a sample of size n are n numbers along the horizontal axis that divide the total area under the standard normal curve into $n + 1$ equal areas. Thus for $n = 5$ the normal scores may be described as the standard normal percentiles corresponding to the fractions $\frac{1}{6}, \frac{2}{6}, \frac{3}{6}, \frac{4}{6}$, and $\frac{5}{6}$, namely, $-0.97, -0.43, 0, +0.43$, and $+0.97$. Note that the fractions or areas are equally spaced but the normal scores are spread out like an ideal normal sample. Exhibit 8.7D gives a similar display for $n = 10$. The normal scores here are $-1.34, -0.91, -0.60, -0.35, -0.11, +0.11, +0.35, +0.60, +0.91$, and $+1.34$.

NORMAL PROBABILITY PLOTS

After the normal scores have been calculated, the smallest normal score is associated with the smallest observation, the next smallest normal score with next smallest observation, and so on until the largest normal score is associated with the largest observation. If the data came from a standard normal distribution, then, apart from

EXHIBIT 8.7C
Normal Scores for $n = 5$

EXHIBIT 8.7D
Normal Scores for
$n = 10$

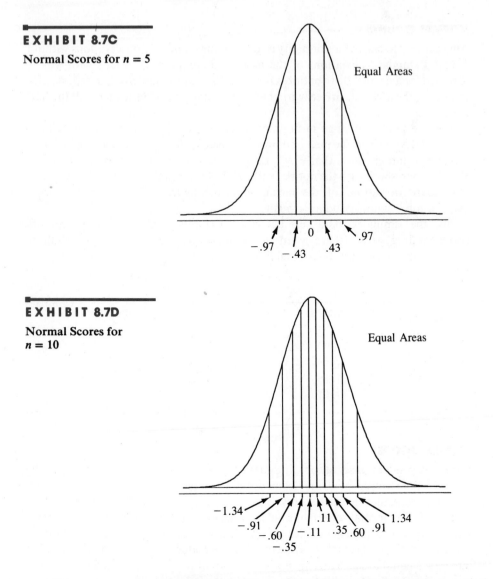

sampling variation, standard normal observations and their associated normal scores should be very similar. If the normal scores are plotted against the associated standard normal observations, an (approximately) 45° line should pass through the origin.

Because any normal variable is linearly related to a standard normal variable [Equations (8.2) and (8.3)], if the data arise from any normal distribution then a plot of normal scores versus observations follows some straight line. A plot of data versus their normal scores is called a **normal probability plot**.[†]

If the sample comes from a nonnormal distribution, then the plot shows curvature. The straighter the plot the better the data fits a normal distribution. For

---
[†] A special graph paper, called *normal probability paper*, that will accomplish essentially the same plot is available. For us, using a package such as Minitab is much easier.

most of us it is much easier to check whether a plot follows a straight line than it is to see if a histogram matches a normal curve.

　　An additional tool for measuring the straightness of the plot is to compute the correlation coefficient between the observations and the normal scores. The closer this correlation is to $+1$ the more the support for normality. Exhibit 8.7E shows this correlation to be 0.994, a strong indication of normality in this case. Compare these results to those in Exhibits 8.1A and 8.7A.

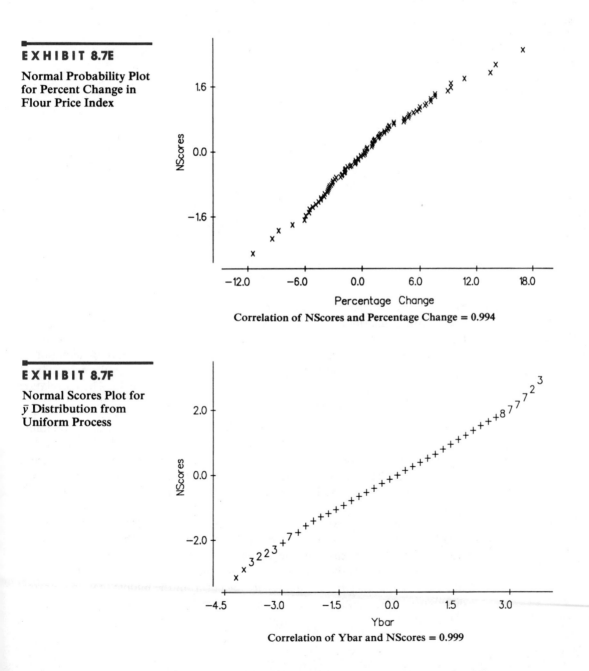

EXHIBIT 8.7E

Normal Probability Plot for Percent Change in Flour Price Index

Correlation of NScores and Percentage Change = 0.994

EXHIBIT 8.7F

Normal Scores Plot for $\bar{y}$ Distribution from Uniform Process

Correlation of Ybar and NScores = 0.999

Exhibits 8.7F and 8.7G give similar output for the $\bar{y}$ distributions for samples of size five from uniform and triangular processes, respectively. These should be compared to the histograms obtained in Exhibits 8.1C and 8.5A. In both cases the assumption of a normal distribution seems warranted.

EXHIBIT 8.7G

Normal Scores Plot for $\bar{y}$ Distribution with $n = 5$ from Triangular Process

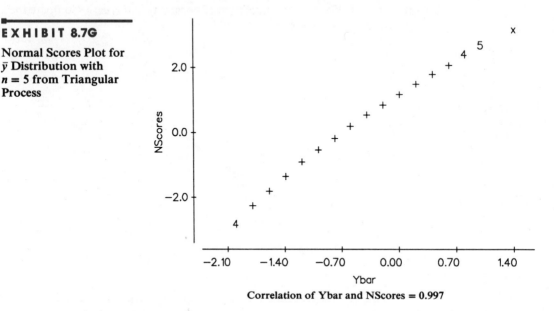

Correlation of Ybar and NScores = 0.997

■ EXAMPLE 8.7A: A regression model is easier to interpret if the residuals follow a normal distribution. (This idea is further explored in Chapters 20 and 21.) Exhibit 8.7H displays the normal scores plot of the residuals from the regression model of Section 7.8 where market value is predicted using a linear combination of square feet, square feet squared, grade, and assessed value. With the exception of the extreme values at both ends, this plot is reasonably straight. The correlation coefficient here is 0.984, confirming the relationship seen in the plot.   ■

But not all distributions are normal. Exhibit 8.7I displays the normal probability plot for the city-size data in Exhibit 4.2H. Their distribution was displayed in Exhibit 4.2I. The normal probability plot in Exhibit 8.7I shows considerable curvature, and normality is not supported. The correlation coefficient in this plot is 0.757. Operating as if this distribution were normal would mislead the decision maker.

The histogram in Exhibit 8.7J is basically symmetric. However, the extreme values are somewhat far away from the bulk of the rest of the data. This can be seen somewhat more easily in the histogram of standardized values given in Exhibit 8.7K. However, the normal scores plot shown in Exhibit 8.7L shows a distinctive *S* shape since both extremes are farther from the middle than in a normal distribution. Distributions like this are said to be *heavy tailed* compared to a normal distribution.

EXHIBIT 8.7H

Normal Scores Plot for
Residuals from Model
of Section 7.8

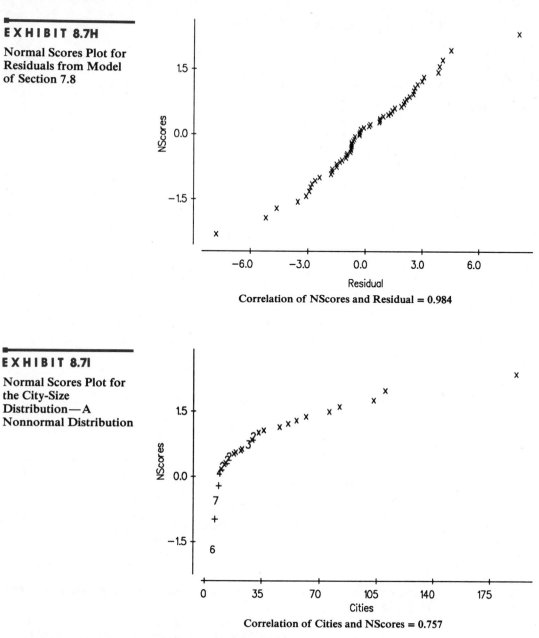

Correlation of NScores and Residual = 0.984

EXHIBIT 8.7I

Normal Scores Plot for
the City-Size
Distribution—A
Nonnormal Distribution

Correlation of Cities and NScores = 0.757

EXHIBIT 8.7J

Histogram of Some
Symmetric but
Nonnormal Data

```
Histogram of Data   N=40

Midpoint   Count
   -5        1    *
   -4        0
   -3        2    **
   -2        4    ****
   -1       11    ***********
    0       15    ***************
    1        5    *****
    2        1    *
    3        0
    4        1    *
```

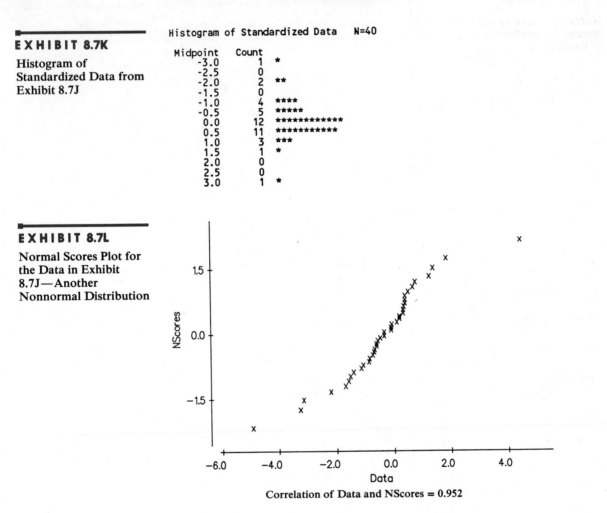

EXHIBIT 8.7K

Histogram of
Standardized Data from
Exhibit 8.7J

```
Histogram of Standardized Data    N=40

Midpoint   Count
  -3.0        1     *
  -2.5        0
  -2.0        2     **
  -1.5        0
  -1.0        4     ****
  -0.5        5     *****
   0.0       12     ************
   0.5       11     ***********
   1.0        3     ***
   1.5        1     *
   2.0        0
   2.5        0
   3.0        1     *
```

EXHIBIT 8.7L

Normal Scores Plot for
the Data in Exhibit
8.7J—Another
Nonnormal Distribution

Correlation of Data and NScores = 0.952

SECTION 8.8

EXERCISES

8.8A Use the Exam 1 scores in Exhibit 4.2J. Their histogram appears in Exhibit 4.2K. Count the number of observations within each of the intervals: mean $\pm$ 1 standard deviation, mean $\pm$ 2 standard deviations, and mean $\pm$ 3 standard deviations. Compare your results to those expected with a normal distribution. (Filename: EXAMS1.DAT.)

8.8B Use the percentage change in the Buffalo, New York, flour price data of Exhibit 2.10A. Count the number of observations within the interval mean $\pm$ 1 standard deviation. Compare your results to those expected with a normal distribution. (Filename: BUFLOUR.DAT.)

8.8C Use the percentage change in the Kansas City flour price data of Exercise 2.10A. Count the number of observations within each of the intervals: mean $\pm$ 1 standard deviation, mean $\pm$ 2 standard deviations, and mean $\pm$ 3 standard deviations. Compare your results to those expected with a normal distribution. (Filename: KCFLOUR.DAT.)

8.8D Use the normal distribution table in Exhibit 8.3G to find the normal scores for a sample of size $n = 4$. Use these scores to produce a plot similar to Exhibit 8.7C.

8.8E Compute and plot a normal scores plot for the Exam 1 scores in Exhibit 4.2J. Exhibit 4.2K gave the histogram. Is this distribution a normal distribution? (Filename: EXAMS1.DAT.)

8.8F Use the percentage change in the Kansas City flour price data of Exercise 2.10A. Display a normal scores plot for these data. Does normality seem appropriate? (Filename: KCFLOUR.DAT.)

8.8G Compute and plot separate normal scores plots for the overall weekday Los Angeles traffic volume and for the minor arterial traffic volume whose histograms were displayed in Exhibits 4.10A and 4.10E, respectively. Also compute the correlation coefficient in the normal scores plots. Which distribution seems better modelled as a normal distribution? Is your conclusion consistent with the histograms displayed earlier? The data are listed in Appendix 2 and available in data file TRAFFIC.DAT.

8.8H Plot normal scores plots for the prediction errors for each of the three prediction rules suggested in Exercise 6.9A. Comment on the approximate normality of each of these sets of prediction errors. (Filename: METALEXP.DAT.)

SECTION 8.9

SUPPLEMENTARY EXERCISES FOR CHAPTER 8

8A The time necessary to complete a certain assembly-line task varies according to many factors: fatigue or freshness, worker skill, whether the required parts are available promptly, and so forth. Suppose that this variation may be adequately modelled using a normal distribution with mean 15 minutes and standard deviation 2 minutes.
(a) Find the fraction of assembly times that are below 13 minutes.
(b) Find the fraction of assembly times that are above 16 minutes.
(c) Find the fraction of assembly times that are between 13 and 16 minutes.
(d) What is the 95th percentile of the assembly-time distribution? Interpret its meaning in this context.

8B From past experience a firm's marketing manager believes that a normal distribution with mean $100,000 and standard deviation $10,000 adequately describes the possible quarterly sales for a computer software product.
(a) How likely are sales to be above $115,000?
(b) What fraction of sales are between $80,000 and $120,000?
(c) Would sales of $135,000 be exceptional?
(d) What level of sales represents the 95th percentile of the sales distribution?

8C Hawkeye Supply Company has randomly selected 100 steel bolts from a large shipment. Suppose that the bolt lengths in the shipment may be described by a normal distribution with mean 3 inches and standard deviation 0.1 inch.
(a) What fraction of the 100 bolts would be expected to have lengths of between 2.7 and 3.3 inches?
(b) What fraction of the 100 bolts would be expected to have lengths of between 2.9 and 3.1 inches?
(c) Consider the average bolt length $\bar{y}$ for the sample of 100. If the sampling procedure were repeated many times, what fraction of the averages would be between 2.9 and 3.1 inches? Between 2.98 and 3.02?

8D A truck carries 40 standard-sized containers. The weight of the containers varies according to many factors but may be described by a distribution with mean 210 pounds and standard deviation 25 pounds. Over many loads, what fraction of loads will exceed the legal load limit of 10,000 pounds?

8E In Exercise 8.2C the distribution of s from a normal process distribution was considered for $n = 5$ and $n = 30$. Display the normal scores plot for each of these distributions and comment on their shapes.

8F In Exercise 8.2E the distribution of the maximum for $n = 5$ and $n = 30$ was investigated. Produce normal scores plots for these distributions and comment on their shapes.

8G Consider a standard normal distribution. Using the normal distribution table in Exhibit 8.3G,
  (a) What are the first and third quartiles?
  (b) What is the interquartile range?
  (c) For a general normal distribution, what is the relation between the interquartile range and the standard deviation?

S E C T I O N 8.10

GLOSSARY FOR CHAPTER 8

Central limit effect	The distribution of a mean or total is approximately normal under many circumstances.
Normal curve	A table of areas under the standard normal curve.
Normal distribution table	The mathematical curve that describes the normal distribution. See Equation (8.1).
Normal probability plot	A plot of normal scores versus values used to support normality of a distribution and to detect lack of normality.
Normal scores	A set of "ideal" values from a normal distribution.
Percentile	A number below which a specified percent of a distributions values lie.
Standard normal curve	A normal curve with mean 0 and standard deviation 1.
z-scores (z-values)	Standardized values or units: $z = (y - \mu)/\sigma$.

## CHAPTER 9

Control Charts for Metric Variables

INTRODUCTION

In 1924 managers at a Chicago plant of Western Electric, then the manufacturing arm of the Bell Telephone System, had a production problem they could not solve: harmful variation in a product. They called on their research division, the Bell Telephone Laboratories in New Jersey, for help. There Dr. Walter A. Shewhart developed the ideas of **statistical process control**, statistical methods used to detect changes in processes, introduced in this chapter. Shewhart's ideas were later published in *Economic Control of Quality of Manufactured Product* (Princeton, N.J.: D. Van Nostrand, 1931). Unfortunately for the United States, his ideas were not widely used here but were exported to Japan after World War II and are credited with starting the quality revolution there. Quality cannot be *inspected* into a product or service. Inspection can only differentiate between the good and the bad *after the fact*. This is very expensive as well as unreliable. Once a defective good or service is produced, the cost of correcting it may be more than 65% of the item's original cost. Resources are used more effectively if the critical processes involved in producing the good or service are individually monitored. If observations on any one process deviate too much from what is expected under usual circumstances, production should be stopped and the problem should be found and fixed. The proper use of control charts is the most important way to document and monitor process control.

With control charts, past behavior of processes is analyzed and current and future behavior is monitored. Special problems and trends that lead to poor quality are detected. Control charts also show what a process is capable of and when a potential improvement in a process has been successful. But to use control charts effectively, the concept of statistical control must first be understood.

WHAT IS STATISTICAL CONTROL?

Processes were introduced in Chapter 2. There we saw that process results vary in spite of the best efforts to produce the same thing every time. For example, reconsider the assembly-line process in Section 2.6. In the ideal situation, every microwave oven assembled would be of the highest quality. In the real world, variation is inevitable. However, if the many processes involved in manufacturing can be "controlled" so that the values of various dimensions are within *acceptable limits*, then reliable, high-quality products that meet customers' needs can be produced.

In 1944 W. Edwards Deming wrote

> *There is no such thing as constancy in real life. There is, however, such a thing as a constant-cause system. The results produced by a constant-cause system vary, and in fact may vary over a wide band or a narrow band. They vary, but they exhibit an important feature called stability. Why apply the terms constant and stability to a cause system that produces results that vary? Because the same percentage of these varying results continues to fall between any given pair of limits hour after hour, day after day, so long as the constant-cause system continues to operate. It is the distribution of results that is constant or stable. When a manufacturing process behaves like a constant-cause system, producing inspection results that exhibit stability, it is said to be in statistical control. The control chart will tell you whether your process is in statistical control.*[†]

COMMON AND SPECIAL CAUSES OF VARIATION

Control charts display information that permits the differentiation among causes of variation in process results. In a constant-cause system the variations in a measured variable are considered to be due to chance and to remain in the system unless the process itself is altered. Such causes are referred to as **common causes** or **chance causes**. The variation observed is considered to be the effect of the combination of many, individually small, unobserved influences. Shewhart likened this to the many forces that cause a coin to come up heads when tossed.

[†] W. Edwards Deming, "Some Principles of the Shewhart Methods of Quality Control," *Mechanical Engineering* 66 (March 1944): 173–177.

Processes are also subject to the influence of special or assignable causes. **Special causes** are individually important and affect process results only some of the time. They arise because of special circumstances. In a manufacturing setting, the introduction of a low-quality batch of raw materials into an otherwise stable process would be considered a special cause of variation. In the monitoring of overtime hours in a municipal police department, the fourth of July holiday could be considered a special (but easily predictable) cause of variation. In general, typical examples of special causes of variation include

- Differences among machines
- Differences among raw materials
- Differences among environmental variables such as temperature or humidity
- Differences among shifts
- Differences among worker training
- Differences among methods

A process is considered to be in control if only common causes are operating and no special causes are influencing the variability of process results. Only when a process is brought into control can process improvement be considered. Because of their underlying differences, dealing with the two kinds of causes requires different techniques. Overreacting to common-cause variation usually leads to "tampering" with a process that may already be in control. This in turn leads to *increased* variation in the process results. On the other hand, failing to detect and deal with a special cause of variation means a lost opportunity to eliminate variation in the process or at least to understand and appreciate the variation in the process. Some special causes can be explained but not removed. Special causes that affect the mean of a process can be detected by analyzing a **mean chart**, a statistical process control chart designed to detect changes in the mean of a process.

SECTION 9.3

MEAN CHARTS FOR PROCESS CONTROL

To study the variation of process results over time, sequence plots of process data are needed. To assess both the mean level and the dispersion of the process over time, a group of data values taken reasonably closely in time is required. For instance, to control the thickness of processed meat products, such as bologna, it is common practice to cut and measure the thickness of five slices from one "log" of meat each hour. In some processes it is possible to measure the variable of interest on a sample of n items at regular times. Each of these samples is called a **subgroup**.[†] The subgroups may be selected from all the product produced in the last hour, produced in one shift, and so on. In other processes it may be necessary to take n measurements spread out over a day or week to produce the subgroup. In any case $\bar{y}_i$

[†] The statistical quality control literature addresses the question of selecting rational subgroups to a much greater extent than in this brief introduction. One good reference is J. M. Juran, *Quality Control Handbook*, 3rd ed. (New York: McGraw-Hill, 1974).

denotes the mean of the ith subgroup and k subgroups are assumed to be available. From the central limit effect of Chapter 8 we know that the distribution of $\bar{y}_i$ will be approximately normal when enough measurements from a stable process are averaged even if the underlying variable is not exactly normally distributed. From Chapter 8 we also know that an n as small as five may lead to a workable approximation. If a constant-cause system is in effect, then we know what to expect of $\bar{y}_i$, and unusual behavior of $\bar{y}_i$ should lead us to question whether a constant-cause system is really operating. A graphical display of the sequence plot of $\bar{y}_i$'s for $i = 1, 2, 3, \ldots, k$ helps point out unusual values.

We begin with the data in Exhibit 9.3A. Twenty-five samples each of size five are given in the rows. The means, $\bar{y}_i$, and standard deviations, s_i, of each sample are also shown. Here $n = 5$ and $k = 25$. (The data and statistics in rows 26 through 30 are for later use.)

EXHIBIT 9.3A

Control Chart Data: $n = 5$

Sample Number	\multicolumn{5}{c}{Samples}	Means	Standard Deviations
	1	2	3	4	5		
1	101.5	98.5	97.0	102.3	99.4	99.74	2.17
2	101.1	100.2	100.4	97.0	101.8	100.10	1.84
3	98.8	99.9	98.2	101.4	99.1	99.48	1.24
4	100.4	99.8	99.4	99.1	97.3	99.20	1.17
5	99.2	101.7	101.6	100.0	100.5	100.60	1.07
6	96.8	101.9	98.0	102.3	100.0	99.80	2.39
7	102.9	98.1	102.3	100.1	99.9	100.66	1.95
8	97.5	100.1	101.9	95.5	101.1	99.22	2.66
9	98.3	98.4	96.3	98.8	100.2	98.40	1.40
10	98.5	97.0	100.6	103.2	102.7	100.40	2.66
11	100.8	98.2	101.3	102.1	101.3	100.74	1.49
12	103.2	101.0	97.6	100.1	100.8	100.54	2.01
13	99.5	100.1	101.2	100.2	99.6	100.12	0.68
14	100.2	94.9	99.4	103.7	103.0	100.24	3.49
15	97.3	101.8	99.2	101.0	100.7	100.00	1.78
16	100.9	99.6	102.9	100.8	99.4	100.72	1.40
17	99.8	97.9	100.7	100.3	99.3	99.60	1.09
18	99.9	99.3	100.6	101.1	103.3	100.84	1.54
19	96.1	101.1	104.1	97.4	102.1	100.16	3.33
20	98.3	99.2	100.7	98.2	100.9	99.46	1.29
21	98.4	104.7	100.0	98.2	99.2	100.10	2.67
22	101.9	97.8	98.1	103.4	99.0	100.04	2.48
23	101.7	96.8	100.9	100.8	101.8	100.40	2.06
24	101.8	102.9	102.9	98.8	101.5	101.58	1.68
25	102.3	100.9	100.1	99.4	101.1	100.76	1.09
26	97.0	97.9	96.5	100.8	102.9	99.02	2.73
27	99.3	100.9	101.3	99.4	98.5	99.88	1.18
28	98.5	101.4	99.1	98.8	103.0	100.16	1.96
29	101.7	102.4	99.5	102.2	101.4	101.44	1.15
30	101.1	98.1	104.1	99.8	100.4	100.70	2.20

Control charts for means begin with a sequence plot of the means, as shown in Exhibit 9.3B. Variation in process results is expected. However, some guidance concerning the amount of variability to be expected "under stable circumstances," that is, when the process is in control, is needed. Exhibit 9.3C shows the same sequence plot of the means but with a horizontal line drawn in at the grand mean

$$\bar{\bar{y}} = \frac{1}{k} \sum_{i=1}^{k} \bar{y}_i \qquad (9.1)$$

Note that $\bar{\bar{y}}$ is just the mean of *all* the $n \times k$ data points in all the subgroups put together. For the first 25 rows of data in Exhibit 9.3A, $\bar{\bar{y}} = 100.12$. If the process is in control, the sequence plot of $\bar{y}_i$ varies about that line.

EXHIBIT 9.3B

Sequence Plot of Means

EXHIBIT 9.3C

Sequence Plot of Means with Grand Mean Displayed

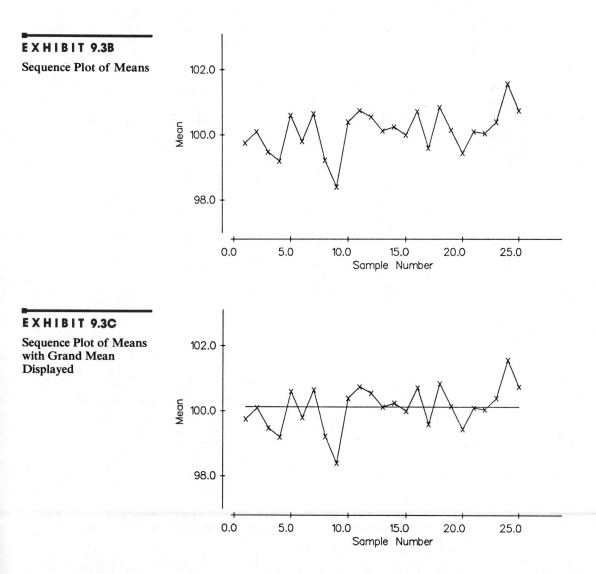

How far might the $\bar{y}_i$'s vary and the process still be considered in control? We know that most of the values in a normal distribution lie in the interval with endpoints at the mean ± 3 standard deviations. In fact, for a true normal distribution, 99.7% of the data points lie in this range. Here we are dealing with averages that are approximately normally distributed with $\mu_{\bar{y}} = \mu$ and standard deviation $\sigma_{\bar{y}} = \sigma/\sqrt{n}$. If the process is in control, then the $\bar{y}_i$'s should for the most part remain within the three-sigma limits $\mu_{\bar{y}} \pm 3\sigma_{\bar{y}} = \mu \pm 3\sigma/\sqrt{n}$. Since μ and σ are not known, in practice they are estimated from the available data. The grand mean $\bar{\bar{y}}$ is our guess at μ, and the average standard deviation, $\bar{s}$, over the k subgroups,

$$\bar{s} = \frac{1}{k} \sum_{i=1}^{k} s_i \tag{9.2}$$

is the estimate[†] of σ.

The factors given in Exhibit 9.3D may then be used to compute limits for the $\bar{y}_i$ sequence within which the subgroup means will almost surely fall *as long as the process remains in statistical control*. The limits are given as $\bar{\bar{y}} \pm a\bar{s}$ and are called

Upper control limit = $UCL = \bar{\bar{y}} + a\bar{s}$
Lower control limit = $LCL = \bar{\bar{y}} - a\bar{s}$

EXHIBIT 9.3D

Factors for Computing Three-Sigma Control Limits[††] for Mean Charts: Subgroup Size n

n	a	n	a
2	2.66	14	0.82
3	1.95	15	0.79
4	1.63	16	0.76
5	1.43	17	0.74
6	1.29	18	0.72
7	1.18	19	0.70
8	1.10	20	0.68
9	1.03	21	0.66
10	0.98	22	0.65
11	0.93	23	0.63
12	0.89	24	0.62
13	0.85	25	0.61

[†] Some authors recommend alternative estimates of the standard deviation σ such as

$$\sqrt{\frac{\sum\limits_{i=1}^{k} (n_i - 1)s_i^2}{\left[\sum\limits_{i=1}^{k} n_i\right] - k}}$$

which arises in certain statistical theory. However, this estimate is more sensitive to extreme values of s_i than ours is.

[††] The factor a is slightly larger than $3/\sqrt{n}$ to adjust for the (theoretical) fact that, on the average, $\bar{s}$ underestimates σ, especially for small values of n. The amount of adjustment is less as n increases.

upper control limits (*UCL*) and lower control limits (*LCL*), respectively. The horizontal line at $\bar{\bar{y}}$ is called the *center line (CL)*. Control limits are *not* related to process objectives or specification limits. The limits say nothing about how the process is *supposed* to perform—only about how it *does* perform.

For the data in Exhibit 9.3A (first 25 rows), $\bar{\bar{y}} = 100.12$ and $\bar{s} = 1.86$. With $n = 5$, Exhibit 9.3D yields control limits of

$$UCL = 100.12 + (1.43 \times 1.86) = 100.12 + 2.66 = 102.78$$

and

$$LCL = 100.12 - (1.43 \times 1.86) = 100.12 - 2.66 = 97.46$$

Exhibit 9.3E gives the sequence plot of the means with horizontal lines at the mean $\bar{\bar{y}}$ and at the estimated "three-sigma" limits. As long as the sequence of subgroup means remains within the control limits, there is no evidence to suggest that special causes are influencing the variation seen in the process results. Exhibit 9.3E indicates that the process is in control.

EXHIBIT 9.3E
Control Chart for
Means

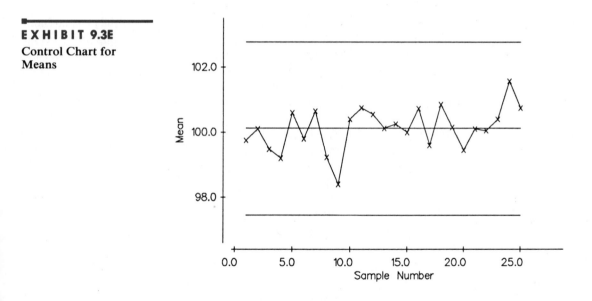

Suppose now that the process continues to operate for five more time periods, producing the results in rows 26 through 30 of Exhibit 9.3A. Does the process remain in control? To check, plot the sequence of 30 subgroup means using the control limits already obtained from the first 25 means and standard deviations, where the process was deemed in control. Exhibit 9.3F shows the resulting graph. Since the sequence remains within the control limits, there is no reason to believe that the process is not still in control.

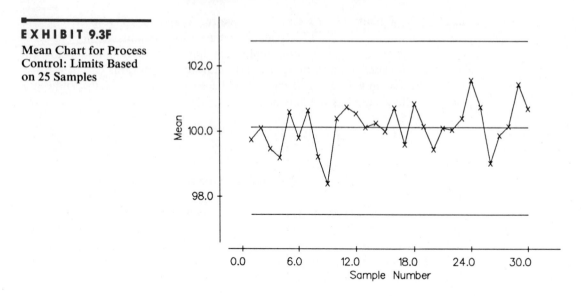

EXHIBIT 9.3F

Mean Chart for Process Control: Limits Based on 25 Samples

CHANGE IN LEVEL

A process may go out of control in many different ways. One of the most common ways is for the mean level to change in an isolated sample or subgroup. In particular, suppose that in the 26th sample a batch of raw materials from a new supplier was used. From the 27th sample on, the usual raw materials were used. Suppose that the effect of the new supplier is to *increase* typical process values, and, in fact, row 26 of the data set in Exhibit 9.3A changes to sample values 101.0, 101.9, 100.5, 104.8, and 106.9, with a mean of 103.02. (For our example the data points for row 26 were each increased by exactly four units.) What will be the effect of such a change on the control chart? Exhibit 9.3G displays the results. Clearly something unusual has

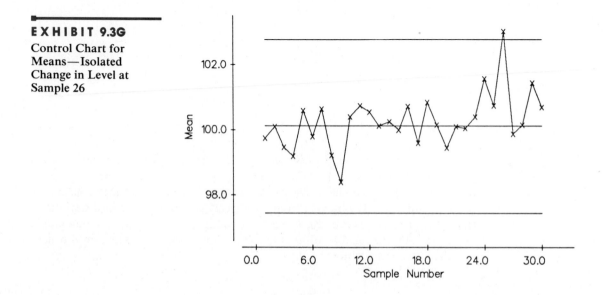

EXHIBIT 9.3G

Control Chart for Means—Isolated Change in Level at Sample 26 happened at sample 26. The mean level of the process has gone out of control at sample 26 and a search for the special cause should be initiated.

Another common out-of-control situation in our example would be to continue using the new (low-quality) supplier from sample 26 on. To simulate that case, the sample values for subgroups 26, 27, 28, 29, and 30 were all increased by four units, leading to a four-unit increase in all of their means. (This alteration will not change the variability in the subgroups, only their mean.) The resulting control chart is shown in Exhibit 9.3H. Again the control limits are based on the first 25 samples known to be in control. The type of change induced in the process is called a *step change*. Exhibit 9.3H shows the effect of this change. Exhibits 9.3F and 9.3H are identical except that in 9.3H the last five means have been increased by four units.

EXHIBIT 9.3H

Control Chart for Means—Change in Level from Sample 26 on

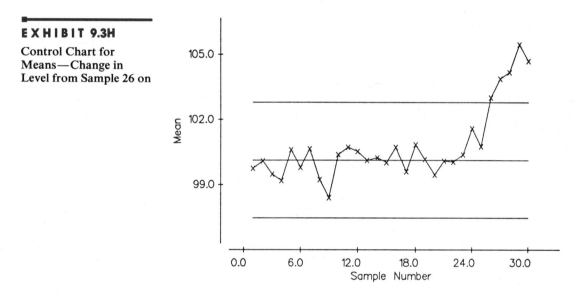

TREND

A third way in which the mean level of a process may go out of control is when the means increase (or decrease) over time. In this case the process is said to have a *time trend* in its mean. An example is given in Exhibit 9.3I. Here the same basic data in Exhibit 9.3A has been used, but it has been altered by adding one unit to the members of sample 26, two units to sample 27,..., and five units to sample 30. The effect will be to increase the means of those samples by the corresponding amount, with no change in their variability. With the aid of the plotted control limits, the time trend is clearly apparent in Exhibit 9.3I, and the chart would warrant searching for special causes of this aberrant behavior in the process.

Processes can exhibit the effects of a nonconstant-cause system in infinitely many ways. Various changes in the mean are the most important cases. However, changes in the process dispersion are also quite prevalent.

EXHIBIT 9.31

Control Chart for
Means—Trend in
Means Starting at
Sample 26

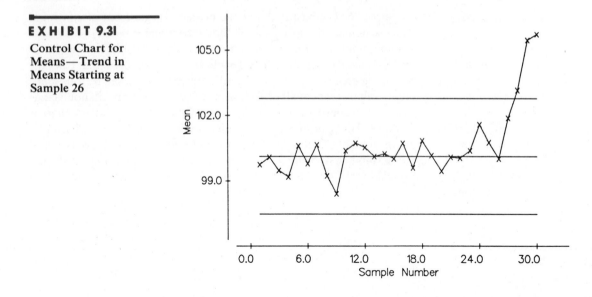

CHANGE IN DISPERSION

Another possibility for going out of control involves changes in dispersion or variability. A change in supplier of raw materials could easily result in changed variability with essentially no change in the mean. As an example, return to the data in Exhibit 9.3A. For this illustration the data in sample 26 are carefully altered to keep the mean unchanged but to double its standard deviation. (Can you think of how to do that?) The new values for sample 26 are 94.98, 96.78, 93.98, 102.58, and 106.78, with mean 99.02 (the same as before) and standard deviation 5.46, which is twice as large as before. What effect will this have on the control chart for the mean? Since the means have not changed, the answer is *no change at all.* The same will be true for any kind of alteration of the dispersion in the samples that leaves the means unchanged. *A control chart for means does not detect changes in variability.* Control charts based on measures of dispersion are needed for that particular purpose.

SECTION 9.4

EXERCISES

9.4A If 25 samples of size 7 yield the statistics $\bar{\bar{y}} = 43.8$ and $\bar{s} = 3.6$, find the UCL and LCL for the corresponding mean chart.

9.4B Observation of 23 samples, each of size 4, on a certain process produced the following data: $n = 4$, $k = 23$, $\sum_{i=1}^{23} \bar{y}_i = 232.2$ inches, and $\sum_{i=1}^{23} s_i = 26.12$ inches.
(a) Find the CL, UCL, and LCL for the mean chart for the data.
(b) Using $\bar{\bar{y}}$ and $\bar{s}$ as estimates of μ and σ, respectively, and assuming that the process is in control, what fraction of the sample means would be expected to fall above 11 inches? Below 10 inches?
(c) As in part (b), and assuming that the individual y values are approximately normally distributed, what fraction of individual y values would be expected to lie above 12 inches? Below 9 inches?

SECTION 9.5

STANDARD DEVIATION CHARTS FOR PROCESS CONTROL

A sequence plot of the subgroup standard deviations, the s_i, forms the basis of the control chart for controlling process dispersion. How should the control limits be determined? Based on large numbers of observations in each subgroup, the distribution of s_i will be *approximately* normally distributed with mean σ and standard deviation $\sigma/\sqrt{2(n-1)}$. But the effect does not hold well for subgroup sizes as small as four or five, which are typical. The true distribution of s_i is quite asymmetric. However, mathematical statisticians have been able to work out the exact distribution of s_i for all sample sizes (at least when the underlying process variable has a normal distribution and the observations are independent).

For our present purpose we need only to be able to apply the factors given in Exhibit 9.5A.[†] In a **standard deviations chart**, or s-chart, a statistical process control chart designed to detect changes in the dispersion of a process, the LCL is obtained by multiplying the estimated process standard deviation $\bar{s}$ by the factor b from the table in Exhibit 9.5A. The UCL is obtained by multiplying by the factor c. Some statistical software will calculate the limits and display the plots without having to reference any tables. The center line, CL, is drawn at $\bar{s}$. In our example $n = 5$ so that the required factors are $b = 0.160$ and $c = 2.286$. With an estimated process standard deviation of $\bar{s} = 1.87$, the control limits are drawn at $LCL = 0.160 \times 1.87 = 0.299$ and $UCL = 2.286 \times 1.87 = 4.27$. Exhibit 9.5B shows the standard deviations control chart for the data in the first 25 rows of Exhibit 9.3A. The process dispersion is clearly shown to be in control—the variation displayed within the subgroups is well within expectations for a constant-cause system.

EXHIBIT 9.5A

Factors for
Constructing Standard
Deviation Control
Charts[††]

$$LCL = b\bar{s},\ UCL = c\bar{s},\ CL = \bar{s}$$
n = subgroup sample size

n	b	c	n	b	c
2	0.002	4.124	14	0.457	1.661
3	0.036	2.966	15	0.474	1.635
4	0.098	2.527	16	0.490	1.612
5	0.160	2.286	17	0.504	1.591
6	0.215	2.129	18	0.517	1.572
7	0.263	2.017	19	0.529	1.555
8	0.303	1.932	20	0.541	1.539
9	0.338	1.864	21	0.551	1.524
10	0.368	1.809	22	0.561	1.511
11	0.394	1.764	23	0.570	1.498
12	0.418	1.725	24	0.578	1.486
13	0.439	1.691	25	0.587	1.476

[†] According to theory for a normal process with mean μ and standard deviation σ and subgroup size n, the factors b and c are determined so that $Pr(b\sigma < s_i < c\sigma) = 0.998$.

[††] Based on the χ^2 distribution of $(n-1)s^2/\sigma^2$ and equal tail probability limits of size 0.001.

EXHIBIT 9.5B

**Standard Deviations
Control Chart**

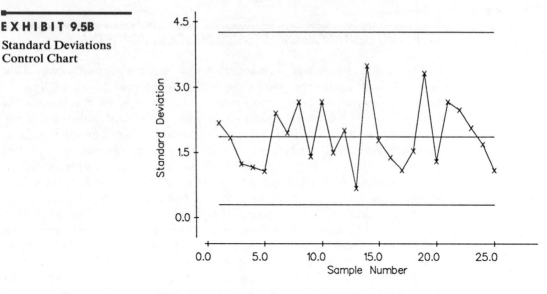

CHANGE IN DISPERSION

What should we expect to see in a standard deviations control chart when dispersion changes? Suppose again that the observations in sample 26 of Exhibit 9.3A are altered so that the sample's standard deviation is doubled but its mean is kept intact. Exhibit 9.5C shows the resulting standard deviations control chart. As before, the limits are based on the statistics calculated from only the first 25 subgroups. The out-of-control dispersion in sample 26 is clearly evident. A search for the special cause that produced the additional dispersion in sample 26 should be initiated.

EXHIBIT 9.5C

**Control Chart for
Dispersion—Special
Cause in Sample 26**

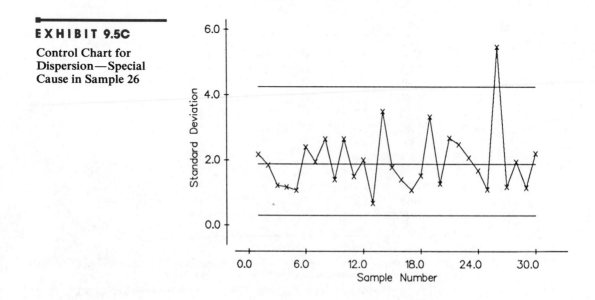

Another possible way dispersion could go out of control is illustrated in Exhibit 9.5D. Here the standard deviations of samples $26, 27, \ldots$, and 30 have been tripled in each case, and the original means in the subgroups have been retained. Again the change in dispersion is quite noticeable although not every point so tripled leads to a value above the *UCL* since several of the original standard deviations were quite small.

EXHIBIT 9.5D

Control Chart for Dispersion—Special Causes from Sample 26 on

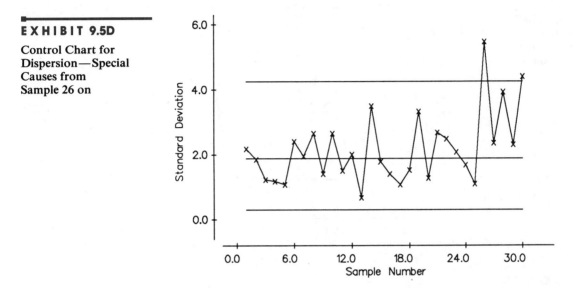

It is almost always true that increased dispersion indicates an out-of-control situation. On the other hand, *decreased* dispersion is usually a desirable goal. Reduced variability means parts fit together better, uncertainty is lessened, or, in general, better control has been achieved. If a new method, technique, tool, and so on is thought to reduce variability, that effect must be documented. The standard deviations chart may be used for this purpose, but now the hope is that after the new method is put into effect the chart will track *below* the *LCL*. Exhibit 9.5E gives such an example. Here the basic process data have been modified so that the standard deviations of the samples from sample 26 on are one-fourth of their previous values (retaining their original means). Only two of the plotted standard deviations actually go below the *LCL*, but the trend is quite evident—the dispersion has been reduced from sample 26 on. Continued process monitoring (together with process analysis, discussed in Section 9.7) will allow us to narrow the control limits by basing them on the new reduced value of the process standard deviation. The process is now capable of better control, and monitoring should reflect the higher expectations in future production.

CHANGE IN LEVEL

Control charts for dispersion will be totally unaffected by changes in level as long as the variability around those new levels is unchanged. For example, standard deviation control charts based on the out-of-control data that produced the mean charts in Exhibits 9.3G, 9.3H, and 9.3I will all be identical to the chart in Exhibit 9.5B since dispersion is in control in all those cases. In general, it will be important to monitor both the mean level and the dispersion in a process to ensure that both are under control.

EXHIBIT 9.5E

Standard Deviations
Chart—Reduced
Dispersion from
Sample 26 on

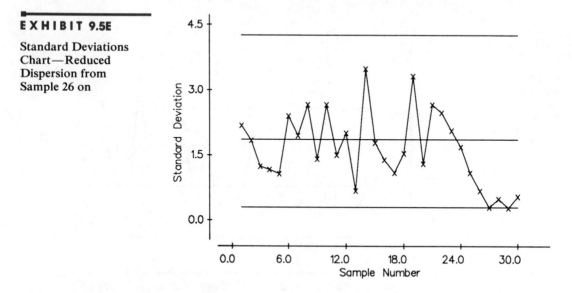

SECTION 9.6

EXERCISES

9.6A Using the information in Exercise 9.4A, find the UCL and LCL for an s-chart for this data set.

9.6B (Continuation of Exercise 9.4B) Observation of 23 samples, each of size 4, on a certain process produced the following data: $n = 4$, $k = 23$, $\sum_{i=1}^{23} \bar{y}_i = 232.2$ inches, and $\sum_{i=1}^{23} s_i = 26.12$ inches.
  (a) Find the CL, UCL, and LCL for the standard deviation chart for the data.
  (b) If the standard deviation for the 10th sample is $s_{10} = 3.49$, would the process be considered in control with respect to dispersion at that point in time? Would the process be in control with respect to mean level at that point in time?

SECTION 9.7

CONTROL CHARTS FOR PROCESS ANALYSIS

In Sections 9.3 and 9.5 we worked under the assumption that the process was initially in control. However, when new processes are developed or old processes are first studied such information will not be available. **Process analysis** involves producing meaningful control charts from historical data to investigate whether or not a process is in control, to estimate the parameters of constant-cause systems, and to detect special causes when control has not been achieved.

STANDARD DEVIATION CHARTS FOR PROCESS ANALYSIS

In process analysis, control charts for dispersion are the starting point, because lack of control of dispersion will affect the charts for detecting control in the mean. A sequence plot of the successive subgroup standard deviations is again created. The process is temporarily assumed to be in control with respect to dispersion, and an overall estimate of the process dispersion is computed by averaging the estimates for dispersion in the subgroups as before. Notice that since each s_i measures dispersion around its own subgroup mean, these standard deviations will not be influenced by changes of level in the process. Of course, $\bar{s}$ will be affected to some degree by subgroups that have unusually high or low variability. For that reason the control limits based on $\bar{s}$ are sometimes called *trial control limits*. Keeping this limitation in mind, control limits based on $\bar{s}$ are calculated.

To illustrate, the full 30 rows of data in Exhibit 9.3A are used. But now suppose no prior knowledge as to whether the process is in control or not. Interest thus centers on process analysis. We find that $\bar{s} = 1.86$, so the center line and control limits will be nearly the same as in Exhibit 9.5B. The new standard deviation chart is displayed in Exhibit 9.7A and supports the hypothesis of a constant-cause system *with respect to dispersion*. As already noted, since this chart depends only on the subgroup standard deviations it will be totally unaffected by changes in subgroup means. For example, an isolated change in the mean of one sample (Exhibit 9.3G), a step change in the means for a sequence of samples (Exhibit 9.3H), or a trend in the means (Exhibit 9.3I) will all produce standard deviations charts exactly as in Exhibit 9.7A.

EXHIBIT 9.7A

Standard Deviations Chart for Process Analysis

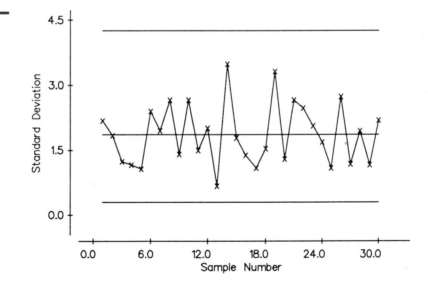

Our present concern is to detect lack of control in dispersion from a process analysis point of view. What will be the effect on the chart if the standard deviation of sample 26 is doubled? Notice that since our statistics are based on *all* the data, $\bar{s}$

will increase and the center line and both control limits will be affected by the abnormal dispersion in sample 26. In the present case, $\bar{s} = 1.95$, compared with 1.87 previously. Thus $LCL = 0.160 \times 1.95 = 0.31$ and $UCL = 2.286 \times 1.95 = 4.46$. The unusual dispersion in sample 26 inflates $\bar{s}$ somewhat, which in turn inflates the UCL. However, Exhibit 9.7B shows that the chart is still able to detect the out-of-control situation. (Compare it with Exhibit 9.5C.)

EXHIBIT 9.7B

Standard Deviation Control Chart for Process Analysis— Increased Dispersion in Sample 26

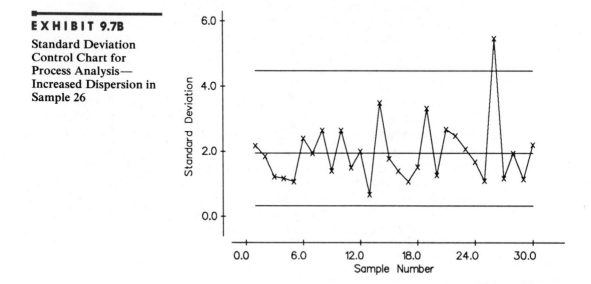

In process analysis, once an out-of-control situation is found and the special cause found and eliminated, then sample 26 should be removed from further consideration and the control limits recalculated. With the special cause eliminated, a better estimate of the process standard deviation is possible. The revised chart will better indicate the process characteristics when in control, and the revised limits are appropriate for use in future process control. In this example, removing sample 26 leads to a new value of $\bar{s} = 1.83$ based on the remaining 29 subgroups and the new control chart in Exhibit 9.7C. If the special cause either cannot be discovered or cannot be eliminated by suitable modification of the process, then the aberrant samples should not be removed from consideration because they must be considered as common causes in future monitoring of the process.

An increase in dispersion for several subgroups will affect the process analysis standard deviation chart more substantially since $\bar{s}$ can be inflated considerably. Suppose the case in which samples 26 through 30 all have their standard deviations tripled but their old mean values retained is investigated again. This causes the value of $\bar{s}$ to increase to 2.17 and the control limits to move to $UCL = 2.286 \times 2.17 = 4.96$ and $LCL = 0.160 \times 2.17 = 0.35$. The resulting control chart is shown in Exhibit 9.7D. Although only one point exceeds the upper control limit, the chart clearly signals trouble that must be investigated. Notice also that many of the standard deviations for samples 1 through 25 are below the center line—another

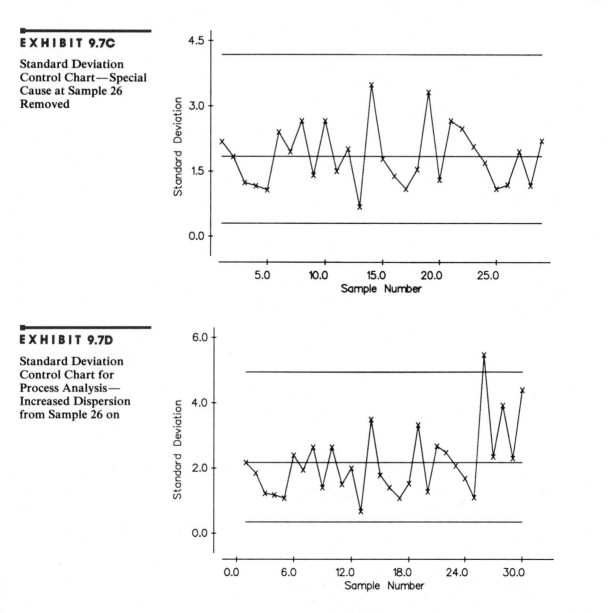

indication of the increased dispersion at the end of the series. If samples 26 through 30 are all omitted from consideration, then $\bar{s} = 1.87$, as in Exhibits 9.7B, 9.7C, and 9.7D. The chart based on this value would be identical to the one in Exhibit 9.7D, where the increased variability is much easier to detect since the control limits are based on a proper measure of dispersion when a constant-cause system is operating.

Process improvement as indicated by reduced variability in results is illustrated in Exhibit 9.7E, where the standard deviations of samples 26 through 30 have been reduced to one-fourth of their previous values. The trial control limits are affected by that reduction, with $\bar{s} = 1.63$ now compared with 1.87 before the reduction.

However, the trend in the standard deviations at the end of the sequence is apparent. Having observed Exhibit 9.7E, we would suspect that a serendipitous special cause was reducing the variability, seek it out, and, if possible, arrange for it to continue in the future. If the reduced variability were due to a planned change in the process, control limits based on the old in-control process as in process control, not process analysis, would be used.

EXHIBIT 9.7E

Standard Deviation Control Chart for Process Analysis—Reduced Variation from Sample 26 on

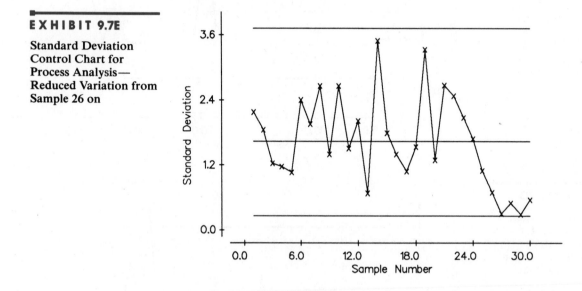

Finally, in process analysis, charts have been considered first to investigate whether process dispersion is in control since assessing possible changes in the subgroup means depends on already having some knowledge of the process dispersion.

MEAN CHARTS FOR PROCESS ANALYSIS

As in process control, the standard method of constructing mean charts for process analysis is to use control limits based on the theoretical limits $\mu \pm 3\sigma_{\bar{y}} = \mu \pm 3\sigma/\sqrt{n}$ where μ and σ are estimated using the data at hand. We use $\bar{\bar{y}} \pm a\bar{s}$ for the trial control limits with $\bar{\bar{y}}$ and $\bar{s}$ computed from the full data set because we have no knowledge about the stability of the process. It is desirable to have first shown the process dispersion to be in control, but more often than not the stability of dispersion and mean value are looked at simultaneously. Again using the full data set in Exhibit 9.3A, the control chart displayed in Exhibit 9.7F is obtained. It shows that the process is in control with respect to the mean.

Now consider the same data set with an isolated change in level of four units at sample 26. Such a change will not affect the standard deviation of that sample and hence will not change $\bar{s}$. The change will increase $\bar{\bar{y}}$ from its original value of 100.12 to 100.27 so that the center line and control limits will all increase similarly. The

EXHIBIT 9.7F

Mean Chart for Process Analysis

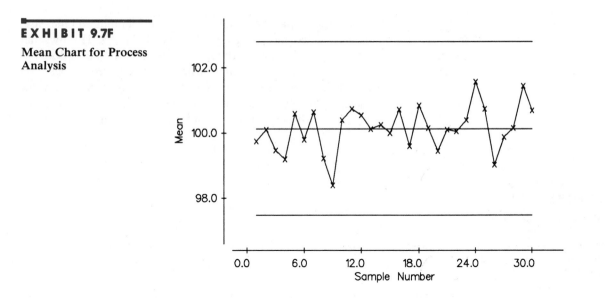

resulting mean chart is shown in Exhibit 9.7G, where the increased level in subgroup 26 is still detected. Compare this chart to Exhibit 9.3G, where the same data are used but the limits are based only on the first 25 data points that are deemed to be in control. If the controls limits are based on the data with sample 26 excluded, a plot very similar to Exhibit 9.3G would result, reinforcing the anomalous nature of the 26th sample.

EXHIBIT 9.7G

Mean Chart for Process Analysis—Special Cause at Sample 26

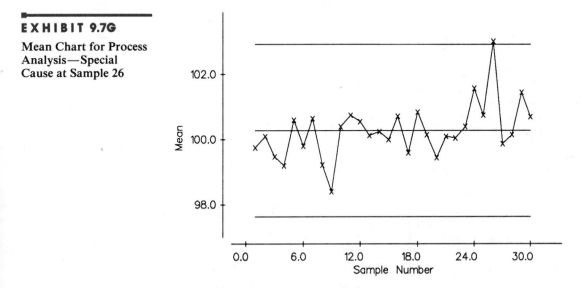

A similar analysis may be carried out on the data with the step change in the mean for samples $26, 27, \ldots, 30$ as in Exhibit 9.3H. In this case $\bar{\bar{y}}$ changes a little more, from

100.12 to 100.80, which implies that the center line and control limits will increase, making it more difficult to detect mean changes. However, Exhibit 9.7H shows that the special cause is still reasonably clear although the mean of sample 26 does not exceed the trial *UCL*. On the basis of this chart the limits should be redone based on data with samples 27, 28, 29, and 30 excluded. With this change $\bar{\bar{y}}$ reverts to a value of 100.23, more in keeping with the mean of the earlier constant-cause data. The control chart in Exhibit 9.7I shows that now even sample 26 is considered out-of-control.

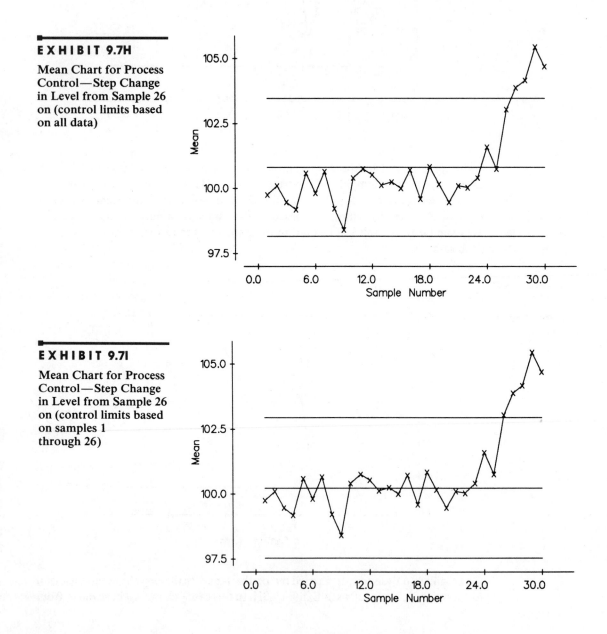

EXHIBIT 9.7H

Mean Chart for Process Control—Step Change in Level from Sample 26 on (control limits based on all data)

EXHIBIT 9.7I

Mean Chart for Process Control—Step Change in Level from Sample 26 on (control limits based on samples 1 through 26)

Finally, consider the data first analyzed in Exhibit 9.3I, whose means begin an upward trend at sample 26. Exhibit 9.7J displays the control chart, which shows that samples 29 and 30 are out of control with respect to the mean. However, we realize that the trending mean affects the trial control limits. Hence, the control limits are recomputed based only on samples 1 through 28, giving the chart in Exhibit 9.7K. We now see that sample 28 is also out of control. Using only the first 27 samples for the limits leads to Exhibit 9.7L, which does not indicate any other out-of-control points. This chart should be compared to Exhibit 9.3I, which gives essentially the same conclusion since it is based on the data only through sample 25.

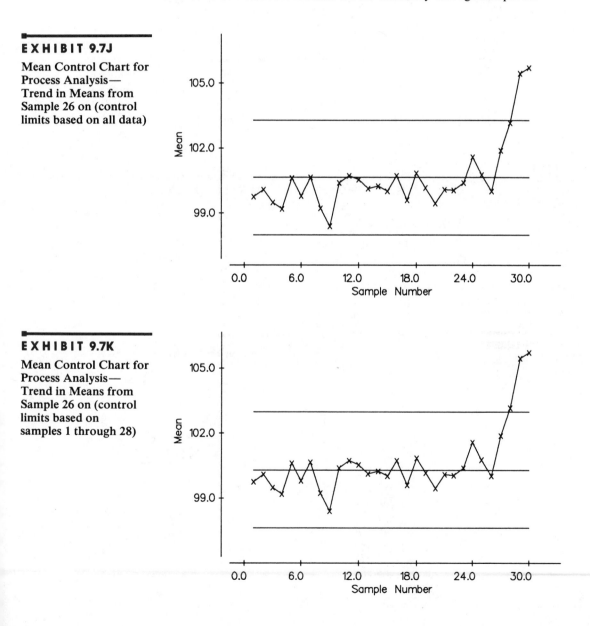

EXHIBIT 9.7J

Mean Control Chart for Process Analysis— Trend in Means from Sample 26 on (control limits based on all data)

EXHIBIT 9.7K

Mean Control Chart for Process Analysis— Trend in Means from Sample 26 on (control limits based on samples 1 through 28)

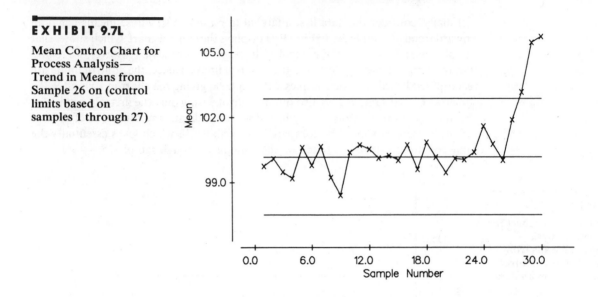

SECTION 9.8

APPLICATIONS OF CONTROL CHARTS IN BUSINESS

FOOD PROCESSING

The food processing industry must closely watch the process of filling containers to the proper amount. Underfilling raises the ire of customers (and may be illegal), and overfilling either raises the cost of the product or erodes company profits. Consider

EXHIBIT 9.8A

Weight of Ice Cream in
200-Ounce Containers

```
# filename: ICECREAM.DAT
# Gross weight in ounces of ice cream fill
# (Source: E.R.Ott, Process Quality Control
# New York: McGraw-Hill, 1975)
# 25 samples of 4 in order of production at 10 minute intervals
# Specifications were 200+-4 ounces
  202 201 198 199
  200 202 212 202
  202 201 208 201
  201 200 200 202
  210 196 200 198
  202 206 205 203
  198 196 202 199
  206 204 204 206
  206 204 203 204
  208 214 213 207
  198 201 199 198
  204 204 202 206
  203 204 204 203
  214 212 206 208
  192 198 204 198
  207 208 206 204
  205 214 215 212
  204 208 196 196
  205 204 205 204
  202 202 208 208
  204 206 209 202
  206 206 206 210
  204 202 204 207
  206 205 204 202
```

the filling of ice cream containers. The process was designed to produce actual fill amounts of between 196 and 204 ounces, with a target of 200 ounces. As a check on the fill process, four containers were taken from production at 10-minute intervals and their weights measured in ounces. Exhibit 9.8A lists the data for 24 such subgroups.[†] The grand mean of these $4 \times 24 = 96$ fills is 203.95 ounces, above the target value of 200 ounces. But of course there is variability to be considered!

Since we are new to this process, process analysis is used to assess fill amount with respect to both dispersion and level over the historical data available. We will look for out-of-control situations and assess the capability of the process as it now stands. Instability of dispersion makes judging the level of the process difficult, so the standard deviation chart is done first. Calculation yields $\bar{s} = 2.72$. Exhibit 9.8B displays the dispersion chart. Fortunately, the chart indicates no problems with respect to dispersion and we may reasonably proceed to the mean chart.

EXHIBIT 9.8B

Standard Deviation Control Chart for Ice Cream Fill Amount

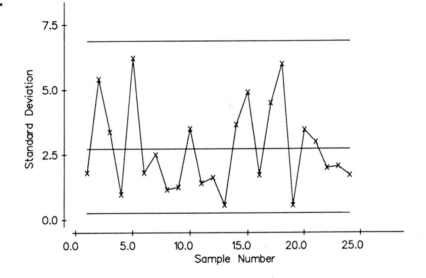

The lack of control in the mean is clear from Exhibit 9.8C. Three points are above the *UCL* and three points are below the *LCL*. Because such variation is extremely unusual for a constant-cause system, we conclude that several special causes must be operating in this process. The pattern of being below the *LCL*, then above the *UCL*, then below, and so on suggests the possibility that the process is being "overcontrolled," that is, when the fill amount is too low the filling equipment is readjusted to increase it. Then when the subsequent fill amount is too high, the equipment is readjusted downward, and so on. Such a hypothesis should be further investigated with the cooperation of the process supervisor and the workers directly associated with the process. As it stands, the process does not meet the criteria of producing containers with between 196 and 204 ounces of ice cream. The process needs to be modified to achieve the range of variation desired.

[†] These data appear in Ellis R. Ott, *Process Quality Control* (New York: McGraw-Hill, 1975), 60, and are attributed to David Lipman, then a graduate student at Rutgers University.

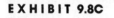

EXHIBIT 9.8C

Mean Control Chart for
Ice Cream Fill Amount

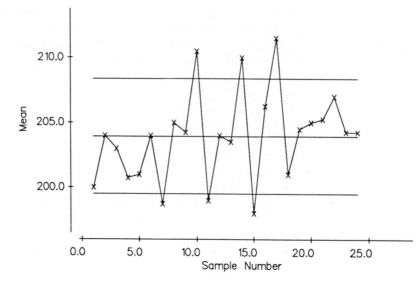

ACCOUNTING PROCESSES

The Winegard Company of Burlington, Iowa, wants to understand the bill-paying behavior of the independent retail distributors of its television reception products. When Winegard receives payment on a bill, it records the number of days since the bill was issued. Suspecting that each distributor has a different paying pattern, Winegard decides to run separate process analyses for different distributors. Three distributors, referred to as ABC, DEF, and XYZ to protect their anonymity, are analyzed. For purposes of constructing control charts, the complete time history over several months is grouped into subgroups of five consecutive bills. For various periods throughout 1986, the three companies paid 260, 130, and 110 bills, respectively.

Company DEF's data are listed in Exhibit 9.8D. Since the complete time history is available, a sequence plot of the series is first done (see Exhibit 9.8E). Two or three suspect values that will likely have a large effect on any further analysis are obvious immediately. The data are arbitrarily placed into subgroups of size 5 (see Exhibit 9.8D) and the control charting is begun. The standard deviation control chart for the subgrouped data is given in Exhibit 9.8F, where the possible outliers have indeed shown up as out-of-control dispersion in samples 13 and 26. In addition, there is unusually small dispersion in subgroup 17 and somewhat small dispersion in subgroup 9. If the mean of a subgroup is at an acceptable level, the small dispersion is a desirable goal. Thus we will proceed with concern about the large dispersion but ignore the small dispersion.

Since the subgrouping was arbitrary we do not want to ignore the "good" data that happen to have been arbitrarily grouped with the outliers. Thus for the next look at the data the two outlying observations in samples 13 and 26 are treated as missing and the data are recharted, noting now that two of the subgroups contain only four observations. Exhibit 9.8G gives the resulting standard deviation chart.

EXHIBIT 9.8D

Days to Pay Account:
DEF Company

```
# filename: DEF.DAT
# Accounts receivable data for DEF Company
# Number of days to collection of account
# (Source: Mark Sellergren, Winegard, Inc.,
# Burlington, Iowa)
# Terms: 1%-10 days, net 30 days
# June 1987 through October 1987
# (Read across, row by row)
  39 39 41 26 28   Jun
  28 25 26 24 38   Jun
  35 38 38 25 38   Jun
  24 38 25 40 38   Jun
  38 25 25 35 35   Jun
  35 32 41 33 31   Jun
  21 21 26 26 28   Jul
  28 28 28 28 20   Jul
  27 25 27 25 28   Jul
  20 28 22 26 34   Jul
  21 21 33 33 21   Jul
  33 22 17 22 20   Jul
  27 20 55 39 26   Jul/Aug
  26 26 39 25 22   Aug
  33 33 19 32 32   Aug
  42 27 37 27 27   Aug
  27 26 26 26 25   Aug
  25 35 35 35 35   Aug
  20 30 25 25 27   Aug
  27 25 25 25 34   Aug
  28 28 21 22 21   Sep
  49 35 28 28 27   Sep
  20 27 27 26 26   Sep
  26 22 22 22 34   Sep/Oct
  26 19 28 19 27   Oct
  16 27 20 63 25   Oct
```

EXHIBIT 9.8E

Sequence Plot of Days
Until Payment:
DEF Company

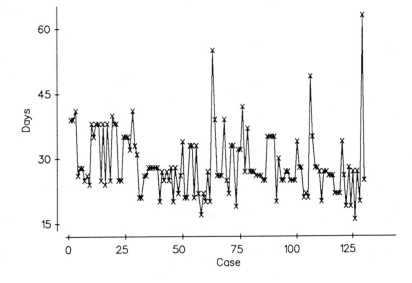

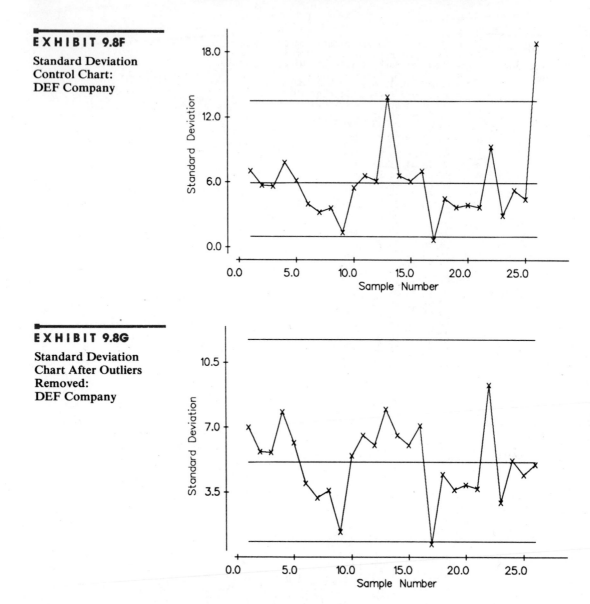

EXHIBIT 9.8F

Standard Deviation
Control Chart:
DEF Company

EXHIBIT 9.8G

Standard Deviation
Chart After Outliers
Removed:
DEF Company

The small dispersion in sample 17 is still observed but otherwise the process variability appears to be in control, so we go on to the mean chart in Exhibit 9.8H. No points lie outside the control limits in this chart and the process is accepted as being in control. The control limits in this chart are equal to $28.1 \pm (1.43)5.13 = 28.1 \pm 7.3$ or $LCL = 20.8$ days and $UCL = 35.4$ days. These limits will serve as control limits for future charts on the process mean and alert the Winegard accounts receivable department to potential difficulties with DEF Company *as they arise.*

EXHIBIT 9.8H

Mean Chart After
Outliers Removed:
DEF Company

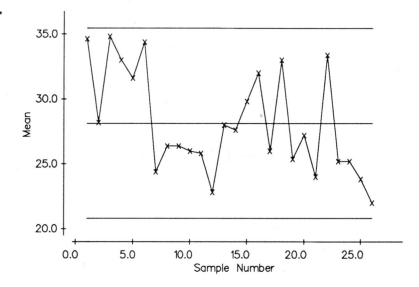

The bill-paying behavior of XYZ Company is considered next. The data are listed in Exhibit 9.8I, and a sequence plot of the individual values is shown in Exhibit 9.8J. (These data first appeared in Exercise 2.9A.)

The sequence plot clearly shows two or three outliers that will greatly affect the subsequent charts, so we set the three values to the missing value code and proceed from that point. The standard deviation chart (with outliers removed) is shown in

EXHIBIT 9.8I

Days to Pay Account:
XYZ Company

```
# filename: XYZ.DAT
# Accounts receivable data for XYZ Company
# Number of days to collection of account
# (Source: Mark Sellergren, Winegard, Inc.,
# Burlington, Iowa)
# Terms: 1%-10 days, net 30 days
# January 1986 through December 1986
# (Read across, row by row)
  29 25 22 21 34   Jan
  29 27 45 22 22   Jan
  41 32 32 30 30   Jan/Feb
  30 30 22 17 15   Feb
  25 28 22 22 22   Feb/Mar
  20 20 18 32 31   Mar
  30 77 22 18 18   Mar
  25 25 24 21 17   Apr
  17 28 42 38 30   Apr/May
  30 30 30 27 21   May
  68 31 23 23 23   May/Jun
   1 20 29 31 31   Jun/Jul
  43 33 38 42 36   Jul/Aug
  48 48 52 49 44   Aug
  51 49 54 50 50   Sep
  50 50 50 49 62   Sep
  62 62 61 60 55   Sep
  61 59 54 54 62   Oct
  57 55 62 62 62   Oct/Nov
  62 62 62 57 57   Nov
  57 57 55 50 50   Nov
  44 44 43 43 41   Dec
```

EXHIBIT 9.8J

Sequence Plot of Days
Until Payment:
XYZ Company

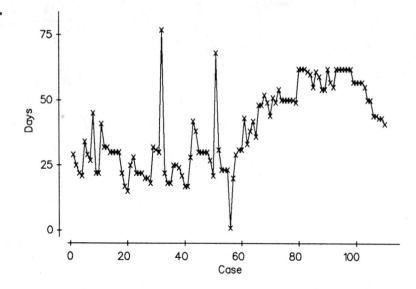

Exhibit 9.8K. Since we see no striking deviation from a stable system with respect to dispersion, we go on to consider the mean chart in Exhibit 9.8L. At this point of the analysis we see the difficulty that was also somewhat apparent in the sequence plot of Exhibit 9.8J. The mean level of the process has increased greatly from sample 14 onward, and the control limits based on the overall mean are essentially meaningless. Exhibit 9.8M shows the mean chart with control limits based only on samples 1 through 13. Clearly an important special cause must have occurred at about the time of the 13th sample. The control limits shown in Exhibit 9.8M have the potential for use in future monitoring of the process. Unfortunately, in

EXHIBIT 9.8K

Standard Deviation
Control Chart:
XYZ Company

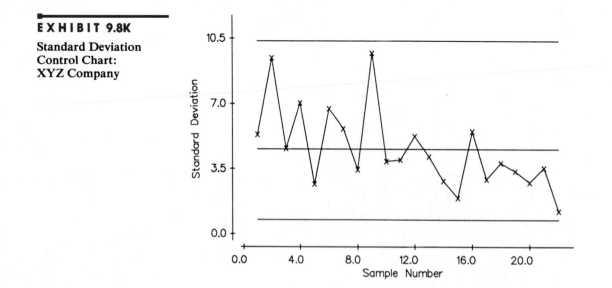

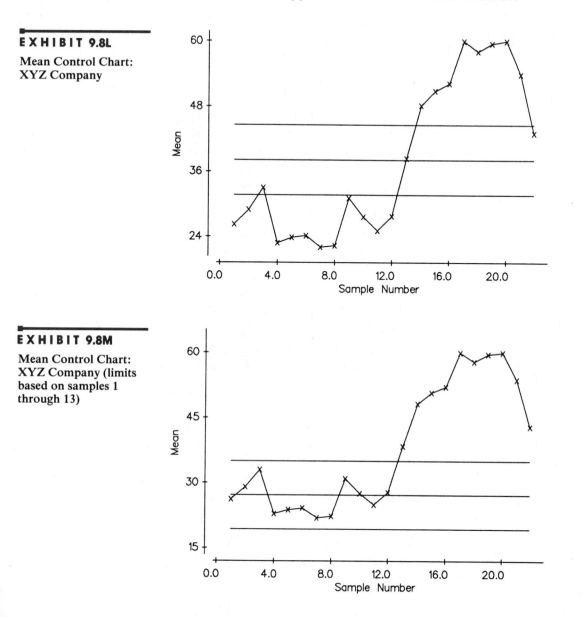

EXHIBIT 9.8L

Mean Control Chart:
XYZ Company

EXHIBIT 9.8M

Mean Control Chart:
XYZ Company (limits
based on samples 1
through 13)

December 1986, XYZ Company filed for bankruptcy. Active charting of the accounting data as it became available to Winegard might have helped them foresee the difficulties that were to come.

Lastly, accounts receivable data from ABC Company is examined. The sequence plot of the 260 observations listed in Exhibit 9.8N is given in Exhibit 9.8O. The sequence plot in Exhibit 9.8O shows immediately that the process variability is unusual and not due to a constant-cause system. Standard deviation and mean charts will not likely produce useful information on this process. However, a little data sleuthing does lead to a possible key to the observed behavior. Referring to the

EXHIBIT 9.8N

Days to Pay Account:
ABC Company

```
# filename: ABC.DAT
# Accounts receivable data for ABC Company
# Number of days to collection of account
# (Source: Mark Sellergren, Winegard, Inc.,
# Burlington, Iowa.)
# Terms: 1%-10 days, net 30 days
# January 1987 through August 1987
# (Read across, row by row)
  53 53 48 47 47  Jan          47 44 42 42 36  May
  47 46 42 41 40  Jan          34 34 34 33 33  May
  40 36 35 33 33  Jan          33 33 33 33 33  May
  33 32 29 29 29  Jan          33 29 28 26 49  May/Jun
  29 29 29 29 29  Jan          47 47 47 47 46  Jun
  29 29 29 29 29  Jan          45 42 41 40 40  Jun
  29 28 49 49 49  Jan/Feb      40 39 39 38 35  Jun
  47 46 46 45 41  Feb          35 34 33 32 28  Jun
  41 39 38 35 32  Feb          28 28 28 28 28  Jun
  32 32 32 32 32  Feb          28 28 28 27 27  Jun
  32 28 28 28 28  Feb          26 25 25 25 53  Jun/Jul
  28 28 28 28 28  Feb          53 52 52 51 51  Jul
  27 27 25 46 45  Feb/Mar      51 46 45 45 44  Jul
  43 38 37 37 36  Mar          43 42 39 38 38  Jul
  28 28 28 28 28  Mar          37 36 36 36 36  Jul
  28 28 28 28 28  Mar          32 32 32 32 32  Jul
  28 28 25 25 24  Mar          32 32 32 32 32  Jul
  24 24 24 24 24  Mar          31 31 31 29 28  Jul
  22 49 42 41 35  Mar/Apr      28 25 25 25 24  Jul
  34 33 32 29 29  Apr          24 48 43 38 35  Jul/Aug
  29 29 29 29 29  Apr          34 34 31 31 31  Aug
  29 29 29 29 29  Apr          31 31 31 31 31  Aug
  29 29 29 29 29  Apr          31 29 29 29 29  Aug
  29 28 27 26 26  Apr          29 29 29 28 28  Aug
  26 25 25 25 25  Apr          28 27 27 27 24  Aug
  22 21 54 50 48  Apr/May      23 23 21 21 20  Aug
```

EXHIBIT 9.8O

Sequence Plot of Days
Until Payment:
ABC Company

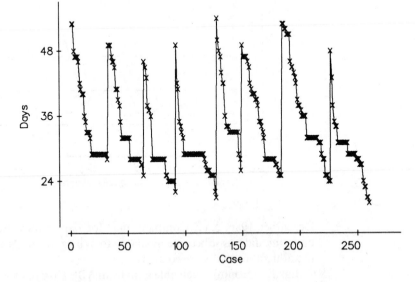

original data in Exhibit 9.8N reveals that the unusually large values always occur at the end of a month and into the beginning of the next month. ABC Company is clearly paying their accounts to Winegard based on a calendar month system. Perhaps some communication between the two companies on this matter can lead to a system that will smooth out the cash flow to the satisfaction of both parties.

SECTION 9.9

EXERCISES

9.9A Procter & Gamble (P&G) is a large worldwide producer of numerous consumer products including Crest toothpaste, Tide laundry detergent, and Prell shampoo. In 1986 a new production line was started in the Iowa City P&G plant to produce and package a hair conditioner. An automatic machine was used to put the caps on the conditioner containers. If the caps are not tight enough the package may leak, but if they are too tight the customer will not be able to open the container easily. A measure of cap tightness is the cap torque, which specifications said should lie in the range from 15 to 40 foot-pounds. Since many out-of-spec caps were found soon after starting the production line, a process analysis was instituted. Cap torques were measured on 18 subgroups, each of size 4. The data are shown below.

```
# filename: P&G1.DAT
# P&G data
# (Source: Jeffrey Enck, Procter & Gamble,
# Iowa City, Iowa)
# Torque on hair conditioner caps
  20 17 40 26
  36 35 34 38
  32 37 31 29
  22 30 18 23
  24 22 24 26
  30 40 34 19
  20 33 16 30
  27 33 36 34
  32 50 43 20
  15 17 31 21
  28 29 36 32
  26 30 20 12
  40 45 27 30
  30 33 53 46
  36 42 31 26
  39 32 35 36
  32 35 36 32
  30 55 57 30
```

(a) Show that $\bar{\bar{y}} = 31.194$ and $\bar{s} = 6.6942$.

(b) Plot the s-chart for these data and show that dispersion of cap torque is in control.

(c) Plot the mean chart for these data and see if the mean level of cap torque is in control.

(d) Display a histogram of the individual measurements and comment on the appearance. Does a mound-shaped distribution appear to fit the histogram? [Based on part (c), should any subgroups be omitted before doing the histogram?]

(e) Form a·plot of the observations versus normal scores and compute the correlation in the plot. Does normality seem to be confirmed?

(f) Using the values given in part (a), estimate the long-run fraction of caps that will *not* meet the specification limits of 15 to 40 foot-pounds. (This process is considered again in Section 10.6.)

9.9B The data on page 280 are reported in Kaoru Ishikawa, *Guide to Quality Control*, 2d rev. ed. (White Plains, N.Y.: UNIPUB, Kraus International Publications, 1986). They are measurements of the moisture content of a textile product taken five times a day for 25 consecutive days.

Day	Time				
Subgroup	6:00	10:00	14:00	18:00	22:00
1	14.0	12.6	13.2	13.1	12.1
2	13.2	13.3	12.7	13.4	12.1
3	13.5	12.8	13.0	12.8	12.4
4	13.9	12.4	13.3	13.1	13.2
5	13.0	13.0	12.1	12.2	13.3
6	13.7	12.0	12.5	12.4	12.4
7	13.9	12.1	12.7	13.4	13.0
8	13.4	13.6	13.0	12.4	13.5
9	14.4	12.4	12.2	12.4	12.5
10	13.3	12.4	12.6	12.9	12.8
11	13.3	12.8	13.0	13.0	13.1
12	13.6	12.5	13.3	13.5	12.8
13	13.4	13.3	12.0	13.0	13.1
14	13.9	13.1	13.5	12.6	12.8
15	14.2	12.7	12.9	12.9	12.5
16	13.6	12.6	12.4	12.5	12.2
17	14.0	13.2	12.4	13.0	13.0
18	13.1	12.9	13.5	12.3	12.8
19	14.6	13.7	13.4	12.2	12.5
20	13.9	13.0	13.0	13.2	12.6
21	13.3	12.7	12.6	12.8	12.7
22	13.9	12.4	12.7	12.4	12.8
23	13.2	12.3	12.6	13.1	12.7
24	13.2	12.8	12.8	12.3	12.6
25	13.1	12.8	12.0	12.3	12.2

(a) Using all the data, prepare standard deviation and mean control charts, with $n = 5$. Assuming you have been asked to do a process analysis, what conclusions about the state of statistical control would you draw from these charts?

(b) Prepare a sequence plot of the data. Use the plotting symbol A or 1 for data collected at 6:00, the symbol B or 2 for data collected at 10:00, and so on. What predictable pattern emerges from the sequence plot? Speculate on possible reasons for this pattern. Does this pattern raise any doubts on your conclusions in part (a)? State why or why not.

(c) Display separate dotplots on the same scale for each of the five times of day. Do these plots reinforce the conclusions drawn in part (b)? (Filename: MOISTURE.DAT.)

SECTION 9.10

DISCUSSION

Sequence plots of subgroup standard deviations and means, together with appropriate control limits, can help us identify and thus perhaps eliminate special causes of variation. The charts can also prevent unnecessary tampering with a process whose variability is due solely to common causes. Monitoring, adjusting, and improving the many individual processes that make up any business are effective ways of ensuring that quality goods and services are produced.

SUPPLEMENTARY EXERCISES FOR CHAPTER 9

9A The Frito-Lay Company uses statistical process control in all of its food processing. In the manufacture of Ruffles, a ridged potato chip, the amount of salt added during the processing is very important. To control the salt levels, the company samples three batches of chips each 15 minutes, measures the salt content of the three batches, and plots the mean of the three batches on control charts. From long experience it has established a known mean salt level of 1.6% as a desirable target value and a known process standard deviation of 0.28%. Any unusual deviation from these known values indicates that the process needs attention. Argue that in this situation control limits for the mean chart should be of the form $1.6 \pm 3(0.28/\sqrt{3})$ rather than as given in this chapter, namely, $\bar{\bar{y}} \pm a\bar{s}$.

9B The data file below gives the thickness of paint-can "ears." Periodically, a sample of five ears is selected from a bin. Thirty samples are available for analysis.

(a) Construct both s-charts and mean charts for these data.

(b) Interpret the charts formed in part (a). Does the process appear to be in control with respect to both variability and mean level?

(c) Now construct displays of the distribution of ear thickness based on all $5 \times 30 = 150$ data points. Use histograms, dotplots, and stem-and-leaf displays. Do all three displays confirm a special shape to the distribution?

(d) The bin contains paint-can ears produced from two different machines. Could this explain the distribution shape?

(e) In light of the results in parts (c) and (d), suggest a better way to collect and analyze data for this situation.

```
# filename: PAINTCAN.DAT
# Thickness of paint can ears
# (Source: R.D.Snee, Graphical Analysis of Process Variation Studies,
# Journal of Quality Technology 15 (April 1983), 76-88)
# Samples of five (rows) are selected periodically from
# a bin of product produced by two different machines
  29 36 39 34 34
  29 29 28 32 31
  34 34 39 38 37
  35 37 33 38 41
  30 29 31 38 29
  34 31 37 39 36
  30 35 33 40 36
  28 28 31 34 30
  32 36 38 38 35
  35 30 37 35 31
  35 30 35 38 35
  38 34 35 35 31
  34 35 33 30 34
  40 35 34 33 35
  34 35 38 35 30
  35 30 35 29 37
  40 31 38 35 31
  35 36 30 33 32
  35 34 35 30 36
  35 35 31 38 36
  32 36 36 32 36
  36 37 32 34 34
  29 34 33 37 35
  36 36 35 37 37
  36 30 35 33 31
  35 30 29 38 35
  35 36 30 34 36
  35 30 36 29 35
  38 36 35 31 31
  30 34 40 28 30
```

9C Exhibit 9.8D contains accounting data for the DEF Company. In the earlier analysis of this data, outliers in samples 13 and 26 were converted to the missing value code before further analysis. There is also a suspicious data point in sample 22 (a value of 49). Change this value to "missing" also and repeat the analysis as in Exhibits 9.8G and 9.8H. Do the conclusions change?

GLOSSARY FOR CHAPTER 9

Common causes (chance causes)	Causes of variation in a measured variable that are due to chance and remain in the system unless the process is fundamentally altered.
Control limits	Limits within which the plotted characteristic (subgroup mean or standard deviation) is expected to vary when the process is in control.
Mean chart	Statistical process control chart designed to detect changes in the mean of a process.
Process analysis	Analysis of past process data to find appropriate limits for future control.
$\bar{s}$	The average of the subgroup standard deviations.
$\bar{s}_i$	Standard deviation for the ith subgroup.
Special causes (assignable causes)	Causes of variation in a measured variable that are individually important and affect process results only some of the time.
Standard deviation chart	Statistical process control chart designed to detect changes in the dispersion of a process.
Statistical process control	Statistical methods used to detect changes in processes.
Subgroups	Small samples of a process variable used to measure the current mean and standard deviation of a process variable.
$\bar{\bar{y}}$	The grand mean of all the subgroups.
$\bar{y}_i$	The mean for the ith subgroup.

## CHAPTER 10

Binomial Distributions

INTRODUCTION

Many situations may be investigated by inspecting each item in a process for some one particular attribute. For example, in a bank a large number of checks are processed each day. Each check must be inspected and the check amount entered into the bank's computer system. It is important to know whether or not the amount was entered correctly. If the amount was entered correctly, the transaction is a success; otherwise it is a failure. In a manufacturing process, a particular item selected from the production line either conforms to the stated product specifications or is nonconforming in some way. In screening loan applicants, the result is either accept or reject. In auditing, a check amount either agrees with the vendor's invoice amount or it does not. If a coin is tossed it either comes up heads or it does not. If a pair of dice is rolled, a seven total is obtained or it is not. Many situations fit into this either-or, yes-no, good-bad, or success-failure framework. For mathematical and computer convenience, success is usually indicated as a 1 and failure as a 0.

ASSUMPTIONS AND SIMULATIONS

Consider a process that at each point in time produces either a 1 (a success) or a 0 (a failure). Each observation is called a *trial*. Two assumptions that simplify the process can be made:

- A constant long-run proportion of successes, denoted by π, applies to each of the trials; that is, π is the probability of a success on each individual trial.

- The trials are statistically independent of one another.[†]

Such success-failure trials are called **Bernoulli trials** or a **Bernoulli process** after James Bernoulli, a probabilist of the early 1700s. Exhibit 10.2A lists the results of a computer simulation of 60 Bernoulli trials with success rate $\pi = 1/2$. Descriptive statistics are also given. Notice that in the 60 trials there were 32 successes, with a mean or sample proportion of $32/60 = 0.5333$ successes per trial. For Bernoulli trials the total number of successes is the statistic from which everything else of interest follows. For binary data a simpler description is given by a tally of the number of successes and failures. Exhibit 10.2B shows the results of the tally for the data in Exhibit 10.2A.

EXHIBIT 10.2A

Sixty Success-Failure Trials with Success Rate $\pi = 1/2$

Rate (0.5)   (Read across, row by row)

1	0	0	0	1	0	1	1	1	1	1	0	1	0	1
0	0	0	1	1	1	1	1	1	1	1	0	0	1	1
1	0	1	0	0	1	0	1	0	0	1	0	0	1	1
1	0	1	0	1	0	0	0	0	1	0	0	1	0	1

	Number	Mean	Standard Deviation
Rate (0.5)	60	0.5333	0.5031

EXHIBIT 10.2B

A Tally for Binary Data

Rate (0.5)	Count	Percent
0	28	47
1	32	53
$n = 60$		

It is also instructive to graph the sequence plot of Bernoulli process results to see how the successes and failures occur over time. Exhibit 10.2C displays the data of Exhibit 10.2A as a sequence plot.

† That is, there is no influence from one trial to any other.

EXHIBIT 10.2C

Sequence Plot—
Bernoulli Process with
$\pi = 1/2$

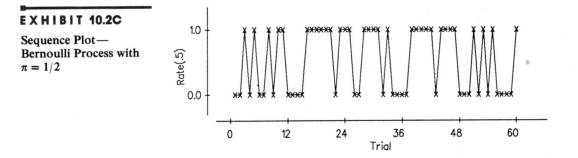

Exhibit 10.2D displays a simulated Bernoulli process with $\pi = 0.2$ along with the relevant statistics. In this case the average number of successes is $13/60 = 0.2167$. Note also that the standard deviation is 0.4155, which is somewhat smaller than that given in Exhibit 10.2A—0.5031 for the case of 32 successes out of 60 trials.

EXHIBIT 10.2D

Sequence Plot and
Statistics—Bernoulli
Process with $\pi = 0.2$

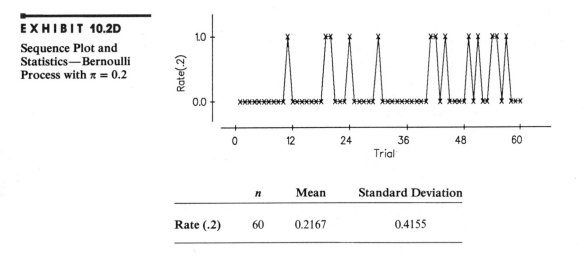

	n	Mean	Standard Deviation
Rate (.2)	60	0.2167	0.4155

A third example simulates a Bernoulli process with $\pi = 0.9$. The results are reported in Exhibit 10.2E. For this particular sequence, 57 successes occurred, so the sample proportion of successes is $57/60 = 0.95$. Furthermore, the standard deviation for this data set is 0.2198, which is even smaller than in the previous two examples. How theory supports these means and standard deviations is discussed in Section 10.7.

One concrete way of picturing a Bernoulli process is to consider a box that contains slips of paper, as in Exhibit 10.2F. A fraction π of the slips have a 1 on them, corresponding to success, and the remaining slips have a 0 on them. For the first trial a slip is selected from the box at random; that is, all the slips have an equal chance of being selected. The trial is recorded either as a success or a failure and the slip is returned to the box and thoroughly remixed with the other slips. For the second,

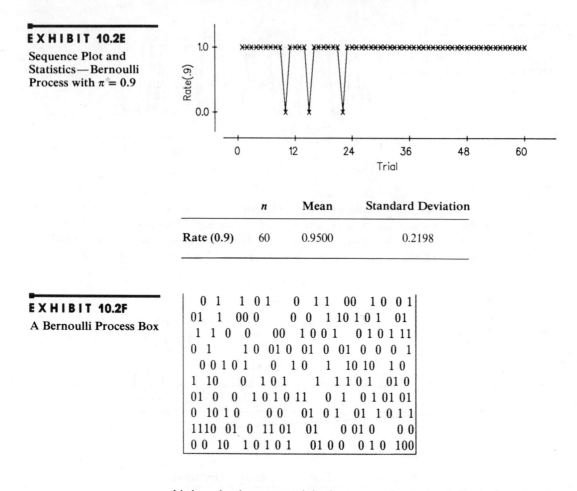

	n	Mean	Standard Deviation
Rate (0.9)	60	0.9500	0.2198

```
 0  1    1 0 1    0   11   00   10  0 1
01  1   00 0      0  0  1 10 1 0 1   01
 1  1 0  0     00  1 0 0 1    0 1 0 1 11
 0  1     1 0  01 0  01  0 01  0 0  0  1
   0 0 1 0 1    0   1 0   1   10 10   1 0
 1 10    0  1 0 1    1   1 1 0 1   01 0
01  0  0  1 0 1 0 11    0  1   0 1 01 01
 0  10 1 0     0 0    01  0 1  01  1 0 1 1
1110  01  0  11 01   01    0 01 0    0 0
 0 0  10   1 0 1 0 1    01 0 0  0 1 0  100
```

third, and subsequent trials the process is repeated. Each time the chosen slip is returned to the box and the slips are mixed thoroughly before the next selection is made. Repeating this procedure for n trials produces a process that satisfies the Bernoulli assumptions.

Whether the assumptions for a Bernoulli process are reasonable or not in real situations depends on the details of the particular situation. Suppose, for example, that households are being surveyed with regard to their television viewing habits. In particular, the survey is interested in whether household members are viewing NBC. If the survey is taken over the day from 8:00 A.M. to 11:00 P.M., then it does not seem reasonable to assume a constant probability of success. The chance of viewing NBC may very well vary over the day, and the success rate, π, could not be assumed to be constant.

As a second example, suppose that a manufacturing process is being observed and conforming and nonconforming product produced is being recorded. If every time a nonconforming item is found the machinery is readjusted, then independence of the trials would be in doubt. Knowledge that a nonconforming item had just been produced would affect the assessment of whether or not a nonconforming item would be produced next; that is, the trials are not independent.

SECTION 10.3

EXERCISES

10.3A The following Minitab commands could be used to produce Exhibit 10.2C.

> RANDOM 60 observations into C1;
> BERNOULLI with rate .5.
> HEIGHT 5 lines
> TSPLOT the series in C1

(a) Use a computer package to produce a similar Bernoulli sequence. Compute the mean and standard deviations of the sequences and note the similarities and dissimilarities between our results and yours.

(b) Repeat part (a) and again note the similarities and dissimilarities.

(c) Repeat part (a) using other success rates, both low and high.

10.3B Simulate 30 Bernoulli trials by tossing a coin and recording the sequence of heads and tails obtained. How many heads did you obtain? What fraction of heads? How many heads did you expect to get?

SECTION 10.4

THE BINOMIAL DISTRIBUTION

Suppose that a fixed number of trials n are under consideration. Let π denote the long-run proportion of successes and let p be the proportion of successes in the n trials. Also let y denote the total number of successes recorded in the n trials. Clearly both p and y will vary from sample to sample, and each of their distributions can be considered. Since $p = y/n$, it will be easy to relate facts about one variable to facts about the other one.

Consider $n = 12$ and $\pi = 0.83$. What total number of successes should be expected? With 12 trials it is possible to get a failure on each trial, giving 0 successes. It is also possible for all trials to produce a success, giving 12 successes. All totals from 0 through 12 are possible, but what is the probability that each of these totals occurs? Simulation can be used to answer this question. Exhibit 10.4A shows a portion of the data generated according to the rules for Bernoulli trials with $\pi = 0.83$. Each row corresponds to 12 trials; row totals are also shown. This sequence of 12 trials was repeated 1000 times so that the distribution of totals could be considered. Exhibit 10.4B shows the histogram of the 1000 totals. Notice that although totals of 0, 1, 2, 3, and 4 are *possible*, they never did occur in the 1000 repetitions of the simulation. Fortunately, not every such situation must be simulated: there is a theoretical model that gives the required distribution in general.

The **binomial probability function** gives the probability that the total number of successes y will take on the value k. If k is an integer value between 0 and n, then the probability of k successes is given by

$$Pr(k \text{ successes}) = \frac{n!}{k!(n-k)!}\pi^k(1-\pi)^{n-k}$$

	Row													Total

EXHIBIT 10.4A

A Simulated Bernoulli Trials and Totals with $n = 12$ and $\pi = 0.83$

Row													Total
1	1	1	1	1	1	1	1	0	1	0	1	0	9
2	1	0	1	1	0	1	1	1	1	1	0	1	9
3	1	1	0	1	1	1	1	1	1	1	1	0	10
4	1	1	1	1	1	1	1	1	1	1	1	1	12
5	1	1	1	1	1	1	1	0	1	0	1	1	10
6	1	0	1	0	1	0	1	1	1	1	1	1	9
7	1	1	0	1	0	1	1	1	1	1	1	1	10
8	1	0	1	1	0	1	1	1	1	1	1	1	10
9	1	1	1	0	1	1	1	1	1	0	0	1	9
10	1	1	1	1	1	1	1	1	1	1	1	1	12
11	1	1	1	0	1	1	1	0	1	1	0	1	9
12	1	0	1	1	1	1	1	1	1	1	0	1	10
13	1	1	1	1	0	1	1	1	1	1	1	1	11
14	1	1	1	0	1	1	1	1	1	0	1	1	10
⋮													⋮
994	1	0	1	1	1	1	0	1	1	0	0	1	8
995	1	1	1	1	1	1	1	0	1	1	1	1	11
996	1	1	1	1	0	0	1	1	1	1	0	1	9
997	1	1	1	1	1	1	1	1	0	1	0	1	10
998	1	0	1	1	1	0	0	0	1	0	0	1	6
999	1	1	1	1	1	1	1	0	1	1	1	1	11
1000	1	1	0	1	1	1	1	1	1	1	1	1	11

EXHIBIT 10.4B

Histogram of 1000 Totals from 12 Bernoulli Trials with $\pi = 0.83$

```
Histogram of Total,  N=1000
Each * represents 10 observations

Midpoint    Count
   5          2    *
   6          4    *
   7         32    ****
   8         80    ********
   9        200    ********************
  10        305    *******************************
  11        276    ****************************
  12        101    **********
```

Recall that factorials are defined for any integer m by the product

$$m! = m(m - 1)(m - 2)\cdots(3)(2)(1)$$

For example, in dealing with $n = 12$ trials suppose that we need to evaluate the chance of observing exactly 10 successes when $\pi = 0.83$ is the long-run fraction of successes. First work out

$$\frac{12!}{10!(12 - 10)!} = \frac{12 \times 11 \times 10 \times 9 \times 8 \times \cdots \times 2 \times 1}{10 \times 9 \times 8 \times \cdots \times 3 \times 2 \times 1 \times 2 \times 1} = \frac{12 \times 11}{2} = 66$$

(In fact there are 66 different sequences of 12 trials, each of which contains exactly 10 successes.) The probability required is then given by

$$66(0.83)^{10}(1 - 0.83)^{12 - 10} = 66(0.83)^{10}(0.17)^2 = 66(0.155156)(0.0289) = 0.296$$

or approximately 30%. If 12 Bernoulli trials with $\pi = 0.83$ were repeated many times, in about 30% of the cases exactly 10 successes would be observed. In our simulation 305 totals of 10 successes were observed.

Most calculators and statistical software can compute any required binomial probability with ease. Exhibit 10.4C shows the results of certain Minitab calculations for both an individual binomial probability and for a whole table of probabilities. Comparing these probabilities with the simulation proportions observed in Exhibit 10.4B, we see that the theoretical model describes the overall situation very well.

EXHIBIT 10.4C

Minitab Results with the Binomial Probability Function with $n = 12$ and $\pi = 0.83$

k	$Pr(y = k)$	
10	0.2960	←This agrees with our hand calculation.

k	$Pr(y = k)$	
0	0.000001	
1	0.000001	
2	0.000001	
3	0.000015	
4	0.000164	
5	0.001280	
6	0.007292	
7	0.030515	
8	0.093116	
9	0.202056	
10	0.295953	←This also agrees with our hand calculation.
11	0.262718	
12	0.106890	

Exhibit 10.4D displays a plot of the full binomial probability function when $n = 12$ and $\pi = 0.83$.

Now consider the distribution of the sample proportion p. For a given number of trials n, the collection of possible values for p is $0 = 0/n, 1/n, 2/n, \ldots, (n-1)/n$, $n/n = 1$. Furthermore, a sample proportion of y/n occurs only when the total number of successes is y. Thus the chance that a proportion y/n occurs is exactly the chance that y successes occur. The binomial probability function gives these probabilities.

For example, the chance that in 12 Bernoulli trials with $\pi = 0.83$ a sample proportion of $10/12 = 0.83333$ is observed is the same as the chance of 10 successes, namely, 0.2960, as shown in Exhibit 10.4C. The full distribution for p can then be obtained by editing the values in Exhibit 10.4C. Exhibit 10.4E shows the results and Exhibit 10.4F plots the resulting distribution.

The binomial distribution can also arise in situations involving metric variables where it is not immediately expected. Suppose a process consists of measuring a metric variable, x, such as length, time, or weight. However, the product being

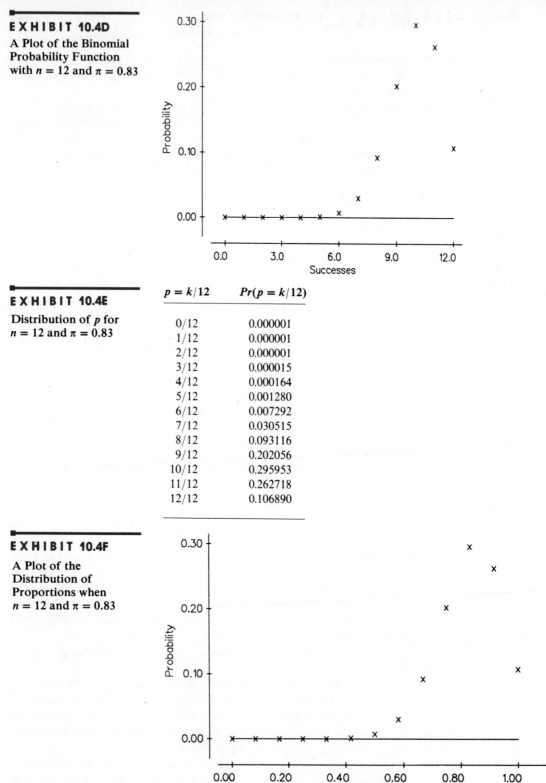

EXHIBIT 10.4D

A Plot of the Binomial Probability Function with $n = 12$ and $\pi = 0.83$

EXHIBIT 10.4E

Distribution of p for $n = 12$ and $\pi = 0.83$

$p = k/12$	$Pr(p = k/12)$
0/12	0.000001
1/12	0.000001
2/12	0.000001
3/12	0.000015
4/12	0.000164
5/12	0.001280
6/12	0.007292
7/12	0.030515
8/12	0.093116
9/12	0.202056
10/12	0.295953
11/12	0.262718
12/12	0.106890

EXHIBIT 10.4F

A Plot of the Distribution of Proportions when $n = 12$ and $\pi = 0.83$

measured is considered "acceptable" only if x lies in the range from a to b. Suppose that when the process is in control the distribution of x is such that the probability is 0.99 that x will lie in the interval $[a, b]$. If n independent values of x are observed and y = the total number of "unacceptable" products is computed, then y will have a binomial distribution with n trials and "success" rate $\pi = 0.01$. Note that the distribution of x is not binomial—it might be a normal distribution, for example. More generally, we might measure several metric variables but count whether or not their sum falls in a specified range. The number of sums falling into the specified range has a binomial distribution.

SECTION 10.5

EXERCISES

10.5A In five Bernoulli trials with success rate 0.5,
  (a) what is the chance of observing exactly two successes?
  (b) what is the chance of observing no successes?
  (c) what number of successes is most likely?

10.5B If $n = 5$ and $\pi = 0.3$, compare $Pr(1 \le y \le 3)$ with $Pr(1 < y < 3)$.
  (a) what is the chance of observing exactly two successes?
  (b) what is the chance of observing no successes?
  (c) what number of successes is most likely?

10.5C If $n = 5$ and $\pi = 0.3$, compare $Pr(1 \le y \le 3)$ with $Pr(1 < y < 3)$.

10.5D A firm maintains 22 cars for business purposes. From past experience it is known that approximately 10% will require major engine service during a one-year period.
  (a) What is the probability that exactly one car will require major engine repair next year?
  (b) Are the Bernoulli trial assumptions reasonable here?

10.5E Use a statistical computer package to create a graph of the binomial probability function for a variety of values of n and π. Comment on the different shapes obtained.

10.5F **(a)** For $n = 7$, compare the binomial probability functions when $\pi = 0.2$ and when $\pi = 0.8$. Do you see any similarities? You may make the comparison either numerically or algebraically.
  (b) Can you generalize this to other n and other pairs of values for π?

10.5G If a balanced coin is tossed five times, what is the chance that the proportion of heads observed is 0.4? Is 0.5? Is less than 0.1?

SECTION 10.6

RUNS (OPTIONAL)

The word *run* is used here in the sense of "a run of good luck," to extend in time, or to continue. Within the context of Bernoulli trials, a *success run* of length k is a sequence of k consecutive successes preceded and followed by at least one failure. The chance of k successes in a row is just π^k. For example, for a fair coin with $\pi = 0.5$, the probability of four heads in a row is $(0.5)^4 = 1/16 = 0.0625$, and the chance of eight consecutive heads is just $(0.5)^8 = 1/256 \simeq 0.004$.

The theory of runs may be applied to control charts to provide useful supplementary rules that indicate an out-of-control situation. In process analysis, where a sequence of means is considered, it is common to look for runs above or below the center line. Since when the process is in control the means are distributed approximately symmetrically about that center line, a value of $\pi = 0.5$ may be used to evaluate the chance of occurrence of various run lengths. Unusually long runs above or below the center line are strong indicators of an out-of-control process. Since runs all along the sequence are being searched for, probability calculations associated with runs are more difficult than those for the binomial distribution. In particular, the chance of observing runs of a given length will also depend on the length of the sequence searched. For sequence lengths in common use for control charts, Mosteller[†] has shown that the following rule provides good protection against tampering with a process that is in control while still offering evidence that the process mean has changed:

■ A run of eight consecutive subgroup means above or below the center line indicates an out-of-control process.

■**EXAMPLE 10.6A:** In Exercise 9.9A a Procter & Gamble process that involved packaging a hair conditioner was introduced. In particular, the tightness of the cap was of concern. The original process was deemed to be in control but not up to specifications. The most likely source of variation was suspected to be the gripper pads that hold the cap during the tightening. The pads were then redesigned to better conform to the grippable surface. The pad material was also changed. A material that had been found to work well in a similar application was used. After these changes the process was again run. The control chart data obtained are given in Exhibit 10.6A.

EXHIBIT 10.6A

A Cap Tightness from Procter & Gamble Hair Conditioner Line

```
# filename: P&G2.DAT
# P&G second data set
# (Source: Jeffrey Enck, Procter & Gamble,
# Iowa City, Iowa)
# Torque on hair conditioner caps after process improvement
  24 14 18 27
  17 32 31 27
  21 27 24 21
  24 26 31 34
  28 32 24 16
  22 37 36 21
  16 17 22 34
  20 19 16 16
  18 30 21 16
  14 15 14 14
  25 15 16 15
  19 15 15 19
  19 30 24 10
  15 17 17 21
  34 22 17 15
  17 20 17 20
  15 17 24 20
```

[†] Fredrick Mosteller, "Note on an Application of Runs to Quality Control Charts," *Annals of Mathematical Statistics* 12 (1941): 228–232.

The standard deviation chart (not shown) gives no indication of an out-of-control situation. However, the mean chart in Exhibit 10.6B does show some unusual behavior. For the first half of the sequence the means are nearly always above the center line; in the last half the tendency is for the means to stay below the center line. Could this be caused by a downward shift in the process mean half-way through? Although such a suspicion is warranted, the data do not provide conclusive evidence that the mean has changed. The initial long run above the center line is of length 6, while the long run below the center line is of length 7. There are no runs of length 8, so special causes of variation are ruled out. In addition, the process improvements have been effective. The fraction of product not meeting specifications of 15 to 40 foot-pounds has been reduced considerably compared with the situation shown in Exercise 9.9A. The company continued to investigate the causes of variation in the capping process with the goal of further stability and reduced variation. Control charts continue to alert them to potential problems and to document process improvements.

EXHIBIT 10.6B

Mean Chart for Cap Tightness

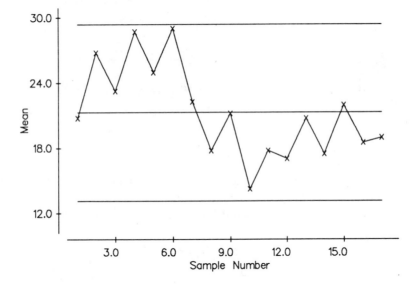

SECTION 10.7

THE MEAN AND STANDARD DEVIATION

In Chapter 8 μ was called the mean of the normal curve, and it was interpreted as a measure of the middle of a distribution. How should the mean of the binomial distribution be defined?

THE MEAN

Consider a particular binomial situation with n trials and success probability π. Repeat this same binomial experiment a large number of times, say m times. Each time the experiment is performed a certain number of successes is observed. Let y_i denote the number of successes in the ith experiment. The data can be laid out as follows:

Experiment Number	Number of Successes Observed
1	y_1
2	y_2
3	y_3
$\vdots$	$\vdots$
m	y_m

Suppose the results of the m experiments were tallied. Each of the y's is either a 0, a 1, a 2,..., or an n. Let $\#(y)$ denote the number of times that the particular value y was observed in the m experiments. Then by grouping the 0's, 1's, 2's,..., together, the mean number of successes can be written as

$$\text{Mean} = \frac{y_1 + y_2 + \cdots + y_m}{m}$$

$$= \frac{[0 \times \#(0)] + [1 \times \#(1)] + \cdots + [n \times \#(n)]}{m}$$

$$= \left[0 \times \frac{\#(0)}{m} \right] + \left[1 \times \frac{\#(1)}{m} \right] + \cdots + \left[n \times \frac{\#(n)}{m} \right]$$

But if m is large, the long run, then the fractions $\#(y)/m$ will be close to the long-run fraction or probability of observing exactly y successes. Thus after repeating the binomial experiment a large number of times, the mean number of successes should be close to

$$0 \times Pr(0 \text{ successes}) + 1 \times Pr(1 \text{ success})$$

$$+ 2 \times Pr(2 \text{ successes}) + \cdots + n \times Pr(n \text{ successes})$$

This defines μ_y, the (theoretical) mean of the binomial distribution. This is also called the mean of y.

Obviously this could amount to a lot of computation! Let the computer calculate the mean in a few cases. Exhibit 10.7A shows the results for the cases ($n = 6, \pi = 0.5$), ($n = 12, \pi = 0.25$), and ($n = 15, \pi = 0.5$). Notice that in each case the mean is numerically equal to $n\pi$ (apart from rounding). This is not just a coincidence. It may be established using mathematical statistics that for a binomial distribution with n trials and success probability π, the mean of the distribution is always equal to

$$\mu_y = n\pi$$

	n = 6, π = .5		n = 12, π = .25		n = 15, π = .5	
k	Probability	Product	Probability	Product	Probability	Product
0	0.015625	0.00000	0.031676	0.000000	0.000031	0.00000
1	0.093750	0.09375	0.126705	0.126705	0.000458	0.00046
2	0.234375	0.46875	0.232293	0.464586	0.003204	0.00641
3	0.312500	0.93750	0.258104	0.774311	0.013885	0.04166
4	0.234375	0.93750	0.193578	0.774311	0.041656	0.16663
5	0.093750	0.46875	0.103241	0.516207	0.091644	0.45822
6	0.015625	0.09375	0.040149	0.240897	0.152740	0.91644
7			0.011471	0.080299	0.196381	1.37466
8			0.002390	0.019119	0.196381	1.57104
9			0.000354	0.003186	0.152740	1.37466
10			0.000035	0.000354	0.091644	0.91644
11			0.000002	0.000024	0.041656	0.45822
12			0.000001	0.000012	0.013885	0.16663
13					0.003204	0.04166
14					0.000458	0.00641
15					0.000031	0.00046
	Total	3.00000		3.000001		7.50000

EXHIBIT 10.7A

The Mean of the Binomial Distribution

Note: k = Number of successes
Probability = Pr(k successes)
Product = k × Pr(k successes)

THE STANDARD DEVIATION

Using a similar motivation, the (theoretical) standard deviation of the binomial distribution can be defined as

$$\text{Standard deviation} = [(0 - n\pi)^2 \times Pr(0 \text{ successes}) + (1 - n\pi)^2 \times Pr(1 \text{ success})$$
$$+ (2 - n\pi)^2 \times Pr(2 \text{ successes}) + \cdots + (n - n\pi)^2$$
$$\times Pr(n \text{ successes})]^{1/2}$$

or $$\text{Standard deviation} = \sigma_y = \sqrt{\sum_{k=0}^{n} [(k - n\pi)^2 \times Pr(k \text{ successes})]}$$

Again theory can be used to show that for a binomial distribution the standard deviation is given by

$$\sigma_y = \sqrt{n\pi(1 - \pi)}$$

For example, for a binomial distribution with $n = 12$ and $\pi = 0.83$, the standard deviation is

$$\sigma_y = \sqrt{12 \times 0.83 \times (1 - 0.83)} = \sqrt{1.6932} = 1.30$$

and the mean is $\mu_y = 12 \times 0.83 = 9.96$.

Exhibit 10.7B shows a plot of $\sqrt{\pi(1 - \pi)}$ as a function of π over the range zero to one. Notice that the curve is symmetric around $\pi = 0.5$. Also notice that the curve has its largest value of 0.5 for $\pi = 0.5$ and decreases as π moves away from 0.5 in either direction. Thus a binomial distribution has its largest variability when $\pi = 0.5$. The variability decreases as π moves away from 0.5 in either direction. These facts help explain the observed standard deviations that were obtained in Exhibits 10.2A, 10.2D, and 10.2E for several different values of π.

EXHIBIT 10.7B
The Curve $\sqrt{\pi(1 - \pi)}$

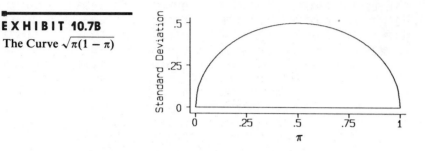

PROPORTIONS

The sample proportion $p = y/n$ is also of interest in analyzing Bernoulli trials. We have already seen how to find its distribution from the binomial distribution. Using facts about linear transformations analogous to those discussed in Section 4.6, the mean of the distribution of p is

$$\mu_p = \pi$$

and the standard deviation of that distribution is

$$\sigma_p = \sqrt{\frac{\pi(1 - \pi)}{n}}$$

With $n = 12$ and $\pi = 0.83$, the mean of p is $\mu_p = 0.83$ and the standard deviation of p is

$$\sigma_p = \sqrt{\frac{0.83(1 - 0.83)}{12}} = \sqrt{0.01175833} = 0.1084$$

SECTION 10.8

EXERCISES

10.8A Use a statistical package as in Exhibit 10.7A to compute the probabilities for various binomial distributions. Evaluate the standard deviation of the distributions numerically from the definition and show that the theoretical formula $\sigma_y = \sqrt{n\pi(1 - \pi)}$ gives the correct answer in these cases.

10.8B Repeat Exercise 10.8A but using the distribution for p and verify numerically that $\sigma_p = \sqrt{\pi(1 - \pi)/n}$.

10.8C If five items are observed at random on a production line where about 5% of the items on average are defective, what are the mean and standard deviation of the proportion of defective items observed? For the number of defectives observed?

10.8D Use a statistical package to simulate a large number (maybe 1000) of binomial variables with $n = 12$ and $\pi = 0.4$. Store the simulated values for use in parts (a) and (b).

(a) Plot a histogram of the simulated values and compare it to the corresponding exact binomial distribution.

(b) Calculate the mean and standard deviation of the simulated values and compare them to the known theoretical values.

10.8E (Calculus required) Show that for π between 0 and 1, $\sqrt{\pi(1 - \pi)}$ increases to a maximum value of 0.5 at $\pi = 0.5$ and then decreases. (*Hint:* Consider $[\sqrt{\pi(1 - \pi)}]^2 = \pi(1 - \pi) = \pi - \pi^2$, differentiate with respect to π, set equal to zero, and solve.)

SECTION 10.9

THE NORMAL APPROXIMATION

Exhibits 10.9A, 10.9B, and 10.9C display a variety of binomial distributions in density histogram form. Only the outer contours of the density histogram are shown to facilitate comparison with a normal curve. The rectangles in the histogram are centered on the values for the number of successes, $0, 1, \ldots, n$, and each rectangle has width one and height equal to the corresponding binomial probability given in Section 10.4. Since the rectangles have width one their *areas* are the probabilities associated with each of the values $0, 1, \ldots, n$. These areas can be compared to areas under a normal curve with the same mean and standard deviation. According to the plots these areas are very nearly the same. As the next paragraph argues, this is no fluke but a consequence of the central limit effect.

Consider n Bernoulli trials with success rate π. The total number of successes y can be thought of as the sum $y_1 + y_2 + \cdots + y_n$ where y_i is a binary variable equal to 1 if the ith trial results in a success and $y_i = 0$ otherwise. In other words, y_i is the

EXHIBIT 10.9A

Binomial Distribution with $n = 20$ and $\pi = 0.5$ (normal distribution overlayed)

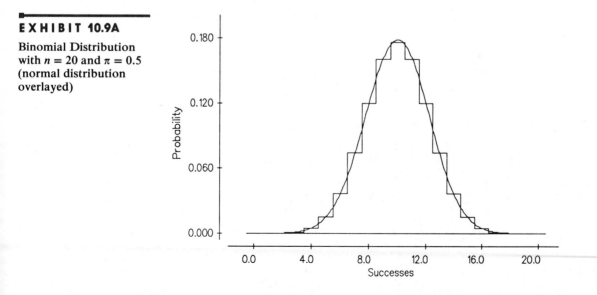

EXHIBIT 10.9B

Binomial Distribution
with $n = 50$ and $\pi = 0.1$
(normal distribution
overlayed)

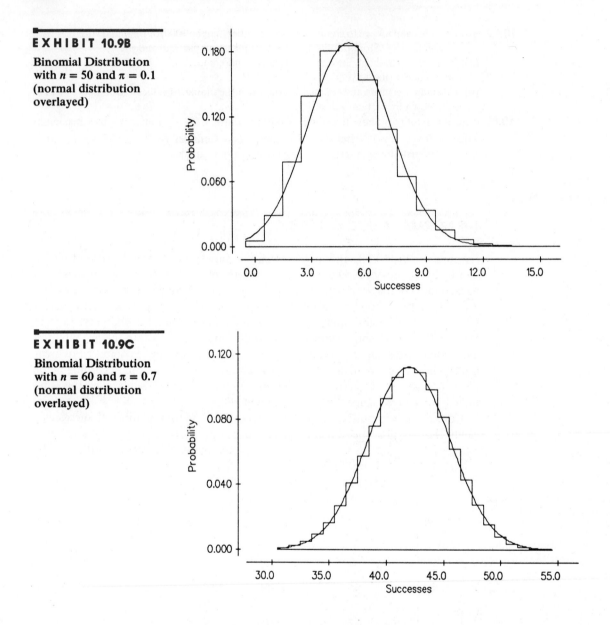

EXHIBIT 10.9C

Binomial Distribution
with $n = 60$ and $\pi = 0.7$
(normal distribution
overlayed)

number of successes on the ith trial. Furthermore, the sample proportion of successes can be expressed as

$$p = \frac{y}{n} = \frac{y_1 + y_2 + \cdots + y_n}{n} = \bar{y}$$

For example, if $n = 5$ and the sequence SFFSF is observed, then $y_1 = 1$, $y_2 = 0$, $y_3 = 0$, $y_4 = 1$, $y_5 = 0$, and $p = \bar{y} = (1 + 0 + 0 + 1 + 0)/5 = 2/5 = 0.4$. The point here is that p is in fact an average, and as such the central limit effect of Section 8.5 applies if n is reasonably large. In this case the process being sampled is the process of the 1's and 0's which has mean π and standard deviation $\sigma = \sqrt{\pi(1-\pi)}$. Thus

$$\sigma_p = \frac{\sigma}{\sqrt{n}} = \frac{\sqrt{\pi(1-\pi)}}{\sqrt{n}} = \sqrt{\frac{\pi(1-\pi)}{n}}$$

and the following rule can be stated:

> *Normal approximation to the distribution of the proportion p: For large n the distribution of p is approximately a normal distribution with mean $\mu_p = \pi$ and standard deviation*
>
> $$\sigma_p = \sqrt{\frac{\pi(1-\pi)}{n}}$$

■**EXAMPLE 10.9A:** Consider a bank loan officer who is interested in investigating missing information on loan applications. Suppose that a random set of 25 loan applications is examined for missing information. A "success" here means that the loan application in question has missing information. From past experience the loan officer knows that about 30% of all applications have information missing. Under these circumstances, what is the chance that the sample contains at most 20% successes, that is, $Pr(p \le 0.2)$? To do the approximation the mean $\mu_p = 0.3$ and the standard deviation $\sigma_p = \sqrt{0.3(1-0.3)/25} = 0.09165$ are needed. The corresponding z-value is $(0.2 - 0.3)/0.09165 = -1.09111$. From Exhibit 8.3G (the normal distribution table), the area below -1.09 is found to be 0.1379. Thus the chance is about 14%.

With computer software this probability can be obtained exactly. Since $n = 25$, $p \le 0.2$ is equivalent to $y \le 25 \times 0.2 = 5$. The probabilities of 0, 1, 2, 3, 4, or 5 successes are added. Exhibit 10.9D gives the probabilities. Adding them yields the

EXHIBIT 10.9D

The Binomial
Probability Function for
$n = 25$ and $\pi = 0.3$

k	$Pr(y = k)$
0	0.0001
1	0.0014
2	0.0074
3	0.0243
4	0.0572
5	0.1030
6	0.1472
7	0.1712
8	0.1651
9	0.1336
10	0.0916
11	0.0536
12	0.0268
13	0.0115
14	0.0042
15	0.0013
16	0.0004
17	0.0001
18	0.0000

exact result $0.0001 + 0.0014 + \cdots + 0.1030 = 0.1934$, or about 19% compared to the normal approximation value of 14%. The normal approximation can actually be improved a bit, as will be shown in "The Continuity Correction" section that follows.

The computer can add the binomial probabilities. This is precisely what the *cumulative distribution function (CDF)* does. The CDF is the probability of k or fewer successes. Exhibit 10.9E displays the answer needed in the loan application problem. (The slight difference between this answer of 0.1935 and the previous one of 0.1934 is due to the fact that rounded probabilities from Exhibit 10.9D were added, but the computer keeps many more digits in its internal calculations to obtain the result in Exhibit 10.9E.)

EXHIBIT 10.9E

The CDF for the Binomial Distribution with $n = 25$, $\pi = 0.3$, and $k = 5$

k	$Pr(y \text{ less or} = k)$	
5	0.1935	←Already accumulated.

■

THE CONTINUITY CORRECTION

Since $p = y/n$, the normal approximation may alternatively be stated in terms of y: For large n, the binomial distribution is approximately a normal distribution with mean $= n\pi$ and standard deviation $= \sqrt{n\pi(1 - \pi)}$.

For the case $n = 25$ and $\pi = 0.3$, the two distributions are displayed in Exhibit 10.9F. The complete normal curve and the outline of a bar chart for the binomial probabilities have been drawn. Since the width of the bars is one, the binomial probabilities can be thought of as areas under the bars and compared directly to the areas under the approximating normal curve.

EXHIBIT 10.9F

Normal Approximation to the Binomial with $n = 25$, $\pi = 0.3$

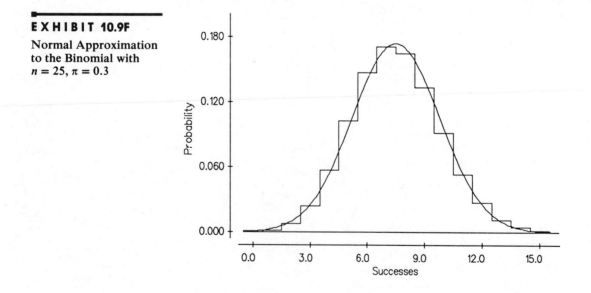

Once we are thinking in terms of areas representing probabilities, it is natural to approximate the probability of five or fewer successes by the area under the normal curve below 5.5 (rather than 5). This is called the *correction for continuity*.

Using the correction for continuity, the new approximation can be obtained using either statistical software or the normal distribution table in Exhibit 8.3G with the z-value $(5.5 - 7.5)/2.2913 = -0.879$. Either way the probability is about 19% when rounded. This agrees exactly with the correct result.

Suppose we need to approximate the chance of getting at least 7 successes but no more than 10, again with $n = 25$ and $\pi = 0.3$. Using the continuity correction the area under the appropriate normal curve from 6.5 to 10.5 is found. With z-values of $(6.5 - 7.5)/2.2913 = -0.44$ and $(10.5 - 7.5)/2.2913 = 1.31$, respectively, the probability $0.9049 - 0.3300 = 0.5749$ is obtained from the normal distribution table. Ignoring the continuity correction would lead to the approximation $Pr(7 \leq y \leq 10) \simeq Pr(-0.22 \leq z \leq 1.09) = 0.4492$. The exact value obtained by adding the values at 7, 8, 9, and 10 from Exhibit 10.9D is 0.5615, and we again see the value of the continuity correction in the normal approximation.

As a final calculation in this example we approximate the probability of exactly nine successes. Notice that without using the continuity correction the approximation would give zero as the answer and would be worthless! With the correction, $Pr(y = 9) = Pr(8.5 \leq y \leq 9.5) \simeq Pr(0.44 \leq z \leq 0.87) \, 0.8078 - 0.6700 = 0.1378$ compared with the exact value from Exhibit 10.9D of 0.1336.

■**EXAMPLE 10.9B:** Suppose that in a marketing process the dollar amount of weekly sales of razor blades in the Midwest is measured. For this stable, nonseasonal product experience has shown that weekly sales are well approximated by a normal distribution with mean $1500 and standard deviation $350. If in any week sales drop below $1000 the company has a policy of looking carefully at market conditions to assess its competitive position. Otherwise the process continues to run without any special intervention or unusual inspection. Supposing that weekly sales amounts are determined independently of each other, what can be said about the number of times the company will go looking for problems when none in fact exist? That is, if the process continues to operate without substantial change, how many "false alarms" might be observed in n weeks using this policy?

Consider a 26-week period. For each week sales either exceed $1000 or they dip below $1000. If y denotes the total number of weeks in which sales go below $1000, then, under our assumptions, y will have a binomial distribution with $n = 26$ trials. The "success" rate will be determined as the chance that a normal variable with mean $1500 and standard deviation $350 falls below $1000. The corresponding z-score is $(1000 - 1500)/350 = -1.43$, and from the normal distribution table in Exhibit 8.3G, $\pi = (1 - 0.9236) = 0.0764$. The mean number of false alarms is then $26 \times 0.0764 = 1.9864$ or about two, and the standard deviation of the number of false alarms is

$$\sqrt{26 \times 0.0764 \times (1 - 0.0764)} = \sqrt{1.8346} = 1.35$$

What is the chance of having two *or more* false alarms in the 26-week period? This is most easily obtained by calculating the chance of 0 or 1 false alarms and subtracting the result from 1. Using the binomial distribution,

$$Pr(0 \text{ successes}) + Pr(1 \text{ success}) = \frac{26!}{0!26!}(0.0764)^0(1 - 0.0764)^{26}$$

$$+ \frac{26!}{1!25!}(0.0764)^1(1 - 0.0764)^{25}$$

$$= 0.1266 + 0.2724 = 0.3990$$

Thus the chance of two or more false alarms in 26 weeks is $1 - 0.399 = 0.601$, or about 60%.

Now approximate this probability with the normal approximation. Using the continuity correction, $Pr(2 \le y) = Pr(1.5 \le y) \simeq Pr[(1.5 - 1.9864)/1.35 \le z] = Pr(-0.36 \le z) = 0.6406$. It is generally agreed that the normal approximation to the binomial distribution will be reasonably accurate if both $n\pi \ge 5$ and $n(1 - \pi) \ge 5$ are satisfied. These inequalities are *not* both satisfied in this example and the approximation could be considered marginally accurate.

Of course the normal approximation and the continuity correction are both of interest only if a statistical computing package is not readily available to do the exact binomial calculations. ▪

SECTION 10.10

EXERCISES

10.10A Consider 25 Bernoulli trials with $\pi = .3$, as in Exhibits 10.10D, 10.10E, and 10.10F.
   (a) Find the exact probability of between 5 and 11 successes inclusive.
   (b) Use the normal approximation without the continuity correction to approximate the probability found in part (a).
   (c) Use the normal approximation *with* the continuity correction to approximate the probability found in part (a) and compare your result to those found in parts (a) and (b).

10.10B If a balanced coin is tossed 50 times, approximate the chance that it comes up heads exactly 25 times. Compare this to the correct binomial value.

10.10C If a production line produces 10% nonconforming items on average and a random set of 100 items is inspected, estimate the chance that more than 20 of the items are nonconforming. Use computer software to compare the approximation with the correct binomial value.

SECTION 10.11

TESTING HYPOTHESES ABOUT π (OPTIONAL)

STATISTICAL HYPOTHESES

We are frequently faced with a process that is quite reasonably modelled as a Bernoulli process but the success probability π is rarely a known number. The π can certainly be estimated using the process proportion p and the accuracy of this estimate can be assessed through the distribution of p, subjects that have been thoroughly discussed earlier in the chapter. However, in some settings a "theory" or perhaps past experience suggests a value for π. For example, a *fair* coin should have $\pi = 1/2$ for heads (or tails) and a *well-balanced* die should have $\pi = 1/6$ for any particular face. In other situations, a range of values may be claimed for the true value of π. For example, a politician may claim that a certain position is held by a majority of her constituents ($\pi > 0.5$) or a company may claim that adults aged 18 to 25 prefer its product to its competitors' ($\pi > 0.5$). For example, the long-run market share for a particular product has been 20% ($\pi = 0.20$). Once a new advertising program is initiated the firm hopes the data will show that $\pi > 0.20$.

In a general Bernoulli setting, a *statistical hypothesis* is a statement about the value of π. The goal of *testing* statistical hypotheses is to determine if the data from the Bernoulli process support the statistical hypothesis postulated.

THE NULL AND ALTERNATIVE HYPOTHESES

Any discussion of hypothesis testing involves the introduction of many new concepts. Instead of presenting the ideas in general terms, we introduce them using a specific example. This quote is from an article in the April 1978 issue of *Consumer Reports*, "Let it be Lowenbrau—American Style":

> *What do you get when you pay a premium for a beer with a grand old European name? We got wind of the controversy involving* Lowenbrau, *a beer that originated in Germany but is now also brewed in the United States under license by Miller Brewing Co.*
>
> *One element of the controversy surfaced when Anheuser-Busch Inc.—brewers of an admittedly domestic premium beer,* Michelob—*asked the Federal Trade Commission to investigate Miller for possible "consumer deception." Anheuser-Busch claims, among other things, that* Lowenbrau *made by Miller in the United States is brewed with different ingredients and under a different process than the German beer.*
>
> *Whether that's true or not, there's another interesting comparison to be made. Miller also brews* Miller High Life *beer. An evident difference between Miller's* Lowenbrau *and* Miller High Life *is price. Miller beer with the German name sells for $2.50 a six-pack; Miller beer with the Miller name sells for $1.80. Miller must believe there's a difference between the two to merit the big price difference.*
>
> *To determine whether there is a difference between domestic* Lowenbrau *and* Miller High Life *that would be discernible to the average beer drinker, we assembled a taste-test panel of 24 staffers. Panelists were given three glasses of beer to taste, two of which were from the same bottle, and asked to identify which glass contained the beer that was different.*[†]

In this example the taste tests to be modelled are considered as 24 Bernoulli trials. "Success" corresponds to a correct identification of the different beer. The symbol π denotes the true but unknown proportion of "average beer drinkers" who, under the conditions of the taste test, would correctly choose the different beer. Again quoting from the article:

> *If the panelists were only guessing which of the three glasses of beer was the correct one, they would be expected to get the right answer about one-third of the time, or 8 of the 24.*

[†] Copyright 1978 by Consumers Union of United States, Inc., Mount Vernon, NY 10553. Reprinted by permission from CONSUMER REPORTS, April 1978.

Skeptics, such as the writers at *Consumer Reports*, might hypothesize that $\pi = 1/3$, which corresponds to random guessing. Miller Brewing Company, on the other hand, might claim that $\pi > 1/3$, corresponding to various degrees of discrimination between the two beers. There are two competing claims here: $\pi = 1/3$ versus $\pi > 1/3$. The hypothesis of "no difference" between the two beers, here $\pi = 1/3$, is called the *null hypothesis*. A null hypothesis is usually denoted H_0 and is frequently read as "H-zero" or "H-nought." The hypothesis that competes with the null hypothesis, here $\pi > 1/3$, is called the *alternative hypothesis* and is denoted H_1. A test of a statistical hypothesis is designed to use the observed data to assess the strength of the evidence against the null hypothesis. In a research setting, the null hypothesis of no difference or no effect is frequently set up as a "straw man" with the hope that the empirical evidence will be sufficient to refute the null hypothesis and establish that a real effect does exist.

Before claiming that any statement is established, supporting evidence from the data must be produced. If $\pi = 1/3$, then the mean number of correct identifications is $(1/3)24 = 8$. Again quoting from *Consumer Reports*, "Only 11 of the total of 24 judgments were correct." Is this evidence sufficient to conclude that the tasters are doing better than random guessing? To address this issue further the errors that decision makers face must be discussed.

THE TWO TYPES OF ERRORS

Intuition suggests that the null hypothesis, $H_0: \pi = 1/3$, should be rejected if the number of correct identifications, y, is large enough. A reasonable *decision rule* is to select a critical number of successes y_0 and decide to reject H_0 if and only if $y \geq y_0$. However, whatever the value of π we know that y will have a binomial distribution over all the values $0, 1, \ldots, 24$ and that any of these values *may* occur. When selecting the value for y_0 the errors displayed in the following table must be considered:

	Truth	
Decision	H_0 **true** ($\pi = 1/3$)	H_0 **false** ($\pi > 1/3$)
Do not reject H_0	Correct decision	Type II error
Reject H_0	Type I error	Correct decision

The table displays four possible situations. If $\pi = 1/3$, we may still observe y_0 or more correct identifications. Our decision then is to reject H_0. This is an incorrect decision and is called a **Type I error**. It is also possible that $\pi > 1/3$ but we observe $y < y_0$ and erroneously declare H_0 to be valid. This is called a **Type II error**. A decision reached using any statistical test may be wrong in either of these two ways.[†]

[†] Some statisticians have recently defined a **Type III error** as the error committed when the wrong problem is solved!

TYPE I ERRORS

Standard practice is to select the critical value y_0 so that the probability of a Type I error is "sufficiently small." Sufficiently small is frequently interpreted to mean 0.05 or even 0.01 or smaller. This is the chance of falsely rejecting a true null hypothesis. We are protecting ourselves against making a Type I error very often.

In the beer-tasting example there are $n = 24$ trials and the null hypothesis says that $\pi = 1/3$. We would choose y_0 so that the total probability in a binomial distribution (with $n = 24$ and $\pi = 1/3$) at y_0 and larger values (the right-hand tail probability) is about 0.05. Exhibit 10.11A shows the required individual binomial probabilities and the sums that need to be considered. To keep the probability of a Type I error at or below 0.05, $y_0 = 13$ must be chosen. That is, the decision rule is to reject H_0 if and only if 13 or more correct identifications are observed in the 24 taste tests. With this choice of critical value, Exhibit 10.11A shows that the exact probability of a Type I error is 0.02844. In general, the maximum Type I error probability is called the **significance level** of the test. The significance level is usually denoted by the Greek letter α (alpha).

	y_0	$Pr(y = y_0)$	$Pr(y \geq y_0)$	
EXHIBIT 10.11A	0	0.000059	1.00000	
	1	0.000713	0.99994	
Binomial Probabilities	2	0.004099	0.99923	
with $n = 24$ and $\pi = 1/3$	3	0.015029	0.99513	
	4	0.039451	0.98010	
	5	0.078903	0.94065	
	6	0.124929	0.86175	
	7	0.160623	0.73682	
	8	0.170661	0.57619	
	9	0.151699	0.40553	
	10	0.113774	0.25383	
	11	0.072401	0.14006	
	12	0.039217	0.06766	← Larger than 0.05
	13	0.018100	0.02844	← First y_0 at which tail probability is ≤ 0.05
	14	0.007111	0.01034	
	15	0.002370	0.00323	
	16	0.000667	0.00086	
	17	0.000157	0.00019	
	18	0.000030	0.00004	
	19	0.000005	0.00001	
	20	0.000001	0.00000	
	21	0.000001	0.00000	
	22	0.000001	0.00000	
	23	0.000001	0.00000	
	24	0.000001	0.00000	

Source: Minitab's PDF and CDF commands with the binomial subcommand.

In the beer-tasting example, remember that only 11 of the total of 24 taste test judgments were correct. *Consumer Reports* interpreted this as follows: "Although the 11 correct choices were an improvement over pure guesswork, we don't consider that to be statistically significant evidence that a beer drinker can tell domestic Lowenbrau from Miller High Life." That is, since 11 is less than the critical value of 13, the evidence is considered insufficient to refute the null hypothesis of random guessing.

TYPE II ERRORS

Since the alternative hypothesis $H_1: \pi > 1/3$ specifies a range of values for π, the probability of a Type II error must be calculated for each value of π of interest in that range. Suppose that in fact beer drinkers are very discriminating so that $\pi = 0.90$. The probability of a Type II error is the chance that 12 or fewer successes are observed in a binomial distribution with $n = 24$ and $\pi = 0.90$. Using computer software, this probability is found to be 0.0000. If drinkers are a little less discriminating, say $\pi = 0.80$, then the chance of a Type II error is 0.0010. Exhibit 10.11B shows a small table of Type II error probabilities.

EXHIBIT 10.11B

Probability of a Type II Error

π	0.40	0.50	0.60	0.70	0.80	0.90
Pr(Type II Error)	0.8857	0.7580	0.2130	0.0314	0.0010	0.0000

Notice that if there is a 50-50 chance of discriminating between the beers then the probability of a Type II error is 0.7580—quite large. In general, the closer the particular value of π ($> 1/3$) is to the null value of $1/3$ the more difficult it is to detect from the data that the null hypothesis is false. However, a value of π just a little larger than $1/3$ does not indicate substantial discrimination among beer drinkers, and a Type II error would have little practical significance.

On the other hand, since the probabilities when $\pi \geq .70$ are very small, we are quite confident that in making our decision to retain H_0 we have not committed a serious Type II error. It is not likely that we have failed to detect the fact that beer drinkers can discriminate quite well.

p VALUES

Some statisticians prefer a related but alternative framework for deciding whether or not the evidence provided by the data is sufficient to refute the null hypothesis. If the observed data are unlikely to have occurred under the supposition that the null hypothesis is true and are more likely to have occurred if the alternative hypothesis is true, then the data represent evidence against the null hypothesis and in favor of the alternative hypothesis. In our example, the more successes obtained, the more the evidence points toward discriminating beer drinkers rather than the null hypothesis of random guessing.

In general, the *p* value of a test is the probability of getting an outcome at least as extreme as the outcome actually observed. The *p* value is computed under the assumption that the null hypothesis is true. *Extreme* is determined according to the alternative hypothesis. In the beer-drinking example 11 successes were observed and the alternative hypothesis suggests that more successes would be observed than under the null hypothesis. The smaller the p value, the stronger the evidence against the null hypothesis. Note, however, that the p value is *not* the probability that the null hypothesis is correct.

In our example extreme means 11 *or more* successes. This is called a *one-sided p* value. The p value is computed from a binomial distribution with $n = 24$ and $\pi = 1/3$ and we have (from the computer)

$$p \text{ value} = Pr(11 \text{ or more successes when } \pi = 1/3) = 0.1401$$

or about 14%. As in our earlier test we usually do not feel that the evidence is sufficient to reject the null hypothesis unless the p value is smaller than 5%, or even less. As quoted earlier, "Although the 11 correct choices were an improvement over pure guesswork, we don't consider that to be statistically significant evidence that a beer drinker can tell domestic Lowenbrau from Miller High Life."

If the p value is smaller than the specified significance level α, the evidence is said to be *statistically significant* at level α. The ideas of significance testing in more general settings and in more detail are presented in Chapter 19.

SECTION 10.12

EXERCISES

10.12A A taste test was designed to compare preferences for Coke versus Pepsi. Twenty tasters were assembled and each was presented with two glasses, labelled A and B, one of which contained Coke and the other Pepsi. The glasses were not otherwise identified but their correct identity was known to the people conducting the test. After sipping from each glass the tasters were asked to identify which glass contained the Pepsi. Let π denote the probability that a person correctly chooses the glass of Pepsi.
  (a) A common null hypothesis in such a situation is that the choice is made at random. State this hypothesis in terms of π.
  (b) In words, the alternative hypothesis is that the tasters can choose the glass of Pepsi better than expected with random guessing. Express this alternative hypothesis in terms of π.
  (c) Would you consider it convincing evidence that people can discriminate between Coke and Pepsi if 15 of the 20 tasters correctly identify the Pepsi?
  (d) Based on the data given in part (c), what is the p value of the test?

10.12B Last season an otherwise star basketball player made only 60% of his foul shots. This season he has made 16 of his first 21 foul shot attempts. Do you find this to be statistically significant evidence that his foul shooting has improved over last year?
  (a) What is the null hypothesis?
  (b) With significance level of about 5%, would you reject the null hypothesis on the basis of these data?
  (c) What is the p value for these data?
  (d) If in fact his true long-run foul shooting probability this year is 80%, what is the chance that a rule that rejects the old value of 60% when 17 or more successes of 21 tries are made

will detect the new, improved percentage? That is, what is the chance of *not* making a Type II error using this decision rule when the percentage has improved from 60% to 80%?

10.12C A coin is suspected of being biased toward heads. It is tossed 11 times. The null hypothesis is that the coin is fair. Find the critical value y_0 for the number of heads at or above which fairness should be rejected. Assume a desired significance level of about 5%.

S E C T I O N 10.13

DISCUSSION

Many two-outcome processes may be adequately modelled as sequences of Bernoulli trials. Recall that the assumptions of constant success rate, π, and independence of the trials must be satisfied, at least approximately, to use the theory described in this chapter. Usually we are interested in either the number of successes y or, equivalently, the proportion of successes p in a fixed number of trials n. The distribution of the number of successes is called the binomial distribution and a formula for it is given in Section 10.4. However, statistical software, such as Minitab, allows easy calculation of any binomial probabilities required.

The mean and standard deviation of the binomial distribution were developed in Section 10.6. The mean is

$$\mu_y = n\pi$$

and the standard deviation is

$$\sigma_y = \sqrt{n\pi(1 - \pi)}$$

For the variable p, the sample proportion, the mean is

$$\mu_p = \pi$$

and the standard deviation is

$$\sigma_p = \sqrt{\frac{\pi(1 - \pi)}{n}}$$

For the Bernoulli distribution, the mean is π and the standard deviation is $\sqrt{\pi(1 - \pi)}$.

Recall that the sample proportion p can be thought of as a sample mean from the 0–1 process. Thus the mean of the distribution of p is the same as the mean of the process, and the standard deviation of the distribution of p is the standard deviation of the process divided by the square root of the number of observations n. If n is reasonably large, the binomial distribution may be meaningfully approximated by a normal distribution with the same mean and standard deviation. Better approximations are obtained if the continuity correction is used. The normal approximation loses some of its traditional value when a statistical computer package is used because exact calculations are easily made in many cases.

SECTION 10.14

SUPPLEMENTARY EXERCISES FOR CHAPTER 10

10A The American College Testing Program in Iowa City, Iowa, designs and produces many tests, including the college entrance exam commonly known as the ACT exam. The scores on the ACT exam for incoming freshmen at The University of Iowa are approximately normally distributed with mean 23.2 and standard deviation 3.1.
  (a) What is the chance that a randomly selected freshman has a score exceeding 26?
  (b) If five freshmen are selected randomly, what is the chance that they all have ACT scores exceeding 26?
  (c) If five freshmen are selected randomly, what is the chance that exactly one of them has an ACT score exceeding 26?
  (d) If five freshmen are selected randomly, what is the mean number of them whose ACT scores exceed 26?

10B According to empirical evidence a polygraph lie-detector test will falsely accuse a person of lying about 20% of the time.
  (a) A firm tests four employees using the polygraph. If in fact they all answer truthfully, what is the probability that at least one of them will be declared a liar?
  (b) Repeat part (a) with the firm testing 50 employees.

10C Compare the standard deviation of a binomial distribution with $n = 100$ and $\pi = 0.01$ with the standard deviation of a binomial distribution with $n = 200$ and $\pi = 0.005$. Can you generalize this comparison?

10D Random testing for illegal drugs is a controversial idea, especially since no drug test is perfect. Suppose a test that produces false positives at a rate of 2% is used. That is, the test will declare about 2% of the people in a large drug-free group to be drug users.
  (a) If 6 drug-free people are tested, what is the chance that there is at least one false positive?
  (b) If 60 drug-free people are tested, what is the chance that there is at least one false positive?

10E Compare the binomial and approximating normal distributions as in Exhibit 10.9A for the cases
  (a) $n = 20, \pi = 0.4$ **(b)** $n = 10, \pi = 0.5$ **(c)** $n = 15, \pi = 0.1$ **(d)** $n = 15, \pi = 0.9$

SECTION 10.15

GLOSSARY FOR CHAPTER 10

Bernoulli process (or Bernoulli trials)	A sequence of independent binary variable trials with constant success rate.
Binomial distribution	The theoretical distribution of the total number of successes in n Bernoulli trials with success probability π.
Binomial mean	$n\pi$
Binomial probability function	The probability of k successes in n Bernoulli trials with success probability π.
Binomial standard deviation	$\sqrt{n\pi(1 - \pi)}$
n	The number of trials considered to obtain a total number of successes.
p	The proportion of successes in n trials.
π	The success probability on each trial.

## CHAPTER 11

Control Charts for Binary Variables

INTRODUCTION

As discussed in Chapter 10, in every business there are many situations in which binary variables are of interest—a loan is approved or rejected, a bank check is input correctly or not, a service is acceptable or not, a dimension on a part is acceptable or not, several dimensions on a product are jointly acceptable or not, and so forth. Can control charts be adapted to monitor binary processes as was done with metric variables? In fact the adaptation is quite straightforward.

In Chapter 10 "success" was used as a generic term for many different specific outcomes in 0–1 processes. In this chapter successes are called "defectives" and π denotes the long-run proportion of defectives in a constant-cause process. Chapter 10 showed that for a constant-cause binary process the distribution of the sample fraction p in a sample of size n is completely determined by π and n. Thus control can be monitored by checking the constancy of π over time. Controlling dispersion and mean level do not have to be considered separately, as they were with metric variables.

p CHARTS

A *p* **chart** is based on a sequence plot of the fraction of defectives in successive subgroups or samples collected from the process over time. We let p_i denote the fraction of defectives in the *i*th subgroup. Similarly, y_i and n_i denote the number of defectives and sample size, respectively, of the *i*th subgroup. Then $p_i = y_i/n_i$, for $i = 1, 2, \ldots, k$.

From Chapter 10 recall that the distribution of a sample fraction *p* has mean $\mu_p = \pi$ and standard deviation $\sigma_p = \sqrt{\pi(1 - \pi)/n}$. Furthermore, if the sample size *n* is not too small, the distribution of *p* can be adequately approximated by a normal distribution. Thus a three-sigma control chart on the fraction of defectives can be constructed by plotting p_i versus *i* for $i = 1, 2, \ldots, k$, using the grand average

$$\bar{p} = \frac{\text{Total number of defectives}}{\text{Total number of trials}} = \frac{\sum_{i=1}^{k} y_i}{\sum_{i=1}^{k} n_i} = \frac{\sum_{i=1}^{k} n_i p_i}{\sum_{i=1}^{k} n_i} \tag{11.1}$$

as an estimate of π and displaying the center line at $CL = \bar{p}$ and control limits for the *i*th sample at

$$UCL_i = \bar{p} + 3\sqrt{\frac{\bar{p}(1 - \bar{p})}{n_i}} \tag{11.2}$$

$$LCL_i = \bar{p} - 3\sqrt{\frac{\bar{p}(1 - \bar{p})}{n_i}} \tag{11.3}$$

Notice that we allow for possible unequal sample sizes in the various subgroups. This situation is very common in applications. Notice also that, depending on the values of $\bar{p}$ and n_i, it is quite possible for the lower control limit to be negative. (The distribution of *p* is only *approximately* normal.) In such a case the lower limit is set equal to zero.

▪ **EXAMPLE 11.2A:** As a first example consider the data in Exhibit 11.2A. The exhibit shows the results of 25 samples each of size 50 from a binary process. The value of p_i for each sample is also given. The overall fraction defective is $\bar{p} = (7 + 9 + 1 + \cdots + 7 + 3)/(25 \times 50) = 129/1250 = 0.1032$. So

$$\sqrt{\frac{\bar{p}(1 - \bar{p})}{n_i}} = \sqrt{\frac{0.1032(1 - 0.1032)}{50}} = 0.043023$$

and the control limits are given by

$$UCL = 0.1032 + (3 \times 0.043023) = 0.232$$

and $\qquad LCL = 0.1032 - (3 \times 0.043023) = -0.0259$

which we increase to zero.

EXHIBIT 11.2A

Number of Defectives: Samples Each of Size 50

Sample	Number of Defectives	p
1	7	0.14
2	9	0.18
3	1	0.02
4	5	0.10
5	7	0.14
6	2	0.04
7	6	0.12
8	9	0.18
9	3	0.06
10	4	0.08
11	5	0.10
12	5	0.10
13	3	0.06
14	6	0.12
15	4	0.08
16	6	0.12
17	5	0.10
18	5	0.10
19	3	0.06
20	6	0.12
21	3	0.06
22	10	0.20
23	5	0.10
24	7	0.14
25	3	0.06

EXHIBIT 11.2B

Fraction Defective Control Chart: Process in Control

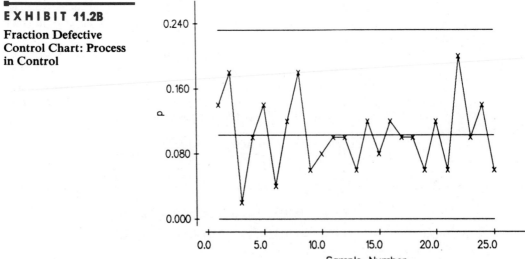

The p chart for these data is in Exhibit 11.2B. It shows there is no reason to doubt that the process is driven by a constant-cause system.

In contrast suppose that the 25th sample had produced 13 defects. Then the overall $\bar{p}$ increases to 0.1112 and the (trial) control limits become $UCL = 0.1112 + (3 \times 0.04446) = 0.24458$ and $LCL = 0.1112 - (3 \times 0.04446) = -0.02218$ (which is again replaced by zero). The control chart shown in Exhibit 11.2C clearly indicates the out-of-control situation in sample 25.

EXHIBIT 11.2C

Fraction Defective Control Chart: Process Out of Control at Sample 25

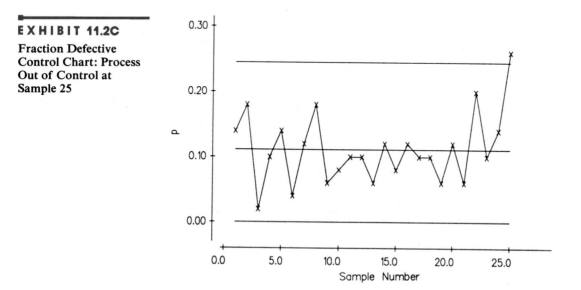

SECTION 11.3

EXERCISES

11.3A In 20 samples each of size 60, a total of 36 defectives were observed.
    (a) What is the value of $\bar{p}$?
    (b) What are the control limits for the p chart based on samples of size 60?
    (c) If five defectives are observed in one sample, would the process be considered out of control?

11.3B Twenty samples of various sizes produced a total of 36 defectives out of 1200 total observations.
    (a) What is the value of $\bar{p}$?
    (b) What are the control limits for the p chart for a sample of size 60?
    (c) What are the control limits for the p chart for a sample of size 40?
    (d) If five defectives are observed in a sample of size 40, would the process be considered out of control at that point?

APPLICATIONS

BANKING — CHECK PROCESSING

Since the mid-1950s nearly all U.S. banks have automated their check processing using magnetic ink character recognition (MICR) technology. Although almost all MICR characters printed on checks can be read automatically, a few are misread because of defects in the characters. When this happens, the automatic reader rejects the check and it must be processed by hand. Needless to say, the rejects are much more costly to handle. Statistical process control has been found to be very effective in monitoring the process and minimizing such costs.[†]

Exhibit 11.4A presents data on defective checks for four weeks of weekday values. Notice that the sample sizes vary over the four-week period from a low of 930 to a high of 1080. The control chart for fraction defective is shown in Exhibit 11.4B. For sample 18 the fraction exceeds the upper control limit, so the process would be declared out of control at that time. Notice that the control limits vary since they are based on differing sample sizes.

EXHIBIT 11.4A

Number of Defective Checks

```
# filename: BADCHEKS.DAT
# Number of defective checks
# (Source: W.J.Latzko, Quality and Productivity for
# Bankers and Financial Managers, Marcel Dekker,
# New York, 1986)
# Four weeks of daily data
# Sample size, Defects
   930    8
  1080   12
  1050   16
  1020    4
  1050    8
  1040   14
   920   11
  1000   16
   990    4
   950    8
   970   13
   950    4
  1030    6
   980   13
  1050    4
  1070   12
   980   11
   940   19
  1050   11
   950    6
```

MANUFACTURING

The Winegard Company uses an automated process to manufacture printed circuit boards that are used in pay telephones. Each board contains 236 positions, each of which must be properly soldered for the board to work correctly. Exhibit 11.4C gives data on the number of defective solder joints per board for a trial production run of

[†] More details may be found in William J. Latzko, *Quality and Productivity for Bankers and Financial Managers* (New York: Marcel-Dekker, 1986).

EXHIBIT 11.4B

Control Chart for
Defective Checks

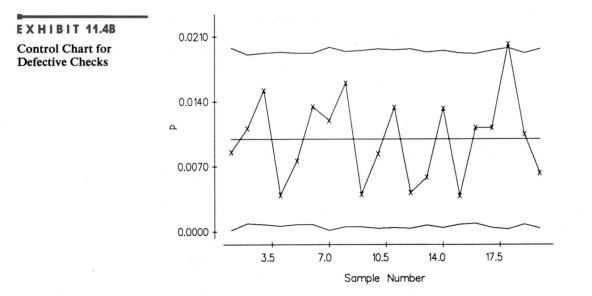

EXHIBIT 11.4C

Defective Solder Joint
Data

Sample	Defects	p
1	14	0.059
2	5	0.021
3	7	0.030
4	10	0.042
5	10	0.042
6	6	0.025
7	10	0.042
8	6	0.025
9	18	0.076
10	9	0.038
11	9	0.038
12	9	0.038
13	6	0.025
14	22	0.093
15	12	0.051
16	19	0.081
17	38	0.161
18	14	0.059
19	23	0.097
20	15	0.064
21	10	0.042
22	29	0.123
23	13	0.055
24	14	0.059
25	18	0.076
26	20	0.085

26 boards in December 1986. The defective joints contain no solder and must be resoldered by hand—a very costly process. Exhibit 11.4D displays the p chart for the 26 boards. Here $\bar{p} = 0.060$ and two points appear above the upper control limit. More important, most of the first 13 values of p_i are below the center line while most of the last 13 values are above the center line.

EXHIBIT 11.4D

Control Chart for
Defective Solder Joints

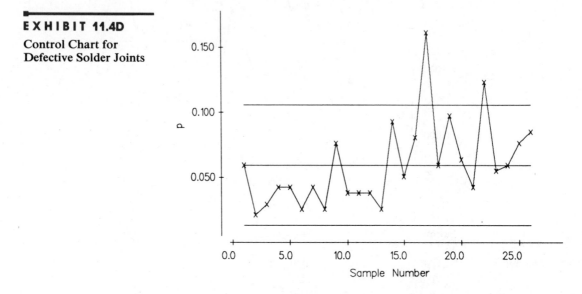

A review of the process with the research and development department revealed that the first 13 runs were done at a belt speed of 12 feet per minute through the automated soldering machine while the last 13 were run at 16 feet per minute. Exhibit 11.4E gives a control chart for just the first 13 values, which shows that the initial portion of the process appears to be in control with $\bar{p} = 0.039$.

EXHIBIT 11.4E

Control Chart for
Defective Solder Joints:
First 13 Samples Only

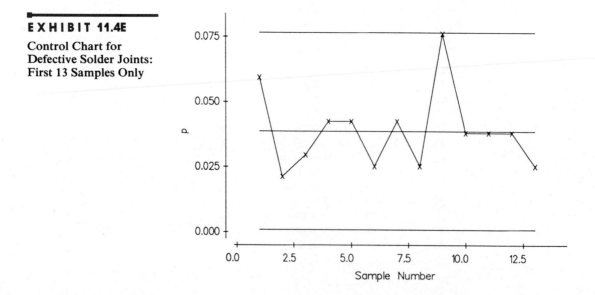

Finally, Exhibit 11.4F displays a control chart for the full sequence but with control limits based only on samples 1 through 13. The change in the last half of the series is more evident than before in this graph. Clearly the 12-feet-per-minute belt speed produces substantially fewer bad solder joints.

EXHIBIT 11.4F

Control Chart for
Defective Solder Joints:
Limits Based on
Samples 1–13 Only

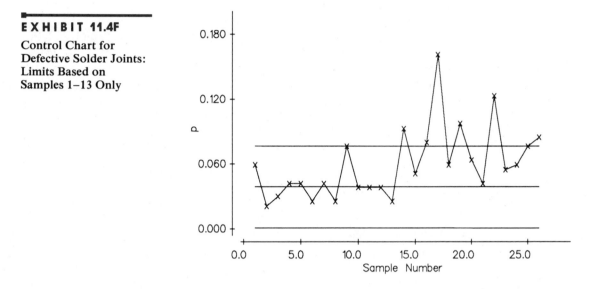

SECTION 11.5

EXERCISES

11.5A The following data give the number of new car loan applications that contained missing information at a particular large bank. The data were collected for 20 weeks, with each week's data based on a sample of 30 applications.
(a) What percentage (overall) of the applications contain missing information?
(b) Does the application system seem to be in control with respect to missing information?

```
# filename: LOANS.DAT
# Number of new car loans with missing information
# 20 weeks of data, samples of size 30 each week
    9 7 6 7 5 7 3 5 4 9 6 7 4 7 5 7 4 7 6 2
```

11.5B The data set below gives the number of defectives in 30 samples each of size 50. The defectives refer to plating defects of assembled parts in a manufacturing process.
(a) Display a p chart for the data and note whether the process is or is not in control.
(b) Redo the chart basing the control limits only on data that are deemed in control. What value of $\bar{p}$ should be used to compute the control limits for future use?

```
# filename: PLATING.DAT
# Plating defects on assembled parts
# (Source: K.Ishakawa, Guide to Quality Control,
#   2nd rev. ed., Asian Productivity Organization
#   White Plains, New York: UNIPUB 1986)
# 30 samples of size 100 each
1 6 5 5 4 3 2 2 4 6 2 1 3 1 4 5 4 1 6 15 12 6 3 4 3 3 2 5 7 4
```

OTHER CONTROL CHARTS

Control charts for defectives are sometimes based on the total number of defectives or on the percent defectives instead of the fraction or proportion defectives. If total defectives are used, then the y_i are plotted with control limits given by $\bar{y} \pm 3\sqrt{n\bar{p}(1-\bar{p})}$ where $\bar{y} = (y_1 + y_2 + \cdots + y_k)/k$. The disadvantage of this approach is that it cannot be used with unequal sample sizes since then $\bar{y}$ makes no sense as a center line.

Charts based on the percent defectives are easily done by plotting percent defectives for the samples, using a center line at $100\bar{p}$ and using the control limits

$$UCL_i = 100\bar{p} + 3\sqrt{\frac{100\bar{p}(100 - 100\bar{p})}{n_i}} \tag{11.4}$$

and
$$LCL_i = 100\bar{p} - 3\sqrt{\frac{100\bar{p}(100 - 100\bar{p})}{n_i}} \tag{11.5}$$

where $100\bar{p}$ is the overall percent defectives. Both these alternative charts will lead to the same decisions about whether the process is or is not in control as p charts do.

SUPPLEMENTARY EXERCISES FOR CHAPTER 11

11A In 15 samples each of size 40, a total of 29 defectives were observed.
(a) What is the value of $\bar{p}$?
(b) What is the value of the lower control limit?
(c) If one of the samples contains only 1 defective, would that sample be declared out of control?

11B The data below give the number of customers served (sample sizes) and number of customer complaints (defectives) about their service over a 25-week period. From week 21 on a new service procedure was implemented with the hope of reducing customer complaints.

```
# filename: IMPROVE.DAT
# Process improvement data
# Starting with sample 21 a new procedure was implemented
# Variables: sample size, number of defects
    48  14              50  15
    46  15              44  21
    45  19              44  14
    47  17              51  12
    44  14              54  11
    43  14              55  18
    43  16              50  13
    42  12              55  14
    55  17              45   4
    46  12              44   5
    51  17              57   5
    60  13              56   4
                        48   3
```

(a) What was the mean number of complaints during the first 20 weeks?
(b) Was the process in control during the first 20 weeks?
(c) Do the data support the claim that the new procedures reduce customer complaints?
(d) Write a one-to-two-page report to management documenting the improvement. Use graphs and descriptive statistics where appropriate but as little technical jargon as possible.

11C Manufacturing television picture tubes is a complex process. The data file below gives information on defective tubes and sample sizes produced daily by General Electric over the period January 2 to 31. Construct a *p* chart for these data and interpret its meaning.

```
# filename: TVTUBES.DAT
# Defective picture tubes at General Electric
# (Source: E.R.Ott, Process Quality Control,
#  New York: McGraw Hill, 1975)
# sample size, number of defectives
  2145   202              3052   226
  2876   104              2874   122
  2607   178              2850   219
  2424   102              2051   205
  2786   170              2379    94
  2239    83              1955    98
  2449   488              1971   125
  2745    97              2120    80
  3268     8              2476   173
  2885    56              2630    59
  2681    46              2948   165
  1414   158              2966    89
  2829   239              2560   117
```

11D The value of $3\sqrt{n\bar{p}(1-\bar{p})}$ enters into the calculation of upper and lower control limits when plotting the numbers of defectives instead of the proportions of defectives. (See Section 11.6.)
(a) Compare the value of $3\sqrt{n\bar{p}(1-\bar{p})}$ when $\bar{p} = 0.01$ and $n = 100$ with the value when $\bar{p} = 0.005$ and $n = 200$.
(b) Can you make any generalizations from part (a)?

SECTION 11.8

GLOSSARY FOR CHAPTER 11

Center line for *p* charts $CL = \bar{p} = \dfrac{\text{Total number of defectives}}{\text{Total number of trials}} = \dfrac{\sum\limits_{i=1}^{k} y_i}{\sum\limits_{i=1}^{k} n_i} = \dfrac{\sum\limits_{i=1}^{k} n_i p_i}{\sum\limits_{i=1}^{k} n_i}$

LCL for *p* charts $LCL_i = \bar{p} - 3\sqrt{\dfrac{\bar{p}(1-\bar{p})}{n_i}}$

p charts   Control charts based on sequence plots of sample proportions.

UCL for *p* charts $UCL_i = \bar{p} + 3\sqrt{\dfrac{\bar{p}(1-\bar{p})}{n_i}}$

Designed
Data Analysis
and Modelling

## PART 3

Data by Design

## CHAPTER 12

Data Collection

In Chapter 1 three tools for collecting data were introduced: simple observation, surveys, and experiments. Further examples of each tool are given in this chapter. The importance of making comparisons possible with the data collected is also stressed. A sequence of steps that constitutes a process for collecting data efficiently and effectively is outlined. The chapter closes with a case study that illustrates important issues in the design of practical data-collection schemes.

SECTION 12.1

SIMPLE OBSERVATION

■ EXAMPLE 12.1A: Electronic data capture has become a characteristic of our computer culture. For example, much of the data that A. C. Nielsen uses to make television program ratings is collected through "people meters," hand-held devices that viewers activate when they watch television and deactivate when they stop watching. Computers are also used to collect data from manufacturing processes, from supermarket checkout stations, from securities markets, and from peoples' brains as they watch advertisements. Computers give us such extensive ability to collect data that the resulting data bases can be overwhelming. One of the challenges of the information age is to learn how to extract relevant information efficiently from huge data bases. Even though the data-collection tools in this example are called "simple," that does not mean to imply that analyzing the data collected with them is a simple matter!

■

■ **EXAMPLE 12.1B:** Cohen et al. report on methods for "accelerated life testing" of the reliability of electronic connectors.[†] Accelerated tests test components at high stress levels because the components rarely fail under "normal" conditions. Engineers try to infer from the performance in the accelerated tests the performance characteristics of the components under normal conditions. Cohen et al. report the need to use "computer-controlled data acquisition systems" to collect as much as hundreds of thousands of measurements during a life test.

Because of the highly focused objectives of this study and the financial and customer-satisfaction implications of the knowledge gained from the study, the collection of vast amounts of data was justified. To analyze enormous data bases, analysts must be able to summarize data using graphical displays and mathematical models that succinctly present the information lurking in millions of bits of data.

■

■ **EXAMPLE 12.1C:** Huge data bases are not necessarily informative. W. Edwards Deming cites the following example.[††] In a manufacturing plant a vast amount of data on plant operations was collected and put into a computer. The computer printed the data in a huge stack of paper, which was laid on a manager's desk each morning. Because the printout was cumbersome and because of the press of the day's activities, the manager never looked at the data. How different it would have been if the computer had been programmed to provide sequence plots that could have shown the manager at a glance the status of his operations! Even more to the point, since the computer was available it could and should have been programmed to make the plots in real time, not to give only a report on yesterday. Modern manufacturing depends on keeping processes in control moment by moment, not day by day or month by month.

■

SECTION 12.2

SURVEYS

Surveys come in a variety of shapes and sizes. The most advanced survey is the probability sample survey. Surveys in general include some of the following characteristics:

- A survey is done during a brief interval of time, called the observation period, and is said to be cross-sectional in focus; that is, the data from a survey are intended to be informative about the characteristics of a population during the observation period.

[†] Howard M. Cohen, Michael J. LuValle, J. Peter Mitchell, and Edward S. Sproles, Jr., "Reliability Evaluations of Interconnection Products," *AT&T Technical Journal* 66(4) (July–August 1987).
[††] W. Edwards Deming, *Quality, Productivity, and Competitive Position* (Cambridge, Mass.: MIT Center for Advanced Engineering Study, 1982) 75–76.

- A relatively large number of elements are collected for observation.
- Many measurements are made on each sample element, usually through the filling out of a questionnaire or checklist.
- Conducting a survey is a complicated process that must be carefully managed to get high-quality results.
- Surveys generate large data bases that must be summarized in charts and tables.

Probability sample surveys have the following additional characteristics:

- The elements are selected according to a probability sampling design whose construction usually requires advanced technical training.
- The successful implementation of a probability sampling design supports rigorous, objective inferences about the characteristics of a population.

▪**E X A M P L E 12.2A:** The December 1, 1987, edition of the *New York Times* reported the results of a *New York Times*/CBS News poll. A probability sample of 1553 adults in the United States were interviewed and asked whether they approved or disapproved of the way then–President Reagan was handling his job. The sample was contacted by telephone, using a random-digit dialing selection technique, between November 20 and 24, 1987. On the basis of this sample the poll estimated that about 45% of adults in the United States approved of Reagan's handling of his job, with a "margin of sampling error" of about three percentage points. Roughly speaking, this means that if all the adults in the United States had been contacted by telephone and interviewed, between 42% and 48% of them would have approved of Reagan's performance.[†]

The data were collected to answer a specific question: What percentage of adult Americans approve of Reagan's handling of his job? The answer was subject to the following limitations:

- It applied only to adults who could be reached by telephone through random-digit dialing.
- It applied only to opinion held between November 20 and 24, 1987.
- It was accurate only to about plus or minus three percentage points.
- It was subject to an unspecified amount of bias not due to probability sampling.

The poll is an example of a *cross-sectional study*. It applies to a fixed period of time and does not convey variation in opinion over time. Because polls are taken weekly, it would be possible to study variation over time if data from previous polls were tracked down. A thorough study of these data would try to account for the sampling variation in each poll (cross-sectional variation) and the longitudinal variation (variation across time). If such a study were done, one might be able to predict with some degree of precision the evolution of opinion about the president's performance of his job. Even with the benefit of a long series of measurements, however, we would probably be unwilling to make any but the most tentative

[†] "Roughly speaking" means that there was about a 5% probability that the margin of sampling error was bigger than three percentage points and that a variety of nonsampling errors could have been at work to cause some degree of bias in the estimates. See Chapters 13 and 14 for a thorough discussion of these more technical points.

predictions because we know how quickly political "situations" develop. Thus, while a sequence plot of poll results may provide a useful context for any particular poll result, it may have little value as a predictive tool. ■

■**EXAMPLE 12.2B:** Contrast the poll in Example 12.2A with the photocopy study introduced in Chapters 1 and 2, which used simple observation. In the photocopy study, complete counts of the number of copies made each day could be plotted and their longitudinal variations searched for clues about future behavior. Both the cross-sectional and the longitudinal issues in the photocopy study are simpler than they are in the poll. As a consequence, the sequence plot in the photocopy study is more informative than the one that might be drawn in the poll study; that is, it is able to communicate more information about the process from which the data were drawn.

The informativeness of the photocopy data has more to do with the longitudinal aspects of the problem than the cross-sectional ones. A sampling scheme that would have collected counts of copies on the machine at several fixed time intervals during the day could have been devised, and this scheme would have yielded quite precise cross-sectional estimates of daily totals. Such a complication was not needed, however, because the machine counted all copies mechanically. Regardless of the means of collecting the cross-sectional data in the photocopy study, making photocopies is a part of normal departmental operations, and this justifies studying the sequence plot not only to understand past behavior but also to gather clues about future behavior. ■

See Chapters 13–16 for more discussion of surveys.

SECTION 12.3

EXERCISES

12.3A As part of a market-research effort, Barbara conducts a random-digit dialing telephone survey during the third week of June. She makes 1500 contacts, but only 1125 of the people answer her questions, so she has 375 nonrespondents. She finds that 720 of the 1125 respondents say they have purchased a certain product in the last three months, so she can say that $64\% [= 100(720/1125)\%]$ of the respondents claim to have purchased the product. She has no evidence concerning the purchase behavior of the nonrespondents, but she can compute the percentage of purchasers out of the 1500 contacts using various assumptions about the nonresponders.

(a) Compute the percentage of purchasers out of the 1500 contacts assuming each of the following conditions:

■ All 375 nonresponders were not purchasers.

■ All 375 nonresponders were purchasers.

■ Of the nonresponders, 64% were purchasers.

(b) Comment on the ambiguity in the percentages created by nonresponse to surveys in light of the calculations you made in part (a).

(c) Redo this exercise assuming there is only a 10% nonresponse rate, that is, that 150 people refused to answer the questions. Continue to assume that 64% of the respondents were purchasers. How does the nonresponse rate affect the ambiguity in the percentages?

12.3B The following table reports monthly unemployment rates for the United States from August 1979 through July 1982.

| | | | | | Month | | | | | | | |
Year	1	2	3	4	5	6	7	8	9	10	11	12
1979								6.9	6.6	6.3	6.4	6.0
1980	7.0	6.8	6.6	5.7	5.4	6.2	6.2	5.8	5.6	5.4	5.5	5.6
1981	6.3	6.4	6.1	5.5	5.1	5.9	5.8	5.8	5.6	5.6	5.6	5.6
1982	6.8	6.8	6.6	6.5	6.9	7.8	7.9					

As a guideline assume that because of sampling error any of these figures could be off by ± 0.3. Sampling errors arise because a sample of about 60,000 households provides the information on unemployment each month. For example, the actual August 1979 figure might be anywhere from 6.6 to 7.2, and the actual September 1979 figure might be anywhere from 6.3 to 6.9. Thus the possibility that actual unemployment rates are the same in the two months cannot be ruled out. Now compare December 1979 with January 1980. The December 1979 figure might be anywhere between 5.7 and 6.3, while the January 1980 figure might be anywhere between 6.7 and 7.3. Even taking sampling error into account, the actual figures are substantially different; that is, they are almost certainly too far apart to be due to sampling error.

(a) Compute the month-to-month changes in the table above. How many of them evidence a substantial change in unemployment rate, after taking sampling error into account? What percentage of the changes provide such evidence?

(b) Sampling theory suggests that if sampling error alone accounted for the month-to-month changes, then at most one or two of them would appear substantial, because sampling error is expected occasionally to generate changes that appear substantial. Given this fact, what do you conclude about the process that generates unemployment rates? Specifically, does it appear that the month-to-month changes are due to sampling error alone?

12.3C Give some examples from your own experience in which sampling was used. Explain why sampling was necessary. Explain the implications of trying to observe the entire population instead of using sampling.

12.3D Explain the importance of the time dimension in decision making. What implications for data collection does the importance of the time dimension have?

EXPERIMENTS

In simple observation and surveying the discovery of characteristics of a process or a population is emphasized. Simple observation and surveys are primarily passive listening devices. Experiments, on the other hand, are active listening devices because with them we attempt to discern what *would be* true of a processs or population if it were changed. An experiment is the study of the effects of change in a limited environment that is to some degree under the experimenter's control.

▪ **E X A M P L E 12.4A:** Baking conditions, such as time and temperature, are important concerns in developing a cake mix that will perform well for a wide variety of users. Consider a mix whose instructions say, "Bake at 325°F for 60 minutes." Because oven and timer settings are known to vary, the mix must bake satisfactorily in *ranges* of temperatures and times.[†]

A typical experimental design is to choose various *combinations* of temperature and time settings, prepare cakes at each of these combinations, submit the cakes to a taste test that yields numerical scores, and analyze the scores for evidence that the mix performs well, or fails to perform well, over the combinations of settings.

To illustrate, assume that the range of temperatures to be studied is 300°F to 350°F and the range of times is 55 minutes to 65 minutes. A possible experimental strategy is to study the recommended times and temperatures and the extremes of the ranges. With this strategy, the three temperature levels to be studied are 300°F, 325°F, and 350°F, and the three time levels are 55 minutes, 60 minutes, and 65 minutes. The choice of levels is up to the experimenter. The two-way table in Exhibit 12.4A shows the nine combinations. The dots mark the nine combinations.

E X H I B I T 12.4A

Two-Way Layout of Combinations of Three Temperatures and Three Times in Cake-Baking Experiment

		Times		
		55 minutes	60 minutes	65 minutes
Temperatures	300°F	·	·	·
	325°F	·	·	·
	350°F	·	·	·

In the terminology of experimental design, a **replication** is a single run of an experiment in which all the planned treatments are run at all the planned levels. In this case the experiment consists of baking cakes at each of the nine combinations and then obtaining taste test scores for each of the nine cakes. Careful implementation of the design would involve at least the following elements:

▪ Use an oven and a timer for which extremely precise settings can be achieved. In the experiment do not try to mimic what actual users do in their kitchens; try to guarantee that the information is collected at the temperatures and times required by the experimenter. Substantial error in the experimental equipment compromises the precision of the experimental findings.

▪ Develop a protocol (that is, a detailed list of instructions) for preparing the cake mix and the oven so that the cakes are prepared under essentially identical conditions.

[†] Products designed to perform well over a range of conditions are said to be *robust*. An example of a robust product is the typical automobile, which must perform in a wide range of environments for a wide range of drivers.

- Prepare the cakes at combinations chosen in a random order. This is done for two reasons. First, if there are effects that carry over systematically from one baking to the next, moving systematically through the table of combinations introduces these carryover effects into the data. Second, the random selection of combinations creates a sound theoretical basis for the use of statistical inference methods in analyzing the data. Tables of random digits are available for making random choices.[†]

- Make sure that the people who taste test the cakes do not know the experimental conditions under which the cakes were prepared. This is called **blinding** the tasters and eliminates bias because of the tasters' prior opinions about "ideal" baking conditions.

- Make sure that the people who conduct the taste tests do not know the experimental conditions under which the cakes were prepared. A person who knows the experimental conditions can transmit clues to the taste tester that can seriously affect the results. The blinding of the conductor as well as the tester is called **double blinding**. Double blinding is one of the most important tools in designing experiments involving human subjects because the opportunities for introducing personal bias are so subtle and so numerous that they defy the most strenuous good-faith efforts of experimenters to avoid them.

- Offer cakes to the taste testers in a random order to avoid carryover effects from test to test.

- Recruit taste testers who can truly discriminate differences between cakes. Some people are much better tasters than others. The difficulties in choosing reliable tasters and strategies for choosing good tasters are ably discussed by Buchanan, Given, and Goldman.[††]   ■

Because experimentation must often be done on a limited scale and because it can be expensive and time consuming, the ability to extract a maximum of information from a minimum of data is important. One of the most useful types of experiment is the **factorial experiment**, an experiment in which all combinations of the treatment levels are run in a replication. It is based on the principle that if the effects of several factors are to be studied, then the most efficient procedure is to vary several factors at once instead of one at a time. Example 12.4A describes an experiment with two *factors*: time and temperature. Three *levels* of each factor are studied, so the experiment involves $3 \times 3 = 9$ combinations in each replication.

■**EXAMPLE 12.4B:** This example continues Example 12.4A by considering the repetition of replications. A single replication of the experiment yields information about the performance of the cake mix at the different temperature/time combinations, but it yields no information about the *variation* induced by the materials, equipment, and tasters. To assess this sort of variation, experimenters conduct a number of replications. Specifically, suppose the experimenter has decided that 12 cakes are to be prepared at each level of each factor. In the context of the factorial experiment this requires four replications. Exhibit 12.4B shows the number of observations obtained for each combination of levels and for each factor. Notice that a total of 36 cakes is baked to conduct the four replications.

[†] See the discussion of randomization in Chapter 1.

[††] Bruce Buchanan, Moshe Given, and Arich Goldman, "Measurement of Discrimination Ability in Taste Tests: An Empirical Investigation," *Journal of Marketing Research* 24 (May 1987): 154–163.

		Times			
		55 minutes	60 minutes	65 minutes	Total
Temperatures	300°F	4	4	4	12
	325°F	4	4	4	12
	350°F	4	4	4	12
	Total	12	12	12	36

EXHIBIT 12.4B

Number of Observations Obtained in Four Replications of a Factorial Experiment Involving Two Factors Each at Three Levels

Now consider the number of cakes required if the experimenter decides to vary the factors one at a time. This means that for each level of temperature, 12 cakes would be baked at each level of time. Then, for each level of time, 12 cakes would be baked at each level of temperature. This yields a total of $3 \times 3 \times 12 = 108$ cakes to be baked and tested. This experimental design actually requires the baking and testing of 36 cakes at each level of each factor, which is three times the number of cakes needed in the factorial experiment. Given that the experimenter requires only 12 cakes per level to be baked in order to discriminate between levels, the use of the one-at-a-time design is clearly very wasteful of time and resources.

Another weakness of the one-at-a-time design is that the combinations of factors cannot be applied in a random order, thus denying the experimenter the opportunity to efficiently control a potential source of bias. This weakness would be present even if the experimenter baked only four cakes at each level of each factor, thus baking the same number of cakes as in the factorial experiment.

The point we are making may seem obvious, but the use of one-at-a-time designs is surprisingly common. The factorial design is usually the much superior design.

Factorial designs also provide a useful framework in which to add and delete factors as a study progresses. For instance, an experimenter may wish to learn the effect of humidity on the cakes. If the humidity of the room can be controlled, this third factor might be studied at two or three levels. The experimental design is then displayed in a three-way table. If the experimenter notices that the quality of the cakes is not much affected by realistic variations in baking time, the time factor could be eliminated and a two-factor study involving temperature and humidity pursued. The collection of relatively small amounts of data over a series of experiments is an economical way to study certain processes, particularly if each small experiment yields information efficiently, as is the case with factorial experiments. ■

SECTION 12.5

EXERCISES

12.5A Identify the two most important factors affecting the shooting of basketball free throws. Design an experiment involving different levels of these factors that could be used to help someone improve his or her free-throwing ability. How would you implement the design?

12.5B Let the process of interest be studying for a class of your choice. Identify the two most important factors affecting the quality of your studying. Design an experiment involving different levels of these factors that could be used to improve this quality. How would you implement the design?

COMPARISONS

Most analyses based on data are comparative because we judge new knowledge or understanding by comparing it to what we already know or understand. Efficient data collection takes this basic fact of human learning explicitly into account.

■ **EXAMPLE 12.6A:** Before-and-after studies play a major role in a variety of applications. If you take a pretest before you start some training and then take a posttest after the training, the difference in the two test scores is a measure of the value of the training. If you maintain data on a quality measure of a process (percent defectives, for example), you may compare the sequence plot of that measure before a quality-improvement program is instituted with the sequence plot that evolves after the quality-improvement program is underway. Comparing measurements taken before and after an intervention is one of the most common methods of analysis. ■

In this section the notion of stratification is introduced and its role in making comparisons with data is discussed. An example of stratification as a tool for identifying sources of variation in process measurements is given. Comparison, especially the comparison of factors, in the context of experiments is also discussed.

STRATIFICATION

Stratification is the separation of observations into groups or categories in order to make comparisons. Stratification is a process you use all the time. You may classify restaurants as expensive, moderately priced, or inexpensive. Or you may classify them as fast food, supper club, haute cuisine, or other. You classify people by the clubs or organizations they belong to, their professions, their ages, their job descriptions, their hair color, and so on. You may classify companies by the quality of the goods and services they offer or by their sales or assets.

Stratification is such a natural and useful activity that calling it a statistical tool may seem pretentious. We do not mean to imply that statistical uses lay a special claim to stratification. Rather, no approach to problem formulation and analysis can ignore the idea of stratification because it is simply fundamental. Our emphasis on stratification serves to make explicit and purposeful a process that is used naturally all the time.

■ **EXAMPLE 12.6B:** Exhibit 12.6A displays family income data by race (also reported in Exhibit 3.6O). Identification of white and black subpopulations of the population of the United States is an example of stratification. Gender and age are other characteristics often used in practice. The income categories in Exhibit 12.6A can be considered income strata. ■

EXHIBIT 12.6A

Numbers of Families in
Income Categories, by
Race, United States,
1982 (numbers in 1000s)

Income Interval ($1000)	Number of Families	
	White Population	Black Population
0– 5	2,399	1,069
5–10	5,452	1,389
10–15	7,007	1,060
15–25	13,615	1,413
25–50	19,628	1,346
Subtotal	48,101	6,277
50 and up	5,168	137
Grand total	53,269	6,414

Source: Current Population Survey, March 1982.   ■

■**EXAMPLE 12.6C:** Geographic region is a popular stratifier. The states in the United States are frequently formed into the following groups:

Region	States Included
Northeast	Connecticut, Maine, Massachusetts, New Hampshire, New Jersey, New York, Pennsylvania, Rhode Island, Vermont
North Central	Illinois, Indiana, Iowa, Kansas, Michigan, Minnesota, Missouri, Nebraska, North Dakota, Ohio, South Dakota, Wisconsin
South	Alabama, Arkansas, Delaware, District of Columbia, Florida, Georgia, Kentucky, Louisiana, Maryland, Mississippi, North Carolina, Oklahoma, South Carolina, Tennessee, Texas, Virginia, West Virginia
West	Alaska, Arizona, California, Colorado, Hawaii, Idaho, Montana, Nevada, New Mexico, Oregon, Utah, Washington, Wyoming

■

■**EXAMPLE 12.6D:** In this example the idea of *sources of variation* is illustrated. Consider an organization with a central purchasing department. You work in a department that heavily uses floppy computer disks, and you get your disks from purchasing. When you first get a disk, you format it and perform some tests on it. If it fails any of the tests, it is sent back to purchasing. Suppose you record the serial numbers of all the disks, the dates on which they are tested, who performs the tests, and whether the disks pass or fail the tests.

On the basis of the data, you compute a failure rate for the disks, that is, the number that fail divided by the number tested. You compute failure rates monthly and put them on a sequence plot that is posted on your bulletin board.

If purchasing gets disks from one supplier, then the overall failure rate and the sequence plot apply to that supplier. But suppose that your purchasing department gets disks from several suppliers, trying always to minimize purchase price. Then the variation displayed in your sequence plot is a mixture of the performances of the various suppliers. The sequence plot does not apply to any one of the suppliers but only to the suppliers as a group.

A solution to this problem, which is an application of stratification, is to keep track of the supplier of a disk and to record this information in your data base. Then you can make sequence plots for each supplier. This separates the sources of variation and forms a basis for making decisions. For example, you may discover that some suppliers have much lower failure rates than others. The suppliers with high failure rates, even if their prices are low, are causing your employees to waste time returning defective disks and testing the replacements. Low price may not be cost-effective in the long run!

If you can find one supplier that is clearly superior to the others, you can encourage purchasing to use that supplier as a sole source. Purchasing can work with that one supplier to improve its quality even further. The goal is to make the supplier so reliable that you can eliminate the testing process from your department. This will save time and money, likely more than enough to pay for a higher initial purchase price of the disks.   ■

Looking for and using data to document sources of variation are basic in process improvement. Typical sources of variation are workers, machines, suppliers, workstations, shifts, and so on. Keeping data on the sources of variation is an application of stratification and is vital for eliminating waste and cutting costs. (See Chapter 25 for further discussion.)

COMPARISON IN EXPERIMENTS

■ **EXAMPLE 12.6E:** Control group and experimental group are important stratifiers in scientific studies. The experimental group receives a new treatment, whereas the control group receives no treatment or a standard treatment. Measurements on the two groups are compared to see if the new treatment makes a difference. In science the control group is the frame of reference against which comparisons are made; studies lacking a control group are rarely considered "scientific." In before-and-after studies, as described in Example 12.6A, the before part is the control group and the after part is the experimental group.

A classic large-scale study that would have faltered without a control group is the one that confirmed the effectiveness of the Salk polio vaccine.[†]   ■

■ **EXAMPLE 12.6F:** In 1958 Wangensteen introduced a new procedure for treating ulcers, called gastric freezing, which was widely adopted. He later published a paper reporting the results of the treatment on 24 patients.[††] Wangensteen did not compare the results with those of a control group.

[†] For a thorough discussion see David Freedman, Robert Pisani, and Roger Purvis, *Statistics* (New York: Norton, 1978), Chapter 1.

[††] O. H. Wangensteen *et al.*, "Achieving 'Physiological Gastrectomy' by Gastric Freezing," *Journal of the American Medical Association* 180 No. 6, May 12 (1962): 439–444.

In 1963 Ruffin performed an experiment in which ulcer patients were divided into two groups.[†] The experimental group, containing 82 patients, received the gastric freezing treatment, while the control group, containing 78 patients, received a **placebo**, a nontreatment disguised so the patients thought it was real. Patients were assigned to the groups at random. The patients were observed for two years after treatment by doctors who did not know which groups the patients were in (so there was double blinding).

Ruffin reported that during the first six weeks of follow-up 47% of the experimental group and 39% of the control group showed improvement, and 29% of the patients in both groups were symptom-free. However, as time passed most patients in both groups became worse. For practical purposes, the two groups behaved the same, casting serious doubt on the value of gastric freezing. Ruffin's and other experiments served to show that gastric freezing was of no use in treating ulcers.[††]

Wangensteen's initial experiment had no control group. Ruffin's experiment showed that gastric freezing had a *placebo effect*. Even though it was of no use, the patients initially responded favorably to the treatment. Unfortunately for Wangensteen, even patients who *thought* they had been treated by gastric freezing responded about as well as those who really had!   ■

Examples 12.4A, 12.4B, 12.6E, and 12.6F illustrate the three basic principles of designed experiments: control, randomization, and replication. Control of experimental factors is needed to make explicit what factors are allowed to have an effect on the response. Randomization is needed to protect against biases due to the effects of unsuspected or uncontrollable factors. Replication is needed to reduce the effects of natural variation to a degree that allows the effects of the experimental factors to be detected.

Lack of control over factors, especially lack of a control group, means that desired comparisons cannot be made. Lack of randomization means that a lurking variable may be the true cause of the variation or relationships observed in the data.[§] Lack of sufficient replication means that natural variation in the experimental units or measuring devices may mask the effect of one or more experimental factors.

The subject of designed experiments is a large and fascinating one, but its further elaboration is beyond the scope of this book. It is one of the most valuable areas of further study you can choose.[∞]

[†] J. M. Ruffin *et al.*, "A Cooperative Double-blind Evaluation of Gastric 'Freezing' in the Treatment of Duodenal Ulcer," *New England Journal of Medicine* 281 (1969): 16–19.

[††] See L. I. Miao, "Gastric Freezing: An Example of the Evaluation of Medical Therapy by Randomized Clinical Trials," in *Costs, Risks, and Benefits of Surgery*, ed. J. P. Bunker, B. A. Barnes, and F. Mosteller (New York: Oxford University Press, 1977), 198–211.

[§] See the discussion of lurking variables in Chapter 6.

[∞] We recommend G. E. P. Box, J. S. Hunter, and W. G. Hunter, *Statistics for Experimenters* (New York: Wiley, 1978) as the place to begin a deeper study of the subject.

EXERCISES

12.7A The August 4, 1988, issue of *U.S.A. Today* reports results from the Department of Transportation's (DOT) monthly study of on-time takeoffs and landings of the 13 largest commercial airlines. On time is defined as within 15 minutes of scheduled time, and the report does not include flights that are delayed because of mechanical failure.

The June 1988 percentage of on-time flights was 84.3%, the highest percentage since the DOT started reporting the figures in September 1987. The previous high was April 1988, with 82.6%. The three top and three bottom airlines, with their percentages of on-time flights, were America West Airlines (92.8), Southwest Airlines (90.8), American (88.2), Pan American (72.2), USAir (76.6), and Trans World Airlines (79).

What might be the value to the individual customer of the stratification by airline? What impact do you think this kind of report might have on the individual airlines? Compare the impacts of the DOT policy with the alternative one of releasing figures for the airline industry as a whole but not for individual airlines.

A potential problem with the DOT report is that in an effort to "look good" in the report an airline will shortcut procedures that are hard to observe, such as maintenance and preflight preparation. Do you think the DOT's policy of not including flights delayed by mechanical failure adequately addresses this issue? If not, what other procedures would you recommend? Try to anticipate the impacts of implementing your recommendations, including costs.

12.7B Choose two grocery stores and keep weekly records of the prices the stores charge for a pound of a certain brand of coffee, a gallon of milk, or some other commodity of your choice. Compare the data from the two stores. A variation on this exercise is to keep track of prices on a "market basket" of commodities, that is, a list of items. This sort of exercise lies behind the construction of the Consumer Price Index, which in turn is used to compute inflation rate.

12.7C If you work in an office or factory, identify a quality measure (such as error rate, failure rate, or service time) for an important process and identify as many sources of variation in this measure as you can. Suggest how data on these items could be collected.

12.7D Consider the sequence plot in Exhibit 2.4A, which displays numbers of copies made daily on a copy machine. The copy machine is available to any member of the department during the workday, and the department members are asked to limit jobs to 25 copies. An honor system is used. Now suppose that on November 23 an auditron system is installed on the machine, and each user must pay for the copies he or she makes. What do you think is the likely appearance of the continuation of the sequence plot? This is an example of a *change in policy*. Describe it in the language of experiments developed in Section 12.6. Cite other examples in which data are or could be used to document the effects of a change in policy.

12.7E In Jesse's business he issues a large number of checks, but some of these checks are never cashed. He plans to follow up on a sample of uncashed checks to try to determine why they are not cashed. He decides to divide the checks into those written for less than $100 and those written for $100 or more. He plans to draw a random sample of size 40 from the first group and a random sample of size 80 from the second group. He has consulted a statistician who assures him that the data so collected can be used to obtain the information he is interested in, as long as he carefully follows up all the checks in his sample. What sources of variation have been eliminated with this sampling design? What sources of variation remain?

12.7F Rita has been commissioned to estimate the number of municipal water towers in Wisconsin. She designs the following sample survey procedure. She divides the state into three geographic regions called upper, middle, and lower. These regions consist of collections of counties. She selects ten counties from each region using a table of random digits. Next she selects three municipalities from each selected county, using a table of random digits. She calls each selected municipality's government office and asks how many water towers are located in the municipality. What sources of variation have been eliminated with this sampling design? What sources of variation remain?

STEPS IN DATA COLLECTION

Data form a basis for action, but the extent to which a given set of data can be relied upon depends on its quality. If we perform or supervise the data collection ourselves, we can judge directly whether they satisfy our quality requirements. If, however, we use data collected by an outside supplier, then we must use indirect means for judging the quality of the data. We may have to rely on a brief technical appendix to a research report or perhaps a telephone conversation with the supplier. Regardless of the situation, two questions about the data collection must be answered satisfactorily:

- **Data design quality:** Was the intent to produce data relevant to the problem we wish to solve?

- **Data production quality:** Were the data collected with sufficient skill and care?

When we do our own data collection we have control over the relevance of the data, so design quality tends to be high. Such data are called **primary source** or simply **primary data**.

Outside sources typically supply general-purpose data. The Census Bureau, for example, collects millions of bits of data each year and publishes them in a variety of formats. The surveys the bureau conducts are so large that they are unlikely to be done by smaller organizations, and they yield data that are national in scope. While valuable for many purposes, such data tend to leave many "microlevel" questions unanswered. The same remarks apply to general-purpose market-research surveys, which tend to emphasize industrywide findings or findings about broad consumer groups. Thus, while the production quality achieved by a large organization like the Census Bureau is high, the design quality of the resulting data can range from high to low, depending on the specific needs of the user. Data collected by a person or organization not the user of the data are called **secondary source** or simply **secondary data**.

Although each attempt at data collection must be tailored to the specific problem being attacked, the following sequence of eight steps provides good guidelines to follow in your planning. If you are not collecting data but are using a secondary source, then you may compare your source's procedures against these guidelines.

STEP 1: STATE THE PURPOSE FOR COLLECTING THE DATA

If you collect the data yourself, you can be specific about the purpose. A secondary source, such as the Census Bureau or a market-research firm, has a general purpose because it has many users with many different specific purposes. The more specific the purpose the better, however. Statements that start out with "To provide information about..." or "To serve the needs of..." are not much use. A statement of purpose should include the universe of elements from which a sample is drawn, define the time period over which the data are collected, state the method of data collection, and give the longitudinal context of the resulting data.

STEP 2: DETERMINE SOURCES

If the source is primary, state the names of the people in your organization who are responsible for collecting the data. If the source is secondary, state the specific publications or electronic data bases used. Also cite the name, address, and telephone number of the data-collection organization. The source actually used may be chosen only after a search of many possible sources. Keep a list of sources considered for future reference.

STEP 3: DETERMINE PRESENTATION METHODS

Data must be relevant to be informative. Part of relevance is collecting data from the right processes. Another part is collecting data that reflect the facts, or are "free of bias," as statisticians say.

An equally important part of relevance is reporting the data so the information they contain is clearly and readily appreciated by those who use them as a basis for action. Data may be reported as lists of numbers, in tables or charts, in equations that define a mathematical model, in a purely verbal description, or in graphical form. Reports frequently consist of a combination of these forms. As you plan data collection it is sound practice to sketch out the formats in which the data will be stored and reported. This will help you focus on what the data will be used for and to anticipate problems.

One of the problems inexperienced analysts run into is incomplete understanding of the construction of computer files and the use of statistical computing programs. We have consulted with analysts who collected data and then set out to find an appropriate program with which to do the data manipulation and analysis. Because they lacked a proper appreciation of what data analysis entails, they did not leave sufficient time to do a careful and thorough job, nor did they collect the data to make its entry into the computer as simple as possible. These analysts suffered from wasted time and frustration that could have been avoided with a little anticipation.

Familiarity with statistical software also allows the analyst to anticipate the kinds of data displays that can be made. A good exercise is to put yourself in the place of the people who will make decisions using the data you collect. What form of presentation will be most useful for these people? If you do not know, ask them. If they cannot tell you, show them some possibilities and get them to commit themselves to a form. Then you will have a concrete objective for your data collection.

If you are in the position of authorizing the collection of data, your familiarity with these guidelines will lead you to provide the information an analyst needs to do a good job. You will also be able to judge the quality of the data you get and appreciate the problems that arose in the data-collection process. We recommend an additional step to gain a full appreciation of the data: involve yourself in the data-collection process.

STEP 4: CONSTRUCT DATA SHEETS AND FILES

Data may be collected on sheets of paper and then transferred to worksheets or computer files for analysis. If you use this method, design the data sheets to ensure the speed and accuracy of each operation. For example, a questionnaire should be easy to read and fill out, and it should make the responses stand out for easy transfer to the computer if this is to be done. Long, disorganized questionnaires discourage respondents and lower the quality of their answers. They also promote errors in data transfer.

Elimination of intermediate steps saves time and increases accuracy.

■ **E X A M P L E 12.8A:** A bank asked credit applicants to fill out a form from which the data were input to a computer file. Many customers complained of errors in documents subsequently received from the bank. Investigation found that the credit application was the culprit. Its design made data transfer difficult. Redesign of the form led to a huge decrease in input errors. Even more errors were eliminated when the application form was done away with altogether. Credit officers began inputting the data on terminals at their desks as they interviewed applicants. Applicants were able to preview the information on the screen and verify its accuracy. ■

Often the data sheet can combine the steps of data collection and data presentation. If, for example, a sequence plot is to be made, it can be constructed on the data sheet as the data are recorded. This saves an intermediate data-transfer step and makes the graph immediately available to support decision making.

When you collect data, record the date and the person or machine who collected it. Failure to do this renders the data useless if they are examined at a later time and no one can determine the circumstances surrounding their collection. The more data collection you supervise, the harder it is to remember when they were collected and who collected them. The data sheet or file should always ask for this basic information, and recording the information should be part of every data collector's job description.

STEP 5: TRAIN PERSONNEL

Training the people who collect the data is essential in assuring the quality of the data. Training includes not only the mechanics of filling out a data sheet or interviewing a respondent but also the importance of the data. Why is it being collected? What decisions will be made and what difference will they make to the organization? What will go wrong if the data contain errors?

Training should also include practice with the data-collection procedures and tools. Trainees must be encouraged to point out problems and make suggestions for improvement. Suggestions that lead to simplification of procedures and improved accuracy of the data should be rewarded concretely. Training should also include what to do if a difficulty (such as an uncooperative interviewee) is encountered.

The more you foster teamwork the more closely the data collectors will follow the prescribed procedures and hence collect the data as intended. An important part of teamwork is an agreement not to pass problems on to other members of the team. If a problem is encountered, it is either solved on the spot or brought to the attention of the team so that countermeasures may be developed.

If data are collected over a long period of time, training should be an ongoing activity. As difficulties are met, procedures for solving the problems must be worked out and shared with the team. Improvements in procedures may be suggested at any time. As these are adopted, they need to be shared with the team. At all times a manager must make sure that all the data collectors know their responsibilities, are following current procedures, and are communicating effectively with other members of the team.

STEP 6: COLLECT THE DATA

Once procedures are established and personnel trained, collect the data.

STEP 7: ERROR CONTROL AND AUDIT

Data collection is a process involving a series of steps. Each step must be conducted correctly if the finished product, the data, are to be of the highest quality. Hence, each step of the process must be controlled. When problems are met in a particular step, they must be solved there and not passed on to the next step. The most effective means of error control is for every worker to be trained to spot and eliminate problems.

If you supervise a long-term data-collection project, you need to do some auditing. This allows you to spot problems that the workers are missing, and it will also allow you to see if your workers need more training. Auditing is usually done by sampling some of the work done at each step. Chapters 13–16 explain how to design and carry out sampling plans. We do not go into details here but simply note the importance of auditing work in progress. It is not sufficient to audit finished product, because then it is too late to counter the problems that led to inferior work.

STEP 8: DOCUMENT THE WORK

Minimal documentation is a data sheet describing the data along with dates of collection and names of data collectors. More elaborate documentation, such as a covering memorandum that states the problem addressed and some background on how the data-collection procedures were arrived at, or a full research report, will often be required. Data displays should be thoroughly labelled so that a user can glean the essential facts needed to make decisions. Fuller explanations may be given in supporting text, but the basic facts about the data should be included in the display itself.

S E C T I O N 12.9

EXERCISES

12.9A Identify as many secondary sources of data as you can by searching a library, talking to a librarian, interviewing an information manager in a company, or any other means you can think of. Here are a few references to get you started:

- H. Webster Johnson, Anthony J. Faria, and Ernest L. Maier, *How to Use the Business Library: With Sources of Business Information*, 5th ed. (Cincinnati: South-Western Publishing, 1984).

- Eleanor G. May, *A Handbook for Business on the Use of Federal and State Statistical Data* (Washington: Department of Commerce, 1979).

- Paul Wasserman, Charlotte Georgi, and James Way, *Encyclopedia of Business Information Sources*, 5th ed., copyright ©1980, 1983 by Paul Wasserman.

- Anthony Kruzas and Linda Varekamp Sullivan, eds., *Encyclopedia of Information Systems and Services*, 6th ed. (Detroit: Gale Research, 1985).

12.9B Choose one of the secondary sources of data you found in completing Exercise 12.9A. Identify the way the source reports the process by which it gathers and reports data. Does the source adequately address the limitations of the data? Justify your conclusions.

12.9C Consider each of the steps in data collection outlined in Section 12.8. Explain the impact on the final results of omitting any step.

12.9D The accounting department is inputting data sets for the marketing department. The marketing department frequently sends over cases that have missing information, and the accounting department keys them in as is. As the missing information is supplied, the data set is updated. Explain why this is a wasteful, inefficient way to process the data. Suggest an appropriate data-collection process that not only eliminates wasted steps but guarantees few or no errors in the final results with high probability. (The procedure outlined above was observed by one of the authors during a consultation with a company!)

12.9E When Jeff audited the data he collected last week, he found that the measurement for one of the items was missed. In order to have the data ready for analysis the next day, Jeff decided to use a measurement collected three weeks ago. Under what circumstances do you think Jeff would be justified in taking the action he did? What could be wrong with what he did? How could Jeff tell if his action was justified?

S E C T I O N 12.10

A CASE STUDY

The response to a request for information can be quite sensitive to the way the request is phrased. The neutral (unbiased) wording of questions is a constant concern in studies based on interviews. Even the user friendliness of a questionnaire can affect the response. This case is based on a simple task that can be performed in a classroom setting or made into a rather elaborate field trial.

The task is to count the number of *e*'s in a sentence. Subjects are shown the sentence and given only a short time (roughly 30 seconds) to perform the task. Usually a subject is asked to count the *e*'s in several sentences. A group of subjects invariably comes up with different counts, thus illustrating the difficulty of a seemingly simple task. The average count for a group is almost always less than the actual number of *e*'s in a sentence, thus documenting a bias in the counting process: a systematic tendency to undercount. If something as simple as counting *e*'s is hard, how much harder is reporting information such as attitude or recollection of events?

Recently one of our colleagues suggested that subjects would produce higher-quality counts if the sentences were held upside down. This case study reports two experiments designed to test our colleague's theory.

THE FIRST EXPERIMENT — A CLASSROOM TRIAL

A class of 67 students was shown four sentences, one at a time, projected on a screen at the front of the room. Two of the sentences were shown right-side up (Rsu), two were upside down (Usd). The students recorded their counts on an index card. The cards were collected and the data keyed into an electronic data base. The top part of Exhibit 12.10A shows tallies of the differences between the reported counts and the actual numbers of e's in the four sentences. These differences are called "errors," with the understanding that a 0 error means a correct count. In the Exhibit, S1 Error stands for the error committed for sentence 1, S2 Error, the error for sentence 2, and so on. Sentences 1 and 2 were shown right-side up and sentences 3 and 4 were shown upside down. The actual number of e's in the sentences were 8, 14, 11, and 10.

EXHIBIT 12.10A

Tallies, Means, and Standard Deviations of Error Distributions in an Experiment in Which Subjects Counted e's in Four Sentences

S1 Error	Count	S2 Error	Count	S3 Error	Count	S4 Error	Count
−2	3	−4	1	−4	1	−2	2
−1	17	−3	9	−2	1	−1	8
0	46	−2	15	−1	12	0	57
3	1	−1	15	0	48	Total	67
Total	67	0	27	1	5		
		Total	67	Total	67		
Mean	−0.3		−1.1		−0.2		−0.2
Standard deviation	0.7		1.1		0.7		0.5

Rsu Error	Count	Usd Error	Count
−5	1	−6	1
−4	8	−2	5
−3	6	−1	13
−2	15	0	44
−1	12	1	4
0	24	Total	67
1	1		
Total	67		
Mean	−1.4		−0.3
Standard deviation	1.5		1.0

The bottom part of Exhibit 12.10A shows tallies for the totals of the errors for the two right-side-up sentences and the total of the errors for the two upside-down sentences. The exhibit also shows means and standard deviations of all the distributions. A mean error not equal to zero suggests bias, while the standard deviation of the errors is a measure of variation, as usual. We see that the right-side-up sentences yielded larger biases *and* larger standard deviations than the upside-down sentences!

While suggestive, these results are hardly conclusive. To be convincing the findings on the orientation of the sentences need to be documented much more extensively.

THE SECOND EXPERIMENT — A FIELD TRIAL

A class of 38 students was asked to perform the following field trial. Each student chose five sentences and wrote them on five index cards. The correct number of *e*'s in each sentence was determined. Each student found six subjects, three of whom were assigned by the flip of a coin to the experimental group. The other three made up the control group. The control group counted the *e*'s in the five sentences held right-side up, while the experimental group counted the *e*'s in the sentences held upside down. For each group the correct total number of *e*'s in the five sentences was subtracted from the number of *e*'s counted to produce an aggregate counting error figure for the group.

The 38 aggregate error figures for each group are the basic data for our analysis. The errors are shown in dotplots, and descriptive statistics are given in Exhibit 12.10B. Not only distributions of the errors for the control (Rsu) and experimental (Usd) groups but also distributions of the differences between the errors for the groups that counted the same sentences (Rsu − Usd) are shown.

The average errors for the control and experimental groups are −10.13 and −8.18, suggesting substantial undercounting on the average. On the other hand,

EXHIBIT 12.10B

Tallies, Means, and Standard Deviations of Error Distributions in an Experiment in Which Subjects Counted *e*'s in Five Sentences

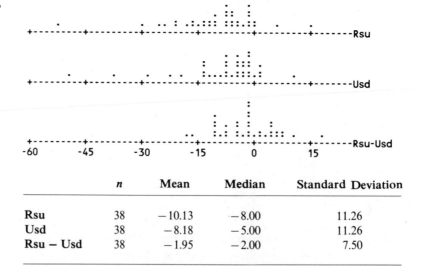

	n	Mean	Median	Standard Deviation
Rsu	38	−10.13	−8.00	11.26
Usd	38	−8.18	−5.00	11.26
Rsu − Usd	38	−1.95	−2.00	7.50

n = 38 cases in control group (Rsu); *n* = 38 cases in experimental group (Usd).
Rsu means right-side up; Usd means upside down.

there appears to be little practical difference between the Rsu and Usd procedures. The average difference between them is -1.95 with a standard deviation of 7.50. The data suggest that both methods produce substantial undercounting and provide little support for the theory that the Usd procedure is superior to the Rsu procedure.

The field trial is implemented quite differently from the classroom exercise reported earlier. For one thing more sentences were involved, which should provide a better test of the theory that Usd is better than Rsu. On the other hand, different sentences were used for each control and experimental group. This undoubtedly contributed some variation to the error distributions. On the other hand,[†] we do not want to base our conclusions on a very limited number of sentences. In other words, we would like our conclusions to be robust to the type of sentences analyzed. Another difference is the use of randomization in the field trial, a step not taken in the classroom exercise. On the whole, the field trial is a sterner test of the theory, and the data do not support the notion of a major difference between Rsu and Usd. We do not find the conclusion conclusive, however. Further experimentation would be required before we would consider the case closed.

Examination of the dotplots in Exhibit 12.10B reveals substantial outliers. To investigate their influence on our conclusions we trimmed (removed) the two extreme outliers from each distribution and redid our plots and calculations. The results are in Exhibit 12.10C. We draw the same conclusions from Exhibit 12.10C as we did from Exhibit 12.10B. The outliers have no substantial effect on the analysis.

EXHIBIT 12.10C

Tallies, Means, and Standard Deviations of Error Distributions in an Experiment in Which Subjects Counted *e*'s in Five Sentences

	n	Mean	Median	Standard Deviation
Tr Rsu	36	-9.67	-8.00	8.10
Tr Usd	36	-7.53	-5.00	8.62
Tr Diff	36	-2.14	-2.00	7.62

Data are as in Exhibit 12.10B with two extreme values removed from each distribution. Tr Rsu means trimmed right-side up. Tr Usd means trimmed upside down. Tr Diff means trimmed differences.

[†] There are at least three hands in this presentation. Some practitioners insist that statisticians consult with one hand tied behind their backs to avoid all the caveats that are preceded by the phrase "on the other hand." We naturally do not favor this practice!

SUPPLEMENTARY EXERCISES FOR CHAPTER 12

12A A colleague of ours once spent a week in a motel with his family. Everyone in his family noticed at breakfast that the motel staff threw away a great deal of food. They began to think of ways that this waste could be reduced. Subsequently, our colleague asked a team of students to consult with the manager of the food operation in the motel to try to reduce waste and at the same time make the service more efficient. Find a food-service establishment whose manager agrees to let you (preferably along with some colleagues) act as a research team whose objective is to eliminate waste and increase efficiency. Identify basic processes and develop data-collection schemes that will provide insight into how the processes work and how they can be improved. (You will find some helpful suggestions on how to do this in Chapter 25.)

12B Repeat Exercise 12A using a different set of processes. Some suggestions include check processing in a bank, the receptionist area in a company, and document examination for certification.

12C An experiment is conducted to measure the impact of three different diets on the growth rate of young rats. Diet A is the "standard" diet and is treated as the control or basis for comparison. Diets B and C are experimental. Fifteen newborn rats are assigned to each diet. The rats are weighed at birth and will be weighed at age 1 month. Difference between birth weight and weight at 1 month will be the measure analyzed for evidence that the diets have different impact. Explain in detail how randomization and double blinding can be incorporated into the experiment. Devise a graphical scheme for displaying the data the experiment will produce that will make it possible to compare the diets at a glance.

12D A consortium of eight business schools agrees to conduct an experiment to measure student satisfaction with the availability of microcomputers. The two factors are type of operating system and method of delivery. Type of operating system has two levels, corresponding to the two most popular operating systems. The brand of hardware used was not considered critical, so this was not used as a factor. Method of delivery also has two levels: micro lab funded by the school and student required to purchase own computer and software. The experimental design is a 2×2 factorial, and there are two business schools at each combination of levels of the two factors. To standardize the evaluation process, 50 MBA students are selected at random from each school and asked to fill out a questionnaire. In return for filling out the questionnaire, each student is given a gift certificate from the local bookstore. One item on the questionnaire asks the students to rate their satisfaction with the computer facilities on a five-point scale, with 1 representing extreme dissatisfaction and 5 representing extreme satisfaction. The average of the 50 responses to this item is the datum provided by a given school. (Other items on the questionnaire can be handled similarly.)
  (a) How many replications of the 2×2 factorial design are used in the experiment?
  (b) What sort of generalization is justified by the randomization used in the experiment?
  (c) Comment on the applicability of the results of this experiment to business schools not included in the experiment.

12E A group of students was asked to analyze a case study that was a report of a regression analysis of variables used to predict energy consumption in large commercial buildings in the Midwest. The students discovered that heating degree days, a measure of how cold a day is, was negatively correlated with energy consumption, a decidedly counter-intuitive result. They discovered that this nonsense correlation was caused by bias in the selection of the buildings: the larger buildings were concentrated in warmer parts of the Midwest, while smaller buldings were concentrated in colder parts of the Midwest. This example illustrates the intimate relationship between data collection and data analysis. Generally speaking even a skillful analysis will not salvage much information from carelessly collected data. Develop some other examples that illustrate this point.

GLOSSARY FOR CHAPTER 12

Blinding	Not allowing subjects in an experiment to know which treatment they receive.
Data design quality	The plan for collecting the data is relevant to the problem to be solved.
Data production quality	Data are collected with sufficient skill and care to be useful.
Double blinding	In addition to blinding the subjects the evaluators are not allowed to know what treatments the subjects receive.
Factorial experiment	An experiment in which all combinations of the treatment levels are run in a replication.
Placebo	A nontreatment disguised so that subjects think it is real.
Primary data	Data collected by the person or organization that also analyzes the data.
Replication	A single run of an experiment in which all the planned treatments are run at all the planned levels.
Secondary data	Data collected by one person or organization and analyzed by another person or organization.
Stratification	Separating observations into groups or categories in order to make comparisons.

## CHAPTER 13

Introduction to Surveys

INTRODUCTION

Much of our information comes from surveys. Opinion polls inform politicians as well as the general public on attitudes and preferences of the electorate. Surveys of populations, business establishments, farms, and consumers inform government and business decision makers, while surveys of academics are used to rate the quality of educational institutions.

Surveys are conducted by government agencies, private survey or polling organizations, survey research groups, and private firms and organizations. Demand for information is supported by dollars. For example, the 1990 Census of the Population of the United States is estimated to cost $2.6 billion. A. C. Nielsen, the largest marketing research firm in the world, reported gross revenues in 1986 of $615 million.

Although it would be impossible to list all the decisions informed by survey data, a few examples are suggestive. A politician tailors his election campaign to appeal to the preferences of his constituents revealed in an opinion poll. A government entitlement program uses population data collected by the Census Bureau to determine eligibility of a county for funds. From a survey conducted in a shopping mall, a mall operator determines the types of tenants most likely to appeal to customers. A company learns from a survey of employees that 16% of the employees spend time caring for elderly friends or relatives and that such employees spend an average of about six hours per week giving care. A service organization learns from a survey of financial contributors that over half of the contributors have made repeated donations. Many other examples could be cited to illustrate the pervasive use of surveys.

Despite the widespread use of surveying, misconceptions, misunderstandings, and ignorance of the fundamentals of surveying are also widespread. As a consequence, opportunities for collecting high-quality data are frequently missed, and data of poor quality receive more credence, not to mention remuneration, than they deserve.

In this and the next two chapters the fundamentals of surveying are presented. Important terms are carefully defined and "do's and don'ts" are illustrated with examples. The emphasis is on probability surveys, though much of what is said also applies to other types of surveys.

S E C T I O N 13.2

DEFINITIONS

In an effort to avoid confusion and misunderstanding, we begin with some carefully worded definitions. A broad definition of the word *survey* is needed first.

SURVEY

A **survey** is a process of systematically obtaining information on a universe of individuals. Almost every word in this definition justifies comment. Remember that surveying is a process. It consists of a sequence of steps. The quality of the final product of the survey is a result of the care that goes into planning and executing each step.

The word *systematically* implies that a survey is conducted to achieve a goal according to a plan that reflects careful and thorough thinking. The word *systematically* is used to distinguish from haphazard or informal methods of obtaining information. The latter methods are the most common ways of obtaining information, but they are not sufficient. Surveys provide information that is difficult or impossible to obtain by less formal methods.

Information is data collected with a purpose and summarized in useful tables, charts, or equations. To be informative, data must answer a question or help solve a problem; in other words, informative data are used as a basis for action. This presupposes a need on the part of the investigator to answer a question or solve a problem, and this presupposes the formulation of the question or problem before the data are collected. Before conducting a survey it is important to formulate the purpose for doing the survey. Otherwise, opportunities for collecting useful data may be missed.

The word *universe* means the collection of elements about which we wish to be informed. This definition is expanded on page 350.

ELEMENTS

The **elements** of a survey are the basic units or individuals about which information is sought. Elements may be people, trees, companies, entries in a book or computer file, and so on. What an element is depends on the study being performed.

UNIVERSE

The **universe** is the collection of all the elements of interest. It is essential that elements are sufficiently well defined so that they can be determined to be in or not in the universe at the time the survey is conducted. If this can be done, we say that we have an *operational definition* of the elements. Obtaining operational definitions is often surprisingly difficult, and compromises frequently need to be made. Moreover, two investigators may legitimately decide on different operational definitions. This, in turn, may mean that they will get different universes and draw different conclusions, even though they supposedly are studying the same problem. In using the results of a survey, you must be clear about the operational definitions used. Inattention to this point leads to unfortunate misunderstandings.

CENSUS

A **census** is a survey conducted with the intention of obtaining information from every element in the universe. The census of a universe of appreciable size or complexity is both time consuming and costly, and detecting and correcting errors sometimes creates intractable difficulties. The main advantage of a census, assuming the errors can be satisfactorily controlled, is the great detail it yields. As discussed below, a well-conducted probability sample survey can be expected to yield higher-quality though less-detailed data than a census. A census should be conducted only if such detail is really needed.

NONPROBABILITY SAMPLE SURVEY

Sample surveys are conducted with the intention of obtaining information from only a portion of the universe. There are two types of sample surveys: those that use probability methods to select the elements to be measured and those that do not. The latter are called **nonprobability surveys**.

A common nonprobability survey is one in which a questionnaire is sent to a large number of elements, possibly the whole universe, and only those questionnaires that are voluntarily returned are analyzed. Such surveys can be quite informative, because the elements that return the questionnaire may be of intrinsic interest. The danger with nonprobability surveys is that an investigator will draw unwarranted conclusions about the universe from the data in the sample.

To illustrate, consider a case in which people who have one opinion about an issue, say those opposed to restrictions on possession of hand guns, are more likely to return the questionnaire than those who have the opposite opinion. The overrepresentation of the former group in the sample would yield a biased picture if the sample were used, without adjustment, as a guide to the composition of the universe.

As a second illustration, consider a survey sent to business establishments. It may be that larger establishments with more resources are more likely to respond than are smaller establishments in which everyone works overtime just to keep up.

If a probability mechanism is not used to draw the sample, inferences from the sample about the universe must be made on the basis of judgment, and different judges may legitimately render different verdicts.

Despite some of the dangers of nonprobability surveys, such surveys, as well as casual or fortuitous observation, are the source of quite a bit of data, even in the scientific world. For example, scientists seriously study dinosaur bones and outcroppings of rocks fortuitously discovered. No scientist would refuse to study a chemical element or an atomic particle discovered by accident. Examples of useful volunteer surveys in the business world include suggestion boards hung in factories or offices and customer suggestion boxes set out in hotel rooms and bank lobbies.

It is unfortunate that data from nonprobability surveys are so often mishandled, usually by treating them as if they were data from probability surveys, with the misguided intention of being "scientific." Do not equate being scientific with using probability surveys. Both probability and nonprobability surveys may be used scientifically; they can equally well be used for trivial or sinister purposes.

PROBABILITY SAMPLE SURVEYS

In **probability surveys** each element of the universe has a known probability of entering the sample. Because of this a sample drawn by probability methods may be used to make predictions within probabilistically specified limits about the whole universe.[†]

Another subtlety is that a probability sample allows inferences about the equal complete coverage of the universe to be made. The **equal complete coverage** is the set of measurements that would be obtained if the survey procedures were used on every element in the universe. Survey procedures include the operational definitions, the measurement methods, the methods of error detection and control, and so forth. A survey that involves one set of procedures will not necessarily yield unbiased information about traits of the universe that would be obtained using another set of procedures, a dilemma analogous to Heisenberg's uncertainty principle in physics. Understanding the procedures used in a survey is essential to understandiing the results of a survey.

■**EXAMPLE 13.2A:** Consider two survey organizations seeking information about purchase behavior of households. One organization selects households at random and uses personal interviews to obtain the information. During the interviews, respondents are asked to recall their last two purchases of certain products. The other organization uses diaries to obtain the information. Selected households are asked to maintain diaries of their purchases of certain products over a period of time. The diaries are then collected and the data extracted from them.

The equal complete coverage for the first organization would be personal interviews conducted at all households in the universe and the information from all these households based on the recall of the respondents. The equal complete coverage for the second organization would be diaries collected from all the

---

[†] The predictions made from a probability sample are analogous to those made from control charts about processes. Remember, however, that the predictions from control charts are longitudinal, whereas the predictions from a probability sample are cross-sectional.

households in the universe. Even assuming exactly the same households in both universes, the equal complete coverages are different because the data-collection methods are different. Data based on recall are subject to different types of error than data based on diaries. Any procedures the organizations use to correct the data become part of the equal complete coverage. Neither organization can be said to have a superior procedure, but they are demonstrably different and would yield different equal complete coverages.   ■

For any given set of procedures, the equal complete coverage of the universe yields a set of numerical characteristics, such as mean age, mean income, mean number of visits to a shopping mall, or proportion of heads of households who are female. Any sample drawn from the universe will also yield a set of numerical characteristics, but in general these will differ from those of the equal complete coverage. They will also be different in different samples. This variation in the numerical characteristics from sample to sample is called **sampling variation**.

S E C T I O N 13.3

EXERCISES

13.3A Go through several issues of your favorite newspaper and clip all the reports of survey results you can find. For each example answer the following questions.
  (a) What organization conducted the survey?
  (b) Who wrote the newspaper report? What organization did the author represent?
  (c) Was the survey a census, nonprobability, or probability survey?
  (d) If it was a probability survey, were the limits of sampling variation reported?
  (e) Were the survey procedures reported in any detail? If so, which ones? Which ones were not reported?
  Develop other pertinent questions that might be asked and answer them. On the basis of your study, what recommendations would you make to the newspaper on the reporting of surveys?

13.3B In a sample-survey class, one of the authors asked the class members to use a probability-survey design to draw a sample of lines from a novel and to count the number of words in each line. On the basis of the sample, each class member was to estimate the number of words in the novel. One problem the class had to solve was to formulate an operational definition of the word *word*. Your job is to attack this operational definition problem. Form a task force to do this. If more than one legitimate definition of *word* emerges, as it did in the class project described, try to anticipate the effects of using the different definitions on the final estimate of the number of words in the novel.

13.3C **(a)** Suppose you manage a fast food restaurant. Develop a customer questionnaire that you believe would provide useful information for the improvement of your service.
  (b) Collect such questionnaires from a number of fast food restaurants in your area and compare them on any set of quality criteria you choose. What types of information do the restaurants seem to be most interested in?
  (c) What groups of people are not likely to fill out such questionnaires? Would the opinions of any such groups be especially valuable to the manager of a fast food restaurant? How might a manager obtain information from such groups?

13.3D The following sentences briefly describe a design commonly used to survey the nation: Divide the country into compact geographic regions, usually large urban/suburban areas and groups of less-populated counties. Further subdivide these geographic regions into blocks, usually the size of several city blocks. Select a sample of large geographic regions. From these select a sample of blocks. Finally, from the blocks select a sample of housing units to be visited. When the household is visited the interviewer may have instructions to obtain information about everyone in the household or to obtain information about a person with certain characteristics, such as a female head of household.

(a) If the interviewer obtains information about every resident of the household, what is the element? What is the universe?

(b) If the interviewer is to obtain information only from female heads of households, what is the element? What is the universe?

13.3E A large industrial firm in Madison, Wisconsin, surveyed its employees to discover the amount of time the employees spent caring for elderly relatives and friends. One problem that arose was how to develop an operational definition of "employee." The sample was drawn from a recent payroll list. For each person on the list, it could be seen whether the person was full- or part-time, whether the person was laid off or working, and the age of the person, among other things. On the basis of the information given, how many operational definitions of "employee" can you come up with? How might the different definitions affect estimates of proportion of employees giving care to elderly persons and of amount of time spent giving care?

SECTION 13.4

CHARACTERISTICS OF PROBABILITY SURVEYS

Probability sample surveys have several distinguishing characteristics. This section fleshes out the bare-bones definitions given earlier.

USING PROBABILITY — UNIFORM RANDOM DIGITS

Probability methods permit portions of the universe to be used to draw conclusions about the whole universe. In earlier discussions the notion of statistical control was introduced. Remember that when a process is in statistical control, data from the process can be used to make predictions within limits about the future behavior of the process. In surveying, the use of probability methods for sample selection imposes a state of statistical control on the data that allows predictions about the universe to be made. In surveying, the universe is fixed in time, and the prediction is an inference about the state of the universe at that fixed time.

How are probability sampling methods carried out in practice? The basic tool needed is a table of random digits.[†] Such a table is given in Exhibit 1.7C. The digits are arranged in numbered rows and columns to make the table easy to use. How to use the table to draw a random sample will be covered in Chapter 14.

THE PRODUCT OF A PROBABILITY SURVEY

The result of a probability survey is not a detailed accounting of all the elements in the universe. That is the product of a census. The probability survey instead yields a

---

[†] If you wish to pursue the question "What is random?" refer to Kevin McKean, "The Orderly Pursuit of Pure Disorder," *Discover*, January 1987, 73–81. A popular table of random digits is *A Million Random Digits with 100,000 Normal Deviates*, published by the RAND Corporation in 1955.

profile of the universe. Usually this profile is a list of estimates of certain numerical characteristics of the elements of the universe. For example, estimates may include average age of employees, average age of inventory of certain parts, or proportion of employees who have taken an adult education course in the last 12 months.

The survey would not allow us to identify *which* employees had taken an adult education course. It would only allow us to infer what *proportion* of the employees had taken a course. A census would provide the more detailed information. Which level of information is needed depends on the decision that is informed or the question that is answered by the survey. If the proportion is all that is needed to make a decision, then doing a census to obtain the information entails a waste of time and money.

DETERMINING SAMPLE DESIGN AND SAMPLE SIZE

In a census the size of the study is determined by the size of the universe because all elements are examined. In sampling, the analyst chooses the size of the study and the design by which the data are collected. The sample design and the sample size are chosen to achieve some level of precision in the inferences about the universe. *Precision* means the width of the limits within which predictions about the universe are made. The narrower the limits the more precise the prediction.

▪**EXAMPLE 13.4A:** You find that the typical opinion poll reported in your newspaper is based on a sample of between 1000 and 1500 people. The limits on the sampling error in such polls are typically reported to be three percentage points. (Find reports of several polls and verify these statements. Can you find any major deviations from the figures reported?) Contrast these figures with the Current Population Survey, which is conducted each month by the Census Bureau for the Bureau of Labor Statistics, and which yields the employment and unemployment figures for the nation. The sample size for the Current Population Survey is roughly 60,000 people. It yields very small limits on sampling error in the overall national estimates. The sample is large so that it can be broken down by such categories as age, race, gender, and geographic region. The estimate of the unemployment rate for black males in the upper Midwest is subject to much larger sampling error than the estimate of the unemployment rate for all workers in the United States. Example 13.4B demonstrates the effect of varying the sample size.   ▪

Precision is not the only consideration in choosing sample size. Because sampling is done to achieve some economy of time and resources, the goal is to achieve either the best precision subject to limits on cost and time expended or a needed level of precision for the least cost. Several approaches to a particular sampling problem are often available. Determining the most efficient approach is not always easy, and compromises are common.

AN ILLUSTRATION OF SIMPLE RANDOM SAMPLING

The fundamental design of probability surveying is called *simple random sampling*. The principles behind this design are explained by working through an example based on an artificially small universe. In realistic problems the universe is much larger, but the basic principles are the same.

■**EXAMPLE 13.4B:** Exhibit 13.4A lists nine residential parcels of land in the small village of Toy, New York. The information shown was obtained from a file kept by the local assessor. A vacant parcel is one that consists of land only. An improved parcel is one on which a residential structure has been erected. Also shown in the exhibit are some numerical characteristics of the universe. Verify these figures.

EXHIBIT 13.4A

Data on Toy, New York

Parcel Number	Address	Vacant or Improved	Assessed Value ($1000s)
1	30 Muir Dr.	Vacant	30
2	12 Dairy La.	Improved	34
3	14 Dairy La.	Vacant	47
4	10 Dairy La.	Improved	50
5	5 Badger St.	Improved	57
6	8 Dairy La.	Improved	67
7	13 Badger St.	Improved	70
8	3 Muir Dr.	Improved	72
9	10 La Follette Blvd.	Improved	105

Proportion vacant = 2/9 = .2222...
Median assessed value = $57,000
Total assessed value = $532,000
Mean assessed value = $59,111.11 = $532,000/9

Now we will create an artificial situation that illustrates probability sampling. Pretend that the last two columns in Exhibit 13.4A are missing. You may select only two parcels at random, and for only those two will the information in the last two columns be revealed. Using that information, you are to make a guess at the figures at the bottom of the exhibit. Before we define "at random," we write down all the samples of two parcels it is possible to get. This is done in Exhibit 13.4B. For each sample the data to be revealed if that sample is chosen are also listed.

There are 36 distinct pairs of parcels that can constitute samples. If each one of these pairs has the same probability of being chosen, then a simple random sampling design is being used.

In Chapter 14 you will see how to implement a simple random sampling design using a table of random digits. But for now we pursue this example assuming that implementation is possible. The simplest characteristic of the universe to estimate is the mean of some variable, such as the mean assessed value. The mean assessed value in the universe is $59,111.11, or roughly 59.111 in $1000 units. Suppose by chance we draw the first sample in Exhibit 13.4B. The mean of the assessed values in this sample is $32,000, or just 32 in $1000 units. This is below the universe mean value by 27.111, a rather large margin of sampling error. The last sample in Exhibit 13.4B has a mean assessed value of $88,500, or 88.5 in $1000 units. The margin of sampling error in this sample is 29.389. The first and last samples

	Parcels in Sample	Number Vacant	Assessed Values	Total Assessed	Mean Assessed
EXHIBIT 13.4B	1 and 2	1	30, 34	64	32
	1 and 3	2	30, 47	77	38.5
All Possible Samples of	1 and 4	1	30, 50	80	40
Two Parcels from Toy,	1 and 5	1	30, 57	87	43.5
New York (values	1 and 6	1	30, 67	97	48.5
expressed in $1000s)	1 and 7	1	30, 70	100	50
	1 and 8	1	30, 72	102	51
	1 and 9	1	30, 105	135	67.5
	2 and 3	1	34, 47	81	40.5
	2 and 4	0	34, 50	84	42
	2 and 5	0	34, 57	91	45.5
	2 and 6	0	34, 67	101	50.5
	2 and 7	0	34, 70	104	52
	2 and 8	0	34, 72	106	53
	2 and 9	0	34, 105	139	69.5
	3 and 4	1	47, 50	97	48.5
	3 and 5	1	47, 57	104	52
	3 and 6	1	47, 67	114	57
	3 and 7	1	47, 70	117	58.5
	3 and 8	1	47, 72	119	59.5
	3 and 9	1	47, 105	152	76
	4 and 5	0	50, 57	107	53.5
	4 and 6	0	50, 67	117	58.5
	4 and 7	0	50, 70	120	60
	4 and 8	0	50, 72	122	61
	4 and 9	0	50, 105	155	77.5
	5 and 6	0	57, 67	124	62
	5 and 7	0	57, 70	127	63.5
	5 and 8	0	57, 72	129	64.5
	5 and 9	0	57, 105	162	81
	6 and 7	0	67, 70	137	68.5
	6 and 8	0	67, 72	139	69.5
	6 and 9	0	67, 105	172	86
	7 and 8	0	70, 72	142	71
	7 and 9	0	70, 105	175	87.5
	8 and 9	0	72, 105	177	88.5

are the extremes. All the other samples have means closer to the universe mean than these.

Another way to look at the data is to display a dotplot of the nine assessed values in the universe of parcels and of the 36 sample mean assessed values in Exhibit 13.4B. This is done in Exhibit 13.4C. The universe mean assessed value, 59.111, is shown as an asterisk (∗). The diagram shows the variation in the sample means, which is the sampling variation of the means.

EXHIBIT 13.4C

Dotplot of
Universe Assessed
Values and Sample Mean
Assessed Values for
Samples of Size 2 and
Size 3

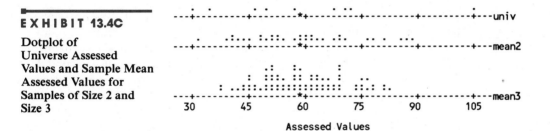

Assessed Values

	Characteristics of		
		Sample Means	
	Universe	Size 2	Size 3
Number	9	36	84
Sum	532	2128	4965.333
Average	59.111	59.111	59.111
Minimum	30	32	37
Maximum	105	88.5	82.333
Median	57	58.5	58
Standard deviation	22.817	14.229	10.756

The descriptive statistics under the diagrams show that the sampling variation in the sample means is less than the variation in the universe assessed values. Whereas the universe values range from 30 to 105 with a standard deviation of 22.82, the sample means range from 32 to 88.5 with a standard deviation of 14.229.

The average value of the assessed values in the universe and the average value of the sample means are the same, namely, 59.111. This is a property of many of the sampling designs studied in statistics. The sample values vary, of course, but their average value is equal to the universe average. This example illustrates the following general property: The average of all the sample means that can be generated from a simple random sampling design is equal to the average of universe values from which the samples are drawn.

Another general property is that the standard deviation of the collection of sample means is less than the standard deviation of the values in the universe. As is explained in Chapter 14, a mathematical formula gives the relationship between these two standard deviations.

Also shown in Exhibit 13.4C are the characteristics of samples of size 3. The detailed calculations are left as Exercise 13.5A, but the results help reinforce the remarks just made. Note that the average value of the means of all the 84 possible means of samples of size 3 is 59.111. For samples of size 3, the sample means range from a low of 37 to a high of 82.333, with a standard deviation of 10.756, which is lower than the universe standard deviation and the standard deviation of the means of samples of size 2. ■

The following analogy should help you understand simple random sampling. Imagine that the elements possible in a random sample are like the cards possible if you are dealt a hand from a deck of cards. The cards you get are subject to chance, beyond your control. But once the cards are dealt, you use your skill and cunning to reap the greatest gain from the cards you have been dealt. How well you do depends on the cards dealt to the other players in the game and how well they play their hands. If all players play skillfully, then some hands are more favorable than others, so there need be no dishonor in defeat if you play your hand in the best way possible.

Likewise, for some random samples it is possible to make estimates that are very close to the equal complete coverage values, whereas for others large sampling errors occur no matter how skillfully estimates are formed. Statistical theory suggests the best way to obtain estimates for a given sampling design and a given characteristic of interest. It also provides a way to place a bound on the magnitude of the sampling error the estimate may be subject to. If you follow the prescribed procedures, you are playing your hand the best way possible, even though by chance you may commit a rather large error. Of course, researchers have some control over the sizes of the errors, because they can choose the design and the sample size. But regardless of the choices, some sampling error will be present, and the card-playing analogy will apply to it.

SECTION 13.5

EXERCISES

13.5A Construct the sampling distribution pictured in the third dotplot in Exhibit 13.4C. It is the distribution of all possible sample mean assessed values of all samples of size 3 from the universe in Exhibit 13.4A. You need to write down the 84 possible samples of size 3, list the assessed values of the three parcels in each sample, and average these values. Finally, you can make a dotplot of the 84 mean values.

13.5B Repeat the analysis for both $n = 2$ and $n = 3$ in Example 13.4B but analyze the variable "Vacant or Improved." Do this by assigning a 0 to vacant parcels and a 1 to improved parcels. Analyze these numerical values just as the assessed values were analyzed in the example. Note that the mean values are just the proportions of parcels that are improved. This example shows that proportions are just means of a binary variable. As part of this exercise, identify the universe, the elements, and the sampling distribution of the sample means. What would be the behavior of samples of size 4? Make a qualitative statement but do not carry out all the calculations for $n = 4$.

SECTION 13.6

PROBLEMS COMMON TO ALL SURVEYS

Some difficulties and problems are common to all surveys, whether they are done by census or by sampling. These problems would arise even if the study did not involve sampling. Probability surveys add one more source of error, namely, sampling error. **Sampling error** is the difference between the value of a sample estimate and a corresponding equal complete coverage value that is due only to the sampling process. How to deal with sampling error will be discussed in Chapter 14. Here the focus is on **nonsampling error**, which is the difference between the value of a sample estimate and a corresponding equal complete coverage value that is due to some other cause than the sampling process.

COVERAGE PROBLEMS

One of the most frustrating problems in surveying is the inability to reach elements that are targeted for measurement. This problem may be caused by defective lists of elements or by a defective design that excludes part of the universe from consideration. For example, because of inadequate preliminary fieldwork a newly developed residential area may not be identified. Or procedures that are not adequate to search out residents of older inner-city areas in which residences are not easy to spot from streets or hallways may be developed. Finally, if shoppers in a mall are asked what stores they would like to see added to the mall, they may give responses different from those obtained from shoppers who do not visit the mall. These latter shoppers are, after all, the source of new visitors to the mall.

Another source of coverage error is inability to find residents at home. This can be an especially serious error if people who are seldom at home have characteristics different from those who are easier to reach. The characteristics of easy-to-reach respondents are overrepresented in surveys in which this problem is not recognized.

Another problem is refusal of respondents to answer even when reached. Sometimes this is due to hostility, sometimes to ignorance or other reasons. A related problem is the respondent who, not knowing an answer or not willing to divulge an answer, makes up one. This is an especially insidious form of error, hard to detect.

Finally, there is interviewer error. This may result from the interviewer not following instructions or from poorly worded instructions. It may also result from an interviewer's reluctance to visit a residence because of its appearance or the presence of a watchdog. An interviewer error may result in a blank questionnaire or one filled out by the interviewer without benefit of questioning a respondent!

Almost every survey, whether census or sample, suffers to some degree from the problem of coverage error, which means that not all the intended elements contribute data to the study. Data that are subject to coverage error are said to be *biased*. Suppose a census of households is taken to obtain information on average age of dwellings. If households in older sections of a city are more difficult to reach than other households, then they will be undercounted in the census and the average age of dwellings will be understated. The average is biased.

Coverage errors are difficult to detect even when we work very hard to detect them; unfortunately, the bias resulting from coverage errors can be quite severe, so the cost of not detecting them can be severe. In a typical survey, therefore, substantial resources are devoted to preventing, detecting, and correcting coverage errors.

PERSONNEL PROBLEMS

A telephone survey may use only a few people to make the calls and enter data into a computer file. An extensive survey that uses personal interviews requires a large field staff and typically a large office staff as well. Careful training and supervision of surveyors is essential to the success of a survey. This is just as important in the clerical processes as in the data-gathering processes. Clerical work can be a major source of errors, even when computers are used, unless it is carefully planned and managed.

Interviewer bias can also be a problem. This results when respondents react to the person asking the questions. In a personal interview, the gender, mannerisms, race, and age of the two people involved can affect the outcome of the interview. In a telephone interview, the gender and voice quality of the interviewer may affect the results. The interviewer effect is subtle. Research shows that interviewers with different characteristics may elicit quite different responses from the same or similar respondents. It is difficult, if not impossible, to say which response is more nearly correct. Probably the best action to take is to have each interviewer talk to as representative a group of respondents as possible. Trying to match interviewers and respondents by their personal characteristics seems to invite biases into the results that would be hard to document.

SURVEY INSTRUMENTS

Survey instruments are the devices used to gather the data. The most obvious example is a questionnaire that is filled out either by the respondent or by an interviewer as the respondent is interviewed. Other examples are diaries, data sheets, and computers that have been programmed to ask questions and receive answers.

The type of instrument used and especially the wording of the questions asked can have a major effect on the responses. Clarity, ease of use, and length are important. Subtle differences such as whether a question is phrased positively or negatively or its location on a questionnaire can have an effect. Because the survey instrument can have such a profound effect, it needs to be field tested carefully.[†]

AUDIT AND ERROR CONTROL

Errors creep into the best surveys. The best defense against errors is to institute rigorous quality-control measures at all stages of the survey process. These measures will include commitment to surveywide quality by everyone, careful training and supervision of workers, adoption of procedures that make the work easy and instill pride in the workers, and the use of statistical methods to monitor the quality of the work. In surveys that require a large work force, a certain amount of auditing is necessary. Usually a sample survey of the work is inspected by supervisors, and if the work is unsatisfactory, retraining or transfer of workers is called for. In surveys in which interviewers visit respondents in their homes, supervisors may revisit a sample of the homes and conduct a second interview to check the quality of the interviewers' work. Likewise, in telephone surveys a sample of numbers can be redialed and the respondents reinterviewed.

The audit and error control aspects of surveying are all too often neglected in practice because they are time consuming and costly; yet they are absolutely

[†] For further discussion of this critical topic, see Howard Schuman and Stanley Presser, *Questions and Answers in Attitude Surveys* (Boston: Academic Press, 1981). Also see the case study at the end of Chapter 12 of this text.

necessary to guarantee high-quality data. The need to perform these steps is one of the main reasons sample surveying is more prevalent than censusing. It is less costly to conduct audits and error controls in a sample of 1000 elements than in a census of 200 million elements. In fact, more stringent quality measures can be imposed on a small study than on a large study, and at less cost. This means that data from a carefully conducted sample survey can actually be of much higher quality than data from a census, while costing less to collect.

THE BIG FOUR

A brochure entitled "What Is a Survey?" appears in the appendix to this chapter. This brochure, prepared by some of the leading exponents of modern sample surveying, rewards careful study. In the "Shortcuts to Avoid" section the authors cite the four most common failings in survey practice: failure to use proper sampling procedures, failure to pretest field procedures, failure to follow up on nonrespondents, and failure to exercise quality control throughout the survey process. Avoid these failings when you are conducting surveys and watch for them in surveys that you are invited to use as a basis for action. Especially note the following sentence: "A low response rate does more damage in rendering a survey's results questionable than a small sample, since there is no valid way of scientifically inferring the characteristics of the [universe] represented by the nonrespondents."

An important practical implication of this remark is that it is better to opt for a small sample and stringent error-control measures, including follow-up on nonrespondents, than for such a large sample that error controls must be relaxed to stay within budget. This implication is sometimes difficult to accept because intuitively it seems that a larger sample must be more informative. In this instance, intuition fails.

The "How a Survey Is Carried Out" section is also important. This section provides a checksheet of steps to follow to conduct a good survey.

SECTION 13.7

EXERCISES

13.7A Suppose you work for an organization that is planning to survey the adult population of the United States, and you are a member of the coverage task force. List some groups that you believe are likely to be hard to reach. Develop strategies for reaching these groups.

13.7B Suppose 800 questionnaires are sent to business establishments in Wisconsin. Suppose further that 150 of the establishments return the questionnaire, and 113 of these say they favor building a business school on Rib Mountain. Which of the following are valid inferences from these data?
(a) 81.25% of the establishments did not return the questionnaire.
(b) 75.33% of those returning the questionnaire favor the Rib Mountain site.
(c) If all 650 of the nonresponding establishments do not favor the Rib Mountain site, then only 14.125% of the 800 surveyed establishments favor the Rib Mountain site.
(d) The survey data as reported contain no information about the 650 nonresponding establishments other than that they did not respond.

13.7C Locate and read Harper W. Boyd, Jr., and Ralph Westfall, "Interviewer Bias Once More Revisited," *Journal of Marketing Research* 7 (May 1970): 249–253. Write a brief memo explaining the problem of interviewer bias and what researchers knew about it, according to Boyd and Westfall, at the time the article was written.

13.7D Locate and read Charles F. Cannell, Lois Oksenberg, and Jean M. Converse, "Striving for Response Accuracy: Experiments in New Interviewing Techniques," *Journal of Marketing Research* 14 (August 1977): 306–315. Write a brief memo explaining the investigated sources of response error and the authors' recommendations for improving response accuracy.

13.7E Suppose you wish to interview a sample of residents of your home town by telephone. What sorts of coverage errors would you encounter if you drew your sample of telephone numbers from the white pages of the telephone book?

SECTION 13.8

THE ERROR TRIANGLE

To summarize the discussion of errors in surveys, a figure called the error triangle is presented in Exhibit 13.8A. The total error present in the data, represented by the hypotenuse of the right triangle, is made up of two parts: sampling error and nonsampling error. These errors are shown in triangular form because in statistical terms

$$(\text{Total error})^2 = (\text{Sampling error})^2 + (\text{Nonsampling error})^2$$

which is literally a Pythagorean theorem for errors.

EXHIBIT 13.8A

The Error Triangle

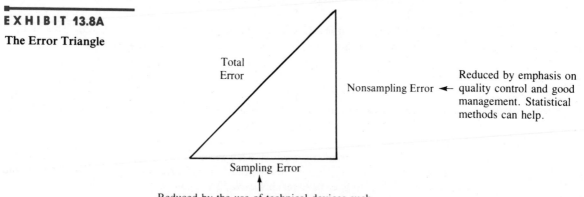

Generally speaking, sampling error is easier to deal with than nonsampling error, because there are a number of technical tools for controlling sampling error at minimum cost. Nonsampling error must be controlled through the institution of good management and process control. As a rule, the positive effects of good management and process control are hard to quantify, but the negative effects are relatively easy to detect. For example, a survey with a high nonresponse rate (say

50% or more) can be subject to so much bias that no reliable inference can be drawn about the universe. The greatest danger in a survey that relies on personal interviews is that different interviewers affect respondents differently. Research suggests that these dangers are so prevalent that to ignore them is to risk the very credibility of the survey, if not the surveyor. See Exercises 13.7C and 13.7D for documentation.

The error triangle shows that the effort that goes into a survey must be appropriately allocated to the two types of error. Perhaps the greatest danger in using probability surveys is that too much effort will be expended on reducing sampling error, because this is relatively easy to do, at the expense of effort that should go toward reducing nonsampling error. To take an extreme case, suppose all the effort were directed toward sampling error, but substantial biases due to nonsampling error were present. Then every reduction in sampling error would magnify the relative contribution of nonsampling error to the degradation of the quality of the data! Of course, failing to adopt a valid probability sampling design would have equally disastrous consequences. Proper attention must be paid to all aspects of the survey process.

SECTION 13.9

EXERCISES

13.9A Newspapers report a steady diet of opinion-poll results in connection with political campaigns, especially presidential campaigns. Survey organizations take polls at regular intervals. Comment on the relevance of such polls to the actual outcome of the election. What sorts of selection and respondent biases are likely to be present in polls taken months, weeks, and days before the election?

13.9B It is a well-established principle of science that the very act of subjecting an element to measurement alters the element. A common but often unstated assumption in surveying is that this fundamental dilemma can be ignored for practical purposes. The following references argue to the contrary. They raise the possibility that surveys, especially opinion polls, are part of a system of opinion and action control imposed by the political elite. Read and comment on these references. In particular, comment on the impact on public opinion of marketing surveys. Take as one example the Nielsen television ratings.

- Edward Walsh, "Polls Are Telling Us More, But Are They Telling It Like It Is?" *Washington Post*, 13 April 1987, weekly edition, 37.

- Benjamin Ginsberg, *The Captive Public: How Mass Opinion Promotes State Power* (New York: Basic Books, 1987). (For a review of this book see Ralph Braccio, "History of Mass Public Opinion and the Political Process," *Christian Science Monitor*, 16 April 1987, 28.)

13.9C Drawing on your reading, your personal experience, or both, make a list of examples in which the results of a survey were used as a basis for action. In each instance state whether the survey was a census, nonprobability, or probability survey.

13.9D Find a recent issue of *Employment and Earnings*, a publication of the Bureau of Labor Statistics. Read the description of the Current Population Survey and the Establishment Survey. Compare and contrast these two surveys in terms of who carries them out, the universes, the types of surveys they are, the data obtained from them, and the way the results are reported.

13.9E Find and read Lester R. Frankel, "Statistics and People—The Statistician's Responsibilities," *Journal of the American Statistical Association* 71 (353) (March 1976): 9–16. According to Frankel, what are a statistician's responsibilities toward the users of the product of a survey? Toward those who supply the raw data? How does Frankel suggest these responsibilities be met?

13.9F Surveys are often done to obtain a count of the number of elements in a universe. If the universe is very large or very complex, or both, the concept of counting is different from the customary notion of matching the elements with the positive integers until the elements are exhausted. For a provocative account of this problem that pays special attention to the management issues involved, read Vincent P. Barabba, Richard O. Mason, and Ian I. Mitroff, "Federal Statistics in a Complex Environment: The Case of the 1980 Census," *The American Statistician* 37 (3) (August 1983): 203–212. Vincent P. Barabba was the director of the Census Bureau when the 1980 census was taken.

Form a discussion group and take this article as a case study. Have the group recommend stategies for managing a census of the United States.

S E C T I O N   13.10

SUGGESTIONS FOR FURTHER READING

A number of references have been suggested in the text and in the exercises. In this section a few more references are provided in case you wish to study the topics of this chapter more deeply.

A good reference on random digits is Mervin E. Muller, "Random Numbers," in *International Encyclopedia of Statistics*, vol. 2, ed. William H. Kruskal and Judith M. Tanur (New York: Free Press, 1978), 839–847.

A remarkable treatment of sampling in business applications is W. Edwards Deming, *Sample Design in Business Research* (New York: Wiley, 1960). See especially Chapter 4 on operational definitions and Chapter 5 on nonsampling errors.

A book whose first five chapters contain a wealth of practical experience and advice on doing surveys is Frank Yates, *Sampling Methods for Censuses and Surveys*, 3rd ed. (New York: Hafner, 1953).

A succinct but rather technical presentation of the field of survey sampling is W. Edwards Deming, "Sample Surveys," in *International Encyclopedia of Statistics*, vol. 2, ed. William H. Kruskal and Judith M. Tanur (New York: Free Press, 1978), 867–885.

An elementary but readable treatment of the field of survey sampling is Richard L. Scheafer, William Mendenhall, and Lyman Ott, *Elementary Survey Sampling*, 4th ed. (Boston: PWS-KENT Publishing Company, 1990).

For a good treatment of nonsampling errors see Frederick Mosteller, "Nonsampling Errors," in *International Encyclopedia of Statistics*, vol. 1, ed. William H. Kruskal and Judith M. Tanur (New York: Free Press, 1978), 208–229.

A superb brief introduction to surveying is David Freedman, Robert Pisani, and Roger Purves, *Statistics* (New York: Norton, 1978), Chapters 19 and 22.

SUPPLEMENTARY EXERCISES FOR CHAPTER 13

13A From a deck of bridge cards take the 2 through the 10 of hearts (a total of nine cards). Let the cards be the elements of your universe, and let the numbers on the cards be the measurements associated with the elements.

    (a) Determine the mean and standard deviation of the whole set of measurements. (*Answer:* mean = 6, standard deviation = $\sqrt{15}/\sqrt{2} = \sqrt{7.5} \simeq 2.739$)

    (b) List all 36 possible samples of size $n = 2$ from the universe and list the measurements associated with the elements in the samples.

    (c) For each sample listed in part (b), compute the mean and standard deviation. Make dotplots of the 36 means and the 36 standard deviations. Compute the mean of the 36 means. (*Answer* = 6) Note that this is equal to the mean of the measurements in the universe. Compute the mean of the 36 standard deviations. (*Answer* = $(10/3)/\sqrt{2} \simeq 2.357$) Note that this is not equal to the standard deviation of the measurements in the universe.

    (d) Describe in general terms the result of repeating parts (b) and (c) for the 84 possible samples of size $n = 3$ from the universe. Do not carry out the computations.

    (e) Carry out the computations in parts (b) and (c) for the 84 samples of size $n = 3$ from the universe. Compare your findings with the predictions you made in part (d).

13B Refer to Exercise 13A, parts (b) and (c).

    (a) Suppose that circumstances prevent you from obtaining the 10 of hearts in your sample, an example of coverage error. Write down the 28 possible samples of size $n = 2$ under these circumstances, and write down the corresponding measurements. Repeat part (c) of Exercise 13A for these samples. Note that the mean of the sample means is not equal to the mean of all the measurements in the universe, namely, 6. Comment on how the coverage error affects the distributions of the sample means and sample standard deviations.

    (b) Repeat part (a) assuming that circumstances prevent you from obtaining the 6 of hearts. Compare the impact of this coverage error with the one you studied in part (a).

13C Come up with some examples of coverage errors and describe the circumstances that caused them. How can a low response rate to a questionnaire have the same effect as coverage error?

13D Coming up with an operational definition of "resident" can be difficult. To illustrate, find out the requirements your state imposes to determine if a person or family is eligible for state welfare benefits. Is there a residency requirement? Now find out the requirements imposed to determine if a student pays in-state tuition at the state university. Come up with other concepts for which operational definitions are difficult. Some suggestions are learning, strong, timely, and cost-effective.

13E Why is the question, "Were you robbed in the last six months?" ambiguous?

GLOSSARY FOR CHAPTER 13

Census　　　　A survey conducted with the intention of obtaining information from every element in the universe.

Elements　　　The basic units or individuals about which information is sought in a survey.

Equal complete coverage	The set of measurements obtained if the survey procedures were used on every element in the universe.
Nonprobability survey	Survey in which probability methods are *not* used to select the elements to be measured.
Nonsampling error	The difference between the value of a sample estimate and a corresponding equal complete coverage value that is due to some cause other than the sampling process.
Probability survey	Survey in which each element of the universe has a known probability of entering the sample.
Sampling error	The difference between the value of a sample estimate and a corresponding equal complete coverage value that is due only to the sampling process.
Sampling variation	The variation of numerical characteristics from sample to sample.
Survey	A process of systematically obtaining information on a universe of individuals.
Universe	The collection of all the elements of interest.

APPENDIX C

WHAT IS A SURVEY?

This document is reprinted with the permission of The American Statistical Association.

AMERICAN STATISTICAL ASSOCIATION WASHINGTON, D.C.

What Is a Survey?

By ROBERT FERBER, Chair, PAUL SHEATSLEY, ANTHONY TURNER, JOSEPH WAKSBERG,
Subcommittee of the Section on Survey Research Methods

INTRODUCTION

The growing popularity of surveys for throwing light on different problems has led to a tendency to overlook the fact that surveys involve many technical problems. Too many surveys seem to be conducted more or less on an ad hoc basis, with the result that the GIGO (garbage in, garbage out) principle is brought into play. This brochure seeks to help the nonstatistician to avoid this danger by providing a nontechnical introduction to sample surveys of human populations and the many different ways in which such surveys are used.

The principal focus is on the design of a survey and on the collection of survey data—two areas in which the many intricacies involved are frequently overlooked. However, attention is also given to the need for proper evaluation of survey data, an essential prerequisite for assessing the value of a survey as well as a basis for proper analysis of the data. (Analysis of survey data is a major topic in itself and is not covered here.)

This brochure can be used in a variety of ways, such as:

• By statisticians and survey agencies, to give prospective clients some appreciation of what is involved in a sample survey.

• By research executives, to help their nonresearch counterparts understand how surveys are conducted.

• By instructors in introductory social science and other courses, to give students a brief introduction to sample surveys.

• By international agencies and others advising in other countries, to give government officials in these other countries an understanding of the various steps of a sample survey.

It should be stressed that this brochure is *not* intended to provide students of statistics or prospective specialists in the field with a comprehensive understanding of survey methods. For this purpose, the books listed at the end of the brochure need to be used, plus many of the specialized sources dealing with the techniques of survey design and data collection. This brochure is meant for nonspecialists, for the users of survey data. If it leads them to have a better appreciation of what is involved in a sample survey, its purpose will have been served.

CHARACTERISTICS OF SURVEYS

The Need

Any observation or investigation of the facts about a situation may be called a survey. But today the word is most often used to describe a method of gathering information from a number of individuals, a "sample," in order to learn something about the larger population from which the sample has been drawn. Thus, a sample of voters is surveyed in advance of an election to determine how the public perceives the candidates and the issues. A manufacturer makes a survey of the potential market before introducing a new product. A government agency commissions a survey to gather the factual information it needs in order to draft new legislation. For example, what medical care do people receive, and how is it paid for? Who uses food stamps? How many people are unemployed?

It has been said that the United States is no longer an industrial society but an "information society." That is, our major problems and tasks no longer focus merely on the production of the goods and services necessary to our survival and comfort. Rather, our major problems and tasks today are those of organizing and managing the incredibly complex efforts required to meet the needs and wishes of nearly 220 million Americans. To do this requires a prompt and accurate flow of information on preferences, needs, and behavior. It is in response to this critical need for information on the part of the government, business, and social institutions that so much reliance is placed upon surveys.

Surveys come in many different forms and have a wide variety of purposes, but they do have certain characteristics in common. Unlike a census, they gather information from only a small sample of people (or farms, businesses, or other units, depending on the purpose of the study). In a bona fide survey, the sample is not selected haphazardly or only from persons who volunteer to participate. It is scientifically chosen so that each individual in the population has a known chance of selection. In this way, the results can be reliably projected to the larger public.

Information is collected by means of standardized questions so that every individual surveyed responds to exactly the same question. The survey's intent is not to describe the particular individuals who by chance are part of the sample but to obtain a statistical profile of the population. Individual respondents are never identified and the survey's results are presented in the form of summaries, such as statistical tables and charts.

The sample size required for a survey will depend on the reliability needed which, in turn, depends on how the results will be used. Consequently, there is no simple rule for sample size that can be used for all surveys. However, analysts usually find that a moderate sample size is sufficient for most needs. For example, the well-known national polls generally use samples of about 1500 persons to reflect national attitudes and opinions. A sample of this size produces accurate estimates even for a country as large as the United States with a population of over 200 million.

When it is realized that a properly selected sample of only 1500 individuals can reflect various characteristics of the total population within a very small margin of error, it is easy to understand the value of surveys in a complex society such as ours. They provide a speedy and economical means of determining facts about our economy and people's knowledge, attitudes, beliefs, expectations, and behavior.

Who Does Surveys?

We all know of the public opinion polls that are reported in the press and broadcast media. The Gallup Poll and the Harris Survey issue reports periodically, describing national public opinion on a wide range of current issues. State polls and metropolitan area polls, often supported by a local newspaper or TV station, are reported regularly in many localities. The major broadcasting networks and national news magazines also conduct polls and report their findings.

But the great majority of surveys are not exposed to public view. The reason is that, unlike the public opinion polls, most surveys are directed to a specific administrative or commercial purpose. The wide variety of issues with which surveys deal is illustrated by the following listing of actual uses:

1. The U.S. Department of Agriculture conducted a survey to find out how poor people use food stamps.

2. Major TV networks rely on surveys to tell them how many and what types of people are watching their programs.

3. Auto manufacturers use surveys to find out how satisfied people are with their cars.

4. The U.S. Bureau of the Census compiles a survey every month to obtain information on employment and unemployment in the nation.

5. The National Center for Health Statistics sponsors a survey every year to determine how much money people are spending for different types of medical care.

6. Local housing authorities make surveys to ascertain satisfaction of people in public housing with their living accommodations.

7. The Illinois Board of Higher Education surveys the interest of Illinois residents in adult education.

8. Local transportation authorities conduct surveys to acquire information on people's commuting and travel habits.

9. Magazine and trade journals utilize surveys to find out what their subscribers are reading.

10. Surveys are used to ascertain what sort of people use our national parks and other recreation facilities.

Surveys of human populations also provide an important source of basic social science knowledge. Economists, psychologists, political scientists, and sociologists obtain foundation or government grants to study such matters as income and expenditure patterns among households, the roots of ethnic or racial prejudice, comparative voting behavior, or the effects of employment of women on family life. (Surveys are also made of nonhuman populations, such as of animals, soils, and housing; they are not discussed here, although many of the principles are the same.)

Moreover, once collected, survey data can be analyzed and reanalyzed in many different ways. Data tapes with identification of individuals removed can be made available for analysis by community groups, scientific researchers, and others.

Types of Surveys

Surveys can be classified in a number of ways. One dimension is by size and type of sample. Many surveys study the total adult population, but others might focus on special population groups: physicians, community leaders, the unemployed, or users of a particular product or service. Surveys may be conducted on a national, state, or local basis and may seek to obtain data from a few hundred or many thousand people.

Surveys can also be classified by their method of data collection. Thus, there are mail surveys, telephone surveys, and personal interview surveys. There are also newer methods of data collection by which information is recorded directly into computers. This includes measurement of TV audiences carried out by devices attached to a sample of TV sets that automatically record in a computer the channels being watched. Mail surveys are seldom used to collect information from the general public because names and addresses are not often available and the response rate tends to be low, but the method may be highly effective with members of particular groups; for example, subscribers to a specialized magazine or members of a professional association. Telephone interviewing is an efficient method of collecting some types of data and is being increasingly used. A personal interview in a respondent's home or office is much more expensive than a telephone survey but is necessary when complex information is to be collected.

Some surveys combine various methods. Survey workers may use the telephone to "screen" for eligible respondents (say, women of a particular age group) and then make appointments for a personal interview. Some information, such as the characteristics of the respondent's home, may be obtained by observation rather than questioning. Survey data are also sometimes obtained by self-administered questionnaires filled out by respondents in groups, e.g., a class of school children or a group of shoppers in a central location.

One can further classify surveys by their content. Some surveys focus on opinions and attitudes (such as a pre-election survey of voters), while others are concerned with factual characteristics or behavior (such as a survey of people's health, housing, or transportation habits). Many surveys combine questions of both types. Thus, a respondent will be asked if s(he) has heard or read about an issue, what s(he) knows about it, his (her) opinion, how strongly s(he) feels and why, interest in the issue, past experience with it, and also certain factual information that will help the survey analyst classify the responses (such as age, sex, marital status, occupation, and place of residence).

The questions may be open-ended ("Why do you feel that way?") or closed ("Do you approve or disapprove?"); they may ask the respondent to rate a political candidate or a product on some kind of scale; they may ask for a ranking of various alternatives. The questionnaire may be very brief—a few questions taking five minutes or less; or it can be quite long—requiring an hour or more of the respondent's time. Since it is inefficient to identify and approach a large national sample for only a few items of information, there are "omnibus" surveys that combine the interests of several clients in a single interview. In such surveys, the respondent will be asked a dozen questions on one subject, half a dozen more on another subject, and so on.

Because changes in attitude or behavior cannot be reliably ascertained from a single interview, some surveys employ a "panel design," in which the same respondents are interviewed two or more times. Such surveys are often used during election campaigns, or to chart a family's health or purchasing pattern over a period of time. They are also used to trace changes in behavior over time, as with the social experiments that study changes by low-income families in work behavior in response to an income maintenance plan.

What Sort of People Work on Surveys?

The survey worker best known to the public is the interviewer who calls on the phone, appears at the door, or stops people at a shopping center. Contrary to the cartoons that typically portray the survey interviewer as a man wearing a hat and carrying a briefcase, the interviewer will usually be a woman between the ages of 30 and 60 who is skilled at approaching strangers, explaining the survey, and conducting the interview. Women interviewers arouse less fear and suspicion than men, and the part-time flexible nature of the work makes the job an attractive form of employment for many women.

Behind the interviewers are the in-house research staff who design the survey, determine the sample design, develop the questionnaire, supervise the data collection, carry out the clerical and computer operations necessary to process the completed interviews, analyze the data, and write the reports. In most survey research agencies, the senior people will have taken courses in survey methods at the graduate level and will hold advanced degrees in sociology, statistics, marketing, or psychology, or they will have the equivalent in business experience. Middle-level supervisors and research associates frequently have similar academic backgrounds, or they have advanced out of the ranks of clerks, interviewers, or coders on the basis of their competence and experience.

Are Responses Confidential?

The privacy of the information supplied by survey respondents is of prime concern to all reputable survey organizations. At the U.S. Bureau of the Census, for example, the confidentiality of much of the data collected is protected by law (Title 13 of the U.S. Code). In Canada, the Statistics Act guarantees the confidentiality of data collected by Statistics Canada. Other countries have similar safeguards. Also, a number of professional organizations that rely on survey methods have codes of ethics that prescribe rules for keeping survey responses confidential. The recommended policy for survey organizations to safeguard such confidentiality includes:

1. Using only code numbers for the identity of a respondent on a questionnaire, and keeping the code separate from that of the questionnaires.

2. Refusing to give names and addresses of survey respondents to anybody outside of the survey organization, including clients.

3. Destroying questionnaires and identifying information about respondents after the responses have been put onto computer tape.

4. Omitting the names and addresses of survey respondents from computer tapes used for analysis.

5. Presenting statistical tabulations by broad enough categories that individual respondents cannot be singled out.

HOW A SURVEY IS CARRIED OUT

As noted earlier, a survey usually has its beginnings when an individual or institution is confronted with an information need and there are no existing data that suffice. A politician may wish to tap prevailing voter opinions in his district about a proposal to build a superhighway through the county. A government agency may wish to assess the impact on the primary recipients and their families of one of its social welfare programs. A university researcher may wish to examine the relationship between actual voting behavior and expressed opinion on some political issue or social concern.

Designing a Survey

Once the information need has been identified and a determination made that existing data are inadequate, the first step in planning a survey is to lay out the objectives of the investigation. This is generally the function of the sponsor of the inquiry. The objectives should be as specific, clear-cut, and unambiguous as possible. The required accuracy level of the data has a direct bearing on the overall survey design. For example, in a sample survey whose main purpose is to estimate the unemployment rate for a city, the approximate number of persons to be sampled can be estimated mathematically when one knows the amount of sampling error that can be tolerated in the survey results.

Given the objectives, the methodology for carrying out the survey is developed. A number of interrelated activities are involved. Rules must be formulated for defining and locating eligible respondents, the method of collecting the data must be decided upon, a questionnaire must be designed and pretested, procedures must be developed for minimizing or controlling response errors, appropriate samples must be designed and selected, interviewers must be hired and trained (except for surveys involving self-administered questionnaires), plans must be made for handling nonresponse cases, and tabulation and analysis must be performed.

Designing the questionnaire represents one of the most critical stages in the survey development process, and social scientists have given a great deal of thought to issues involved in questionnaire design. The questionnaire links the information need to the realized measurement.

Unless the concepts are clearly defined and the questions unambiguously phrased, the resulting data are apt to contain serious biases. In a survey to estimate the incidence of robbery victimization, for example, one might want to ask, "Were you robbed during the last six months?" Though apparently straightforward and clear-cut, the question does present an ambiguous stimulus. Many respondents are unaware of the legal distinction between robbery (involving personal confrontation of the victim by the offender) and burglary (involving breaking and entering but no confrontation), and confuse the two in a survey. In the National Crime Survey, conducted by the Bureau of the Census, the questions on robbery victimization do not mention "robbery." Instead, several questions are used that, together, seek to capture the desired responses by using more universally understood phrases that are consistent with the operational definition of robbery.

Designing a suitable questionnaire entails more than well-defined concepts and distinct phraseology. Attention must also be given to its length, for unduly long questionnaires are burdensome to the respondent, are apt to induce respondent fatigue and hence response errors, refusals, and incomplete questionnaires, and may contribute to higher nonresponse rates in subsequent surveys involving the same respondents. Several other factors must be taken into account when designing a questionnaire to minimize or prevent biasing the results and to facilitate its use both in the field and in the processing center. They include such diverse considerations as the sequencing of sections or individual questions in the document, the inclusion of check boxes or precoded answer categories versus open-ended questions, the questionnaire's physical size and format, and instructions to the respondent or to the interviewer on whether certain questions are to be skipped depending on response patterns to prior questions.

Selecting the proper respondent in a sample unit is a key element in survey planning. For surveys where the inquiry is basically factual in nature, any knowledgeable person associated with the sample unit may be asked to supply the needed information. This procedure is used in the Current Population Survey, where the sample units are households and any responsible adult in a household is expected to be able to provide accurate answers on the employment-unemployment status of the eligible household members.

In other surveys, a so-called household respondent will produce erroneous and/or invalid information. For example, in attitude surveys it is generally accepted that a randomly chosen respondent from among the eligible household members produces a more valid cross section of opinion than does the nonrandomly selected household respondent. This is because a nonrandomly selected individual acting as household respondent is more likely to be someone who is at home during the day, and the working public and their attitudes would be underrepresented.

Another important feature of the survey planning process is devising ways to keep response errors and biases to a minimum. These considerations depend heavily on the subject matter of the survey. For example, memory plays an important role in surveys dealing with past events that the respondent is expected to report accurately, such as in a consumer expenditure survey. In such retrospective surveys, therefore, an appropriate choice of reference period must be made so that the respondent is not forced to report events that may have happened too long ago to remember accurately. In general, attention must be given to whether the questions are too sensitive, whether they may prejudice the respondent, whether they unduly invade the respondent's privacy, and whether the information sought is too difficult even for a willing respondent to provide. Each of these concerns has an important bearing on the overall validity of the survey results.

Sampling Aspects

Virtually all surveys that are taken seriously by social scientists and policy makers use some form of scientific sampling. Even the decennial Censuses of Population and Housing use sampling techniques for gathering the bulk of the data items, although 100 percent enumeration is used for the basic population counts. Methods of sampling are well-grounded in statistical theory and in the theory of probability. Hence, reliable and efficient estimates of a needed statistic can be made by surveying a carefully constructed sample of a population, as opposed to the entire population, provided of course that a large proportion of the sample members give the requested information.

The particular type of sample used depends on the objectives and scope of the survey, including the overall survey budget, the method of data collection, the subject matter, and the kind of respondent needed. A first step, however, in deciding on an appropriate sampling method is to define the relevant population. This target population can be all the people in the entire nation or all the people in a certain city, or it can be a subset such as all teenagers in a given location. The population of interest need not be people; it may be wholesale businesses or institutions for the handicapped or government agencies, and so on.

The types of samples range from simple random selection of the population units to highly complex samples involving multiple stages or levels of selection with stratification and/or clustering of the units into various groupings. Whether simple or complex, the distinguishing characteristic of a properly designed sample is that all the units in the target population have a known, nonzero chance of being included in the sample. It is this feature that makes it scientifically valid to draw inferences from the sample results about the entire population that the sample represents.

Ideally, the sample size chosen for a survey should be based on how reliable the final estimates must be. In practice, usually a trade-off is made between the ideal sample size and the expected cost of the survey. The complexity of a sample plan often depends on the availability of auxiliary information that can be used to introduce efficiencies into the overall design. For example, in a recent federal government survey on characteristics of health-care institutions, existing information about the type of care provided and the number of beds in each institution was useful in sorting the institutions into "strata," or groups by type and size, in advance of selecting the sample. The procedure permitted more reliable survey estimates than would have been possible if a simple random selection of institutions had been made without regard to size or type.

A critical element in sample design and selection is defining the source of materials from which a sample can be chosen. This source, termed the sampling frame, generally is a list of some kind, such as a list of housing units in a city, a list of retail establishments in a county, or a list of students in a university. The sampling frame can also consist of geographic areas with well-defined natural or artificial boundaries, when no suitable list of the target population exists. In the latter instance, a sample of geographic areas (referred to as segments) is selected and an interviewer canvasses the sample "area segments" and lists the appropriate units—households, retail stores, or whatever—so that some or all of them can be designated for inclusion in the final sample.

The sampling frame can also consist of less concrete things, such as all possible permutations of integers that make up banks of telephone numbers, in the case of telephone surveys that seek to include unlisted numbers. The quality of the sampling frame—whether it is up to date and how complete—is probably the dominant feature for ensuring adequate coverage of the desired population.

Conducting a Survey

Though a survey design may be well conceived, the preparatory work would be futile if the survey were executed improperly. For personal or telephone interview surveys, interviewers must be carefully trained in the survey's concepts, definitions, and procedures. This may take the form of classroom training, self-study, or both. The training stresses good interviewer techniques on such points as how to make initial contacts, how to conduct interviews in a professional manner, and how to avoid influencing or biasing responses. The training generally involves practice interviews to familiarize the interviewers

with the variety of situations they are likely to encounter. Survey materials must be prepared and issued to each interviewer, including ample copies of the questionnaire, a reference manual, information about the identification and location of the sample units, and any cards or pictures to be shown to the respondent.

Before conducting the interview, survey organizations frequently send an advance letter to the sample member explaining the survey's purpose and the fact than an interviewer will be calling soon. In many surveys, especially those sponsored by the federal government, information must be given to the respondent regarding the voluntary or mandatory nature of the survey, and how the answers are to be used.

Visits to sample units are scheduled with attention to such considerations as the best time of day to call or visit and the number of allowable callbacks for no-one-at-home situations. Controlling the quality of the field work is an essential aspect of good survey practice. This is done in a number of ways, most often through observation or rechecking of a subsample of interviews by supervisory or senior personnel, and through office editing procedures to check for omissions or obvious mistakes in the data.

When the interviews have been completed and the questionnaires filled out, they must be processed in a form so that aggregated totals, averages, or other statistics can be computed. This will involve clerical coding of questionnaire items that are not already precoded. Occupation and industry categorizations are typical examples of fairly complex questionnaire coding that is usually done clerically. Also procedures must be developed for coding open-ended questions and for handling items that must be transcribed from one part of the questionnaire to another.

Coded questionnaires are keypunched, entered directly onto tape so that a computer file can be created, or entered directly into the computer. Decisions may then be needed on how to treat missing data and "not answered" items.

Coding, keypunching, and transcription operations are subject to human error and must be rigorously controlled through verification processes, either on a sample basis or 100 percent basis. Once a computer file has been generated, additional computer editing, as distinct from clerical editing of the data, can be accomplished to alter inconsistent or impossible entries, e.g., a six-year-old grandfather.

When a "clean" file has been produced, the survey data are in a form where analysts can specify to a computer programmer the frequency counts, cross-tabulations, or more sophisticated methods of data presentation or computation that are needed to help answer the concerns outlined when the survey was initially conceived.

The results of the survey are usually communicated in publications and in verbal presentations at staff briefings or more formal meetings. Secondary analysis is also often possible to those other than the survey staff by making available computer data files at nominal cost.

Shortcuts to Avoid

As we have seen, conducting a creditable survey entails scores of activities, each of which must be carefully planned and controlled. Taking shortcuts can invalidate the results and badly mislead the user. Four types of shortcuts that crop up often are failure to use a proper sampling procedure, no pretest of the field procedures, failure to follow up nonrespondents, and inadequate quality control.

One way to ruin an otherwise well-conceived survey is to use a convenience sample rather than one that is based on a probability design. It may be simple and cheap, for example, to select a sample of names from a telephone directory to find out which candidate people intend to vote for. However, this sampling procedure could give incorrect results since persons without telephones or with unlisted numbers would have no chance to be reflected in the sample, and their voting preferences could be quite different from persons who have listed telephones. This is what happened with the *Literary Digest* presidential poll of 1936 when use of lists of telephone owners, magazine subscribers, and car owners led to a prediction that President Roosevelt would lose the election.

A pretest of the questionnaire and field procedures is the only way of finding out if everything "works," especially if a survey employs a new procedure or a new set of questions. Since it is rarely possible to foresee all the possible misunderstandings or biasing effects of different questions and procedures, it is vital for a well-designed survey plan to include provision for a pretest. This is usually a small-scale pilot study to test the feasibility of the intended techniques or to perfect the questionnaire concepts and wording.

Failure to follow up nonrespondents can ruin an otherwise well-designed survey, for it is not uncommon for the initial response rate to most surveys to be under 50 percent. Plans must include returning to sample households where no one was home, attempting to persuade persons who are inclined to refuse, and, in the case of mail surveys, contacting all or a subsample of the nonrespondents by telephone or personal visit to obtain a completed questionnaire. A low response rate does more damage in rendering a survey's results questionable than a small sample, since there is no valid way of scientifically inferring the characteristics of the population represented by the nonrespondents.

Quality control, in the sense of checking the different facets of a survey, enters in at all stages—checking sample selection, verifying interviews, and checking the editing and coding of the responses, among other things. In particular, sloppy execution of the survey in the field can seriously damage the results. Without proper quality control, errors can occur with disastrous results, such as selecting or visiting the wrong household, failing to ask questions properly, or recording the incorrect answer. Insisting on proper standards in recruitment and training of interviewers helps a great deal, but equally important is proper review, verification, and other quality control measures to ensure that the execution of a survey corresponds to its design.

USING THE RESULTS OF A SURVEY

How Good Is the Survey?

The statistics derived from a survey will rarely correspond exactly with the unknown truth. (Whether "true" values always exist is not important in the present context. For fairly simple measurements—the average age of the population, the amount of livestock on farms, etc.—the concept of a true value is fairly straightforward. Whether true values exist for measurements of such items as attitudes toward political candidates, I.Q.'s, etc., is a more complex matter.)

Fortunately, the value of a statistic does not depend on its being exactly true. To be useful, a statistic need not be exact, but it does need to be sufficiently reliable to serve the particular needs. No overall criterion of reliability applies to all surveys since the margin of error that can be tolerated in a study depends on the actions or recommendations that will be influenced by the data. For example, economists examining unemployment rates consider a change of 0.2 percent as having an important bearing on the U.S. economy. Consequently, in the official U.S. surveys used to estimate unemployment, an attempt is made to keep the margin of error below 0.2 percent. Conversely, there are occasions when a high error rate is acceptable. Sometimes a city will conduct a survey to measure housing vacancies to determine if there is a tight housing supply. If the true vacancy rate is very low, say 1 percent, survey results that show double this percentage will not do any harm; any results in the range of 0 to 2 or 3 percent will lead to the same conclusion—a tight housing market.

In many situations the tolerable error will depend on the kind of result expected. For example, during presidential elections the major television networks obtain data on election night from a sample of election precincts, in order to predict the election results early in the evening. In a state in which a large difference is expected (pre-election polls may indicate that one candidate leads by a substantial majority and is likely to receive 60 percent of the vote), even with an error of 5 or 6 percent it would still be possible to predict the winner with a high degree of accuracy. A relatively small sample size may be adequate in such a state. However, much more precise estimates are required in states where the two candidates are fairly evenly matched and where, say, a 52–48 percent vote is expected.

Thus, no general rule can be laid down to determine the reliability that would apply to all surveys. It is necessary to consider the purpose of the particular study, how the data will be used, and the effect of errors of various sizes on the action taken based on the survey results. These factors will affect the sample size, the design of the questionnaire, the effort put into training and supervising the interview staff, and so on. Estimates of error also need to be considered in analyzing and interpreting the results of the survey.

Sources of Errors

In evaluating the accuracy of a survey, it is convenient to distinguish two sources of errors: (1) sampling errors and (2) nonsampling errors, including the effect of refusals and not-at-homes, respondents providing incorrect information, coding or other processing errors, and clerical errors in sampling.

Sampling Errors Good survey practice includes calculation of sampling errors, which is possible if probability methods are used in selecting the sample. Furthermore, information on sampling errors should be made readily available to all users of the statistics. If the survey results are published, data on sampling errors should be included in the publication. If information is disseminated in other ways, other means of informing the public are necessary. Thus, it is not uncommon to hear television newscasters report on the size of sampling errors as part of the results of some polling activity.

There are a number of ways of describing and presenting data on sampling errors so that users can take them into account. For example, in a survey designed to produce only a few statistics (such as the votes that the candidates for a particular office are expected to get), the results could be stated that Candidate A's votes are estimated at 57 percent with the error unlikely to be more than 3 percent, so that this candidate's votes are expected to fall in the range of 54–60 percent. Other examples can be found in most publications of the principal statistical agencies of the U.S. government, such as the Bureau of the Census.

Nonsampling Errors Unfortunately, unlike sampling errors, there is no simple and direct method of estimating the size of nonsampling errors. In most surveys, it is not practical to measure the possible effect on the statistics of the various potential sources of error. However, in the past 30 or 40 years, there has been a considerable amount of research on the kinds of errors that are likely to arise in different kinds of surveys. By examining the procedures and operations of a specific survey, experienced survey statisticians will frequently be able to assess its quality. Rarely will this produce actual error ranges, as for sampling errors. In most cases, the analyst can only state that, for example, the errors are probably relatively small and will not affect most conclusions drawn from the survey, or that the errors may be fairly large and inferences are to be made with caution.

Nonsampling errors can be classified into two groups— random types or errors whose effects approximately cancel out if fairly large samples are used, and biases that tend to create errors in the same direction and thus cumulate over the entire sample. With large samples, the possible biases are the principal causes for concern about the quality of a survey.

Biases can arise from any aspect of the survey operation. Some of the main contributing causes of bias are:

1. *Sampling operations.* There may be errors in sample selection, or part of the population may be omitted from the sampling frame, or weights to compensate for disproportionate sampling rates may be omitted.

2. *Noninterviews.* Information is generally obtained for only part of the sample. Frequently there are differences between the noninterview population and those interviewed.

3. *Adequacy of respondent.* Sometimes respondents cannot be interviewed and information is obtained about them from others, but the "proxy" respondent is not always as knowledgeable about the facts.

4. *Understanding the concepts.* Some respondents may not understand what is wanted.

5. *Lack of knowledge.* Respondents in some cases do not know the information requested, or do not try to obtain the correct information.

6. *Concealment of the truth.* Out of fear or suspicion of the survey, respondents may conceal the truth. In some instances, this concealment may reflect a respondent's desire to answer in a way that is socially acceptable, such as indicating that s(he) is carrying out an energy conservation program when this is not actually so.

7. *Loaded questions.* The question may be worded to influence the respondents to answer in a specific (not necessarily correct) way.

8. *Processing errors.* These can include coding errors, data keying, computer programming errors, etc.

9. *Conceptual problems.* There may be differences between what is desired and what the survey actually covers. For example, the population or the time period may not be the one for which information is needed, but had to be used to meet a deadline.

10. *Interviewer errors.* Interviewers may misread the question or twist the answers in their own words and thereby introduce bias.

Obviously, each survey is not necessarily subject to all these sources of error. However, a good survey statistician will explore all of these possibilities. It is considered good practice to report on the percent of the sample that could not be interviewed and as many of the other factors listed as practicable.

BUDGETING A SURVEY

We have seen from the preceding sections that many different stages are involved in a survey. These include tasks such as planning, sample design, sample selection, questionnaire preparation, pretesting, interviewer hiring and training, data collection, data reduction, data processing, and report preparation. From a time point of view, these different stages are not necessarily additive since many of them overlap. This is illustrated in the diagram on page 375 which portrays the sequence of steps involved in a typical personal interview survey. Some steps, such as sample design and listing housing units in the areas to be covered in the survey, can be carried out at the same time a questionnaire is being revised and put into final form. Although they are not additive, all of these steps are time consuming, and one of the most common errors is to underestimate the time needed by making a global estimate without considering these individual stages.

How much time is needed for a survey? This varies with the type of survey and the particular situation. Sometimes a survey can be done in two or three weeks, if it involves a brief questionnaire and if the data are to be collected by telephone from a list already available. More usually, however, a survey of several hundred or a few thousand individuals will take anywhere from a few months to more than a year, from initial planning to having results ready for analysis.

A flow diagram for a particular survey is very useful in estimating the cost of such a survey. Such a diagram ensures that allowance is made for the expense involved in the different tasks, as well as for quality checks at all stages of the work. Thus, among the factors that enter into an expense budget are the following:

1. Staff time for planning the study and steering it through the various stages.

2. Labor and material costs for pretesting the questionnaire and field procedures.

3. Supervisory costs for interviewer hiring, training, and supervision.

4. Interviewer labor costs and travel expense (and meals and lodging, if out of town).

5. Labor and expense costs of checking a certain percentage of the interviews (by reinterviews).

6. Cost of preparing codes for transferring information from the questionnaire.

7. Labor and material costs for editing, coding, and keypunching the information from the questionnaire onto computer tape.

8. Cost of spot-checking to assure the quality of the editing, coding, and keypunching.

9. Cost of "cleaning" the final data tapes, that is, checking the tapes for inconsistent or impossible answers.

10. Programming costs for preparing tabulations and special analyses of the data.

11. Computer time for the various tabulations and analyses.

12. Labor time and material costs for analysis of the data and report preparation.

13. Telephone charges, postage, reproduction, and printing costs.

An integral part of a well-designed survey, both in terms of time and of costs, is allowance for quality checks all along the way. For example, checks have to be made that the sample was selected according to specifications, that the interviewers did their work properly, that the information from the questionnaires was coded accurately, that the keypunching was done correctly, and that the computer programs used for data analysis work properly. For these reasons, a good survey does not come cheap, although some are more economical than others. As a rule, surveys made by personal interview are more expensive than by mail or by telephone; and costs will increase with the complexity of the questionnaire and the amount of analysis to be carried out. Also, surveys that involve more interviews tend to be cheaper on a per interview basis than surveys with fewer interviews. This is particularly so where the sample size is less than about a thousand because "tooling up" is involved for just about any survey, except one that is to be repeated on the same group.

WHERE TO GET MORE INFORMATION

Several professional organizations have memberships heavily involved in survey research. They also frequently have workshops or sessions on surveys as parts of their regional and annual meetings. The principal organizations are the following:

1. The American Statistical Association is concerned with survey techniques and with general application of survey data. It has a separate Section on Survey Research Methods that sponsors sessions on surveys at the annual

Stages of a Survey

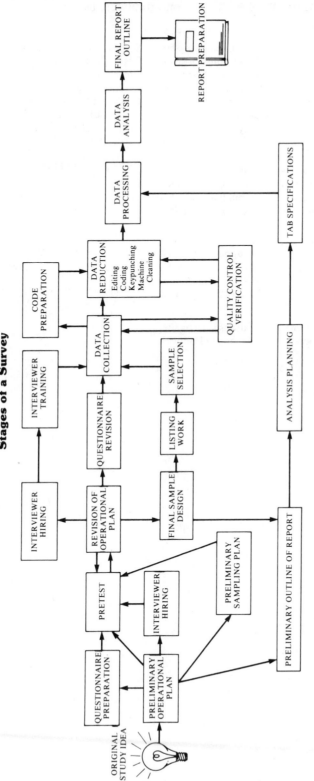

meetings of the association. The many chapters of the association in the various parts of the country also periodically have meetings and workshops on survey methods, and its publications, the *Journal of the American Statistical Association* and the *American Statistician*, carry numerous articles about surveys.

2. The American Marketing Association is concerned, among other things, with the application of survey methods to marketing problems. Like the American Statistical Association, it sponsors sessions on survey methods at its annual meetings, and still other sessions are sponsored by its local chapters. Its publications, the *Journal of Marketing* and the *Journal of Marketing Research*, frequently contain articles on surveys.

3. The American Association for Public Opinion Research focuses on survey methods as applied to social and media problems. Its journal, the *Public Opinion Quarterly*, regularly carries articles on survey techniques and on the application of survey methods to political and social problems.

A number of other professional associations such as the American Sociological Association, the American Political Science Association, the Association for Consumer Research, the American Public Health Association, the American Psychological Association, the Canadian Psychological Association, and the Statistical Society of Canada, place emphasis periodically on survey methods. There are also various business-oriented associations such as the Advertising Research Foundation and the American Association of Advertising Agencies, that give attention to survey methods as applied to business. These and other associations publish a number of journals that carry a great deal of material on survey methods.

There are many good books on survey methods written for nontechnical readers. A few of these are:

1. Judith Tanur et al., *Statistics: A Guide to the Unknown* (San Francisco: Holden-Day, 1972).

2. Philip Hauser, *Social Statistics in Use* (New York: Russell Sage Foundation, 1975).

3. William H. Williams, *A Sampler on Sampling* (New York: Wiley, 1978).

## CHAPTER 14

Survey Design and Simple Random Sampling

INTRODUCTION

This chapter begins the technical study of probability sampling. Chapter 13 was mostly conceptual. In this chapter basic methods for designing surveys and forming estimates of important quantities are introduced.

Consider a project that was done by the word processing department of a large government agency.[†] As the quality-improvement team began to meet to identify the problems they felt were important, they surveyed the employees in the other departments of the agency that were heavy users of word processing. They were quite surprised to find that their work was perceived to be of rather high quality in terms of error rate but that their turnaround time was too long. This finding prompted them to determine the causes of slow turnaround and to work on ways to

[†] William Hunter, Jan O'Neill, and Carol Wallen, "Doing More with Less in the Public Sector: A Progress Report from Madison, Wisconsin," Report No. 13, Center for Quality and Productivity Improvement, University of Wisconsin-Madison, June 1986.

speed up their service without increasing the error rate. Their work ultimately led to a reduction of average turnaround from two weeks to eight hours *and* a reduction in error rate! The survey of customers helped the quality-improvement team quickly identify the most important part of their service that needed improvement.

The message we hope to convey is that surveying is not the exclusive property of large survey outfits. When you encounter work done by these outfits, though, you need to be able to interpret the reports correctly. Thus the interpretation of the report of a complex survey is presented in Chapter 15.

Three fundamental probability sampling designs are explained in this chapter and Chapter 16: simple random sampling, stratified sampling, and cluster sampling. This chapter presents simple random sampling. Chapter 16 covers stratification and clustering. The first two designs are covered in some detail; the third is only sketched. Clustering, while pervasive in practice, is technically complicated, so references in which you may pursue this topic if you desire are given.

As you plan and carry out a survey, you need to pay careful attention to a large number of detailed steps. Chapters 14–16 concentrate on the design steps and the estimation steps. As discussed in Chapter 13, steps must also be devoted to tasks such as error prevention, detection, and correction; personnel recruitment, training, and supervision; and report preparation.

SECTION 14.2

STRUCTURE OF SIMPLE RANDOM SAMPLING

The most elementary sampling design is simple random sampling. Although it can be used in small studies, its primary use is in conjunction with other techniques, such as stratification and clustering.

THE SAMPLING PLAN

A **simple random sample** is a sample taken so that each possible sample of size *n* has the same chance of being selected. To implement simple random sampling a list of the elements of the universe from which the sample will be drawn is needed. The list is called a **frame**. Ideally, each element is shown on the list once and only once. In practice, constructing a frame can be quite difficult, and the frame may have errors. Some elements may be left off the list; others may appear more than once. Although the probabilities of drawing elements from the frame are known, they cannot be attributed to the elements of the universe unless there is an exact correspondence between the universe and the frame. Thus frame construction is a critical step in simple random sampling.

Part of frame construction is the numbering of the elements. A number can be written next to each element in the frame. A rule for working through the frame such that each element is assigned a unique number must be used. The numbering starts with 0 and is consecutive. This is done to make it easy to use random digits to draw the sample.

The way to draw elements at random from the frame is described in the following subsection. Once the drawing is done, the elements must be contacted and measured. This could mean contacting a household in person or by phone and interviewing a designated member of the household, or it could mean driving to a telephone pole and measuring a number of its physical characteristics. The way the data are collected depends on the plan developed for the particular survey.

HOW TO DRAW A SIMPLE RANDOM SAMPLE

■ **E X A M P L E 14.2A:** Suppose the frame lists 2164 elements, and a sample of 50 elements is desired. Fifty numbers between 0000 and 2163 need to be selected at random. The elements associated with these numbers are drawn into the sample. The first element is associated with the number 0000, the second element with 0001, and so on. The last element is associated with 2163.

How are the 50 numbers selected at random? A table of uniform random digits such as the one presented in Exhibit 1.7C is used. The simplest way to use the table is to pick an arbitrary starting point in the table, then work across the rows of the table, grouping the digits in groups of four. Any such four-digit number that falls between 0000 and 2163 draws an element into the sample. Elements are allowed to appear only once in a given sample, so if a random number is repeated, the number is ignored and the corresponding element is not entered into the sample a second time. This is called *sampling without replacement*. Likewise, numbers that do not fall between 0000 and 2163 are ignored.

The table of random digits in Exhibit 1.7C is repeated in Exhibit 14.2A. It has 50 rows and 20 columns. We asked a colleague to pick any number between 1 and 50. He picked 23. We asked another colleague to pick a number between 1 and 20. He picked 5. We started our list of random digits in row 23 and column 5 of Exhibit 14.2A. Reading across the row, the first four-digit number is 0320, which is between 0000 and 2163. This number brings element 321 into the sample. The next four-digit number is 4125. This is greater than 2163, so it does not draw an element into the sample. The next few four-digit random numbers are 3535, 5852, 9645, 4460, 9798, 5525, 2614, 3415, and 1302. The process continues until 50 elements have been drawn from the frame. A larger table than the one shown in Exhibit 14.2A may be needed to complete the sample. The procedure outlined above assigns the same probability of being drawn to each possible sample of 50 elements from the frame, approximately 9×10^{-103}. Even though such a probability is unfathomably small, it applies to each possible sample of size 50. Of course, one such sample is certainly selected by the random sampling procedure. Each element has 50 chances out of 2164 of being included in the sample. This probability, $50/2164 = .0231$, about 23 chances out of 1000, is not beyond comprehension and is intuitively reasonable, since there are 50 elements drawn from 2164. ■

This example illustrates the approach to use in drawing a simple random sample from any frame. The number of digits that need to be grouped into random numbers is determined by the number of elements in the frame. If there are 100 elements, digits need to be grouped two at a time: $00, 01, \ldots, 99$. If there are 10,000 elements, digits need to be grouped four at a time: $0000, 0001, \ldots, 9999$.

EXHIBIT 14.2A

Table of Random Digits

Row	1	2	3	4	5	6	7	8	9	10	11	12	13	14	15	16	17	18	19	20
1	2	1	9	4	6	3	9	5	5	5	7	1	7	2	4	4	6	7	1	7 8
2	9	5	5	6	6	0	3	0	7	3	5	5	7	0	8	4	2	8	9	6
3	2	5	2	3	2	0	0	4	5	3	1	4	8	1	3	7	7	6	4	0
4	3	9	4	4	3	8	5	4	3	9	0	2	8	4	6	4	9	7	7	6
5	6	4	0	9	4	6	8	0	5	5	7	6	1	1	9	8	1	5	4	1
6	1	3	7	3	8	1	9	9	8	7	5	8	0	3	7	0	1	4	2	1
7	0	3	0	9	9	6	9	1	2	1	4	7	4	7	5	5	2	3	1	9
8	9	7	8	2	2	1	1	6	7	6	0	9	7	8	0	1	2	5	2	1
9	9	9	3	6	1	3	3	9	7	6	8	5	9	1	2	4	9	7	0	1
10	7	5	0	3	6	8	9	5	4	9	9	4	6	5	0	4	9	7	4	9
11	7	8	5	7	1	7	9	3	7	1	1	7	1	9	1	5	7	8	1	1
12	4	2	6	8	1	1	8	7	6	0	5	6	7	1	2	1	9	8	3	4
13	0	0	7	5	9	4	1	8	6	4	4	0	6	6	8	4	0	9	7	8
14	0	4	6	0	5	3	8	7	9	0	7	1	0	2	4	7	4	7	5	7
15	0	4	0	1	8	0	6	8	8	7	5	5	1	2	1	5	8	7	7	4
16	5	4	8	5	3	4	1	9	1	5	0	1	9	5	3	0	3	3	9	1
17	0	5	4	8	7	9	0	4	9	9	0	0	5	0	8	8	1	4	0	3
18	6	2	4	8	9	9	0	2	2	5	0	1	6	0	8	7	7	6	4	0
19	0	1	8	4	2	2	3	5	9	2	5	7	8	0	6	1	9	4	9	0
20	8	9	8	2	4	1	0	0	9	6	8	9	5	4	3	9	1	4	9	6
21	4	9	8	1	1	9	0	6	0	6	9	9	7	3	7	0	4	2	7	2
22	2	9	4	1	8	2	9	3	3	8	2	8	3	5	0	3	5	4	3	
23	5	3	4	1	0	3	2	0	4	1	2	5	3	5	3	5	5	8	5	2
24	9	6	4	5	4	4	6	0	9	7	9	8	5	5	2	5	2	6	1	4
25	3	4	1	5	1	3	0	2	1	3	3	1	2	9	4	8	9	8	2	8
26	7	7	2	9	6	2	4	6	3	2	1	3	6	7	3	9	4	1	6	7
27	5	3	9	2	7	8	2	6	7	6	6	9	1	5	9	2	5	4	4	3
28	6	7	7	8	7	7	8	1	0	4	1	7	0	6	4	3	6	8	0	6
29	6	4	6	0	6	0	2	3	3	0	6	7	3	5	0	7	3	9	8	7
30	0	7	2	6	5	9	1	7	4	2	2	7	9	2	9	5	2	9	5	0
31	1	3	7	8	4	5	2	4	2	6	7	3	2	9	9	3	5	1	6	4
32	1	8	5	6	6	3	7	7	0	0	1	9	2	6	1	4	2	1	0	9
33	0	7	6	5	0	3	8	2	6	0	1	0	4	4	0	1	1	4	9	7
34	7	1	7	3	2	6	6	4	4	5	0	6	2	6	6	9	3	6	8	8 4
35	1	0	5	9	9	6	7	7	6	3	5	1	3	3	7	4	4	0	6	1
36	9	9	6	7	7	2	8	3	9	8	8	0	1	8	8	8	0	2	1	2
37	5	3	4	9	7	9	2	9	2	9	9	1	1	1	5	3	5	0	6	5
38	0	4	6	6	8	5	2	9	3	5	2	9	2	0	0	7	3	1	3	6
39	6	9	8	4	0	3	4	2	8	2	8	0	9	1	7	3	0	8	9	6
40	3	0	3	0	5	0	7	8	0	9	1	3	0	7	8	6	8	6	0	8
41	9	5	1	2	8	1	8	2	6	3	9	9	0	1	0	7	7	2	3	3
42	5	3	2	2	2	4	0	0	3	9	6	8	9	1	7	4	2	7	6	8
43	2	1	6	1	3	3	1	6	5	7	7	3	5	1	7	4	5	7	3	8
44	5	7	1	4	4	7	1	2	9	1	8	5	9	9	7	7	9	8	7	9
45	9	0	0	5	4	6	3	6	1	5	0	0	4	8	3	5	9	5	3	2
46	0	5	0	0	0	2	1	9	2	3	0	1	0	2	8	6	6	3	6	7
47	0	2	4	1	1	5	0	2	5	5	7	7	8	2	2	9	0	4	0	9
48	4	0	1	7	9	7	7	3	0	2	0	7	0	0	1	2	3	2	2	6
49	1	6	0	8	0	7	8	6	6	6	6	5	2	7	1	1	8	2	1	7
50	5	9	9	9	5	0	7	4	7	1	1	5	4	6	3	5	9	7	5	6 4

Certain notation is used frequently in simple random sampling. The number of elements in the frame is denoted by N, the size of the sample by n. The ratio n/N is called the *sampling fraction* and is denoted by f, that is, $f = n/N$. This is the probability of including any given element in the sample. It is also the proportion of the frame elements included in the sample.

DATA

Suppose we want to draw a sample of size 50 from a group of employees. A recent payroll list that can be used as a frame is available, and it has 2164 names on it. After the sample is drawn, the selected employees will be contacted and asked 20 questions. If all goes well, 20 responses from each of the 50 employees, a total of 1000 responses, will constitute the data set. Now consider 2 of the 20 questions:

- Question 1: Are you male or female?
- Question 2: How many hours per week do you spend caring for elderly parents or friends?

Males are numerically coded with a 0 and females with a 1. The data set, in skeleton form, would then look like this:

Employee Number	Gender	Hours	xxxx	xxxx
1	1	5	xxxx	xxxx
2	0	0	xxxx	xxxx
3	1	0	xxxx	xxxx
⋮	⋮	⋮	⋮	⋮
50	1	10	xxxx	xxxx

The symbol xxxx stands for other variables and values not explicitly considered in this example. The vertical ellipsis points indicate items left out of the display to save space. Our job is to use the data to estimate characteristics of the universe. For instance, what proportion of all employees are female? This information is on hand for a sample of 50 employees. But what about for the whole group? We would also like to know the average of reported hours per week the whole group spent on caring. The information gathered from the 50 employees allows us to estimate the group average within limits. How is this done? These questions are answered in Section 14.4. Before turning to them, though, some additional notation must be introduced.

POPULATIONS AND PARAMETERS

To distinguish between the universe and the samples drawn from it, notation that refers to the universe and notation that refers to the sample must be used. Exhibit 14.2B shows the structure of a universe of individual elements, denoted by $I_1, I_2, \ldots, I_N$, from which two measurements are obtained: gender and number of hours. The responses to the question of gender are assumed to be coded 0 for male and 1 for female. The notation for these responses is $Y_1, Y_2, \ldots, Y_N$. In other words, Y_1 stands for the numerical code attached to the response of the first individual, Y_2 for the second individual, and so on. The responses to the question of number of hours are denoted by $X_1, X_2, \ldots, X_N$. The numerical values are simply those that would be reported by the employees. The measurements in Exhibit 14.2B are hypothetical because they stand for what the employees would report if responses

	Elements (employees)	y measurements (0 = male, 1 = female)	x measurements (number of hours)
	I_1	Y_1	X_1
	I_2	Y_2	X_2
	$\vdots$	$\vdots$	$\vdots$
	I_N	Y_N	X_N
Total		τ_y	τ_x
Mean (average)		μ_y	μ_x
Standard deviation		S_y	S_x

$$\tau_x = \sum_{i=1}^{N} X_i \qquad \mu_x = \frac{\tau_x}{N} \qquad S_x = \sqrt{\frac{1}{N-1} \sum_{i=1}^{N} (X_i - \mu_x)^2}$$

$$\tau_y = \sum_{i=1}^{N} Y_i \qquad \mu_y = \frac{\tau_y}{N} \qquad S_y = \sqrt{\frac{1}{N-1} \sum_{i=1}^{N} (Y_i - \mu_y)^2}$$

were elicited from them in the manner in which responses are elicited in the survey. In other words, they are equal complete coverage measurements.

At the bottom of the columns of measurements, the sums, averages, and standard deviations of the measurements are shown. These are called parameters because they are characteristics of the equal complete coverage of the universe. The measured characteristics are called **variables**. In Exhibit 14.2B there are two variables: gender and number of hours. The set of all equal complete coverage measurements on a variable is called a **population**. Exhibit 14.2B displays two populations: the gender population and the hours-of-caring population.

Populations also have parameters. For example, the sum and average under the gender measurements are two of the parameters of the gender population. The usual statistical notation for a total is the Greek letter t, which is called tau. The symbol is τ. The statistical symbol for an average, or mean, is the Greek m, called mu. The symbol is μ, as noted earlier (Chapter 8, for instance). Any numerical characteristic of a population is called a **parameter**. Statistical notation for parameters tends to use Greek letters. In survey literature, the standard deviation is an exception to this rule, as is shown in Exhibit 14.2B and emphasized further below.

The numerical values in the gender population are denoted by Y's, the values in the hours-of-caring population by X's. As shorthand, these populations are sometimes referred to as the y population and the x population. Such terminology enables us to speak abstractly about populations. For example, think of an arbitrary universe for which x, y, q, r, and t populations have been defined. Numerical characteristics of the x population are parameters of that population; numerical characteristics of the q population are parameters of that population; and so on. The symbols denoting the parameters of a population may be subscripted with the letter denoting the population. For example, the mean of the y population may be denoted by μ_y.

Characteristics may be shared by two or more of the populations. For example, suppose the correlation coefficient between the values of the x population and the q population were computed. The correlation coefficient would be called a parameter of the joint x,q population. Statistical notation for the correlation co-efficient of a joint population is the Greek r, called rho. The symbol is ρ.

Suppose y is the variable indicating gender. We might compute the correlation coefficient for all x,q values associated with females and then compute the correlation coefficient for all x,q values associated with males. Technically speaking, these correlation coefficients are parameters of the joint q,x,y population. As a final example, consider making a cross-tabulation involving the levels of several of the variables. The numerical characteristics in the table would be parameters of a joint population of many variables.

Statisticians commonly use the standard deviation as a measure of variation. For any population the standard deviation may be computed by the formula given in Chapter 4. For example, for the y population the standard deviation is, in symbols,

$$S_y = \sqrt{\frac{1}{N-1} \sum_{i=1}^{N} (Y_i - \mu_y)^2} \tag{14.1}$$

where the index of summation runs from 1 to N, the number of numbers in the population.[†]

At this stage, only one final parameter needs to be defined: a population proportion. Interpret the y population in Exhibit 14.2B as measurements on the variable gender. Then each Y_i is equal to either 0 or 1, depending on whether the gender of the employee is male or female. The sum of this column of Y_i values is just the number of females in the frame, and the average of the column is just the proportion of females. For finite populations, counts and proportions are simply totals and means. Nevertheless, it is traditional to denote proportions by the Greek p, called pi. The symbol is π.

It can be shown (see Exercise 14.3F) that the standard deviation of a population of 0's and 1's is

$$\sqrt{\pi(1 - \pi)\frac{N}{N-1}} \tag{14.2}$$

For large values of N, the ratio $N/(N-1)$ is close to 1, so the standard deviation is close to $\sqrt{\pi(1 - \pi)}$, which is the standard deviation of the Bernoulli distribution introduced in Chapter 10. The Bernoulli distribution is a mathematical model for a process, whereas the expression in Equation (14.2) is the standard deviation of a finite binary population. That is why the Bernoulli formula is not exactly equal to the finite population formula.

NOTATION FOR DATA AND STATISTICS

Exhibit 14.2C gives a format for the data collected by simple random sampling. Remember that a simple random sample of size n means that each possible sample of size n has the same probability of being selected. Once a sample is drawn and the data collected, the data may be displayed as in Exhibit 14.2C. The first column shows the elements drawn into the sample. These are denoted by $i_1, i_2, \ldots, i_n$. In the exhibit two measurements were taken from each element, a y measurement and

---

[†] In some discussions authors use another definition of the standard deviation. They divide the sum of squares by N instead of $N - 1$ and denote the resulting quantity by σ.

EXHIBIT 14.2C

Data Format for Simple Random Sampling

Elements (employees)	y measurements (0 = male, 1 = female)	x measurements (number of hours)
i_1	y_1	x_1
i_2	y_2	x_2
$\vdots$	$\vdots$	$\vdots$
i_n	y_n	x_n

	y measurements	x measurements
Total	$\sum\limits_{i=1}^{n} y_i$	$\sum\limits_{i=1}^{n} x_i$
Mean (average)	$\bar{y} = p$	$\bar{x}$
Standard deviation	$s_y = \sqrt{p(1-p)\dfrac{n}{n-1}}$	$s_x = \sqrt{\dfrac{1}{n-1}\sum\limits_{i=1}^{n}(x_i - \bar{x})^2}$
Standard error	$se_p = \dfrac{s_y}{\sqrt{n}} fpc$	$se_{\bar{x}} = \dfrac{s_x}{\sqrt{n}} fpc$

where fpc = finite population correction = $\sqrt{\dfrac{N-n}{N}} = \sqrt{1-f}$ and $f = \dfrac{n}{N}$

an x measurement. For concreteness, you can think of the y variable as gender, coding males as 0 and females as 1, and the x variable as number of hours. Notice that sample measurements are denoted by lowercase letters, whereas population measurements are denoted by uppercase letters (see Exhibit 14.2B). Below the columns of data a number of numerical characteristics are shown: totals, means, standard deviations, and standard errors. Only the standard errors are unfamiliar at this point; they are discussed in Section 14.4.

SECTION 14.3

EXERCISES

14.3A Suppose you wish to survey private residences in your city or town. Comment on the use of the telephone directory as a sampling frame. What items in the directory do not correspond to elements in your universe? What elements of your universe are not included in the frame? Suggest another possible frame for this study.

14.3B You wish to survey the employees over the age of 30 in your organization by sampling, and you decide to use a payroll list as your frame. What sorts of problems might this choice of frame entail? Suggest another possible frame for this study.

14.3C Your building manager wishes to study uses of various parts of the building, which is very large. The manager has detailed floor plans for all parts of the building. Suggest how she might draw a sample of locations from her plans. Discuss how to design the study so that building use may be studied by time of day and day of the week.

14.3D Your firm has 6273 employees, and you wish to draw a simple random sample of 400 employees from a payroll file. Set up a scheme to use a table of random digits to draw the sample.

14.3E Exhibit 13.4A displayed a small universe with two populations: Vacant or Improved and Assessed Value. For the Vacant or Improved population, code vacant as 0 and improved as 1. Attach to each item in Exhibit 13.4A an appropriate piece of notation as defined in Exhibit 14.2B. For example, $N = 9$. If Y_i is defined as 0 if parcel i is vacant and 1 if parcel i is improved, then $Y_1 = 0$ would be written in place of the word vacant for the parcel at 30 Muir Dr. Once all the notation has been assigned, compute the population parameters defined at the bottom of Exhibit 14.2B and record them.

14.3F A certain population consists of 22 0's and 29 1's. Verify that Equations (14.1) and (14.2) both yield the same numerical value for the standard deviation of this population. Now do the calculation assuming there are M 0's and $N - M$ 1's.

14.3G The data below are actual responses to a student survey done in a statistics class of about 250 students. For this exercise the first 20 responses were chosen from the data base. The rows correspond to students (elements); the columns correspond to questions on the questionnaire (variables). Responses are shown for these five items:

(1) What is your gender? (0 = male, 1 = female)

(2) I won't have much use for statistics beyond this course.

(3) I am worried about how well I will do in this course.

(4) I think statistics is a boring subject to learn.

(5) Large lecture courses offer little opportunity for individual attention.

For the last four questions, students responded with one of the numbers from 1 to 5. Response 1 meant "strongly agree" with the statement, 2 meant "agree," 3 meant "neutral," 4 meant "disagree," and 5 meant "strongly disagree."

04122	04221
13422	04423
04122	12131
12211	03213
15432	05111
05433	04513
04141	13211
03411	04543
02222	11311
04544	03111

For this exercise, treat these data as a universe with 20 elements, for which five variables have been measured. Put the data into the format of Exhibit 14.2B and perform all the calculations required to complete the format.

14.3H Consider a universe consisting of $N = 5$ elements with associated X and Y values as defined below.

Case	Element	X_i	Y_i
1	I_1	8	1
2	I_2	9	1
3	I_3	10	0
4	I_4	10	1
5	I_5	13	0

(a) Verify that $\mu_x = 10$, $S_x = \sqrt{3.5}$, and $\mu_y = \pi = 0.6$.

(b) List the 10 possible samples of size $n = 2$, along with the associated values for X and Y. Compute the sample means $\bar{x}$ and $\bar{y} = p$ for each sample. Verify that the average of the 10 $\bar{x}$'s is $10 (= \mu_x)$ and of the 10 $\bar{y}$'s is $0.6 (= \pi)$. Construct dotplots of the $\bar{x}$'s and $\bar{y}$'s. These are the sampling distributions of the sample means. Compare the variability of these sampling distributions with the variability in the X and Y populations.

(c) Repeat part (b) for samples of size $n = 3$.

(d) Suppose a third variable (Z) may be measured, and its population values are $Z_1 = 8$, $Z_2 = 9$, $Z_3 = 9$, $Z_4 = 10$, and $Z_5 = 12$. Compute ρ_{xz}, the population correlation coefficient between X and Z. For each possible sample of size $n = 3$, compute the sample correlation coefficient r_{xz}. Construct a dotplot of the sampling distribution of this statistic. Compute the mean of this distribution. Is it equal to ρ_{xz}?

INTERVAL ESTIMATION

Numerical characteristics of samples, such as totals, means, and standard deviations, are called **statistics**. The statistics of random samples make it possible to make probabilistic inferences about the parameters of populations. Inference means the statistics are used to predict, or infer, within limits, the values of population parameters.

MEANS

The sample mean may be treated as an estimate of the population mean. But different samples have different means because of sampling variation. Thus any sample mean is unlikely to be equal to the population mean. How different can the sample mean and the population mean be? Using statistical theory, limits to the difference can be established provided the sample is drawn by a probability method such as simple random sampling.

To illustrate, we estimate the population mean of the x sample in Exhibit 14.2C. Statistical theory holds that the difference between the sample mean and the population mean is almost certainly less (in absolute value) than three standard errors. A **standard error** is the standard deviation of the sampling distribution of a statistic. The formula for the standard error of $\bar{x}$ is given in Exhibit 14.2C. In symbols,

$$|\mu_x - \bar{x}| \leq 3se_{\bar{x}}$$

or
$$\bar{x} - 3se_{\bar{x}} \leq \mu_x \leq \bar{x} + 3se_{\bar{x}}$$

Thus if an interval whose endpoints are the sample mean minus 3 standard errors and the sample mean plus 3 standard errors is computed, this interval almost certainly contains the population mean. Because of this property, the interval is called a **confidence interval** for μ_x.

Think of constructing all possible samples of size n from the universe, taking the x measurements and computing the sample means for all these samples. This program was carried out for a small universe in Exhibit 13.4B. The focus of attention is now the distribution of all the sample means. In practice this distribution is not constructed, but in theory it exists and its properties can be studied. For moderately large sample sizes, n, and small to moderate sampling fraction, f, the distribution is well approximated by a normal curve with mean μ_x and standard deviation

$$SE_{\bar{x}} = \frac{S_x}{\sqrt{n}} \, fpc \tag{14.3}$$

The normal approximation comes from a central limit effect, which can be derived theoretically and demonstrated empirically. Even the small samples in Exhibits 13.4B and 13.4C show some evidence of a central limit effect. For larger, and more practical, sample sizes, the effect is even more pronounced.

Because of the normal approximation, practically all the sample means obtained by simple random sampling differ from the population mean by no more than 3 of the standard errors given in Equation (14.3). This is a property of the normal curve. Other properties of the normal curve may also be used. For example, roughly 95% of the sample means differ from the population mean by no more than 2 of the standard errors given in Equation (14.3).

As noted, the standard error of the sample means is nothing more than the standard deviation of the distribution of all possible sample means. The standard error of sample means is a function of S_x, N, and n, that is, the standard deviation of the population, the population size, and the sample size. The standard error decreases as the sample size increases. In the example in Exhibit 13.4C, the distribution of means with $n = 3$ was less spread out than the distribution of means with $n = 2$. This makes intuitive sense: more information should decrease uncertainty.

In practice, only one of the many possible samples is obtained. The information in that sample must be used to make estimates of population parameters. As noted above, the sample mean is used to estimate the population mean. The standard error in Equation (14.3) must also be estimated because it depends on the parameter S_x, which is typically unknown. As with means, the sample standard deviation is used to estimate the population standard deviation. Thus in practice,

$$se_{\bar{x}} = \frac{S_x}{\sqrt{n}} \, fpc \tag{14.4}$$

This is the formula for the standard error of the x sample mean given in Exhibit 14.2C.

A variety of confidence intervals may be computed, but the format of all the intervals is the same:

[Sample mean $- z \times$ Standard error,   Sample mean $+ z \times$ Standard error]

The sample mean and standard error are computed from the sample. The value of z is chosen to achieve the level of confidence required. For example, $z = 3$ is associated with a 99.7% level of confidence because 0.997 is the area under a normal curve over the interval that runs from the mean minus 3 standard deviations to the mean plus 3 standard deviations. The value $z = 2$ (or 1.96) is associated with a 95%

level of confidence, and so on. As the value of z increases the level of confidence increases, but so does the length of the interval. On the other hand, the length of the interval decreases as the value of n increases.

In practice, the length of the interval is interpreted as a measure of precision in the estimate. The narrower the interval the more precisely the population mean has been estimated. Many practitioners use half the length of the interval as a measure of precision, since this is a bound on the absolute value of the difference between the sample and population means. We also follow this practice.

Once a sample is obtained and the data are collected, a confidence interval is computed using the value of z believed to be appropriate. The interval is interpreted as an estimate of the population mean. Half the length of the interval measures the precision with which the population mean has been estimated. This procedure involves estimating the population standard deviation with the sample standard deviation.

The procedure outlined for the x sample can be repeated for the y sample. All the formulas and interpretations apply except y's are substituted for x's.

PROPORTIONS

It is traditional to distinguish samples of 0's and 1's from samples of measurements, even though the procedures for analyzing the two types of samples are exactly the same. Only the notation changes to reflect the two types of data. Assume the y sample is from a population of 0's and 1's and look at the notation. Instead of using the symbols $\bar{y}$ and s_y for the sample mean and standard deviation, the symbols p and $\sqrt{p(1-p)n/(n-1)}$ are used.[†]

The symbol p stands for the sample mean, which is just the proportion of 1's in the sample. The formula for the standard deviation is an algebraic result that can be derived from the definition of the standard deviation and the definition of p (see Exercise 14.6I). It also follows algebraically that the sample standard error is

$$se_p = \frac{s_y}{\sqrt{n}} fpc = fpc \frac{\sqrt{p(1-p)\dfrac{n}{n-1}}}{\sqrt{n}} = \sqrt{\frac{p(1-p)}{n-1}} \, fpc \qquad \textbf{(14.5)}$$

where $fpc = \sqrt{1-f} = \sqrt{1-n/N}$. This form of the standard error is used in Exhibit 14.2C, where it is assumed that the y population is a 0–1 population.

EFFECT OF SAMPLE SIZE AND UNIVERSE (POPULATION) SIZE

In all the standard error formulas, the factor $\sqrt{(N-n)/N} = \sqrt{1-f}$ appears.[††] This is called the **finite population correction factor** (fpc). It appears as a consequence of drawing a simple random sample from a finite population of numbers. If N is a very large number, as it is for large universes like the population of the United States, then the finite population correction is virtually equal to one and can be dropped

---

[†] These formulas are similar to the formulas encountered in Chapter 10 in the discussion of the distribution of the proportion of successes.

[††] Note that $1-f$ is the proportion of the universe elements *not* sampled.

from the formulas for practical purposes. But if n is a substantial fraction of N, say $f = 0.10$ or more, then the finite population correction makes a difference. Its presence serves to decrease the standard error and hence to decrease the length of the confidence interval and to increase the measure of precision of the estimate.

Although the universe size, N, sometimes affects the standard error of estimates, it plays a relatively minor role. The sample size and the population standard deviation are the main determinants of precision. Once the population is targeted and simple random sampling is chosen as the sampling design, only the sample size may be manipulated to achieve a desired level of precision. Section 14.11 discusses choosing sample sizes.

SECTION 14.5

NUMERICAL ILLUSTRATION

Suppose the employee study described in earlier sections has been carried out. A project such as this was done by a sample-survey class in the spring semester of 1987. The study was much larger than the one described in this example, but the data in the example are based on the actual study. In the study, nonresponse occurred and corrections for nonresponse bias had to be made. For purposes of illustration in the example, the sample is treated as if no nonresponse occurred. Assume that a simple random sample of size $n = 30$ was drawn from the group of 2164 employees.

A questionnaire was mailed to the randomly selected group of employees, who filled out the questionnaires and returned them. In this illustration only the gender of the employee and the number of hours per week spent giving care are treated as the measured variables. The study included many more questions, but here we are simply illustrating the basic computations. The data are in Exhibit 14.5A. Some statistics are displayed at the bottom of the exhibit.

The computation of the totals, means, and standard deviations may be done by hand or by computer. Here are the computations needed to obtain the standard errors.

For the x sample (hours), $n = 30$, $s_x = 17.96$, and $N = 2164$. So

$$se_{\bar{x}} = \frac{17.96}{\sqrt{30}} \sqrt{\frac{2164 - 30}{2164}} = 3.26$$

For the y sample (gender), $n = 30$, $p = 0.2$, and $N = 2164$. So

$$s_y = \sqrt{\frac{p(1 - p)n}{n - 1}} = \sqrt{\frac{0.2(0.8)(30)}{29}} = 0.4068$$

and $$se_p = \sqrt{\frac{p(1 - p)}{n - 1}} \, fpc = \sqrt{\frac{0.16}{29}} \sqrt{\frac{2134}{2164}} = (0.0743)(0.9930) = 0.0738$$

The computation of confidence intervals is now quite straightforward. The 99.7% confidence interval for the x population mean, that is, the mean of the population of

EXHIBIT 14.5A

Data from a Survey
of Employees at a
Madison, Wisconsin,
Company

Element	Gender	Hours	Element	Gender	Hours
1	0	0	16	0	14
2	1	98	17	0	0
3	0	0	18	0	0
4	0	0	19	1	0
5	0	0	20	0	0
6	0	0	21	0	0
7	1	0	22	1	1.5
8	0	0	23	0	0
9	0	0	24	0	0
10	0	7	25	0	0
11	1	0	26	0	0
12	0	0	27	0	0
13	0	0	28	0	0
14	1	4	29	0	0
15	0	0	30	0	0
Total				6	124.5
Average				0.2	4.15
Standard deviation				0.4068	17.96
Standard error				0.0738	3.26

Note: Respondents reported giving care to elderly relatives or friends in the spring of
1987. The sampling design was simple random; the frame size was 2164; and the sample size
was 30.

reported number of hours per week spent giving care, is

$$\bar{x} \pm 3se_{\bar{x}} = 4.15 \text{ hours} \pm 3(3.26 \text{ hours}) = 4.15 \text{ hours} \pm 9.78 \text{ hours}$$

We interpret the interval as follows: If we had surveyed the whole universe of
employees using the same mail out/mail back procedure, the same questionnaire,
and the same data processing techniques that were used to obtain data from the
sample, the average of the reported hours spent for the whole group would almost
certainly have been between −5.6 hours and 13.9 hours.

In this illustration the lower endpoint of the interval is negative, which is impossible. A 0 should certainly be an absolute lower bound on a number of hours.
The negative endpoint is a consequence of a relatively large standard error, indicating very little precision in the estimate of average number of hours. This lack
of precision is due to the large standard deviation (17.96) and the small sample
size (30). In the study conducted by the sample-survey class, a sample of size 350
was drawn and interviewed, which naturally led to much greater precision in the
estimates.

Remember that this example is designed to illustrate computations and so is
small in scale. Actual surveys usually involve hundreds or even thousands of
participants.

The 99.7% confidence interval for the proportion of female employees is

$$p \pm 3se_p = 0.2 \pm 3(0.0738) = 0.2 \pm 0.2214$$

Again a negative left endpoint is obtained, which would be reported as zero in practice. The interval shows that the proportion of female employees in the company is almost certainly less than 0.42 (that is, 42%). A larger sample would have allowed for more precision about the proportion of female employees. For example, in the actual study, which used a sample of size 350, the proportion of female employees was estimated to be 0.27 with a standard error of 0.038, so the 99.7% confidence interval for the proportion of female workers was 0.27 ± 0.11. We were almost certain that between 16% and 38% of the universe of employees were females.

SECTION 14.6

EXERCISES

14.6A Draw a simple random sample of size $n = 4$ from the universe in Exercise 14.3G. Use the sample to estimate the mean response for each variable; construct 90% confidence intervals. Do any of your confidence intervals fail to contain the actual population mean? There are 4845 possible samples of size 4 from this universe. Approximately how many of them produce 90% confidence intervals that do not contain the population mean of a specified variable?

14.6B A questionnaire was sent to a simple random sample of 50 customers, who filled it out and returned it. Thirty-eight of the customers responded that your delivery times were too slow. Estimate the proportion of all your customers who feel your delivery times are too slow, using a 99.7% confidence interval. (Assume the frame size is very large so that the finite population correction may be ignored.) Give a precise statement of the meaning of the interval. What interval would you get if the sample size were 100 (assuming $p = 0.76$)? What is the percentage reduction in interval length resulting from the doubling of the sample size?

14.6C The numerical illustration in Section 14.5 is based on an actual survey of 350 employees. The frame, which was a payroll list, contained 2164 entries. In the sample, 27% of the employees said they were females.
(a) Compute the standard error and the 99.7% confidence interval for $N = 2164$, $n = 350$, and $p = 0.27$, assuming a simple random sampling design. (*Answer:* 0.022, [0.20, 0.34])
(b) The results reported from the survey are proportion of females $= 0.27$ with a standard error of 0.038. The standard error is higher than the standard error you got in part (a). This is due to the necessary correction for nonresponse in the actual survey. How much precision was lost because some of the employees did not respond?

14.6D For simple random sampling, the standard error of a sample proportion is

$$se_p = \sqrt{[p(1 - p)/(n - 1)][(N - n)/N]}$$

For given N and n, what value of p maximizes this standard error? (*Answer:* $\frac{1}{2}$) In designing a survey, you often place a bound on the sampling error, which is usually measured by half the width of some confidence interval.
(a) Let B denote the specified upper bound on the sampling error in a 95% confidence interval, so $B = 2se_p$. Let *semax* denote the standard error with $\frac{1}{2}$ substituted for p. If we set $B = 2semax$ and solve for n, then we have a "safe" value for n. It is safe because it corresponds to a bound on the worst possible value of the standard error. Your job in this part is to solve the resulting equation

$$B = 2\sqrt{[(\tfrac{1}{2})(\tfrac{1}{2})/(n - 1)][(N - n)/N]}$$

for n. [*Answer:* $N(1 + B^2)/(NB^2 + 1)$]

(b) In this part you are to solve for a safe value of n for an arbitrary level of confidence. Let z denote the number of standard errors required to achieve the desired level of confidence. Then set $B = zsemax$ and solve for n. [*Answer:* $N(z^2/4 + B^2)/(NB^2 + z^2/4)$.]

14.6E You plan to draw a sample of employees from an agency that is divided into a number of departments as follows:

Department	Number of Employees
A	349
B	278
C	181
D	82
E	42
F	12
G	4
Total	948

Each department manager wants to have at least one member of his or her department in the sample, and two of the managers (of departments F and G) insist that all their employees be surveyed. Your study group has set a target to estimate proportions in each department to within eight percentage points. You have the resources to include about 10% of all employees in the sample. How would you try to satisfy the constraints? (This is based on an actual experience.)

14.6F In Exercise 14.6E, suppose the sample sizes finally decided on were, by department, 30, 25, 18, 8, 4, 12, and 4.
(a) Compute the finite correction factors for each department.
(b) Suppose the sampled employees are asked a 0–1 type question, and in every department the proportion of 1's is .8, rounded to one decimal place. Compute the standard errors of the estimated proportions for each department. Comment on the relative impacts of department size and sample size on these standard errors.
(c) On the basis of your analysis so far, do you feel that the proposed sample sizes are reasonable? If not, what would you recommend?

14.6G Suppose you have sampled from a frame with N elements and obtained an estimated proportion of p with a standard error of se_p. You have been asked to estimate the total number of elements responding with a 1 (to the 0–1 question).
(a) Develop an appropriate estimate, standard error, and confidence interval. (*Answer:* Np, Nse_p, and $Np \pm zNse_p$)
(b) For the data in Exercise 14.6B, estimate the number of customers who feel your delivery times are too slow if the frame has $N = 3000$ elements.

14.6H Suppose you have sampled from a frame with N elements and obtained an estimated mean of $\bar{x}$ with a standard error of $se_{\bar{x}}$. You have been asked to estimate the population total value of x. Develop an appropriate estimate, standard error, and confidence interval. (*Answer:* $N\bar{x}$, $Nse_{\bar{x}}$, $N\bar{x} \pm zNse_{\bar{x}}$)

14.6I Suppose a sample of size n from a 0–1 population yields m 1's and $n - m$ 0's. Let $p = m/n$ denote the sample proportion. Show that the sample mean is equal to p and the sample standard deviation is equal to $\sqrt{p(1 - p)n/(n - 1)}$.

RANDOM VERSUS REPRESENTATIVE SAMPLES

Some people use the word *representative* when referring to samples. For example, a lawyer trying to discredit evidence collected by probability sampling may say a sample cannot be representative of a population. Presumably the lawyer means that the sample is not a mirror image of the universe. This is certainly factual. The sample may have 20% females, whereas the universe may have 25% females. If a case turns on knowing precisely the number of females in a universe, then there is no choice but to census the universe! The probability sample only predicts characteristics of the universe within limits.

What is fundamental is not the representativeness of the probability sample but the type of information required. If only a census will answer the question, then using a sample is inappropriate. On the other hand, if the information needed can be obtained by sampling, then to census is to engage in waste.

Base arguments on important issues! The validity of a probability sample is a legitimate issue, but if the sample is obtained by a correct process, then it is both superficial and a waste of time to argue about its representativeness.

Another unfortunate use of representativeness is **quota sampling**. This involves constructing a sample whose characteristics match some demographic targets. For example, interviewers might be sent into a shopping mall and told to interview 100 people who satisfy the following quotas:

Women	Totals 60
Teenagers	15
With young children	20
Wearing business suits	15
Over 50	10
Men	**40**
Wearing business suits	10
Wearing Hawaiian shorts	5
With young children	10
Teenagers	15

The quotas may make the sample representative of some universe, but they fail to satisfy more constraints than they satisfy, so the sample will be unrepresentative in some way. Samples cannot completely mirror a universe. At least probability samples can be used to make valid inferences about the universe. The use of probability makes the question of representativeness irrelevant to inference making.

Another misuse of representativeness arises in the treatment of nonresponse in nonprobability surveys. Suppose a nonprobability survey sample has been collected, and 20% of the people to whom questionnaires were sent returned them. A favorite pastime of people who conduct nonprobability surveys is to compute demographic characteristics (such as age, gender, and geographic location) of the sample and to compare them to those of published censuses or other surveys. If there is a close correspondence, then the people say their sample is representative. That is their operational definition. But then they take a fatal step. They use the sample as if it were a probability sample. They compute estimates, standard errors, and confidence intervals and publish them as if they had the same meaning they would have had if the sample had been drawn by a probability method. There is no logical foundation in sampling theory for doing this.

SECTION 14.8

EXERCISES

14.8A State U has about 40,000 students. One of the student newspapers interviews a sample of 100 students. They set up a booth on the library mall and tell a reporter to start interviewing people at 10:00 A.M. on Wednesday morning and to gather interviews until 100 interviews are conducted. The newspaper prepares an article reporting the results of the survey. They claim that the sample was random and quote standard errors of the estimates. What does statistical theory say about these results?

14.8B Quota sampling has led to some dramatically bad results. See Frederick Mosteller et al., *The Pre-election Polls of 1948* (New York: Social Research Council, 1949); and David Freedman, Robert Pisani, and Roger Purves, *Statistics* (New York: Norton, 1978), Chapter 19, Section 3, 305ff. F. F. Stephan and P. J. McCarthy, *Sampling Opinions* (New York: Wiley, 1958), gives an excellent comparison of quota and random sampling methods. See also Alan Stuart, "Nonprobability Sampling," in *International Encyclopedia of Statistics*, vol. 2, ed. William H. Kruskal and Judith M. Tanur (New York: Free Press, 1978), 885–889. Read these references, plus any others you can find, and prepare a memo on the dangers of quota sampling. Why is it that a sample can satisfy a large number of constraints and still yield badly biased results?

SECTION 14.9

SURVEYS AND FORECASTING

The successful forecasting of winners on election nights is a familiar phenomenon. These predictions are based on surveys of "key precincts" that have successfully helped to predict elections in the past. More speculative forecasts made on the basis of polls taken before election day asking people how they plan to vote are also familiar. The more sophisticated of such polls also try to forecast the probability with which a respondent will actually vote.

The more time that elapses between when a survey is done and when a forecasted event will occur, the more speculative the forecast is. If a particular survey is part of a series of surveys, then the whole series of results is needed to assess the relevance of the particular survey to some future event.

The reason for this is somewhat subtle but absolutely crucial for a correct use of survey information. Sampling variation and measures of it, such as standard errors, refer only to errors due to observing only part of the universe during the sampling period. The difference between an estimate and the equal complete coverage value is a sampling error, and the standard error of the estimate gives us an idea of the likely magnitude of the difference. The difference between an estimate from a particular survey and an estimate that will occur in some future survey, for example, is an error about which the standard error has no information. A time series analysis of a series of survey results may be informative on the magnitude of the latter error. But to develop information about longitudinal errors, longitudinal data must be analyzed. Analyzing a single cross section does not yield information about forecasting errors.

One implication of this realization is that a long-term perspective is needed to do sensible forecasting. Data collected in a standardized fashion over a long period of time are needed to get good insights into the longitudinal behavior of a process. A hodgepodge of surveys collected by different methods and with varying degrees of quality is a poor basis for forecasting, or any other decision making.

Another implication is that we need to be realistic about what can be learned from a survey. For example, a market researcher once studied powdered instant fruit-flavored drinks for a large U.S. foods corporation. The market researcher did a large number of studies to determine the marketability of the new product. An advanced analysis of these studies suggested to the research team that the new product was a winner, but after a brief initial success the product's sales decreased quickly and it was removed from the market. The researcher concluded, "If we had only studied the question of repeat sales!" The researchers learned of the initial attractiveness of their product but not of the second thoughts of people who actually tried it. A longitudinal study might have produced the warning signals that could have led to better product development.

SECTION 14.10

EXERCISES

14.10A Recommend a design for a longitudinal study that might have helped the market researcher whose story appears at the end of Section 14.9.

14.10B An exit survey of shoppers in a mall results in a 99.7% confidence interval for the average expenditure at the mall of [$2.74, $10.95]. An analyst concludes that a randomly encountered shopper at the mall will almost certainly spend between $2.74 and $10.95 at the mall.
   (a) What is wrong with the analyst's argument?
   (b) What is wrong with the statement that the average shopper spends between $2.74 and $10.95 at the mall?
   (c) Use your intuition to construct a typical distribution of expenditures at the mall. Think of a group of 10,000 shoppers. What fraction of them spend nothing? What fraction spend something but less than $5. Continue in this fashion. Try to construct a distribution you think is reasonable and has a mean between $2.74 and $10.95.
   (d) This problem describes an attempt by an analyst to use a survey estimate of a mean to make a prediction about individual behavior, a fallacious use of the estimate. It is possible to use survey data to make predictions about individuals, but a measure of variation that applies to individuals must be used to do this. For example, let y denote the

reported expenditure variable. The survey yields a standard deviation of the individual expenditures, denoted by s_y. Let the standard error of the mean expenditure be denoted by $se_{\bar{y}}$. To estimate the expenditure of an individual shopper, use the sample mean, $\bar{y}$. When the mean is used as a predictor of individual behavior, the standard error of the prediction error is $\sqrt{s_y^2 + se_{\bar{y}}^2}$. Denote the latter standard error by the symbol ise_y, for *individual standard error*. A 99.7% confidence interval for an individual expenditure is $\bar{y} \pm 3ise_y$. Other multiples of the standard error yield other levels of probability, in the usual way.

14.10C This is a numerical illustration of the theory outlined in part (d) of Exercise 14.10B. Suppose the survey yields a standard deviation of expenditures of $27.40 and a standard error of mean expenditure of $2.70. The mean reported expenditure is $6.80. Compute a 99.7% confidence interval for the expenditure of a randomly encountered shopper. To what universe of individuals does this interval apply? Now compute the 99.7% confidence interval for the mean expenditure. Explain why the two intervals are different.

SECTION 14.11

A NOTE ON SAMPLE SIZES

As discussed earlier in the chapter, sample size is important in reducing sampling variation. In simple random sampling, the standard error of a sample mean is $(fpc)s/\sqrt{n}$, where $fpc = \sqrt{(N - n)/N}$. The fpc varies somewhat with sample size n, but the main impact of the sample size is revealed in the term $s/\sqrt{n}$. Three observations need to be made here:

(1) The standard error decreases as sample size increases because $\sqrt{n}$ divides s.

(2) As sample size increases, the standard error decreases as the square root of the sample size, so the rate of decrease in the standard error is much slower than the rate of increase in the sample size. But since the cost of sampling typically increases in proportion to the sample size, a rather severe decreasing marginal return to investment in sample size results.

(3) Decreases in s result in direct decreases in the standard error. Thus strategies that reduce s pay off better than increases in sample size. One such strategy is stratification, which is discussed in Chapter 16. Stratification is the separation of the elements into groups on the basis of characteristics that can be identified at the design stage. For example, if the gender of individuals is shown in the frame, it may pay to draw separate samples from the males and females. This will reduce overall variation if males and females respond very differently to the questions in the survey.

There are cogent arguments in sampling theory to keep sample sizes to a minimum. There are also good arguments based on minimizing total survey costs. As noted in Chapter 13, preventing and detecting nonsampling error consume resources. The larger the sample size, the more effort is required to manage nonsampling errors, not to mention recruiting and training workers. A survey must be judged not only on precision but also on quality and cost. If an acceptable level of precision cannot be delivered without sacrificing quality, then all the resources devoted to the survey are wasted. Thus one of the most important factors in deciding to do a survey is whether the survey will produce sufficient precision and quality to justify doing the survey at all.

One aspect of planning is to compute the sample size needed to achieve a given level of precision. In Exercise 14.6D you were asked to develop the sample-size formula for the estimation of a proportion, using simple random sampling. This formula gives a sample size appropriate for the case where sampling error is the only source of error. In practice, where surveys suffer from nonresponse, interviewer error, clerical error, and other defects, the nominal level of precision in the formula is rarely achieved.

Planning a survey involves guesswork. Sample-size formulas are helpful guidelines, but they need to be used in conjunction with other knowledge to come up with a final plan. One way to use them is to propose a sample size and then work out the standard error and bound on the sampling error implied by that sample size. Testing several sample-size choices gives you an appreciation for the sensitivity of the precision of the estimates to sample size. Finally, remember that there is never a "correct" survey design for a given problem. Different investigators may develop different plans, all of which are reasonable. The important thing is to execute the plan as faithfully as possible. Then, provided that nonsampling errors are not overwhelming, the survey's results will be valid, even if the standard errors are bigger than desired. Validity is important, even when desired levels of precision are not achieved, because a survey can be a valuable source of information that will help in planning the next survey. It also may become part of a collection of high-quality surveys that all point to a very important conclusion, even though no one of them is conclusive by itself.

SECTION 14.12

EXERCISES

14.12A In simple random sampling the theoretical standard deviation of the mean is $(fpc)S/\sqrt{n}$, and the theoretical bound on the sampling error between the population and sample means is $B = z(fpc)S/\sqrt{n}$, where z is chosen to achieve a given level of confidence. Assuming B, z, and S are given, solve this equation for n. [*Answer:* $z^2NS^2/(NB^2 + z^2S^2)$]

Notice that to use this formula we need a guess at S, the population standard deviation. Guessing at S must be part of the survey design process. Various methods for doing this are discussed in books on surveying. Here we simply ask you to develop a feel for the implications of the formula by doing some numerical calculations. To keep things simple, assume $fpc = 1$ and take $B = 1$. Set up a two-way table with rows corresponding to $z = 1.645$, 2, and 3, and columns corresponding to $S = 0.5$, 1.0, 2.0, and 10.0. Now fill in the table with the values of n corresponding to these choices of z and S. Comment on the behavior of n as the two factors z and S vary. Compute rates of change. Which factor has the greater impact?

14.12B A service organization has a list of members and a list of contributors who are not members. The membership list has 3000 names; the contributor list has 10,000 names. The organization plans to draw a simple random sample from each list. A sample of size 300 is planned for the membership list. One of the planners argues that a sample between 3 and 3.5 times this size from the contributors list is needed to achieve the same level of precision as planned for the membership list. What do you recommend? Why?

14.12C A simple random sample of $n = 49$ observations yields a sample mean of 1556 and a standard deviation of 91. Compute the standard error of the mean. (*Answer:* 13)

SUPPLEMENTARY EXERCISES FOR CHAPTER 14

14A Use the restaurant section of the yellow pages of your local telephone book as a frame. Draw a simple random sample of 30 entries. Determine whether or not the entry corresponds to a chain of restaurants. To do this you must form an operational definition of "chain." Estimate the proportion of chain restaurants in your area using a 99.7% confidence interval. What sort of biases may be present in your estimate? Why does the confidence interval not account for the biases? What does it account for? What could you do to reduce the biases if you did this study again?

14B A marketing department draws a simple random sample of 1000 households from a city and attempts to conduct personal interviews with the heads of these households. After much effort, the department finds that they have found only 815 heads to interview, the others having never been home at the time of call. They decide to draw a random sample of 500 additional households and to interview heads of these households until 185 interviews have been completed. The resulting sample of 1000 interviews is then to be analyzed. What biases are introduced by this procedure? What types of households are likely to be overrepresented in the sample? Underrepresented?

14C A very large organization of analysts has asked each analyst to draw an independent random sample of size 30 from a gigantic population of numbers that has mean 100 and standard deviation 10. The analysts are to compute the means of their samples and bring them to their annual meeting. At the meeting the analysts plan to construct a histogram of their sample means and compute the mean and standard deviation of their sample means. Describe in as much detail as you can what the analysts will observe.

14D An agricultural organization wishes to survey a sample of farms in Texas. One proposed method of sampling farms is to select points at random on a state map. The three farms closest to each point will be surveyed. What sort of bias might this sampling design cause?

14E Which of the following five statements does *not* describe a consequence of using probability methods in surveying?

(1) Probability methods mean that each individual in the universe has a specified probability of entering the sample.

(2) Probability selection of samples imposes a state of statistical control that allows prediction within limits.

(3) Probability methods allow prediction within limits of the equal complete coverage.

(4) The intent of a probability survey is to obtain a statistical profile of a population rather than detailed information on individuals.

(5) With probability methods, one does not have to worry about coverage errors because these are incorporated into the standard errors of the estimates.

14F A simple random sample of $n = 25$ observations yields a sample mean of 26.23 and a standard deviation of 13.91. Compute the standard error of the mean.

14G An analyst has received a survey of households from a certain city that reports a 99.7% confidence interval for the average household income of [$15,372, $31,928]. The analyst writes in her report to management that if a household were drawn at random from the city and its income determined, it would almost certainly be between $15,372 and $31,928. What is wrong with her argument? How would you help her formulate a correct statement?

GLOSSARY FOR CHAPTER 14

Confidence interval	An interval computed from a sample such that the collection of such intervals from all possible samples has a specified probability of containing a parameter.
f	Sampling fraction, $f = n/N$.
Finite population correction factor, (fpc)	$fpc = \sqrt{(N - n)/N}$
Frame	The list of elements of the universe from which a sample is drawn.
N	Number of elements in a frame.
n	Size of the sample.
Parameter	Numerical characteristic of a population, for example, the mean, denoted by μ.
Population	The set of measurements on a variable that the whole universe would yield were a census taken.
Quota sample	A sample drawn so that some of its characteristics match predetermined targets, for example, percentage female is 50.
Simple random sample	A sample taken so that each possible sample of size n has the same chance of being selected.
Standard error	The standard deviation of the sampling distribution of a statistic.
Statistics	Numerical characteristics of a sample, usually thought of as estimates of population parameters.
Variable	A measured characteristic of elements.

## CHAPTER 15

Reading the Results of a Survey

INTRODUCTION TO THE REPORT

In this chapter a published report is used to show how to interpret the results of a survey. The report is "Diagnosis-Related Groups Using Data from the National Hospital Discharge Survey: United States, 1982," by Robert Pokras and Kurt K. Kubishke. It was published January 18, 1985, by the National Center for Health Statistics (NCHS) as part of the series *advancedata* from Vital and Health Statistics.[†] The whole publication appears in the appendix to this chapter.

The report is relatively brief because it presents only a portion of the information gathered in a large survey called the National Hospital Discharge Survey (NHDS), which is conducted annually by the NCHS. The data in the report are taken from the 1982 NHDS.

Take a few minutes to look through the report to develop a feel for its contents. The body consists of only two parts: Introduction and Highlights. It contains

[†] The National Center for Health Statistics is part of the Public Health Service, which is located at 3700 East-West Highway, Hyattsville, MD 20782.

four tables, numbered 1 through 4, which make up over 50% of its contents. The References section, which follows the body, is followed by the Technical Notes section, which consists of almost two pages of text and two tables numbered I and II.

Our focus will be on the tables and the technical notes. But first, we outline the problem the report addresses: estimating characteristics of diagnostic-related groups (DRGs). As noted in the Introduction of the report, DRGs were formed to help set uniform reimbursement rates for care of Medicare inpatients. Such patients compose about 30% of all discharges from short-stay nonfederal hospitals.

Two behavioral characteristics are studied in this report:

(1) Number of discharges

(2) Average length of stay in the hospital

Understanding these characteristics is important not only for the administration of Medicare but also for the administration of organizations that compete for health care dollars. For example, one thing you will learn from this report is that the average length of stay in hospital is different in different parts of the country and in hospitals of different size. Yet the purpose of DRGs is to support a uniform reimbursement schedule for Medicare. What are the causes of the variation in length of stay? Are they related to quality of care, costs of materials, or ways of doing business that could be changed? Do they appear simply because the data were collected during a period when hospitals were just learning to deal with the reimbursement system based on DRGs? The report raises these and other important questions for further study and thought.

If you were working in a hospital that tended to keep patients longer than average, your hospital would be allocating more of its Medicare reimbursement to patient care than a hospital with shorter lengths of stay. You would want to look at the differences in the hospitals and to make sure the differences in lengths of stay had sound medical causes. On the basis of your study you might decide to lobby for changes in the Medicare reimbursement system. Or you might want to use some of the differences you find in a marketing effort to highlight the quality characteristics of your hospital.

SECTION 15.2

INITIAL EXPLORATION OF TABLES

Before getting into the technical details it is usually a good idea to form some initial impressions by treating the data in the tables as purely descriptive. This creates a useful context for the inferential statistical analysis to follow.

Look at Table 1 first. It displays numbers of discharges and average lengths of stay of patients under the age of 65, overall and by four geographic regions. These figures are given for all discharges and for discharges in 20 DRGs. The DRGs are listed down the page according to decreasing numbers of discharges for all regions combined. The major source of discharges for people under the age of 65 is "Vaginal delivery without complicating diagnoses," that is, normal childbirth. The number of discharges reported is 2784 thousand, which we call about 2.8 million for convenience and clarity. The second largest source of discharges is "Medical back problems," with 790,000 discharges, and so on. Total discharges in 1982 are estimated at almost 28 million.

The four geographic regions are Northeast, North Central, South, and West. The states belonging to each region are given in the Technical Notes section under the heading "Definition of Terms." The regions are listed across the page according to decreasing average lengths of stay, for all DRGs combined. The lengths of stay in the South and West appear to be substantially less than those in the Northeast and North Central. The national average length of stay is estimated at 5.9 days.

It is useful to compare the trends within subgroups to overall trends. For example, Exhibit 15.2A compares numbers of discharges and average lengths of stay for total discharges and vaginal delivery without complicating diagnoses. Notice that the orders of the average lengths of stay are the same for both All Discharges and Vaginal Delivery but that there is a reversal between the Northeast and West in the Number of Discharges. A reversal occurs when regions change places in the two rankings. What other reversals do you find in Table 1 of the report?

EXHIBIT 15.2A

Comparison of All Discharges and Vaginal Delivery Without Complicating Diagnoses for Four Regions of the United States, 1982

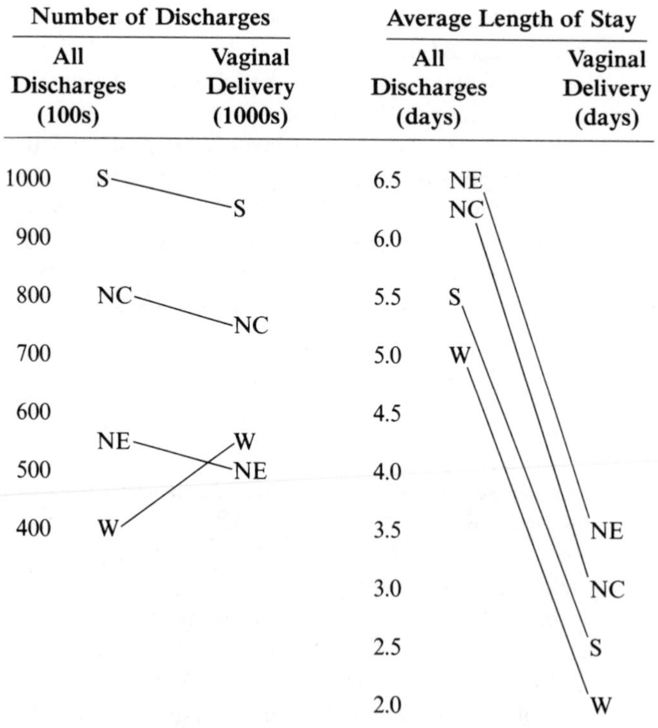

Number of Discharges		Average Length of Stay	
All Discharges (100s)	Vaginal Delivery (1000s)	All Discharges (days)	Vaginal Delivery (days)

Note: NE = Northeast; NC = North Central; S = South; W = West

Source: National Hospital Discharge Survey, National Center for Health Statistics.

Look down the column of DRGs for a given geographic region and notice that the numbers of discharges are not always ordered the same way they are for national figures. There is some variation by geographic region.

The data could be ordered in other ways. For example, DRGs could be listed in decreasing order of average length of stay. Exhibit 15.2B shows the top five DRGs on this criterion, along with the averages for all regions and by individual region.

EXHIBIT 15.2B

Top Five DRGs
According to Overall
Average Length of Stay
(in days), by Geographic
Region, 1982

| Diagnosis-Related Group | Average Length of Stay | | | | |
	All Regions	Northeast	North Central	South	West
Psychoses	16.5	19.1	19.7	13.8	11.6
Unrelated operating room procedures	11.2	13.8	12.0	9.7	10.1
Alcohol- and substance-induced organic mental syndrome	10.6	9.8	11.9	10.7	10.9
Diabetes, age greater than 35 years	8.2	9.9	8.7	7.4	6.4
Total cholecystectomy with common bile duct exploration, age less than 70 years without substantial comorbidity and/or complication	7.8	8.1	7.9	8.1	6.7

Source: National Hospital Discharge Survey, National Center for Health Statistics.

Within a given geographic region, the top five DRGs may not correspond to those given in Exhibit 15.2B. Our examination reveals variation among regions of the country in terms of both numbers of discharges and average lengths of stay.

Age is another source of variation. Table 2 of the report shows the same information as Table 1 except that it applies to people 65 years of age and over. It is no surprise that vaginal deliveries fail to make the list of important DRGs! Lens procedures account for the largest number of discharges nationwide, though they are not the greatest source of discharges in every region of the country.

Now compare average lengths of stay for "Unrelated operating room procedures" for the two age groups by region. This is done in Exhibit 15.2C.

For a given region, the average length of stay for the two age groups can be compared. The simplest way to compare is to subtract the length of stay for one group from the length of stay for the other group. The last column in Exhibit 15.2C shows these subtractions. The average lengths of stay are greater for the older age group, but the differences vary by geographic region. The smallest difference is in the West (4.9 days), the largest in the Northeast (6.2 days).

EXHIBIT 15.2C

Comparison of Lengths
of Stay (in days) Due to
Unrelated Operating
Room Procedures in
Short-Stay Nonfederal
Hospitals, by Age
Grouping and by
Geographic Region,
United States, 1982

| | Age | | | | | |
| | Under 65 Years | | 65 Years or More | | |
Region	Length of Stay	Difference	Length of Stay	Difference	Difference
All	11.2	—	17.3	—	6.1
Northeast	13.8		20.0		6.2
North Central	12.0	1.8	17.5	2.5	5.5
West	10.1	1.9	15.0	2.5	4.9
South	9.7	0.4	15.8	−0.8	6.1

Source: National Hospital Discharge Survey, National Center for Health Statistics.

For a given age group average lengths of stay for different regions can be
compared. Again this is done by subtracting. Take the group aged under 65 years.
The average length of stay for the Northeast region is 13.8 days; for the North
Central region it is 12.0 days. The difference is 1.8 days, and this is recorded in the
first Difference column in the exhibit. The second entry in that same column is
$1.9 = 12.0 - 10.1$, the difference between the average lengths of stay in the North
Central region and the West region. The other differences are calculated likewise.
Comparing the differences between regions for the two age groups shows that the
regional differences are somewhat larger for the older age group.

In this section, we have studied two of the tables in the report looking for
interesting patterns of variation, and we have not been disappointed. The most
striking finding is in the regional differences in average length of stay. It is also
interesting that the South, which is far from the most densely populated region of the
country, produces the largest numbers of discharges in both age groups.

Findings of similar magnitude and interest can be found in Tables 3 and 4; this
search is left to you as an exercise. We also invite you to more fully explore Tables 1
and 2.

Our enthusiasm for our findings must be tempered by the realization that the
numbers in the tables we have examined are estimates based on probability samples
and so are subject to sampling error. They may also suffer from biases caused by
nonsampling errors. How much impact do these sources of error have on the
tentative conclusions we have drawn from the numbers treated strictly descriptively? That question is answered in the next section.

SECTION 15.3

SOME SIMPLE INTERVAL ESTIMATES

STRUCTURE OF TECHNICAL NOTES

Before computing some simple interval estimates, we examine the Technical Notes
of the report. We need to learn from these notes how to compute the standard errors
of the estimates in the tables so we can compute confidence intervals.

The standard errors of the estimates in this report are computed by a much more complicated process than the one you have learned for simple random sampling, because the design used to collect the data is much more complicated than simple random sampling.

In the report of a complicated survey, we have to depend on the competence of the surveyor to produce proper standard errors as well as to indicate to what extent the data have or have not been adjusted for nonsampling error biases. In this case, the NCHS is quite a reliable source of information, and we have faith in their work. We nevertheless have some concerns that subtle problems with the data may not be presented in a brief report. We are prepared to question findings that do not correspond to our common sense! If such findings emerge, we would call NCHS to get our questions answered.

The Technical Notes are in two sections: Survey Methodology and Definition of Terms. The methodology section gives a brief sketch of the survey design and the estimation results, especially standard errors. Notice that the design involved stratification, the subject of Chapter 16, and probability sampling techniques much more subtle than simple random sampling. Such techniques are vital in conducting a large-scale survey of national scope. In the Data Collection and Estimation section we read that the estimates have been adjusted for nonresponse, so we know not all the chosen hospitals participated in the survey. The definition section sets forth the operational definitions used in the survey. For example, read the definitions of *Hospitals* and *Bed size of hospital.* Think about how the definitions might have been formulated differently, but still plausibly. Think about how these definitions would have been employed in the survey. What sorts of problems might have arisen? Definitions are crucial, especially if you compare the results of this survey with another survey that uses different definitions.

The techniques required to compute standard errors for such a survey have not yet been presented. Fortunately, the Sampling Errors and Rounding of Numbers section tells us how to get standard errors from Tables I and II. Table I is used for estimates of number of discharges, Table II for estimates of average lengths of stay.

STANDARD ERRORS

Look at Table I first. The table reports relative standard errors, that is, standard errors divided by the estimate. To convert a relative standard error to a standard error, the relative standard error must be multiplied by the estimate. That is why the table gives a range of sizes of the estimate. Note carefully that the relative standard errors are reported as percents. Thus they have the form $rse = 100(se/\text{Estimate})$, where rse is the relative standard error and se is the standard error. We see that

$$se = (rse)(\text{Estimate})/100 \qquad \textbf{(15.1)}$$

To illustrate, consider the number of discharges in the Northeast region due to vaginal deliveries without complicating diagnoses. This is reported in Table 1 as 524,000. How much sampling variation is present in this number? Table I is used to get the standard error. The estimate is approximately 500,000, so that line in the table is used. The corresponding relative standard error is 5.9. Formula (15.1) says the standard error is, therefore,

$$se = (5.9)(524{,}000)/100 = 30{,}916 \qquad \textbf{(15.2)}$$

The actual reported estimate was used in this calculation, not the approximate one of 500,000. A confidence interval will be computed and interpreted below.

If the size of the estimate is not close to any of the values in Table I, interpolation can be used to get relative standard errors. If the estimate is larger than 4 million, it is safe to treat the number as essentially exact, having no sampling error.

Now try your hand at a calculation. In Table 2, the number of discharges for lens procedures in the North Central region is reported as 127,000. Find the standard error of this estimate. You'll get slightly different answers depending on whether or not you decide to interpolate in Table I. If you interpolate, you get a standard error of about 10,414. If you do not interpolate but instead use the size of estimate = 100,000 in Table I, you get a standard error of about 10,795. The difference in the two standard errors is of little practical importance.

Now look at Table II. This table gives standard errors of estimates of average lengths of stay measured in days. The standard errors depend on the number of discharges reported and the average length of stay reported. To illustrate, look at the average length of stay for medical back problems in the North Central region. This is reported in Table 1 as 7.3 days. The number of discharges, also reported in Table 1, is 245,000. The crudest way to use Table II is to find the values nearest the reported values and use the standard error given in the table. To do this you would use number of discharges = 100,000 (the value nearest to 245,000) and average length of stay in days = 6 (the value nearest to 7.3). The corresponding standard error is 0.6 day.

A more precise way to use the table is to interpolate. Here is a format for interpolating in a two-way table:

Number of Discharges	Average Length of Stay		
	6	7.3	10
100,000	0.6		0.9
245,000		?	
500,000	0.5		0.8

The question mark shows the standard error we are after. Numerical analysts have developed many two-way interpolation schemes, but the rather small adjustments that we require do not warrant learning a sophisticated approach. Informally, we see that we need to go about 60% of the way between 100,000 and 500,000 in the Number of Discharges column and 33% of the way between 6 and 10 in the Average Length of Stay row. We enter 0.54 in the slot corresponding to number of discharges = 245,000 and average length of stay = 6. We enter 0.84 in the slot corresponding to number of discharges = 245,000 and average length of stay = 10. The value 33% of the way between these two numbers is about 0.64, and this will be used as our standard error. Notice that it is only slightly different from our crude value of 0.6.

Now you try a calculation. In Table 2, the average length of stay for unrelated operating room procedures in the North Central region is reported as 17.5 days, and the number of discharges is reported as 65,000. Use Table II to find a standard error for the estimated average length of stay. You will find the interpolated value is very little different from the crude value of 1.4.

CONFIDENCE INTERVALS

Many confidence intervals have the form

$$\text{Estimate} \pm (\text{Factor})(\text{Standard error})$$

where the factor used determines the level of confidence. As a rule, a factor of 3, which corresponds to a 99.7% confidence level, is preferred. A 0.3% risk of misestimating a parameter is acceptable, as a guideline, in an environment in which many estimations are made. Each estimation is made with a 0.997 probability of being correct, but this probability does not apply to a set of estimations.

If the estimations are made on independent samples, then the binomial distribution presented in Chapter 10 can be used to compute characteristics of sets of estimates. Let n denote the number of confidence intervals in the set, and assume for simplicity that all the confidence coefficients are 0.997. Then the probability that all n of the intervals contains the corresponding parameters of interest is the probability of n successes, namely, $(0.997)^n$. The probability that at least one of the intervals does not contain the parameter of interest is $1 - (0.997)^n$. The probability that exactly one of the intervals does not contain the parameter of interest is

EXHIBIT 15.3A

Probabilistic Behavior of Sets of n Independent Confidence Intervals

Number of Intervals n	Probability All Intervals Correct $(0.997)^n$	Probability One Interval Incorrect $n(0.997)^{n-1}(0.003)$	Probability at Least One Interval Incorrect $1 - (0.997)^n$
1	.997000	.0030000	.0030000
2	.994009	.0059820	.0059910
3	.991027	.0089461	.0089731
4	.988054	.0118924	.0119462
5	.985090	.0148209	.0149104
6	.982134	.0177317	.0178657
7	.979188	.0206250	.0208121
8	.976250	.0235007	.0237496
9	.973322	.0263589	.0266784
10	.970402	.0291999	.0295984
11	.967490	.0320235	.0325096
12	.964588	.0348299	.0354121
13	.961694	.0376192	.0383059
14	.958809	.0403914	.0411910
15	.955932	.0431467	.0440675
16	.953065	.0458848	.0469350
17	.950206	.0486063	.0497940
18	.947355	.0513110	.0526450

$n(0.997)^{n-1}(0.003)$. Values of these probabilities for selected values of n are given in Exhibit 15.3A.

■**EXAMPLE 15.3A:** Look at the $n = 18$ line in Exhibit 15.3A. The figures say that if 18 independent 99.7% confidence intervals are made, there is a 94.7% chance that all the intervals are correct, a 5.1% chance that exactly one interval is incorrect, and a 5.3% chance that at least one interval is incorrect.

People who engage in scientific studies tend to use a factor of 2 in the confidence interval formula, which corresponds to about a 95% level of confidence. This is scientific tradition, but it is not without its critics. For example, if 18 independent 95% confidence intervals are made, there is a 39.7% chance that all the intervals are correct, a 37.6% chance that exactly one interval is incorrect, and a 60.3% chance that at least one interval is incorrect. These probabilities are distinctly inferior to the ones for $n = 18$ in Exhibit 15.3A.   ■

In practical applications, intervals are often constructed for parameters of many variables for which the same sample provides data. In such situations, the confidence intervals are not independent. The characteristics of dependent intervals are more difficult to calculate than those for independent intervals because a simple model like the binomial cannot be used. We therefore simply state the most useful practical result: if n $100(1 - \alpha)$% confidence intervals are computed, then the probability that they are all correct is at least $1 - n\alpha$, and the probability that at least one is incorrect is no more than $n\alpha$.[†]

■**EXAMPLE 15.3B:** To illustrate the result stated in the previous paragraph, consider two decision makers who have made 18 dependent confidence interval estimates, one using 3 standard error intervals, the other 2 standard error intervals. The probability that the former has constructed 18 correct intervals is at least $1 - 18(0.003) = 1 - 0.054 = 0.946$. This is very close to the probability that would have applied if the intervals had been independent, which is reported as 0.947 in Exhibit 15.3A. The probability that the decision maker who makes 2 standard error intervals makes 18 correct ones is at least $1 - 18(0.05) = 1 - 0.9 = 0.1$, not a very reassuring guarantee.   ■

Even 3 standard error confidence intervals can prove inadequate in the face of a large number of applications. In practice, we recommend using 3 standard error intervals as a guideline, but you need to keep track of the number of intervals you compute and make sure that $1 - n\alpha$ does not get too small. As n increases you need to decrease α to control the risk of making too many incorrect intervals.

Numerically, the computation of a confidence interval is quite simple once the value of the estimate and the value of the standard error are known. For example, in the Northeast region the number of discharges due to vaginal deliveries without

---

[†] This result is based on Bonferroni's inequality. It can be generalized to say that if n confidence intervals with confidence coefficients $1 - \alpha_1, 1 - \alpha_2, \ldots, 1 - \alpha_n$ are made, then the chance that they are all correct is at least $1 - \alpha_1 - \alpha_2 - \cdots - \alpha_n$, and the chance that at least one is incorrect is at most $\alpha_1 + \alpha_2 + \cdots \alpha_n$.

complicating diagnoses was estimated as 524,000 with a standard error of 30,916. A 99.7% confidence interval for the number of discharges is thus

$$524,000 \pm 3(30,916) = 524,000 \pm 92,748.$$

Because the original estimate was given to only three significant figures (524), the confidence limits should also be rounded to three significant figures. Thus our final report is that the number of discharges is (almost certainly)

$$524,000 \pm 93,000$$

We are quite confident that if sampling error were the only source of error, then the equal complete coverage number of discharges is somewhere between 431,000 and 617,000.

Because we are told that the estimates have been adjusted for nonresponse, we feel that at least one source of bias has been minimized. We do not know what other sources of bias may be present in the data, so we do not want to make an unqualified statement about the total number of discharges. That is why we said *if sampling error were the only source of error*. Since the report mentions no major source of nonsampling bias, we feel that the confidence interval in fact deserves roughly the 99.7% level of confidence.

Keep in mind that we are estimating the equal complete coverage number of discharges, that is, the number we would have gotten if we had applied the survey methods to the whole universe of hospitals.

Confidence intervals for average length of stay are handled in exactly the same way, so a detailed example is not given. Instead we turn to making comparisons, a more interesting, but slightly more complicated, process.

SECTION 15.4

COMPARISON OF GROUPS: ESTIMATES, STANDARD ERRORS, AND CONFIDENCE INTERVALS

In exploring Tables 1 and 2 in Section 15.2, most of our time was spent making comparisons. In Exhibit 15.2A regional trends in a DRG were compared with the trends in all DRGs combined. A number of DRGs that did not behave exactly like the combined category were noted in Table 1. This showed variation among DRGs with respect to regions. In Exhibit 15.2B DRGs were compared and ranked with respect to average length of stay. Again regional differences were found, this time in the rankings. In Exhibit 15.2C average lengths of stay for unrelated operating room procedures were compared across four geographic regions and two age groups. The geographic differences appeared to be more pronounced for the older age group than for the younger.

Every number in the three exhibits is an estimate, so each one is subject to sampling and nonsampling errors. This means that a part of every difference computed is error. Our job is to discover what part of any difference we have calculated is error and what part points to a genuine difference in the equal complete coverage values associated with the universe.

This is done by computing standard errors of the numbers obtained when estimates are subtracted. Some of the rules for computing standard errors of functions of estimates are quite simple. Fortunately, these simple rules often suffice, and they will be the focus here. Formulas for standard errors of more complicated functions can be found in more advanced books on statistics.

SUMS AND DIFFERENCES OF TWO ESTIMATES

The easiest and most useful rule is the Pythagorean rule for sums and differences of independent estimates.[†]

> *Whether two independent estimates are added or subtracted, the standard error of the result is computed by taking the square root of the sum of the squares of the standard errors of the estimates.*

The rule can also be stated symbolically. Let E_1 and E_2 be two estimates whose standard errors are se_1 and se_2. Then the standard error of either $E_1 + E_2$ or $E_1 - E_2$ is

$$se = \sqrt{se_1^2 + se_2^2}$$

You see why this is called the Pythagorean rule. It is the same formula used to find the length of the hypotenuse of a right triangle! Exhibit 15.4A shows the result geometrically.

EXHIBIT 15.4A

The Pythagorean Rule for Computing the Standard Error of a Sum or Difference

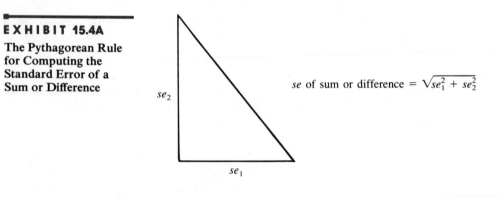

se of sum or difference $= \sqrt{se_1^2 + se_2^2}$

EXAMPLES

To illustrate the result numerically, some standard errors are attached to the differences shown in Exhibit 15.2C. The difference between the Northeast and North Central regions for people under the age of 65 is

$$1.8 = 13.8 - 12.0 \tag{15.3}$$

[†] Estimates are independent if different random numbers are used to select the data used to form the estimates. This will typically be the case when, as in the NHDS, the universe is stratified, that is, broken into several distinct groups. Fresh random numbers are used to draw data from each group. Technically speaking, the DRGs are poststratification groups and so are only conditionally independent. For practical purposes, their standard errors may be computed as if they were completely independent.

To compute the standard error for the difference we first find standard errors of the estimates that are subtracted. Table II provides a standard error of 1.0 for the estimate 13.8 and a standard error of 0.9 for the estimate 12.0. The standard errors have been computed crudely and rounded to one significant decimal place. Equation (15.3) is repeated, with standard errors placed in parentheses under the estimates:

$$1.8 = 13.8 - 12.0$$
$$(\quad) \quad (1.0) \quad (0.9)$$

(15.4)

We must now compute the standard error of the difference 1.8 and insert it under the estimate. Using the Pythagorean rule,

$$se = \sqrt{(1.0)^2 + (0.9)^2} = \sqrt{1.81} = 1.3 \tag{15.5}$$

We can now state that we estimate the difference in the equal complete coverage lengths of stay in the Northeast and North Central regions to be 1.8 days with a standard error of 1.3 days. A 99.7% confidence interval for the difference is

$$1.8 \pm 3(1.3) = 1.8 \pm 3.9 = [-2.1, 5.7] \tag{15.6}$$

days.

The confidence interval says the equal complete coverage difference could be positive or negative. A positive difference indicates a longer average length of stay in the Northeast than in the North Central. A negative difference indicates a longer average length of stay in the North Central than in the Northeast. The sampling error in the estimate does not allow us to rule out either possibility conclusively. The average length of stay in the Northeast may be as much as 5.7 days longer than the average length of stay in the North Central, or the average length of stay in the North Central may be as much as 2.1 days longer than the average length of stay in the Northeast. Larger samples from these regions would have been needed to get more conclusive information.

Now try your hand at a calculation. The difference between the Northeast and North Central for patients over the age of 65 is

$$2.5 = 20.0 - 17.5$$

Compute the confidence interval for the difference in the equal complete coverage values. Do the data allow you to conclude that one region almost certainly has a longer average length of stay than the other?

As another example, compute the standard error of the difference between average lengths of stay for the two age groups in the North Central region. The desired difference is

$$5.5 = 17.5 - 12.0$$
$$(\quad) \quad (1.4) \quad (0.9)$$

(15.7)

The standard errors of the estimates have been found in the usual way from Table II. The computation of the standard error of the difference is

$$se = \sqrt{(1.4)^2 + (0.9)^2} = \sqrt{2.77} = 1.7 \tag{15.8}$$

Thus a 99.7% confidence interval for the difference in the equal complete coverage values is

$$5.5 \pm 3(1.7) = 5.5 \pm 5.1 = [0.4, 10.6] \tag{15.9}$$

days. The evidence is fairly conclusive that in the North Central region the average length of stay for people over age 65 is greater than the average length of stay for people under the age of 65. The difference could be as small as 0.4 day and as large as 10.6 days.

Exhibit 15.4B is a repeat of Exhibit 15.2C with the standard errors of all the numbers shown in parentheses. You may wish to verify a few of the calculations just to internalize the process. Try to compute a confidence interval or two and give interpretations. Remember, it is the confidence interval that conveys the information. The calculations are simply an intermediate step.

EXHIBIT 15.4B

Repeat of Exhibit 15.2C
with Standard Errors

		Age			
		Under 65 Years		65 Years or More	
Region	Length of Stay	Difference	Length of Stay	Difference	Difference
All	11.2		17.3		6.1
	(0.8)		(1.0)		(1.3)
Northeast	13.8		20.0		6.2
	(1.0)		(1.4)		(1.7)
		1.8		2.5	
		(1.3)		(2.0)	
North Central	12.0		17.5		5.5
	(0.9)		(1.4)		(1.7)
		1.9		2.5	
		(1.3)		(2.1)	
West	10.1		15.0		4.9
	(1.0)		(1.6)		(1.9)
		0.4		−0.8	
		(1.3)		(1.9)	
South	9.7		15.8		6.1
	(0.9)		(1.1)		(1.4)

SECTION 15.5

EXERCISES

15.5A Refer to Exhibit 15.4B. Verify each of the estimates and standard errors for the West region. For the West region compute the 99.7% confidence interval for the difference between the average length of stay for persons over age 65 and for persons under age 65. Give a precise verbal interpretation of the interval. Now compute the 95% confidence interval for the same difference and give a precise verbal interpretation of that interval. One interval contains zero while the other does not. How do you explain this apparent contradiction?

15.5B Refer to Exhibit 15.4B. For patients under age 65, compute the 99.7% confidence interval for the difference between the average length of stay in the Northeast region and in the West region. Does there appear to be a conclusive difference in the two regions? Repeat the exercise for patients 65 years of age and older.

15.5C Independent simple random samples are selected from two large groups of people and measurements on a variable y collected. These are the descriptive statistics:

Group	Sample Size	Mean ($\bar{y}$)	Standard Deviation
A	75	110	8.7
B	120	107	10.2

Compute the standard error of the difference between the group means. Compute a 99.7% confidence interval for the difference in the equal complete coverage means. An analyst claims the data conclusively show that group A has a larger mean than group B. What is your response?

15.5D In a large company, a simple random sample of managers is selected and the managers are asked if they favor a certain change in the company's pension plan. An independent simple random sample of hourly workers is also selected and asked the same question. The results are displayed below.

Group	Sample Size	Number in Favor of Change	Proportion in Favor of Change
Managers	50	32	0.64
Hourly workers	100	51	0.51

An analyst claims the data show that a substantially higher proportion of managers than hourly workers favor the change. Compute the 99.7% confidence interval for the difference in the equal complete coverage proportions and comment on the analyst's claim in the light of the confidence interval. Do the data provide conclusive evidence that a majority of all managers favor the change? A majority of all hourly workers?

15.5E Locate a published report of a probability survey. Examine the report for discussion of sampling design, standard errors, treatment of nonsampling errors, and operational definitions. How fully and clearly are these issues discussed? On the basis of your study, formulate a judgment on the credibility and usefulness of the report. Formulate at least one comparison for which the report provides sufficient information to compute a confidence interval. Formulate at least one comparison for which the report does *not* provide sufficient information to compute a confidence interval.

SECTION 15.6

SUPPLEMENTARY EXERCISES FOR CHAPTER 15

15A An auditor must examine two sets of accounts and determine the dollar amount of the difference between the amount recorded in the account and the amount the auditor considers correct. She does not have time to examine every account and so examines simple random samples from each set of accounts. Here are the results of her work. The data are reported in $1000 units.

Set	Number[†]	Sample Size	Mean	Standard Deviation
A	4,000	75	110	8.7
B	10,000	120	107	10.2

[†] This is the total number of accounts in the set.

(a) Compute a 99.7% confidence interval for the total amount of difference between recorded and correct values in set A.

(b) Compute a 99.7% confidence interval for the total amount of difference between recorded and correct values in set B.

(c) Compute a 99.7% confidence interval for the total amount of difference between recorded and correct values in the two sets.

15B An instructor teaches two sections of the same class. At the end of the class each student is asked to rate the instructor on her overall performance on a five-point scale, with 1 indicating poor performance and 5 indicating outstanding performance. Here is a summary of the responses from the two classes:

Section	Section Size	Mean	Standard Deviation
A	75	3.9	0.9
B	120	4.1	1.2

The instructor believes that student ratings are subject to a certain amount of subjectivity that can be approximated by assuming that they behave *as if* they were obtained by simple random sampling from a population of ratings. She therefore feels justified in computing confidence intervals using the data. The confidence intervals display the range of average ratings possible provided her assumption is valid.

(a) Accepting the instructor's assumption, compute the 99.7% confidence interval for the average rating from section 1.

(b) Accepting the instructor's assumption, compute the 99.7% confidence interval for the average rating from section 2.

(c) Accepting the instructor's assumption, compute the 99.7% confidence interval for the average rating from the two sections combined.

(d) Accepting the instructor's assumption, compute the 99.7% confidence interval for the difference between the average ratings from the two sections. Do the sections seem to have rated her differently?

15C A random-digit dialing survey of city residents was conducted to estimate use of natural and artificial Christmas trees. A survey of 800 residences produced 693 residences that set up Christmas trees in their homes last year. These residences were asked if the tree was natural or artificial. There were 245 artificial trees and 448 natural trees. Using a sample size of $n = 693$, compute the 99.7% confidence interval for the difference between the proportion of the city population that uses artificial trees and the proportion of the city population that uses natural trees. Also compute the 99.7% confidence interval for the proportion of city residents who display no tree at all.

APPENDIX D

DIAGNOSIS-RELATED GROUPS USING DATA FROM THE NATIONAL HOSPITAL DISCHARGE SURVEY: UNITED STATES, 1982

From Vital and Health Statistics of the National Center for Health Statistics, Number 105, January 18, 1985. Used with permission.

NCHS ADVANCE DATA REPORT

Diagnosis-Related Groups Using Data from the National Hospital Discharge Survey: United States, 1982

by Robert Pokras and Kurt K. Kubishke, Division of Health Care Statistics

INTRODUCTION

This report presents selected estimates for 1982 of diagnosis-related groups (DRGs) based on data from the National Hospital Discharge Survey (NHDS). A similar report has been published for 1981.[1] The current plan is to publish reports on DRGs regularly because they determine the reimbursement rates of Medicare inpatients, about 30 percent of all discharges from short-stay nonfederal hospitals.[2]

Developed at the Yale School of Organization and Management, DRGs are being used by the Health Care Financing Administration, some states, and some third-party payers to reimburse hospitals for inpatient care on a prospective basis.[3] This approach to health care reimbursement operates on the principle that patients with similar medical conditions should receive similar care and use approximately the same amount of resources; therefore, in general a hospital should be reimbursed the same amount for each patient in a DRG. While there is variation in resource consumption among individuals within a DRG, these are expected to balance across all patients.

DRGs were developed under the guiding principle that "The primary objective in the construction of DRGs was

a definition of case type, each of which could be expected to receive similar outputs or services from a hospital."[4] Their formulation was accomplished using clinical judgment and statistical procedures that classify patients by measuring resource utilization. The first step in this process was to cluster the universe of medical diagnoses into broad, mutually exclusive categories. These groups were formed to be consistent in their anatomical or physiopathological classification, or in a manner in which they are clinically managed. Once these major diagnostic groups were formed, an interactive statistical program (AUTOGROUP[4]) was used to further classify each major group into discrete DRGs. This process incorporated patient information regarding diagnoses (primary and secondary), procedures, sex, and age to explain maximally a patient's length of stay. In all, there currently are 470 DRGs.

Prospective reimbursement was authorized under the Tax Equity and Fiscal Responsibility Act of 1983. Under this act hospitals participating in the Medicare program were brought into this system beginning with their fiscal year as of October 1, 1983. The Health Care Financing Administration, which operates the Medicare program, is allowing several years for hospitals to make a transition to prospective reimbursement by adjusting DRG payments based on certain hospital characteristics and geographic location. At the end of this phase-in period, care provided to a Medicare inpatient will translate into a preestablished payment based solely on the patient's DRG.

There is an important issue related to the NHDS and the implementation of this prospective reimbursement system: how this system may affect the selection of a patient's principal diagnosis and/or comorbidities. Because the NHDS is designed to collect data on the morbidity of the hospital inpatient population, any external influence on diagnostic practices may affect NHDS data. For example, two patients admitted to a hospital for treatment of chest pain—one diagnosed as having chest pain and the other diagnosed as having angina—will be placed into different DRGs and have different reimbursement rates. There is speculation that in cases such as this prospective reimbursement may influence the selection of a diagnosis,[3] which in turn may affect estimates produced from the NHDS. After prospective payment has been in place for a few years, it may be possible to examine trends in NHDS data and determine the magnitude, if any, of this type of effect.

The statistics in this report are based on data collected by means of the NHDS, a continuous survey conducted by the National Center for Health Statistics since 1965. Data for this survey are sampled from short-stay nonfederal general and specialty hospitals in the 50 states and the District of Columbia. The sample for 1982 contained approximately 214,000 medical records from 426 hospitals. The relevant variables required to produce DRGs (diagnoses, procedures, sex, age, and other variables) were abstracted from the face sheet of each sampled medical record, and NHDS data thereby could be used to produce national estimates of DRGs. These estimates may be of value for hospitals to compare their experience with that of other hospitals. For this reason, statistics in this report are frequency estimates and associated average length of stay for DRGs by hospital bed size and region of the country.

HIGHLIGHTS

The frequency and average length of stay for the most common DRGs are presented by age, region of the country, and hospital bed size (Tables 1–4). Age is dichotomized as under 65 years of age and 65 years of age and older. This allows a comparison with the Medicare population because Medicare covers most hospital costs for approximately 94 percent of discharges 65 years of age and over. Tables 1 and 2 provide regional data, while Tables 3 and 4 provide bed-size data for these DRGs. Within each of these sets of tables, the first (Tables 1 and 3) are for patients under 65 years of age, and the second (Tables 2 and 4) are for patients 65 years of age and over.

By definition, some DRGs are only for patients in a specific age range. In such a case the DRG title and the table title (Tables 1–4) together define the age group of the estimate. That is, the most restrictive case of either the

TABLE 1 Number of Discharges and Average Length of Stay of Patients under 65 Years of Age Discharged from Short-Stay Hospitals, by Selected Diagnosis-Related Groups and Geographic Regions: United States, 1982 (Discharges from nonfederal short-stay hospitals. Excludes newborn infants.)

Diagnosis-Related Group	All Regions	Northeast	North Central	South	West	All Regions	Northeast	North Central	South	West
	Number in Thousands					**Average Length of Stay in Days**				
All discharges	27,896	5,564	7,929	9,804	4,598	5.9	6.5	6.3	5.6	5.0
Vaginal delivery without complicating diagnoses	2,784	524	765	937	559	2.9	3.4	3.3	2.7	2.2
Medical back problems	790	121	245	298	125	7.2	9.0	7.3	6.8	6.2
Esophagitis, gastroenteritis, and miscellaneous digestive disorders, age 18–69 years without substantial comorbidity and/or complication	673	97	178	320	78	4.1	4.5	4.2	4.2	3.3
Cesarean section without substantial comorbidity and/or complication	649	125	145	258	121	5.7	6.7	6.2	5.3	4.8

(Continued)

TABLE 1 *(Continued)*

Diagnosis-Related Group	All Regions	Northeast	North Central	South	West	All Regions	Northeast	North Central	South	West
	Numbers in Thousands					Average Length of Stay in Days				
Nonradical hysterectomy, age less than 70 years without substantial comorbidity and/or complication	495	70	128	212	85	7.2	7.9	7.6	7.1	6.2
Unrelated operating room procedures	401	75	116	145	65	11.2	13.8	12.0	9.7	10.1
Esophagitis, gastroenteritis, and miscellaneous digestive disorders, age 0–17 years	392	69	111	173	39	3.8	3.9	3.8	3.8	3.3
Psychoses	388	95	118	108	68	16.5	19.1	19.7	13.8	11.6
Alcohol- and substance-induced organic mental syndrome	360	157	90	68	45	10.6	9.8	11.9	10.7	10.9
Dilation and curettage of uterus; conization except for malignancy	345	111	85	118	32	1.8	1.7	1.9	2.0	1.2
Abortion with dilation and curettage of uterus	325	136	65	86	39	1.3	1.0	1.7	1.5	1.1
Bronchitis and asthma, age 0–17 years	313	65	96	118	34	3.9	4.6	3.8	3.8	3.3
Simple pneumonia and pleurisy, age 0–17 years	279	36	86	131	28	4.7	5.3	5.0	4.6	4.1
Tonsillectomy and/or adenoidectomy, age 0–17 years	279	43	106	83	48	1.8	1.7	1.9	2.1	1.2
Inguinal and femoral hernia procedures, age 18–69 years without substantial comorbidity and/or complication	271	76	74	80	42	4.2	4.0	4.4	4.7	3.0
Diabetes, age greater than 35 years	259	52	72	104	30	8.2	9.9	8.7	7.4	6.4
Vaginal delivery with sterilization and/or dilation and curettage of uterus	247	44	57	110	37	3.6	4.2	4.1	3.3	2.8
Other factors influencing health status	242	53	68	75	46	3.5	3.6	3.8	3.2	3.4
Total cholecystectomy with common bile duct exploration, age less than 70 years without substantial comorbidity and/or complication	233	48	63	83	39	7.8	8.1	7.9	8.1	6.7
Bronchitis and asthma, age 18–69 years without substantial comorbidity and/or complication	227	45	62	81	38	5.3	5.9	5.8	4.9	4.6

TABLE 2 Number of Discharges and Average Length of Stay of Patients 65 Years of Age and Over Discharged from Short-Stay Hospitals, by Selected Diagnosis-Related Groups and Geographic Regions: United States, 1982 (Discharges from nonfederal short-stay hospitals. Excludes newborn infants.)

Diagnosis-Related Group	All Regions	Northeast	North Central	South	West	All Regions	Northeast	North Central	South	West
	Numbers in Thousands					Average Length of Stay in Days				
All discharges	10,697	2,283	3,008	3,631	1,774	10.1	12.3	10.3	9.4	8.2
Lens procedures	429	81	127	119	102	2.9	3.0	3.3	3.0	2.4
Atherosclerosis, age greater than 69 years and/or substantial comorbidity and complication	427	99	109	157	62	8.7	10.9	9.0	8.2	6.3
Heart failure and shock	387	88	108	132	59	9.7	11.8	10.3	8.8	7.7
Esophagitis, gastroenteritis, and miscellaneous digestive disorders, age greater than 69 years and/or substantial comorbidity and complication	376	63	102	169	42	6.7	8.3	6.9	6.3	5.8
Chronic obstructive pulmonary disease	300	54	76	117	54	9.8	11.9	10.2	8.8	9.2
Specific cerebrovascular disorders except transient ischemic attack	295	64	76	103	52	15.4	20.4	16.2	13.2	12.2
Simple pneumonia and pleurisy, age greater than 69 years and/or substantial comorbidity and complication	276	51	80	106	38	10.7	11.8	10.6	10.7	9.5
Unrelated operating room procedures	226	59	65	72	29	17.3	20.0	17.5	15.8	15.0
Diabetes, age greater than 35 years	208	49	56	77	24	10.0	13.9	9.7	8.4	8.1
Angina pectoris	195	49	47	67	32	6.6	8.0	6.4	6.6	4.9
Medical back problems	186	38	58	63	27	9.3	11.5	9.7	7.7	8.8
Cardiac arrhythmia and conduction disorders, age greater than 69 years and/or substantial comorbidity and complication	181	35	51	65	30	7.1	9.1	7.2	7.1	4.8
Circulatory disorders with acute myocardial infarction without cardiovascular complications, discharged alive	174	44	44	62	24	12.2	13.6	12.9	11.8	9.4
Hypertension	158	28	43	70	17	7.9	8.8	7.7	7.6	8.4
Transient ischemic attacks	155	39	42	52	22	7.6	9.6	7.8	7.3	4.3

TABLE 2 (*Continued*)

Diagnosis-Related Group	All Regions	Northeast	North Central	South	West	All Regions	Northeast	North Central	South	West
	Numbers in Thousands					Average Length of Stay in Days				
Bronchitis and asthma, age greater than 69 years and/or substantial comorbidity and complication	148	22	38	59	29	8.3	9.2	8.0	8.3	8.0
Transurethral prostatectomy, age greater than 69 years and/or substantial comorbidity and complication	144	29	42	45	28	9.3	11.1	9.5	9.4	6.8
Kidney and urinary tract infections, age greater than 69 years and/or substantial comorbidity and complication	142	23	34	67	17	8.5	9.9	8.8	8.1	7.1
Respiratory neoplasms	137	36	34	43	24	10.9	11.0	11.9	11.2	9.0
Hip and femur procedures except major joint, age greater than 69 years and/or substantial comorbidity and complication	135	27	45	38	25	19.5	25.1	19.9	18.5	14.3

TABLE 3 Number of Discharges and Average Length of Stay of Patients under 65 Years of Age Discharged from Short-Stay Hospitals, by Selected Diagnosis-Related Groups and Hospital Bed Size: United States, 1982 (Discharges from nonfederal short-stay hospitals. Excludes newborn infants.)

Diagnosis-Related Group	All Hospitals	6–99 Beds	100–199 Beds	200–299 Beds	300–399 Beds	500 or More Beds	All Hospitals	6–99 Beds	100–199 Beds	200–299 Beds	300–399 Beds	500 or More Beds
	Number in Thousands						Average Length of Stay in Days					
All discharges	27,896	4,664	4,906	4,459	6,909	6,958	5.9	4.5	5.3	5.7	6.2	6.8
Vaginal delivery without complicating diagnoses	2,784	425	466	433	700	759	2.9	2.4	2.8	2.8	3.1	3.2
Medical back problems	790	170	137	150	185	149	7.2	6.3	7.0	7.5	7.6	7.6
Esophagitis, gastroenteritis, and miscellaneous digestive disorders, age 18–69 years without substantial comorbidity and/or complication	673	191	116	115	143	108	4.1	3.3	4.3	4.6	4.2	4.8
Cesarean section without substantial comorbidity and/or complication	649	75	123	93	175	183	5.7	5.4	5.2	5.5	5.8	6.1

(*Continued*)

TABLE 3 *(Continued)*

Diagnosis-Related Group	All Hospitals	6–99 Beds	100– 199 Beds	200– 299 Beds	300– 399 Beds	500 or More Beds	All Hospitals	6–99 Beds	100– 199 Beds	200– 299 Beds	300– 399 Beds	500 or More Beds
	Number in Thousands						Average Length of Stay in Days					
Nonradical hysterectomy, age less than 70 years without substantial comorbidity and/or complication	495	51	111	80	126	125	7.2	7.1	6.5	7.4	7.3	7.5
Unrelated operating room procedures	401	50	65	65	98	123	11.2	6.9	7.7	12.8	13.0	12.5
Esophagitis, gastroenteritis, and miscellaneous digestive disorders, age 0–17	392	82	97	60	78	75	3.8	2.7	3.7	3.8	4.0	4.8
Psychoses	388	34	74	40	137	103	16.5	12.0	14.5	15.1	15.8	20.9
Alcohol- and substance-induced organic mental syndrome	360	105	59	39	97	60	10.6	9.6	13.5	12.9	9.9	9.4
Dilation and curettage of uterus; conization except for malignancy	345	56	78	43	81	87	1.8	1.8	1.7	2.1	1.9	1.6
Abortion with dilation and curettage of uterus	325	36	68	41	78	102	1.3	1.6	1.4	1.5	1.2	1.1
Bronchitis and asthma, age 0–17 years	313	59	79	50	70	56	3.9	3.4	3.8	4.5	4.1	3.8
Simple pneumonia and pleurisy, age 0–17 years	279	85	63	48	49	35	4.7	4.1	4.9	5.0	5.2	4.9
Tonsillectomy and/or adenoidectomy, age 0–17 years	279	52	55	63	68	41	1.8	1.6	1.8	1.9	1.7	1.9
Inguinal and femoral hernia procedures, age 18–69 years without substantial comorbidity and/or complication	271	40	50	45	72	64	4.2	4.2	3.9	4.4	4.2	4.2
Diabetes, age greater than 35 years	259	57	43	53	56	50	8.2	6.2	7.2	8.2	9.4	9.7
Vaginal delivery with sterilization and/or dilation and curettage of uterus	247	47	47	41	47	65	3.6	3.4	3.3	3.5	3.7	3.8
Other factors influencing health status	242	35	38	39	58	73	3.5	3.1	4.0	3.5	3.6	3.4
Total cholecystectomy with common bile duct exploration, age less than 70 years without substantial comorbidity and/or complication	233	44	41	34	65	48	7.8	7.2	7.5	8.4	8.4	7.4
Bronchitis and asthma, age 18–69 years without substantial comorbidity and/or complication	227	60	37	38	45	46	5.3	4.8	5.3	5.0	5.7	5.8

TABLE 4 Number of Discharges and Average Length of Stay of Patients 65 Years of Age or Over Discharged from Short-Stay Hospitals, by Selected Diagnosis-Related Groups and Hospital Bed Size: United States, 1982 (Discharges from nonfederal short-stay hospitals. Excludes newborn infants.)

Diagnosis-Related Group	Number in Thousands						Average Length of Stay in Days					
	All Hospitals	6–99 Beds	100–199 Beds	200–299 Beds	300–399 Beds	500 or More Beds	All Hospitals	6–99 Beds	100–199 Beds	200–299 Beds	300–399 Beds	500 or More Beds
All discharges	10,697	2,172	1,832	1,907	2,638	2,148	10.1	8.1	9.6	10.2	10.8	11.5
Lens procedures	429	32	94	85	118	99	2.9	2.9	3.0	2.6	3.0	3.1
Atherosclerosis, age greater than 69 years and/or substantial comorbidity and complication	427	90	87	80	107	63	8.7	7.3	8.1	8.8	9.6	10.2
Heart failure and shock	387	113	70	68	82	54	9.7	8.1	9.3	10.5	10.8	11.0
Esophagitis, gastroenteritis, and miscellaneous digestive disorders, age greater than 69 years and/or substantial comorbidity and complication	376	123	60	64	78	51	6.7	5.6	7.2	6.9	8.3	6.5
Chronic obstructive pulmonary disease	300	76	48	58	71	48	9.8	8.1	9.5	10.7	10.6	10.5
Specific cerebrovascular disorders except transient ischemic attack	294	66	54	60	63	50	15.4	11.2	15.8	16.1	14.9	20.1
Simple pneumonia and pleurisy, age greater than 69 years and/or substantial comorbidity and complication	276	98	45	42	56	36	10.7	9.3	10.9	11.7	11.8	11.6
Unrelated operating room procedures	226	29	42	45	58	52	17.3	14.1	17.3	16.0	17.5	19.9
Diabetes, age greater than 35 years	208	50	,37	44	44	33	10.0	8.2	9.2	10.3	10.9	12.1
Angina pectoris	195	54	34	40	44	23	6.6	5.9	6.3	6.3	7.6	7.4
Medical back problems	186	45	33	36	41	31	9.3	7.8	8.3	8.5	11.6	10.2
Cardiac arrhythmia and conduction disorders, age greater than 69 years and/or substantial comorbidity and complication	181	49	31	33	37	30	7.1	5.7	6.6	7.8	7.8	8.5
Circulatory disorders with acute myocardial infarction without cardiovascular complications, discharged alive	174	35	27	31	46	35	12.2	11.2	11.6	12.1	12.9	12.9
Hypertension	158	39	31	29	27	32	7.9	6.2	7.3	9.3	7.7	9.6
Transient ischemic attacks	155	36	34	30	32	24	7.6	5.5	7.5	7.6	9.7	8.2

(Continued)

TABLE 4 (Continued)

Diagnosis-Related Group	All Hospitals	6–99 Beds	100–199 Beds	200–299 Beds	300–399 Beds	500 or More Beds	All Hospitals	6–99 Beds	100–199 Beds	200–299 Beds	300–399 Beds	500 or More Beds
	Number in Thousands						**Average Length of Stay in Days**					
Bronchitis and asthma, age greater than 69 years and/or substantial comorbidity and complication	148	47	31	25	28	17	8.3	6.9	9.6	8.7	8.8	8.2
Transurethral prostatectomy, age greater than 69 years and/or substantial comorbidity and complication	144	14	31	27	38	33	9.3	9.2	8.3	10.2	9.2	9.5
Kidney and urinary tract infections, age greater than 69 years and/or substantial comorbidity and complication	142	48	26	20	31	18	8.5	7.2	9.2	8.5	9.2	9.4
Respiratory neoplasms	137	22	19	19	40	37	10.9	7.7	10.8	10.0	11.8	12.4
Hip and femur procedures except major joint, age greater than 69 years and/or substantial comorbidity and complication	135	16	23	24	40	32	19.5	18.3	18.1	17.9	20.3	21.3

table or DRG title determines the age group of the estimate. For example, "Diabetes, age greater than 35 years" in Table 2 only refers to patients 65 years of age and over because of the table title; whereas "Simple pneumonia and pleurisy, age greater than 69 years and/or substantial comorbidity and complication" in Table 2 would not include a patient under 70 years of age because of the restriction in the DRG title.

The most common DRG for patients under 65 years of age was "Vaginal delivery without complicating diagnoses" (Table 1), with an estimated 2.8 million discharges in 1982. "Cesarean section without substantial comorbidity and/or complication," with 649,000 discharges, also was among the most frequent DRGs in this age group. For patients 65 years of age and older (Table 2), "Lens procedures" was the most common DRG, 429,000, and "Atherosclerosis, age greater than 69 years and/or substantial comorbidity and complication," 427,000, was the second most common DRG for the elderly.

The average length of stay for specific DRGs in the four regions of the country generally reflects the pattern found for all patients: the Northeast and North Central have the longest average length of stay and the West has the shortest. Regional length-of-stay differences were greater for patients 65 years of age or more than for younger patients. The West had an average length of stay of 5.0 days for patients under 65 years of age, and the Northeast had an average length of stay of 6.5 days, a difference of 1.5 days, or 30 percent greater. For older patients, however, the Northeast had an average length of stay 4.1 days greater than the elderly patients in the West (12.3 versus 8.2 days), a difference of 50 percent.

Overall there was a tendency for length of stay to increase with hospital bed size (Tables 3 and 4) for patients under 65 years of age as well as for older patients, but this pattern is not consistent for some of the individual DRGs for which average length of stay in small and medium-size hospitals is equal to or greater than the average length of stay in large hospitals (500 or more beds).

The average length of stay associated with a DRG (Tables 1–4) allows hospitals to compare their experience with that of other hospitals. While comparison is tenuous on a case-by-case basis, a hospital with an average length of stay 2, 3, or more days longer than the national average for a specific DRG may need to examine why it is so far from the norm. This kind of comparison may be worthwhile as a starting point, but even within a DRG, average length of stay is not an exact measure of resource consumption.

The change to prospective payment for Medicare inpatient reimbursement is likely to affect areas such as cost savings, quality of care, medical records keeping, and certain areas of medical practice. However, for at least two reasons data currently available on DRGs from the NHDS (this report and a similar report using 1981 data[1]) should not be used to evaluate the success of prospective payment. First, the prospective payment program was not implemented until October 1983, and, second, historical trends must be studied to shed light on short-term changes in hospital utilization.

For example, from 1981 to 1982 average length of stay decreased 0.4 day for patients 65 years of age and over, and some specific DRGs also showed a reduction in average length of stay. However, length of stay in short-stay nonfederal hospitals has been decreasing for over a decade (the average length of stay for patients 65 years of age and over was 12.2 days in 1972[5] compared with 10.1 days in 1982), and it will take more time to understand the effects prospective payment will have, if any, on hospital utilization.

REFERENCES

[1] National Center for Health Statistics, R. Pokras: Diagnosis-related groups using data from the National Hospital Discharge Survey, United States, 1981. *Advance Data From Vital and Health Statistics*. No. 98. DHHS Pub. No. (PHS) 84–1250. Public Health Service. Hyattsville, Md., July 20, 1984.

[2] National Center for Health Statistics, E. J. Graves: Utilization of short-stay hospitals, United States, 1982 Annual Summary. *Vital and Health Statistics*. Series 13, No. 78. DHHS Pub. No. (PHS) 84–1739. Public Health Service. Washington. U.S. Government Printing Office, Aug. 1984.

[3] J. Alsofrom: Playing the numbers. *Medical World News*, Oct. 24, 1983, pp. 38–55.

[4] R. B. Fetter, S. Youngsoo, J. L. Freeman, and others: Case mix definition by diagnostic related groups. *Medical Care* 18(2), Supplement. (Copyright 1980: Used with the permission of *Medical Care*.)

[5] National Center for Health Statistics, W. F. Lewis: Utilization of short-stay hospitals, summary of nonmedical statistics, United States, 1972. *Vital and Health Statistics*. Series 13, No. 19. DHEW Pub. No. (HRA) 75–1770. Health Resources Administration. Washington. U.S. Government Printing Office, June 1975.

[6] National Center for Health Statistics, M. G. Sirken: Utilization of short-stay hospitals, summary of nonmedical statistics, United States, 1965. *Vital and Health Statistics*. Series 13, No. 2. PHS Pub.

No. 1000. Public Health Service. Washington. U.S. Government Printing Office, Aug. 1967.

[7] National Center for Health Statistics, M. J. Witkin: Utilization of short-stay hospitals by characteristics of discharged patients, United States, 1965. *Vital and Health Statistics*. Series 13, No. 3. PHS Pub. No. 1000. Public Health Service. Washington. U.S. Government Printing Office, Dec. 1967.

[8] National Center for Health Statistics, R. Pokras: Surgical and non-surgical procedures in short-stay hospitals, United States, 1979. *Vital and Health Statistics*. Series 13, No. 70. DHHS Pub. No. (PHS) 83–1731. Public Health Service. Washington. U.S. Government Printing Office, Feb. 1983.

[9] U.S. Public Health Service and Health Care Financing Administration: *International Classification of Diseases, 9th Revision, Clinical Modification*. DHHS Pub. No. (PHS) 80–1260. Public Health Service. Washington. U.S. Government Printing Office, Sept. 1980.

[10] *Federal Register*, Vol. 48, No. 171, Part II, Rules and Regulations, Sept. 1, 1983.

TECHNICAL NOTES

Survey Methodology

Source of Data The National Hospital Discharge Survey (NHDS) encompasses patients discharged from short-stay hospitals, exclusive of military and Veterans Administration hospitals, located in the 50 states and the District of Columbia. Only hospitals with six or more beds and an average length of stay of less than 30 days for all patients are included in the survey. Discharges of newborn infants are excluded from this report.

The universe of the survey consisted of 6965 short-stay hospitals contained in the 1963 Master Facility Inventory of Hospitals and Institutions. New hospitals were sampled for inclusion in the survey in 1972, 1975, 1977, and 1981. The sample for 1982 consisted of 550 hospitals. Of these, 71 refused to participate and 53 were out of scope either because the hospital had gone out of business or because it failed to meet the definition of a short-stay hospital. Thus 426 hospitals participated in the survey during 1982 and provided approximately 214,000 abstracts of medical records.

Sample Design All hospitals with 1000 or more beds in the universe of short-stay hospitals were selected with certainty in the sample. All hospitals with fewer than 1000 beds were stratified, the primary strata being 24 size-by-region classes. Within each of these 24 primary strata, the allocation of the hospitals was made through a controlled selection technique so that hospitals in the sample would be properly distributed with regard to type of ownership and geographic division. Sample hospitals were drawn with probabilities ranging from certainty for the largest hospitals to 1 in 40 for the smallest hospitals.

Sample discharges were selected within the hospitals using the daily listing sheet of discharges as the sampling frame. These discharges were selected by a random technique, usually on the basis of the terminal digit or digits of the patient's medical record number, a number assigned when the patient was admitted to the hospital. The within-hospital sampling ratio for selecting sample discharges varied inversely with the probability of selection of the hospital.

Data Collection and Estimation   The sample selection and the transcription of information from the hospital records for abstract forms were performed by the hospital staff or by representatives of the National Center for Health Statistics or by both. The data were abstracted from the face sheets of the medical records. All discharge diagnoses were listed on the abstract in the order of the principal one, or the first-listed one if the principal one was not identified, followed by the order in which all other diagnoses were entered on the face sheet of the medical record.

Statistics produced by NHDS are derived by a complex estimating procedure. The basic unit of estimation is the sample inpatient discharge abstract. The estimating procedure used to produce essentially unbiased national estimates in NHDS has three principal components: inflation by reciprocals of the probabilities of sample selection, adjustment or nonresponse, and ratio adjustment to fixed totals. These components of estimation are described in appendix I of two earlier publications.[6,7]

Diagnosis-Related Groups   The diagnosis-related groups (DRGs) used in this report were produced using the most current DRG program available at the time (summer of 1983). This is a computer program that groups patients into DRGs based on diagnostic, surgical, and patient information. The program is maintained and is commercially available at Health Systems International (DRG Support Group, 100 Broadway, New Haven, Conn. 06511). However, the actual program used to produce estimates in this report was obtained from the Health Care Financing Administration.

To help interpret the data in this report, two points are worth mentioning. First, the entire NHDS file was used to produce estimates, including outliers. None of the data was excluded, or trimmed, because of an abnormally long length of stay. Second, the NHDS only codes three ICD-9-CM Class 4 procedures[8,9]: circumcision, code 64.0; episiotomy, code 73.6; and removal of intrauterine contraceptive device, code 97.71. In certain instances Class 4 procedures can alter the DRG designation for a patient. The effect of not coding these procedures in the NHDS on determining DRGs is unknown but probably quite small. In all other respects, the DRGs presented

in this report are consistent with those in the *Federal Register* of Thursday, September 1, 1983.[10]

In publications from the National Center for Health Statistics using NHDS data, several schemes have been used to group patients into categories based on either their diagnoses or the procedures performed. These groups were developed to report general purpose statistics to the many users of NHDS data, and any similarity between the titles of those categories and DRG titles is coincidental.

Sampling Errors and Rounding of Numbers

The standard error is a measure of the sampling variability that occurs by chance because only a sample, rather than an entire universe, is surveyed. The relative standard error of the estimate is obtained by dividing the standard error by the estimate itself and is expressed as a percent of the estimate. Table I shows relative standard errors for discharges and first-listed diagnoses for 1982. The standard errors for average lengths of stay are shown in Table II. Estimates have been rounded to the nearest thousand. For this reason detailed figures within tables do not always add to the totals.

TABLE I Approximate Relative Standard Errors of Estimated Number of Discharges and First-Listed Diagnoses: United States, 1982

Size of Estimate	Relative Standard Error (%)
10,000	16.3
50,000	10.2
100,000	8.5
300,000	6.6
500,000	5.9
1,000,000	5.1
4,000,000	4.0

TABLE II Approximate Standard Errors of Average Lengths of Stay by Number of Discharges: United States, 1982

Number of Discharges	Average Length of Stay in Days			
	2	6	10	20
	Standard error in days			
10,000	0.7	1.2	1.7	2.2
50,000	0.3	0.7	1.0	1.4
100,000	0.3	0.6	0.9	1.2
500,000	0.2	0.5	0.8	0.9
1,000,000	0.2	0.5	0.8	0.7
5,000,000	0.2	0.5	0.8	—

Tests of Significance In this report, the determination of statistical inference is based on the two-tailed Bonferroni test for multiple comparisons. Terms relating to differences, such as "higher" and "less," indicate that the differences are statistically significant. Terms such as "similar" or "no difference" mean that no statistically significant difference exists between the estimates being compared. A lack of comment on the difference between any two estimates does not mean that the difference was tested and found to be not significant.

Definition of Terms

Patient—A person who is formally admitted to the inpatient service of a short-stay hospital for observation, care, diagnosis, or treatment. In this report the number of patients refers to the number of discharges during the year, including any multiple discharges of the same individual from one or more short-stay hospitals.

Average length of stay—The total number of patient days accumulated at time of discharge by patients discharged during the year divided by the number of patients discharged.

Age—Patient's age refers to age at birthday prior to admission to the hospital inpatient service.

Discharge—Discharge is the formal release of a patient by a hospital; that is, the termination of a period of hospitalization by death or by disposition to place of residence, nursing home, or another hospital. The terms "discharges" and "patients discharged" are used synonymously.

Geographic region—Hospitals are classified by location in one of the four geographic regions of the United States that correspond to those used by the U.S. Bureau of the Census:

Region	States Included
Northeast	Maine, New Hampshire, Vermont, Massachusetts, Rhode Island, Connecticut, New York, New Jersey, and Pennsylvania
North Central	Michigan, Ohio, Illinois, Indiana, Wisconsin, Minnesota, Iowa, Missouri, North Dakota, South Dakota, Nebraska, and Kansas
South	Delaware, Maryland, District of Columbia, Virginia, West Virginia, North Carolina, South Carolina, Georgia, Florida, Kentucky, Tennessee, Alabama, Mississippi, Arkansas, Louisiana, Oklahoma, and Texas
West	Montana, Idaho, Wyoming, Colorado, New Mexico, Arizona, Utah, Nevada, Washington, Oregon, California, Hawaii, and Alaska

Hospitals—Short-stay special and general hospitals have six beds or more for inpatient use and an average length of stay of less than 30 days. Federal hospitals and hospital units of institutions are not included.

Bed size of hospital—Size is measured by the number of beds, cribs, and pediatric bassinets regularly maintained (set up and staffed for use) for patients; bassinets for newborn infants are not included. In this report the classification of hospitals by bed size is based on the number of beds at or near midyear reported by the hospitals.

## CHAPTER 16

Stratified, Cluster, and Systematic Sampling[†]

In practice, populations are usually quite complex and hard to sample, and the methods used to extract information from them must be correspondingly advanced. Although not all the complexities of sampling designs are considered here, three fundamental tools of sampling are presented: stratification, clustering, and systematic sampling. Acquaintance with these tools will give you a better appreciation of sampling in practice.

SECTION 16.1

STRATIFICATION IN SAMPLING

WHAT IS STRATIFICATION?

Stratification is the grouping of elements in a frame according to some common characteristic or characteristics. **Stratified sampling** is a design in which random samples are drawn from strata in the frame.

[†] This is an optional section.

■ E X A M P L E   16.1A:[†] A supplier of paper that is made into corrugated board uses three different production lines to produce the paper. Although the three lines are considered identical, a study shows that paper produced by one of the lines is consistently stronger than that produced by the other two lines. The study of output by production line is an example of stratification.   ■

■ E X A M P L E   16.1B: One of the fundamental tenets of marketing is market segmentation, which is the formation of groups of potential customers according to such characteristics as age, geographic location, psychological traits, and so on. The grouping of customers is an example of stratification.   ■

■ E X A M P L E   16.1C: In the DRG study in Chapter 15, hospitals were grouped by geographic region and size, another illustration of stratification.   ■

In each of the examples stratification was chosen to help solve a problem: finding sources of variation in a paper product, identifying a target market, and studying the feasibility of a uniform reimbursement plan. Statistically speaking, an important result of stratification is a reduction in the sampling variability of estimates of important parameters.[††] The intuitive explanation for this is that grouping elements by a common characteristic removes some variation from the population that would otherwise show up in the estimates. Thus stratification is both a natural strategy in the study of groups and a helpful statistical device for controlling variation.

HOW IS STRATIFIED SAMPLING PERFORMED?

To introduce stratification into a sampling design, there must be a frame that shows the stratum to which each element belongs. For example, the sample may come from a list of names of people who are either members of an organization or non-members who have made a financial contribution. A sample of members and a sample of nonmembers are drawn, which gives stratification by membership status. In Example 16.1A it is natural to stratify because output is obtained from each production line. In Example 16.1C the job of compiling lists of hospitals and attaching geographic and bed-size codes is clearly a massive one. Yet it is necessary to carry out the stratification done in the study.

Once the frame is constructed, a separate probability sample is drawn from each stratum. Using a fresh set of random numbers in sampling each stratum guarantees the independence of the samples. After the samples are drawn, the measurement of the selected elements takes place and the data are ready for analysis.

HOW ARE ESTIMATES FORMED FROM STRATIFIED SAMPLES?

A sample from a single stratum is analogous to a sample from a single population. If a simple random sample is drawn from a stratum, then that sample is used just as in

---

[†] This example is adapted from P. G. Moore, *Statistics and the Manager* (London: MacDonald, 1966), 5–7.

[††] Reducing variability is not always the primary objective of stratification. If the comparison of certain groups is an objective of the survey, these groups may be used as strata even though the stratification may do little to further the reduction of sampling variability.

Chapter 14 to estimate the stratum mean, total, or proportion. No new theory is required for this.

To estimate the difference between two strata means, totals, or proportions, the Pythagorean rule for computing the standard errors of differences between estimates, discussed in Chapter 15, is used. Comparisons also require no new theory.

But if a stratified random sample is drawn from a population and we wish to estimate the overall population mean, total, or proportion, some new theory is needed. This problem has not been encountered before. The theory for it is presented in Section 16.2.

SECTION 16.2

MECHANICS OF STRATIFIED SAMPLING

NOTATION FOR TWO STRATA

In this section the notation for two strata is developed. Once you master the problem with two strata, you will find it easy to deal with any number of strata. Independent simple random samples are taken from the strata.

The existence of a frame of elements designated as belonging to stratum 1 or stratum 2 is taken for granted. Let N_1 denote the number of stratum 1 elements in the frame and N_2 the number of stratum 2 elements in the frame. Denote by $N = N_1 + N_2$ the total number of elements in the frame. Let n_1 denote the number of elements drawn into the sample from stratum 1, and n_2 the number of elements from stratum 2. The total number of elements in the two samples is $n = n_1 + n_2$. Let $f_1 = n_1/N_1$ and $f_2 = n_2/N_2$ denote the sampling fractions for the two strata. The total sampling fraction is

$$f = \frac{n}{N} = \frac{(n_1 + n_2)}{N} = \left(\frac{N_1}{N}\right)\left(\frac{n_1}{N_1}\right) + \left(\frac{N_2}{N}\right)\left(\frac{n_2}{N_2}\right) = \left(\frac{N_1}{N}\right)f_1 + \left(\frac{N_2}{N}\right)f_2$$

The quantities $\sqrt{1 - f_1}, \sqrt{1 - f_2}$, and $\sqrt{1 - f}$ are the finite population corrections.

Equal complete coverage of stratum 1 would yield a set of N_1 measurements whose mean and standard deviation are denoted by μ_1 and S_1. Similarly, equal complete coverage of stratum 2 would yield a set of N_2 measurements whose mean and standard deviation are denoted by μ_2 and S_2.

The simple random sample from stratum 1 yields data from which any statistics may be computed. To keep the presentation concrete, assume that the objective is to estimate means. Thus from the data from stratum 1, the mean, standard deviation, and standard error of the mean, which are denoted by $\bar{y}_1$, s_1, and

$$\sqrt{\frac{(1 - f_1)s_1^2}{n_1}} = \frac{(fpc_1)s_1}{\sqrt{n_1}}$$

would be computed.

Similarly, the mean, standard deviation, and standard error of the mean from the data from stratum 2 are denoted by $\bar{y}_2$, s_2, and

$$\sqrt{\frac{(1 - f_2)s_2^2}{n_2}} = \frac{(fpc_2)s_2}{\sqrt{n_2}}$$

The goal is to estimate the population mean, which is denoted by μ. First observe that the relationship between μ, μ_1, and μ_2 is

$$\mu = \left(\frac{N_1}{N}\right)\mu_1 + \left(\frac{N_2}{N}\right)\mu_2 \tag{16.1}$$

which is analogous to the relationship between the overall sampling fraction and the stratum sampling fractions. The overall mean is a weighted average of the stratum means, where the weights are the proportions of stratum 1 and stratum 2 elements in the frame. See Exercise 16.3A for a sketch of the proof of Equation (16.1).

Because $\bar{y}_1$ and $\bar{y}_2$ are estimates of μ_1 and μ_2, it is natural to estimate μ with

$$\bar{y}_{st} = \left(\frac{N_1}{N}\right)\bar{y}_1 + \left(\frac{N_2}{N}\right)\bar{y}_2 \tag{16.2}$$

The mean estimate based on the stratified sample is denoted by $\bar{y}_{st}$. The theoretical standard error of this estimate is

$$S_{\bar{y}.st} = \sqrt{\left(\frac{N_1}{N}\right)^2 (1 - f_1)\frac{S_1^2}{n_1} + \left(\frac{N_2}{N}\right)^2 (1 - f_2)\frac{S_2^2}{n_2}} \tag{16.3}$$

The derivation of this expression will be studied later. For now we complete the outline of the estimation procedure that would be used in practice. The theoretical standard error in Equation (16.3) could not be computed in practice because the stratum standard errors would not be known. As is usual in such cases, sample standard errors are substituted to produce an estimated standard error. This yields

$$s_{\bar{y}.st} = \sqrt{\left(\frac{N_1}{N}\right)^2 (1 - f_1)\frac{s_1^2}{n_1} + \left(\frac{N_2}{N}\right)^2 (1 - f_2)\frac{s_2^2}{n_2}} \tag{16.4}$$

An approximate 99.7% confidence interval for the population mean is then

$$\bar{y}_{st} \pm 3s_{\bar{y}.st} \tag{16.5}$$

provided n_1 and n_2 are large enough.

A NUMERICAL ILLUSTRATION

A frame consists of elements divided into two strata, stratum 1 having $N_1 = 700$ elements and stratum 2 having $N_2 = 2100$ elements. Simple random samples of size $n_1 = 42$ and $n_2 = 63$ are drawn from the two strata, yielding means and standard deviations $\bar{y}_1 = 117$, $s_1 = 9$, $\bar{y}_2 = 109$, and $s_2 = 10$. Construct 99.7% confidence intervals for the population mean and for the difference between the two strata means.

To construct the confidence interval for the population mean, the quantities in Equations (16.2) and (16.4) must be computed. Note that $f_1 = 42/700 = 0.06$, and $f_2 = 63/2100 = 0.03$. The mean estimate in Equation (16.2) is

$$\bar{y}_{st} = \left[\frac{700}{2800} \times 117\right] + \left[\frac{2100}{2800} \times 109\right] = (.25)(117) + (.75)(109) = 111$$

The standard error estimate in Equation (16.4) is

$$s_{\bar{y}.st} = \sqrt{\frac{(.25)^2(1-.06)(9)^2}{42} + \frac{(.75)^2(1-.03)(10)^2}{63}}$$

$$= \sqrt{0.11330 + 0.86607} = 0.99$$

approximately. These quantities are now substituted into Equation (16.5) to get

$$111 \pm 3(0.99) = 111 \pm 3.0 = [108, 114]$$

as the 99.7% confidence interval for the population mean.

To estimate the difference between the strata means, the theory learned in Chapter 15 is applied. The formula is

$$\bar{y}_1 - \bar{y}_2 \pm 3\sqrt{(1-f_1)\frac{s_1^2}{n_1} + (1-f_2)\frac{s_2^2}{n_2}}$$

Compute

$$117 - 109 \pm 3\sqrt{(.94)\frac{81}{42} + (.97)\frac{100}{63}} = 8 \pm 3\sqrt{1.81286 + 1.53968}$$

$$= 8 \pm 3(1.83) = 8 \pm 5.5 = [1.5, 13.5]$$

to get a 99.7% confidence interval for the difference between the strata means.

The first confidence interval tells us we may know the population mean to within about 3.0 units of measurement. The second interval tells us we may know the difference between the strata means to within about 5.5 units of measurement. This teaches the useful lesson that in a given probability sample not all parameters are estimated with the same level of precision. In the illustration, all the data are pooled to yield a relatively precise estimate of the population mean, but the samples from the two strata must be used separately, in a sense, to estimate the difference in the strata means. The estimated standard errors are essential to a proper interpretation of the survey data.

DERIVATION OF STANDARD ERROR OF THE MEAN ESTIMATE (OPTIONAL)

The estimate in Equation (16.2) may be written

$$\bar{y}_{st} = W_1\bar{y}_1 + W_2\bar{y}_2 \qquad \text{(16.6)}$$

where $W_i = N_i/N$, $i = 1, 2$, which is the sum of two random quantities. The Pythagorean formula for computing standard errors may be applied to this relationship because it has the form $E = E_1 + E_2$, where E is the stratified mean estimate, and E_1 and E_2 are the two quantities on the right-hand side of Equation (16.6). The Pythagorean formula in Chapter 15 yields

$$SE = \sqrt{SE_1^2 + SE_2^2} \qquad \text{(16.7)}$$

where SE_i denotes the standard error of E_i. Using these definitions, each E_i is a constant times a sample mean.

Statistical theory shows how to compute standard deviations of any quantity whose form is a constant multiplying a random quantity. To state this general result, we define a random quantity $U = cV$, where c denotes a constant and V denotes a random quantity. Then theory shows that the standard deviation of U is

$$SD(U) = |c|SD(V) \qquad \text{(16.8)}$$

where $|c|$ denotes the absolute value of c, and SD is the notation for standard deviation.

To apply Equation (16.8) to the specific problem, let $U = E_1$, let $c = W_1$, and let V denote the sample mean from stratum 1. The relationship $U = cV$ becomes $E_1 = W_1 \bar{y}_1$ and Equation (16.8) becomes

$$SD(E_1) = W_1 SD(\bar{y}_1) = W_1 \sqrt{(1 - f_1)\frac{s_1^2}{n_1}} \qquad \text{(16.9)}$$

because W_1 is positive and the standard deviation of a sample mean is its standard error. A completely analogous argument yields the standard error of E_2. Substituting these results into Equation (16.7) yields Equation (16.3).

FORMULAS FOR ANY NUMBER OF STRATA

Let I denote the number of strata, let $N_1, N_2, \ldots, N_I$ denote the number of elements in the strata, and let $n_1, n_2, \ldots, n_I$ denote the number of elements drawn into the samples from each stratum. Let $W_i = N_i/N$ and $f_i = n_i/N_i$, $i = 1, 2, \ldots, I$, denote the proportion of elements and the sampling fraction from stratum i. Let $\bar{y}_1, \bar{y}_2, \ldots, \bar{y}_I$ and $s_1, s_2, \ldots, s_I$ denote the sample means and standard deviations of the data from the various strata. Then the estimate of the population mean is

$$\bar{y}_{st} = W_1 \bar{y}_1 + W_2 \bar{y}_2 + \cdots + W_I \bar{y}_I \qquad \text{(16.10)}$$

and the estimated standard error of this mean is

$$s_{\bar{y}.st} = \sqrt{W_1^2(1 - f_1)\frac{s_1^2}{n_1} + W_2^2(1 - f_2)\frac{s_2^2}{n_2} + \cdots + W_I^2(1 - f_I)\frac{s_I^2}{n_I}} \qquad \text{(16.11)}$$

Equation (16.10) is a generalization of Equation (16.6), and Equation (16.11) is a generalization of Equation (16.4).

A 99.7% confidence interval for the population mean is

$$\bar{y}_{st} \pm 3s_{\bar{y}.st} \qquad \text{(16.12)}$$

SECTION 16.3

EXERCISES

16.3A Prove Equation (16.1). [*Hint:* The total y value in stratum i is $N_i \mu_i$, $i = 1, 2$, so the total y value in the population is $N_1 \mu_1 + N_2 \mu_2$. The population mean is the total y value in the population divided by the number of elements in the population, which is N. In other words, $\mu = (N_1 \mu_1 + N_2 \mu_2)/N$, from which Equation (16.1) follows immediately.]

16.3B You are given the following data concerning a stratified sampling problem with two strata.

Stratum (i)	1	2
N_i	2,000	3,000
n_i	50	50
$\bar{y}_i$	10,000	7,000
s_i	2,000	1,500

Construct a 99.7% confidence interval for the population mean μ. Construct a 99.7% confidence interval for the difference in the strata means. Which of the two confidence intervals is shorter? By how much?

16.3C Redo Exercise 16.2B with the following choices of n_1 and n_2, and with all other values the same.

Case	n_1	n_2
1	25	75
2	10	90
3	90	10
4	75	25
5	20	180
6	50	150
7	100	100
8	150	50
9	180	20

Comment on the effects of changing the allocation of sample sizes and on the effect of doubling the total sample size. Try to give intuitive explanations of these effects. (*Hint:* You will probably want to computerize your solution to this problem to avoid tedious calculations.)

16.3D Let V denote the time (in hours) it takes Cindy to commute to work. V is a random quantity with mean 1.1 hours and standard deviation 0.25 hour. If Cindy wished to convert her commuting times to minutes, she would have to make the transformation $U = 60V$. Compute the mean and standard deviation of U.

16.3E Let U and V denote random quantities related by the equation $U = b + V$, where b is a constant. Explain why the standard deviation of U must equal the standard deviation of V. (*Hint:* A simple numerical illustration will help. Suppose V may assume only one of the values 2, 8, or 12. Compute the mean and standard deviation of this set of three numbers. Add a constant to each of the resulting numbers, for example, 7. Compute the mean and standard deviation of this new set of numbers. Show that the standard deviation of the new set is equal to the standard deviation of the original set.)

16.3F Equation (16.8) can be generalized to take into account the addition of a constant in the transformation. Show that if $U = b + cV$, then $SD(U) = |c|SD(V)$.

16.3G Let V denote the number of items produced by a workstation in a day, and assume V is a random quantity with mean 50 and standard deviation 7. Suppose that fixed expense of production in a day is $500 and variable expense is $1.25 per item. Then total expense for a day's production of V items is $U = \$500 + \$1.25V$. Compute the mean and standard deviation of daily total expense.

16.3H (Continuation of Exercise 16.3G) A second workstation has a fixed expense of $300 and a variable expense of $2.50. Let X denote the daily output, and assume the mean and standard deviation of X are 80 and 10. Write an expression for the total expense associated with the output of the two workstations. Find the mean of the total expense. Compute the standard deviation of this total expense assuming the outputs from the workstations are independent of each other. (*Answer:* Total expense $= \$800 + \$1.25V + \$2.50X$, mean $= \$1062.50$, standard deviation $= \$26.49$)

16.3I You are given the following data for a stratified sampling problem involving three strata, that is, $I = 3$.

Stratum (i)	1	2	3
N_i	500	700	800
n_i	50	70	80
$\bar{y}_i$	89	50	43
s_i	200	210	180

Find a 99.7% confidence interval for the population mean. Use several difference choices of $n_1, n_2,$ and n_3, and comment on the effects of these choices.

CLUSTERING

WHAT IS CLUSTERING?

Clustering is a type of grouping that groups elements according to their "nearness to each other. In contrast to stratification, clustering tends to increase the variability of estimates based on probability samples. As compensation, clustering tends to reduce the costs of sampling because clusters of elements tend to be near one another.

▪ **E X A M P L E   16.4A:** You wish to give a test to children in a school. To minimize disruption, you agree to choose five classes of children and to give the test to every child in those five classes. The classes are clusters. The students in a class have much in common that may be quite different from the other students in the school—the teacher, for example. A stratified design could have been constructed using classes as strata. This would have required you to draw a sample of children from each class, which would have been too disruptive. ▪

▪ **E X A M P L E   16.4B:** If personal interviews are to be conducted in a large geographic region, a cluster design is often used to cut down on the travel time of the interviewers. The region is divided into small subregions, the clusters. A sample of clusters is selected and households from these subregions are selected for interview. The households are also clusters, so this example illustrates multistage clustering. Multistage clustering is very common in large-scale surveys. ▪

▪ **E X A M P L E   16.4C:** A fast food company sells franchises to local entrepreneurs. Part of the franchise agreement is that the parent company may inspect a local establishment without warning. The parent may choose local establishments at random for inspection. The establishments are clusters. ▪

■ **EXAMPLE 16.4D:** In random-digit dialing surveys, blocks of telephone numbers are chosen at random and all the numbers in a block are called. This is done because telephone companies typically issue numbers in blocks and will make the block information available to researchers. ■

Clustering may be combined with stratification.

■ **EXAMPLE 16.4E:** As a continuation of Example 16.4B, the clusters may be formed into strata and a sample of clusters taken from each stratum. This is typically done in large-scale surveys. ■

These examples show that **cluster sampling**, a design in which a random sample of clusters is selected, is quite different from simple random sampling of elements. Because the elements within a cluster have similar characteristics, they do not provide independent bits of information as do the elements in a simple random sample. Thus, an estimate based on a cluster sample is usually less precise than an estimate based on a simple random sample with the same number of elements. On the other hand, a simple random sample may be very expensive to obtain because of the costs of frame construction, travel time, or both. Thus for many surveys, clustering is the only affordable course of action. Sometimes, as in Example 16.4A, it can be the only course of action.

NOTATION FOR A SIMPLE CLUSTER SAMPLING DESIGN

The formulas for general cluster sampling are too complicated to present in this elementary introduction. A very simple case that has some practical applications is presented instead. Consult a book on sample surveys for a complete treatment of cluster sampling.[†]

Assume that the population elements have been arranged into N clusters of equal size; the clusters are assumed to have equal numbers of elements. A simple random sample of n clusters is selected, and all the elements in the selected clusters are measured. Let $\bar{y}_1, \bar{y}_2, \ldots, \bar{y}_n$ denote the means of the observations from the sampled clusters. The estimate of the population mean is the average of these sample means:

$$y_{cl} = (\bar{y}_1 + \bar{y}_2 + \cdots + \bar{y}_n)/n \tag{16.13}$$

which is just the mean of the cluster means.

The estimated standard error of the estimate is

$$s_{\bar{y}_{cl}} = \sqrt{\frac{(N - n) \sum_{i=1}^{n} (\bar{y}_i - \bar{y}_{cl})^2}{Nn(n - 1)}} \tag{16.14}$$

which is just the standard error of the sample mean displayed in Equation (16.13).

The results in Equations (16.13) and (16.14) are simple only because very restrictive assumptions were made. In practice the clusters are rarely of equal size, and the cluster sizes show up in the general formulas. The formulas above also assume every element in a cluster is measured, but in practice elements are often sampled from clusters, which greatly complicates the formulas. These important complications are not discussed in this text.

[†] W. G. Cochran, *Sampling Techniques*, 2nd ed. (New York: Wiley, 1953).

SECTION 16.5

SYSTEMATIC SAMPLING

Systematic sampling, a design in which elements are chosen systematically from the frame after a random start (or starts) has been chosen, often replaces simple random sampling in practice. It can be much easier to implement than simple random sampling, and it can produce more precise estimates under certain conditions. Systematic sampling is ideally suited to the sampling of lists.

WHAT IS SYSTEMATIC SAMPLING?

Suppose the frame consists of a list of items stored in a book, card file, or electronically stored file. Let M denote the number of items in the file, and suppose a 10% sample is desired, that is, $m = 0.1M$, where sample size is denoted by m. For simplicity assume m is an integer. A systematic sample is drawn using these steps:

(1) Select a starting digit between 1 and 10 at random.

(2) Choose the item in the file corresponding to the randomly chosen starting digit.

(3) Choose every tenth item thereafter in the file.

To illustrate, suppose the file has 3000 items, and a 10% sample, that is, a sample of size 300, is desired. Choose an integer between 1 and 10 at random; suppose it turns out to be 2. The sample would then consist of items $2, 12, 22, 32, \ldots, 2992$ from the file.

The systematic sample is easy to draw because it is a simple matter for a clerk or computer to step through the file and select the sample items.

More generally, let f denote a number between 0 and 1 such that $m = fM$ and $1/f$ are integers. Then a $100f\%$ systematic sample is drawn using these steps:

(1) Select a starting digit between 1 and $1/f$ at random.

(2) Choose the item in the file corresponding to the randomly chosen starting digit.

(3) Choose every $1/f$th item thereafter in the file.

CHARACTERISTICS OF A SYSTEMATIC SAMPLE

The systematic sampling design described above makes limited use of randomization. The design assigns equal probabilities of $f = m/M$ to each element in the frame because the number of possible samples is $1/f$, and each element appears in one and only one sample. In systematic sampling, most combinations of m elements cannot be drawn as samples, whereas with simple random sampling all possible combinations of m elements are possible. On the other hand, if the elements are placed in the frame in random order, systematic sampling is equivalent to simple random sampling. In the latter case, the estimation formulas of simple random sampling may be used for a systematic sample.

In general, though, the simple random sample formulas cannot be reliably used with a systematic sample. One way to see this is to note that the systematic sampling design is a form of cluster sampling in which only one cluster is drawn at random. Equations (16.13) and (16.14) apply to this case with $N = M/m$ and $n = 1$. Equation (16.14) for the estimated standard error is undefined for $n = 1$ because of the resulting division by zero.

Statistical theory shows that the theoretical standard error of the systematic sample mean is

$$SE(\bar{y}_{sys}) = \sqrt{\frac{S^2}{m}[1 + (m-1)\rho]} \qquad \textbf{(16.15)}$$

where ρ is the correlation coefficient between all possible pairs of elements from the frame. If the elements in the frame are randomly shuffled, then $\rho = 0$, and the standard formulas apply; otherwise we may have $\rho > 0$ or $\rho < 0$, depending on the arrangement of the elements in the frame. If the value of ρ is not known a priori, then the standard error in Equation (16.15) is difficult to estimate. Yates suggests the estimate

$$\sqrt{\frac{\sum_{i=1}^{m-1}(y_{i+1} - y_i)^2}{2m(m-1)}} \qquad \textbf{(16.16)}$$

which is a sensible practical approximation.[†]

SECTION 16.6

REPLICATED SYSTEMATIC SAMPLING

Systematic sampling is attractive because it is simple to implement, but it creates difficulties in the computation of standard errors unless the researcher has a rather detailed knowledge of the arrangement of elements in the frame. W. Edwards Deming advocates the use of replicated sampling designs in practical work and presents several examples of the use of replicated systematic sampling.[††] This design maintains the virtue of simplicity and does not suffer from the inability to compute estimated standard errors.

An elementary discussion of the replicated systematic sampling design is presented below. For a more detailed exposition of replicated designs in general, see Deming's book cited in the footnote. This book is strongly recommended.

In the discussion that follows assume that the frame is a list of sampling elements.

DESCRIPTION OF DESIGN WITH $n = 2$ REPLICATIONS

The simplest version of the design uses two replications. Let $2m$ denote the total sample size, and for simplicity suppose the frame consists of mN elements. If the number of elements in the frame is slightly less than mN, "blank" elements are added to bring the number up to mN. This simple device purchases a great deal of simplification at no cost.

Designate the first N elements in the frame as Zone 1. Designate the second N elements in the frame as Zone 2. Continue in this fashion until the frame has

---

[†] Frank Yates, *Sampling Methods for Censuses and Surveys*, 2nd ed. (New York: Hafner Publishing, 1953), 229–230.

[††] W. Edwards Deming, *Sample Design in Business Research* (New York: Wiley, 1960).

been divided into m zones, each consisting of N consecutive elements in the frame.

Now, using a table of random digits, select two digits at random from the digits $1, 2, \ldots, N$. These are the two random starts. For concreteness, suppose the random starts are 2 and 11. Then the first systematic sample consists of the 2nd element and every Nth element thereafter, and the second systematic sample consists of the 11th element and every Nth element thereafter. These two systematic samples of size m constitute the total sample of size $2m$. Notice that in drawing a systematic sample, one element is drawn from each zone. In general, the two random starts, whatever they may be, define two systematic samples having an element from each zone.

It now becomes obvious why the replication of the systematic samples improves on the simple systematic design described in Section 16.5. The design with two systematic samples is a cluster sampling design in which two clusters are selected at random, so that Equations (16.13) and (16.14) can be used because $n = 2$. The device of adding blanks to the frame serves to make all the clusters of equal size. When a blank element is drawn into one of the systematic samples, it is simply ignored in the computations. This introduces an approximation into the formulas, but the practical effect is slight in most cases.

DESCRIPTION OF DESIGN WITH $n = 10$ REPLICATIONS

The most common version of the design uses 10 replications. Let $10m$ denote the total sample size, and for simplicity suppose the frame consists of mN elements. If the number of elements in the frame is slightly less than mN, add blank elements to bring the number up to mN.

Designate the first N elements in the frame as Zone 1. Designate the second N elements in the frame as Zone 2. Continue in this fashion until the frame has been divided into m zones, each consisting of N consecutive elements in the frame.

Now, using a table of random digits, select 10 digits at random from the digits $1, 2, \ldots, N$. These are the 10 random starts. Draw 10 systematic samples, choosing each of the 10 random starts and every Nth element thereafter. These 10 systematic samples of size m constitute the total sample of size $10m$. Notice that in drawing the systematic samples, one element is drawn from each zone.

The design with 10 systematic samples is a cluster sampling design in which 10 clusters are selected at random, so that Equations (16.13) and (16.14) can be used because $n = 10$. The device of adding blanks to the frame serves to make all the clusters of equal size. When a blank element is drawn into one of the systematic samples, it is simply ignored in the computations.

COMPUTATION OF ESTIMATES

Now consider the case in which the estimate of the population mean is computed. Other estimates are computed in similar fashion. In the discussion that follows, wherever a cluster sample mean appears, another estimate, such as a total or proportion, could take its place and the formula would remain valid. This illustrates the generality of the replicated samples method.

Let $\bar{y}_1, \bar{y}_2, \ldots, \bar{y}_n$ denote the means of the n systematic samples. The estimate of the population mean and its standard error are given by Equations (16.13) and (16.14). A 99.7% confidence interval for the population mean is given by

$$\bar{y}_{cl} \pm 3s_{\bar{y}_{cl}} \qquad\qquad \textbf{(16.17)}$$

SECTION 16.7

SUPPLEMENTARY EXERCISES FOR CHAPTER 16

16A　Choose a building near you that experiences a lot of traffic. If you attend a college or university, the student union is a good choice. Design a sampling plan to estimate the number of occupants of the building at 10:00 A.M. on a specified day. (This exercise will help you appreciate the task of the Census Bureau, which must estimate the number of "occupants" of the United States on April 1 of a census year!)

16B　If you attend a college or university, design a stratified sampling scheme using faculty as one stratum and students as the other stratum. What will you use as a frame? Decide on a question of interest, for example, degree of satisfaction with computer facilities or athletic facilities. Carry out the sampling scheme. Compare faculty and student responses on the question. Estimate the average response of faculty and students combined.

16C　Select a replicated systematic sample of size $2m = 10$ with two replications from the list of cases in Exhibit 6.2A. Use the sample to estimate the average market value for the whole set of cases, using a 99.7% confidence interval. Does the confidence interval contain the average market value for all the cases?

16D　Refer to Exercise 16C. How many possible replicated systematic samples of size $2m = 10$ with two replications are there? Display each one and estimate average market value for each one, using 90% confidence intervals. How many of the intervals fail to contain the average market value of all the cases?

16E　Refer to Exhibit 6.2A. Let each successive group of five parcels displayed there be a cluster. Select two clusters at random and use the resulting sample to estimate the average market value of the whole set of cases with a 99.7% confidence interval. Does the interval contain the average market value of the whole set of cases?

16F　Refer to Exercise 16E. How many possible cluster samples of size 2 are there? Display each one and compute the 90% confidence interval for average market value for each one. How many of the intervals do not contain the actual average market value for all the cases?

SECTION 16.8

GLOSSARY FOR CHAPTER 16

Clustering	Grouping elements according to their "nearness" to each other.
Cluster sampling	A design in which a random sample of clusters is selected.
Stratification	Grouping elements in a frame according to some common characteristic or characteristics.
Stratified sampling	A design in which random samples are drawn from strata in the frame.
Systematic sampling	A design in which elements are chosen systematically from the frame after a random start (or starts) has been chosen.

## PART 4

Principles of Probabilistic Inference

## CHAPTER 17

Simulation[†]

SECTION 17.1

INTRODUCTION

Because statistical methods deal with variation, they are always applied in an environment of uncertainty.[††] Rude surprises can stymie the cleverest attempts to overcome the undesirable effects of uncertainty because the degree of reliability or the relevance of the data can never be completely known. One way to prepare for some of these surprises is to study statistical calculations in environments where uncertainty is deliberately and artificially introduced. This is done by generating **randomness**, a property of uncertain outcomes that can be modelled using the mathematics of probability. In such experiments the researcher has more knowledge and control of the process creating the uncertainty than in practice. Thus the consequences of randomness can be isolated and the insights gained can be applied to the analysis of data from real processes. Models for randomness are discussed in Section 17.2.

Whether we are balancing our checkbooks or managing company accounts, computing our total points in a course or computing monthly sales for offices

---

[†] This is an optional chapter.
[††] This chapter gives technical background on simulation techniques that is not needed to understand the simulation applications presented elsewhere in the text.

around the world, our livelihoods depend critically on the arithmetic we perform. Many numbers are not completely accurate because of uncertainties in the data-collection process, rounding off, or inherent limitations of computing machinery. In Section 17.4 the effects of doing arithmetic on uncertain quantities are studied so you will be better able to draw prudent conclusions from "fuzzy numbers."

Section 17.6 introduces the random-walk model. A number of practical processes resemble random walks or generalizations of random walks. Here are just four examples:

- Daily stock prices
- Daily or annual sales
- Annual total claims on policies held by an insurance company
- Many accounting figures such as expenses, income, and so on

The theoretical study of random walks has yielded valuable insights into such practical processes. Some properties of random walks are illustrated with simulations.

SECTION 17.2

RANDOMNESS

In Chapter 1 the notion of randomization was introduced. The distinction between surveys and experiments that employed randomization and those that did not was emphasized. In Chapters 8 and 10 two important models for random variation were presented: normal distributions and binomial distributions. Chapters 12–16 showed how to make probabilistic inferences from data collected with the aid of randomization. All these instances illustrate the practical utility of the concept of random variation. In this chapter further examples of models that use randomness are given to help you gain insight into the variations encountered in practical data analysis.

The theory and practical implementation of randomness in this text are based on the random drawing of numbers from the unit interval [0, 1), the set of real numbers between 0 and 1, 0 included, 1 excluded. A physical model for such drawings is the "spinner" pictured in Exhibit 17.2A. Ideally, imagine that all the numbers between 0 and 1 are represented on the circle. When the circle is spun, it finally comes to rest

EXHIBIT 17.2A

An Ideal Spinner That Chooses Numbers at Random from [0, 1)

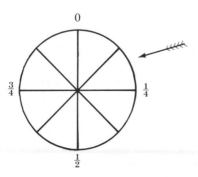

and the pointer points at a number that can be read off the circle. This is an idealization because in reality there is no infinitely thin pointer, and an infinitely fine scale cannot be read off the circle.

Theorists have developed computer algorithms that approximate the implementation of the ideal spinner to sufficient accuracy for practical use. Some algorithms programmed in statistical software are used here to illustrate important practical facts about randomness.

Exhibit 17.2B shows a frequency histogram of 500 drawings generated by an algorithm designed to produce random drawings from the numbers in the interval $[0, 1)$.[†] The histogram groups the 500 numbers into 10 subintervals of length 0.1. Intuition about randomness suggests that each of the subintervals should contain about $\frac{1}{10}$, or 50, of the numbers drawn. The frequencies of the subintervals are close to 50, though only two subintervals contain exactly 50 numbers. The deviations of the frequencies from the expected, or "ideal," number of 50 are one of the effects of randomness.

EXHIBIT 17.2B

Histogram of 500
Random Drawings from
$[0, 1)$ Performed by
Minitab and Histogram
of the Ideal Uniform
Distribution

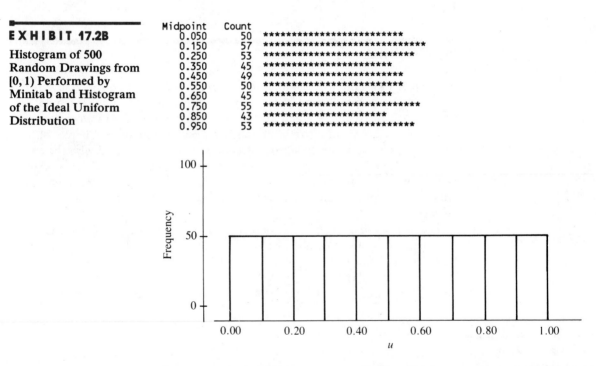

```
Midpoint   Count
  0.050       50    **************************
  0.150       57    ******************************
  0.250       53    ***************************
  0.350       45    ***********************
  0.450       49    *************************
  0.550       50    **************************
  0.650       45    ***********************
  0.750       55    *****************************
  0.850       43    **********************
  0.950       53    ***************************
```

[†] The illustrations in this chapter were done using Minitab. The output in Exhibit 17.2B comes from the commands

```
RANDOM 500 C1;
  UNIFORM 0 1.
HISTOGRAM C1;
  START 0.05;
  INCREMENT 0.1.
```

The UNIFORM 0 1 subcommand implements 500 spins of the ideal spinner and places the 500 outcomes in column C1 of the Minitab worksheet.

The ideal distribution of the random drawings from [0, 1) is called the **uniform distribution**. Exhibit 17.2B also shows this distribution.

Although the frequencies based on a set of random drawings are expected to deviate from the ideal frequencies, not all deviations would conform to our intuition about randomness. For example, if the frequencies in the 10 subintervals were 90, 80, 70, 60, 50, 50, 30, 30, 20, 20, we would conclude the drawings were not made randomly because there would be a clear bias in favor of the first four subintervals and against the last four.

Not all deviations from randomness are this blatant. Statistical tools are needed to help evaluate the hypothesis of randomness in less clear-cut practical cases.

Exhibit 17.2B shows a cross-sectional analysis of the 500 random drawings. But randomness also has longitudinal impact. Think of the *sequence* of drawings: the first, followed by the second, followed by the third, and so on. Intuition suggests that at a given stage in the sequence, knowledge of the outcomes of the drawings up to that stage should provide no help in predicting the outcome of the next drawing. This intuitive hypothesis may be tested by looking at the scatterplot of the adjacent values in the sequence and by computing the first lag autocorrelation coefficient of the sequence, as discussed in Section 6.8. Exhibit 17.2C displays these items. There is essentially no first lag autocorrelation in the sequence, a finding consistent with the hypothesis of randomness. Further analysis of the sequence not presented here shows there is no autocorrelation at any lag.

EXHIBIT 17.2C

First Lag
Autocorrelation
Analysis of Sequence of
500 Random Drawings
from [0, 1) Made by
Minitab

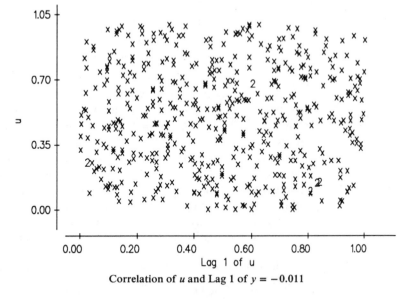

Correlation of u and Lag 1 of $y = -0.011$

For practical purposes the Minitab software, like many other software packages, produces an adequate approximation to random drawings from [0, 1). From such a set of drawings, random drawings may be constructed from virtually any other distribution.

▪**EXAMPLE 17.2A:** The following transformation was applied to each of the 500 random drawings reported in Exhibit 17.2B: $v = 2u - 1$, where u stands for one of the outcomes from $[0, 1)$. This results in a new set of 500 numbers (the v's) that range from -1 to 1 because the u's range from 0 to 1. Exhibit 17.2D shows a histogram of the 500 new numbers. Notice that the new numbers behave randomly. All the transformation did was to change the range of the numbers from $[0, 1)$ to $[-1, 1)$.

The transformation has an effect on the descriptive statistics of the numbers. Exhibit 17.2D shows the means and standard deviations for the two sets of numbers. The mean of the original set of numbers is 0.494, while the mean of the transformed set is -0.012. The standard deviation of the original set is 0.29, while the standard deviation of the transformed set is 0.58.[†]

EXHIBIT 17.2D

Histogram and Descriptive Statistics of 500 Numbers Created by the Transformation $v = 2u - 1$, where u is Randomly Drawn from $[0, 1)$

```
Midpoint   Count
 -0.900      50   **************************
 -0.700      57   *****************************
 -0.500      53   ***************************
 -0.300      45   ***********************
 -0.100      49   *************************
  0.100      50   **************************
  0.300      45   ***********************
  0.500      55   ****************************
  0.700      43   **********************
  0.900      53   ***************************
```

	n	Mean	Standard Deviation
u	500	0.4939	0.2903
$v = 2u - 1$	500	-0.0121	0.5807

If the ideal uniform distribution with 50 observations in each of the 10 classes had been used, the original set of numbers would have had a mean of 0.5 and a standard deviation of $\sqrt{1/12} = 0.29$. The mean and standard deviation of the new set of numbers formed by the transformation $v = 2u - 1$ would then be 0 and $2\sqrt{1/12} = 0.58$, using the rule in the footnote at the bottom of the page. You see that these "ideal" results are close to those obtained with the 500 numbers randomly drawn from $[0, 1)$. This is another indication that the random number algorithm in the software produces plausible results.

Theory justifies treating the new set of numbers as random drawings from the interval $[-1.0, 1.0)$.[††] If such a set of drawings is needed for problem solving, a set of

---

[†] The standard deviation of the new set is twice the standard deviation of the original set of numbers. This conforms to a mathematical property of linear transformations of random quantities. If a set of numbers, denoted by u, has standard deviation denoted by σ, then the set of numbers denoted by $v = a + bu$ has standard deviation $|b|\sigma$, where $|b|$ denotes the absolute value of b. Also, if the mean of the original set of numbers is denoted by μ, then the mean of the transformed set is $a + b\mu$. In this illustration, $\mu = 0.494$, $\sigma = 0.29$, $a = -1$, and $b = 2$. See Section 18.8 for a more complete discussion.

[††] Minitab will produce such a set of numbers directly with the command

RANDOM 500 C1;
UNIFORM -1.0 1.0.

random drawings from $[0, 1)$ may be chosen and transformed. In Section 17.4 such a set of numbers is used to study the effects of randomness on arithmetic operations.

■

■ **EXAMPLE 17.2B:** In Example 17.2A the effects of a linear transformation on numbers drawn at random from $[0, 1)$ were illustrated. This example shows the effects of a nonlinear transformation, the natural logarithm, which is denoted by log. Because all the values of u are fractions, their natural logarithms are negative. To make the new numbers positive, they are defined by the transformation $w = -\log(u)$, where u stands for one of the numbers drawn at random from $[0, 1)$. The histogram of the new set of numbers in Exhibit 17.2E shows that their distribution is not uniform. The nonlinear logarithmic transformation has changed uniformly distributed numbers into numbers that have an **exponential distribution**, a probability distribution on $[0, \infty)$ such that the probability assigned to the intervals of the form $[0, w)$ is $1 - e^{-w}$. Exhibit 17.2E also shows a plot of the function $g(w) = e^{-w}$ for positive values of w. Notice the resemblance of this curve to the shape of the histogram.

EXHIBIT 17.2E

Histogram of 500 Random Drawings from an Exponential Distribution and a Graph of the Exponential Curve

```
Midpoint   Count
  0.250      193   *****************************************
  0.750      116   ************************
  1.250       70   **************
  1.750       59   ************
  2.250       21   *****
  2.750       15   ***
  3.250       11   ***
  3.750        5   *
  4.250        2   *
  4.750        4   *
  5.250        3.  *
  5.750        1   *
```

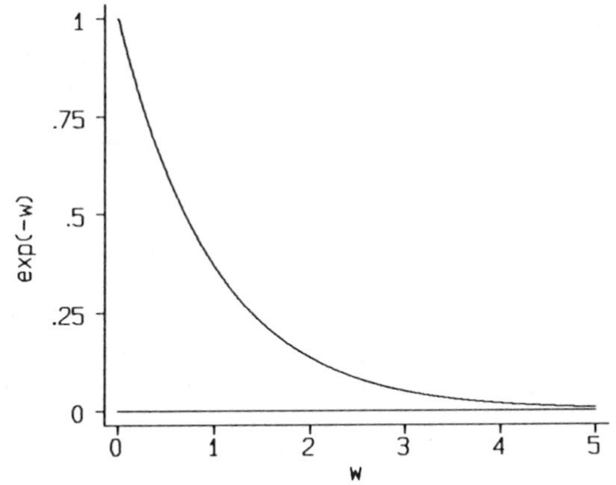

Theory justifies treating the new numbers, denoted by w's, as random drawings from a population of numbers with the exponential distribution pictured in Exhibit 17.2E. Generally speaking, numbers drawn randomly from $[0, 1)$, that is, numbers with a uniform distribution, can be transformed into numbers with other distributions by making suitable transformations of them.

■

In practice transformations of numerical data that are subject to variation are constantly performed. The theory presented in this chapter provides insight into the consequences of these transformations and therefore helps us draw prudent conclusions from the data. A concrete illustration is presented in Section 17.4.

SECTION 17.3

EXERCISES

17.3A You are given three nonnegative fractions, $u_1 = 0.582$, $u_2 = 0.220$, and $u_3 = 0.396$.
(a) Apply the transformation $v = 2u - 1$ to each fraction, obtaining values v_1, v_2, and v_3.
(b) Apply the transformation $w = -\log(u)$ to each fraction, obtaining values w_1, w_2, and w_3.

17.3B Using computer software, generate 200 random drawings from $[0, 1)$. Denote the numbers by $u_1, u_2, \ldots, u_{200}$.
(a) Make a frequency histogram of the 200 numbers. Compare and contrast your histogram with the one in Exhibit 17.2B. Roughly how many observations do you expect in each class of your histogram? Why?
(b) Compute the mean and standard deviation of your 200 numbers. What theoretical values should they be close to? Why?
(c) Do an autocorrelation analysis of your numbers. Is their behavior consistent with the hypothesis of randomness?
(This exercise is continued in Exercises 17.3C, 17.3D, and 17.3E.)

17.3C Apply the transformation $v = 2u - 1$ to the 200 numbers generated in Exercise 17.3B.
(a) Make a frequency histogram of the v's. Compare it to the histogram of the u's.
(b) Compute the mean and standard deviation of the v's. How are they related to the mean and standard deviation of the u's? Verify these relationships numerically.
(c) Compare and contrast your findings in this exercise with those reported in Exhibit 17.2D.

17.3D Apply the transformation $x = u^2$ to each number in Exercise 17.3B.
(a) Make a frequency histogram and describe its shape.
(b) Compute the mean and standard deviation of the x's. Verify that $\bar{x} \neq (\bar{u})^2$. There is no simple relationship between $\bar{x}$ and $\bar{u}$ as there is for linear functions of the u's.

17.3E Apply the transformation $y = -2\log(u)$ to the numbers in Exercise 17.3B.
(a) Make a frequency histogram of the y's and describe its shape.
(b) Compare the shape of the histogram with the one in Exhibit 17.2E.

17.3F Apply the transformation $x = v^2$ to the numbers obtained in Exercise 17.3C. Make a histogram of the x's and compare it to the one you made in Exercise 17.3D. Why are they different? Now apply the transformation $y = -\log(x)$ to the x's. Make a histogram and describe its shape.

17.3G Write a two-to-three-page essay on transforming random data. Why are transformations important? Compare and contrast linear and nonlinear transformations.

SECTION 17.4

RANDOM ARITHMETIC (OPTIONAL)

In this section the effects of randomness on the arithmetic operations of addition and multiplication are discussed. Arithmetic is usually thought of as a deterministic process that leads to a right answer if carried out correctly. In an environment of uncertainty, however, even arithmetic can yield answers far from the truth.

ANALYSIS OF TOTALS: ADDING TWO RANDOM QUANTITIES

Suppose you add two figures that are accurate only to the nearest dollar. If a $100 figure is recorded, its actual value may be any figure between, say, $99.50 and $100.49. Thus the difference between the actual figure and the recorded one could be any of the 100 numbers $-\$0.50$, $-\$0.49, \ldots, \$0.49$. For purposes of discussion, now assume that each of these numbers has an equal chance, namely, $1/100$, of being the difference.

With little loss of realism and a good deal of practical simplification, the cents can be treated as *random drawings* from the interval $[-0.5, 0.5]$. This is the model for the uncertainty in the figures. The $100 figure will be written as $y = 100 + v$, where v is randomly drawn from $[-0.5, 0.5)$.[†] In the model equation, the $ symbol is understood, not written explicitly. The symbol y stands for the recorded figure.

To implement the idea of adding two uncertain quantities, let y denote the first quantity and write, in general, $y = \mu_1 + v$, where μ_1 denotes the actual value of the figure. In the preceding paragraph, $\mu_1 = 100$, meaning $100. This general notation allows the actual value to be any amount that might come up in practice.

The notation for the second quantity to be added is $z = \mu_2 + w$, where μ_2 denotes the actual value, w denotes the difference between the recorded and actual values, and z denotes the recorded value. We assume that w is drawn randomly from $[-0.5, 0.5)$, completely independently of v. We refer to v and w as *random errors*. They could be interpreted as round-off errors or as errors that occur because the recorded numbers are determined with uncertainty.

Now consider the consequences of adding two recorded numbers y and z that are actual numbers plus the random errors described above. To be concrete, assume both μ_1 and μ_2 are equal to 100. An appropriate computer algorithm allows two numbers, one the value of v, the other the value of w, to be drawn. Such an algorithm was used to draw the two numbers $v = -0.455$ and $w = -0.395$. Thus the values of y and z are

$$y = 100 + (-0.455) = 99.545$$

representing about $99.54, and

$$z = 100 + (-0.395) = 99.605$$

representing about $99.60.

Now when y and z are added, the result is $y + z = 99.545 + 99.605 = 199.15$, which differs from the actual total of 200 by the amount 0.85. In this particular realization of the process, the random errors result in a reported total that is $0.85 less than the actual sum of $200. The process described is a *simulation* of the actual process of adding two uncertain quantities. The model for the random errors is called the *simulation model*.

In general, if $y = \mu_1 + v$ and $z = \mu_2 + w$, then

$$y + z = (\mu_1 + \mu_2) + (v + w) \tag{17.1}$$

[†] We may construct v from a random drawing u from $[0, 1)$ by the transformation $v = u - 0.5$. A Minitab command to generate 1000 v's is

RANDOM 1000 C1;
UNIFORM -0.5 0.5.

which is equal to the actual total plus the total of the random errors. Thus to study the effect of the random errors on the total of two numbers, we need only to look at the total of the random errors. The distribution of the total of the errors is superimposed on the actual total.

The process might have yielded a recorded total as much as \$1 less than the actual total of \$200. This would have happened if both the random errors had been -0.50. How likely is this, given the assumptions made so far about the random errors? How likely is it that the random errors cancel each other out, that is, that $v = -w$? Although answers to these questions could be developed mathematically, the behavior of the process can be demonstrated more easily by summarizing many simulations of the process. To get 1000 simulations, the computer software is asked to draw 1000 v's and 1000 w's from $[-0.5, 0.5)$ and add the resulting pairs of v's and w's. A histogram and descriptive statistics of the 1000 resulting totals are then prepared. These items are estimates of the theoretical items that could be derived mathematically. The larger the number of simulations summarized, the closer the empirical items are to the theoretical ones. And, in principle, any desired degree of accuracy can be achieved by doing enough simulations.

This is the basic idea behind most simulation studies: summarizing a large number of realizations from a model of a process to gain insights into the implications of the model. Mathematical analysis of the model may yield the same insights if the researcher is sophisticated enough to derive them, but simulations typically make fewer demands on mathematical sophistication. Recent research has revealed that simulations yield insights into processes that are so complex that their mathematical analysis defies even the efforts of well-trained mathematicians. Thus simulation methods have become part of the advanced analysis of such processes.

Exhibit 17.4A shows histograms, means, and standard deviations of the set of 1000 v's, the set of 1000 w's, and the set of 1000 totals $v + w$ derived from the simulations of our simple model. The means of the three distributions are all close to 0, which agrees with intuition and is predicted by theory. The standard deviations of the v's and the w's are both close to $\sqrt{1/12} \simeq 0.289$, as predicted by theory.

Intuition may also suggest that the standard deviation of the totals should be close to the total of the standard deviations of the v's and the w's, but this is not correct. In theory, the standard deviation of the total is equal to the square root of the total of the squares of the standard deviations of the u's and the v's. This Pythagorean rule is the same one used in Chapter 15 to compute standard errors of totals and differences of estimates from probability survey data.

For the data reported in Exhibit 17.4A, the standard deviation of the total is $0.41 = \sqrt{(0.29)^2 + (0.29)^2}$, which is close to the value

$$0.408 \simeq \sqrt{(1/\sqrt{12})^2 + (1/\sqrt{12})^2} = \sqrt{1/6}$$

predicted by theory.

The standard deviation of the total $v + \omega$ is greater than the standard deviation of either of the components v and w. Adding two numbers subject to uncertainty means greater uncertainty in the result, as measured by the standard deviation. This

EXHIBIT 17.4A   Histogram and Descriptive Statistics for the Totals of 1000 Pairs of Numbers Randomly Drawn from $[-0.5, 0.5)$ and the Components of the Totals

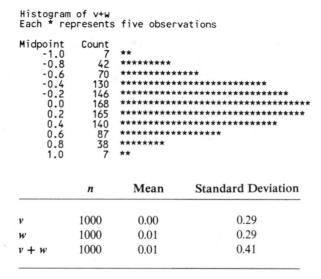

```
Histogram of v in [-0.5, 0.5)
Each * represents five observations

Midpoint   Count
  -0.450      96   ********************
  -0.350     100   *******************
  -0.250      99   ********************
  -0.150     105   *********************
  -0.050     111   ***********************
   0.050      88   *****************
   0.150      99   ********************
   0.250     105   *********************
   0.350     100   *******************
   0.450      97   *******************
```

```
Histogram of w in [-0.5, 0.5)
Each * represents five observations

Midpoint   Count
  -0.450      97   ********************
  -0.350      97   ********************
  -0.250      79   ***************
  -0.150     105   *********************
  -0.050     106   **********************
   0.050     108   ********************
   0.150      82   ****************
   0.250     107   **********************
   0.350     116   ************************
   0.450     103   *********************
```

```
Histogram of v+w
Each * represents five observations

Midpoint   Count
   -1.0       7   **
   -0.8      42   *********
   -0.6      70   **************
   -0.4     130   **************************
   -0.2     146   *****************************
    0.0     168   **********************************
    0.2     165   *********************************
    0.4     140   ****************************
    0.6      87   ******************
    0.8      38   ********
    1.0       7   **
```

	n	Mean	Standard Deviation
v	1000	0.00	0.29
w	1000	0.01	0.29
$v + w$	1000	0.01	0.41

corresponds to intuition because the reported total can differ from the actual total by as much as \$1, whereas the reported components can differ from the actual components by no more than \$0.50. The triangularly shaped histogram of the totals in Exhibit 17.4A suggests that smaller errors are more likely than large errors.

Using mathematical theory, the fact that the theoretical distribution of the total of two uniformly distributed errors is *triangular* can be derived. Exhibit 17.4B shows the theoretical triangular distribution. Mathematical analysis of the theoretical distributions involved in this illustration reveals the following results. For a uniform distribution on $[-0.5, 0.5)$, 50% of the values are in the interval $[-0.25, 0.25)$. For the triangular distribution of the total of the random errors, 75% of the values are in the interval $[-0.25, 0.25)$. Thus the likelihood of an error less than \$0.25 is actually *greater* in the reported total than it is in either of the reported components! To state it another way, an error greater than \$0.25 in one of the reported components is more likely than in the reported total.

EXHIBIT 17.4B

Graph of Triangular
Distribution

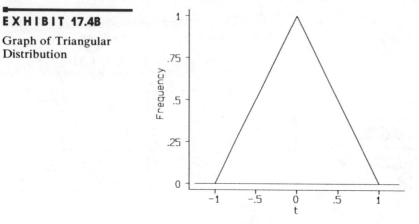

ANALYSIS OF TOTALS: ADDING MORE THAN TWO RANDOM QUANTITIES

Suppose five numbers whose cents are determined by independent random
drawings from $[-0.5, 0.5)$ are added. The resulting total is the actual value plus
the total of the random error. Exhibit 17.4C displays the first five in a series of
1000 simulations of the five random errors along with the total of the errors.

EXHIBIT 17.4C

Five Simulations of
Totals of Five Random
Errors and a Histogram
and Descriptive
Statistics for 1000
Simulations

Case	v_1	v_2	v_3	v_4	v_5	$\sum_{i=1}^{5} v_i$
1	0.127413	0.058220	−0.134160	−0.166290	−0.238235	−0.35305
2	−0.073335	0.277525	0.230049	0.213799	0.220666	0.86870
3	−0.166918	−0.309363	−0.243884	−0.275121	−0.416725	−1.41201
4	0.135300	0.329591	−0.485515	−0.390095	−0.090572	−0.50129
5	−0.087534	0.198927	0.310670	0.238094	−0.321446	0.33871

```
Histogram of 1000 sums of five components
Each * represents five observations

Midpoint   Count
   -2.0        1   *
   -1.6       15   ***
   -1.2       55   ***********
   -0.8      123   *************************
   -0.4      201   *****************************************
    0.0      236   ************************************************
    0.4      190   **************************************
    0.8      114   ***********************
    1.2       42   *********
    1.6       19   ****
    2.0        4   *
```

	Number	Mean	Standard Deviation	Minimum	Maximum
$\sum_{i=1}^{5} v_i$	1000	−0.0136	0.6709	−2.1960	2.0047

The exhibit also shows a histogram of all 1000 totals, along with some descriptive statistics.

Such a simulation is familiar: it is like the one used to illustrate the central limit effect in Chapter 8. It is not surprising that the histogram in Exhibit 17.4C resembles a normal curve, because the central limit effect for totals says it must. Moreover, the mean and standard deviation are expected to be close to the theoretical values of $\mu = 0$ and $\sqrt{n}\sigma = \sqrt{5} \times \sqrt{1/12} \simeq 0.6455$.

Errors in individual totals cannot be predicted, but because the errors follow, to a good approximation, a normal curve with mean 0 and standard deviation 0.6455, it can be predicted that about 68% of the errors in all such totals are in $(0 - 0.6455, 0 + 0.6455) \simeq (-0.65, 0.65)$, about 95% of the errors are in $(0 - 2 \times 0.6455, 0 + 2 \times 0.6455) \simeq (-1.29, 1.29)$, and about 99.7% of the errors are in $(0 - 3 \times 0.6455, 0 + 3 \times 0.6455) \simeq (-1.94, 1.94)$. On average, the errors in totals of five numbers subject to the assumptions of the model are zero, but it would not be surprising to find occasional errors as large as $-\$1.94$ or $\$1.94$. There is better than a 50% chance that the errors are between $-\$0.65$ and $\$0.65$.

Because of the central limit effect, the following general statement can be made: If $y_i = \mu_i + v_i$, $i = 1, 2, \ldots, n$, is a set of recorded values of sums of actual values, denoted by μ's, and random errors, denoted by v's, and if the random errors are independently drawn from a distribution with mean 0 and standard deviation σ, then the distribution of totals of the form $\sum_{i=1}^{n} y_i$ is approximately normal with mean $\sum_{i=1}^{n} \mu_i$ and standard deviation $\sqrt{n}\sigma$. Because the total of the errors has mean 0, the mean of the total of the recorded values is just the total of the actual values. The random variation comes from the random errors, which have an approximate normal distribution with standard deviation $\sqrt{n}\sigma$.

In the statement above, a distribution for the random errors does not have to be specified. The central limit effect says that totalling overwhelms the impact of the individual error distributions and yields the normal approximation for the total. In this case, then, regardless of the distribution the random errors are simulated from, an approximately normal total is expected. There is one proviso: The normal approximation appears when n is chosen sufficiently large. When a uniform distribution for the random errors is used, $n = 5$ is sufficiently large. If drawing from a very skewed distribution, an n larger than 5 might have to be picked to get a satisfactory normal approximation. Practically speaking, however, simulations do not need to be done to understand distributions of totals. The main facts about them are known through the central limit effect.

ANALYSIS OF PRODUCTS: MULTIPLYING TWO RANDOM QUANTITIES

The effects of randomness on the process of multiplication are not so well understood as they are on addition. Rather than quote theory, simulations will be used to explore the behavior of products of random quantities.

If $y_1 = \mu_1 + v_1$ and $y_2 = \mu_2 + v_2$, then the product of the recorded values is

$$y_1 y_2 = (\mu_1 + v_1)(\mu_2 + v_2) = \mu_1\mu_2 + \mu_1 v_2 + v_1 \mu_2 + v_1 v_2 \qquad \textbf{(17.2)}$$

which is the product of the actual values plus the product of the random errors *plus* two additional products involving the actual values and the random errors. This means that the characteristics of the product $y_1 y_2$ depend on the interaction between the actual values and the random errors. Contrast this with totals, in which the actual values and the random errors entered additively. [See Equation (17.1).] The behavior of products is inherently more complicated than the behavior of totals.

Four cases, as outlined in the following table, are studied.

		Error Distributions	
		Uniform on $[-0.5, 0.5)$	Normal, Mean 0 $\sigma = \sqrt{1/12}$
Means	$\mu_1 = \mu_2 = 0$	Example 17.4A	Example 17.4C
	$\mu_1 = \mu_2 = 100$	Example 17.4B	Example 17.4D

▪ **EXAMPLE 17.4A:** In this example, $y_1 = v_1$ and $y_2 = v_2$, and the v's are drawn randomly from $[-0.5, 0.5)$. Exhibit 17.4D shows a histogram and descriptive statistics for 1000 simulated outcomes $v_1 v_2$. The distribution ranges from -0.25 to 0.25 and is symmetric about 0. Notice that 353, or 35.3%, of the observations are in the interval $(-0.025, 0.025)$. Also notice that 699, or 69.9%, of the observations are in the interval $(-0.075, 0.075)$. The middle 50% of the distribution lies in the interval $(Q_1, Q_3) = (-0.041, 0.047)$. The distribution is highly concentrated about 0. ▪

EXHIBIT 17.4D

Histogram and Descriptive Statistics for 1000 Simulations of the Product of Two Numbers Drawn Randomly from $[-0.5, 0.5)$

	Number	Mean	Standard Deviation
v_1	1000	-0.01092	0.28101
v_2	1000	0.01131	0.28556
$v_1 v_2$	1000	0.00339	0.07909

```
Histogram of v1*v2
Each * represents 10 observations

Midpoint    Count
  -0.25        1   *
  -0.20       14   **
  -0.15       42   *****
  -0.10       81   *********
  -0.05      174   ******************
   0.00      353   ************************************
   0.05      172   ******************
   0.10       88   *********
   0.15       48   *****
   0.20       25   ***
   0.25        2   *
```

▪ **EXAMPLE 17.4B:** In this example, $y_1 = 100 + v_1$ and $y_2 = 100 + v_2$. The effects of multiplying two numbers whose actual values are $100.00 but whose cents are randomly determined are studied. Exhibit 17.4E shows histograms of $y_1 y_2$ and

$y_1 y_2 - 10,000$ and associated descriptive statistics. The quantity $y_1 y_2 - 10,000$ is the set of reported products minus the theoretical product $10,000 = 100 \times 100$. The histogram of this quantity shows the distribution of errors in the reported products and helps illustrate the effects of the random errors on multiplication. The errors range from about -100 to 100. This means that the product could be in error by almost \$100 even though y_1 and y_2 are in error by no more than \$0.50! The interaction between the random errors and the actual values makes possible large errors in the products.

EXHIBIT 17.4E

Histograms of 1000 Simulations of $y_1 y_2$ and $y_1 y_2 - 10,000$, Where $y_i = 100 + v_i$, $i = 1, 2$, and v_i is Randomly Drawn from $[-0.5, 0.5)$

```
Histogram of y1*y2
Each * represents five observations

Midpoint   Count
   9900        3   *
   9920       39   ********
   9940       90   ******************
   9960      119   ************************
   9980      161   *********************************
  10000      180   ************************************
  10020      154   *******************************
  10040      135   ***************************
  10060       77   ****************
  10080       32   *******
  10100       10   **
```

```
Histogram of y1*y2-10,000
Each * represents five observations

Midpoint   Count
   -100        3   *
    -80       39   ********
    -60       90   ******************
    -40      119   ************************
    -20      161   *********************************
      0      180   *********************************************
     20      154   *******************************
     40      135   ***************************
     60       77   ****************
     80       32   *******
    100       10   **
```

	n	Mean	Standard Deviation
y_1	1000	99.89	0.281
y_2	1000	100.01	0.29
$y_1 y_2$	1000	10000.0	40.9
$y_1 y_2 - 10,000$	1000	0.04	40.93

The middle 50% of the products lies in $(Q_1, Q_3) = (-30.28, 30.67)$. Because of this the errors in the products will be less than about \$30.50, in absolute value, about half the time.

Notice also that the shape of the distribution in Exhibit 17.4E is quite different from the shape of the distribution in Exhibit 17.4D. The subtlety of the effects of randomness on multiplication begin to become apparent. ■

■**EXAMPLE 17.4C:** This example repeats Example 17.4A except that the random errors are drawn from a normal distribution with mean 0 and standard deviation $\sigma = \sqrt{1/12} \simeq 0.29$, which is the standard deviation of the uniform distribution on $[-0.5, 0.5)$.[†] The observations from the normal distribution are not

---

EXHIBIT 17.4F

Histograms and Descriptive Statistics of Products of 1000 Pairs of Numbers Drawn at Random from a Normal Distribution wth Mean 0 and Standard Deviation $\sqrt{1/12}$ and the Components

```
Histogram of v1                              Histogram of v2
Each * represents 10 observations            Each * represents 10 observations

Midpoint   Count                             Midpoint   Count
   -1.0       1  *                              -1.0       1  *
   -0.8       6  *                              -0.8       5  *
   -0.6      30  ***                            -0.6      37  ****
   -0.4     107  ***********                    -0.4     103  **********
   -0.2     218  **********************         -0.2     194  *******************
    0.0     300  ******************************  0.0     277  ****************************
    0.2     183  ******************              0.2     224  **********************
    0.4     113  ************                    0.4     122  *************
    0.6      35  ****                            0.6      25  ***
    0.8       6  *                               0.8      11  **
    1.0       1  *                               1.0       1  *
```

```
                    Histogram of v1*v2
                    Each * represents 10 observations

                    Midpoint    Count
                     -0.4500        1  *
                     -0.4000        0
                     -0.3500        2  *
                     -0.3000        3  *
                     -0.2500       10  *
                     -0.2000       14  **
                     -0.1500       24  ***
                     -0.1000       64  *******
                     -0.0500      162  *****************
                     -0.0000      462  ****************************************************
                      0.0500      141  ***************
                      0.1000       56  ******
                      0.1500       29  ***
                      0.2000       16  **
                      0.2500        8  *
                      0.3000        1  *
                      0.3500        3  *
                      0.4000        1  *
                      0.4500        2  *
                      0.5000        1  *
```

	n	Mean	Standard Deviation
v_1	1000	0.00214	0.28554
v_2	1000	0.01012	0.29143
$v_1 v_2$	1000	0.00017	0.08521

[†] Minitab commands that accomplish the simulation are

```
LET K1 = SQRT(1/12)
RANDOM 1000 C1 C2;
   NORMAL MEAN = 0 AND STD DEV = K1.
LET C3 = C1*C2
```

limited to the interval $[-0.5, 0.5)$, so more variation in the product $y_1 y_2$ is expected. The histogram of the products in Exhibit 17.4F confirms this expectation. The products range from about -0.50 to 0.50. Their standard deviation is 0.085, whereas the standard deviation of the products of uniformly distributed numbers is 0.079 (see Exhibit 17.4D). About 976, or 97.6%, of the products fall in the interval $[-0.25, 0.25)$, which is the range of the products of the uniformly distributed numbers.

The middle 50% of the distribution of the products lies in $(Q_1, Q_3) = (-0.03, 0.03)$, which is *smaller* than the middle 50% interval for the products of the uniformly distributed numbers! Thus, while the distribution of products of the numbers with normal errors is more spread out overall than the distribution of products of the numbers with uniform errors, the middle 50% of the former distribution is less spread out than the middle 50% of the distribution of the latter. Although this result could have been derived mathematically, it would have been a major technical tour de force. With simulation, it is easily observed. ■

■**EXAMPLE 17.4D:** This example repeats Example 17.4B but with normally distributed errors. Thus $y_1 = 100 + v_1$ and $y_2 = 100 + v_2$, but v_1 and v_2 are drawn randomly from a normal distribution with mean 0 and standard deviation $\sigma = \sqrt{1/12}$. Exhibit 17.4G shows the histograms of $y_1 y_2$, the products, and $y_1 y_2 - 10,000$, the errors in the products. The errors in the products range from about -150 to 150 and have a standard deviation of 40.8. The middle 50% of the errors lies in $(Q_1, Q_3) = (-25.75, 27.34)$. This is a shorter interval than the middle 50% interval for products of uniformly distributed numbers. ■

Examples 17.4A, 17.4B, 17.4C, and 17.4D are instructive. They show that computer simulations can quickly produce results that may take a long time or be impossible to derive. In general, simulations can be used to illustrate results that are beyond our capacity to derive mathematically.

Does this mean that mathematically derived results are not important? We believe not, for two reasons. First, and perhaps most important, mathematical results are general, whereas simulations are specific to the assumptions built into the simulation model. For example, the central limit effect is based on mathematical theorems that hold that the underlying distribution of the data is virtually irrelevant to the fact that totals and means have approximate normal distributions. To derive this result with simulation, we would have to generate data from every conceivable distribution and notice that the totals and means always displayed a normal shape! Moreover, central limit theorems in mathematics apply to many complex processes. To simulate from all such processes would take many lifetimes.

Second, mathematics is explicit about the assumptions that make a result true. If a process fails to satisfy the assumptions of a known theorem, then the conclusions of the theorem may or may not apply to the process. Simulations may be used to see if the theorem *seems* to hold for the process, but if they do, then ultimately a theorem that says so would be useful because it might apply to other interesting new processes as well. (We may try to interest a mathematician in proving such a theorem.)

Practical problems often suggest a mathematical discovery. Simulations of new processes may well be the beginning of new mathematical investigations that yield

EXHIBIT 17.4G

Histograms of Products
and Errors in Products
of 1000 Pairs of
Numbers $y_i = 100 + v_i$,
$i = 1, 2$, Where v_i Is
Drawn at Random from
a Normal Distribution
with Mean 0 and
Standard Deviation
$\sqrt{1/12}$

```
Histogram of y1*y2
Each * represents five observations

Midpoint   Count
   9860      1    *
   9880      2    *
   9900      9    **
   9920     28    ******
   9940     69    **************
   9960    112    ***********************
   9980    160    ********************************
  10000    205    *****************************************
  10020    190    **************************************
  10040    107    **********************
  10060     67    **************
  10080     38    ********
  10100      7    **
  10120      3    *
  10140      2    *
```

```
Histogram of y1*y2-10,000
Each * represents five observations

Midpoint   Count
   -140      1    *
   -120      2    *
   -100      9    **
    -80     28    ******
    -60     69    **************
    -40    112    ***********************
    -20    160    **********************************
      0    205    *****************************************
     20    190    **************************************
     40    107    **********************
     60     67    **************
     80     38    ********
    100      7    **
    120      3    *
    140      2    *
```

	n	Mean	Standard Deviation
y_1	1000	100.00	0.29
y_2	1000	100.01	0.29
$y_1 y_2$	1000	10001.2	40.8
$y_1 y_2 - 10{,}000$	1000	1.23	40.8

theorems like the central limit theorems. The original central limit theorem was discovered by mathematicians who were consulted by gamblers hoping to confirm their intuitive conclusions drawn from playing games of chance in casinos. The games were the original "simulations." The resulting mathematics has had a profound impact on every branch of applied science.

ANALYSIS OF PRODUCTS: MULTIPLYING MANY RANDOM QUANTITIES

Multiplication of more than two random quantities creates a very complex situation that is difficult to study in general. Some illustrative simulations are suggested in the following exercises, but no abstract statements are offered.

EXERCISES

17.5A Let $y_1 = \mu + v_1$ and $y_2 = \mu + v_2$ be two recorded values subject to random errors v_1 and v_2. Carry out a simulation study of the effects of randomness on the difference $y_1 - y_2 = (\mu + v_1) - (\mu + v_2) = v_1 - v_2$, assuming
(a) the v's are randomly drawn from $[-0.5, 0.5)$.
(b) the v's are normal with mean 0 and standard deviation $\sqrt{1/12}$.
Choose the number of simulations and construct histograms and compute descriptive statistics. Compare your findings with the analysis of sums presented in the text.

17.5B Suppose you observe numbers that are correct to the nearest 10th. Thus a recorded value of 100.10 could actually be any number between 100.05 and 100.15. Develop a model for this situation and do a simulation study on the effects of this kind of error on the addition and subtraction of the recorded values.

17.5C Let $y_i = 100 + v_i$, $i = 1, 2$. Study the effects of randomness on the formation of ratios y_1/y_2 assuming
(a) the v's are randomly drawn from $[-0.5, 0.5)$.
(b) the v's are normal with mean 0 and standard deviation $\sqrt{1/12}$.

17.5D Let $y_i = 100 + z_i$, $i = 1, 2$, denote recorded values consisting of fixed components of 100 and random components z_1 and z_2, which are independently drawn from normal distribution with mean 0 and standard deviation 1. Do a simulation study of the sum $y_1 + y_2$, the difference $y_1 - y_2$, the product $y_1 y_2$, and the ratio y_1/y_2.

17.5E Consider the same setup as in Exercise 17.5D but assume the recorded values are $y_i = 100 + z_i + v_i$, where v_1 and v_2 are randomly drawn from $[-0.5, 0.5)$. This is a model that allows for round-off errors as well as other random errors. Do a simulation study of the sum, difference, product, and ratio of the y's and compare your findings to those in Exercise 17.5D.

17.5F Suppose the recorded values have the form $y_i = 100 + 1 + v_i$, $i = 1, 2$, where 100 is interpreted as the theoretical value and 1 as the bias in the measurement. On average the recorded values overstate the theoretical values by 1. The recorded values are also subject to random errors v_1 and v_2. Do a simulation study of the sum, difference, product, and ratio of y_1 and y_2 assuming the random errors
(a) are drawn randomly from $[-0.5, 0.5)$.
(b) are drawn randomly from a normal distribution with mean 0 and standard deviation $\sqrt{1/12}$.

17.5G Let v_1, v_2, and v_3 denote three independent random quantities. Do a simulation study of the product $v_1 v_2 v_3$ assuming the v's
(a) are drawn randomly from $[-0.5, 0.5)$.
(b) are drawn randomly from a normal distribution with mean 0 and standard deviation $\sqrt{1/12}$.
(c) are drawn randomly from a normal distribution with mean 0 and standard deviation 1.

17.5H Let $y_i = 10 + v_i$, $i = 1, 2, 3$, where the v's are defined in Exercise 17.5G. Do a simulation study of the product $y_1 y_2 y_3$.

17.5I Let $y_i = \mu_i + v_i$, $i = 1, 2, 3, 4, 5$, denote random quantities, where v_i is drawn from a normal distribution with mean 0 and standard deviation σ_i, and the μ_i are fixed components. Specify the values of the parameters as in the following table:

i	μ_i	σ_i
1	1	1
2	2	2
3	3	3
4	4	2
5	5	1

With these specifications, do a simulation study of the sum $y_1 + y_2 + y_3 + y_4 + y_5$ and the product $y_1 y_2 y_3 y_4 y_5$. In this study you examine the effects of randomness on arithmetic operations on components that do not all have the same distribution.

17.5J For $i = 1, 2, 3, 4, 5$, let y_i have a binomial distribution with parameters n_i and π_i, where the values of the parameters are as follows:

i	n_i	π_i
1	4	$\frac{1}{5}$
2	2	$\frac{2}{5}$
3	3	$\frac{3}{5}$
4	4	$\frac{2}{5}$
5	5	$\frac{1}{5}$

With these specifications, do a simulation study of the sum $y_1 + y_2 + y_3 + y_4 + y_5$ and the product $y_1 y_2 y_3 y_4 y_5$.

SECTION 17.6

SIMULATING RANDOM WALKS

A pure **random walk** is the running totals of independent outcomes from a stable process with mean 0 and standard deviation σ. As noted in Section 17.1, random walks are useful models for many practical processes.

To introduce the topic of random walks, consider a simple gambling game: matching pennies. You and a friend each toss a penny into the air and let the pennies fall. If the pennies match, that is, they both show heads or both show tails, you win your friend's penny. If they do not match, then your friend wins your penny. You keep playing until one of you runs out of pennies or you tire of the game. The following table shows the possible outcomes of the game and the probabilities of the outcomes:

		Your Penny	
		Head	Tail
Your Friend's Penny	Head	1/4	1/4
	Tail	1/4	1/4

The chance of both pennies showing heads is 1/4, as is the chance of both pennies showing tails. Thus the chance of a match is 1/2. This means that the chance of the pennies not matching is also 1/2. Each of you has a 50-50 chance of winning a penny.

Consider a sequence of plays of the game, keeping track not only of the result of each play but also of your net gain over the sequence. Exhibit 17.6A shows the result of 19 plays. In the Outcome column a -1 means you lost a penny, whereas a 1 means you won a penny. The numbers in the Net Gain column are the running totals of the numbers in the Outcome column. For example, for play number 5, you won a penny, and your net gain after play number 5 is 3, meaning that in the first 5 plays you won three more pennies than you lost. At the end of the sequence of 19 plays you are ahead by 5 pennies.

EXHIBIT 17.6A

Results of 19 Plays of the Matching-Pennies Game

Play	Outcome	Net Gain
1	-1	-1
2	1	0
3	1	1
4	1	2
5	1	3
6	-1	2
7	-1	1
8	-1	0
9	-1	-1
10	1	0
11	1	1
12	-1	0
13	-1	-1
14	1	0
15	1	1
16	1	2
17	1	3
18	1	4
19	1	5

The game is essentially a sequence of Bernoulli trials. If your winning a penny is called a "success," and your friend's winning a penny a "failure," then the probability of success is $\pi = 1/2$. If success is coded as $u = 1$ and failure as $u = 0$, then the outcome of a play is

$$y = 2u - 1 \qquad \textbf{(17.3)}$$

And if $y_1, y_2, \ldots, y_n$ is a sequence of n outcomes, then your net gain over the sequence is

$$y_1 + y_2 + \cdots + y_n = \sum_{i=1}^{n} y_i \qquad \textbf{(17.4)}$$

These formulas make it easy to simulate the matching-pennies game on a computer, which can play much faster than you and your friend can with real pennies. A good understanding of the properties of the game can be gained by studying the data from simulations.

To illustrate, 360 Bernoulli (0–1) trials were generated with $\pi = 1/2$. The result of each trial, u, was transformed by $2u - 1$ to obtain the outcome of that play of the game. This yielded a sequence of -1's and $+1$'s. The latter sequence was cumulated to obtain the sequence of net gains, which is plotted in a sequence plot in Exhibit 17.6B.[†]

The process plotted in Exhibit 17.6B meanders. Between trials 1 and 50 it hovers about 0; in the next 120 trials it stays mostly below 0; and in the remaining trials it stays strictly above 0. There are long stretches where one player is ahead. This is rather surprising behavior for a process that is generated by a stable Bernoulli process. The *cumulation* of stable Bernoulli outcomes produces a wildly unstable process!

Now in the 360 plays represented in Exhibit 17.6B, you win 186 times, and your friend wins 174 times; almost an even split, as is expected from a Bernoulli process with $\pi = 1/2$. The average of your winnings is $\bar{y} = [186(1) + 174(-1)]/360 = 0.03 \simeq 0$, the long-run average of the Bernoulli-like winnings process. A game with 0 long-run average winnings for each player is called "fair" in mathematical literature.

The average of the cumulative winnings, or your net gain, is 0.494, which is also close to 0. The mathematical theory of random walks says that, for a fair game, the long-run average of the net gains is 0. In other words, in the long run the swings above and below 0 tend to cancel each other out in such a way that the average net gain is zero. Neither player should expect to gain much in a very long sequence of plays.

However, the sequence plot in Exhibit 17.6B shows that both players can expect to win or lose substantial amounts at some point during the long sequence of plays. If the game had stopped at the "right time," you would have had a net gain of 17 pennies. Your friend could have won 16 pennies if the game had stopped at a "right time" for her. Moreover, the theory says that the longer you play, the larger the excursions away from 0 will be! In theory, the only limit to your winnings, provided you stop at the "right time," is your friend's total assets, and vice versa.

You can confirm this result by thinking about Equation (17.4). Your net gain is a total of n independent observations from a stable Bernoulli-like process with mean

---

[†] Minitab commands to accomplish this are

```
RANDOM 360 C1;
  BERNOULLI, PI = 0.5.
LET C2 = 2*C1 - 1
PARSUM C2 C3
TSPLOT C3
```

A high resolution plot is obtained by replacing TSPLOT by

```
SET C4
  1:360
GPLOT;
  LINE C3 C4.
```

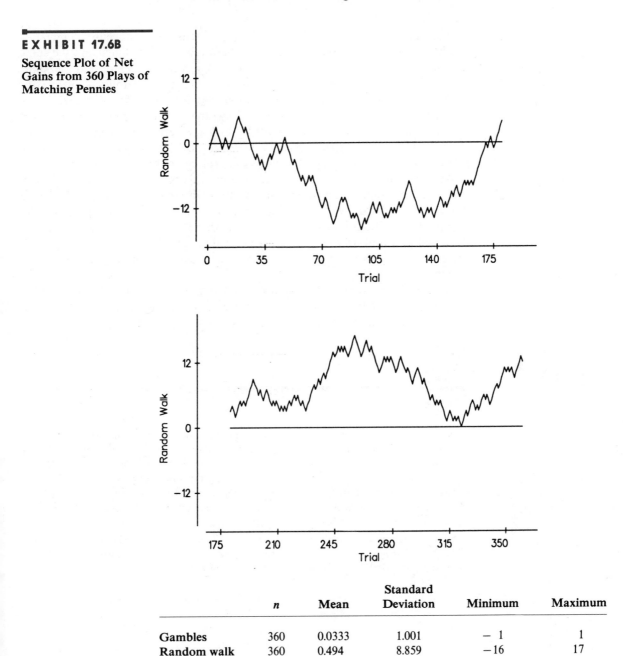

	n	Mean	Standard Deviation	Minimum	Maximum
Gambles	360	0.0333	1.001	− 1	1
Random walk	360	0.494	8.859	−16	17

$\mu = 0$ and standard deviation $\sigma = 1.$[†] From the discussion of the central limit effect in Chapter 8, we know that the mean of the total is $n\mu = n(0) = 0$ and the standard deviation of the total is $\sqrt{n}\sigma = \sqrt{n}(1) = \sqrt{n}$, which gets larger as the number of plays, n, gets larger. This is why, in principle, there is no limit to the sizes of the excursions away from the mean of 0 in very long sequences of plays.

The general definition of random walk shows that any stable process with mean 0 and standard deviation σ can be substituted for the Bernoulli-like process used to illustrate the matching-pennies game. Different distributions are appropriate for different applications. Some possibilities are explored in the exercises.

An important generalization of the random walk is the *random walk with drift*. This process is obtained by assuming that the y variables in Equation (17.4) have nonzero mean δ (the lowercase Greek d, called delta). The parameter δ is called the *drift parameter*. If δ is positive and very small, then the random walk will appear to drift gradually upward over a long period of time. This is the case for many stock prices, so the random walk with drift rather than the pure random walk is often used as a model for stock prices.

Another important generalization assumes that the y variables in Equation (17.4) are not independent. This gets into the topic of time series analysis, which is discussed in more detail in Chapters 23 and 24.

SECTION 17.7

EXERCISES

17.7A Let $z_i, i = 1, 2, 3, \ldots, 360$ denote a sequence of random quantities drawn independently from a normal distribution with mean 0 and standard deviation 1. Let $\sum_{i=1}^{n} z_i$ denote the sums of the first n z's, $n = 1, 2, 3, \ldots, 360$. Use computer software to generate a sequence of z's and the corresponding sequence of sums. Make sequence plots of the two sequences. Compute descriptive statistics of the two sequences. Compare and contrast your findings with the matching-pennies simulation presented in the text. Repeat the simulation several times. Note similarities and differences between the various simulations.

17.7B Let a sequence of z's be defined as in Exercise 17.7A, and let $y_i = 0.001 + z_i$ for each i. Then $\sum_{i=1}^{n} y_i = n(0.001) + \sum_{i=1}^{n} z_i$ is a random walk with drift. Simulate several such random walks and compare their behavior with that of the random walks simulated in Exercise 17.7A.

17.7C Let p_t denote the price of a security at time t, and suppose the model for the price is the following random walk with drift:

$$p_t = t\delta + z_0 + z_1 + z_2 + \cdots + z_t$$

This implies that the price of the security at time $t + n$ is

$$p_{t+n} = (t + n)\delta + z_0 + z_1 + z_2 + \cdots + z_{t+n}$$

[†] The underlying Bernoulli process variable u has $\pi = 0.5$, mean $1 \cdot \pi = 0.5$, and standard deviation $\sqrt{1 \cdot \pi(1 - \pi)} = 0.5$. The winnings variable is $y = 2u - 1 = a + b \cdot u$, where $a = -1$ and $b = 2$. From the footnote on page 444, the mean of the winnings variable is $2(0.5) - 1 = 0$, and the standard deviation of the winnings variable is $2(0.5) = 1$.

In finance research, prices are often converted to rates of return by the formula

$$r_{t+n} = \left(\frac{p_{t+n} - p_t}{p_{t+n}} \right)$$

which, according to the model, may be written

$$r_{t+n} = \frac{n\delta + z_{t+1} + \cdots + z_{t+n}}{(t+n)\delta + z_0 + z_1 + z_2 + \cdots + z_{t+n}}$$

Choose an appropriate value for δ and an appropriate distribution for the z's and do a simulation study of the behavior of rates of return defined in this way.

17.7D Your grade in a course is to be determined by your score on a 100-question true/false test. You decide to flip a coin to determine your answers to the questions, giving yourself a 50% chance of getting the correct answer on each question. To pass the test, you must score above 70%. Let y_i denote the outcome of your guess on the ith question, coded so that $y_i = 1$ if your answer is correct, $y_i = 0$ if your answer is incorrect. This means that $y_1, y_2, \ldots, y_{100}$ is a sequence of Bernoulli trials with $\pi = 0.5$. Define the random walk with drift

$$S_n = \sum_{i=1}^{n} y_i - 0.7n$$

This quantity is positive if your accumulated performance up to the nth question is "passing," that is, the percentage of correct guesses is greater then 70%. You pass the exam if $S_{100} > 0$.

(a) Use your knowledge of the binomial distribution to compute the theoretical mean and standard deviation of S_n.

(b) Simulate a sequence of answers from the corresponding random walk. Make a sequence plot of the random walk. At how many points in the sequence is S_n positive? Is it positive at the end of the sequence?

(c) Simulate 50 sequences of answers. For how many of the sequences do you pass the exam?

(d) Use your knowledge of the binomial distribution to compute the probability that you will pass the exam using the coin-tossing strategy. (Use the normal approximation to the binomial.)

17.7E You invest in a 36-month instrument whose interest rate changes monthly according to market conditions. Let $r_1, r_2, \ldots, r_{36}$ denote the 36 monthly rates. Then \$1 invested in the instrument will be worth \$$(1 + r_1)(1 + r_2) \cdots (1 + r_{36})$ at the end of the 36-month period. The equivalent constant monthly rate of return is found by solving for r in the equation

$$(1 + r)^{36} = (1 + r_1)(1 + r_2) \cdots (1 + r_{36})$$

which yields

$$\log(1 + r) = \frac{1}{36} \sum_{i=1}^{36} \log(1 + r_i) - 1$$

or

$$r = e^{(1/36) \sum_{i=1}^{36} \log(1 + r_i)} - 1$$

(a) Assume the interest rates $r_1, r_2, \ldots, r_{36}$ are drawn randomly from the interval $[-0.004, 0.018]$. Simulate 100 sequences of 36 rates, calculating the value of r for each sequence. Prepare a dotplot and compute descriptive statistics of the distribution of r's.

(b) Make a different assumption about the r's. The choice of distribution is yours. Redo the simulation in part (a). How has the change in assumptions changed the distribution of r's?

SUPPLEMENTARY EXERCISES FOR CHAPTER 17

17A Use computer software to generate 200 random drawings from $[-0.5, 0.5)$. Denote the numbers by $u_1, u_2, \ldots, u_{200}$. Compute a new set of 199 numbers using the transformations $v_2 = u_2 - 0.5u_1$, $v_3 = u_3 - 0.5u_2$, and so on. Note that v_i is equal to u_i minus half the first lag value u_{i-1}. Make a histogram of the 199 v's. Compute the means and standard deviations of the u's and the v's. How do they compare? Do a first lag autocorrelation analysis of the u's and the v's like the one displayed in Exhibit 17.2C. How do they compare?

17B An auditor has examined 100 accounts and determined that five of them are in error as shown below. The figures are in dollars.

Account	Reported Value	Correct Value	Error
12	4381	5011	630
33	872	875	3
35	1222	1322	100
84	66	72	6
91	297	302	5
		Total	744

Suppose that the auditor's "correct" values are accurate only to within $10. Set up a simulation to show the distribution of total errors possible, assuming the mistakes in the correct values are random drawings from $[-\$10, \$10)$. Your simulation needs to consider all 100 accounts because any "correct" value can be in error. You need to make up a complete list of reported and correct values.

17C In preparing a value of inventory report, Carl summarizes his findings on five items as follows.

Item	Number of Items	Price	Value = Number × Price
A	234	$1.25	$292.50
B	61	0.75	45.75
C	187	2.50	467.50
D	43	0.50	21.50
E	38	3.00	114.00
		Total	$941.25

The counts of the numbers of items are subject to random error, simply because the counting process is not completely accurate. (For one thing, the counters get bored and do not keep track of the count very well.) Assume the counts could be off by as much as $-5, -4, -3, -2, -1, 0, 1, 2, 3, 4$, or 5 with equal probability. (An error of 0 represents an accurate count.) Do a simulation to show the variation in the value of inventory possible with this assumption.

17D A business school has maintained a faculty of about 75 professors over a 10-year period. During that period the faculty have produced an average of 70 research papers per year with a standard deviation of 1 paper per year. Assuming the number of papers per year is approximately normal with mean 70 and standard deviation 1, simulate 100 random walks of cumulative production over the 10-year period for this faculty. Make sequence plots of the 100 random walks. Summarize the distribution of the total production of the faculty from these 100 random walks, that is, the final values of the 100 random walks.

S E C T I O N 17.9

GLOSSARY FOR CHAPTER 17

Exponential distribution	A probability distribution on $[0, \infty)$ such that the probability assigned to intervals of the form $[0, w)$ is $1 - e^{-w}$.
Randomness	A property of uncertain outcomes that can be modelled using the mathematics of probability.
Random walk	The sequence of running totals of independent outcomes from a stable process.
Uniform distribution on $[0, 1)$	A distribution of probability that assigns equal probabilities to subintervals of equal length on $[0, 1)$.
$[0, 1)$	The interval of real numbers between 0 and 1, 0 included, 1 excluded.

## CHAPTER 18

Distribution Functions and Moments[†]

INTRODUCTION

The most fundamental comparison of two variables is a comparison of the distributions that describe their variability. In Section 18.2 tools for describing and comparing distributions of variables observed as data are presented. In Section 18.4 tools for describing and comparing theoretical distributions are discussed. Section 18.2 is fundamental; but the rest of this chapter goes into some mathematics of distributions that is not essential for most practical applications. It is pertinent for those who wish to work within an abstract framework, but it is not essential for most. Sections 18.6 and 18.8 deal with the concept of moments within the abstract framework.

[†] This is an optional chapter.

SECTION 18.2

CUMULATIVE DISTRIBUTIONS FOR DATA

EMPIRICAL CUMULATIVE DISTRIBUTION FUNCTIONS

Consider a sample of 10 numbers drawn at random from $[0, 1)$ and rounded to four decimal places: 0.0301, 0.1418, 0.2626, 0.3719, 0.4562, 0.5590, 0.6491, 0.7317, 0.8258, 0.9285.[†] The numbers are in numerical order rather than the order in which they were drawn. What fraction of the sample items is less than or equal to 0.0301? The answer is clearly 1/10. What fraction of the sample items is less than or equal to 0.1418? The answer is clearly 2/10. Continue in this way so that the numbers $1/10, 2/10, \ldots, 10/10$ are associated with the ordered sample items.

Plotting these fractions versus the sample items results in the graph in Exhibit 18.2A. This is an empirical cumulative distribution function graph. It associates with each item in the sample the fraction of sample items less than or equal to that item.

EXHIBIT 18.2A

Graph of ecdf of a Sample of 10 Items from $[0, 1)$

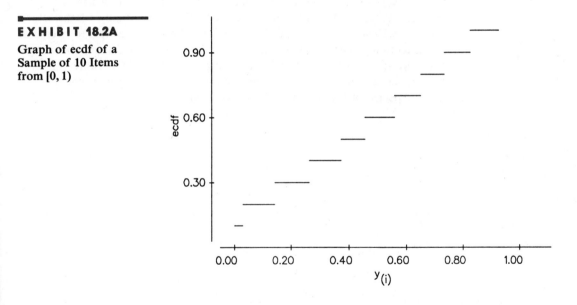

Notice that the graph does even more by displaying horizontal lines between the ordered sample items. In effect, it associates the value 1/10 with each value between the first and second ordered sample items, namely, 0.0301 and 0.1418. It associates the value 2/10 with each value between the second and third ordered sample items, namely, 0.1418 and 0.2626. The continuation of this argument is obvious.

Finally, the graph associates the value 0 with each value less than the smallest sample item, namely, 0.0301, and the value 1 with each value greater or equal to the largest sample item, namely, 0.9285. Thus it graphs a function that associates a

---

[†] It may help to think of the numbers as the ratio (expense for rental car)/(total expense) computed from the expense accounts of 10 members of a travelling sales force.

unique value with each real number. This function is called the **empirical cumulative distribution function (ecdf)** of the sample, which, as a function of y, is the proportion of sample items less than or equal to y.

The ecdf's of samples from different distributions have different characteristic shapes, so graphing ecdf's helps us to visualize the underlying distributions and to compare samples from different distributions. For example, two samples that have roughly equal ecdf's could be treated as having come from the same underlying distribution, but if the ecdf's of the two samples are quite different, this is clear evidence that the samples come from different underlying distributions.

QUANTILE FUNCTIONS AND GRAPHS

Even though the ecdf is a useful tool, especially for discrete distributions, its graph is inconvenient in problems that involve metric data, because of its "stair-step" appearance. For example, in the illustration in the preceding subsection, a larger sample would tend to yield shorter intervals because the observations would tend to distribute themselves uniformly throughout $[0, 1)$. Moreover, in a larger sample, values smaller than 0.0301 and larger than 0.9285 are likely, so associating 0 with values below 0.0301 and 1 with values above 0.9285 is conceptually unsatisfactory.

Exhibit 18.2B shows a graph, called a **quantile plot**, that attempts to overcome these shortcomings. The graph assigns 0 to numbers less than 0, 1 to numbers larger than 1, and values between 0 and 1 to numbers that fall in the interval $[0, 1)$. Moreover, the graph increases continually over $[0, 1)$. This graph emulates the behavior expected of the ecdf with a very large sample.

E X H I B I T 18.2B

Quantile Plot of 10 Items Drawn at Random from [0, 1)

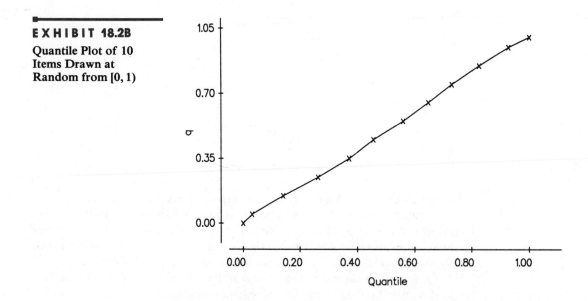

The quantile plot is simple to construct. Use the following general rule: If $y_{(i)}$ is the ith smallest item in a sample of size n, associate the value $q_i = (i - 1/2)/n$ with it. If L is the *smallest possible value* of a sample item, associate the value 0 with it. If U is the *largest possible value* of a sample item, associate the value 1 with it. Plot the points $(L, 0), (y_{(i)}, q_i)$ for $i = 1, 2, \ldots, n$, and $(U, 1)$. Finally, join the plotted points with straight lines.

Quantile is a general term that contains quartile and percentile as special cases. The number $y_{(i)}$ is the $100q_i$th quantile of the sample, and for large samples about $100q_i\%$ of the underlying distribution from which the sample has been drawn lies below $y_{(i)}$.

Any comparison made with the ecdf can also be made with the quantile plot. The quantile plot is frequently preferred in practice, especially for graphical analysis of metric data, because of its intuitively appealing behavior. For count or categorical data, however, the ecdf is more natural because these types of data do not vary over a continuous scale.

■ **EXAMPLE 18.2A:** A sample of 200 numbers drawn from $[0, 1)$ was simulated and the quantile plot shown in Exhibit 18.2C was prepared. Notice that the plot closely resembles a straight line.

EXHIBIT 18.2C

Quantile Plot of a Sample of 200 Items Drawn Randomly from $[0, 1)$

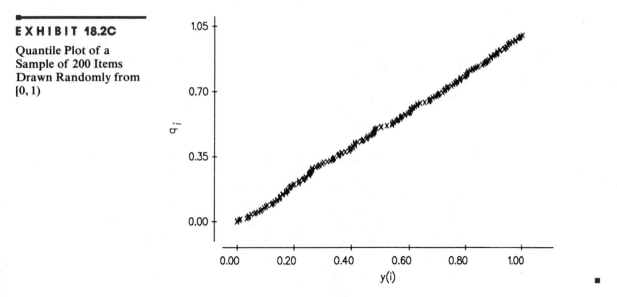

■ **EXAMPLE 18.2B:** A sample of 200 items from a normal distribution with mean 0 and standard deviation 1 was simulated and the quantile plot shown in Exhibit 18.2D was prepared. Notice that the graph has an S shape, quite distinct from the graph in Exhibit 18.2C. This demonstrates that the cumulative distributions of samples from different distributions exhibit distinctive behaviors. The S shape of the quantile plot of a sample from a normal distribution would not be mistaken for the shape of a sample drawn randomly from a uniform distribution!

A small technical difficulty arises when constructing the quantile plot for the normal sample because the normal distribution has no smallest or largest values. In this case, simply start the quantile plot with $(y_{(1)}, q_1)$, the point with the smallest y value, and end it with $(y_{(n)}, q_n)$ the point with the largest y value.

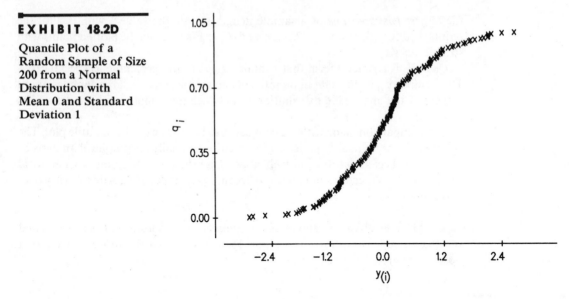

QUANTILE-QUANTILE PLOTS

Examples 18.2A and 18.2B suggest one way to compare metric data sets: compare their quantile plots. The **quantile-quantile plot** carries this idea one step further by making the comparison in a single graph. The quantiles of one data set versus the quantiles of the other are plotted. If the two data sets have about the same distributions, the points in their quantile-quantile plot fall very close to a 45° straight line.

Data sets may come from the same family of distributions but have different descriptive statistics, such as means or standard deviations. If the distributions come from the same family but have different descriptive statistics, their quantile-quantile plots fall close to a straight line whose slope is different from 45°.

This idea was used in Chapter 8 when normal probability plots were introduced. There we wanted to see how closely a data set's distribution resembled a normal distribution. Let $(y_{(1)}, q_1), \ldots, (y_{(n)}, q_n)$ denote the ordered values of the data set and the corresponding q values. To make the normal probability plot, construct the "data set" $(z_{(1)}, q_1), \ldots, (z_{(n)}, q_n)$, where $z_{(i)}$ is the $100q_i$th quantile of a standard normal distribution. Then plot the pairs $(z_{(i)}, y_{(i)})$, $i = 1, 2, \ldots, n$, and judge the closeness of this plot to a straight line.

Quantile-quantile plots can be constructed to compare any two distributions. The two sets of quantiles can be based on data collected from empirical processes or from theoretical distributions such as the normal. The data used depends on the problem being studied.

■**EXAMPLE 18.2C:** Exhibit 18.2E shows weekly sales (in $100s) for two salespeople of computer equipment for 20 consecutive weeks. Also shown are dotplots and descriptive statistics for the two distributions of sales. The descriptive statistics suggest substantial differences in the means and some difference in standard

EXHIBIT 18.2E

Sales ($100s) for
Two Salespeople,
20 Consecutive Weeks

Week	Sale 1	Sale 2
1	145	135
2	156	126
3	207	118
4	180	151
5	163	95
6	168	175
7	158	131
8	206	213
9	185	142
10	178	153
11	94	139
12	213	180
13	135	134
14	165	164
15	198	115
16	122	147
17	163	138
18	216	118
19	225	137
20	140	98

```
        .           .     . . .    .. :...    .. .     .   .. ..
   ----+---------+---------+---------+---------+---------+--------+ Sale 1
    ..         .:   . . :::. ...      .   . .            .
   ----+---------+---------+---------+---------+---------+--------+ Sale 2
      100       125       150       175       200       225
```

	n	Mean	Standard Deviation	Minimum	Maximum
Sale 1	20	170.8	34.1	94	225
Sale 2	20	140.4	27.9	95	213

deviations, but it is difficult to tell from the dotplots if the two distributions could be from the same family. To implement a quantile-quantile plot, the two sets of sales are ordered separately and the numbers $q_i = (i - 0.5)/20$, $i = 1, 2, \ldots, 20$, are associated with the ordered data. Exhibit 18.2F shows the results of this procedure. Exhibit 18.2G is a letter plot of Sale 1 versus q_i (plotting symbol A) and Sale 2 versus q_i (plotting symbol B). The vertical distances between the A's and B's are differences between the corresponding quantiles of the two distributions. This plot confirms that the two distributions differ substantially in location, which explains the difference in the means.

Could the two distributions be from the same family of distributions, despite the difference in means? To check, the quantile-quantile plot of ordered Sale 1 (denoted

Case	Order 1	Order 2	q_i
1	94	95	0.025
2	122	98	0.075
3	135	115	0.125
4	140	118	0.175
5	145	118	0.225
6	156	126	0.275
7	158	131	0.325
8	163	134	0.375
9	163	135	0.425
10	165	137	0.475
11	168	138	0.525
12	178	139	0.575
13	180	142	0.625
14	185	147	0.675
15	198	151	0.725
16	206	153	0.775
17	207	164	0.825
18	213	175	0.875
19	216	180	0.925
20	225	213	0.975

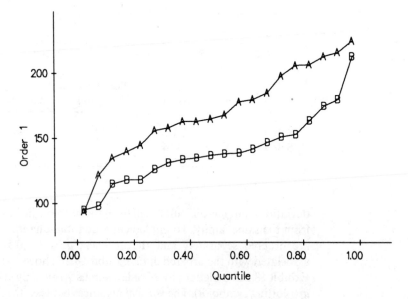

by Order 1) versus ordered Sale 2 (denoted by Order 2) shown in Exhibit 18.2H is
prepared. The points display some curvature, especially in the extremes of the plot,
but the amount of curvature is not great. It is possible that the two distributions
come from the same family. Examination of more data might lead to a more
conclusive result.

EXHIBIT 18.2H

Quantile-Quantile Plot
of Sales Data in
Exhibit 18.2E

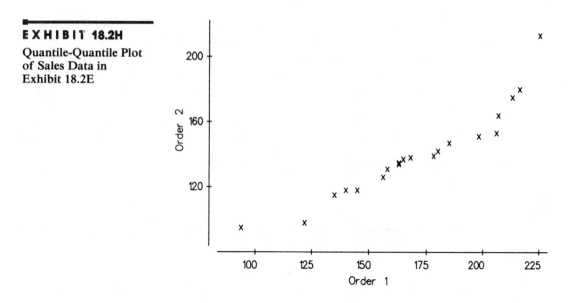

If we accept as a working hypothesis that the two distributions of sales come from the same family, then we compare the distributions using simple descriptive statistics such as the mean and the standard deviation. If we conclude that the two distributions are from different families, then we need to display more detail about them, such as the quantile plots. The first case is one in which substantial simplification is possible; the second is more complex. ▪

SECTION 18.3

EXERCISES

18.3A You are given this sample of 10 numbers:

96.371	100.819	108.429	106.814	93.536
82.600	116.153	104.275	110.511	111.410

(a) Plot the ecdf of the sample.
(b) Prepare a quantile plot of the sample items.
(c) Do the data behave as if they are uniformly distributed? Why or why not?
(d) Prepare a normal probability plot. Do the data appear to have come from a normal distribution?

18.3B (a) Repeat Exercise 18.2A with the following sample:

0.6598	0.7564	−0.8997	−0.5124	0.5531
0.3312	−1.1795	15.8208	−0.0365	−6.6554

(b) Make up a sample and repeat Exercise 18.3A.

18.3C Simulate 100 random drawings from $[0, 1)$, denoted by $u_1, u_2, \ldots, u_{100}$. Form new numbers by the transformation $y_i = u_i^2$. Make a quantile plot and a histogram of the u's and the y's. Compare the distributions of the two sets of numbers. Make a quantile-quantile plot. Make a normal probability plot of the y's. Do they appear to be normally distributed?

18.3D Redo Exercise 18.3C using any transformation from u to y that you would like to study. Some suggestions: $y = u^3$, $y = -\text{Log}(u)$, and $y = 1$ if $u < 0.5$ and $y = 0$ if $u \geq 0.5$.

18.3E Redo Exercise 18.3C but draw the u's from a normal distribution with mean 0 and standard deviation 1. Consider also some of the transformations you considered in Exercise 18.3D.

18.3F Write a two-to-three-page essay on the effects of transformations on random data. Use numerical examples to illustrate your points.

18.3G Choose some data sets you have analyzed previously and diagnose the distributions of the variables using quantile plots, quantile-quantile plots, and normal probability plots, as appropriate.

18.3H Refer to the sales data in Exhibit 18.3E. Prepare normal probability plots for each of the sales distributions. Do the distributions appear to be normal?

SECTION 18.4

THEORETICAL CUMULATIVE DISTRIBUTION FUNCTIONS

Cumulative distribution functions are like fingerprints. Each distribution has a unique cumulative distribution, so distributions can be compared and distinguished by comparing and distinguishing their cumulative distribution functions. So far cumulative distribution functions have been discussed in terms of data sets; but they can also be discussed in terms of theoretical distributions, such as the normal.

Theoretically, any function that assigns values to the set of real numbers such that the smallest value is 0, the largest value is 1, and the function is nondecreasing is a **cumulative distribution function (cdf)** of some distribution. The empirical cumulative distribution functions and quantile functions defined earlier also satisfy these conditions.

■ **EXAMPLE 18.4A:** The function F defined by

$$F(y) = 0, \quad \text{for } y < 0$$
$$= y^2, \quad \text{for } 0 \leq y < 1$$
$$= 1, \quad \text{for } y \geq 1$$

satisfies the conditions of a cdf. Verify this statement and sketch a graph of the function. ■

■ **EXAMPLE 18.4B:** Let $f(z)$ be the function whose graph is the standard normal curve, as defined in Chapter 8, and define the function F by

$$F(y) = \int_{-\infty}^{y} f(z)\,dz \tag{18.1}$$

Then, using a standard interpretation of definite integrals from calculus, $F(y)$ is the *area* bounded by the horizontal axis, a vertical line between y and $f(y)$, and the curve defined by the set of points $\{f(z): -\infty < z \leq y\}$. You can easily verify that $0 \leq F(y) \leq 1$ for all values of y, and F is nondecreasing. You can also see that

$$\lim_{y \to -\infty} F(y) = 0 \quad \text{and} \quad \lim_{y \to \infty} F(y) = 1,$$

so at least in the limit, F satisfies the conditions of making 0 and 1 the minimum and maximum values of the function.   ▪

Example 18.4B illustrates a general technique for constructing cdf's. Start with a function f such that

- $f(z) \geq 0$ for all values of z.
- The integral of f exists.
- The integral of f over the real line is 1.

Then $F(y) = \int_{-\infty}^{y} f(z)\, dz$ is a cdf. The corresponding distribution is said to be a **continuous distribution**, a distribution in which the variable y assumes an infinite number of values in a continuous manner. By the fundamental theorem of calculus, the derivative of F exists for all but at most a finite number of values in any finite subinterval of the real line, and when its derivative F' does exist, $F'(y) = f(y)$. For distributions of the continuous type, the function f is called the **probability density function (*pdf*)** of the distribution.

The distribution in Example 18.4A is of the continuous type. You can show that F is differentiable except at $y = 0$ and $y = 1$, and that the pdf is

$$f(y) = F'(y) = 2y, \text{ for } 0 < y < 1 \quad \text{and} \quad f(y) = 0, \text{ for } y < 0 \text{ and } y > 1 \quad \textbf{(18.2)}$$

The definitions of $f(0)$ and $f(1)$ are immaterial because they do not enter into the calculation of F. It is conventional to define $f(0) = f(1) = 0$ in such cases.

▪ **EXAMPLE 18.4C:** Consider a binomial distribution with $n = 4$ and $\pi = 0.6$. Define $f(y) = Pr(\text{number of successes} = y)$. Then unless $y = 0, 1, 2, 3,$ or 4, $f(y) = 0$. The following table of probabilities is obtained from the formula for the binomial distribution.

y	$f(y)$
0	0.0256
1	0.1536
2	0.3456
3	0.3456
4	0.1296

The cdf for this probability distribution is defined by

$$
\begin{aligned}
F(y) &= 0,   &&\text{for } y < 0 \\
     &= 0.0256,   &&\text{for } 0 \leq y < 1 \\
     &= 0.1792,   &&\text{for } 1 \leq y < 2 \\
     &= 0.5248,   &&\text{for } 2 \leq y < 3 \\
     &= 0.8704,   &&\text{for } 3 \leq y < 4 \\
     &= 1.0000,   &&\text{for } 4 \leq y
\end{aligned}
$$

You can verify that $F(y)$ is the probability that four Bernoulli trials, with $\pi = 0.6$, yield y or fewer successes. You can also verify that $f(y) = F(y) - F(y^-)$,

where
$$F(y^-) = \lim_{x \uparrow y} F(x),$$

the limit of F from the left of y.

■

Example 18.4C illustrates a **discrete distribution**. This type of distribution arises if the cdf is a step function with at most a countable number of jumps. The typical cases are distributions with jumps at the nonnegative integers (called *count distributions*) and jumps at only a finite number of values. The corresponding *mass function* defined by

$$f(y) = F(y) - F(y^-) \tag{18.3}$$

assigns positive masses (interpreted as probabilities) to the set of jump points. The symbol J is used to denote the set of points where the mass function has positive values. This is also the set of points where the cdf jumps. The mass function has value 0 for all real numbers not in J.

All ecdf's are of the discrete type. They are the types of distributions obtained when data from real-world processes are used. Distributions of the continuous type allow us to work with somewhat idealized distributions using the methods of calculus.

SECTION 18.5

EXERCISES

18.5A You are given the pdf $f(y) = 2y$ for $0 \le y < 1$, $= 0$ for $y < 0$ and $y \ge 1$. Find the corresponding cdf $F(y)$. Graph $f(y)$ and $F(y)$.

18.5B Redo Exercise 18.5A using the pdf $f(y) = e^{-y}$ for $0 \le y < \infty$, $= 0$ for $y < 0$.

18.5C Redo Exercise 18.5A using the pdf $f(y) = \frac{1}{2} e^{-|y|}$ for all real y.

18.5D You are given the cdf

$$F(y) = \frac{e^y}{1 + e^y}$$

Find the corresponding pdf.

18.5E Consider binomial distributions with $n = 3$ and $\pi = 1/3, 1/2$, and $2/3$. Plot the mass functions and cdf's of these distributions. Describe how the functions change as π changes. Repeat the exercise with $n = 5$.

18.5F Consider a discrete mass function of the form $f(y) = (1 - \pi)\pi^y$ for $y = 0, 1, 2, \ldots$. The parameter π is any number between 0 and 1 (for example, $\frac{1}{2}$). Use the formula $(1 - x)^{-1} = 1 + x + x^2 + \cdots$ to show that $f(y)$ sums to 1.

SECTION 18.6

MOMENTS

In Section 18.4 two types of distributions were introduced: continuous and discrete. As mentioned there, because different distributions have different cumulative distribution functions, the cdf's act like fingerprints for distributions. Some useful characteristics of the corresponding distribution can be extracted from a cdf. Perhaps the most commonly studied characteristics are the moments. In Chapter 4 such important **moments** as the mean, the standard deviation, and the measure of skewness were introduced. This section shows how moments are related to cdf's and gives some general definitions.

MOMENTS OF THEORETICAL DISTRIBUTIONS

If F is of the continuous type, we work with the corresponding pdf f. If F is of the discrete type, we work with the corresponding mass function f. For a discrete distribution, J is the set of jump points of F, that is, the set of y values at which F takes a step up.

■ **DEFINITION**

The mean of a theoretical distribution is denoted by μ and defined by

$$\mu = \int_{-\infty}^{+\infty} yf(y)\,dy \qquad \text{in the continuous case}$$

$$\mu = \sum_{y \in J} yf(y) \qquad \text{in the discrete case}$$

If either the integral or the sum above does not exist, we say that the mean does not exist.[†] ■

The mean of a distribution is also called the *first moment about zero*. This terminology comes from the following general definition.

■ **DEFINITION**

The pth moment about zero of a theoretical distribution is denoted by μ'_p and defined by

$$\mu'_p = \int_{-\infty}^{+\infty} y^p f(y)\,dy \qquad \text{in the continuous case}$$

$$\mu'_p = \sum_{y \in J} y^p f(y) \qquad \text{in the discrete case}$$

provided the integral or sum is finite. If either is not finite, then the corresponding moment does not exist.[††] ■

From these definitions it follows that $\mu = \mu'_1$, that is, that the mean is the first moment about zero. The phrase *moment about zero* is mysterious until the next definition of a moment about an arbitrary value is introduced.

[†] Technically, for the mean to exist the sum or integral has to be absolutely convergent.

[††] Technically, the definition requires the integral or sum of the pth power of the absolute value of y times $f(y)$ to be finite.

■ **DEFINITION**

For a theoretical distribution the pth moment about an arbitrary point a is denoted by $\mu'_p(a)$ and defined by

$$\mu'_p(a) = \int_{-\infty}^{+\infty} (y - a)^p f(y)\,dy \qquad \text{in the continuous case}$$

$$\mu'_p(a) = \sum_{y \in J} (y - a)^p f(y) \qquad \text{in the discrete case}$$

provided the integral or sum is finite. If either is not finite, then the corresponding moment does not exist.   ■

From this definition we see that $\mu'_p = \mu'_p(0)$, that is, the notation for the pth moment about zero has been simplified by dropping the "(0)." The moments about zero have special importance in statistical theory and so have acquired this special notation. Other moments of special importance are the moments about the mean.

■ **DEFINITION**

The pth moment about the mean is denoted by $\bar{\mu}_p$ and defined by

$$\bar{\mu}_p = \mu_p(\mu) = \int_{-\infty}^{+\infty} (y - \mu)^p f(y)\,dy \qquad \text{in the continuous case}$$

$$\bar{\mu}_p = \mu_p(\mu) = \sum_{y \in J} (y - \mu)^p f(y) \qquad \text{in the discrete case}$$

provided the mean is finite and the sum or integral exists.   ■

■ **DEFINITION**

The variance of a distribution is the second moment about the mean, provided the mean is finite. The variance is denoted by σ^2, that is, $\sigma^2 = \bar{\mu}_2$. The standard deviation is the positive square root of the variance, provided the variance exists. The standard deviation is denoted by σ.   ■

■ **DEFINITION**

A measure of skewness of a distribution is $\gamma_1 = \bar{\mu}_3/\sigma^3$. A measure of kurtosis of a distribution is $\gamma_2 = \bar{\mu}_4/\sigma^4$. These definitions assume the needed moments exist.   ■

■ **THEOREM 1**

If a distribution is symmetric, then the measure of skewness $\gamma_1 = 0$, when it exists. For any normal distribution, the measure of kurtosis is $\gamma_2 = 3$.   ■

■ **THEOREM 2**

$$\sigma^2 = \mu'_2 - (\mu'_1)^2 = \mu'_2 - \mu^2$$

For a proof, see Exercise 18.7A.   ■

■ **EXAMPLE 18.6A:** The pdf of the distribution introduced in Example 18.4A is given in Equation (18.2). Some moments of the distribution are calculated below for illustrative purposes.

The pth moment about 0 is

$$\mu_p' = \int_{-\infty}^{+\infty} y^p f(y)\, dy = \int_0^1 y^p 2y\, dy = 2\int_0^1 y^{p+1}\, dy = \frac{2}{p+2}$$

Setting $p = 1$ gives the mean $\mu = \frac{2}{3}$. Using Theorem 2 gives the variance $\sigma^2 = \mu_2' - \mu^2 = \frac{2}{4} - (\frac{2}{3})^2 = \frac{1}{18}$. This yields a standard deviation of $\sqrt{\frac{1}{18}} \simeq 0.2357$.

The pth moment about the arbitrary value a is

$$\mu_p'(a) = \int_{-\infty}^{+\infty} (y-a)^p f(y)\, dy$$

$$= \int_0^1 (y-a)^p 2y\, dy$$

$$= 2\int_0^1 (y-a)^p (y - a + a)\, dy$$

$$= 2\int_0^1 (y-a)^{p+1}\, dy + 2\int_0^1 (y-a)^p (a)\, dy$$

Setting $a = \mu$ and $p = 3$,

$$\bar\mu_3 = 2\int_0^1 \left(y - \frac{2}{3}\right)^4 dy + 2\int_0^1 \left(y - \frac{2}{3}\right)^3 \left(\frac{2}{3}\right) dy = -\frac{1}{135}$$

From this we can compute the measure of skewness

$$\gamma_1 = \frac{\bar\mu_3}{\sigma^3} = \frac{(-\frac{1}{135})}{(\sqrt{\frac{1}{18}})^3} \simeq -0.57$$

The measure indicates mild skewness to the left. Try to compute the measure of kurtosis. ■

■ **EXAMPLE 18.6B:** A very simple discrete mass function is

$$f(y) = (\tfrac{1}{2})^{y+1} \quad \text{for } y = 0, 1, 2, \ldots$$
$$f(y) = 0 \qquad\quad \text{for all other values of } y$$

Sketch the graph of this function and graph the corresponding cdf. The mass function is nonnegative and

$$\sum_{y=0}^{\infty} f(y) = \frac{1}{2}\left[1 + \left(\frac{1}{2}\right) + \left(\frac{1}{2}\right)^2 + \left(\frac{1}{2}\right)^3 + \cdots\right] = \frac{1}{2}\left(\frac{1}{1-\frac{1}{2}}\right) = \frac{1}{2} \cdot 2 = 1$$

The power series expansion

$$\frac{1}{1-x} = 1 + x + x^2 + x^3 + \cdots$$

which is valid for fractional values of x, has been used. In our application, we set $x = \frac{1}{2}$. To compute the first moment of the distribution, recall from calculus that a convergent power series may be differentiated term by term. This means, for example, that

$$\frac{d}{dx}\left[\frac{1}{1-x}\right] = \frac{d}{dx}(1 + x + x^2 + x^3 + \cdots) = 1 + 2x + 3x^2 + \cdots$$

But

$$\frac{d}{dx}\left[\frac{1}{1-x}\right] = -1(1-x)^{-2}(-1) = \frac{1}{(1-x)^2}$$

so

$$\frac{1}{(1-x)^2} = 1 + 2x + 3x^2 + \cdots$$

Now the mean of the distribution under study is

$$\sum_{y=0}^{\infty} yf(y) = (\tfrac{1}{2})^2[1 + 2(\tfrac{1}{2}) + 3(\tfrac{1}{2})^2 + 4(\tfrac{1}{2})^3 + \cdots] = \tfrac{1}{4} \cdot 4 = 1$$

applying the result above with $x = \frac{1}{2}$. Other moments can be computed using other mathematical tricks, which are pursued in Exercise 18.7E. ▪

MATHEMATICAL EXPECTATION

The calculations presented in this section can be summarized by defining **mathematical expectation**. Consider the continuous case first.

▪ **DEFINITION**

Let y be a variable with cdf F and pdf f, of the continuous type. Let $g(y)$ denote a function of y. Then the integral

$$\int_{-\infty}^{+\infty} [g(y)]f(y)\,dy$$

provided the integral exists, is called the mathematical expectation of $g(y)$ and is denoted by the symbol $E[g(y)]$. ▪

Now consider the discrete case.

▪ **DEFINITION**

Let y be a variable with cdf F and mass function f, of the discrete type. Let $g(y)$ denote a function of y. Then the sum

$$\sum_{y \in J} [g(y)]f(y)$$

provided the sum exists, is called the mathematical expectation of $g(y)$ and is denoted by the symbol $E[g(y)]$. ▪

Except for the distinction between continuous and discrete cases, these two definitions are identical. The notation $E[g(y)]$ applies to both cases. The *concept* of expectation is the same regardless of whether the *implementation* is with the continuous or discrete case. In more advanced treatments the notation $E[g(y)]$ can apply to cases more general than continuous or discrete. Thus it has great unifying power.

The moments just defined are obtained with different specifications of g:

Specification of g	Moment
$g(y) = y$	mean μ
$g(y) = y^p$	pth moment about 0
$g(y) = (y - a)^p$	pth moment about a
$g(y) = (y - \mu)^2$	variance σ^2

Theorem 2 can be expressed as $\sigma^2 = E[y^2] - \mu^2$, which can also be written $E[y^2] = \sigma^2 + \mu^2$, that is, the second moment about zero is the variance plus the square of the mean. This is a general principle of mathematical statistics. The notation of mathematical expectation allows us to express it succinctly without referring to specific implementations like the continuous or discrete cases.

MOMENTS OF EMPIRICAL DISTRIBUTIONS

As discussed earlier, the ecdf is the cdf of a discrete distribution. The mass function, $f_n(y)$, associates the value $1/n$ with each ordered sample item $y_{(i)}, i = 1, 2, 3, \ldots$, and 0 to all other values of y. The ecdf is defined by

$$F_n(y) = (\text{number of sample items less than or equal to } y)/n$$

The first moment about zero is

$$\sum_{i=1}^{n} y_{(i)} f(y_{(i)}) = (y_{(1)} + y_{(2)} + \cdots + y_{(n)}) \cdot \left(\frac{1}{n}\right) = \left(\frac{1}{n}\right) \cdot (y_1 + y_2 + \cdots + y_n) = \bar{y}$$

which is just the sample mean. Even though the formula is written as a function of the ordered sample, the items of the data set may be summed in any order. There is no need to order the sample before the mean is calculated. The second moment about the mean is

$$\sum_{i=1}^{n} (y_{(i)} - \bar{y})^2 f(y_{(i)}) = \sum_{i=1}^{n} (y_i - \bar{y})^2 \left(\frac{1}{n}\right) = \left(\frac{n-1}{n}\right) s^2$$

where s^2 is the square of the sample standard deviation. The quantity s^2 is referred to as the *sample variance*. For large sample sizes, n, the second moment about the mean is about equal to the sample variance, and hence its square root is about equal to the sample standard deviation. In a similar way, other sample moments can be derived from the ecdf.

Theorem 2 may be specialized to the empirical distribution to get

$$\left(\frac{n-1}{n}\right) s^2 = \left[\frac{1}{n} \sum_{i=1}^{n} y_i^2\right] - (\bar{y})^2$$

Multiplying both sides of this equation by n yields

$$\sum_{i=1}^{n}(y_i - \bar{y})^2 = \sum_{i=1}^{n} y_i^2 - n(\bar{y})^2 = \sum_{i=1}^{n} y_i^2 - \left(\sum_{i=1}^{n} y_i\right)^2 \bigg/ n \qquad \text{(18.4)}$$

SECTION 18.7

EXERCISES

18.7A Prove Theorem 2. (*Hint:* Consider the continuous case, so that

$$\sigma^2 = \int_{-\infty}^{+\infty} (y - \mu)^2 f(y)\, dy$$

$$= \int_{-\infty}^{+\infty} (y^2 - 2y\mu + \mu^2) f(y)\, dy$$

$$= \int_{-\infty}^{+\infty} y^2 f(y)\, dy - 2\mu \int_{-\infty}^{+\infty} y f(y)\, dy + \mu^2 \int_{-\infty}^{+\infty} f(y)\, dy$$

$$= \mu_2' - 2\mu \cdot \mu + \mu^2 \cdot 1$$

and the result follows.)

18.7B Compute the kurtosis of the distribution in Example 18.4A.

18.7C Sketch the graph of the mass function $f(y)$ and cdf $F(y)$ in Example 18.6B.

18.7D Show that

$$\mu_2' - \mu = \int_{-\infty}^{+\infty} y(y - 1) f(y)\, dy \qquad \text{in the continuous case}$$

$$\mu_2' - \mu = \sum_{y \in J} y(y - 1) f(y) \qquad \text{in the discrete case}$$

18.7E For the distribution in Example 18.6B, use Exercise 18.7D to show that $\mu_2' - \mu = 2$. Now since $\sigma^2 = \mu_2' - \mu^2 = \mu_2' - \mu + \mu - \mu^2$, you can show that the variance of the distribution is also 2.

18.7F Given $y_1 = 2$, $y_2 = 8$, $y_3 = 9$, and $y_4 = 1$, compute $\bar{y}$, $\sum_{i=1}^{4}(y_i - \bar{y})^2$, $\sum_{i=1}^{4} y_i^2$, and $\sum_{i=1}^{4} y_i$, and verify Equation (18.4) numerically.

18.7G (a) Compute the mean of the distribution in Exercise 18.5A.
　　　　(b) Compute the variance of the distribution in part (a).
　　　　(c) Compute the skewness of the distribution in part (a).
　　　　(d) Compute the kurtosis of the distribution in part (a).

18.7H Redo Exercise 18.7G for the distributions in Exercises 18.5B and 18.5C.

18.7I You are given the discrete mass function listed in this table:

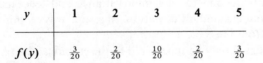

y	1	2	3	4	5
$f(y)$	$\frac{3}{20}$	$\frac{2}{20}$	$\frac{10}{20}$	$\frac{2}{20}$	$\frac{3}{20}$

Compute μ, μ_2', σ^2, γ_1, and γ_2.

MOMENTS OF TRANSFORMED VARIABLES

EMPIRICAL DISTRIBUTIONS

Let $y_1, y_2, \ldots, y_n$ denote a data set with mean $\bar{y}$, variance s_y^2, and standard deviation $s_y = +\sqrt{s_y^2}$. We first investigate the effect of making the same linear transformation of each item in the data set. Specifically, define a new data set $x_1, x_2, \ldots, x_n$ by $x_i = a + by_i$ for each $i = 1, 2, \ldots, n$. Assume that $b \neq 0$. Let the mean, variance, and standard deviation of the x data set be denoted by $\bar{x}$, s_x^2, and $s_x = +\sqrt{s_x^2}$. The relationship between the means, variances, and standard deviations of the two data sets are given in Theorem 3.

■ **THEOREM 3**

$$\bar{x} = a + b\bar{y}$$

$$s_x^2 = b^2 s_y^2$$

$$s_x = |b|s_y, \text{ where } |b| \text{ denotes the absolute value of } b$$

A proof of this theorem is outlined in Exercise 18.9A. These results were presented in Chapter 4 without proof. ■

■ **E X A M P L E 18.8A:** Standardization is a linear transformation, that is,

$$x_i = \frac{y_i - \bar{y}}{s_y} = -\left(\frac{\bar{y}}{s_y}\right) + \left(\frac{1}{s_y}\right) \cdot y_i \qquad \text{for } i = 1, 2, \ldots, n$$

In our general notation, $a = -(\bar{y}/s_y)$ and $b = (1/s_y)$. Applying Theorem 3, we find that $\bar{x} = 0$ and $s_x^2 = 1 = s_x$. Standardization is a transformation that yields a data set with mean 0 and standard deviation 1. ■

Now consider a data structure with n cases and observations on two variables for each case, as indicated below.

Case (i)	x_i	y_i	$w_i = x_i + y_i$	$v_i = x_i - y_i$
1	x_1	y_1	$w_1 = x_1 + y_1$	$v_1 = x_1 - y_1$
2	x_2	y_2	$w_2 = x_2 + y_2$	$v_2 = x_2 - y_2$
$\vdots$	$\vdots$	$\vdots$	$\vdots$	$\vdots$
n	x_n	y_n	$w_n = x_n + y_n$	$v_n = x_n - y_n$

Also shown in the table are columns of case-by-case sums and differences of the x and y observations. The sums are denoted by w's, the differences by v's. How are the means and variances of the w's and the v's related to the means and variances of the x's and y's? Theorem 4 explains.

▪ **THEOREM 4**

$$\bar{w} = \bar{x} + \bar{y}$$
$$\bar{v} = \bar{x} - \bar{y}$$
$$s_w^2 = s_x^2 + s_y^2 + 2s_{xy}$$
$$s_v^2 = s_x^2 + s_y^2 - 2s_{xy}$$

where $(n-1)s_{xy} = \sum_{i=1}^{n}(x_i - \bar{x})(y_i - \bar{y}) = \sum_{i=1}^{n} x_i y_i - n\bar{x}\bar{y}$ ▪

The quantity denoted by s_{xy} is called the **covariance** between the x observations and the y observations. As its name implies, it is a measure of covariation between the two data sets. To bring this idea home, refer to the definition of the correlation coefficient in Chapter 6. It can now be seen that r, the correlation coefficient, may be expressed as

$$r = \frac{s_{xy}}{s_x s_y} \tag{18.5}$$

that is, the covariance divided by the product of the standard deviations of the x observations and the y observations. From this, the correlation coefficient is 0 whenever the covariance is equal to 0. When $r = 0$, the x and y variables are said to be uncorrelated.

THEORETICAL DISTRIBUTIONS

Consider a theoretical distribution that is either continuous with pdf $f(y)$ or discrete with mass function $f(y)$. Let $g(y)$ denote a function that maps the values of the y variable into some set of real numbers. The transformation creates a new variable, say, $x = g(y)$, which has a distribution. Let $h(y)$ denote the pdf or mass function of the new x distribution. Then there is a natural relationship between the moments of the x distribution and a certain function of the y distribution, which is spelled out in Theorem 5.

▪ **THEOREM 5**

Given the definitions above, and subject to some mild restrictions on the function g, the following conditions exist:

If the y and x distributions are both continuous, then

$$\int_{-\infty}^{+\infty} x^p h(x)\,dx = \int_{-\infty}^{+\infty} [g(y)]^p f(y)\,dy$$

provided the second integral exists.

If the y distribution is discrete, then the x distribution is necessarily discrete, and the pth moment of the x distribution is

$$\sum_{x \in J_x} x^p h(x) = \sum_{y \in J_y} [g(y)]^p f(y)$$

provided the second sum exists. The symbols J_x and J_y denote the sets for which $h(x)$ and $f(y)$ are positive.

It is possible for the y distribution to be continuous and the x distribution to be discrete, as Example 18.8B shows. ■

■ **EXAMPLE 18.8B:** Let the y distribution be of the continuous type, and define

$$g(y) = \begin{cases} 1 \text{ if } y \in [25, 50) \\ 0 \text{ if } y \notin [25, 50) \end{cases}$$

Then the x distribution is that of a single Bernoulli trial with $\pi = \int_{25}^{50} f(y) \, dy$. Thus the mean of the x variable is $\mu_x = \pi = \int_{-\infty}^{+\infty} g(y) f(y) \, dy$, which is an application of Theorem 5. ■

Theorem 5 may be expressed in the notation of mathematical expectation as $E[x^p] = E[g(y)^p]$, where $x = g(y)$. This notation succinctly states a general principle of mathematical statistics. For example, Example 18.8B shows how to handle transformation from a continuous distribution to a discrete distribution. Theorem 5 covers this case, but the implementation is messy. The notion of mathematical expectation expresses the truth quite simply.

■ **EXAMPLE 18.8C:** Let μ_y and σ_y denote the mean and standard deviation of the y variable, and let $x = g(y) = (y - \mu_y)/\sigma_y$, the standardizing transformation. Theorem 5 can be used to show that the mean and standard deviation of the x variable are $\mu_x = 0$ and $\sigma_x = 1$. ■

Theorem 5 can be applied to derive the following result: the mathematical expectation of a linear function of y is that linear function of the mathematical expectation. Simply use $x = g(y) = a + by$. In the notation of mathematical expectation, $E[a + by] = a + bE[y]$.

The last case covered is computing the sum or difference of two variables and asking for the mean and variance of the sum or difference. Let x and y be two variables that are either both of the continuous type or both of the discrete type. (Although the theory also covers the case where the variables are not both of the same type, that case is not discussed here.) Define new variables $w = x + y$ and $v = x - y$.

■ **THEOREM 6**

$$\mu_w = \mu_x + \mu_y$$
$$\mu_v = \mu_x - \mu_y$$
$$\sigma_w^2 = \sigma_x^2 + \sigma_y^2 + 2\sigma_{xy}$$
$$\sigma_v^2 = \sigma_x^2 + \sigma_y^2 - 2\sigma_{xy}$$

where σ_{xy} denotes the covariance between the x and y variables. The technical definition of the covariance of a theoretical joint distribution of two variables is beyond the scope of this text. The theoretical quantity is analogous to the sample quantity defined in Theorem 4. ■

The theoretical **product-moment correlation coefficient** between two variables, x and y, is denoted by ρ and defined by $\rho = \sigma_{xy}/\sigma_x\sigma_y$, which is the covariance divided by the product of the standard deviations of the two variables. When the covariance is 0, the correlation coefficient is 0, and the variables are said to be uncorrelated. Theorem 6 is a special case of the following general result.

■ **THEOREM 7**

Let x and y be variables with theoretical distributions having means μ_x and μ_y, variances σ_x^2 and σ_y^2, and covariance σ_{xy}. Define the new variable $w = ax + by$. Then the mean and variance of the theoretical distribution of w are

$$\mu_w = a\mu_x + b\mu_y$$

and
$$\sigma_w^2 = a^2\sigma_x^2 + b^2\sigma_x^2 + 2ab\sigma_{xy}$$

■

SECTION 18.9

EXERCISES

18.9A Let $y_1, y_2, \ldots, y_n$ be a set of numbers with mean $\bar{y}$ and variance s_y^2. Let a new set of numbers be defined by $x_i = a + by_i$, $i = 1, 2, \ldots, n$. Show that $\bar{x} = a + b\bar{y}$ and $s_x^2 = b^2 s_y^2$.

[*Hint:*
$$n\bar{x} = \sum_{i=1}^{n} x_i = \sum_{i=1}^{n} (a + by_i) = na + b\sum_{i=1}^{n} y_i = na + bn\bar{y}$$

and the first equation results from dividing both sides by n. In a similar way,

$$(n-1)s_x^2 = \sum_{i=1}^{n} (x_i - \bar{x})^2 = \sum_{i=1}^{n} (a + by_i - a - b\bar{y})^2 = b^2 \sum_{i=1}^{n} (y_i - \bar{y})^2$$

and the second equation follows from dividing by $n - 1$.]

18.9B As a numerical illustration of Exercise 18.9A, let $y_1 = 1$, $y_2 = 8$, and $y_3 = 9$. Define $x_1 = 1 + 2y_1 = 3$, $x_2 = 1 + 2y_2 = 17$, and $x_3 = 1 + 2y_3 = 19$. Verify numerically that the results stated in Exercise 18.9A are true.

18.9C Let $(x_1, y_1) = (1, 2)$, $(x_2, y_2) = (2, 1)$, and $(x_3, y_3) = (3, 3)$. Let $w_i = x_i + y_i$ and $v_i = x_i - y_i$ for $i = 1, 2, 3$. Verify Theorem 4 numerically for this case.

18.9D Let (x_i, y_i), $i = 1, 2, \ldots, n$, denote data on the pair of variables (x, y), and denote the product-moment correlation coefficient by r_{xy}. Form two new variables t and u by the transformations $t = a + bx$ and $u = c + dy$, applied to each (x, y) pair. Let r_{tu} denote the product-moment correlation coefficient of the new set of pairs. Show that

$$r_{tu} = \frac{bd}{|b| \cdot |d|} r_{xy},$$

where $| \ |$ stands for absolute value. Show also that this implies that if $bd > 0$, then $r_{tu} = r_{xy}$, and if $bd < 0$, then $r_{tu} = -r_{xy}$. Thus the linear transformations may or may not change the sign of the correlation coefficient, depending on the sign of bd. Note also that $|r_{tu}| = |r_{xy}|$ in any event.

18.9E Theorem 4 is a special case of the following result: Let $w_i = ax_i + by_i$ and $v_i = cx_i + dy_i$. Then

$$\bar{w} = a\bar{x} + b\bar{y}$$
$$\bar{v} = c\bar{x} + d\bar{y}$$
$$s_w^2 = a^2 s_x^2 + b^2 s_y^2 + 2abs_{xy}$$
$$s_v^2 = c^2 s_x^2 + d^2 s_y^2 + 2cds_{xy}$$
$$s_{wv} = acs_x^2 + bds_y^2 + (ad + bc)s_{xy}$$

(a) Make up a very simple numerical example and verify this result.
(b) Set $a = b = c = 1$ and $d = -1$ in the equations above. Compare your results with those given in Theorem 4. What additional information do you get from the equations in this exercise?
(c) Use part (b) to show that with the choices of a, b, c, and d given there, and with $s_{xy} = 0$, $(s_x^2) - (s_y^2)/(s_x^2) + (s_y^2)$.
Under what condition is $r_{wv} = 0$?
(d) Show that with the choices of a, b, c, and d in part (b),

$$s_x^2 + s_y^2 = (s_w^2 + s_v^2)/2 \quad \text{and} \quad s_{xy} = (s_w^2 - s_v^2)/4$$

(e) Make up at least three different choices for the set of parameters a, b, c, and d and substitute them into the equations given at the beginning of the exercise. For each set also compute r_{xy} and r_{wv}.
(f) Identify conditions under which $r_{xy} \neq 0$ and $r_{wv} = 0$.
(g) Identify conditions under which $r_{xy} = 0$ and $r_{wv} \neq 0$.

18.9F You are given the data on five (x, y) pairs:

i	x_i	y_i
1	-2	4
2	-1	1
3	0	0
4	1	1
5	2	4

Make a scatterplot of the five (x, y) pairs. Compute $\bar{x}$, $\bar{y}$, s_x^2, s_y^2, s_{xy}, and r_{xy}. Interpret the information about the relationship between the x and y variables conveyed by the graph and the statistics.

SECTION 18.10

SUPPLEMENTARY EXERCISES FOR CHAPTER 18

18A A class of MBA students was broken into nine teams. Each team was asked to prepare oral and written reports on a case study. The scores given to the nine teams in reward for their work are shown below (maximum possible score was 35):

$$28.0, \quad 28.3, \quad 29.9, \quad 28.2, \quad 27.9, \quad 26.2, \quad 29.1, \quad 28.7, \quad 29.2$$

Repeat Exercise 18.3A for these nine scores.

18B You are given the pdf $f(y) = 2(1 - y)$ for $0 \leq y < 1$, $= 0$ for $y < 0$ and $y \geq 1$. Find the corresponding cdf $F(y)$. Graph $f(y)$ and $F(y)$.

18C You are given the pdf $f(y) = \frac{1}{2}$ for $-1 \leq y < 1$, $= 0$ for $y < -1$ and $y \geq 1$. Find the corresponding cdf $F(y)$. Graph $f(y)$ and $F(y)$.

18D You are given the discrete mass function $f(y) = \frac{1}{11}$ for $y = -5, -4, -3, -2, -1, 0, 1, 2, 3, 4, 5$, and $= 0$ for all other values of y. Find the corresponding cdf $F(y)$. Graph $f(y)$ and $F(y)$.

18E Find the mean and variance of the distribution given in
(a) Exercise 18B. (b) Exercise 18C. (c) Exercise 18D.

18F Find the mean and variance of the distribution of the transformed variable $x = 3y - 8$, where the distribution of y is given in
(a) Exercise 18B. (b) Exercise 18C. (c) Exercise 18D.

18G Let x and y be two variables whose distributions have the following characteristics: $\mu_x = 18$, $\sigma_x = 5$, $\mu_y = 28$, $\sigma_y = 2$, and $\sigma_{xy} = 5$. Compute the following quantities.
(a) The correlation coefficient between x and y, denoted by ρ
(b) The mean and standard deviation of w, where $w = x + y$
(c) The mean and standard deviation of v, where $v = x - y$
(d) The correlation coefficient between w and v defined in parts (b) and (c)
(e) The mean and standard deviation of r, where $r = 5x - 3y$
(f) The mean and standard deviation of s, where $s = 10x + 0.5y$
(g) The correlation coefficient between r and s defined in parts (e) and (f)

SECTION 18.11

GLOSSARY FOR CHAPTER 18

Continuous distribution	The variable y assumes an infinite number of values in a continuous manner.
Covariance	$\sigma_{xy} = E[(x - \mu_x)(y - \mu_y)]$
Cumulative distribution function (cdf)	Any function that assigns values to the set of real numbers such that the smallest value is 0, the largest value is 1, and the function is non decreasing.
Discrete distribution	The variable y assumes at most a countable number of values.
Empirical cumulative distribution function (ecdf)	As a function of y, it is the proportion of sample items less than or equal to y.
L	Notation for the smallest possible value for a sample item.
Mathematical expectation	$E[g(y)]$: the weighted average of $g(y)$, where the weights come from the pdf (continuous case) or mass function (discrete case); more general definitions are covered by the notation.
Moment	The most general moment is $E[g(y)^p]$; all others are special cases.
Probability density function (pdf)	Any function f such that $f(x) \geq 0$ for all x, the integral of f exists and the integral of f over the real line is 1.
Product-moment correlation coefficient	$\rho = \sigma_{xy}/\sigma_x\sigma_y$
q_i	Notation for the quantity $(i - 0.5)/n$
Quantile plot	The points $(L, 0)$, $(y_{(i)}, q_i)$, $i = 1, 2, \ldots, n$, $(U, 1)$, joined by straight lines.
Quantile-quantile plot	Scatterplot of the quantiles of two distributions, one versus the other.
U	Notation for the largest possible value for a sample item.
$y_{(i)}$	Notation for the ith largest sample item, the $100q_i\%$ quantile.

## CHAPTER 19

Sampling Distributions and Significance Testing

INTRODUCTION

Chapter 17 showed how simulation is used to gain concrete experience with randomness. The impact of randomness on arithmetic operations was studied, and the ways in which simple random data can be transformed into paradoxically behaving processes like random walks were discussed. Simulation is a valuable tool for practitioners who wish to gain deep insights into data analysis. In this chapter this aspect of simulation is further probed. Simulations are used to introduce statistics that form the foundation of many probabilistic inferences used in practice.

SECTION 19.2

THE *t* STATISTIC FOR A SINGLE SAMPLE MEAN

This section discusses the standardization of the sample mean. Introducing notation, let $y_1, y_2, \ldots, y_n$ denote a sample of n numbers, let $\bar{y}$ denote the mean of the sample, and let s denote the sample standard deviation. Assume the sample is from a process or from a very large population so that in either case the question of a finite population correction factor can be ignored. The long-run process or population mean is denoted by μ, which is the theoretical mean. Then the sample standard error of the sample mean is $s/\sqrt{n}$, and the standardized mean is

$$t = \frac{\bar{y} - \mu}{s/\sqrt{n}} = \frac{\sqrt{n}(\bar{y} - \mu)}{s} \qquad \textbf{(19.1)}$$

This is the difference between the sample and theoretical means divided by the sample standard error. Usual statistical notation for this quantity is the letter t, and the quantity is called a t statistic. Many statistics are referred to as t statistics because the idea of dividing the difference between a sample and theoretical quantity by a sample standard error is pervasive in statistical applications. This type of calculation is also called *Studentizing*. The British statistician who discovered the t statistic, W. S. Gossett, wrote a paper about his discovery under the pseudonym Student because the management of the brewery he worked for did not want their competitors to know they possessed the discovery or how they used it.[†]

The impact of randomness on the t statistic defined in Equation (19.1) is first explored. A sample size $n = 5$ is used and 500 samples of size 5 from a normal distribution with mean $\mu = 0$ and standard deviation $\sigma = 1$ are simulated. For each of the 500 samples, a new mean $\bar{y}$, a new standard deviation s, and a new t statistic t are computed. Suppose the first sample consisted of the following five values:

$$-1.20873 \quad -0.11594 \quad -2.14575 \quad 0.78050 \quad -0.38638 \qquad \textbf{(19.2)}$$

You may verify that $\bar{y} = -0.615$, $s = 1.112$, $s/\sqrt{n} = 1.112/\sqrt{5} = 0.497$, and the value of the t statistic is

$$t = (-0.615 - 0)/0.497 \simeq -1.24$$

The process above was simulated 500 times using Minitab software.[††] Exhibit 19.2A shows a dotplot of the 500 t statistics generated by the simulation. Notice that the distribution appears quite symmetric and mound shaped, which suggests that it may be normal. But that is not the case! To show the lack of normality, Exhibit 19.2B displays the normal probability plot of the 500 t statistics. The deviation from the straight line that should have been obtained if the distribution had been normal is clear. The theoretical distribution of the t statistics has more area in the tails than a normal distribution, and it is less peaked at the center.

In comparison, Exhibit 19.2A shows the 500 simulated sample means standardized by the actual process standard deviation of 1, that is, it shows a dotplot of

---

[†] For a complete discussion, see Stigler, S. M., *The History of Statistics*, Cambridge MA: Harvard University Press, 1986.

[††] Minitab commands to do the simulation are

```
RANDOM 500 C1-C5
RMEAN C1-C5    C6
RSTDEV C1-C5   C7
LET C8=SQRT(5)*C6/C7
```

EXHIBIT 19.2A

Dotplot of 500 Simulated *t* Statistics from 500 Random Samples of Size $n = 5$ from a Standard Normal Distribution. Also shown is a dotplot of the 500 sample means standardized by the process standard deviation of $\sigma = 1$. The exhibit includes descriptive statistics for both sets of numbers.

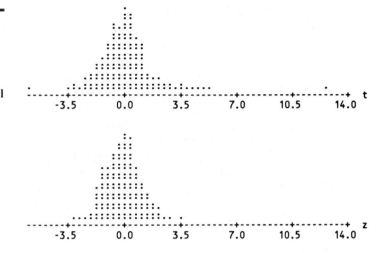

Descriptive Statistics

	n	Mean	Median	Standard Deviation	Minimum	Maximum
t	500	0.11	0.08	1.50	−5.85	12.85
z	500	0.05	0.07	1.03	−3.28	3.45

EXHIBIT 19.2B

Normal Probability Plot of 500 Simulated *t* Statistics with 4 Degrees of Freedom

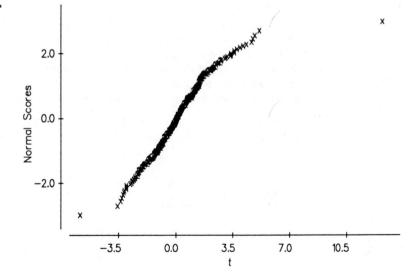

quantities computed by the formula

$$z = \frac{\sqrt{5}(\bar{y} - 0)}{1} = \sqrt{5}\,\bar{y}$$

The theoretical distribution of the t statistic is called the t distribution with 4 degrees of freedom. The name suggests that the distribution depends on a parameter that is one less than the sample size $n = 5$, and this is correct. If a different sample size n, had been used, a t distribution would have been simulated, but it would have had a degrees of freedom parameter equal to $n - 1$.

The theoretical distribution of the 500 t statistics is an example of what statisticians call a **sampling distribution**, a distribution of values of a statistic in repeated drawings from a stable process or random samples from a fixed universe. Sampling distributions were used in the discussion of probabilistic inference in surveys in Chapters 13–16 and in the presentation of the central limit effect in Chapter 8.

■ DEFINITION

Let $y_1, y_2, \ldots, y_n$ denote a sample of size n drawn randomly from a normal distribution with mean μ and standard deviation σ. Let $\bar{y}$ and s denote the sample mean and standard deviation. Then the sampling distribution of the t statistic defined in Equation (19.1) is the t distribution with $n - 1$ degrees of freedom.   ■

The results in Theorem 1 can be derived mathematically.

■ THEOREM 1

A t distribution with $n - 1$ degrees of freedom is symmetric and mound shaped.[†] Provided $n - 1 \geq 2$, the mean of the t distribution is 0. Provided $n - 1 \geq 3$, the standard deviation of the t distribution is $\sqrt{(n - 1)/(n - 3)}$. When $n - 1 = 1$, the mean and standard deviation of the t distribution do not exist. When $n - 1 = 2$, the mean exists but the standard deviation does not. As n grows large without bound, the t distribution converges to the standard normal distribution.   ■

To illustrate the computation of the standard deviation, consider a t distribution with 4 degrees of freedom, that is, $n - 1 = 4$. The standard deviation is

$$\sqrt{\frac{n - 1}{n - 3}} = \sqrt{\frac{4}{5 - 3}} = \sqrt{\frac{4}{2}} \simeq 1.414$$

For a t distribution with $n - 1 = 20$,

$$\sqrt{\frac{n - 1}{n - 3}} = \sqrt{\frac{20}{21 - 3}} = \sqrt{\frac{20}{18}} \simeq 1.054$$

[†] The t distribution with $n - 1$ degrees of freedom is a continuous-type distribution with pdf

$$f(t) = c\left(1 + \frac{t^2}{(n - 1)}\right)^{-n/2} \qquad \textbf{(19.3)}$$

where c is a constant, depending on n, that makes the total area under the pdf equal to 1 (see Section 18.4).

Exhibit 19.2C shows plots of *t* distributions with 4 and 20 degrees of freedom. Also shown are the means, standard deviations, and 95th percentiles of *t* distributions with 4, 20, and 60 degrees of freedom, and the mean, standard deviation, and 95th percentile of the standard normal distribution. All of these distributions have mean 0, which is also the median because of symmetry. The *t* distribution with 4 degrees of freedom has standard deviation 1.414, and the distribution with 20 degrees of freedom has standard deviation 1.054, indicating a decrease in variability with increase in degrees of freedom. Because the distribution with 4 degrees of freedom is more spread out, its 95th percentile is larger than that of the distribution with 20 degrees of freedom.

EXHIBIT 19.2C

Graphs of pdf's of Two *t* Distributions and a Table of Means, Standard Deviations, and 95th Percentiles

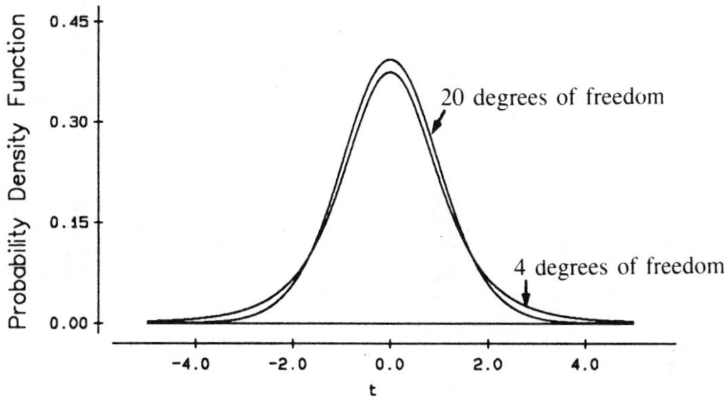

	t Distribution with Degrees of Freedom			Standard Normal Distribution
	4	**20**	**60**	
Mean	0	0	0	0
Standard deviation	1.414	1.054	1.017	1
95th percentile	2.132	1.725	1.671	1.645

One implication of Theorem 1 is that as degrees of freedom are increased, the listed characteristics of the *t* distribution get closer and closer to those of the standard normal distribution. Exhibit 19.2D gives a table of selected percentiles of *t* distributions for selected degrees of freedom. Notice that for degrees of freedom greater than 30, the percentiles of the *t* distributions are little different from those of the standard normal.

In Exhibit 19.2D the degrees of freedom parameter is denoted by v, so $v = n - 1$. This is standard statistical notation for degrees of freedom. It is convenient because in other applications of the *t* distribution, the degrees of freedom parameter is not equal to $n - 1$ but some other function of n. Using the general notation v for degrees of freedom allows the table in Exhibit 19.2D to be used for a large number of applications.

EXHIBIT 19.2D

Percentiles of Selected t Distributions with v Degrees of Freedom

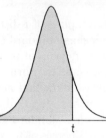

t

v	0.550	0.600	0.650	0.700	0.750	0.800	0.850	0.900	0.950	0.975	0.990	0.995	0.997	0.998	0.999
1	0.158	0.325	0.510	0.727	1.000	1.376	1.963	3.078	6.314	12.706	31.821	63.657	106.100	159.156	318.317
2	0.142	0.289	0.445	0.617	0.816	1.061	1.386	1.886	2.920	4.303	6.965	9.925	12.852	15.764	22.327
3	0.137	0.277	0.424	0.584	0.765	0.978	1.250	1.638	2.353	3.182	4.541	5.841	6.994	8.053	10.215
4	0.134	0.271	0.414	0.569	0.741	0.941	1.190	1.533	2.132	2.776	3.747	4.604	5.321	5.951	7.173
5	0.132	0.267	0.408	0.559	0.727	0.920	1.156	1.476	2.015	2.571	3.365	4.032	4.570	5.030	5.893
6	0.131	0.265	0.404	0.553	0.718	0.906	1.134	1.440	1.943	2.447	3.143	3.707	4.152	4.524	5.208
7	0.130	0.263	0.402	0.549	0.711	0.896	1.119	1.415	1.895	2.365	2.998	3.499	3.887	4.207	4.785
8	0.130	0.262	0.399	0.546	0.706	0.889	1.108	1.397	1.860	2.306	2.896	3.355	3.705	3.991	4.501
9	0.129	0.261	0.398	0.543	0.703	0.883	1.100	1.383	1.833	2.262	2.821	3.250	3.573	3.835	4.297
10	0.129	0.260	0.397	0.542	0.700	0.879	1.093	1.372	1.812	2.228	2.764	3.169	3.472	3.716	4.144
11	0.129	0.260	0.396	0.540	0.697	0.876	1.088	1.363	1.796	2.201	2.718	3.106	3.393	3.624	4.025
12	0.128	0.259	0.395	0.539	0.695	0.873	1.083	1.356	1.782	2.179	2.681	3.055	3.330	3.550	3.930
13	0.128	0.259	0.394	0.537	0.694	0.870	1.079	1.350	1.771	2.160	2.650	3.012	3.278	3.489	3.852
14	0.128	0.258	0.393	0.537	0.692	0.868	1.076	1.345	1.761	2.145	2.624	2.977	3.234	3.438	3.787
15	0.128	0.258	0.393	0.536	0.691	0.866	1.074	1.341	1.753	2.131	2.602	2.947	3.197	3.395	3.733
16	0.128	0.258	0.392	0.535	0.690	0.865	1.071	1.337	1.746	2.120	2.583	2.921	3.165	3.358	3.686
17	0.128	0.257	0.392	0.534	0.689	0.863	1.069	1.333	1.740	2.110	2.567	2.898	3.138	3.326	3.646
18	0.127	0.257	0.392	0.534	0.688	0.862	1.067	1.330	1.734	2.101	2.552	2.878	3.113	3.298	3.610
19	0.127	0.257	0.391	0.533	0.688	0.861	1.065	1.328	1.729	2.093	2.539	2.861	3.092	3.273	3.579
20	0.127	0.257	0.391	0.533	0.687	0.860	1.064	1.325	1.725	2.086	2.528	2.845	3.073	3.251	3.552
21	0.127	0.257	0.391	0.532	0.686	0.859	1.063	1.323	1.721	2.080	2.518	2.831	3.056	3.231	3.527
22	0.127	0.256	0.390	0.532	0.686	0.858	1.061	1.321	1.717	2.074	2.508	2.819	3.041	3.214	3.505
23	0.127	0.256	0.390	0.532	0.685	0.858	1.060	1.319	1.714	2.069	2.500	2.807	3.027	3.198	3.485
24	0.127	0.256	0.390	0.531	0.685	0.857	1.059	1.318	1.711	2.064	2.492	2.797	3.014	3.183	3.467
25	0.127	0.256	0.390	0.531	0.684	0.856	1.058	1.316	1.708	2.060	2.485	2.787	3.003	3.170	3.450
26	0.127	0.256	0.390	0.531	0.684	0.856	1.058	1.315	1.706	2.056	2.479	2.779	2.992	3.158	3.44
27	0.127	0.256	0.389	0.531	0.684	0.855	1.057	1.314	1.703	2.052	2.473	2.771	2.982	3.147	3.42
28	0.127	0.256	0.389	0.530	0.683	0.855	1.056	1.313	1.701	2.048	2.467	2.763	2.973	3.136	3.408
29	0.127	0.256	0.389	0.530	0.683	0.854	1.055	1.311	1.699	2.045	2.462	2.756	2.965	3.127	3.396
30	0.127	0.256	0.389	0.530	0.683	0.854	1.055	1.310	1.697	2.042	2.457	2.750	2.957	3.118	3.385
31	0.127	0.256	0.389	0.530	0.682	0.853	1.054	1.309	1.696	2.040	2.453	2.744	2.950	3.109	3.375
32	0.127	0.255	0.389	0.530	0.682	0.853	1.053	1.309	1.694	2.037	2.449	2.738	2.943	3.102	3.365
33	0.127	0.255	0.389	0.530	0.682	0.853	1.053	1.308	1.692	2.035	2.445	2.733	2.937	3.094	3.356
34	0.127	0.255	0.389	0.529	0.682	0.852	1.052	1.307	1.691	2.032	2.441	2.728	2.931	3.088	3.348
35	0.127	0.255	0.389	0.529	0.682	0.852	1.052	1.306	1.690	2.030	2.438	2.724	2.926	3.081	3.340
40	0.126	0.255	0.388	0.529	0.681	0.851	1.050	1.303	1.684	2.021	2.423	2.704	2.902	3.055	3.307
50	0.126	0.255	0.388	0.528	0.679	0.849	1.047	1.299	1.676	2.009	2.403	2.678	2.870	3.018	3.261
60	0.126	0.255	0.387	0.527	0.679	0.848	1.045	1.296	1.671	2.000	2.390	2.660	2.849	2.994	3.232
120	0.126	0.254	0.386	0.526	0.677	0.845	1.041	1.289	1.658	1.980	2.358	2.617	2.798	2.935	3.160
inf	0.126	0.253	0.385	0.524	0.674	0.842	1.036	1.282	1.645	1.960	2.326	2.576	2.748	2.878	3.090

Note: The body of the table contains values of t corresponding to areas a. The parameter a is the area bounded by the horizontal axis, a vertical line through t, and the pdf of the t distribution with v degrees of freedom.

EXERCISES

19.3A Simulate a random sample of size $n = 7$ from a standard normal distribution and compute the value of the sample mean, the sample standard deviation, the t statistic in Equation (19.1), and the z statistic, $z = \sqrt{7} \cdot \bar{y}$. Repeat the simulation 100 times, storing the 100 values of $\bar{y}, s, t$, and z. Make dotplots and compute descriptive statistics of each of these variables. Relate your findings to those discussed in the text.

19.3B Suppose $n = 25$, $\mu = 0$, $\bar{y} = -4.27$, and $t = -2.1$. What is the value of s?

19.3C Suppose $\bar{y} = 4.27$, $\mu = 3$, $s = 0.79$, and $t = 8.04$. What is the value of n?

19.3D Suppose $n = 18$, $\bar{y} = 97.6$, $\mu = 100$, and $s = 5.3$. What is the value of t?

19.3E For each case below, find the requested percentile of the t distribution with the indicated degrees of freedom v.

Case	v	Percentile
a	10	90th
b	10	40th
c	15	95th
d	15	97.5th
e	15	20th
f	30	99.9th
g	30	99.5th
h	30	0.5th

19.3F You plan to draw a random sample of size $n = 20$ from a process in statistical control and with a normal cross-sectional distribution whose mean is $\mu = 100$.
(a) For what percentage of such samples will the value of the t statistic $t = \sqrt{n}(\bar{y} - 100)/s$ be greater than 2.093?
(b) For what percentage of such samples will the value of the t statistic be between -2.861 and 2.861?

19.3G Find a value b such that with probability 0.99 the values of the t statistic with 7 degrees of freedom are between $-b$ and b.

19.3H Write a one-to-two-page essay on the differences between $z = \sqrt{n}(\bar{y} - \mu)/\sigma$ and $t = \sqrt{n}(\bar{y} - \mu)/s$. Use simulations to illustrate your points.

APPLICATION TO SIGNIFICANCE TESTING

INFORMAL INTRODUCTION

Significance testing is a process of probabilistic inference that uses sampling distributions to compare behavior in data with theories about the process that generated the data. Consider a situation in which data from a process in statistical control whose cross-sectional distribution is normal are drawn, the value of the long-run process mean, denoted by μ, is in doubt, and the value of the long-run process standard deviation σ is not known. One way to approach inference about μ is to venture a guess, called a theory or hypothesis, about the value of μ. After the data are collected, the value of the guess is compared with the value of the sample mean.

Because sample means vary from sample to sample, a criterion for determining whether a specific sample mean deviates from the guess by more than an amount that can be attributed to natural sampling variation is needed. The t statistic in Equation (19.1) and its associated t distribution with $n-1$ degrees of freedom provide such a criterion.

■ **E X A M P L E 19.4A:** Suppose you plan to take a sample of size $n = 5$ from the process. Also assume that you have formulated a hypothesis that $\mu = 1$. This is the guess at μ. From the theory presented above, you know that if the guess coincides with the actual long-run process mean, then the statistic

$$t = \frac{\bar{y} - 1}{s/\sqrt{5}} = \frac{\sqrt{5}(\bar{y} - 1)}{s} \qquad \textbf{(19.4)}$$

has a t sampling distribution with 4 degrees of freedom. This distribution describes the variation inherent in the random sampling of the process. The table in Exhibit 19.2D shows that the 99.5th percentile of this distribution is 4.604. This means that if the long-run process mean is indeed 1, then 99% of the values of the t statistics in Equation (19.4) that could be obtained by random sampling of the process are between -4.604 and 4.604.

How might this result be used? Significance testing uses it as follows:

(1) Draw a random sample of five items from the process.

(2) Compute the sample mean $\bar{y}$, standard deviation s, and t statistic t.

(3) If $|t| \leq 4.604$, declare the difference between the sample mean and the hypothesized mean of 1 to be due to random variation.

(4) If $|t| > 4.604$, declare the difference between the sample mean and the hypothesized mean of 1 to be *statistically significant* at the 1% significance level.

Step 4 requires elaboration. The reference to a 1% significance level comes from the fact that 4.604 is the 99.5th percentile of the t distribution with 4 degrees of freedom. As noted above, if the hypothesized value of 1 and the actual long-run value of the process mean coincide, then there is only a 1% chance that the t statistic value falls outside the interval defined by $|t| \leq 4.604$. If a value outside this interval is observed, it is tempting to conclude that there is a discrepancy between the hypothesized value and the actual long-run process mean. This is the reasoning behind the phrase **statistically significant**.

In more informal terms, an outcome $|t| > 4.604$ in this case is not likely to be due to chance alone; there is likely a "cause" other than pure chance of the result. The cause that most readily comes to mind is that the hypothesis is defective.   ■

The reasoning introduced in Example 19.4A assumes certain things that may not stand up under scrutiny. For example, the process sampled from may not be in statistical control. Or the sampling process may be defective, so that the data do not really satisfy the assumption of randomness. Or the data may contain measurement errors that bias the value of $\bar{y}$. Finally, the cross-sectional distribution of the process may seriously deviate from the normal form assumed. The reasoning behind significance testing presupposes that none of these problems is present. Before a conclusion based on significance testing can be reached, the experimenter must be satisfied that none of the problems mentioned seriously affect the data. Otherwise, completely unwarranted conclusions could be drawn with significance testing.

The point in the preceding paragraph is profoundly important for practical applications. The mechanics and interpretation of significance testing are so appealing that practitioners are tempted to apply them without thinking deeply about the assumptions that must be satisfied to obtain valid inferences. There are many slippery curves to negotiate when performing inference!

For the moment, think about inferential situations in which a significance test would be appropriate, that is, situations in which none of the serious problems mentioned above are present. Consider two variations on the significance test outlined above. One variation is to use a different sample size. The sample size $n = 5$ was chosen for illustration. In practice the sample size is one of the important design choices available to the investigator.

Your intuition probably suggests, and rightly so, that the choice of n affects the performance of a significance test. In particular, tests based on larger values of n ought to be better able than those based on smaller values of n to detect a given amount of discrepancy between the hypothesized and actual values of the process mean, a conclusion that statistical theory confirms.

This result should not lead you to conclude that large sample sizes are necessarily better than small ones. Remember that collecting data is costly, and the larger the sample the greater the chance that nonsampling errors will creep undetected into the data.

Another caution is that statistical significance does not automatically imply *practical* importance. A significance test based on a large sample will signal statistical significance for a small deviation from a hypothesized mean. If such a small deviation from a hypothesized mean has no useful practical implication, then the temptation to celebrate the statistically significant finding must be resisted. The researcher must understand the process under study well enough to know the magnitude of a practically important deviation. Estimating the magnitude of the deviation from a hypothesized mean, using confidence intervals, then yields the most directly useful information from the data. More than the concept of statistical significance is needed as a guide to practical action.

Another variation on the significance test introduced above is to change the level of significance. A 1% level of significance was obtained by choosing a 99.5th percentile of the t distribution as the dividing line between sampling variation and special-cause variation. In theory, there is no single dividing line that is better than any other. The 95th percentile, which is 2.132 for a t distribution with 4 degrees of freedom, could have been chosen just as easily. Had this been done, the significance level would have been 10%. This means that if the hypothesized value and the long-run process mean coincide, then 10% of all t statistics that can possibly be obtained by random sampling of the process are outside the interval $|t| \leq 2.132$. If this criterion is chosen, 10% of the time statistically significant results will be obtained even though the hypothesis coincides with the long-run process mean.

FORMAL INTRODUCTION

In this subsection some of the formal terminology and notation of the theory of significance testing is introduced. A brief introduction in the context of the binomial distribution appears in Section 10.11, which you may wish to reread. Here a normal process in statistical control is sampled to test the validity of a guess at the long-run process mean μ.

The numerical value of the guess is called the **null hypothesis** and is denoted by H_0. If μ_0 denotes the numerical guess at μ, then $H_0: \mu = \mu_0$ defines the null hypothesis. Once a null hypothesis is defined, the notation H_0 is used to refer to it.

To conduct a test of significance, a **test statistic** that forms a comparative link between some function of the data and the long-run process mean μ is defined. The researcher must be able to state the sampling distribution of the test statistic when the null hypothesis is assumed to be true. Saying that the null hypothesis is true means that a "good guess" has been made, that is, that μ_0 and the actual long-run value of μ coincide.

The test statistic must be constructed so that if a good guess is not made, the statistic sends an appropriate signal, which is exactly what the t statistic does. Here is the logic. Because the sampling distribution of the t statistic is known when H_0 is true, an interval of values expected to be observed, called the interval of plausible values, can be constructed. Now if after the data are collected and the value of the t statistic

$$t = \frac{\bar{y} - \mu_0}{s/\sqrt{n}} = \frac{\sqrt{n}(\bar{y} - \mu_0)}{s} \qquad \textbf{(19.5)}$$

is computed, and the t statistic falls outside the interval of plausible values, then there is reason to suspect that the hypothesis was not really a good guess. Notice that the value of t is obtained by dividing the difference between the sample mean obtained from the data and the null hypothesis value μ_0 by the sample standard error of the mean.

When the value of the t statistic computed for actual data falls outside the interval of plausible values, it has fallen into the **critical region** of the test and the value is statistically significant. If the researcher believes the signal the test gives and concludes that the hypothesis is not a good guess, then *the null hypothesis is rejected.* The implication of this language is that if the actual value of the t statistic falls *in* the interval of plausible values, then *the null hypothesis is not rejected.*

The interval of plausible values plays a fundamental role. Values of the t statistic not in this interval are deemed to be "critical" and to signal rejection of the null hypothesis. The interval of plausible values is chosen to make it unlikely that the test statistic rejects the null hypothesis when it is true. More formally, the interval of plausible values is chosen so that when the null hypothesis is true, an acceptably small proportion of possible t statistics falls outside the interval, according to the sampling t distribution with $n - 1$ degrees of freedom.

In Exhibit 19.2A, when the null hypothesis was assumed to be true, the t statistics had a t distribution with 4 degrees of freedom. This implied that when the null hypothesis was assumed to be true, 99% of the possible t statistic values were between -4.604 and 4.604, and the interval between these values was used as the interval of plausible values. The probability of rejecting a true null hypothesis was therefore only 0.01 (or 1%). Since only one out of a hundred possible t statistic values would lead to rejecting a true null hypothesis, the researcher would feel confident that the test of significance is not misleading. Put another way, if a t statistic value outside the interval of plausible values (and therefore inside the critical region) is observed, this justifies doubts about the truth of the null hypothesis. The 1% probability that the t statistic falls in the critical region is called the **significance level** of the test. It is a measure of the risk of incorrectly concluding that the null hypothesis is false.

There is no purely objective way to choose the interval of plausible values. In Example 19.4A it would have been just as valid to have chosen the interval between -2.776 and 2.776 as the interval of plausible values. From the table in Exhibit 19.2D, you learn that when the null hypothesis is true, 95% of the possible t statistics fall in this interval. This means that when the null hypothesis is true, the probability that a t statistic falls in the critical region is 0.05 (or 5%). The significance level of this test is 5%. This test is riskier than the test with the 1% significance level because there is a higher probability of rejecting a true null hypothesis.

So should the test with the smallest possible significance level always be used? If this were the whole story, the best test would never reject a null hypothesis, yielding a significance level of 0. But this is clearly ridiculous. There is more to the story!

The risk of rejecting a true null hypothesis is only one kind of risk. Another is the risk of not rejecting a false null hypothesis. It is the trade-off between these two risks that forces researchers to use nonzero significance levels. A test that never rejects a null hypothesis cannot signal that the guess at μ is no good. Researchers run some risk of rejecting a true null hypothesis to discover a false one. Such is the trade-off inherent in trying to discover new truth from imperfect or incomplete data.

As stated before, there is no completely objective method for choosing the significance level of a significance test. A thorough analysis of approaches to the choice leads into a long and arduous theoretical discussion that is beyond the scope of this book. The prevailing practice is to choose significance levels more or less by convention, the most common choices being 10%, 5%, and 1%. The smaller the significance level, the larger the interval of plausible values, and the larger the t statistic has to be, in absolute value, to fall in the critical region and signal rejection of the null hypothesis.

Another approach, used frequently but seldom stated formally, is to use a fixed dividing line between plausible and critical values of the t statistic. Statisticians in practice often consider $|t| > 2$ critical for moderate to large sample sizes. For samples of size 31 or more, this corresponds to about a 5% significance level, as you can confirm by looking at Exhibit 19.2D. Although we appreciate this approach because it avoids cumbersome reference to tables, we prefer to use $|t| > 3$ as the fixed critical region. This corresponds to about a 0.3% significance level for moderate to large samples. Accepting a 5% risk of rejecting a true null hypothesis, on the other hand, implies little confidence in the null hypothesis to begin with, which raises the question of why pay to test it?

In practice the analysis of data leads to formulating and testing many hypotheses. If 10 true null hypotheses are independently tested at the 5% significance level, then the probability that all 10 tests correctly fail to reject the null hypotheses is only $(0.95)^{10} \simeq 0.60$. On the other hand, if the hypotheses are tested at the 0.3% significance level, the probability that all 10 tests correctly fail to reject the null hypotheses is $(0.997)^{10} \simeq 0.97$. The risk of making errors is much lower for the smaller significance level.

Three types of errors are possible in significance testing: Type I, Type II, and Type III. **Type I error** is rejecting a true null hypothesis. This means that the significance level is the probability of committing a Type I error. Type II error is not rejecting a false null hypothesis. In some problems it is possible to compute probabilities of Type II errors, but their calculation is usually a formidable technical exercise.[†]

Type III error refers to answering an irrelevant question. In formulating problems researchers usually try to define the problem in terms that make it easy to solve. Doing this creates the risk of "defining away" the real problem, that is, setting up a problem that can be solved but whose salient features do not match the real problem. The resulting solution may be quite impressive in its technical detail and in the slickness of its presentation, but it does not help improve the process that needs improving. There is a double cost to Type III errors: the cost of the resources spent in deriving a "solution," and the cost of still having to deal with the fundamental problem that has not been solved.

A test of significance based on the t statistic defined in Equation (19.5) is called a **t test for the process mean**. There are many other t tests, one of which is introduced in Section 19.10.

▪ **E X A M P L E 19.4B:** Example 19.4A showed that for a test of significance based on the t distribution with 4 degrees of freedom, a 1% significance level test consists of rejecting the null hypothesis if the value of the t statistic falls outside the interval $[-4.604, 4.604]$. Using the sample in display (19.2) and assuming the null hypothesis $H_0: \mu = 0$, the value of the t statistic was found to be $t \simeq -1.24$, so for this sample the t test says not to reject the null hypothesis that the underlying process mean is 0, at the 1% significance level.

[†] The null hypothesis is false whenever the actual value of μ is not equal to μ_0. The probability of a Type II error is different for different values of the actual process mean μ. Rather than report probabilities of Type II errors, most investigators prefer to report probabilities of rejecting the null hypothesis for different values of μ. The resulting function is called the *power function* of the significance test. A value of μ that is not equal to μ_0 is called an **alternative hypothesis** to the null hypothesis. The probability of rejecting the null hypothesis when the actual process mean has alternative value μ is called the **power** of the test at that alternative. Power refers to the test's ability to reject a false null hypothesis. The higher the power, the better the test is able to detect that the corresponding alternative, rather than the null, hypothesis is true.

What if $H_0: \mu = 1$ had been used as the null hypothesis? Then the t statistic would have been

$$t = (-0.615 - 1)/0.497 \simeq -3.25$$

which is also in the interval of plausible values. This t test says not to reject the null hypothesis that the underlying process mean is 1, at the 1% significance level. On the basis of the data in display (19.2) and a t test at the 1% significance level, neither 0 nor 1 can be rejected as plausible values of the underlying process mean!

What if $H_0: \mu = 1.7$ had been used as the null hypothesis? Then the t statistic would have been

$$t = (-0.615 - 1.7)/0.497 \simeq -4.66$$

which is outside the interval of plausible values and is therefore statistically significant at the 1% significance level. The t test says to reject the hypothesis that the underlying process mean is 1.7. ▪

This example emphasizes that a t statistic is a function of both the data and the null hypothesis; it is a vehicle for comparing a hypothesized value of the process mean with data drawn from the process. For a given sample of data, some hypotheses yield significant t statistics and some do not.

▪ **EXAMPLE 19.4C:** The set of null hypotheses that are not rejected by the significance test can be obtained as follows. Use the sample in display (19.2) as given. Then the set of null hypotheses μ_0 not rejected by the t test at the 1% significance level is the set that yields t statistics in the interval of plausible values, namely, those for which

$$-4.604 \leq \frac{(-0.615 - \mu_0)}{0.497} \leq 4.604$$

or those for which

$$(-4.604)(0.497) \leq -0.615 - \mu_0 \leq (4.604)(0.497)$$

or for which
$$-2.90 \leq \mu_0 \leq 1.673$$

The interval of null hypotheses that cannot be rejected using a specific sample and using the t test at the 1% significance level is a **confidence interval** for the process mean with a 99% confidence coefficient. The **confidence coefficient**, one minus the significance level of the test upon which a confidence interval is based, is just 100% minus 1%. The confidence interval is interpreted as the set of plausible guesses at the process mean, given the sample. ▪

The argument in Example 19.4C could have been repeated for a 5% significance level test, in which case the confidence coefficient would have been 95%. The argument can be repeated for any sample and any given significance level. In principle, a confidence interval can always be obtained by considering a sample, a significance test, and a significance level. This principle applies in general, not just to the t test.

EXERCISES

19.5A Assume you have drawn a random sample of size $n = 15$ observations from a normal process with unknown mean μ and unknown standard deviation σ. The sample mean and standard deviation are $\bar{y} = 33.6$ and $s = 5.2$. You have been asked to comment on the null hypothesis $H_0 : \mu = 36.5$.
(a) Perform the t test at the 5% significance level.
(b) Perform the t test at the 1% significance level.
(c) Compare the conclusions of the two tests in parts (a) and (b).
(d) Construct the 99% confidence interval for μ.
(e) Discuss the meaning of the confidence interval in part (d).

19.5B Repeat Exercise 19.5A with $n = 9$, $\bar{y} = 102.4$, $s = 9.8$, and $H_0 : \mu = 100$.

19.5C Repeat Exercise 19.5B with $n = 900$, $\bar{y} = 102.4$, $s = 9.8$, and $H_0 : \mu = 100$.

19.5D Compare the results of Exercises 19.5B and 19.5C.

19.5E Repeat Exercise 19.5A with $n = 900$, $\bar{y} = 3.9$, $s = 1.0$, and $H_0 : \mu = 3$.

19.5F Explain why different analysts can draw opposite conclusions from the same data using significance tests. What are some of the considerations that go into choosing a significance level? Can there be a completely objective way of choosing a significance level?

19.5G Write a two-to-three-page essay interpreting mean control charts as applications of the t test for a process mean. What role does statistical control play in this application? What impact does lack of statistical control have on the validity of the significance test?

19.5H Write a three-to-five-page essay that outlines the rationale of significance testing using the t test for a process mean. Use simulations to illustrate your points. Why must researchers risk drawing wrong conclusions?

19.5I Find an article in a publication in your field in which a t test is reported. Write a brief essay on the problem addressed by the article. Does the article discuss clearly the process used to collect data? Was it in statistical control? Are you convinced that the conclusions drawn from the test are valid? Why or why not? What significance level was used? Why?

t STATISTICS FOR NONNORMAL PROCESSES[†]

Sections 19.2 and 19.4 investigated the sampling variation of t statistics when random samples were drawn from processes with normal cross-sectional distributions. In this section the behavior of t statistics when the cross-sectional distribution of a process is not normal is discussed. Understanding such behavior is of practical interest because nonnormal processes are common. If we choose to use a significance test or confidence interval based on the t statistic when the process is not normal, do we run a substantial risk that the significance test or confidence interval responds differently to the nonnormal process than to the normal one? If so, the nature of the nonnormality must be diagnosed and a test statistic appropriate for the process developed. If not, the t statistic can be used *as if* the process were normal. Statistical theory and practice support the latter case.

[†] This section deals with advanced topics and should be treated as optional reading.

For moderate to large sample sizes, the sampling distribution of the t statistic is about the same regardless of the cross-sectional distribution of the underlying process. Because of this behavior, statisticians call the t statistic *robust*. The secret to the robustness of the t statistic is doing the sampling at random. Failure to obtain a random sample much more seriously compromises the performance of the t statistic than mild departures from normality in the underlying process. The simulations in this section illustrate the robust behavior of the t statistic.

■**EXAMPLE 19.6A:** As a first illustration, the drawing of random samples of size 50 from a Bernoulli process with $\pi = 0.7$ is simulated. The Bernoulli distribution is a discrete, skewed distribution very different from a continuous, symmetric normal

EXHIBIT 19.6A

Histogram and Descriptive Statistics for 200 t Statistics Based on Random Samples of Size 50 from a Bernoulli Process with $\pi = 0.7$

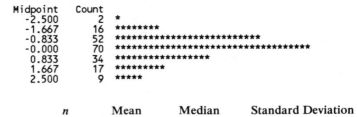

```
Histogram of t    N=200
Each * represents two observations

Midpoint    Count
 -2.500       2    *
 -1.667      16    ********
 -0.833      52    **************************
 -0.000      70    ***********************************
  0.833      34    *****************
  1.667      17    *********
  2.500       9    *****
```

	n	Mean	Median	Standard Deviation
t	200	-0.0012	0.0000	1.0005

EXHIBIT 19.6B

Normal Probability Plot for 200 t Statistics Based on Random Samples of Size 50 from a Bernoulli Process with $\pi = 0.7$

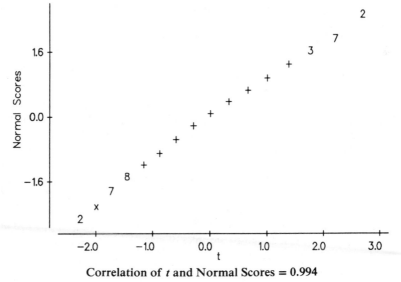

Correlation of t and Normal Scores = 0.994

distribution. For each sample the t statistic

$$t = \frac{\bar{y} - 0.7}{s/\sqrt{50}} = \frac{\sqrt{50}(\bar{y} - 0.7)}{s}$$

is computed, which is the t statistic computed if the null hypothesis coincides with the long-run process mean of 0.7. Exhibit 19.6A shows a histogram of 200 simulated samples. Exhibit 19.6B shows a normal probability plot of the 200 t statistics. This plot is appropriate because with 49 degrees of freedom, the t sampling distribution is essentially a standard normal distribution. The 200 t statistics computed from data from a Bernoulli process behave remarkably like t statistics from a normal process.

▪

▪**EXAMPLE 19.6B:** This example uses data reported in J. O. Ramsay, "Monotone Regression Splines in Action," *Statistical Science* 3(4) (November 1988): 425–441. Below are makes of 21 automobiles and their weights in 100-kilogram units. The data were originally reported in 1986 issues of *Consumer Reports*.

Make	Weight (100 kg)
Chevrolet Spectrum	8.7
Dodge Omni	9.5
Dodge Colt	9.9
Chevrolet Chevette	10.0
Chevrolet Nova	10.2
Ford Escort	10.9
Dodge Aires	11.5
Pontiac Fiero	11.5
Chevrolet Cavalier	11.6
Chrysler Le Baron	11.7
Ford Tempo	11.8
Oldsmobile Calais	12.0
Buick Century	12.6
Pontiac 6000	12.6
Chrysler Laser	12.7
Dodge Lancer	12.7
Mercury Cougar	14.1
Buick Electra	15.0
Oldsmobile Cutlass	15.2
Chrysler Fifth Avenue	16.2
Chevrolet Caprice	16.5

Exhibit 19.6C shows a dotplot of the 21 weights, which have a mean of 12.233 100s of kilograms. The distribution of the weights will be used as a population from which to draw samples of size 21 *with replacement*. In other words, on each of the 21

draws each of the weights in the list of automobiles will have a 1/21 probability of being drawn. With this scheme, any of the weights can be drawn into the sample several times.

EXHIBIT 19.6C

Dotplot of Weights of 21 Automobiles Listed in Exhibit 19.6B

```
                      .              .
  . .  .   . ...  .  :...  ::    .      ..     . .
----:-+-------:----+---------:--+--------+---------+---------:-+-  Weight
    9.0     10.5      12.0       13.5      15.0      16.5
```

The sampling scheme outlined here is an example of **bootstrapping**. The idea is this: Use the sample actually obtained from the process as a basis for simulating possible samples from the process and studying the sampling variation in statistics computed from these samples. The simulated samples are called *bootstrap samples*. By drawing these samples with replacement from the data, many variations on the actual sample can be obtained. If the empirical cumulative distribution function of the actual sample is a good estimate of the cumulative distribution function of the underlying process, then the distribution of a statistic computed from the bootstrap samples should be a good estimate of the sampling distribution of the statistic. Recent statistical research has shown that bootstrapping does work this way in certain situations. It is especially effective in studying the behavior of statistics computed from data drawn from nonnormal processes. Consequently, bootstrapping is a tool that can be used when the *t* distribution is not appropriate.

From the automobile weights above, 250 bootstrap samples of size 21 were generated. For each sample the sample mean $\bar{y}$, the sample standard deviation s, and the *t* statistic

$$t = \frac{\bar{y} - 12.233}{s/\sqrt{21}} = \frac{\sqrt{21}(\bar{y} - 12.233)}{s}$$

were computed.[†]

Exhibit 19.6D shows a quantile-quantile plot of the 250 *t* statistics. (Quantile-quantile plots are explained in Section 18.2.) The quantiles on the vertical axis are taken from a *t* distribution with 20 degrees of freedom. If the 250 bootstrapped *t* statistics were from a *t* distribution with 20 degrees of freedom, the quantile-quantile plot would display a straight line. The similarity to a straight line over most of the plot is remarkable; only in the left-hand tail is there a serious departure from

---

[†] With the weights in column C1 and 1/21 in each row of column C2, Minitab commands to simulate the samples are

```
RANDOM 250 C11-C31;
DISCRETE C1 C2.
RMEAN C11-C31 C32
RSTAN C11-C31 C33
LET C34 = SQRT(21)*(C32 – 12.233)/C33
```

linearity. Some descriptive statistics for the two sets of quantiles are also given. These statistics show that the bootstrap distribution is slightly skewed to the left, not centered on 0, and slightly less variable than the *t* distribution with 20 degrees of freedom.

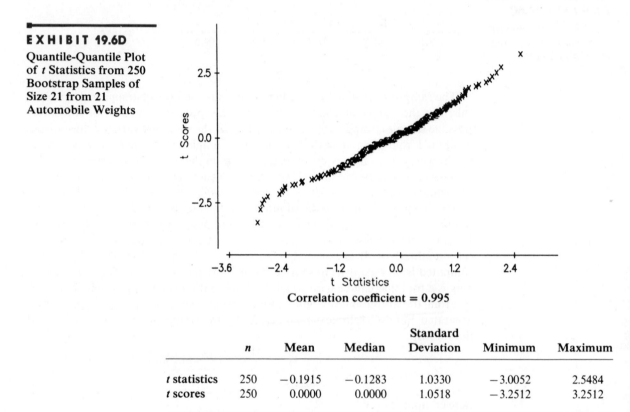

EXHIBIT 19.6D

Quantile-Quantile Plot of *t* Statistics from 250 Bootstrap Samples of Size 21 from 21 Automobile Weights

Correlation coefficient = 0.995

	n	Mean	Median	Standard Deviation	Minimum	Maximum
t statistics	250	−0.1915	−0.1283	1.0330	−3.0052	2.5484
t scores	250	0.0000	0.0000	1.0518	−3.2512	3.2512

Note: Quantiles on the vertical axis are from a *t* distribution with 20 degrees of freedom. Also shown are selected descriptive statistics.

The *t* distribution with 20 degrees of freedom is a "fair-to-good" first approximation to the bootstrap distribution, one that could be considered for practical use. Some recent mathematical results on bootstrapping indicate that the bootstrap is an even better approximation to the actual sampling distribution of the *t* statistics. The bootstrap distribution allows for the skewness of the sampling distribution, whereas the *t* distribution approximation imposes symmetry. With access to a computer and appropriate software, the cost of simulating this distribution is relatively small, though it would be wise to do 500 to 1000 simulations in a practical application, especially if you wanted a good estimate of extreme percentiles, such as the 0.5th, 2.5th, 97.5th, or 99.5th percentiles. ▪

Example 19.6B is illuminating. It shows that with appropriate computing power an approximation to a sampling distribution that would be tedious if not impossible to get mathematically can be obtained. On the other hand, if a computer was unavailable but a t table was available, you could appeal with some justification to the robustness of the t statistic in this case. In fact, this underlines the idea behind robustness. Using the t statistic as if it came from a normal process is justified even though the data may not come from a normal process. Doing this avoids the need to do special analysis for each problem encountered. If statistical tools like the t statistic were not robust, the practice of statistics would be tedious indeed!

SECTION 19.7

EXERCISES

19.7A Simulate 200 random samples of size $n = 15$ from a uniform distribution on $[-0.5, 0.5)$. Compute the t statistic for $H_0: \mu = 0$ for each sample. Prepare a histogram, compute descriptive statistics, and prepare a quantile-quantile plot with quantiles from a t distribution with 14 degrees of freedom on the vertical axis. How closely do the t statistics conform to the t distribution? Why is exact conformance not expected?

19.7B Repeat Exercise 19.7A drawing data from an exponential distribution.

19.7C Repeat Exercise 19.7A drawing data from any distribution you choose.

19.7D Apply the bootstrap procedure to the data in Exhibit 4.2A. Do the t statistics appear to be well approximated by the t distribution? Why or why not?

19.7E Write a one-to-two-page essay on the robustness of the t statistic and the implications robustness has for significance testing in practice.

SECTION 19.8

CHI-SQUARE STATISTICS

In Chapter 5 the analysis of multi-way tables was introduced, and in Sections 6.10, 6.12, and 6.15 Pearson's X^2 statistic as a measure of association for multi-way tables was discussed. Practitioners use Pearson's statistic heavily, both descriptively and inferentially. In this section its sampling distribution is studied, with an eye on the inferential uses.

Pearson's statistic is often referred to as a *chi-square statistic. Chi-square* is a transliteration of the mathematical symbol χ^2, which is the Greek letter *chi* to the second power. This notation is used to stand for the family of mathematical curves that describe the sampling distribution of Pearson's statistic under certain conditions. In particular, the **chi-squared distribution** is the approximate sampling distribution of Pearson's X^2 statistic when the null hypothesis of no association is true. In this section the connection between χ^2 distributions and sample variances of samples from normal populations is also discussed.

PEARSON'S χ^2 FOR 2 × 2 TABLES

Recall the notation for 2 × 2 tables introduced in Exhibit 6.10:

		W		
		W_1	W_2	Total
V	V_1	a	c	$a + c = n_{1.}$
	V_2	b	d	$b + d = n_{2.}$
	Total	$a + b = n_{.1}$	$c + d = n_{.2}$	$a + b + c + d = n$

The two categorical variables are V and W, the counts in each cell of the cross-classification are denoted by a, b, c, and d, and the row, column, and grand totals are denoted by n's with appropriate subscripts. The value of Pearson's chi-square statistic, denoted by X^2, is given by the formula

$$X^2 = \frac{n(ad - bc)^2}{(n_{.1})(n_{.2})(n_{1.})(n_{2.})} \tag{19.6}$$

As a numerical example consider the two tables displayed in Exhibit 19.8A. The computation of X^2 is shown for each table.

EXHIBIT 19.8A

Two 2 × 2 Tables and Corresponding Values of X^2

	W_1	W_2	Total		W_1	W_2	Total
V_1	40	40	80	V_1	48	36	84
V_2	60	60	120	V_2	54	62	116
Total	100	100	200	Total	102	98	200

$$X^2 = \frac{200[(40 \times 60) - (60 \times 40)]^2}{100 \times 100 \times 80 \times 120}$$

$$= 0$$

$$X^2 = \frac{200[(48 \times 62) - (54 \times 36)]^2}{102 \times 98 \times 84 \times 116}$$

$$= 2.19689$$

We wish to study instances in which tables like those in Exhibit 19.8A arise by chance because the data are a sample drawn at random from a universe. The simulations assume that the universe is very large or that sampling is done with replacement, so there is no finite population correction. The elements in the universe have a V characteristic and a W characteristic, so each element belongs to one and only one of the cells of the 2 × 2 table.

If the table on the left-hand side of Exhibit 19.8A described the universe, it would reveal that 20% [= 100 × (40/200)%] of the universe elements fall in the $V_1 \times W_1$ and $V_1 \times W_2$ cells, and 30% [= 100 × (60/200)%] of the universe elements fall in the $V_2 \times W_1$ and $V_2 \times W_2$ cells. Because the rows of this table are proportional to one another, there is no association between the variables V and W.

In the first simulation random samples of size $n = 200$ elements are drawn from such a universe. The cell counts differ in different samples because of randomness. The goal is to gain an appreciation of the amount of variation that randomness can cause. In particular, we wish to observe the sampling distribution of Pearson's chi-square statistic, because this will provide a basis for forming a significance test.

Exhibit 19.8B shows the numerical values and a dot diagram of X^2 statistics resulting from 51 independent random samples of size 200.[†] The values are reported in increasing numerical order rather than in the order drawn. Also shown are some descriptive statistics for the 51 values of X^2. Notice that the frequency distribution is quite skewed to the right. If a very large number of samples were drawn and a dot-plot of the resulting X^2 statistics were made, then for practical purposes, the χ^2 distribution with 1 degree of freedom would be obtained, because there is 1 degree of freedom associated with a 2×2 table.[††]

The graph of the χ^2 with 1 degree of freedom is the continuous curve shown at the bottom of Exhibit 19.8B. It looks somewhat like a J that has been rotated clockwise $90°$, so it is sometimes called a J-shaped curve.

The mean and standard deviation of the theoretical χ^2 distribution with 1 degree of freedom are 1 and $\sqrt{2} \simeq 1.414$. The descriptive statistics in Exhibit 19.8B show that the sample mean and standard deviation of the 51 simulated values of X^2 are 1.146 and 1.536, quite close to the theoretical values. As usual, the discrepancies between empirical and theoretical values are due to sampling error. Only 51 observations from the sampling distribution have been observed, so substantial sampling errors are possible.

The next simulation is of 51 random samples drawn from a different universe, one in which 20% of the elements are in the $V_1 \times W_1$ cell, 30% are in the $V_2 \times W_1$ cell, 40% are in the $V_1 \times W_2$ cell, and 10% are in the $V_2 \times W_2$ cell. In contrast to the first simulation, the rows of the table in this universe are not proportional to each other, so there is association between the variables. The simulation will show that this fact changes the sampling distribution of X^2. Because of this, X^2 is a useful test statistic for a significance test that attempts to distinguish among different types of behaviors

---

[†] A simple Minitab program that simulates a table is

```
READ INTO C1 AND C2
1    0.2
2    0.3
3    0.2
4    0.3
END
RANDOM 200 C3;
  DISCRETE C1 C2.
INDICATOR C3 C4 C5 C6 C7
LET C8(1)=SUM(C4)
LET C8(2)=SUM(C5)
LET C9(1)=SUM(C6)
LET C9(2)=SUM(C7)
```

The 2×2 table is in the first two rows of columns C8 and C9.

[††] A general $r \times c$ table has degrees of freedom

$$v = (r - 1)(c - 1)$$

that is, (number of rows minus 1)(number of columns minus 1).

EXHIBIT 19.8B

Simulation of 51 Values of X^2 from a Universe with No Association and Graph of a χ^2 Distribution with 1 Degree of Freedom

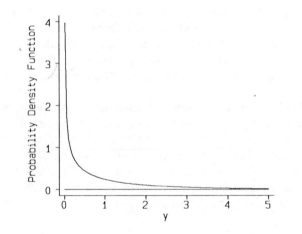

0.00092	0.00334	0.00975	0.04500	0.05493	0.06616	0.06903
0.09280	0.13629	0.16148	0.16168	0.16344	0.16991	0.27397
0.29173	0.32471	0.34189	0.34189	0.43544	0.44891	0.47406
0.53534	0.54657	0.57716	0.59064	0.63179	0.66289	0.68396
0.70105	0.70267	0.71286	0.78210	0.94481	1.00917	1.06999
1.12234	1.21828	1.23058	1.30559	1.45631	1.70366	1.82185
1.84174	1.88783	2.01587	2.97641	3.27336	3.97379	4.89745
6.65738	6.85251					

```
          ::. :.
          ::.:: .
          ::::::.::....::       .  .      .         . .
        -+---------+---------+---------+---------+---------+- χ²
        0.0       1.5       3.0       4.5       6.0       7.5
```

	n	Mean	Median	Standard Deviation	Minimum	Maximum
X^2	51	1.146	0.632	1.536	0.001	6.853

of categorical variables. The significance test will be explained in more detail later in the section.

Exhibit 19.8C shows the values and a dotplot of X^2 resulting from 51 random samples of size $n = 200$ from the universe described above. The association in the variables causes the distribution of X^2 to shift to the right, that is, the values of X^2 tend to be larger, on the whole, than they were when the samples were from variables with no association. Notice that the mean and standard deviation of the 51 values of X^2 are 10.284 and 5.854.

The observed shift is a theoretically predictable property of X^2. A shift to the right would have occurred no matter what type of association had been built into the simulation. Some associations cause bigger shifts than others, but the shift always tends to make X^2 bigger, on the whole, than it is when the variables do not interact.

EXHIBIT 19.8C

Simulation of 51 Values of X^2 from a Universe with Association

1.5552	2.7653	2.9091	3.1258	3.1988	3.2613	4.5779
4.8878	5.2342	5.7155	5.7385	6.2780	6.4195	6.4826
6.5455	6.6724	6.8990	6.9588	6.9977	7.0546	7.2062
7.8561	7.8785	8.0867	8.3162	8.3162	8.5633	8.6642
8.8820	9.4762	9.6526	10.6065	12.1062	12.8348	12.9884
13.0288	13.5032	13.5254	13.6999	14.6089	14.7625	15.2312
16.5431	16.5748	17.4088	18.7754	19.6966	20.3407	21.7815
24.1635	26.1516					

```
                    ..
          :       :: .:
    .  :. .:: :: ::.:. .   ..
  .  :.  .:: :: ::.:.  . .:: .: :  .  ..   .     .     .     x²
  +---------+---------+---------+---------+---------+---------+---
 0.0       5.0      10.0      15.0      20.0      25.0
```

	n	Mean	Median	Standard Deviation	Minimum	Maximum
X^2	51	10.284	8.316	5.854	1.555	26.152

The principle stated in the preceding paragraph is the basis for a significance test in which the null hypothesis is that the categorical variables do not interact in the universe. When this null hypothesis is true and the table is 2×2, then the sampling distribution of X^2 is approximately χ^2 with 1 degree of freedom. We know that if the variables do interact in the universe, then the values of X^2 tend to be shifted to the right, so sufficiently large values of X^2 should be taken as evidence against the null hypothesis.

It can be shown theoretically that the 95th percentile of the χ^2 distribution with 1 degree of freedom is 3.841. If a 5% significance level is desired, the null hypothesis is rejected whenever the value of X^2 is greater than 3.841. If this rule is followed, there is a 5% risk of declaring a true null hypothesis false. It can also be shown that the 99th percentile of the χ^2 distribution with 1 degree of freedom is 6.635, so if a 1% significance level is desired, the null hypothesis is rejected whenever the value of X^2 is greater than 6.635.

How do the results in Exhibits 19.8B and 19.8C compare to theoretical predictions? In Exhibit 19.8B there are four values of X^2 greater than 3.841. This yields a percentage of Type I errors of $100(4/51)\% \simeq 8\%$, which is reasonably close to the theoretical value of 5%. In Exhibit 19.8C there are only six values of X^2 less than 3.841, yielding a percentage of Type II errors of $100(6/51)\% \simeq 12\%$. The significance test seems quite capable of signalling the type of association represented in the second simulation at the 5% significance level.

In Exhibit 19.8B there are two values of X^2 greater than 6.635. This yields a percentage of Type I errors of $100(2/51)\% \simeq 4\%$, which is somewhat close to the theoretical value of 1%. In Exhibit 19.8C there are 15 values of X^2 less than 6.635, yielding a percentage of Type II errors of $100(15/51)\% \simeq 29\%$.

Keep in mind that only 51 replications were done in the simulations. This number is too small to achieve the results predicted by mathematical theory, but the discrepancies between the simulated and theoretical results are well within the bounds of sampling error. Moreover, the example provides some insight into the practical application of significance tests. Hundreds of significance tests are not performed in the same environment, or probably even over an entire career. Thus the "long-run" results of theory must be viewed as theoretical characteristics of the procedures used, not as hard-and-fast predictions of success when a relatively small number of significance tests are performed. The simulations help point out the real risks inherent in making inferences from incomplete data!

The mathematical theory for Pearson's chi-square statistic says that as the sample size, n, gets larger, the sampling distribution of X^2 becomes more nearly like a χ^2 distribution with 1 degree of freedom, provided the null hypothesis of no association is true. This type of statement also occurs in the central limit effect, which guarantees approximate normality of totals and means, provided the sample size is large enough. As seen in Chapter 8, for some processes even small samples yield totals and means that are essentially normal. For the chi-square approximation, however, fairly large sample sizes are needed.

Guidelines on how large the sample size needs to be have been debated extensively in the statistical literature, but no universally accepted advice is available. A conservative rule that is easy to apply is recommended here: Do not rely on the χ^2 approximation unless the sample size is at least 50 and all the cell frequencies are at least 5.

Another thorny question in applications of Pearson's chi-square statistic is that of sampling design. The theory discussed here assumes simple random sampling with replacement, but in practice this design is rare. Recent research on complex sampling designs shows clearly that Pearson's X^2 statistic has different sampling distributions when different sampling designs are used, and the differences seriously affect the significance levels of significance tests. Because of this, X^2 should be used cautiously when making probabilistic inferences.

PEARSON'S CHI-SQUARE FOR $r \times c$ TABLES

The chi-square test of the null hypothesis of no association in a general $r \times c$ two-way table is very simple to perform. First compute the value of X^2, using the formula given in Chapter 6. Then compute the associated degrees of freedom

$$v = (r - 1)(c - 1) \tag{19.7}$$

Next choose the level of significance, which is denoted by α. Now there is a different χ^2 distribution for each value of the degrees of freedom, so you must have a table of percentiles of χ^2 distributions or access to a computer program that outputs the appropriate percentiles.

Exhibit 19.8D is a small table of percentiles of selected χ^2 distributions. Suppose you want to perform a chi-square test for a 5×3 table. Here $r = 5$ and $c = 3$, so the degrees of freedom is equal to $v = 4 \times 2 = 8$. If a 5% significance level is desired, use the 95th percentile of the χ^2 distribution with 8 degrees of freedom, which is 15.507. If a 1% significance level is desired, find the 99th percentile, which is 20.090. The degrees of freedom determine which row of the table is used. The experimenter chooses the significance level to reflect the appropriate amount of risk associated with the Type I error.

EXHIBIT 19.8D   Selected Percentiles of Chi-Square Distributions with v Degrees of Freedom

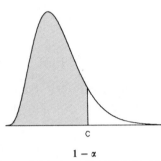

$1 - \alpha$

v	0.010	0.050	0.100	0.300	0.500	0.700	0.900	0.950	0.990	0.999
1	0.0002	0.0039	0.0158	0.1485	0.4549	1.0742	2.7055	3.8415	6.6349	10.8277
2	0.0201	0.1026	0.2107	0.7133	1.3863	2.4079	4.6052	5.9915	9.2103	13.8155
3	0.1148	0.3518	0.5844	1.4237	2.3660	3.6649	6.2514	7.8147	11.3449	16.2663
4	0.2971	0.7107	1.0636	2.1947	3.3567	4.8784	7.7794	9.4877	13.2767	18.4669
5	0.5543	1.1455	1.6103	2.9999	4.3515	6.0644	9.2364	11.0705	15.0863	20.5150
6	0.8721	1.6354	2.2041	3.8276	5.3481	7.2311	10.6446	12.5916	16.8119	22.4578
7	1.2390	2.1674	2.8331	4.6713	6.3458	8.3834	12.0170	14.0671	18.4753	24.3220
8	1.6465	2.7326	3.4895	5.5274	7.3441	9.5245	13.3616	15.5073	20.0902	26.1246
9	2.0879	3.3251	4.1682	6.3933	8.3428	10.6564	14.6837	16.9190	21.6660	27.8771
10	2.5582	3.9403	4.8652	7.2672	9.3418	11.7807	15.9872	18.3070	23.2093	29.5884
11	3.0535	4.5748	5.5778	8.1479	10.3410	12.8987	17.2750	19.6751	24.7250	31.2642
12	3.5706	5.2260	6.3038	9.0343	11.3403	14.0111	18.5493	21.0261	26.2170	32.9097
13	4.1069	5.8919	7.0415	9.9257	12.3398	15.1187	19.8119	22.3620	27.6882	34.5278
14	4.6604	6.5706	7.7895	10.8215	13.3393	16.2221	21.0641	23.6848	29.1413	36.1235
15	5.2293	7.2609	8.5468	11.7212	14.3389	17.3217	22.3071	24.9958	30.5779	37.6973

Note: The body of the table shows values of c such that $1 - \alpha$ is the area bounded by the horizontal axis, a vertical line located at c, and the chi-square curve.

Once the correct percentile of the appropriate χ^2 distribution has been found, simply compare the sample value of X^2 to that percentile. If X^2 is greater than the chosen percentile, the test says to reject the null hypothesis; the X^2 is statistically significant. If X^2 is less than the chosen percentile, the test says not to reject the null hypothesis of no association. If you do not reject the null hypothesis, you conclude that knowledge of one of the variables for a particular element in the universe provides very little information about the value of the other variable for that element. That is the practical effect of the no-association hypothesis.

Again, use X^2 cautiously to make probabilistic inferences. The major practical question is the sampling design. Unless the use of simple random sampling can be substantiated, the theory discussed above should be used with extreme caution.

SAMPLE VARIANCES OF NORMAL SAMPLES (OPTIONAL)

In the previous subsection an application in which the χ^2 distribution emerged as an approximation to the sampling distribution of Pearson's chi-square test statistic was presented. This subsection presents a case in which the χ^2 distribution is an exact sampling distribution. This case arises when the question, What is the sampling distribution of the sample variance? is asked.

Let $y_1, y_2, \ldots, y_n$ denote data from a simple random sample from a process that is normally distributed with mean μ and standard deviation σ. Recall that the sample variance is just the square of the standard deviation, so the variance is

$$s^2 = \frac{1}{n-1} \sum_{i=1}^{n} (y_i - \bar{y})^2 \qquad \text{(19.8)}$$

The mathematical theory of statistics shows that the sampling distribution of the random quantity $(n-1)s^2/\sigma^2$ is χ^2 with $n-1$ degrees of freedom. This is an exact result and is appropriately used only when the underlying process distribution is normal. It is not a robust result like the central limit effect or the robustness of the t statistic. In the exercises in Section 19.9 you are asked to construct a simulation study to illustrate this result and to study its lack of robustness.

S E C T I O N 19.9

EXERCISES

19.9A For each of the 2×2 tables below compute the value of X^2 and perform the chi-square test of the null hypothesis of no association at the 5% and 1% significance levels.
(a) $a = 5, b = 50, c = 175, d = 1750$ (b) $a = 25, b = 50, c = 175, d = 350$
(c) $a = 5, b = 50, c = 175, d = 350$ (d) $a = 25, b = 50, c = 175, d = 1750$
(e) $a = 50, b = 50, c = 175, d = 350$

19.9B For each of the 3×2 tables below compute the value of X^2 and perform the chi-square test of the null hypothesis of no association at the 5% and 1% significance levels.
(a) 14 78 (b) 14 28 (c) 28 78
     8 37   8 16   16 37
    23 92   23 46   46 92

19.9C Find the values from the χ^2 table that yield 5% and 1% significance levels of the chi-square test of no association when the dimensions of the two-way table are
(a) 4×4 (b) 5×4 (c) 8×3 (d) 3×6

19.9D Find an article in a publication in your field in which a chi-square test is reported. Write a brief essay on the problem addressed by the article. Does the article discuss clearly the process used to collect data? Was it in statistical control? Are you convinced that the conclusions drawn from the test are valid? Why or why not? What significance level was used? Why?

19.9E (a) Show that

$$\sum_{i=1}^{n} y_i^2 = n\bar{y}^2 + \sum_{i=1}^{n} (y_i - \bar{y})^2.$$

This is the simplest possible example of what statisticians call the analysis of variance. Note that $\sum_{i=1}^{n}(y_i - \bar{y})^2 = (n-1)s^2$.

(b) Show that

$$\sum_{i=1}^{n}(y_i - \mu)^2 = n(\bar{y} - \mu)^2 + \sum_{i=1}^{n}(y_i - \bar{y})^2 = n(\bar{y} - \mu)^2 + (n-1)s^2$$

Part (a) is a special case of this result for $\mu = 0$.

(c) Divide each member of the equation in part (b) by σ^2 to show that

$$\sum_{i=1}^{n}\left(\frac{y_i - \mu}{\sigma}\right)^2 = \left(\frac{\bar{y} - \mu}{\sigma/\sqrt{n}}\right)^2 + \frac{1}{\sigma^2}\sum_{i=1}^{n}(y_i - \bar{y})^2$$

$$= \left(\frac{\bar{y} - \mu}{\sigma/\sqrt{n}}\right)^2 + \frac{(n-1)s^2}{\sigma^2}$$

The result in part (a) is a special case of this result with $\mu = 0$ and $\sigma = 1$.

19.9F (Continuation of 19.9E) Here is a theoretical result: If $y_1, y_2, \ldots, y_n$ is a random sample from a normal distribution with mean μ and standard deviation σ, then the quantity on the left-hand side of the equation in part (c) of Exercise 19.9E has a χ^2 distribution with n degrees of freedom, the first quantity on the right-hand side has a χ^2 distribution with 1 degree of freedom, and the second quantity on the right-hand side has a χ^2 distribution with $n - 1$ degrees of freedom.

(a) Simulate the drawing of 200 samples of size $n = 9$ from a standard normal distribution and compute each of the quantities displayed in part (a) of Exercise 19.9E for each sample. Make dotplots and quantile plots and compute descriptive statistics for each set of 200 quantities so calculated. Do the quantities appear to have χ^2 distributions?

(b) Simulate the drawing of 200 samples of size $n = 9$ from a normal distribution with mean 100 and standard deviation 10. Compute each of the quantities displayed in part (c) of Exercise 19.9E for each sample. Make dotplots and quantile plots and compute descriptive statistics for each set of 200 quantities so calculated. Do the quantities appear to have χ^2 distributions?

(c) Do quantile-quantile plots of comparable quantities simulated in parts (a) and (b). The plots should be close to straight lines. Why?

19.9G Repeat part (a) of Exercise 19.9F drawing the samples from a uniform distribution on the interval $[-\sqrt{3}, \sqrt{3}]$. The simulated quantities should not appear to have χ^2 distributions, thus illustrating the lack of robustness of the sampling distribution of s^2.

19.9H Repeat part (a) of Exercise 19.9F drawing the samples from an exponential distribution. The simulated quantities should not appear to have χ^2 distributions, thus illustrating the lack of robustness of the sampling distribution of s^2.

SECTION 19.10

TWO-SAMPLE *t* STATISTICS
FOR THE DIFFERENCES BETWEEN TWO SAMPLE MEANS

One of the more common applications of inferential statistics is to use two sample means to infer differences in process means. Under certain conditions, the two-sample *t* procedure can be used to make the inferences.

▪ **EXAMPLE 19.10A:** A process in statistical control is to be improved. A control chart of some quality characteristic has been kept during the period prior to improvement efforts. A new method of operating is now standardized and the process is brought into statistical control. The control chart kept after standardizing the improvement is compared to the control chart kept before improvement in hopes of documenting a measurable effect. If the new mean level of the characteristic is significantly different from the old mean level, then a measurable effect can be claimed. Two-sample t significance tests can be used to document the effect. ▪

▪ **EXAMPLE 19.10B:** An insurance company wishes to measure the impact of two advertising documents on potential buyers of insurance. A mailing list of prospects is divided into two groups at random. One group receives one advertising document, the other group receives the other document. The prospects are followed up in the company's usual way by telephone and personal visit, if appropriate. After one year the amounts of insurance sold to members of the two groups are recorded. Among other comparisons, the means of the two sets of amounts are compared. Because the groups were formed at random, a state of statistical control that justifies the procedure discussed in this section is imposed on the experiment. ▪

Both examples have the following elements in common:

▪ Metric data

▪ Two groups to be compared

▪ Data generated independently from two groups

▪ The processes generating the data in statistical control

If these elements are present, then the two-sample t procedure usually works quite well for practical purposes. The details of the testing procedure are presented below.

TWO-SAMPLE t TEST OF NO DIFFERENCE BETWEEN GROUP MEANS

Let n_1 denote the number of items of data in the first group, and let $\bar{y}_1$ and s_1 denote the sample mean and standard deviation of the data. Let n_2, $\bar{y}_2$, and s_2 denote the same quantities for the second group. A **two-sample t statistic** is formed by computing[†]

$$t = \frac{\bar{y}_1 - \bar{y}_2}{\sqrt{\dfrac{s_1^2}{n_1} + \dfrac{s_2^2}{n_2}}}$$

(19.9)

[†] Theorem 6 in Section 18.8 yields some insight into the origin of the formula in Equation (19.9). In the notation of Theorem 6, let $x = \bar{y}_1$, $y = \bar{y}_2$, and $v = \bar{y}_1 - \bar{y}_2$. If the data from the two groups are independent random samples, then the covariance between $\bar{y}_1$ and $\bar{y}_2$ is zero, that is, $\sigma_{\bar{y}_1,\bar{y}_2} = 0$. Thus $\mu_{\bar{y}_1 - \bar{y}_2} = \mu_1 - \mu_2$ and

$$\sigma_{\bar{y}_1 - \bar{y}_2} = \sqrt{\sigma_{\bar{y}_1}^2 + \sigma_{\bar{y}_2}^2} = \sqrt{\frac{\sigma_1^2}{n_1} + \frac{\sigma_2^2}{n_2}}$$

Now if $\mu_1 = \mu_2$, then $\mu_1 - \mu_2 = 0$, and the difference in the sample means standardized by subtracting this theoretical mean 0 and the *estimated* standard deviation (with σ's replaced by s's) is given by Equation (19.9).

■EXAMPLE 19.10C: As a numerical illustration, suppose the data yield the following statistics:

i	$\bar{y}_i$	s_i	n_i
1	21.0	2.2	32
2	22.5	1.9	13

The numerator of the *t* statistic is

$$\bar{y}_1 - \bar{y}_2 = 21.0 - 22.5 = -1.5$$

The denominator of the *t* statistic is

$$\sqrt{\frac{s_1^2}{n_1} + \frac{s_2^2}{n_2}} = \sqrt{\frac{2.2^2}{32} + \frac{1.9^2}{13}} = \sqrt{0.15125 + 0.27769} \simeq 0.655$$

Finally, the value of the *t* statistic is

$$t = \frac{-1.5}{0.655} = -2.29$$

■

The theory in the next paragraph underlies the use of the *t* statistic as a significance test statistic for comparing two means. The theory is exact if the cross-sectional distributions of the underlying processes are normal. Otherwise we appeal to the robustness of the *t* statistic. In the latter case, the reliability of the *t* distribution approximation is enhanced by having large sample sizes. When the two sample sizes are both small, say, less than 15 or 20, then robustness is enhanced by making the two sample sizes equal.

Let μ_1 and μ_2 denote the means of the two underlying processes. Adopt a null hypothesis of equality of these two means, that is H_0: $\mu_1 = \mu_2$. If this hypothesis cannot be rejected, the evidence for a difference between the process means is very weak. Given the assumptions outlined above, the following statement can be asserted:

If the null hypothesis H_0: $\mu_1 = \mu_2$ is true, then the sampling distribution of the *t* statistic in Equation (19.9) is a *t* distribution with degrees of freedom v computed by the formula

$$\frac{1}{v} = \frac{a^2}{n_1 - 1} + \frac{(1 - a)^2}{n_2 - 1} \tag{19.10}$$

where the parameter a is computed from the formula

$$a = \frac{\dfrac{s_1^2}{n_1}}{\dfrac{s_1^2}{n_1} + \dfrac{s_2^2}{n_2}} \tag{19.11}$$

This result allows the following significance test to be conducted:

(1) Compute the t statistic in Equation (19.9).

(2) Compute the degrees of freedom v in Equation (19.10).

(3) Choose a significance level α.

(4) Determine the $100(1 - \alpha/2)$th percentile of the t distribution with v degrees of freedom, denoted by $t_{1-\alpha/2}(v)$.

(5) Reject H_0 at the $100\alpha\%$ significance level if $|t| > t_{1-\alpha/2}(v)$; otherwise, do not reject H_0.

In implementing this test, you will find that the degrees of freedom parameter v is seldom an integer, but tables of the t distribution report only integer values of the degrees of freedom. For practical applications, simply use the smallest integer degrees of freedom that is greater than v. As an alternative, computer software that gives percentiles of the t distribution can compute the exact percentile for degrees of freedom that are not integers.

▪ **EXAMPLE 19.10D:** Continuing Example 19.10C, compute the degrees of freedom and perform the significance test. The value of the parameter a is

$$a = \frac{\dfrac{2.2^2}{32}}{\dfrac{2.2^2}{32} + \dfrac{1.9^2}{13}} = \frac{0.15125}{0.15125 + 0.27769} = 0.352612$$

Thus $\dfrac{1}{v} = \left[\dfrac{0.3522612^2}{31}\right] + \dfrac{(1 - 0.3522612)^2}{12} = 0.004003 + 0.034964 = 0.038967$

and $v = 1/0.038967 \simeq 25.66 \simeq 26$. Using the t-table row corresponding to 26 degrees of freedom, the 97.5th percentile is 2.056 and the 99.5th percentile is 2.779. These are the tabled values needed to perform significance tests at the 5% and 1% significance levels.

Using the data in Example 19.10C, the value of the t statistic is -2.29. Because $|t| = 2.29 > 2.056$, the null hypothesis would be rejected at the 5% significance level. Because $|t| = 2.29 < 2.779$, the null hypothesis would not be rejected at the 1% significance level. This example underlines the importance of having some idea of the desired level of risk when doing the significance test. The t statistic signals different actions depending on the level of significance, which is a parameter chosen by the experimenter. It is impossible to use the test as a basis for action if you have no idea what significance level is appropriate.

This example also shows how different analysts can reach different conclusions after looking at the same data. Two analysts with different significance levels can actually come to opposite conclusions about the implications of a statistic! When this happens, the analysts may

(1) Negotiate a significance level they can both agree on

(2) Agree to seek more data and perform the test again to see if the conclusion is clear-cut

(3) Simply agree to disagree ▪

TWO-SAMPLE *t* TEST FOR ARBITRARY DIFFERENCE OF GROUP MEANS

Occasionally, researchers need to test whether the difference between two group means is equal to a nonzero quantity. Then the null hypothesis is

$$H_0: \mu_1 - \mu_2 = \delta$$

where δ denotes the specified difference between the theoretical means. The significance testing procedure exactly parallels that outlined in the preceding subsection except that the *t* statistic is computed from the formula

$$t = \frac{\bar{y}_1 - \bar{y}_2 - \delta}{\sqrt{\dfrac{s_1^2}{n_1} + \dfrac{s_2^2}{n_2}}} \tag{19.12}$$

instead of the formula in Equation (19.9).

CONFIDENCE INTERVALS FOR A DIFFERENCE IN MEANS

The *t* statistic in Equation (19.12) can be used as a basis for an approximate confidence interval for the difference in the theoretical means of the two groups. Theory says that under appropriate conditions, to a good approximation, the statistic in Equation (19.12) has a *t* distribution with v degrees of freedom, where v is given by Equation (19.10). Thus, solving the inequality

$$|t| < t_{1-\alpha/2}(v) \tag{19.13}$$

for δ provides an interval of differences that cannot be rejected by the significance test at the $100\alpha\%$ significance level. This interval of values is a $100(1-\alpha)\%$ confidence interval for the difference between the theoretical means of the two groups. The interval can be shown to be

$$\bar{y}_1 - \bar{y}_2 - t_{1-\alpha/2}(v)\sqrt{\frac{s_1^2}{n_1} + \frac{s_2^2}{n_2}} < \delta < \bar{y}_1 - \bar{y}_2 + t_{1-\alpha/2}(v)\sqrt{\frac{s_1^2}{n_1} + \frac{s_2^2}{n_2}} \tag{19.14}$$

■ **EXAMPLE 19.10E:** Example 19.10C displayed data for which

$$\bar{y}_1 - \bar{y}_2 = -1.5 \quad \text{and} \quad \sqrt{\frac{s_1^2}{n_1} + \frac{s_2^2}{n_2}} = 0.655$$

To get a 99% confidence interval for the difference in the theoretical means of the two groups, use $t_{0.005}(26) = 2.779$ and compute the interval

$$-1.5 - 2.779(0.655) < \delta < -1.5 + 2.779(0.655)$$

or

$$-1.5 - 1.8 < \delta < -1.5 + 1.8$$

or

$$-3.3 < \delta < 0.3$$

In this instance, we have 99% confidence that the difference between the first and second group means is between -3.3 and $+0.3$, indicating that we cannot conclusively conclude, with this level of confidence, that one mean is larger than the other. ■

EXERCISES

19.11A For each case below use the two-sample t test to test the null hypothesis that the two process means are equal, at both the 5% and 1% significance levels.
   (a) $n_1 = 20$, $n_2 = 20$, $\bar{y}_1 = 30.4$, $\bar{y}_2 = 18.9$, $s_1 = 25.1$, $s_2 = 27.8$
   (b) $n_1 = 20$, $n_2 = 20$, $\bar{y}_1 = 30.4$, $\bar{y}_2 = 18.9$, $s_1 = 40.6$, $s_2 = 27.8$
   (c) $n_1 = 200$, $n_2 = 200$, $\bar{y}_1 = 30.4$, $\bar{y}_2 = 18.9$, $s_1 = 25.1$, $s_2 = 27.8$
   (d) $n_1 = 20$, $n_2 = 10$, $\bar{y}_1 = 30.4$, $\bar{y}_2 = 18.9$, $s_1 = 25.1$, $s_2 = 27.8$
   (e) $n_1 = 10$, $n_2 = 20$, $\bar{y}_1 = 30.4$, $\bar{y}_2 = 18.9$, $s_1 = 40.6$, $s_2 = 27.8$

19.11B For each case in Exercise 19.11A, use the two-sample t test at both the 5% and the 1% significance levels to test $H_0\colon \mu_1 - \mu_2 = 10$.

19.11C For each case in Exercise 19.11A, use the two-sample t statistic to construct 95% and 99% confidence intervals for $\mu_1 - \mu_2$. Which of the intervals contain the value 0? Which of the intervals contain the value 10?

19.11D Explain the meaning of the confidence intervals obtained in Exercise 19.11C. For fixed sample sizes, what is the practical effect of decreasing the confidence coefficient?

19.11E Find an article in a publication in your field in which a two-sample t test is reported. Write a brief essay on the problem addressed by the article. Does the article discuss clearly the processes used to collect data? Were they in statistical control? Are you convinced that the conclusions drawn from the test are valid? Why or why not? What significance level was used? Why?

19.11F Using the notation of Section 19.10, show that if $a = 1/2$, then $v = 4(n_1 - 1)(n_2 - 1)/(n_1 + n_2 - 1)$. Show further that if $n_1 = n_2 = n/2$, then $v = n - 2$. Under what conditions does $a = 1/2$?

19.11G Write a two-to-three-page essay discussing how a comparison of two mean control charts could be conducted using the two-sample t test.

F STATISTICS

F statistics are used when probabilistic inferences about sources of variation are made. Statisticians call these inferences the analysis of variance. You may recall that an analysis of variance was part of the output from a regression command in Chapter 7. Here the F distribution is defined and an elementary sampling illustration of it is given. Later applications will show the variety of occasions for which F statistics are appropriate.

In the mathematical theory of statistics a random quantity has an **F distribution** with v_1 and v_2 degrees of freedom if it is a ratio of two independent chi-square random quantities divided by their degrees of freedom. In symbols,

$$F = \frac{U_1/v_1}{U_2/v_2} \tag{19.15}$$

where U_1 and U_2 are independent, U_1 has a chi-square distribution with v_1 degrees of freedom, and U_2 has a chi-square distribution with v_2 degrees of freedom. The parameter v_1 is called the numerator degrees of freedom; v_2 the denominator degrees of freedom.

▪**EXAMPLE 19.12A:** Equation (19.15) can be illustrated using a simulation. Degrees of freedom $v_1 = 10$ and $v_2 = 5$ were chosen. A computer was used to draw an observation from a chi-square distribution with 10 degrees of freedom: 5.75539 was obtained. An independent observation from a chi-square distribution with 5 degrees of freedom was then drawn, which yielded 7.43531. The ratio $F = (5.75539/10)/(7.43531/5) = 0.387031$ was then formed. This process was repeated 500 times. Exhibit 19.12A shows a dotplot and some descriptive statistics of the 500 values of F. Notice that the F distribution is skewed to the right. Its mean is 1.6656, and its standard deviation is 2.2231. These are close to the theoretical mean and standard deviation of an F distribution with 10 and 5 degrees of freedom, which are $5/3 \simeq 1.67$ and $\sqrt{65/9} \simeq 2.69$.

EXHIBIT 19.12A

Dotplot and Descriptive Statistics for 500 Simulated Values from the F Distribution with 10 and 5 Degrees of Freedom

	n	Mean	Median	Standard Deviation	Minimum	Maximum
F	500	1.6656	1.1009	2.2231	0.1473	24.5211

A printout of the 500 F values (not shown here) shows that the 476th largest value is 4.5701. This is the sample estimate of the 95th percentile of the F distribution with 10 and 5 degrees of freedom. The actual 95th percentile of the theoretical distribution is 4.74, so the sample estimate is too low by about 0.17. The 496th largest value in the sample, which is an estimate of the 99th percentile of the F distribution with 10 and 5 degrees of freedom, is 12.4746. The actual 99th percentile of the F distribution is 10.05, so the estimate is too high by about 2.42. Had more values been simulated, more reliable estimates of the percentiles would have been obtained. ▪

Mathematical statistics shows that the mean and standard deviation of the F distribution with v_1 and v_2 degrees of freedom are

$$\mu = \frac{v_2}{v_2 - 2} \quad \text{and} \quad \sigma = \sqrt{\frac{2v_2^2(v_1 + v_2 - 2)}{v_1(v_2 - 2)^2(v_2 - 4)}} \tag{19.16}$$

Note that the mean does not exist if v_2 is less than or equal to 2, and the standard deviation does not exist if v_2 is less than or equal to 4.

Tables of F distributions are complicated because they must display distributions for each possible combination of the numerator and denominator degrees of freedom. Exhibit 19.12B shows a limited F distribution table, which gives only the

EXHIBIT 19.12B   Table of 95th and 99th Percentiles of Selected *F* Distributions

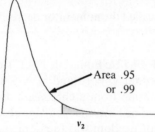

v_2

v_1	1	2	3	4	5	6	7	8	9	10
1	161.44	18.5121	10.1282	7.7086	6.6079	5.9874	5.5913	5.3176	5.1174	4.9646
	4052.18	98.5057	34.1169	21.1977	16.2579	13.7452	12.2462	11.2587	10.5614	10.0443
2	199.50	19.0000	9.5522	6.9443	5.7860	5.1431	4.7373	4.4590	4.2566	4.1029
	4999.50	99.0001	30.8156	18.0000	13.2739	10.9246	9.5464	8.6490	8.0215	7.5594
3	215.69	19.1634	9.2769	6.5913	5.4094	4.7570	4.3469	4.0661	3.8625	3.7083
	5403.35	99.1692	29.4571	16.6946	12.0600	9.7796	8.4514	7.5909	6.9920	6.5523
4	224.57	19.2468	9.1169	6.3881	5.1923	4.5337	4.1203	3.8379	3.6331	3.4780
	5624.58	99.2495	28.7099	15.9771	11.3920	9.1482	7.8465	7.0061	6.4221	5.9944
5	230.16	19.2971	9.0135	6.2559	5.0502	4.3874	3.9715	3.6876	3.4816	3.3259
	5763.65	99.2982	28.2374	15.5215	10.9670	8.7460	7.4605	6.6319	6.0570	5.6363
6	233.98	19.3294	8.9405	6.1632	4.9503	4.2839	3.8660	3.5806	3.3738	3.2172
	5858.99	99.3317	27.9105	15.2071	10.6721	8.4661	7.1913	6.3707	5.8018	5.3858
7	236.78	19.3533	8.8867	6.0942	4.8758	4.2067	3.7870	3.5004	3.2928	3.1355
	5928.36	99.3545	27.6723	14.9757	10.4556	8.2601	6.9929	6.1777	5.6128	5.2001
8	238.89	19.3716	8.8450	6.0412	4.8184	4.1468	3.7258	3.4382	3.2296	3.0717
	5981.07	99.3772	27.4889	14.7987	10.2893	8.1016	6.8400	6.0289	5.4671	5.0566
9	240.55	19.3854	8.8122	5.9989	4.7724	4.0990	3.6767	3.3881	3.1789	3.0204
	6022.47	99.3896	27.3453	14.6591	10.1577	7.9762	6.7187	5.9106	5.3512	4.9424
10	241.89	19.3959	8.7854	5.9643	4.7351	4.0599	3.6365	3.3472	3.1373	2.9783
	6055.85	99.4035	27.2289	14.5460	10.0512	7.8740	6.6201	5.8144	5.2565	4.8492
11	242.97	19.4042	8.7634	5.9359	4.7040	4.0275	3.6030	3.3130	3.1024	2.9430
	6083.32	99.4069	27.1327	14.4522	9.9626	7.7896	6.5382	5.7344	5.1779	4.7715
12	243.91	19.4124	8.7448	5.9118	4.6776	3.9999	3.5747	3.2839	3.0730	2.9130
	6106.32	99.4132	27.0510	14.3736	9.8882	7.7182	6.4691	5.6667	5.1114	4.7058
13	244.67	19.4190	8.7288	5.8912	4.6552	3.9763	3.5504	3.2590	3.0476	2.8871
	6125.86	99.4260	26.9824	14.3066	9.8250	7.6575	6.4100	5.6088	5.0545	4.6496
14	245.35	19.4243	8.7149	5.8732	4.6358	3.9559	3.5293	3.2374	3.0254	2.8647
	6142.67	99.4311	26.9244	14.2485	9.7700	7.6049	6.3590	5.5589	5.0052	4.6008
15	245.97	19.4287	8.7028	5.8578	4.6189	3.9380	3.5108	3.2183	3.0061	2.8450
	6157.28	99.4288	26.8723	14.1982	9.7221	7.5591	6.3144	5.5151	4.9621	4.5581

Note: Rows are numerator degrees of freedom; columns are denominator degrees of freedom. Entries in a cell are the 95th on top of the 99th percentile.

EXHIBIT 19.12B   (*Continued*)

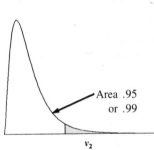

v_1	11	12	13	14	15	16	17	18	19	20
1	4.84422	4.74720	4.66725	4.60006	4.54315	4.49401	4.45122	4.41398	4.38066	4.35128
	9.64599	9.33015	9.07371	8.86159	8.68315	8.53096	8.39981	8.28537	8.18505	8.09599
2	3.98223	3.88526	3.80552	3.73883	3.68235	3.63378	3.59151	3.55452	3.52194	3.49283
	7.20570	6.92666	6.70103	6.51497	6.35891	6.22627	6.11207	6.01283	5.92587	5.84890
3	3.58741	3.49026	3.41049	3.34388	3.28741	3.23893	3.19681	3.15990	3.12740	3.09836
	6.21668	5.95250	5.73935	5.56388	5.41692	5.29215	5.18499	5.09190	5.01024	4.93822
4	3.35670	3.25921	3.17917	3.11226	3.05559	3.00695	2.96472	2.92777	2.89508	2.86605
	5.66834	5.41194	5.20533	5.03540	4.89317	4.77257	4.66896	4.57903	4.50031	4.43073
5	3.20392	3.10588	3.02541	2.95824	2.90131	2.85239	2.81004	2.77286	2.74009	2.71089
	5.31599	5.06433	4.86162	4.69495	4.55560	4.43739	4.33595	4.24784	4.17077	4.10268
6	3.09466	2.99607	2.91528	2.84776	2.79045	2.74135	2.69870	2.66129	2.62834	2.59895
	5.06922	4.82063	4.62035	4.45583	4.31829	4.20165	4.10150	4.01464	3.93860	3.87141
7	3.01231	2.91335	2.83212	2.76418	2.70664	2.65717	2.61433	2.57669	2.54356	2.51399
	4.88613	4.63949	4.44098	4.27785	4.14154	4.02596	3.92672	3.84061	3.76528	3.69874
8	2.94796	2.84858	2.76695	2.69863	2.64082	2.59112	2.54798	2.51018	2.47679	2.44708
	4.74445	4.49936	4.30206	4.13997	4.00443	3.88955	3.79093	3.70541	3.63052	3.56444
9	2.89622	2.79641	2.71438	2.64576	2.58762	2.53767	2.49431	2.45626	2.42270	2.39281
	4.63151	4.38749	4.19110	4.02970	3.89477	3.78043	3.68223	3.59706	3.52253	3.45668
10	2.85358	2.75341	2.67105	2.60215	2.54368	2.49352	2.44993	2.41167	2.37795	2.34791
	4.53927	4.29607	4.10023	3.93937	3.80498	3.69089	3.59307	3.50817	3.43384	3.36817
11	2.81789	2.71732	2.63466	2.56550	2.50684	2.45639	2.41253	2.37413	2.34023	2.31002
	4.46247	4.21978	4.02449	3.86403	3.72989	3.61614	3.51850	3.43376	3.35962	3.29412
12	2.78753	2.68667	2.60369	2.53423	2.47533	2.42468	2.38066	2.34206	2.30796	2.27760
	4.39744	4.15524	3.96034	3.80012	3.66628	3.55267	3.45517	3.37063	3.29653	3.23112
13	2.76140	2.66021	2.57690	2.50727	2.44810	2.39724	2.35306	2.31431	2.28004	2.24952
	4.34163	4.09984	3.90521	3.74524	3.61155	3.49813	3.40070	3.31620	3.24220	3.17688
14	2.73864	2.63712	2.55362	2.48373	2.42440	2.37333	2.32896	2.29003	2.25562	2.22493
	4.29320	4.05175	3.85731	3.69754	3.56398	3.45065	3.35334	3.26891	3.19492	3.12961
15	2.71861	2.61684	2.53308	2.46304	2.40345	2.35222	2.30767	2.26862	2.23404	2.20330
	4.25082	4.00965	3.81538	3.65568	3.52222	3.40898	3.31169	3.22730	3.15335	3.08802

Note: Rows are numerator degrees of freedom; columns are denominator degrees of freedom. Entries in a cell are the 95th on top of the 99th percentile.

95th and 99th percentiles for selected distributions. Access to computer software is essential for practical uses of the F distribution. There is no use limiting yourself to the percentiles shown in the typical tables.

S E C T I O N 19.13

EXERCISES

19.13A **(a)** For an F distribution with 7 and 13 degrees of freedom, find the 95th and 99th percentiles.

(b) Simulate 300 values from an F distribution with 7 and 13 degrees of freedom. Put them in numerical order and print them out. What fraction of them are above the 95th percentile you found in part (a)? What fraction of them are above the 99th percentile?

(c) Use the simulated values in part (b) to estimate the 50th percentile of the F distribution with 7 and 13 degrees of freedom.

19.13B For each case below, find the mean, standard deviation, 95th percentile, and 99th percentile of the indicated F distribution.

(a) $v_1 = 2, v_2 = 5$ **(b)** $v_1 = 2, v_2 = 10$ **(c)** $v_1 = 4, v_2 = 20$
(d) $v_1 = 8, v_2 = 12$ **(e)** $v_1 = 8, v_2 = 8$

19.13C Let $t_{1-\alpha/2}(v)$ denote the $100(1 - \alpha/2)$th percentile of the t distribution with v degrees of freedom. Let $F_{1-\alpha}(1, v)$ denote the $100(1 - \alpha)$th percentile of the F distribution with 1 and v degrees of freedom. Mathematical theory shows that $F_{1-\alpha}(1, v) = [t_{1-\alpha/2}(v)]^2$. Verify this fact numerically for $v = 2, 4, 6, 8$, and 10. Use $\alpha = .05$.

S E C T I O N 19.14

ORDER STATISTICS

Order statistics result from putting the items in a sample in increasing numerical order. Ordering the data is the basic operation behind making frequency distributions, computing descriptive statistics such as the quartiles, and so on. This section shows how to use simulation to study the impact of sampling variation on the ordering operation. The focus is on the "extreme" order statistics, that is, the maximum and minimum values of a sample. Other order statistics are suggested in the exercises in Section 19.15.

▪**E X A M P L E 19.14A:** Consider the behavior of the largest and smallest sample items in random samples of size 5 from a normal distribution with mean $\mu = 100$ and standard deviation $\sigma = 10$. One thousand such samples were simulated and the largest and smallest items in each sample were recorded. Exhibit 19.14A shows the dotplot and some descriptive statistics for the 1000 maxima. The distribution is roughly symmetric and moundshaped with a mean of 111.65 and a standard deviation of 6.7. The smallest sample maximum was 90.93 and the largest was 136.59, quite a range of variation. In particular notice that several of the samples had maxima that fell below the theoretical process mean of 100. In small samples, the extreme sample values can vary a lot.

EXHIBIT 19.14A

Dotplot and Descriptive
Statistics for 1000
Simulated Maxima from
Samples of Size 5 from a
Normal Distribution
with $\mu = 100$ and $\sigma = 10$

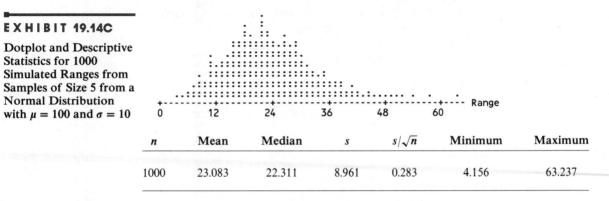

n	Mean	Median	s	$s/\sqrt{n}$	Minimum	Maximum
1000	111.65	111.31	6.70	0.21	90.93	136.59

Exhibit 19.14B tells a similar story for the sample minima. The distribution exhibits a bit more skewness than the distribution of the maxima. The mean is 88.56 and the standard deviation is 6.982. The largest and smallest minima were 107.52 and 53.69, again quite a range. Several of the sample minima fell above the theoretical process mean of 100.

EXHIBIT 19.14B

Dotplot and Descriptive
Statistics for 1000
Simulated Minima from
Samples of Size 5 from a
Normal Distribution
with $\mu = 100$ and $\sigma = 10$

n	Mean	Median	s	$s/\sqrt{n}$	Minimum	Maximum
1000	88.563	89.038	6.982	0.221	53.692	107.521

As a final illustration, the range of each of the 1000 samples was computed, that is, the smallest item was subtracted from the largest item in each sample. Exhibit 19.14C shows the dotplot and descriptive statistics for the 1000 ranges. The

EXHIBIT 19.14C

Dotplot and Descriptive
Statistics for 1000
Simulated Ranges from
Samples of Size 5 from a
Normal Distribution
with $\mu = 100$ and $\sigma = 10$

n	Mean	Median	s	$s/\sqrt{n}$	Minimum	Maximum
1000	23.083	22.311	8.961	0.283	4.156	63.237

average value of the ranges is about 23, with a standard deviation of about 9. The smallest sample range was 4.156, and the largest was 63.237. The variability in the extreme order statistics translates into considerable variability in the sample range. For this reason, the sample range is seldom used in practice to make probabilistic inferences.   ▪

TESTING A HYPOTHESIS ABOUT THE MEDIAN

Extreme order statistics can be used to perform a significance test about the underlying process median, provided the process is in statistical control and the data items are collected independently. Let n denote the size of the sample taken from the process, let η denote the long-run process median, and let the null hypothesis be $H_0: \eta = \eta_0$.

The simplest test of H_0 is based on the maximum and minimum values of the sample. The null hypothesis will be rejected if either the sample maximum is below η_0 or the sample minimum is above η_0. The simulation in Example 19.14A showed that either of these events can happen, but they happen relatively rarely if the null hypothesis is true.

Given these assumptions, the binomial distribution can be used to compute the probabilities of the events defined above when the null hypothesis is true. The event "largest sample item less than the median" is equivalent to the event "all sample items less than the median." If "success" is defined as a sample item less than the median, then "all sample items less than the median" is also the event "n successes in a sample of size n." When the long-run process median is η_0, then the probability of a success, that is, the probability that a sample item falls below η_0, is simply 1/2, by the definition of median. The Bernoulli parameter "probability of success" is therefore used as $\pi = 1/2$. The probability of n successes is just $\pi^n = (\frac{1}{2})^n$. This is the probability that the largest sample item is less than η_0 when the null hypothesis is true.

Using a completely analogous argument, it can be shown that the probability that the smallest sample item falls above η_0 when the null hypothesis is true is also $(\frac{1}{2})^n$. The null hypothesis is rejected if either of the two events in question occurs. The probability that either occurs is just the sum of their probabilities, because the events cannot occur simultaneously. Thus the significance level of the test is

$$(\tfrac{1}{2})^n + (\tfrac{1}{2})^n = 2(\tfrac{1}{2})^n = (\tfrac{1}{2})^{n-1}$$

The table below shows some sample sizes and values of the significance level computed from this formula.

n	Significance Level
2	0.5
3	0.25
4	0.125
5	0.0625
6	0.03125
7	0.015625
8	0.0078125
9	0.00390625

With samples of size 9 the probability of Type I error is almost negligible. Moreover, the simulation in Example 19.14A showed that extreme order statistics tend to be quite variable. These two observations suggest that it is possible to use less extreme order statistics in samples of 10 or more items. You are asked to show in the exercises in Section 19.15 that this indeed is the case. For moderate-sized samples, acceptably small significance levels can be achieved while using less volatile order statistics, a neat illustration of statistical efficiency.

CONFIDENCE INTERVALS USING ORDER STATISTICS

The theory given above also yields confidence intervals for the long-run process median. For example, the smallest and largest items in a sample could be used as endpoints of a confidence interval for the median η. The table of significance levels in the table on page 526 yields the corresponding confidence coefficients. Simply subtract the significance levels from 1 and you get the probability that the endpoints bracket η. The table shows that for a sample of size 9, the smallest and largest sample items form a 99.6% confidence interval for the process median.

SECTION 19.15

EXERCISES

19.15A (a) Draw 200 random samples of size 10 from a normal distribution with mean 1 and standard deviation 1. Prepare dotplots and descriptive statistics for the sample minima, sample maxima, and sample ranges. The median of the theoretical normal distribution is 1 (equal to the mean by symmetry). Count the number of simulated sample minima greater than 1. Count the number of simulated sample maxima that are less than 1.

(b) Repeat part (a) drawing samples from an exponential distribution.

(c) Repeat part (a) drawing samples from a uniform distribution on $[1 - \sqrt{3}, 1 + \sqrt{3})$.

(d) Compare the distributions of minima, maxima, and ranges obtained in parts (a), (b), and (c). What impacts do the differing theoretical distributions have on these distributions?

19.15B Consider the following test for a process median, with $H_0: \eta = \eta_0$: Reject H_0 if either the second largest sample item is less than η_0 or the second smallest item is greater than η_0.

(a) Show that the significance level of this test is $(n + 1)(\frac{1}{2})^{n-1}$. [*Hint:* The second largest sample item is less than η_0 if either all the sample items are less than η_0 or if exactly $n - 1$ sample items are less than η_0. Using the binomial distribution, defining "success" as an item below η_0, the probability of either n or $n - 1$ successes is $(\frac{1}{2})^n + n(\frac{1}{2})^n$. Repeat this argument for the second smallest sample item and combine the results to obtain the required formula.]

(b) Evaluate the formula given in part (a) for $n = 5, 6, \ldots, 15$.

(c) Use the results in parts (a) and (b) to derive confidence intervals for the process median based on the second and smallest second largest order statistics.

19.15C Two analysts disagree about the value of the median of monthly fringe-benefit payments to a large pool of workers. Computing the benefits is complicated, so only a small sample of eight employee records can be used to make the estimate. Researcher 1 maintains the null hypothesis $H_0: \eta = 400$. Researcher 2 maintains the null hypothesis $H_0: \eta = 500$. The random sample of employee records yields the following amounts (in dollars): 68.42, 423.10, 362.36, 260.45, 681.18, 105.74, 15.02, 376.14.

(a) Test both researchers' null hypotheses at the 0.8% significance level. Can they resolve their disagreement with these data?

(b) Compute the 99.2% confidence interval for the theoretical median of fringe benefits.

(c) Redo parts (a) and (b) using a significance level of 7% and a confidence coefficient of 93%.

19.15D Redo parts (a) and (b) of Exercise 19.15C assuming $n = 10$, a significance level of 2%, and a confidence coefficient of 98%. The sample items are 389.40, 607.41, 388.03, 386.03, 192.15, 457.75, 87.96, 450.92, 287.02, 2.99.

S E C T I O N 19.16

p VALUES

In presenting significance tests, the importance of choosing the significance level to reflect the investigator's attitude toward the risk of making a Type I error has been stressed. As mentioned, investigators with different attitudes toward this risk can reach opposite conclusions from the outcome of a significance test, which makes the reporting of findings based on significance tests to others delicate. A result cannot be simply declared statistically significant, because other investigators might not have found it so. On the other hand, there is usually pressure to report results as compactly as possible, either to keep a report short or to ensure speedy assimilation of the information. The scientific community has developed a style of reporting that conveys the essential findings of significance tests while allowing people with differing attitudes toward risk to apply their own significance levels to the findings. The reporting style uses **p values**, empirical significance levels.

The essential ingredients of a significance test include

- A model for the underlying process
- A sampling plan that takes account of or imposes a state of statistical control on the data
- A null hypothesis to be tested
- A test statistic
- The sampling distribution of the test statistic when the null hypothesis is true
- A criterion for deciding when to reject the null hypothesis
- Ability to compute the significance level, which is the probability that the test rejects a true null hypothesis.

The last two ingredients are the ones that are modified to produce p values. Rather than begin with an abstract discussion, p values are introduced by examples.

▪ **EXAMPLE 19.16A:** Consider the t test introduced in Section 19.4. Specifically, recall the discussion in Examples 19.4A and 19.4B concerning the sample of size $n = 5$ in display (19.2). If the null hypothesis is $H_0: \mu = 0$, then a t statistic of -1.24, which is not statistically significant at either the 1% or 5% significance levels, is obtained.

To obtain the p value associated with this outcome, the observed value of $t = -1.24$ is treated *as if* it were on the boundary of the plausible values. In other words, we act as if the interval of plausible values of t were $[-1.24, 1.24]$. The p value is the significance level associated with this interval, namely, the probability that a t statistic value outside this interval would be observed when the null hypothesis is true. The table of *t*-distribution percentiles is not extensive enough to show the required probability. Statistical software is used to do the calculation. Minitab was used to obtain the *p* value of 0.2827.[†]

The interpretation of the *p* value is as follows. If a significance level greater than 28.27% had been chosen, then the *t* statistic actually obtained, $t = -1.24$, would have been declared statistically significant. Any investigator whose significance level is less than 28.27% will not find the actual *t*-statistic value statistically significant. This style of reporting leaves it up to the person receiving the report to draw a conclusion from the test. The conclusion drawn will depend on the receiver's attitude toward risk. Few people who have given significance testing any thought will have significance levels as high as 28.27%, so it would be fairly safe to assume that there will be general agreement about the meaning of the test in this case. On the other hand, if a test yields a *p* value between 0.05 and 0.01, there is considerable potential for investigators to disagree. Current practice suggests that *p* values less than 0.01 command general agreement that the result is statistically significant. ■

■ **EXAMPLE 19.16B:** In Section 19.8 a significance test for the null hypothesis of no association between two categorical variables displayed in an $r \times c$ table was introduced. The test was based on Pearson's chi-square statistic, denoted by X^2, and the assumption that the sampling distribution of X^2 under the null hypothesis was sufficiently well approximated by a χ^2 distribution with $v = (r - 1)(c - 1)$ degrees of freedom. To see how *p* values could be developed in this context, suppose that the test is performed on data in a 3×5 table and that the value of X^2 turns out to be 17.971. To develop a *p* value, we assume that the value $X^2 = 17.971$ is on the borderline between significant and nonsignificant values of X^2. Recall that for the chi-square test, the null hypothesis is rejected if the value of X^2 is greater than the chosen critical value. Adopting 17.971 as the critical value of the test, the probability that a variable with a χ^2 distribution with $v = 2 \times 4 = 8$ degrees of freedom is greater than 17.971 must be computed. Minitab was used to obtain 0.04 for this probability.[††] An investigator with a 5% significance level would find the result statistically significant and reject the null hypothesis of no association between the variables. On the other hand, any investigator with a significance level less than 4% would not reject the null hypothesis. ■

[†] The *t* distribution has 4 degrees of freedom, and we want to compute 1 minus the area bounded by the horizontal axis, vertical lines through -1.24 and $+1.24$, and the pdf of the *t* distribution. Appropriate Minitab commands are

```
SET C1
−1.24 1.24
END
CDF C1 C2;
  T 4.
LET K1 = 1 + C2(1) − C2(2)
PRINT K1
```

[††] Appropriate Minitab commands are

```
CDF 17.971 K1;
  CHIS 8.
LET K2 = 1 − K1
PRINT K2
```

Keeping these two examples in mind, a general procedure for computing p values is presented. First, set up and perform the test of interest. Then make the value of the test statistic obtained from the data a boundary between significant and nonsignificant values of the test statistic. In other words, act as if the obtained value had been used to set up the critical region of the test in the first place. On the basis of this assumption, compute the significance level associated with this "empirical" critical region, which is the p value sought. Reporting the p values along with the other essential information about the test allows other investigators to draw conclusions in light of their attitudes toward risk.

But p values are subject to subtle misinterpretation. It is tempting, and few have resisted the temptation, to conclude that if a p value is very small, say, less than 0.001, then the result of the test is "more significant" than a result associated with a higher p value, say, 0.01. Some investigators have even attempted to use p values to rank the importance of results! This practice is at least indefensible and misleading and at worst wasteful of valuable research resources.

To illustrate the fallacy concretely, consider the very simple significance test for the median of a process presented in Section 19.14. Let the null hypothesis be $H_0: \eta = \eta_0$, where η_0 is the guess at the process median. The analysis in Section 19.14 shows that if you take a random sample of size 9 from the process and all the items are less than η_0, then you reject the null hypothesis at the 0.4% significance level. If you take a sample of size 9, and all the items do indeed fall below η_0, then the p value of the test is 0.004. All investigators with significance levels greater than 0.4% will reject the null hypothesis.

Now suppose another investigator performs the same test with a sample of size 18 and all 18 items in the sample fall below η_0. Then that investigator can claim a p value of $(\frac{1}{2})^{17} = 0.000007629$. Now this clearly means that all investigators with significance levels greater than 0.000007629 will reject the null hypothesis. Is this result "more significant" than the result based on a sample of size 9? It is difficult to attach much meaning to the phrase "more significant." The literal comparison of the two results is that the second result will convince people who have significance levels between 0.004 and 0.000007629 to reject the null hypothesis, whereas the first result will not convince such people to reject the null hypothesis. This would be a notable comparison if you felt there were many such people and they were worth convincing. But the vast majority of investigators use significance levels higher than 0.04%, so the first test is just as convincing as the second. The extra nine observations in the second sample are essentially wasted. If they were expensive, then the money spent on them was wasted.

A more economical way to use the larger sample is to perform a test that achieves a sensible significance level, say, approximately 0.04%, and reduces the probability of Type II error relative to the smaller test. This objective is achieved by the following test:

(1) Take a random sample of size 18.

(2) Reject $H_0: \eta = \eta_0$ if either exactly three sample items are above η_0 or exactly three sample items fall below η_0.

The significance level of this test is 0.0075, which is also the p value if one of the events in item 2 occurs. Moreover, the test is much less likely to lead to a specified Type II error than the best based on a sample of size 9.

The moral of the story is that p values can be made very small simply by using very large samples, even when the null hypothesis is true. Since very small p values lead to rejection of the null hypothesis, and, even more disturbing, to the temptation to treat the test result with unusual reverence, be on guard that p values are reported sensibly. In particular, make sure that the sample size has been thoughtfully chosen.

SECTION 19.17

EXERCISES

19.17A An investigator uses a random sample of size $n = 15$ to test $H_0: \mu = 100$ using a t test. Suppose $\bar{y} = 102.7$ and $s = 10.4$. Compute the p value of the outcome.

19.17B Explain the interpretation of the p value obtained in Exercise 19.17A.

19.17C An investigator performs a chi-square test for no association on a 4×3 table and obtains $X^2 = 14.38$. Compute the p value of the outcome.

19.17D Explain the interpretation of the p value obtained in Exercise 19.17C.

19.17E Find the p values of the tests in the following exercises:
(a) Exercises 19.5A, 19.5B, 19.5C, and 19.5E   (b) Exercises 19.8A and 19.8B
(c) Exercises 19.11A and 19.11B   (d) Exercises 19.15C and 19.15D

19.17F Find an article in a publication in your field in which a p value is reported. Write a brief essay on the problem addressed by the article. Does the article discuss clearly the process used to collect data? Was it in statistical control? Are you convinced that the conclusions drawn from the test are valid? Why or why not? Do you feel the p value was used appropriately?

19.17G Give an illustration of the misuse of p values.

SECTION 19.18

SUPPLEMENTARY EXERCISES FOR CHAPTER 19

19A Use the nine scores recorded in Exercise 18A. Compute the value of the one-sample t statistic for each of the following values of μ:
(a) $\mu = 0$ (b) $\mu = 10$ (c) $\mu = 15$
(d) $\mu = 20$ (e) $\mu = 25$ (f) $\mu = 30$
What value of μ minimizes the value of the t statistic?

19B Use the nine scores recorded in Exercise 18A.
(a) Perform a significance test of the hypothesis $H_0: \mu = 27$ at the 5% significance level.
(b) Compute the p value of the test in part (a) and interpret the meaning of the p value.
(c) Find the largest value of μ you could use as a null hypothesis and still find that the p value is greater than 0.05.
(d) Compute the 99.7% confidence interval for μ based on the t statistic.

19C For each of the 3×2 tables below, perform the χ^2 test for no association at the 5% and 1% significance levels. Compute the p values for each test.
(a) 14 37 92 (b) 14 46 78 (c) 28 37 46
   8 23 78   8 23 28   78 16 92

19D For each case below use the two-sample t test to test the null hypothesis that the two process means are equal, at both the 5% and the 1% significance levels. Also compute the p value for each test and interpret its meaning.
   (a) $n_1 = 15, n_2 = 15, \bar{y}_1 = 29, s_1 = 3, \bar{y}_2 = 27, s_2 = 2.8$
   (b) $n_1 = 25, n_2 = 15, \bar{y}_1 = 29, s_1 = 3, \bar{y}_2 = 27, s_2 = 2.8$

19E For each case in Exercise 19D compute the 99% confidence interval for $\mu_1 - \mu_2$. Interpret the meaning of the intervals.

19F Use the data in Exercise 15A. Use the two-sample t test to test the null hypothesis $H_0: \mu_1 - \mu_2 = 0$, where μ_1 is the population mean of Set A and μ_2 is the population mean of Set B.

19G Use the data in Exercise 15B. Use the two-sample t test to test the null hypothesis $H_0: \mu_1 - \mu_2 = 0$, where μ_1 is the theoretical mean response of Section A and μ_2 is the theoretical mean response of Section B.

19H According to the footnote on page 516, the theoretical standard deviation of the difference between two sample means, when two independent simple random samples are drawn, is

$$\sigma_{\bar{y}_1 - \bar{y}_2} = \sqrt{\frac{\sigma_1^2}{n_1} + \frac{\sigma_2^2}{n_2}}$$

Thus $3\sigma_{\bar{y}_1 - \bar{y}_2}$ is the theoretical bound on the error in a 99.7% confidence interval for $\mu_1 - \mu_2$. In practice, knowledge of the process of interest can be used to determine a difference of practical significance. In other words, knowledge of the process places a bound on $\mu_1 - \mu_2$ without the expense of taking any more data from the process. To justify data collection and analysis, therefore, we must have assurance that the statistical bound, $3\sigma_{\bar{y}_1 - \bar{y}_2}$, will probably yield more precise information than we already possess. Let B denote an error bound that would be an improvement over current knowledge. If we knew σ_1 and σ_2, we could set

$$B = 3\sigma_{\bar{y}_1 - \bar{y}_2} \tag{19.17}$$

and solve for values of n_1 and n_2 that would yield this bound. In practice, we again appeal to knowledge of the process of interest to obtain rough estimates of σ_1 and σ_2 and then solve the equation. Solve Equation (19.17) under the following different circumstances:
   (a) $\sigma_1 = \sigma_2 = \sigma$ and $n_1 = n_2 = n$ (d) $\sigma_1 = k\sigma_2$ and $n_1 = n_2 = n$, for some $k > 0$
   (b) $\sigma_1 = 2\sigma_2$ and $n_1 = n_2 = n$ (e) $\sigma_1 = k\sigma_2$ and $n_1 = kn_2$, for some $k > 0$
   (c) $\sigma_1 = 2\sigma_2$ and $n_1 = 2n_2$ (f) $\sigma_1 = k_1\sigma_2$ and $n_1 = k_2n_2$, for $k_1 > 0$ and $k_2 > 0$

19I Use the nine scores in Exercise 18A. Compute the 99.6% confidence interval for the process median using order statistics. Compare the interval with the one you obtained in Exercise 19B, part (d). Explain clearly the distinction between the parameters for which the two intervals provide estimates.

SECTION 19.19

GLOSSARY FOR CHAPTER 19

Alternative hypothesis	A hypothesis other than the null hypothesis.
Bootstrapping	A technique that derives an empirical sampling distribution for a statistic by drawing random samples with replacement from a real sample.
Chi-square distribution	The approximate sampling distribution of Pearson's X^2 statistic when the null hypothesis of no association is true.
Confidence coefficient	One minus the significance level of the test upon which a confidence interval is based.

Confidence interval	The set of parameter values that a significance test does not reject in response to a given set of data.
Critical region	Those values of a test statistic that cause rejection of the null hypothesis
F distribution	The sampling distribution formed from the ratio of two independent chi-square variables divided by their degrees of freedom.
Null hypothesis	The hypothesis assumed to be true when deriving the sampling distribution of a test statistic used to compute the significance level.
Order statistics	The items of a sample of measurements arranged in increasing numerical order.
Power	Probability of rejecting the null hypothesis when an alternative hypothesis is true.
p values	Empirical significance levels.
Sampling distribution	Distribution of values of a statistic in repeated drawings from a stable process or random samples from a fixed universe.
Significance level	The probability that the test statistic falls outside the critical region when the null hypothesis is true.
Significance testing	A process of probabilistic inference that uses sampling distributions to compare behavior in data with theories about the process that generated the data.
Statistically significant	A phrase used when the value of a test statistic is an extreme value in the appropriate sampling distribution that assumes the null hypothesis to be true.
t distribution with $n - 1$ degrees of freedom	The sampling distribution of the t statistic for the sample mean when the data come from a normal distribution.
Test statistic	A statistic used in a significance test.
t statistic for the process mean	$$t = \frac{\bar{y} - \mu_0}{s/\sqrt{n}} = \frac{\sqrt{n}(\bar{y} - \mu_0)}{s}$$
Two-sample t statistic	$$t = \frac{\bar{y}_1 - \bar{y}_2}{\sqrt{\dfrac{s_1^2}{n_1} + \dfrac{s_2^2}{n_2}}}$$
Type I error	Rejecting a true null hypothesis.
Type II error	Failing to reject a false null hypothesis.
Type III error	Giving a sophisticated answer to an irrelevant question.

## PART 5

Modelling
Many Variables

## CHAPTER 20

Inference
in Regression Models

A STATISTICAL MODEL FOR REGRESSION ANALYSIS

In Chapter 7 the basics of multiple regression models were presented and many of the concepts about them were illustrated with specific examples and data sets. In this chapter and Chapters 21 and 22, multiple regression models are covered in more detail and their more advanced aspects are explored. Recall that regression models involve both a mathematical curve that describes the global behavior of the response variable y under a range of settings of the predictor variables $x_1, x_2, \ldots, x_k$ and also a notion of the variability in the response to be expected for particular settings of the k predictor variables $x_1, x_2, \ldots, x_k$. Regression analysis has several general objectives:

- To determine whether relationships exist between variables
- To describe the relationships if they exist
- To assess the accuracy in the descriptions of the relationships
- To assess the importance of each of the predictors in a relationship

Formally, the multiple regression model assumes that the relationship may be expressed as

$$y = \beta_0 + \beta_1 x_1 + \beta_2 x_2 + \cdots + \beta_k x_k + e \qquad \textbf{(20.1)}$$

where $\beta_0, \beta_1, \beta_2, \ldots, \beta_k$ are unknown **regression parameters** and e is the **error** term.[†] The error term is not observed, and it encompasses all the variation in the response y that is *not* modelled by the linear function of the predictor variables $x_1, x_2, \ldots, x_k$. As in Chapter 7, some of the **predictor variables**, the variables used to predict or explain the response variable, may be squares or cross-products of other variables, logarithms of other variables, or binary indicator variables. (The **response variable** is the variable to be predicted or explained.)

The data set consists of n cases (or observations) with values for the predictor variables for the ith case denoted $x_{i1}, x_{i2}, \ldots, x_{ik}$ and the corresponding response denoted y_i. The multiple regression model for the full data set may then be expressed through the n equations

$$y_i = \beta_0 + \beta_1 x_{i1} + \beta_2 x_{i2} + \cdots + \beta_k x_{ik} + e_i \qquad \text{for } i = 1, 2, \ldots, n \qquad \textbf{(20.2)}$$

To support the inference procedures that will be developed in this chapter, several assumptions about the statistical nature of the error terms must be made. The following formal assumptions will be needed in various stages of inference:

The errors are independent of one another, that is, the size of any one error has no influence on the size of any other error, and have a normal distribution with 0 mean and standard deviation σ.

It can be argued that these assumptions are equivalent to assuming that the y's arise independently with y_i coming from a normal distribution with mean $\beta_0 + \beta_1 x_{i1} + \beta_2 x_{i2} + \cdots + \beta_k x_{ik}$ and standard deviation σ. The parameter σ will also be unknown and will be estimated from the observed data.

For the case of a single predictor x, Exhibit 20.1A depicts some of the model assumptions in a graphical display.

EXHIBIT 20.1A

The Simple Linear Regression Model

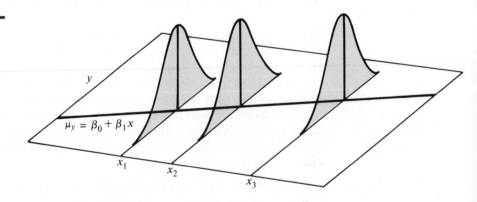

[†] Notice the use of the term *error* in the sense of *statistical error* rather than in the sense of a *mistake*.

INTERPRETING THE REGRESSION PARAMETERS

The parameter β_0 is the *intercept* or *constant term* that represents the value of y expected when all the predictors are zero. However, in many examples, zero values for all the predictors would be quite meaningless as the observed ranges of the predictors are all far from zero. In those cases the intercept parameter does not have a useful literal interpretation. The regression parameters $\beta_1, \ldots, \beta_k$ are most easily interpreted when there are no squared or cross-product terms in the model. The parameters $\beta_1, \ldots, \beta_k$ are sometimes called *partial slopes* in the sense that β_i is the change in the mean of y with respect to a unit change in the predictor variable x_i with all other predictors, $x_1, x_2, \ldots, x_{i-1}, x_{i+1}, \ldots, x_k$ held constant. Of course, if one of the other predictors is x_i^2 this interpretation fails. Also, in many applications the predictor variables are themselves related, so again it is unrealistic to consider changing one predictor without changing another one. The problem of related predictors is introduced later in this chapter. This topic is also covered more completely in the Chapter 22 discussion of collinearity.

In most applications of regression, the model represents only a convenient approximation of the "truth." Data collected on the same variables over a different range of predictor values may very well be modelled by a somewhat different mathematical function so that the parameters $\beta_0, \beta_1, \ldots, \beta_k$ would have different meanings. Every regression model must be interpreted within its own context, which includes the range of values for the predictors and response.

Again excluding models with square and cross-product predictors, the sign of β_i indicates the *direction* of the relationship between the mean of the response y and the predictor x_i, all other predictors being held constant. A positive value for β_i implies a direct relationship; a negative value implies an inverse relationship.

The units of each coefficient β_i will depend on the units of the response y and the predictor x_i. For example, if the response is measured as market value of a house in thousands of dollars and the predictor is square footage of the house, then the corresponding regression coefficient has units of thousands of dollars per square foot. If the assessed value of the house (in thousands of dollars) is used as an additional predictor, then its regression coefficient has units of thousand dollars in market value per thousand dollars of assessed value. The large-sample example in Section 7.2 relating market value to square footage for 60 parcels produced the regression coefficient estimate of 0.018362. Thus for each additional square foot of living area the market value is predicted to increase by about $18. The more complicated model in Section 7.8 gave

$$\text{Predicted market value} = 1.111 + 0.0448883 \text{ Sq.ft} - 0.000015064 \, (\text{Sq.ft})^2$$
$$+ 4.15 \text{ Med} + 5.216 \text{ Hi} + 0.22337 \text{ Assessed} \qquad \textbf{(20.3)}$$

where Med and Hi are binary indicator variables for the grade of the house. Here the coefficient 4.15 indicates that a medium-grade house has a predicted market value of $4150 *above* a low-grade house, while the 5.216 coefficient translates to an increase of about $5216 in predicted market value for a high-grade house above that for a low-grade house with the Sq.ft (and hence Sq.ft.sq) and Assessed variables held constant. Also, each dollar in assessed value is reflected in about a $0.22 increase in predicted market value (all other variables being held constant). The regression coefficients associated with square footage cannot be interpreted separately since square feet and square feet squared *must* change together.

SECTION 20.3

EXERCISES

20.3A Use Equation (20.3) to find the predicted market value for a house with 1100 square feet of living space, medium grade, and assessed value of $40,000. (Remember that assessed value is measured in thousands of dollars.)

20.3B Use Equation (20.3) to find the predicted market value for a high-grade house with assessed value of $42,100 and with 1300 square feet of living space.

20.3C Use Equation (20.3) to find the predicted market value for a house with 900 square feet of living space, low grade, and assessed value of $31,000.

20.3D According to Equation (20.3), is the relationship between market value and assessed value direct or inverse?

20.3E The following model was used by a chain of audio-video retail stores to predict profits:

$$y = \beta_0 + \beta_1 x_1 + \beta_2 x_2 + \beta_3 x_3 + e$$

where y is profit, x_1 is dollar sales of audio items, x_2 is dollar sales of video items, and x_3 is the store size in hundreds of square feet. Interpret each of the coefficients β_0, β_1, β_2, and β_3.

20.3F The following regression model was investigated to predict a building's energy consumption:

$$y = \beta_0 + \beta_1 x_1 + \beta_2 x_2 + \beta_3 x_3 + \beta_4 x_4 + e$$

where y represents energy consumption (in thousands of BTUs), x_1 is the total outside wall area (in hundreds of square feet), x_2 is the total outside window area (in hundreds of square feet), x_3 is the total roof area (in hundreds of square feet), and x_4 is a binary variable indicating whether the building is fully insulated ($x_4 = 1$) or not ($x_4 = 0$). Interpret each of the coefficients β_0, β_1, β_2, β_3, and β_4.

20.3G A telemarketing firm is experimenting with two different training programs (I and II) for its current sales employees. They propose testing the effectiveness of the program by measuring each employee's sales production for the three months following the training and using the model

$$\widehat{\text{Sales}} = \beta_0 + \beta_1 \text{ Training}$$

where Training = 0 for training program I and Training = 1 for training program II.
(a) Interpret the model in the special case where $\beta_1 = 0$.
(b) Interpret the parameters β_0 and $\beta_0 + \beta_1$.
(c) Sketch a scatterplot of sales versus training that would support the contention that the two training programs led to different sales results.
(d) Sketch a scatterplot of sales versus training that would support the contention that there was no discernible difference between the training programs.

20.3H The telemarketing firm in Exercise 20.3G decides to use a more realistic model since they believe that the length of time (in months) that the employee has been with their firm will also affect sales performance. So they formulate the two-predictor model

$$\widehat{\text{Sales}} = \beta_0 + \beta_1 \text{ Time} + \beta_2 \text{ Training}$$

where again Training = 0 for training program I and Training = 1 for training program II.
   (a) Interpret the model in the special case where $\beta_2 = 0$.
   (b) Interpret the parameters β_0 and $\beta_0 + \beta_2$.
   (c) Sketch a scatterplot of sales versus time that would support the contention that there was a discernible difference between the two training programs. Indicate on the plot by different plotting symbols which points correspond to which training program.
   (d) Sketch a scatterplot of sales versus training that would support the contention that there was no discernible difference between the two training programs. Indicate on the plot by different plotting symbols which points correspond to which training program.

SECTION 20.4

ESTIMATING PARAMETERS

In Chapter 7 the basic ideas of least squares were introduced. Within the formal regression model framework just introduced, the least squares method is an intuitive and reasonable method for producing estimates for the unknown regression parameters $\beta_0, \beta_1, \ldots, \beta_k$. The **least squares estimates** $b_0, b_1, \ldots, b_k$ are the values for the parameters $\beta_0, \beta_1, \ldots, \beta_k$ that minimize the sum of squares

$$\sum_{i=1}^{n} [y_i - \beta_0 - \beta_1 x_{i1} - \beta_2 x_{i2} - \cdots - \beta_k x_{ik}]^2 \tag{20.4}$$

The appendix to this chapter shows that $b_0, b_1, \ldots, b_k$ may be found by solving a certain system of linear equations called the *normal equations*. As noted in Chapter 7, computer software is readily available for solving these equations and thus obtaining the estimates.

Once estimates for the regression parameters are available, the **residuals** are obtained as

$$\text{Residual} = \text{Observation} - \text{Fit}$$

or
$$\hat{e}_i = y_i - \hat{y}_i \tag{20.5}$$

where the ith **fitted value**, $\hat{y}_i$, is

$$\hat{y}_i = b_0 + b_1 x_{i1} + b_2 x_{i2} + \cdots + b_k x_{ik} \tag{20.6}$$

Finally, the **residual standard deviation**, s, where

$$s = \sqrt{\frac{1}{n-k-1} \sum_{i=1}^{n} \hat{e}_i^2} \tag{20.7}$$

with $n - k - 1$ degrees of freedom, is interpreted as an estimate of the standard deviation σ of the error terms.

EXERCISES

20.5A Use Equation (20.3) to find the residual for the house with 890 square feet of living space, medium grade, $20,200 assessed value, and market value of $35,000.

20.5B Interpret, geometrically, the process of finding least squares estimates of β_0 and β_1 when the model contains only one predictor. A stylized scatterplot should be used in the description.

20.5C Consider the three (x, y) pairs $(0, 5)$, $(1, 3)$, and $(2, 1)$. Argue *without calculation* that the least squares estimate of the slope parameter is -2.

20.5D Use the following small data set:

x	y
1	1
2	1
3	2
4	2

(a) Verify that the least squares line of y versus x is

$$y = 0.5 + 0.4x$$

(b) Verify that the least squares line when the roles of x and y are reversed is

$$x = -0.5 + 2y$$

(c) Plot the scatterplot of the data and graph both lines on the plot. Why are these different lines?

INFERENCE FOR MODELS WITH ONE PREDICTOR

SIGNIFICANCE TESTS ON REGRESSION COEFFICIENTS

The property data of Chapter 7 and some simulated data will be used to illustrate the inferences appropriate in regression models. The first example uses the one-predictor model

$$y = \beta_0 + \beta_1 x + e \qquad \textbf{(20.8)}$$

such as was used initially to model Market value in terms of Sq.ft. In such a model it is important to assess whether or not the parameter β_1 is zero. If $\beta_1 = 0$, the model becomes $y = \beta_0 + e$, which says that the response varies randomly around the level β_0 but its variation is *not* different for different values of x. In the terminology of significance tests, we need to assess whether the estimate b_1 of β_1 is significantly different from zero.

In the one-predictor model the test may equally well be based on either the **t ratio** for b_1, that is, $b_1/se(b_1)$, or on the F ratio of regression mean square to residual (or error) mean square introduced in Section 7.10. Exhibit 20.6A shows the Minitab output for this regression. The display gives many useful statistics, including the parameter estimates (under Coef), the standard errors of those estimates (under Stdev) and the ratios of these two quantities (under t-ratio). The t ratio required is given by

$$t \text{ ratio for } b_1 = \frac{b_1}{se(b_1)} = \frac{0.018362}{0.002134} = 8.60 \qquad \textbf{(20.9)}$$

For the one-predictor model the standard error, $se(b_1)$, has a reasonably simple formula.[†] However, the specific formula is of little interest. Software is used for all computations, including standard errors.

EXHIBIT 20.6A

Minitab Output for Market Regressed on Sq.ft

```
The regression equation is

Market = 20.5 + 0.0184 Sq.ft

Predictor       Coef       Stdev     t-ratio         p
Constant      20.508       2.075        9.88     0.000
Sq.ft       0.018362    0.002134        8.60     0.000

s = 3.981      R-sq = 56.1%      R-sq(adj) = 55.3%

Analysis of Variance

SOURCE        DF          SS          MS        F         p
Regression     1      1173.1      1173.1    74.01     0.000
Error         58       919.3        15.8
Total         59      2092.4
```

Statistical theory establishes that, under the regression assumptions, the sampling distribution of $(b_1 - \beta_1)/se(b_1)$ is a t distribution with $n - 2$ degrees of freedom. Hence, under the hypothesis that $\beta_1 = 0$, the t ratio $b_1/se(b_1)$ may be used to test $\beta_1 = 0$. The hypothesis $\beta_1 = 0$ is rejected if the corresponding t ratio is too large in magnitude. In this example the t ratio of 8.60 with $60 - 2 = 58$ degrees of freedom indicates clear statistical significance. The Minitab output also shows a p value of 0.000, meaning the p value is less than 0.0005, which further signals the clear significance of b_1.

Statistical theory, again under the standard regression assumptions, shows that the sampling distribution of the F ratio of regression mean square to residual (or error) mean square is an F distribution with 1 and $n - 2$ degrees of freedom if indeed $\beta_1 = 0$ is true. Otherwise, the F tends to be inflated and the hypothesis $\beta_1 = 0$ should be rejected for large values of F. The observed F ratio of 74.01 with 1 and 24 degrees of freedom and p value of 0.000 indicates the strong statistical significance of the predictor Sq.ft in predicting Market value.

[†] For the one-predictor model it may be shown that the standard error of the slope coefficient estimate is given by

$$se(b_1) = \frac{s}{\sqrt{\sum_{i=1}^{n}(x_i - \bar{x})^2}}$$

Note also that, to within rounding error,

$$F \text{ ratio} = 74.01 \approx (0.018362/0.002134)^2 = (t \text{ ratio for } b_1)^2.$$

With a one-predictor model it may be shown that the F ratio will always equal the square of this t ratio so that either significance test may be used to assess the usefulness of the predictor.

As demonstrated in earlier chapters, simulation is a valuable technique for learning (and sometimes discovering) complex statistical theory. Regression theory is no exception. Standard regression theory will be illustrated using 25 cases from the following regression model:

$$y = 10 + 3x + e \qquad \textbf{(20.10)}$$

EXHIBIT 20.6B

Data for One Regression Simulation of $y = 10 + 3x + e$ **with** $n = 25$

Case	x	y	$e/2$
1	6.1	27.1550	−0.57250
2	7.0	30.6433	−0.17837
3	7.5	31.9737	−0.26315
4	7.9	35.2806	0.79029
5	8.2	34.5976	−0.00122
6	8.5	38.8857	1.69283
7	8.9	36.2589	−0.22055
8	8.9	34.8010	−0.94948
9	9.2	38.8264	0.61318
10	9.4	38.8036	0.30181
11	9.6	39.6669	0.43345
12	9.8	41.0976	0.84881
13	10.0	37.5849	−1.20753
14	10.2	40.5016	−0.04919
15	10.4	36.7930	−2.20347
16	10.7	42.8571	0.37857
17	10.7	41.2343	−0.43284
18	11.1	42.4704	−0.41479
19	11.1	44.8549	0.77746
20	11.5	47.0112	1.25562
21	11.8	46.0120	0.30599
22	12.1	44.6774	−0.81130
23	12.5	47.2986	−0.10070
24	13.0	48.1982	−0.40091
25	13.9	50.1098	−0.79508

Variable	n	Mean	Standard Deviation
x	25	10.000	1.914

```
Dotplot of x

        .       .   .   . . . : :. .... .... : :   . . . .          .
  -+---------+---------+---------+---------+---------+----- x
  6.0       7.5       9.0       10.5      12.0      13.5
```

with $\sigma = 2$. Exhibit 20.6B displays the 25 x values used for all the simulations. The x's range from a minimum of 6.1 to a maximum of 13.9, with a mean value of 10.000 and a standard deviation of 1.914. The full dotplot of the x's is also shown in the display. The exhibit also shows the result of *one* simulation. The e's were created as independent normally distributed variables with 0 mean and standard deviation of 2. (Actually, standard normal variables were first created and then each was multiplied by 2.) Then the y's were obtained as indicated in Equation (20.10). Finally, for this one data set a regression of y on x was carried out, with the results as shown in Exhibit 20.6C. Notice that the slope estimate is 2.89 compared with the known value of 3 and the intercept estimate is 11.0 compared with the true model value of 10. According to the p values shown, both of these estimates are significantly different from zero. The t statistics $(b_1 - 3)/se(b_1) = (2.8896 - 3)/0.1805 = -0.61$ and $(b_0 - 10)/se(b_0) = (11.008 - 10)/1.836 = 0.55$ may also be computed. These statistics show that these estimated values are not close to being significantly different from the values 3 and 10 used in the simulation.

EXHIBIT 20.6C

Regression on Simulated Data

```
The regression equation is

y = 11.0 + 2.89 x

Predictor       Coef       Stdev     t-ratio        p
Constant      11.008       1.836        5.99    0.000
x             2.8896      0.1805       16.01    0.000

s = 1.693      R-sq = 91.8%      R-sq(adj) = 91.4%

Analysis of Variance

SOURCE        DF          SS         MS         F        p
Regression     1      734.29     734.29    256.30    0.000
Error         23       65.89       2.86
Total         24      800.18
```

Exhibit 20.6D gives the scatterplot of the data, the estimated regression line shown as a solid line, and (since this is a simulation) the true regression line shown as a dashed line. Notice that the underestimation of the slope is partially compensated for by the overestimation of the intercept term.

Using these same 25 predictor values for x and the model in Equation (20.10), the regression simulation was repeated 500 times, each time obtaining a new set of errors and hence responses y. For each of the 500 data sets the regression calculations were performed and the results such as b_0, b_1, s, and R^2 saved for further analysis. In particular, Exhibit 20.6E shows the histogram of the 500 values of b_1 obtained. Notice that there were a few simulated data sets where the estimated slope was as small as 2.3 or 2.4 and others where the slope estimates were as large as 3.5 or 3.6. However, the majority of the simulations gave slopes in the range of about 2.8 to 3.2. Furthermore, the distribution is nicely symmetric with a mean of 3.0047 compared to the true value of 3.

According to statistical theory the sampling distribution of b_1 is a normal distribution with mean 3 and certain known standard deviation depending on σ and the values for x. To illustrate the correctness of this theory, the histogram of the

EXHIBIT 20.6D

Estimated Regression
Line with True Line
Overlayed

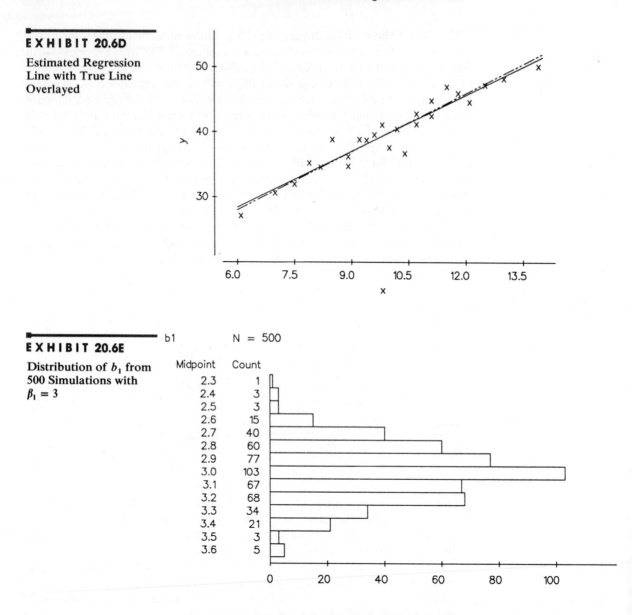

EXHIBIT 20.6E

Distribution of b_1 from
500 Simulations with
$\beta_1 = 3$

standardized b_1 values has been plotted in Exhibit 20.6F, which should be compared to a standard normal distribution. Finally, in Exhibit 20.6G the distribution of the t statistic $(b_1 - 3)/se(b_1)$ is shown. Theory says that this distribution is a t distribution with $25 - 2 = 23$ degrees of freedom. Such a distribution is difficult to distinguish from a standard normal distribution but it should contain a few more extreme values. These can be seen if Exhibits 20.6F and 20.6G are compared. Calculation shows that the standard deviations of these two distributions are 1.0184 and 1.0476, respectively, again indicating the slightly wider spread in the t distribution. From Theorem 1 in Section 19.1, the corresponding theoretical values are 1 for a standard normal distribution and 1.0465 for a t distribution with 23 degrees of freedom. Exhibits 20.6H and 20.6I show the normal scores plots for the standardized b_1 values and for the t statistic $(b_1 - 3)/se(b_1)$ values. Again, the graph in Exhibit 20.6H is a fairly straight line, but the one in Exhibit 20.6I shows more deviation from a straight line, especially in the extremes or tails. The t distribution with 23 degrees of freedom is nearly normal but not quite. Similar plots could be done for the estimates of the intercept parameter, but the slope parameter is of much more practical interest.

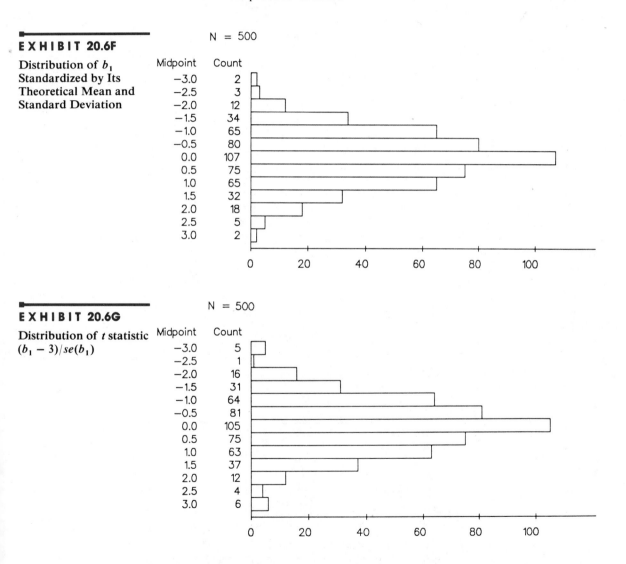

EXHIBIT 20.6F

Distribution of b_1 Standardized by Its Theoretical Mean and Standard Deviation

N = 500

Midpoint	Count
−3.0	2
−2.5	3
−2.0	12
−1.5	34
−1.0	65
−0.5	80
0.0	107
0.5	75
1.0	65
1.5	32
2.0	18
2.5	5
3.0	2

EXHIBIT 20.6G

Distribution of t statistic $(b_1 - 3)/se(b_1)$

N = 500

Midpoint	Count
−3.0	5
−2.5	1
−2.0	16
−1.5	31
−1.0	64
−0.5	81
0.0	105
0.5	75
1.0	63
1.5	37
2.0	12
2.5	4
3.0	6

In Exhibits 20.6C and 20.6D the underestimated slope was compensated for somewhat by an overestimated intercept. This was not a fluke of that particular simulation. The pairs of estimates of slope and intercept are strongly negatively

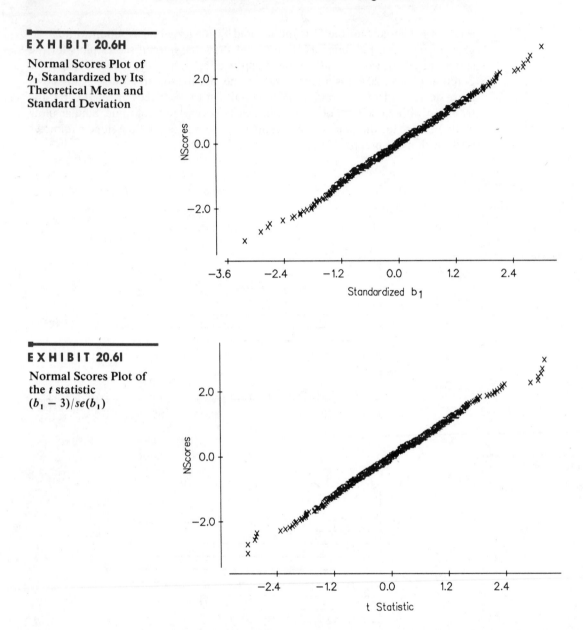

E X H I B I T 20.6I

Normal Scores Plot of
the t statistic
$(b_1 - 3)/se(b_1)$

correlated over the 500 simulations. Exhibit 20.6J displays the scatterplot of the 500 pairs of b_0 and b_1. Notice that when the slope is overestimated the intercept usually is underestimated to compensate, and vice versa.

Once the 500 simulations have been carried out and the results saved, a great many distributions and relationships can be investigated. Exhibit 20.6K gives the distribution of s. Theory predicts that s will be nearly normally distributed for large degrees of freedom but that the distribution will be skewed to the right for smaller sample sizes. In our example the degrees of freedom are 23, but Exhibit 20.6K still shows some of this skewness. Notice that even though the true value of σ is 2, one sample produced a value for s as large as about 3.4.

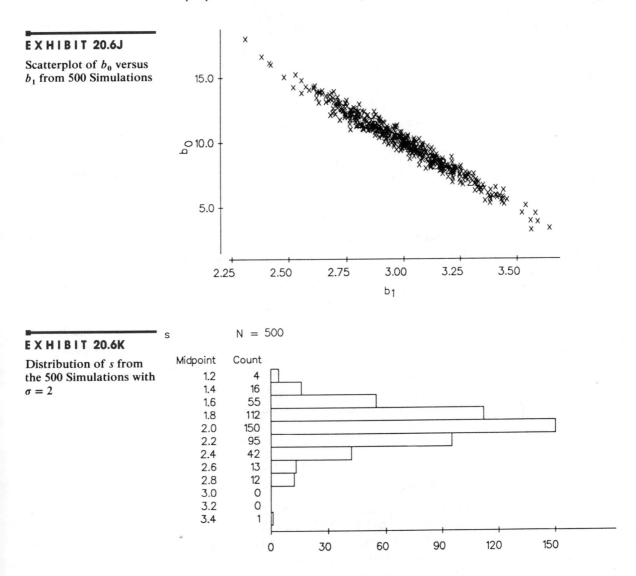

EXHIBIT 20.6J

Scatterplot of b_0 versus b_1 from 500 Simulations

EXHIBIT 20.6K

Distribution of s from the 500 Simulations with $\sigma = 2$

Exhibit 20.6L displays the scatterplot of slope estimates and corresponding estimates of σ. The lack of correlation between these two quantities, which may be established by statistical theory, is seen clearly in this plot. An under-, over-, or accurate estimate of the slope has no effect whatsoever on the estimate of σ.

EXHIBIT 20.6L

Scatterplot of b_1 versus s from the 500 Simulations

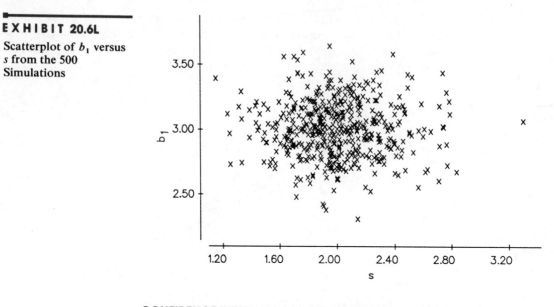

CONFIDENCE INTERVALS FOR THE REGRESSION COEFFICIENTS

Rather than testing for significance, estimates of unknown parameters are frequently given together with appropriate error bounds. In general, confidence intervals for individual regression parameters β_i are calculated as

$$b_i \pm t \cdot se(b_i)$$

where the multiplier t is either a convenient predetermined value like 3, which balances the confidence level and sample size n, or else is determined from the t distribution with $n - 2$ degrees of freedom to achieve a prescribed confidence level.

The information given in Exhibit 20.6A allows a confidence interval for the true but unknown slope in regressing Market value on Sq.ft to be obtained quickly. Using a multiplier of 3,

$$0.018362 \pm 3(0.002134)$$

or 0.018362 ± 0.006402

or, now rounding, 0.0184 ± 0.0064

Stated otherwise, we can be quite confident that the true slope lies somewhere in the interval from 0.012 to 0.025 or that the true change in predicted market value per square foot of living area is in the range from \$12 to \$25. Notice that this interval does *not* include the value of zero. Thus the confidence interval is consistent with rejecting the hypothesis $\beta_1 = 0$.

For the regression in Exhibit 20.6C on the simulated data, the 3-standard-error confidence interval for the slope is

$$2.8896 \pm 3(0.1805)$$

or 2.8896 ± 0.5415

or 2.89 ± 0.54

In interval form this is 2.35 to 3.43, which nicely surrounds the true value of 3 in this simulation. For a given t multiplier or prescribed confidence level, each of the 500 replications from this model produces its own confidence interval for the slope. In fact, 22, or 4.4%, of the 95% confidence intervals so produced failed to include the true value of 3. Only 7 out of the 500, or 1.4%, did not cover the true slope value when the intervals were based on plus or minus 3 standard errors. The t distribution with 23 degrees of freedom predicts that 0.6% will miss, so that theory is substantiated reasonably well in this simulation.

PREDICTION INTERVALS

In prediction the future value of the response is "guessed" when the predictor variable is set at a particular value x^*. For example, suppose you are considering selling a house that has 1000 square feet of living space. What is the predicted market value of this house and how precise is the prediction? Let the value of the future response be denoted y^*. As discussed in Chapter 7, the prediction is given by $\hat{y}^* = b_0 + b_1 x^*$. Furthermore, the precision of the forecast is assessed by looking at the properties of the **prediction error** $y^* = \hat{y}^* = y^* - b_0 - b_1 x^*$. Under the regression assumptions it may be shown that the prediction error has a normal distribution with mean 0 and a certain standard deviation. The estimate of this standard deviation is called the **prediction standard error** (*predse*) and is given by a certain formula[†] For our purposes, only the following facts concerning conditions of the prediction standard error are important:

■ It is proportional to s.
■ It is always larger than s.
■ It is close to s if n is large and x^* is not too far from $\bar{x}$.
■ It is smallest when $x^* = \bar{x}$ and increases as x^* moves away from $\bar{x}$ in either direction.

Prediction intervals are formed just like confidence intervals for regression parameters, namely,

$$\text{Prediction} \pm t \cdot predse$$

or

$$b_0 + b_1 x^* \pm t \cdot predse$$

where t is selected either as a convenient multiplier such as 3 or else to achieve a prescribed confidence level using the t distribution with $n - 2$ degrees of freedom.

Exhibit 20.6M gives a plot of the 60 market values versus square footage values with the 95% prediction limits also displayed. The prediction limits were obtained by computing the limits at each observed x value and then connecting the limits with straight lines. The prediction limits displayed are not themselves straight lines, as

[†] For the simple one-predictor model it may be shown that under the assumptions on page 538 the prediction standard error is given by

$$predse = s \sqrt{1 + \frac{1}{n} + \frac{(x^* - \bar{x})^2}{\sum_{i=1}^{n} (x_i - \bar{x})^2}}$$

EXHIBIT 20.6M

95% Prediction Limits
for Market in Terms of
Sq.ft

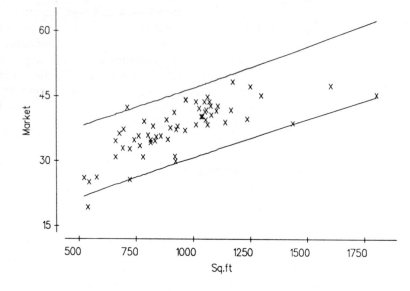

you may verify by measuring the vertical distance between the curves. The limits widen out a little as x^* moves away from $\bar{x}$ in either direction. This is caused by the increase in *predse*. The effect is most prominent on the extreme right-hand side of the plot.

The simulation of the model in Equation (20.10) may also be used to illustrate the theoretical properties of the predictions from regression models. Recall that 500 replications of the model were obtained, each with a sample size of 25, $\bar{x} = 10.0$, and largest x value of 13.9. For prediction purposes both a middle value for x^*, namely, 10, and an extreme value of $x^* = 14$, where prediction is somewhat more difficult, will be considered. For each of the 500 replications additional values for the response y were obtained according to the model $y = 10 + 3x + e$ for both $x = 10$ and $x = 14$. Once the regression parameters are estimated for a given sample of 25 observations, the predictions and prediction limits for these two x values are produced. There are then, for each of these two x values, 500 actual values, predicted values, and upper and lower prediction limits. The predictions may then be compared to the actual values obtained for y in several ways.

In the first analysis simply count the number of replications where the prediction limits failed to surround the actual value. Since 95% prediction intervals are being computed, we should miss about 5% of the time, or 25 out of 500. With $x = 10$ the simulation process actually missed 27 times, and with $x = 14$, 26 failures were observed, both of which agree well with theory. Exhibits 20.6N and 20.6O display the actual values and 95% prediction limits for the first 80 replications. Here replications 30, 53, and 59 correspond to misses for the middle x case, and replications 29, 35, and 50 are misses for the extreme x case. In addition, the prediction-limit widths vary with replication, because these widths are determined by the varying estimates of σ. Also, generally speaking, the prediction-interval widths are wider when attempting to predict at the extreme x value.

EXHIBIT 20.6N

EXHIBIT 20.6N

95% Prediction Limits
and Simulated Actual
Values—Middle x Case

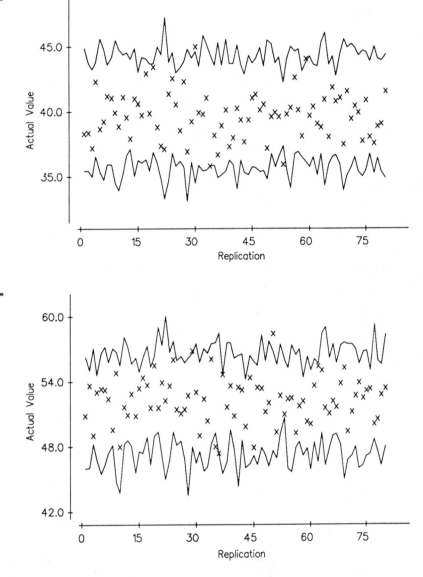

EXHIBIT 20.6O

95% Prediction Limits
and Simulated Actual
Values—Extreme x
Case

Rather than just counting the number of misses, the distribution of the actual prediction error could also be considered in both prediction situations. This error has a normal distribution with mean 0 and a theoretical standard deviation. Exhibit 20.6P shows this distribution for the 500 replications with $x = 10$. Exhibit 20.6Q gives a similar display with $x = 14$. Both distributions are quite symmetric and centered around zero, but the second distribution is slightly more spread out, as theory predicts. The standard deviations of the two distributions are, in fact, 2.0131 and 2.2062, respectively, which compare well with the corresponding theoretical values of 2.0396 and 2.2108.

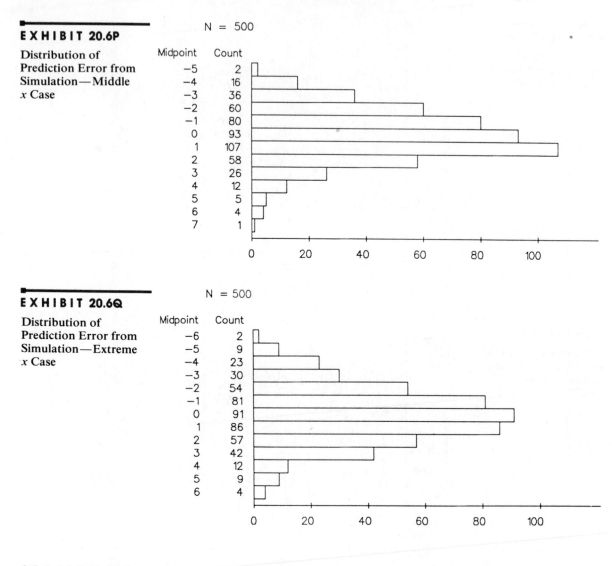

EXHIBIT 20.6P

Distribution of
Prediction Error from
Simulation—Middle
x Case

N = 500

Midpoint	Count
−5	2
−4	16
−3	36
−2	60
−1	80
0	93
1	107
2	58
3	26
4	12
5	5
6	4
7	1

EXHIBIT 20.6Q

Distribution of
Prediction Error from
Simulation—Extreme
x Case

N = 500

Midpoint	Count
−6	2
−5	9
−4	23
−3	30
−2	54
−1	81
0	91
1	86
2	57
3	42
4	12
5	9
6	4

SECTION 20.7

EXERCISES

20.7A Use the information provided in Exhibit 20.6A to obtain a confidence interval on the intercept parameter β_0 for Market regressed on Sq.ft. Use a multiplier of 3.

20.7B Use the computer output shown in Exhibit 20.6C.
   (a) Find a confidence interval for the slope parameter β_1 (which is known to be 3). Use a multiplier of 2 so that the interval has a confidence level of about 95%.
   (b) Does the interval include the true value of 3?
   (c) If the simulations were repeated 1000 times, approximately what percentage of the confidence intervals constructed as in part (a) would *not* include the number 3?

20.7C Use Exhibit 20.6C to verify that in simple linear regression the F ratio for regression is the same as the square of the t ratio for the slope coefficient.

20.7D Based on Exhibit 20.6J, if you were told that the intercept estimate was 5.0, what would you predict for the corresponding slope estimate?

20.7E Based on Exhibit 20.6L, if you were told that the slope estimate was 3.50, what would you predict for the corresponding estimate of σ?

20.7F Consider a regression situation such as reported in Exhibit 20.6B. Two predictions are to be made: one with $x = 6.9$ and the other with $x = 10.1$. Which of these two predictions will have *wider* 95% prediction intervals?

20.7G The data set below gives the average height of girls by age. (These data are used in several later exercises.)

(a) Use age to predict height in a simple linear regression model.

(b) Test whether age is significant as a predictor of girls' average height.

(c) The response in this data set is the *average* height for girls at each age. Would it be reasonable to use the regression equation developed in part (a) to predict an *individual* girl's height? Would s be useful as a measure of the precision of that prediction? Why or why not?

```
# filename: AGEHGT_G.DAT
# Age and height data for girls
# (Source: The World Almanac and Book of Facts: 1985 edition
# Their source: Physicians' Handbook, 1983)
# age (in years), height (in inches)
 .5    26
  1    29
  2    33
  3    36
  4    39
  5    41
  6    44
  7    47
  8    50
  9    52
 10    54
 11    56
 12    58
 13    60
 14    62
```

20.7H The data set below gives boys' average heights by age. Use age to predict height in a simple regression model.

(a) Test whether age is significant as a predictor of boys' height.

(b) Compare the prediction equation for boys' height with the prediction equation for girls' height found in Exercise 20.7G.

```
# filename: AGEHGT_B.DAT
# Age and height data for boys
# (Source: The World Almanac and Book of Facts: 1985 edition
# Their source: Physicians' Handbook, 1983)
# age (in years), height (in inches)
 .5    26
  1    29
  2    33
  3    36
  4    39
  5    42
  6    45
  7    47
  8    50
  9    52
 10    54
 11    56
 12    58
 13    60
 14    62
```

20.7I The data file below lists the capacities of a collection of ice chests and coolers as stated by the manufacturers versus the actual size as measured by the staff at Consumers Union and reported in *Consumer Reports*, June 1989.

(a) Using the stated size as the predictor variable, fit a simple linear regression to the actual size.

(b) Test the significance of the estimated regression coefficient.

(c) Predict the actual size of a cooler that claims to be 12 cubic feet. Find a 2-standard-error prediction interval for the actual size.

```
# filename: COOLERS.DAT
# Capacity of ice chests and coolers
# (Source: Consumer Reports, June 1989)
# Stated capacity, actual capacity (cubic feet)
    17     15.5
    18     15.5
    15     16.75
    15     15.5
    12     13.5
    15     13.5
     8      8.25
    12     10.75
     8      7.5
     6      6.75
     6      6.5
     6      6.75
  13.5     13.5
    12     12.5
    12     12.25
    12     12.25
    12     12
```

20.7J Hardwood trees are harvested in a selective manner for the manufacture of fine furniture. The volume of lumber in a selected tree is critical in determining the worth of the tree to the buyer and determines the price paid to the grower. However, volume is not easily measured before the tree is harvested. Two common measurements made before cutting down the tree are DBH (the diameter of the tree at breast height, 4.5 feet off the ground) and the height of the tree measured with sighting instruments. After the tree is harvested the volume of lumber may be measured. A regression model relating volume to diameter and/or height will be helpful to the lumber buyers. The data file below and on page 557 gives the diameters, heights, and volumes of 31 trees harvested in the Allegheny National Forest in Pennsylvania. (This data set is used in several later exercises.)

(a) Fit a regression model that predicts volume from diameter.

(b) Fit a regression model that predicts volume from height.

(c) Compare the models fit in parts (a) and (b).

```
# filename: TREES.DAT
# Data on black cherry trees
# Allegheny National Forest, Pennsylvania
# (Source: B.F.Ryan, B.L.Joiner and T.A.Ryan, Minitab Handbook,
# 2d ed., PWS-KENT, Boston, 1986)
# Diameter in inches at 4.5 feet above ground level
# Height of tree in feet
# Volume of tree in cubic feet
# Diameter, Height, Volume
     8.3      70      10.3
     8.6      65      10.3
     8.8      63      10.2
    10.5      72      16.4
    10.7      81      18.8
    10.8      83      19.7
```

(Continued)

11.0	66	15.6
11.0	75	18.2
11.1	80	22.6
11.2	75	19.9
11.3	79	24.2
11.4	76	21.0
11.4	76	21.4
11.7	69	21.3
12.0	75	19.1
12.9	74	22.2
12.9	85	33.8
13.3	86	27.4
13.7	71	25.7
13.8	64	24.9
14.0	78	34.5
14.2	80	31.7
14.5	74	36.3
16.0	72	38.3
16.3	77	42.6
17.3	81	55.4
17.5	82	55.7
17.9	80	58.3
18.0	80	51.5
18.0	80	51.0
20.6	87	77.0

SECTION 20.8

INFERENCE FOR MODELS WITH MANY PREDICTORS

SIGNIFICANCE TESTS ON REGRESSION COEFFICIENTS

Consider the real-property data set once more. In Chapter 7 several models involving many predictor variables were developed. How is the usefulness of the predictors assessed in these more complex situations? The F test based on the ratio of the regression mean square to the residual mean square is a place to start. This ratio is appropriate for testing the hypothesis $H_0: \beta_1 = \beta_2 = \cdots = \beta_k = 0$. If true, this of course would say that the variation in the response y is simply chance variation. Statistical theory says that if H_0 is true, then the sampling distribution of the F ratio is an F distribution with k and $n - k - 1$ degrees of freedom. If H_0 is not true, then the F ratio tends to be larger than it is under H_0. Thus large values for the F ratio argue against H_0. Notice that "H_0 *not* true" only means that *some* of the coefficients $\beta_1, \beta_2, \ldots, \beta_k$ are not zero—not necessarily that *all* of them are nonzero.

Exhibit 20.8A shows the regression results for predicting Market value using both Sq.ft and Sq.ft.sq. The analysis of variance table gives the F ratio as 58.26 with 2 and 57 degrees of freedom. The p value of 0.000 indicates that this is indeed a large F ratio, and we can confidently conclude that at least one of the coefficients on Sq.ft or Sq.ft.sq is not zero.

However, is the inclusion of the extra predictor Sq.ft.sq really important in the model? Does $\beta_2 = 0$? Notice here that nothing at all is being said about β_1. The question is not whether Sq.ft.sq is an important predictor but rather whether or not it is an important predictor *in addition to* the Sq.ft variable. The hypothesis $\beta_2 = 0$ (with β_1 arbitrary) may be tested by looking at the t ratio, $b_2/se(b_2)$, associated with the x_2 variable. If indeed $\beta_2 = 0$ is true, it may be shown that the sampling distribution of this t ratio is a t distribution with $n - k - 1 = 57$ degrees of freedom. Exhibit 20.8A shows that the t ratio for Sq.ft.sq is -4.39, which leads to a p value

EXHIBIT 20.8A

Regression of Market
on Sq.ft and Sq.ft.sq

```
The regression equation is

Market = 0.07 + 0.0597 Sq.ft - 0.000020 Sq.ft.sq

Predictor         Coef        Stdev      t-ratio         p
Constant         0.073        4.998         0.01     0.988
Sq.ft         0.059729     0.009614         6.21     0.000
Sq.ft.sq  -0.00001960   0.00000447        -4.39     0.000

s = 3.473        R-sq = 67.2%    R-sq(adj) = 66.0%

Analysis of Variance

SOURCE       DF         SS          MS         F         p
Regression    2    1405.07      702.54     58.26     0.000
Error        57     687.33       12.06
Total        59    2092.40
```

of 0.000. Thus Sq.ft.sq is a useful predictor even when Sq.ft is already included in the prediction model.

A formula for computing the standard error of an estimated regression coefficient for models with more than one predictor is given in the appendix to this chapter [Equation (A10)] but such detail is not needed here. As usual, statistical software supplies the necessary standard errors.

In general the significance of an individual regression coefficient b_i in a multiple regression model with k predictors can be tested by looking at the magnitude of the corresponding t ratio, $b_i/se(b_i)$. If indeed $\beta_i = 0$ is true, it may be shown that the sampling distribution of this t ratio is a t distribution with $n - k - 1$ degrees of freedom. Otherwise, the t ratio will tend to be larger in magnitude and the null hypothesis $\beta_i = 0$ should be rejected for values of the t ratio that are far enough from zero.

Exhibit 20.8B gives the multiple regression results of Market on Sq.ft, Sq.ft.sq, Grade (through the binary indicator variables Med and Hi), and Assessed. The F ratio of 45.80 with 5 and 54 degrees of freedom is very large with a p value of 0.000. At least some of these predictors are of value in predicting Market. The t ratios for the individual coefficients all indicate significance of the predictors even

EXHIBIT 20.8B

Market Regressed on
Sq.ft, Sq.ft.sq, Med, Hi,
and Assessed

```
The regression equation is

Market = 1.11 + 0.0449 Sq.ft - 0.000015 Sq.ft.sq + 4.15 Med
                              + 5.22 Hi + 0.223 Assessed

Predictor         Coef        Stdev      t-ratio         p
Constant         1.111        4.242         0.26     0.794
Sq.ft         0.044883     0.008073         5.56     0.000
Sq.ft.sq  -0.00001506   0.00000366        -4.12     0.000
Med              4.150        1.081         3.84     0.000
Hi               5.216        1.926         2.71     0.009
Assessed       0.22337      0.06940         3.22     0.002

s = 2.719        R-sq = 80.9%    R-sq(adj) = 79.2%

Analysis of Variance

SOURCE       DF         SS          MS         F         p
Regression    5    1693.16      338.63     45.80     0.000
Error        54     399.24        7.39
Total        59    2092.40
```

when the other variables are in the model. Assuming that the model assumptions are reasonably well satisfied, this multiple regression model looks very useful for predicting market value. In Chapter 21 important techniques for assessing the reasonableness of the model assumptions are considered. In Chapter 22 the problem of selecting the best set of predictor variables is discussed.

CONFIDENCE INTERVALS FOR REGRESSION COEFFICIENTS

Confidence intervals for an individual regression coefficient β_i in models with several predictors can be constructed just as they were for simpler models. We use $b_i \pm t \cdot se(b_i)$, the only added complication being the computation of $se(b_i)$. Since statistical software provides this computation, no new difficulties are encountered. As examples, consider the model results presented in Exhibit 20.8B. We can be quite confident that the partial slope coefficient associated with the Assessed predictor lies in the interval

$$0.22337 \pm 3(0.06940)$$

or
$$0.22337 \pm 0.2082$$

Rounding gives the final interval of $(0.015, 0.432)$. Notice that this interval does *not* include zero, again indicating that Assessed is a useful predictor in addition to the other predictors in this model.

The 3-standard-error confidence interval for the binary predictor variable Med, indicating the effect of a medium-grade property compared with a low-grade one, is

$$4.150 \pm 3(1.081)$$

or
$$4.150 \pm 3.243$$

which rounds to the interval $(0.91, 7.39)$. We are confident that, on average, a medium-grade house will have a market value above a low-grade house of between about \$900 and \$7400, all other predictor variables being equal.

PREDICTION INTERVALS

The facts about prediction intervals for a future response y^* in regression models with one predictor generalize quite easily to the more complicated models. The predictions are obtained from $b_0 + b_1 x_1^* + b_2 x_2^* + \cdots + b_k x_k^*$ and the prediction error is $y^* - (b_0 + b_1 x_1^* + b_2 x_2^* + \cdots + b_k x_k^*)$. The corresponding prediction intervals are formed as

$$\text{Prediction} \pm t \cdot predse$$

or
$$b_0 + b_1 x_1^* + b_2 x_2^* + \cdots + b_k x_k^* \pm t \cdot predse$$

where t is selected either as a convenient multiplier such as 3 or else to achieve a prescribed confidence level using the t distribution with $n - k - 1$ degrees of freedom. As mentioned earlier, the specific formula for the prediction standard error is not necessary here but can be found in the appendix to this chapter [Equation (A12)]. The following basic properties of the prediction standard error are important:

- It is proportional to s.
- It is always larger than s.

▪ It is close to *s* if *n* is large and all of the predictor variables are near their respective means.

▪ It is smallest when all the predictor variables are set to their respective means.

Exhibit 20.8C shows 95% prediction intervals for the market value response based on the two variable quadratic curve model using Sq.ft and Sq.ft.sq. (The estimates for this model may be reviewed in Exhibit 20.8A.) In this display the widening of the prediction limits for more extreme values of the predictors is noticeable. Compare the predictions and prediction limits here to those in Ex-

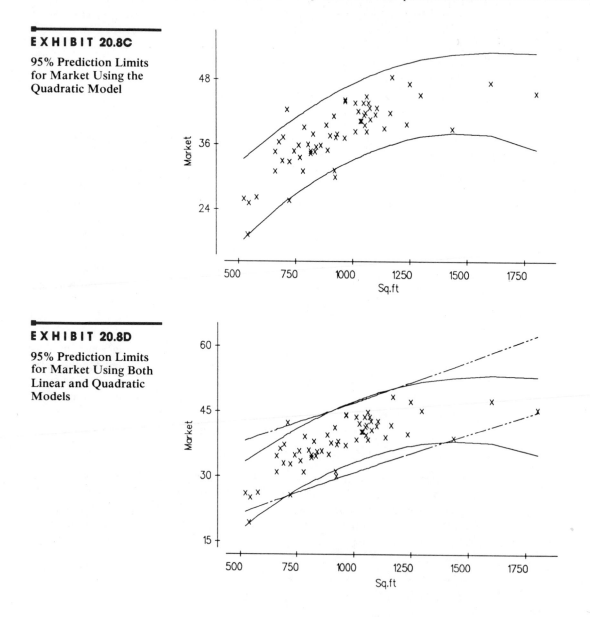

EXHIBIT 20.8C

95% Prediction Limits for Market Using the Quadratic Model

EXHIBIT 20.8D

95% Prediction Limits for Market Using Both Linear and Quadratic Models

hibit 20.6M, where the simpler straight line model was considered. Such a comparison is facilitated by overlaying the two sets of prediction limits as in Exhibit 20.8D. In this display it is clear that the quadratic model produces prediction limits that are narrower and better follow the shape of the scatterplot.

Now consider predictions based on the full set of predictors, Sq.ft, Sq.ft.sq, Med, Hi, and Assessed. Since two of the predictors are binary, a considerable amount of information can be displayed in a single plot. Exhibit 20.8E shows the scatterplot of the market values versus square feet with the grade variable coded as L = low grade, M = medium grade, and H = high grade. Exhibit 20.8E also displays the 95% prediction limits for this full model. The effect of every variable but assessed value can be seen in this plot.

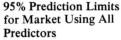

EXHIBIT 20.8E

95% Prediction Limits for Market Using All Predictors

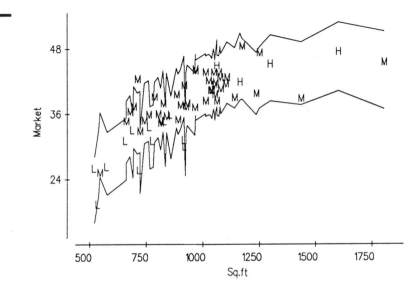

SECTION 20.9

EXERCISES

20.9A Use the regression results presented in Exhibit 20.8B to test whether or not Sq.ft.sq is an important predictor variable even after Sq.ft, Med, Hi, and Assessed are included in the model for Market.

20.9B The data file on page 562 gives 28 cases on 11 potential predictor variables for predicting the selling price of houses in Erie, Pennsylvania, in the early 1970s. (This data set is used in later exercises.)

(a) Use taxes, number of baths, and square feet as predictors and test the overall model using the *F* ratio statistic.

(b) Using the same model as in part (a), test whether the number-of-baths variable is an important predictor in addition to the other two predictors, taxes and square feet.

(c) Using the model of part (a), find a 3-standard-error confidence interval for the regression coefficient associated with square feet.

(d) Predict the sales price of a house that has 1.5 baths, taxes of $850, and 1500 square feet of living space. What are the 2-standard-error prediction limits for this prediction?

```
# filename: HOUSEPRI.DAT
# Sale price of homes with 11 predictors
# (Source: Narula and Wellington, Technometrics (1977): 185-190.)
# Variables: price ($100), taxes ($), number of baths, lot size,
# square feet living space, number of garages, number of rooms,
# number of bedrooms, age in years,
# type(1=brick, 2=brick and frame, 3=aluminum and frame, 4=frame)
# style (1=two story, 2=one and one-half story, 3=ranch)
# number of fireplaces
259  492 1.0  3472  998 1.0   7 4 42 3 1 0
295  502 1.0  3531 1500 2.0   7 4 62 1 1 0
279  454 1.0  2275 1175 1.0   6 3 40 2 1 0
259  456 1.0  4050 1232 1.0   6 3 54 4 1 0
299  506 1.0  4455 1121 1.0   6 3 42 3 1 0
299  389 1.0  4455  988 1.0   6 3 56 2 1 0
309  590 1.0  5850 1240 1.0   7 3 51 2 1 1
289  560 1.0  9520 1501 0.0   6 3 32 1 1 0
849 1542 2.5  9800 3420 2.0  10 5 42 2 1 1
829 1446 2.5 12800 3000 2.0   9 5 14 4 1 1
359  583 1.0  6435 1225 2.0   6 3 32 1 1 0
315  530 1.0  4988 1552 1.0   6 3 30 1 2 0
310  627 1.0  5520  975 1.0   5 2 30 1 2 0
309  596 1.0  6666 1121 2.0   6 3 32 2 1 0
300  505 1.0  5000 1020 0.0   5 2 46 4 1 1
289  560 1.0  9520 1501 0.0   6 3 32 1 1 0
369  825 1.5  5150 1664 2.0   8 4 50 4 1 0
419  670 1.5  6902 1488 1.5   7 3 22 1 1 1
405  778 1.5  7102 1376 1.0   6 3 17 2 1 0
439  904 1.0  7800 1500 1.5   7 3 23 3 3 0
375  599 1.0  5520 1256 2.0   6 3 40 4 1 1
379  754 1.5  4000 1690 1.0   6 3 22 1 1 0
445  880 1.5  9890 1820 2.0   8 4 50 1 1 1
379  609 1.5  6726 1652 1.0   6 3 44 4 1 0
389  836 1.5  9150 1777 2.0   8 4 48 1 1 1
369  814 1.0  8000 1504 2.0   7 3  3 1 3 0
458  914 1.5  7326 1831 1.5   8 4 31 4 1 0
410 1200 1.5  5000 1200 2.0   6 3 30 3 1 1
```

20.9C Consider the house-price data in Exercise 20.9B. Regression analysis may also be used to investigate relationships among various predictor variables.

(a) Fit a model that uses lot size and number of rooms to predict the square feet in the house.

(b) What percentage of the variation in house square footage values is explained by these two variables?

(c) Are both of these predictors important once the other is in the model?

20.9D The data file on page 563 lists sales and advertising data for Crest toothpaste over the years 1967 through 1980. Crest sales are to be related to Crest advertising dollars, the ratio of Crest advertising to Colgate advertising (the major Crest competitor), and U.S. disposable family income for those years.

(a) Estimate a regression model that predicts Crest sales using a linear combination of Crest advertising dollars, advertising ratio, and disposable income.

(b) Test the overall worth of the model using the F ratio.

(c) Procter & Gamble, the manufacturer of Crest toothpaste, is especially interested in the effect of its advertising on Crest sales. Test whether or not the Crest advertising dollars contribute substantially to the prediction equation given that the other variables are in the model.

```
# filename: CREST.DAT
# Crest toothpaste sales and advertising data
# (Source: C.I.Allmon, Business Economics (1982))
# Variables: year, Crest sales ($1000s),
# advertising ($1000s), advertsing ratio (Crest to Colgate),
# personal disposable income ($billion)
1967  105000  16300  1.25   547.9
1968  105000  15800  1.34   593.4
1969  121600  16000  1.22   638.9
1970  113750  14200  1.00   695.3
1971  113750  15000  1.15   751.8
1972  128925  14000  1.13   810.3
1973  142500  15400  1.05   914.5
1974  126000  18250  1.27   998.3
1975  162000  17300  1.07  1096.1
1976  191625  23000  1.17  1194.4
1977  189000  19300  1.07  1311.5
1978  210000  23056  1.54  1462.9
1979  224250  26000  1.59  1641.7
1980  245000  28000  1.56  1821.7
```

20.9E Consider the tree data from Exercise 20.7J.

(a) Fit a model that predicts volume with a linear combination of diameter and height.

(b) Evaluate the worth in the model of the height predictor after diameter is in the model.

(c) Compare the model in part (a) to models that use diameter and height separately.

(d) Predict the volume of a tree that has a diameter of 14 inches and a height of 80 feet.

(e) Predict the volume of a tree with diameter 9 inches and height 76 feet.

(f) Is 9 inches an unusual diameter? Is 75 feet an unusual height? Is this combination of diameter and height unusual in this data set?

(g) Compare the widths of the prediction intervals associated with the predictions found in parts (d) and (e).

(Other multiple regression models for these data are considered in Chapters 21 and 22.) (Filename: TREES.DAT.)

SECTION 20.10

THE REGRESSION FALLACY

Exhibit 20.10A gives a scatterplot of first and second exam scores for 39 students in a statistics class.[†] As is typical there is quite a lot of scatter in these data. Some students who did poorly on the first exam managed to score better on the second, and some who scored well on the first exam did less well on the second one. The mean score on the first exam for the 10 lowest students is 44.8; these same students averaged 50.1 on the second exam. Similarly, the 10 best students on the first test had a mean score of 94.4 on that exam and only 82.4 on the second. The word *regression* was introduced by Sir Francis Galton because he perceived this effect as a *regression toward the mean* or even regression toward mediocrity.[††]

Actually the students have not regressed at all. There will always be differences between the two scores due at least to measurement error. The *regression fallacy*

[†] Both sets of exam scores were standardized and then relocated and scaled so that they have the same mean and standard deviation.

[††] Galton's *Natural Inheritance* was published in London in 1889 by Macmillan. A modern critique of Galton's work may be found in Stephen M. Stigler, *The History of Statistics* (Boston: Harvard University Press, 1986).

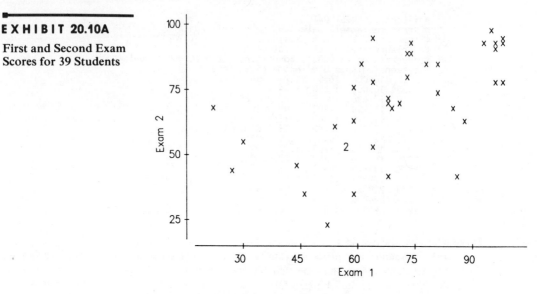

EXHIBIT 20.10A

First and Second Exam
Scores for 39 Students

occurs if this "regression" is interpreted as an important effect—not simply due to the spread of the data points around the regression line. Exhibit 20.10B shows the same scatterplot of exam scores with the solid regression line and dashed 45° line also displayed. The regression line has a slope of about 0.6 compared to the slope of 1 for the 45° line. The 45° line represents the naive prediction that a student will score the same on the second exam as she did on the first.

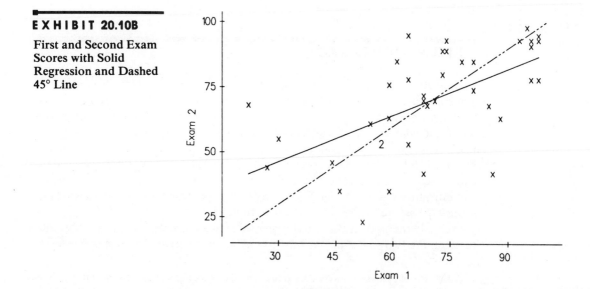

Although regression analysis is one of the most useful statistical techniques, it must be interpreted and used carefully. Section 20.11 illustrates other difficulties in interpreting these models.

As a second example of this fallacy, consider introducing a new product into 10 different regions of the country. Presumably sales may differ in the regions due to real factors such as different age or income distributions in the regions. But there will also be chance variation of sales not explained by these factors. Suppose that after one year regions 2 and 5 have outstanding sales while regions 8 and 9 have the lowest sales. Should the sales managers in regions 2 and 5 be praised and those in regions 8 and 9 be reprimanded? If the chance component of sales is substantial, then there is every reason to believe that next year's sales will be lower in regions 2 and 5 and higher in regions 8 and 9 regardless of the skill of the sales managers. Without statistical reasoning, including the understanding of chance variation, the regression fallacy can be very misleading.

SECTION 20.11

SAMPLING MODELS (OR HOW TO INFLATE R^2)

Regression analysis may be carried out on data that have been obtained from a designed experiment where the values of the predictor variables are under the researcher's control or on data that are observational or happenstance. The exam scores on the first exam used in the preceding section were not determined in advance by the analyst. In any case, all the formal inferences assume that the values for the predictor variables are fixed. What are the implications of selecting different values for the predictors?

THE POPULATION

A collection of 200 pairs of data whose scatterplot is shown in Exhibit 20.11A is used to illustrate. These data will be treated as a population from which various kinds of samples of size 30 are selected. Here are some relevant facts about this population: the regression line $\hat{y} = -75.7 + 0.857x$, $s = 0.6435$, and $R^2 = 62.4\%$.

EXHIBIT 20.11A

Population of Regression Data

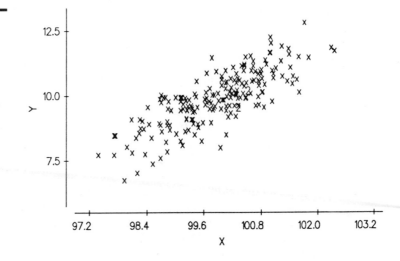

A RANDOM SAMPLE

Now suppose that a random sample of 30 cases is selected from the 200 predictor values carrying along the corresponding 30 response values. Exhibit 20.11B displays the scatterplot of the 30 selected cases and Exhibit 20.11C gives the regression results for this sample. The parameter estimates based on this sample reproduce the corresponding values in the population quite well:

$$\hat{Y}\text{sample} = -72.4 + 0.825 \text{ Xsample}, s = 0.5616, \quad \text{and} \quad R^2 = 60.1\%.$$

E X H I B I T 20.11B

A Random Sample of the Regression Data in Exhibit 20.11A

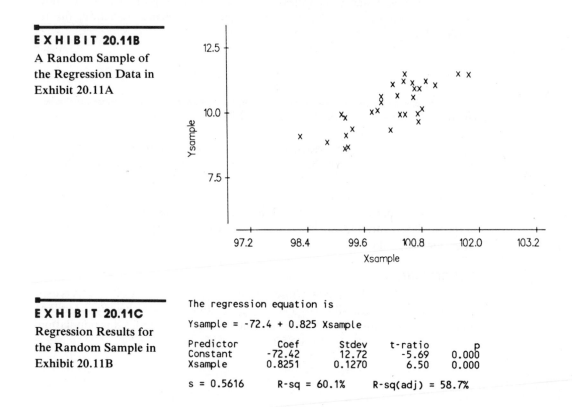

E X H I B I T 20.11C

Regression Results for the Random Sample in Exhibit 20.11B

```
The regression equation is

Ysample = -72.4 + 0.825 Xsample

Predictor        Coef        Stdev      t-ratio          p
Constant       -72.42        12.72        -5.69      0.000
Xsample         0.8251       0.1270        6.50      0.000

s = 0.5616       R-sq = 60.1%       R-sq(adj) = 58.7%
```

AN OUTER SAMPLE

Suppose now that the population is "sampled" by selecting the 15 cases with the smallest values for the predictor and the 15 cases with the largest values for the predictor—an "outer" sample. Exhibit 20.11D gives the scatterplot of the 30 pairs and Exhibit 20.11E the regression results. Here the estimated regression line and estimate of σ are quite reasonable ($\hat{Y}$outer $= -75.2 + 0.851$ Xouter, and $s = 0.6717$) but the $R^2 = 84.8\%$ value is substantially inflated compared to the population value of 62.4%. By omitting all the middle-sized x values we have also omitted all the middle-sized y values and thus increased the spread of the y values relative to their spread in the population. But the spread around the regression line has been kept nearly the same as in the population. Since R^2 is 100 times one minus

EXHIBIT 20.11D

An Outer Sample of the
Regression Data in
Exhibit 20.11A

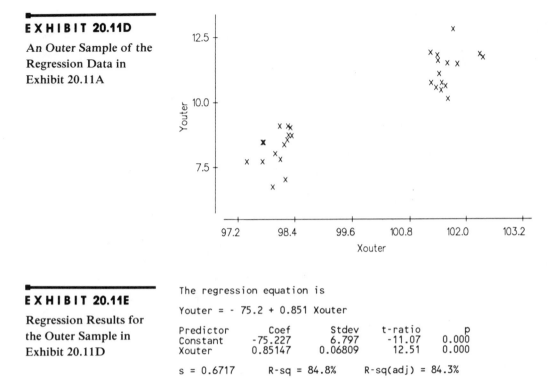

EXHIBIT 20.11E

Regression Results for
the Outer Sample in
Exhibit 20.11D

```
The regression equation is

Youter = - 75.2 + 0.851 Xouter

Predictor       Coef      Stdev    t-ratio       p
Constant     -75.227      6.797     -11.07   0.000
Xouter       0.85147    0.06809      12.51   0.000

s = 0.6717      R-sq = 84.8%      R-sq(adj) = 84.3%
```

the ratio of the spread around the regression line to the spread in the response
values, the effect is the inflated R^2 value.

A MIDDLE SAMPLE

In this illustration 30 cases whose x values are in the middle range of the 200 x values
are selected. When the cases are ordered according to the value of the x values, cases
86 through 115 are used. A scatterplot in which the scales were chosen to fill the plot
in both the vertical and horizontal directions is shown in Exhibit 20.11F. Our initial
reaction is that the plot is quite boring, showing very little if any relationship
between x and y. To keep this plot in perspective, the same data are replotted in
Exhibit 20.11G but using the same scales on the axes as in the original scatterplot of
Exhibit 20.11A.

From this exhibit it is apparent that it will be difficult to estimate the true
regression line! Exhibit 20.11H gives the results of the regression calculations.
Although the results look disastrous (nothing is "significant" and the R^2 value is
0.1%), the fitted line does give good predictions but only for x values very near the
mean of the x's ($\simeq 100$). For example, the fitted value at $x = 100$ is $\hat{y} = -6.3 +
0.162(100) = 9.9$, which compares well with the population y values for x's near
100 (see Exhibit 20.11A). In addition, the estimate of σ given as $s = 0.7523$ is not too
bad when compared to the population value of 0.6435. These special nonrandom
samples of predictor values should be kept in mind when interpreting R^2 values.

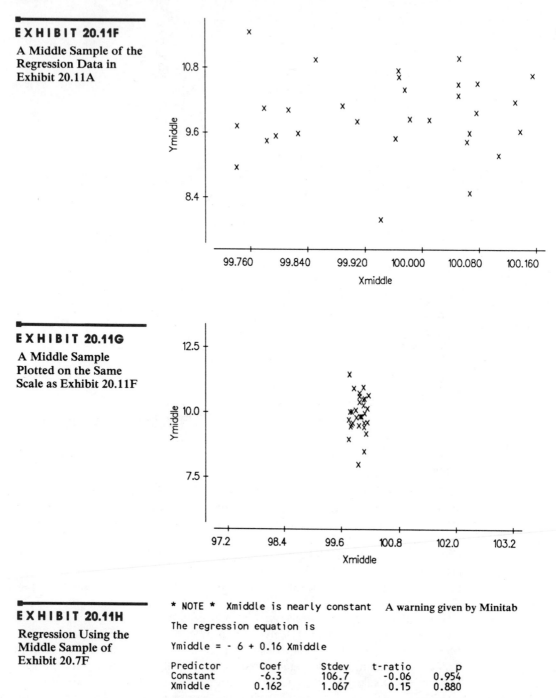

E X H I B I T 20.11F

A Middle Sample of the
Regression Data in
Exhibit 20.11A

E X H I B I T 20.11G

A Middle Sample
Plotted on the Same
Scale as Exhibit 20.11F

E X H I B I T 20.11H

Regression Using the
Middle Sample of
Exhibit 20.7F

* NOTE * Xmiddle is nearly constant   A warning given by Minitab

The regression equation is

Ymiddle = - 6 + 0.16 Xmiddle

Predictor	Coef	Stdev	t-ratio	p
Constant	-6.3	106.7	-0.06	0.954
Xmiddle	0.162	1.067	0.15	0.880

s = 0.7523   R-sq = 0.1%   R-sq(adj) = 0.0%

EXERCISE

20.12A The population of *x, y* values whose scatterplot is shown in Exhibit 20.11A is listed in Appendix 2 and is available in the file named RSQUARE.DAT.

(a) Select a new random sample of 30 of the *x, y* pairs and scatterplot the pairs selected. Compare your plot to Exhibit 20.11B.

(b) Perform a simple linear regression using your sample and compare your results to those reported in Exhibit 20.11C.

(c) Using the ordered *x* values, select a systematic sample by selecting every sixth pair until 30 pairs have been selected.

(d) Scatterplot the pairs selected in part (c) and compare this to the results in part (a) and to Exhibit 20.11B.

(e) For the systematic sample, perform a linear regression and compare the results to those in part (b) and Exhibit 20.11C.

BINARY RESPONSE VARIABLES AND DISCRIMINANT ANALYSIS

In some situations regression-like problems with a binary-valued response variable are studied. This type of problem is usually discussed under the topic of **discriminant analysis**, analysis of a model whose response is binary (or, more generally, categorical) for the purpose of separating or discriminating among response values on the basis of the predictor variables. For example, banks have large data bases of people who have applied for loans, people who have been given loans, and those who have defaulted and those who have not. They would like to build a model that would predict the credit worthiness of a customer on the basis of variables such as family income, current indebtedness, amount of savings, home ownership status, and marital status. The binary response here is either to make the loan (success) or not (failure). Or a human resources manager would like to predict whether a job candidate will be successful at a job using variables such as MBA grade point average, a measure of computer skills, and so forth. Graduate schools of business attempt to predict a student's potential for success in an MBA program using GMAT scores, undergraduate GPA, and grades in specified courses as predictors.

The Internal Revenue Service receives millions of tax returns each year and they audit a select few of them. Some of these audits yield a lot of return in additional taxes; some yield very little. Based on past data the IRS uses discriminant analysis to predict whether or not an audit of an individual's tax return would be likely to find errors large enough to make the audit cost-effective. The predictor variables in this example include quantities such as the amounts claimed as charitable giving and as medical and business expenses. This section shows how regression techniques can be applied to produce this special type of prediction.

The data set in Exhibit 20.13A is used to illustrate. These data were gleaned from *Moody's Industrial Manuals* from 1968 to 1972 and contain annual financial data on 21 firms that went bankrupt approximately two years later and 25 firms that were financially sound at the end of the same period. The goal is to obtain predictions of bankruptcy worthiness that may be applied to firms in the future. Good predictions allow us to avoid investing in businesses whose future looks bleak. Based on financial theory, four variables were selected as potentially useful predictor variables. They are four ratios: cash flow to total debt (CF/TD), net income to total assets (NI/TA), current assets to current liabilities (CA/CL), and current assets to net sales (CA/NS). The objective is to determine the linear combination of these predictors that best discriminates between the bankrupt firms and the sound firms. However, the simpler problem of discrimination based on a single predictor is first considered.

EXHIBIT 20.13A

Financial Data on Bankrupt and Financially Sound Firms

```
# filename: BANKRUPT.DAT
# Bankrupcy financial data
# 21 bankrupt firms and 25 sound firms
# (Source: R.A.Johnson and D.W.Wichern, Applied Multivariate Analysis,
# 2d ed., Engelwood Cliffs, N.J.: Prentice-Hall, 1988
# Their source: Moody's Industrial Manuals, 1968-1972)
# Variables: 1=bankrupt,0=not;CF/TD;NI/TA;CA/CL;CA/NS
# CF=cash flow, TD=total debt, NI=net income, TA=total assets
# CA=current assets, CL=current liabilities, NS=net sales,
  1  -.4485  -.4106  1.0865   .4526        0   .3776   .1075  3.2651  .3548
  1  -.5633  -.3114  1.5134   .1642        0   .1933   .0473  2.2506  .3309
  1   .0643   .0156  1.0077   .3978        0   .3248   .0718  4.2401  .6279
  1  -.0721  -.0930  1.4544   .2589        0   .3132   .0511  4.4500  .6852
  1  -.1002  -.0917  1.5644   .6683        0   .1184   .0499  2.5210  .6925
  1  -.1421  -.0651   .7066   .2794        0  -.0173   .0233  2.0538  .3484
  1   .0351   .0147  1.5046   .7080        0   .2169   .0779  2.3489  .3970
  1  -.0653  -.0566  1.3737   .4032        0   .1703   .0695  1.7973  .5174
  1   .0724  -.0076  1.3723   .3361        0   .1460   .0518  2.1692  .5500
  1  -.1353  -.1433  1.4196   .4347        0  -.0985  -.0123  2.5029  .5778
  1  -.2298  -.2961   .3310   .1824        0   .1398  -.0312   .4611  .2643
  1   .0713   .0205  1.3124   .2497        0   .1379   .0728  2.6123  .5151
  1   .0109   .0011  2.1495   .6969        0   .1486   .0564  2.2347  .5563
  1  -.2777  -.2316  1.1918   .6601        0   .1633   .0486  2.3080  .1978
  1   .1454   .0500  1.8762   .2723        0   .2907   .0597  1.8381  .3786
  1   .3703   .1098  1.9941   .3828        0   .5383   .1064  2.3293  .4835
  1  -.0757  -.0821  1.5077   .4215        0  -.3330  -.0854  3.0124  .4730
  1   .0451   .0263  1.6756   .9494        0   .4785   .0910  1.2444  .1847
  1   .0115  -.0032  1.2602   .6038        0   .5603   .1112  4.2918  .4443
  1   .1227   .1055  1.1434   .1655        0   .2029   .0792  1.9936  .3018
  1  -.2843  -.2703  1.2722   .5128        0   .4746   .1380  2.9166  .4487
  0   .5135   .1001  2.4871   .5368        0   .1661   .0351  2.4527  .1370
  0   .0769   .0195  2.0069   .5304        0   .5808   .0371  5.0594  .1268
```

Exhibit 20.13B displays the dotplots of each of the four potential predictor variables broken down by bankrupt firms and financially sound firms. A good predictor of bankruptcy would be such that its distribution for bankrupt firms would be quite separated from its distribution for financially sound firms—the distributions would not overlap at all. Of course in the real world, predictors are not perfect. The dotplots show that CA/CL (cash assets to cash liabilities) seems to best separate the bankrupt firms from the nonbankrupt firms. Thus the problem of predicting bankruptcy is considered based on this single predictor.

Although a binary response variable does *not* meet the standard regression assumptions (since it is not even approximately normally distributed, for example), it is still reasonable to consider predicting the binary response with a linear function of the predictor(s) and choosing the linear combination using the principle of least

EXHIBIT 20.13B

Distributions of
Predictors for Bankrupt
and Sound Firms

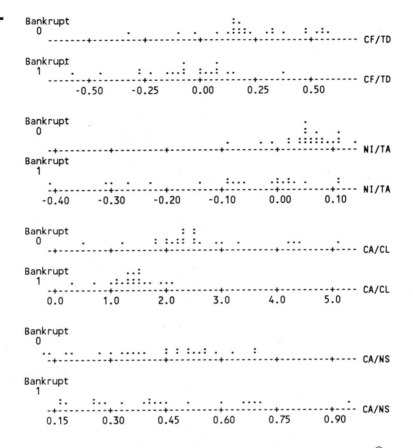

EXHIBIT 20.13B

Distributions of
Predictors for Bankrupt
and Sound Firms

squares. If this regression is carried out, the regression equation is $\widehat{\text{Bankrupt}} = 1.08 - 0.307\ \text{CA/CL}$. Exhibit 20.13C gives the Fitted values from this model. The fitted values from bankrupt firms are attempting to predict the value 1, while the fitted values for the sound firms are predicting the value 0. A simple discrimination rule is to predict that a firm will go bankrupt if its fitted value is closer to 1 than to 0, that is, if its fitted value is greater than 0.5. Similarly, a firm is predicted to be sound if its fitted value is less than 0.5. (In the unlikely event that a fitted value is exactly 0.5, the decision must be made rather arbitrarily, say by flipping a coin.)

Using this decision rule, Exhibit 20.13C shows that among the 21 bankrupt firms, firms 13 and 16 are misclassified. Similarly, among the 25 sound firms, firms 31, 34, 38, and 41 are misclassified. Exhibit 20.13D gives the dotplots of the fitted values for both the bankrupt and sound firms. Again notice the separation between the two distributions.

For use in the future we will calculate the value of CA/CL for a firm, plug it into the expression $1.08 - 0.307\ \text{CA/CL}$, and predict that the firm will go bankrupt if the resulting value is greater than 0.5; otherwise, we will predict that the firm is financially sound.

Discriminant analysis can also be used when several predictors are available. With four predictors it is, of course, an impossible task to separate the joint

E X H I B I T 20.13C

Fitted Values from
Regressing Bankrupt on
CA/CL

ROW	Bankrupt	CA/CL	Fitted	
1	1	1.0865	0.747617	
2	1	1.5134	0.616465	
3	1	1.0077	0.771826	
4	1	1.4544	0.634591	
5	1	1.5644	0.600797	
6	1	0.7066	0.864330	
7	1	1.5046	0.619168	
8	1	1.3737	0.659383	
9	1	1.3723	0.659814	
10	1	1.4196	0.645282	
11	1	0.3310	0.979722	
12	1	1.3124	0.678216	
13	1	2.1495	0.421042	← misclassified
14	1	1.1918	0.715267	
15	1	1.8762	0.505005	
16	1	1.9941	0.468784	← misclassified
17	1	1.5077	0.618216	
18	1	1.6756	0.566634	
19	1	1.2602	0.694253	
20	1	1.1434	0.730136	
21	1	1.2722	0.690566	
22	0	2.4871	0.317324	
23	0	2.0069	0.464851	
24	0	3.2651	0.078306	
25	0	2.2506	0.389982	
26	0	4.2401	-0.221234	
27	0	4.4500	-0.285719	
28	0	2.5210	0.306909	
29	0	2.0538	0.450443	
30	0	2.3489	0.359782	
31	0	1.7973	0.529245	← misclassified
32	0	2.1692	0.414990	
33	0	2.5029	0.312470	
34	0	0.4611	0.939753	← misclassified
35	0	2.6123	0.278860	
36	0	2.2347	0.394867	
37	0	2.3080	0.372347	
38	0	1.8381	0.516710	← misclassified
39	0	2.3293	0.365804	
40	0	3.0124	0.155941	
41	0	1.2444	0.699107	← misclassified
42	0	4.2918	-0.237117	
43	0	1.9936	0.468937	
44	0	2.9166	0.185373	
45	0	2.4527	0.327893	
46	0	5.0594	-0.472939	

E X H I B I T 20.13D

Distributions of Fitted
Values Using a Single
Predictor CA/CL

```
Bankrupt                                         .
   0      .          . ..          . ..  .:::::.:....   .        .
       +---------+---------+---------+---------+---------+------ Fitted
Bankrupt                                      :..
   1                              . .. ..:::::..   .    .
       +---------+---------+---------+---------+---------+------ Fitted
     -0.60     -0.30      0.00      0.30     ↑ 0.60      0.90
                                           0.5
```

distributions of those predictors as to bankrupt and sound firms. However, using regression the four variables can be reduced to one manageable variable through the fitted values. The binary response is regressed on all the predictors and the resulting fitted values are used to provide the discrimination values. Using all four financial variables in Exhibit 20.13A as predictors produces the regression equation

$$\widehat{Bankrupt} = 0.793 - 0.160\ CF/TD - 1.14\ NI/TA - 0.226\ CA/CL + 0.300\ CA/NS$$

The fitted values are listed in Exhibit 20.13E. Among the 21 bankrupt firms, firms 15, 16, and 20 are misclassified. Similarly, among the 25 sound firms, one firm (34) is misclassified. Exhibit 20.13F gives the dotplots of the fitted values for both the bankrupt and sound firms. Once more notice the good separation between the two distributions.

EXHIBIT 20.13E

Fitted Values from Regression of Bankrupt on Four Predictors

ROW	Bankrupt	CF/TD	NI/TA	CA/CL	CA/NS	Fitted	
1	1	-0.4485	-0.4106	1.0865	0.4526	1.22269	
2	1	-0.5633	-0.3114	1.5134	0.1642	0.94515	
3	1	0.0643	0.0156	1.0077	0.3978	0.65694	
4	1	-0.0721	-0.0930	1.4544	0.2589	0.65979	
5	1	-0.1002	-0.0917	1.5644	0.6683	0.76093	
6	1	-0.1421	-0.0651	0.7066	0.2794	0.81422	
7	1	0.0351	0.0147	1.5046	0.7080	0.64362	
8	1	-0.0653	-0.0566	1.3737	0.4032	0.67883	
9	1	0.0724	-0.0076	1.3723	0.3361	0.58120	
10	1	-0.1353	-0.1433	1.4196	0.4347	0.78780	
11	1	-0.2298	-0.2961	0.3310	0.1824	1.14681	
12	1	0.0713	0.0205	1.3124	0.2497	0.53697	
13	1	0.0109	0.0011	2.1495	0.6969	0.51404	
14	1	-0.2777	-0.2316	1.1918	0.6601	1.03020	
15	1	0.1454	0.0500	1.8762	0.2723	0.37104	← misclassified
16	1	0.3703	0.1098	1.9941	0.3828	0.27358	← misclassified
17	1	-0.0757	-0.0821	1.5077	0.4215	0.68476	
18	1	0.0451	0.0263	1.6756	0.9494	0.66272	
19	1	0.0115	-0.0032	1.2602	0.6038	0.69165	
20	1	0.1227	0.1055	1.1434	0.1655	0.44488	← misclassified
21	1	-0.2843	-0.2703	1.2722	0.5128	1.01291	
22	0	0.5135	0.1001	2.4871	0.5368	0.19667	
23	0	0.0769	0.0195	2.0069	0.5304	0.46473	
24	0	0.3776	0.1075	3.2651	0.3548	-0.02033	
25	0	0.1933	0.0473	2.2506	0.3309	0.29953	
26	0	0.3248	0.0718	4.2401	0.6279	-0.10935	
27	0	0.3132	0.0511	4.4500	0.6852	-0.11411	
28	0	0.1184	0.0499	2.5210	0.6925	0.35611	
29	0	-0.0173	0.0233	2.0538	0.3484	0.41022	
30	0	0.2169	0.0779	2.3489	0.3970	0.25859	
31	0	0.1703	0.0695	1.7973	0.5174	0.43630	
32	0	0.1460	0.0518	2.1692	0.5500	0.38616	
33	0	-0.0985	-0.0123	2.5029	0.5778	0.43123	
34	0	0.1398	-0.0312	0.4611	0.2643	0.78143	← misclassified
35	0	0.1379	0.0728	2.6123	0.5151	0.25303	
36	0	0.1486	0.0564	2.2347	0.5563	0.36761	
37	0	0.1633	0.0486	2.3080	0.1978	0.24991	
38	0	0.2907	0.0597	1.8381	0.3786	0.37729	
39	0	0.5383	0.1064	2.3293	0.4835	0.20515	
40	0	-0.3330	-0.0854	3.0124	0.4730	0.40543	
41	0	0.4785	0.0910	1.2444	0.1847	0.38743	
42	0	0.5603	0.1112	4.2918	0.4443	-0.25867	
43	0	0.2029	0.0792	1.9936	0.3018	0.31097	
44	0	0.4746	0.1380	2.9166	0.4487	0.03633	
45	0	0.1661	0.0351	2.4527	0.1370	0.21390	
46	0	0.5808	0.0371	5.0594	0.1268	-0.44628	

EXHIBIT 20.13F

Distributions of Fitted Values Using Four Predictors

For future use we evaluate

$$0.793 - 0.160 \text{ CF}/\text{TD} - 1.14 \text{ NI}/\text{TA} - 0.226 \text{ CA}/\text{CL} + 0.300 \text{ CA}/\text{NS}$$

for a firm and predict that it will go bankrupt only if this value is greater than 0.5.

This material has introduced you to discriminant analysis. To do a high-quality discriminant analysis, additional topics must be considered. For example, the accuracy of the discrimination must be evaluated. Procedures for selecting good predictors and assessing the worth of each predictor are also needed.

Generalizations of discriminant analysis as discussed here are also important. For example, the response variable may be categorical but with more than two values to be discriminated among. In addition the costs of making various kinds of errors and the probabilities, prior to looking at the predictors, of an observation belonging to a particular group may be brought into the problem.

SECTION 20.14

EXERCISES

20.14A   Using the house-selling price data of Exercise 20.9B, consider discriminating among houses with and without fireplaces.

(a) Use the variables taxes, rooms, bedrooms, and style to predict the number of fireplaces.

(b) Use the fitted values from the regression in part (a) to check each case for misclassification. (Filename: HOUSEPRI.DAT.)

20.14B   Exploration for natural resources such as oil, gas, or mineral deposits is expensive and time consuming. It is important to be able to discriminate between productive and nonproductive areas on the basis of measurements that can be made at reasonable expense. The data in Exhibit 20.14A give the values of 13 variables believed to help predict whether or not a particular region will be productive for mining a certain heavy metal in heavily forested areas in Sweden. The measurements are made in stream sediments from areas known to be either productive or nonproductive. A set of six measurements are also available for areas whose productivity is unknown.

(a) Using a binary response variable, which is 1 for productive areas and 0 for nonproductive areas, fit a multiple regression using all 13 of the listed predictors.

(b) Use the fitted values from the regression results of part (a) to classify each of the observations where the productivity of the area is known. Which observations are misclassified?

(c) Use the regression results of part (a) to classify each of the observations whose productivity is unknown. (Filename: DISCRIM.DAT.)

EXHIBIT 20.14A

Trace-Element Analyses
of Stream Sediments
Collected in Two Areas
in Sweden

```
# filename: DISCRIM.DAT
# Trace element analysis of stream sediment in Sweden
# (Source: J.C.Davis, Statistics and Data Analysis in Geology
# Wiley, New York, 1973)
# Variables:group (0=productive, 1=nonproductive, 2=productivity unknown)
#    Ti  Mn   Ag    Ba  Co  Cr  Cu  Ni  Pb   Sr   V  Zn Au
  0  728  13 30.0   720  30  15  73   5   7    6   7  19  2
  0 1030  12  0.7  1280  20  16  25   5   7    9   5   5  2
  0  650   7  1.0  1070  20  20  48  70  10   21   5  17  1
  0  700  15  0.7   760  30  16  70  40  11   24   4  25  1
  0  510  10  0.5   740  20  14  39   5   8    5   6  13  2
  0 1060  21  0.3   980  30   5  25   3   7   15  16  11  1
  0 1420  20  0.2   690  30   7  25   5   6   16   7  18  1
  0  970   9  0.2   680  35   7  38   3   7    8  11  25  1
  0  230  15  0.2   710   5  11  50   2   7    8   3  12  1
  0 1210  63  0.1  1520  30   3  24   3   8   32  16  19  2
  0  300  11  0.2   510   5   3  15   3   3   24   3   5  2
  0  750  24  0.7   690  30   3  31   1  10   21   4  28  3
  0  780  18  4.0   730  55   4  24   3   2    9  32   9  1
  0  690  15  1.0   326  30   5  25   1   9    7  20   7  4
  0 1120  31  1.5   660  50   4  20   4   5   14  28   9  1
  0  520  14  0.8   680  35   5  42   2   5    3  15  15  1
  0  510  15  0.9   700  25   6  67   4   8    4  19   9  1
  0 1060  29  0.4  1640  25   2  21   3   3   32   9  20  1
  0 1150  32  0.7   710  30   3  15   2   2   26  27  18  1
  0  710  18  0.9   490  75   5   8   1   3    8  18  10  2
  1  482   5  0.1   160  20   7  30   1   0   72  14  20  1
  1  304   5  0.2   150  20   3  82   1   2  158  16   7  1
  1   89   6  0.1    50  10   1  61   1   0   34   4   5  2
  1  210   5  0.1   100  15   3  77   1   0   65   9   8  2
  1  506   7  0.3   140  20   5 154   2   0  124  14   8  1
  1  198   7  0.1    80  15   2  63   2   0   72   8  11  0
  1  322   6  0.2   160  20   3  45   2   1  110  12   6  1
  1  328   8  0.2    90  15   1  40   3   2  148   7   4  0
  1  202   7  0.1     8  15   2 104   2   0   42   8   7  0
  1  460   7  0.3   160  20   6  48   1   2   78  15   5  2
  1  310   5  0.2   100  15   3  65   1   2   71  10   4  1
  1  302   6  0.2     9  15   1  69   0   3  131  11   3  2
  1  186   5  0.1    70  10   2  63   0   1   48   8   5  0
  1  280   7  0.1   110  15   2  58   1   2   73  12   8  1
  1  104  16  0.1    20   5   1  37   0   1   14   3   8  1
  1  464   8  0.3   220  15   2 121   2   2  120  21  16  0
  1  499   9  0.3   190  20   4  59   2   3   48  23  12  2
  1  283   8  0.2   120  15   2   4   1   2   69  14   6  0
  1  450   7  0.2   140  20   3  82   2   1   71  17   7  0
  1  290   6  0.1    80  15   1  99   0   0   76   8   9  1
  2  426   8  0.3   180  20   6 128   3   3   46  11   8  2
  2  650  12  0.5   380  30   4  72   5   2   32   9  16  1
  2 1220  52  1.5   630  25   8  39   4   9   21  20  18  1
  2  108  16  0.2    80   5   1 120   0   1   16   3   8  0
  2  382   5  0.2   170  25   4  60   2   1  110  16   4  2
  2  102  24  0.1    20   0   1  28   0   0  132   2   6  0
```

SECTION 20.15

SUPPLEMENTARY EXERCISES FOR CHAPTER 20

20A Exercise 7.9C dealt with the time it took to assemble an electronic printed circuit board in terms of seven predictor variables.

(a) Carry out the regression of completion time on the seven predictors.

(b) Interpret each of the estimated regression coefficients obtained.

(c) Use the F ratio to test the overall worth of the model.

(d) What is the value of the t ratio for the variable Total Number of Components? (Filename: BOARDS.DAT.)

20B Section 4.10 presented actual Los Angeles traffic data for freeways, minor arterial streets, and major arterial streets (including Ventura Boulevard). In an attempt to predict traffic volumes at a particular location, traffic planners build complicated models that incorporate demographic information such as housing density, income levels, and employment levels near that location. Barton-Aschman Associates of Pasadena, California, constructed such a model and are interested in comparing their model predictions with actuality. A small portion of the large data set that contains 396 observations is shown below. The full data set is in Appendix 2 and is available in the file named TRAFFIC.DAT.

```
# Los Angeles traffic data: 396 observations
# (Source: Lee Cryer, Barton-Aschman Associates
# Pasadena, CA)
# Variables: road type (1=freeway,2=minor arterial
# 3=major arterial,4=Ventura Boulevard)
# estimated traffic volume, actual traffic volume
  1   106848   126000
  1   121121   126000
  1   109751   126000
  1   129345   126000
  :      :        :
  3    22920    14942
  3    16712    13232
  2     5220     7097
  2     9664     4925
  2     7531     5204
  2     5853     8174
  4    12967    11727
  2     7657     5677
  4    16242    21622
  4    16135    20071
```

(a) If the model were perfect then the actual volume would equal the estimated volume, and a 45° line through the origin would describe the relationship between actual and estimated traffic volumes. Display the scatterplot of actual volume versus estimated volume. Does a 45° line seem to fit the plot?

(b) Perform the regression of actual volume on estimated volume and interpret the output.

(c) Plot the residuals versus fitted values for the regression model fit in part (a). Interpret.

(d) Now consider a model that allows different intercepts for different road types. That is,

$$\text{Actual} = \hat{\beta}_0 + \beta_1 \text{ Freeway} + \beta_2 \text{ Major} + \beta_3 \text{ Estimated}$$

where Freeway $= 1$ for freeways and 0 otherwise and Major $= 1$ for major arterials (including Ventura Boulevard) and 0 otherwise. Estimate this model and interpret the coefficients.

(e) Plot the residuals versus fitted values for the regression model fit in part (d) and interpret.

(f) Now consider each of the road types separately. Display scatterplots of actual volumes against estimated volumes for each of the three road types.

(g) Estimate separate regression models for the three road types and interpret the scatterplots of residuals versus fitted values in each case.

(h) What can be concluded from the preceding analyses? Does the traffic planner's model seem to predict actual volumes well? Overall? Separately by road types?

GLOSSARY FOR CHAPTER 20

Discriminant analysis	Analysis of a model whose response is binary (or, more generally, categorical) for the purpose of separating or discriminating among response values on the basis of the predictor variables.
Error term	The part of the response that is not modelled by the linear function of the predictor variables.
Fitted value	The value predicted by the model $\hat{y}_i = b_0 + b_1 x_{i1} + \cdots + b_k x_{ik}$.
Least squares estimates	The estimates $b_0, b_1, \ldots, b_k$ of the unknown parameters $\beta_0, \beta_1, \ldots, \beta_k$.
Prediction error	The new response value minus the prediction based on the model.
Prediction standard error	The estimated standard deviation of the difference between a new response value and the predicted value.
Predictor variables	The variables used to predict or explain the response variable.
Regression parameters	The coefficients $\beta_0, \beta_1, \ldots, \beta_k$.
Residual	The actual response value minus the value predicted by the model.
Residual standard deviation	$s = \sqrt{\dfrac{1}{n-k-1} \sum_{i=1}^{n} \hat{e}_i^2}$
Response variable	The variable to be predicted or explained.
t ratio for b_i	The ratio $b_i / se(b_i)$.

APPENDIX E

THE MATRIX APPROACH TO MULTIPLE REGRESSION

The multiple regression model that has been written as the n equations

$$y_i = \beta_0 + \beta_1 x_{i1} + \beta_2 x_{i2} + \cdots + \beta_k x_{ik} + e_i \qquad \text{for } i = 1, 2, \ldots, n \qquad \textbf{(A1)}$$

may also be expressed very economically in vector-matrix notation. First define the column vectors

$$\underset{(n \times 1)}{y} = \begin{bmatrix} y_1 \\ y_2 \\ \vdots \\ y_n \end{bmatrix}, \qquad \underset{[(k+1) \times 1]}{\beta} = \begin{bmatrix} \beta_0 \\ \beta_1 \\ \vdots \\ \beta_k \end{bmatrix}, \qquad \underset{(n \times 1)}{e} = \begin{bmatrix} e_1 \\ e_2 \\ \vdots \\ e_n \end{bmatrix}$$

and the matrix

$$\underset{[n \times (k+1)]}{X} = \begin{bmatrix} 1 & x_{11} & x_{12} & \cdots & x_{1k} \\ 1 & x_{21} & x_{22} & \cdots & x_{2k} \\ \vdots & \vdots & \vdots & & \vdots \\ 1 & x_{n1} & x_{n2} & \cdots & x_{nk} \end{bmatrix}$$

Then, recalling the definition of matrix multiplication, Equations (A1) may be written compactly as

$$y = X\beta + e \tag{A2}$$

The principle of ordinary least squares says to estimate the components of β by minimizing the quantiy

$$S(\beta) = \sum_{i=1}^{n} [y_i - \beta_0 - \beta_1 x_{i1} - \beta_2 x_{i2} - \cdots - \beta_k x_{ik}]^2 = (y - X\beta)'(y - X\beta) \tag{A3}$$

This may be accomplished by solving the system of $k + 1$ linear equations obtained from computing the partial derivatives and setting

$$\frac{\partial}{\partial \beta} S(\beta) = 0$$

This in turn yields the so-called *normal equations*:

$$X'X\beta = X'y \tag{A4}$$

Here X' denotes the transpose of the matrix X.

A proof using algebra (but not calculus) that a solution of the normal equations provides the least squares estimates may be obtained as follows: Let b be any solution of the normal equations (A4). Then

$$
\begin{aligned}
S(\beta) &= (y - X\beta)'(y - X\beta) \\
&= [(y - Xb) - X(\beta - b)]'[(y - Xb) - X(\beta - b)] \\
&= (y - Xb)'(y - Xb) + [X(\beta - b)]'[X(\beta - b)] \\
&\quad + (y - Xb)'X(\beta - b) + [X(\beta - b)]'(y - Xb)
\end{aligned}
$$

But since b satisfies the normal equations (A4) it is easy to see that the final two "cross-product" terms are each zero. Thus we have the identity

$$S(\beta) = (y - Xb)'(y - Xb) + [X(\beta - b)]'[X(\beta - b)] \tag{A5}$$

The first term on the right-hand side of Equation (A5) does not involve β; the second term is the sum of squares of the elements of the vector $X(\beta - b)$. This sum of squares can never be negative and is clearly smallest (namely, zero) when $\beta = b$. Thus a solution to the normal equations will provide ordinary least squares estimates of the components of β.

If the $(k + 1) \times (k + 1)$ dimensional matrix $X'X$ is invertible, then Equation (A4) has a unique solution, which may be written as

$$b = (X'X)^{-1}X'y \tag{A6}$$

The column vector of *fitted values* is then

$$\hat{y} = Xb = X(X'X)^{-1}X'y \tag{A7}$$

and the column vector of *residuals* is

$$\hat{e} = y - \hat{y} = [I - X(X'X)^{-1}X']y \tag{A8}$$

By direct calculation it is easy to see that the matrix $H = X(X'X)^{-1}X'$ has the special property $H'H = H$ so that H is an *idempotent* matrix. It may also be argued that H is a symmetric matrix so that $H' = H$. The matrix H is sometimes called the *hat matrix* since the observation vector y is premultiplied by H to produce $\hat{y}$ (y hat). It is easy to show that $I - H$ is also symmetric and idempotent.

The estimate of σ is then

$$s = \sqrt{\frac{\hat{e}'\hat{e}}{n-k-1}} = \sqrt{\frac{(y-\hat{y})'(y-\hat{y})}{n-k-1}} = \sqrt{\frac{y'(I-H)y}{n-k-1}} \qquad \textbf{(A9)}$$

with $n - k - 1$ degrees of freedom.

Under the usual regression assumptions, it may be shown that the individual regression coefficient, b_i, has a normal distribution with mean β_i. The standard deviation of the distribution of b_i is given by σ times the square root of the ith diagonal element of the matrix $(X'X)^{-1}$. The standard error of b_i is obtained similarly by replacing σ by s. That is,

$$se(b_i) = s\sqrt{[(X'X)^{-1}]_{ii}} \qquad \textbf{(A10)}$$

Let $x^* = (1, x_1^*, x_2^*, \ldots, x_k^*)$ be a row vector containing specific values for the k predictor variables for which we want to predict a future value for the response, y^*. The prediction is given by x^*b and the *prediction error* is $y^* - x^*b$. The standard deviation of the prediction error can be shown to be

$$\sigma_{y^* - x^*b} = \sigma\sqrt{1 + x^*(X'X)^{-1}x^{*'}} \qquad \textbf{(A11)}$$

The *prediction standard error*, denoted *predse*, is obtained by replacing σ by s in Equation (A11). That is,

$$predse = s\sqrt{1 + x^*(X'X)^{-1}x^{*'}} \qquad \textbf{(A12)}$$

Finally, the breakdown of the total sum of squares may be expressed as

$$(y - \bar{y})'(y - \bar{y}) = (\hat{y} - \bar{y})'(\hat{y} - \bar{y}) + (y - \hat{y})'(y - \hat{y}) \qquad \textbf{(A13)}$$

[Total SS = Regression SS + Residual SS]

with degrees of freedom $n - 1$, k, and $n - k - 1$, respectively. Here $\bar{y}$ is a column vector with the mean $\bar{y}$ in all positions.

## CHAPTER 21

Regression Diagnostics and Transformations

INTRODUCTION

All the regression theory and methods presented in Chapter 20 and earlier rely to a certain extent on the standard regression assumptions. In particular it was assumed that the data were generated by a process that could be modelled according to

$$y_i = \beta_0 + \beta_1 x_{i1} + \beta_2 x_{i2} + \cdots + \beta_k x_{ik} + e_i \qquad \text{for } i = 1, 2, \ldots, n \qquad \textbf{(21.1)}$$

where the error terms $e_1, e_2, \ldots, e_n$ are independent of one another and are each normally distributed with mean 0 and common standard deviation σ. But in any practical situation, assumptions are always in doubt and can only hold approximately at best. The second part of any statistical analysis is to stand back and criticize the model and its assumptions. This phase is frequently called **model diagnostics**. If under close scrutiny the assumptions seem to be approximately satisfied, then the model can be used to predict and to understand the relationship between the response and the predictors. Otherwise, ways to improve the model are sought, once more checking the assumptions of the new model. This process is continued until either a satisfactory model is found or it is determined that none of the models are completely satisfactory.[†] Ideally, the adequacy of the model is assessed by checking it with a new set of data. However, that is a rare luxury; most often diagnostics based on the original data set must suffice. The study of diagnostics begins with the important topic of residuals.

SECTION 21.2

RESIDUALS

STANDARDIZED RESIDUALS

Most of the regression assumptions apply to the error terms $e_1, e_2, \ldots, e_n$. However, the error terms cannot be obtained, and the assessment of the errors must be based on the *residuals* obtained as actual value minus the fitted value that the model predicts with all unknown parameters estimated from the data. Recall that in symbols the ith residual is

$$\hat{e}_i = y_i - b_0 - b_1 x_{i1} - b_2 x_{i2} - \cdots - b_k x_{ik} \qquad \text{for } i = 1, 2, \ldots, n \qquad \text{(21.2)}$$

To analyze residuals (or any other diagnostic statistic), their behavior when the model assumptions *do* hold and, if possible, when at least some of the assumptions *do not* hold must be understood. If the regression assumptions all hold, it may be shown that the residuals have normal distributions with 0 means. It may also be shown that the distribution of the ith residual has the standard deviation $\sigma\sqrt{1 - h_{ii}}$ where h_{ii} is the ith diagonal element of the "hat matrix" determined by the values of the set of predictor variables. This matrix may be found in Appendix E to Chapter 20, but the particular formula given there is not needed here. In the simple case of a single predictor model it may be shown that

$$h_{ii} = \frac{1}{n} + \frac{(x_i - \bar{x})^2}{\sum_{j=1}^{n} (x_j - \bar{x})^2} \qquad \text{(21.3)}$$

Note in particular that the standard deviation of the distribution of the ith residual is *not* σ, the standard deviation of the distribution of the ith error term e_i. It may be shown that, in general,

$$\frac{1}{n} \leq h_{ii} \leq 1 \qquad \text{(21.4)}$$

so that
$$0 \leq \sigma\sqrt{1 - h_{ii}} \leq \sigma\sqrt{1 - \frac{1}{n}} < \sigma \qquad \text{(21.5)}$$

It may be seen from Equation (21.3) and also argued in the general case that h_{ii} is at its minimum value, $1/n$, when the predictors are all equal to their mean values. On the other hand, h_{ii} approaches its maximum value, 1, when the predictors are very far from their mean values. Thus residuals obtained from data points that are far from

---

[†] Sometimes answers are required immediately and a model with known deficiencies must suffice.

the center of the data set will tend to be smaller than the corresponding error terms. Curves fit by least squares will usually fit better at extreme values for the predictors than in the central part of the data. Exhibit 21.2A displays the h_{ii} values (along with many other diagnostic statistics that will be discussed) for the regression of Market values on the single predictor of Sq.ft. Notice that h_{ii} is equal to $1/60 \simeq 0.017$ for

EXHIBIT 21.2A

Diagnostic Statistics for the Regression of Market on Sq.ft

ROW	Sq.ft	Market	Resids	Std Res	t-Resid	hii	CookD
1	521	26.0	-4.07	-1.06	-1.06	0.068	0.041
2	538	19.4	-10.99	-2.85	-3.05	0.064	0.276
3	544	25.2	-5.30	-1.37	-1.38	0.062	0.063
4	577	26.2	-4.90	-1.27	-1.27	0.055	0.047
5	661	31.0	-1.65	-0.42	-0.42	0.039	0.004
6	662	34.6	1.94	0.50	0.49	0.039	0.005
7	677	36.4	3.46	0.89	0.88	0.037	0.015
8	691	33.0	-0.20	-0.05	-0.05	0.035	0.000
9	694	37.4	4.15	1.06	1.06	0.034	0.020
10	712	42.4	8.82	2.25	2.34	0.032	0.083
11	721	32.8	-0.95	-0.24	-0.24	0.031	0.001
12	722	25.6	-8.17	-2.08	-2.15	0.031	0.068
13	743	34.8	0.65	0.17	0.16	0.028	0.000
14	760	35.8	1.34	0.34	0.34	0.026	0.002
15	767	33.6	-0.99	-0.25	-0.25	0.025	0.001
16	780	31.0	-3.83	-0.97	-0.97	0.024	0.012
17	787	39.2	4.24	1.08	1.08	0.024	0.014
18	802	36.0	0.77	0.19	0.19	0.022	0.000
19	814	34.8	-0.65	-0.17	-0.16	0.021	0.000
20	815	34.4	-1.07	-0.27	-0.27	0.021	0.001
21	825	38.0	2.34	0.59	0.59	0.021	0.004
22	834	34.6	-1.22	-0.31	-0.31	0.020	0.001
23	838	35.6	-0.30	-0.07	-0.07	0.020	0.000
24	858	35.8	-0.46	-0.12	-0.12	0.019	0.000
25	883	39.6	2.88	0.73	0.73	0.018	0.005
26	890	35.0	-1.85	-0.47	-0.47	0.017	0.002
27	899	37.6	0.58	0.15	0.15	0.017	0.000
28	918	41.2	3.84	0.97	0.97	0.017	0.008
29	920	31.2	-6.20	-1.57	-1.59	0.017	0.021
30	923	30.0	-7.46	-1.89	-1.93	0.017	0.030
31	926	37.4	-0.11	-0.03	-0.03	0.017	0.000
32	931	38.0	0.40	0.10	0.10	0.017	0.000
33	965	37.2	-1.03	-0.26	-0.26	0.017	0.001
34	966	44.0	5.75	1.46	1.47	0.017	0.018
35	967	44.2	5.94	1.50	1.52	0.017	0.019
36	1011	43.6	4.53	1.15	1.15	0.018	0.012
37	1011	38.4	-0.67	-0.17	-0.17	0.018	0.000
38	1024	42.2	2.89	0.73	0.73	0.019	0.005
39	1033	40.4	0.92	0.23	0.23	0.019	0.001
40	1040	40.4	0.80	0.20	0.20	0.019	0.000
41	1047	43.6	3.87	0.98	0.98	0.020	0.010
42	1051	41.4	1.59	0.40	0.40	0.020	0.002
43	1052	39.6	-0.22	-0.06	-0.06	0.020	0.000
44	1056	41.8	1.90	0.48	0.48	0.020	0.002
45	1060	44.8	4.83	1.23	1.23	0.021	0.016
46	1060	38.4	-1.57	-0.40	-0.40	0.021	0.002
47	1070	43.6	3.44	0.87	0.87	0.021	0.008
48	1075	42.8	2.55	0.65	0.65	0.022	0.005
49	1079	40.6	0.28	0.07	0.07	0.022	0.000
50	1100	41.6	0.89	0.23	0.23	0.024	0.001
51	1106	42.8	1.98	0.50	0.50	0.024	0.003
52	1138	39.0	-2.40	-0.61	-0.61	0.028	0.005
53	1164	41.8	-0.08	-0.02	-0.02	0.031	0.000
54	1171	48.4	6.39	1.63	1.66	0.032	0.044
55	1237	39.8	-3.42	-0.88	-0.88	0.042	0.017
56	1249	47.2	3.76	0.97	0.96	0.044	0.021
57	1298	45.2	0.86	0.22	0.22	0.053	0.001
58	1435	38.8	-8.06	-2.12	-2.19	0.087	0.213
59	1602	47.4	-2.52	-0.68	-0.68	0.142	0.039
60	1804	45.4	-8.23	-2.36	-2.46	0.230	0.832

middle values of Sq.ft. The largest value for h_{ii}, 0.230, occurs at the largest value of the predictor. These values of h_{ii} lead to multipliers $\sqrt{1 - 0.017} = 0.992$ and $\sqrt{1 - 0.230} = 0.8775$, respectively, for the standard deviations of the corresponding residuals.

To compensate for the differences in dispersion among the distributions of the different residuals, it is usually better to consider the **standardized residuals** defined by[†]

$$i\text{th standardized residual} = \frac{\hat{e}_i}{s\sqrt{1 - h_{ii}}} \qquad \text{for } i = 1, 2, \ldots, n \qquad \textbf{(21.6)}$$

Notice that the unknown σ has been estimated by s. If n is large and if the regression assumptions are all approximately satisfied, then the standardized residuals should behave about like standard normal variables. Exhibit 21.2A also lists the residuals and standardized residuals for all 60 cases.

Even if all the regression assumptions are met, the residuals (and standardized residuals) are not independent. For example, the residuals for a model that includes an intercept term always add to zero. This alone implies they are negatively correlated. It may be shown that, in fact, the theoretical correlation coefficient between the ith and jth residuals (or standardized residuals) is

$$\frac{-h_{ij}}{\sqrt{(1 - h_{ii})(1 - h_{jj})}} \qquad \textbf{(21.7)}$$

where h_{ij} is the ijth element of the hat matrix. Again, the general formula for these elements is not needed here. For the simple single-predictor case it may be shown that

$$h_{ij} = \frac{1}{n} + \frac{(x_i - \bar{x})(x_j - \bar{x})}{\displaystyle\sum_{i=1}^{n} (x_i - \bar{x})^2} \qquad \textbf{(21.8)}$$

From Equations (21.3), (21.7), and (21.8) (and in general) we see that the correlations will be small except for small data sets and/or for residuals associated with data points very far from the central part of the predictor values. From a practical point of view this small correlation can usually be ignored, and the assumptions on the error terms can be assessed by comparing the properties of the standardized residuals to those of independent, standard normal variables.

RESIDUAL PLOTS

Plots of the standardized residuals against other variables are very useful in detecting departures from the standard regression assumptions. Exhibit 21.2B shows an ideal residual plot in which standardized residuals versus case number have been plotted for 25 cases. If the regression assumptions are met, then the

---

[†] Unfortunately, the terminology used here has not been standardized. The term *studentized* residual is used by some authors. Others call $\hat{e}_i/s$ standardized residuals. We reserve the term *studentized* residual for another form given in Section 21.4.

EXHIBIT 21.2B

Plot of Ideal
Standardized Residuals
versus Case Number

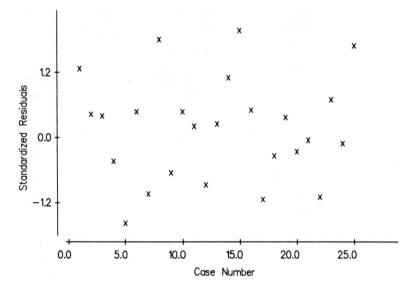

distributions of all the standardized residuals are approximately standard normal distributions and the residuals are approximately uncorrelated. Thus no patterns should be apparent in such a plot.

Departures from the standard regression assumptions may, in principle, occur in many different ways—in fact, in infinitely many ways. What is needed are diagnostic procedures that will detect the most common of those departures. Useful diagnostic plots include plotting residuals against fitted values, against individual predictors, or against time.

Many of the most common problems may be seen by plotting (standardized) residuals against the corresponding fitted values. In this plot, residuals associated with approximately equal-sized fitted values are visually grouped together. In this way it is relatively easy to see if mostly negative (or mostly positive) residuals are associated with the largest and smallest fitted values. Such a plot would indicate curvature that the chosen regression curve did not capture. Exhibit 21.2C gives an example of such a residual plot. Here the residuals for the four smallest and three largest fitted values are all negative, indicating the curvature that is lacking in the model. Exhibit 21.2D displays the corresponding residual plot when the quadratic model is used for the same data set. Now the residuals for extreme values of fitted values are a mixture of positives and negatives and show no general model inadequacies.

Another important use for the plot of residuals versus fitted values is to detect lack of a common standard deviation among different error terms. Contrary to the assumption of common standard deviation, it is not uncommon for variability to increase as the values for the response variable increase. Exhibit 21.2E gives an example of the residual plot in such a situation. Here the city miles per gallon values for 45 cars have been regressed on their weight and a binary variable giving their

EXHIBIT 21.2C

Standardized Residuals versus Fitted Values—Market on Sq.ft

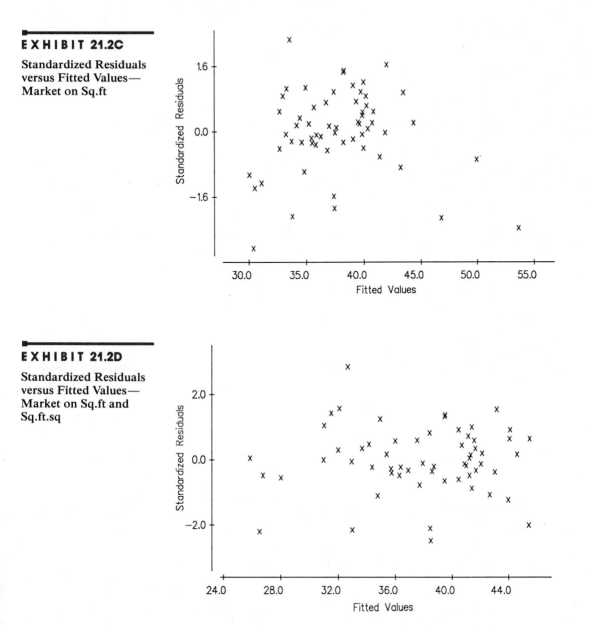

EXHIBIT 21.2D

Standardized Residuals versus Fitted Values—Market on Sq.ft and Sq.ft.sq

type of transmission—automatic or manual. For this type of data the variability of city gas mileage is larger for the more efficient cars. This is reflected in the residual plot as greater variability in the residuals as the fitted values increase. This example is used again in Section 21.8 when transformations that will correct this problem of lack of common standard deviation are discussed. Autocorrelation in residuals, another problem that may be detected with various residual plots, is discussed in Chapter 23.

E X H I B I T 21.2E

Standardized Residuals
versus Fitted Values—
City MPG on Weight
and Transmission Type

SECTION 21.3

EXERCISES

21.3A Consider the data of Exercise 20.7G giving the average height of girls at various ages and the regression of height in terms of age.
(a) Plot the residuals versus the fitted values. Comment on the shape of the plot.
(b) Plot the residuals versus the age variable. Comment on the shape of this plot compared to the one in part (a).
(c) Plot the standardized residuals versus the fitted values and comment on the display.
(d) Fit a new model that includes age and age squared as predictors of height.
(e) Plot the residuals versus the fitted values for the model estimated in part (d). Comment on this plot. (Filename: AGEHGT_G.DAT.)

21.3B Use the tree data of Exercise 20.7J to predict volume using a linear combination of diameter and height. Plot the standardized residuals versus the fitted values and comment on the information about the quality of the model conveyed in this plot. (Filename: TREES.DAT.)

21.3C Consider the house selling price data in Exercise 20.9B. In that exercise you fit the model that predicts selling price using taxes, number of baths, and square feet as predictors.
(a) Plot the standardized residuals versus the fitted values and comment on the plot.
(b) Plot the standardized residuals versus taxes and comment on the plot.
(c) Plot the standardized residuals versus bedrooms and comment on the plot.
(d) Plot the standardized residuals versus square feet and comment on the plot. (Filename: HOUSEPRI.DAT.)

21.3D Consider the regression model that related Crest toothpaste sales to Crest advertising, advertising ratio (Crest to Colgate), and family disposable income. The data are reported in Exercise 20.9D.
(a) Plot the standardized residuals versus the fitted values and comment on the plot.

(b) Plot the standardized residuals versus advertising and comment on the plot.
(c) Plot the standardized residuals versus advertising ratio and comment on the plot.
(d) Plot the standardized residuals versus disposable income and comment on the plot.
(e) Plot the standardized residuals versus year and comment on the plot. (Filename: CREST.DAT.)

SECTION 21.4

OUTLIERS

In regression analysis the model is assumed to be appropriate for all the observations. However, it is not unusual for one or two cases to be inconsistent with the general pattern of the data in one way or another. When a single predictor is used such cases may be easily spotted in the scatterplot of the data. When several predictors are employed such cases will be much more difficult to detect. The nonconforming data points are usually called **outliers**. Sometimes it is possible to retrace the steps leading to the suspect data point and isolate the reason for the outlier. For example, it could be the result of a recording error. If this is the case the data can be corrected. At other times the outlier may be due to a response obtained when variables not measured were quite different than when the rest of the data were obtained. Regardless of the reason for the outlier, its effect on regression analysis can be substantial.

Outliers that have unusual response values are the focus here. (Other types of outliers are considered in Section 21.6.) Unusual responses should be detectable by looking for unusual residuals, preferably by checking for unusually large standardized residuals. If the normality of the error terms is not in question (see Section 21.8), then a standardized residual larger than 3 in magnitude certainly is unusual and the corresponding case should be investigated for a special cause for this value. Minitab warns you by flagging all cases with standardized residuals outside of ± 2. This warning must be considered with care since with data sets of, say, 60 observations, standardized residuals this large are not that unusual even if the regression assumptions are all met.

STUDENTIZED RESIDUALS

A difficulty with looking at standardized residuals is that an outlier, if present, will also affect the estimate of σ that enters into the denominator of the standardized residual. Typically, an outlier will inflate s and thus deflate the standardized residuals and mask the outlier. One way to circumvent this problem is to estimate the value of σ used in calculating the ith standardized residual using all the data *except* the ith case. Let $s_{(i)}$ denote such an estimate where the subscript (i) indicates that the ith case has been deleted. This leads to the **studentized residuals** defined by

$$i\text{th studentized residual} = \frac{\hat{e}_i}{s_{(i)}\sqrt{1 - h_{ii}}} \qquad \text{for } i = 1, 2, \ldots, n \qquad \textbf{(21.9)}$$

These are sometimes called externally studentized residuals, externally standardized residuals, studentized deleted residuals, or t residuals.[†]

THE EFFECT OF OUTLIERS

A small artificial data set is used to illustrate the detection of outliers and their effect on analysis. Exhibit 21.4A shows a scatterplot that will be considered the "correct" data against which results will be compared when an outlier is introduced. Exhibit 21.4B shows the standard regression results for these data. Then $\hat{y} = 31.114 + 1.66781x$ and $s = 1.001$ are considered the "correct" values for the regression line and residual standard deviation. The exhibit also lists the standardized and studentized residuals; no anomalies are observed.

E X H I B I T 21.4A

A Scatterplot with "Correct" Data

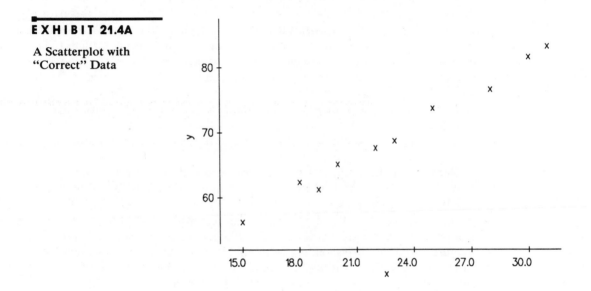

Now suppose that case 7 with $x = 25$ and $y = 73.8$ is misrecorded as $y = 80.1$. With a single predictor variable the outlier in Exhibit 21.4C is quite easy to see. However, with several predictors this would not be true. Suppose y is regressed on x with the outlier present. Exhibit 21.4D shows the results with $\hat{y} = 30.667 + 1.7133x$ and $s = 2.638$. The outlier has pulled the regression equation slope up and grossly inflated the value of s. The large value for s is especially disturbing since the standard errors of the regression coefficients and prediction standard errors are all proportional to s. The widths of all confidence intervals and prediction intervals will be greatly increased and the precision of the inferences will be misleading. Notice

[†] On first thought it would appear that these residuals would be very tedious to calculate since a new regression problem with $n - 1$ cases must be solved for each studentized residual. However, clever methods that allow them to be obtained without extensive calculation have been discovered. Modern statistical software packages calculate them routinely. In Minitab they are available through the REGRESS command and TRESIDS subcommand.

EXHIBIT 21.4B

Regression and
Diagnostic Statistics for
"Correct" Data

The regression equation is

y = 31.1 + 1.67 x

Predictor	Coef	Stdev	t-ratio	p
Constant	31.114	1.477	21.07	0.000
x	1.66781	0.06245	26.71	0.000

s = 1.001   R-sq = 98.9%   R-sq(adj) = 98.8%

ROW	x	y	std res	t-resid	hii	CookD
1	15	56.2	0.09	0.08	0.36	0.002
2	18	62.4	1.42	1.53	0.20	0.252
3	19	61.2	-1.75	-2.09	0.17	0.304
4	20	65.1	0.68	0.65	0.14	0.037
5	22	67.6	-0.22	-0.20	0.10	0.003
6	23	68.7	-0.81	-0.80	0.10	0.037
7	25	73.8	1.05	1.06	0.11	0.071
8	28	76.6	-1.35	-1.44	0.19	0.218
9	30	81.6	0.53	0.51	0.29	0.057
10	31	83.2	0.47	0.45	0.34	0.059

EXHIBIT 21.4C

Scatterplot with Outlier
at x = 25

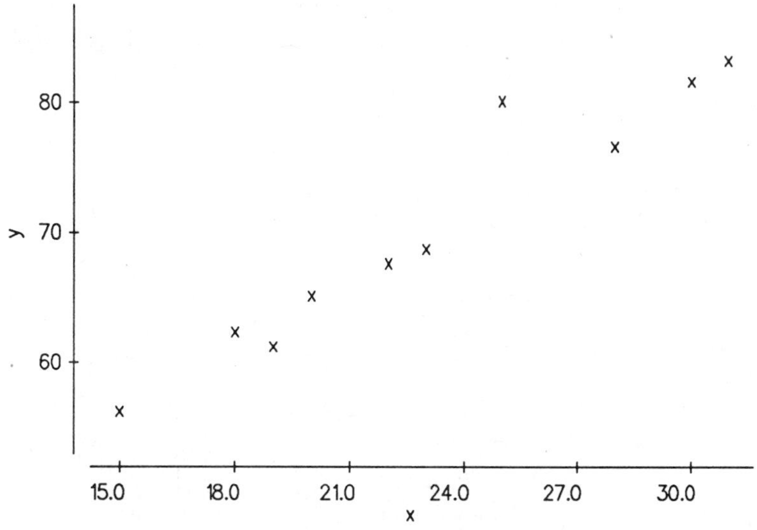

that Minitab warns you when it finds a standardized residual exceeding 2. The corresponding studentized residual (t residual) is equal to 7.03 and more clearly indicates the magnitude of the problem data point. Looking for large studentized residuals is an effective method for spotting individual outlying response values.

Once we are convinced that case 7 is unusual, we may, if possible, go back to the data-collection process and correct the data point. Otherwise, we may have to be content with deleting that case from the data set and proceeding from there. The regression results with case 7 deleted are shown in Exhibit 21.4E. Now the regression line and value of s are nearly equal to the corresponding values for the "correct" data, and the diagnostic statistics indicate no further difficulties.

EXHIBIT 21.4D

Regression with Outlier
at $x = 25$

The regression equation is

$y = 30.7 + 1.71 x$

Predictor	Coef	Stdev	t-ratio	p
Constant	30.667	3.892	7.88	0.000
x	1.7144	0.1646	10.42	0.000

$s = 2.638$ R-sq = 93.1%   R-sq(adj) = 92.3%

Unusual Observations

Obs.	x	y	Fit	Stdev.Fit	Residual	St.Resid
7	25.0	80.100	73.527	0.891	6.573	2.65R

R denotes an observation with a large St. Resid.   (← Minitab warning)

ROW	x	y	std res	t-resid	hii	CookD
1	15	56.2	-0.09	-0.08	0.36	0.002
2	18	62.4	0.37	0.35	0.20	0.017
3	19	61.2	-0.85	-0.83	0.17	0.071
4	20	65.1	0.06	0.06	0.14	0.000
5	22	67.6	-0.31	-0.30	0.10	0.006
6	23	68.7	-0.56	-0.53	0.10	0.017
7	25	80.1	2.65	7.03	0.11	0.451
8	28	76.6	-0.87	-0.86	0.19	0.092
9	30	81.6	-0.22	-0.21	0.29	0.010
10	31	83.2	-0.29	-0.27	0.34	0.022

EXHIBIT 21.4E

Regression After
Deleting Case 7

The regression equation is

$y = 31.2 + 1.66 x$

Predictor	Coef	Stdev	t-ratio	p
Constant	31.193	1.467	21.26	0.000
x	1.65953	0.06246	26.57	0.000

$s = 0.9933$ R-sq = 99.0%   R-sq(adj) = 98.9%

ROW	x	y	std res	t-resid	hii	CookD
1	15	56.2	0.14	0.13	0.36	0.006
2	18	62.4	1.51	1.70	0.21	0.295
3	19	61.2	-1.69	-2.02	0.17	0.293
4	20	65.1	0.78	0.76	0.14	0.051
5	22	67.6	-0.11	-0.10	0.11	0.001
6	23	68.7	-0.71	-0.68	0.11	0.031
7	*	*	*	*	*	*
8	28	76.6	-1.20	-1.25	0.21	0.198
9	30	81.6	0.75	0.73	0.31	0.128
10	31	83.2	0.71	0.69	0.37	0.150

How do these diagnostic methods work with real data? The property data example is used to illustrate. Exhibit 21.4F lists diagnostic statistics for the quadratic regression of Market value on Sq.ft and Sq.ft.sq. Notice that for most cases the standardized and studentized residuals differ by very little. However, in row 10 the standardized residual is 2.86, whereas the studentized residual is 3.06, giving a clear

EXHIBIT 21.4F

Diagnostic Statistics—
Quadratic Model of
Market on Sq.ft and
Sq.ft.sq

ROW	Sq.ft	Market	Resids	Std Res	t-Resid	hii	CookD
1	521	26.0	0.13	0.04	0.04	0.144	0.000
2	538	19.4	-7.13	-2.20	-2.28	0.128	0.236
3	544	25.2	-1.56	-0.48	-0.48	0.122	0.011
4	577	26.2	-1.81	-0.55	-0.55	0.096	0.011
5	661	31.0	0.01	0.00	0.00	0.051	0.000
6	662	34.6	3.58	1.06	1.06	0.051	0.020
7	677	36.4	4.87	1.44	1.45	0.045	0.033
8	691	33.0	1.01	0.30	0.30	0.041	0.001
9	694	37.4	5.32	1.56	1.58	0.040	0.034
10	712	42.4	9.74	2.86	3.06	0.035	0.100
11	721	32.8	-0.15	-0.04	-0.04	0.033	0.000
12	722	25.6	-7.38	-2.16	-2.24	0.033	0.053
13	743	34.8	1.17	0.34	0.34	0.029	0.001
14	760	35.8	1.66	0.48	0.48	0.027	0.002
15	767	33.6	-0.75	-0.22	-0.22	0.026	0.000
16	780	31.0	-3.74	-1.09	-1.09	0.024	0.010
17	787	39.2	4.26	1.24	1.25	0.024	0.012
18	802	36.0	0.63	0.18	0.18	0.022	0.000
19	814	34.8	-0.90	-0.26	-0.26	0.022	0.001
20	815	34.4	-1.33	-0.39	-0.38	0.022	0.001
21	825	38.0	1.99	0.58	0.58	0.021	0.002
22	834	34.6	-1.65	-0.48	-0.48	0.021	0.002
23	838	35.6	-0.76	-0.22	-0.22	0.021	0.000
24	858	35.8	-1.09	-0.32	-0.31	0.020	0.001
25	883	39.6	2.07	0.60	0.60	0.020	0.003
26	890	35.0	-2.70	-0.79	-0.78	0.021	0.004
27	899	37.6	-0.33	-0.09	-0.09	0.021	0.000
28	918	41.2	2.82	0.82	0.82	0.021	0.005
29	920	31.2	-7.23	-2.11	-2.17	0.021	0.032
30	923	30.0	-8.50	-2.48	-2.60	0.021	0.045
31	926	37.4	-1.17	-0.34	-0.34	0.022	0.001
32	931	38.0	-0.69	-0.20	-0.20	0.022	0.000
33	965	37.2	-2.26	-0.66	-0.65	0.023	0.003
34	966	44.0	4.52	1.32	1.33	0.023	0.014
35	967	44.2	4.70	1.37	1.38	0.023	0.015
36	1011	43.6	3.18	0.93	0.93	0.026	0.008
37	1011	38.4	-2.02	-0.59	-0.59	0.026	0.003
38	1024	42.2	1.52	0.44	0.44	0.027	0.002
39	1033	40.4	-0.45	-0.13	-0.13	0.027	0.000
40	1040	40.4	-0.59	-0.17	-0.17	0.028	0.000
41	1047	43.6	2.48	0.72	0.72	0.028	0.005
42	1051	41.4	0.21	0.06	0.06	0.028	0.000
43	1052	39.6	-1.61	-0.47	-0.47	0.028	0.002
44	1056	41.8	0.51	0.15	0.15	0.029	0.000
45	1060	44.8	3.44	1.01	1.01	0.029	0.010
46	1060	38.4	-2.96	-0.86	-0.86	0.029	0.007
47	1070	43.6	2.06	0.60	0.60	0.030	0.004
48	1075	42.8	1.17	0.34	0.34	0.030	0.001
49	1079	40.6	-1.10	-0.32	-0.32	0.030	0.001
50	1100	41.6	-0.46	-0.13	-0.13	0.032	0.000
51	1106	42.8	0.65	0.19	0.19	0.032	0.000
52	1138	39.0	-3.66	-1.07	-1.07	0.035	0.014
53	1164	41.8	-1.24	-0.36	-0.36	0.037	0.002
54	1171	48.4	5.26	1.55	1.56	0.037	0.031
55	1237	39.8	-4.16	-1.23	-1.23	0.044	0.023
56	1249	47.2	3.11	0.92	0.91	0.046	0.013
57	1298	45.2	0.63	0.19	0.18	0.053	0.001
58	1435	38.8	-6.62	-2.00	-2.06	0.096	0.141
59	1602	47.4	1.95	0.64	0.64	0.228	0.040
60	1804	45.4	1.37	0.65	0.65	0.628	0.237

signal that the 10th case is unusual. In fact, the response of 42.4 is exceptionally large for a square footage of 712. Perhaps a predictor other than square footage will help explain the market value for this case. Also note that case 10 lies above the 95% upper prediction limit for this model (see Exhibit 20.8C). No other cases have studentized residuals larger than 3 in magnitude.

EXERCISES

21.5A Calculate and examine the studentized residuals for the regression of average girls' height in terms of age. The data are given in Exercise 20.7G. Are any outliers apparent? (Filename: AGEHGT_G.DAT.)

21.5B Calculate and examine the studentized residuals for the regression of actual capacity of ice chests in terms of stated capacity. The data appear in Exercise 20.7I. Are any outliers indicated from the studentized residuals? (Filename: COOLERS.DAT.)

21.5C The data in Exercise 20.9B gave house prices and several predictor variables. Consider the regression of house price in terms of taxes, number of baths, and square feet. Find the studentized residuals for this model. Are any outliers apparent in this regression? (Filename: HOUSEPRI.DAT.)

21.5D Exercise 20.9D gave data on Crest toothpaste sales and several potential predictors. For the model that uses advertising dollars, advertising ratio, and personal disposable income to predict sales, calculate the studentized residuals. Are any of these residuals exceptionally large? (Filename: CREST.DAT.)

INFLUENTIAL OBSERVATIONS

The principle of ordinary least squares gives equal weight to each case. On the other hand, each case does not have the same effect on the fitted regression curve. For example, observations with extreme predictor values can have a substantial impact on the slope of a fitted value. Such data are said to have great **influence** on the regression analysis. A number of diagnostic statistics have been invented to quantify the amount of influence (or at least potential influence) that individual cases have in a regression analysis. The first measure of influence is provided by the diagonal elements of the hat matrix.

LEVERAGE

When considering the influence of individual cases on regression analysis, the ith diagonal element of the hat matrix, h_{ii}, is often called the **leverage** for the ith case, which means a measure of the ith data point's influence in a regression with respect to the predictor variables. In what sense does h_{ii} measure influence? It may be shown that $\hat{y}_i = h_{ii}y_i + \Sigma_{j \neq i}h_{ij}y_j$ so that $\partial \hat{y}_i / \partial y_i = h_{ii}$, that is, h_{ii} is the rate of change of the ith fitted value with respect to the ith response value. If h_{ii} is small, then a small change in the ith response results in a small change in the corresponding fitted value. However, if h_{ii} is large, then a small change in the ith response produces a large change in the corresponding $\hat{y}_i$.

Further interpretation of h_{ii} as leverage is based on the material in Section 21.2. There it was shown that the standard deviation of the sampling distribution of the ith residual is not σ but $\sigma\sqrt{1 - h_{ii}}$. Furthermore, h_{ii} is equal to its smallest value, $1/n$, when all the predictors are equal to their mean values. These are the values for the predictors that have the least influence on the regression curve and imply, in general, the largest residuals. On the other hand, if the predictors are far from their means, then h_{ii} approaches its largest value of 1 and the standard deviation of such residuals is quite small. In turn this implies a tendency for small residuals, and the regression curve is pulled toward these influential observations.

Exhibit 21.6A shows a scatterplot and fitted regression line for which the observation at $x = 6$ has a great deal of influence on the resulting line. The numerical regression results and diagnostic statistics for these data are given in Exhibit 21.6B. Notice that all the values of h_{ii} are about 0.1 *except* for the influential

EXHIBIT 21.6A

Scatterplot and
Regression Line to
Illustrate Influence of
Case with $x = 6$ and
$y = 6$

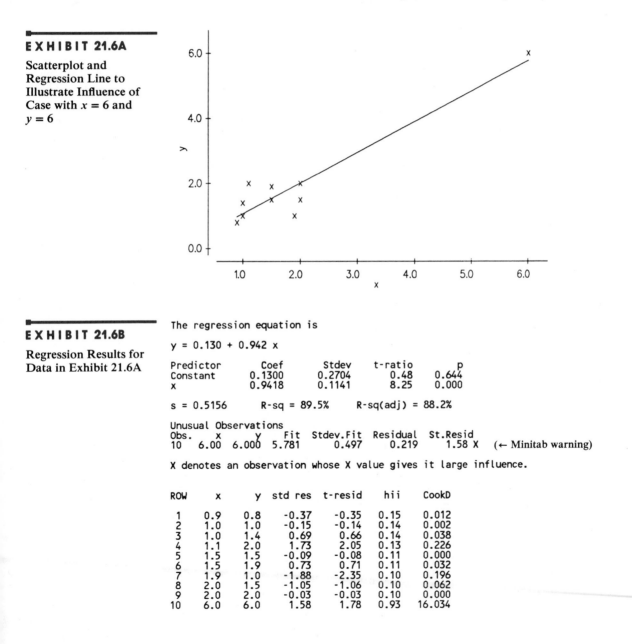

EXHIBIT 21.6B

Regression Results for
Data in Exhibit 21.6A

The regression equation is

y = 0.130 + 0.942 x

Predictor	Coef	Stdev	t-ratio	p
Constant	0.1300	0.2704	0.48	0.644
x	0.9418	0.1141	8.25	0.000

s = 0.5156   R-sq = 89.5%   R-sq(adj) = 88.2%

Unusual Observations

Obs.	x	y	Fit	Stdev.Fit	Residual	St.Resid	
10	6.00	6.000	5.781	0.497	0.219	1.58 X	(← Minitab warning)

X denotes an observation whose X value gives it large influence.

ROW	x	y	std res	t-resid	hii	CookD
1	0.9	0.8	-0.37	-0.35	0.15	0.012
2	1.0	1.0	-0.15	-0.14	0.14	0.002
3	1.0	1.4	0.69	0.66	0.14	0.038
4	1.1	2.0	1.73	2.05	0.13	0.226
5	1.5	1.5	-0.09	-0.08	0.11	0.000
6	1.5	1.9	0.73	0.71	0.11	0.032
7	1.9	1.0	-1.88	-2.35	0.10	0.196
8	2.0	1.5	-1.05	-1.06	0.10	0.062
9	2.0	2.0	-0.03	-0.03	0.10	0.000
10	6.0	6.0	1.58	1.78	0.93	16.034

case 10, where $h_{10,10} = 0.93$. The influence of this case may be dramatically revealed by omitting it from the data and refitting the regression line. Exhibit 21.6C displays both the original line and the (dashed) line obtained from the reduced data set—a substantial difference. The numerical regression results corresponding to the nine cases is shown in Exhibit 21.6D. Once case 10 is removed, everything in the analysis changes completely, emphasizing the influence of that one case.

How large might a leverage value be before a case is considered to have large influence? It may be shown algebraically that the average leverage over all cases is $(k + 1)/n$, that is,

$$\frac{1}{n} \sum_{i=1}^{n} h_{ii} = \frac{k + 1}{n} \qquad (21.10)$$

where k is the number of predictors in the model. On the basis of this result, many authors suggest marking cases as influential if their leverage exceeds two or three times $(k + 1)/n$. In Exhibit 21.6B, $k = 1$ and $n = 10$ so that $(k + 1)/n = 2/10 = 0.2$. Thus case 10 with $h_{10,10} = 0.93$ is quite influential according to this criterion.

Returning to the property data, Exhibit 21.2A lists the leverage values for the simple straight-line regression of Market on Sq. ft. Here $k = 1, n = 60$, and $(k + 1)/n = 2/60 = 0.033$. Using $2(0.033) = 0.066$ and $3(0.033) = 0.099$ as guides, cases 1

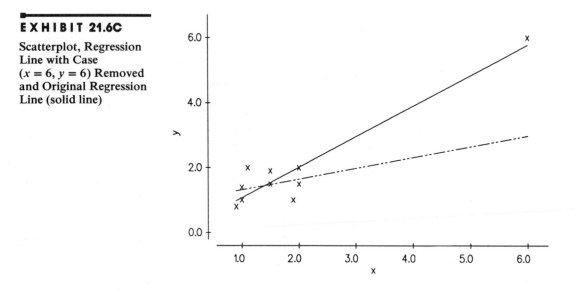

EXHIBIT 21.6C

Scatterplot, Regression Line with Case $(x = 6, y = 6)$ Removed and Original Regression Line (solid line)

EXHIBIT 21.6D

Regression Results for Data in Exhibit 21.6C

The regression equation is

y = 0.981 + 0.331 x

Predictor	Coef	Stdev	t-ratio	p
Constant	0.9807	0.5337	1.84	0.109
x	0.3313	0.3569	0.93	0.384

s = 0.4570   R-sq = 11.0%   R-sq(adj) = 0.0%

and 58 should be considered influential and cases 59 and 60 very influential. When the quadratic model is used, the criteria are based on $(2 + 1)/60 = 0.05$. According to Exhibit 21.4F, cases 1, 2, and 3 exceed twice that amount and cases 59 and 60 exceed three times that amount.

COOK'S DISTANCE

As good as large leverage values are in detecting cases influential on the regression analysis, this criterion is not without its faults. Leverage values are completely determined by the values of the predictor variables and do not involve the response values at all. A data point that possesses large leverage but also lies close to the trend of the other data will not have undue influence on the regression results. Exhibits 21.6E and 21.6F give an example in which high leverage does *not* imply that an observation is truly influential in a regression analysis. Exhibit 21.6F shows a leverage value of 0.78 for case 10 with $x = 10$. However, as shown in Exhibits 21.6G and 21.6H, when the case with $x = 10$ is omitted from the data set the regression results change very little. The fitted regression lines and the values of s are nearly the same with or without case 10. A better criterion for measuring influence would involve both the response and predictor values.

Several statistics have been proposed to better measure the influence of individual cases. One of the most popular is called **Cook's distance**, which is a measure of a data point's influence on regression results that considers both the predictor variables and the response variable.[†] The basic idea is to compare the predictions of the model when the ith case is and is not included in the calculations.

EXHIBIT 21.6E

Scatterplot and Regression Line: Potential Influence of Case with $x = 10$

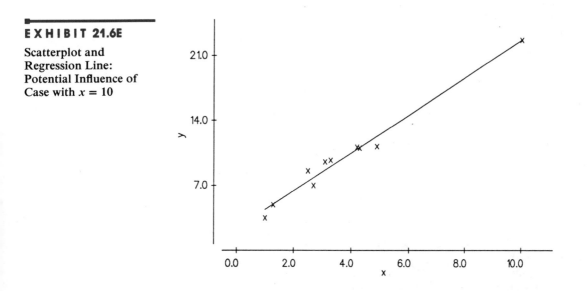

[†] The statistic that later became known as Cook's distance was first proposed by R. D. Cook in "Detection of Influential Observations in Linear Regression," *Technometrics* 19 (1977): 15–18.

EXHIBIT 21.6F

Regression Results
for the Data in
Exhibit 21.6E

The regression equation is

y = 2.33 + 2.04 x

Predictor	Coef	Stdev	t-ratio	p
Constant	2.3287	0.4740	4.91	0.000
x	2.0352	0.1068	19.05	0.000

s = 0.8118   R-sq = 97.8%   R-sq(adj) = 97.6%

Analysis of Variance

SOURCE	DF	SS	MS	F	p
Regression	1	239.16	239.16	362.88	0.000
Error	8	5.27	0.66		
Total	9	244.44			

Unusual Observations

Obs.	x	y	Fit	Stdev.Fit	Residual	St.Resid
10	10.0	22.700	22.681	0.717	0.019	0.05 X

X denotes an observation whose X value gives it large influence.

ROW	x	y	std res	t-resid	hii	CookD
1	1.0	3.5	-1.21	-1.25	0.23	0.218
2	1.3	4.9	-0.10	-0.10	0.20	0.001
3	2.5	8.6	1.56	1.75	0.13	0.176
4	2.7	7.0	-1.08	-1.09	0.12	0.078
5	3.1	9.5	1.12	1.15	0.11	0.076
6	3.3	9.7	0.85	0.84	0.10	0.042
7	4.2	11.1	0.29	0.27	0.10	0.005
8	4.3	11.0	-0.10	-0.10	0.11	0.001
9	4.9	11.2	-1.45	-1.58	0.12	0.148
10	10.0	22.7	0.05	0.05	0.78	0.005

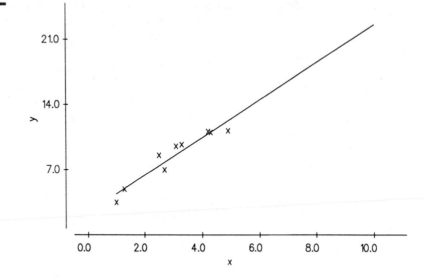

The regression equation is

y = 2.36 + 2.03 x

9 cases used: 1 case contained missing values

Predictor	Coef	Stdev	t-ratio	p
Constant	2.3557	0.7592	3.10	0.017
x	2.0256	0.2314	8.75	0.000

s = 0.8677   R-sq = 91.6%   R-sq(adj) = 90.4%

In particular, Cook's distance, D_i, for the ith case is defined to be

$$D_i = \frac{\sum_{j=1}^{n} (\hat{y}_j - \hat{y}_{j(i)})^2}{(k+1)s^2} \qquad \textbf{(21.11)}$$

where $\hat{y}_{j(i)}$ is the predicted or fitted value for case j using the regression curve obtained when case i is omitted.[†] Large values of D_i indicate that case i has large influence on the regression results, as then $\hat{y}_j$ and $\hat{y}_{j(i)}$ differ substantially for many cases. The deletion of a case with a large value of D_i will alter conclusions substantially. If D_i is not large, regression results will not change dramatically even if the leverage for the ith case is large.

The data and analyses given in Exhibits 21.6E–H provide an example. Case 10 has already shown high leverage even though the results do not change much when that case is deleted. Exhibit 21.6F displays the values of Cook's distance for all cases. Case 10 should not be singled out as having a large value for D_{10}.

In contrast, return to the earlier data and analysis given in Exhibits 21.6A–D. Here case 10 had a substantial impact on the regression results and, indeed, the values of D_i listed in Exhibit 21.6B show a very large value for that influential case.

One interpretation of Cook's distance suggests using the F distribution to decide when to consider D_i large. Some authors have suggested that cases with D_i larger than the median of an F distribution with $k+1$ and $n-k-1$ degrees of freedom should be investigated further with regard to their true influence on the regression analysis. With one predictor (and 2 numerator degrees of freedom) the median of the relevant F distribution ranges from 0.76 with 10 cases to 0.70 with 102 cases. With five predictors the medians are 0.9 for typical sample sizes. In general, if the largest value of D_i is substantially less than 1, then no cases are especially influential. On the other hand, cases with D_i greater than 1 should certainly be investigated further to more carefully assess their influence on the regression analysis results.

Exhibit 21.6I gives the diagnostic statistics for the full model of the property data. Here Market was regressed on Sq.ft, Sq.ft.sq, grade based on the indicator variables Med and Hi, and Assessed value. With respect to influence, cases 2 and 60 have the largest values of Cook's distance: 0.448 and 0.326, respectively. Neither value indicates excessive influence contrary to the high leverage value of 0.70 for case 60. However, the data should be investigated for possible outliers in cases 2 and 10 with studentized residuals (t-resids) of -3.55 and 3.35, respectively. Contrary to the conclusions with earlier simpler models, cases 59 and 60 do not appear to have unusual response values in this final model.

What is next once influential observations have been detected? If the influential observation is due to incorrect recording of the data point, an attempt to correct that observation should be made and the regression analysis rerun. If the data point

---

[†] There are many relationships among the various diagnostic statistics that are useful for motivation or computation. An alternative form useful for computational purposes is

$$D_i = \frac{1}{(k+1)} \frac{\hat{e}_i^2}{s^2} \frac{h_{ii}}{(1-h_{ii})^2}$$

EXHIBIT 21.6I   Diagnostic Statistics for the Full Regression Model of Market on Sq.ft, Sq.ft.sq, Med, Hi, and Assessed

ROW	Sq.ft	Market	Std Res	t-Resids	hii	CookD	ROW	Sq.ft	Market	Std Res	t-Resids	hii	CookD
1	521	26.0	1.61	1.64	0.23	0.127	31	926	37.4	-0.22	-0.22	0.05	0.000
2	538	19.4	-3.22	-3.55	0.21	0.448	32	931	38.0	-0.55	-0.55	0.03	0.001
3	544	25.2	-2.12	-2.20	0.19	0.174	33	965	37.2	-0.23	-0.23	0.09	0.001
4	577	26.2	-0.30	-0.29	0.13	0.002	34	966	44.0	1.02	1.02	0.05	0.009
5	661	31.0	0.58	0.57	0.11	0.007	35	967	44.2	1.42	1.44 ·	0.03	0.010
6	662	34.6	0.72	0.71	0.10	0.009	36	1011	43.6	0.79	0.79	0.04	0.004
7	677	36.4	0.98	0.98	0.08	0.013	37	1011	38.4	-0.99	-0.99	0.03	0.005
8	691	33.0	1.17	1.17	0.10	0.024	38	1024	42.2	0.28	0.28	0.03	0.000
9	694	37.4	0.76	0.76	0.08	0.008	39	1033	40.4	-0.29	-0.29	0.03	0.000
10	712	42.4	3.07	3.35	0.06	0.107	40	1040	40.4	-0.09	-0.09	0.03	0.000
11	721	32.8	-0.69	-0.69	0.06	0.005	41	1047	43.6	0.44	0.43	0.05	0.002
12	722	25.6	-0.69	-0.69	0.16	0.016	42	1051	41.4	-0.11	-0.11	0.03	0.000
13	743	34.8	-0.51	-0.50	0.05	0.002	43	1052	39.6	-0.27	-0.27	0.04	0.001
14	760	35.8	-0.31	-0.30	0.05	0.001	44	1056	41.8	0.07	0.07	0.03	0.000
15	767	33.6	0.76	0.76	0.10	0.010	45	1060	44.8	0.57	0.56	0.28	0.021
16	780	31.0	-0.39	-0.39	0.10	0.003	46	1060	38.4	-1.07	-1.08	0.03	0.007
17	787	39.2	1.10	1.11	0.04	0.008	47	1070	43.6	0.92	0.92	0.04	0.005
18	802	36.0	-0.47	-0.46	0.04	0.001	48	1075	42.8	-0.04	-0.03	0.05	0.000
19	814	34.8	-0.12	-0.12	0.09	0.000	49	1079	40.6	-0.36	-0.36	0.03	0.001
20	815	34.4	-0.25	-0.25	0.09	0.001	50	1100	41.6	-0.57	-0.57	0.05	0.003
21	825	38.0	-0.13	-0.13	0.04	0.000	51	1106	42.8	-0.28	-0.28	0.07	0.001
22	834	34.6	0.97	0.97	0.10	0.017	52	1138	39.0	-1.33	-1.34	0.04	0.012
23	838	35.6	-0.90	-0.90	0.03	0.004	53	1164	41.8	-1.26	-1.27	0.27	0.096
24	858	35.8	0.88	0.88	0.11	0.017	54	1171	48.4	1.55	1.57	0.08	0.033
25	883	39.6	0.26	0.25	0.03	0.000	55	1237	39.8	-0.67	-0.67	0.10	0.008
26	890	35.0	-1.04	-1.05	0.04	0.007	56	1249	47.2	1.70	1.73	0.06	0.033
27	899	37.6	-0.38	-0.38	0.03	0.001	57	1298	45.2	0.31	0.31	0.27	0.006
28	918	41.2	0.09	0.09	0.07	0.000	58	1435	38.8	-1.83	-1.87	0.14	0.088
29	920	31.2	-1.22	-1.22	0.12	0.035	59	1602	47.4	0.42	0.41	0.36	0.016
30	923	30.0	-0.31	-0.31	0.25	0.006	60	1804	45.4	0.91	0.91	0.70	0.326

is known to be faulty but cannot be corrected, then that observation should be excluded from the data set. If it is determined that the influential data point is indeed accurate, it is likely that the proposed regression model is not appropriate for the problem at hand. Perhaps an important predictor variable has been neglected or the form of the regression curve is not adequate. The problem of selecting appropriate predictors is discussed in Chapter 22. Section 21.8 discusses transformations as a method to obtain better regression curves in some situations.

Several other alternative influence statistics have been studied recently, but most behave quite similarly to Cook's distance. They are discussed in more specialized books on regression analysis.

SECTION 21.7

EXERCISES

21.7A Calculate and examine the leverage values and Cook's distance for the regression of average girls' height in terms of age. The data are given in Exercise 20.7G. Are any outliers apparent from either of these diagnostic statistics? If so, what do they suggest about the model? (Filename: AGEHGT_G.DAT.)

21.7B Calculate and examine the leverage values and Cook's distances for the regression of actual capacity of ice chests in terms of stated capacity. The data appear in Exercise 20.7I. Are any outliers indicated from these statistics? (Filename: COOLERS.DAT.)

21.7C The data in Exercise 20.9B gave house prices and several predictor variables. Consider the regression of house price in terms of taxes, number of baths, and square feet. Find the leverage values and Cook's distances for this model. Do these statistics indicate any outliers in this regression? (Filename: HOUSEPRI.DAT.)

21.7D Exercise 20.9D gave data on Crest toothpaste sales and several potential predictors. For the model that uses advertising dollars, advertising ratio, and personal disposable income to predict sales, calculate the leverage values and Cook's distances. Are any of these leverage values or Cook's distance values exceptionally large? (Filename: CREST.DAT.)

SECTION 21.8

TRANSFORMATIONS

So far a variety of methods for detecting the failure of some of the underlying assumptions of regression analysis have been discussed. Transformations of the data, either of the response and/or the predictor variables, provide a powerful method for turning marginally useful regression models into quite valuable models in which the assumptions are much more credible and hence the predictions much more reliable. Some of the most common and most useful transformations include logarithms, square roots, and reciprocals. Careful consideration of various transformations for data can clarify and simplify the structure of relationships among variables.

Sometimes transformations occur "naturally" in the ordinary reporting of data. As an example, consider a bicycle computer that displays, among other things, the current speed of the bicycle in miles per hour. What is really measured is the time it takes for each revolution of the wheel. Since the exact circumference of the tire is stored in the computer, the reported speed is calculated as a constant divided by the measured time per revolution of the wheel. The speed reported is basically a reciprocal transformation of the measured variable.

As a second example, consider gasoline consumption in a car. Usually these values are reported in miles per gallon. However, they are obtained by measuring the fuel consumption on a test drive of fixed distance. Miles per gallon are then calculated by computing the reciprocal of the gallons per mile figure. In *Consumer Reports* they specifically state,

> *We take each group of vehicles on a 195-mile "open-road" trip.... The trip consists of circuits on a 33-mile loop of road.... A precision gauge monitors fuel consumption during the 195-mile trip, again at a steady 55 mph on an interstate highway, and finally on a one-mile circuit that simulates city driving.*[†]

Many more commonplace uses of transformations are described by David Hoaglin.[††]

[†] Copyright 1989 by Consumers Union of United States, Inc., Mount Vernon, NY 10553. Reprinted by permission from CONSUMER REPORTS, April 1989.

[††] David C. Hoaglin, "Transformations in Everyday Experience," *Chance* 1 (1988): 40–45.

NONCONSTANT STANDARD DEVIATION

Recall that Exhibit 21.2E presented an example in which the plot of residuals versus fitted values suggested that the variability in the response was not constant over different values of the predictor variables. This plot is based on the multiple regression of city miles per gallon values for 45 cars on weight and transmission type (automatic = 1, manual = 0) of the car. The data are listed in Exhibit 21.8A and are part of a much larger set of variables that is considered in Chapter 22.

Exhibit 21.8B gives the scatterplot of city miles per gallon versus weight. The

E X H I B I T   21.8A

City MPG, Weight, and Transmission Type: Car Data for 1987–1988

```
# filename: CARS1.DAT
# Car data from Consumer Reports, 1987-1988
# Variables: city MPG, weight and
# transmission type (1=automatic, 0=manual)
  22  2365  0  Acura Integra RS          21  2695  0  Ford Probe
  22  2430  0  Toyota Corolla FX16       18  2885  0  Dodge Daytona
  29  1895  0  Honda Civic 2dr           13  3310  1  Ford Mustang LX
  21  2320  1  Chevrolet Nova            13  3430  1  Chevy Camaro RS
  18  2330  1  Mercury Tracer            18  2670  1  Plymouth Sundance
  20  2255  1  Plymouth Colt             19  2925  1  Toyota Camry LE
  18  2350  1  Pontiac Le Mans           16  2735  1  Pontiac Grand AM LE
  28  1635  0  Ford Festiva              15  3155  1  Ford Taurus
  24  2070  0  Mazda 323                 16  2995  1  Eagle Premier
  22  2115  0  Mitsubishi Precis         15  3150  1  Dodge Dynasty
  23  1840  0  Yugo GVS                  16  2950  1  Buick Century
  27  1970  0  Toyota Tercel             15  3295  1  Mercury Cougar
  31  1575  0  Chevrolet Sprint          16  2915  1  Chrysler Le Baron Coupe
  24  2185  0  Hundai Excel              16  3220  1  Buick Regal Coupe
  24  2115  0  VW Fox                    16  2900  1  Chrysler New Yorker Turbo
  16  3040  1  Mazda 626 4ws turbo       15  3205  1  Toyota Camry wagon
  19  2620  1  Audi 80                   16  2930  1  Eagle Medallion wagon
  14  3230  1  Mitsubishi Galant Sigma   14  3320  1  Nissan Maxima wagon
  18  2745  1  Mitsubishi Galant         16  3080  1  Volvo 240 wagon
  17  2573  1  Peugeot 405 DL            13  3625  1  Plymouth Gran Voyager
  17  2802  1  Ford Tempo GLS            12  3665  1  Ford Aerostar
  18  2699  1  Chevrolet Corsica LT      13  3625  1  Nissan GXE van
                                        14  3415  1  Mitsubishi van
```

E X H I B I T   21.8B

Scatterplot of City MPG versus Weight and Transmission Type

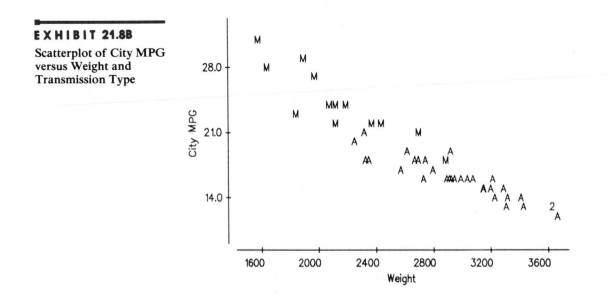

binary predictor variable transmission type is indicated by using A as the plotting symbol for the cars with automatic transmissions and M for those with manual transmissions. The lack of a constant standard deviation for different levels of predictors is only barely perceptible in this plot. The residual plot of Exhibit 21.2E is much clearer in this regard.

As noted above, miles per gallon is not necessarily the most natural way to measure gasoline consumption. It would be just as easy to go back to the original data of gallons per mile by taking reciprocals of the reported miles per gallon (MPG) figures. Exhibit 21.8C shows the scatterplot of gallons per mile (GPM) versus the weight of the cars, with transmission type again indicated by the plotting symbols A and M. Comparing this display to that given in Exhibit 21.8B shows that the situation of nonconstant standard deviation is improved. The residual plot for this regression, shown in Exhibit 21.8D, presents the situation quite clearly. Here there are no striking difficulties with the assumption of constant variability over the full range of cases. This residual plot should be compared to the corresponding plot in Exhibit 21.2E when using the original response of miles per gallon.

Another common transformation is the **logarithm transformation**. It may be shown that a logarithm transformation will tend to correct the problem of nonconstant standard deviation in case the standard deviation of e_i is proportional to the mean of y_i. If the mean of y doubles, then so does the standard deviation of e, and so forth. Exhibit 21.8E gives an example where log transformation is warranted.

Winnebago Industries, Inc., of Forest City, Iowa, is a widely known maker of recreational vehicles. In fact, the name "Winnebago" has become a generic term for recreational vehicle. From 1966 to 1972, Winnebago experienced a tremendous growth in sales. The data are listed in Exercise 23B and are available in data file WINNEBAG.DAT. Exhibit 21.8E displays a sequence plot of the monthly sales from November 1966 through February 1972. The sequence plot also clearly

EXHIBIT 21.8C

Scatterplot of City GPM versus Weight and Transmission Type

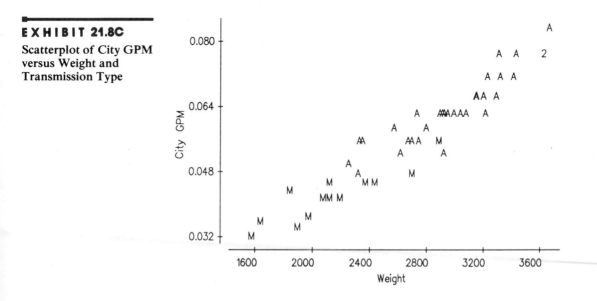

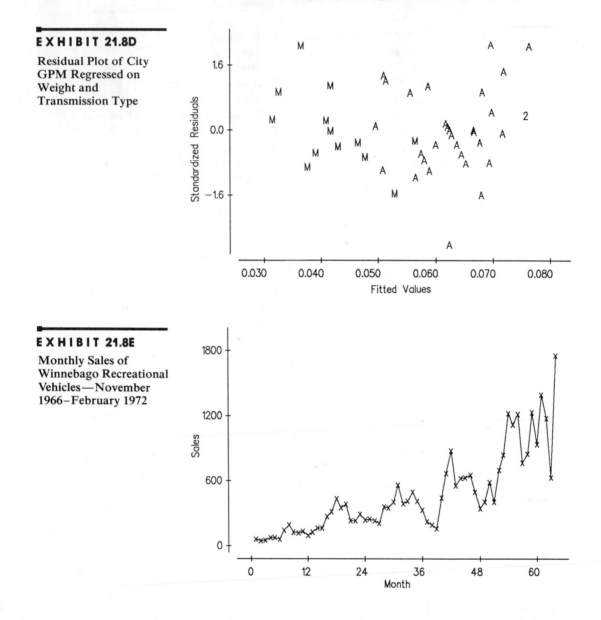

E X H I B I T 21.8D

Residual Plot of City
GPM Regressed on
Weight and
Transmission Type

E X H I B I T 21.8E

Monthly Sales of
Winnebago Recreational
Vehicles—November
1966–February 1972

shows the greater monthly variation in sales values as the general level of the series increases. However, the sequence plot of the logarithm of sales shown in Exhibit 21.8F shows a much more equal monthly variability for high and low levels of log sales. This example and many others where logarithms are helpful will be referred to in the discussion of time series models in Chapters 23 and 24.

The natural logarithm curve for values of y from 1 to 100 is displayed in Exhibit 21.8G. Notice how the rate of increase in the curve gets less and less as y gets larger and larger. This effect is what allows the log transformation to correct the problem of increasing standard deviation with increasing mean y. Exhibit 21.8H

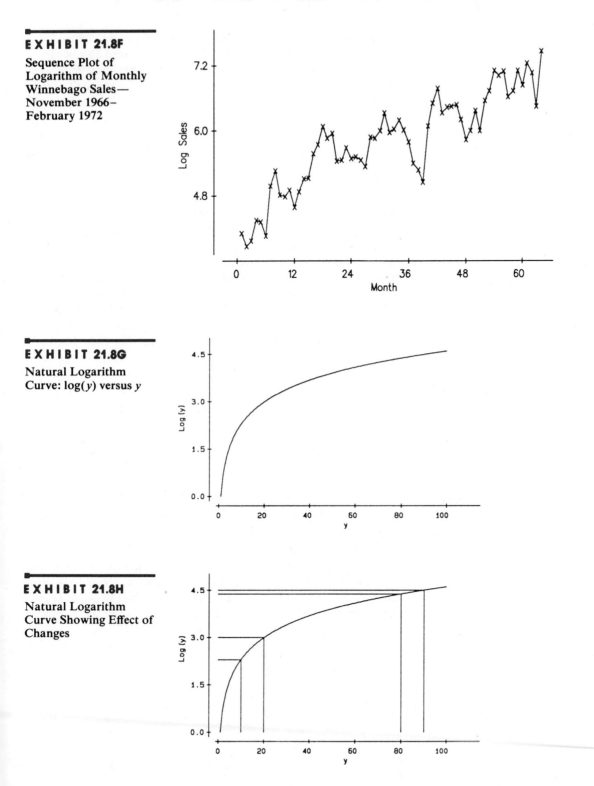

EXHIBIT 21.8F

Sequence Plot of
Logarithm of Monthly
Winnebago Sales—
November 1966–
February 1972

EXHIBIT 21.8G

Natural Logarithm
Curve: log(y) versus y

EXHIBIT 21.8H

Natural Logarithm
Curve Showing Effect of
Changes

shows the same log curve with lines indicating the effect of certain changes in y. Note that when y changes 10 units from 10 to 20 a certain change also occurs in the $\log(y)$ values, but when y changes 10 units from 80 to 90 a much smaller change occurs in $\log(y)$. This display gives additional evidence as to why the log transformation works so well in equalizing the variability under the conditions described in this chapter.

In general, the **power** (or **Box-Cox**) **transformations** defined as

$$y = x^\lambda \tag{21.12}$$

for some choice of constant power λ, are quite useful transformations in statistical practice. They have become known as Box-Cox transformations because of the important work of George Box and David Cox.[†] Notice that $\lambda = -1$ corresponds to the reciprocal transformation, $\lambda = 0.5$ is the square root transformation, and $\lambda = 2$ provides the square transformation. Putting Equation (21.12) into a slightly different but equivalent form, one can argue that the logarithm transformation is obtained as the limiting transformation when λ tends to zero. Usually it suffices to proceed by trial and error and consider the effects of each of the transformations defined by powers of -1, -0.5, -0.25, 0, 0.25, 0.5, 1, and 2 where $\lambda = 0$ is interpreted as the log transformation. As already seen, sometimes these power transformations have intuitive or physical appeal in addition to their empirical justification.

NONLINEARITY

Transformations are also quite useful in turning curved relationships into simpler straight-line relationships.

Exponential growth or exponential decay models are such that a response y is related to a predictor x by the equation

$$y = c_1 e^{c_2 x} \tag{21.13}$$

where c_1 and c_2 are constants and e is the base for the natural logarithms. **Exponential growth** is described by Equation (21.13) with c_2 positive. **Exponential decay** is described by Equation (21.13) with c_2 negative. For example, this equation describes the growth of a savings account with initial value c_1, rate of interest c_2 per time unit, continuous compounding for x time units, and no additional deposits to the account over the time period considered. In other applications the constant c_2 is negative and thus the curve displays exponential decay. Exhibit 21.8I shows graphs of both exponential growth and exponential decay using as examples the curves $y = 10e^{0.2x}$ and $y = 50e^{-0.5x}$.

[†] George E. P. Box and David R. Cox, "An Analysis of Transformations," *Journal of the Royal Statistical Society* B(26)(1964): 211–243. The form

$$y = \frac{x^\lambda - 1}{\lambda}$$

produces $\log(y)$ as $\lambda \to 0$.

EXHIBIT 21.8I

Two Exponential Curves: $y = 10e^{0.2x}$ and $y = 50e^{-0.5x}$

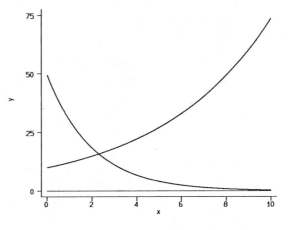

In statistical applications Equation (21.13) represents the mean of response y for a predictor with value x, and the constants c_1 and c_2 are unknown parameters to be estimated from observed data. If the statistical errors are added to Equation (21.13), the resulting model is *not* linear in the parameters. However, taking (natural) logarithms of both sides of the equation and recalling the laws for logarithms and exponents yields

$$\log(y) = \log(c_1) + c_2 x \tag{21.14}$$

Exhibit 21.8J shows the graphs of $\log(y)$ versus x for the curves displayed in Exhibit 21.8I. (This is the same as plotting the functions used in Exhibit 21.8I on a log scale.) The log transformation straightens out the exponential curves perfectly.

Assuming that for the relationship defined by Equation (21.14) the errors are additive and reverting to the standard notation for parameters, the result is the model

$$\log(y_i) = \beta_0 + \beta_1 x_i + e_i \tag{21.15}$$

EXHIBIT 21.8J

Log(y) versus x for Curves Displayed in Exhibit 21.8I

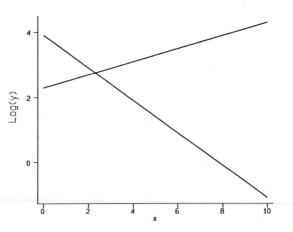

The parameters β_0 and β_1 could then be estimated by regressing $\log(y)$ on x. Note that additive errors in the $\log(y)$ model translate back to *multiplicative* errors in the original relationship.

In economic analysis, a common model relating quantity produced, Q, to capital, C, and labor, L, input to a system is the *Cobb-Douglas production function*

$$Q = \alpha C^{\beta_1} L^{\beta_2} \tag{21.16}$$

where α, β_1, and β_2 are parameters. Again this is nonlinear in the parameters, but taking logs and then assuming an additive error term produces the multiple linear regression model

$$\log(Q) = \beta_0 + \beta_1 \log(C) + \beta_2 \log(L) + e \tag{21.17}$$

with response $\log(Q)$ regressed on the predictors $\log(C)$ and $\log(L)$.[†]

Some other applications suggest relationships of "diminishing returns" such as depicted in Exhibit 21.8K. Here the curve $y = x/(1 + 0.5x)$ has been plotted.

EXHIBIT 21.8K

A Hyperbolic Curve: $y = x/(1 + 0.5x)$

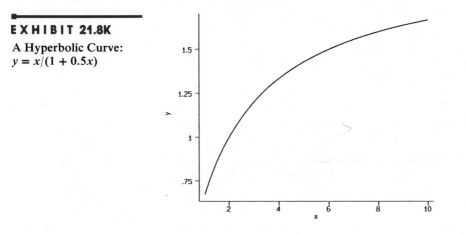

Exhibit 21.8L shows, however, that a straight line is obtained if for the same function displayed in Exhibit 21.8K $1/y$ versus $1/x$ is graphed. In general the curve $y = x/(c_1 + c_2 x)$ may be straightened by taking reciprocals of both sides of the equation to obtain

$$\frac{1}{y} = \frac{c_1 + c_2 x}{x} = c_2 + c_1 \left(\frac{1}{x}\right) \tag{21.18}$$

That is, in the reciprocals of y and x there is a straight line with slope c_1 and intercept c_2. Again assuming that additive errors apply to the relationship defined by Equation (21.18), the reciprocal of y would be regressed on the reciprocal of x to obtain estimates of the unknown parameters and the regression assumptions in the transformed variables would then be further assessed.

[†] In economics, β_1 is called the *capital elasticity* and β_2 is the *labor elasticity*.

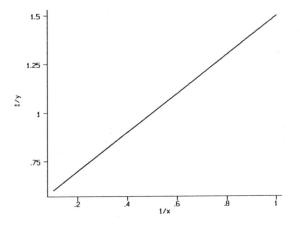

Exhibit 21.8M summarizes some of the common transformations that simplify a variety of curved relationships found in practice. Be aware that not all relationships can be made even approximately linear by transformation. For example, if β_0, β_1, and β_2 are unknown, then the function $y = \beta_0 + \beta_1 e^{\beta_2 x}$ cannot be transformed so that it is linear in the parameters. If such a curve must be fit to data, more advanced techniques in nonlinear regression analysis are used. Also keep in mind that the error terms are always assumed to be additive in the final transformed model—not in the original model. In the case study in Section 21.10, and in Chapter 22, several transformations are illustrated.

EXHIBIT 21.8M

Linearizing
Transformations

Transformation	Original Relationship	Transformed Relationship	
$\log(y)$, x	$y = c_1 e^{c_2 x}$	$\log(y) = \beta_0 + \beta_1 x$	$(\beta_0 = \log c_1, \beta_1 = c_2)$
$\log(y)$, $\log(x)$	$y = c_1 x^{c_2}$	$\log(y) = \beta_0 + \beta_1 \log(x)$	$(\beta_0 = \log c_1, \beta_1 = c_2)$
$\dfrac{1}{y}$, $\dfrac{1}{x}$	$y = \dfrac{x}{c_1 + c_2 x}$	$\dfrac{1}{y} = \beta_0 + \beta_1 \left(\dfrac{1}{x}\right)$	$(\beta_0 = c_2, \quad \beta_1 = c_1)$

NONNORMALITY

In the regression context, the assumption of normal distributions for the error terms justifies the use of t and F distributions for the significance tests and confidence intervals that were discussed in Chapter 20. However, the ordinary least squares estimates of the regression parameters, $\beta_0, \beta_1, \ldots, \beta_k$, are usually quite reasonable regardless of normality *as long as there are no outliers in the data set.* As mentioned earlier in this chapter, outliers must be detected and dealt with if the regression analysis is to be meaningful. Normality of the errors is also required for the proper interpretation of prediction intervals.

Normality of the error terms is studied by looking at the distribution of the residuals or standardized residuals using any or all of the following tools: histograms, dotplots, stem-and-leaf diagrams, or normal scores plots. Recall that normal scores plots are the easiest to consider, as we then need to compare the plot to a straight line to "test" for normality. Also, specific departures from a straight line depict certain specific characteristics in the error distribution. Exhibit 21.8N shows several possible departures and the implications. A heavy-tailed error distribution means that more extreme values (both large and small) than would be expected in a normal distribution are present. This can be especially bothersome because it may indicate outliers in the data set. Light-tailed distributions, on the other hand, have fewer extreme values than a normal distribution.

EXHIBIT 21.8N
Normal Scores Plots and Their Interpretation

(a) Normal Errors   (b) Light-Tailed Errors   (c) Heavy-Tailed Errors

(d) Light Left Tail
Heavy Right Tail

(e) Heavy Left Tail
Light Right Tail

Fortunately, in many practical analyses a transformation can be found that will improve many, if not all, of the problems of nonlinearity of the relationship, lack of constant standard deviation, and normality of the error terms simultaneously!

SECTION 21.9

EXERCISES

21.9A Review the regression of actual ice chest values in terms of their stated values. The data are given in Exercise 20.7I. The scatterplot of standardized residuals versus fitted values indicated that somewhat larger dispersion appeared with residuals that correspond to larger fitted values.

(a) Transform both the actual and stated values using their reciprocals. Display the scatterplot of these transformed values and interpret.

(b) Perform the regression of 1/actual in terms of 1/stated. Compare the results to those obtained in Exercise 20.7I where the model was actual in terms of stated. In particular, consider the plot of standardized residuals versus fitted values. (Filename: COOLERS.DAT.)

21.9B Consider the real estate data that first appeared in Exhibit 6.2A. Curvature was noticed in the scatterplot of market versus square feet in Exhibit 6.2C. The curvature was modelled earlier using square feet squared as an additional predictor. Consider some alternative methods based on transformations.

(a) Plot market against the logarithm of square feet. Does this transformation of the predictor help straighten the relationship?

(b) Plot market against the reciprocal of square feet. Does this transformation of the predictor improve the linearity of the relationship?

(c) Compare four models: market versus square feet, market versus square feet and square feet squared, market versus log(Sq.ft), and market versus 1/Sq.ft. Compare residual standard deviations, R-squared values, residual versus fitted plots, leverage values, and Cook's distance.

(d) Now consider a multiple regression model that models Market in terms of 1/Sq.ft, Med, Hi, and Assessed. Compare the results of this model to those shown in Exhibits 20.8B and 21.8I. (Filename: REALPROP.DAT.)

21.9C The data below report three variables: Expressway MPG, Weight, and Number of transmission gears for the same 45 cars reported in Exhibit 21.8A.

(a) Prepare a scatterplot of Expressway MPG against weight. Does the plot suggest a linear model or should a transformation be considered?

(b) Plot Expressway GPM against Weight. Does a straight-line model seem more tenable in these terms?

(c) Fit a model that predicts Expressway GPM in terms of Weight and Number of transmission gears. Are the regression coefficients significantly different from zero for both predictors?

(d) Plot the residuals versus the fitted values for the model in part (c). Would the plot be best described as random scatter?

(e) Plot the residuals versus each of the predictor variables Weight and Number of transmission gears. Would each of these plots be best described as random scatter?

(f) Display a normal scores plot for the residuals from the model in part (c). Does the plot support the normality assumption for the error terms?

```
# filename: CARS2.DAT
# Car data from Consumer Reports, 1987-1988
# Variables: expressway MPG, weight, and
# number of transmission gears
  36   2365   5   Acura Integra RS
  38   2430   5   Toyota Corolla FX16
  51   1895   4   Honda Civic 2dr
  38   2320   3   Chevrolet Nova
  35   2330   3   Mercury Tracer
  36   2255   3   Plymouth Colt
  43   2350   3   Pontiac Le Mans
  47   1635   4   Ford Festiva
  38   2070   4   Mazda 323
  39   2115   4   Mitsubishi Precis
  39   1840   4   Yugo GVS
  49   1970   4   Toyota Tercel
  58   1575   5   Chevrolet Sprint
  41   2185   4   Hundai Excel
  41   2115   4   VW Fox
  35   3040   4   Mazda 626 4ws turbo
  35   2620   3   Audi 80
```

(Continued)

(Continued)

```
29  3230  4  Mitsubishi Galant Sigma
35  2745  4  Mitsubishi Galant
32  2573  4  Peugeot 405 DL
32  2802  3  Ford Tempo GLS
39  2699  3  Chevrolet Corsica LT
43  2695  5  Ford Probe
43  2885  5  Dodge Daytona
28  3310  4  Ford Mustang LX
32  3430  4  Chevy Camaro RS
34  2670  3  Plymouth Sundance
44  2925  4  Toyota Camry LE
36  2735  3  Pontiac Grand AM LE
37  3155  4  Ford Taurus
36  2995  4  Eagle Premier
34  3150  3  Dodge Dynasty
33  2950  3  Buick Century
33  3295  4  Mercury Cougar
34  2915  3  Chrysler Le Baron Coupe
37  3220  4  Buick Regal Coupe
31  2900  3  Chrysler New Yorker Turbo
33  3205  4  Toyota Camry wagon
30  2930  3  Eagle Medallion wagon
31  3320  4  Nissan Maxima wagon
31  3080  4  Volvo 240 wagon
28  3625  3  Plymouth Gran Voyager
28  3665  4  Ford Aerostar
27  3625  4  Nissan GXE van
27  3415  4  Mitsubishi van
```

21.9D Consider the data set of average girls' height by age given in Exercise 20.7G.

  (a) Transform both height and age using logarithms. Plot log(height) versus log(age) and describe the plot. Would a straight-line model seem appropriate in these terms?

  (b) Fit a linear model that predicts log(height) with log(age) and test the significance of the model using the F ratio.

  (c) For the model estimated in part (b), plot the residuals against the fitted values and comment on the plot. (Filename: AGEHGT_G.DAT.)

S E C T I O N 21.10

A CASE STUDY—SEX DISCRIMINATION IN THE WORKPLACE?

THE PROBLEM

Salary discrimination on the basis of gender, whether overt or otherwise, is a serious problem in our society. It is also illegal. However, detecting and measuring it are not easy. Even in entry-level jobs, many valid factors other than gender may and should be considered in setting salaries. In 1978 a discrimination lawsuit was brought against the Harris Bank of Chicago. As a result of this suit the data in Exhibit 21.10A were made public by the defense statisticians.[†] The data give beginning salaries together with several valid measures of job qualifications, such as educational level and previous experience, for 61 female and 32 male "skilled entry-level" clerical employees. The beginning salaries for males and females will be

---

[†] H. V. Roberts, *Harris Trust and Savings Bank: An Analysis of Employee Compensation.* Report 7946, CMSBE, Graduate School of Business, University of Chicago, 1979. A recent discussion of the relevant issues can be found in A. P. Dempster, "Employment Discrimination and Statistical Science," *Statistical Science* 3 (2) (1988): 149–195.

EXHIBIT 21.10A   Salary Data from the Harris Bank of Chicago—1970

```
# Salary data from J. Bus. & Econ. Stats, Oct. 1987
# Variables: beginning salary, years of education
# previous experience (in months)
# time of hire (months after Jan. 1, 1969)
# gender (1=female, 0=male)
```

3900	12	0.0	1	1	5220	12	127.0	29	1	5040	15	14.0	3	0
4020	10	44.0	7	1	5280	8	90.0	11	1	5100	12	180.0	15	0
4290	12	5.0	30	1	5280	8	190.0	1	1	5100	12	315.0	2	0
4380	8	6.2	7	1	5280	12	107.0	11	1	5220	12	29.0	14	0
4380	8	7.5	6	1	5400	8	173.0	34	1	5400	12	7.0	21	0
4380	12	0.0	7	1	5400	8	228.0	33	1	5400	12	38.0	11	0
4380	12	0.0	10	1	5400	12	26.0	11	1	5400	12	113.0	3	0
4380	12	4.5	6	1	5400	12	26.0	33	1	5400	15	17.5	8	0
4440	15	75.0	2	1	5400	12	38.0	22	1	5400	15	359.0	11	0
4500	8	52.0	3	1	5400	12	82.0	29	1	5700	15	36.0	5	0
4500	12	8.0	19	1	5400	12	169.0	27	1	6000	8	320.0	21	0
4620	12	52.0	3	1	5400	12	244.0	1	1	6000	12	24.0	2	0
4800	8	70.0	20	1	5400	15	24.0	13	1	6000	12	32.0	17	0
4800	12	6.0	23	1	5400	15	49.0	27	1	6000	12	49.0	8	0
4800	12	11.0	12	1	5400	15	51.0	21	1	6000	12	56.0	33	0
4800	12	11.0	17	1	5400	15	122.0	33	1	6000	12	252.0	11	0
4800	12	63.0	22	1	5520	12	97.0	17	1	6000	12	272.0	19	0
4800	12	144.0	24	1	5520	12	196.0	32	1	6000	15	25.0	13	0
4800	12	163.0	12	1	5580	12	132.5	30	1	6000	15	35.5	32	0
4800	12	228.0	26	1	5640	12	55.0	9	1	6000	15	56.0	12	0
4800	12	381.0	1	1	5700	12	90.0	23	1	6000	15	64.0	33	0
4800	16	214.0	15	1	5700	12	116.5	25	1	6000	15	108.0	16	0
4980	8	318.0	25	1	5700	15	51.0	17	1	6000	16	45.5	3	0
5100	8	96.0	33	1	5700	15	61.0	11	1	6300	15	72.0	17	0
5100	12	36.0	15	1	5700	15	241.0	34	1	6600	15	64.0	16	0
5100	12	29.0	14	1	6000	12	121.0	30	1	6600	15	84.0	33	0
5100	15	115.0	1	1	6000	15	78.5	13	1	6600	15	215.5	16	0
5100	15	165.0	4	1	6120	12	208.5	21	1	6840	15	41.5	7	0
5100	16	123.0	12	1	6300	12	86.5	33	1	6900	12	175.0	10	0
5160	12	18.0	12	1	6300	15	231.0	15	1	6900	15	132.0	24	0
5220	8	102.0	29	1	4620	12	11.5	22	0	8100	16	54.5	33	0

compared after taking individual qualifications into account. If after adjusting for these valid qualifications there is still a real difference between the beginning salaries for males and females, then sex discrimination may justifiably be claimed.[†]

TRANSFORMATIONS OF RESPONSE AND PREDICTOR VARIABLES

Variables available as predictors of beginning salaries were years of education at the time of hiring, years of previous work experience, and time of hire. All of these employees were hired between 1969 and 1971. To account for the general effect of beginning salaries increasing over this two-year period (inflation), a time variable measured as month of hire since January 1, 1969, was also included as a predictor. Exhibit 21.10B gives some basic descriptive statistics of the various variables. Notice that mean beginning salaries for women were lower than those for men but that the men had larger mean years of education and months of experience. Also, most of the employees' education had spanned either 8, 12, or 15 years.

[†] Daniel W. Schafer, "Measurement-error Diagnostics and the Sex Discrimination Problem," *Journal of Business and Economic Statistics* 5 (4) (October 1987): 529ff.

EXHIBIT 21.10B

Descriptive Statistics of
Salary Variables by
Gender (1 = female,
0 = male)

	Gender	N	Mean	Median	Standard Deviation
Salary	0	32	5957	6000	691
	1	61	5139	5220	540
Education (years)	0	32	13.5	15	1.9
	1	61	12.0	12	2.3
Experience (months)	0	32	103	56	102
	1	61	99	82	86
Time of hire	0	32	15	14.5	9.7
	1	61	17	17.0	10.5

Education	Count
8	12
10	1
12	49
15	27
16	4
(N=93)	

How should salaries depend on variables such as amount of education, experience, and time of hire? Most would agree that an additional year of education might be reflected in a certain percentage increase in beginning salary. Similarly, an additional year of experience would lead, up to a point, to another percentage increase. For these reasons it is quite natural to use a log transformation on salary before beginning the regression analysis. Thus the response is log(salary).

Exhibit 21.10C shows the scatterplot of log(salary) versus education. There is a slight upward trend, and no compelling reason to rule out a linear trend is observed. Similarly, Exhibit 21.10D displays the relationship between log(salary) and time of hire. A slow upward drift of salaries over the 35-month study period is discernible in the plot.

EXHIBIT 21.10C

Scatterplot of
Log(Salary) versus
Education

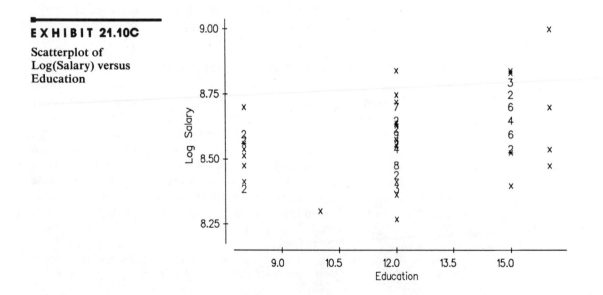

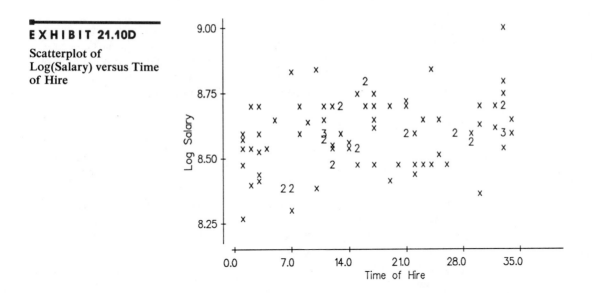

Finally, Exhibit 21.10E gives the scatterplot of log(salary) against experience. Males and females are distinguished with appropriate plotting symbols. Notice that at all experience levels the males generally have the higher log salaries and thus higher salaries. This plot does not reveal the effect of the other predictors, however, so the full regression analysis must be done.

Since only entry-level jobs are being considered, there is an effect of diminishing returns in the relationship of experience on beginning salary. From Exhibit 21.10E, there is an evident increase of beginning (log) salaries up to about 70 or 80 months of

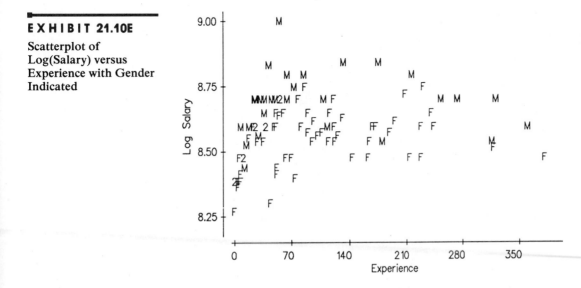

prior experience. But then the relationship seems to level off. For an entry-level position, very large amounts of experience do not correspond to large beginning salaries. One approach to modelling this relationship would be to use a quadratic curve in the experience variable as was done in Chapter 7 with the square footage variable. However, other viable possibilities include using logs or reciprocals of the experience variable.

Trying to take logs of the experience variable results in an immediate problem. It is not possible to take the logarithm of zero! A similar difficulty arises when trying to calculate the reciprocal of zero. When zero occurs as a predictor value it is customary to add a small constant to all of the values before taking logs or reciprocals. What value should be added? The goal is to produce a relationship between log(salary) and a transformed experience variable that is reasonably modelled by a straight line. With a computer it is easy to try several different transformations and compare the results. For this data set, 1, 6, and 12 months were added before taking both logs and reciprocals. A quadratic function of experience was also tried. In each case the resulting regression equation and the significance of the regression coefficients were considered. The adequacy of the model with respect to model assumptions through diagnostics was also considered. Although the regression results were not very different, the reciprocal of (experience + 12 months) was finally chosen because it produced the best model with respect to nearly all criteria. Exhibit 21.10F gives the scatterplot of log(salary) versus this transformed predictor. Now the relationship is approximately linear but with plenty of scatter. Note that since 75 months of experience transforms into a value of $1/(75 + 12) = 1/87 = 0.0115$, all the people with 75 or more months of experience are grouped together with transformed predictors between 0 and 0.0115. Thus the desired effect is achieved by this transformation.

EXHIBIT 21.10F

Scatterplot of
Log(Salary) versus
1/(Experience + 12) with
Gender Indicated

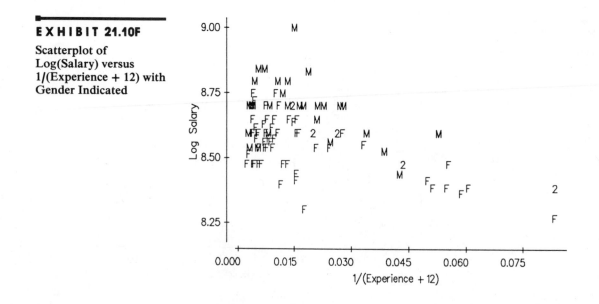

REGRESSION CALCULATIONS

The regression of log(salary) can now be done using the predictor variables: education, time, 1/(experience + 12), and gender. If the model explains a large portion of the variation in beginning salaries and if sex discrimination has not taken place, then it would be expected that the regression coefficient associated with gender would not be significantly different from zero. On the other hand, if that coefficient is significant (and if subsequent analysis reveals a good model), then the model suggests that sex discrimination has occurred in setting beginning salaries. Exhibit 21.10G displays the initial regression results for this data set. All the regression coefficients are significantly different from zero with t statistics (t ratios) greater than 3 and p values 0.001 or smaller. An R^2 of 62.5% indicates that a substantial portion of the variation in beginning salaries is explained by these predictors. The regression coefficient associated with gender is -0.123 with a corresponding t ratio of -6.54, indicating a real effect of gender on beginning salaries even after allowing for the effect of education, experience, and time of hire (inflation). Since the coding of the binary gender variable is female = 1 and male = 0, the regression coefficient of -0.123 corresponds to reduced log(salary) for females of -0.123, all other qualifications (as measured by education, experience, and time of hire) being equal. In original salary terms this corresponds to a factor of $e^{-0.123} = 0.88$. Thus salaries for females are generally only 88% of the salaries of males with comparable qualifications.

EXHIBIT 21.10G

Regression of Log(Salary) on Education, Time, 1/(Experience + 12) and Gender

```
The regression equation is

Log(Salary)=8.49+0.0138Educa.+0.00336Time-2.70(1/(Exp+12))-0.123Gender

Predictor        Coef       Stdev    t-ratio        p
Constant      8.49315     0.05840     145.44    0.000
Educa.       0.013757    0.003922       3.51    0.001
Time        0.0033629   0.0008507       3.95    0.000
1/(Exp+12)    -2.7045      0.4661      -5.80    0.000
Gender       -0.12318     0.01883      -6.54    0.000

s = 0.08093     R-sq = 62.5%     R-sq(adj) = 60.8%

Analysis of Variance

SOURCE        DF        SS         MS          F        p
Regression     4   0.95966    0.23991      36.63    0.000
Error         88   0.57638    0.00655
Total         92   1.53604

Unusual Observations
Obs.   Educa. Log(Salary)    Fit Stdev.Fit  Residual   St.Resid
  2     10.0     8.29904  8.48278   0.01606  -0.18374     -2.32R
 62     12.0     8.43815  8.61712   0.02095  -0.17897     -2.29R
 91     12.0     8.83928  8.67739   0.01750   0.16189      2.05R
 93     16.0     8.99962  8.78356   0.02305   0.21606      2.79R

R denotes an observation with a large St. Resid.
```

DIAGNOSTICS

The discussion in the preceding paragraph assumes that the model assumptions are satisfied at least approximately. Model diagnostics are used to check this out. Exhibit 21.10H shows the scatterplot of standardized residuals against fitted values.

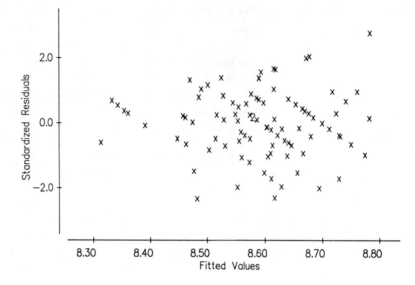

There are no obvious difficulties revealed in this display. With the exception of the smallest fitted values, the variability appears to be quite similar across all levels of fitted values. Exhibit 21.10I gives a similar display of standardized residuals plotted against the time-of-hire predictor variable. Here again constant variability across all values for the time-of-hire predictor is supported.

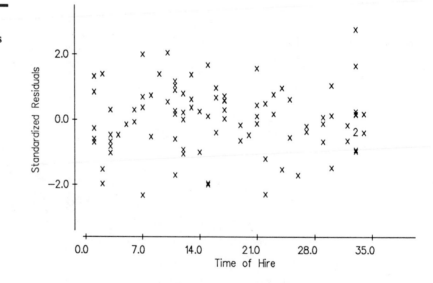

Exhibit 21.10J gives a similar plot for the experience predictor. Again this plot does not suggest any weaknesses of the model with respect to nonconstant variability. Exhibit 21.10K shows residuals versus education level. There appear to

EXHIBIT 21.10J

Standardized Residuals
versus Experience—
Salary Discrimination
Data

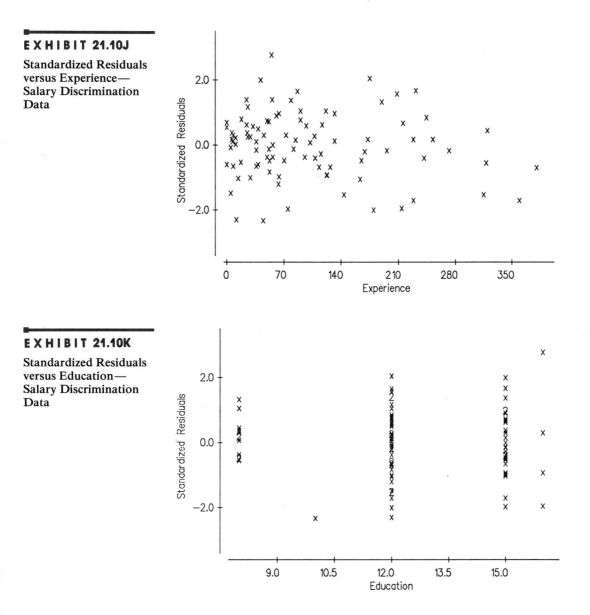

EXHIBIT 21.10K

Standardized Residuals
versus Education—
Salary Discrimination
Data

be some differences of variability in residuals for different levels of education, but the effect is not severe. Checks of normality are the next step.

The histogram of the standardized residuals is presented in Exhibit 21.10L. The distribution is quite symmetric and generally mound-shaped. However, to better assess the normality a normal probability or normal scores plot is done, as discussed in Chapter 8. Exhibit 21.10M gives the normal probability plot of the standardized residuals for this model. Recall that normality is supported by a straight-line plot. Here the results are quite good, and the correlation coefficient between normal scores and the standardized residuals is .996.

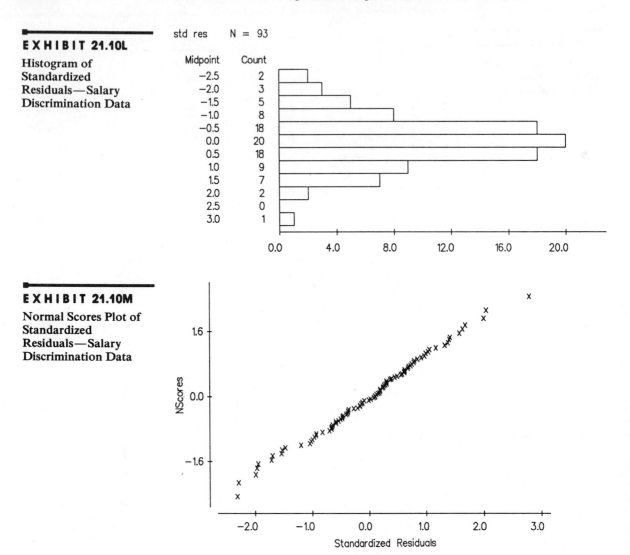

EXHIBIT 21.10L

Histogram of
Standardized
Residuals—Salary
Discrimination Data

EXHIBIT 21.10M

Normal Scores Plot of
Standardized
Residuals—Salary
Discrimination Data

Finally, diagnostics for outliers and influential cases are considered. Among other things, Exhibit 21.10G lists the largest standardized residuals. Recall that there are 93 cases so that the largest standardized residual of 2.79 should not be considered as too unusual. As a further check on outliers, the studentized residuals (also known as deleted studentized residuals or t residuals) are calculated. After deleting case 93, the corresponding studentized residual increases only to 2.9 so that again there is no indication of an outlier for this case. Exhibit 21.10N displays a dotplot of all the studentized residuals No case presents a serious outlier problem.

Exhibit 21.10N also displays the dotplot of Cook's distances for the 93 cases. Again it is case 93 that corresponds to the most extreme value for Cook's distance. However, it is only equal to 0.137, which is considerably smaller than 1, and no difficulty with influential cases occurs in this regression model.

EXHIBIT 21.10N

Studentized Residuals and Cook's Distance— Salary Discrimination Data

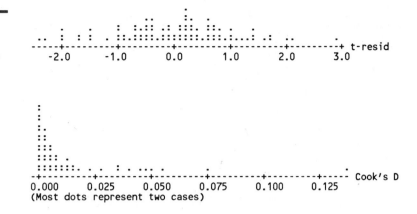

In summary, the assumptions of constant variability and normality of the error terms seem very reasonable for this choice of regression model. Exercise 22.9E provides additional practice in evaluating the reasonableness of the assumptions when alternative transformations of the response and predictor variables are used.

SECTION 21.11

LOGISTIC REGRESSION (OPTIONAL)

In Chapter 20 situations in which the response was binary and discrimination of the two groups based on the values of the predictors was the goal were considered. In other situations, it may be of more interest to carefully model the mean response in terms of several predictor variables. If y_i denotes a binary response variable, then, from Chapter 10, the response has mean π_i where π_i is the probability of "success" for the ith case. Of course, π_i will depend in some way on the predictor variables. In many cases the simple approach using the model

$$\pi_i = \beta_0 + \beta_1 x_{i1} + \beta_2 x_{i2} + \cdots + \beta_k x_{ik} \qquad \text{for } i = 1, 2, \ldots, n \qquad \textbf{(21.19)}$$

will fail if the range of predictor variables is so large as to produce estimates of π_i that lie outside the acceptable range of 0 to 1 for probabilities. In addition, as noted in Chapter 20, additive errors in such a model cannot be normally distributed nor have constant standard deviation since $\sigma_{y_i} = \pi_i(1 - \pi_i)$.

To achieve a model satisfying reasonable properties, a popular approach is to use the *logit curve*, which is defined as

$$\text{logit}(\pi) = \log\left[\frac{\pi}{1 - \pi}\right] \qquad \text{for } 0 < \pi < 1 \qquad \textbf{(21.20)}$$

The logit curve gives the logarithm of the *odds ratio* of success probability to the failure probability. Its graph is given in Exhibit 21.11A. The logit curve is undefined at the extreme values of 0 and 1 for π, but as π varies from a little above 0 to almost 1 the logit curve increases and, in theory, varies from (almost) $-\infty$ to (almost) $+\infty$.

EXHIBIT 21.11A

The Logit Curve:
$y = \log[\pi/(1 - \pi)]$

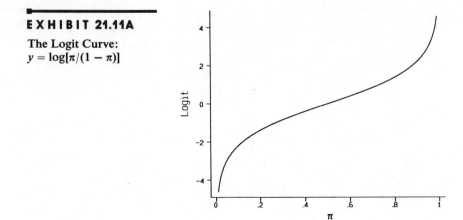

The key to using the logit curve is now to assume the relationship

$$\text{logit}(\pi_i) = \beta_0 + \beta_1 x_{i1} + \beta_2 x_{i2} + \cdots + \beta_k x_{ik} \tag{21.21}$$

to link the probability π_i to the predictor variables through the nonlinear logit curve. With a little algebra, Equation (21.21) may be solved for π_i to obtain the equation

$$\pi_i = \frac{1}{1 + e^{-[\beta_0 + \beta_1 x_{i1} + \beta_2 x_{i2} + \cdots + \beta_k x_{ik}]}} \tag{21.22}$$

This relationship is then used to define a regression model for the binary response y_i by adding an error term to obtain the *logistic regression model*

$$y_i = \frac{1}{1 + e^{-[\beta_0 + \beta_1 x_{i1} + \beta_2 x_{i2} + \cdots + \beta_k x_{ik}]}} + e_i \tag{21.23}$$

Unfortunately, this model is not linear in the parameters $\beta_0, \beta_1, \ldots, \beta_k$. Furthermore, the logistic regression model cannot be converted into a linear regression model by transforming the response or the predictors. Special nonlinear regression methods have been developed to cover the fitting of these important models.[†]

S E C T I O N 21.12

SUPPLEMENTARY EXERCISES FOR CHAPTER 21

21A Exercise 7.9C and Exercise 20A dealt with the time it takes to assemble an electronic printed circuit board in terms of seven predictor variables.
   (a) Plot the residuals of the model against the fitted values and interpret the plot.
   (b) Plot the residuals of the model against each of the predictor variables and interpret each plot.
   (c) Display the normal scores plot for the residuals of the model. Interpret this plot.

[†] See D. M. Bates and D. G. Watts, *Nonlinear Regression Analysis and its Applications* (New York: Wiley, 1988) for a discussion of these models and methods.

   (d) Plot the standardized residuals of the model against each of the predictor variables. Interpret the plot.

   (e) Calculate leverage values for each case and interpret their magnitudes.

   (f) Calculate Cook's distance statistics for each case and interpret their magnitudes. (Filename: BOARDS.DAT.)

21B Consider the Los Angeles traffic data that first appeared in Section 4.10 and was further analyzed in Exercise 20B. Using the full data set (ignoring road type), consider transforming both actual and estimated traffic volumes using a square root transformation.

   (a) Display the scatterplot of the transformed variables. Does a 45° line seem appropriate here?

   (b) Estimate the simple regression of square root actual volume on square root estimated volume.

   (c) Display the scatterplot of residuals versus fitted values and interpret.

   (d) Calculate leverage values for each case and interpret their magnitudes. A dotplot of the leverage values would be helpful.

   (e) Calculate Cook's distance statistics for each case and interpret their magnitudes. (Again a dotplot of the distance statistics would be helpful.)

   (f) Check the residuals with respect to normality. (Filename: TRAFFIC.DAT.)

SECTION 21.13

GLOSSARY FOR CHAPTER 21

Box-Cox transformation A transformation from the power family $y = x^\lambda$ for some choice of constant power λ.

Cook's distance A measure of a data point's influence on regression results that considers both the predictor variables and the response variable.

Exponential decay Described by the curve $y = c_1 e^{c_2 x}$ with c_2 negative.

Exponential growth Described by the curve $y = c_1 e^{c_2 x}$ with c_2 positive.

Influence A measure of the effect each data point has on the regression results.

Leverage A measure of a data point's influence in a regression with respect to the predictor variables.

Logarithm transformation A transformation useful for simplifying certain curved relationships and for stabilizing variability when the standard deviation of a response is proportional to the mean of the response.

Model diagnostics Testing the assumptions of a model.

Outliers Data that are inconsistent with the general pattern of the other data.

Standardized residuals Residuals that have been corrected to have a standard deviation of 1.

Studentized residuals Residuals that have been standardized using data that exclude the ith case.

## CHAPTER 22

Regression Model Selection

INTRODUCTION

In the regression work in previous chapters it has been assumed that the "correct" predictor variables are available. If this is so, the analyst merely carries out the regression calculations after discovering appropriate transformations of the response and/or predictor variables and dealing with outliers and influential data points. In practice, though, many potentially useful predictor variables are available, some that are useful and others of dubious value. How are the best predictor variables and best model selected?

Exhibit 22.1A displays data from *Consumer Reports* on the gas mileage of 45 cars tested and reported on over the period of January 1987 through February 1989. The goal is to construct a regression model that will predict gasoline efficiency in terms of other easily measured variables. Three different gas mileage ratings—city, trip, and expressway—are given together with eight potential predictor variables: weight, engine displacement, number of cylinders, horsepower, a binary type of transmission variable (0 = manual or 1 = automatic), number of gears in the transmission (3, 4, or 5), a size categorical variable (1, 2, 3, 4, or 5), and a binary variable for foreign or U.S. domestic manufacture (1 = foreign, 0 = domestic). A small portion of these data were reported in Chapter 21. The gas mileage figures were obtained by *Consumer Reports* as follows:

> *We take each group of vehicles on a 195-mile "open-road" trip.... The trip consists of circuits on a 33-mile loop of road.... A precision gauge monitors fuel consumption during the 195-mile trip, again at a steady 55 mph on an interstate highway, and finally on a one-mile circuit that simulates city driving.*[†]

EXHIBIT 22.1A

Car Mileage Data

```
# filename: CARS.DAT
# Car data from Consumer Reports
# January 1987 through February 1989 issues
# 11 variables and 45 cases
# MPG: city, trip and expressway; weight; displacement
# number of cylinders; horsepower
# transmission:1=auto,0=manual; number of transmission gears
# size/type: 1=small, 2=compact, 3=medium, 4=wagon, 5=minivan
# foreign/domestic: 1=foreign, 0=domestic
  22 32 36 2365 1.6 4 113 0 5 1 1  Acura Integra RS
  22 33 38 2430 1.6 4 108 0 5 1 1  Toyota Corolla FX16
  29 42 51 1895 1.3 4  60 0 4 1 1  Honda Civic 2dr
  21 36 38 2320 1.6 4  74 1 3 1 0  Chevrolet Nova
  18 32 35 2330 1.6 4  82 1 3 1 1  Mercury Tracer
  20 34 36 2255 1.5 4  68 1 3 1 1  Plymouth Colt
  18 36 43 2350 1.6 4  74 1 3 1 1  Pontiac Le Mans
  28 41 47 1635 1.3 4  58 0 4 1 1  Ford Festiva
  24 36 38 2070 1.6 4  82 0 4 1 1  Mazda 323
  22 34 39 2115 1.5 4  68 0 4 1 1  Mitsubishi Precis
  23 35 39 1840 1.1 4  52 0 4 1 1  Yugo GVS
  27 43 49 1970 1.5 4  78 0 4 1 1  Toyota Tercel
  31 51 58 1575 1.0 3  48 0 5 1 1  Chevrolet Sprint
  24 37 41 2185 1.5 4  68 0 4 1 1  Hundai Excel
  24 36 41 2115 1.8 4  81 0 4 1 1  VW Fox
  16 28 35 3040 2.2 4 145 1 4 2 1  Mazda 626 4ws turbo
  19 34 35 2620 2.0 4 108 1 3 2 1  Audi 80
  14 25 29 3230 3.0 6 142 1 4 2 1  Mitsubishi Galant Sigma
  18 29 35 2745 2.0 4 102 1 4 2 1  Mitsubishi Galant
  17 28 32 2573 1.9 4 110 1 4 2 1  Peugeot 405 DL
  17 27 32 2802 2.3 4 100 1 3 2 0  Ford Tempo GLS
  18 31 39 2699 2.0 4  90 1 3 2 0  Chevrolet Corsica LT
  21 36 43 2695 2.2 4 110 0 5 2 0  Ford Probe
  18 31 43 2885 2.5 4 100 0 5 2 0  Dodge Daytona
  13 23 28 3310 5.0 8 225 1 4 2 0  Ford Mustang LX
  13 23 32 3430 5.0 8 170 1 4 2 0  Chevy Camaro RS
  18 29 34 2670 2.2 4  97 1 3 2 0  Plymouth Sundance
  19 35 44 2925 2.0 4 115 1 4 2 1  Toyota Camry LE
  16 28 36 2735 2.5 4  98 1 3 2 0  Pontiac Grand AM LE
  15 29 37 3155 3.0 6 140 1 4 3 0  Ford Taurus
  16 30 36 2995 3.0 6 150 1 4 3 0  Eagle Premier
  15 27 34 3150 3.0 6 136 1 3 3 0  Dodge Dynasty
  16 29 33 2950 2.8 6 125 1 3 3 0  Buick Century
  15 26 33 3295 3.8 6 140 1 4 3 0  Mercury Cougar
  16 28 34 2915 2.5 4 100 1 3 3 0  Chrysler Le Baron Coupe
  16 29 37 3220 2.8 6 125 1 4 3 0  Buick Regal Coupe
  16 26 31 2900 2.2 4 146 1 3 3 0  Chrysler New Yorker Turbo
  15 27 33 3205 2.5 4 153 1 4 4 1  Toyota Camry wagon
  16 26 30 2930 2.2 4 103 1 3 4 0  Eagle Medallion wagon
  14 25 31 3320 3.0 6 157 1 4 4 1  Nissan Maxima wagon
  16 26 31 3080 2.3 4 114 1 4 4 1  Volvo 240 wagon
  13 24 28 3625 3.0 6 136 1 3 5 0  Plymouth Gran Voyager
  12 23 28 3665 3.0 6 145 1 4 5 0  Ford Aerostar
  13 22 27 3625 2.4 4 106 1 4 5 1  Nissan GXE van
  14 23 27 3415 2.4 4 107 1 4 5 1  Mitsubishi van
```

[†] Copyright 1989 by Consumers Union of United States, Inc., Mount Vernon, NY 10553. Reprinted by permission from CONSUMER REPORTS, April, 1989.

For the reasons discussed in Chapter 21, all of the miles per gallon figures are transformed to their reciprocals, gallons per mile (GPM), before further analysis. Thus the gallons per mile variables will be modelled as functions of the weight of the car, displacement of the engine, and other available predictor variables. Here the city gallons per mile are modelled; you are asked to model both trip and expressway gallons per mile in the exercises.

Exhibits 22.1B and 22.1C display the scatterplots of city GPM versus weight and versus horsepower. Because there is a direct relationship between city GPM and each of these predictors, a regression of city GPM in terms of either predictor is potentially useful. However, our interest is in the one multiple regression model that

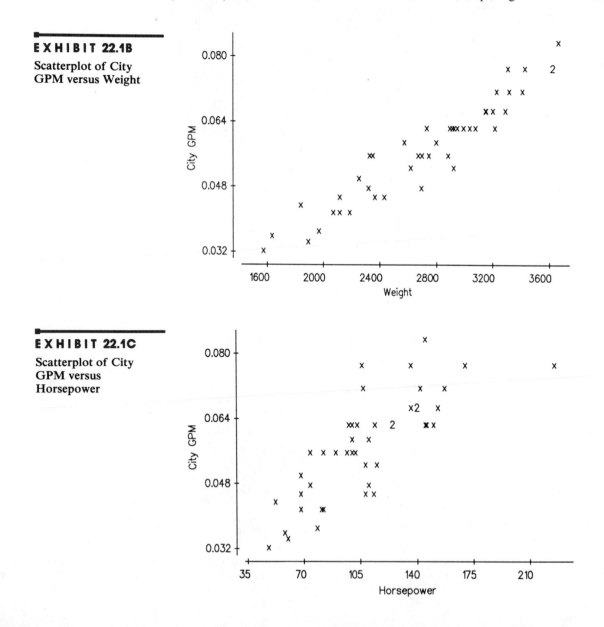

EXHIBIT 22.1B

Scatterplot of City GPM versus Weight

EXHIBIT 22.1C

Scatterplot of City GPM versus Horsepower

includes the best set of predictors. Perhaps car weight and horsepower provide similar information about the response GPM. A scatterplot of city GPM against either horsepower or weight need not show the relationship between city GPM and a linear combination of horsepower and weight. What is needed is a measure and graphical display of the *additional* effect of a predictor, such as horsepower, to a model that already includes other predictors, such as weight.

Exhibit 22.1D shows the results of three regressions: city GPM on weight, city GPM on horsepower, and city GPM on both weight and horsepower. The exhibit shows that weight alone explains 90.9% of the variation in GPM, and horsepower alone explains 63.1% of that same variation. The best linear combination of these two predictors explains 91.0% of the variation—a very small increase from the 90.9% explained by weight alone. As noted in Section 20.8, in the two-predictor case the *t* ratio for horsepower provides a measure of the additional usefulness of that predictor after weight is already in the model. In Exhibit 22.1D the *t* ratio for horsepower *when weight is in the model* is only 0.83, showing that horsepower is of little additional use. A graphical display of the added variable effect is provided by the added variable plot.

EXHIBIT 22.1D

Regression of City
GPM on Weight, on
Horsepower, and on
Weight and Horsepower

```
The regression equation is

city GPM = -0.00346 + 0.000022 weight

Predictor        Coef        Stdev      t-ratio        p
Constant     -0.003462     0.002996      -1.16      0.254
weight      0.00002220   0.00000107      20.68      0.000

s = 0.003881     R-sq = 90.9%     R-sq(adj) = 90.7%


The regression equation is

city GPM = 0.0264 + 0.000283 HP

Predictor        Coef        Stdev      t-ratio        p
Constant      0.026447     0.003787       6.98      0.000
HP          0.00028319   0.00003303       8.57      0.000

s = 0.007800     R-sq = 63.1%     R-sq(adj) = 62.2%


The regression equation is

city GPM = -0.00263 + 0.000021 weight + 0.000023 HP

Predictor        Coef        Stdev      t-ratio        p
Constant     -0.002627     0.003171      -0.83      0.412
weight      0.00002096   0.00000184      11.42      0.000
HP          0.00002334   0.00002810       0.83      0.411

s = 0.003895     R-sq = 91.0%     R-sq(adj) = 90.6%
```

SECTION 22.2

ADDED VARIABLE PLOTS

Exhibits 22.1B and 22.1C show that city GPM is directly related to both weight and horsepower. However, Exhibit 22.2A shows that weight and horsepower are themselves closely related—the heavier the car the higher its engine horsepower.

EXHIBIT 22.2A

Scatterplot of
Horsepower versus
Weight

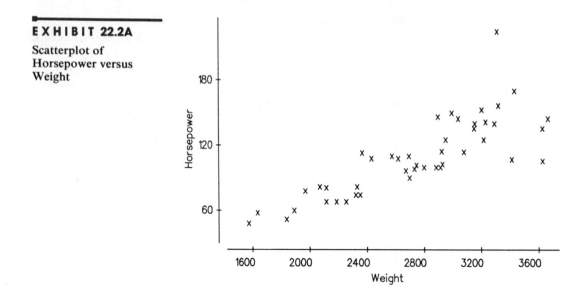

Since many regression calculations with different variables must be considered, it is convenient to introduce some common regression terminology. If the regression calculations for a response variable y with predictor variables $x_1, x_2, \ldots, x_k$ are carried out, we say that y has been regressed on $x_1, x_2, \ldots, x_k$. Using this terminology, suppose city GPM is regressed on weight and the residuals are saved. These residuals may be interpreted as the part of city GPM that is *not* explained by the predictor weight. Now perform the regression with horsepower as response and weight as predictor, that is, regress horsepower on weight. Save these residuals also. These residuals are the portion of the horsepower variable *not* explained by weight. Now plot the first set of residuals against the second set. This is the **added variable plot** and shows the relationship, if any, between city GPM and horsepower *after adjusting for the effect of weight*. If the plot shows a trend of some sort, then horsepower should be included in the model to account for this. If, on the other hand, the relationship shown in the added variable plot is very weak, then adding horsepower to the model that already includes weight will be fruitless. The added variable plot shown in Exhibit 22.2B shows no useful relationship between the two sets of residuals ($r = 0.13$) and confirms the conclusions based on Exhibit 22.1D. The correlation coefficient in an added variable plot is called the *partial correlation coefficient*. In particular, the partial correlation coefficient between city GPM and horsepower after adjusting for the effect of weight is 0.13.

The roles of the predictors weight and horsepower may be reversed and the added variable plot for weight considered after using horsepower in the model. Exhibit 22.2C displays the plot. Here there is a strong relationship (partial $r = 0.87$), indicating that weight is indeed a useful predictor in addition to horsepower. At this point weight appears to be a clear winner as a predictor of city GPM, but since horsepower has little additional predictive power another predictor to use with weight is sought. Exhibit 22.2D displays the added variable plot for transmission type after including weight in the model. The (partial) correlation coefficient in this

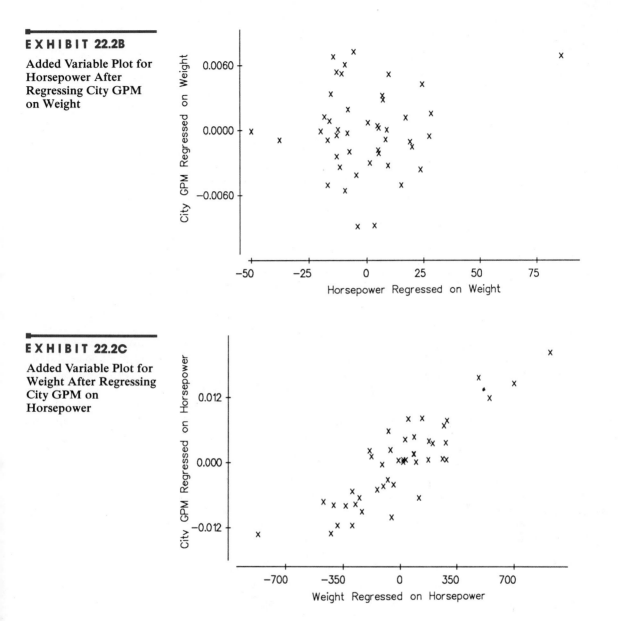

EXHIBIT 22.2B

Added Variable Plot for
Horsepower After
Regressing City GPM
on Weight

EXHIBIT 22.2C

Added Variable Plot for
Weight After Regressing
City GPM on
Horsepower

plot is 0.44, which supports the visual perception of a weak upward trend. On the basis of this plot a model with two predictors, weight and transmission type, is considered, and more predictors are sought.

With more variables involved, how is the added variable plot defined? An example will illustrate. Consider adding the predictor displacement after weight and transmission type are in the model. City GPM is first regressed on weight and transmission type and the residuals are saved. Then displacement is regressed on weight and transmission type, obtaining a second set of residuals. As expected, the

EXHIBIT 22.2D

Added Variable Plot for Transmission Type After Regressing City GPM on Weight

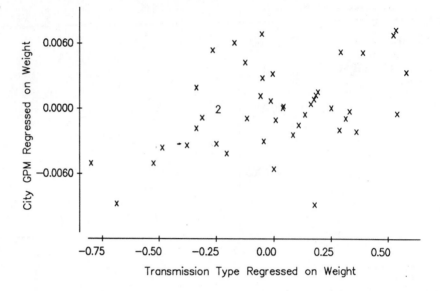

added variable plot for displacement is the plot of the first set of residuals against the second. As before, any trend indicates the usefulness of displacement in addition to weight and transmission type. The absence of trend shows the futility of using displacement in addition to the other two variables. For our data set the added variable plot given in Exhibit 22.2E indicates that displacement has little additional predictive power (partial $r = 0.34$) in a model already containing weight and transmission type. This correlation is called the partial correlation coefficient

EXHIBIT 22.2E

Added Variable Plot for Displacement After Regressing City GPM on Weight and Transmission Type

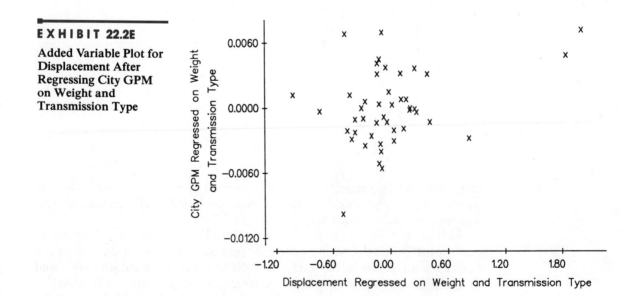

between city GPM and displacement after adjusting for the effects of both weight and transmission type. This plot also displays two possible outliers with residual values on the horizontal axis of about 1.8 and 2.0. These two residuals correspond to the Camaro and Mustang, each with a large engine displacement of 5.0 liters, in the original data. If these two cases are omitted from the correlation calculation, the value of (partial) r drops to 0.065, reinforcing the perception of no real relationship in Exhibit 22.2E.

SUPPRESSOR VARIABLES

In a multiple regression setting the combined effect of several predictors may be difficult to discern. Scatterplots of the response versus each of the predictors may not be very helpful. Frequently, the added effect of another predictor improves the regression only marginally in the sense that the R^2 value for the multiple regression is less than the sum of the R^2 values for the regressions of y on each predictor individually. Exhibit 22.1D provides an example. Here weight alone produces an R^2 of 90.7% and horsepower produces an R^2 of 63.1%, but the multiple regression including both variables has an R^2 of 91.0%.

However, in some situations it is possible that the R^2 value for the multiple regression is *larger* than the sum of the R^2 values from each of the simple regressions. An example is based on the data given in Exhibit 22.2F.

EXHIBIT 22.2F

Suppressor Variable
Example

```
# filename: SUPPRESS.DAT
# Data for supressor variable example
#   y     x1    x2
  197.4  20.8  29.3
  194.2  18.9  29.8
  199.8  20.5  30.3
  199.9  19.7  30.9
  195.7  19.8  29.7
  198.4  19.9  30.0
  197.1  19.0  30.9
  197.9  19.8  30.2
  198.5  19.1  31.2
  198.1  21.8  28.2
  196.5  20.6  28.6
  198.8  19.3  31.3
  200.0  21.8  28.7
  195.5  19.3  30.0
  199.0  19.1  31.9
  200.7  20.4  30.7
  196.8  19.8  29.4
  197.5  21.3  27.6
  197.1  19.2  30.6
  201.1  21.1  30.5
  196.5  19.3  30.0
  199.3  19.6  31.0
  198.4  19.8  29.8
  196.0  19.9  28.7
  197.3  18.6  31.1
```

Scatterplots of the response y versus each of the predictor variables are provided in Exhibits 22.2G and 22.2H. Neither plot shows a strong relationship between the response and the predictor when the predictors are considered separately. This impression is confirmed by the simple regression results shown in Exhibit 22.2I.

EXHIBIT 22.2G

Scatterplot of y versus x_1

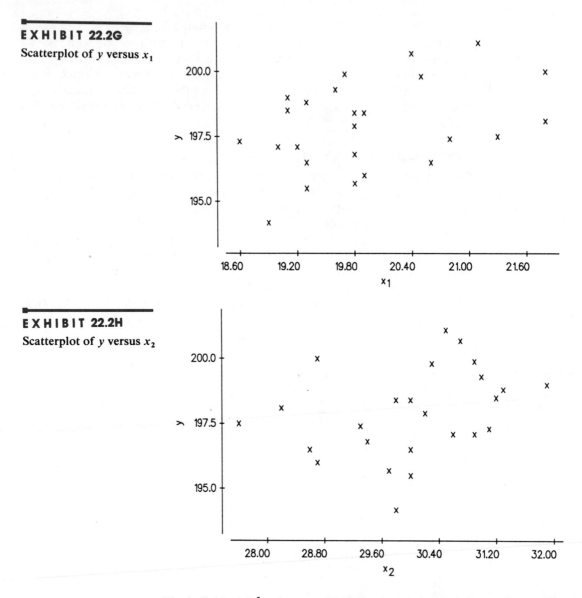

EXHIBIT 22.2H

Scatterplot of y versus x_2

The individual R^2 values are 15.5% and 10.4%, respectively. The t ratios for the coefficients of x_1 and x_2 in the simple regressions are quite small: 2.05 and 1.63, respectively.

However, when a model that contains both predictors is considered the results change dramatically. Exhibit 22.2J shows the results. Here the value of R^2 has jumped to 84.9%—considerably larger than the sum of the individual R^2s. The t ratios for each predictor are now large, 10.41 and 10.05, respectively. The added variable plot in Exhibit 22.2K clearly shows the usefulness of the x_2 variable after x_1 is in the model.

EXHIBIT 22.2I

Regressions of y on x_1 and y on x_2

```
The regression equation is

y = 183 + 0.755 x1

Predictor       Coef       Stdev     t-ratio       p
Constant     182.847       7.342       24.90   0.000
x1             0.7551      0.3679        2.05   0.052

s = 1.605       R-sq = 15.5%     R-sq(adj) = 11.8%

Analysis of Variance

SOURCE        DF          SS          MS        F       p
Regression     1      10.843      10.843     4.21   0.052
Error         23      59.217       2.575
Total         24      70.060
```

```
The regression equation is

y = 182 + 0.518 x2

Predictor       Coef       Stdev     t-ratio       p
Constant     182.358       9.522       19.15   0.000
x2             0.5178      0.3171        1.63   0.116

s = 1.652       R-sq = 10.4%     R-sq(adj) = 6.5%

Analysis of Variance

SOURCE        DF          SS          MS        F       p
Regression     1       7.280       7.280     2.67   0.116
Error         23      62.780       2.730
Total         24      70.060
```

EXHIBIT 22.2J

Multiple Regression of y on x_1 and x_2

```
The regression equation is

y = 95.7 + 2.31 x1 + 1.87 x2

Predictor       Coef       Stdev     t-ratio       p
Constant      95.735       9.232       10.37   0.000
x1             2.3123      0.2221       10.41   0.000
x2             1.8679      0.1859       10.05   0.000

s = 0.6939      R-sq = 84.9%     R-sq(adj) = 83.5%

Analysis of Variance

SOURCE        DF          SS          MS        F       p
Regression     2      59.467      29.734    61.75   0.000
Error         22      10.593       0.481
Total         24      70.060
```

In situations such as this one predictor is said to *suppress* or *mask* the effect of the other predictor.[†]

Although added variable plots are useful tools for assessing the additional usefulness of predictor variables, a large number of regression calculations must be carried out and a large number of plots considered to discover the important predictors.

[†] Further details and examples of suppressor variables may be found in David Hamilton, "Sometimes $R^2 > r_{yx_1}^2 + r_{yx_2}^2$," *The American Statistician* 41 (2) (May 1987): 129–132.

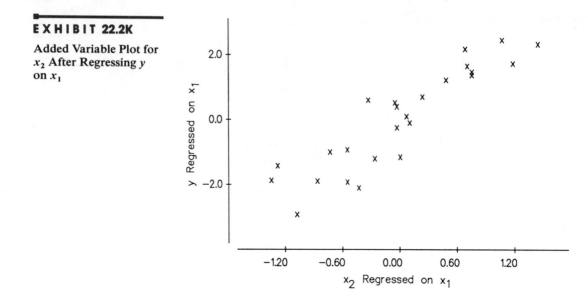

Could a large regression model that includes any and all possible predictors be constructed? Are there any difficulties with such an approach? Section 22.4 considers these questions in detail.

S E C T I O N 22.3

EXERCISES

22.3A Consider the car mileage data in Exhibit 22.1A. Display and interpret the added variable plot for displacement after regressing city GPM on weight. (Filename: CARS.DAT.)

22.3B Use the car mileage data in Exhibit 22.1A again but consider expressway GPM as the response variable.
   (a) Plot the scatterplot of expressway GPM versus weight.
   (b) Plot the scatterplot of expressway GPM versus gears.
   (c) Display and interpret the added variable plot for the number of gears after weight is in the regression model.
   (d) Display and interpret the added variable plot for weight after number of gears is in the regression model. (Filename: CARS.DAT.)

22.3C For the suppressor variable example in Exhibit 22.2F, display the added variable plot of y on x_1 given x_2. (Filename: SUPPRESS.DAT.)

22.3D Use the house price data listed in Exhibit 20.8B.
   (a) Construct and interpret the added variable plot for square feet after taxes are used to predict house price.
   (b) Construct and interpret the added variable plot for number of rooms after taxes, number of baths, and square feet are used to predict house price. (Filename: HOUSEPRI.DAT.)

COLLINEARITY

DETECTION

Suppose that in the car data the car weight in kilograms in addition to the car weight in pounds is used as a predictor variable. Let x_1 denote the weight in pounds and let x_2 denote the weight in kilograms. Now since one kilogram is the same as 2.2046 pounds,

$$\beta_1 x_1 + \beta_2 x_2 = \beta_1(2.2046 x_2) + \beta_2 x_2 = (2.2046\beta_1 + \beta_2)x_2 = \gamma x_2$$

with $\gamma = 2.2046\beta_1 + \beta_2$. Here γ represents the "true" regression coefficient associated with the predictor weight when measured in kilograms. Regardless of the value of γ, there are infinitely many different values for β_1 and β_2 that produce the same value for γ. If both x_1 and x_2 are included in the model, then β_1 and β_2 cannot be uniquely defined and cannot be estimated from the data.

The same difficulty occurs if there is a linear relationship among any of the predictor variables. If for some set of predictor variables $x_1, x_2, \ldots, x_m$ and some set of constants $c_1, c_2, \ldots, c_{m+1}$ not all zero,

$$c_1 x_1 + c_2 x_2 + \cdots + c_m x_m = c_{m+1} \tag{22.1}$$

for all values of $x_1, x_2, \ldots, x_m$ in the data set, then the predictors $x_1, x_2, \ldots, x_m$ are said to be **collinear**. Exact collinearity rarely occurs with actual data, but approximate collinearity occurs when predictors are nearly linearly related. As discussed later, approximate collinearity also causes substantial difficulties in regression analysis. Variables are said to be collinear even if Equation (22.1) holds only approximately. Setting aside for the moment the assessment of the effect of collinearity, how is it detected?

The search for collinearity begins by displaying scatterplots of one predictor against another, as was done in Exhibit 22.2A. That exhibit showed that horsepower and weight were related quite substantially. With many potential predictors, a large number of scatterplots must be considered. With some computer packages it is possible to display many small scatterplots all on one screen in what is called a *scatterplot matrix*. Exhibit 22.4A gives such a display for nine variables in the car data set. In this display each of the nine variables (including the response) is plotted against each of the other variables. For example, the first row of scatterplots plots city GPM against each of the potential predictors. In the second row, weight is plotted against each other variable. Note that the first plot in the second row is weight versus city GPM—the inverse of the plot of city GPM versus weight.

With categorical variables, many points usually pile up on top of one another and disappear in the plot. A technique called *jittering*, which adds a small random amount to these variables in a random direction so they will be slightly separated and all points will appear on the plot distinctly, can be used to circumvent this difficulty. The scatterplots of the response and of the metric predictors versus the categorical predictors are useful, but very little information is obtained when one categorical variable is plotted against another categorical variable. Relationships among categorical variables are best seen in tables.

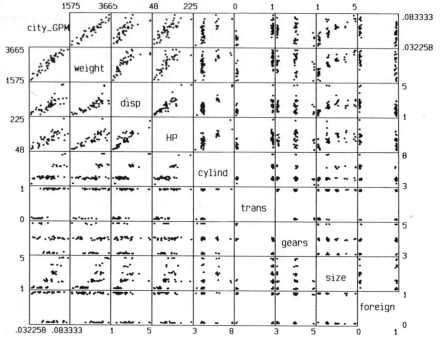

Note: Plot produced with the Stata statistical package.

Many such relationships are also assessed by calculating the correlation coefficients between all pairs of predictor variables and displaying them in a table as in Exhibit 22.4B. Here, for example, horsepower and weight have a correlation of 0.810, and number of cylinders and displacement have a correlation of 0.889. The upper part of the table need not be filled in because the correlation between weight and number of cylinders is the same as the correlation between number of cylinders and weight.

	weight	disp	cylind	HP	trans	size	gears
disp	0.791						
cylind	0.611	0.889					
HP	0.810	0.880	0.775				
trans	0.713	0.532	0.384	0.546			
size	0.838	0.493	0.333	0.535	0.575		
gears	-0.125	-0.052	-0.031	0.033	-0.615	-0.144	
foreign	-0.462	-0.575	-0.478	-0.417	-0.373	-0.328	0.324

However, these scatterplots and correlations are only between pairs of predictors and cannot assess more complicated (near) linear relationships among several predictors as expressed in Equation (22.1). To do so the multiple coefficient of determination, R_j^2, obtained from regressing the jth predictor variable on all the other predictor variables is calculated. That is, x_j is temporarily treated as the response in this regression, as was done in added variable plots. The closer this R_j^2 is to 1 (or 100%), the more serious the collinearity problem is with respect to the jth predictor. As an example, if weight is regressed on the other seven predictors, an R^2 value of 93% is obtained, indicating a collinearity problem that needs to be considered further.

EFFECT ON PARAMETER ESTIMATES

The effect of collinearity on the estimates of the regression coefficients may be best seen from the expression giving the standard errors of those coefficients. Standard errors give a measure of expected variability for the coefficient estimates—the smaller the standard error the better the coefficient tends to be estimated. It may be shown that the standard error of the jth coefficient, b_j, is given by

$$se(b_j) = s \sqrt{\frac{1}{1 - R_j^2} \cdot \frac{1}{\sum\limits_{i=1}^{n} (x_{ij} - \bar{x}_j)^2}} \qquad \text{(22.2)}$$

where, as before, R_j^2 is the R^2 value obtained from regressing the jth predictor variable on all other predictors. Equation (22.2) shows that, with respect to collinearity, the standard error will be smallest when R_j^2 is zero, that is, the jth predictor is not linearly related to the other predictors. Conversely, if R_j^2 is near 1, then the standard error of b_j is large and the estimate is much more likely to be far from the true value of β_j. The quantity

$$\text{VIF}_j = \frac{1}{1 - R_j^2} \qquad \text{(22.3)}$$

is called the **variance inflation factor (VIF)**. The larger the value of VIF for a predictor x_j, the more severe the collinearity problem. As a guideline, many authors recommend that a VIF greater than 10 suggests a collinearity difficulty worthy of further study. This is equivalent to flagging predictors with R_j^2 greater than 90%.

Exhibits 22.4C and 22.4D display regression results for two models: city GPM on weight and transmission type, and city GPM on all seven predictors. In each printout the corresponding VIF value is also given for each predictor. As we shall see, the simpler model is excellent. With the simpler model the regression coefficient for weight is estimated as 0.00001903 with standard error 0.00000139. In the more complicated model the corresponding estimate is 0.00001445 with standard error 0.00000341. The latter standard error is about three times larger. Looking further, the estimate of the regression coefficient for transmission type and its standard error are 0.005286 and 0.001650, respectively, for the simple model, while they change to 0.003541 and 0.002529 in the large model. Again these changes are substantial and lead to confusion about the true effect of an automatic versus manual transmission on gas mileage.

```
The regression equation is

city GPM = 0.00146 + 0.000019 weight + 0.00529 trans

Predictor        Coef        Stdev      t-ratio        p      VIF
Constant     0.001455    0.003121         0.47    0.644
weight       0.00001903  0.00000139      13.71    0.000     2.0
trans        0.005286    0.001650         3.20    0.003     2.0

s = 0.003520    R-sq = 92.7%    R-sq(adj) = 92.3%

Analysis of Variance

SOURCE        DF        SS           MS          F         p
Regression     2    0.0065673    0.0032837    265.02    0.000
Error         42    0.0005204    0.0000124
Total         44    0.0070877
```

```
The regression equation is

city GPM = 0.00845 + 0.000014 weight + 0.00265 disp
         + 0.00102 cylind - 0.000010 HP + 0.00354 trans
         - 0.00179 gears + 0.00115 size + 0.00224 foreign

Predictor        Coef         Stdev      t-ratio        p      VIF
Constant      0.008454    0.006493         1.30    0.201
weight        0.00001445  0.00000341       4.23    0.000    14.4
disp          0.002650    0.002053         1.29    0.205    12.9
cylind        0.001024    0.001019         1.00    0.322     5.6
HP           -0.00001006  0.00003423      -0.29    0.770     6.2
trans         0.003541    0.002529         1.40    0.170      .6
gears        -0.001786    0.001386        -1.29    0.206     3.2
size          0.0011498   0.0008478        1.36    0.183     4.8
foreign       0.002241    0.001349         1.66    0.105     1.9

s = 0.003250    R-sq = 94.6%    R-sq(adj) = 93.4%


Analysis of Variance

SOURCE        DF        SS           MS          F         p
Regression     8    0.00670755   0.00083844    79.39    0.000
Error         36    0.00038018   0.00001056
Total         44    0.00708774
```

EFFECT ON INFERENCE

If collinearity affects parameter estimates and their standard errors then it follows that t ratios will also be affected. Exhibits 22.4C and 22.4D show that the t ratios associated with weight in the two models are 13.71 and 4.23, respectively, both of which indicate that weight is an important variable. However, the t ratios for transmission type change from 3.20 to 1.40, apparently showing in the latter case that transmission type is *not* important. The collinearity has confused the effects of the various predictors. Note that the estimated regression coefficient for horsepower is negative, seemingly indicating that an increase in horsepower leads to *lower* gallons per mile and better fuel economy!

EFFECT ON PREDICTION

The effect of collinearity on prediction depends on the particular values specified for the predictors. If the relationships among the predictors used in fitting the model are preserved in the predictor values used for prediction, then the predictions will be little affected by collinearity. On the other hand, if the specified predictor values are contrary to the observed relationships among the predictors in the model, then the predictions will be poor.

For example, in June 1989, *Consumer Reports* tested a Mazda 929 that weighed 3480 pounds and had a 3.0 liter V6 engine with 158 horsepower. In addition, the tested car had an automatic transmission with four gears, was size 3, and was of foreign manufacture. The city MPG tested out at 14 MPG. Using the small model with only weight and transmission type as predictors, the predicted city GPM is 0.07335 GPM, which translates to 13.6 MPG. Using the full model with eight predictors yields a similar prediction of 13.7 MPG. Both of these predictions are quite reasonable and both produce 3-standard-error prediction intervals that contain the true value of 14 MPG.

In contrast, consider a fictitious car that weighs 2800 pounds and has a 5.0 liter engine that generates 100 horsepower. The car has an automatic transmission with three gears, is size 4, and is of foreign manufacture. The predictor values for weight and transmission type are similar to the actual data and lead to a prediction of 16.7 MPG. However, the other predictor values are dissimilar from those in the data set. In particular, the large engine (5.0 liters) has only four cylinders and 100 horsepower. The full eight-predictor model predicts a city MPG of 14.9, which is rather different from the prediction of 16.7 based on the smaller model. Collinearity may place hidden restrictions on the predictor variables, and values well within the ranges of the individual predictors may be far from the given predictors when their values are considered jointly. For example, for the fictitious car each of the individual predictor values, weight = 2800, cylinders = 4, displacement = 5.0, HP = 100, automatic transmission with three gears, size = 3, and foreign = 0, is within the range of the predictors in the data set. However, this *combination* of values is far from any combination in the data set.

WHAT TO DO ABOUT COLLINEARITY

The best defense against the problems associated with collinear predictors is to keep models as simple as possible. Variables that add little to the usefulness of a regression model should be deleted from the model. Sections 22.6 and 22.8 present methods for selecting the better predictor variables. When collinearity is detected among variables, none of which can reasonably be deleted from a regression model, avoid extrapolation and beware of inferences on individual regression coefficients.

SECTION 22.5

EXERCISES

22.5A Consider the car mileage data of Exhibit 22.1A and let expressway GPM be the response of interest.

(a) Compare a model that uses weight and number of gears as predictors with a model that uses all the predictors in the data set. In particular, look at *t* ratios for the predictors and VIF values.

    (b) Compare the models considered in part (a) in terms of predicting the expressway GPM of the Ford Probe. (Filename: CARS.DAT.)

22.5B Look once more at the house price data given in Exercise 20.9B.

    (a) Compare a model that uses taxes, number of baths, and square feet to predict house price with a model that uses all the predictors available. Interpret the t ratios for the predictors in both models. Also compare VIF values.

    (b) Use both models in part (a) to predict the price of the first house in the data set. (Filename: HOUSEPRI.DAT.)

SECTION 22.6

EFFECTS OF MODEL MISSPECIFICATION

Most regression problems require decisions on which of the many potential predictors to include in the model. In addition to the initial predictors, possible transformed predictors such as their logarithms, reciprocals, and squares must be considered. Cross-products of initial predictors or transformations of initial predictors may also need to be studied. A model that does not include the "correct" predictor variables is called a **misspecified model**. Empirical analysis based on various scatterplots and careful consideration of potential theoretical relationships in the particular area of application provide a pool of potential predictors. The challenge is to choose predictors from that pool that avoid model misspecification.

EFFECT OF UNDERSPECIFICATION

Suppose you want to estimate the effect on city GPM of having a car with an automatic transmission. A first approach might be to fit a regression model that uses only the binary transmission-type variable. Exhibit 22.6A displays the results from this fit and gives the estimate of about 0.021 gallon per mile as the price for having an automatic transmission. The standard error of this estimate is about 0.0027, which leads to a 3-standard-error confidence interval for the automatic transmission price of $[0.021 - 3(0.0027), 0.021 + 3(0.0027)] = [0.0129, 0.0291]$ gallons per mile.

EXHIBIT 22.6A

An Underspecified Model

```
The regression equation is

city GPM = 0.0421 + 0.0214 trans

Predictor       Coef        Stdev      t-ratio        p
Constant    0.042116     0.002258       18.65      0.000
trans       0.021408     0.002678        7.99      0.000

s = 0.008142    R-sq = 59.8%    R-sq(adj) = 58.8%
```

However, there is now substantial empirical and theoretical evidence that weight is an important variable in determining city GPM. Exhibit 22.4C showed that in a model that contains both weight and transmission type as predictors, the estimated effect of transmission type is 0.005286 gallon per mile with a standard error of 0.001650. This standard error is nearly half of the previous value of 0.002678. The 3-standard-error confidence interval for the automatic transmission price in this more complete model is

$$[0.0053 - 3(0.0016), 0.0053 + 3(0.0016)] = [0.0005, 0.00101]$$

gallons per mile. Note that this interval does not even overlap the corresponding interval based on the model that uses only transmission type as a predictor. Leaving out the important predictor of weight has the effect of overestimating the price of having an automatic transmission.

An **underspecified model** is a model that fails to include important predictor variables. In general, omitting important predictor variables will

- Produce inaccurate estimates of the regression coefficients
- Produce inaccurate predictions of new response values
- Overestimate σ with s
- Overestimate the standard errors of the regression coefficients since s is too large
- Overestimate the prediction standard error since s is too large

An important exception to the first two statements occurs when all the predictor variables are uncorrelated among themselves. However, even in that case, s tends to overestimate σ, which leads to overestimation of standard errors of regression coefficients and standard errors of prediction.

EFFECT OF OVERSPECIFICATION

When extra predictors are included in a model, the most important effect, beyond the difficulty with possible collinearity, is that the standard errors of the regression coefficients and the standard errors of prediction are larger than they need be. An **overspecified model** is a model that includes extra predictor variables. This effect may be seen by again comparing the results given in Exhibits 22.4C and 22.4D. In the two-predictor model the estimated regression coefficient for weight is 0.00001903 with a standard error of 0.00000139. In the eight predictor model the regression coefficient changes only a little, to 0.00001445, but the standard error nearly triples to 0.00000341. Similarly the regression coefficient for the transmission-type variable and its standard error change from 0.005286 and 0.001650 in the two-predictor model to 0.003541 and 0.002529 in the overspecified model. Here again the standard error is substantially larger in the latter case.

For a variety of reasons, then, it is important to find the "best" predictor variables in a multiple regression model.

SECTION 22.7

EXERCISE

22.7A Consider again the expressway MPG data given in Exercise 21.9C. First transform the response to GPM using the reciprocal transformation. Consider using three different models to predict expressway GPM: weight alone, number of gears alone, and using a linear combination of weight and gears.

(a) Compare the residual standard deviations of the three models. Which is smallest?

(b) Compare the coefficient on weight in the simple linear regression model with the corresponding coefficient in the multiple regression model. Are they similar or different?

(c) Compare the coefficient on number of gears in the simple linear regression model with the corresponding coefficient in the multiple regression model. Are they similar or different?

(d) Interpret the regression coefficient associated with number of transmission gears in the simple linear regression model and then in the multiple regression model. (Filename: CARS2.DAT.)

SECTION 22.8

BEST SUBSET METHODS

CRITERIA FOR SELECTING PREDICTOR VARIABLES

Several statistics already discussed form the basis for criteria for selecting predictor variables. Generally speaking, models with smaller values of the residual standard deviation, s, are preferred over models with larger values of s. Similarly, larger values of R^2 correspond to preferable models. Here, however, recall the discussion of R^2 in Sections 7.10 and 20.11. Interpretation of the multiple coefficient of determination, R^2, depends on the sampling method and *always increases* as more variables are added to a model. Furthermore, R^2 does not have a predictive interpretation. The adjusted R^2, $R^2(\text{adj}) = 100[1 - (s^2/s_y^2)]\%$, can be used to compare models with different numbers of predictors but, since s_y is fixed, large values for $R^2(\text{adj})$ correspond exactly to small values of s. You may just as well choose a model on the basis of values of s. **Best subset regression** is a method for choosing the best predictor variables by considering all possible subsets of predictors and one or more criteria. Two statistics that lead to criteria based on selecting variables that improve the predictive power of the model are Mallows' C_p criterion and *PRESS*.

MALLOWS' C_p CRITERION

Suppose k variables are in the pool of potential predictors. Let s be the residual standard deviation obtained from the regression model that includes all k predictors—the full model. Now consider a model that includes only a particular subset of predictors and let p be the number of regression coefficients (including β_0, if present) in the subset model. For this subset model let RSS_p denote the sum of squares of the residuals. Then the C_p statistic for this subset model is defined as[†]

$$C_p = \frac{RSS_p}{s^2} + 2p - n \tag{22.4}$$

If the subset model contains all the important predictors, then it may be shown that, on average, $C_p = p$. On the other hand, if the subset model is missing important predictors, then C_p will tend to be larger than p. In general, smaller values for C_p indicate more desirable models. Two subset models may be compared by comparing their values of C_p. Mallows suggested that good models have $C_p \simeq p$.

[†] C. L. Mallows, "Some Comments on C_p," *Technometrics* 15 (1973): 661–676.

A plot of C_p versus p can be used to look for the models that satisfy this criterion. Note that there will be k different one-variable models and thus k values of C_p for one-variable models. These values should all be plotted above $p = 2$. There are $k(k - 1)/2$ different choices of predictors for models with two predictors, plus an intercept, and each of these will have its own value for C_p. The better of these models will have C_p near 3. In general, models with fewer predictors and with C_p near p will be the better models. Once a small number of models has been singled out, they are studied carefully with respect to outliers, influential observations, normality of the errors, and constancy of the standard deviation of the errors before choosing a final model for use.

PRESS

Another model-selection criterion is based on prediction and on the diagnostic ideas presented in Section 21.4. For a model based on a particular subset of predictor variables, consider estimating the regression equation with the ith case deleted from the data set. Now use this estimated regression equation to predict the response for the ith case. Let $\hat{y}_{(i)}$ denote this prediction. Since the actual response for the ith case is available,

$$PRESS = \sum_{i=1}^{n} (y_i - \hat{y}_{(i)})^2 \tag{22.5}$$

can be computed as a measure of the predictive power of the present model. **PRESS** stands for predicted residual sum of squares; models with smaller values for $PRESS$ are preferred. In the terms of Section 23.4, $PRESS$ is the sum of squares of the studentized residuals.[†]

If k is not too large each of the required regressions can be computed and the various statistics (s, R^2, R^2(adj), C_p, and $PRESS$) obtained and compared. However, for problems with many potential predictors, the number of models that must be considered in this way is prohibitive. In these situations it is important that clever computation methods that minimize the time needed to find the best models be used. Most statistical software takes advantage of these computational "tricks" and makes variable selection according to the criteria above feasible. If you are interested in the details of these methods, consult one of the standard books on regression analysis and the references contained in them.[††]

To illustrate these selection methods the car data with eight potential predictors are again used. Exhibit 22.8A gives the Minitab output from the command BREGRESS (best regression). Here the summary results for each of the five "best" models of each possible size are displayed. "Best" is in the sense of smallest value of s^2. The values of R^2, R^2(adj), and C_p are also given for each model reported. The X's under the predictor variable names indicate that those predictors are

---

[†] Minitab does not give $PRESS$ directly but its value can be obtained once the studentized residuals have been calculated through the TRESIDUALS subcommand to REGRESS. If the studentized residuals have been stored in 't resid' then $PRESS = SSQ('t resid')$.

[††] R. H. Meyers, *Classical and Modern Regression Analysis*, 2d ed. (Boston: PWS-KENT, 1990); or Sanford Weisberg, *Applied Linear Regression Analysis*, 2d ed. (New York: Wiley, 1985).

EXHIBIT 22.8A

Best Subset Regression of City GPM

Vars	R-sq	Adj. R-sq	Cp	s	Weight	Disp	Cylind	HP	Trans	Gears	Size	Foreign
1	90.9	90.7	20.3	0.0038806	X							
1	64.8	64.0	195.1	0.0076156		X						
1	63.4	62.6	204.3	0.0077619							X	
1	63.1	62.2	206.7	0.0078001				X				
1	59.8	58.8	228.9	0.0081423					X			
2	92.7	92.3	10.3	0.0035200	X			X				
2	92.5	92.2	11.3	0.0035546	X						X	
2	91.7	91.3	16.5	0.0037359	X	X						
2	91.6	91.2	17.7	0.0037746	X	X						
2	91.0	90.6	21.3	0.0038947	X		X					
3	93.8	93.3	4.8	0.0032797	X		X	X				
3	93.5	93.1	6.4	0.0033437	X	X		X				
3	93.5	93.1	6.5	0.0033459	X		X				X	
3	93.4	92.9	7.4	0.0033814	X	X					X	
3	93.0	92.5	10.0	0.0034780	X			X			X	
4	94.1	93.5	4.9	0.0032457	X		X	X			X	
4	94.0	93.4	5.0	0.0032504	X	X					X	X
4	94.0	93.4	5.4	0.0032678	X		X				X	X
4	93.9	93.3	5.7	0.0032785	X			X	X	X		
4	93.9	93.3	6.0	0.0032901	X	X		X			X	
5	94.2	93.5	5.6	0.0032336	X	X				X	X	X
5	94.2	93.5	5.8	0.0032423	X		X		X		X	X
5	94.2	93.4	6.0	0.0032509	X	X		X	X			X
5	94.2	93.4	6.2	0.0032562	X		X	X			X	X
5	94.1	93.4	6.3	0.0032621	X	X	X		X		X	
6	94.5	93.6	6.0	0.0032083	X	X		X	X	X	X	
6	94.4	93.5	6.7	0.0032364	X		X	X	X	X	X	
6	94.3	93.5	7.0	0.0032481	X	X	X		X	X	X	
6	94.3	93.4	7.1	0.0032520	X	X	X	X	X			X
6	94.3	93.4	7.1	0.0032525	X	X	X	X		X	X	
7	94.6	93.6	7.1	0.0032093	X	X	X		X	X	X	X
7	94.5	93.4	8.0	0.0032501	X	X		X	X	X	X	X
7	94.4	93.3	8.7	0.0032786	X	X	X	X		X	X	X
7	94.4	93.3	8.7	0.0032789	X		X	X	X	X	X	X
7	94.4	93.3	8.8	0.0032864	X	X	X	X	X	X		X
8	94.6	93.4	9.0	0.0032497	X	X	X	X	X	X	X	X

EXHIBIT 22.8B

Plot of C_p versus p for City GPM (omitting models with C_p values above 22)

Vertical axis (C_p) tick labels: 21.0, 14.0, 7.0, 0.0

Horizontal axis (p) tick labels: 2.0, 4.0, 6.0, 8.0

included in the corresponding model. For example, the best model with three predictors uses weight, transmission type, and number of cylinders as predictors. For this model, $s = 0.0032797$, $C_p = 4.8$, and $p = 3 + 1 = 4$. Exhibit 22.8B displays the plot of C_p versus p with the p versus p "45°" line overlayed.

Since models with C_p, small, near p, and with the least number of predictors are preferred, this plot confirms the superiority of this three-predictor model.

SECTION 22.9

EXERCISES

22.9A Use the car mileage data of Exhibit 22.1A with expressway GPM as the response. Use a best subsets regression package to compare different possible sets of predictors.
  (a) Which model produces the smallest value for residual standard deviation?
  (b) Which model gives the largest value for adjusted R^2?
  (c) Which model gives the smallest value for C_p? (Filename: CARS.DAT.)

22.9B Use the car mileage data of Exhibit 22.1A with trip GPM as the response. Use a best subsets regression package to compare different possible sets of predictors.
  (a) Which model produces the smallest value for residual standard deviation?
  (b) Which model gives the largest value for adjusted R^2?
  (c) Which model gives the smallest value for C_p? (Filename: CARS.DAT.)

22.9C Return to the house price data of Exercise 20.9B. Use a best subsets regression package to compare different possible sets of predictors.
  (a) Which model produces the smallest value for residual standard deviation?
  (b) Which model gives the largest value for adjusted R^2?
  (c) Which model gives the smallest value for C_p? (Filename: HOUSEPRI.DAT.)

22.9D Consider the tree data listed in Exercise 20.7J. Two predictors are given: diameter and height. Create three more predictors: diameter^2, height^2, and diameter × height.
  (a) Use a best subsets regression program to select among models that may include any linear combination of the five predictors: diameter, diameter^2, height, height^2, and diameter × height.
  (b) Trees are roughly cylindrical in shape. The volume of a cylinder is given by the area of the base times the height. Since the area of a circle is proportional to its diameter squared, our simple geometrical argument suggests that diameter^2 × height might be a useful predictor of a tree's volume. Fit the one-predictor model volume = β_0 + β_1(diameter^2 × height) + e and compare it to all of the possible models based on subsets of the predictors: diameter, diameter^2, height, height^2, and diameter × height considered in part (a). (Filename: TREES.DAT.)

22.9E Consider the Harris Bank salary data presented in Section 21.10. The model presented there contains four predictors: educational level, time of hire, 1/(experience + 12), and gender. Create additional predictors: log(experience + 1), log(experience + 6), log(experience + 12), 1/(experience + 1), and 1/(experience + 6).
  (a) Plot log(salary) against each of these transformed experience predictors and interpret the plots.
  (b) Use a best subsets regression package to compare all possible subsets among the predictors: educational level, time of hire, log(experience + 1), log(experience + 6), log(experience + 12), 1/(experience + 1), 1/(experience + 6), and 1/(experience + 12). (Filename: SALARY.DAT.)

THE F TEST FOR SUBSETS OF COEFFICIENTS (OPTIONAL)

In some settings researchers want to test whether certain groups of regression parameters are zero. If they are, then the corresponding predictors may be safely omitted from the model. For example, we may ask if the grade (med and hi) variables and assessed value variables as a group are important in modelling market value once square feet and square feet squared are in the regression model we have been considering throughout this book. In general, the model

$$y = \beta_0 + \beta_1 x_1 + \cdots + \beta_k x_k + e \qquad \textbf{(22.6)}$$

is considered to be reasonable on the basis of theory or earlier regression work. But the question centers on whether or not the p additional predictor variables x_{k+1}, $x_{k+2}, \ldots, x_{k+p}$ should also be included in the model. That is, the expanded model

$$y = \beta_0 + \beta_1 x_1 + \cdots + \beta_k x_k + \beta_{k+1} x_{k+1} + \cdots + \beta_{k+p} x_{k+p} + e \qquad \textbf{(22.7)}$$

is being considered but statistical confirmation of the added complication is needed. Formally, the hypothesis $H_0: \beta_{k+1} = \beta_{k+2} = \cdots = \beta_{k+p} = 0$ needs to be tested. The model of Equation (22.7) must yield a smaller residual sum of squares, and a statistical test may be based on the reduction in the sum of squares of residuals obtained when going from the reduced model of Equation (22.6), $SSE_{reduced}$, to the full model of Equation (22.7), SSE_{full}. A large reduction goes against the null hypothesis, while a more moderate reduction supports the null hypothesis. Under the usual regression assumptions it may be established that, when H_0 is true, the F ratio

$$F = \frac{(SSE_{reduced} - SSE_{full})/p}{SSE_{full}/(n - k - p - 1)} \qquad \textbf{(22.8)}$$

will follow an F distribution with p and $n - k - p - 1$ degrees of freedom for the numerator and the denominator, respectively. The null hypothesis $H_0: \beta_{k+1} = \beta_{k+2} = \cdots = \beta_{k+p} = 0$ is rejected if the observed F ratio is *larger* than an appropriate cut-off value obtained from the F distribution or if the p value obtained from the upper tail of the F distribution is small enough.

■ **EXAMPLE 22.10A:** Exhibit 20.8A displays the regression results when fitting market value using square feet and square feet squared as predictors. The exhibit shows that $SSE_{reduced} = 687.33$. Exhibit 20.8B gives the regression results for the full model, which includes, in addition, the grade variables (med and hi) and the assessed variable. Here $SSE_{full} = 399.24$ with 54 degrees of freedom, and the current question may be phrased as, Is the reduction from an SSE of 687.33 to 399.24 *significant*? The F ratio of Equation (22.8) is given as

$$F = \frac{(687.33 - 399.24)/3}{399.24/(60 - 2 - 3 - 1)} = 12.99$$

with 3 and 54 degrees of freedom. Using a statistical package such as Minitab, the exact p value is 0.0000 and we conclude that the additional predictors are indeed useful additions to the model. ■

SECTION 22.11

EXERCISES

22.11A Consider the simple real estate model that relates market value linearly to square feet of living space. The regression results are in Exhibit 20.6A. Use the method of this section to assess the value of adding the set of variables square feet squared, grade variables med and hi, and assessed value to the model. The required regression results for the full model appear in Exhibit 20.8B.

22.11B Use the F ratio described in Section 22.10 to test whether square feet squared should be included in the market value model in addition to square feet. The SSE for the reduced model is given in Exhibit 20.6A and the SSE for the full model is in Exhibit 20.8A. In addition, show that the F ratio obtained is the square of the t ratio for testing $H_0: \beta_2 = 0$ in the full model. This t ratio is shown in Exhibit 20.8A. When only *one* additional predictor is considered, that is, $p = 1$, it may be shown that the square of the t ratio for this parameter in the full model will always equal the F ratio of Equation (22.8). Thus a one-sided test based on the F ratio will be equivalent to a two-sided test based on the t ratio.

22.11C Consider the Harris Bank salary data presented in Section 21.10. The model presented there contains four predictors: educational level, time of hire, $1/(\text{experience} + 12)$, and gender. Use the F test of Section 22.10 to evaluate the worth of adding the variables $1/(\text{experience} + 12)$ and gender to a simpler model that uses just educational level and time of hire to predict log(salary). (Filename: SALARY.DAT.)

SECTION 22.12

STEPWISE REGRESSION (OPTIONAL)

Methods classified as stepwise regression were developed to find good subsets of predictors but with less computation than best subset methods. These methods are useful when a very large number of potential predictors makes calculating the best subset regression prohibitively time-consuming or expensive. The modelling proceeds sequentially by adding or deleting variables from the current model according to one of the criteria discussed previously. First, all one-predictor models are examined and the best one selected. Then the next model is obtained from the preceding one either by adding or deleting variables. Three somewhat different variations of the required steps are commonly considered: forward selection, backward elimination and stepwise regression.

Starting with the best one-predictor model, **forward selection** selects additional predictor variables by adding variables one at a time to the model. At each step of the selection process the variable in the collection of predictors not already in the model that gives the largest decrease in the residual sum of squares is added to the model. A rule based on one of the criteria for good models is chosen to decide when to stop adding variables to the model.

Backward elimination begins with a model that contains all the predictors. Variables are then eliminated one by one on the basis of their t ratios. The variable with the *smallest* t ratio is dropped first. The multiple regression model is then reestimated and again the variable with the smallest t ratio is dropped. This process is continued until some predetermined criterion is met.

Stepwise regression combines the previous two ideas. In forward selection a variable that enters the model can never be dropped later in the process. In backward elimination, once a variable is dropped it can never reenter the model. Neither method takes into account the fact that the addition or deletion of a variable affects the contributions of the other variables in the model. A variable dropped in backward elimination may become important later after other variables are dropped, and a variable added in forward selection may become unimportant later after other variables have entered the model. Stepwise regression begins with the best one-predictor model, proceeds with forward selection, but rechecks at each stage to see if variables should be dropped from the model once other variables have entered. Criteria for keeping or deleting variables are based on the F test of Section 22.10.

Exhibit 22.12A shows the output from Minitab's STEPWISE command (slightly edited and with subcommands to force forward selection). Weight is the best single predictor. Transmission type was added second and number of cylinders third. According to the criteria used by Minitab, no further predictors should be added. Note that this final model agrees with our earlier choice of model based on looking at all subsets of predictors and using the C_p plot.

EXHIBIT 22.12A

Forward Selection of Predictors with City GPM

```
Forward selection of city GPM on eight predictors, with N=45

   Step            1         2         3
   Constant   -3.46E-03 0.0014551 0.0001472

   weight       0.00002   0.00002   0.00002
   t-ratio        20.68     13.71     11.15

   trans                   0.0053    0.0057
   t-ratio                   3.20      3.67

   cylind                            0.00150
   t-ratio                              2.72

   s            0.00388   0.00352   0.00328
   R-sq           90.86     92.66     93.78
```

Exhibit 22.12B gives the regression results when backward elimination is used. Horsepower is the first variable to be deleted. In the third step the number of cylinders is eliminated. The final model presented includes weight, displacement, gears, and foreign. Unfortunately, this is far from the best model, which contains weight, transmission type, and number of cylinders. None of the stepwise procedures are guaranteed to find the best models.

Finally, Exhibit 22.12C presents the results of the full stepwise regression method. In fact, for this data set, stepwise regression leads to the same model as forward selection in Exhibit 22.12A. Such agreement is not guaranteed in general. All "automatic" selection procedures must be used with caution. Automatic procedures can never replace the skill and subject-matter knowledge that the analyst brings to any given regression problem.

EXHIBIT 22.12B

Backward Elimination
for Predictors of City
GPM

Backward elimination for city GPM on eight predictors, with N=45

Step	1	2	3	4	5
Constant	0.008454	0.009095	0.012001	0.013141	0.009591
weight	0.00001	0.00001	0.00001	0.00002	0.00002
t-ratio	4.23	4.34	4.26	5.92	12.69
disp	0.0027	0.0024	0.0039	0.0039	0.0032
t-ratio	1.29	1.28	3.33	3.28	3.09
cylind	0.0010	0.0010			
t-ratio	1.00	0.99			
HP	-0.00001				
t-ratio	-0.29				
trans	0.0035	0.0034	0.0031		
t-ratio	1.40	1.39	1.27		
gears	-0.00179	-0.00189	-0.00206	-0.00336	-0.00336
t-ratio	-1.29	-1.42	-1.57	-4.04	-4.02
size	0.00115	0.00118	0.00119	0.00098	
t-ratio	1.36	1.42	1.43	1.19	
foreign	0.0022	0.0022	0.0024	0.0028	0.0027
t-ratio	1.66	1.66	1.81	2.20	2.09
s	0.00325	0.00321	0.00321	0.00323	0.00325
R-sq	94.64	94.62	94.48	94.25	94.04

EXHIBIT 22.12C

Stepwise Regression of
City GPM on Eight
Potential Predictors

Stepwise regression of city GPM on eight predictors, with N=45

Step	1	2	3
Constant	-3.46E-03	0.0014551	0.0001472
weight	0.00002	0.00002	0.00002
t-ratio	20.68	13.71	11.15
trans		0.0053	0.0057
t-ratio		3.20	3.67
cylind			0.00150
t-ratio			2.72
s	0.00388	0.00352	0.00328
R-sq	90.86	92.66	93.78

SECTION 22.13

EXERCISES

22.13A Use the car mileage data of Exhibit 22.1A with expressway GPM as the response. Use a stepwise regression package to compare different possible sets of predictors. Compare the results to those obtained in Exercise 22.9A. (Filename: CARS.DAT.)

22.13B Use the car mileage data of Exhibit 22.1A with trip GPM as the response. Use a stepwise regression package to compare different possible sets of predictors. Compare the results to those obtained in Exercise 22.9B. (Filename: CARS.DAT.)

22.13C Return to the house price data of Exercise 20.9B. Use a best subsets regression package to compare different possible sets of predictors. Compare the results to those obtained in Exercise 22.9C. (Filename: HOUSEPRI.DAT.)

22.13D Consider the tree data listed in Exercise 20.7J. Use a stepwise regression program to select among models, which may include any linear combination of these predictors: diameter, $diameter^2$, height, $height^2$, diameter $\times$ height, and $diameter^2 \times$ height. Compare the results to those obtained in Exercise 22.9D. (Filename: TREES.DAT.)

SECTION 22.14

SUPPLEMENTARY EXERCISES FOR CHAPTER 22

22A Exercise 7.9C, Exercise 20A, and Exercise 21A dealt with the time it takes to assemble an electronic printed circuit board in terms of seven predictor variables.
  (a) Calculate the correlation coefficients between all the predictor variables and interpret.
  (b) Calculate the variance inflation factors for each predictor variable in the full regression model and interpret their magnitudes.
  (c) Display the added variable plot for assessing the added effect of the variable Number of Transistors after adjusting for the effect of the variable Number of Components. Interpret this plot.
  (d) Use a best subsets regression program to select the best regression models with one, two, ..., seven predictor variables. Use the C_p criterion to select the best model. (Filename: BOARDS.DAT.)

22B The Chevrolet Lumina APV was a new domestic model in 1990, a rather radical, plastic bodied, ultrastreamlined all-purpose vehicle (minivan). It weighs 3630 pounds, has a 3.1 liter V6, 120 horsepower engine, and transmits its power to the front wheels through an automatic, three-gear transmission.
  (a) Use the results displayed in Exhibit 22.4C to predict the city GPM for this vehicle.
  (b) Use the results displayed in Exhibit 22.4D to predict the city GPM for this vehicle and compare your answer to the one in part (a).
  (c) In the January 1990 issue of *Consumer Reports* the Lumina APV test results gave a city MPG of 12. Compare this to the predictions found in parts (a) and (b).

22C The data file below gives additional car data that was not available when the data set in Exhibit 22.1A was constructed.
  (a) Using the models displayed in Exhibits 22.4C and 22.4D, predict the city GPM for each of these new cases.
  (b) Compare the external predictive power of the two models by computing the RMSPE (root mean square prediction error) based on these additional data only.

```
# filename CARS3.DAT
# More car data from Consumer Reports
# March 1989 through June 1989
# Variables: MPG (city, trip, expressway), weight, displacement,
# number of cylinders, horsepower,
# transmission type (1=automatic, 0=manual)
# size, foreign/domestic
   14 26 35 3300 3.0 6 141 1 4 3 0   Dodge Dynatsy
   15 27 38 3325 3.8 6 165 1 4 3 0   Oldsmobile 88 Royale Brougham
   13 24 30 3790 5.0 8 150 1 4 5 0   Ford LTD Crown Victoria
   12 21 29 3855 5.0 8 170 1 4 5 0   Chevrolet Caprice Classic
   25 37 43 2340 1.5 4  81 0 5 1 1   Eagle Summit LX
   24 37 44 2275 1.6 4  90 0 5 1 1   Nissan Sentra XE
   26 38 46 2075 1.5 4  78 0 5 1 1   Toyota Tercel Deluxe
   23 38 47 2345 1.9 4  90 0 5 1 0   Ford Escort LX
   13 25 29 3265 2.7 6 160 1 4 3 1   Acura Legend L
   14 24 30 3480 3.0 6 158 1 4 3 1   Mazda 929
   15 26 33 3200 3.0 6 160 1 4 3 1   Nissan Maxima GXE
   16 26 32 3480 3.0 6 190 1 4 3 1   Toyota Cressida
```

GLOSSARY FOR CHAPTER 22

Added variable plot	Plot for assessing the effect of a predictor variable after adjusting for the effect of another predictor variable.
Backward elimination	A special stepwise regression method that eliminates more and more predictors to find the "best" model.
Best subset regression	A method for choosing the best predictor variables by considering all possible subsets of predictors.
Collinear	Predictor variables that are approximately linearly related.
Forward selection	A special stepwise regression method that selects more and more predictors to find the "best" model.
Mallows' C_p criterion	A criterion for choosing the better predictor variables.
Misspecified model	A model that does not include the "correct" predictor variables.
Overspecified model	A model that includes extra predictor variables.
PRESS	The predicted residual sum of squares.
Stepwise regression	A sequential method for choosing the best predictor variables.
Underspecified model	A model that fails to include important predictor variables.
Variance inflation factor (VIF)	A measure of an individual predictors' collinearity with the other predictors.

## CHAPTER 23

Time Series Data

INTRODUCTION

Data are often measurements of a variable taken at regular intervals, such as weekly, monthly, quarterly, or yearly. Stock prices are reported daily, interest rates are posted weekly, and sales figures are given monthly, quarterly, and annually. Inventory and production levels are also recorded at regular time periods. The list goes on and on. The sequence plots of Chapter 2 and the notion of autocorrelation introduced in Section 6.8 are important aspects of the longitudinal analysis of time series data that will be expanded on in this chapter.

Data collected from a process over time provide a unique opportunity for predicting future values of the series. If an adequate statistical model for past series behavior can be found and if the process continues to operate similarly in the future, then predictions can be made on the basis of the model. But predictions alone are not enough. If the model adequately describes the series behavior, then a measure of accuracy can be attached to the predictions. Prediction intervals that are likely to contain future values are an important aspect of the prediction process. Regression model ideas are first extended to time series data.

650

TIME SERIES REGRESSION

TIME AS A PREDICTOR

For time series that exhibit a strong upward or downward trend, a regression model with time as a predictor may be considered. The simplest such case is a **linear time trend** model, which is a trend modelled as a straight line. Here it is assumed that the series y_t at time t can be expressed as

$$y_t = \beta_0 + \beta_1 t + e_t \qquad \textbf{(23.1)}$$

This method is illustrated using the data in Exhibit 23.2A. Six years of monthly data are available, but the last year's data are held out to check the prediction accuracy of the model. That is, the June 1986 observation will be treated as the last value available. The 60 observations from July 1981 through June 1986 are then used to fit the model and predict values for the 12 months following. The predictions can then be compared with the actual values to assess the forecasting performance of the model. A linear time trend model seems plausible based on the sequence plot in Exhibit 23.2B.

EXHIBIT 23.2A

Hourly Wages in the Apparel and Textile Industry by Month— 1981–1987

```
# filename: APAWAGES.DAT
# Hourly wages - apparel and other textile products
# (Source: Survey of Current Business, September issues, 1981-1987)
# July 1981 through June 1987
#  Jul  Aug  Sep  Oct  Nov  Dec  Jan  Feb  Mar  Apr  May  Jun
  4.92 4.96 5.04 5.05 5.04 5.04 5.18 5.13 5.15 5.18 5.16 5.18 # 1981-1982
  5.19 5.20 5.23 5.21 5.24 5.28 5.33 5.33 5.33 5.35 5.33 5.36 # 1982-1983
  5.35 5.35 5.39 5.40 5.43 5.44 5.50 5.46 5.48 5.49 5.48 5.50 # 1983-1984
  5.53 5.55 5.63 5.61 5.61 5.68 5.73 5.70 5.73 5.74 5.69 5.70 # 1984-1985
  5.70 5.69 5.75 5.74 5.75 5.80 5.82 5.79 5.80 5.81 5.78 5.79 # 1985-1986
  5.79 5.83 5.91 5.87 5.87 5.90 5.94 5.93 5.93 5.94 5.89 5.91 # 1986-1987
```

EXHIBIT 23.2B

Sequence Plot of Hourly Wages in Apparel and Textile Industry—1981–1986

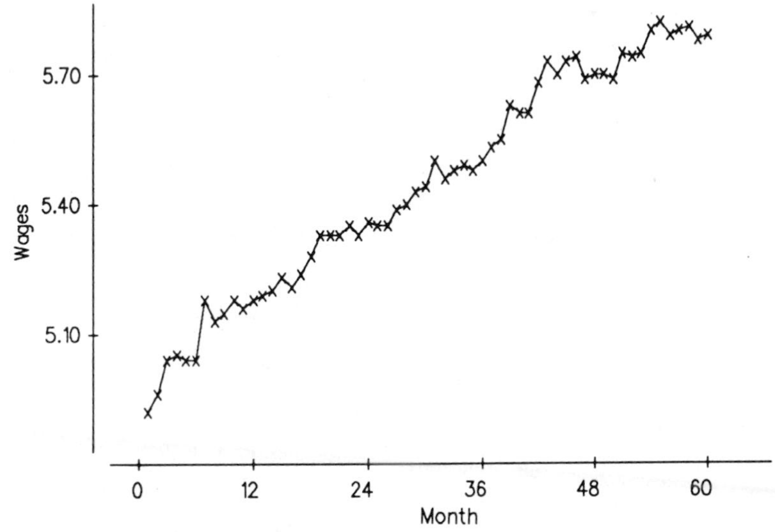

The regression results are shown in Exhibit 23.2C. Notice that wages tend to increase by about 0.0146 dollars per month. Also notice that the regression coefficient on the time predictor has a t ratio of 49.62, which most would deem highly significant. The R^2 value of 97.7% is also extremely large. Exhibit 23.2D displays the sequence plot with the straight-line fit overlayed. Surely this is a "good model," and it is used to forecast the 12 values for the coming year.

EXHIBIT 23.2C

Wages Regressed on Time

```
The regression equation is

Wages = 5.00 + 0.0146time

Predictor        Coef       Stdev     t-ratio        p
Constant      5.00218     0.01030      485.58    0.000
time        0.0145735   0.0002937       49.62    0.000

s = 0.03940      R-sq = 97.7%      R-sq(adj) = 97.7%
```

EXHIBIT 23.2D

Sequence Plot of Wages with Straight-Line Fit

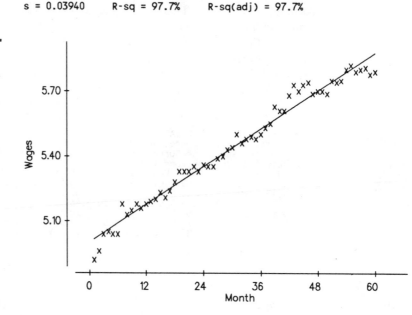

Exhibit 23.2E lists the actual values along with predictions and the 95% prediction intervals obtained from standard regression calculations. More digits are displayed here than would be appropriate for a final report. These should be considered as working values obtained from standard computer results.

EXHIBIT 23.2E

Predictions and Prediction Intervals Based on Straight-Line Model

Month	Prediction	Prediction Interval	Actual Value
61	5.89116	[5.80962, 5.97269]	5.79
62	5.90573	[5.82406, 5.98740]	5.83
63	5.92031	[5.83850, 6.00211]	5.91
64	5.93488	[5.85294, 6.01682]	5.87
65	5.94945	[5.86737, 6.03154]	5.87
66	5.96403	[5.88179, 6.04626]	5.90
67	5.97860	[5.89621, 6.06098]	5.94
68	5.99317	[5.91063, 6.07571]	5.93
69	6.00775	[5.92505, 6.09045]	5.93
70	6.02232	[5.93946, 6.10518]	5.94
71	6.03689	[5.95387, 6.11992]	5.89
72	6.05147	[5.96827, 6.13467]	5.91

A better perspective on the predictions may be seen through various graphs. Exhibit 23.2F shows the original sequence plot with the wage data plotted as A's, the fitted straight line as a solid line, the future-wage data plotted as B's, and the future predictions shown as a dashed line. This exhibit shows that the predictions are uniformly too high. But how wide are the prediction intervals and how are they placed relative to the actual values? Perhaps the intervals include all or most of the future data. Again, graphic displays readily show the facts.

EXHIBIT 23.2F

Predictions and Actual Values from Straight-Line Model

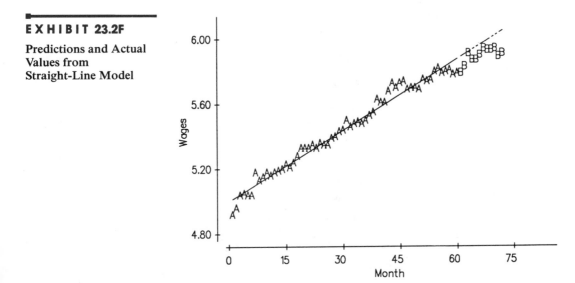

Exhibit 23.2G displays the actual wage values for the year preceding the forecasts (A's), the year of the forecasts (also A's), the forecast (B's), and the upper and lower 95% prediction limits. Three of the 12 actual values are outside the intervals. In particular, the first month's prediction interval missed the actual value. This model is clearly inadequate for forecasting the wage rate series.

One approach to improving the forecasts is to use a model that allows for curvature in the trend in a manner similar to what was done with regression models for cross-sectional data. The simplest such model includes an additional term with time squared as a predictor. This defines a model with **quadratic time trend**:

$$y_t = \beta_0 + \beta_1 t + \beta_2 t^2 + e_t \tag{23.2}$$

The quadratic trend regression results for the wages time series are given in Exhibit 23.2H, and they show that both the linear and quadratic terms are highly significant and the R^2 value is 98.2%. The adjusted R^2 has increased to 98.1%, and the value of s has decreased to 0.03504 when compared to the results for the straight-line model displayed in Exhibit 23.2C. Exhibit 23.2I shows the 60 actual series values, the fitted quadratic trend, the prediction curve based on the quadratic trend, and the actual future year's values. The last year's values used in model fitting, the predictions and prediction limits, and the future year's values are displayed in Exhibit 23.2J.

E X H I B I T 23.2G

**Actual Values,
Predictions, and
Prediction Limits from
Straight-Line Model**

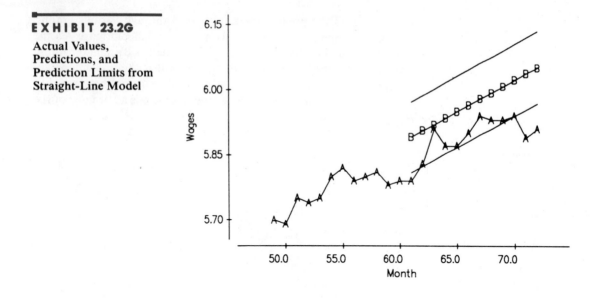

E X H I B I T 23.2H

**Wages Regressed on
Time and Time Squared**

The regression equation is

Wages = 4.96 + 0.0187time -0.000068time^2

Predictor	Coef	Stdev	t-ratio	p
Constant	4.95919	0.01404	353.34	0.000
time	0.018733	0.001062	17.65	0.000
time^2	-0.00006819	0.00001687	-4.04	0.000

s = 0.03504   R-sq = 98.2%   R-sq(adj) = 98.1%

E X H I B I T 23.2I

**Predictions and Actual
Values from Quadratic
Trend Model**

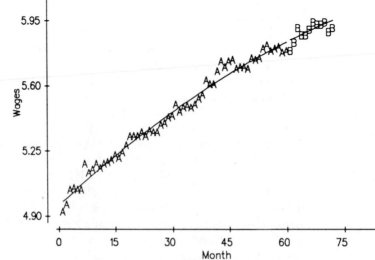

EXHIBIT 23.2J

Predictions, Prediction Limits, and Actual Values from Quadratic Curve Model

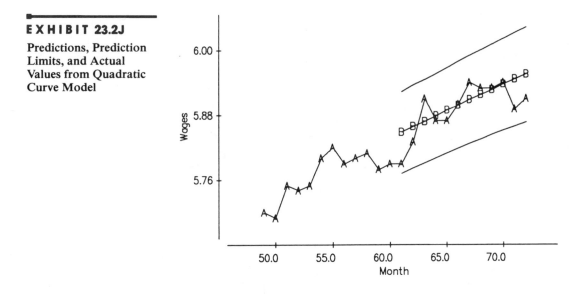

These results should be compared to those given in Exhibits 23.2F and 23.2G, in which the straight-line model was used. The quadratic model does a much better job of following the trend in the series. However, as we will soon see the regression assumption of independent error terms is seriously violated with both the straight-line and quadratic trend models. Although these models are extremely simple, there are very few applications of them in the social sciences where the standard regression assumptions are reasonably well satisfied. Other models that take account of the autocorrelation in the data are usually much more appropriate. This series is used again in Exercise 24.6G; a considerably better model is illustrated there.

DIAGNOSTICS: AUTOCORRELATION REVISITED

Autocorrelation is present in nearly all time series data. Even after modelling the general trend with a line, a quadratic curve, or other curve, the errors around that curve are generally autocorrelated. When modelling time series data, an important diagnostic tool is a sequence plot of the residuals. As always, we hope to see no patterns in this plot. Any trends here indicate the inadequacy of the model. In particular, autocorrelation indicates that relationships among variables that have not been captured by the model are present. By accounting for the autocorrelation in the model, we should be able to better predict future values of the series.

Exhibit 23.2K shows the sequence plot of residuals when fitting the wages series with a straight-line trend model. Two things are apparent from this plot. The residuals at both ends of the series are all negative. This indicates the curvature in the general trend that was not captured in the straight-line model. As important, however, is the fact that residuals that are close together in time are nearly always of the same sign, either both positive or both negative. That is, they lie on the same side of the mean residual of zero. The residuals are at least moderately autocorrelated at lag 1. This autocorrelation may be more easily seen in the scatterplot of residuals versus residuals lagged one month shown in Exhibit 23.2L. The correlation in this

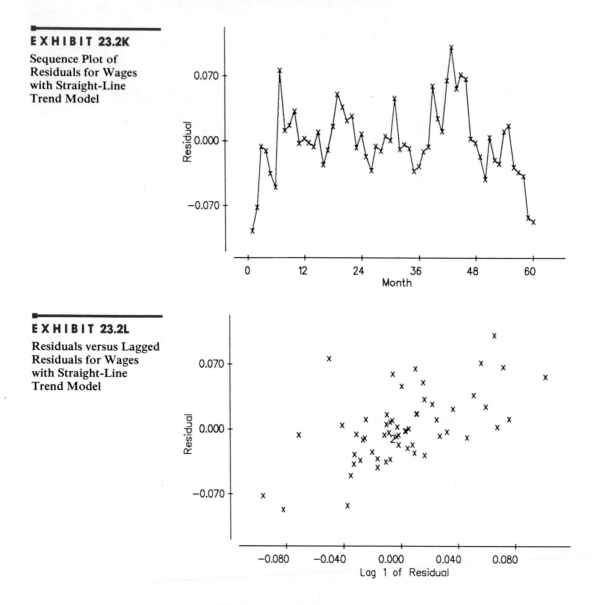

EXHIBIT 23.2K

Sequence Plot of
Residuals for Wages
with Straight-Line
Trend Model

EXHIBIT 23.2L

Residuals versus Lagged
Residuals for Wages
with Straight-Line
Trend Model

plot is 0.597, documenting the relationship seen in the plot. Of course, it is possible that the perceived autocorrelation is not real but only an artifact of using the wrong trend model for this data set.

Similar plots for the quadratic trend model are considered next. Exhibit 23.2M gives the sequence plot of residuals for the wage series when modelled with the quadratic trend. The problem of numerous negative residuals at both ends of the series has now been addressed. However, the residuals are still autocorrelated. This can be seen more readily in the scatterplot of residuals versus lagged residuals in Exhibit 23.2N. The correlation in this display is 0.520, again showing moderate autocorrelation in the residuals at lag one month.

EXHIBIT 23.2M

Sequence Plot of
Residuals for Wages
with Quadratic Trend
Model

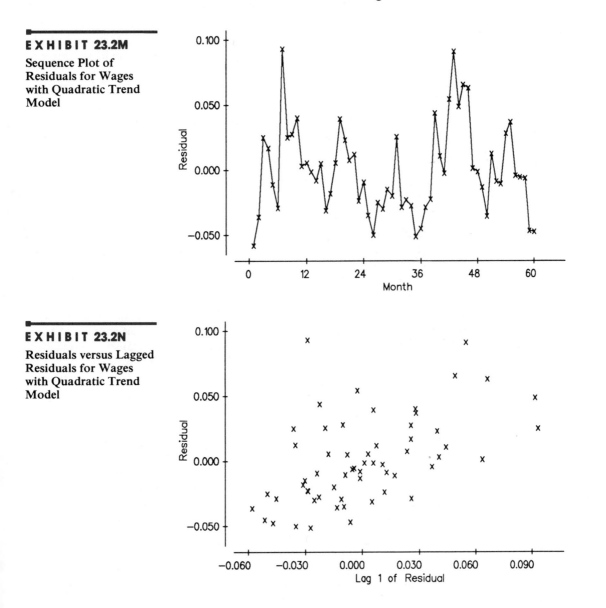

EXHIBIT 23.2N

Residuals versus Lagged
Residuals for Wages
with Quadratic Trend
Model

To better assess the magnitude of autocorrelations in residuals, the theoretical results obtained by Bartlett are used.[†] He showed that for independent data and large n, the sampling distribution of an autocorrelation coefficient is approximately normal with mean zero and standard deviation $1/\sqrt{n}$. Thus an autocorrelation larger than $2/\sqrt{n}$ or $3/\sqrt{n}$ in magnitude would be considered statistically significant and independence would be strongly questioned. In the present example, $n = 60$ so

---

[†] M. S. Bartlett, "On the Theoretical Specification of Sampling Properties of autocorrelated Time Series,"*Journal of the Royal Statistical Society*, B, 8 (1946): 27–41.

that $3/\sqrt{60} = 0.387$ and the observed autocorrelation of 0.520 is excessive for independent data. As noted earlier, Exercise 24.6G suggests a model for this wage series that substantially improves on those considered here.

THE DURBIN–WATSON STATISTIC [†]

Another statistic frequently used to detect autocorrelation in regression residuals is the Durbin–Watson statistic, which is calculated as

$$DW = \frac{\sum_{t=2}^{n}(\hat{e}_t - \hat{e}_{t-1})^2}{\sum_{t=1}^{n}\hat{e}_t^2}$$

By straightforward algebra it can be shown that, to a good first approximation, $DW \simeq 2(1 - r_1)$ where r_1 is the lag 1 autocorrelation in the residuals. Thus if the residuals are not autocorrelated so that $r_1 \simeq 0$, DW is expected to be about 2. If the residuals are strongly positively autocorrelated with $r_1 \simeq 1$, then $DW \simeq 0$; if the residuals are strongly negatively autocorrelated with $r_1 \simeq -1$, then $DW \simeq 4$. Values of DW near 2 support independence of the error terms; values of DW away from 2 and nearer the extremes of 0 or 4 support an hypothesis of autocorrelated errors. Nearly all statistical software calculates the Durbin–Watson statistic automatically.

Consider the linear time trend model for wages reported in Exhibit 23.2C and with residuals plotted in Exhibit 23.2K. For these residuals, $DW = 0.73$, which is reasonably close to $2(1 - r_1) = 2(1 - 0.597) = 0.81$. This value being closer to 0 than to 2 signals the problem with positively autocorrelated residuals mentioned earlier. Similarly, considering the quadratic trend model with regression results in Exhibit 23.2H and residuals sequence plotted in Exhibit 23.2M, DW of 0.93 is found. Although 0.93 is slightly closer to 2 than 0.73, this still indicates that important positive autocorrelation exists in the errors for this model.

Formal tests of significance of lag 1 autocorrelation in the errors may be based on DW. However, the sampling distribution of DW, even when the errors are independent, *depends on the specific values for the predictor variables in the regression problem being considered*. It is not feasible to tabulate or even computerize the percentiles of all these distributions. It is possible to tabulate upper and lower bounds on the critical percentiles so that unambiguous conclusions may be reached in many cases. However, the possibility always exists that the test may be inconclusive. In the quadratic trend model for wages with 60 cases and two predictors (time and time squared) and under the hypothesis of independent errors, the first percentile of the distribution of DW is between 1.35 and 1.48.[††] Thus the observed value of $DW = 0.93$, which is below 1.35, provides conclusive evidence of positive autocorrelation at lag 1 in the errors of the quadratic trend model.

[†] This statistic was proposed in a series of three papers by J. Durbin and G. S. Watson, "Testing for Serial Correlation in Least Squares Regression, I, II and III," *Biometrika* 37 (1950): 409–428; 38 (1951): 159–178; and 58 (1971): 1–19.

[††] Further discussion of these tests and tables of the bounds on the critical percentiles may be found, for example, in R. B. Miller and D. W. Wichern, *Intermediate Business Statistics* (New York: Holt, Rinehart and Winston, 1977).

The most serious difficulty with the Durbin–Watson statistic is that it only checks for autocorrelation in the errors at lag 1. For this reason the autocorrelations of the residuals at several lags, including scatterplots of residuals versus lagged residuals and especially lags at which autocorrelation is suspected, should also be considered.

DIFFERENCES

In some applications, two or more time series have been collected over the same time period and interest centers on the relationship between the series. An example that introduces some subtle issues in longitudinal data analysis will illustrate.

Exhibit 23.2O shows annual figures on the index of industrial production (IIP) and the unemployment rate (Unemployment) for the United States from 1973 to 1982. A scatterplot of Unemployment versus IIP is shown in Exhibit 23.2P. The IIP is a measure of output from the manufacturing sector of the economy. Consequently, it is expected to be strongly negatively correlated with Unemployment. In other words, when industrial production is high, the demand for workers is expected to keep the unemployment rate low, and vice versa. The scatterplot shows a disappointingly weak negative correlation. On the basis of the scatterplot, it would be reasonable to conclude that Unemployment is virtually unrelated to IIP. Because this flies in the face of intuition and economic theory, we may be tempted to conclude that at least one of the two measures does not accurately reflect reality. This conclusion, however, is faulty. The difficulty with the analysis put forward so far is an inappropriate interpretation of the scatterplot and a mishandling of the time dimension.

EXHIBIT 23.2O

Annual Index of Industrial Production and the Unemployment Rate

Year	IIP	Unemployment
1973	130	4.8
1974	129	5.5
1975	118	8.3
1976	131	7.6
1977	138	6.9
1978	146	6.0
1979	153	5.8
1980	147	7.0
1981	151	7.5
1982	139	9.5

Source: U.S. Bureau of the Census, *Statistical Abstract of the United States: 1984,* 104th ed. (Washington, D.C.: U.S. Government Printing Office, 1983).

The plotting symbols A, B,..., J in Exhibit 23.2P show time order; that is, A denotes 1973, B denotes 1974, and so on. Connecting these symbols in alphabetical order yields the scatterplot in Exhibit 23.2Q. The line segment running from A to B shows that there was a decrease in IIP and an increase in Unemployment between

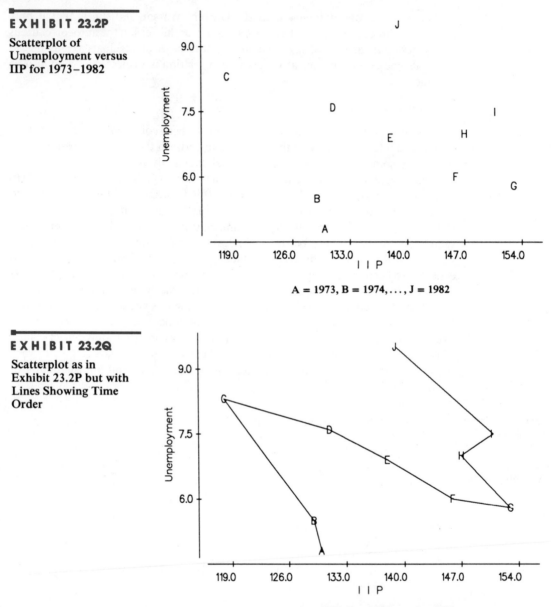

A = 1973, B = 1974, . . . , J = 1982

E X H I B I T 23.2Q

Scatterplot as in
Exhibit 23.2P but with
Lines Showing Time
Order

A = 1973, B = 1974, . . . , J = 1982

1973 and 1974. Similar changes occurred between 1974 and 1975. The line running from C to D shows that there was an increase in IIP and a decrease in Unemployment.

These changes correspond to our intuitive understanding of the relationship between IIP and Unemployment. The table in Exhibit 23.2R shows the annual changes in the two variables. The change variables (differences) are labelled DIIP and DUnemployment because the annual changes are called *first differences* of the original series. Notice that except for 1981, the changes in IIP and Unemployment are of opposite sign!

EXHIBIT 23.2R

First Differences of IIP and Unemployment

Year	IIP	Unemployment	DIIP	DUnemployment
1973	130	4.8	*	*
1974	129	5.5	−1	0.7
1975	118	8.3	−11	2.8
1976	131	7.6	13	−0.7
1977	138	6.9	7	−0.7
1978	146	6.0	8	−0.9
1979	153	5.8	7	−0.2
1980	147	7.0	−6	1.2
1981	151	7.5	4	0.5
1982	139	9.5	−12	2.0

Exhibit 23.2S shows the scatterplot of DUnemployment versus DIIP. The correlation of $r = -0.95$ shows a very strong negative linear relationship between the two variables, suggesting that *changes* in the index of industrial production should be useful in predicting *changes* in unemployment rate.

EXHIBIT 23.2S

Scatterplot of Differences of Unemployment versus Differences of IIP

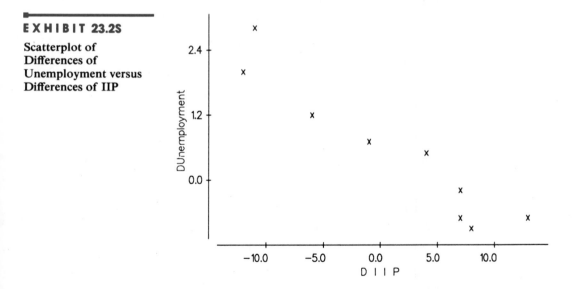

The analysis of the first differences suggests that IIP and Unemployment do a good job of documenting changes. Fortunately, if changes can be predicted accurately, then the level of a series can be tracked; the predicted change could be added to the current level of the series to get a prediction of the next level of the series. If the analysis of levels in Exhibit 23.2P had been used, the opportunity to predict via the changes would have been missed.

To examine the predictiveness of the relationship in Exhibit 23.2S, a straight line was fitted by *OLS* and the following results were obtained:

$$\text{DUn\hat{e}mployment} = 0.660 - 0.138\text{DIIP} \qquad \textbf{(23.3)}$$

with $s = 0.4302$ and $R^2 = 90.3\%$. Residual analysis is quite tenuous here since there are only nine data points after differencing. However, the sequence plot in Exhibit 23.2T and the plot of residuals versus lagged residuals in Exhibit 23.2U do not indicate any difficulties with the assumption of independent error terms.

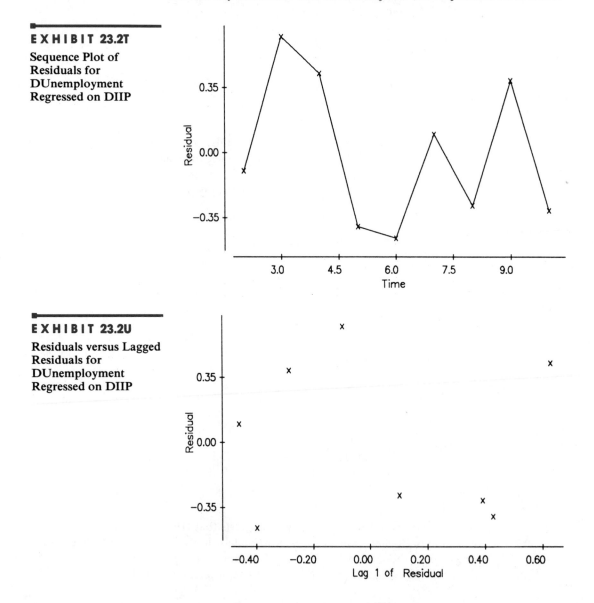

E X H I B I T 23.2T

Sequence Plot of Residuals for DUnemployment Regressed on DIIP

E X H I B I T 23.2U

Residuals versus Lagged Residuals for DUnemployment Regressed on DIIP

Since the standard deviation of DUnemployment is 1.29, the regression model should produce substantially better predictions than the observed differences in unemployment rate. This statement is subject to a major condition, however. To achieve the promised accuracy in the prediction of DUnemployment, the estimate of the value of DIIP must be accurate. To predict DUnemployment for the next year (1983) using the regression model, a value for DIIP for that year must be selected.

Inspection of the differenced data in Exhibit 23.2R shows that DIIP is much more variable than DUnemployment. You may verify that DIIP has a mean of 1 and a standard deviation of 9, whereas the mean and standard deviation of DUnemployment are 0.522 and 1.294, respectively. Thus using the past data on DIIP gives very little accuracy in predicting future values of DIIP. The choice of the value for DIIP to use in the regression prediction must come from other considerations. If there is a great deal of uncertainty in the changes in industrial production, then this will increase the uncertainty in the prediction of future changes. One way to convey this notion is to list several values of DIIP and the corresponding 2-standard-deviation prediction intervals for DUnemployment, as in the table below.

$x = $ DIIP	$\hat{y} = 0.66 - 0.138x$	2-Standard-Deviation Prediction Interval for $y = $ DUnemployment
-11	2.178	[1.2, 3.2]
-5	1.350	[0.5, 2.3]
1	0.522	[-0.4, 1.4]
7	-0.306	[-1.2, 0.6]
13	-1.134	[-2.1, -0.0]

You see that the value of DIIP chosen has a substantial impact on the prediction DUnemployment and a modest impact on the length of the prediction interval. With this display the importance of choosing DIIP as well as possible is obvious immediately. And because the past history of the DIIP gives little information about the future, knowledge of other aspects of the economy would have to be analyzed in trying to come up with the best choice of DIIP. If a reliable choice of DIIP remains elusive, one may fall back on the prediction interval based on the unemployment series alone, namely,

$$\bar{y} \pm 2s_y = [0.522 - 2(1.294), 0.522 + 2(1.294)]$$
$$= [-2.1, 3.1]$$

which virtually contains the union of the intervals produced by the regression model displayed above. Since the interval predicts that the unemployment rate may record anything between a decrease of 2.1 percentage points to an increase of 3.1 percentage points, it conveys little if any definitive information.

In this section examples have illustrated the use of the relationship between two time series to create a prediction model. The time series that were analyzed showed that even though the series of *levels* may be only weakly correlated, the series of *changes* may well be highly correlated. Be on the lookout for this phenomenon when analyzing time series, because when it occurs the changes allow a good predictive model to be built, whereas the levels are not a reliable basis for a predictive model.

The model in this section relates values of two variables *in the same year*. This means that to predict a future value of y, a good estimate of a future value of x must be chosen—a task that may prove difficult in practice. In some time series applications, current values of y can be related to past values of x. If so, current values of x can be used to predict future values of y. Such models are of great practical value and will be discussed in Section 23.4.

EXERCISES

23.3A Calculate the autocorrelation coefficients at lags 1 and 2 for the time series 4, 5, 7, 5, 6, 8, 7.

23.3B Consider the flour price index for Buffalo, New York, listed in Exhibit 2.10A and plotted in Exhibit 2.10B and the flour price index for Kansas City given in Exercise 2.11A. These monthly series were obtained for the same period of time but at different geographic locations.

(a) Investigate a model that predicts the Buffalo value using the Kansas City value for the same month. Are the residuals autocorrelated?

(b) Comment on the applicability of the model obtained in part (a) for predicting the Buffalo value from the Kansas City value. (Filenames: BUFLOUR.DAT and KCFLOUR.DAT.)

23.3C You are given that the current level of a time series is 600 and you are given the following 2-standard-deviation prediction interval for the next *change* in the series: $[-25, 31]$. What is the prediction interval for the next *level* of the series?

LAGGED VARIABLES

DISTRIBUTED LAGS

Market researchers have long been interested in the longitudinal relationship between advertising and sales. However, in the absence of controlled experimentation, causal relationships are difficult, if not impossible, to establish. Data often arise haphazardly in the normal course of business. Correlation between two variables *could* reflect causation from one to the other but could also be due to causation in the reverse direction or to a relationship with a third variable. The goal, then, is not to establish causative relationships but simply to build models that help *predict* one variable from another.

The data set in Exhibit 23.4A is used to illustrate the ideas in this section. Sales for a dietary weight control product were measured monthly in multiples of equivalent serving units (to account for the different sizes of packages sold). Advertising for this product was also measured in monthly dollars of advertising. Advertising dollars were attributed to the actual month in which the advertising appeared rather than to the month in which the advertising bills were sent or paid. Considerable variability over time in both sales and advertising is shown in the sequence plots given in Exhibits 23.4B and 23.4C.

EXHIBIT 23.4A

Monthly Sales and
Advertising
Expenditures for
36 Months

```
# filename: SALESADS.DAT
# Sales and advertising for 36 months
# (Source: F.M.Bass and D.G.Clarke, "Testing Distributed Lag Models
# of Advertising Effect," J. Marketing Research (1972) 298-308.)
# Variables: sales, advertising
  12.0  15          30.5  33
  20.5  16          28.0  62
  21.0  18          26.0  22
  15.5  27          21.5  12
  15.3  21          19.7  24
  23.5  49          19.0   3
  24.5  21          16.0   5
  21.3  22          20.7  14
  23.5  28          26.5  36
  28.0  36          30.6  40
  24.0  40          32.3  49
  15.5   3          29.5   7
  17.3  21          28.3  52
  25.3  29          31.3  65
  25.0  62          32.2  17
  36.5  65          26.4   5
  36.5  46          23.4  17
  29.6  44          16.4   1
```

EXHIBIT 23.4B

Sequence Plot
of Advertising
Expenditures for a
Dietary Weight
Control Product

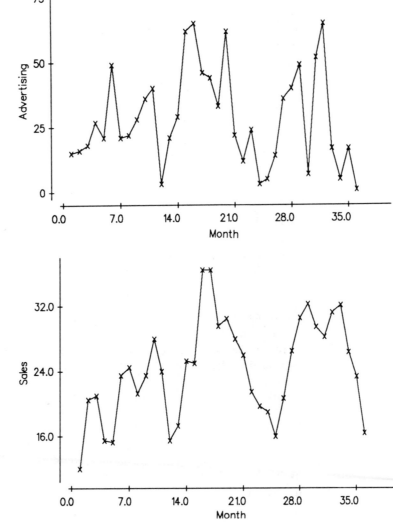

EXHIBIT 23.4C

Sequence Plot of Sales
of a Dietary Weight
Control Product

To begin to understand the relationships between Sales and Advertising, consider the combined sequence plot shown in Exhibit 23.4D. Here standardized versions of both sequences have been plotted on the same graph but 3 has been added to each standardized Advertising value so that the sequences will not plot on top of each other. In this plot the series generally go up and down together, although this pattern is not completely regular. There are time periods in which Sales increase despite no increase in Advertising, and there are other time periods in which Sales do not increase even when Advertising dollars increase. The drop in Advertising at month 30 is not reflected in a corresponding drop in Sales.

EXHIBIT 23.4D

Overlaid Sequence Plots of Standardized Sales and Standardized Advertising +3

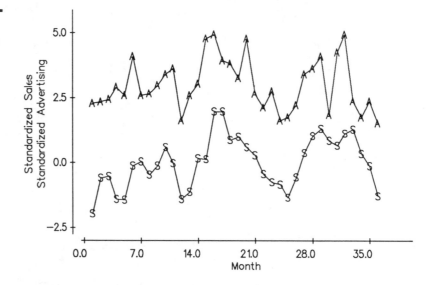

To further investigate the relationships, Sales versus Advertising is scatterplotted in Exhibit 23.4E. The relationship shown here is roughly linear but somewhat disappointing in that the correlation coefficient is only 0.631. If Sales is regressed on Advertising, the prediction equation

$$\widehat{\text{Sales}} = 18.3 + 0.208 \text{ Advertising} \qquad \textbf{(23.4)}$$

with $s = 4.863$ and $R^2 = 39.9\%$ is obtained. However, the residuals are far from random. Exhibit 23.4F shows the sequence plot of the residuals based on Equation (23.4). The autocorrelation at lag one month is 0.317, which indicates lack of independence. We proceed to models that account for the relationship between Sales and Advertising in a more complicated way.

Market researchers have postulated that the effects of advertising may carry over beyond the month in which the ad is viewed or heard. That is, advertising seen in March may affect March, April, and May sales to some extent. The scatterplot shown in Exhibit 23.4G displays the approximate linear relationship between Sales and Advertising lagged one month. Here the correlation is 0.674 so that it is reasonable to consider a model that also includes lagged Advertising as a predictor variable.

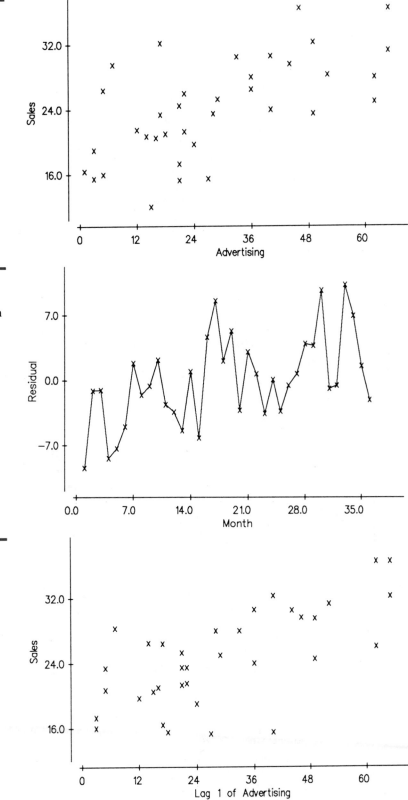

In general, a model of the form

$$y_t = \beta_0 + \beta_1 x_t + \beta_2 x_{t-1} + \cdots + \beta_k x_{t-k} + e_t \qquad \textbf{(23.5)}$$

involving k lags on the predictor variable x_t might be considered. Such models are called **distributed lag models**. However, this model may involve many regression coefficients, each of which must be estimated from the data. Because typical series lengths will not permit accurate estimation of a large number of parameters, a simplification of the model is necessary.

KOYCK MODEL

Frequently the general distributed lag model may be simplified by assuming that $\beta_1, \beta_2, \ldots, \beta_k$ are of the special form $\beta_1 = \alpha_0$, $\beta_2 = \alpha_0 \lambda$, $\beta_3 = \alpha_0 \lambda^2$, $\beta_4 = \alpha_0 \lambda^3, \ldots,$ $\beta_k = \alpha_0 \lambda^{k-1}$. This particular distributed lag model is called the **Koyck** or **geometric distributed lag model**:

$$y_t = \beta_0 + \alpha_0 x_t + \alpha_0 \lambda x_{t-1} + \alpha_0 \lambda^2 x_{t-2} + \cdots + \alpha_0 \lambda^k x_{t-k} + e_t \qquad \textbf{(23.6)}$$

Only three parameters, β_0, α_0, and λ, need to be estimated in this model. In most cases the parameter λ is restricted to lie between 0 and 1 so that the coefficients on lagged x_t decay in magnitude geometrically as the lag increases. In our example, this corresponds to advertising in March having an effect on March sales but a diminished effect on April sales, a further diminished effect on May sales, and so on.

If k is large enough that λ^{k+1} can be considered negligibly small, then Equation (23.6) can be rewritten as

$$y_t = \beta_0^* + \lambda y_{t-1} + \alpha_0 x_t + e_t^* \qquad \textbf{(23.7)}$$

where $\beta_0^* = \beta_0(1 - \lambda)$ and $e_t^* = e_t - \lambda e_{t-1}$. If the errors in the model of Equation (23.6) are independent, then it may be shown that the errors in the model of Equation (23.7) are correlated at lag 1. However, the method of least squares will still produce reasonable, if not ideal, estimates of the parameters and diagnostic tools will always be used to check on the model assumptions after fitting the model.

To estimate the parameters in the model defined by Equation (23.7), y_t is regressed on two predictors: y_{t-1} and x_t. The results of such a regression for the Sales and Advertising series are shown in Exhibit 23.4H. The estimated model uses $\hat{\lambda} = 0.528$ and $\hat{\alpha}_0 = 0.146$, both of which would be deemed highly significant by the usual t ratio tests. In addition, the estimated (transformed) intercept term is 7.45 and the residual standard deviation is 3.480 with an R^2 of 67.2%. Exhibit 23.4I displays overlaid sequence plots of the actual Sales series (plotted as S's) and the

---

EXHIBIT 23.4H

Estimation of Koyck Distributed Lag Model of Sales on Advertising

```
The regression equation is

Sales = 7.45 + 0.528 Lag1Sales + 0.146 Advertising

35 cases used; one case contained missing values

Predictor        Coef       Stdev     t-ratio       p
Constant        7.453      2.467       3.02       0.005
Lag1Sales       0.5276     0.1021      5.17       0.000
Advertising     0.14650    0.03305     4.43       0.000

s = 3.480       R-sq = 67.2%      R-sq(adj) = 65.2%
```

EXHIBIT 23.4I
Sequence Plot of Actual
and Fitted Values for
Sales

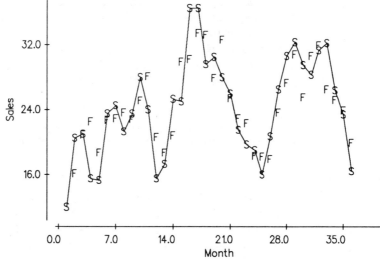

series of fitted values (plotted as F's). Notice how well the fitted values track the actual values.

Shortly the usual diagnostic tests will be discussed. Assuming for now that the diagnostics support the postulated model, notice how easy it is to forecast with this model. Suppose that n denotes the time of the last available data: x_n and y_n. According to Equation (23.7), the next value of y satisfies

$$y_{n+1} = \beta_0^* + \lambda y_n + \alpha_0 x_{n+1} + e_{n+1}^* \qquad (23.8)$$

Since e_{n+1}^* is a future error, the best prediction for its value is its mean of zero. In our example, Advertising is under our control so that x_{n+1} may be chosen for next month according to our budget and sales goals. The forecast of next month's sales is then given by

$$\hat{y}_{n+1} = \beta_0^* + \lambda y_n + \alpha_0 x_{n+1} \qquad (23.9)$$

where the parameters are replaced by their estimates based on the data.

In our example the value for Sales at month 36 is 16.4, and Advertising ranges from a low of 1 to a high of about 60. For illustration suppose 30 is budgeted for next month's advertising. Then the predicted sales are Sales $= 7.45 + 0.528(16.4) + 0.146(30) = 20.4892$, or 20.5. For planning purposes a variety of trial values may be considered for next month's advertising and the predicted sales consequences investigated. As always, the associated prediction intervals should also be presented so that the precision of the predictions may be assessed. Three scenarios are given in the following table:

Advertising	Predicted Sales	95% Prediction Interval	Interval Length
10	17.57	[10.16, 24.98]	14.82
30	20.50	[13.11, 27.89]	14.78
60	24.90	[17.09, 32.70]	15.61

Notice that the prediction interval is least precise, that is, widest, when we attempt to predict using an extreme value for the Advertising variable.

To forecast two months ahead, Equation (23.8) is used but n is increased by 1. The error term in this equation is forecast as zero, and x_{n+2} must be specified, but what should be done with y_{n+1}? Simply use the forecast given in Equation (23.9). Thus, the two-month-ahead forecast is obtained from

$$\hat{y}_{n+2} = \beta_0^* + \lambda \hat{y}_{n+1} + \alpha_0 x_{n+2} \tag{23.10}$$

Similarly, forecasts for l time units into the future are produced using

$$\hat{y}_{n+l} = \beta_0^* + \lambda \hat{y}_{n+l-1} + \alpha_0 x_{n+l} \tag{23.11}$$

To complete this example, diagnostic analysis of the fitted model is done. Exhibit 23.4J gives the sequence plot of the residuals and Exhibit 23.4K displays the scatterplot of residuals versus fitted values. No special patterns are apparent in these plots, and this perception is reinforced by the small lag 1 autocorrelation of -0.05.

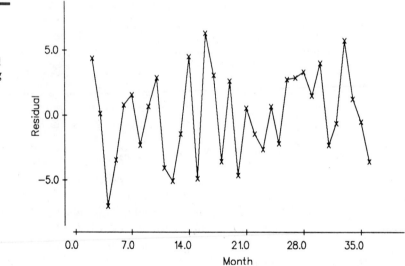

Finally, we look at the normality of the error terms. The histogram of standardized residuals is shown in Exhibit 23.4L. The mound shape of the histogram is further substantiated in the straightness of the normal scores plot given in Exhibit 23.4M. The correlation coefficient in the normal scores plot is a strong 0.993. On all accounts, the Koyck distributed lag model provides an excellent model for the Sales-Advertising time series data.

EXHIBIT 23.4K

Residuals versus Fitted Values for Distributed Lag Model of Sales on Advertising

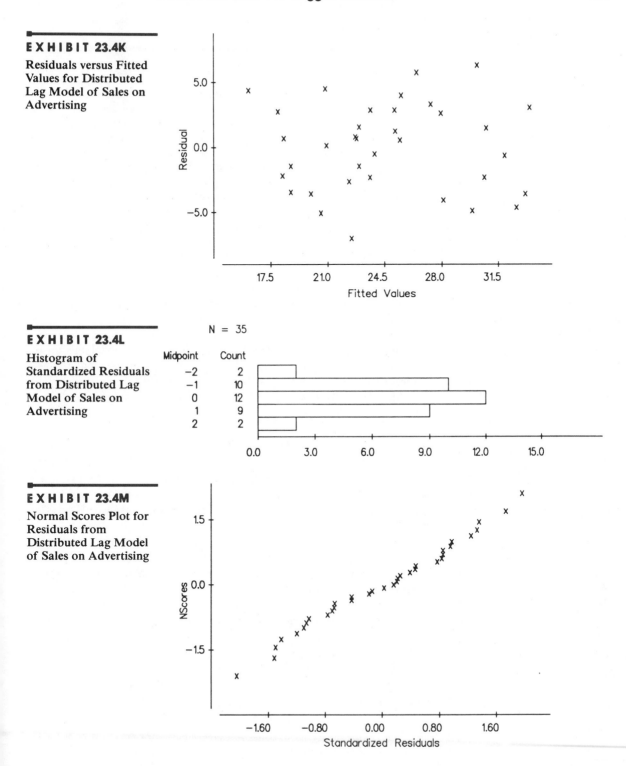

EXHIBIT 23.4L

Histogram of Standardized Residuals from Distributed Lag Model of Sales on Advertising

N = 35

Midpoint	Count
-2	2
-1	10
0	12
1	9
2	2

EXHIBIT 23.4M

Normal Scores Plot for Residuals from Distributed Lag Model of Sales on Advertising

EXERCISE

23.5A Consider the flour price index for Buffalo, New York, listed in Exhibit 2.10A and plotted in Exhibit 2.10B and the flour price index for Kansas City given in Exercise 2.11A. These monthly series were obtained for the same months but at different geographic locations.

   (a) Fit the Koyck model using the Buffalo series as the response and Kansas City series as the predictor. Check the residuals for autocorrelation.

   (b) Comment on the usefulness of the model considered in part (a) for prediction purposes.

   (c) Consider a Koyck distributed lag model that uses the Kansas City flour price index *lagged one month* as the predictor and the Buffalo index as the response. That is, replace x_t by x_{t-1} in Equation (23.7). Estimate this model and test the significance of the regression coefficients.

   (d) Comment on the practicality of the model considered in part (c) for prediction purposes. (Filenames: BUFLOUR.DAT and KCFLOUR.DAT.)

AUTOREGRESSION

With many time series no accompanying predictor time series is available nor is a distinctive time trend evident in the data. In such cases the single available series may be modelled in terms of its own past behavior using an autoregressive model. A series y_t is said to follow an **autoregressive model** of order p if for each time point t

$$y_t = \beta_0 + \beta_1 y_{t-1} + \beta_2 y_{t-2} + \cdots + \beta_p y_{t-p} + e_t \qquad \textbf{(23.12)}$$

where e_t is an error term that is independent of past series values $y_{t-1}, y_{t-2}, \ldots$. The terminology *autoregression* is self-evident: y has been regressed on itself at lagged time values. For short, y_t is said to satisfy an AR(p) model. The general theory and application of autoregressive models is beyond the scope of this book.[†] Here the focus is on the simpler AR(1) and AR(2) cases. They are treated as special regression problems.

Exhibit 23.6A lists the 57 values for a certain industrial time series. The values given are deviations from a desired target value of a dimension of a product produced by a complex machine tool. In this process a control mechanism is employed to reset some of the parameters of the machine tool depending on the magnitude of the deviation of the dimension from the target value on the last item produced. Exhibit 23.6B shows the sequence plot of the series. The series wanders about the desired target deviation of zero but tends to stay on the same side of zero for deviations that are close together in time. Such behavior reflects positive autocorrelation for small time lags.

The scatterplot of deviations versus lag 1 deviations shown in Exhibit 23.6C confirms the autocorrelation graphically. Here the correlation is 0.533.

[†] The interested reader may consult G. E. P. Box and G. M. Jenkins, *Time Series Analysis*, rev. ed. (San Francisco: Holden-Day, 1976). More accessible accounts are given in B. L. Bowerman and R. T. O'Connell, *Time Series Forecasting*, 2d ed. (Boston: Duxbury Press, 1987); and J. D. Cryer, *Time Series Analysis* (Boston: Duxbury Press, 1986).

EXHIBIT 23.6A

Data from an Industrial Machining Process— Deere & Co.

```
# filename: DEERE3.DAT
# Machining data from Deere & Co.
# (Source: Jerri Matchinsky, M.S. thesis,
# University of Iowa, 1988)
# Deviations from target value in ten millionths of an inch
# (Read across, row by row)
 -500 -1250  -500 -3000 -2375 2000 2375  1500  -625  250
    0   625  3125  2125  2250 3875 1000   250   750  750
 -375  -625  -875 -1125   250 -250 -125 -1750   625  125
  625  -375   875  -500   250  625 -250  2375 -2000  125
  125 -1000   375 -1250   500 1625 1875  1875  3000 3625
  750 -1125 -2875 -5750 -1750 -750 -750
```

EXHIBIT 23.6B

Sequence Plot of Deviations from Target—Deere & Co. Machining Operation

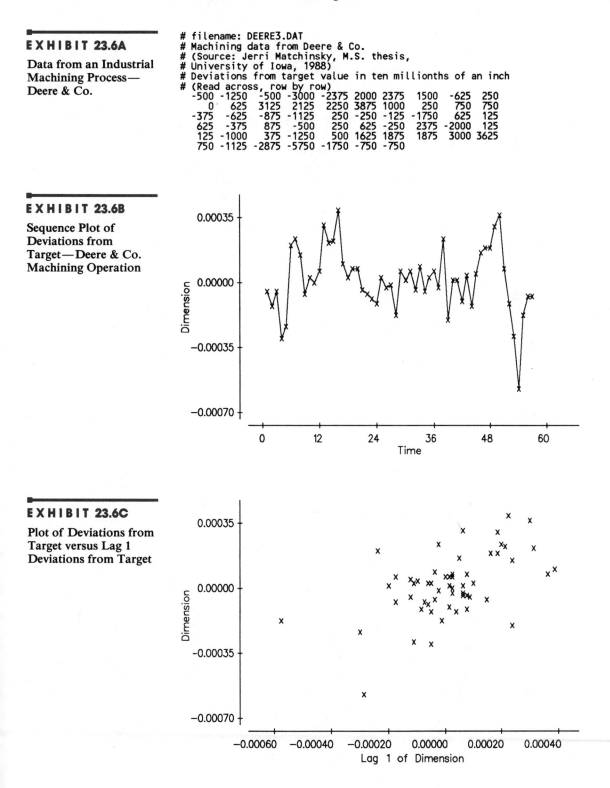

EXHIBIT 23.6C

Plot of Deviations from Target versus Lag 1 Deviations from Target

AR(1) MODELS

An **AR(1) model** is an autoregressive model in which the predictor variable is the response variable at the previous time point. Consider the AR(1) model

$$y_t = \beta_0 + \beta_1 y_{t-1} + e_t \tag{23.13}$$

Exhibit 23.6D gives the regression results of fitting this model to our series. The t ratio associated with β_1 is 4.62 so the regression coefficient on the lagged deviation is statistically different from zero and the lag 1 deviation should help in the prediction of the next deviation. Notice that the intercept term is not significantly different from zero. This should not be surprising since deviations from a desired target value are being measured and the machine is constantly readjusted in an attempt to achieve the target value. Also note that the value of R^2 is only 28.4%. Initially this may seem disappointing, but to what should the predictions produced by this model be compared? What alternative model might be used for prediction?

EXHIBIT 23.6D

Regression Results for the AR(1) Model of the Machining Process

```
The regression equation is

Dimension = 0.000007 + 0.533 Lag1Dimension

56 cases used; 1 case contained missing values

Predictor        Coef       Stdev     t-ratio      p
Constant      0.00000747  0.00001982    0.38     0.708
Lag1Dimension    0.5332      0.1153      4.62     0.000

s = 0.0001476    R-sq = 28.4%    R-sq(adj) = 27.0%
```

For a series that behaves such as this one, an alternative model would be that of a purely random process with a mean of 0.00002 inch and standard deviation of 0.00017 inch. These correspond to the mean and standard deviation of the series values. Based on a purely random process, predictions for all future deviations are the mean deviation of 0.00002 inch. The precision of these predictions is measured by the standard deviation of the process 0.00017 inch.

On the other hand, the AR(1) model bases its predictions on the equation

$$\hat{y}_{n+1} = 0.000007 + 0.533 y_n \tag{23.14}$$

and, more generally,

$$\hat{y}_{n+l} = 0.000007 + 0.533 \hat{y}_{n+l-1} \qquad \text{for } l \geq 1 \tag{23.15}$$

The prediction standard error here is proportional to 0.0001476, which should be compared to the standard deviation of 0.00017 of the deviations series. This amounts to a very worthwhile improvement over the alternative simpler model.

To complete the analysis, the sequence plot of the residuals from the AR(1) model is given in Exhibit 23.6E. There are no trends evident here, and this perception is confirmed by the lag 1 autocorrelation in the residuals of only -0.009. Further analysis of the residuals confirms their approximate normality.

Exhibit 23.6F displays the series values (plotted with A's) with the sequence of fitted values (F's) from the AR(1) model overlaid. Notice how, to a large extent, the fitted values trace the path of the actual values.

EXHIBIT 23.6E

Sequence Plot of
Residuals from the
AR(1) Model for the
Machining Process

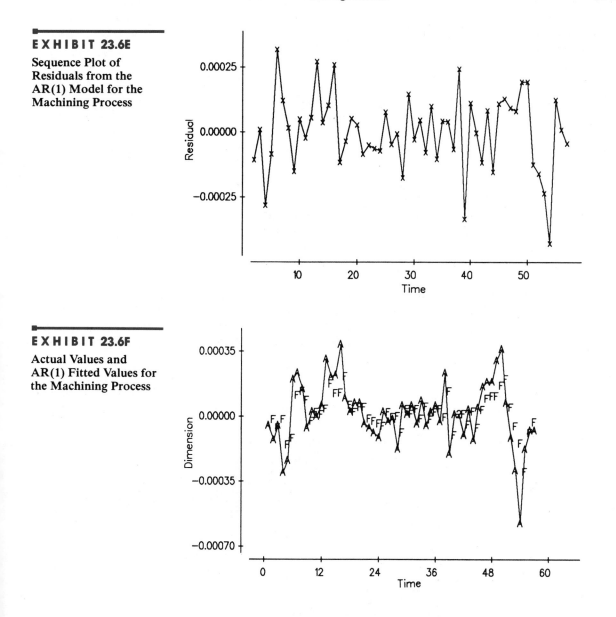

EXHIBIT 23.6F

Actual Values and
AR(1) Fitted Values for
the Machining Process

As a final check on the AR(1) model, suppose that an additional lagged term, y_{t-2}, is added to the model. Exhibit 23.6G displays the regression results. First note that the regression coefficient for lag 2 is not statistically significant: the t ratio is only 0.06. Furthermore, the estimate of the regression coefficient for lag 1 is essentially unchanged from the AR(1) model and is still highly significant. Clearly, adding an additional lagged value to the model is not helpful, and the AR(1) model is supported by this further check.

In other cases adding additional lagged y values can be very helpful. We proceed to the AR(2) model.

■───────
EXHIBIT 23.6G

Regression Results for an AR(2) Model for the Machining Process

```
The regression equation is

Dimension = 0.000009 + 0.525 Lag1Dimension + 0.008 Lag2Dimension

55 cases used; 2 cases contained missing values

Predictor         Coef       Stdev    t-ratio       p
Constant     0.00000941  0.00002033     0.46   0.646
Lag1Dimension   0.5246      0.1381       3.80   0.000
Lag2Dimension   0.0079      0.1383       0.06  0.954

s = 0.0001497   R-sq = 28.2%   R-sq(adj) = 25.4%
```

AR(2) MODELS

An **AR(2) model** is an autoregressive model in which the two predictor variables are the response variable at the previous two time points. An autoregressive model of order two satisfies the relationship

$$y_t = \beta_0 + \beta_1 y_{t-1} + \beta_2 y_{t-2} + e_t \tag{23.16}$$

where the error term e_t at time t is independent of earlier series values $y_{t-1}, y_{t-2}, \dots$. An example of a series that is well modelled by an AR(2) model is the sequence of quarterly U.S. unemployment rates for the period first quarter 1948 through first quarter 1978. The series values are given in Exhibit 23.6H and the sequence plot is shown in Exhibit 23.6I.

■───────
EXHIBIT 23.6H

U.S. Quarterly Unemployment Rates: First Quarter 1948 through First Quarter 1978

```
# filename: UNEMP.DAT
# U.S. quarterly unemployment rates (seasonally adjusted)
# (Source: J.D.Cryer, Time Series Analysis,
# Boston: PWS-Kent, 1986)
# First quarter 1948 through first quarter 1978, n=121
# (Read across, row by row)
3.73 3.67 3.77 3.83 4.67 5.87 6.70 6.97 6.40 5.57 4.63 4.23
3.50 3.10 3.17 3.37 3.07 2.97 3.23 2.83 2.70 2.57 2.73 3.70
5.27 5.80 5.97 5.33 4.73 4.40 4.10 4.23 4.03 4.20 4.13 4.13
3.93 4.10 4.23 4.93 6.30 7.37 7.33 6.37 5.83 5.10 5.27 5.60
5.13 5.23 5.53 6.27 6.80 7.00 6.77 6.20 5.63 5.53 5.57 5.53
5.77 5.73 5.50 5.57 5.47 5.20 5.00 5.00 4.90 4.67 4.37 4.10
3.87 3.80 3.77 3.70 3.77 3.83 3.83 3.93 3.73 3.57 3.53 3.43
3.37 3.43 3.60 4.17 4.80 5.17 5.87 5.93 5.97 5.97 5.97 5.97
5.83 5.77 5.53 5.27 5.03 4.93 4.77 4.67 5.17 5.13 5.50 6.57
8.37 8.90 8.37 8.40 7.63 7.43 7.83 7.93 7.37 7.07 6.90 6.63
6.20
```

Neighboring unemployment rates are quite similar. Large changes do not occur over short periods of time. However, larger changes do take place over longer periods. How can this autocorrelation be modelled? Exhibits 23.6J and 23.6K display the scatterplots of the unemployment rates versus lag 1 and versus lag 2 unemployment rates, respectively. The autocorrelation at lag 1 is 0.943 and at lag 2 is 0.815. Perhaps, an AR(2) will account for this autocorrelation structure.

The regression results of fitting an AR(2) model to this series are given in Exhibit 23.6L. Notice that both the lag 1 and lag 2 predictors are shown to have coefficients that are significantly different from zero. You are asked to do the residual analysis of this model in the exercises in Section 23.7. Assuming that the analysis indicates that the model is adequate, the model is used for prediction purposes.

EXHIBIT 23.6I

Sequence Plot of
Quarterly U.S.
Unemployment Rates:
1948–1978

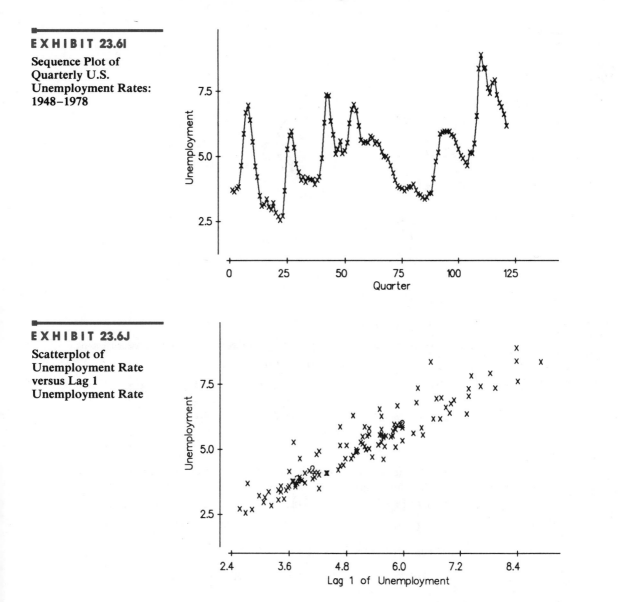

EXHIBIT 23.6I

Sequence Plot of
Quarterly U.S.
Unemployment Rates:
1948–1978

EXHIBIT 23.6J

Scatterplot of
Unemployment Rate
versus Lag 1
Unemployment Rate

Forecasts from this model for one time unit ahead are obtained from

$$\hat{y}_{n+1} = \beta_0 + \beta_1 y_n + \beta_2 y_{n-1} \qquad \textbf{(23.17)}$$

To forecast two steps ahead, use

$$\hat{y}_{n+2} = \beta_0 + \beta_1 \hat{y}_{n+1} + \beta_2 y_n \qquad \textbf{(23.18)}$$

where $\hat{y}_{n+1}$ is the one-step-ahead forecast obtained in Equation (23.17). Finally, for l steps ahead, use

$$\hat{y}_{n+l} = \beta_0 + \beta_1 \hat{y}_{n+l-1} + \beta_2 \hat{y}_{n+l-2} \qquad \text{for } l > 2 \qquad \textbf{(23.19)}$$

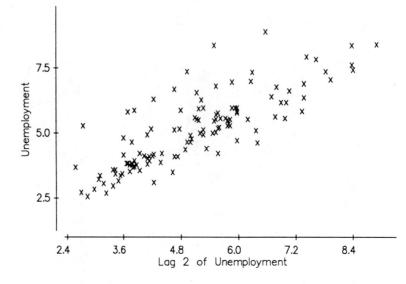

EXHIBIT 23.6L

Regression Results for
the AR(2) Model of
Unemployment Rates

```
The regression equation is

Unemployment = 0.505 + 1.55 Lag1Unemployment - 0.651 Lag2Unemployment

119 cases used; 2 cases contained missing values

Predictor           Coef      Stdev    t-ratio        p
Constant          0.5051     0.1267       3.99    0.000
Lag1Unemployment  1.55368    0.07074     21.96    0.000
Lag2Unemployment -0.65148    0.07081     -9.20    0.000

s = 0.3632      R-sq = 93.5%     R-sq(adj) = 93.4%
```

to calculate the forecasts one after the other. In our series the last two values are 6.63 for the fourth quarter of 1977 and 6.20 for the first quarter of 1978. The unemployment rate for the second quarter of 1978 is then forecast as

$$\text{Un\hat{e}mployment}_{n+1} = 0.505 + 1.55(6.20) - 0.651(6.63) = 5.80$$

The forecast for the third quarter of 1978 is then

$$\text{Un\hat{e}mployment}_{n+2} = 0.505 + 1.55(5.80) - 0.651(6.20) = 5.4588$$

and the forecast for the next quarter is

$$\text{Un\hat{e}mployment}_{n+3} = 0.505 + 1.55(5.4588) - 0.651(5.80) = 5.19034$$

In this way as many forecasts as desired may be calculated one after the other.

As a final example, consider the series of monthly AA railroad bond yields given in Exhibit 23.6M. The sequence plot in Exhibit 23.6N again shows a strong tendency for neighboring values to be quite similar. There is strong autocorrelation in this series. The lag 1 autocorrelation coefficient is 0.96 and at lag 2 it is 0.92. By lag 3 it is still 0.86. These high autocorrelations at several lags are a sign that models for the *changes* in the series should be considered. Exhibit 23.6O displays the sequence plot of the monthly changes.

EXHIBIT 23.6M

Monthly Bond Yields
on Railroad Bonds—
January 1968 through
June 1976

```
# filename: RRBONDS.DAT
# Monthly AA railroad bond yields (%X100)
# (Source: J.D.Cryer, Time Series Analysis,
# Boston: PWS-Kent, 1986)
# January 1968 through June 1976, n=102
# (Read across, row by row)
  639 643 640 653 667 667 663 654 649 651 659 672 # 1968
  670 675 692 702 706 710 722 729 740 755 763 788 # 1969
  818 826 821 819 827 848 881 879 878 878 868 856 # 1970
  844 824 820 819 813 815 822 818 815 792 769 775 # 1971
  771 773 780 779 774 772 775 770 766 771 773 772 # 1972
  767 775 777 777 776 779 787 790 791 792 802 799 # 1973
  792 780 790 799 810 814 828 862 874 892 872 869 # 1974
  870 859 857 870 867 856 854 862 861 855 846 847 # 1975
  845 838 828 823 814 812                         # 1976
```

EXHIBIT 23.6N

Sequence Plot of
Monthly Railroad
Bond Yields

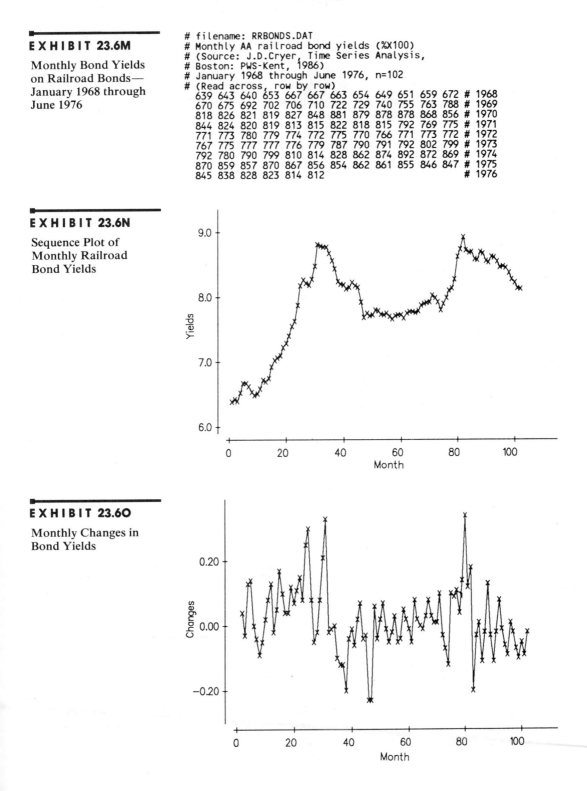

EXHIBIT 23.6O

Monthly Changes in
Bond Yields

Now consider the changes as a time series and evaluate the autocorrelations in this transformed series. The autocorrelation at lag 1 is 0.468, but at other higher lags the autocorrelations are negligible. Perhaps an AR(1) model *for the series of changes* will produce a reasonable model for the behavior of this series. Exhibit 23.6P shows the results of the estimation of parameters in the model. You are asked to do a residual analysis in the exercises in Section 23.7.

EXHIBIT 23.6P

Regression Results for
AR(1) Model for
Changes in Bond Yields

```
The regression equation is

Changes = 0.00871 + 0.468 Lag1Changes

100 cases used; 2 cases contained missing values

Predictor        Coef      Stdev     t-ratio        p
Constant      0.008707   0.009413      0.93      0.357
Lag1Changes   0.46814    0.08931       5.24      0.000

s = 0.09282     R-sq = 21.9%     R-sq(adj) = 21.1%
```

If y_t represents the bond yield at time t then the AR(1) model for changes says that

$$y_t - y_{t-1} = \beta_0 + \beta_1(y_{t-1} - y_{t-2}) + e_t \qquad \textbf{(23.20)}$$

or
$$y_t = \beta_0 + (\beta_1 + 1)y_{t-1} - \beta_1 y_{t-2} + e_t \qquad \textbf{(23.21)}$$

which looks like an AR(2) model. However, here the two regression coefficients on the response lagged one and two time units are related to the *same* parameter β_1 rather than being two separate parameters. In Section 23.7 you are asked to estimate a general AR(2) model for the bond yields and verify that the AR(2) results confirm the simpler analysis of the changes in the yields. As suggested by Equation (23.21), forecasting with this AR(1) model for the changes will proceed just as it did for the AR(2) model in Equations (23.17–23.19).

Selecting appropriate autoregressive models for time series or their changes is a difficult task. See the specialized time series books referred to earlier in this chapter for more details.

SECTION 23.7

EXERCISES

23.7A Consider the flour price index for Buffalo, New York, listed in Exhibit 2.10A and plotted in Exhibit 2.10B.
  (a) Fit an AR(1) model to this series and investigate the autocorrelation in the residuals.
  (b) Fit an AR(1) model to the logarithm of this series. Investigate the autocorrelation in the residuals from this model.
  (c) Which of these two models fits the series better? (Filename: BUFLOUR.DAT.)

23.7B Refer to the metal exports data given in Exercise 6.9A. Fit an AR(1) model. What prediction rule does your fitted model suggest? What predictive performance do you expect it to have in future years, assuming the process remains stable? (Filename: STEELEXP.DAT.)

23.7C Fit an AR(2) model to the Buffalo flour price index series. The data are in Exhibit 2.10A.

Compare this model to the AR(1) model obtained in Exercise 23.7A. (Filename: BUFLOUR.DAT.)

23.7D Consider the time series of hourly wages shown in Exhibit 23.2A. Models for this series with fixed linear or quadratic trend contain substantial residual autocorrelation. Fit an AR(1) model to this series and compare the results to those obtained earlier. In particular, look at the autocorrelation in the residuals and especially at lags 1, 2, 12, 24, and 36. This series is considered again in Exercise 24.6G. (Filename: APAWAGES.DAT.)

23.7E The time series given below gives the final position in the "x direction" after an industrial robot is finished with a planned set of movements. The measurements are expressed as deviations from a desired position. The robot is put through this planned set of exercises many times with the hope that its behavior will be repeatable and thus predictable.

```
# filename: ROBOT.DAT
# Robot data: x position after "exercising"
# (Source: William Fulkerson, Deere & Co.
#  Technical Center, Moline, Illinois)
# (Read across, row by row)
 -1  42   4  35  -4   0  14  34    2  24 -12
 25  24  -9  40   1 -13  49  -6   -3  -9   3
-13  10  33  12  31  20  -6 -17   28   0  12
 12  38  10   4   1  17  -4  20    0  22   3
 37  58  28   0  -8  -4  -4  27  -24 -20 -35
-15 -14 -31  11 -39 -43 -37  -4  -31 -47 -12
-28 -72 -75 -21 -35 -41 -32 -24  -49 -69 -60
-64 -78 -64 -81 -54 -90 -80 -92 -103 -70 -91
-62 -90 -74 -52 -70 -79 -39 -54  -69 -71 -77
-75 -37 -69 -90 -75 -64 -76 -65  -54 -73 -90
-87 -47 -52 -46 -48 -67 -22 -63  -64 -58
```

(a) Construct a sequence plot of the data. Describe the plot. Are there any evident patterns? Would a model that says that the successive positions arise independently from some common distribution seem appropriate?

(b) Find the autocorrelation at lag 1 and at lag 2.

(c) Fit an AR(1) model to this series and comment on the results.

(d) Check the residuals from the AR(1) fit with respect to autocorrelation and normality.

23.7F Consider the AR(2) model that was suggested for the quarterly U.S. unemployment rates in Exhibit 23.6H. The estimation results appear in Exhibit 23.6L.

(a) Analyze the scatterplot of residuals versus fitted values for model inadequacies.

(b) Check the residuals for autocorrelation at lags 1, 2, and 3. Compare their magnitudes to $3/\sqrt{n}$.

(c) Check the residuals for normality by inspecting their histogram and normal scores plot.

(d) Fit an AR(3) model to this series and compare the resulting coefficients to those of the AR(2) model. Do the results confirm the AR(2) model? (Filename: UNEMP.DAT.)

23.7G Return to the AA railroad bond yields given in Exhibit 23.6M. An AR(1) model was fit to the changes of this series and the results reported in Exhibit 23.6L.

(a) Analyze the scatterplot of residuals versus fitted values for model inadequacies.

(b) Check the residuals for autocorrelation at lags 1, 2, and 3. Compare their magnitudes to $3/\sqrt{n}$.

(c) Check the residuals for normality by inspecting their histogram and normal scores plot.

(d) Fit an AR(2) model to the changes in this series and compare the resulting coefficients to those of the AR(1) model. Do the results confirm the AR(1) model? (Filename: RRBONDS.DAT.)

EXPONENTIAL SMOOTHING

SIMPLE EXPONENTIAL SMOOTHING

Exponential smoothing is a technique for smoothing out the random variation in a series. It developed from very practical considerations.[†] Some of the variation in a time series must be smoothed out so that the general trend, if any, may be seen without being masked by the short-term, irregular variation of the series. This method is illustrated using the quarterly percent changes in Iowa nonfarm income per capita.

The original data and the percent changes shown in Exhibit 23.8A extend over the period from the first quarter of 1948 through the third quarter of 1975. (If the

EXHIBIT 23.8A   Iowa Nonfarm Income per Capita and Growth Rates—1948–1975

Income	Percent Change	Quarter	Year	Income	Percent Change	Quarter	Year	Income	Percent Change	Quarter	Year
601	*	1	1948	1013	1.19880	2	1957	1760	2.62391	3	1966
604	0.49917	2	1948	1021	0.78973	3	1957	1812	2.95455	4	1966
620	2.64901	3	1948	1028	0.68560	4	1957	1809	-0.16556	1	1967
626	0.96774	4	1948	1027	-0.09728	1	1958	1828	1.05030	2	1967
641	2.39617	1	1949	1048	2.04479	2	1958	1871	2.35230	3	1967
642	0.15601	2	1949	1070	2.09924	3	1958	1892	1.12239	4	1967
645	0.46729	3	1949	1095	2.33645	4	1958	1946	2.85412	1	1968
655	1.55039	4	1949	1113	1.64384	1	1959	1983	1.90134	2	1968
682	4.12214	1	1950	1143	2.69542	2	1959	2013	1.51286	3	1968
678	-0.58651	2	1950	1154	0.96238	3	1959	2045	1.58967	4	1968
692	2.06490	3	1950	1173	1.64645	4	1959	2069	1.17359	1	1969
707	2.16763	4	1950	1178	0.42626	1	1960	2107	1.83664	2	1969
736	4.10184	1	1951	1183	0.42445	2	1960	2144	1.75605	3	1969
753	2.30978	2	1951	1205	1.85968	3	1960	2183	1.81903	4	1969
763	1.32802	3	1951	1208	0.24896	4	1960	2231	2.19881	1	1970
775	1.57274	4	1951	1209	0.08278	1	1961	2304	3.27208	2	1970
775	0.00000	1	1952	1223	1.15798	2	1961	2343	1.69271	3	1970
783	1.03226	2	1952	1238	1.22649	3	1961	2377	1.45113	4	1970
794	1.40485	3	1952	1245	0.56543	4	1961	2393	0.67312	1	1971
813	2.39295	4	1952	1258	1.04418	1	1962	2461	2.84162	2	1971
823	1.23001	1	1953	1278	1.58983	2	1962	2494	1.34092	3	1971
826	0.36452	2	1953	1294	1.25196	3	1962	2532	1.52366	4	1971
829	0.36320	3	1953	1314	1.54560	4	1962	2565	1.30332	1	1972
831	0.24125	4	1953	1323	0.68493	1	1963	2631	2.57310	2	1972
830	-0.12034	1	1954	1336	0.98262	2	1963	2682	1.93843	3	1972
838	0.96386	2	1954	1355	1.42216	3	1963	2782	3.72856	4	1972
854	1.90931	3	1954	1377	1.62362	4	1963	2849	2.40834	1	1973
872	2.10773	4	1954	1416	2.83224	1	1964	2930	2.84310	2	1973
882	1.14679	1	1955	1430	0.98870	2	1964	3029	3.37884	3	1973
903	2.38095	2	1955	1455	1.74825	3	1964	3102	2.41004	4	1973
919	1.77187	3	1955	1480	1.71821	4	1964	3181	2.54674	1	1974
937	1.95865	4	1955	1514	2.29730	1	1965	3282	3.17510	2	1974
927	-1.06724	1	1956	1545	2.04756	2	1965	3391	3.32115	3	1974
962	3.77562	2	1956	1589	2.84790	3	1965	3488	2.86051	4	1974
975	1.35135	3	1956	1634	2.83197	4	1965	3568	2.29358	1	1975
995	2.05128	4	1956	1669	2.14198	1	1966	3657	2.49439	2	1975
1001	0.60302	1	1957	1715	2.75614	2	1966	3705	1.31255	3	1975

[†] E. S. Gardner, "Exponential Smoothing: The State of the Art," *Journal of Forecasting* 4 (1985): 1–28, provides a review of these techniques, which originated with R. G. Brown for the U.S. Navy during World War II.

percent changes were being reported they would be rounded off to around the nearest tenth of a percent. For this analysis, however, several more decimal places are retained, as shown in the exhibit.) Exhibit 23.8B shows the sequence plot of the percent changes and shows a great deal of variation over the time period displayed. The series shows no seasonality or consistent trends upward or downward. However, the mean level of the series appears to change over time, being higher at the end of the series than at the beginning. The objective of smoothing is to estimate the current mean level of the series in situations where the mean is suspected of changing over time. Exhibit 23.8C shows the sequence plot of the percent changes with a plot of the exponentially smoothed series overlaid.

E X H I B I T 23.8B

Sequence Plot of Percent Change in Iowa Nonfarm Income

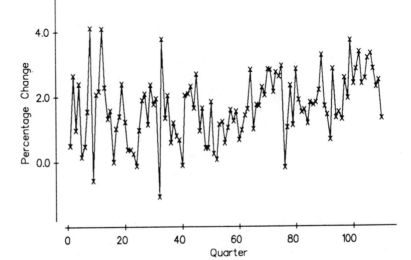

E X H I B I T 23.8C

Sequence Plot of Series and Smoothed Sequence Plot ($\alpha = 0.1$)

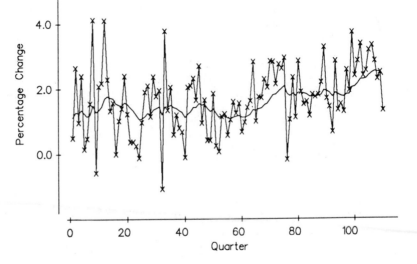

The equations governing the exponential smoothing method may be expressed many different equivalent ways. The smoothed series at time t is defined by

$$\hat{\beta}_t = \alpha y_t + \alpha(1 - \alpha)y_{t-1} + \alpha(1 - \alpha)^2 y_{t-2} + \cdots + \alpha(1 - \alpha)^{t-1}y_1 \quad \textbf{(23.22)}$$

where α is a **smoothing constant** that is selected in the range $0 < \alpha < 1$. Since $0 < \alpha < 1$, the weights that are applied to the current and past observations, α, $\alpha(1 - \alpha)$, $\alpha(1 - \alpha)^2, \ldots$, decrease *exponentially* (or geometrically) with increasing time lag and at a rate determined by the discount factor $1 - \alpha$. For example, if $\alpha = 0.1$, then the weights are $\alpha = 0.1$, $\alpha(1 - \alpha) = 0.09$, $\alpha(1 - \alpha)^2 = 0.081$, $\alpha(1 - \alpha)^3 = 0.0729$, and so on. If the weight on the current observation is increased to $\alpha = 0.4$, then the sequence of weights 0.4, 0.24, 0.144, 0.0864, ... decreases more rapidly and relatively more weight is given to the most recent observations. It may be shown that the weights (nearly) add to 1 so that the smoothed value at time t is an *exponentially weighted average* of current and past observations. The smoothed value at time t, $\hat{\beta}_t$, is the forecast of the value for the series for time $t + 1$.

The smooth curve given in Exhibit 23.8C was obtained using a smoothing constant of $\alpha = 0.1$. Exhibit 23.8D shows the same series smoothed with $\alpha = 0.5$. Here the current observation is given much more weight than the others and the smoothed curve, to a much greater extent, follows the variation in the series rather than smoothing it out. To better see the effect of the larger smoothing constant, just the last portion of the sequence plot is plotted in Exhibit 23.8E. Here it is easier to see that the smoothed series (plotted as S's) is attempting to follow the individual variations in the actual series (A's) too much. If the series has a large swing upward, then the smoothed series is frequently pulled up too much at the next time point when the series of percent changes tends to revert to a lower value.

The calculation of the smoothed series is not usually accomplished using the definition in Equation (23.22). Rather, rewriting the right-hand side of Equa-

EXHIBIT 23.8D

Sequence Plot of Series
and Smoothed Sequence
Plot ($\alpha = 0.5$)

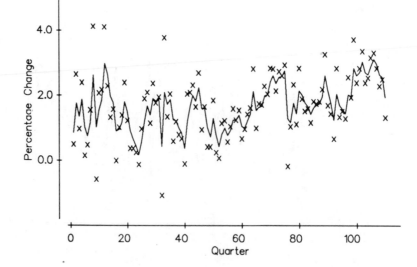

EXHIBIT 23.8E

Expanded Sequence Plot
of Percent Changes and
Smoothed Sequence
Plot ($\alpha = 0.5$)

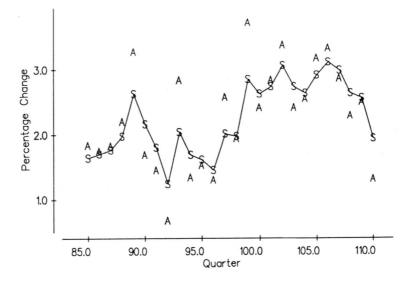

tion (23.22) as

$$\hat{\beta}_t = \alpha y_t + (1 - \alpha)[\alpha y_{t-1} + \alpha(1 - \alpha)y_{t-2} + \cdots + \alpha(1 - \alpha)^{t-2}y_1]$$

it can be seen that

$$\hat{\beta}_t = \alpha y_t + (1 - \alpha)\hat{\beta}_{t-1} \qquad \textbf{(23.23)}$$

which provides a convenient recursive expression for calculation. Equation (23.23)
also shows that the smoothed series at time t can be expressed as a weighted average
of the current observation, y_t with weight α, and the previous smoothed series value
with weight $1 - \alpha$.

To use Equation (23.23) an initial value $\hat{\beta}_0$ is needed. A variety of choices have
been advocated in the literature. Some authors use $\hat{\beta}_0 = y_1$, while others use $\hat{\beta}_0 = \bar{y}$
or more complicated calculations. A simple compromise is to set $\hat{\beta}_0$ equal to the
average of the first six series values. Once the value of $\hat{\beta}_0$ is determined, the next
smoothed value is obtained from

$$\hat{\beta}_1 = \alpha y_1 + (1 - \alpha)\hat{\beta}_0$$

In turn, the smoothed value at $t = 2$ is

$$\hat{\beta}_2 = \alpha y_2 + (1 - \alpha)\hat{\beta}_1$$

and so forth.

For our illustration series, the average of the first six data points is 1.18923 so that
with $\alpha = 0.1$,

$$\hat{\beta}_1 = 0.1(0.49917) + 0.9(1.18923) = 1.120224$$

and $\qquad \hat{\beta}_2 = 0.1(2.64901) + 0.9(1.120224) = 1.2731026$

and so forth. Several of the smoothed values for both $\alpha = 0.1$ and $\alpha = 0.5$ are given
in Exhibit 23.8F. (They were obtained with computer software.)

		Percent Change	Smoothed	Smoothed
	t	y_t	$\alpha = 0.1$	$\alpha = 0.5$
	0		1.18923	1.18923
	1	0.49917	1.12022	0.84420
	2	2.64901	1.27310	1.74660
	3	0.96774	1.24257	1.35717
	4	2.39617	1.35793	1.87667
	5	0.15601	1.23773	1.01634
	6	0.46729	1.16069	0.74181
	7	1.55039	1.19966	1.14610
	8	4.12214	1.49191	2.63412
	9	−0.58651	1.28407	1.02380
	10	2.06490	1.36215	1.54435
	11	2.16763	1.44270	1.85599
	⋮	⋮	⋮	⋮
	106	3.32115	2.48498	3.11443
	107	2.86051	2.52253	2.98747
	108	2.29358	2.49964	2.64052
	109	2.49439	2.49911	2.56746
	110	1.31255	2.38046	1.94001

EXHIBIT 23.8F

Exponential Smoothing Results with $\alpha = 0.1$ and $\alpha = 0.5$

A statistical model that leads to exponential smoothing as an optimal forecasting method may be defined as follows. Assume that the observed time series can be expressed as the "regression"

$$y_t = \beta_t + e_t \tag{23.24}$$

where the unobserved (and slowly changing) "mean" component, β_t, follows a random walk ("autoregressive") model:

$$\beta_t = \beta_{t-1} + a_t \tag{23.25}$$

Here a_t is another sequence of error terms independent of the e_t error terms. Then the changes or differences in y_t may be written as

$$y_t - y_{t-1} = e_t - e_{t-1} + a_t = e_t^* \tag{23.26}$$

where the sequence e_t^* contains negative autocorrelation at lag 1 but no autocorrelation at any other lags. A series y_t that satisfies Equation (23.26) is called an *integrated moving average* (IMA) series. More specifically, this is an IMA $(1, 1)$ series. The first 1 refers to the first differencing and the second 1 refers to the fact that the differenced series has nonzero autocorrelation only at lag 1.

The IMA model described here is a special case of a much more general class of models called ARIMA (AutoRegressive-Integrated-Moving Average) models. A general discussion of these models is beyond the scope of this book. They are explored extensively in the specialized time series books cited earlier.

CHOICE OF SMOOTHING CONSTANT

Some authors have suggested that the smoothing constant be selected rather arbitrarily, say, as $\alpha = 0.1$. Others have suggested choosing α based on a subjective assessment of the variation in the series being smoothed. If the perceived changes in the level of the series seem to dominate the short-term variations, then a large value of α should be used. However, if the short-term variation is more prominent than the level changes, then a small value for the smoothing constant is advised.

A more objective approach is to select a smoothing constant that leads to good "forecasts" of the observed series. That is, use $\hat{\beta}_t$ to forecast y_{t+1} for a range of values of t and choose α to minimize the root mean square prediction error, RMSPE, introduced in Chapter 6. Recall that RMSPE is defined as

$$RMSPE = \sqrt{(\text{Mean prediction error})^2 + (\text{Standard deviation of prediction error})^2}$$

Since the forecasts involve powers of α, this minimization cannot be accomplished directly. Rather, the smoothed series and the corresponding RMSPE are computed for a range of α values and the α chosen for the final smoothing is the one that produces the smallest value for RMSPE.

Since we recommend using the average of the first six series values to initialize the smoothing and the smoothing procedure needs several values to "warm up," we skip over the first six observations and begin calculating the one-step-ahead forecasts at the seventh observation. Prediction errors are then obtained from the seventh series value through the end of the series, and the RMSPE is based on these errors. Exhibit 23.8G displays some of these calculations for $\alpha = 0.1$ and

EXHIBIT 23.8G

Calculation of
Prediction Errors and
RMSPE

		$\alpha = 0.1$		$\alpha = 0.5$	
t	Percentage Change y_t	Smoothed (at $t - 1$)	Prediction Error	Smoothed (at $t - 1$)	Prediction Error
1	0.49917	1.18923	(-0.69006)	1.18923	(-0.69006)
2	2.64901	1.12022	(1.52878)	0.84420	(1.80481)
3	0.96774	1.27310	(-0.30536)	1.74660	(-0.77886)
4	2.39617	1.24257	(1.15360)	1.35717	(1.03899)
5	0.15601	1.35793	(-1.20192)	1.87667	(-1.72066)
6	0.46729	1.23773	(-0.77044)	1.01634	(-0.54905)
7	1.55039	1.16069	0.38970	0.74181	0.80857
8	4.12214	1.19966	2.92248	1.14610	2.97604
9	-0.58651	1.49191	-2.07842	2.63412	-3.22063
10	2.06490	1.28407	0.78083	1.02380	1.04109
11	2.16763	1.36215	0.80548	1.54435	0.62328
⋮	⋮	⋮	⋮	⋮	⋮
106	3.32115	2.39207	0.92907	2.90772	0.41343
107	2.86051	2.48498	0.37553	3.11443	-0.25392
108	2.29358	2.52253	-0.22896	2.98747	-0.69389
109	2.49439	2.49964	-0.00524	2.64052	-0.14613
110	1.31255	2.49911	-1.18656	2.56746	-1.25491

for $\alpha = 0.5$. For example, the prediction error when using $\alpha = 0.1$ at time $t = 7$ is $1.55039 - 1.16069 = 0.38970$. At the next time point the prediction error is $4.12214 - 1.19966 = 2.92248$, and so on. After obtaining all of the prediction errors the mean and standard deviation of the prediction errors and finally the RMSPE are calculated. In our example with $\alpha = 0.1$ the mean prediction error is 0.11729 and the standard deviation is 0.96177, which leads to RMSPE = $\sqrt{(0.11729)^2 + (0.96177)^2} = 0.9689$. Similar calculations using $\alpha = 0.5$ produce a smaller mean prediction error of 0.023042 but a larger standard deviation of prediction errors of 1.0417. These combine to give a larger RMSPE = 1.0419.

Exhibit 23.8H lists the RMSPE corresponding to a variety of values of α for the percent changes of the Iowa income series. A plot of these values is presented in Exhibit 23.8I, showing that the best choice for α is 0.10 or 0.11. Notice, however, that the value for RMSPE is nearly constant over the range from $\alpha = 0.07$ to $\alpha = 0.15$, and any value in this range would provide about the same amount of smoothing.

EXHIBIT 23.8H

RMSPE for Various
Smoothing Constants

α	RMSPE	α	RMSPE
0.01	1.05039	0.12	0.96915
0.02	1.01453	0.13	0.96960
0.03	0.99561	0.14	0.97021
0.04	0.98473	0.15	0.97096
0.05	0.97814	0.20	0.97620
0.06	0.97406	0.25	0.98342
0.07	0.97155	0.30	0.99228
0.08	0.97005	0.35	1.00264
0.09	0.96924	0.40	1.01440
0.10	0.96890	0.45	1.02750
0.11	0.96890	0.50	1.04193

EXHIBIT 23.8I

Plot of RMSPE versus
Smoothing Constant

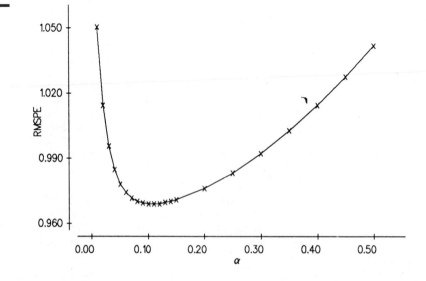

DOUBLE EXPONENTIAL SMOOTHING

Single exponential smoothing provides good forecasts for series that in the short run vary around a reasonably constant mean but for which the mean level changes over longer time periods. Equations (23.24) and (23.25) present a specific statistical model for such behavior. Other series may be better modelled by a process that assumes that the short-term behavior is approximated by a linear time trend but with the slope and intercept changing over a longer time horizon. Double exponential smoothing leads to estimates in this case. The model is written as

$$y_t = \beta_{0,t} + \beta_{1,t}t + e_t \tag{23.27}$$

where the intercept $\beta_{0,t}$ and slope $\beta_{1,t}$ are varying over time. Estimates of the intercept and slope are obtained by smoothing the time series twice, hence the name *double exponential smoothing*.

For double exponential smoothing S_t' denotes the smoothed value at time t for the series y_t:

$$S_t' = \alpha y_t + (1 - \alpha)S_{t-1}' \tag{23.28}$$

Then the smoothed values are smoothed a second time to obtain S_t'' where

$$S_t'' = \alpha S_t' + (1 - \alpha)S_{t-1}'' \tag{23.29}$$

Finally, based on algebra not given here, the estimates of the changing intercept and slope are obtained from

$$\hat{\beta}_{0,t} = 2S_t' - S_t'' \tag{23.30}$$

and

$$\hat{\beta}_{1,t} = \frac{\alpha}{1 - \alpha}(S_t' - S_t'') \tag{23.31}$$

If n denotes the time of the last available series value, then the forecast l time units into the future is given by extrapolating the linear time trend using the current

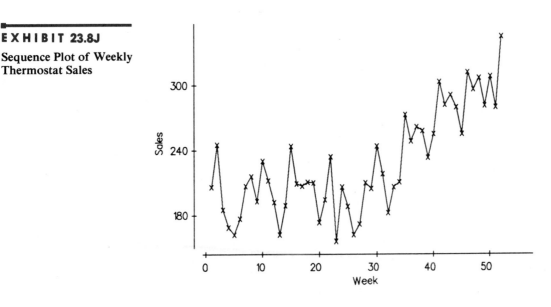

EXHIBIT 23.8J

Sequence Plot of Weekly Thermostat Sales

estimates of the intercept and slope:

$$\hat{y}_{n+l} = \hat{\beta}_{0,n} + \hat{\beta}_{1,n}l \qquad \text{for } l = 1, 2, \ldots \qquad \textbf{(23.32)}$$

For illustration the series displayed in Exhibit 23.8J is used. These data of weekly thermostat sales are reported in Exhibit 23.8K.

EXHIBIT 23.8K

Weekly Thermostat
Sales Data

```
# filename: THERMOST.DAT
# Weekly thermostat sales
# (Source: R.G.Brown, Smoothing, Forecasting and Prediction of
# Discrete Time Series, Engelwood Cliffs, NJ: Prentice-Hall, 1962)
# (Read across, row by row)
  206 245 185 169 162 177 207 216 193 230 212 192 162
  189 244 209 207 211 210 173 194 234 156 206 188 162
  172 210 205 244 218 182 206 211 273 248 262 258 233
  255 303 282 291 280 255 312 296 307 281 308 280 345
```

INITIALIZING DOUBLE EXPONENTIAL SMOOTHING

As with single exponential smoothing, the recursive calculations of Equations (23.28) and (23.29) must be started with initial values S_0' and S_0''. Although several different initializations are advocated in the smoothing literature, we recommend fitting a straight-line trend to the first six series values. Solving Equations (23.30) and (23.31) for S_0' and S_0'' in terms of $\hat{\beta}_0$ and $\hat{\beta}_1$ leads to the expressions

$$S_0' = \hat{\beta}_{0,0} - \frac{\alpha}{1-\alpha}\hat{\beta}_{1,0} \qquad \textbf{(23.33)}$$

and

$$S_0'' = \hat{\beta}_{0,0} - 2\frac{\alpha}{1-\alpha}\hat{\beta}_{1,0} \qquad \textbf{(23.34)}$$

Here $\hat{\beta}_{0,0}$ and $\hat{\beta}_{1,0}$ are the intercept and slope of the linear time trend fitted to the first six values of the series by regressing $y_1, y_2, \ldots, y_6$ on $1, 2, \ldots, 6$.

For illustration consider smoothing the thermostat sales series. Exhibit 23.8L gives the time trend fit to the first six series values. Using a smoothing constant of $\alpha = 0.24$, Equations (23.30) and (23.31) yield

$$S_0' = 231.67 - \frac{.76}{.24}(-11.714) = 268.764$$

and

$$S_0'' = 231.67 - 2\left[\frac{.76}{.24}\right](-11.714) = 305.859$$

EXHIBIT 23.8L

Initial Value
Calculations—Linear
Time Trend Fitted to
First Six Values

```
The regression equation is

Sales = 232 - 11.7 week

Predictor      Coef       Stdev     t-ratio        p
Constant      231.67      22.30       10.39     0.000
week          -11.714      5.727      -2.05     0.110
```

Exhibit 23.8M shows the results of double exponential smoothing for the weekly sales series using these initial values and $\alpha = 0.24$. Here the fitted value at time t is the one-step-ahead forecast considering y_t as the last series value.[†]

EXHIBIT 23.8M

Double Exponential Smoothing of Weekly Thermostat Sales Data

Week	Sales	S'	S''	Fitted
0	*	268.762	305.857	*
1	206	253.699	293.339	219.952
2	245	251.611	283.324	201.541
3	185	235.625	271.877	209.883
4	169	219.635	259.338	187.925
5	162	205.802	246.490	167.393
6	177	198.890	235.066	152.266
7	207	200.836	226.851	151.290
8	216	204.476	221.481	166.607
9	193	201.721	216.738	182.100
10	230	208.508	214.763	181.962
11	212	209.346	213.463	200.278
12	192	205.183	211.476	203.929
⋮	⋮	⋮	⋮	⋮
42	282	263.329	243.481	284.038
43	291	269.970	249.838	289.445
44	280	272.377	255.248	296.459
45	255	268.207	258.358	294.916
46	312	278.717	263.244	281.166
47	296	282.865	267.953	299.076
48	307	288.657	272.922	302.486
49	281	286.820	276.257	309.362
50	308	291.903	280.012	300.717
51	280	289.046	282.180	307.548
52	345	302.475	287.051	298.080

The choice of the smoothing constant can again be based on minimizing the RMSPE for the observed series values. Exhibits 23.8N and 23.8O give the calculated values and a plot showing that $\alpha = 0.24$ provides the best fit. As seen with other data sets, a range of values of the smoothing constant provide nearly equivalent values for the RMSPE.

In the exercises in Section 23.9 you are asked to examine the residuals from the double exponential smoothing with regard to their autocorrelation, normality, and so forth. For now, it is assumed that the diagnostics checks have been performed and that the model appears to be acceptable.

[†] The minor differences between the initial values here and those calculated earlier are due to round-off error. The smoothing was done with computer software that uses many more digits internally.

	α	RMSPE	α	RMSPE

EXHIBIT 23.8N

**RMSPE Values for
Double Exponential
Smoothing of
Thermostat Sales Series**

α	RMSPE	α	RMSPE
0.10	42.6330	0.22	30.2193
0.11	39.2751	0.23	30.1682
0.12	36.8230	0.24	30.1530
0.13	35.0195	0.25	30.1676
0.14	33.6841	0.26	30.2072
0.15	32.6899	0.27	30.2678
0.16	31.9476	0.28	30.3464
0.17	31.3934	0.29	30.4403
0.18	30.9819	0.30	30.5475
0.19	30.6799	0.35	31.2316
0.20	30.4633	0.40	32.0816
0.21	30.3143	0.50	34.0968

EXHIBIT 23.8O

**RMSPE Values for
Double Exponential
Smoothing of
Thermostat Sales Series**

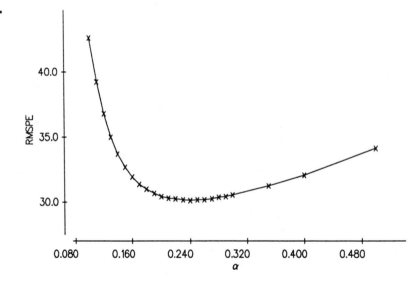

After the double smoothing is complete, forecasts are obtained using Equations (23.30), (23.31), and (23.32) for a set of lead values $l = 1, 2, \ldots$ into the future. For example, with the sales data $S'_{52} = 287.051$ and $S''_{52} = 302.475$ that, in turn, yield intercept and slope coefficients of

$$\hat{\beta}_{0,52} = 2S'_{52} - S''_{52} = (2 \times 302.475) - 287.051 = 317.899$$

and $$\hat{\beta}_{1,52} = \frac{\alpha}{1-\alpha}(S'_{52} - S''_{52}) = \frac{.24}{.76}(302.475 - 287.051) = 4.8707$$

Forecasts l weeks ahead are given by

$$\hat{y}_{52+l} = 317.899 + 4.8707l$$

which are listed in Exhibit 23.8P for leads $l = 1, 2, \ldots, 6$.

EXHIBIT 23.8P

Forecasts for the Next
Six Weeks' Thermostat
Sales

t	l	$\hat{y}_{52+l}$
53	1	322.770
54	2	327.640
55	3	332.511
56	4	337.382
57	5	342.253
58	6	347.123

Exhibit 23.8Q displays a sequence plot of the actual sales series (plotting symbol A), the fitted values (symbol F) based on double exponential smoothing, and the predictions (symbol P) for six weeks into the future.

EXHIBIT 23.8Q

Sequence Plot of Actual
Sales Values, Fitted
Values, and Forecasts
for Six Weeks

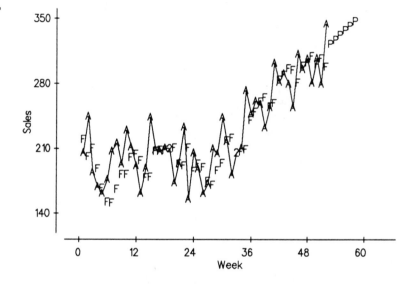

In direct analogy with the model described by Equations (23.25) and (23.26), a time series model for which double exponential smoothing produces optimal forecasts can be described as

$$y_t = \beta_t + e_t \qquad \text{(23.35)}$$

where

$$\beta_t = \beta_{t-1} + \alpha_t \qquad \text{(23.36)}$$

and

$$\alpha_t = \alpha_{t-1} + u_t \qquad \text{(23.37)}$$

Here u_t is a sequence of independent errors that are also independent of the e_t errors. Notice that α_t is the *rate of change* or slope of the β_t sequence at time t so that the slope of the "trend" β_t is changing according to a random walk model. This is another example of an integrated moving-average process, specifically, an IMA(2, 2) process: the second difference of the y_t series has nonzero autocorrelation only at lags 1 and 2. A general study of these types of models is beyond the scope of this text. Refer to books specializing in time series models for more information.

EXERCISES

23.9A A time series begins with values 5, 7, 6, 9, 6, 5, 6, and 7.
  (a) Using an initial value of $\hat{\beta}_0 = 6$ and a smoothing constant of $\alpha = 0.1$, find the smoothed series values.
  (b) Plot the series and overlay the series of smoothed values.

23.9B The time series given in Exercise 23.7E gave the final position in the "x direction" after an industrial robot finished a planned set of movements. The measurements are expressed as deviations from a desired position.
  (a) Use simple exponential smoothing with $\alpha = 0.1$ to smooth the series. Compare the fit of this model to that of the AR(1) model considered in Exercise 23.7E.
  (b) Use simple exponential smoothing with $\alpha = 0.05, 0.15$, and 0.2 in addition to $\alpha = 0.1$ in part (a) on the series. Which smoothing constant provides the smallest RMSPE? (Filename: ROBOT.DAT.)

23.9C Use the Deere & Co. machining data of Exhibit 23.6A.
  (a) Exponentially smooth the series using $\alpha = 0.1$.
  (b) Plot the sequence plot of the series and overlay the smoothed series. Comment on the plot.
  (c) Exponentially smooth the series using $\alpha = 0.7$.
  (d) Plot the sequence plot of the series and overlay the smoothed series obtained in part (c). Comment on the plot. (Filename: DEERE3.DAT.)

23.9D Use double exponential smoothing on the AA railroad bond yields of Exhibit 23.6M.
  (a) Use a smoothing constant of $\alpha = 0.1$.
  (b) Overlay the smoothed series on the sequence plot of the bond yields. Comment on the appearance of the plot.
  (c) Now use a smoothing constant of $\alpha = 0.6$.
  (d) Again overlay the smoothed series from part (c) on the sequence plot of the bond yields. Comment on the appearance of this plot. (Filename: RRBONDS.DAT.)

SUPPLEMENTARY EXERCISES FOR CHAPTER 23

23A Sequence data from an industrial process at Deere & Co. were first encountered in Exercise 2A. Using those data
  (a) Compute the autocorrelations at lags 1, 2, and 3 and comment on their magnitudes.
  (b) Construct scatterplots of the series versus the series lagged one time unit. Does the plot suggest that the lag 1 autocorrelation is a useful measure of the dependence in the series?
  (c) Fit an AR(1) model to this series. Check the residuals for any lack of fit or lack of normality.
  (d) Fit an AR(2) model to the series. Does this model confirm the AR(1) model estimated and checked in part (c)?
  (e) Perform simple exponential smoothing on this series. Use smoothing coefficients of 0.1, 0.4, and 0.8. Plot the resulting smoothed series and compare them to the original series. (Filename: DEERE2.DAT.)

23B Monthly unit sales of motor homes by Winnebago Industries are listed below. A sequence plot of the logarithms of these data was presented in Exhibit 21.8F.

(a) Display a sequence plot of the month-to-month changes in log(sales). Are any patterns apparent?

(b) Now construct the sequence plot using plotting symbols that indicate the months as in Exhibit 2.12B. Are any patterns apparent now?

(c) Calculate the autocorrelation of log(sales) at lag 12 and interpret its magnitude. (These data are used again in Exercise 24C.)

```
# filename: WINNEBAG.DAT
# Monthly unit sales of motor homes
# Winnebago Industries, Forest City, Iowa
# November 1966 through February 1972
# (Source: H.V.Roberts, Data Analysis for Managers,
# Redwood City, CA: The Scientific Press, 1988)
# Jan  Feb  Mar  Apr  May  Jun  Jul  Aug  Sep  Oct  Nov  Dec
                                                    61   48 # 1966
    53   78   75   58  146  193  124  120  134   99  130  166 # 1967
   168  267  314  432  355  384  232  235  293  242  248  236 # 1968
   209  358  352  406  562  389  416  493  409  328  222  195 # 1969
   156  439  671  874  558  621  628  652  495  344  405  586 # 1970
   403  700  837 1224 1117 1214  762  846 1228  937 1396 1174 # 1971
   628 1753                                              # 1972
```

23C The data file below gives the number of new passenger cars registered in the United States annually for the years 1950 through 1988.

(a) Display the sequence plot of these data.

(b) Fit a quadratic time trend model to these data and check the residuals for autocorrelation at lag 1.

(c) Now display the sequence plot of the percent changes from year to year.

(d) Show that the mean rate of growth per year is 3.01% and the standard deviation of the growth rates is 14.75%.

(e) Show that the percent changes have roughly a normal-shaped distribution.

(f) Calculate the autocorrelation in the percent changes at lags 1, 2, and 3 and argue that these are small correlations. Combining the results of parts (c), (d), (e), and (f), the percent changes are said to behave as if they were drawn randomly and independently from a normal distribution with mean 3.01% and standard deviation 14.75%.

```
# filename: NEWCARS.DAT
# Annual new passenger car registrations in the U.S.
# 1951-1988, in 100,000s
# (Source: Survey of Current Business, various issues)
# (Read across, row by row)
  5061  4158  5739  5535  7170  5955  5982  4655  6041
  6577  5855  6939  7557  8065  9314  9009  8357  9404
  9447  8388  9831 10409 11351  8701  8262  9752 10826
 11946 10357  8761  8444  7754  8924 10129 10889 11140
 10122 10480
```

GLOSSARY FOR CHAPTER 23

AR(1) model	An autoregressive model in which the predictor variable is the response variable at the previous time point.
AR(2) model	An autoregressive model in which the two predictor variables are the response variable at the previous two time points.
Autocorrelation	Correlation between a series and its lagged values.

Autoregressive model	A time series model using lagged values of the response variable as predictor variables.
Differences	The series of changes from one time period to the next.
Distributed lag model	A model relating a response variable to the lagged values of a predictor variable.
Exponential smoothing	An ad hoc technique for smoothing out the random variation in a series.
Koyck (or geometric) model	A particular distributed lag model in which a response is related to an exponentially weighted combination of the predictor variable at many lags.
Lagged variable	A variable given by the value at a previous time point.
Linear time trend	Trend modelled as a straight line.
Quadratic time trend	Trend modelled as a quadratic curve in time.
Smoothing constant	The constant in exponential smoothing that determines the extent of the smoothing.

## CHAPTER 24

Seasonal Time Series

SEASONALITY

A *seasonal* phenomenon is one that occurs (more or less) with a regular period, such as every 12 months. Some seasonal phenomena are directly related to the seasons of the year. In the northern parts of the United States, the level of building construction is generally higher during the summer months when temperatures are more favorable to outdoor work. Other seasonal phenomena, such as the Christmas holidays, have a dramatic influence on economic series such as retail sales and levels of employment in certain industries. Employment levels are also affected by the seasonal influx of students into the summer job market. Since the seasonal phenomenon is frequently quite predictable, models that reflect seasonality should help analysts forecast the behavior of processes affected by seasonality.

A time series of average monthly temperatures in Dubuque, Iowa, over the years 1964 through 1975 is used to illustrate. The last year, 1975, is held out from all model building so that the model forecasts can be compared with the actual series values for that year. The data are listed in Exhibit 24.1A and the sequence plot is shown in Exhibit 24.1B. The seasonal pattern for this series is very regular, but no other patterns are apparent in the plot.

EXHIBIT 24.1A

Average Monthly
Temperatures for
Dubuque, Iowa—
1964–1975

```
# filename: TEMPDUB.DAT
# Average monthly temperatures in Dubuque, Iowa
# (Source: J.D.Cryer, Time Series Analysis,
# Boston: Duxbury, 1986)
# January 1964 through December 1975, n=144
# Jan  Feb  Mar  Apr  May  Jun  Jul  Aug  Sep  Oct  Nov  Dec
 24.7 25.7 30.6 47.5 62.9 68.5 73.7 67.9 61.1 48.5 39.6 20.0 # 1964
 16.1 19.1 24.2 45.4 61.3 66.5 72.1 68.4 60.2 50.9 37.4 31.1 # 1965
 10.4 21.6 37.4 44.7 53.2 68.0 73.7 68.2 60.7 50.2 37.2 24.6 # 1966
 21.5 14.7 35.0 48.3 54.0 68.2 69.6 65.7 60.8 49.1 33.2 26.0 # 1967
 19.1 20.6 40.2 50.0 55.3 67.7 70.7 70.3 60.6 50.7 35.8 20.7 # 1968
 14.0 24.1 29.4 46.6 58.6 62.2 72.1 71.7 61.9 47.6 34.2 20.4 # 1969
  8.4 19.0 31.4 48.7 61.6 68.1 72.2 70.6 62.5 52.7 36.7 23.8 # 1970
 11.2 20.0 29.6 47.7 55.8 73.2 68.0 67.1 64.9 57.1 37.6 27.7 # 1971
 13.4 17.2 30.8 43.7 62.3 66.4 70.2 71.6 62.1 46.0 32.7 17.3 # 1972
 22.5 25.7 42.3 45.2 55.5 68.9 72.3 72.3 62.5 55.6 38.0 20.4 # 1973
 17.6 20.5 34.2 49.2 54.8 63.8 74.0 67.1 57.7 50.8 36.8 25.5 # 1974
 20.4 19.6 24.6 41.3 61.8 68.5 72.0 71.1 57.3 52.5 40.6 26.2 # 1975
```

EXHIBIT 24.1B

Sequence Plot of
Average Monthly
Temperatures—
1964–1974

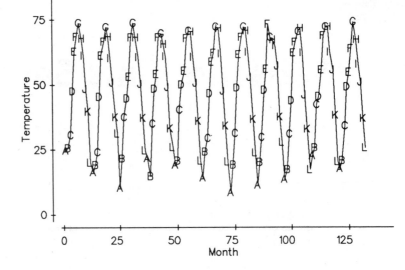

SECTION 24.2

EXERCISES

24.2A The data file below gives the monthly production of milk in pounds per cow for the period January 1962 through December 1975. Plot and interpret the sequence plot of this time series. Use appropriate plotting symbols so that seasonality may be looked for. Is there a general trend of any sort beyond seasonality?

```
# filename: MILKPROD.DAT
# Milk production in pounds per cow per month
# (Source: J.D.CRYER, Time Series Analysis,
# Boston: Duxbury, 1986)
# January 1962 through December 1975, n=168
 589 561 640 656 727 697 640 599 568 577 553 582 # 1962
 600 566 653 673 742 716 660 617 583 587 565 598 # 1963
 628 618 688 705 770 736 678 639 604 611 594 634 # 1964
 658 622 709 722 782 756 702 653 615 621 602 635 # 1965
```

```
677  635  736  755  811  798  735  697  661  667  645  688 # 1966
713  667  762  784  837  817  767  722  681  687  660  698 # 1967
717  696  775  796  858  826  783  740  701  706  677  711 # 1968
734  690  785  805  871  845  801  764  725  723  690  734 # 1969
750  707  807  824  886  859  819  783  740  747  711  751 # 1970
804  756  860  878  942  913  869  834  790  800  763  800 # 1971
826  799  890  900  961  935  894  855  809  810  766  805 # 1972
821  773  883  898  957  924  881  837  784  791  760  802 # 1973
828  778  889  902  969  947  908  867  815  812  773  813 # 1974
834  782  892  903  966  937  896  858  817  827  797  843 # 1975
```

24.2B The data set below gives the monthly bus ridership values for Portland, Oregon, during the period January 1973 through June 1982.

(a) Plot the sequence plot. Does there appear to be seasonality in the series? Are there any general trends upward or downward?

(b) Plot the sequence plot for the logarithms of the ridership values. Comment on the seasonality and other patterns shown in this plot.

```
# filename: PORTBUS.DAT
# Portland, Oregon, average monthly bus ridership (/100)
# (Source: J.D.Cryer, Time Series Analysis,
# Boston: Duxbury, 1986.)
# January 1973 through June 1982, n=114
# Jan  Feb  Mar  Apr  May  Jun  Jul  Aug  Sep  Oct  Nov  Dec
  648  646  639  654  630  622  617  613  661  695  690  707 # 1973
  817  839  810  789  760  724  704  691  745  803  780  761 # 1974
  857  907  873  910  900  880  867  854  928 1064 1103 1026 # 1975
 1102 1080 1034 1083 1078 1020  984  952 1033 1114 1160 1058 # 1976
 1209 1200 1130 1182 1152 1116 1098 1044 1142 1222 1234 1155 # 1977
 1286 1281 1224 1280 1228 1181 1156 1124 1152 1205 1260 1188 # 1978
 1212 1269 1246 1299 1284 1345 1341 1308 1448 1454 1467 1431 # 1979
 1510 1558 1536 1523 1492 1437 1365 1310 1441 1450 1424 1360 # 1980
 1429 1440 1414 1424 1408 1337 1258 1214 1326 1417 1417 1329 # 1981
 1461 1425 1419 1432 1394 1327                               # 1982
```

24.2C The data below are the total U.S. air passenger miles for the period January 1960 through December 1977.

(a) Display the sequence plot for this time series. Comment on any apparent seasonality. Are there any other general trends or patterns?

(b) Display the sequence plot of the logarithms of the series. Comment on the patterns seen here.

```
# filename: AIRMILES.DAT
# Monthly U.S. air passenger miles (millions)
# (Source: J.D.Cryer, Time Series Analysis,
# Boston, Duxbury, 1986)
# January 1960 through December 1977, n=216
# (Read across, row by row)
  2.42  2.14  2.28  2.50  2.44  2.72  2.71  2.74  2.55  2.49  2.13  2.28 # 1960
  2.35  1.82  2.40  2.46  2.38  2.83  2.68  2.81  2.54  2.54  2.37  2.54 # 1961
  2.62  2.34  2.68  2.75  2.66  2.96  2.66  2.93  2.70  2.65  2.46  2.59 # 1962
  2.75  2.45  2.85  2.99  2.89  3.43  3.25  3.59  3.12  3.16  2.86  3.22 # 1963
  3.24  2.95  3.32  3.29  3.32  3.91  3.80  4.02  3.53  3.61  3.22  3.67 # 1964
  3.75  3.25  3.70  3.98  3.88  4.47  4.60  4.90  4.20  4.20  3.80  4.50 # 1965
  4.40  4.00  4.70  5.10  4.90  5.70  3.90  4.20  5.10  5.00  4.70  5.50 # 1966
  5.30  4.60  5.90  5.50  5.40  6.70  6.80  7.40  6.00  5.80  5.50  6.40 # 1967
  6.20  5.70  6.40  6.70  6.30  7.80  7.60  8.60  6.60  6.50  6.00  7.60 # 1968
  7.00  6.00  7.10  7.40  7.20  8.40  8.50  9.40  7.10  7.00  6.60  8.00 # 1969
 10.45  8.81 10.61  9.97 10.69 12.40 13.38 14.31 10.90  9.98  9.20 10.94 # 1970
 10.53  9.06 10.17 11.17 10.84 12.09 13.66 14.06 11.14 11.10 10.00 11.98 # 1971
 11.74 10.27 12.05 12.27 12.03 13.95 15.10 15.65 12.47 12.29 11.52 13.08 # 1972
 12.50 11.05 12.94 13.24 13.16 14.95 16.00 16.98 13.15 12.88 11.99 13.13 # 1973
 12.99 11.69 13.78 13.70 13.57 15.12 15.55 16.73 12.68 12.65 11.18 13.27 # 1974
 12.64 11.01 13.30 12.19 12.91 14.90 16.10 17.30 12.90 13.36 12.26 13.93 # 1975
 13.94 12.75 14.19 14.67 14.66 16.21 17.72 18.15 14.19 14.33 12.99 15.19 # 1976
 15.09 12.94 15.46 15.39 15.34 17.02 18.85 19.49 15.61 16.16 14.84 17.04 # 1977
```

SEASONAL INDICATORS

A common method for incorporating seasonal effects into time series models is to use a regression model with **seasonal indicators**, which are binary (or indicator) predictor variables for the various months of the year. If their use appears warranted, other predictors such as linear time trends may be used in combination with the seasonal indicators.

For the temperature series, consider the model

$$y_t = \beta_0 + \gamma_1 \text{Jan}_t + \gamma_2 \text{Feb}_t + \gamma_3 \text{Mar}_t + \cdots + \gamma_{11} \text{Nov}_t + e_t \qquad \textbf{(24.1)}$$

where the binary seasonal indicators are defined as

$$\text{Jan}_t = \begin{cases} 1 & \text{if } t = \text{January} \\ 0 & \text{if } t \neq \text{January} \end{cases}$$

$$\text{Feb}_t = \begin{cases} 1 & \text{if } t = \text{February} \\ 0 & \text{if } t \neq \text{February} \end{cases}$$

$$\vdots$$

and
$$\text{Nov}_t = \begin{cases} 1 & \text{if } t = \text{November} \\ 0 & \text{if } t \neq \text{November} \end{cases}$$

Here $t = $ January means that time t corresponds to a January in some year. Similarly, $t = $ February, and so forth. Notice that a binary variable for December has not been included. The intercept term, β_0, provides the estimate of the December effect in the model. Then γ_1 is the adjustment to β_0 to be made for all Januarys. Similarly, γ_2 is the differential effect, either positive or negative, for all Februarys relative to the December level of β_0.

The basic results from fitting the model of Equation (24.1) to the temperature series are shown in Exhibit 24.3A. Here the intercept is estimated as 23.4°, which is interpreted as the predicted value for all Decembers. Januarys are predicted to be 7.15° colder than Decembers; Julys are predicted to be 48.3° warmer than

EXHIBIT 24.3A

Regression on Seasonal Indicator Variables— Monthly Temperature Series

The regression equation is

```
temperature = 23.4 - 7.15 Jan - 2.66 Feb + 9.78 Mar + 23.6 Apr
              + 34.3 May + 44.0 Jun + 48.3 Jul + 45.8 Aug
              + 38.0 Sep + 27.4 Oct + 12.9 Nov
```

Predictor	Coef	Stdev	t-ratio	p
Constant	23.409	1.018	23.00	0.000
Jan	-7.145	1.439	-4.96	0.000
Feb	-2.664	1.439	-1.85	0.067
Mar	9.782	1.439	6.80	0.000
Apr	23.591	1.439	16.39	0.000
May	34.345	1.439	23.86	0.000
Jun	44.000	1.439	30.57	0.000
Jul	48.282	1.439	33.55	0.000
Aug	45.764	1.439	31.80	0.000
Sep	37.955	1.439	26.37	0.000
Oct	27.427	1.439	19.06	0.000
Nov	12.882	1.439	8.95	0.000

s = 3.375   R-sq = 97.2%   R-sq(adj) = 97.0%

Decembers; and so on. This seasonal indicators model accounts for 97.2% of the variation in the observed temperature series.

A sequence plot of the residuals from this model is shown in Exhibit 24.3B. No seasonal patterns or other patterns are detected here. This conclusion is reinforced by the absence of autocorrelation in the residual series, which you may verify.

EXHIBIT 24.3B

Sequence Plot of Residuals from Seasonal Indicators Model for Temperature Series

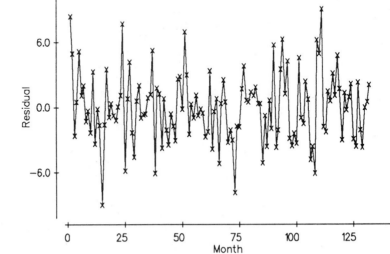

Forecasting is the next step. Forecasts for any month are easily obtained from the estimated regression coefficients as described above. The predictions, 2-standard-deviation prediction intervals, and the actual 1975 values are listed in Exhibit 24.3C. Only one actual value, an unusually cold March, misses being covered by the 12 prediction intervals. A graphic display of the prediction intervals is presented in Exhibit 24.3D.

EXHIBIT 24.3C

Predictions and Prediction Intervals for Temperature Series

Month	Prediction	Prediction Interval Lower	Prediction Interval Upper	1975 Actual Value	
Jan	16.264	9.282	23.245	20.4	
Feb	20.745	13.764	27.727	19.6	
Mar	33.191	26.209	40.173	24.6	← miss
Apr	47.000	40.018	53.982	41.3	
May	57.755	50.773	64.736	61.8	
Jun	67.409	60.427	74.391	68.5	
Jul	71.691	64.709	78.673	72.0	
Aug	69.173	62.191	76.155	71.1	
Sep	61.364	54.382	68.345	57.3	
Oct	50.836	43.855	57.818	52.5	
Nov	36.291	29.309	43.273	40.6	
Dec	23.409	16.427	30.391	26.2	

The seasonal indicators model implies a very regular and unchanging seasonality for a time series. Most series exhibit less seasonal regularity. Consider the time series of bus ridership in Iowa City, Iowa. The monthly averages of weekday ridership

EXHIBIT 24.3D

Actual Values,
Predictions, and
Prediction Intervals for
the Temperature Series

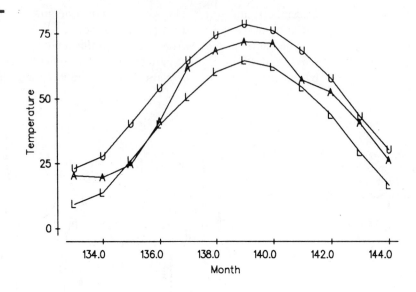

over the period September 1971 through December 1982 are listed in Exhibit 24.3E, and the corresponding sequence plot is shown in Exhibit 24.3F. Weather is an important seasonal factor affecting bus ridership. During warmer months potential bus riders have the option of walking or bicycling, but in winter their transportation options are reduced. Lower ridership in summer months is also due, in part, to the lower summer enrollment at the University of Iowa. Again, the last year of data, 1982, is held out from all of the model fitting so that the actual series values can be compared with the forecasts.

EXHIBIT 24.3E

Weekday Bus Ridership
in Iowa City, Iowa—
September 1971–
December 1982

```
# filename: ICBUS.DAT
# Weekday bus ridership, Iowa City, Iowa (monthly averages)
# (Source: J.D.Cryer, Time Series Analysis,
# Boston: Duxbury, 1986)
# September 1971 through December 1982, n=114
# (Read across, row by row)
  3603  4448  4734  4353  5438  5954  4838  4532  3599  3248  3230  2790
  4738  5043  5367  5262  5065  5824  4612  4823  3564  3651  3625  3170
  5022  5018  5326  5412  6345  6698  5605  5260  3789  4023  3775  3384
  5303  5506  5645  5168  6173  6776  5957  5777  3833  4200  3891  3595
  5862  5719  5957  5226  6467  6383  5589  5296  3943  4188  3673  3475
  5392  5583  5738  4944  6552  6451  5354  5081  3874  3973  3751  3621
  5328  5427  5419  5983  6568  8346  6800  6308  4857  4663  4499  3878
  6031  6325  6764  6929  7557  8182  6892  6860  5181  5462  5328  4331
  7279  7772  8262  7499  8081 10121  8745  8045  5906  5274  5283  4956
  7879  8289  8422  7832  7857 10008  8057  7791  6147  5438  5494  5253
  8154  8604  8832  7815 10179 11460  9641  9243  6824  6149  6161  5962
  9068  9538  9988  7916
```

The sequence plot in Exhibit 24.3F displays several important features. First, notice the upward trend in the general level of ridership over this time period. Second, notice that the variation in ridership levels over the later portion of the time period is much greater than in the earlier part of the series. This signals that a logarithm transformation should be used to try to equalize the variability around

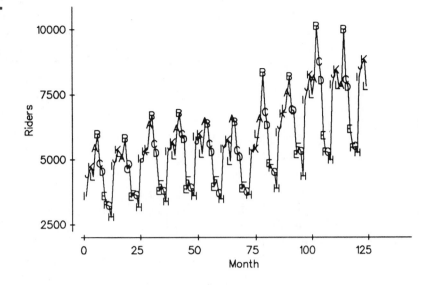

the general upward trend. Finally, a careful reading of the plot reveals that ridership values 12 months apart are quite similar relative to the general upward trend. Summer months are generally associated with lower ridership, and winter months are nearly always high ridership periods. This is seasonality.

Exhibit 24.3G gives the sequence plot of the logarithms of ridership values. Now the variation is quite similar in magnitude over the whole time period but the upward linear trend and the seasonality are still apparent. To better isolate the seasonality, a linear time trend is fit to log(ridership) and the nature of the residual series is considered.

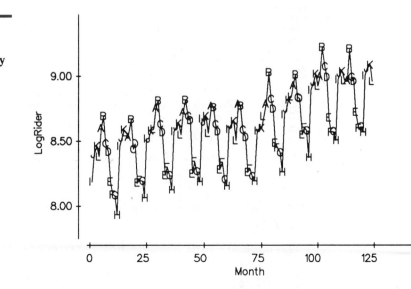

The sequence plot of residuals shown in Exhibit 24.3H shows that the seasonality accounts for a substantial portion of the variation in the series after the linear time trend has been fit to the series. It may be verified that for these residuals the autocorrelation is 0.829 at lag 12, 0.720 at lag 24, and 0.601 at lag 36. Models that account for this seasonality should lead to substantial improvement in forecasting

EXHIBIT 24.3H

Sequence Plot of
Residuals from Linear
Time Trend of Log
Ridership

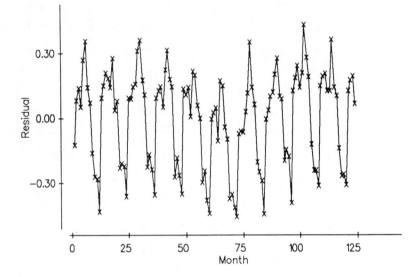

EXHIBIT 24.3I

Regression of Log
Ridership on Time
Trend and Seasonal
Indicator Variables

```
The regression equation is

LogRider = 8.37 + 0.00499 time + 0.125 Jan  + 0.233 Feb
              + 0.0475 Mar    + 0.0007 Apr - 0.297 May
              - 0.308 Jun     - 0.352 Jul  - 0.460 Aug
              - 0.0194 Sep    + 0.0262 Oct + 0.0618 Nov

Predictor      Coef        Stdev     t-ratio        p
Constant    8.36736      0.02634     317.72     0.000
time        0.0049891    0.0001936    25.76     0.000
Jan         0.12461      0.03369       3.70     0.000
Feb         0.23313      0.03368       6.92     0.000
Mar         0.04749      0.03368       1.41     0.161
Apr         0.00073      0.03368       0.02     0.983
May        -0.29683      0.03367      -8.81     0.000
Jun        -0.30835      0.03367      -9.16     0.000
Jul        -0.35235      0.03367     -10.46     0.000
Aug        -0.45976      0.03368     -13.65     0.000
Sep        -0.01935      0.03287      -0.59     0.557
Oct         0.02620      0.03286       0.80     0.427
Nov         0.06177      0.03286       1.88     0.063

s = 0.07707    R-sq = 93.0%    R-sq(adj) = 92.3%

Time    Fit     Stdev.Fit   95% Prediction Interval
125   9.11560    0.02752     (8.95341,9.27780)
126   9.22912    0.02752     (9.06692,9.39132)
127   9.04847    0.02752     (8.88627,9.21067)
128   9.00669    0.02752     (8.84449,9.16889)
129   8.71412    0.02752     (8.55192,8.87632)
130   8.70759    0.02752     (8.54539,8.86979)
131   8.66858    0.02752     (8.50638,8.83077)
132   8.56616    0.02752     (8.40396,8.72836)
133   9.01156    0.02710     (8.84964,9.17348)
134   9.06210    0.02710     (8.90018,9.22402)
135   9.10265    0.02710     (8.94073,9.26457)
136   9.04587    0.02710     (8.88395,9.20780)
```

and, more generally, will explain considerably more of the variation in such time series.

Exhibit 24.3I gives the regression results for the linear time trend, seasonal indicators model applied to the Log Ridership series. This exhibit also gives the predicted values and 2-standard-deviation prediction intervals for the next year corresponding to $t = 125, 126, \ldots, 136$. (Many more digits are shown here than would be reported in a summary of the results.) In Exhibit 24.3J the sequence of fitted values is plotted to graphically demonstrate how the seasonality is superimposed on the upward linear trend.

Forecasts (plotted with F's) and actual series values (A's) for the held-out year are plotted in Exhibit 24.3K. As expected, the forecasts mimic the seasonality plus

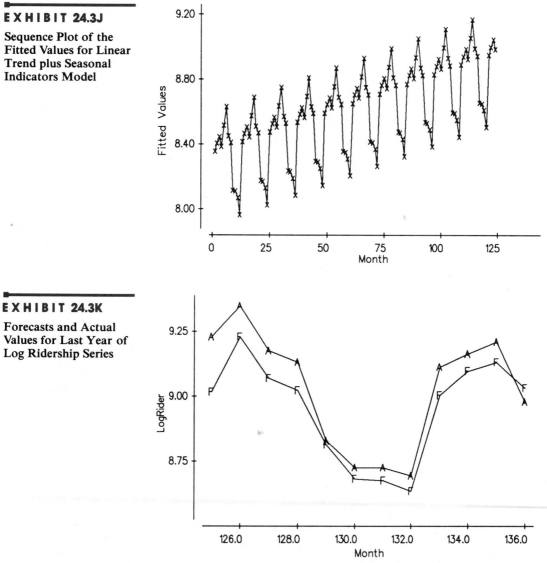

EXHIBIT 24.3J

Sequence Plot of the Fitted Values for Linear Trend plus Seasonal Indicators Model

EXHIBIT 24.3K

Forecasts and Actual Values for Last Year of Log Ridership Series

upward drift of the series. Unfortunately, the residuals from this model behave rather badly. The sequence plot of residuals appears in Exhibit 24.3L. The autocorrelation is 0.7 at lag 1, 0.6 at lag 2, 0.5 at lag 3, and so on. Given this behavior of the residuals, prediction intervals are not presented since their justification rests partly on the assumption of independent error terms. The seasonality and trend in this series are not regular enough to be adequately modelled by the seasonal indicators plus trend model. Other models for this series must be considered.

EXHIBIT 24.3L

Sequence Plot of
Residuals from Seasonal
Indicators Model of
Log Ridership Series

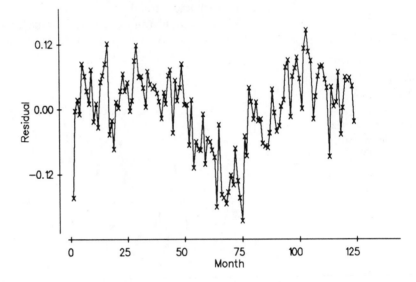

SECTION 24.4

EXERCISES

24.4A Refer to the milk production data set of Exercise 24.2A.
  (a) Fit a model to these data consisting of seasonal indicator variables. Plot a sequence plot of the residuals. Does this model capture most of the features of this time series?
  (b) Consider a model with seasonal indicators plus a linear time trend. Display the sequence plot of the residuals from this model. Of the models in parts (a) and (b), which captures the features of the data better?
  (c) Calculate the autocorrelations at lags 1 and 2 of the residuals from the model considered in part (b). Does the model considered in part (b) seem to adequately describe the series? (Filename: MILKPROD.DAT.)

24.4B Use the logarithms of the Portland, Oregon, bus ridership data given in Exercise 24.2B.
  (a) Fit a model that includes seasonal indicators and a linear time trend. Plot a sequence plot that overlays the log(series) and the fitted values. Do the fitted values follow the observed series?
  (b) Plot the sequence plot of the residuals. Do they appear random or are there patterns in them over time?
  (c) Evaluate the autocorrelations in the residuals at lags 1 and 2 and comment on their magnitude. (Filename: PORTBUS.DAT.)

24.4C Consider the U.S. air passenger miles data set in Exercise 24.2C. Use the logarithms of the data throughout this exercise.

(a) Fit a model that includes seasonal indicators plus a linear time trend. Plot a sequence plot that overlays the log(series) and the fitted values. Do the fitted values follow the observed series?

(b) Comment on the sequence plot of the residuals. Do they appear random or are there patterns in them over time?

(c) Calculate the autocorrelations in the residuals at lags 1 and 2 and comment on their size. (Filename: AIRMILES.DAT.)

SECTION 24.5

SEASONAL AUTOREGRESSION

Seasonal autoregressive models allow for seasonality differently than seasonal indicator models do. As in the earlier autoregressive models, the series y_t is regressed on itself at various lags, but now the seasonal lags $12, 24, \ldots$ play a special role. In **seasonal autoregression** the predictor variable is lagged at multiples of the seasonal period. A purely seasonal autoregressive model of order 1 (season) is expressed as

$$y_t = \beta_0 + \beta_{12} y_{t-12} + e_t \tag{24.2}$$

This model relates the behavior of y_t to the behavior of the series 12 months ago but only indirectly to the values $24, 36, \ldots$ months ago.

In addition to seasonality, the Log Ridership series also drifts upward over time. To account for this type of nonseasonal behavior, the model given in Equation (24.2) is extended:

$$y_t = \beta_0 + \beta_1 y_{t-1} + \beta_{12} y_{t-12} + e_t \tag{24.3}$$

This model incorporates both a seasonal relationship at lag 12 and a short-term relationship at lag 1.

Exhibit 24.5A displays the results of fitting such a model to the Log Ridership series. The seasonal autoregressive model estimated here says that the current value of Log Ridership is explained (predicted) by taking about 85% of the ridership of one year ago plus 13% of last month's value plus a constant term of 0.239. This simple three-parameter model (including the intercept term) accounts for 89.8% (adjusted) of the variation in the series. This should be compared to the 13-parameter seasonal indicators model, which had an R^2(adjusted) of 92.3%.

EXHIBIT 24.5A

Seasonal Autoregression
for Log Ridership Series

```
The regression equation is

LogRider = 0.239 + 0.127Lag1LogRider + 0.852Lag12LogRider

112 cases used; 12 cases contained missing values

Predictor           Coef      Stdev    t-ratio        p
Constant          0.2392     0.2779       0.86    0.391
Lag1LogRider      0.12693    0.04344      2.92    0.004
Lag12LogRider     0.85152    0.04456     19.11    0.000

s = 0.08507     R-sq = 90.0%     R-sq(adj) = 89.8%
```

Forecasts from the seasonal autoregressive model are obtained in a manner similar to those for earlier autoregressive models. Equation (24.3) is updated to time $t + 1$ as

$$y_{t+1} = \beta_0 + \beta_1 y_t + \beta_{12} y_{t-11} + e_{t+1} \tag{24.4}$$

Then, since e_{t+1} is independent of all observations up to time t, it is forecast by its mean of zero. At time t both y_t and y_{t-11} are available and the forecast one step ahead from time t is given by

$$\hat{y}_{t+1} = \beta_0 + \beta_1 y_t + \beta_{12} y_{t-11} \tag{24.5}$$

Replacing $t + 1$ by $t + 2$ in Equation (24.4) yields

$$y_{t+2} = \beta_0 + \beta_1 y_{t+1} + \beta_{12} y_{t-10} + e_{t+2} \tag{24.6}$$

However, at time t, y_{t+1} has not been observed. Two steps ahead is thus forecast using

$$\hat{y}_{t+2} = \beta_0 + \beta_1 \hat{y}_{t+1} + \beta_{12} y_{t-10} \tag{24.7}$$

In a similar fashion, forecasts any number of steps into the future may be produced one at a time.

Consider forecasting the bus ridership series:

$$
\begin{aligned}
\hat{y}_{124+1} &= 0.2392 + 0.12693 y_{124} + 0.85152 y_{113} \\
&= 0.2392 + 0.12693(8.96380) + 0.85152(8.96916) \\
&= 9.01439
\end{aligned}
$$

and

$$
\begin{aligned}
\hat{y}_{124+2} &= 0.2392 + 0.12693 \hat{y}_{124+1} + 0.85152 y_{114} \\
&= 0.2392 + 0.12693(9.01439) + 0.85152(9.21114) \\
&= 9.22687
\end{aligned}
$$

and so forth. Exhibit 24.5B lists the forecasts and actual values for a full year; the sequence plot is shown in Exhibit 24.5C. These results should be compared to those obtained with the seasonal indicators model, which were displayed in Exhibit 24.3K.

		1982
EXHIBIT 24.5B	Month	Forecast	Actual Value

EXHIBIT 24.5B

Forecasts and Actual Values for Log Ridership in 1982

Month	Forecast	Actual Value
Jan	9.01439	9.22808
Feb	9.22687	9.34662
Mar	9.06919	9.17378
Apr	9.02058	9.13162
May	8.81260	8.82820
Jun	8.68185	8.72404
Jul	8.67398	8.72599
Aug	8.63478	8.69316
Sep	9.00422	9.11251
Oct	9.09686	9.16304
Nov	9.13089	9.20914
Dec	9.03104	8.97664

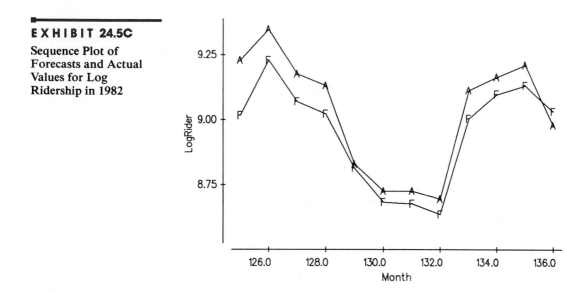

Exhibit 24.5D gives the sequence plot of the residuals from the fitted seasonal autoregressive model. Unfortunately, they are unacceptably autocorrelated. The autocorrelation is 0.51 at lag 1, 0.45 at lag 2, and 0.26 at lag 3. In the autoregression there are 112 cases after lagging, and these estimated autocorrelations of the residuals may be compared to their approximate standard error of $1/\sqrt{112} = 0.09$. Although the seasonal autoregression is an improvement over the seasonal indicators model, the search for a better model continues.

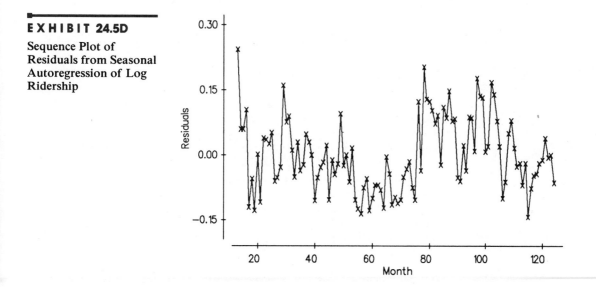

EXERCISES

24.6A Using the data for Deere & Co. monthly sales of oil filters given in Exhibits 2.6A and 6.8A, fit the seasonal AR model $\hat{y}_t = \beta_0 + \beta_1 y_{t-12}$. Compare the residual standard deviation s with the RMSPE of 837 for the model $\hat{y}_t = y_{t-12}$ suggested in Section 6.8. Does this model appear to be superior to the earlier one? If so, state how you expect the model to perform predictively. (Filename: OILFILT.DAT.)

24.6B Refer to the Deere & Co. oil-filter sales data of Exhibits 2.6A and 6.8A. Fit the mixed AR model $\hat{y}_t = \beta_0 + \beta_1 y_{t-1} + \beta_2 y_{t-12}$. Compare the fitted values, residuals, and residual standard deviation s of this model to those of the model in Exercise 24.6A. Does this model appear superior? (Filename: OILFILT.DAT.)

24.6C Use the milk production time series listed in Exercise 24.2A.
(a) Fit the model $y_t = \beta_0 + \beta_2 y_{t-1} + \beta_{12} y_{t-12} + e_t$.
(b) Check the sequence plot of the residuals from the model for lack of randomness.
(c) Calculate the autocorrelations of the residuals at lag 1 and 2 and comment on their magnitude. (Filename: MILKPROD.DAT.)
(d) Compare the model of this exercise to the one considered in Exercise 24.4A. Which does a better job of capturing the structure in the observed time series?

24.6D Use the logarithms of the Portland, Oregon, bus ridership series given in Exercise 24.2B.
(a) Fit the seasonal autoregressive model $y_t = \beta_0 + \beta_1 y_{t-1} + \beta_{12} y_{t-12} + e_t$.
(b) Check the sequence plot of the residuals for patterns indicating lack of randomness.
(c) Calculate the autocorrelations of the residuals at lag 1 and 2 and comment on their size.
(d) Compare the autoregressive model of this exercise to the seasonal indicators model of Exercise 24.4B. Which does a better job of capturing the structure in the observed time series? (Filename: PORTBUS.DAT.)

24.6E Use the logarithms of the U.S. air passenger miles time series given in Exercise 24.2C.
(a) Fit the model $y_t = \beta_0 + \beta_1 y_{t-1} + \beta_{12} y_{t-12} + e_t$.
(b) Check the sequence plot of the residuals for patterns indicating lack of randomness.
(c) Calculate the autocorrelations of the residuals at lag 1 and 2 and comment on their size.
(d) Compare the autoregressive model of this exercise to the seasonal indicators model of Exercise 24.4C. Which does a better job of capturing the structure in the observed time series? (Filename: AIRMILES.DAT.)

24.6F Consider the monthly Dubuque temperature series listed in Exhibit 24.1A.
(a) Fit a seasonal autoregression of the form $y_t = \beta_0 + \beta_1 y_{t-1} + \beta_{12} y_{t-12} + e_t$. Compare the results to those given in Exhibit 24.3A, where a seasonal indicators model is used.
(b) Now fit the model $y_t = \beta_0 + \beta_{12} y_{t-12} + \beta_{24} y_{t-24} + e_t$ [a seasonal AR(2) model]. Compare this model to the one obtained in part (a) and to the model reported in Exhibit 24.3A. (Filename: TEMPDUB.DAT.)

24.6G Consider the hourly wages time series shown in Exhibit 23.2A. In Exercise 23.7D you saw that an AR(1) model fit the series better than a model with a fixed linear or quadratic trend but that the residuals showed signs of seasonality. Now fit the seasonal autoregressive model: $y_t = \beta_0 + \beta_1 y_{t-1} + \beta_{12} y_{t-12} + e_t$. Compare this model to earlier models. In particular, check the autocorrelation in the residuals at the seasonal lags 12 and 24. (Filename: APAWAGES.DAT.)

24.6H Fit a simple AR(1) model, $y_t = \beta_0 + \beta_1 y_{t-1} + e_t$, to the logarithms of the bus ridership series given in Exhibit 24.3E.

(a) Plot the sequence of residuals. Are any patterns evident?
(b) Calculate the autocorrelation in the residuals obtained in part (a) at lags 12 and 24. Comment. (Filename: ICBUS.DAT.)

SECTION 24.7

SEASONAL EXPONENTIAL SMOOTHING

The ideas of exponential smoothing can be extended to seasonal time series without difficulty. **Winter's additive model** for seasonal exponential smoothing assumes that the series may be written as

$$y_t = \beta_{0,t} + \beta_{1,t}t + S_t + e_t \tag{24.8}$$

where $\beta_{0,t}$ is a (slowly) changing intercept term, $\beta_{1,t}$ is a (slowly) changing slope, S_t is a seasonal term that changes (slowly) from year to year, and e_t is the error term. For definiteness, the seasonal terms are assumed to add to zero over any given consecutive 12 months so that they measure the seasonal effect around the overall level of $\beta_{0,t}$.

As in our previous encounter with exponential smoothing, initial estimates for the parameters are obtained based on the initial behavior of the series and the estimates are then smoothed according to equations that put a certain amount of weight on old estimates of the parameters and complementary weight on the current information. In seasonal exponential smoothing there are three smoothing equations:

$$\hat{\beta}_{0,t+1} = \alpha_1(y_{t+1} - \hat{S}_{t-11}) + (1 - \alpha_1)(\hat{\beta}_{0,t} + \hat{\beta}_{1,t}) \tag{24.9}$$

$$\hat{\beta}_{1,t+1} = \alpha_2(\hat{\beta}_{0,t+1} - \hat{\beta}_{0,t}) + (1 - \alpha_2)\hat{\beta}_{1,t} \tag{24.10}$$

and $$\hat{S}_{t+1} = \alpha_3(y_{t+1} - \hat{\beta}_{0,t+1}) + (1 - \alpha_3)\hat{S}_{t-11} \tag{24.11}$$

where α_1, α_2, and α_3 are three smoothing constants each chosen in the interval $(0, 1)$. Each of these equations has an intuitive meaning. The intercept at time $t + 1$, $\hat{\beta}_{0,t+1}$, is updated by smoothing the current, deseasonalized observation, $y_{t+1} - \hat{S}_{t-11}$, with what would have been the new "intercept," $\hat{\beta}_{0,t} + \hat{\beta}_{1,t}$, at time $t + 1$. The new slope at time $t + 1$, $\hat{\beta}_{1,t+1}$, is updated by smoothing the old slope, $\hat{\beta}_{1,t}$, with a new estimate of slope, $\hat{\beta}_{0,t+1} - \hat{\beta}_{0,t}$. Finally, the seasonal effect at time $t + 1$ is updated by combining the old seasonal effect of one year ago, $\hat{S}_{t-11}$, with a current estimate of the seasonal effect, $y_{t+1} - \hat{\beta}_{0,t+1}$.

Forecasts of future values from time t using this model are obtained from the equations

$$\hat{y}_{t+l} = \hat{\beta}_{0,t} + \hat{\beta}_{1,t}l + \hat{S}_{t+l-12} \quad \text{for } l = 1, 2, \ldots, 12 \tag{24.12}$$

$$\hat{y}_{t+l} = \hat{\beta}_{0,t} + \hat{\beta}_{1,t}l + \hat{S}_{t+l-24} \quad \text{for } l = 12, 13, \ldots, 24 \tag{24.13}$$

and so forth. In words, the current linear time trend is projected and then adjusted according to the appropriate seasonal effect corresponding to the month being forecast.

INITIALIZATION OF SEASONAL EXPONENTIAL SMOOTHING

Seasonal exponential smoothing, exponential smoothing that accounts for seasonality, may be initialized by several different methods. We recommend fitting a seasonal indicators plus linear trend model to the first 24 observations. The seasonal indicator variables are modified by subtracting the binary variable Dec_t from each of the binary variables Jan_t, Feb_t,..., Nov_t and regressing on $Jan(mod)_t = Jan_t - Dec_t$, $Feb(mod)_t = Feb_t - Dec_t$,..., $Nov(mod)_t = Nov_t - Dec_t$ in addition to the time variable $1, 2,..., 24$. With this modification the initial December seasonal $\hat{S}_{12,0}$ is the negative of the sum of the other initial seasonals, that is

$$\hat{S}_{12,0} = -(\hat{S}_{1,0} + \hat{S}_{2,0} + \cdots + \hat{S}_{11,0})$$

This ensures that the seasonals add to zero and have the proper interpretation as seasonal effects above or below the general level of β_0. The initial values $\hat{\beta}_{0,0}$ and $\hat{\beta}_{1,0}$ are taken as the intercept and slope estimates from the initial regression.

Exhibit 24.7A displays the regression results needed to initialize seasonal exponential smoothing of the Log Ridership series. The values $\hat{\beta}_{0,0} = 8.28176$, $\hat{\beta}_{1,0} = 0.006848$, $\hat{S}_{1,0} = -0.00325$, $\hat{S}_{2,0} = 0.12644$,..., $\hat{S}_{11,0} = -0.26025$ are in the left-hand column. Then $\hat{S}_{12,0} = -(-0.00325 + 0.12644 + \cdots - 0.26025) = -0.40738$ is obtained. Since this process can be computer automated, little thought or hand calculation is needed in the end.

E X H I B I T 24.7A

Initialization of
Seasonal Exponential
Smoothing for Log
Ridership

```
The regression equation is

LogRider = 8.28 + 0.00685 time - 0.0033 Jan(mod)
          + 0.126 Feb(mod)  + 0.182 Mar(mod) + 0.123 Apr(mod)
          + 0.209 May(mod)  + 0.317 Jun(mod) + 0.0896 Jul(mod)
          + 0.0724 Aug(mod) - 0.201 Sep(mod) - 0.247 Oct(mod)
          - 0.260 Nov(mod)
```

Predictor	Coef	Stdev	t-ratio	p
Constant	8.28176	0.03433	241.23	0.000
time	0.006848	0.002476	2.77	0.018
Jan(mod)	-0.00325	0.05112	-0.06	0.950
Feb(mod)	0.12644	0.05052	2.50	0.029
Mar(mod)	0.18188	0.05003	3.64	0.004
Apr(mod)	0.12320	0.04966	2.48	0.031
May(mod)	0.20855	0.04941	4.22	0.001
Jun(mod)	0.31685	0.04929	6.43	0.000
Jul(mod)	0.08955	0.04929	1.82	0.097
Aug(mod)	0.07241	0.04941	1.47	0.171
Sep(mod)	-0.20095	0.04966	-4.05	0.002
Oct(mod)	-0.24705	0.05003	-4.94	0.000
Nov(mod)	-0.26025	0.05052	-5.15	0.000

```
s = 0.07278    R-sq = 94.4%    R-sq(adj) = 88.3%
```

CHOICE OF SMOOTHING CONSTANTS

Values for three **smoothing constants**, constants that control the degree of smoothing in exponential smoothing procedures, need to be selected to carry out Winter's seasonal exponential smoothing procedure. Even with modern computers, calculating the RMSPE for a large number of values of *all three* smoothing constants can be prohibitive. Recall that in nonseasonal situations the RMSPE is usually quite flat over a broad range of values of the smoothing constant. (Review Exhibit 23.8I and

23.8O.) The choice of value of the smoothing constant is not extremely critical to the smoothing procedure. However, since smoothing of the seasonal effects takes place over several years rather than over several months, past information on seasonal effects should not be discounted too quickly; that is, a larger smoothing constant is suggested for seasonal effects than for nonseasonal effects. A compromise which we recommend consists of simply using $\alpha_1 = \alpha_2 = 0.1$ and $\alpha_3 = 0.4$.

With this choice the Log Ridership series has been smoothed as shown in Exhibit 24.7B. The calculations proceed according to Equations (24.9–24.11) with the initial values obtained earlier. From Equation (24.9),

$$\hat{\beta}_{0,1} = 0.1(y_1 - \hat{S}_{-11,0}) + 0.9(\hat{\beta}_{0,0} + \hat{\beta}_{1,0})$$
$$= 0.1[8.18952 - (-0.003251)] + 0.9(8.28176 + 0.0068476) = 8.27902$$

EXHIBIT 24.7B

Seasonal Exponential Smoothing with $\alpha_1 = 0.1$, $\alpha_2 = 0.1$, and $\alpha_3 = 0.4$

t	LogRider	Intercept	Slope	Seasonal	Fitted
-11	*	*	*	-0.003251	*
-10	*	*	*	0.126439	*
-9	*	*	*	0.181883	*
-8	*	*	*	0.123204	*
-7	*	*	*	0.208551	*
-6	*	*	*	0.316846	*
-5	*	*	*	0.089554	*
-4	*	*	*	0.072405	*
-3	*	*	*	-0.200952	*
-2	*	*	*	-0.247050	*
-1	*	*	*	-0.260249	*
0	*	8.28176	0.0068476	-0.407378	*
1	8.18952	8.27903	0.0058892	-0.037753	8.28536
2	8.40021	8.28380	0.0057777	0.122426	8.41136
3	8.46253	8.28869	0.0056883	0.178665	8.47146
4	8.37862	8.29048	0.0052988	0.109179	8.41758
5	8.60117	8.30546	0.0062671	0.243413	8.50433
6	8.69182	8.31805	0.0068995	0.339614	8.62857
7	8.48426	8.33193	0.0075971	0.114664	8.41451
8	8.41892	8.34022	0.0076670	0.074921	8.41193
9	8.18841	8.35204	0.0080817	-0.186022	8.14694
10	8.08579	8.35739	0.0078089	-0.256869	8.11307
11	8.08024	8.36273	0.0075617	-0.269146	8.10495
12	7.93380	8.36738	0.0072705	-0.417860	7.96291
13	8.46337	8.38730	0.0085352	0.007778	8.33690
14	8.52576	8.39658	0.0086102	0.125126	8.51826
15	8.58802	8.40561	0.0086518	0.180166	8.58386
16	8.56827	8.41874	0.0091002	0.125317	8.52344
17	8.53011	8.41373	0.0076887	0.192600	8.67126
18	8.66974	8.41229	0.0067758	0.306750	8.76103
19	8.43642	8.40933	0.0058027	0.079632	8.53373
20	8.48115	8.41424	0.0057137	0.071715	8.49006
21	8.17864	8.41443	0.0051606	-0.205929	8.23394
22	8.20276	8.42359	0.0055609	-0.242456	8.16272
23	8.19561	8.43271	0.0059169	-0.256329	8.16001
24	8.06149	8.44270	0.0063240	-0.403201	8.02077
⋮	⋮	⋮	⋮	⋮	⋮
115	8.99430	8.91975	0.0049058	0.126249	9.09004
116	8.96072	8.91868	0.0043082	0.074322	9.02050
117	8.72372	8.92384	0.0043932	-0.204710	8.71522
118	8.60117	8.91974	0.0035443	-0.272733	8.68606
119	8.61141	8.91960	0.0031756	-0.288288	8.64827
120	8.56656	8.92645	0.0035432	-0.379744	8.52980
121	9.00626	8.93119	0.0036625	0.068632	8.99433
122	9.05998	8.93700	0.0038773	0.111383	9.03850
123	9.08614	8.94230	0.0040193	0.136170	9.07193
124	8.96380	8.94102	0.0034900	0.051367	9.01674

Similarly, for the slope update,

$$\hat{\beta}_{1,1} = 0.1(\hat{\beta}_{0,1} - \hat{\beta}_{0,0}) + 0.9\hat{\beta}_{1,0}$$
$$= 0.1(8.27902 - 8.28176) + 0.9(0.0068476) = 0.0058888.$$

Finally, the first seasonal update is

$$\hat{S}_1 = 0.4(y_1 - \hat{\beta}_{0,1}) + 0.6\hat{S}_{-11,0}$$
$$= 0.4(8.18952 - 8.27902) + 0.6(-0.003251) = -0.037751$$

At each time point the updating is continued until the end of the series is reached.

The *fitted value at time t* is given by the one-step-ahead forecast using data only through time $t - 1$. From Equation (24.12) the fitted value is

$$\hat{y}_t = \hat{\beta}_{0,t-1} + \hat{\beta}_{1,t-1} + \hat{S}_{t-12} \qquad \textbf{(24.14)}$$

Once seasonal exponential smoothing is complete, a forecast may be made using Equation (24.12):

$$\hat{y}_{124+1} = \hat{\beta}_{0,124} + 1\hat{\beta}_{1,124} + \hat{S}_{124-11}$$
$$= 8.94102 + 0.0034900 + 0.138557 = 9.083067$$

and $\qquad \hat{y}_{124+2} = \hat{\beta}_{0,124} + 2\hat{\beta}_{1,124} + \hat{S}_{124-10}$
$$= 8.94102 + 2(0.0034900) + 0.317979 = 9.265979$$

and so on. Forecasts and actual values for 1982 are listed in Exhibit 24.7C and plotted in Exhibit 24.7D.

EXHIBIT 24.7C

Actual Values and Forecasts from Seasonal Exponential Smoothing

Month	Forecast	1982 Actual Value
Jan	9.08307	9.22808
Feb	9.26598	9.34662
Mar	9.07774	9.17378
Apr	9.02930	9.13162
May	8.75376	8.82820
Jun	8.68923	8.72404
Jul	8.67716	8.72599
Aug	8.58920	8.69316
Sep	9.04106	9.11251
Oct	9.08731	9.16304
Nov	9.11558	9.20914
Dec	9.03427	8.97664

Again the forecasts nicely follow the seasonal pattern and upward trend in the historic data. The residual standard deviation here is 0.0738, which is marginally smaller than the corresponding quantity for the time trend, seasonal indicators model of Exhibit 24.3I. The residual standard deviation for the seasonal autoregressive model of Exhibit 24.5A was a little larger, at 0.08507. However, the residuals here still contain significant autocorrelation. The sequence plot of the residuals is shown in Exhibit 24.7E. The autocorrelation is 0.42 at lag 1 and 0.33 at lag 2.

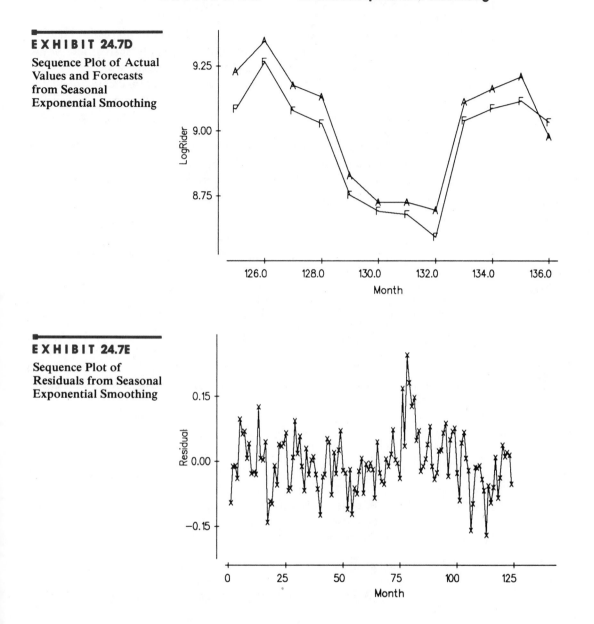

EXHIBIT 24.7D

Sequence Plot of Actual Values and Forecasts from Seasonal Exponential Smoothing

EXHIBIT 24.7E

Sequence Plot of Residuals from Seasonal Exponential Smoothing

EXTERNAL RMSPE

To compare the forecasting ability of the three models considered for the Log Ridership series, the external RMSPE for each of them must be evaluated. Since data are reasonably plentiful, the 12 months of 1982 have been held out from the model-building process. The true test of a forecasting model is its ability to generate accurate forecasts on new data. The RMSPE applied to new data is called the **external RMSPE**. Using December 1981 as the last available observation, each of the 12 months of 1982 is forecast. The prediction errors are the actual values for 1982 minus the values that the model forecasts. RMSPE is then obtained as always for these external prediction errors. Exhibit 24.7F lists the external RMSPE for each method considered in this chapter: regression with seasonal indicator predictor variables, seasonal autoregression, and seasonal exponential smoothing. On the basis of external RMSPE, the seasonal autoregression is slightly better than regression with seasonal indicators, and the seasonal exponential smoothing is better than either of the other methods by a worthwhile margin. Recall, however, that all three of these methods have substantial autocorrelation in their residuals. A model incorporating seasonal differencing that produces acceptable residuals for these data is discussed in Section 24.9.

EXHIBIT 24.7F

External RMSPE for Three Methods

Method	Mean PE	Standard Deviation PE	RMSPE
Seasonal indicators	0.086193	0.058651	0.104376
Seasonal autoregression	0.076298	0.065186	0.100352
Seasonal exponential smoothing	0.072430	0.049662	0.087820

SECTION 24.8

EXERCISES

24.8A Consider the milk production series of Exercise 24.2A.
  (a) Using the smoothing constants $\alpha_1 = \alpha_2 = 0.1$ and $\alpha_3 = 0.4$, find the exponentially smoothed series.
  (b) Plot the smoothed series and the original on the same sequence plot. Comment on the appearance.
  (c) Plot the sequence of residuals from the smoothed series. Do they appear random? (Filename: MILKPROD.DAT.)

24.8B Use the series of logarithms of bus ridership values for Portland, Oregon. The data are in Exercise 24.2B.
  (a) Using the smoothing constants $\alpha_1 = \alpha_2 = 0.1$ and $\alpha_3 = 0.4$, find the exponentially smoothed series.
  (b) Plot the smoothed series and the original on the same sequence plot. Comment on the appearance.
  (c) Plot the sequence plot of residuals from the smoothed series. Do they appear random? (Filename: PORTBUS.DAT.)

24.8C The series of monthly U.S. air passenger miles is given in Exercise 24.2C. Use the logarithms of these values.
  (a) Find the exponentially smoothed series using smoothing constants $\alpha_1 = \alpha_2 = 0.1$ and $\alpha_3 = 0.4$.
  (b) Overlay the smoothed series and the original on the same sequence plot. Comment on the appearance.
  (c) Display the sequence plot of residuals from the smoothed series. Do they appear random? (Filename: AIRMILES.DAT.)

SEASONAL DIFFERENCING

Chapter 23 and earlier chapters showed that month-to-month changes in some series are more easily modelled than the original series values. These changes are commonly called *differences*. Series with moderate to strong seasonality, but not as regular as the seasonality shown in the temperature series of Exhibit 24.1B, may frequently be better modelled by considering season-to-season changes called **seasonal differences**. That is, the changes from one January to the next, one February to the next, and so forth are considered. In symbols the seasonally differenced series is

$$z_t = y_t - y_{t-12} \tag{24.15}$$

The seasonally differenced series may then be modelled using any of the previous models, such as autoregression on lagged variables or seasonal indicators and trends.

Usually such series also exhibit some slow drift or nonseasonal trend. In those cases a nonseasonal, month-to-month difference will also be necessary to obtain a series that may be adequately modelled. Calculating a nonseasonal difference of the series z_t, the doubly dfferenced series w_t is obtained:

$$w_t = z_t - z_{t-1} = (y_t - y_{t-12}) - (y_{t-1} - y_{t-13}) \tag{24.16}$$

A model that works well for a large variety of seasonal series and captures any short-term and seasonal variation remaining after differencing is given by

$$w_t = \beta_0 + \beta_1 w_{t-1} + \beta_{12} w_{t-12} + e_t \tag{24.17}$$

that is, *after* taking seasonal and nonseasonal differences, the series satisfies a mixed nonseasonal, seasonal AR model as in Equation (24.3).

Exhibit 24.9A displays the autoregression results when Equation (24.17) is estimated for the Log Ridership series. Both the lag 1 and lag 12 predictors are statistically significant with large t ratios. The residual standard deviation of $s = 0.06641$ is smaller than that obtained earlier in Exhibit 24.5A for the seasonal autoregressive model ($s = 0.08507$), for the time trend plus seasonal indicators model of Exhibit 24.3I ($s = 0.07707$), and for exponential smoothing ($s = 0.0738$).

In addition, the residuals are well behaved with regard to autocorrelation. Exhibit 24.9B shows the sequence plot of residuals. No patterns are indicated there. Calculation shows that the autocorrelation in the residuals at lag 1 is only -0.087 and only -0.088 at lag 12. Further investigation, which is left for the exercises, shows that no important autocorrelation exists at any lags and that the assumption of normal errors is quite plausible.

Forecasting using the model in Equation (24.17) proceeds as with earlier autoregressive models. Using Equations (24.16) and (24.17) with t replaced by $t + 1$ yields

$$(y_{t+1} - y_t) - (y_{t-11} - y_{t-12}) = \beta_0 + \beta_1[(y_t - y_{t-1}) - (y_{t-12} - y_{t-13})]$$
$$+ \beta_{12}[(y_{t-11} - y_{t-12}) - (y_{t-23} - y_{t-24})] + e_t \tag{24.18}$$

EXHIBIT 24.9A

A Model for
Log Ridership
After Seasonal
and Nonseasonal
Differencing

```
The regression equation is

DDLogRider = - 0.00151 - 0.308 Lag1 - 0.281 Lag12

99 cases used; 25 cases contained missing values

Predictor      Coef       Stdev     t-ratio      p
Constant    -0.001513   0.006678     -0.23     0.821
Lag1        -0.30788    0.09116      -3.38     0.001
Lag12       -0.28111    0.08293      -3.39     0.001

s = 0.06641     R-sq = 20.1%     R-sq(adj) = 18.4%

Analysis of Variance

SOURCE       DF        SS          MS        F        p
Regression    2     0.106281   0.053141    12.05    0.000
Error        96     0.423443   0.004411
Total        98     0.529724
```

Note: DDLogRider is the seasonal and nonseasonal difference of the Log Ridership series.

EXHIBIT 24.9B

Sequence Plot of
Residuals from Seasonal
Difference Model

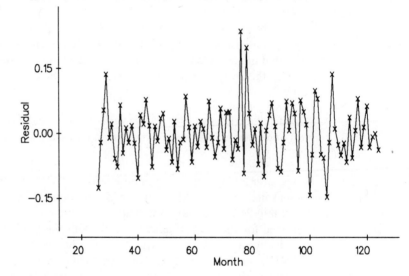

Then rewriting in forecast terms,

$$\hat{y}_{t+1} = \beta_0 + (1 + \beta_1)y_t - \beta_1 y_{t-1} + (1 + \beta_2)y_{t-11} - (1 + \beta_1 + \beta_2)y_{t-12}$$
$$+ \beta_1 y_{t-13} - \beta_2 y_{t-23} + \beta_2 y_{t-24}$$

(24.19)

This expression is long but easily implemented for forecasting purposes. Once $\hat{y}_{t+1}$ is available, forecasting two steps ahead uses a new version of Equation (24.19) with $t + 1$ replacing t throughout.

Exhibit 24.9C shows the forecasts and actual values for the 12 months of 1982 for the Log Ridership series. This should be compared to Exhibits 24.3K, 24.5C, and 24.7D for the earlier models. The mean prediction error for these 12 predictions is 0.12067, while the standard deviation of the prediction errors is 0.05006, leading to an RMSPE of 0.1306, which is somewhat larger than the values given in Ex-

EXHIBIT 24.9C

Actual and Forecast
Values for 1982 Log
Ridership: Seasonal
Differences Model

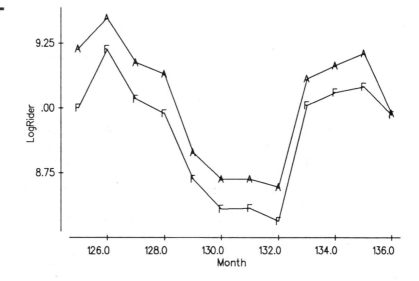

hibit 24.7F for the earlier models. Forecasts with the seasonal difference model could be described as giving biased predictions but with little variability in the prediction errors. All of the models considered seem to underpredict most of the time. In general, there is no guarantee that the model that performs best internally (here the seasonal difference model) will also perform best externally. All forecasting models must be monitored with regard to their ongoing performance in real forecasting and modified or updated as their real-world performance is observed.

SECTION 24.10

EXERCISES

24.10A Consider the seasonal differences model for the Log Ridership series of Exhibit 24.3E.
   (a) Carry out the regression calculations shown in Exhibit 24.9A. Check the autocorrelations in the residuals at lags 2, 3, 24, and 36.
   (b) Evaluate the normality of the error terms by looking at the residuals. In particular, display a histogram of the standardized residuals and a normal scores plot of the residuals. Comment on the plots.
   (c) Display the scatterplot of residuals versus fitted values and comment. (Filename: ICBUS.DAT.)

24.10B Use the logarithms of Portland, Oregon, bus ridership given in Exercise 24.2B.
   (a) Fit a seasonal differences model as in Equation (24.17).
   (b) Evaluate the autocorrelations in the residuals at lags 1, 2, 12, and 24. Comment.
   (c) Evaluate the normality of the error terms by looking at the residuals. In particular, display a histogram of the standardized residuals and a normal scores plot of the residuals. Comment on the plots.
   (d) Display the scatterplot of residuals versus fitted values and comment. (Filename: PORTBUS.DAT.)

24.10C Use the milk production series given in Exercise 24.2A.
   (a) Fit a seasonal differences model as in Equation (24.17).
   (b) Evaluate the autocorrelations in the residuals at lags 1, 2, 12, and 24. Comment.
   (c) Evaluate the normality of the error terms by looking at the residuals. In particular, display a histogram of the standardized residuals and a normal scores plot of the residuals. Comment on the plots.
   (d) Display the scatterplot of residuals versus fitted values and comment. (Filename: MILKPROD.DAT.)

24.10D Use the logarithms of the U.S. air passenger miles series as given in Exercise 24.2C.
   (a) Fit a seasonal differences model as in Equation (24.17).
   (b) Evaluate the autocorrelations in the residuals at lags 1, 2, 12, and 24. Comment.
   (c) Evaluate the normality of the error terms by looking at the residuals. In particular, display a histogram of the standardized residuals and a normal scores plot of the residuals. Comment on the plots.
   (d) Display the scatterplot of residuals versus fitted values and comment. (Filename: AIRMILES.DAT.)

S E C T I O N 24.11

SEASONAL ADJUSTMENT

In April 1982, then President Ronald Reagan announced that unemployment had just fallen by 88,000 workers in the preceding month. However, the Bureau of Labor Statistics (BLS) had reported an increase of 98,000 in the unemployment ranks. The president had reported actual numbers but the BLS was using so-called seasonally adjusted figures in an attempt to take into account the fact that unemployment typically increases from February to March. Seasonal adjustment is a somewhat controversial procedure. A rise in weekly hours worked in December does not necessarily mean an upturn in the economy has occurred, since increased hours are almost always worked in December. To avoid this misinterpretation, the BLS reports **seasonally adjusted** values, which attempt to compensate for this known seasonal variation. Exhibit 2.12B gave the sequence plot of the *unadjusted* monthly hours worked per week in the manufacturing sector. Exhibit 24.11A lists the corresponding seasonally adjusted values and Exhibit 24.11B displays the series values after seasonal adjustment. The 1982 recession is still apparent, but notice how the December values have been brought more into line with other monthly values.

E X H I B I T 24.11A

Seasonally Adjusted
Average Hours Worked
per Week in
Manufacturing

```
# filename: MANHRSSA.DAT
# Seasonally adjusted average hours worked per week (X10)
# Manufacturing, July 1982 through June 1987
# (Source: Survey of Current Business, September issues, 1982-1987.)
# Jul Aug Sep Oct Nov Dec Jan Feb Mar Apr May Jun
  391 390 388 389 390 390 397 392 395 401 400 401 # 1982-1983
  402 403 407 406 406 409 409 409 407 411 406 406 # 1983-1984
  405 405 406 405 405 406 406 401 404 402 404 404 # 1984-1985
  404 406 407 407 407 409 408 407 407 407 407 406 # 1985-1986
  406 408 408 407 408 408 409 411 409 406 410 410 # 1986-1987
```

EXHIBIT 24.11B

Seasonally Adjusted
Average Hours Worked
per Week

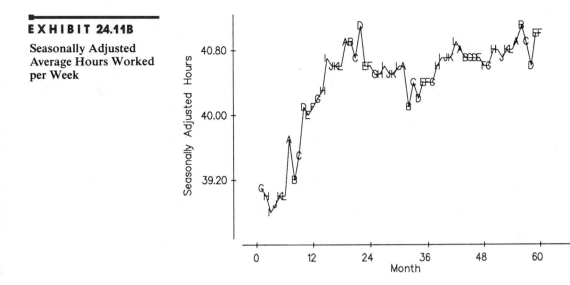

The actual adjustment procedures are complicated and a considerable current research effort is devoted to discovering better adjustment procedures. An idea of the size and direction of the adjustment may be seen by computing the ratios of unadjusted values to the adjusted values. Exhibit 24.11C gives the sequence plot of these ratios for the weekly hours data. December figures, which are typically higher than values for other months, are adjusted downward by 1.5% to 2%, whereas January, February, and July figures, typically low values, are adjusted upward by up to 1%. August, September, and October values are changed very little since their adjustment factors are about 1.

EXHIBIT 24.11C

Seasonal Adjustment
Factors

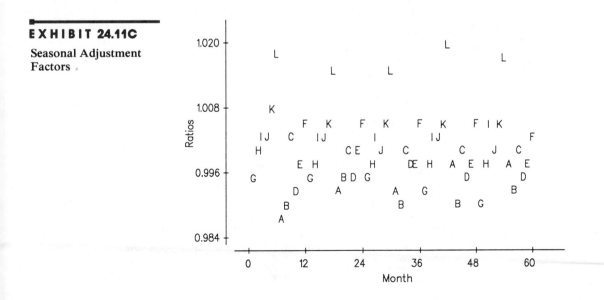

SUPPLEMENTARY EXERCISES FOR CHAPTER 24

24A Use the monthly total U.S. retail sales (in billions of dollars) for 1983 through 1987 first considered in Exercise 2B.

    (a) Fit a model to these data using 12 seasonal indicators plus a linear time trend and save the residuals from the model for further analysis.

    (b) Consider the autocorrelation in the residuals at lags 1, 2, and 12 and comment on their magnitude.

    (c) Construct a sequence plot of the residuals and comment on its appearance.

    (d) Does a normal scores plot of the residuals suggest a normal distribution for the errors in the model? (Filename: RETAIL.DAT.)

24B Consider the monthly retail sales data in Exercise 2B and Exercise 24A.

    (a) Fit a seasonal autoregressive model of the form $y_t = \beta_0 + \beta_1 y_{t-1} + \beta_{12} y_{t-12} + e_t$ to these data. Save the residuals from the model for further analysis.

    (b) Consider the autocorrelation in the residuals at lags 1, 2, and 12 and comment on their magnitude.

    (c) Construct a sequence plot of the residuals and comment on its appearance.

    (d) Does a normal scores plot of the residuals support the assumption of a normal distribution for the errors in the model?

    (e) Compare this model to the one discussed in Exercise 24A. (Filename: RETAIL.DAT.)

24C In Exercise 23B seasonality in the monthly unit sales of Winnebago motor homes was discovered. Consider a model based on ordinary and seasonal differences of the log(sales) data as in Equations (24.16) and (24.17).

    (a) Use regression to fit such a model to the sales data.

    (b) Assess the significance of both of the predictor variables.

    (c) On the basis of your results in part (b), drop one of the predictors and reestimate the simpler model, saving the residuals for further analysis.

    (d) Assess the adequacy of this model by looking at the scatterplot of residuals versus fitted values, checking the normality assumption, and calculating the autocorrelations of the residuals at lags 1 and 12. (Filename: WINNEBAG.DAT.)

24D The data file below gives monthly electric power usage in the United States over the period January 1983 through July 1989.

    (a) Compare the sequence plots of power usage and logarithms of power usage. Which should be used for further modelling?

    (b) Fit a model that predicts log(power) with lag 12 log(power). Interpret the output.

    (c) Check the residuals by plotting them against fitted values and by looking at their normality.

```
# filename: POWER.DAT
# Monthly electric power usage in the U.S.
# billions of kilowatt-hours, January 1983 to July 1989
# (Source: Survey of Current Business, various issues)
# (Read across, row by row)
#  Jan   Feb   Mar   Apr   May   Jun   Jul   Aug   Sep   Oct   Nov   Dec
  166.3 144.5 152.2 140.4 143.2 160.4 192.0 203.6 173.7 161.4 158.2 180.5
  186.9 161.7 169.7 151.1 160.4 180.9 193.8 204.2 174.3 170.1 168.1 174.2
  200.2 172.3 170.3 160.5 170.4 181.5 205.4 206.1 183.7 174.7 169.5 193.9
  195.9 169.1 168.4 159.6 171.1 188.8 218.6 204.0 185.5 176.3 173.3 213.6
  222.7 194.0 201.8 189.5 206.1 225.6 247.9 247.6 213.0 203.0 200.3 220.5
  237.6 216.8 213.8 195.8 208.2 232.5 257.2 267.4 220.0 210.4 209.4 232.6
  231.3 219.1 226.4 207.7 219.8 235.4 256.7
```

GLOSSARY FOR CHAPTER 24

External RMSPE	Root mean square prediction error for data external to the model building process.
Seasonal adjustment	A procedure applied to a time series in an attempt to account for known seasonality.
Seasonal autoregression	An autoregressive model with the predictor variable lagged at multiples of the seasonal period.
Seasonal differences·	The series of season to season changes.
Seasonal exponential smoothing	Exponential smoothing that accounts for seasonality.
Seasonal indicators	Binary variables indicating the various seasons.
Smoothing constants	Constants that control the degree of smoothing in exponential smoothing procedures.
Winter's additive model	A model that leads to seasonal exponential smoothing.

Statistics
in Organizations

## CHAPTER 25

A Perspective on Statistics in Organizations

SECTION 25.1

INTRODUCTION

People form organizations to achieve objectives. As time passes an organization's objectives are likely to increase in number and complexity.

■ **EXAMPLE 25.1A:** A local chess club may start as a group of chess enthusiasts who meet once a week in someone's living room. As the group grows, it seeks a larger meeting place. In time it may decide to join a national association, promote chess education in schools, sponsor tournaments, and invite chess masters to give lectures and exhibitions. Achieving these objectives requires increasing levels of organizational, fund-raising, and promotional activity. ■

Businesses also grow in this fashion. Examples are computer hardware and software companies that started with inventions created in someone's basement, and a hamburger stand that decided to specialize in fast, reliable service. Other organizations, such as governments, churches, not-for-profit hospitals, and so on, have similar histories.

Members of organizations typically achieve personal objectives, as when an employee earns a salary to support a family. However, if members gain little satisfaction from helping the organization to achieve its objectives, the basis for membership is weak. The discussion in this chapter is in terms of business firms. And it is a working assumption that employees want to help the firm achieve its objectives, at least because the employee may lose his or her job should the firm falter.

Effective management encourages never-ending improvement in the organization by helping employees find pride in their work and by valuing their participation in improvement efforts. From this point of view there is mutual reinforcement in the objectives of the firm and the objectives of its members.

SECTION 25.2

ORGANIZATIONAL STRUCTURE

Even though business firms vary widely in size, complexity, and organizational details, a few general terms apply to most firms. For example, a firm often has four levels of employees: top management, middle management, supervisors, and hourly workers. Not all firms have employees in these four categories, and some firms may find it necessary to define other levels. Such details are not pertinent here. Abstract theories invariably require modification when they are applied to specific cases. The concern here is to develop connections between management and science that will serve as useful guides to action.

Top management primarily seeks to find ways and means of ensuring the long-term survival and growth of the firm. This means finding new markets for existing products and services and finding new products and services that the firm can successfully offer for sale. It also means supporting the never-ending improvement of quality of all aspects of the firm's business. Top management creates, communicates, and supports the implementation of policy. Ideally, this means being in constant dialogue with all levels of the organization concerning the improvement of performance.

Middle management oversees the implementation of policy, including its communication throughout the firm. Middle managers make short-term decisions in the light of the long-term objectives set forth by top management. Middle management also plays a critical role in fostering communication throughout the organization. This includes identifying needs for training and authorizing the training that enables members of the firm to perform effectively and efficiently.

Supervisors oversee the daily activities of hourly workers. They help workers adhere to established procedures, at the same time encouraging workers to make suggestions for improvement. They also see that workers have proper training and materials to do their jobs. This includes clear instructions on what people's jobs are and what is considered acceptable performance in the job. In many cases, they are given responsibility for implementing policy as communicated by middle management.

Hourly workers primarily follow established work procedures. If given the opportunity, they may form groups to identify and work on solutions to problems (quality-control circles, for example). They may also be encouraged to make individual suggestions for improvement.

Large firms are divided into departments. For example, a manufacturer has, in addition to a production department, departments of design, marketing, accounting, finance, service, personnel, purchasing, and so on. Each department consists of specialists and a variety of supporting staff. A large department can take on a life of its own, that is, it can operate as an autonomous organization with its own set of specialized objectives. It may even look upon the parent firm as a "client," whose existence may be threatened if the department's expert advice is not followed. This sort of situation is difficult to avoid in large firms, but the energies of the departments can be channelled constructively through forceful policy deployment by top management.

It is important to identify the productive activities of a firm and to see how the firm's departments contribute to the efficient conduct of these activities. The concept of a process helps do this. Exhibit 25.2A is a process diagram introduced by W. Edwards Deming in his teaching in Japan in the 1950s. It helps us visualize the productive activity of a manufacturing firm. Notice that the components of the diagram are not confined to agents within the firm. Suppliers of raw materials and tools, as well as paying customers (purchasers of final product) are part of the process. Deming asserts that paying customers are the most important part of the process, because the firm's success depends on not only supplying a product customers will buy today but also persuading the customer to buy the product again and discovering new products that customers will buy in the future.

EXHIBIT 25.2A

Deming's Process Diagram

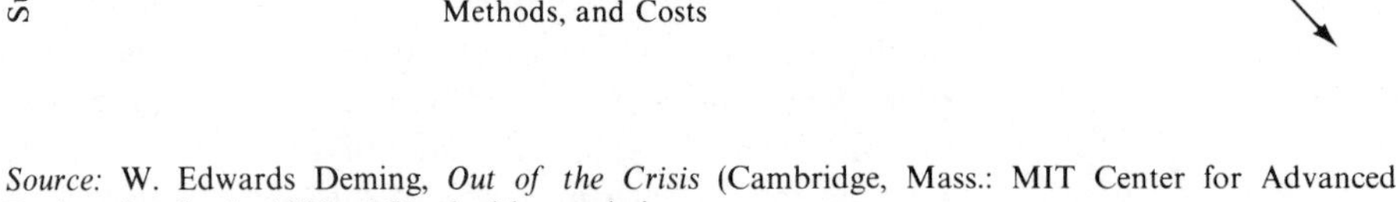

Source: W. Edwards Deming, *Out of the Crisis* (Cambridge, Mass.: MIT Center for Advanced Engineering Study, 1986), 4. Used with permission.

Deming's diagram suggests many crucial interactions among the firm's departments and between the firm and agents outside the firm. For example, people involved in sales, distribution, and service often learn from personal contact with customers what they like or do not like about their dealings with the firm. This knowledge is valuable if it is brought back to the firm and treated as data that can be used for improvement. Yet many firms do not encourage people to share such information, or, if it is shared, it is treated as evidence that the customer is too demanding.

Another critical interaction is that between the design and engineering departments and the production department. It is easy to fall into the situation in which a design presented to the production department is either difficult or impossible to make. It is much more time- and cost-effective to require cooperation between the departments from the beginning.

Finally, the firm and its suppliers interact. A firm can substantially reduce its costs by insisting on the practice of good quality control by its suppliers. This may even require setting up training courses for the suppliers and giving "report cards" to the suppliers, informing them on how the quality, cost, and scheduling of their products meet the expectations of the firm. Such practices have become common in the automobile industry.

Deming's diagram is emphasized to show the importance of identifying processes that matter. This almost invariably cuts across departmental lines and demonstrates the importance of communication between components in a process and among processes in systems.

The need for communication implies the need for a common language. This language must be precise and suitable for the discussion of problems that arise in making business processes work. Experience suggests that scientific method is such a language and that statistics is an indispensable part of it.

S E C T I O N 25.3

SCIENCE IN ORGANIZATIONS

Ideally, the primary objective of a business firm is to provide goods and services of such quality, affordability, and timeliness as to exceed the expectations of paying customers. From a scientific point of view, a business is a network of processes, where a process is viewed as a sequence of steps taken to achieve a goal. To pursue its primary objective, a business firm engages in a never-ending effort to improve its processes, because no process works perfectly. Because science helps us think formally about processes, it is a natural tool to use to attack business problems.

Scientific methods taken together constitute a systematic approach to learning, using theory and observation. In business and industry the motivation for learning is the solution of problems that arise from a firm's attempts to offer desirable products and services as economically as possible.

In Chapter 1 Deming's wheel, PDCA, was suggested as a model for "practical science," that is, science with decision making and action as the goal. In this chapter questions of implementation and organization are discussed. In the complex organizations of our "information society," implementation is a constant struggle against barriers to achievement and communication.

Mistakes are inevitable, and the good decision of today may appear as the short-sighted blunder of tomorrow. Every mistake, and every problem, represents an opportunity to seek improvements in the processes that produced the mistake or problem. Yet no organization has the resources to launch major improvement projects for every process. Seeking the *fundamental* processes, whose improvement has a sizable impact on the goals of the organization, and making their control the priority of the organization is the key to successful management. In this sense the goals of effective management and science are the same, because science also searches for fundamental, unifying processes.

A number of authors recommend that quality improvement be the guide in seeking the fundamental processes of an organization. This attitude is accessibly presented by Imai.[†] He asserts that the secret to world-class performance is unflagging commitment to quality improvement (Q), cost control (C), and timely scheduling (S). Actions taken to enhance QCS add value to the organization; other actions constitute waste. If cost control and timely scheduling are considered part of the quality of the organization's performance, then quality improvement can be seen as the driving principle behind world-class performance.

Another part of success is producing goods and services that can be sold! Holding the patent on a high-quality product with no perceived value is not an attractive prospect. Thus achieving a profitable share of the market must be at the heart of an organization's activities.

These two principles, quality improvement and market share, are affirmed by a report from PIMS (Profit Impact of Market Strategy).[††] The report is the result of a worldwide study of factors that make business firms competitive. Here are two of its most significant conclusions:

> *In the long run, the most important single factor affecting a Business Unit's performance is the Quality of its products and services relative to those of competitors.*

and

> *[M]arket share is key to a company's growth and profitability . . . one factor above all others, quality, drives market share. And when superior quality and large market share are both present, profitability is virtually guaranteed.*

The PIMS report suggests that quality is the key to market share and profitability as well. From this and other writing it is obvious that a rigorous focus on quality improvement promises tangible rewards.

STATISTICAL TOOLS IN PROBLEM FORMULATION

Complex organizations, faced with complex problems, inevitably form task forces, committees, or teams to attack the problems. Because teamwork is so valuable, this discussion assumes that a team has been formed to find ways to improve some step

[†] Imai, Masaaki, *Kaizen: The Key to Japan's Competitive Success*, New York: Random House, 1986.

[††] PIMS is a system of study housed in the Strategic Planning Institute, a nonprofit corporation governed by its member companies. It originated in the planning department of General Electric in the 1960s and was developed in the 1970s by the Marketing Science Institute. The report quoted from is Robert D. Buzzell and Bradley T. Gale, *The PIMS Principles* (New York: Free Press, 1987).

in a process.[†] How might the team proceed? An approach that has proven successful in practice is presented here. In the course of the presentation some useful tools are introduced and some tools that were discussed earlier come into play. Do not think of this presentation as a recipe that must be followed in every problem. The approach can, and indeed should, be modified as circumstances warrant.

The approach recommended is based on the experience of companies that are recognized as leaders in quality improvement. An interesting piece of documentation is the record of quality-improvement tools used by Yokohama Hewlett-Packard (HP) in its drive to win the Deming Prize in Japan.[††] Yokohama HP was the first subsidiary of a U.S. firm to win the Deming Prize. Exhibit 25.4A shows a list of quality-improvement tools and the number of users of these tools in Yokohama HP.

A number of statistical tools are listed in Exhibit 25.4A. The late Kaoru Ishikawa, one of the early leaders of the quality-improvement thrust in Japan, has stated that in more than 90% of the problems attacked with statistical tools only the following seven tools need be used: cause-and-effect diagrams, Pareto diagrams, graphs, checksheets, histograms, scatter diagrams (scatterplots), and stratification.[§] Some of these tools have been presented elsewhere in the text. The presentation here covers the rest plus some others that are especially useful.

EXHIBIT 25.4A

Numbers of Users of Selected Statistical Tools at Yokohama Hewlett-Packard

Statistical Tool	Number of Users
Cause-and-effect diagram	996
Pareto diagram	885
Brainstorming	807
Graph	672
Checksheet	628
Flow diagram	586
Histogram	424
Affinity diagram	326
Control chart	216
Scatter diagram	117
Analysis of variance	75
Binomial probability analysis	42
Weibull analysis	37
Industrial engineering	32
Other	250

[†] For a modern treatment of teamwork in organizations, see Peter Scholtes, *The Team Handbook*, 1988, Joiner Associates, Inc., P.O. Box 5445, Madison, WI 53705–0445.

[††] The Deming Prize, developed in Japan, is given to companies in recognition of high achievement in quality improvement. The competition for the prize is extremely stiff. In 1989 Florida Power and Light became the first company on U.S. soil to win this coveted prize.

[§] Kaoru Ishikawa, ed., "Special Issue: Seven Management Tools for QC," *Statistical Application Research, Union of Japanese Scientists and Engineers*, 33(2) (June 1986). See K. Ishikawa, *Guide to Quality Control* (Ann Arbor, Mich.: UNIPUB, 1986) for an elementary presentation of the seven tools in a manufacturing setting.

STEP 1: FLOW DIAGRAMS

Flow diagrams rank sixth in Exhibit 25.4A. A **flow diagram** is simply a series of boxes connected by arrows that show the flow of work in the step. If several activities take place in a step, a flow diagram for each activity may be constructed and then the way in which the activities relate to each other can be shown. Exhibit 25.4B shows a flow diagram for the construction of a density histogram. Exhibit 25.4C shows a flow diagram for a student moving through a registration station in a university department.

E X H I B I T   25.4B

Flow Diagram of the Construction of a Density Histogram (see Section 3.6 for an explanation of the process)

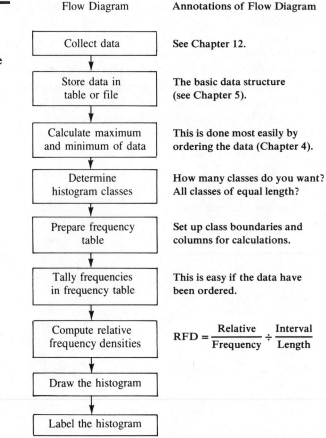

Flow Diagram — Annotations of Flow Diagram

Flow Diagram	Annotations of Flow Diagram
Collect data	See Chapter 12.
Store data in table or file	The basic data structure (see Chapter 5).
Calculate maximum and minimum of data	This is done most easily by ordering the data (Chapter 4).
Determine histogram classes	How many classes do you want? All classes of equal length?
Prepare frequency table	Set up class boundaries and columns for calculations.
Tally frequencies in frequency table	This is easy if the data have been ordered.
Compute relative frequency densities	$\text{RFD} = \dfrac{\text{Relative Frequency}}{} \div \dfrac{\text{Interval Length}}{}$
Draw the histogram	
Label the histogram	

Exhibit 25.4B illustrates the technique of annotating a flow diagram. The annotation space can also be used to make note of problems that arise in implementing the process. Suppose a flow diagram that shows how the process should work ideally is drawn. In practice, the flow diagram of the actual process may contain many more steps than shown in the ideal diagram. Are the extra steps necessary? If so, they must be shown in the "ideal" flow diagram. If not, then eliminating them eliminates waste and results in increased quality. In this application, the ideal

EXHIBIT 25.4C

Flow Diagram of
Movement Through a
Registration Site in a
School of Business

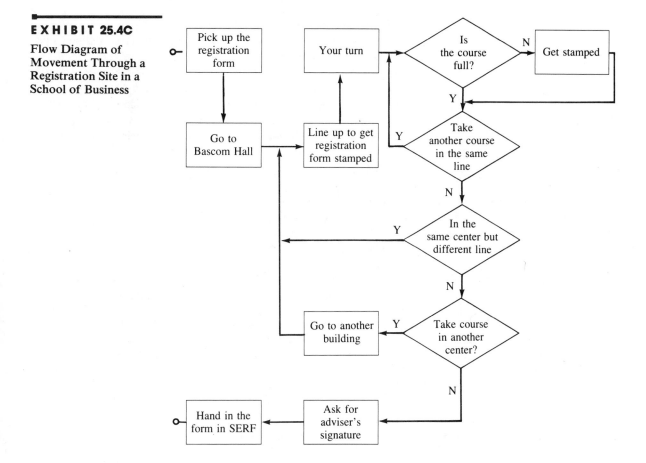

diagram is a theory that is tested against the data coming from the actual process. By expanding the ideal diagram where necessary and eliminating unnecessary steps in the actual process, theory and practice are brought together and tighter control is exerted over the process.

Exhibit 25.4C illustrates the technique of using different shaped boxes to display types of steps. The diamond-shaped boxes indicate decision steps, or branches, in which the direction taken depends on the answer to a yes-or-no question. The rectangles indicate steps that must be taken to get through the process.

Construction of the flow diagram yields valuable insights. Steps that are taken almost unconsciously in practice are documented and exposed to scrutiny. It is not unusual to discover unnecessary steps in the process that can be eliminated, resulting in immediate gains in quality. Discussion of the flow diagram in a team meeting often yields consensus on which step in the flow diagram should be improved first.

STEP 2: OPERATIONAL DEFINITIONS

For each activity in the flow diagram, what takes place must be defined operationally. What constitutes satisfactory work? Exactly how is the work done? What constitutes unsatisfactory work? Who is the customer for the work? Are the customer's needs clear? Are there deadlines or quotas to meet? Are they essential? How does the work add value to the final product or service? The **operational definition** answers who, what, when, where, why, and how. If any of these questions cannot be answered, an activity is not well defined and is therefore not in control.

▪ **E X A M P L E 25.4A:** Suppose the job is to count the number of words on this page. How do you operationally define "word"? Is a numeral a word? The page number? What about hyphenated words? What about abbreviations?

Select an operational definition of "word." Give the definition to three people and ask them to perform the job, that is, to count the words on this page. Usually, when this is done, the people get different numbers of words because the job is complex and requires a great deal of concentration. Given that different people get different answers, how do you come to a conclusion about the number of words on this page? Can you suggest a counting process that would tend to eliminate the differences? ▪

This example illustrates variation in a process. Even a job that has a theoretically correct outcome, such as the number of words on this page, will exhibit variation in practice.

▪ **E X A M P L E 25.4B:** What does it mean for a commercial airline flight to be "on time"? Does it mean that the plane always arrives at the gate on or before the stated time of arrival? Does it mean that over a series of, say, 30 arrivals its average time of arrival is equal to the stated time of arrival? ▪

▪ **E X A M P L E 25.4C:** What does it mean for a commercial airline to be "safe"?

▪

Concepts such as safety, timeliness, color, roundness, and so on, are difficult to define operationally. Doing so requires statistical analysis, because of variation. A detailed discussion of operational definitions appears in Chapter 9 of W. Edwards Deming, *Out of the Crisis* (Cambridge, Mass.: MIT Center for Advanced Engineering Study, 1986). Deming notes that creating operational definitions improves the efficiency of operations because workers who understand their jobs work confidently toward common goals and tend to exhibit less variation in their work.

STEP 3: CONFORMANCE ANALYSIS

Operational definitions are a basis for deciding if output conforms to standards. Sometimes lack of conformance is obvious to casual observation. In most cases, it is necessary to collect data over a period of time to determine lack of conformance. In the latter case, statistical methods come into play. **Conformance analysis** is the collection of data to determine if standards for a process are met. For example, a commercial airline flight may be considered "on time" if its average arrival time in 30 flights is within five minutes of its stated arrival time. To operationalize this definition, "arrival" must be specifically defined. Does it mean touchdown time on the runway, time of parking at the gate, or time when the first passenger deplanes? The proposed definition of "on time" leaves plenty of room for *variation* in the arrival times because only the mean is required to conform. A definition that also involves limits on the amount of deviation from stated arrival time on each flight is more stringent.

If several activities show lack of conformance, then the team must decide which activity or activities to improve first—activities with implications for worker safety receive top priority. Activities with important economic implications also receive high priority. The priorities are set with reference to policies deployed by top management.

STEP 4: CAUSE-AND-EFFECT ANALYSIS

Suppose one activity has been chosen for study and a measure of performance, such as being on time, has been chosen. To improve performance, the factors that influence (or cause) performance must be understood. To do this involves intense study of the activity. One stage of cause-and-effect analysis is a brainstorming session in which team members' ideas about causes are recorded. Brainstorming sessions can be free-wheeling or structured. The nominal group technique is a structured format designed to give all members of the team equal opportunity to share ideas.[†] Brainstorming is tool number 3 in Exhibit 25.4A.

Another stage of cause-and-effect analysis is intensive observation of workers performing the activity, with an eye to spotting unsuspected causes of variation in the performance measure. The measurement process itself can be a source of variation. For example, if inspectors examine parts for defects, different inspectors might use different criteria unless the question of standardization is carefully addressed.

A useful guideline in cause-and-effect analysis is to keep asking "Why?" or as it is sometimes said, "Ask why five times," because fundamental causes are not obvious. A tool that can help in this effort is the **cause-and-effect diagram**, or CE diagram, an example of which appears in Exhibit 25.4D. The diagram is also known as an Ishikawa diagram, after its inventor Kaoru Ishikawa, and as a fishbone chart, because the diagram reminds some observers of the skeleton of a fish. It is tool number 1 in Exhibit 25.4A.

The CE diagram in Exhibit 25.4D was constructed in a brainstorming session with some students who were asked, "What factors contribute to variation in your final grade in a course?" The characteristic of interest, in this case "final grade," is placed in a box at the right-hand side of the chart, and a horizontal line, emanating from the center of the box, is drawn across the chart. The major direct factors are displayed in boxes around the border of the diagram: Exams, Other Students' Performance, Lecture Attendance, Professor's Attitude, and Homework or Projects.

[†] This is especially important if the team has introverted and extroverted members. See Andre L. Delbecq, Andrew H. Van de Ven, and David H. Gustafson, *Group Techniques for Program Planning, A Guide to Nominal Group and Delphi Processes* (Glenview, Ill.: Scott Foresman, 1975).

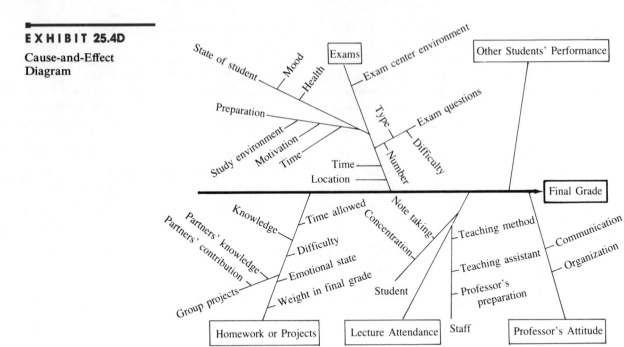

For each major direct factor, the question "Why does this factor cause variation?" was asked. In response to this question about exams, the most important factors were Exam questions, State of student, Preparation, Location, Time, and Exam center environment. These are shown as branches (or fish bones!) coming off of the line connecting the Exams box with the central line. For each of these factors, the question "Why does this factor contribute to variation in the exam score?" is asked. The answers to this question for Exam questions yielded: Difficulty, Type, and Number of questions. This questioning process is continued until all the causes of variation the group can think of are displayed on the chart.

Because cause-and-effect diagrams are used in brainstorming sessions, they are typically written on flip charts, blackboards, or overhead projector transparencies. They are typically modified at successive meetings or by people who are assigned the job of "cleaning them up." The presentation of a diagram in printed form, as in Exhibit 25.4D, does not convey the dynamic way the diagram is used in practice. The best way to appreciate the value of cause-and-effect diagrams is to create them in real problem-solving environments.[†]

[†] For a more detailed presentation of cause-and-effect diagrams, see K. Ishikawa, *Guide to Quality Control*, Chapter 3 and Section 13.3.

STEP 5: PARETO ANALYSIS

The cause-and-effect analysis typically produces a large list of causes, some of which have an important bearing on performance, many of which do not. The **Pareto principle** states that only a few causes are responsible for most of the variation.

The next step is therefore to select the important causes and to set aside the less important ones, possibly for future study. The important causes are not always obvious. Sometimes they can be selected through further brainstorming or by collecting votes from team members. It is often necessary to collect data on the causes and the performance measure to discover which causes are really important.

■ **E X A M P L E 25.4D:** Exhibit 25.4E shows part of a checksheet that might be used to collect data on a commercial airline flight.[†] The performance measures are time of touchdown in destination airport and time of arrival at gate in destination airport. Among the causes, not all of which are listed in the exhibit, are time of departure from gate at originating airport, time of takeoff at originating airport, pilot, copilot, aircraft, windspeed, and condition of sky. An important step in analyzing these data is the construction of scatterplots with a performance measure on the vertical axis and a cause on the horizontal axis.[††]

EXHIBIT 25.4E

Excerpt from a Checksheet Used to Monitor Airline Flight Arrivals

Flight Number	Date	Recorder	Aircraft	Gate Departure Time	Takeoff
4407	3/18	JBR	47083219	8:00 A.M.	8:30 A.M.
4321	3/18	JBR	47083219	12:20 P.M.	1:00 P.M.

Causes showing the greatest degree of correlation with the performance measures are of special interest. If these causes can be brought under control, that is, made predictable, and if the amount of variation in them can be reduced, then the variation in the performance measures will also be made predictable and reduced.

Here is an actual case. It was discovered that the time between departure from gate and takeoff at the originating airport was quite variable, so this time became the focus of a cause-and-effect study. Why was the time so variable? What steps might be taken to reduce the variation? A study of traffic patterns at the originating airport turned up a lull in departures near the established departure time of the flight under study. A slight schedule change resulted in a substantial reduction in variation. This translated into a decrease in the variation of arrival times, making life easier for employees and making customers happier. A survey of customers showed the number of repeat trips up, and customers said they were recommending the flight to friends. ■

This case shows how the study of one process leads naturally to the study of another process. Study of arrival at one airport led to the study of takeoff at another airport. Looking from one step in a process to an earlier step for sources of

---

[†] Checksheets are tool number 5 in Exhibit 25.4A.
[††] Scatter diagrams (or scatterplots) are tool number 10 in Exhibit 25.4A.

improvement is called *moving upstream*. Solving problems *upstream* means that those problems will not be transmitted *downstream*, which means that they will not reach any of the customers in the process, including the all-important paying customer. The point of Pareto analysis is that the most important problems should be tackled first because solving them will yield the largest return.

A typical step in Pareto analysis is the construction of a Pareto diagram.[†] A **Pareto diagram** displays the important causes of variation, as reflected in data collected on the causes. Diagrams constructed before and after process improvement efforts take place, document the effects of improvements and suggest causes of variation that need attention next. This application fits into Step 4 of the Shewhart cycle introduced in Chapter 1, namely, deciding what to do next.

■ **EXAMPLE 25.4E:** Fuller describes a study of a marketing department that was filling telephone orders.[††] A study of their activities revealed that they were spending a great deal of time on nonproductive work. The data were collected by having employees record their activities at randomly chosen times during the workday. Exhibit 25.4F displays a table and a Pareto diagram showing the number of times an employee engaged in one of four nonproductive activities during a three-day study

EXHIBIT 25.4F

Pareto Analysis of Fuller's Marketing Group Data (three-day study period)

Activity	Number	Percent
PR	20	49
CB	8	20
ES	7	16
COS	6	15
	41	100

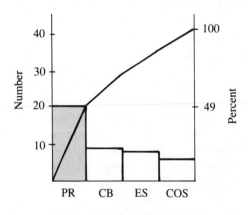

[†] Pareto diagrams are tool number 2 in Exhibit 25.4A.

[††] The data for this example are from F. Timothy Fuller, "Eliminating Complexity from Work: Improving Productivity by Enhancing Quality," *National Productivity Review* (Autumn 1985): 327–344.

period.[†] These activities were processing returns (PR), converting backlog (CB), expediting shipments (ES), and checking order status (COS). All these activities were undertaken because of orders not filled correctly or not shipped on time.

Constructing a Pareto diagram is quite simple. The first step is to prepare a table that shows the activities recorded, the numbers of times the activities were observed, and the percentage of the total number of times represented by each count. In Exhibit 25.4F, the total number of times is 41, and the number of times processing returns was observed is 20. Thus $100(20/41) = 49\%$. Similar calculations complete the table.

The Pareto diagram has two vertical axes, the left one corresponding to the Number column in the table, the right one corresponding to the Percent column in the table. On the horizontal axis, the activities are listed, creating bases of equal length for the rectangles shown in the diagram. The activities are listed in decreasing order of occurrence. Doing this means that the most frequently observed activity lies on the left extreme of the diagram, and the least frequently observed activity lies on the right extreme. The heights of the rectangles are drawn to show the frequencies of the activities, and then the sides of the rectangles are drawn.

EXHIBIT 25.4G

Pareto Analysis of Hypothetical Before and After Analysis Based on Fuller's Marketing Group Data (three-day study period)

Activity	Before		After	
	Number	Percent	Number	Percent
PR	20	49	7	24
CB	8	20	5	17
ES	7	16	10	35
COS	6	15	7	24
	41	100	29	100

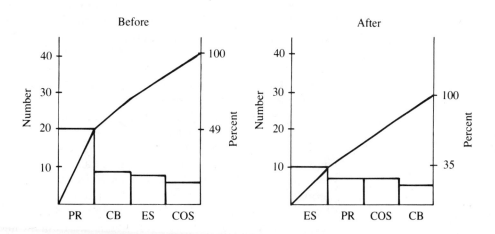

[†] Employees were reassured that they were not at fault for engaging in unproductive activities; they were part of the process. The purpose of the study was to find and eliminate unproductive work so that the employees could contribute more effectively to the marketing effort.

The next step is to locate the *cumulative percents* of the activities using the right-hand axis. The cumulative percent for the first rectangle is, of course, 49; for the second it is $49 + 20 = 69$. The 69 is plotted over the right-hand side of the rectangle labelled CB. The next cumulative percent is $49 + 20 + 16 = 69 + 16 = 85$, which is plotted over the right-hand side of the rectangle labelled ES. The last cumulative percent is, of course, 100, and it is plotted over the right-hand side of the last rectangle. Now draw straight lines between the plotted cumulative percents as shown in the exhibit. The next step is to label the axes and add a title to the diagram. In Exhibit 25.4F the tallest rectangle is lightly shaded to highlight the most frequent activity, suggesting the one that may deserve first priority in problem solving.

As a hypothetical continuation of Fuller's study, suppose that efforts to reduce unnecessary activities are made. During a later three-day period, Fuller's study is repeated with the results shown in Exhibit 25.4G. The new Pareto diagram is also displayed next to the old one in Exhibit 25.4G. Comparison of the "arms" showing the cumulative percentages of unnecessary work clearly shows the beneficial results of the improvement efforts. Comparison of the activities ranked on the horizontal axis shows that old sources of unnecessary work have been brought under better control (PR and CB), and a new one (ES) now deserves priority.   ▪

The example from Fuller's article reinforces the idea behind Pareto analysis: the majority of problems are due to a small number of identifiable causes. The Pareto diagram in Exhibit 25.4F shows the four major sources of unproductive activity found in Fuller's study and also shows that the single source "processing returns" accounted for almost half of the instances recorded. Such a finding helps to channel improvement efforts where they will do the most good. As Exhibit 25.4G demonstrates, the Pareto diagrams from a series of studies helps to document the effects of improvement efforts and points to the most productive direction for the next round of efforts.

When Pareto diagrams are to be compared, you must be sure that the data were collected on comparable bases. In our example, this was done by suggesting that Fuller's study be replicated literally, that is, that three-day study periods be used in both the Before and After studies. It was also assumed that the two three-day periods were comparable in terms of overall level of activity. Comparisons across studies that have different time periods or different data-collection methods are difficult at best, though sometimes sophisticated adjustments can be performed to obtain rough comparability. For routine practical work, however, it is best to stick to comparing the obviously comparable and avoid comparing data from studies with obvious substantive differences.

Many authorities recommend that Pareto analysis take the *costs* of the activities into account. The concern is that a very frequent problem may nevertheless imply less overall cost than a relatively rare but disastrous problem. For example, you are probably willing to put up with a little static in your telephone line in return for being able to count on the line's availability. If the telephone company spent its resources trying to eliminate the last bit of static from the line but failed to keep the lines in good repair, it would not be acting rationally.

As another example, consider the problem of round-off error in calculations on an electronic computer. Theoretically, most calculations involve some error because of the finiteness of the machine, but reliable methods of controlling this error are available. Although it might be useful for someone to develop even better methods for controlling round-off error, it is much more important for most people to learn to write programs accurately. A "bug" in a program, while rare, spoils the whole program, whereas round-off error, while common, is a relatively harmless threat.

Before basing a Pareto analysis on frequencies, as we did in our example, we need to decide that the seriousness of the problems is roughly proportional to the frequencies. If seriousness fails to satisfy this criterion, then activities should be measured in some other way. A possible modification of the Fuller study is to keep track of *how much time* employees spend on each activity. Then time spent would replace the frequencies in the table in Exhibit 25.4F. Notice that measuring time spent is more difficult and costly than simply counting instances, so using time spent would have to be justified on economic grounds. Our example underlines the importance of judging the *relevance* of the measurements used in a Pareto analysis.

SECTION 25.5

EXERCISES

25.5A Sit in a diner or fast food restaurant and write down all the processes you observe. Draw flow diagrams of some of the processes. At what points do the processes seem to have problems? List some of the causes of the problems you see. If possible, persuade the manager of the establishment to discuss some problems he or she perceives. Again, if possible, try to obtain permission to ask some of the employees about barriers to achievement and communication in the establishment. (You often find that employees know about problems that have not been shared with the manager!)

25.5B Repeat Exercise 25.5A for any business establishment of your choice.

25.5C Choose a process that interests you and that you can observe. Draw a flow diagram of how you think the process should work. Then draw a flow diagram of how the process actually works. Suggest improvements in the process. How would you go about collecting data from the process? How would these data help you find the fundamental steps in the process?

25.5D If possible collect data on problems that occur in the process you studied in Exercises 25.5A, 25.5B, and 25.5C. Make a Pareto diagram of the problems and identify the most frequent problem. How would you try to counteract this problem?

25.5E In your place of work, or in your classroom, organize a quality team. Have the team brainstorm on the problems they face. Decide on the most important problem and work on countermeasures to the problem. This exercise will be most successful if the manager or classroom instructor supports the effort.

SECTION 25.6

ORGANIZING FOR QUALITY IMPROVEMENT

Quality improvement does not just happen; it takes commitment, effort, and organizational skill. A scientific approach to quality improvement requires the timely flow of precisely formulated information, that is, high-quality *communication*. A scientific approach also requires that, so far as possible, communication be based on the collection, analysis, and presentation of data; in other words, the use of statistics. Two organizational principles follow from these remarks:

(1) Barriers to communication must be identified and eliminated.

(2) Statistics must be part of the everyday vocabulary of the organization.

At this point, some key points made earlier are reiterated and a model for the effective introduction of statistics into a firm is offered.

Barriers to communication are so numerous that they defy any attempt to list them. Common ones are departmentalization, fear, mistrust, laziness, failure to appreciate the importance of communication, and lack of commitment to the concept of never-ending improvement. Imai cites a number of organizational countermeasures to the barriers, among them cross-functional management, quality function deployment, management by policy, and the firmwide training of employees in statistical methods.[†] The point we stress here is that knowledge of statistical methods is fundamental to organizing for quality. This does not mean knowledge by a few specialists, but by *all* members of the firm. Naturally, statistical specialists are responsible for learning, and creating, new methodology to solve new problems, but they also need to be involved in training nonspecialists and in helping them to apply statistical methods to the solution of their everyday problems.

Adopting the methods of science to help solve business problems means adopting statistical tools. Firmwide training in statistical tools is important, but whose job is it to see that the training is done so that the following conditions are met:

(1) The training is understandable.

(2) The use of statistical tools is taught as part of a scientific approach to problem formulation and solution.

(3) The training is put to use to solve important problems in the firm.

These objectives cannot be left to chance. Someone who is answerable to top management and is well trained in statistics must have responsibility for coordinating all the statistical activities of the firm. Otherwise the use of statistics will be sporadic.

Even very skillful applications of statistics have less than full impact if they are not fitted into a strategic plan within the firm. The gains from the applications need to be communicated to the rest of the firm. If the techniques that have worked in one part of the firm can be applied successfully in another part, the second application may go much more quickly than the first, provided the appropriate learning is communicated. In addition, new procedures need to be standardized to achieve maximum gain. Finally, a statistical coordinator with support from top management must have authority to seek out problems that can be attacked scientifically and whose solution will result in important improvements. This type of activity is not possible for a statistician who is assigned to a department, for he or she then faces the familiar barriers to communication. The organizational step of creating a person, or office, in charge of statistical coordination helps to break down the barriers to communication while at the same time encouraging maximum use of

[†] Imai, *Kaizen.*

statistical methods for process improvement and hence increased productivity of the firm.

Exhibit 25.6A shows a model presented by W. Edwards Deming in *Out of the Crisis* and based on a model originated by Morris Hansen at the Census Bureau. Here the statistical coordinator answers to top management and oversees the statistical activities in all areas of the firm. One of the most important of these activities is training, so that all members of the firm can work effectively to improve the processes for which they are responsible. Only in this way can firmwide, never-ending improvement take place. It is too big a job for any one person or small group of people. It must involve everyone!

EXHIBIT 25.6A

Deming's Model for Location of Statistical Coordinator in an Organization

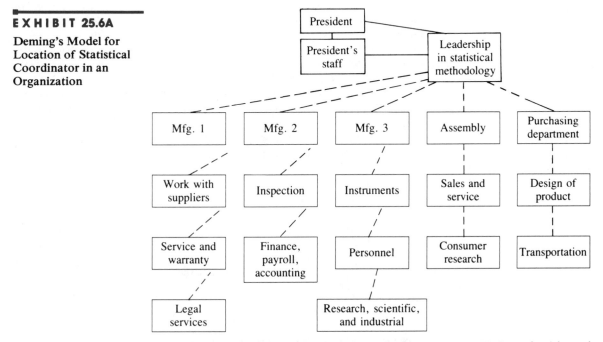

Source: W. Edwards Deming, *Out of the Crisis* (Cambridge, Mass.: MIT Center for Advanced Engineering Study, 1986), 467. Used with permission.

SECTION 25.7

EXERCISES

25.7A Read Vernon R. Alden, "Who Says You Can't Crack Japanese Markets?" *Harvard Business Review* 87(1) (January–February 1987): 52–56.

(a) State the four myths about Japan that Alden cites.

(b) State Alden's three suggestions for breaking the legal barriers to the Japanese market.

(c) State Alden's three suggestions for breaking the social and cultural barriers to the Japanese market.

(d) Make a list of all the Western companies that Alden uses as examples of firms that have overcome trade barriers with Japan.

25.7B Locate a business in your community that engages in international trade. Make an appointment with one of the top managers of the company and discuss the difficulties and rewards of foreign trade.

25.7C This exercise emphasizes the value of new technology in furthering the development of the discipline of statistics. It also illustrates the role of competition. The reading shows the torturous path required to get the technology "accepted." The improvement and acceptance of the technology grew in parallel.

Find a copy of Joel Shurkin, *Engines of the Mind: A History of the Computer* (New York: Norton, 1984). Read Chapter 3, pages 86–92. It is the story of Herman Hollerith, who was able to adapt the idea of machines driven by punch cards to the processing of data from the U.S. Census. Hollerith created the Tabulating Machine Company, but ill health forced him to allow the company to be merged with some others by Charles Ranlett Flint in 1911. The new company was called Computing-Tabulating-Recording Company (CTR). The new company also increased Hollerith's ability to compete with Powers's company, which got started because the Census Bureau did not believe in a sole supplier. Powers's company eventually merged with Remington Rand, which later became Sperry Rand, maker of the UNIVAC. In May 1914 CTR hired Thomas Watson as general manager. Watson soon took control of the company and in 1924 changed its name to International Business Machines (IBM). Hollerith died in 1929.

Comment on how each of the following ideas is touched on in this story: never-ending improvement, management of technology, Hollerith as an employer, and basing decisions on data.

25.7D Collect at least three articles from newspapers, magazines, or journals concerning quality and productivity improvement in business. Find articles that explicitly mention management techniques or philosophies. Articles that simply say that quality is a good thing are not acceptable! Write a two-page essay summarizing these articles. Try to highlight a common theme that runs through the articles, or, if the articles contain conflicting ideas, compare and contrast them. Conclude your essay with a recommendation of a specific quality issue that warrants further study, on the basis of the material in the articles.

SECTION 25.8

SUPPLEMENTARY EXERCISES FOR CHAPTER 25

25A Develop, preferably in the context of a study team, operational definitions of the concepts of quality, cost control, and scheduling in one or more of the following areas:
(a) Providing care in a nursing home
(b) Running a purchasing department
(c) Designing a research project
(d) Forming a study team
(e) Developing an action plan for introducing new hardware and software into a clerical office
(f) Developing a pilot quality improvement project
(g) Writing a paper

25B Read and summarize Chapter 6 of Robert D. Buzzell and Bradley T. Gale, *The PIMS Principles* (New York: Free Press, 1987).

25C What are the Deming Prize and the Baldrige Prize? How do companies win them? Which companies have won them?

25D Do a study to find out why the accounting profession treats capital equipment, such as desks and chairs, as assets and treats people, in terms of their salaries and fringe benefits, as liabilities. A quality perspective treats people, and their ability to improve processes, as assets. Think about how to bring this perspective into the accounting profession.

25E Read F. Timothy Fuller, "Eliminating Complexity from Work: Improving Productivity by Enhancing Quality," *National Productivity Review* (Autumn 1985): 327–344. Apply the ideas in this article to a process of interest to you. This could be your own schedule of daily activities or a process at work.

25F Explain why quality improvement is a never-ending process of PDCA.

SECTION 25.9

GLOSSARY FOR CHAPTER 25

Cause-and-effect diagram	A "fishbone" diagram that shows causes of causes of causes, and so on, so that truly fundamental causes of variation are documented.
Conformance analysis	Collection of data to determine if standards for a process are met; part of the check step in the PDCA cycle.
Flow diagram	A series of boxes connected by arrows that show the flow of work in a step in a process.
Hourly workers	Those whose primary responsibility is to follow established work procedures.
Middle management	Those who oversee the implementation of policy.
Operational definition	The result of answering who, what, when, where, why, and how.
Pareto diagram	A diagram that displays causes of variation ranked by importance.
Pareto principle	Only a few causes are responsible for most of the variation in a process.
Supervisors	Those who oversee the daily activities of hourly workers.
Top management	Those responsible for seeking ways and means of ensuring the long-term survival and growth of an organization.

Tables

TABLE 1

Percentiles of Selected t Distributions with v Degrees of Freedom

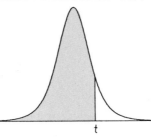

t

Note: The body of the table contains values of t corresponding to areas a. The parameter a is the area bounded by the horizontal axis, a vertical line through t, and the pdf of the t distribution with v degrees of freedom.

$a = $ **area**

v	0.550	0.600	0.650	0.700	0.750	0.800	0.850	0.900	0.950	0.975	0.990	0.995	0.997	0.998	0.999
1	0.158	0.325	0.510	0.727	1.000	1.376	1.963	3.078	6.314	12.706	31.821	63.657	106.100	159.156	318.317
2	0.142	0.289	0.445	0.617	0.816	1.061	1.386	1.886	2.920	4.303	6.965	9.925	12.852	15.764	22.327
3	0.137	0.277	0.424	0.584	0.765	0.978	1.250	1.638	2.353	3.182	4.541	5.841	6.994	8.053	10.215
4	0.134	0.271	0.414	0.569	0.741	0.941	1.190	1.533	2.132	2.776	3.747	4.604	5.321	5.951	7.173
5	0.132	0.267	0.408	0.559	0.727	0.920	1.156	1.476	2.015	2.571	3.365	4.032	4.570	5.030	5.893
6	0.131	0.265	0.404	0.553	0.718	0.906	1.134	1.440	1.943	2.447	3.143	3.707	4.152	4.524	5.208
7	0.130	0.263	0.402	0.549	0.711	0.896	1.119	1.415	1.895	2.365	2.998	3.499	3.887	4.207	4.785
8	0.130	0.262	0.399	0.546	0.706	0.889	1.108	1.397	1.860	2.306	2.896	3.355	3.705	3.991	4.501
9	0.129	0.261	0.398	0.543	0.703	0.883	1.100	1.383	1.833	2.262	2.821	3.250	3.573	3.835	4.297
10	0.129	0.260	0.397	0.542	0.700	0.879	1.093	1.372	1.812	2.228	2.764	3.169	3.472	3.716	4.144
11	0.129	0.260	0.396	0.540	0.697	0.876	1.088	1.363	1.796	2.201	2.718	3.106	3.393	3.624	4.025
12	0.128	0.259	0.395	0.539	0.695	0.873	1.083	1.356	1.782	2.179	2.681	3.055	3.330	3.550	3.930
13	0.128	0.259	0.394	0.537	0.694	0.870	1.079	1.350	1.771	2.160	2.650	3.012	3.278	3.489	3.852
14	0.128	0.258	0.393	0.537	0.692	0.868	1.076	1.345	1.761	2.145	2.624	2.977	3.234	3.438	3.787
15	0.128	0.258	0.393	0.536	0.691	0.866	1.074	1.341	1.753	2.131	2.602	2.947	3.197	3.395	3.733
16	0.128	0.258	0.392	0.535	0.690	0.865	1.071	1.337	1.746	2.120	2.583	2.921	3.165	3.358	3.686
17	0.128	0.257	0.392	0.534	0.689	0.863	1.069	1.333	1.740	2.110	2.567	2.898	3.138	3.326	3.646
18	0.127	0.257	0.392	0.534	0.688	0.862	1.067	1.330	1.734	2.101	2.552	2.878	3.113	3.298	3.610
19	0.127	0.257	0.391	0.533	0.688	0.861	1.065	1.328	1.729	2.093	2.539	2.861	3.092	3.273	3.579
20	0.127	0.257	0.391	0.533	0.687	0.860	1.064	1.325	1.725	2.086	2.528	2.845	3.073	3.251	3.552
21	0.127	0.257	0.391	0.532	0.686	0.859	1.063	1.323	1.721	2.080	2.518	2.831	3.056	3.231	3.527
22	0.127	0.256	0.390	0.532	0.686	0.858	1.061	1.321	1.717	2.074	2.508	2.819	3.041	3.214	3.505
23	0.127	0.256	0.390	0.532	0.685	0.858	1.060	1.319	1.714	2.069	2.500	2.807	3.027	3.198	3.485
24	0.127	0.256	0.390	0.531	0.685	0.857	1.059	1.318	1.711	2.064	2.492	2.797	3.014	3.183	3.467
25	0.127	0.256	0.390	0.531	0.684	0.856	1.058	1.316	1.708	2.060	2.485	2.787	3.003	3.170	3.450
26	0.127	0.256	0.390	0.531	0.684	0.856	1.058	1.315	1.706	2.056	2.479	2.779	2.992	3.158	3.44
27	0.127	0.256	0.389	0.531	0.684	0.855	1.057	1.314	1.703	2.052	2.473	2.771	2.982	3.147	3.42
28	0.127	0.256	0.389	0.530	0.683	0.855	1.056	1.313	1.701	2.048	2.467	2.763	2.973	3.136	3.408
29	0.127	0.256	0.389	0.530	0.683	0.854	1.055	1.311	1.699	2.045	2.462	2.756	2.965	3.127	3.396
30	0.127	0.256	0.389	0.530	0.683	0.854	1.055	1.310	1.697	2.042	2.457	2.750	2.957	3.118	3.385
31	0.127	0.256	0.389	0.530	0.682	0.853	1.054	1.309	1.696	2.040	2.453	2.744	2.950	3.109	3.375
32	0.127	0.255	0.389	0.530	0.682	0.853	1.053	1.309	1.694	2.037	2.449	2.738	2.943	3.102	3.365
33	0.127	0.255	0.389	0.530	0.682	0.853	1.053	1.308	1.692	2.035	2.445	2.733	2.937	3.094	3.356
34	0.127	0.255	0.389	0.529	0.682	0.852	1.052	1.307	1.691	2.032	2.441	2.728	2.931	3.088	3.348
35	0.127	0.255	0.389	0.529	0.682	0.852	1.052	1.306	1.690	2.030	2.438	2.724	2.926	3.081	3.340
40	0.126	0.255	0.388	0.529	0.681	0.851	1.050	1.303	1.684	2.021	2.423	2.704	2.902	3.055	3.307
50	0.126	0.255	0.388	0.528	0.679	0.849	1.047	1.299	1.676	2.009	2.403	2.678	2.870	3.018	3.261
60	0.126	0.255	0.387	0.527	0.679	0.848	1.045	1.296	1.671	2.000	2.390	2.660	2.849	2.994	3.232
120	0.126	0.254	0.386	0.526	0.677	0.845	1.041	1.289	1.658	1.980	2.358	2.617	2.798	2.935	3.160
inf	0.126	0.253	0.385	0.524	0.674	0.842	1.036	1.282	1.645	1.960	2.326	2.576	2.748	2.878	3.090

TABLE 2

Normal Distribution Table

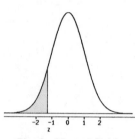

Plot for Normal Table

Each entry is the total area under the standard normal curve to the left of z.
Values were obtained by rounding the results from Minitab's CDF command.

z	0.00	0.01	0.02	0.03	0.04	0.05	0.06	0.07	0.08	0.09
-3.9	0.0000	0.0000	0.0000	0.0000	0.0000	0.0000	0.0000	0.0000	0.0000	0.0000
-3.8	0.0001	0.0001	0.0001	0.0001	0.0001	0.0001	0.0001	0.0001	0.0001	0.0001
-3.7	0.0001	0.0001	0.0001	0.0001	0.0001	0.0001	0.0001	0.0001	0.0001	0.0001
-3.6	0.0002	0.0002	0.0001	0.0001	0.0001	0.0001	0.0001	0.0001	0.0001	0.0001
-3.5	0.0002	0.0002	0.0002	0.0002	0.0002	0.0002	0.0002	0.0002	0.0002	0.0002
-3.4	0.0003	0.0003	0.0003	0.0003	0.0003	0.0003	0.0003	0.0003	0.0003	0.0002
-3.3	0.0005	0.0005	0.0005	0.0004	0.0004	0.0004	0.0004	0.0004	0.0004	0.0003
-3.2	0.0007	0.0007	0.0006	0.0006	0.0006	0.0006	0.0006	0.0005	0.0005	0.0005
-3.1	0.0010	0.0009	0.0009	0.0009	0.0008	0.0008	0.0008	0.0008	0.0007	0.0007
-3.0	0.0013	0.0013	0.0013	0.0012	0.0012	0.0011	0.0011	0.0011	0.0010	0.0010
-2.9	0.0019	0.0018	0.0018	0.0017	0.0016	0.0016	0.0015	0.0015	0.0014	0.0014
-2.8	0.0026	0.0025	0.0024	0.0023	0.0023	0.0022	0.0021	0.0021	0.0020	0.0019
-2.7	0.0035	0.0034	0.0033	0.0032	0.0031	0.0030	0.0029	0.0028	0.0027	0.0026
-2.6	0.0047	0.0045	0.0044	0.0043	0.0041	0.0040	0.0039	0.0038	0.0037	0.0036
-2.5	0.0062	0.0060	0.0059	0.0057	0.0055	0.0054	0.0052	0.0051	0.0049	0.0048
-2.4	0.0082	0.0080	0.0078	0.0075	0.0073	0.0071	0.0069	0.0068	0.0066	0.0064
-2.3	0.0107	0.0104	0.0102	0.0099	0.0096	0.0094	0.0091	0.0089	0.0087	0.0084
-2.2	0.0139	0.0136	0.0132	0.0129	0.0125	0.0122	0.0119	0.0116	0.0113	0.0110
-2.1	0.0179	0.0174	0.0170	0.0166	0.0162	0.0158	0.0154	0.0150	0.0146	0.0143
-2.0	0.0227	0.0222	0.0217	0.0212	0.0207	0.0202	0.0197	0.0192	0.0188	0.0183
-1.9	0.0287	0.0281	0.0274	0.0268	0.0262	0.0256	0.0250	0.0244	0.0239	0.0233
-1.8	0.0359	0.0351	0.0344	0.0336	0.0329	0.0322	0.0314	0.0307	0.0301	0.0294
-1.7	0.0446	0.0436	0.0427	0.0418	0.0409	0.0401	0.0392	0.0384	0.0375	0.0367
-1.6	0.0548	0.0537	0.0526	0.0516	0.0505	0.0495	0.0485	0.0475	0.0465	0.0455
-1.5	0.0668	0.0655	0.0643	0.0630	0.0618	0.0606	0.0594	0.0582	0.0571	0.0559
-1.4	0.0808	0.0793	0.0778	0.0764	0.0749	0.0735	0.0721	0.0708	0.0694	0.0681
-1.3	0.0968	0.0951	0.0934	0.0918	0.0901	0.0885	0.0869	0.0853	0.0838	0.0823
-1.2	0.1151	0.1131	0.1112	0.1093	0.1075	0.1056	0.1038	0.1020	0.1003	0.0985
-1.1	0.1357	0.1335	0.1314	0.1292	0.1271	0.1251	0.1230	0.1210	0.1190	0.1170
-1.0	0.1587	0.1562	0.1539	0.1515	0.1492	0.1469	0.1446	0.1423	0.1401	0.1379
-0.9	0.1841	0.1814	0.1788	0.1762	0.1736	0.1711	0.1685	0.1660	0.1635	0.1611
-0.8	0.2119	0.2090	0.2061	0.2033	0.2005	0.1977	0.1949	0.1921	0.1894	0.1867
-0.7	0.2420	0.2389	0.2358	0.2327	0.2296	0.2266	0.2236	0.2206	0.2177	0.2148
-0.6	0.2743	0.2709	0.2676	0.2643	0.2611	0.2578	0.2546	0.2514	0.2483	0.2451
-0.5	0.3085	0.3050	0.3015	0.2981	0.2946	0.2912	0.2877	0.2843	0.2810	0.2776
-0.4	0.3446	0.3409	0.3372	0.3336	0.3300	0.3264	0.3228	0.3192	0.3156	0.3121
-0.3	0.3821	0.3783	0.3745	0.3707	0.3669	0.3632	0.3594	0.3557	0.3520	0.3483
-0.2	0.4207	0.4168	0.4129	0.4090	0.4052	0.4013	0.3974	0.3936	0.3897	0.3859
-0.1	0.4602	0.4562	0.4522	0.4483	0.4443	0.4404	0.4364	0.4325	0.4286	0.4247
-0.0	0.5000	0.4960	0.4920	0.4880	0.4840	0.4801	0.4761	0.4721	0.4681	0.4641

(Continues)

TABLE 2 *(Continued)*

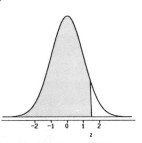

Plot for Normal Table

Each entry is the total area under the standard normal curve to the left of z.
Values were obtained by rounding the results from Minitab's CDF command.

z	0.00	0.01	0.02	0.03	0.04	0.05	0.06	0.07	0.08	0.09
0.0	0.5000	0.5040	0.5080	0.5120	0.5160	0.5199	0.5239	0.5279	0.5319	0.5359
0.1	0.5398	0.5438	0.5478	0.5517	0.5557	0.5596	0.5636	0.5675	0.5714	0.5753
0.2	0.5793	0.5832	0.5871	0.5910	0.5948	0.5987	0.6026	0.6064	0.6103	0.6141
0.3	0.6179	0.6217	0.6255	0.6293	0.6331	0.6368	0.6406	0.6443	0.6480	0.6517
0.4	0.6554	0.6591	0.6628	0.6664	0.6700	0.6736	0.6772	0.6808	0.6844	0.6879
0.5	0.6915	0.6950	0.6985	0.7019	0.7054	0.7088	0.7123	0.7157	0.7190	0.7224
0.6	0.7257	0.7291	0.7324	0.7357	0.7389	0.7422	0.7454	0.7486	0.7517	0.7549
0.7	0.7580	0.7611	0.7642	0.7673	0.7704	0.7734	0.7764	0.7794	0.7823	0.7852
0.8	0.7881	0.7910	0.7939	0.7967	0.7995	0.8023	0.8051	0.8078	0.8106	0.8133
0.9	0.8159	0.8186	0.8212	0.8238	0.8264	0.8289	0.8315	0.8340	0.8365	0.8389
1.0	0.8413	0.8438	0.8461	0.8485	0.8508	0.8531	0.8554	0.8577	0.8599	0.8621
1.1	0.8643	0.8665	0.8686	0.8708	0.8729	0.8749	0.8770	0.8790	0.8810	0.8830
1.2	0.8849	0.8869	0.8888	0.8907	0.8925	0.8944	0.8962	0.8980	0.8997	0.9015
1.3	0.9032	0.9049	0.9066	0.9082	0.9099	0.9115	0.9131	0.9147	0.9162	0.9177
1.4	0.9192	0.9207	0.9222	0.9236	0.9251	0.9265	0.9279	0.9292	0.9306	0.9319
1.5	0.9332	0.9345	0.9357	0.9370	0.9382	0.9394	0.9406	0.9418	0.9429	0.9441
1.6	0.9452	0.9463	0.9474	0.9484	0.9495	0.9505	0.9515	0.9525	0.9535	0.9545
1.7	0.9554	0.9564	0.9573	0.9582	0.9591	0.9599	0.9608	0.9616	0.9625	0.9633
1.8	0.9641	0.9649	0.9656	0.9664	0.9671	0.9678	0.9686	0.9693	0.9699	0.9706
1.9	0.9713	0.9719	0.9726	0.9732	0.9738	0.9744	0.9750	0.9756	0.9761	0.9767
2.0	0.9772	0.9778	0.9783	0.9788	0.9793	0.9798	0.9803	0.9808	0.9812	0.9817
2.1	0.9821	0.9826	0.9830	0.9834	0.9838	0.9842	0.9846	0.9850	0.9854	0.9857
2.2	0.9861	0.9864	0.9868	0.9871	0.9875	0.9878	0.9881	0.9884	0.9887	0.9890
2.3	0.9893	0.9896	0.9898	0.9901	0.9904	0.9906	0.9909	0.9911	0.9913	0.9916
2.4	0.9918	0.9920	0.9922	0.9925	0.9927	0.9929	0.9931	0.9932	0.9934	0.9936
2.5	0.9938	0.9940	0.9941	0.9943	0.9945	0.9946	0.9948	0.9949	0.9951	0.9952
2.6	0.9953	0.9955	0.9956	0.9957	0.9959	0.9960	0.9961	0.9962	0.9963	0.9964
2.7	0.9965	0.9966	0.9967	0.9968	0.9969	0.9970	0.9971	0.9972	0.9973	0.9974
2.8	0.9974	0.9975	0.9976	0.9977	0.9977	0.9978	0.9979	0.9979	0.9980	0.9981
2.9	0.9981	0.9982	0.9982	0.9983	0.9984	0.9984	0.9985	0.9985	0.9986	0.9986
3.0	0.9987	0.9987	0.9987	0.9988	0.9988	0.9989	0.9989	0.9989	0.9990	0.9990
3.1	0.9990	0.9991	0.9991	0.9991	0.9992	0.9992	0.9992	0.9992	0.9993	0.9993
3.2	0.9993	0.9993	0.9994	0.9994	0.9994	0.9994	0.9994	0.9994	0.9995	0.9995
3.3	0.9995	0.9995	0.9995	0.9996	0.9996	0.9996	0.9996	0.9996	0.9996	0.9997
3.4	0.9997	0.9997	0.9997	0.9997	0.9997	0.9997	0.9997	0.9997	0.9997	0.9998
3.5	0.9998	0.9998	0.9998	0.9998	0.9998	0.9998	0.9998	0.9998	0.9998	0.9998
3.6	0.9998	0.9998	0.9999	0.9999	0.9999	0.9999	0.9999	0.9999	0.9999	0.9999
3.7	0.9999	0.9999	0.9999	0.9999	0.9999	0.9999	0.9999	0.9999	0.9999	0.9999
3.8	0.9999	0.9999	0.9999	0.9999	0.9999	0.9999	0.9999	0.9999	0.9999	0.9999
3.9	1.0000	1.0000	1.0000	1.0000	1.0000	1.0000	1.0000	1.0000	1.0000	1.0000

TABLE 3

Table of 95th and 99th Percentiles of Selected F Distributions

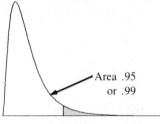

Area .95
or .99

Note: Rows are numerator degrees of freedom; columns are denominator degrees of freedom. Entries in a cell are the 95th on top of the 99th percentile.

v_2

v_1	1	2	3	4	5	6	7	8	9	10
1	161.44	18.5121	10.1282	7.7086	6.6079	5.9874	5.5913	5.3176	5.1174	4.9646
	4052.18	98.5057	34.1169	21.1977	16.2579	13.7452	12.2462	11.2587	10.5614	10.0443
2	199.50	19.0000	9.5522	6.9443	5.7860	5.1431	4.7373	4.4590	4.2566	4.1029
	4999.50	99.0001	30.8156	18.0000	13.2739	10.9246	9.5464	8.6490	8.0215	7.5594
3	215.69	19.1634	9.2769	6.5913	5.4094	4.7570	4.3469	4.0661	3.8625	3.7083
	5403.35	99.1692	29.4571	16.6946	12.0600	9.7796	8.4514	7.5909	6.9920	6.5523
4	224.57	19.2468	9.1169	6.3881	5.1923	4.5337	4.1203	3.8379	3.6331	3.4780
	5624.58	99.2495	28.7099	15.9771	11.3920	9.1482	7.8465	7.0061	6.4221	5.9944
5	230.16	19.2971	9.0135	6.2559	5.0502	4.3874	3.9715	3.6876	3.4816	3.3259
	5763.65	99.2982	28.2374	15.5215	10.9670	8.7460	7.4605	6.6319	6.0570	5.6363
6	233.98	19.3294	8.9405	6.1632	4.9503	4.2839	3.8660	3.5806	3.3738	3.2172
	5858.99	99.3317	27.9105	15.2071	10.6721	8.4661	7.1913	6.3707	5.8018	5.3858
7	236.78	19.3533	8.8867	6.0942	4.8758	4.2067	3.7870	3.5004	3.2928	3.1355
	5928.36	99.3545	27.6723	14.9757	10.4556	8.2601	6.9929	6.1777	5.6128	5.2001
8	238.89	19.3716	8.8450	6.0412	4.8184	4.1468	3.7258	3.4382	3.2296	3.0717
	5981.07	99.3772	27.4889	14.7987	10.2893	8.1016	6.8400	6.0289	5.4671	5.0566
9	240.55	19.3854	8.8122	5.9989	4.7724	4.0990	3.6767	3.3881	3.1789	3.0204
	6022.47	99.3896	27.3453	14.6591	10.1577	7.9762	6.7187	5.9106	5.3512	4.9424
10	241.89	19.3959	8.7854	5.9643	4.7351	4.0599	3.6365	3.3472	3.1373	2.9783
	6055.85	99.4035	27.2289	14.5460	10.0512	7.8740	6.6201	5.8144	5.2565	4.8492
11	242.97	19.4042	8.7634	5.9359	4.7040	4.0275	3.6030	3.3130	3.1024	2.9430
	6083.32	99.4069	27.1327	14.4522	9.9626	7.7896	6.5382	5.7344	5.1779	4.7715
12	243.91	19.4124	8.7448	5.9118	4.6776	3.9999	3.5747	3.2839	3.0730	2.9130
	6106.32	99.4132	27.0510	14.3736	9.8882	7.7182	6.4691	5.6667	5.1114	4.7058
13	244.67	19.4190	8.7288	5.8912	4.6552	3.9763	3.5504	3.2590	3.0476	2.8871
	6125.86	99.4260	26.9824	14.3066	9.8250	7.6575	6.4100	5.6088	5.0545	4.6496
14	245.35	19.4243	8.7149	5.8732	4.6358	3.9559	3.5293	3.2374	3.0254	2.8647
	6142.67	99.4311	26.9244	14.2485	9.7700	7.6049	6.3590	5.5589	5.0052	4.6008
15	245.97	19.4287	8.7028	5.8578	4.6189	3.9380	3.5108	3.2183	3.0061	2.8450
	6157.28	99.4288	26.8723	14.1982	9.7221	7.5591	6.3144	5.5151	4.9621	4.5581

(Continues)

TABLE 3   (*Continued*)

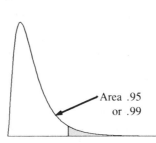

Area .95
or .99

Note: Rows are numerator degrees of freedom; columns are denominator degrees of freedom. Entries in a cell are the 95th on top of the 99th percentile.

v_2

v_1	11	12	13	14	15	16	17	18	19	20
1	4.84422	4.74720	4.66725	4.60006	4.54315	4.49401	4.45122	4.41398	4.38066	4.35128
	9.64599	9.33015	9.07371	8.86159	8.68315	8.53096	8.39981	8.28537	8.18505	8.09599
2	3.98223	3.88526	3.80552	3.73883	3.68235	3.63378	3.59151	3.55452	3.52194	3.49283
	7.20570	6.92666	6.70103	6.51497	6.35891	6.22627	6.11207	6.01283	5.92587	5.84890
3	3.58741	3.49026	3.41049	3.34388	3.28741	3.23893	3.19681	3.15990	3.12740	3.09836
	6.21668	5.95250	5.73935	5.56388	5.41692	5.29215	5.18499	5.09190	5.01024	4.93822
4	3.35670	3.25921	3.17917	3.11226	3.05559	3.00695	2.96472	2.92777	2.89508	2.86605
	5.66834	5.41194	5.20533	5.03540	4.89317	4.77257	4.66896	4.57903	4.50031	4.43073
5	3.20392	3.10588	3.02541	2.95824	2.90131	2.85239	2.81004	2.77286	2.74009	2.71089
	5.31599	5.06433	4.86162	4.69495	4.55560	4.43739	4.33595	4.24784	4.17077	4.10268
6	3.09466	2.99607	2.91528	2.84776	2.79045	2.74135	2.69870	2.66129	2.62834	2.59895
	5.06922	4.82063	4.62035	4.45583	4.31829	4.20165	4.10150	4.01464	3.93860	3.87141
7	3.01231	2.91335	2.83212	2.76418	2.70664	2.65717	2.61433	2.57669	2.54356	2.51399
	4.88613	4.63949	4.44098	4.27785	4.14154	4.02596	3.92672	3.84061	3.76528	3.69874
8	2.94796	2.84858	2.76695	2.69863	2.64082	2.59112	2.54798	2.51018	2.47679	2.44708
	4.74445	4.49936	4.30206	4.13997	4.00443	3.88955	3.79093	3.70541	3.63052	3.56444
9	2.89622	2.79641	2.71438	2.64576	2.58762	2.53767	2.49431	2.45626	2.42270	2.39281
	4.63151	4.38749	4.19110	4.02970	3.89477	3.78043	3.68223	3.59706	3.52253	3.45668
10	2.85358	2.75341	2.67105	2.60215	2.54368	2.49352	2.44993	2.41167	2.37795	2.34791
	4.53927	4.29607	4.10023	3.93937	3.80498	3.69089	3.59307	3.50817	3.43384	3.36817
11	2.81789	2.71732	2.63466	2.56550	2.50684	2.45639	2.41253	2.37413	2.34023	2.31002
	4.46247	4.21978	4.02449	3.86403	3.72989	3.61614	3.51850	3.43376	3.35962	3.29412
12	2.78753	2.68667	2.60369	2.53423	2.47533	2.42468	2.38066	2.34206	2.30796	2.27760
	4.39744	4.15524	3.96034	3.80012	3.66628	3.55267	3.45517	3.37063	3.29653	3.23112
13	2.76140	2.66021	2.57690	2.50727	2.44810	2.39724	2.35306	2.31431	2.28004	2.24952
	4.34163	4.09984	3.90521	3.74524	3.61155	3.49813	3.40070	3.31620	3.24220	3.17688
14	2.73864	2.63712	2.55362	2.48373	2.42440	2.37333	2.32896	2.29003	2.25562	2.22493
	4.29320	4.05175	3.85731	3.69754	3.56398	3.45065	3.35334	3.26891	3.19492	3.12961
15	2.71861	2.61684	2.53308	2.46304	2.40345	2.35222	2.30767	2.26862	2.23404	2.20330
	4.25082	4.00965	3.81538	3.65568	3.52222	3.40898	3.31169	3.22730	3.15335	3.08802

TABLE 4   Selected Percentiles of Chi-Square Distributions with *v* Degrees of Freedom

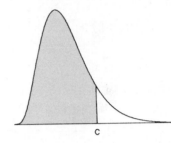

Note: The body of the table shows values of *c* such that $1 - \alpha$ is the area bounded by the horizontal axis, a vertical line located at *c*, and the chi-square curve.

$1 - \alpha$

v	0.010	0.050	0.100	0.300	0.500	0.700	0.900	0.950	0.990	0.999
1	0.0002	0.0039	0.0158	0.1485	0.4549	1.0742	2.7055	3.8415	6.6349	10.8277
2	0.0201	0.1026	0.2107	0.7133	1.3863	2.4079	4.6052	5.9915	9.2103	13.8155
3	0.1148	0.3518	0.5844	1.4237	2.3660	3.6649	6.2514	7.8147	11.3449	16.2663
4	0.2971	0.7107	1.0636	2.1947	3.3567	4.8784	7.7794	9.4877	13.2767	18.4669
5	0.5543	1.1455	1.6103	2.9999	4.3515	6.0644	9.2364	11.0705	15.0863	20.5150
6	0.8721	1.6354	2.2041	3.8276	5.3481	7.2311	10.6446	12.5916	16.8119	22.4578
7	1.2390	2.1674	2.8331	4.6713	6.3458	8.3834	12.0170	14.0671	18.4753	24.3220
8	1.6465	2.7326	3.4895	5.5274	7.3441	9.5245	13.3616	15.5073	20.0902	26.1246
9	2.0879	3.3251	4.1682	6.3933	8.3428	10.6564	14.6837	16.9190	21.6660	27.8771
10	2.5582	3.9403	4.8652	7.2672	9.3418	11.7807	15.9872	18.3070	23.2093	29.5884
11	3.0535	4.5748	5.5778	8.1479	10.3410	12.8987	17.2750	19.6751	24.7250	31.2642
12	3.5706	5.2260	6.3038	9.0343	11.3403	14.0111	18.5493	21.0261	26.2170	32.9097
13	4.1069	5.8919	7.0415	9.9257	12.3398	15.1187	19.8119	22.3620	27.6882	34.5278
14	4.6604	6.5706	7.7895	10.8215	13.3393	16.2221	21.0641	23.6848	29.1413	36.1235
15	5.2293	7.2609	8.5468	11.7212	14.3389	17.3217	22.3071	24.9958	30.5779	37.6973

Selected Data Set Listings

These four large data sets are not listed in the text chapters:

Amana Microwave Oven Assembly Line Data (AMANA.DAT), used in Chapter 2.

Population of 200 Regression Data (RSQUARE.DAT), used in Chapter 20.

Restaurant Survey Data (RESTRNT.DAT), used in Chapters 5 and 6.

Los Angeles Traffic Data (TRAFFIC.DAT), used in Chapters 4 and 20.

Amana Microwave Oven Assembly Line Data

Left and Right distances between the oven wrapper edge and the waveguide measured on microwave ovens produced by Amana Refrigeration, Inc. There are observations on 120 ovens. Further description of the data is given in Chapter 2 on pages 42 and 43.

```
# filename: AMANA.DAT
# Microwave oven assembly data, 1986
# (Source: Robert Cech, Amana Refrigeration, Amana, Iowa)
# Left and Right measurements on waveguide position
  56   54      48   58      60    48      36   44      44   47
  70   58      40   46      68    78      45   40      50   48
  71   74      50   56      80    72      50   39      48   56
  58   50      48   58      73    90      56   47      44   50
  52   32      44   54      64    73      48   35      47   54
  58   54      50   58      80   121      58   50      41   50
  38   32      54   55      78    96      60   39      50   44
  60   60      32   56      81    78      60   48      45   39
  60   54      58   56      66    78      51   61      48   51
  70   82      60   52      50    56      64   60      47   64
  48   42      56   64      84    71      59   60      50   49
  52   40      70   72      89    86      51   46      46   51
  68   68      80   94      71    80      50   59      55   57
  48   52      74   68      69    78      60   64      56   51
  50   51      58   62      73    79      54   59      48   46
  48   46      72   42      80    66      58   45      51   48
  52   62      44   44      79    81      41   47
  56   66      55   68      64    70      40   49
  65   80      40   50      45    59      51   54
  45   54      74   78      22    27      56   58
  50   62      50   58      42    44      28   39
  56   66      80   85      66    56      55   41
  51   58      70   83      56    71      44   50
  44   50      92   67      69    69      50   39
  56   58      90   59      34    35      51   44
  50   50      81   74      36    40      54   48
```

Population of 200 Regression Data

These data are used in Section 20.11 to illustrate difficulties in interpreting R^2.

```
# filename: RSQUARE.DAT
# Population of 200 Y and X values
#     Y         X
```

Y	X	Y	X	Y	X
7.7216	97.390	9.4082	99.398	10.5848	100.342
8.4778	97.719	10.0677	99.404	9.9352	100.364
7.7187	97.724	9.9640	99.424	10.4771	100.383
8.4557	97.740	10.5509	99.434	11.1437	100.384
6.7515	97.935	9.5574	99.456	10.0875	100.411
8.0277	97.981	8.9212	99.470	10.9831	100.428
9.0801	98.086	8.7668	99.473	11.2113	100.440
7.8140	98.099	8.2434	99.547	10.3640	100.442
8.3641	98.179	8.9679	99.574	11.1437	100.443
7.0371	98.206	9.8732	99.615	9.9331	100.462
8.5759	98.240	9.6428	99.626	11.4849	100.466
9.1042	98.256	10.1303	99.639	9.8936	100.466
8.7486	98.262	9.9066	99.651	10.5048	100.483
9.0460	98.305	10.8610	99.653	9.9248	100.485
8.7265	98.335	9.7618	99.656	10.1802	100.520
7.7648	98.366	9.7667	99.712	10.1911	100.524
9.5704	98.413	10.2679	99.719	11.5284	100.570
8.9114	98.439	9.5005	99.722	10.1004	100.573
8.3608	98.489	8.9544	99.740	10.9566	100.586
7.3781	98.515	9.7174	99.742	10.5631	100.599
8.9414	98.656	11.4663	99.759	11.1717	100.623
9.8830	98.670	10.0461	99.779	11.3292	100.630
8.8700	98.675	9.4557	99.783	10.6046	100.635
7.6031	98.677	9.5380	99.795	10.9252	100.667
10.0445	98.691	10.0226	99.813	9.6129	100.683
9.7655	98.693	9.5913	99.827	10.5870	100.729
8.6292	98.700	10.9460	99.852	9.9740	100.735
9.9338	98.751	10.0910	99.889	10.8506	100.739
9.9384	98.785	9.8073	99.909	9.6707	100.750
8.2317	98.803	8.0018	99.941	10.5250	100.753
9.0142	98.827	9.4913	99.962	10.4211	100.753
8.8822	98.828	10.7485	99.967	10.9387	100.772
7.8507	98.832	10.6406	99.968	10.8419	100.786
9.4946	98.838	10.3909	99.976	11.0124	100.801
9.7688	98.856	9.8486	99.983	10.6489	100.813
8.6732	98.878	9.8353	100.010	10.1225	100.816
8.8615	98.879	10.5057	100.051	10.1457	100.825
9.4466	98.910	10.2935	100.052	9.5475	100.849
9.9286	99.002	10.9814	100.052	10.4423	100.865
8.5382	99.009	9.4287	100.063	11.3707	100.881
9.9369	99.104	9.6036	100.067	11.2337	100.912
9.9029	99.108	8.4918	100.067	11.6613	100.973
8.2602	99.109	9.9808	100.076	12.2551	100.984
9.4517	99.110	10.5207	100.079	11.6505	100.986
9.7667	99.111	9.1734	100.107	12.0307	100.996
9.9274	99.139	10.1677	100.131	9.7924	101.022
8.1069	99.147	9.6243	100.138	10.9549	101.024
9.7023	99.157	10.6597	100.156	10.6963	101.047
9.5023	99.166	9.3408	100.162	10.8563	101.049
8.6325	99.196	9.9286	100.163	11.0482	101.107
9.9136	99.199	10.2979	100.168	11.3591	101.213
9.7994	99.208	10.0891	100.184	11.8929	101.226
9.0986	99.222	11.0848	100.214	10.7626	101.238
9.1281	99.224	10.6025	100.235	10.5514	101.341
9.4777	99.237	9.6156	100.244	11.8054	101.379
9.4478	99.242	9.2066	100.261	11.5956	101.391
9.5831	99.255	10.1315	100.269	11.1049	101.412
8.6809	99.271	10.0666	100.269	10.4703	101.453
9.8395	99.284	10.5068	100.281	10.7383	101.467
9.6125	99.317	10.8306	100.284	10.6276	101.542
9.5515	99.327	10.0337	100.286	11.5006	101.583
9.0917	99.332	10.2038	100.291	10.1321	101.599
9.4938	99.342	9.9186	100.308	12.8224	101.712
9.3727	99.359	10.6547	100.309	11.4666	101.793
9.0947	99.363	9.5292	100.317	11.8573	102.278
8.9342	99.375	9.6373	100.319	11.7150	102.341
8.4906	99.395	9.5195	100.324		

Restaurant Survey Data

These data are from a 1980 survey conducted by the University of Wisconsin Small Business Development Center. The data are used extensively in Chapters 5 and 6.

```
# filename: RESTRNT.DAT
# Wisconsin restaurant survey data
# Variable: Description
# ID number
# Business Outlook categorized as
#        1 = very unfavorable...6 = very favorable
# Sales: Gross 1979 sales in $1000's
# New capital: New capital invested in 1979
# Value: Estimated market value of business ($1000's)
# Cost of goods: Cost of goods sold as % of sales
# Wages: Wages as % of sales
# Advertising: $ as % of sales
# Type: 1=fast food, 2=supper club, 3=other
# Seats: number of dining seats
# Owner: 1=sole proprietorship, 2=partnership, 3=corp.
# Full Time: # of full time employees
# Part Time: # of part time employees
# Size: Size of restaurant categorized as
#        1 = 1 to 9.5 full time equivalent employees
#        2 = 10 to 20 full time equivalent employees
#        3 = more than 20 full time equivalent employees
#        (Full time equivalent=full time + 1/2part time)
```

ID	Outlook	Sales	NewCap	Value	Cost	Wages	Adv	Type	Seats	Owner	FullT	PartT	Size
1	2	480	0	600	35	25	2	2	200	3	8	30	3
2	4	507	22	375	59	20	5	2	150	1	6	25	2
3	5	210	25	275	40	24	3	1	46	1	0	17	1
4	5	246	*	80	43	30	1	1	28	3	2	13	1
5	2	148	*	85	45	35	1	3	44	1	*	*	*
6	3	50	*	135	40	30	10	2	50	3	2	*	*
7	2	72	0	125	85	10	5	2	50	1	0	5	1
8	3	99	7	150	43	25	1	2	130	1	1	8	1
9	4	160	5	85	*	*	*	*	*	2	2	10	1
10	4	243	7	150	38	15	2	2	50	2	2	19	2
11	4	200	3	225	42	22	2	1	64	1	3	12	1
12	4	1000	20	1500	20	20	10	1	240	3	30	40	3
13	4	350	*	*	31	35	*	1	111	3	10	19	2
14	3	550	0	410	50	26	2	2	125	3	6	16	2
15	3	500	10	1000	50	40	10	2	120	1	4	28	2
16	4	1100	8	900	*	*	*	*	3	13	47	3
17	3	416	0	400	40	21	4	1	92	3	7	15	2
18	2	650	*	*	63	32	5	1	90	3	20	25	3
19	5	292	0	425	42	13	1	2	150	3	1	16	1
20	3	400	10	350	30	25	5	2	90	1	15	10	2
21	3	42	0	15	64	35	1	3	15	2	0	0	1
22	2	100	15	185	50	15	1	2	80	3	0	7	1
23	4	75	0	160	*	*	*	2	76	1	0	10	1
24	3	180	0	180	50	20	2	2	65	1	1	14	1
25	4	201	0	250	70	27	3	2	178	1	0	20	2
26	6	273	60	300	32	28	10	3	110	3	7	13	2
27	4	150	0	150	*	*	*	2	60	*	51	80	3
28	5	60	4	100	*	*	*	1	0	1	0	0	1
29	4	1200	50	800	35	32	3	3	150	3	35	45	3
30	3	247	4	*	38	*	2	1	60	3	4	8	1
31	2	290	3	200	39	29	1	1	85	3	16	14	3
32	2	58	2	75	45	28	5	2	25	3	2	2	1
33	4	400	0	100	40	35	1	3	85	3	18	15	3
34	3	75	*	26	40	40	5	3	20	2	4	4	1
35	5	*	*	*	32	40	4	2	200	*	*	*	*
36	4	144	0	25	45	25	0	3	0	1	6	3	1
37	4	65	0	25	48	20	1	1	0	1	2	2	1
38	3	*	*	*	*	*	*	1	210	*	*	*	*
39	4	465	0	75	38	28	7	1	111	3	6	32	3
40	5	*	*	*	50	40	10	3	0	3	10	5	2
41	5	510	3	750	35	29	4	1	152	3	30	25	3
42	3	440	0	*	38	20	5	1	62	3	9	16	2
43	4	608	30	395	31	28	2	3	165	3	30	12	3
44	3	200	3	350	43	21	4	1	68	2	3	18	2
45	1	90	5	40	60	30	10	1	60	1	3	3	1
46	5	45	3	40	40	20	3	3	0	1	0	7	1
47	6	36	1	*	65	25	5	1	0	2	3	0	1
48	4	249	6	275	65	30	5	1	52	1	8	10	2
49	5	200	5	60	35	20	2	3	24	3	4	20	2
50	2	80	0	150	60	30	5	2	70	1	1	4	1
51	1	500	5	350	40	30	3	1	72	3	20	6	3
52	2	125	10	140	50	20	5	2	68	3	0	8	1
53	2	101	0	140	54	13	1	2	58	1	2	3	1
54	4	110	2	160	60	20	1	2	46	1	0	6	1
55	3	1200	*	2500	37	29	3	1	200	3	80	45	3
56	1	*	*	*	33	25	25	3	120	3	25	5	3
57	4	4700	20	1500	50	20	4	1	200	3	15	50	3
58	3	48	0	45	45	25	2	3	10	3	0	12	1
59	2	150	20	150	45	25	5	3	0	3	10	20	2
60	1	185	40	*	40	40	4	1	62	3	2	18	2
61	4	157	2	250	*	*	*	1	99	1	3	8	1
62	6	621	9	0	36	23	3	1	120	3	5	45	3
63	2	257	10	365	40	22	0	1	100	1	14	3	2
64	2	137	0	75	55	30	3	1	0	3	1	3	1
65	1	190	0	400	60	40	0	1	125	1	2	11	1
66	1	*	*	*	*	*	*	*	*	0	*	*	*
67	2	320	6	350	50	20	3	2	96	1	10	10	2
68	5	650	*	*	50	30	1	2	140	3	20	15	3
69	5	610	61	*	38	19	5	1	100	3	10	30	3
70	5	385	4	150	36	29	4	3	48	3	20	28	3
71	5	360	75	325	29	23	3	1	120	3	4	15	2
72	1	276	*	200	65	30	5	1	0	3	20	3	3
73	6	600	20	500	38	22	2	2	125	3	28	5	3
74	2	330	0	100	45	25	2	1	0	1	2	14	1
75	3	215	10	125	45	30	2	1	15	1	11	0	2
76	3	425	15	1750	39	27	12	3	250	1	2	70	3
77	4	250	10	10	40	40	10	2	80	3	10	4	2
78	2	120	0	80	*	*	*	3	30	1	1	2	1
79	3	60	30	45	60	30	10	1	16	2	0	4	1
80	3	141	6	80	85	10	5	1	34	2	0	4	1
81	5	800	50	500	50	25	5	3	120	2	35	13	3
82	3	207	4	200	48	20	1	1	0	*	*	*	*
83	5	1016	16	1000	40	36	1	3	200	3	20	40	3
84	3	60	0	40	50	30	20	3	80	3	2	4	1
85	3	309	10	500	52	18	2	2	80	1	6	14	2
86	2	960	20	400	54	22	2	3	0	3	7	40	3
87	3	150	*	650	70	20	10	2	220	3	3	18	2
88	4	56	5	125	40	20	10	2	44	1	0	2	1
89	6	250	5	100	33	30	2	1	55	3	10	15	2
90	4	275	10	295	50	25	5	2	85	3	10	3	2
91	5	150	50	300	30	30	0	1	77	3	4	13	2
92	4	325	2	175	45	25	5	3	125	3	20	6	3

Restaurant Survey Data (*Continued*)

```
 93 5  110    5   235 50 30 20 2  65 2   2  10 1
 94 3  250    5   230 50 30  4 2  90 3   4  12 2
 95 3  550    0   500 48 22  2 2 100 3  13   6 2
 96 1  100    3   200 35 25  0 1  50 3   0   6 1
 97 3   32    1    42 35 10  2 1  30 1   3   0 1
 98 7  366   10   300 42 25  1 2 150 3  12  40 3
 99 5   70    3   150 50  7  2 2  50 3   3   2 1
100 3  531    2   450 46 30  1 3  72 3   1  39 3
101 4  225    0   300 50 40  0 1  43 1  10   4 2
102 3  108    5   110  *  *  * *   *  2   0   8 1
103 3  100    *     * 86 14  0 3   0 1   3   2 1
104 4   40    4    75 30  1  1 3  20 1   *   2 *
105 4  750    0  1000 40 22  5 2 140 2  15  25 3
106 2  312    *   250 40 34  2 3 110 3   6  20 2
107 2   50    5    75 40 20  5 3  56 1   0   5 1
108 5  163    3   115 50 28  5 2  75 3   5   4 1
109 1   75    1    55  *  *  * 3  32 1   0   0 1
110 6  550    6   600 48 24  1 2  76 2   3  30 2
111 1 3450    8   100  *  *  * 2  80 3   3   9 1
112 3   50    4   305 45  9  4 2  60 1   4   6 1
113 5   80    0    50 43 18  2 3   0 1   0   6 1
114 3  435   10   250 30 14  5 3  36 1   1  11 1
115 1   70    2    75 30 35  0 1   0 1   1   2 1
116 1   78    1   125 90  0 10 3  62 1   5   0 1
117 5  210   20   225 80 18  2 1  28 1   0   5 1
118 4  280    *   300 40 16  8 1  50 3   2  18 2
119 4  192    *   300 35 85  5 2  82 3   8   4 2
120 4  116   15   135 50  *  * 1  28 1   2   7 1
121 5  245    0   450 36 24  2 2 100 3   7  20 2
122 1  110    *   160  *  *  * 2  80 1   0   0 1
123 3  229    *   150 35 25  5 1  72 3   7   8 2
124 4  275    *  1100 60 40  0 1  96 3   4   7 1
125 1  100    *    75 50 20  2 3  46 1   4   4 1
126 4  647   10   350 50 30  5 1  90 3   5  12 2
127 4  300    1   100  *  *  * * 3   *   *   * 
128 7   54    0     * 35 20 15 3  70 *   0   0 1
129 5  400    *   300  *  *  * 3  78 3   3  25 2
130 2  120    2   100 84 15  1 2  55 1   1   5 1
131 5    *    *     * 30 15  9 1  40 3  10  15 2
132 1  179    6    70 43 23  2 1  27 1   1  15 1
133 4  300    3   175 35 30  1 1  30 3   7   8 2
134 3  500  125   300 45 78  5 1 125 3  10  22 3
135 2  150   12   210 45 15  2 2  60 1   0  10 1
136 3  135    2    90 60 18  2 1  42 1   3   4 1
137 5  400    4   250 42 35  1 1  36 3  13   3 2
138 1  480    *   450 57 38  0 2 200 2  30   8 3
139 3  530   40   200 40 30  8 2 180 3  25  12 3
140 5    *    *     *  *  *  * 3  20 1   0   2 1
141 5  600   12    90 35 30  5 1  30 3  36   4 3
142 4    *    4   150 42  0  2 3  50 1   7   3 1
143 2  125    1     * 55 20  2 1  35 3   3   8 1
144 1  382    0   190  *  *  * 1  51 3   4   0 1
145 5    *    *   400 30 13  4 1 100 3   2   7 1
146 3  200   10   200 30 30  5 3  50 3   4  12 2
147 5  800   21   750 38 25  3 3 144 3  20  21 3
148 4  144    *   200 40 20  1 2  50 1   2   5 1
149 4  130    1   150  0 40  1 2  60 3   3   9 1
150 2 1010   50     * 50 25  3 2 127 3  25  35 3
151 5   60    5   150  *  *  * 3  25 1   0   2 1
152 4  292   20   100 49 30  8 2  75 2   6  24 2
153 3  100   56     * 45 25  5 2  75 3   6  14 2
154 3   98    0    70 70 28  2 1  32 1   0   7 1
155 2  250    6   250 50 25  1 2  90 3   7   7 2
156 4  172    1   200 35 14  3 1   0 1   0  20 2
157 3  145   12   155  *  *  * 2  74 1   1   9 1
158 4    *    *     *  *  *  * 2   0 3   *   0 *
159 1    *    *     *  *  *  * *   * *   *   * *
160 4    *    *     *  *  *  * 1   0 3   3   1 1
161 3   37    1    20 45 10  1 3  12 1   1   1 1

162 3    *    *     *  *  *  3 1  82 2   5  22 2
163 4   77    0   150  *  *  * 1  35 2   4   1 1
164 3  400    *   400  *  *  * 3  44 3   6   8 2
165 4 1000   20     * 40 34  2 2   * 2   *   * *
166 2  250   15   750 40 20  5 2  95 3  26  13 3
167 4   50    *    90  *  *  * 3  24 1   0   0 1
168 1  120    6     * 80 15  5 1  70 1   1   6 1
169 4  750   78     0 30 32  3 3  94 2  40   6 3
170 5  190    8    75 42 31  1 3  60 3   6   3 1
171 1  140    5   180 40  5  5 2  87 1   3   3 1
172 4   80   52    60 36 23  1 2 100 1   0   8 1
173 5   55    0    50 50 20 10 3  40 3   0   6 1
174 5  690    0   250 45 21  3 3 196 3   8  35 3
175 4  200    1   175 49 19  2 1 100 1   0  18 1
176 4   28    2    55 33  0  1 3  34 3   0   0 1
177 5   40    1     0  *  *  * 3  24 3   1   3 1
178 4    2    0     2 30  5  0 1  10 3   0   2 1
179 2  217    0   750 51 29  4 2  95 3   3  25 2
180 4  250    0   300 40 30 10 1  20 3  10  10 2
181 3  990    *  1500 40 29  5 1 175 3  12  43 3
182 4    2    2     * 90 10  0 1   0 2   0   4 1
183 3   50   20   325 50 30 20 2  75 3   2   3 1
184 7  290  150   450 51 59  3 2 110 1   5  14 2
185 1   75   10   140  *  *  * 1   0 1   0   0 1
186 1    *    *     *  *  *  * 1   0 1   0   0 1
187 5  400   10   300 20 25  5 2  85 3  10  10 2
188 3   30    0    60 49 30  1 1   0 2   2   4 1
189 2   70    0    32 40 30  1 3  65 1   2   3 1
190 2  250    0     0 37 14  4 1  16 3   3  13 1
191 5 1600   20  1000 34 32  4 1  52 3  20  55 3
192 2  290    0   125 60 35  5 1  70 3   6   2 1
193 4  203    2    40 39 31  4 1   0 1   8   4 2
194 5    *    *     * 60 30  0 1  16 1   0   3 1
195 2  100    5   300 60  0  1 2  50 2   0   0 1
196 3  551    0  1500  *  *  * 1 100 3  10  25 3
197 3  220   10    70 42 40  4 1  85 3   6   7 1
198 3  225   10   550 50 15  5 1 200 3   1  15 1
199 3  140   14   175 33 10  5 1   0 1   0   4 1
200 1  154    0    20 45 28  0 *  80 3   6   5 1
201 4   39    0    65 42 42  0 1  75 1   0  30 2
202 4  565    0   500  *  *  * 2  85 3  15  35 3
203 3    0    2     0 43 15  2 2  75 1   1   4 1
204 2 1096   73  2000 34 29  1 1 142 3  42  30 3
205 4   35    1     0 90 10  0 1  60 1   4   0 1
206 5   53   20   125 40 20  5 1  30 3   5   7 1
207 2  390    8   450  *  *  * * 3  30  16 3
208 3    *    *     * 32 34  2 1 104 3   2  16 2
209 4    *    *    80  *  *  * 3  45 1   1   9 1
210 5  500   25   450 45 35  1 2 132 3  18  20 3
211 4  180    5   300 58 40  2 3  30 3   8   3 1
212 6   89    4   120 45 15  2 1   0 1   1   2 1
213 1   77   10   175 35 10  1 3   0 1   0   5 1
214 1  460    3    75 40 23  6 1  94 3   2  35 2
215 3  440   35  1000 38 39  3 3 110 3  40  30 3
216 5   56    8   125 40 33  2 3   0 1  12   0 2
217 4   15   23    30 52 46  2 1   0 1   0   0 1
218 5  150    *   150  *  *  * * 2   0   7 1
219 5 8064  300 12000 37 31  3 1 550 3 250  60 3
220 3  200    *     * 20 20  1 2  20 3   1   8 1
221 3   30    0   350 50 20  5 1  80 3   0   4 1
222 5   71    0   185 40  8  0 3   0 1   0   3 1
223 4   11    0     0 99  0  0 1   4 1   0   0 1
224 1  267    2   125 40 25  5 1  44 3   2  13 1
225 7  325   10   400 46 25  4 2  70 1   3   9 1
226 1  155    0    85 35 35  5 3  70 1  10   3 2
227 4 1000  100  5000 35 20  7 1 180 3  30  20 3
228 3   85   30    45 45 25  2 1  54 1   1   6 1
229 3  250   50  1000 35 35  0 3 150 3  25  30 3
230 2   30    5    40 30 30  3 3  55 1   1   4 1
```

(*Continues*)

Restaurant Survey Data (*Continued*)

```
231 2   20    1      0 45 20  2 3    0 3    0   3 1
232 *    *    *      * 40 10  5 1   40 *    *   * *
233 2  125    5    125 50 30 10 1   65 1    0   6 1
234 4  720   13    650 37 24  6 1  150 3    6  25 2
235 4    *    *      * 40 30  5 3  150 3   25 100 3
236 1  240    3    225 50 20  2 2   30 1    5   6 1
237 4   10    *     10 50 38  2 3   35 2    3  10 1
238 5  240    0    125 45 25  1 1    0 1    7   3 1
239 6   59    *      *  *  *  * 3    0 2    2   4 1
240 3 1080   20   1000 32 30  5 3  170 3   40  50 3
241 1  225    1    150 34 22  4 3  120 3   18   5 3
242 3    *    *      *  *  *  * 3    4   20   2
243 2   70    7    225 25 35 10 3   43 1    4   2 1
244 1  430   35    500 42 26  2 2    0 3    6  30 3
245 4  198    *    130 45 21  1 1   62 1    5   8 1
246 5   65   12    150 35 30  2 1   35 1   10   4 2
247 2   69    3     18 44 26  1 3   43 1    0   9 1
248 4  230    0      0 35 36  3 3  150 3   20  12 3
249 4  250   25    850 40 15  1 1   40 3    0   * *
250 5  140   80    140  *  *  * *    * 1    2  12 1
251 5  180    5    150 40 25  5 1  130 3    2   6 1
252 3   60    7      * 40 10  2 1   18 1    1   0 1
253 1   80    0    150 51 18  0 1    0 1    1   2 1
254 1   42    0     75 65 25 10 1   36 1    0   3 1
255 4    8    0     14 25 15  0 3    0 1    *   2 *

256 3  210    *    350  *  *  * 2  100 1    0  16 1
257 3   95    0     70 45 25  2 3   42 1    4   1 1
258 4   55   50     89 65 30  5 3   32 3    0   2 1
259 5  121    1    160 55 30  5 1   30 1    3   2 1
260 3   75   10     80 40 26  5 3   26 1    2   2 1
261 1    *    *      * 45 21  4 3  205 3    8  32 3
262 6  250   10    300 38 29  4 1   50 3    5  20 2
263 4  220   10    350 55 25 10 2   70 1    0  15 1
264 4  120   10     80 35 60  2 1   80 1    2  22 2
265 2   25    1     40 40 10  6 1    0 *    *   * *
266 1  500    0    175 75 20  5 2  200 3   32   1 3
267 3    *    *    475 45 20 10 2   80 1    2  15 1
268 3  200   10     70 45 20 25 1   70 3    0  10 1
269 4  250    3      5 35 50  0 3   15 2    1   3 1
270 5  215    1    100 36 33  2 3   98 3    5  17 2
271 4    *    *      *  *  *  * 2   36 2    7   6 2
272 3  733   35    500 53 21  0 1    0 1    6  40 3
273 1    *    *      *  *  *  * 3    0 1    0   0 1
274 1  200    1    210 50 20  5 2   70 *    *   * *
275 5  305    0    450 58 27  2 2   85 3    3  25 2
276 1  110    5    175  *  *  * 2   99 1    0   7 1
277 2    *    *    100  *  *  * 3   45 1    3   6 1
278 3  100   20    250 24 30 10 3  100 3    0   7 1
279 4  355    *     95 40 20  5 1  130 3    8  12 2
```

Los Angeles Traffic Data

Only the roadtype and actual volume variables are used in Chapter 4. All variables in this data set are used in the Chapter 20 exercises. There are 396 observations. The data are described further on page 99.

```
# filename: TRAFFIC.DAT
# Los Angeles traffic data: 396 observations
# (Source: Lee Cryer, Barton-Aschman Associates,
#  Pasadena, CA)
# Variables: roadtype (1=freeway, 2=minor arterial
# 3=major arterial, 4=Ventura Boulevard),
# actual traffic volume, estimated traffic volume
```

roadtype	actual	estimated	roadtype	actual	estimated	roadtype	actual	estimated	roadtype	actual	estimated
1	126000	106848	4	15130	13651	1	52000	68028	1	92000	94674
1	126000	121121	4	14785	13310	1	55000	65378	1	92000	98295
1	126000	109751	2	6164	12953	1	86000	98437	1	92000	96779
1	126000	129345	4	19482	13195	1	82000	97375	1	90000	93243
1	137000	136049	4	14481	12211	1	52000	68326	1	90000	92994
1	137000	143882	4	14245	12779	1	55000	65972	1	88000	88755
1	137000	134221	4	15963	12016	1	55000	59788	1	88000	88303
1	126000	93397	4	11860	11906	1	55000	60150	1	88000	88755
1	126000	105125	4	16259	12219	1	56000	60593	1	88000	88303
1	126000	103249	4	16971	13474	1	57000	55432	1	80000	85058
1	92000	97804	4	18252	13183	1	56000	60523	1	80000	81959
1	113000	118250	4	17714	12831	1	57000	55259	1	80000	83251
1	92000	76863	4	20819	11915	1	84000	107808	1	110000	122229
1	92000	86452	4	19001	13186	1	36000	52664	1	110000	112271
1	66000	90369	4	24525	14664	1	86000	98117	1	110000	105969
1	114000	113392	4	20151	16947	1	84000	107923	1	102000	88226
1	110000	108444	2	3676	9858	1	82000	97731	1	102000	96531
4	13186	11789	4	21074	14776	1	77000	97022	1	99000	87493
4	11623	13566	4	21775	16272	1	77000	97259	1	72000	79312
4	11628	11241	4	15162	10960	1	77000	94923	1	66000	76186
1	110000	111046	4	14843	11028	1	77000	95199	1	72000	79303
1	110000	99858	4	14530	13285	1	80000	80506	1	72000	77541
1	102000	96531	2	8007	5947	1	113000	122218	1	72000	77659
1	102000	92448	1	99000	105257	1	92000	101705	1	71000	74996
1	66000	83263	1	104000	108749	1	92000	108603	1	71000	75182
1	66000	93756	1	112000	110769	1	92000	97227	1	69000	73461
4	2970	2018	1	112000	107599	1	92000	91056	1	69000	74287

Los Angeles Traffic Data (*Continued*)

1	60000	70425	1	119000	115522	3	16872	16844	2	4084	1309
1	60000	71140	1	119000	115599	3	17432	15558	3	7247	8301
1	49000	62060	1	126000	131159	2	6147	7335	2	5365	2062
1	49000	62809	1	126000	132824	3	14398	14766	2	4147	3103
1	42000	57395	1	127000	131829	3	16451	15841	3	11731	9574
1	36000	52376	1	127000	131578	2	8351	7756	2	5237	4900
1	42000	56657	1	137000	133549	2	6115	9795	2	1158	3667
1	56000	60523	1	137000	142886	3	13502	10874	2	4043	5025
1	56000	60593	1	137000	134546	2	8512	6688	3	18961	13640
3	7773	16333	1	92000	72623	3	7789	3644	2	12699	4629
3	17124	22100	1	126000	89910	3	4671	9958	2	5212	8723
3	6993	12333	1	126000	120187	3	7228	9178	3	15278	15360
3	3522	1052	1	125000	112790	3	7287	13605	2	3098	3200
3	10671	12140	1	125000	113059	3	15813	16201	2	9417	7610
3	13376	13258	1	124000	111572	3	10034	4455	3	15475	18756
4	5957	16455	1	124000	110727	4	29370	15569	2	2646	2479
4	12721	9332	1	116000	110103	2	4371	6900	2	5428	6922
4	16915	15245	1	116000	110067	4	16502	13352	3	8950	11600
4	14782	10053	1	116000	110103	4	14836	14495	2	9339	9472
4	13447	11982	1	112000	110466	4	15667	14474	3	13121	10932
4	12624	11883	1	116000	110067	3	6453	7841	2	7494	16452
4	21918	15386	1	112000	107666	3	5975	4170	3	23179	33268
4	9489	11789	1	99000	89273	3	9494	7776	3	19141	15736
4	10604	6907	1	66000	75046	3	11017	8450	2	954	1679
3	11302	13691	4	21506	17036	3	7077	2402	3	17500	21588
3	10188	12420	3	14829	15955	3	8308	16020	3	13324	14762
2	2322	9656	3	18746	12346	2	3672	3872	4	12739	13309
3	13253	11313	3	10572	14018	4	6552	2520	4	15237	12473
3	12560	14170	2	7128	3738	4	15880	10401	3	16195	14673
3	16147	14641	2	10010	9918	2	1514	642	3	13397	14530
2	8238	3559	4	24719	9432	2	6568	8845	2	5038	8505
2	1671	6228	3	22254	19463	3	16441	17594	2	12511	9873
3	15549	17968	3	29230	16436	2	2387	3548	2	12403	11355
3	16807	13174	4	15995	9442	2	2831	2622	3	17458	13861
3	10026	12988	3	17317	23548	2	5923	1845	2	15262	11320
3	12143	14888	2	12904	7892	2	8483	1818	2	7087	11137
2	7135	2639	2	4038	1050	2	8986	5160	2	8896	8100
3	18515	11974	2	9113	4766	2	7236	3811	3	12899	15672
3	14218	15198	3	12603	12244	2	5883	6994	2	9846	8048
3	14525	11642	2	12814	19933	3	20446	19538	4	14564	14660
3	12781	11602	3	15993	17664	2	1263	1787	4	13821	11435
3	8025	10798	3	16658	16887	3	18710	13122	2	3041	3811
3	13271	16717	4	14425	10840	2	8783	5973	3	4940	13114
3	19267	14430	2	9564	3045	2	9715	10917	2	5433	4645
3	17481	16247	3	13453	19106	2	14516	10564	2	3521	6625
3	15762	16838	3	16535	14482	2	10579	11763	3	15488	16514
3	9077	1749	3	18456	17075	2	6258	9328	2	11663	10421
2	1405	1669	3	14714	14507	3	15284	11367	2	9422	10158
2	16555	2263	2	9275	3056	2	8527	5158	2	15238	10709
2	5537	9183	2	15274	11414	2	7494	7459	2	9449	11523
3	14437	18769	2	2971	7639	2	3289	2845	2	8796	7900
3	12908	17581	3	8355	7441	2	3717	2533	2	9807	14105
3	6189	5481	2	16233	7928	2	3198	2351	3	15204	18214
3	16453	15482	2	7316	5501	3	11743	9526	3	15670	20317
3	14960	14277	2	8236	9493	2	9549	4256	2	7095	10225
3	14783	17624	2	10615	14381	2	5277	2344	2	8570	9181
3	11804	8017	3	12074	12363	2	11258	1696	2	11156	18525
2	5891	1345	2	11914	4071	3	12189	13576	3	7875	14109
3	7434	13402	2	4426	4447	3	17440	16570	2	11771	8945
1	66000	85274	3	13290	14224	3	17208	19671	2	18989	13914
1	76000	87077	2	4218	6386	3	24300	21643	3	12203	15842
1	76000	88032	3	9799	14296	2	9416	10525	3	15256	24588
1	86000	101423	3	4000	1064	2	6003	4169	3	14942	22920
1	99000	104076	3	11548	12494	2	10100	10509	3	13232	16712
1	86000	102346	2	8353	4805	2	7397	3566	2	7097	5220
1	104000	109166	2	4815	9585	2	5153	750	2	4925	9664
1	110000	111935	3	28777	19910	2	8259	8109	2	5204	7531
1	114000	107083	3	20446	20088	2	15481	4696	2	8174	5853
1	110000	112307	3	12058	13581	3	18530	27195	4	11727	12967
1	114000	113386	3	12614	14635	2	10099	6849	4	5677	7657
1	114000	113315	2	8319	8841	3	17616	17932	4	21622	16242
1	114000	113309	2	5361	6416	3	16106	14997	4	20071	16135

References

A Million Random Digits with 100,000 Normal Deviates. Santa Monica, CA: RAND Corporation, 1955.

Alden, Vernon R. "Who Says You Can't Crack Japanese Markets?" *Harvard Business Review* 87, no. 1 (January–February 1987): 52–56.

Allmon, Carolyn I. "Advertising and Sales Relationships for Toothpaste: Another Look." *Business Economics* 17, no. 4 (September 1982): 55–61.

Anscombe, Frank, "Graphs in Statistical Analysis." *American Statistician* 27 (February 1973): 17–21.

Assael, H. *Consumer Behavior and Marketing Action.* 3d ed. Boston: PWS-KENT, 1987.

Barabba, Vincent P., Richard O. Mason, and Ian I. Mitroff. "Federal Statistics in a Complex Environment: The Case of the 1980 Census." *American Statistician* 37, no. 3 (August 1983): 203–12.

Bartlett, M. S. "On the Theoretical Specification of Sampling Properties of Autocorrelated Time Series." *Journal of the Royal Statistical Society* B, 8 (1946): 27–41.

Bass, Frank M., and Darral G. Clarke. "Testing Distributed Lag Models of Advertising Effect." *Journal of Marketing Research* 9, no. 3 (August 1972): 298–308.

Bates, Douglas M., and Donald G. Watts. *Nonlinear Regression Analysis and its Applications.* New York: John Wiley & Sons, 1988.

Blattberg, Robert C., and Abel P. Jeuland. "Micromodeling Approach to Investigate the Advertising-Sales Relationship." *Management Science* 27, no. 9 (September 1981): 988–1005.

Bowerman, Bruce L., and R. T. O'Connell. *Time Series Forecasting.* 2d ed. Boston: PWS-KENT, 1987.

Box, G. E. P. "Robustness in the Strategy of Scientific Model Building." In *Robustness in Statistics*, edited by R. L. Lanner and G. N. Wilkerson. New York: Academic Press, 1979.

Box, G. E. P., and David R. Cox. "An Analysis of Transformations." *Journal of the Royal Statistical Society* B, 26 (1964): 211–43.

Box, G. E. P., J. S. Hunter, and W. G. Hunter. *Statistics for Experimenters.* New York: John Wiley & Sons, 1978.

Box, G. E. P., and G. M. Jenkins. *Time Series Analysis.* rev. ed. San Francisco: Holden-Day, 1976.

Boyd, Harper W., Jr., and Ralph Westfall. "Interviewer Bias Once More Revisited." *Journal of Marketing Research* 7, (May 1970): 249–53.

Braccio, Ralph. "History of Mass Public Opinion and the Political Process." *Christian Science Monitor*, 16 April 1987, 28.

Brown, R. G. *Smoothing, Forecasting and Prediction of Discrete Time Series.* Englewood Cliffs, N.J.: Prentice Hall, 1962.

Buchanan, Bruce, Moshe Given, and Arich Goldman. "Measurement of Discrimination Ability in Taste Tests: An Empirical Investigation." *Journal of Marketing Research* 24, (1987): 154–63.

Buzzell, Robert D., and Bradley T. Gale. *The PIMS Principles.* New York: Free Press, 1987.

Cannell, Charles F., Lois Oksenberg, and Jean M. Converse. "Striving for Response Accuracy: Experiments in New Interviewing Techniques." *Journal of Marketing Research* 14, (August 1977): 306–15.

Cochran, William G. *Sampling Techniques.* 2d ed. New York: John Wiley & Sons, 1953.

Cohen, Howard M., Michael J. LuValle, J. Peter Mitchell, and Edward S. Sproles, Jr. "Reliability Evaluations of Interconnection Products." *AT&T Technical Journal* 66, no. 4 (July–August 1987): 70–80.

Cook, R. Dennis. "Detection of Influential Observations in Linear Regression." *Technometrics* 19, no. 2 (1977): 15–18.

Cryer, Jonathan D. *Time Series Analysis.* Boston: PWS-KENT, 1986.

Davis, John C. *Statistics and Geology.* New York: John Wiley & Sons, 1973.

Delbecq, Andre L., Andrew H. Van de Ven, and David H. Gustafson. *Group Techniques for Program Planning: A Guide to Nominal Group and Delphi Processes.* Glenview, Ill.: Scott Foresman, 1975.

Deming, W. Edwards. "Some Principles of the Shewhart Methods of Quality Control." *Mechanical Engineering* 66 (March 1944): 173–77.

Deming, W. Edwards. *Sample Design in Business Research.* New York: John Wiley & Sons, 1960.

Deming, W. Edwards. "Sample Surveys." In *International Encyclopedia of Statistics*, vol. 2, edited by William H. Kruskal and Judith M. Tanur, 867–85. New York: Free Press, 1978.

Deming, W. Edwards. *Quality, Productivity, and Competitive Position.* Cambridge, Mass.: MIT Center for Advanced Engineering Study, 1982.

Deming, W. Edwards. *Out of the Crisis.* New York: John Wiley & Sons, 1986.

Dempster, Arthur P. "Employment Discrimination and Statistical Science." *Statistical Science* 3, no. 2 (1988): 149–95.

Drucker, Peter F. "The Coming of the New Organization." *Harvard Business Review* 88, no. 1: 45–53.

Durbin, J., and G. S. Watson. "Testing for Serial Correlation in Least Squares Regression, I." *Biometrika* 37 (1950): 409–28.

Durbin, J., and G. S. Watson. "Testing for Serial Correlation in Least Squares Regression, II." *Biometrika* 38 (1951): 159–78.

Durbin, J., and G. S. Watson. "Testing for Serial Correlation in Least Squares Regression, III." *Biometrika* 58 (1971): 1–19.

Ehrenberg, A. S. C. *Primer in Data Reduction.* New York: John Wiley & Sons, 1982.

Frankel, Lester R. "Statistics and People—The Statistician's Responsibilities." *Journal of the American Statistical Association* 71, no. 353 (March 1976): 9–16.

Freedman, David, Robert Pisani, and Roger Purvis. *Statistics.* New York: W. W. Norton, 1978.

Fuller, F. Timothy. "Eliminating Complexity from Work: Improving Productivity by Enhancing Quality." *National Productivity Review* (Autumn 1985): 327–44.

Galton, Francis. *Natural Inheritance.* London: Macmillan, 1889.

Gardner, E. S. "Exponential Smoothing: The State of the Art." *Journal of Forecasting* 4 (1985): 1–28.

Ginsberg, Benjamin. *The Captive Public: How Mass Opinion Promotes State Power.* New York: Basic Books, 1987.

Goodman, Leo A., and William H. Kruskal. "Measures of Association for Cross-classifications." *Journal of the American Statistical Association* 49 (1954): 732–64.

Gundaker, Bruce F., David E. Martinich, and Michael J. Tortorella. "Quality Technology in Product Realization Systems." *AT&T Technical Journal* 66, no. 5 (September–October 1987): 5–20.

Hamilton, David. "Sometimes $R^2 > r_{yx_1}^2 + r_{yx_2}^2$." *American Statistician* 41, no. 2 (May 1987): 129–32.

Hellevik, Ottar. *Introduction to Causal Analysis: Exploring Survey Data by Crosstabulation.* London: George Allen & Unwin, 1984.

Hoaglin, David C. "Transformations in Everyday Experience." *Chance* 1 (1988): 40–45.

Homans, George C. *Social Behavior: Its Elementary Forms.* New York: Harcourt Brace Jovanovich, 1961.

Hunter, William, Jan O'Neill, and Carol Wallen. "Doing More with Less in the Public Sector: A Progress Report from Madison, Wisconsin." Report No. 13, Center for Quality and Productivity Improvement, University of Wisconsin–Madison, June 1986.

Imai, Masaaki. *Kaizen: The Key to Japan's Competitive Success.* New York: Random House, 1986.

Ishikawa, Kaoru. *Guide to Quality Control.* 2d rev. ed. White Plains, N.Y.: Kraus International Publications, 1986.

Ishikawa, Kaoru, ed. *Statistical Application Research, Union of Japanese Scientists and Engineers (Special Issue: Seven Management Tools for QC)* 33, no. 2 (June 1986).

Jaffe, A. J., and Spirer, H. F. *Misused Statistics: Straight Talk for Twisted Numbers.* New York: Marcel Dekker, 1987.

Johnson, H. Webster, Anthony J. Faria, and Ernest L. Maier. *How to Use the Business*

Library: With Sources of Business Information. 5th ed. Cincinnati: South-Western Publishing, 1984.

Johnson, Richard A., and Dean W. Wichern. *Applied Multivariate Analysis.* 2d ed. New York: John Wiley & Sons, 1988.

Juran, J. M., and F. M. Gryna, eds. *Juran's Quality Control Handbook*, 4th ed. New York: McGraw-Hill (ASQC Quality Press), 1988.

Kruzas, Anthony, and Linda Varekamp Sullivan, eds. *Encyclopedia of Information Systems and Services.* 6th ed. Detroit: Gale Research, 1985.

Latzko, William J. *Quality and Productivity for Bankers and Financial Managers.* New York: Marcel Dekker, 1986.

Mallows, Colin L. "Some Comments on C_p." *Technometrics* 15 (1973): 661–76.

Mann, J. I., M. P. Vessey, M. Thorogood, and R. Doll. "Myocardial Infarction in Young Women with Special Reference to Oral Contraceptive Practice." *British Medical Journal* 2 (1975): 241–45.

Maritz/Rogers. "Early Model New Car Buyers' Study." As quoted in *PC Week*, 28 June 1988, 1.

Matchinsky, Jerri Marie. "Methods in Simultaneous Comparison Charts: Means and Standard Deviations." Master of Science thesis, University of Iowa, 1988.

May, Eleanor G. *A Handbook for Business on the Use of Federal and State Statistical Data.* Washington, D.C.: Department of Commerce, 1979.

McKean, Kevin. "The Orderly Pursuit of Pure Disorder." *Discover*, January 1987, 73–81.

Meyers, Raymond H. *Classical and Modern Regression Analysis.* 2d ed. Boston: PWS-KENT, 1990.

Miao, L. I. "Gastric Freezing: An Example of the Evaluation of Medical Therapy by Randomized Clinical Trials." In *Costs, Risks, and Benefits of Surgery*, edited by J. P. Bunker, B. A. Barnes, and F. Mosteller, 198–211. New York: Oxford University Press, 1977.

Miller, Robert B. *Minitab Handbook for Business and Economics.* Boston: PWS-KENT, 1988.

Miller, Robert B., and Dean W. Wichern. *Intermediate Business Statistics.* New York: Holt, Rinehart and Winston, 1977.

Moore, P. G. *Statistics and the Manager.* London: MacDonald, 1966.

Mosteller, Frederick. "Note on an Application of Runs to Quality Control Charts." *Annals of Mathematical Statistics* 12 (1941): 228–32.

Mosteller, Frederick. "Nonsampling Errors." In *International Encyclopedia of Statistics*, vol. 1, edited by William H. Kruskal and Judith M. Tanur, 208–29. New York: Free Press, 1978.

Mosteller, Frederick, et alia. *The Pre-election Polls of Nineteen Forty-Eight.* New York: Social Research Council, 1949.

Mosteller, Frederick, and John W. Tukey. *Data Analaysis & Regression: A Second Course in Statistics.* Reading, Mass.: Addison-Wesley, 1977.

Muller, Mervin E. "Random Numbers." In *International Encyclopedia of Statistics*, vol. 2, edited by William H. Kruskal and Judith M. Tanur, 839–47. New York: Free Press, 1978.

Narula, Subash C., and John F. Wellington. "Prediction, Linear Regression and the Minimum Sum of Relative Errors." *Technometrics* 19, no. 2 (1977): 185–90.

Ott, Ellis R. *Process Quality Control*. New York: McGraw-Hill, 1975.

Pearson, Karl. "Mathematical Contributions to the Theory of Evolution, III. Regression, Heredity, and Panmixia." *Philosophical Transcriptions of the Royal Society* A, 187 (1896): 253–318.

Pearson, Karl. "On a Criterion that a Given System of Deviations from the Probable in the Case of a Correlated System of Variables is Such That It Can be Reasonably Supposed to Have Arisen from Random Sampling." *Philosophical Magazine* 50, no. 5 (1990): 157–75.

Pokras, Robert, and Kurt K. Kubishke. "Diagnosis-related Groups Using Data for the National Hospital Discharge Survey: United States, 1982." Washington, D.C.: National Center for Health Statistics, January 18, 1985.

Ramsay, James O. "Monotone Regression Splines." *Statistical Science* 3, no. 4 (November 1988): 425–41.

Roberts, Harry V. "Harris Trust and Savings Bank: An Analysis of Employee Compensation." Report 7946, CMSBE, Graduate School of Business, University of Chicago, 1979.

Roberts, Harry V. *Data Analysis for Managers*. Redwood City, Calif.: Scientific Press, 1988.

Rogers, R. Mark. "Tracking the Economy: Fundamentals for Understanding Data." *Economic Review*, Federal Reserve Bank of Atlanta (March–April 1989): 30–48.

Ruffin, Julian M., et al. "A Cooperative Double-blind Evaluation of Gastric "Freezing" in the Treatment of Duodenal Ulcer." *New England Journal of Medicine* 281 (1969): 16–19.

Ryan, Barbara F., Brian L. Joiner, and Thomas A. Ryan, Jr. *Minitab Handbook*. 2d ed. Boston: PWS-KENT, 1988.

Schafer, Daniel W. "Measurement-error Diagnostics and the Sex Discrimination Problem." *Journal of Business and Economic Statistics* 5, no. 4 (October 1987): 529–37.

Scheaffer, Richard L., Willliam Mendenhall and Lyman Ott, *Elementary Survey Sampling*. 4th ed. Boston: PWS-KENT, 1990.

Scholtes, Peter. *The Team Handbook*. Madison, Wis.: Joiner Associates, 1987.

Schuman, Howard, and Stanley Presser. *Questions and Answers in Attitude Surveys*. New York: Academic Press, 1981.

Shewhart, Walter A. *Economic Control of Quality of Manufactured Product*. New York: Van Nostrand, 1931.

Shurkin, Joel. *Engines of the Mind: A History of the Computer*. New York: W. W. Norton, 1984.

Snee, Ronald D. "Graphical Analysis of Process Variation." *Journal of Quality Technology* 15 (April 1983): 76–88.

Stephan, F. F., and P. J. McCarthy, *Sampling Opinions*. New York: John Wiley & Sons, 1958.

Stigler, Stephen M. *The History of Statistics*. Cambridge, Mass.: Harvard University Press, 1986.

Stuart, Alan. "Nonprobability Sampling." In *International Encyclopedia of Statistics*, vol. 2, edited by William H. Kruskal and Judith M. Tanur, 885–89. New York: Free Press, 1978.

Sugiman, Toshio, and Jyuji Misumi. "Development of a New Evacuation Method for Emergencies: Control of Collective Behavior by Emergent Small Groups." *Journal of Applied Psychology* 73, no. 1 (1988): 3–10.

Tiao, George C., and Ruey S. Tsay. "Model Specification in Multivariate Time Series." Technical Report No. 61, Graduate School of Business, University of Chicago, August 14, 1987.

Tufte, E. R. *The Visual Display of Quantitative Information.* Cheshire, Conn.: Graphics Press, 1983.

U.S. Bureau of the Census. *Statistical Abstract of the United States: 1984.* 104th ed. Washington, D.C.: Government Printing Office, 1984.

U.S. Bureau of the Census. *Statistical Abstract of the United States: 1989.* 109th ed. Washington, D.C.: Government Printing Office, 1988.

Wagner, Clifford H. "Simpson's Paradox in Real Life." *American Statistician* 36 (1982): 46–48.

Walsh, Edward. "Polls Are Telling Us More, But Are They Telling It Like It Is?" *Washington Post*, weekly edition, 13 April 1987, 37.

Wangensteen, Owen H., et al., "Achieving 'Physiological Gastrectomy' by Gastric Freezing." *Journal of the American Medical Association* 180, no. 6 (May 12, 1962): 439–44.

Wasserman, Paul, Charlotte Georgi, and James Way. *Encyclopedia of Business Information Sources.* 5th ed. Copyright ©1980, 1983 by Paul Wasserman.

Weisberg, Sanford. *Applied Linear Regression Analysis.* 2d ed. New York: John Wiley & Sons, 1985.

Yates, Frank. *Sampling Methods for Censuses and Surveys.* 3d ed., rev. and enl. New York: Hafner, 1953.

Glossary

Added variable plot	Plot for assessing the effect of a predictor variable after adjusting for the effect of another predictor variable.
Alternative hypothesis	An hypothesis other than the null hypothesis.
AR(1) model	An autoregressive model in which the predictor variable is the response variable at the previous time point.
AR(2) model	An autoregressive model in which the two predictor variables are the response variable at the previous two time points.
Autocorrelation	Correlation between a time series and its lagged values.
Autoregressive model	A time series model using lagged values of the response variable as predictor variables.
Backward elimination	A special stepwise regression method that eliminates more and more predictors to find the "best" model.
Bernoulli process (Bernoulli trials)	A sequence of independent binary variable trials with constant success rate.
Best subset regression	A method for choosing the best predictor variables by considering all possible subsets of predictors.
Binomial distribution	The theoretical distribution of the total number of successes in n Bernoulli trials with success probability π.
Binomial mean	$n\pi$
Binomial probability function	The probability of k successes in n Bernoulli trials with success probability π.

Binomial standard deviation	$\sqrt{n\pi(1-\pi)}$
Blinding	Not allowing subjects in an experiment to know which treatment they receive.
Body of a table	The cells defined by all the combinations of categories of the variables in a table of categorical data.
Bootstrapping	A technique that derives an empirical sampling distribution for a statistic by drawing random samples with replacement from a real sample.
Box–Cox transformation	A transformation from the power family $y = x^\lambda$ for some choice of constant power λ.
Cases	Rows in a data table.
Categorical data	Data that are arranged in classes or categories.
Cause-and-effect diagram	A "fishbone" diagram that shows causes of causes of causes, and so on, so that truly fundamental causes of variation are documented.
Cell	Location in a table defined by the intersection of a category of one variable with a category of another variable.
Census	A survey conducted with the intention of obtaining information from every element in the universe.
Central limit effect	The distribution of a mean or total is approximately normal under many circumstances.
Chi-square distribution	The approximate sampling distribution of Pearson's X^2 statistic when the null hypothesis of no association is true.
Class frequencies	The frequencies or counts of data values within the class intervals.
Class intervals	Intervals dividing up the values of a variable.
Clustering	Grouping elements according to their "nearness" to each other.
Cluster sampling	A design in which a random sample of clusters is selected.
Coded data	Replacing data by a code for simplicity.
Collapsing	Combining categories of a categorical variable to create a variable with fewer categories.
Collinearity	Approximate linear relationships among predictor variables.
Common causes (chance causes)	Causes of variation in a measured variable that are due to chance and remain in a system unless the process is fundamentally altered.
Conditions	Fixed levels of predictor variables.
Confidence coefficient	One minus the significance level of the test upon which a confidence interval is based.
Confidence interval	An interval computed from a sample such that the collection of such intervals from all possible samples has a specified probability of containing a parameter.
Conformance analysis	Collection of data to determine if standards for a process are met. Part of the check step in the PDCA cycle.
Consequences	Responses to a set of conditions in a model.
Control limits	Limits within which the plotted process characteristic (subgroup mean or standard deviation) is expected to vary when the process is in control.
Cook's distance	A measure of a data point's influence on regression results that considers both the predictor variables and the response variable.
Critical region	Those values of a test statistic that cause rejection of the null hypothesis.
Cross-sectional data	Data where the time dimension is either absent or ignored.

Data design quality	The plan for collecting the data is relevant to the problem to be solved.
Data production quality	Data are collected with sufficient skill and care to be useful.
Density histogram	A graphical display of a distribution especially useful with unequal width class intervals.
Designed experiment	A designed study in which a randomization device is used to determine which treatment is applied to which elements.
Designed study	A study in which the elements are chosen or assigned by a randomization device.
Differences	The series of changes from one time period to the next.
Discriminant analysis	Analysis of a model whose response is binary (or, more generally, is categorical) for the purpose of separating or discriminating among response values on the basis of the predictor variables.
Distributed lag model	A model relating a response variable to the lagged values of a predictor variable.
Dotplot	The display of a distribution on a number line with no grouping.
Double blinding	In addition to blinding the subjects the evaluators are not allowed to know what treatments the subjects receive.
Ecological correlation	Correlation computed from data that are aggregates of smaller units of study.
Elements	The basic units or individuals about which information is sought in a survey.
Equal complete coverage	The set of measurements obtained if the survey procedures are used on every element in the universe.
Error term	The part of the response that is not modelled by the linear function of the predictor variables in a regression model.
Experiment	The study of the effects of change in an environment that is, to some degree, under the control of the experimenter.
Exponential smoothing	An ad hoc technique for smoothing out the random variation in series.
External RMSPE	Root mean square prediction error for data external to the model building process.
f	Sampling fraction, $f = n/N$.
Factorial experiment	An experiment in which all combinations of the treatment levels are run in a replication.
Finite population correction factor	$fpc = \sqrt{(N - n)/N}$
First differences	The sequence of changes from one data value to the next.
First quartile	The data value one-quarter from the bottom of the ordered list.
Fitted value	The value predicted by the model.
Flow diagram	A series of boxes connected by arrows that show the flow of work in a step in a process.
Forward selection	A special stepwise regression method that selects more and more predictors to find the "best" model.
Frame	The list of elements of the universe from which a sample is actually drawn.
Frequency histogram	A graphical display of a frequency distribution.
General linear model (GLM)	$\hat{y} = b_0 + b_1 x_1 + b_2 x_2 + \cdots + b_k x_k$
Influence	A measure of the effect each data point has on the regression results.
Interquartile range	The difference between the third quartile and the first quartile.
Koyck (or geometric) model	A particular distributed lag model in which a response is related to an exponentially (or geometrically) weighted combination of the predictor variable at many lags.

Lag	An interval of time between observations in a time series.
Lagged variable	A variable given by the value at a previous time point.
Levels	The actual values of a sequence where the first differences or changes may be of primary interest.
Leverage	A measure of a data point's influence in a regression with respect to the predictor variables.
Linear time trend	Trend modelled as a straight line over time.
Linear transformation	Replacing a variable y by $a + by$ for some choice of constants a and b.
Logarithm transformation	A transformation useful for simplifying certain curved relationships and for stabilizing variability when the standard deviation of a response is proportional to the mean of the response.
Longitudinal study	A study of the evolution of a process over time.
Lurking variable	A third variable whose influence plausibly explains the correlation between two other variables.
Mallows' C_p criterion	A criterion for choosing the better predictor variables in a regression model.
Mean	The arithmetic average of the data values.
Mean chart	Statistical process control chart designed to detect changes in the mean of a process.
Meandering series	A series whose observations close in time are also close in value but whose observations far apart in time may be quite different.
Median	The middle value for a data set ordered in magnitude.
Misspecified model	A model that does not include the "correct" predictor variables.
Model diagnostics	The testing of a model with respect to assumptions.
Moment	A statistic formed as the average of a power of the data values.
N	Number of elements in a frame.
n	Sample size, number of cases in a regression data set, or number of trials considered to obtain a total number of successes in Bernoulli trials.
Nonprobability survey	Survey in which probability methods are not used to select the elements to be measured.
Nonsampling error	The difference between the value of a sample estimate and a corresponding equal complete coverage value that is due to some other cause than the sampling process.
Normal curve	The mathematical curve that describes the normal distribution. See Equation (8.1).
Normal distribution table	A table of areas under the standard normal curve.
Normal probability plot	A plot of normal scores versus values used to support normality of a distribution and to detect lack of normality.
Normal scores	A set of "ideal" values from a normal distribution.
Null hypothesis	The hypothesis assumed to be true when deriving the sampling distribution of a test statistic used to compute the significance level.
Observational study	A study in which randomization is not used to select elements for observation.
Operational definition	The result of answering who, what, when, where, why, and how.
Ordered categories	Those categories that cannot be displayed in an arbitrary order without losing some information.
Ordinary least squares (OLS)	A method that fits a curve to data pairs $(x_1, y_1), (x_2, y_2), \ldots, (x_n, y_n)$ by minimizing the sum of squared vertical distances between the y-values and the curve.

Outlier	An observation that is separated from the main body of the data.
Overspecified model	A model that includes unnecessary predictor variables.
p	The proportion of successes in n trials.
π	The success probability on each trial.
Parameter	Numerical characteristic of a population, for example, the mean, denoted by μ.
Pareto diagram	A diagram that displays causes of variation ranked by importance.
Pareto principle	Only a few causes are responsible for most of the variation in a process.
p-chart	A control chart based on sequence plots of sample proportions.
PDCA	Plan, Do, Check, Act. The steps in Deming's wheel taken over and over again to bring about improvements in processes.
Pearson's X^2	$$X^2 = \sum \frac{(\text{OBSERVED} - \text{FITTED})^2}{\text{FITTED}} = \sum \frac{(\text{RESIDUAL})^2}{\text{FITTED}}$$
Percentage changes	The relative changes from one data value to the next data value on a percentage basis and relative to the previous data value.
Percentile	A number below which a specified percent of a distribution's values lie.
Period	Time span at which a sequence *may* tend to repeat its general behavior — 12 for monthly data, 4 for quarterly data, and so on.
Placebo	A nontreatment disguised so that subjects think it is real.
Population	The set of all measurements on a variable that the whole universe would yield were a census taken.
Prediction error	The new response value minus the prediction based on the model.
Prediction standard error	The estimated standard deviation of the difference between a new response value and the predicted value.
Predictor variables	The variables used to predict or explain the response variable.
predsd	Notation for the estimated standard deviation of a prediction error in a regression model.
Primary data	Data collected by the person or organization that also analyzes the data.
Probability	The hypothesized limiting value of the proportion of occurrences of an event in a large number of repetitions of a process that may yield the event.
Probability survey	Survey in which each element of the universe has a known probability of entering the sample.
Process	A sequence of steps taken to achieve a goal or outcome.
Process analysis	Activities undertaken to understand and model the steps in a process and the relationships among the steps or analysis of past process data to find appropriate limits for future control.
Process control	Activities undertaken to keep process outcomes as close as possible to a predetermined target or to effect an improvement in the performance of the process.
Product-moment correlation coefficient	$$r = \frac{1}{n-1} \sum_{i=1}^{n} \left[\left(\frac{x_i - \bar{x}}{s_x} \right) \left(\frac{y_i - \bar{y}}{s_y} \right) \right]$$
p-values	Empirical significance levels.
Quadratic time trend	Trend modelled as a quadratic curve in time.
Quantile plot	A plot used to assess the shape of a distribution.
Quantile-quantile plot	Scatterplot of the quantiles of two distributions, one versus the other, used to assess the similarity of the two distributions.

Quasi-experimental design	An intervention is applied to a process; then the behavior of the process before the intervention is compared to the behavior of the process after the intervention.
Quota sample	A sample drawn so that some of its characteristics match predetermined targets, for example, percentage female is 50.
r	Symbol for the correlation coefficient. Also used for the number of rows in a two-way table.
R^2	Notation for the multiple coefficient of determination.
R^2(adj)	Notation for the adjusted coefficient of determination.
Randominess	A property of uncertain outcomes that can be modelled using the mathematics of probability.
Random walk	The sequence of running totals of independent outcomes from a stable process.
Range	The difference between the largest and smallest data value.
Regression model	A mathematical curve summarizing a relationship among variables together with measures of variation from the curve.
Relative frequency histogram	A graphical display of a relative frequency distribution especially useful for comparing distributions of different-sized data sets.
Replication	A single run of an experiment in which all the planned treatments are run at all the planned levels.
Residual	The actual response value minus the value predicted by the model.
Response variable	The variable to be predicted or explained.
Root mean square prediction error	$RMSPE = \sqrt{(\text{Mean of } PE)^2 + (\text{Standard Deviation of } PE)^2}$ where PE denotes prediction error.
s	Notation for standard deviation.
Sample	A collection of elements from a universe or process.
Sampling distribution	Distribution of values of a statistic in repeated drawings from a stable process or random samples from a fixed universe.
Sampling error	The difference between the value of a sample estimate and a corresponding equal complete coverage value that is due only to the sampling process.
Sampling variation	The variation of numerical characteristics from sample to sample.
Scatterplot	An (x, y) plot that displays the statistical relationship between the two variables.
Seasonal adjustment	A procedure applied to a time series in an attempt to account for known seasonality.
Seasonal autoregression	An autoregressive model with the predictor variable lagged at multiples of the seasonal period.
Seasonal differences	The series of season to season changes.
Seasonal exponential smoothing	Exponential smoothing that accounts for seasonality.
Seasonal indicators	Binary variables indicating the various seasons.
Seasonality	The tendency of a sequence to repeat its general behavior at regular time periods.
Secondary data	Data collected by one person or organization and analyzed by another person or organization.
Sequence plot	A graph of a time series with time displayed on the horizontal axis and values of the variable of interest on the vertical axis.
Significance level	Probability of rejecting a true null hypothesis.

Significance testing	A process of probabilistic inference that uses sampling distributions to compare behavior in data with theories about the process that generated the data.
Simple observation	Observation of every outcome from a process or outcomes taken systematically at predetermined instants.
Simple random sample	A sample taken so that each possible sample of size n has the same chance of being selected.
Simpson's paradox	A paradox where an overall average changes in a way opposite to the changes in the averages for component parts.
Skewed distribution	An asymmetric distribution with values stretched out on either the high or low end.
Smoothing constants	The constants in exponential smoothing that determine the extent of the smoothing.
Special causes (assignable causes)	Causes of variation in a measured variable that are individually important and affect process results only some of the time.
Standard deviation	The square root of the number obtained from the sum of squared deviations of the observations from their mean divided by $n - 1$.
Standard deviation chart	Statistical process control chart designed to detect changes in the dispersion of a process.
Standard error	The standard deviation of the sampling distribution of a statistic.
Standard normal curve	A normal curve with mean 0 and standard deviation 1.
Standardization	Replacing a variable y by $(y - \bar{y})/s$, case by case.
Standardized residuals	Residuals that have been corrected to have a standard deviation of 1.
Statistical process control	Statistical methods used to detect changes in processes.
Statistically significant	A phrase used when the value of a test statistic is an extreme value in the appropriate sampling distribution that assumes the null hypothesis to be true.
Statistics	Numerical characteristics of a sample, usually thought of as estimates of population parameters.
Stem-and-leaf display	A display of a distribution using the digits of the data to form the groupings and graphical display of frequencies.
Stepwise regression	A sequential method for choosing the best predictor variables.
Stratification	Separating observations into groups or categories in order to make comparisons or grouping elements in a frame according to some common characteristic or characteristics.
Stratified sampling	A design in which random samples are drawn from strata in the frame.
Studentized residuals	Residuals that have been standardized using data that excludes the ith case.
Subgroups	Samples of a process variable used to measure the current mean and standard deviation for process analysis.
Survey	A data collection tool in which a sample of elements is selected from a universe of elements for measurement.
Symmetric distribution	A distribution whose left and right sides are mirror-images of one another.
Systematic sampling	A design in which elements are chosen systematically from the frame after a random start (or starts) has been chosen.
Table of random digits	A table of the digits $0, 1, \ldots, 9$ constructed so that each of the digits has an equal chance of occurring in any location in the table.
Tally	A count of the number of cases in each category of a variable.

t **distribution with** $n - 1$ **degrees of freedom**	The sampling distribution of the *t* statistic for the sample mean when the data come from a normal distribution.
Test statistic	A statistic used in a significance test.
Third quartile	The data value one-quarter from the top of the ordered list.
Time series	A sequence of observations collected from a process at fixed epochs of time.
Treatment	A set of conditions set up by an experimenter and applied to an element.
t **statistic for the process mean**	$t = \dfrac{\bar{y} - \mu}{s/\sqrt{n}} = \dfrac{\sqrt{n}(\bar{y} - \mu)}{s}$
Two-sample *t* **statistic**	$t = \dfrac{\bar{y}_1 - \bar{y}_2}{\sqrt{\dfrac{s_1^2}{n_1} + \dfrac{s_2^2}{n_2}}}$
Two-way table	A breakdown of the number of respondents (or counts) in each category formed by intersecting the categories of two variables.
Type I error	Rejecting a true null hypothesis.
Type II error	Failing to reject a false null hypothesis.
Type III error	Solving the wrong problem.
Underspecified model	A model which fails to include important predictor variables.
Universe	The collection of all elements that might be drawn into a sample for a survey.
Variable	A measured characteristic of elements.
Variance inflation factors (VIF)	A measure of an individual predictors' collinearity with the other predictors.
z-**scores (***z*-**values)**	Standardized values or units: $z = (y - \mu)/\sigma$

Answers to Selected Exercises

CHAPTER 4

4.3A	Q_1	Median	Q_3	Interquartile Range	Range
(a)	5	7	11	6	11
(b)	5	7	11	6	38
(c)	4	7	13	9	11

4.3B $28,000 **4.3C** No

4.5A	Mean	Standard Deviation
(a)	7.9	3.8
(b)	9.1	14.1
(c)	8.0	4.2

4.5B $28,060   **4.5C** Yes

4.5H

n	Mean	Standard Deviation
30	512.1	189.3
29	488.4	140.3
Percent reduction	5	26

4.5I $576.45   **4.5J** $563.57

4.7A (b)

	Mean	Standard Deviation
Coded	1.420	4.393
Inches	0.0000355	0.000100009825

4.7C Median = 1,462,240 yen, $Q_3 - Q_1$ = 323,380 yen
4.7D Mean = $340.15, standard deviation = $85.04
4.9B Standard deviation$_{before}$ = 0.0011 inches, standard deviation$_{after}$ = 0.0009 inches

4.9D

	Mean	Standard Deviation
Left	56.61	13.54
Right	57.87	15.20

CHAPTER 5

5.3C

Outlook	Size	Cases
2	1	7
2	3	1
3	1	8
4	1	9
4	2	2, 10
5	1	3, 4

5.3D (a)

	Grade	
	−1	0
Sq.ft	597.6	657.8
Assess	20.92	22.96
Market	27.12	35.20
A/M	0.811	0.672

5.5A

Size	Count	Percent
1	5	62.5
2	2	25.0
3	1	12.5
$N=$	8	100
$*=$	2	

This is *not* the presentation quality version of the table.

5.7B (a)

	Future Use Counts				
	1	2	3	4	5
Male	0	1	3	8	2
Female	1	2	2	0	1

	Future Use Percents				
	1	2	3	4	5
Male	0	7	22	57	14
Female	17	33	33	0	17

(b)

		Anxiety				
		1	2	3	4	5
Future Use	1	0	0	1	0	0
	2	1	2	0	0	0
	3	1	2	0	2	0
	4	3	1	0	1	3
	5	1	0	0	2	0

(c)

		Anxiety	
		1–3	4–5
Future Use	1–3	7	2
	4–5	5	6

A slight tendency for anxiety to be associated with low future use.

5.7D Percent responding favorably to question concerning economic outlook for the coming year, by type of ownership

Outlook	Sole Proprietorship	Partnership	Corporation	Overall
% favorable	43	63	51	49

Source: 1980 Wisconsin Restaurant Survey conducted by the University of Wisconsin Small Business Development Center. A mail survey of a random sample of 1000 restaurants in 19 Wisconsin counties yielded 269 responses to the table. There were 106 sole proprietorships, 27 partnerships, and 136 corporations.

5.11C (a) Table of counts:

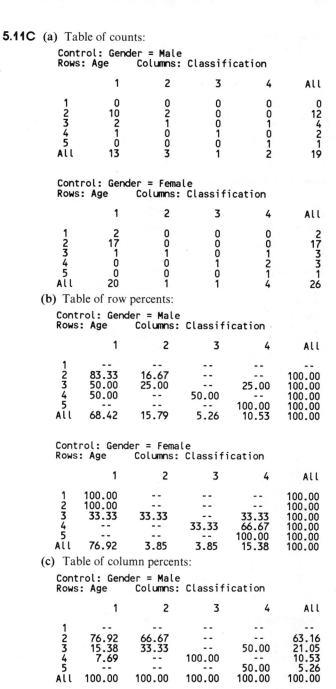

```
Control: Gender = Male
Rows: Age      Columns: Classification

               1       2       3       4      All

    1          0       0       0       0        0
    2         10       2       0       0       12
    3          2       1       0       1        4
    4          1       0       1       0        2
    5          0       0       0       1        1
   All        13       3       1       2       19


Control: Gender = Female
Rows: Age      Columns: Classification

               1       2       3       4      All

    1          2       0       0       0        2
    2         17       0       0       0       17
    3          1       1       0       1        3
    4          0       0       1       2        3
    5          0       0       0       1        1
   All        20       1       1       4       26
```

(b) Table of row percents:

```
Control: Gender = Male
Rows: Age      Columns: Classification

               1       2       3       4      All

    1         --      --      --      --       --
    2      83.33   16.67      --      --    100.00
    3      50.00   25.00      --   25.00    100.00
    4      50.00      --   50.00      --    100.00
    5         --      --      --  100.00    100.00
   All     68.42   15.79    5.26   10.53    100.00


Control: Gender = Female
Rows: Age      Columns: Classification

               1       2       3       4      All

    1     100.00      --      --      --    100.00
    2     100.00      --      --      --    100.00
    3      33.33   33.33      --   33.33    100.00
    4         --      --   33.33   66.67    100.00
    5         --      --      --  100.00    100.00
   All     76.92    3.85    3.85   15.38    100.00
```

(c) Table of column percents:

```
Control: Gender = Male
Rows: Age      Columns: Classification

               1       2       3       4      All

    1         --      --      --      --       --
    2      76.92   66.67      --      --     63.16
    3      15.38   33.33      --   50.00     21.05
    4       7.69      --  100.00      --     10.53
    5         --      --      --   50.00      5.26
   All    100.00  100.00  100.00  100.00    100.00
```

```
Control: Gender = Female
Rows: Age     Columns: Classification

          1       2       3       4      All

  1      10.00    --      --      --     7.69
  2      85.00    --      --      --    65.38
  3       5.00   100.00   --     25.00  11.54
  4       --      --     100.00  50.00  11.54
  5       --      --      --     25.00   3.85
 All     100.00  100.00  100.00 100.00 100.00
```

CHAPTER 6

6.3E The cross-sectional distribution of sales is roughly the same from year to year. If there had been a strong upward trend over years, then the cross-sectional distributions would also show an upward trend. The converse would be true for a downward trend.

6.3F A roughly linear relationship; quite similar to the first plot suggested; a slight linear tendency with much more scatter than observed in the first two plots.

6.5B $r = -0.765$. The plot below uses letters A, B, C, and D to denote sales in the four years, so that some of the longitudinal behavior is displayed. In a raw scatterplot the longitudinal effects are usually masked.

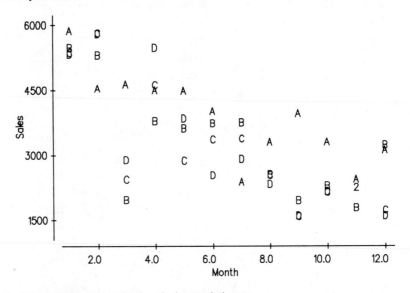

6.5D Each data set has the same descriptive statistics.

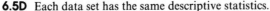

	Mean	Standard Deviation	Correlation between x and y
x	9	3.37	0.816
y	7.501	2.03	0.816

Because the scatterplots are very different and the descriptive statistics are the same, just looking at descriptive statistics is not sufficient for data analysis. Graphical techniques must be used to learn about processes.

6.5F All standardization does is change the scales of the x- and y-axes. It does not affect the relationship between the variables.

6.5G

	N	Mean	Median	Standard Deviation
Sq.ft	5	1478	1435	228
Assessed	5	25.72	23.60	4.71
Market	5	44.80	45.40	3.50

The correlations between the various variables are given in the following table:

	Sq.ft	Assessed
Assessed	.853	
Market	.048	.497

6.9A (c)

	Steel	Lag1stee
Lag1stee	0.474	
Lag2stee	0.107	0.479

(d)

Rule	RMSPE
(1)	1.754
(2)	1.819
(3)	1.562

The average of rules (1) and (2) performs better than either of the rules alone. The technique of combining forecasts in this way often produces good practical results. Each forecasting rule captures a slightly different feature of the process, and combining the rules takes advantage of the good points of both. The analysis should be a good guide to future performance provided the process remains stable. Do not expect the RMSPE to be as small when computed from real future data. The RMSPEs computed in this exercise use the same data for constructing the rules and evaluating them. This makes the calculations too optimistic.

6.11A (a) The tables show the same degree but opposite "directions" of association.

(b) For Table I, $a/b = 1/2$ and $c/d = 2$. For Table II, $a/b = 2$ and $c/d = 1/2$.

(c) $X^2 = 100/3$ for both tables. The maximum value for X^2 in this case is 300, so the degree of association is modest at best.

6.11C (a) Row percents: Yes: 35, 65; No: 16, 84; Total: 27, 73. There is a moderate degree of association. Smokers have a higher risk of heart attacks than nonsmokers, according to these data.

(b) $a = 35$, $b = 24$, $c = 93$, $d = 64$. $a/b = c/d = 1.45$

(c) $a/b = 3.2143$, $c/d = 1.1216$

(d) For the table given in the exercise, $X^2 = 9.73$. For table in part (b), $X^2 = 0$. The data table exhibits a degree of association nearer the minimum value of 0 than to the maximum value of 216.

6.13A (a) Using (6.2), $X^2 = 9.66 \approx 9.7$.

(b) Using (6.3), $X^2 = 9.6616$.

(c) They could have been made closer by retaining more decimals, but they are "exact" when rounded to one decimal place, and this is all that is required for most practical purposes.

6.15A (a) Expected counts are printed below observed counts

		Columns		
	1	**2**	**3**	**Total**
1	20	7	16	43
	17.34	12.14	13.52	
Rows 2	20	11	8	39
	15.73	11.01	12.27	
3	10	17	15	42
	16.94	11.85	13.21	
Total	50	35	39	124

(b) $X^2 = 0.408 + 2.174 + 0.453 +$
$1.162 + 0.000 + 1.484 +$
$2.840 + 2.233 + 0.243 = 10.997$
The degree of association is relatively slight.

(c) 10.9983. Round-off error.

6.15C (a) Expected counts are printed below observed counts

		Fast Food		
	S	**M**	**L**	**Total**
Prop	32	9	1	42
	22.56	11.67	7.78	
Part	6	2	0	8
	4.30	2.22	1.48	
Corp	20	19	19	58
	31.15	16.11	10.74	
Total	58	30	20	108

$X^2 = 3.955 + 0.610 + 5.906 +$
$0.676 + 0.022 + 1.481 +$
$3.990 + 0.518 + 6.351 = 23.509$

Expected counts are printed below observed counts
Supper Clubs

	S	M	L	Total
Prop	23	7	0	30
	14.37	10.14	5.49	
Part	2	4	2	8
	3.83	2.70	1.46	
Corp	9	13	11	33
	15.80	11.15	6.04	
Total	34	24	13	71

$$X^2 = 5.189 + 0.973 + 5.493 +$$
$$0.875 + 0.621 + 0.196 +$$
$$2.928 + 0.305 + 4.068 = 20.648$$

Expected counts are printed below observed counts
Other

	S	M	L	Total
Prop	26	2	1	29
	16.29	4.37	8.34	
Part	5	0	2	7
	3.93	1.05	2.01	
Corp	10	9	18	37
	20.78	5.58	10.64	
Total	41	11	21	73

$$X^2 = 5.791 + 1.285 + 6.462 +$$
$$0.290 + 1.055 + 0.000 +$$
$$5.593 + 2.104 + 5.084 = 27.665$$

CHAPTER 7

7.3A (a) The same output occurs for *each* data set:

```
The regression equation is

y1 = 3.00 + 0.500 x1

Predictor      Coef      Stdev    t-ratio        p
Constant      3.000      1.125       2.67    0.026
x1            0.5001     0.1179      4.24    0.002

s = 1.237      R-sq = 66.7%     R-sq(adj) = 62.9%

Analysis of Variance

SOURCE       DF          SS         MS        F        p
Regression    1      27.510     27.510    17.99    0.002
Error         9      13.763      1.529
Total        10      41.273
```

7.3E For Data set 1, $\hat{y} = 0.10 + 1.30x$, and both of the plots of the residuals versus fitted values and residuals versus x look the same. For Data set 2, $\hat{y} = 7.90 - 1.30x$, so the slope has the same magnitude and opposite sign with the slope in Data set 1. The plot of the residuals versus fitted values is the same as in Data set 1, but the plot of residuals versus x is reversed. This is the effect of the negative slope.

7.3F $\hat{y} = 3.76 + 0.688x$, with $s = 1.73$. The residual plot shows that Illinois is an outlier that casts doubt on the adequacy of the straight-line model.

7.5B To avoid some round-off error problems, the values of x have all been divided by 1000, so the data look like this.

Row	x	y	x^2
1	0.544	25.2	0.29594
2	0.694	37.4	0.48164
3	0.767	33.6	0.58829
4	0.825	38.0	0.68062
5	0.899	37.6	0.80820
6	0.965	37.2	0.93122
7	1.033	40.4	1.06709
8	1.060	44.8	1.12360
9	1.106	42.8	1.22324
10	1.298	45.2	1.68480

The regression equation is $\hat{y} = -1.5 + 64.8x - 22.3x^2$ with $s = 2.637$. The sum of the y's is 382.20, as is the sum of the fitted values. This makes the sum of the residuals equal to zero. The sum of the products of the residuals and x is 0.0000050142, which is essentially zero. The sum of the products of the residuals and x^2 is 0.0000049211, which is also essentially zero.

7.5C (a) $\hat{y} = 25.5 - 0.268x$, $s = 40.71$. The residual plot shows a rainbow, so the straight-line model is inadequate.

(b) Only 1 y value falls outside the prediction intervals, but the intervals are huge.

(c) $\hat{y} = 0.1 + 0.0047x + 0.00246x^2$, $s = 7.553$. The residual plot suggests no obvious model inadequacy.

(d) Only 1 y value falls outside the prediction intervals, but the intervals are much narrower than those in part (b).

7.5D The inadequate model may produce huge prediction intervals. See Exercise 7.5C for an example. A model that predicts perfectly is rare, unless processes with no random variation are predicted! An imperfect model may be quite useful. Perfect predictions are rarely essential to success. The weather forecast on the nightly news is seldom "right," but it is a useful guide to planning for the next day.

7.7D When $x_2 = 0$, we get the equation $\hat{y} = b_0 + b_1x$, relating salary to years of employment for females. When $x_2 = 1$, we get the equation $\hat{y} = (b_0 + b_2) + b_1x$, relating salary to years of employment for males. Thus the model implies the same slope coefficient for both genders. The difference between the genders is captured entirely in the y intercept term. In particular, b_2 represents the difference between the male and female y intercepts. If it is positive, then the model predicts higher salaries for males, with the difference between males and females being the same for all values of x.

7.9A When $x_3 = 0$, $\hat{y} = b_0 + b_1x_1 + b_2x_2$, and when $x_3 = 1$, $\hat{y} = (b_0 + b_3) + b_1x_1 + b_2x_2$. The model assumes the female and male salaries follow the same model except for the y intercept. The coefficient b_3 is the difference in intercepts.

7.9B $\hat{y} = b_0 + b_1x_1 + b_2x_2 + b_3x_3 + b_4x_4$, where y = sales, x_1 = wages, x_2 = advertising, x_3 = 1 if fast food and = 0 if not, x_4 = 1 if supper club and = 0 if not. $\hat{y} = b_0 + b_1x_1 + b_2x_2 + b_3x_3 + b_4x_4 + b_5x_5$, where y = sales, x_1 = new capital, x_2 = wages, x_3 = number of full-time employees, x_4 = 1 if sole proprietorship and = 0 if not, x_5 = 1 if partnership and = 0 if not.

7.11A See the answer to Exercise 7.3A.

7.11C For the straight line, the regression equation is $y = 25.5 - 0.268x$.

```
Predictor      Coef      Stdev    t-ratio      p
Constant     25.467      9.154       2.78    0.012
x           -0.26842    0.08511      -3.15    0.005

s = 40.71      R-sq = 35.6%    R-sq(adj) = 32.0%

Analysis of Variance

SOURCE       DF        SS        MS        F        p
Regression    1      16482     16482     9.95    0.005
Error        18      29831      1657
Total        19      46313
```

For the quadratic curve, the regression equation is $y = 0.10 + 0.0047x + 0.00246x^2$.

```
Predictor       Coef        Stdev     t-ratio      p
Constant       0.100        2.039        0.05    0.961
x            0.00473      0.01992        0.24    0.815
x.sq       0.0024600    0.0001094       22.49    0.000

s = 7.553      R-sq = 97.9%    R-sq(adj) = 97.7%

Analysis of Variance

SOURCE       DF        SS        MS        F         p
Regression    2      45343     22672    397.41    0.000
Error        17       970        57
Total        19      46313
```

7.11D

Source	Sum of Squares	Degrees of Freedom	Mean Square	F
Regression	510.90	3	170.3	8.0
Error	127.33	6	$21.22 = s^2$	
Total	638.23	9	$70.97 = s_y^2$	

$s = 4.61$ $s_y = 8.43$ $R^2 = 80\%$ $R^2(\text{adj}) = 70\%$

7.11E When $df = 12$, $s^2 = 10.61$, $F = 16$, and $R^2(\text{adj}) = 75\%$. Note that R^2 does not change. When $df = 24$, $s^2 = 5.3054$, $F = 32$, and $R^2(\text{adj}) = 77.6\%$. Replication can be used to increase error df.

7A.B

Row	x	y	pred_x
1	−1	−1.00	−0.8
2	0	1.00	−0.4
3	1	0.75	0.0
4			0.4
5			0.8

	N	Mean	Median	Standard Deviation	Standard Error of Mean
x	3	0.000	0.000	1.000	0.577
y	3	0.250	0.750	1.090	0.629

Correlation of x and y = .803

```
The regression equation is

y = 0.250 + 0.875 x

Predictor       Coef      Stdev     t-ratio        p
Constant      0.2500     0.5303       0.47      0.720
x             0.8750     0.6495       1.35      0.407

s = 0.9186     R-sq = 64.5%     R-sq(adj) = 28.9%

Analysis of Variance

SOURCE       DF          SS          MS          F        p
Regression    1      1.5313      1.5313       1.81    0.407
Error         1      0.8438      0.8438
Total         2      2.3750
```

Predictions made for x values in column labelled 'pred_x' on the previous page:

Prediction	predse	95% Prediction Interval
−0.450	1.181	(−2.765, 1.865)
−0.100	1.092	(2.240, 2.040)
0.250	1.061	(−1.829, 2.329)
0.600	1.091	(−1.540, 2.740)
0.950	1.181	(−1.365, 3.265)

CHAPTER 8

8.4A (a) 0.8413 (b) 0.9904 (c) 0.3085 (d) 0.1359 (e) 0.1587 (f) 0.0107
8.4B (a) 0 (b) 2.3 (c) 1.96 (d) 0.8413 **8.4D** (a) 1.5 (b) −1 (c) 2.4
8.4G (a) 0.2417 (b) 0.1587 (c) 0.2743 (d) 0.4013 (e) 0.1915 (f) 0.5914
8.4H (a) 136.8 (b) 100 (c) 109.2 (d) 90.8
 8.4I $15,000 is 3 standard deviations above the mean. Such an extreme value should not be expected for quite a long time. $8,000 is really an implausible value. It is hard to imagine that the stated normal distribution applies to the process.
8.6A 0.13% **8.6C** 0.11% **8.8D** −0.84, −0.253, 0.253, 0.84

CHAPTER 9

9.4A [39.6, 48.0] **9.4B** (a) $LCL = 8.2, CL = 10.1, UCL = 11.9$ (b) 0.0571 (c) 0.0475
9.6A $LCL = 0.95, UCL = 7.26$ **9.6B** $LCL = 0.1, CL = 1.1, UCL = 2.9$

CHAPTER 10

10.5A (a) 0.3125 (b) 0.03125 (c) 2.5, 2, and 3 have the same probability of 0.3125
10.5B (a) 0.3456 (b) 0.0778 (c) 2 is most likely
10.5C $Pr(1 \leq y \leq 3) = 0.80115$ and $Pr(1 < y < 3) = Pr(y = 2) = 0.3087$ **10.5D** (a) 0.24072
10.5F $Pr(\text{proportion} = 0.4) = 0.3125$, $Pr(\text{proportion} = 0.5) = 0$, $Pr(\text{proportion} < 0.1) = 0.03125$

10.8C

	Mean	Standard Deviation
Proportion	0.05	0.09747
Number	0.25	0.48734

10.10A (a) 0.8653 (b) 0.7991 (%error = 7.7% too low) (c) 0.8648 (%error = 0.06% too low).
The continuity correction makes a whale of a difference.
10.12A (a) $H_0: \pi = \frac{1}{2}$ (b) $H_0: \pi > \frac{1}{2}$ (c) $Pr(y \geq 15 \mid \pi = 0.5) = 0.02069$ (d) same as part (c)
10.12B (a) $H_0: \pi = .6$ (b) No (c) 0.0967 (d) $Pr(y \geq 17 \mid \pi = 0.8) = 0.3704$
10.12C 8

CHAPTER 11

11.3A (a) $CL = 0.03$ (b) $LCL = 0$, $UCL = 0.096$ (c) No
11.3B (a) 0.03 (b) $[0, 0.096]$ (c) $[0, 0.111]$ (d) Yes

CHAPTER 12

12.3A (a) 48%, 73%, 64%
(c) 57.6%, 67.6%, 64%. There is less variation between extremes when the nonresponse rate
is lower.

CHAPTER 13

13.3D (a) A person in a household; all people living in a household.
(b) A female head of household; all female heads of households.
13.7B A, B, C, and D are all true.

CHAPTER 14

14.6B Doubling the sample size reduces the length of the interval by a factor of $\sqrt{2}$. This is a 41%
reduction in interval length.

14.6F (a)

Department	N	n	fpc	se_p	$3se_p$
A	349	30	0.956	0.07	0.21
B	278	25	0.954	0.08	0.24
C	181	18	0.949	0.09	0.27
D	82	8	0.950	0.13	0.39
E	42	4	0.951	0.19	0.57
F	12	12	0	0	0
G	4	4	0	0	0
Total	948	101	—	—	—

The sample size is much more important than the department size.

(c) The group will fall woefully short of its goal of estimating within 8 percentage points in each department. If the agency as a whole is sampled, using simple random sampling, then the goal of an 8% error margin is attainable because the standard error will be approximately $\sqrt{0.9} \times \sqrt{(0.8)(0.2)/101} \simeq 0.8$.

14.10C For an individual, the prediction interval is [$0, $89.40], while for the average, the confidence interval is [$0, $14.90].

14.12A $n = z^2 S^2 / B^2$. For reference take $B = 1$. Then the table of sample sizes is

z	S	n
1.645	0.5	1
	1.0	3
	2.0	11
	10.0	271
2	0.5	1
	1.0	4
	2.0	16
	10.0	400
3	0.5	3
	1.0	9
	2.0	36
	10.0	900

For a value of B not equal to 1, just divide the n values in the table by the value of B^2 to get the sample size required for the given value of B.

CHAPTER 15

15.5B For ages less than or equal to 65, the confidence interval is $[-1.5, 6.9]$. For ages greater than 65, the confidence interval is $[-1.4, 11.4]$. In neither case is there a conclusive difference. The data do not support a claim that the average length of stay is longer in the Northeast than in the West or vice versa.

15.5C $[-1.11, 7.11]$

15.5D Confidence interval for difference $= [-0.12, 0.38]$. Confidence interval for proportion of managers $= [0.44, 0.84]$. Confidence interval for proportion of hourly workers $= [0.36, 0.66]$. Neither group is decisively in favor.

CHAPTER 16

16.3B Confidence interval for $\mu = 8,200 \pm 507$. Confidence interval for $\mu_1 - \mu_2 = 3,000 \pm 729$

16.3D $E(U) = 66$ minutes, $SD(U) = 15$ minutes

16.3G Mean $= \$562.50$, standard deviation $= \$8.75$ **16.3I** 56.95 ± 4.47

CHAPTER 17

17.3A

i	v_i	w_i
1	0.164	0.541
2	-0.560	1.514
3	-0.208	0.926

CHAPTER 18

18.5A $F(y) = 0, y \le 0; = y^2, 0 \le y < 1; = 1, y \ge 1$ **18.5B** $F(y) = 0, y < 0; = 1 - e^{-y}, y \ge 0$

18.5D $f(y) = e^y/(1 + e^y)^2, -\infty < y < \infty$ **18.7B** $\gamma_2 = 2.4$

18.7F

i	y_i	$y_i - \bar{y}$	$(y_i - \bar{y})^2$	y_i^2
1	2	-3	9	4
2	8	3	9	64
3	9	4	16	81
4	1	-4	16	1
Sum	20	0	50	150
Mean	5	—	—	—

$50 = 150 - 4(5)^2 = 150 - (20)^2/4$

18.7G (a) $2/3$ (b) $1/18$ (c) -2.577 (d) 2.4

18.7I $\mu = 3, \mu'_1 = 10.4, \sigma^2 = 1.4, \gamma_1 = 0, \gamma_2 = 2.551$

CHAPTER 19

19.3B 10.167   **19.3C** 5   **19.3D** -1.921

19.3E (a) 1.372   (b) -0.260 (c) 1.753   (d) 2.131   (e) -0.866 (f) 3.38518   (g) 2.45727
(h) -2.45727

19.3F (a) 2.5%   (b) 99%

19.3G 3.499

19.5A $t = -2.16$
(a) Reject the null hypothesis at the 5% significance level.
(b) Do nöt reject the null hypothesis at the 1% significance level.

(c) They yield opposite inferences.

(d) [29.6, 37.6]

19.5E $t = 27$

(a) Reject the null hypothesis at the 5% significance level.

(b) Reject the null hypothesis at the 1% significance level.

(c) They yield the same inference.

(d) [3.8, 4.0]

19.9A (a) $X^2 = 0$, not significant

(b) $X^2 = 0$, not significant

(c) $X^2 = 13.67$, significant at both levels

(d) $X^2 = 47.138$, significant at both levels

(e) $X^2 = 10.127$, significant at both levels

19.9B (a) 0.798 (b) 0 (c) 1.359 None is statistically significant.

19.9C (a)

df	95th Percentile	99th Percentile
9	16.9190	21.6660
12	21.0261	26.2170
14	23.6848	29.1413
10	18.3070	23.2093

19.11A (a) $t = 1.4$, $df = 38$, do not reject the null hypothesis

(c) $t = 4.34$, df large implies use of normal distribution, reject the null hypothesis

(d) $t = 1.1$, $df = 28$, do not reject the null hypothesis

(e) $t = 1.14$, do not reject the null hypothesis

19.11B (a) $t = 0.18$, not significant (c) $t = 0.91$, not significant (d) $t = 0.14$ (e) $t = 0.15$

19.11C (a) 11.5 ± 14.1, contains 0 and 10; 11.5 ± 20.2, contains 0 and 10

(c) 11.5 ± 5.3 and 11.5 ± 8.0, contain 10 but not 0

(d) 11.5 ± 17.7 and 11.5 ± 26.1

19.13A (a) For the F distribution with 7 and 13 degrees of freedom, the 95th percentile is 3.5504 and the 99th percentile is 6.4100.

19.13B

	Mean	Standard Deviation	95th Percentile	99th Percentile
(a)	5/3	$5\sqrt{5}/3$	19.2971	99.2982
(b)	5/4	$5\sqrt{15}/12$	19.3959	99.4035
(c)	10/9	$5\sqrt{11}/18$	2.8661	4.4307
(d)	6/5	$0.9\sqrt{2}$	3.2839	5.6667
(e)	4/3	$\sqrt{14}/3$	3.4382	6.0289

19.15C (a) There is no disagreement; the hypotheses are indistinguishable with these data

(b) [$15.02, $681.18]

(c) Use $[y_{(1)}, y_{(7)}] = [\$68.42, \$423.10]$. Reject $\eta = \$500$ but not $\eta = \$400$ at the 7% significance level.

19.15D Use $[y_{(2)}, y_{(8)}] = [\$87.96, \$457.75]$. Reject $\eta = \$500$ but not $\eta = \$400$.

19.17A 0.3318 **19.17C** 0.0256

CHAPTER 20

20.3A $45,350   **20.3B** $48,628   **20.3D** Direct   **20.5A** $2791   **20.7A** 20.5 ± 6.2

20.7B (a) [2.53, 3.25]   (b) Yes   (c) 5%

20.7C $t^2 = (16.01)^2 = 256.3 = F$

20.7F The prediction for $x = 6.9$ because it is farther from the mean of the x values than is 10.1.

20.7G (a) Height $= 27.6 + 2.58$ age, $s = 1.34$, $R^2 = 98.7\%$

(b) The standard error of the slope estimate is 0.08163, yielding a t statistic of 31.66 and a p value of 0.000. The relationship is statistically significant.

(c) The regression of average ages vastly understates the variability in individual heights, even though the regression based on averages might be useful in predicting individual heights.

20.7H Height $= 27.8 + 2.57$ age, $s = 1.468$, $R^2 = 98.5\%$ (a) The standard error of the slope estimate is 0.08881, yielding a t statistic of 28.97 and a p value of 0.000.

20.9A The t ratio is -4.12 with a p value of 0.000. The contribution of square feet squared is statistically significant.

20.9D (a)   Sales $= 34,105 + 375$ advert $- 30,046$ ratio $+ 85.9$ pdi

t ratios   1.90 -1.31 4.80

$s = 9574$, $R^2 = 96.9\%$

Only the coefficient on pdi is statistically significant.

(b) $F = 104.51$ with p value 0.000. The overall relationship is statistically significant.

(c) $t = 1.90$ with p value 0.087. The contribution of advertising is not statistically significant at the 5% level in the presence of the other variables.

CHAPTER 21

21.7A   The regression equation is

Height = 27.6 + 2.58 Age

Predictor	Coef	Stdev	t-ratio	p
Constant	27.6242	0.6716	41.13	0.000
Age	2.58424	0.08163	31.66	0.000

s = 1.349   R-sq = 98.7%   R-sq(adj) = 98.6%

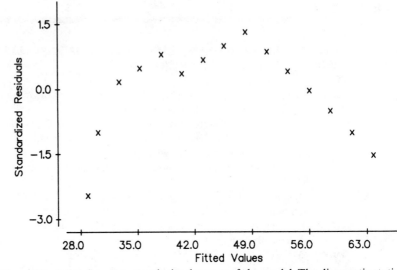

The residual plot demonstrates the inadequacy of the model. The diagnostic statistics below only hint at the inadequacy.

Row	Age	Height	Std Res	Fitted	Leverage	Cook's D
1	0.5	26	-2.45171	28.9163	0.222886	0.862001
2	1.0	29	-1.00121	30.2084	0.199890	0.125216
3	2.0	33	0.16759	32.7927	0.159388	0.002663
4	3.0	36	0.49400	35.3769	0.126205	0.017623
5	4.0	39	0.81170	37.9611	0.100342	0.036742
6	5.0	41	0.35160	40.5454	0.081798	0.005507
7	6.0	44	0.66908	43.1296	0.070575	0.016997
8	7.0	47	0.98662	45.7139	0.066671	0.034767
9	8.0	50	1.30795	48.2981	0.070087	0.064468
10	9.0	52	0.86395	50.8823	0.080822	0.032816
11	10.0	54	0.41645	53.4666	0.098878	0.009515
12	11.0	56	-0.04024	56.0508	0.124253	0.000115
13	12.0	58	-0.51257	58.6350	0.156948	0.024456
14	13.0	60	-1.00836	61.2193	0.196962	0.124695
15	14.0	62	-1.53753	63.8035	0.244297	0.382106

21.9D (a)

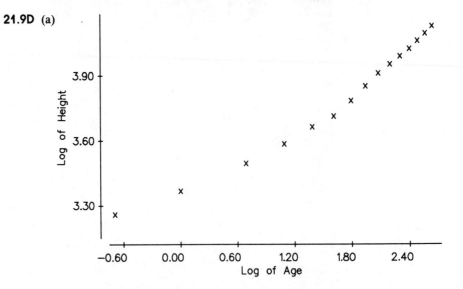

(b)

```
The regression equation is

Log Height = 3.35 + 0.271 Log Age

Predictor      Coef       Stdev     t-ratio       p
Constant    3.34988     0.02713     123.50     0.000
Log Age     0.27056     0.01435      18.86     0.000

s = 0.05290     R-sq = 96.5%     R-sq(adj) = 96.2%
```

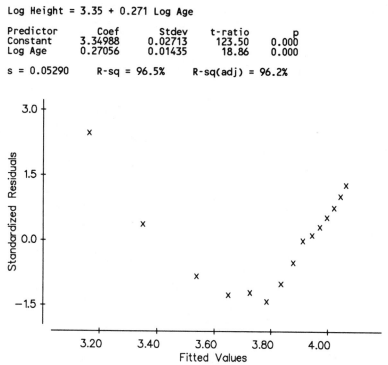

The plot demonstrates the inadequacy of the transformation. The statistics reported below only hint at the problem.

ROW	Log Height	Log Age	Std Res	Fitted	Leverage	Cook's D
1	3.25810	-0.69315	2.47479	3.16234	0.464936	2.66094
2	3.36730	0.00000	0.38353	3.34988	0.262961	0.02624
3	3.49651	0.69315	-0.82998	3.53742	0.131700	0.05224
4	3.58352	1.09861	-1.25885	3.64712	0.087698	0.07617
5	3.66356	1.38629	-1.20430	3.72496	0.071153	0.05555
6	3.71357	1.60944	-1.40423	3.78533	0.066708	0.07047
7	3.78419	1.79176	-0.98860	3.83466	0.068517	0.03594
8	3.85015	1.94591	-0.51506	3.87637	0.073863	0.01058
9	3.91202	2.07944	-0.00932	3.91250	0.081321	0.00000
10	3.95124	2.19722	0.13637	3.94436	0.090077	0.00092
11	3.98898	2.30259	0.32107	3.97287	0.099641	0.00570
12	4.02535	2.39790	0.53485	3.99866	0.109699	0.01762
13	4.06044	2.48491	0.77076	4.02220	0.120049	0.04052
14	4.09434	2.56495	1.02366	4.04385	0.130555	0.07867
15	4.12713	2.63906	1.28980	4.06391	0.141122	0.13667

CHAPTER 23

23.3A 0.262 and −0.237   **23.3C** [575, 631]

23.7B

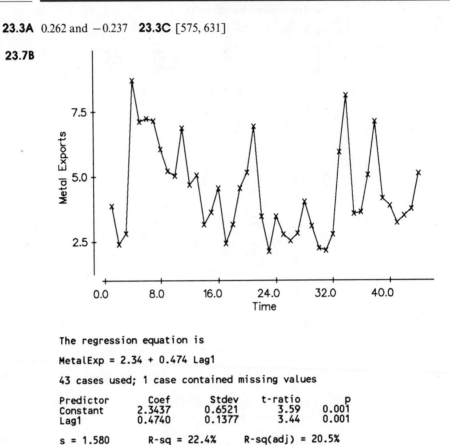

```
The regression equation is

MetalExp = 2.34 + 0.474 Lag1

43 cases used; 1 case contained missing values

Predictor      Coef      Stdev     t-ratio      p
Constant     2.3437     0.6521       3.59     0.001
Lag1         0.4740     0.1377       3.44     0.001

s = 1.580      R-sq = 22.4%     R-sq(adj) = 20.5%
```

The prediction for the next observation is 0.474 times the current observation plus 2.34. The residual autocorrelations suggest no model inadequacy.

	Lag1	Lag2	Lag3
Residual autocorrelations	0.066	−0.159	−0.037

The standard deviation of future prediction errors should be about 1.58. Compare this to the standard deviation of future predictions based on the sample mean, namely, 1.754.

	n	**Mean**	**Median**	**Standard Deviation**
Metalexp	44	4.418	3.875	1.754

23.9A (a) 5.90, 6.01, 6.01, 6.31, 6.28, 6.15, 6.13, 6.22

CHAPTER 24

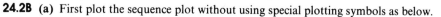

24.2B **(a)** First plot the sequence plot without using special plotting symbols as below.

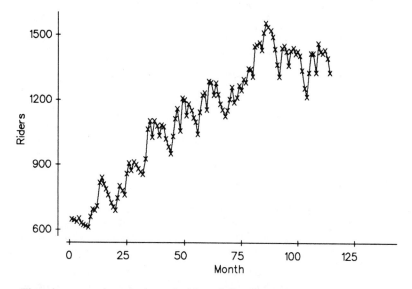

There is a general upward trend with variation along the way. The variation around the overall trend is somewhat larger where the series values are larger. This suggests considering the logarithm of the series for further analysis. Near the end of the series there seems to be a downturn or at least a leveling off of the series values. Without special plotting symbols seasonal patterns are difficult to spot. The plot is repeated using plotting symbols A = January, B = February,..., L = December.

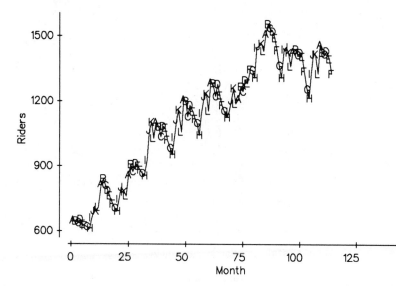

In this plot the seasonal pattern becomes more apparent. Ridership is generally low in August (symbol H) and higher during the winter months (December = K, January = A). The logarithms of the series are then considered. The sequence plot follows.

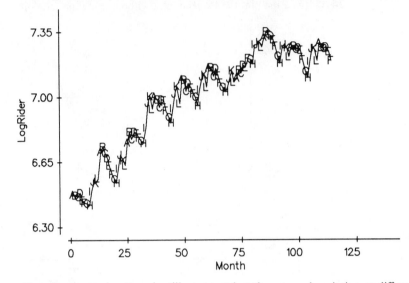

Here the seasonal pattern is still apparent but the unequal variation at different series levels has been corrected. The logarithm of the series will be used for all further analysis.

24.4B (a) After setting up the required time variable and binary seasonal indicator variables the regression results are as follows:

```
The regression equation is

LogRider = 6.54 + 0.00743 Time + 0.0651 Jan + 0.0685 Feb + 0.0322 Mar
                + 0.0472 Apr + 0.0169 May - 0.0207 Jun - 0.0349 Jul
                - 0.0705 Aug + 0.0015 Sep + 0.0526 Oct + 0.0546 Nov
```

Predictor	Coef	Stdev	t-ratio	p
Constant	6.54267	0.03694	177.13	0.000
Time	0.0074345	0.0002810	26.46	0.000
Jan	0.06505	0.04532	1.44	0.154
Feb	0.06848	0.04532	1.51	0.134
Mar	0.03221	0.04531	0.71	0.479
Apr	0.04715	0.04530	1.04	0.300
May	0.01691	0.04530	0.37	0.710
Jun	-0.02072	0.04530	-0.46	0.648
Jul	-0.03494	0.04650	-0.75	0.454
Aug	-0.07054	0.04649	-1.52	0.132
Sep	0.00147	0.04649	0.03	0.975
Oct	0.05257	0.04648	1.13	0.261
Nov	0.05462	0.04648	1.18	0.243

s = 0.09859   R-sq = 87.7%   R-sq(adj) = 86.3%

Analysis of Variance

SOURCE	DF	SS	MS	F	p
Regression	12	7.01846	0.58487	60.17	0.000
Error	101	0.98182	0.00972		
Total	113	8.00027			

Only the time variable appears to be significant in the regression equation. The sequence plot of fitted values traces out the linear time trend with the small seasonal effect added on top. The fitted values are consistently too high in the early and later parts of the series. This model completely misses the changing nature of the last part of the series.

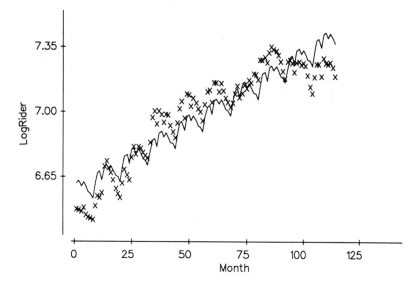

The connected line shows the fitted values. X's mark the actual series values.
(b) Sequence plot of the residuals from the fitted model.

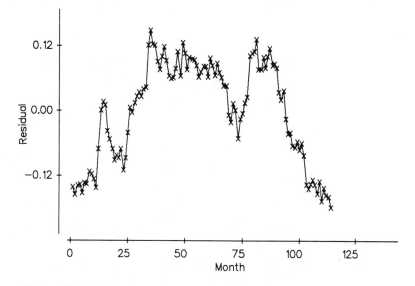

This residual plot does not appear to be close to random.

(c) The autocorrelation in the residuals is 0.957 at lag 1 and 0.910 at lag 2. These are very large correlations and give further indications of the nonrandom nature of the residuals.

24.6D (a) Using the model of Equation (24.3) yields the following regression results:

```
The regression equation is

LogRider = 0.676 + 0.651 Lag1 + 0.256 Lag12

102 cases used; 12 cases contained missing values

Predictor       Coef        Stdev      t-ratio        p
Constant       0.6760      0.1567         4.31     0.000
Lag1           0.65149     0.05663       11.50     0.000
Lag12          0.25635     0.04561        5.62     0.000

s = 0.04538     R-sq = 95.5%     R-sq(adj) = 95.4%

Analysis of Variance

SOURCE        DF          SS          MS         F          p
Regression     2       4.2833      2.1416    1039.92     0.000
Error         99       0.2039      0.0021
Total        101       4.4871
```

In this regression both the lag 1 and lag 12 predictors are quite important (t ratios of 4.31 and 5.62, respectively).

(b) The sequence plot of the residuals shows no indication of model inadequacy.

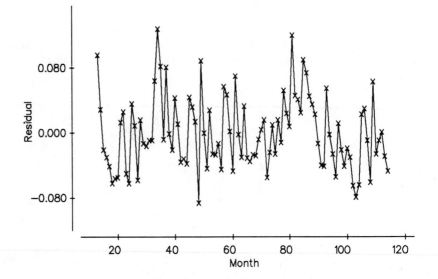

(c) The autocorrelations in the residuals are 0.265 at lag 1 and 0.088 at lag 2. These are much smaller than the corresponding autocorrelations for the model considered in Exercise 24.4B.

(d) This model contains only three regression parameters, the constant or intercept term, the lag 1 term, and the lag 12 term. In contrast, the model in Exercise 24.4B used 13 regression coefficients. In the present model all of the predictors are statistically significant. The residual standard deviation for the present model is 0.04538, which is smaller than the value of 0.09859 obtained with the previous model.

In addition, the present model is less rigid than the time trend plus seasonal indicators model. This can be seen graphically by plotting the fitted and actual series values.

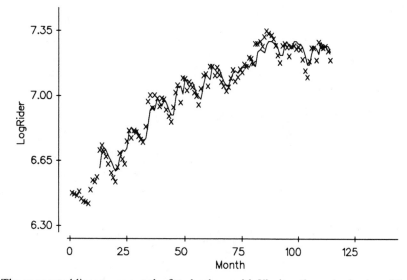

The connected lines trace out the fitted values, with X's denoting actual values. Notice how the values fitted from the seasonal autoregressive model follow the actual values better than those with the previous model. (Note that no fitted values are available for the first 12 months due to the nature of the lagged regression model.) All in all, this simpler model does a much better job of explaining the behavior of the time series.

24.8B **(b)** Sequence plot of actual series values (X's) and exponentially smoothed values (connected lines). The smoothed series follows the actual series quite well most of the time but seems to have difficulty near the end of the series where the series nature appears to be changing.

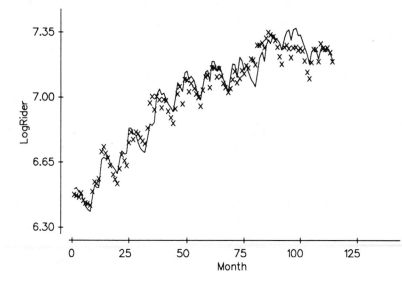

(c) The sequence plot of the residuals from exponential smoothing does not support randomness in the residuals.

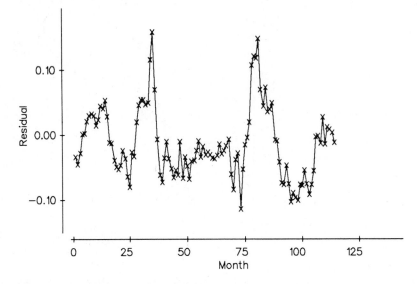

24.10B (a) After computing the required differences the regression calculations give the results:

```
The regression equation is

W(t) = - 0.00153 + 0.021 W(t-1) - 0.273 W(t-12)

89 cases used; 25 cases contained missing values

Predictor      Coef      Stdev      t-ratio      p
Constant    -0.001533    0.003503    -0.44      0.663
W(t-1)       0.0212      0.1073       0.20      0.844
W(t-12)     -0.2727      0.1072      -2.54      0.013

s = 0.03282    R-sq = 7.9%    R-sq(adj) = 5.7%

Analysis of Variance

SOURCE       DF      SS         MS        F      p
Regression    2    0.007910   0.003955   3.67   0.030
Error        86    0.092650   0.001077
Total        88    0.100560
```

In this regression the lag 12 predictor is marginally significant but the lag 1 predictor is not significant at all.

(b) Very little autocorrelation is present in the residuals as shown in the following table:

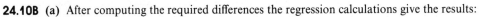

	Lag1	Lag2	Lag12	Lag24
Autocorrelation	0.015	−0.053	−0.101	−0.262

(c) The histogram and normal scores plot for the standardized residuals give good support for normality of the error terms in the model.

Std Res   N = 89   N* = 25

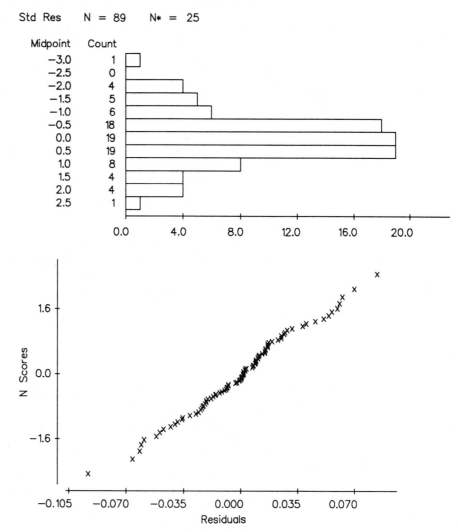

Midpoint	Count
−3.0	1
−2.5	0
−2.0	4
−1.5	5
−1.0	6
−0.5	18
0.0	19
0.5	19
1.0	8
1.5	4
2.0	4
2.5	1

(d) The scatterplot of residuals versus the corresponding fitted values gives no indications that the model assumptions are violated.

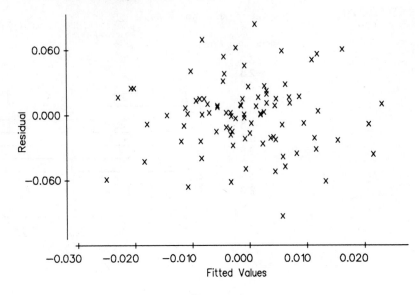

Data Set Index

If a data set is listed in the text, then it is simply indexed by page number here. The page number given is the page on which the data set is listed. If the data set is not listed in the text, then it is indexed here and listed in Appendix 2: Selected Data Set Listings. All data sets are on disk provided by the publisher. The index is in alphabetical order based on the computer filename.

Index